# *Elements of Literature*

Fifth Canadian Edition

# *Elements of Literature*

## Fiction • Poetry • Drama

Edited by **Robert Scholes** • **Nancy R. Comley**
**Carl H. Klaus** • **David Staines**

OXFORD
UNIVERSITY PRESS

**OXFORD**
UNIVERSITY PRESS

Oxford University Press is a department of the University of Oxford. It furthers the University's objective of excellence in research, scholarship, and education by publishing worldwide. Oxford is a registered trade mark of Oxford University Press in the UK and in certain other countries.

Published in Canada by
Oxford University Press
8 Sampson Mews, Suite 204,
Don Mills, Ontario M3C 0H5 Canada

www.oupcanada.com



First Canadian Edition published in 1987
Second Canadian Edition published in 1990
Third Canadian Edition published in 2004
Fourth Canadian Edition published in 2010

*Elements of Literature 3: Fiction, Poetry, Drama* was originally published in English in 1982 by Oxford University Press, Inc., 198 Madison Avenue, New York, N.Y. 10016-4314, USA, with the ISBN 9780195030716. This adapted edition is published by arrangement. Oxford University Press Canada is solely responsible for this adaptation from the original work. Copyright © Oxford University Press, Inc. 1982.



**Library and Archives Canada Cataloguing in Publication**

Elements of literature : fiction, poetry, drama / edited by Robert Scholes, Nancy R. Comley, Carl H. Klaus, and David Staines. — Fifth Canadian edition.

Includes bibliographical references and index.
ISBN 978-0-19-901489-7 (pbk.)

1. English literature. 2. American literature. 3. Canadian literature (English). I. Comley, Nancy R., editor II. Klaus, Carl H., editor III. Scholes, Robert, 1929–, editor IV. Staines, David, 1946–, editor

PN6014.E44 2015 820.8 C2015-900353-9

Oxford University Press is committed to our environment. Wherever possible, our books are printed on paper which comes from responsible sources.

Printed and bound in the United States of America

1 2 3 4 — 18 17 16 15

# Contents

# DRAMA

# From the Publisher

Oxford University Press is delighted to present the fifth Canadian edition of *Elements of Literature*, edited by Robert Scholes, Nancy R. Comley, Carl H. Klaus, and David Staines. Like its predecessors, the new edition is designed to introduce students to the greatest works of short fiction, poetry, and drama written in (or translated into) English from the Golden Age of classical Greek theatre to the twenty-first century. Each writer is introduced by a short biocritical headnote to set his or her work within the context of the literary canon. In addition, each of the three major sections begins with an essay that introduces students to the key characteristics of the genre—fiction, poetry, or drama—while providing an overview of approaches to critical analysis.

The fifth edition includes new selections by Margaret Atwood, Aphra Behn, Christian Bök, Leonard Cohen, Tamas Dobozy, Seamus Heaney, Alice Munro, Robert Pinsky, Madeleine Thien, and William Butler Yeats. The selection and comprehensive treatment of authors, along with the genre introductions and the outstanding coverage of Canadian writers, continue to give *Elements of Literature* a depth of coverage that is unmatched in any single-volume anthology on the market.

## ONLINE RESOURCES

*Elements of Literature* is supported by an online instructor's manual that includes

- a thematic table of contents,
- introductory essays on writing about literature and on critical approaches,
- reading guides for each genre (short fiction, poetry, and drama), and
- links to audio and video clips and to original manuscripts of selected poems and short stories.

**www.oupcanada.com/ScholesStaines5Ce**

## REVIEWERS

We would like to thank the reviewers, both named and anonymous, whose thoughtful comments and suggestions have helped to shape this and earlier editions of the anthology.

### Current Edition

Lesley Choyce, Dalhousie University
Ronald W. Cooley, University of Saskatchewan
Andre Furlani, Concordia University
David Grant, MacEwan University
Geoff Hamilton, Mount Allison University
Eugenia Zuroski Jenkins, McMaster University
Jo-Ann Wallace, University of Alberta

**Previous Editions**

Bert Almon, University of Alberta
Anne Blott, Vanier College
Stewart Blott, Vanier College
Roy Campbell, University of Manitoba
Rhiannon Don, Nipissing University
Candace Fertile, Camosun College
Debbie Hlady, Camosun College
Kathleen James-Cavan, University of Saskatchewan
Mike Matthews, Vancouver Island University
Robert J. Merrett, University of Alberta
David J. Parkinson, University of Saskatchewan
Barry Popowich, University of Saskatchewan

# Preface

This fifth edition of *Elements of Literature* brings together outstanding works of fiction, poetry, and drama in a collection designed to aid those who want to learn how to understand and appreciate works of literature. There are introductory discussions for each of the literary forms represented, genre-specific glossaries of critical terms, and biographical headnotes for each author.

The stories, poems, and plays presented here have been chosen for their suitability in introducing the work of their authors. Fiction writers, poets, and playwrights are presented chronologically by date of birth. They range in time and place from Sophocles and the world of classical Greek tragedy to such contemporary writers as Tamas Dobozy and Madeleine Thien, Margaret Atwood and Michael Ondaatje, and Sharon Pollock and Michel Tremblay. The date of its earliest publication follows each story, poem, and play. The collection is not a history of literature in English. It is a textbook of significant fiction, poetry, and drama of American, British, and Canadian literatures.

I wish to take this occasion to thank four people from Oxford University Press who stand behind this new edition. Phyllis Wilson invited me to rethink the original text, Eric Sinkins provided his careful editorial suggestions, Dave Ward marshalled from across the country critical commentaries for this new edition, and Leah-Ann Lymer oversaw its final production with authority. My thanks to them for their advice and unfailing support.

David Staines
Ottawa, Ontario
March 2015

# FICTION

# The Elements of Fiction

## FICTION, FACT, AND TRUTH

A fiction is a made-up story. This definition covers a lot of territory. It includes the 'white' lies we tell to protect ourselves from scrutiny and the jokes and anecdotes we hear and re-tell in casual conversation. It also covers great visionary works of literature like John Milton's *Paradise Lost* and even the Bible. To call something a fiction does not mean that it necessarily lacks truth, or that it may not contain fact. The relationship between fact and fiction is by no means simple, and, since it is important to an understanding of fiction, it must be considered with some care.

Fact and fiction are old acquaintances. Both derive from Latin words: 'fact' comes from *facere*, 'to make or do'; 'fiction' comes from *fingere*, 'to make or shape'. Plain enough words, one would think—not necessarily loaded with overtones of approval or disapproval. But their fortunes in the world of words have not been equal. In ordinary use, fact is associated with those pillars of verbal society 'reality' and 'truth'. Fiction, on the other hand, is known to consort with such suspicious characters as 'unreality' and 'falsehood'. But if we look deeper into the matter, we can see that the relation of fact and fiction to 'the real' and 'the untrue' is not exactly what it appears on the surface. Fact still means literally 'a thing done', and fiction has never lost its meaning of 'a thing made'. But in what sense do things done or things made partake of truth or reality?

We can observe the relationship between fact and fiction clearly if we consider one place where the two come together: in history. The word 'history' itself hides a double meaning. It comes from a Greek word that originally meant 'inquiry' or 'investigation', but it soon acquired the two meanings that interest us here. On the one hand, history can mean 'things that have happened'; on the other, it can refer to 'a recorded version of things that are supposed to have happened'. In other words, history can mean both the events of the past and the story of those events: fact—or fiction. The word 'story' lurks in the word 'history' and is derived from it. Fact, in order to survive, must become fiction. Seen in this way, fiction is not the opposite of fact but its complement: it gives a more lasting shape to the vanishing deeds of women and men.

This is just one aspect of fiction. We *do* think of it also as something different from historical records or mere data. We think of it not just as made but made up, a product of the imagination. It is helpful to see fiction in both ways outlined here: it can be factual, maintaining the closest possible correspondence between its story and events that have actually happened, or it can be fanciful, defying our sense of life's ordinary possibilities.

If we take these two extremes of fiction as opposite ends of a spectrum—the infra red of pure history and the ultraviolet of pure imagination—we can distinguish many shades of coloration. All are fragments of the white radiance of truth, which is present in both history books and fairy tales—though only partly present in each—fragmented by the prism of fiction, without which we could not see it at all. For truth is like ordinary light, present everywhere but invisible, and we must break it to behold it. To fracture truth in a purposeful and pleasing way—that is the job of the writer of fiction, with whatever shades from the spectrum he or she chooses to work.

## THE SPECTRUM OF FICTION

The fictional spectrum can be a useful way to analyze fiction as long as we remember that it is just a metaphor, a handy linguistic tool to be discarded when it becomes more of a hindrance to understanding than a help. In terms of this metaphor, we may think of fiction as resembling the spectrum of colour found in ordinary light, with history and fantasy as its ends. Of course, only a recording angel, taking notes of all the deeds of humankind without distorting or omitting anything, could be called a 'pure' historian. All recorded history becomes fictional, just as all human fantasy involves some resemblance—however far-fetched—to real life. For the student of fiction, then, the way historical and imaginative materials are combined becomes crucial. This is because our understanding of fiction depends on our grasping the way in which any particular work is related to life.

Life itself is neither tragic nor comic, neither sentimental nor ironic. It is a sequence of sensations, actions, thoughts, and events that we try to tame with language. Every time we say a word about our existence, we are engaged in this taming process. The art of fiction is like a highly developed method of domestication, in which life is not merely brought under control but asked to perform tricks as well. The tricks, if well done, please us in a complicated way. In the first place, they please us because their order and intelligibility are a welcome relief from the confusions and pressures of daily life. In the second place, this artificial order may be mastered and used to help us make sense of our own experience. We recognize aspects of ourselves and our situations in the more ordered perspectives of fiction, and having read Flannery O'Connor or Alice Munro, we begin to recognize certain situations in our existence as having a family resemblance to situations these authors describe. At the same time, fiction presents us with ideal and debased extremes of existence—both possible and impossible—that are interesting in themselves and interestingly different from our own experience. In this way, literature offers us an 'escape' from life, but also provides us with new equipment for our inevitable return. It also offers us an 'imitation' of life that helps us to understand it, just as life helps us to understand fiction. Our experience of fiction, then, involves both pleasure and understanding. We may think of understanding either as a result of the pleasurable experience of fiction or as a necessary preliminary to that pleasure. But no matter how we view the complicated relationship between pleasure and understanding, we must recognize that the two are inseparable in the reading of fiction.

Understanding a work of fiction begins with recognizing what kind of fiction it is. Here, again, the notion of fiction as a spectrum may be useful: we can adjust to the special qualities of any given work more easily if we begin with a clear and flexible view of fictional possibilities. Any attempt to give *every* shade of fiction its own place would be cumbersome and misleading, but we can imagine the 'spectrum of fiction' as a rough scale, showing the primary possibilities located in relation to one another. Between the extremes of history and fantasy on such a scale we might locate two major points of reference: *realism* and *romance*. Realism and romance represent the two principal ways that fiction can be related to life.

Realism is a matter of perception. The realist presents impressions of the world of experience. These impressions are part of the vocabulary and other technical instruments the realist shares with social scientists—especially psychologists and sociologists. The realistic writer sets out to give the reader a sense of the way things are, but feels that a made-up structure of character and event can do better justice to the way things are than any attempt to copy real life directly. The realist's truth is a bit more general and typical than the reporter's 'fact'. It may also be more vivid and memorable.

Romance is a matter of vision. The writer of romance presents not so much impressions of the world as ideas about it. The ordinary world is seen at a greater distance, and its shape and colour are deliberately altered by the lenses and filters of philosophy and fantasy. In the world of romance, ideas are given freedom to play without being encumbered by data. Yet although 'what is' often gives way in romance to 'what ought to be' or 'what might be', *ought* and *might* always hint at what is by their distortion of it.

Realism and romance are not absolutely different: they have some qualities in common. Realism itself is more romantic than history or journalism. (It is not reality, after all, but real*ism*.) And romance is more realistic than fantasy. Many important works of fiction are rich and complicated blends of romance and realism. In fact, it is possible to say that the greatest works are those that successfully blend the realist's perception and the romance writer's vision, giving us fictional worlds remarkably close to our sense of the actual, but skilfully shaped to make us intensely aware of the meaningful potential of existence.

## FICTIONAL MODES AND PATTERNS

The usefulness of the concept of a fictional spectrum depends on our ability to adapt it to different works of fiction. Before we can begin to do this, we need to add to our scale certain fictional modes and patterns.

The spectrum assumes that romance diverges from realism in one way only along the line that leads from history to fantasy. But we gain a fuller view of this divergence by recognizing that there are two different modes of what we have been calling romance. These two modes represent two obvious ways that reality can be distorted by fiction: it can be made to appear better or worse than we believe it to be. These distortions are ways of seeing certain aspects of reality more clearly at the expense of others. A fictional work that presents a world better than the real world is in the mode of romance; a work that presents a fictional world worse than the real world is in the mode of 'anti-romance', or satire. Because they represent certain potentialities that we recognize as present in our world, both views depend on our sense of the actual to achieve their effects.

The world of romance emphasizes beauty and order. The world of satire emphasizes ugliness and disorder. The ways in which individual characters relate to their distorted worlds constitute a crucial element of fiction, for these relations determine certain patterns, or master plots, that affect the shaping of the particular plot of every story. One of these master plots deals with the kind of character who begins out of harmony with his world and is gradually educated or initiated into a harmonious situation in it. This pattern may operate in either the ordered world of romance or the chaotic world of satire, but the same pattern will have quite a different effect on us when we observe it working out in such different situations. Education that adapts the inept or foolish character for a role in the orderly world presents a comic rise that we observe with approval and pleasure. An initiation into a world of ugliness and disorder amounts to corruption, an ironic rise to what Milton called a 'bad eminence', and we react with disapproval or even disgust.

Another master plot reverses this process of accommodation and presents us with a character who begins in harmony with his world but is ultimately rejected or destroyed by it. Our reaction again depends on our view of the world presented. The heroic figure who falls from a lofty position in the orderly world through some flaw in character is *tragic*. The lowly creature whose doom is the result of his unfortunate virtue or delicacy is *pathetic*. The latter's fall is, ironically, a kind of rise.

The *comic* rise and the *tragic* fall are straightforward, because the values of the orderly world represent human virtue raised to a heroic power. The *satiric* rise and *pathetic* fall are ironic because of the inverted values of the debased world. Satire and pathos debase the world in order to criticize it; tragedy and comedy elevate it to make it acceptable. The two romantic patterns promote resignation, the two satiric patterns opposition.

One other pair of fictional patterns may be added to the two already considered. When characters begin and end in a harmonious relation to their worlds, the fictional pattern is one not of change but of movement. These characters will have adventures or encounters, but they will not make any fundamental change in themselves or in their relation to the world around them. In this kind of story the hero will not be as important as the things he or she meets. In the romantic world the adventures of the (traditionally male) hero will take the form of a quest or voyage that ends with his triumphant return and/or his marriage to the heroine. This pattern moves us to admiration of the wonderful, offering us more an escape from the actual than a criticism of it. In the satiric world, the adventures of a born anti-hero or rogue will parody the quest pattern, typically reflecting the chaos of the debased world by becoming endless themselves. Stories of this kind are likely to end when the rogue heads for new territory or another tour of the familiar chaos. This picaresque pattern moves us to recognition and acceptance of the chaotic.

We have, then, distinguished three pairs of fictional patterns, or six kinds in all: the comic and the satiric rise; the tragic and the pathetic fall; the heroic (romantic) and the anti-heroic (picaresque) quest. But we have done this only with regard to the fantasy worlds of romance and satire. When these patterns are applied to a more realistic fictional world, the results become complicated: the neat, schematic distinctions fade; the various patterns combine and interact; and values themselves are called into question. Rise and fall, success and failure, all become problematic. This problematic quality is one of the great sources of interest in realistic fiction. Realism uses the familiar patterns of education, expulsion, and quest, but often in such a way as to call into question the great issues of whether the education is beneficial, the expulsion or death justified, the quest worthwhile. Our recognition of the traces of traditional patterns in realistic fiction is useful mainly in helping us to see what questions are being raised.

Viewed historically, realism developed later than romance and satire, and it is useful to see realistic fiction as combining elements of its predecessors in various ways. It would be a mistake, though, to think of realism as superseding the earlier forms just because it uses some of their elements in a new way. In fact, the rise of realism led to a kind of counterflow of realistic elements into the older forms of fiction, reinvigorating them with its problematical qualities. The reader of contemporary fiction in particular will require the flexibility of response that can be attained through careful attention to the workings of traditional patterns in modern fiction. But our ability to identify these patterns in any work of fiction will depend on our grasp of the specific elements of that work. We must be alert to the way that its plots, its characters, and its point of view adapt the traditional elements we have been considering.

## Plot

Fiction is movement. A story is a story because it tells about a process of change: a character changes, or his or her situation changes, or our understanding of the character changes. These are the essential movements of fiction. Before we can begin to interpret what we are reading, we must be able to recognize these movements and follow them. The points below offer some advice about how to perceive and follow fictional plotting. Keep in mind that not all stories follow a linear chronology. For instance, a story could begin with a character speaking in the present and recounting an event through a series of flashbacks. Nevertheless, although the movement may appear to be disjointed, the story still traces a process of change.

1. *Look at beginnings and endings.* Movement in fiction is always movement *from* and *to.* A good grasp of a story's start and finish should give you a sense of its overall direction.

2. *Isolate the central characters.* The things that happen in fiction happen to somebody. A few major characters or even a single central character may be the real focus of our concern. Consider the situation of each of the central characters at the start and at the end of the story. The changes the characters have undergone will give a good indication of what the story is about.

3. *Note the stages in all important changes.* If a character has moved from one situation to another, or from one state of mind to another, the steps leading to the completed change should be illuminating. By examining each step in the process, the reader can get to the 'hows' and 'whys' of the change.

4. *Note the things working against the movement of the story.* The interest generated in a story is often the product of two forces: the things that work to move a story toward its end, and those that work against that movement, delaying its completion. If the main characters in a story are advancing towards a particular destination, for

example, consider what things delay the journey. When we see the obstacles clearly, we gain a better sense of the direction of the plot itself.

5. *In a long story or novel, consider the various lines of action.* A complex fiction is likely to involve a number of actions, each with its own central character or characters. The actions may not interact, and the central character in one line of action may be insignificant in another. But by isolating the various lines of action, we should gain a better sense of those things that connect them. Often these connections will lead us to related themes that cast light on the meaning of the fiction as a whole.

6. *Take note of characters or events that seem to make no contribution to plot or movement.* This advice is a way of moving from the story's plot to its meaning. Elements that are not important in the plot often have a special thematic importance.

Some of the strategies suggested here can be applied either during or following a first reading. It is worth remembering that a good story may be experienced pleasurably many times, and that a second or third reading will often be more satisfying in every respect than the first.

### Character

No character in a book is a real person. Characters in fiction are *like* real people, but they are also unlike them. In realistic fiction, which includes most novels and short stories, writers emphasize the lifelikeness of their characters. They do this by surrounding these characters with details drawn from contemporary life, and by trying to restrict the events of their narrative to things likely to happen in ordinary life. As a result, writers of realistic fiction have to abandon certain kinds of plots that are too fanciful for characters supposed to typify ordinary life. In this way, they try to draw the reader away from an interest in the movement of fiction and toward an interest in character for its own sake.

Realistic writers draw on psychology and sociology to offer instruction in human nature. The motivation of characters, the workings of conscience and consciousness, are the focal point of most novels and short stories. The best example of this is writing based on a stream-of-consciousness narrative, through which fiction writers offer us a version of mental process at the level where impressions of things seen and heard converge with confused thoughts and longings arising from the subconscious mind. In reading this kind of fiction we must check the validity of its characterization against our own sense of the way people behave. The best realists always offer us a shock of recognition through which we share their perception of human behaviour.

It may be useful to think of character as a function of two impulses: the impulse to individualize and the impulse to typify. Great and memorable characters are the result of a powerful combination of these two impulses. We remember the special, individualizing quirks—habitual patterns of speech, action, or appearance—and we remember the way the character represents something larger than herself. These individualizing touches are part of the storyteller's art. They amuse us or engage our sympathy for the character. The typifying touches are part of a story's meaning. In realistic fiction a character is likely to be representative of a social class, a race, a profession. Or the character may be a recognizable psychological type, who can be analyzed in terms of a particular complex or syndrome. The character may even be a mixture of social and psychological qualities. In allegorical fiction the characters are more likely to represent philosophical positions. In a story of adventure we will encounter types belonging to the traditional pattern of romantic quest: hero, heroine, villain, monster.

The important thing for a reader to remember about characterization is that there are many varieties—and many combinations of the varieties. An adventure story may have an important realistic or allegorical dimension that can be observed in its characterizations. Characters in realistic novels may also be meaningful as illustrations of philosophical ideas or attitudes. As readers, we must be alert and ready to respond to different kinds of characterization on their own terms. A story by James Joyce and a story by Rohinton Mistry are not likely to yield equally to the same kind of reading. It is the reader's business to adapt to whatever fictional world is being entered; it is the writer's business to make the reader's business worthwhile.

### Themes

More often than not, when we discuss a story after reading it, we talk about its meaning. In the classroom, 'What are the themes of this work?' is a favourite question. This interpretive aspect of literary analysis is the most difficult, because in order to attempt it we must look carefully not only at the work but also away from the work to the world of ideas and experiences. Discovering themes in a story involves making connections between the work and the world outside it. These connections *are* the meaning. The great problem for the reader, then, surrounds the validity of the thematic elements he or she discovers. *Are these ideas really there?* we want to know. Are they being 'read out' of the story or 'read into' it? Is any given set of connections between story and world necessarily implied by the story itself? Or are they arbitrarily imposed by an overzealous reader?

A story is always particular, always an instance. How do we properly move from any given instance to a general notion? When, for example, is it legitimate to conclude from the presence of a husband and wife in a story that the story is 'about' marriage—that it makes a statement or raises a question about this aspect of human relations? It is impossible to provide a single method that will always work, but there are certain procedures that will frequently prove helpful.

If we isolate everything that is not just narration, description, or dialogue, some clues are likely to appear. The title of a work is a good example. Sometimes it will point our thinking about the work in a particular direction, or else it may emphasize the importance of a particular element in the work. Like the title, passages in the writing that are themselves commentary or interpretation are of particular importance for thematic discussion. Often interpretive passages will not be presented directly by omniscient and objective narrators with all their authority behind them. They may be spoken instead by a narrator who is also a participant in the action described, and who is therefore not objective, or they may be presented by another character in speech reported by the narrator. In this case, we must assess the reliability of the character before we decide to accept the character's interpretation as valid. Sometimes the narrator herself will be characterized to the extent that we must question her reliability. In similar ways narration and description may also be coloured by thematic materials. The author may present a character or a scene in a manner that leads us to think about the materials presented in a particular way. A character called 'Dean Drone' is introduced to us with a name that carries some not too subtle advice about how we are to understand the presentation.

In less obvious cases, where the author refrains from direct commentary, we must look for subtler clues. Patterns of repetition, ironic juxtaposition, the tone of the narration—devices such as these must lead us to the connections between the particular world of the book and the generalized world of ideas. And the more delicate and subtle the story is, the more delicate our interpretation must be. Thus, taking care that our interpretation is rooted in the work itself is only one aspect of the problem.

The other aspect involves the outside knowledge that the reader brings to the work. If the story is realistic, it will be understood best by those readers whose experience has equipped them with information about the aspect of reality the story points to. This does not mean that one must be the transplanted son of a Cape Breton fisherman to understand Alistair MacLeod's 'The Boat', or the observant daughter in a splintering family to understand Madeleine Thien's 'Simple Recipes'. But interpreting the story depends on the reader's having some understanding of family ties and cultural displacement and some sense of the way nature can act destructively upon individuals or even whole groups of human beings.

Often a realistic story may point to an aspect of life we have encountered but never understood, and the fiction may help us clarify and organize that experience. Madeleine Thien's story can teach us something about personal relations, and Thien requires us to bring some experience of family life to that story, for without that it must remain meaningless for the reader.

Tamas Dobozy's 'The Ghosts of Budapest and Toronto' is an exciting story about dreamers in Toronto and in Budapest, but it is also a marked criticism of a superstitious society, a society brought over from the old country and still subject to the superstitions and nightmarish fears that haunt their consciousness. Modern allegories of this kind are often called 'fabulation', and they trace their roots to the simple fable and the homely parable. Modern fabulation may contain many realistic details, but in such modern fables as Nathaniel Hawthorne's 'My Kinsman, Major Molineux' or John Cheever's 'The Swimmer' there is at least one break with what we recognize as normal or probable; there is some moving away from realism for the sake of ideas that may ordinarily be concealed by the surface of reality. Modern fables try to unsettle, to disturb patterns of thought and action that have become so habitual they conceal important dimensions of existence. In studying such tales we must ask what ideas are being called into question. Often the best way to do this is to locate the most fabulous elements in each work and ask why the author chose to break with ordinary probabilities or possibilities where they occur. With this question in mind, it should be possible to examine the way any given feature of a fable relates to the larger concerns of the whole story.

Fiction generates its meanings in innumerable ways, but always in terms of some movement from the particular characters and events of the story to general ideas or human situations suggested by them. Readers come to an understanding of a fictional work by sifting their store of general notions drawn from experience or systematic thought to find those appropriate to the particular materials of the story, then applying these general notions to the story in order to test their relevance. In this way, readers look for the ways the story refines, qualifies, questions, or reinforces those notions. This process—performed not a single time but in rapid oscillation into the work and back out—should leave readers with an understanding of the story and with an enriched store of general notions they have been led to develop in order to understand. In addition to acquiring new notions, readers may have refined their attitudes toward their old notions and toward experience itself. Fiction is justified not as a means of conveying ideas but as a means of generating attitudes toward ideas. The meaning of fiction must finally be seen in terms of emotions directed toward impressions of experience or toward ideas about life.

## Point of View: Perspective and Language

'Point of view' is a technical term for the way a story is told. A stage play normally has no particular point of view: no one stands between the audience and the action. But if we *read* a play, the stage directions—the words of someone who is not a character—offer a special point of view. Similarly, a story told entirely through dialogue would be without a point of view, but as soon as a descriptive phrase is added—such as 'he said *cruelly*' or 'she *complained bitterly*'—we as readers begin to have access to a special viewpoint. A voice outside the action is shaping our attitude toward the events being presented. In our experience of fiction, the attitude we develop toward the events, and our understanding of those events, will usually be controlled by the author through his or her technical management of point of view.

The concept of fictional viewpoint can be conveniently divided into two related parts: one dealing with the storyteller in any given fiction, the other dealing with language. Obviously the two are not really separate. Certain kinds of narration require certain kinds of language—the narrator of Thomas King's 'Borders', for instance, must talk like an Aboriginal Canadian—but we may consider them apart for analytical purposes.

The nature of the storyteller is far from a simple matter. We need to consider such things as the extent to which the storyteller is presenting a character whose personality affects our understanding of the storyteller's statements, and the extent to which the storyteller's view of events is limited in time and space or in the storyteller's ability to see into the minds of various characters. The reader's problem comes down to knowing how to take the things presented. This means paying special attention to any limitations in the narrator's viewpoint. If the viewpoint in the story is 'partial'—if it is either incomplete or biased—the reader must be ready to compensate in appropriate ways.

The language of narration presents a similar problem for the reader—that is, a problem of adjustment and compensation. Of all the dimensions of language that can be considered, two are especially important for the reader of fiction. Both may be seen as ways in which wit—or artistic intelligence—operates through language. One has to do with *tone*, or the way unstated attitudes are conveyed through language. The other has to do with *metaphor*, or the way language can convey the richest and most delicate kinds of understanding by bringing together different images and ideas. Consider first this short passage from 'The Marine Excursion of the Knights of Pythias', from Stephen Leacock's *Sunshine Sketches of a Little Town*:

> Dr Gallagher, who knew Canadian history, said to Dean Drone that it was strange to think that Champlain had landed there with his French explorers three hundred years ago; and Dean Drone, who didn't know Canadian history, said it was stranger still to think that the hand of the Almighty had piled up the hills and rocks long before that; and Dr Gallagher said it was wonderful how the French had found their way through such a pathless wilderness; and Dean Drone said that it was wonderful also to think that the Almighty had placed even the smallest shrub in its appointed place. Dr Gallagher said it filled him with admiration. Dean Drone said it filled him with awe. Dr Gallagher said he'd been full of it ever since he was a boy and Dean Drone said so had he.

The tone of this passage is clearly sarcastic. The paragraph asks us to be critical of the two characters, but it does not do so directly. It uses the indirection of verbal irony, in which the real meaning is different from the apparent sense of the words. The last sentence might be read aloud with a particular emphasis on the phrase 'full of it', accompanied by a knowing smirk. How do we know this? How do we supply the appropriate tone of voice for words that we see on the page but do not hear pronounced? We pay attention to the clues given. Dean Drone and Dr Gallagher appear in a similar light several times in this story. For example, when confronted with a report that the *Mariposa Belle* is sinking, Dr Gallagher 'said no, that he had thought so earlier in the day but that he didn't now think that she was.' To the same fact, 'Dean Drone, of course, and some others were quieter about it, and said that one must make allowances and that naturally there were two sides to everything.' Both men are befuddled, clearly out of touch with reality. Their responses to the sinking parallel their responses in their conversation: they speak at cross-purposes to each other, each trying to show off knowledge and expertise with inaccurate information that is meaningless to the other. The 'He said . . . He said . . .' sentence pattern of the first passage shows that neither is interested in what the other has to say. The final statement, if read literally, conflicts both with the actions narrated and with the tone of the narration. It is difficult to believe that Dean Drone's or Dr Gallagher's comments have anything to do with awe or admiration. On the contrary, the two characters seem motivated by one-upmanship. We resolve the conflict by reading the sentence as *ironic*, meaning something other than what it seems to say, and acquiring thereby a sarcastic tone. The additional connotations of the phrase 'full of it' show that Dean Drone and Dr Gallagher are equally objects of the author's sympathetic but nonetheless real irony.

Catching the tone of this passage is a matter of paying attention to clues in sentence pattern and choice of words, and also of keeping in mind the whole context of the story we are reading. The more we read a particular author, the better we become at catching his tone—at perceiving the emotional shades that colour the sense of his words. In *Sunshine Sketches of a Little Town*, Dean Drone and Dr Gallagher are presented in a similar way often enough that by this appearance, we have been prepared to regard them unsympathetically. But on the strength of these sentences we should be able to catch the tone.

The second key dimension of the language of narration, *metaphor*, is illustrated well in Sinclair Ross's 'The Painted Door'. In the following passage, Ann watches her husband set off to visit his father on a prairie winter morning:

> From the bedroom window she watched him nearly a mile along the road. The fire had gone down when at last she turned away, and already through the house there was an encroaching chill. A blaze sprang up again when the drafts were opened, but as she went on clearing the table her movements were furtive and constrained. It was the silence weighing upon her—the frozen silence of the bitter fields and sun-chilled sky—lurking outside as if alive, relentlessly in wait, mile-deep between her now and John. She listened to it, suddenly tense, motionless. The fire crackled and the clock ticked. Always it was there. 'I'm a fool,' she whispered hoarsely, rattling the dishes in defiance, going back to the stove to put in another fire. 'Warm and safe—I'm a fool. It's a good chance when he's away to paint. The day will go quickly. I won't have time to brood.'
>
> Since November now the paint had been waiting warmer weather. The frost in the walls on a day like this would crack and peel it as it dried, but she needed something to keep her hands occupied, something to stave off the gathering cold and loneliness. 'First of all,' she said aloud, opening the paint and mixing it with a little turpentine, 'I must get the house warmer. Fill up the stove and open the oven door so that all the heat comes out. Wad something along the window sills to keep out the drafts. Then I'll feel brighter. It's the cold that depresses.'

The word 'depress' has been used so often to mean 'dispirit' or 'sadden' that it is possible to use it without any sense that it is metaphorical. But the notion of pressing or pushing down is present in the expression. A writer who, like Ross, is sensitive to metaphor can pick up the implications of such an expression and use them to strengthen his meaning. The somewhat uncharacteristic syntax of the final line—it would be more common to say 'It's the cold that depresses people' or 'It's the cold people find depressing'—draws our attention to this word and lets us know that the author wants us to notice it. Throughout the passage, the cold outside is associated with the quiet of the small house. The 'frozen silence', which represents Ann's fear and loneliness, is characterized as 'encroaching', 'gathering', 'lurking'. In the line, 'It was the silence weighing upon her', the author uses another metaphor for depression—'weighing upon'—that, like 'depresses', has as its literal meaning the idea of pressing or forcing down. In a paragraph that comes shortly after this passage, we read the following:

> Suddenly her movements became precise, deliberate, her posture self-conscious, as if someone had entered the room and were watching her. It was the silence again, aggressive, hovering.

Here the 'frozen silence' of the earlier line returns as something 'hovering' over Ann, reinforcing the idea that fear and loneliness are depressing or 'weighing upon her'.

The combined effect of these lines is a powerful metaphor that presents intangible ideas—loneliness and fear—as something physical, a sort of malevolent being waiting to pounce. The image, however, takes on added significance, by way of contrast, later in the same story. The following passage recounts Ann's reaction to the arrival of a family friend, Steven:

> . . . suddenly at the assurance of his touch and voice the fear that had been gripping her gave way to an hysteria of relief. Scarcely aware of herself she seized his arm and sobbed against it. He remained still a moment, unyielding, then slipped his other arm around her shoulder. It was comforting and she relaxed against it, hushed by a sudden sense of lull and safety. Her shoulders trembled with the easing of the strain, then fell limp and still. 'You're shivering,'—he drew her gently towards the stove. 'There's nothing to be afraid of now, though. . . .'

Note the contrasts between this passage and the one cited previously. No longer is Ann's 'posture self-conscious': now she is 'scarcely aware of herself', and her shoulders are now 'limp'. Her fear, once again described metaphorically as 'gripping', gives way to relief, and the last line, in which Steven addresses Ann's cold and fear, confirms that his arrival represents a brief end to the 'frozen silence' that has been 'weighing upon her'.

### Design: Juxtaposition and Repetition in the Structure of Fiction

When we look at a painting up close, we can see clearly its details and the texture of its brush strokes, but we cannot see it as a whole. When we back away, we lose our perception of these minute qualities but gain, with this new perspective, a sense of its design. Similarly, as we read a story, we are involved in its details. And in a story we are involved especially because we experience it as a flow of words in time, bringing us impressions and ideas, moving us emotionally and stirring us intellectually. It is natural to back away from a painting and see it as a whole. But it is less natural and more difficult to gain a similar perspective on a book. We can never 'see' it all at once. Yet design is an important part of the writer's art, and a sense of design is essential to a thorough assessment of the text.

Design in fiction takes many forms, but these may be seen as mainly of two kinds. One has to do with *juxtaposition*, with what is put next to what in the arrangement of the story. The other has to do with *repetition*, with images, ideas, or situations that are repeated—often with interesting variations—in the course of the narrative. Juxtaposition is more important in some kinds of fiction than it is in others. If a single action is presented in a simple, chronological arrangement, the order of events is not likely to assume any special significance. But if the action is rearranged in time so that we encounter events out of their chronological sequence—through flashbacks, for example—the order should be given some attention. We must look for reasons behind the author's manipulation of chronology. Why has the author chosen to place this particular scene from the narrative past next to this particular scene in the narrative present? Similarly, if we are following two actions in one story, we should look for reasons why an incident from one plot line has been placed next to a particular incident in the other.

This method of examination often uncovers interesting parallels: similar situations that amount to a kind of repetition with variation. If character *A* gets into a situation and takes one kind of action, while character *B*, in a similar situation, takes a different action, we should compare the two and contrast their distinctive behaviour, which will help us learn more about both. This kind of comparison can also lead us to generalizations about the meaning of a work as a whole.

Significant kinds of repetition occur also in sections of a story that are not placed next to one another. This kind of repetition, an important element of design, serves to tie separate parts of a story together, enriching and strengthening the whole structure. Structure in fiction is a complicated notion because it involves so many factors. We can think of structure in one sense as the elements that shape our experience as we move through the story; in this sense structure is close to plot. We can also think of structure as the elements that enable us to see a meaningful pattern in the whole work; in this sense structure is close to design. If plot has to do with the *dynamics*, or movement, of fiction, design has to do with the *statics* of fiction—the way we see a whole story after we have stopped moving through it. When we become aware of design in reading, so that one part of a story reminds us of parts we have read earlier, we are involved in a movement counter to our progress from beginning to end. Plot wants to move us along; design wants to delay our movement, to make us pause and 'see'. The opposition of these two forces is one of the things that enrich our experience of fiction.

Design is often a matter of repeating images or metaphors. In considering the metaphors in 'The Painted Door', we have already begun an examination of the way metaphoric design can tie together different characters and situations. The following example is a striking illustration of a rather different use of repetition in the design of a story. This is a case in which two episodes in the life of the same character—separated both by pages of our reading and by weeks in the life of the character—are brought together into powerful contrasts by means of repetition with variation.

At the end of the second chapter of James Joyce's first published novel, *A Portrait of the Artist as a Young Man*, the young man of the title, Stephen Dedalus, has been led by the urgings of physical desire into the arms of a prostitute. This is the last paragraph of that chapter:

> With a sudden movement she bowed his head and joined her lips to his and he read the meaning of her movements in her frank uplifted eyes. It was too much for him. He closed his eyes, surrendering himself to her, body and mind, conscious of nothing in the world but the dark pressure of her softly parting lips. They pressed upon his brain as upon his lips as though they were the

> vehicle of vague speech; and between them he felt an unknown and timid pressure, darker than the swoon of sin, softer than sound or odour.

By the end of the third chapter, Joyce has taken Stephen Dedalus through a period of disgust, remorse, and repentance. In the last paragraphs of the chapter we find Stephen receiving Holy Communion:

> He knelt before the altar with his classmates, holding the altar cloth with them over a living rail of hands. His hands were trembling, and his soul trembled as he heard the priest pass with the ciborium from communicant to communicant.
>
> —*Corpus Domini nostri.*
>
> Could it be? He knelt there sinless and timid: and he would hold upon his tongue the host and God would enter his purified body.
>
> —*In vitam eternam. Amen.*
>
> Another life! A life of grace and virtue and happiness! It was true.
>
> —*Corpus Domini nostri.*
>
> The ciborium had come to him.

In the last sentence of the second chapter, Stephen felt the woman's tongue, pressing through her kiss—'an unknown and timid pressure'. In the last lines of the third chapter, his tongue receives the body of Christ, making a contrast that is striking and rich in emotional and intellectual implications. Design here is carrying out Joyce's intention, which is to make us see Stephen poised between the extremes of sin and redemption, both of which attract him powerfully but neither of which can hold him finally—as the later chapters demonstrate. The focus on tongues in these two episodes is the crucial repeated element that makes the contrast Joyce wishes. And in the context of the whole story, it reminds us that tongues are not only for kissing or receiving the sacrament. They are also instruments of expression. Stephen ultimately must strive to express himself as an artist of languages, using his gift of tongues. In these two episodes, Stephen has been passive, the receiver. Later he will learn to speak out.

What we have been considering is the way that an object—in this case the tongue—can by its use in a fictional design acquire a metaphorical value that points in the direction of meaning. When this happens, the object becomes a symbol.

A fiction, we noted at the beginning, is a made-up story, and this anthology reveals a myriad of fascinating stories that will challenge you, disturb you, and entertain you. All fiction invites and demands your complete involvement in the story, and what you must bring to your careful reading is a flexibility of response. As you examine the designs of the individual stories, you are entering the worlds of contemporary fiction.

## A GUIDE TO OUR SELECTIONS

> So when I write a story I want to make a certain kind of structure, and I know the feeling I want to get from being inside that structure. This is the hard part of the explanation, where I have to use a word like 'feeling', which is not very precise, because if I attempt to be more intellectually respectable I will have to be dishonest. 'Feeling' will have to do.

So states Alice Munro, one of the preeminent writers of short fiction in the English-speaking world. To write a short story is to create a structure for this 'feeling'. But as Munro goes on to say, there is no blueprint, no plan, for the structure of a story.

> It's not a question of, 'I'll make this kind of house because if I do it right it will have this effect.' I've got to make, I've got to build up, a house, a story, to fit around the indescribable 'feeling' that is like the soul of a story, and which I must insist upon in a dogged, embarrassed way, as being no more definable than that. And I don't know where it comes from. It seems to be already there, and some unlikely clue, such as a shop window or a bit of conversation, makes me aware of it. Then I start accumulating the material and putting it together. Some of the material I may have lying around already, in memories and observations, and some I invent, and some I have to go diligently looking for (factual details), while some is dumped in my lap (anecdotes, bits of speech). I see how this material might go together to make the shape I need, and I try it. I keep trying and seeing where I went wrong and trying again.[1]

For a writer to talk about the structure of the writing, there are many handicaps. A writer can talk about the craft of writing, yet no sense emerges of just what the writer is doing, apart from piecing together the fragments that ultimately become the completed story.

The word 'novel' comes from a word meaning 'new', a word that, in the plural, is used to mean 'news', news of the day or news of the period. The English novel begins with the august figure of Daniel Defoe, the author of such books as *Robinson Crusoe* (1719), a work of fiction based on 'a real life story' of a round-the-world voyage described to him by the returned traveller. Defoe stitched this together with material he had gathered from another written account. All of Defoe's novels pretend to be factual accounts or factual documents, and so the English novel, by his hand, came into being as a long prose account of true happenings. It is then not surprising that many novelists were first of all journalists, newspaper people who specialized in reporting. Defoe was a journalist, and so were other celebrated novelists, people like Charles Dickens, Ernest Hemingway, and Morley Callaghan. For this reason, the novel has its roots in a love of fact, and we speak of the novel's penchant for realism, its commitment to mirroring its society and the realities of its time.

The short story begins with Edgar Allan Poe, who never wrote a novel but wrote many stories where brevity and a sense of mystery are the dominant features of his style. He conceived of the mystery story as his own creation, and he became a seminal influence on the writing of detective fiction.

For Herman Melville, fiction was a true story, rooted closely in the world it was meant to depict. His classic novel *Moby-Dick*, the gruesome tale of Captain Ahab and his maniacal pursuit of the great white whale, includes a compendium on whaling, complete with many chapters that contain truths 'stranger than fiction'. These chapters of verifiable fact are a bridge to the credibility of the pursuit. In Melville's short story 'Bartleby the Scrivener: A Story of Wall Street', we encounter in a downtown New York office 'a rather elderly man', who tells us the story of Bartleby. We believe what we read because the narrator describes what he has seen and heard. At the same time, Nathaniel Hawthorne, also rooting his stories in a fixed time and place, strove to create what he called 'tales', stories that move well beyond the surface reality to explore the hidden inner life of his characters.

In Canada the short story first emerged in the animal stories of Charles G.D. Roberts and Ernest Thompson Seton. This was the medium in which these writers, for the first time, described their world in fictional form, and in their hands it differed markedly from the animal story of contemporary American and British writers. American animal stories are confrontations between human beings and animals, where the latter symbolize nature's hostility. British animal stories are thinly disguised fables, acted out by animals to illuminate human problems. Canadian animal stories, on the other hand, focus on animals, and we are often invited to sympathize with their plight.

In the writings of Kate Chopin and Charlotte Perkins Gilman, the female voice produces stories that are deliberately strong and pointed, in Chopin through a third-person narrator, in Gilman through a first-person narrator who introduces an autobiographical dimension to the fiction. The stories of these writers represent the fiction of the 1890s.

Stephen Leacock ushers in the new century with his classic comic story 'The Marine Excursion of the Knights of Pythias'. It is perhaps the finest illustration of his talent as a humorist. Leacock wrote almost a volume of comic stories and sketches every year from 1910 until his death in 1944; he never wrote a novel.

James Joyce introduced the concept of the 'epiphany', or 'moment of illumination', in his fiction. A moment like the appearance of Mangan's sister to the 13-year-old narrator in 'Araby' is a revelatory incident that suggests the nature of their encounter and its aftermath. Katherine Mansfield employs an objective narrator who indulges in terse irony as she dissects the relationships of her main characters.

For the American writers, F. Scott Fitzgerald and Ernest Hemingway, the short story was a vehicle for conveying much of the tension and the regret that are also present in their novels. In their selections here, Fitzgerald paints the dreary world of an exile during the Depression, while Hemingway casts his eye on the equally dreary world of cafés and bodegas. Both writers use the omniscient third-person narrator to illuminate their depictions of their individualistic worlds.

The literature of the American South comes to especial prominence in the short story form. Eudora Welty, a native Mississippian, takes a humorous view of her fellow Southerners. And Flannery O'Connor, from Georgia, looks with her concentrated and Catholic vision on the prejudices of the people around her.

Canadian writer Morley Callaghan fashioned short stories out of his highly objective style. In his autobiographical *That Summer in Paris*, he states his own artistic purpose: 'Strip the language, and make the style, the method, all the psychological ramifications, the ambience of the relationships, all the one thing, so the reader couldn't make separations. Cézanne's apples. The appleness of apples. Yet just apples.' He sent a short story to the *New Yorker*, and it became the first piece of fiction the magazine printed. At the same time, Sinclair Ross was writing, as he does in 'The Painted Door', about the windswept plains, the drought of the Depression, and the lives of people caught in this immensely forbidding landscape of the Prairies.

Sheila Watson's 'Antigone' marks a dramatic change from the short story worlds of, for example, Fitzgerald, and Callaghan. Her novel *The Double Hook* marks the beginning of modern Canadian fiction, and her short story here is mythic in its structure, employing classical mythology—the story of Antigone and her sister Ismene—to organize contemporary reality and to endow seemingly homely actions with the significance usually associated with myth. So, too, does John Cheever's 'The Swimmer' turn the story of one man's homeward journey into a mythic return through the grass-lined suburbs of New York City.

More recent writers have continued to fashion their stories to reflect their own real or imagined worlds. Doris Lessing paints an astonishing sunrise on her African landscape, and Mavis Gallant, like Fitzgerald and Hemingway earlier in the century, records with penetrating insight the pathetic lives of exiled North Americans in Europe.

Margaret Laurence paints the threatening world of Manawaka, Manitoba, for the young Vanessa MacLeod, the narrator of 'A Bird in the House'; Alice Munro depicts, in a complex way, the painful search for forgiveness; and Alistair MacLeod looks back, again through a first-person narrator, on the summer long ago when he was only 15. These three Canadian authors write of distant incidents through the prism of their carefully delineated narrators.

In the contemporary world, we meet many writers from many worlds who bring their ethnic roots to bear on their fiction. Bernard Malamud brings Jewish characters into the mainstream of American fiction, Bharati Mukherjee and Rohinton Mistry bring their Indian backgrounds to their stories of an interracial affair and a young boy's seeming obsession with stamp collecting, and Aboriginal authors Thomas King and Louise Erdrich bring their roots to the surface of their writings. Tamas Dobozy searches into his ancestral roots to chronicle the harsh lives of Hungarians in post–Second World War Budapest and Toronto. And Madeleine Thien studies the fracturing family bonds of an immigrant family in contemporary Canada.

The stories presented in this anthology run the gamut from the comic to the tragic. All of them reflect the time, locations, and cultural backgrounds of their authors, and in doing so they also represent the variegated short story itself, taking on many forms all under the single term of 'the short story'.

Just as we began this brief tour through the stories with Alice Munro, we will close with the words of the same writer. Reflecting on her purpose in writing, she concludes:

> It seems to me this is what writing is, when it's real—a straining of something immense and varied, a whole dense vision of the world, into whatever confines the writer has learned to make for it, and this process, unless you are Shakespeare or Tolstoy, must be accompanied by regret; fortunately it is often accompanied by gleeful satisfactions as well.[2]

## Notes

1. 'What Is Real?' in *Making it New: Contemporary Canadian Stories*, edited by John Metcalf (Toronto: Methuen, 1982), p. 224.
2. 'Author's Commentary', in *Sixteen by Twelve: Short Stories by Canadian Writers*, edited by John Metcalf (Toronto: The Ryerson Press, 1970), p. 126.

# Nathaniel Hawthorne

## 1804–1864

Born in Salem, Massachusetts, at a time when the American Revolution was still living history and the Puritan heritage of Salem was very much alive, Nathaniel Hawthorne absorbed its preoccupation with sin and its remembrance of witch hunts. Four years at Bowdoin College in Maine, a job at the Boston Custom House, and a short stay at Brook Farm—an idealistic commune that ran into practical problems—broadened his horizons, but his best work came from brooding over the past more than from observation of his own time. He called his short fiction 'tales' and his longer works 'romances', insisting that his imagination have a certain latitude in which to work. *The Scarlet Letter* (1850) has become a classic of world literature, and many of his shorter tales, such as the one reprinted here, have proven equally durable.

'My Kinsman, Major Molineux', which was first published in 1832 but not collected until *The Snow-Image, and Other Tales* (1851), pushes beyond surface reality to focus intently on the complex inner life of the individual. The story probes this inner life and becomes a warning against simplistic moral judgments.

## My Kinsman, Major Molineux

After the kings of Great Britain had assumed the right of appointing the colonial governors, the measures of the latter seldom met with the ready and generous approbation which had been paid to those of their predecessors, under the original charters. The people looked with most jealous scrutiny to the exercise of power which did not emanate from themselves, and they usually rewarded their rulers with slender gratitude for the compliances by which, in softening their instructions from beyond the sea, they had incurred the reprehension of those who gave them. The annals of Massachusetts Bay will inform us, that of six governors in the space of about forty years from the surrender of the old charter, under James II, two were imprisoned by a popular insurrection; a third, as Hutchinson inclines to believe, was driven from the province by the whizzing of a musket-ball; a fourth, in the opinion of the same historian, was hastened to his grave by continual bickerings with the House of Representatives; and the remaining two, as well as their successors, till the Revolution, were favoured with few and brief intervals of peaceful sway. The inferior members of the court party, in times of high political excitement, led scarcely a more desirable life. These remarks may serve as a preface to the following adventures, which chanced upon a summer night, not far from a hundred years ago.[1] The reader, in order to avoid a long and dry detail of colonial affairs, is requested to dispense with an account of the train of circumstances that had caused much temporary inflammation of the popular mind.

1 The time of this tale is the eve of the American Revolution. The place is Boston.

It was near nine o'clock of a moonlight evening, when a boat crossed the ferry with a single passenger, who had obtained his conveyance at that unusual hour by the promise of an extra fare. While he stood on the landing-place, searching in either pocket for the means of fulfilling his agreement, the ferryman lifted a lantern, by the aid of which, and the newly risen moon, he took a very accurate survey of the stranger's figure. He was a youth of barely eighteen years, evidently country-bred, and now, as it should seem, upon his first visit to town. He was clad in a coarse grey coat, well worn, but in excellent repair; his under garments were durably constructed of leather, and fitted tight to a pair of serviceable and well-shaped limbs; his stockings of blue yarn were the incontrovertible work of a mother or a sister; and on his head was a three-cornered hat, which in its better days had perhaps sheltered the graver brow of the lad's father. Under his left arm was a heavy cudgel formed of an oak sapling, and retaining a part of the hardened root; and his equipment was completed by a wallet, not so abundantly stocked as to incommode the vigorous shoulders on which it hung. Brown, curly hair, well-shaped features, and bright, cheerful eyes were nature's gifts, and worth all that art could have done for his adornment.

The youth, one of whose names was Robin, finally drew from his pocket the half of a little province bill of five shillings, which, in the depreciation in that sort of currency, did but satisfy the ferryman's demand, with the surplus of a sexangular piece of parchment, valued at three pence. He then walked forward into town, with as light a step as if his day's journey had not already exceeded thirty miles, and with as eager an eye as if he were entering London city, instead of the little metropolis of a New England colony. Before Robin had proceeded far, however, it occurred to him that he knew not whither to direct his steps; so he paused, and looked up and down the narrow street, scrutinizing the small and mean wooden buildings that were scattered on either side.

'This low hovel cannot be my kinsman's dwelling,' thought he, 'nor yonder old house, where the moonlight enters at the broken casement; and truly I see none hereabouts that might be worthy of him. It would have been wise to inquire my way of the ferryman, and doubtless he would have gone with me, and earned a shilling from the Major for his pains. But the next man I meet will do as well.'

He resumed his walk, and was glad to perceive that the street now became wider, and the houses more respectable in their appearance. He soon discerned a figure moving on moderately in advance, and hastened his steps to overtake it. As Robin drew nigh, he saw that the passenger was a man in years, with a full periwig of grey hair, a wide-skirted coat of dark cloth, and silk stockings rolled above his knees. He carried a long and polished cane, which he struck down perpendicularly before him at every step; and at regular intervals he uttered two successive hems, of a peculiarly solemn and sepulchral intonation. Having made these observations, Robin laid hold of the skirt of the old man's coat, just when the light from the open door and windows of a barber's shop fell upon both their figures.

'Good evening to you, honoured sir,' said he, making a low bow, and still retaining his hold of the skirt. 'I pray you tell me whereabouts is the dwelling of my kinsman, Major Molineux.'

The youth's question was uttered very loudly; and one of the barbers, whose razor was descending on a well-soaped chin, and another who was dressing a Ramillies wig, left their occupations, and came to the door. The citizen, in the mean time, turned a long-favoured countenance upon Robin, and answered him in a tone of excessive anger and annoyance. His two sepulchral hems, however, broke into the very centre of his rebuke, with most singular effect, like a thought of the cold grave obtruding among wrathful passions.

'Let go my garment, fellow! I tell you, I know not the man you speak of. What! I have authority, I have—hem, hem—authority; and if this be the respect you show for your betters, your feet shall be brought acquainted with the stocks[2] by daylight, tomorrow morning!'

Robin released the old man's skirt, and hastened away, pursued by an ill-mannered roar of laughter from the barber shop. He was at first considerably surprised by the result of his question, but, being a shrewd youth, soon thought himself able to account for the mystery.

'This is some country representative', was his conclusion, 'who has never seen the inside of my kinsman's door, and lacks the breeding to answer a stranger civilly. The man is old, or verily—I might be tempted to turn back and smite him on the nose. Ah, Robin, Robin! even the barber's boys laugh at you for choosing such a guide! You will be wiser in time, friend Robin.'

He now became entangled in a succession of crooked and narrow streets, which crossed each other, and meandered at no great distance from the water-side. The smell of tar was obvious to his nostrils, the masts of vessels pierced the moonlight above the tops of the buildings, and the numerous signs, which Robin paused to read, informed him that he was near the centre of business. But the streets were empty, the shops were closed, and lights were visible only in the second storeys of a few dwelling-houses. At length, on the corner of a narrow lane, through which he was passing, he beheld the broad countenance of a British hero swinging before the door of an inn, whence proceeded the voices of many guests. The casement of one of the lower windows was thrown back, and a very thin curtain permitted Robin to distinguish a party at supper, round a well-furnished table. The fragrance of the good cheer steamed forth into the outer air, and the youth could not fail to recollect that the last remnant of his travelling stock of provision had yielded to his morning appetite, and that noon had found and left him dinnerless.

'Oh, that a parchment three-penny might give me a right to sit down at yonder table!' said Robin, with a sigh. 'But the Major will make me welcome to the best of his victuals; so I will even step boldly in, and inquire my way to his dwelling.'

He entered the tavern, and was guided by the murmur of voices and the fumes of tobacco to the public-room. It was a long and low apartment, with oaken walls, grown dark in the continual smoke, and a floor which was thickly sanded, but of no immaculate purity. A number of persons—the larger part of whom appeared to be mariners, or in some way connected with the sea—occupied the wooden benches, or leather-bottomed chairs, conversing on various matters, and occasionally lending their attention to some topic of general interest. Three or four little groups were draining as many bowls of punch, which the West India trade had long since made a familiar drink in the colony.

2 The stocks were an outdoor engine of imprisonment.

Others, who had the appearance of men who lived by regular and laborious handicraft, preferred the insulated bliss of an unshared potation, and became more taciturn under its influence. Nearly all, in short, evinced a predilection for the Good Creature in some of its various shapes, for this is a vice to which, as Fast Day sermons of a hundred years ago will testify, we have a long hereditary claim. The only guests to whom Robin's sympathies inclined him were two or three sheepish countrymen, who were using the inn somewhat after the fashion of a Turkish caravansary; they had gotten themselves into the darkest corner of the room, and heedless of the Nicotian atmosphere, were supping on the bread of their own ovens, and the bacon cured in their own chimney-smoke. But though Robin felt a sort of brotherhood with these strangers, his eyes were attracted from them to a person who stood near the door, holding a whispered conversation with a group of ill-dressed associates. His features were separately striking almost to grotesqueness, and the whole face left a deep impression on the memory. The forehead bulged out into a double prominence, with a vale between; the nose came boldly forth in an irregular curve, and its bridge was of more than a finger's breadth; the eyebrows were deep and shaggy, and the eyes glowed beneath them like fire in a cave.

While Robin deliberated of whom to inquire respecting his kinsman's dwelling, he was accosted by the innkeeper, a little man in a stained white apron, who had come to pay his professional welcome to the stranger. Being in the second generation from a French Protestant, he seemed to have inherited the courtesy of his parent nation; but no variety of circumstances was ever known to change his voice from the one shrill note in which he now addressed Robin.

'From the country, I presume, sir?' said he, with a profound bow. 'Beg leave to congratulate you on your arrival, and trust you intend a long stay with us. Fine town here, sir, beautiful buildings, and much that may interest a stranger. May I hope for the honour of your commands in respect to supper?'

'The man sees a family likeness! the rogue has guessed that I am related to the Major!' thought Robin, who had hitherto experienced little superfluous civility.

All eyes were now turned on the country lad, standing at the door, in his worn three-cornered hat, grey coat, leather breeches, and blue yarn stockings, leaning on an oaken cudgel, and bearing a wallet on his back.

Robin replied to the courteous innkeeper, with such an assumption of confidence as befitted the Major's relative. 'My honest friend,' he said, 'I shall make it a point to patronize your house on some occasion, when'—here he could not help lowering his voice—'when I may have more than a parchment three-pence in my pocket. My present business', continued he, speaking with lofty confidence, 'is merely to inquire my way to the dwelling of my kinsman, Major Molineux.'

There was a sudden and general movement in the room, which Robin interpreted as expressing the eagerness of each individual to become his guide. But the innkeeper turned his eyes to a written paper on the wall, which he read, or seemed to read, with occasional recurrences to the young man's figure.

'What have we here?' said he, breaking his speech into little dry fragments. '"Left the house of the subscriber, bounden servant, Hezekiah Mudge,—had on, when he went away, grey coat, leather breeches, master's third-best hat. One pound currency reward to whosoever shall lodge him in any jail of the province." Better trudge, boy; better trudge!'

Robin had begun to draw his hand towards the lighter end of the oak cudgel, but a strange hostility in every countenance induced him to relinquish his purpose of breaking the courteous innkeeper's head. As he turned to leave the room, he encountered a sneering glance from the bold-featured personage whom he had before noticed; and no sooner was he beyond the door, than he heard a general laugh, in which the innkeeper's voice might be distinguished, like the dropping of small stones into a kettle.

'Now, is it not strange,' thought Robin, with his usual shrewdness,—'is it not strange that the confession of an empty pocket should outweigh the name of my kinsman, Major Molineux? Oh, if I had one of those grinning rascals in the woods, where I and my oak sapling grew up together, I would teach him that my arm is heavy though my purse be light!'

On turning the corner of the narrow lane, Robin found himself in a spacious street, with an unbroken line of lofty houses on each side, and a steepled building at the upper end, whence the ringing of a bell announced the hour of nine. The light of the moon, and the lamps from the numerous shop-windows, discovered people promenading on the pavement, and amongst them Robin had hoped to recognize his hitherto inscrutable relative. The result of his former inquiries made him unwilling to hazard another, in a scene of such publicity, and he determined to walk slowly and silently up the street, thrusting his face close to that of every elderly gentleman, in search of the Major's lineaments. In his progress, Robin encountered many gay and gallant figures. Embroidered garments of showy colours, enormous periwigs, gold-laced hats, and silver-hilted swords glided past him and dazzled his optics. Travelled youths, imitators of the European fine gentlemen of the period, trod jauntily along, half dancing to the fashionable tunes which they hummed, and making poor Robin ashamed of his quiet and natural gait. At length, after many pauses to examine the gorgeous display of goods in the shop-windows, and after suffering some rebukes for the impertinence of his scrutiny into people's faces, the Major's kinsman found himself near the steepled building, still unsuccessful in his search. As yet, however, he had seen only one side of the thronged street; so Robin crossed, and continued the same sort of inquisition down the opposite pavement, with stronger hopes than the philosopher seeking an honest man, but with no better fortune. He had arrived about midway towards the lower end, from which his course began, when he overheard the approach of someone who struck down a cane on the flagstones at every step, uttering at regular intervals, two sepulchral hems.

'Mercy on us!' quoth Robin, recognizing the sound.

Turning a corner, which chanced to be close at his right hand, he hastened to pursue his researches in some other part of town. His patience now was wearing low, and he seemed to feel more fatigue from his rambles since he crossed the ferry, than from his journey of several days on the other side. Hunger also pleaded loudly within him, and Robin began to balance the propriety of demanding, violently, and with lifted cudgel, the necessary guidance from the first solitary passenger whom he should meet. While a resolution to this effect was gaining strength, he entered a street of mean appearance, on either side of which a row of ill-built houses was straggling towards the harbour. The moonlight fell upon no passenger along the whole extent, but in the third domicile which Robin passed there was a half-opened door, and his keen glance detected a woman's garment within.

'My luck may be better here,' said he to himself.

Accordingly, he approached the door, and beheld it shut closer as he did so; yet an open space remained, sufficing for the fair occupant to observe the stranger, without a corresponding display on her part. All that Robin could discern was a strip of scarlet petticoat, and the occasional sparkle of an eye, as if the moonbeams were trembling on some bright thing.

'Pretty mistress,' for I may call her so with a good conscience, thought the shrewd youth, since I know nothing to the contrary,—'my sweet pretty mistress, will you be kind enough to tell me whereabouts I must seek the dwelling of my kinsman, Major Molineux?'

Robin's voice was plaintive and winning, and the female, seeing nothing to be shunned in the handsome country youth, thrust open the door, and came forth into the moonlight. She was a dainty little figure, with a white neck, round arms, and a slender waist, at the extremity of which her scarlet petticoat jutted out over a hoop, as if she were standing in a balloon. Moreover, her face was oval and pretty, her hair dark beneath the little cap, and her bright eyes possessed a sly freedom, which triumphed over those of Robin.

'Major Molineux dwells here,' said this fair woman.

Now, her voice was the sweetest Robin had heard that night, yet he could not help doubting whether that sweet voice spoke Gospel truth. He looked up and down the mean street, and then surveyed the house before which they stood. It was a small, dark edifice of two storeys, the second of which projected over the lower floor, and the front apartment had the aspect of a shop for pretty commodities.

'Now, truly, I am in luck,' replied Robin, cunningly, 'and so indeed is my kinsman, the Major, in having so pretty a housekeeper. But I prithee trouble him to step to the door; I will deliver him a message from his friends in the country, and then go back to my lodgings at the inn.'

'Nay, the Major has been abed this hour or more,' said the lady of the scarlet petticoat; 'and it would be to little purpose to disturb him tonight, seeing his evening draught was of the strongest. But he is a kind-hearted man, and it would be as much as my life's worth to let a kinsman of his turn away from the door. You are the good old gentleman's very picture, and I could swear that was his rainy-weather hat. Also he has garments very much resembling those leather small-clothes. But come in, I pray, for I bid you hearty welcome in his name.'

So saying, the fair and hospitable dame took our hero by the hand; and the touch was light, and the force was gentleness, and though Robin read in her eyes what he did not hear in her words, yet the slender-waisted woman in the scarlet petticoat proved stronger than the athletic country youth. She had drawn his half-willing footsteps nearly to the threshold, when the opening of a door in the neighbourhood startled the Major's housekeeper, and, leaving the Major's kinsman, she vanished speedily into her own domicile. A heavy yawn preceded the appearance of a man, who, like the Moonshine of Pyramus and Thisbe, carried a lantern, needlessly aiding his sister luminary in the heavens. As he walked sleepily up the street, he turned his broad, dull face on Robin, and displayed a long staff, spiked at the end.

'Home, vagabond, home!' said the watchman, in accents that seemed to fall asleep as soon as they were uttered. 'Home, or we'll set you in the stocks by peep of day!'

'This is the second hint of the kind,' thought Robin. 'I wish they would end my difficulties, by setting me there tonight.'

Nevertheless, the youth felt an instinctive antipathy towards the guardian of midnight order, which at first prevented him from asking his usual question. But just when the man was about to vanish behind the corner, Robin resolved not to lose the opportunity, and shouted lustily after him,—

'I say, friend! will you guide me to the house of my kinsman, Major Molineux?'

The watchman made no reply, but turned the corner and was gone; yet Robin seemed to hear the sound of drowsy laughter stealing along the solitary street. At that moment, also, a pleasant titter saluted him from the open window above his head; he looked up, and caught the sparkle of a saucy eye; a round arm beckoned to him, and next he heard light footsteps descending the staircase within. But Robin, being of the household of a New England clergyman, was a good youth, as well as a shrewd one; so he resisted temptation, and fled away.

He now roamed desperately, and at random, through the town, almost ready to believe that a spell was on him, like that by which a wizard of his country had once kept three pursuers wandering, a whole winter night, within twenty paces of the cottage which they sought. The streets lay before him, strange and desolate, and the lights were extinguished in almost every house. Twice, however, little parties of men, among whom Robin distinguished individuals in outlandish attire, came hurrying along; but, though on both occasions, they paused to address him, such intercourse did not at all enlighten his perplexity. They did but utter a few words in some language of which Robin knew nothing, and perceiving his inability to answer, bestowed a curse upon him in plain English and hastened away. Finally, the lad determined to knock at the door of every mansion that might appear worthy to be occupied by his kinsman, trusting that perseverance would overcome the fatality that had hitherto thwarted him. Firm in this resolve, he was passing beneath the walls of a church, which formed the corner of two streets, when, as he turned into the shade of its steeple, he encountered a bulky stranger, muffled in a cloak. The man was proceeding with the speed of earnest business, but Robin planted himself full before him, holding the oak cudgel with both hands across his body as a bar to further passage.

'Halt, honest man, and answer me a question,' said he, very resolutely. 'Tell me, this instant, whereabouts is the dwelling of my kinsman, Major Molineux!'

'Keep your tongue between your teeth, fool, and let me pass!' said a deep, gruff voice, which Robin partly remembered. 'Let me pass, I say, or I'll strike you to the earth!'

'No, no, neighbour!' cried Robin, flourishing his cudgel, and then thrusting its larger end close to the man's muffled face. 'No, no, I'm not the fool you take me for, nor do you pass till I have an answer to my question. Whereabouts is the dwelling of my kinsman, Major Molineux?'

The stranger, instead of attempting to force his passage, stepped back into the moonlight, unmuffled his face, and stared full into that of Robin.

'Watch here an hour, and Major Molineux will pass by,' said he.

Robin gazed with dismay and astonishment on the unprecedented physiognomy of the speaker. The forehead with its double prominence, the broad hooked nose, the shaggy eyebrows, and fiery eyes were those which he had noticed at the inn, but the man's complexion had undergone a singular, or more properly, a twofold change. One side of the face blazed an intense red, while the other was black as midnight, the division line being in the broad bridge of the nose; and a mouth which seemed to extend from ear to ear was black or red, in contrast to the colour of the cheek.[3] The effect was as if two individual devils, a fiend of fire and a fiend of darkness, had united themselves to form this infernal visage. The stranger grinned in Robin's face, muffled his party-coloured features, and was out of sight in a moment.

'Strange things we travellers see!' ejaculated Robin.

He seated himself, however, upon the steps of the church-door, resolving to wait the appointed time for his kinsman. A few moments were consumed in philosophical speculations upon the species of man who had just left; but having settled this point shrewdly, rationally, and satisfactorily, he was compelled to look elsewhere for his amusement. And first he threw his eyes along the street. It was of more respectable appearance than most of those into which he had wandered; and the moon, creating, like the imaginative power, a beautiful strangeness in familiar objects, gave something of romance to a scene that might not have possessed it in the light of day. The irregular and often quaint architecture of the houses, some of whose roofs were broken into numerous little peaks, while others ascended, steep and narrow, into a single point, and others again were square; the pure snow-white of some of their complexions, the aged darkness of others, and the thousand sparklings, reflected from bright substances in the walls of many; these matters engaged Robin's attention for a while, and then began to grow wearisome. Next he endeavoured to define the forms of distant objects, starting away, with almost ghostly indistinctness, just as his eye appeared to grasp them; and finally he took a minute survey of an edifice which stood on the opposite side of the street, directly in front of the church-door, where he was stationed. It was a large, square mansion, distinguished from its neighbours by a balcony, which rested on tall pillars, and by an elaborate Gothic window, communicating therewith.

'Perhaps this is the very house I have been seeking,' thought Robin.

Then he strove to speed away the time, by listening to a murmur which swept continually along the street, yet was scarcely audible, except to an unaccustomed ear like his; it was a low, dull, dreamy sound, compounded of many noises, each of which was at too great a distance to be separately heard. Robin marvelled at this snore of a sleeping town, and marvelled more whenever its continuity was broken by now and then a distant shout, apparently loud where it originated. But altogether it was a sleep-inspiring sound, and, to shake off its drowsy influence, Robin arose, and climbed a window-frame, that he might view the interior of the church. There the moonbeams

3 The disguise of an Indian in war paint was much used by the early revolutionaries, as in the Boston Tea Party.

came trembling in, and fell down upon the deserted pews, and extended along the quiet aisles. A fainter yet more awful radiance was hovering around the pulpit, and one solitary ray had dared to rest upon the open page of the great Bible. Had nature, in that deep hour, become a worshipper in the house which man had builded? Or was that heavenly light the visible sanctity of the place,—visible because no earthly and impure feet were within the walls? The scene made Robin's heart shiver with a sensation of loneliness stronger than he had ever felt in the remotest depths of his native woods; so he turned away and sat down again before the door. There were graves around the church, and now an uneasy thought obtruded into Robin's breast. What if the object of his search, which had been so often and so strangely thwarted, were all the time mouldering in his shroud? What if his kinsman should glide through yonder gate, and nod and smile to him in dimly passing by?

'Oh that any breathing thing were here with me!' said Robin.

Recalling his thoughts from this uncomfortable track, he sent them over forest, hill, and stream, and attempted to imagine how that evening of ambiguity and weariness had been spent by his father's household. He pictured them assembled at the door, beneath the tree, the great old tree, which had been spared for its huge twisted trunk and venerable shade, when a thousand leafy brethren fell. There, at the going down of the summer sun, it was his father's custom to perform domestic worship, that the neighbours might come and join with him like brothers of the family, and that the wayfaring man might pause to drink at that fountain, and keep his heart pure by freshening the memory of home. Robin distinguished the seat of every individual of the little audience; he saw the good man in the midst, holding the Scriptures in the golden light that fell from the western clouds; he beheld him close the book and all rise up to pray. He heard the old thanksgivings for daily mercies, the old supplications for their continuance, to which he had so often listened in weariness, but which were now among his dear remembrances. He perceived the slight inequality of his father's voice when he came to speak of the absent one; he noted how his mother turned her face to the broad and knotted trunk; how his elder brother scorned, because the beard was rough upon his upper lip, to permit his features to be moved; how the younger sister drew down a low hanging branch before her eyes; and how the little one of all, whose sports had hitherto broken the decorum of the scene, understood the prayer for her playmate, and burst into clamorous grief. Then he saw them go in at the door; and when Robin would have entered also, the latch tinkled into its place, and he was excluded from his home.

'Am I here, or there?' cried Robin, starting; for all at once, when his thoughts had become visible and audible in a dream, the long, wide, solitary street shone out before him.

He aroused himself, and endeavoured to fix his attention steadily upon the large edifice which he had surveyed before. But still his mind kept vibrating between fancy and reality; by turns, the pillars of the balcony lengthened into the tall, bare stems of pines, dwindled down to human figures, settled again into their true shape and size, and then commenced a new succession of changes. For a single moment, when he deemed himself awake, he could have sworn that a visage—one which he seemed to remember, yet could not absolutely name as his kinsman's—was looking towards him from the Gothic window. A deeper sleep wrestled with and nearly overcame him, but fled at the sound of footsteps along the opposite pavement. Robin rubbed his eyes, discerned a man passing at the foot of the balcony, and addressed him in a loud, peevish, and lamentable cry.

'Hallo, friend! must I wait here all night for my kinsman, Major Molineux?'

The sleeping echoes awoke, and answered the voice; and the passenger, barely able to discern a figure sitting in the oblique shade of the steeple, traversed the street to obtain a nearer view. He was himself a gentleman in his prime, of open, intelligent, cheerful, and altogether prepossessing countenance. Perceiving a country youth, apparently homeless and without friends, he accosted him in a tone of real kindness, which had become strange to Robin's ears.

'Well, my good lad, why are you sitting here?' inquired he. 'Can I be of service to you in any way?'

'I am afraid not, sir,' replied Robin, despondingly; 'yet I shall take it kindly, if you'll answer me a single question. I've been searching, half the night, for one Major Molineux; now, sir, is there really such a person in these parts, or am I dreaming?'

'Major Molineux! The name is not altogether strange to me,' said the gentleman, smiling. 'Have you any objection to telling me the nature of your business with him?'

Then Robin briefly related that his father was a clergyman, settled on a small salary, at a long distance back in the country, and that he and Major Molineux were brothers' children. The Major, having inherited riches, and acquired civil and military rank, had visited his cousin, in great pomp, a year or two before; had manifested much interest in Robin and an elder brother, and, being childless himself, had thrown out hints respecting the future establishment of one of them in life. The elder brother was destined to succeed to the farm which his father cultivated in the interval of sacred duties; it was therefore determined that Robin should profit by his kinsman's generous intentions, especially as he seemed to be rather the favourite, and was thought to possess other necessary endowments.

'For I have the name of being a shrewd youth,' observed Robin, in this part of the story.

'I doubt not you deserve it,' replied his new friend, good-naturedly; 'but pray proceed.'

'Well, sir, being nearly eighteen years old, and well grown, as you see,' continued Robin, drawing himself up to his full height, 'I thought it high time to begin in the world. So my mother and sister put me in handsome trim, and my father gave me half the remnant of his last year's salary, and five days ago I started for this place, to pay the Major a visit. But, would you believe it, sir! I crossed the ferry a little after dark, and have yet found nobody that would show me the way to his dwelling; only, an hour or two since, I was told to wait here, and Major Molineux would pass by.'

'Can you describe the man who told you this?' inquired the gentleman.

'Oh, he was a very ill-favoured fellow, sir,' replied Robin, 'with two great bumps on his forehead, a hook nose, fiery eyes; and, what struck me as the strangest, his face was of two different colours. Do you happen to know such a man, sir?'

'Not intimately,' answered the stranger, 'but I chanced to meet him a little time previous to your stopping me. I believe you may trust his word, and that the Major will very shortly pass through this street. In the mean time, as I have a singular curiosity to witness your meeting, I will sit down here upon the steps and bear you company.'

He seated himself accordingly, and soon engaged his companion in animated discourse. It was but of brief continuance, however, for a noise of shouting, which had long been remotely audible, drew so much nearer that Robin inquired its cause.

'What may be the meaning of this uproar?' asked he. 'Truly, if your town be always as noisy, I shall find little sleep while I am an inhabitant.'

'Why, indeed, friend Robin, there do appear to be three or four riotous fellows abroad tonight,' replied the gentleman. 'You must not expect all the stillness of your native woods here in our streets. But the watch will shortly be at the heels of these lads and'—

'Ay, and set them in the stocks by peep of day,' interrupted Robin, recollecting his own encounter with the drowsy lantern-bearer. 'But, dear sir, if I may trust my ears, an army of watchmen would never make head against such a multitude of rioters. There were at least a thousand voices went up to make that one shout.'

'May not a man have several voices, Robin, as well as two complexions?' said his friend.

'Perhaps a man may; but Heaven forbid that a woman should!' responded the shrewd youth, thinking of the seductive tones of the Major's housekeeper.

The sounds of a trumpet in some neighbouring street now became so evident and continual, that Robin's curiosity was strongly excited. In addition to the shouts, he heard frequent bursts from many instruments of discord, and a wild and confused laughter filled up the intervals. Robin rose from the steps, and looked wistfully towards the point whither people seemed to be hastening.

'Surely some prodigious merry-making is going on,' exclaimed he. 'I have laughed very little since I left home, sir, and should be sorry to lose an opportunity. Shall we step round the corner by that darkish house, and take our share of the fun?'

'Sit down again, sit down, good Robin,' replied the gentleman, laying his hand on the skirt of the grey coat. 'You forget that we must wait here for your kinsman; and there is reason to believe that he will pass by, in the course of a very few moments.'

The near approach of the uproar had now disturbed the neighbourhood; windows flew open on all sides; and many heads, in the attire of the pillow, and confused by sleep suddenly broken, were protruded to the gaze of whoever had leisure to observe them. Eager voices hailed each other from house to house, all demanding the explanation, which not a soul could give. Half-dressed men hurried towards the unknown commotion, stumbling as they went over the stone steps that thrust themselves into the narrow foot-walk. The shouts, the laughter, and the tuneless bray, the antipodes of music, came onwards with increasing din, till scattered individuals, and then denser bodies, began to appear round a corner at a distance of a hundred yards.

'Will you recognize your kinsman, if he passed in this crowd?' inquired the gentleman.

'Indeed, I can't warrant it, sir; but I'll take my stand here, and keep a bright look-out,' answered Robin, descending to the outer edge of the pavement.

A mighty stream of people now emptied into the street, and came rolling slowly towards the church. A single horseman wheeled the corner in the midst of them, and close behind him came a band of fearful wind-instruments, sending forth a fresher discord now that no intervening buildings kept it from the ear. Then a redder light disturbed the moonbeams, and a dense multitude of torches shone along the street, concealing, by their glare, whatever object they illuminated. The single horseman, clad in a military dress, and bearing a drawn sword, rode onward as the leader, and, by his fierce and variegated countenance, appeared like war personified; the red of one cheek was an emblem of fire and sword; the blackness of the other betokened the mourning that attends them. In his train were wild figures in the Indian dress, and many fantastic shapes without a model, giving the whole march a visionary air, as if a dream had broken forth from some feverish brain, and were sweeping visibly through the midnight streets. A mass of people, inactive, except as applauding spectators, hemmed the procession in; and several women ran along the sidewalk, piercing the confusion of heavier sounds with their shrill voices of mirth or terror.

'The double-faced fellow has his eye upon me,' muttered Robin, with an indefinite but an uncomfortable idea that he was himself to bear a part in the pageantry.

The leader turned himself in the saddle, and fixed his glance full upon the country youth, as the steed went slowly by. When Robin had freed his eyes from those fiery ones, the musicians were passing before him, and the torches were close at hand; but the unsteady brightness of the latter formed a veil which he could not penetrate. The rattling of wheels over the stones sometimes found its way to his ear, and the confused traces of a human form appeared at intervals, and then melted into the vivid light. A moment more, and the leader thundered a command to halt: the trumpets vomited a horrid breath, and then held their peace; the shouts and laughter of the people died away, and there remained only a universal hum, allied to silence. Right before Robin's eyes was an uncovered cart. There the torches blazed the brightest, there the moon shone out like day, and there, in tar-and-feathery dignity,[4] sat his kinsman, Major Molineux!

He was an elderly man, of large and majestic person, and strong, square features, betokening a steady soul; but steady as it was, his enemies had found means to shake it. His face was pale as death, and far more ghastly; the broad forehead was contracted in his agony, so that his eyebrows formed one grizzled line; his eyes were red and wild, and the foam hung white upon his quivering lip. His whole frame was agitated by a quick and continual tremor, which his pride strove to quell, even in those circumstances of overwhelming humiliation. But perhaps the bitterest pang of all was when his eyes met those of Robin; for he evidently knew him on the instant, as the youth stood witnessing the foul disgrace of a head grown grey in honour. They stared at each other in silence, and Robin's knees shook, and his hair bristled, with a mixture of pity and terror. Soon, however, a bewildering excitement began to seize upon his mind; the preceding adventures of the night, the unexpected appearance of the crowd,

4 In this rough punishment a man was stripped naked, covered with hot tar, and sprinkled with feathers. It was frequently visited upon those suspected of resisting the Revolution.

the torches, the confused din and the hush that followed, the spectre of his kinsman reviled by that great multitude,—all this, and more than all, a perception of tremendous ridicule in the whole scene, affected him with a sort of mental inebriety. At that moment a voice of sluggish merriment saluted Robin's ears; he turned instinctively, and just behind the corner of the church stood the lantern-bearer, rubbing his eyes, and drowsily enjoying the lad's amazement. Then he heard a peal of laughter like the ringing of silvery bells; a woman twitched his arm, a saucy eye met his, and he saw the lady of the scarlet petticoat. A sharp, dry cachinnation appealed to his memory, and, standing on tiptoe in the crowd, with his white apron over his head, he beheld the courteous little innkeeper. And lastly, there sailed over the heads of the multitude a great, broad laugh, broken in the midst by two sepulchral hems; thus, 'haw, haw, haw,—hem, hem,—haw, haw, haw, haw!'

The sound proceeded from the balcony of the opposite edifice, and thither Robin turned his eyes. In front of the Gothic window stood the old citizen, wrapped in a wide gown, his grey periwig exchanged for a nightcap, which was thrust back from his forehead, and his silk stockings hanging about his legs. He supported himself on his polished cane in a fit of convulsive merriment, which manifested itself on his solemn old features like a funny inscription on a tombstone. Then Robin seemed to hear the voices of the barbers, of the guests of the inn, and of all who had made sport of him that night. The contagion was spreading among the multitude, when all at once, it seized upon Robin, and he sent forth a shout of laughter that echoed through the street,—every man shook his sides, every man emptied his lungs, but Robin's shout was the loudest there. The cloud-spirits peeped from their silvery islands, as the congregated mirth went roaring up the sky! The Man in the Moon heard the far bellow. 'Oho,' quoth he, 'the old earth is frolicsome tonight!'

When there was a momentary calm in that tempestuous sea of sound, the leader gave the sign, the procession resumed its march. On they went, like fiends that throng in mockery around some dead potentate, mighty no more, but majestic still in his agony. On they went, in counterfeited pomp, in senseless uproar, in frenzied merriment, trampling all on an old man's heart. On swept the tumult, and left a silent street behind.

'Well, Robin, are you dreaming?' inquired the gentleman, laying his hand on the youth's shoulder.

Robin started, and withdrew his arm from the stone post to which he had instinctively clung, as the living stream rolled by him. His cheek was somewhat pale, and his eye not quite as lively as in the earlier part of the evening.

'Will you be kind enough to show me the way to the ferry?' said he, after a moment's pause.

'You have, then, adopted a new subject of inquiry?' observed his companion, with a smile.

'Why, yes, sir,' replied Robin, rather dryly. 'Thanks to you, and to my other friends, I have at last met my kinsman, and he will scarce desire to see my face again. I begin to grow weary of a town life, sir. Will you show me the way to the ferry?'

'No, my good friend Robin,—not tonight, at least,' said the gentleman. 'Some few days hence, if you wish it, I will speed you on your journey. Or, if you prefer to remain with us, perhaps, as you are a shrewd youth, you may rise in the world without the help of your kinsman, Major Molineux.'

1832

# Edgar Allan Poe

1809–1849

Born in Boston into a theatrical family, Edgar Allan Poe became an orphan at an early age and was adopted and raised by John Allan, a Virginia tobacco exporter. He began his schooling in England but returned to the United States to attend the University of Virginia. Expelled for drinking and gambling, he entered the army for two years and later attended the United States Military Academy at West Point, from which he was also expelled.

Poet and short-story writer, critic and editor, he aimed for a 'unity of effect' in all his writings. In his essay 'The Poetic Principle', he suggests that brevity, a sense of mystery, some degree of verbal magic, and immediate emotional effect are the qualities he seeks in poetry. These are also the qualities he brings to his own short fiction. In 'The Purloined Letter', he makes the mystery story his own unique creation. He became a major influence on the detective story.

## The Purloined Letter

*Nil sapientiae odiosius acumine nimio.*[1]

—Seneca

At Paris, just after dark one gusty evening in the autumn of 18—, I was enjoying the twofold luxury of meditation and a meerschaum, in company with my friend, C. Auguste Dupin, in his little back library, or book-closet, *au troisième*, No. 33 *Rue Dunôt, Faubourg St Germain.*[2] For one hour at least we had maintained a profound silence; while each, to any casual observer, might have seemed intently and exclusively occupied with the curling eddies of smoke that oppressed the atmosphere of the chamber. For myself, however, I was mentally discussing certain topics which had formed matter for conversation between us at an earlier period of the evening; I mean the affair of the Rue Morgue, and the mystery attending the murder of Marie Rogêt.[3] I looked upon it, therefore, as something of a coincidence, when the door of our apartment was

1 Nothing is more offensive to the wise than an excess of trickery.
2 On the third floor in a fashionable district in Paris.
3 These are the subjects of previous detective stories by Poe.

thrown open and admitted our old acquaintance, Monsieur G——, the Prefect of the Parisian police.

We gave him a hearty welcome; for there was nearly half as much of the entertaining as of the contemptible about the man, and we had not seen him for several years. We had been sitting in the dark, and Dupin now rose for the purpose of lighting a lamp, but sat down again, without doing so, upon G.'s saying that he had called to consult us, or rather to ask the opinion of my friend, about some official business which had occasioned a great deal of trouble.

'If it is any point requiring reflection,' observed Dupin, as he forbore to enkindle the wick, 'we shall examine it to better purpose in the dark.'

'That is another of your odd notions,' said the Prefect, who had the fashion of calling everything 'odd' that was beyond his comprehension, and thus lived amid an absolute legion of 'oddities'.

'Very true,' said Dupin, as he supplied his visitor with a pipe, and rolled toward him a comfortable chair.

'And what is the difficulty now?' I asked. 'Nothing more in the assassination way I hope?'

'Oh, no; nothing of that nature. The fact is, the business is *very* simple indeed, and I make no doubt that we can manage it sufficiently well ourselves; but then I thought Dupin would like to hear the details of it because it is so excessively *odd*.'

'Simple and odd,' said Dupin.

'Why, yes; and not exactly that either. The fact is, we have all been a good deal puzzled because the affair *is* so simple, and yet baffles us altogether.'

'Perhaps it is the very simplicity of the thing which puts you at fault,' said my friend.

'What nonsense you *do* talk!' replied the Prefect, laughing heartily.

'Perhaps the mystery is a little *too* plain,' said Dupin.

'Oh, good heavens! who ever heard of such an idea?'

'A little *too* self-evident.'

'Ha! ha! ha!—ha! ha! ha!—ho! ho! ho!' roared our visitor, profoundly amused, 'oh, Dupin, you will be the death of me yet!'

'And what, after all, *is* the matter on hand?' I asked.

'Why, I will tell you,' replied the Prefect, as he gave a long, steady, and contemplative puff, and settled himself in his chair. 'I will tell you in a few words; but, before I begin, let me caution you that this is an affair demanding the greatest secrecy, and that I should most probably lose the position I now hold, were it known that I confided it to anyone.'

'Proceed,' said I.

'Or not,' said Dupin.

'Well, then; I have received personal information, from a very high quarter, that a certain document of the last importance has been purloined from the royal apartments. The individual who purloined it is known; this beyond a doubt; he was seen to take it. It is known, also, that it still remains in his possession.'

'How is this known?' asked Dupin.

'It is clearly inferred', replied the Prefect, 'from the nature of the document, and from the non-appearance of certain results which would at once arise from its passing *out* of the robber's possession—that is to say, from his employing it as he must design in the end to employ it.'

'Be a little more explicit,' I said.

'Well, I may venture so far as to say that the paper gives its holder a certain power in a certain quarter where such power is immensely valuable.' The Prefect was fond of the cant of diplomacy.

'Still I do not quite understand,' said Dupin.

'No? Well; the disclosure of the document to a third person, who shall be nameless, would bring in question the honour of a personage of most exalted station; and this fact gives the holder of the document an ascendancy over the illustrious personage whose honour and peace are so jeopardized.'

'But this ascendancy', I interposed, 'would depend upon the robber's knowledge of the loser's knowledge of the robber. Who would dare—'

'The thief', said G., 'is the Minister D——, who dares all things, those unbecoming as well as becoming a man. The method of the theft was not less ingenious than bold. The document in question—a letter, to be frank—had been received by the personage robbed while in the royal *boudoir*. During its perusal she was suddenly interrupted by the entrance of the other exalted personage from whom especially it was her wish to conceal it. After a hurried and vain endeavour to thrust it in a drawer, she was forced to place it, open as it was, upon a table. The address, however, was uppermost, and, the contents thus unexposed, the letter escaped notice. At this juncture enters the Minister D——. His lynx eye immediately perceives the paper, recognizes the handwriting of the address, observes the confusion of the personage addressed, and fathoms her secret. After some business transactions, hurried through in his ordinary manner, he produces a letter somewhat similar to the one in question, opens it, pretends to read it, and then places it in close juxtaposition to the other. Again he converses, for some fifteen minutes, upon the public affairs. At length, in taking leave, he takes also from the table the letter to which he had no claim. Its rightful owner saw, but, of course, dared not call attention to the act, in the presence of the third personage who stood at her elbow. The Minister decamped; leaving his own letter—one of no importance—upon the table.'

'Here, then,' said Dupin to me, 'you have precisely what you demand to make the ascendancy complete—the robber's knowledge of the loser's knowledge of the robber.'

'Yes,' replied the Prefect; 'and the power thus attained has, for some months past, been wielded, for political purposes, to a very dangerous extent. The personage robbed is more thoroughly convinced, every day, of the necessity of reclaiming her letter. But this, of course, cannot be done openly. In fine, driven to despair, she has committed the matter to me.'

'Than whom', said Dupin, amid a perfect whirlwind of smoke, 'no more sagacious agent could, I suppose, be desired, or even imagined.'

'You flatter me,' replied the Prefect; 'but it is possible that some such opinion may have been entertained.'

'It is clear,' said I, 'as you observe, that the letter is still in the possession of the Minister; since it is this possession, and not any employment of the letter, which bestows the power. With the employment the power departs.'

'True,' said G.; 'and upon this conviction I proceeded. My first care was to make thorough search of the Minister's hotel;[4] and here my chief embarrassment lay in the necessity of searching without his knowledge. Beyond all things, I have been warned of the danger which would result from giving him reason to suspect our design.'

'But,' said I, 'you are quite *au fait* in these investigations. The Parisian police have done this thing often before.'

'Oh, yes; and for this reason I did not despair. The habits of the Minister gave me, too, a great advantage. He is frequently absent from home at night. His servants are by no means numerous. They sleep at a distance from their master's apartment, and, being chiefly Neapolitans, are readily made drunk. I have keys, as you know, with which I can open any chamber or cabinet in Paris. For three months a night has not passed, during the greater part of which I have not been engaged, personally, in ransacking the D—— Hotel. My honour is interested, and, to mention a great secret, the reward is enormous. So I did not abandon the search until I had become fully satisfied that the thief is a more astute man than myself. I fancy that I have investigated every nook and corner of the premises in which it is possible that the paper can be concealed.'

'But is it not possible', I suggested, 'that although the letter may be in possession of the Minister, as it unquestionably is, he may have concealed it elsewhere than upon his own premises?'

'This is barely possible,' said Dupin. 'The present peculiar condition of affairs at court, and especially of those intrigues in which D—— is known to be involved, would render the instant availability of the document—its susceptibility of being produced at a moment's notice—a point of nearly equal importance with its possession.'

'Its susceptibility of being produced?' said I.

'That is to say, of being *destroyed*,' said Dupin.

'True,' I observed; 'the paper is clearly then upon the premises. As for its being upon the person of the Minister, we may consider that as out of the question.'

'Entirely,' said the Prefect. 'He has been twice waylaid, as if by footpads, and his person rigidly searched under my own inspection.'

'You might have spared yourself this trouble,' said Dupin. 'D——, I presume, is not altogether a fool, and, if not, must have anticipated these waylayings, as a matter of course.'

'Not *altogether* a fool,' said G., 'but then he is a poet, which I take to be only one remove from a fool.'

'True,' said Dupin, after a long and thoughtful whiff from his meerschaum, 'although I have been guilty of certain doggerel myself.'

'Suppose you detail', said I, 'the particulars of your search.'

'Why, the fact is, we took our time, and we searched *everywhere*. I have had long experience in these affairs. I took the entire building, room by room; devoting the

4 'hotel' in the French sense: a large building; in this case a private house in the city

nights of a whole week to each. We examined, first, the furniture of each apartment. We opened every possible drawer; and I presume you know that, to a properly trained police agent, such a thing as a "*secret*" drawer is impossible. Any man is a dolt who permits a "secret" drawer to escape him in a search of this kind. The thing is so plain. There is a certain amount of bulk—of space—to be accounted for in every cabinet. Then we have accurate rules. The fiftieth part of a line could not escape us. After the cabinets we took the chairs. The cushions we probed with the fine long needles you have seen me employ. From the table we removed the tops.'

'Why so?'

'Sometimes the top of a table, or other similarly arranged piece of furniture, is removed by the person wishing to conceal an article; then the leg is excavated, the article deposited within the cavity, and the top replaced. The bottoms and tops of bedposts are employed in the same way.'

'But could not the cavity be detected by sounding?' I asked.

'By no means, if, when the article is deposited, a sufficient wadding of cotton be placed around it. Besides, in our case, we were obliged to proceed without noise.'

'But you could not have removed—you could not have taken to pieces *all* the articles of furniture in which it would have been possible to make a deposit in the manner you mention. A letter may be compressed into a thin spiral roll, not differing much in shape or bulk from a large knitting needle, and in this form it might be inserted into the rung of a chair, for example. You did not take to pieces all the chairs?'

'Certainly not; but we did better—we examined the rungs of every chair in the hotel, and, indeed, the jointings of every description of furniture, by the aid of a most powerful microscope. Had there been any traces of recent disturbance we should not have failed to detect it instantly. A single grain of gimlet dust, for example, would have been as obvious as an apple. Any disorder in the gluing—any unusual gaping in the joints—would have sufficed to insure detection.'

'I presume you looked to the mirrors, between the boards and the plates, and you probed the beds and the bedclothes, as well as the curtains and carpets.'

'That of course; and when we had absolutely completed every particle of furniture in this way, then we examined the house itself. We divided its entire surface into compartments, which we numbered, so that none might be missed; then we scrutinized each individual square inch throughout the premises, including the two houses immediately adjoining, with the microscope, as before.'

'The two houses adjoining!' I exclaimed; 'you must have had a great deal of trouble.'

'We had; but the reward offered is prodigious.'

'You included the *grounds* about the houses?'

'All the grounds are paved with brick. They gave us comparatively little trouble. We examined the moss between the bricks, and found it undisturbed.'

'You looked among D——'s papers, of course, and into the books of the library?'

'Certainly; we opened every package and parcel; we not only opened every book, but we turned over every leaf in each volume, not contenting ourselves with a mere shake, according to the fashion of some of our police officers. We also measured the thickness of every book *cover*, with the most accurate admeasurement, and applied to each the most jealous scrutiny of the microscope. Had any of the bindings been recently meddled with, it would have been utterly impossible that the fact should have escaped observation. Some five or six volumes, just from the hands of the binder, we carefully probed, longitudinally, with needles.'

'You explored the floors beneath the carpets?'

'Beyond a doubt. We removed every carpet, and examined the boards with the microscope.'

'And the paper on the walls?'

'Yes.'

'You looked into the cellars?'

'We did.'

'Then', I said, 'you have been making a miscalculation, and the letter is *not* upon the premises, as you suppose.'

'I fear you are right there,' said the Prefect. 'And now, Dupin, what would you advise me to do?'

'To make a thorough research of the premises.'

'That is absolutely needless,' replied G., 'I am not more sure that I breathe than I am that the letter is not at the hotel.'

'I have no better advice to give you,' said Dupin. 'You have, of course, an accurate description of the letter?'

'Oh, yes!'—And here the Prefect, producing a memorandum book, proceeded to read aloud a minute account of the internal, and especially of the external, appearance of the missing document. Soon after finishing the perusal of this description, he took his departure, more entirely depressed in spirits than I had ever known the good gentleman before.

In about a month afterward he paid us another visit, and found us occupied very nearly as before. He took a pipe and a chair and entered into some ordinary conversation. At length I said:

'Well, but G., what of the purloined letter? I presume you have at last made up your mind that there is no such thing as overreaching the Minister?'

'Confound him, say I—yes; I made the re-examination, however, as Dupin suggested—but it was all labour lost, as I knew it would be.'

'How much was the reward offered, did you say?' asked Dupin.

'Why, a very great deal—a *very* liberal reward—I don't like to say how much, precisely; but one thing I *will* say, that I wouldn't mind giving my individual cheque for fifty thousand francs to any one who could obtain me that letter. The fact is, it is becoming of more and more importance every day; and the reward has been lately doubled. If it were trebled, however, I could do no more than I have done.'

'Why, yes,' said Dupin, drawlingly, between the whiffs of his meerschaum, 'I really—think, G., you have not exerted yourself—to the utmost in this matter. You might—do a little more, I think, eh?'

'How?—in what way?'

'Why—puff, puff—you might—puff, puff—employ counsel in the matter, eh?—puff, puff, puff. Do you remember the story they tell of Abernethy?'

'No; hang Abernethy!'

'To be sure! hang him and welcome. But, once upon a time, a certain rich miser conceived the design of spunging upon this Abernethy for a medical opinion. Getting up, for this purpose, an ordinary conversation in a private company, he insinuated his case to the physician, as that of an imaginary individual.

' "We will suppose", said the miser, "that his symptoms are such and such; now, doctor, what would you have directed him to take?"

' "Take!" said Abernethy, "why, take *advice*, to be sure." '

'But,' said the Prefect, a little discomposed, '*I* am *perfectly* willing to take advice, and to pay for it. I would *really* give fifty thousand francs to anyone who would aid me in the matter.'

'In that case,' replied Dupin, opening a drawer, and producing a chequebook, 'you may as well fill me up a cheque for the amount mentioned. When you have signed it, I will hand you the letter.'

I was astounded. The Prefect appeared absolutely thunder-stricken. For some minutes he remained speechless and motionless, looking incredulously at my friend with open mouth, and eyes that seemed starting from their sockets; then apparently recovering himself in some measure, he seized a pen, and after several pauses and vacant stares, finally filled up and signed a cheque for fifty thousand francs, and handed it across the table to Dupin. The latter examined it carefully and deposited it in his pocketbook; then, unlocking an *escritoire*, took thence a letter and gave it to the prefect. This functionary grasped it in a perfect agony of joy, opened it with a trembling hand, cast a rapid glance at its contents, and then, scrambling and struggling to the door, rushed at length unceremoniously from the room and from the house, without having uttered a syllable since Dupin had requested him to fill up the cheque.

When he had gone, my friend entered into some explanations.

'The Parisian police', he said, 'are exceedingly able in their way. They are persevering, ingenious, cunning, and thoroughly versed in the knowledge which their duties seem chiefly to demand. Thus, when G. detailed to us his mode of searching the premises at the Hotel D——, I felt entire confidence in his having made a satisfactory investigation—so far as his labours extended.'

'So far as his labours extended?' said I.

'Yes,' said Dupin, 'The measures adopted were not only the best of their kind, but carried out to absolute perfection. Had the letter been deposited within the range of their search, these fellows would, beyond a question, have found it.'

I merely laughed—but he seemed quite serious in all that he said.

'The measures, then,' he continued, 'were good in their kind, and well executed; their defect lay in their being inapplicable to the case and to the man. A certain set of highly ingenious resources are, with the Prefect, a sort of Procrustean bed, to which he forcibly adapts his designs. But he perpetually errs by being too deep or too shallow for the matter at hand; and many a schoolboy is a better reasoner than he. I knew one about eight years of age, whose success at guessing in the game of "even and odd" attracted universal admiration. This game is simple, and is played with marbles. One player holds in his hand a number of these toys, and demands of another whether that number is even or odd. If the guess is right, the guesser wins one; if wrong, he loses one. The boy to whom I allude won all the marbles at school. Of course he had some principle of guessing; and this lay in mere observation and admeasurements of the astuteness of his opponents. For example, an arrant simpleton is his opponent, and holding up his closed hand, asks, "Are they even or odd?" Our schoolboy replies, "Odd," and loses; but upon the second trial he wins, for he then says to himself: "The simpleton had them even upon the first trial, and his amount of cunning is just sufficient to make him have them odd upon the second; I will therefore guess odd";—he guesses odd, and wins. Now, with a simpleton a degree above the first, he would have reasoned thus: "This fellow finds that in the first instance I guessed odd, and, in the second, he will propose to himself, upon the first impulse, a simple variation from even to odd, as did the first simpleton; but then a second thought will suggest that this is too simple a variation, and finally he will decide upon putting it even as before. I will therefore guess even";—he guesses even, and wins. Now this mode of reasoning in the schoolboy, whom his fellows termed "lucky",—what, in its last analysis, is it?'

'It is merely', I said, 'an identification of the reasoner's intellect with that of his opponent.'

'It is,' said Dupin; 'and, upon inquiring of the boy by what means he effected the *thorough* identification in which his success consisted, I received answer as follows; "When I wish to find out how wise, or how stupid, or how good, or how wicked is anyone, or what are his thoughts at the moment, I fashion the expression of my face, as accurately as possible, in accordance with the expression of his, and then wait to see what thoughts or sentiments arise in my mind or heart, as if to match or correspond with the expression." This response of the schoolboy lies at the bottom of all the spurious profundity which has been attributed to Rochefoucault, to La Bougive, to Machiavelli, and to Campanella.'

'And the identification', I said, 'of the reasoner's intellect with that of his opponent, depends, if I understand you aright, upon the accuracy with which the opponent's intellect is admeasured.'

'For its practical value it depends upon this,' replied Dupin; 'and the Prefect and his cohort fail so frequently, first, by default of this identification and, secondly, by ill-admeasurement, or rather through non-admeasurement, of the intellect with which they are engaged. They consider only their *own* ideas of ingenuity; and, in searching for anything hidden, advert only to the modes in which *they* would have hidden it. They are right in this much—that their own ingenuity is a faithful representative of that of the *mass*; but when the cunning of the individual felon is diverse in character from their own, the felon foils them, of course. This always happens when it is above their own, and very usually when it is below. They have no variation of principle in their investigations; at best, when urged by some unusual emergency—by some extraordinary reward—they extend or exaggerate their old modes of *practice*, without touching their principles. What, for example, in this case of D——, has been done to vary the principle of action? What is all this boring, and probing, and sounding, and scrutinizing with the microscope, and dividing the surface of the building into registered square inches—what is it all but an exaggeration *of the application* of the one principle or set of principles of search, which are based upon the one set of notions regarding human ingenuity, to which the Prefect, in the long routine of his duty, has been accustomed? Do you not see he has taken it for granted that *all* men proceed to conceal a letter, not exactly in a gimlet-hole bored in a chair leg, but, at least, in *some* out-of-the-way hole or corner suggested by the same tenor of thought which would urge a man to secrete a letter in a gimlet-hole bored in a chair leg? And do you not see also, that such *recherchés* nooks for concealment are adapted only for ordinary occasions, and would be adopted only by ordinary intellects; for, in all cases of concealment, a disposal of the article concealed—a disposal of it in this *recherché* manner,—is, in the very first instance, presumable and presumed; and thus its discovery depends, not at all upon the acumen, but altogether upon the mere care, patience, and determination of the seekers; and where the case is of importance—or, what amounts to the same thing in the political eyes, when the reward is of magnitude,—the qualities in question have *never* been known to fail. You will now understand what I mean in suggesting that, had the purloined letter been hidden anywhere within the limits of the Prefect's examination—in other words, had the principle of its concealment been comprehended within the principles of the Prefect—its discovery would have been a matter altogether without question. This functionary, however, has been thoroughly mystified; and the remote source of his defeat lies in the supposition that the Minister is a fool, because he has acquired renown as a poet. All fools are poets; this the Prefect *feels*; and he is merely guilty of a *non distributio medii* in thence inferring that all poets are fools.'

'But is this really the poet?' I asked. 'There are two brothers, I know; and both have attained reputation in letters. The Minister I believe has written learnedly on the Differential Calculus. He is a mathematician, and no poet.'

'You are mistaken; I know him well; he is both. As poet *and* mathematician, he would reason well; as mere mathematician, he could not have reasoned at all, and thus would have been at the mercy of the Prefect.'

'You surprise me', I said, 'by these opinions, which have been contradicted by the voice of the world. You do not mean to set at naught the well-digested idea of centuries. The mathematical reason has long been regarded as the reason *par excellence.*'

'"*Il y a à parier*"', replied Dupin, quoting from Chamfort, '"*que toute idée publique, toute convention reçue, est une sottise, car elle a convenu au plus grand nombre.*"[5] The mathematicians, I grant you, have done their best to promulgate the popular error to which you allude, and which is none the less an error for its promulgation as truth. With an art worthy a better cause, for example, they have insinuated the term "analysis" into application to algebra. The French are the originators of this particular deception; but if a term is of any importance—if words derive any value from applicability—then "analysis" conveys "algebra" about as much as, in Latin, "ambitus" implies "*ambition*", "*religio*" "*religion*", or "*hommes honesti*" a set of *honourable* men.'

'You have a quarrel on hand, I see,' said I, 'with some of the algebraists of Paris; but proceed.'

5 'The odds are that any public idea or accepted opinion is stupid, because it has suited the majority of people.'

'I dispute the availability, and thus the value, of that reason which is cultivated in any especial form other than the abstractly logical. I dispute, in particular, the reason educed by mathematical study. The mathematics are the science of form and quantity; mathematical reasoning is merely logic applied to observation upon form and quantity. The great error lies in supposing that even the truths of what is called *pure* algebra are abstract or general truths. And this error is so egregious that I am confounded at the universality with which it has been received. Mathematical axioms are *not* axioms of general truth. What is true of *relation*—of form and quantity—is often grossly false in regard to morals, for example. In this latter science it is very usually *un*true that the aggregated parts are equal to the whole. In chemistry also the axiom fails. In the consideration of motive it fails; for two motives, each of a given value, have not, necessarily, a value when united, equal to the sum of their values apart. There are numerous other mathematical truths which are only truths within the limits of *relation*. But the mathematician argues from his *finite truths*, through habit, as if they were of an absolutely general applicability—as the world indeed imagines them to be. Bryant, in his very learned "Mythology", mentions an analogous source of error, when he says that "although the pagan fables are not believed, yet we forget ourselves continually, and make inferences from them as existing realities." With the algebraists, however, who are pagans themselves, the "pagan fables" *are* believed and the inferences are made, not so much through lapse of memory as through an unaccountable addling of the brains. In short, I never yet encountered the mere mathematician who would be trusted out of equal roots, or one who did not clandestinely hold it as a point of his faith that $x2 + px$ was absolutely and unconditionally equal to $q$. Say to one of these gentlemen, by way of experiment, if you please, that you believe occasions may occur where $x2 + px$ is *not* altogether equal to $q$, and, having made him understand what you mean, get out of his reach as speedily as convenient, for, beyond doubt, he will endeavour to knock you down.

'I mean to say', continued Dupin, while I merely laughed at his last observations, 'that if the Minister had been no more than a mathematician, the Prefect would have been under no necessity of giving me this cheque. I knew him, however, as both mathematician and poet, and my measures were adapted to his capacity, with reference to the circumstances by which he was surrounded. I knew him as a courtier, too, and as a bold *intriguant*. Such a man, I considered, could not fail to be aware of the ordinary police modes of action. He could not have failed to anticipate—and events have proved that he did not fail to anticipate—the waylayings to which he was subjected. He must have foreseen, I reflected, the secret investigations of his premises. His frequent absences from home at night, which were hailed by the Prefect as certain aids to his success, I regarded only as ruses, to afford opportunity for thorough search to the police, and thus the sooner to impress them with the conviction to which G., in fact, did finally arrive—the conviction that the letter was not upon the premises. I felt, also, that the whole train of thought, which I was at some pains in detailing to you just now, concerning the invariable principle of policial action in searches for articles concealed—I felt that this whole train of thought would necessarily pass through the mind of the Minister. It would imperatively lead him to despise all the ordinary *nooks* of concealment. *He* could not, I reflected, be so weak as not to see that the most intricate and remote recess of his hotel would be as open as his commonest closets to the eyes, to the probes, to the gimlets, and to the microscopes of the Prefect. I saw, in fine, that he would be driven, as a matter of course, to *simplicity*, if not deliberately induced to it as a matter of choice. You will remember, perhaps, how desperately the Prefect laughed when I suggested, upon our first interview, that it was just possible this mystery troubled him so much on account of its being so *very* self-evident.'

'Yes,' said I, 'I remember his merriment well. I really thought he would have fallen into convulsions.'

'The material world', continued Dupin, 'abounds with very strict analogies to the immaterial; and thus some colour of truth has been given to the rhetorical dogma, that metaphor, or simile, may be made to strengthen an argument as well as to embellish a description. The principle of the *vis inertiae*, for example, seems to be identical in physics and metaphysics. It is not more true in the former, that a large body is with more difficulty set in motion than a smaller one, and that its subsequent *momentum* is commensurate with this difficulty, than it is, in the latter, that intellects of the vaster capacity, while more forcible, more constant, and more eventful in their movements than those of inferior grade, are yet the less readily moved, and more embarrassed, and full of hesitation in the first few steps of their progress. Again: have you ever noticed which of the street signs, over the shop doors, are the most attractive of attention?'

'I have never given the matter a thought,' I said.

'There is a game of puzzles,' he resumed, 'which is played upon a map. One party playing requires another to find a given word—the name of a town, river, state, or empire—any word, in short, upon the motley and perplexed surface of the chart. A novice in the game generally seeks to embarrass his opponents by giving them the most minutely lettered names; but the adept selects such words as stretch, in large characters, from one end of the chart to the other. These, like the over-largely lettered signs and placards of the street, escape observation by dint of being excessively obvious; and here the physical oversight is precisely analogous with the moral inapprehension by which the intellect suffers to pass unnoticed those considerations which are too obtrusively and too palpably self-evident. But this is a point, it appears, somewhat above or beneath the understanding of the Prefect. He never once thought it probable, or possible, that the Minister had deposited the letter immediately beneath the nose of the whole world, by way of best preventing any portion of that world from perceiving it.

'But the more I reflected upon the daring, dashing, and discriminating ingenuity of D——; upon the fact that the document must always have been *at hand*, if he intended to use it to good purpose; and upon the decisive evidence, obtained by the Prefect, that it was not hidden within the limits of the dignitary's ordinary search—the more satisfied I became that, to conceal this letter, the Minister had resorted to the comprehensive and sagacious expedient of not attempting to conceal it at all.

'Full of these ideas, I prepared myself with a pair of green spectacles, and called one fine morning, quite by accident, at the Ministerial hotel. I found D—— at home, yawning, lounging, and dawdling, as usual, and pretending to be in the last extremity of *ennui*. He is, perhaps, the most really energetic human being now alive—but that is only when nobody sees him.

'To be even with him, I complained of my weak eyes, and lamented the necessity of the spectacles, under cover of which I cautiously and thoroughly surveyed the whole apartment, while seemingly intent only upon the conversation of my host.

'I paid especial attention to a large writing-table near which he sat, and upon which lay confusedly, some miscellaneous letters and other papers, with one or two musical instruments and a few books. Here, however, after a long and very deliberate scrutiny, I saw nothing to excite particular suspicion.

'At length my eyes, in going the circuit of the room, fell upon a trumpery filigree card-rack of pasteboard, that hung dangling by a dirty blue ribbon, from a little brass knob just beneath the middle of the mantelpiece. In this rack, which had three or four compartments, were five or six visiting cards and a solitary letter. This last was much soiled and crumpled. It was torn nearly in two, across the middle—as if a design, in the first instance, to tear it entirely up as worthless, had been altered, or stayed, in the second. It had a large black seal, bearing the D—— cipher *very* conspicuously, and was addressed, in a diminutive female hand, to D——, the Minister himself. It was thrust carelessly, and even, as it seemed, contemptuously, into one of the uppermost divisions of the rack.

'No sooner had I glanced at this letter than I concluded it to be that of which I was in search. To be sure, it was, to all appearance, radically different from the one of which the Prefect had read us so minute a description. Here the seal was large and black, with the D—— cipher; there it was small and red, with the ducal arms of the S—— family. Here, the address, to the Minister, was diminutive and feminine; there the superscription, to a certain royal personage, was markedly bold and decided; the size alone formed a point of correspondence. But, then, the *radicalness* of these differences, which was excessive; the dirt; the soiled and torn condition of the paper, so inconsistent with the *true* methodical habits of D——, and so suggestive of a design to delude the beholder into an idea of the worthlessness of the document;—these things, together with the hyperobtrusive situation of this document, full in the view of every visitor, and thus exactly in accordance with the conclusions to which I had previously arrived; these things, I say, were strongly corroborative of suspicion, in one who came with the intention to suspect.

'I protracted my visit as long as possible, and, while I maintained a most animated discussion with the Minister, upon a topic which I knew well had never failed to interest and excite him, I kept my attention really riveted upon the letter. In this examination, I committed to memory its external appearance and arrangement in the rack; and also fell, at length, upon a discovery which set at rest whatever trivial doubt I might have entertained. In scrutinizing the edges of the paper, I observed them to be more *chafed* than seemed necessary. They presented the *broken* appearance which is manifested when a stiff paper, having been once folded and pressed with a folder, is refolded in a reversed direction, in the same creases or edges which had formed the original fold. This discovery was sufficient. It was clear to me that the letter had been turned, as a glove, inside out, re-directed and re-sealed. I bade the Minister good-morning, and took my departure at once, leaving a gold snuff-box upon the table.

'The next morning I called for the snuff-box, when we resumed, quite eagerly, the conversation of the preceding day. While thus engaged, however, a loud report, as if of a pistol, was heard immediately beneath the windows of the hotel, and was succeeded by a series of fearful screams, and the shoutings of a terrified mob. D—— rushed to a casement, threw it open, and looked out. In the meantime I stepped to the card-rack, took the letter, put it in my pocket, and replaced it by a *facsimile*, (so far as regards externals) which I had carefully prepared at my lodgings—imitating the D—— cipher, very readily, by means of a seal formed of bread.

'The disturbance in the street had been occasioned by the frantic behaviour of a man with a musket. He had fired it among a crowd of women and children. It proved, however, to have been without ball, and the fellow was suffered to go his way as a lunatic or a drunkard. When he had gone, D—— came from the window, whither I had followed him immediately upon securing the object in view. Soon afterward I bade him farewell. The pretended lunatic was a man in my own pay.'

'But what purpose had you', I asked, 'in replacing the letter by a *facsimile*? Would it not have been better, at the first visit, to have seized it openly, and departed?'

'D——', replied Dupin, 'is a desperate man, and a man of nerve. His hotel, too, is not without attendants devoted to his interests. Had I made the wild attempt you suggest, I might never have left the Ministerial presence alive. The good people of Paris might have heard of me no more. But I had an object apart from these considerations. You know my political prepossessions. In this matter, I act as a partisan of the lady concerned. For eighteen months the Minister has had her in his power. She has now him in hers—since, being unaware that the letter is not in his possession, he will proceed with his exactions as if it was. Thus will he inevitably commit himself, at once, to his political destruction. His downfall, too, will not be more precipitate than awkward. It is all very well to talk about the *facilis descensus Averni*;[6] but in all kinds of climbing, as Catalani said of singing, it is far more easy to get up than to come down. In the present instance I have no sympathy—at least no pity—for him who descends. He is that *monstrum horrendum*, an unprincipled man of genius. I confess, however, that I should like very well to know the precise character of his thoughts, when, being defied by her whom the Prefect terms "a certain personage", he is reduced to opening the letter which I left for him in the card-rack.'

'How? did you put any thing particular in it?'

'Why—it did not seem altogether right to leave the interior blank—that would have been insulting. D——, at Vienna once, did me an evil turn, which I told him, quite good-humouredly, that I should remember. So, as I knew he would feel some curiosity in regard to the identity of the person who had outwitted him, I thought it a pity not to give him a clue. He is well acquainted with my MS.,[7] and I just copied into the middle of the blank sheet the words—

6 'the easy descent to Hell' as described by Virgil in *The Aeneid*
7 MS—handwriting.

"——Un dessein si funeste,
S'il n'est digne d'Atrée, est digne de Thyeste."[8]

They are to be found in Crébillon's "Atrée".'

1845

8 'A scheme so horrible, / If it is unworthy of Atreus, is worthy of Thyestes.' The allusion is to a particularly revolting episode of revenge in Greek mythology.

# Herman Melville

1819–1891

A native of New York City, Herman Melville attended the Albany Academy and the Albany Classical School, then worked as a bank clerk and as a schoolteacher before deciding to seek his fortune at sea. He signed on a packet ship bound for Liverpool in 1839; the experience, however, proved disillusioning, and he went back to teaching. But in 1841 he returned to life on the sea, signing on the whaler Acushnet, bound for the South Seas. There he jumped ship to live in Tahiti before ultimately returning as a sailor to the United States.

In his fiction, Melville often sought to record and recreate his experiences at sea; among his novels of the sea are *White-Jacket* (1850), *Moby-Dick* (1851), and the posthumously published novella *Billy Budd* (1924). Deeply distressed, like his contemporary Walt Whitman, by the American Civil War, he turned to poetry to record his reflections in the collection *Battle-Pieces* (1866); it was the first of four volumes of poetry he would write.

In his own lifetime Melville's writings met with little critical and even less popular success, and he never made enough money to support himself and his family.

## Bartleby, the Scrivener: A Story of Wall Street

I am a rather elderly man. The nature of my avocations, for the last thirty years, has brought me into more than ordinary contact with what would seem an interesting and somewhat singular set of men, of whom, as yet, nothing, that I know of, has ever been written—I mean, the law-copyists, or scriveners. I have known very many of them professionally and privately, and, if I pleased, could relate divers histories, at which good-natured gentlemen might smile, and sentimental souls might weep. But I waive the biographies of all other scriveners, for a few passages in the life of Bartleby, who was a scrivener, the strangest I ever saw, or heard of. While, of other law-copyists, I might write the complete life, of Bartleby nothing of that sort can be done. I believe that no materials exist for a full and satisfactory biography of this man. It is an irreparable loss to literature. Bartleby was one of those beings of whom nothing is ascertainable, except from the original sources, and, in his case, those are very small. What my own astonished eyes saw of Bartleby, *that* is all I know of him, except, indeed, one vague report, which will appear in the sequel.

Ere introducing the scrivener, as he first appeared to me, it is fit I make some mention of myself, my *employés*, my business, my chambers, and general surroundings; because some such description is indispensable to an adequate understanding of the chief character about to be presented. Imprimis: I am a man who, from his youth upwards, has been filled with a profound conviction that the easiest way of life is the best. Hence, though I belong to a profession proverbially energetic and nervous, even to turbulence, at times, yet nothing of that sort have I ever suffered to invade my peace. I am one of those unambitious lawyers who never address a jury, or in any way draw down public applause; but, in the cool tranquility of a snug retreat, do a snug business among rich men's bonds, and mortgages, and title deeds. All who know me, consider me an eminently *safe* man. The late John Jacob Astor, a personage little given to poetic enthusiasm, had no hesitation in pronouncing my first grand point to be prudence; my next, method. I do not speak it in vanity, but simply record the fact, that I was not unemployed in my profession by the late John Jacob Astor; a name which, I admit, I love to repeat; for it hath a rounded and orbicular sound to it, and rings like unto bullion. I will freely add, that I was not insensible to the late John Jacob Astor's good opinion.

Some time prior to the period at which this little history begins, my avocations had been largely increased. The good old office, now extinct in the State of New York, of a Master in Chancery, had been conferred upon me. It was not a very arduous office, but very pleasantly remunerative. I seldom lose my temper; much more seldom indulge in dangerous indignation at wrongs and outrages; but I must be permitted to be rash here and declare, that I consider the sudden and violent abrogation of the office of Master in Chancery, by the new Constitution, as a—premature act; inasmuch as I had counted upon a life-lease of the profits, whereas I only received those of a few short years. But this is by the way.

My chambers were upstairs, at No. — Wall Street. At one end, they looked upon the white wall of the interior of a spacious skylight shaft, penetrating the building from top to bottom.

This view might have been considered rather tame than otherwise, deficient in what landscape painters call 'life'. But, if so, the view from the other end of my chambers offered, at least, a contrast, if nothing more. In that direction, my windows commanded an unobstructed view of a lofty brick wall, black by age and everlasting shade; which wall required no spy-glass to bring out its lurking beauties, but, for the benefit of all near-sighted spectators, was pushed up to within ten feet of my window panes. Owing to the great height of the surrounding buildings, and my chambers being on the second floor, the interval between this wall and mine not a little resembled a huge square cistern.

At the period just preceding the advent of Bartleby, I had two persons as copyists in my employment, and a promising lad as an office-boy. First, Turkey; second, Nippers;

third, Ginger Nut. These may seem names, the like of which are not usually found in the Directory. In truth, they were nicknames, mutually conferred upon each other by my three clerks, and were deemed expressive of their respective persons or characters. Turkey was a short, pursy Englishman, of about my own age—that is, somewhere not far from sixty. In the morning, one might say, his face was of a fine florid hue, but after twelve o'clock, meridian—his dinner hour—it blazed like a grate full of Christmas coals; and continued blazing—but, as it were, with a gradual wane—till six o'clock, p.m., or thereabouts; after which, I saw no more of the proprietor of the face, which, gaining its meridian with the sun, seemed to set with it, to rise, culminate, and decline the following day, with the like regularity and undiminished glory. There are many singular coincidences I have known in the course of my life, not the least among which was the fact, that, exactly when Turkey displayed his fullest beams from his red and radiant countenance, just then, too, at that critical moment, began the daily period when I considered his business capacities as seriously disturbed for the remainder of the twenty-four hours. Not that he was absolutely idle, or averse to business then; far from it. The difficulty was, he was apt to be altogether too energetic. There was a strange, inflamed, flurried, flighty recklessness of activity about him. He would be incautious in dipping his pen into his inkstand. All his blots upon my documents were dropped there after twelve o'clock, meridian. Indeed, not only would he be reckless, and sadly given to making blots in the afternoon, but, some days, he went further, and was rather noisy. At such times, too, his face flamed with augmented blazonry, as if canned coal had been heaped on anthracite. He made an unpleasant racket with his chair; spilled his sand-box; in mending his pens, impatiently split them all to pieces, and threw them on the floor in a sudden passion; stood up, and leaned over his table, boxing his papers about in a most indecorous manner, very sad to behold in an elderly man like him. Nevertheless, as he was in many ways a most valuable person to me, and all the time before twelve o'clock, meridian, was the quickest, steadiest creature, too, accomplishing a great deal of work in a style not easily to be matched—for these reasons, I was willing to overlook his eccentricities, though, indeed, occasionally, I remonstrated with him. I did this very gently, however, because, though the civilest, nay, the blandest and most reverential of men in the morning, yet, in the afternoon, he was disposed, upon provocation, to be slightly rash with his tongue—in fact, insolent. Now, valuing his morning services as I did, and resolved not to lose them—yet, at the same time, made uncomfortable by his inflamed ways after twelve o'clock—and being a man of peace, unwilling by my admonitions to call forth unseemly retorts from him, I took upon me, one Saturday noon (he was always worse on Saturdays) to hint to him, very kindly, that, perhaps, now that he was growing old, it might be well to abridge his labours; in short, he need not come to my chambers after twelve o'clock, but, dinner over, had best go home to his lodgings, and rest himself till tea-time. But no; he insisted upon his afternoon devotions. His countenance became intolerably fervid, as he oratorically assured me—gesticulating with a long ruler at the other end of the room—that if his services in the morning were useful, how indispensable, then, in the afternoon?

'With submission, sir,' said Turkey, on this occasion, 'I consider myself your right-hand man. In the morning I but marshal and deploy my columns; but in the afternoon

I put myself at their head, and gallantly charge the foe, thus'—and he made a violent thrust with the ruler.

'But the blots, Turkey,' intimated I.

'True; but, with submission, sir, behold these hairs! I am getting old. Surely, sir, a blot or two of a warm afternoon is not to be severely urged against grey hairs. Old age—even if it blot the page—is honourable. With submission, sir, we *both* are getting old.'

This appeal to my fellow-feeling was hardly to be resisted. At all events, I saw that go he would not. So, I made up my mind to let him stay, resolving, nevertheless, to see to it that, during the afternoon, he had to do with my less important papers.

Nippers, the second on my list, was a whiskered, sallow, and, upon the whole, rather piratical-looking young man, of about five-and-twenty. I always deemed him the victim of two evil powers—ambition and indigestion. The ambition was evinced by a certain impatience of the duties of a mere copyist, an unwarrantable usurpation of strictly professional affairs, such as the original drawing up of legal documents. The indigestion seemed betokened in an occasional nervous testiness and grinning irritability, causing the teeth to audibly grind together over mistakes committed in copying; unnecessary maledictions, hissed, rather than spoken, in the heat of business; and especially by a continual discontent with the height of the table where he worked. Though of a very ingenious mechanical turn, Nippers could never get this table to suit him. He put chips under it, blocks of various sorts, bits of pasteboard, and at last went so far as to attempt an exquisite adjustment, by final pieces of folded blotting-paper. But no invention would answer. If, for the sake of easing his back, he brought the table lid at a sharp angle well up towards his chin, and wrote there like a man using the steep roof of a Dutch house for his desk, then he declared that it stopped the circulation in his arms. If now he lowered the table to his waistbands, and stooped over it in writing, then there was a sore aching in his back. In short, the truth of the matter was, Nippers knew not what he wanted. Or, if he wanted anything, it was to be rid of a scrivener's table altogether. Among the manifestations of his diseased ambition was a fondness he had for receiving visits from certain ambiguous-looking fellows in seedy coats, whom he called his clients. Indeed, I was aware that not only was he, at times, considerable of a ward-politician, but he occasionally did a little business at the Justices' courts, and was not unknown on the steps of the Tombs. I have good reason to believe, however, that one individual who called upon him at my chambers, and who, with a grand air, he insisted was his client, was no other than a dun, and the alleged title-deed, a bill. But, with all his failings, and the annoyances he caused me, Nippers, like his compatriot Turkey, was a very useful man to me; wrote a neat, swift hand; and, when he chose, was not deficient in a gentlemanly sort of deportment. Added to this, he always dressed in a gentlemanly sort of way; and so, incidentally, reflected credit upon my chambers. Whereas, with respect to Turkey, I had much ado to keep him from being a reproach to me. His clothes were apt to look oily, and smell of eating-houses. He wore his pantaloons very loose and baggy in summer. His coats were execrable; his hat not to be handled. But while the hat was a thing of indifference to me, inasmuch as his natural civility and deference, as a dependent Englishman, always led him to doff it the moment he entered the room, yet his coat was another matter. Concerning his coats, I reasoned with him; but with no effect. The truth was, I suppose, that a man with so small an income could not afford to sport such a lustrous face and a lustrous coat at one and the same time. As Nippers once observed, Turkey's money went chiefly for red ink. One winter day, I presented Turkey with a highly respectable-looking coat of my own—a padded grey coat, of a most comfortable warmth, and which buttoned straight up from the knee to the neck. I thought Turkey would appreciate the favour, and abate his rashness and obstreperousness of afternoons. But no; I verily believe that buttoning himself up in so downy and blanket-like a coat had a pernicious effect upon him—upon the same principle that too much oats are bad for horses. In fact, precisely as a rash, restive horse is said to feel his oats, so Turkey felt his coat. It made him insolent. He was a man whom prosperity harmed.

Though, concerning the self-indulgent habits of Turkey, I had my own private surmises, yet, touching Nippers, I was well persuaded that, whatever might be his faults in other respects, he was, at least, a temperate young man. But, indeed, nature herself seemed to have been his vintner, and, at his birth, charged him so thoroughly with an irritable, brandy-like disposition, that all subsequent potations were needless. When I consider how, amid the stillness of my chambers, Nippers would sometimes impatiently rise from his seat, and stopping over his table, spread his arms wide apart, seize the whole desk, and move it, and jerk it, with a grim, grinding motion on the floor, as if the table were a perverse voluntary agent, intent on thwarting and vexing him, I plainly perceive that, for Nippers, brandy-and-water were altogether superfluous.

It was fortunate for me that, owing to its peculiar cause—indigestion—the irritability and consequent nervousness of Nippers were mainly observable in the morning, while in the afternoon he was comparatively mild. So that, Turkey's paroxysms only coming on about twelve o'clock, I never had to do with their eccentricities at one time. Their fits relieved each other, like guards. When Nippers's was on, Turkey's was off; and *vice versa.* This was a good natural arrangement under the circumstances.

Ginger Nut, the third on my list, was a lad, some twelve years old. His father was a carman, ambitious of seeing his son on the bench instead of a cart, before he died. So he sent him to my office, as student at law, errand-boy, cleaner, and sweeper, at the rate of one dollar a week. He had a little desk to himself, but he did not use it much. Upon inspection, the drawer exhibited a great array of the shells of various sorts of nuts. Indeed, to this quick-witted youth, the whole noble science of the law was contained in a nut-shell. Not the least among the employments of Ginger Nut, as well as one which he discharged with the most alacrity, was his duty as cake and apple purveyor for Turkey and Nippers. Copying law papers being proverbially a dry, husky sort of business, my two scriveners were fain to moisten their mouths very often with Spitzenbergs, to be had at the numerous stalls nigh the Custom House and Post Office. Also, they sent Ginger Nut very frequently for that peculiar cake—small, flat, round, and very spicy—after which he had been named by them. Of a cold morning, when business was but dull, Turkey would gobble up scores of these cakes, as if they were mere wafers—indeed, they sell them at the rate of six or eight for a penny—the scrape of his pen blending with the crunching of the crisp particles in his mouth.

Of all the fiery afternoon blunders and flurried rashnesses of Turkey, was his once moistening a ginger-cake between his lips, and clapping it on to a mortgage, for a seal. I came within an ace of dismissing him then. But he mollified me by making an oriental bow, and saying—

'With submission, sir, it was generous of me to find you in stationery on my account.'

Now my original business—that of a conveyancer and title hunter, and drawer-up of recondite documents of all sorts—was considerably increased by receiving the Master's office. There was now great work for scriveners. Not only must I push the clerks already with me, but I must have additional help.

In answer to my advertisement, a motionless young man one morning stood upon my office threshold, the door being open, for it was summer. I can see that figure now—pallidly neat, pitiably respectable, incurably forlorn! It was Bartleby.

After a few words touching his qualifications, I engaged him, glad to have among my corps of copyists a man of so singularly sedate an aspect, which I thought might operate beneficially upon the flighty temper of Turkey, and the fiery one of Nippers.

I should have stated before that ground-glass folding doors divided my premises into two parts, one of which was occupied by my scriveners, the other by myself. According to my humour, I threw open these doors, or closed them. I resolved to assign Bartleby a corner by the folding doors, but on my side of them, so as to have this quiet man within easy call, in case any trifling thing was to be done. I placed his desk close up to a small side-window in that part of the room, a window which originally had afforded a lateral view of certain grimy back-yards and bricks, but which, owing to subsequent erections, commanded at present no view at all, though it gave some light. Within three feet of the panes was a wall, and the light came down from far above, between two lofty buildings, as from a very small opening in a dome. Still further to a satisfactory arrangement, I procured a high green folding screen, which might entirely isolate Bartleby from my sight, though not remove him from my voice. And thus, in a manner, privacy and society were conjoined.

At first, Bartleby did an extraordinary quantity of writing. As if long famishing for something to copy, he seemed to gorge himself on my documents. There was no pause for digestion. He ran a day and night line copying by sunlight and by candle-light. I should have been quite delighted with his application, had he been cheerfully industrious. But he wrote on silently, palely, mechanically.

It is, of course, an indispensable part of a scrivener's business to verify the accuracy of his copy, word by word. Where there are two or more scriveners in an office, they assist each other in this examination, one reading from the copy, the other holding the original. It is a very dull, wearisome, and lethargic affair. I can readily imagine that, to some sanguine temperaments, it would be altogether intolerable. For example, I cannot credit that the mettlesome poet, Byron, would have contentedly sat down with Bartleby to examine a law document of, say five hundred pages, closely written in a crimpy hand.

Now and then, in the haste of business, it had been my habit to assist in comparing some brief document myself, calling Turkey or Nippers for this purpose. One object I had, in placing Bartleby so handy to me behind the screen, was, to avail myself of his services on such trivial occasions. It was on the third day, I think, of his being with me, and before any necessity had arisen for having his own writing examined, that, being much hurried to complete a small affair I had in hand, I abruptly called to Bartleby. In my haste and natural expectancy of instant compliance, I sat with my head bent over the original on my desk, and my right hand sideways, and somewhat nervously extended with the copy, so that, immediately upon emerging from his retreat, Bartleby might snatch it and proceed to business without the least delay.

In this very attitude did I sit when I called to him, rapidly stating what it was I wanted him to do—namely, to examine a small paper with me. Imagine my surprise, nay, my consternation, when, without moving from his privacy, Bartleby, in a singularly mild, firm voice, replied, 'I would prefer not to.'

I sat awhile in perfect silence, rallying my stunned faculties. Immediately it occurred to me that my ears had deceived me, or Bartleby had entirely misunderstood my meaning. I repeated my request in the clearest tone I could assume; but in quite as clear a one came the previous reply, 'I would prefer not to.'

'Prefer not to,' echoed I, rising in high excitement, and crossing the room with a stride. 'What do you mean? Are you moon-stuck? I want you to help me compare this sheet here—take it,' and I thrust it towards him.

'I would prefer not to,' said he.

I looked at him steadfastly. His face was leanly composed; his grey eye dimly calm. Not a wrinkle of agitation rippled him. Had there been the least uneasiness, anger, impatience, or impertinence in his manner; in other words, had there been anything ordinarily human about him, doubtless I should have violently dismissed him from the premises. But as it was, I should have soon thought of turning my pale plaster-of-paris bust of Cicero out of doors. I stood gazing at him awhile, as he went on with his own writing, and then reseated myself at my desk. This is very strange, thought I. What had one best do? But my business hurried me. I concluded to forget the matter for the present, reserving it for my future leisure. So, calling Nippers from the other room, the paper was speedily examined.

A few days after this, Bartleby concluded four lengthy documents, being quadruplicates of a week's testimony taken before me in my High Court of Chancery. It became necessary to examine them. It was an important suit, and great accuracy was imperative. Having all things arranged, I called Turkey, Nippers, and Ginger Nut, from the next room, meaning to place the four copies in the hands of my four clerks, while I should read from the original. Accordingly, Turkey, Nippers, and Ginger Nut had taken their seats in a row, each with his document in his hand, when I called to Bartleby to join this interesting group.

'Bartleby! quick, I am waiting.'

I heard a slow scrape of his chair legs on the uncarpeted floor, and soon he appeared standing at the entrance of his hermitage.

'What is wanted?' said he, mildly.

'The copies, the copies,' said I, hurriedly. 'We are going to examine them. There'—and I held towards him the fourth quadruplicate.

'I would prefer not to,' he said, and gently disappeared behind the screen.

For a few moments I was turned into a pillar of salt, standing at the head of my seated column of clerks. Recovering myself, I advanced towards the screen, and demanded the reason for such extraordinary conduct.

'*Why* do you refuse?'

'I would prefer not to.'

With any other man I should have flown outright into a dreadful passion, scorned all further words, and thrust him ignominiously from my presence. But there was something about Bartleby that not only strangely disarmed me, but, in a wonderful manner, touched and disconcerted me. I began to reason with him.

'These are your own copies we are about to examine. It is labour saving to you, because one examination will answer for your four papers. It is common usage. Every copyist is bound to help examine his copy. Is it not so? Will you not speak? Answer!'

'I prefer not to,' he replied in a flute-like tone. It seemed to me that, while I had been addressing him, he carefully revolved every statement that I made; fully comprehended the meaning; could not gainsay the irresistible conclusion; but, at the same time, some paramount consideration prevailed with him to reply as he did.

'You are decided, then, not to comply with my request—a request made according to common usage and common sense?'

He briefly gave me to understand, that on that point my judgment was sound. Yes: his decision was irreversible.

It is not seldom the case that, when a man is browbeaten in some unprecedented and violently unreasonable way, he begins to stagger in his own plainest faith. He begins, as it were, vaguely to surmise that, wonderful as it may be, all the justice and all the reason is on the other side. Accordingly, if any disinterested persons are present, he turns to them for some reinforcement for his own faltering mind.

'Turkey,' said I, 'what do you think of this? Am I not right?'

'With submission, sir,' said Turkey, in his blandest tone, 'I think you are.'

'Nippers,' said I, 'what do *you* think of it?'

'I think I should kick him out of the office.'

(The reader of nice perceptions will here perceive that, it being morning, Turkey's answer is couched in polite and tranquil terms, but Nippers's replies in ill-tempered ones. Or, to repeat a previous sentence, Nippers's ugly mood was on duty, and Turkey's off.)

'Ginger Nut,' said I, willing to enlist the smallest suffrage in my behalf, 'what do *you* think of it?'

'I think, sir, he's a little *luny*,' replied Ginger Nut, with a grin.

'You hear what they say,' said I, turning towards the screen, 'come forth and do your duty.'

But he vouchsafed no reply. I pondered a moment in sore perplexity. But once more business hurried me. I determined again to postpone the consideration of this dilemma to my future leisure. With a little trouble we made out to examine the papers without Bartleby, though at every page or two Turkey deferentially dropped his opinion, that this proceeding was quite out of the common; while Nippers, twitching in his chair with a dyspeptic nervousness, ground out, between his set teeth, occasional hissing maledictions against the stubborn oaf behind the screen. And for his (Nippers's) part, this was the first and the last time he would do another man's business without pay.

Meanwhile Bartleby sat in his hermitage, oblivious to everything but his own peculiar business there.

Some days passed, the scrivener being employed upon another lengthy work. His late remarkable conduct led me to regard his ways narrowly. I observed that he never went to dinner; indeed, that he never went anywhere. As yet I had never, of my personal knowledge, known him to be outside of my office. He was a perpetual sentry in the corner. At about eleven o'clock though, in the morning, I noticed that Ginger Nut would advance toward the opening in Bartleby's screen, as if silently beckoned thither by a gesture invisible to me where I sat. The boy would then leave the office, jingling a few pence, and reappear with a handful of ginger-nuts, which he delivered in the hermitage, receiving two of the cakes for his trouble.

He lives, then, on ginger-nuts, thought I; never eats a dinner, properly speaking; he must be a vegetarian, then, but no; he never eats even vegetables, he eats nothing but ginger-nuts. My mind then ran on in reveries concerning the probable effects upon the human constitution of living entirely on ginger-nuts. Ginger-nuts are so called, because they contain ginger as one of their peculiar constituents and the final flavoring one. Now, what was ginger? A hot, spicy thing. Was Bartleby hot and spicy? Not at all. Ginger, then, had no effect upon Bartleby. Probably he preferred it should have none.

Nothing so aggravates an earnest person as a passive resistance. If the individual so resisted be of a not inhumane temper, and the resisting one perfectly harmless in his passivity, then, in the better moods of the former, he will endeavour charitably to construe to his imagination what proves impossible to be solved by his judgment. Even so, for the most part, I regarded Bartleby and his ways. Poor fellow! thought I, he means no mischief; it is plain he intends no insolence; his aspect sufficiently evinces that his eccentricities are involuntary. He is useful to me. I can get along with him. If I turn him away, the chances are he will fall in with some less indulgent employer, and then he will be rudely treated, and perhaps driven forth miserably to starve. Yes. Here I can cheaply purchase a delicious self-approval. To befriend Bartleby; to humour him in his strange wilfulness, will cost me little or nothing, while I lay up in my soul what will eventually prove a sweet morsel for my conscience. But this mood was invariable with me. The passiveness of Bartleby sometimes irritated me. I felt strangely goaded on to encounter him in a new opposition—to elicit some angry spark from him answerable to my own. But, indeed, I might as well have essayed to strike fire with my knuckles against a bit of Windsor soap. But one afternoon the evil impulse in me mastered me, and the following little scene ensued:

'Bartleby,' said I, 'when those papers are all copied, I will compare them with you.'

'I would prefer not to.'

'How? Surely you do not mean to persist in that mulish vagary?'

No answer.

I threw open the folding doors near by, and, turning upon Turkey and Nippers, exclaimed:

'Bartleby a second time says, he won't examine his papers. What do you think of it, Turkey?'

It was afternoon, be it remembered. Turkey sat glowing like a brass boiler; his bald head steaming; his hands reeling among his blotted papers.

'Think of it?' roared Turkey. 'I think I'll just step behind his screen, and black his eyes for him!'

So saying, Turkey rose to his feet and threw his arms into a pugilistic position. He was hurrying away to make good his promise, when I detained him, alarmed at the effect of incautiously rousing Turkey's combativeness after dinner.

'Sit down, Turkey,' said I, 'and hear what Nippers has to say. What do you think of it, Nippers? Would I not be justified in immediately dismissing Bartleby?'

'Excuse me, that is for you to decide, sir. I think his conduct quite unusual, and, indeed, unjust, as regards to Turkey and myself. But it may only be a passing whim.'

'Ah,' exclaimed I, 'you have strangely changed your mind, then—you speak very gently of him now.'

'All beer,' cried Turkey; 'gentleness is effects of beer—Nippers and I dined together today. You see how gentle I am, sir. Shall I go and black his eyes?'

'You refer to Bartleby, I suppose. No, not today, Turkey,' I replied; 'pray, put up your fists.'

I closed the doors, and again advanced towards Bartleby. I felt additional incentives tempting me to my fate. I burned to be rebelled against again. I remembered that Bartleby never left the office.

'Bartleby,' said I, 'Ginger Nut is away; just step around to the Post Office, won't you?' (it was but a three minutes' walk) 'and see if there is anything for me.'

'I would prefer not to.'

'You *will* not?'

'I *prefer* not.'

I staggered to my desk, and sat there in a deep study. My blind inveteracy returned. Was there any other thing in which I could procure myself to be ignominiously repulsed by this lean, penniless wight?—my hired clerk? What added thing is there, perfectly reasonable, that he will be sure to refuse to do?

'Bartleby!'

No answer.

'Bartleby,' in a louder tone.

No answer.

'Bartleby,' I roared.

Like a very ghost, agreeably to the laws of magical invocation, at the third summons, he appeared at the entrance of his hermitage.

'Go to the next room, and tell Nippers to come to me.'

'I prefer not to,' he respectfully and slowly said, and mildly disappeared.

'Very good, Bartleby,' said I, in a quiet sort of serenely severe self-possessed tone, intimating the unalterable purpose of some terrible retribution very close at hand. At the moment I half intended something of the kind. But upon the whole, as it was drawing towards my dinner-hour, I thought it best to put on my hat and walk home for the day, suffering much from perplexity and distress of mind.

Shall I acknowledge it? The conclusion of this whole business was, that it soon became a fixed fact of my chambers, that a pale young scrivener, by the name of Bartleby, had a desk there; that he copied for me at the usual rate of four cents a folio (one hundred words); but he was permanently exempt from examining the work done by him, that duty being transferred to Turkey and Nippers, out of compliment, doubtless, to their superior acuteness; moreover, said Bartleby was never, on any account, to be dispatched on the most trivial errand of any sort; and that even if entreated to take upon him such a matter, it was generally understood that he would 'prefer not to'—in other words, that he would refuse point-blank.

As days passed on, I became considerably reconciled to Bartleby. His steadiness, his freedom from all dissipation, his incessant industry (except when he chose to throw himself into a standing reverie behind his screen) his great stillness, his unalterableness of demeanour under all circumstances, made him a valuable acquisition. One prime thing was this—*he was always there*—first in the morning, continually through the day, and the last at night. I had a singular confidence in his honesty. I felt my most precious papers perfectly safe in his hands. Sometimes, to be sure, I could not, for the very soul of me, avoid falling into sudden spasmodic passions with him. For it was exceeding difficult to bear in mind all the time those strange peculiarities, privileges, and unheard-of exemptions, forming the tacit stipulations on Bartleby's part under which he remained in my office. Now and then, in the eagerness of dispatching pressing business, I would inadvertently summon Bartleby, in a short, rapid tone, to put his finger, say, on the incipient tie of a bit of red tape with which I was about compressing some papers. Of course, from behind the screen the usual answer, 'I prefer not to,' was sure to come; and then, how could a human creature, with the common infirmities of our nature, refrain from bitterly exclaiming upon such perverseness—such unreasonableness? However, every added repulse of this sort which I received only tended to lessen the probability of my repeating the inadvertence.

Here it must be said, that, according to the custom of most legal gentlemen occupying chambers in densely populated law buildings, there were several keys to my door. One was kept by a woman residing in the attic, which person weekly scrubbed and daily swept and dusted my apartments. Another was kept by Turkey for convenience sake. The third I sometimes carried in my own pocket. The fourth I knew not who had.

Now, one Sunday morning I happened to go to Trinity Church, to hear a celebrated preacher, and finding myself rather early on the ground I thought I would walk round to my chambers for a while. Luckily I had my key with me; but upon applying it to the lock, I found it resisted by something inserted from the inside. Quite surprised, I called out; when to my consternation a key was turned from within; and thrusting his lead visage at me, and holding the door ajar, the apparition of Bartleby appeared, in his shirt-sleeves, and otherwise in a strangely tattered déshabillé, saying quietly that he was sorry, but he was deeply engaged just then, and—preferred not admitting me at present. In a brief word or two, he moreover added, that perhaps I had better walk round the block two or three times, and by that time he would probably have concluded his affairs.

Now, the utterly unsurmised appearance of Bartleby, tenanting my law-chambers of a Sunday morning, with his cadaverously gentlemanly *nonchalance*, yet withal firm and self-possessed, had such a strange effect upon me, that incontinently I slunk away from my own door, and did as desired. But not without sundry twinges of impotent rebellion against the mild effrontery of this unaccountable scrivener. Indeed, it was his wonderful mildness chiefly, which not only disarmed me, but unmanned me, as it were. For I consider that one, for the time, is a sort of unmanned when he tranquilly permits his hired clerk to dictate to him, and order him away from his own premises. Furthermore, I was full of uneasiness as to what Bartleby could possibly be doing in my office in his shirt-sleeves, and in an otherwise dismantled condition of a Sunday morning. Was anything amiss going on? Nay, that was out of the question. It was not to be thought of for a moment that Bartleby was an immoral person. But what could he be doing there—copying? Nay again, whatever might be his eccentricities, Bartleby was an eminently decorous person. He would be the last man to sit down to his desk in any state approaching to nudity. Besides, it was Sunday; and there was something about Bartleby that forbade the supposition that he would by any secular occupation violate the proprieties of the day.

Nevertheless, my mind was not pacified; and full of a restless curiosity, at last I returned to the door. Without hindrance I inserted my key, opened it, and entered. Bartleby was not to be seen. I looked round anxiously, peeped behind his screen; but it was very plain that he was gone. Upon more closely examining the place, I surmised that for an indefinite period Bartleby must have ate, dressed, and slept in my office, and that too without plate, mirror, or bed. The cushioned seat of a rickety old sofa in one corner bore the faint impress of a lean, reclining form. Rolled away under his desk, I found a blanket; under the empty grate, a blacking box and brush; on a chair, a tin basin, with soap and a ragged towel; in a newspaper a few crumbs of ginger-nuts and a morsel of cheese. Yes, thought I, it is evident enough that Bartleby had been making his home here, keeping bachelor's hall all by himself. Immediately then the thought came sweeping across me, what miserable friendlessness and loneliness are here revealed? His poverty is great; but his solitude, how horrible! Think of it. Of a Sunday, Wall Street is deserted as Petra; and every night of every day it is an emptiness. This building, too, which of weekdays hums with industry and life, at nightfall echoes with sheer vacancy, and all through Sunday is forlorn. And there Bartleby makes his home; sole spectator of a solitude which he has seen all populous—a sort of innocent and transformed Marius brooding among the ruins of Carthage!

For the first time in my life a feeling of overpowering stinging melancholy seized me. Before, I had never experienced aught but a not unpleasing sadness. The bond of a common humanity now drew me irresistibly to gloom. A fraternal melancholy! For both I and Bartleby were sons of Adam. I remembered the bright silks and sparkling faces I had seen that day, in gala trim, swan-like sailing down the Mississippi of Broadway; and I contrasted them with the pallid copyist, and thought to myself, Ah, happiness courts the light, so we deem the world is gay; but misery hides aloof, so we deem that misery there is none. These sad fancyings—chimeras, doubtless of a sick and silly brain—led on to other and more special thoughts, concerning the eccentricities of Bartleby. Presentiments of strange discoveries hovered round me. The scrivener's pale form appeared to me laid out, among uncaring strangers, in its shivering winding-sheet.

Suddenly I was attracted by Bartleby's closed desk, the key in open sight left in the lock.

I mean no mischief, seek the gratification of no heartless curiosity, thought I; besides, the desk is mine, and its contents, too, so I will make bold to look within. Everything was methodically arranged, the papers smoothly placed. The pigeon-holes were deep, and removing the files of documents, I groped into their recesses. Presently I felt something there, and dragged it out. It was an old bandanna handkerchief, heavy and knotted. I opened it, and saw it was a saving's bank.

I now recalled all the quiet mysteries which I had noted in the man. I remembered that he never spoke but to answer; that, though at intervals he had considerable time to himself, yet I had never seen him reading—no, not even a newspaper; that for long periods he would stand looking out, at his pale window behind the screen, upon the dead brick wall; I was quite sure he never visited any refectory or eating-house; while his pale face clearly indicated that he never drank beer like Turkey, or tea and coffee even, like other men; that he never went anywhere in particular that I could learn; never went out for a walk, unless, indeed, that was the case at present; that he had declined telling who he was or whence he came, or whether he had any relatives in the world; that though so thin and pale, he never complained of ill-health. And more than all, I remembered a certain unconscious air of pallid—how shall I call it?—of pallid haughtiness, say, or rather an austere reserve about him which had positively awed me into my tame compliance with his eccentricities, when I had feared to ask him to do the slightest incidental thing for me, even though I might know, from his long-continued motionlessness, that behind his screen he must be standing in one of those dead-wall reveries of his.

Revolving all these things, and coupling them with the recently discovered fact, that he made my office his constant abiding place and home, and not forgetful of his morbid moodiness; revolving all these things, a prudential feeling began to steal over me. My first emotions had been those of pure melancholy and sincerest pity; but just in proportion as the forlornness of Bartleby grew and grew to my imagination, did that same melancholy merge into fear, that pity into repulsion. So true it is, and so terrible, too, that up to a certain point the thought or sight of misery enlists our best affections; but, in certain special cases, beyond that point it does not. They err who would assert that invariably this is owing to the inherent selfishness of the human heart. It rather proceeds from a certain hopelessness of remedying excessive and organic ill. To a sensitive being, pity is not seldom pain. And when at last it is perceived that such pity cannot lead to effectual succour, common sense bids the soul be rid of it. What I saw that morning persuaded me that the scrivener was the victim of innate and incurable disorder. I might give alms to his body; but his body did not pain him; it was his soul that suffered, and his soul I could not reach.

I did not accomplish the purpose of going to Trinity Church that morning. Somehow, the things I had seen disqualified me for the time from church-going. I walked homeward, thinking what I would do with Bartleby. Finally, I resolved upon this—I would put certain calm questions to him the next morning, touching his history, etc., and if he declined to answer them openly and unreservedly (and I supposed he would prefer not), then to give him a twenty dollar bill over and above whatever I might owe him, and tell him his services are no longer required; but that if in any other way I could assist him, I would be happy to do so, especially if he desired to return to his native place, wherever that might be, I would willingly help to defray the expenses. Moreover, if, after reaching home, he found himself at any time in want of aid, a letter from him would be sure of reply.

The next morning came.

'Bartleby,' said I, gently calling to him behind his screen.

No reply.

'Bartleby,' said I, in a still gentler tone, 'come here; I am not going to ask you to do anything you would prefer not to do—I simply wish to speak to you.'

Upon this he noiselessly slid into view.

'Will you tell me, Bartleby, where you were born?'

'I would prefer not to.'

'Will you tell me *anything* about yourself?'

'I would prefer not to.'

'But what reasonable objection can you have to speak to me? I feel friendly towards you.'

He did not look at me while I spoke, but kept his glance fixed upon my bust of Cicero, which, as I then sat, was directly behind me, some six inches above my head.

'What is your answer, Bartleby?' said I, after waiting a considerable time for a reply, during which his countenance remained immovable, only there was the faintest conceivable tremor of the white attenuated mouth.

'At present I prefer to give no answer,' he said, and retired into his hermitage.

It was rather weak of me I confess, but his manner, on this occasion, nettled me. Not only did there seem to lurk in it a certain calm disdain, but his perverseness seemed ungrateful, considering the undeniable good usage and indulgence he had received from me.

Again I sat ruminating what I should do. Mortified as I was at his behaviour, and resolved as I had been to dismiss him when I entered my office, nevertheless I strangely felt something superstitious knocking at my heart, and forbidding me to carry out my purpose, and denouncing me for a villain if I dared to breathe one bitter word against this forlornest of mankind. At last, familiarly drawing my chair behind his screen, I sat down and said: 'Bartleby, never mind, then, about revealing your history; but let me entreat you, as a friend, to comply as far as may be with the usages of this office. Say now, you will help to examine papers tomorrow or next day: in short, say now, that in a day or two you will begin to be a little reasonable:—say so, Bartleby.'

'At present I would prefer not to be a little reasonable,' was his mildly cadaverous reply.

Just then the folding doors opened, and Nippers approached. He seemed suffering from an unusually bad night's rest, induced by severer indigestion than common. He overhead those final words of Bartleby.

'*Prefer not,* eh?' gritted Nippers—'I'd *prefer* him, if I were you, sir,' addressing me—'I'd *prefer* him; I'd give him preferences, the stubborn mule! What is it, sir, pray, that he *prefers* not to do now?'

Bartleby moved not a limb.

'Mr Nippers,' said I, 'I'd prefer that you would withdraw for the present.'

Somehow, of late, I had got into the way of involuntarily using this word 'prefer' upon all sorts of not exactly suitable occasions. And I trembled to think that my contact with the scrivener had already and seriously affected me in a mental way. And what further and deeper aberration might it not yet produce? This apprehension had not been without efficacy in determining me to summary measures.

As Nippers, looking very sour and sulky, was departing, Turkey blandly and deferentially approached.

'With submission, sir,' said he, 'yesterday I was thinking about Bartleby here, and I think that if he would but prefer to take a quart of good ale every day it would do much towards mending him, and enabling him to assist in examining his papers.'

'So you have got the word, too,' said I, slightly excited.

'With submission, what word, sir?' asked Turkey, respectfully crowding himself into the contracted space behind the screen, and by so doing, making me jostle the scrivener. 'What word, sir?'

'I would prefer to be left alone here,' said Bartleby, as if offended at being mobbed in his privacy.

'*That's* the word, Turkey,' said I—'*that's* it.'

'Oh, *prefer*? oh yes—queer word. I never use it myself. But, sir, as I was saying, if he would but prefer—'

'Turkey,' interrupted I, 'you will please withdraw.'

'Oh certainly, sir, if you prefer that I should.'

As he opened the folding door to retire, Nippers at his desk caught glimpse of me, and asked whether I would prefer to have certain paper copied on blue paper or white. He did not in the least roguishly accent the word 'prefer'. It was plain that it involuntarily rolled from his tongue. I thought to myself, surely I must get rid of a demented man, who already has in some degree turned the tongues, if not the heads of myself and clerks. But I thought it prudent not to break the dismission at once.

The next day I noticed that Bartleby did nothing but stand at his window in his dead-wall revery. Upon asking him why he did not write, he said that he had decided upon doing no more writing.

'Why, how now? what next?' exclaimed I, 'do no more writing?'

'No more.'

'And what is the reason?'

'Do you not see the reason for yourself?' he indifferently replied.

I looked steadfastly at him, and perceived that his eyes looked dull and glazed. Instantly it occurred to me, that his unexampled diligence in copying by his dim window for the first few weeks of his stay with me might have temporarily impaired his vision.

I was touched. I said something in condolence with him. I hinted that of course he did wisely in abstaining from writing for a while; and urged him to embrace that opportunity of taking wholesome exercise in the open air. This, however, he did not do. A few days after this, my other clerks being absent, and being in a great hurry to dispatch certain letters by the mail, I thought that, having nothing else earthly to do, Bartleby would surely be less inflexible than usual, and carry these letters to the post office. But he blankly declined. So, much to my inconvenience, I went myself.

Still added days went by. Whether Bartleby's eyes improved or not, I could not say. To all appearance, I thought they did. But when I asked him if they did, he vouchsafed no answer. At all events, he would do no copying. At last, in reply to my urgings, he informed me that he had permanently given up copying.

'What!' exclaimed I; 'suppose your eyes should get entirely well—better than ever before—would you copy then?'

'I have given up copying,' he answered, and slid aside.

He remained as ever, a fixture in my chamber. Nay—if that were possible—he became still more of a fixture than before. What was to be done? He would do nothing in the office; why should he stay there? In plain fact, he had now become a millstone to me, not only useless as a necklace, but afflictive to bear. Yet I was sorry for him. I speak less than truth when I say that, on his own account, he occasioned me uneasiness. If he would but have named a single relative or friend, I would instantly have written, and urged their taking the poor fellow away to some convenient retreat. But he seemed alone, absolutely alone in the universe. A bit of wreck in the mid-Atlantic. At length, necessities connected with my business tyrannized over all other considerations. Decently as I could, I told Bartleby that in six days' time he must unconditionally leave the office. I warned him to take measures, in the interval, for procuring some other abode. I offered to assist him in this endeavour, if he himself would but take the first step towards a removal. 'And when you finally quit me, Bartleby,' added I, 'I shall see that you go not away entirely unprovided. Six days from this hour, remember.'

At the expiration of that period, I peeped behind the screen, and lo! Bartleby was there.

I buttoned up my coat, balanced myself; advanced slowly towards him, touched his shoulder, and said, 'The time has come; you must quit this place; I am sorry for you; here is money; but you must go.'

'I would prefer not,' he replied, with his back still towards me.

'You *must*.'

He remained silent.

Now I had an unbounded confidence in this man's common honesty. He had frequently restored to me sixpences and shillings carelessly dropped upon the floor, for I am apt to be very reckless in such shirt-button affairs. The proceeding, then, which followed will not be deemed extraordinary.

'Bartleby,' said I, 'I owe you twelve dollars on account; here are thirty-two, the odd twenty are yours—Will you take it?' and I handed the bills towards him.

But he made no motion.

'I will leave them here, then,' putting them under a weight on the table. Then taking my hat and cane and going to the door, I tranquilly turned and added—'After you have removed your things from these offices, Bartleby, you will of course lock the door—since everyone is now gone for the day but you—and if you please, slip your key underneath the mat, so that I may have it in the morning. I shall not see you again; so good-bye to you. If, hereafter, in your new place of abode, I can be of any service to you, do not fail to advise me by letter. Good-bye, Bartleby, and fare you well.'

But he answered not a word; like the last column of some ruined temple, he remained standing mute and solitary in the middle of the otherwise deserted room.

As I walked home in a pensive mood, my vanity got the better of my pity. I could not but highly plume myself on my masterly management in getting rid of Bartleby. Masterly I call it, and such it must appear to any dispassionate thinker. The beauty of my procedure seemed to consist in its perfect quietness. There was no vulgar bullying, no bravado of any sort, no choleric hectoring, and striding to and fro across the apartment, jerking out vehement commands for Bartleby to bundle himself off with his beggarly traps. Nothing of the kind. Without loudly bidding Bartleby depart—as an inferior genius might have done—I *assumed* the ground that depart he must; and upon that assumption built all I had to say. The more I thought over my procedure, the more I was charmed with it. Nevertheless, next morning, upon awakening, I had my doubts—I had somehow slept off the fumes of vanity. One of the coolest and wisest hours a man has, is just after he awakes in the morning. My procedure seemed as sagacious as ever—but only in theory. How it would prove in practice—there was the rub. It was truly a beautiful thought to have assumed Bartleby's departure; but, after all, that assumption was simply my own, and none of Bartleby's. The great point was, not whether I had assumed that he would quit me, but whether he would prefer so to do. He was more a man of preferences than assumptions.

After breakfast, I walked downtown, arguing the probabilities *pro* and *con.* One moment I thought it would prove a miserable failure, and Bartleby would be found all alive at my office as usual; the next moment it seemed certain that I should find his chair empty. And so I kept veering about. At the corner of Broadway and Canal Street, I saw quite an excited group of people standing in earnest conversation.

'I'll take odds he doesn't,' said a voice as I passed.

'Doesn't go?—done!' said I, 'put up your money.'

I was instinctively putting my hand in my pocket to produce my own, when I remembered that this was an election day. The words I had overheard bore no reference to Bartleby, but to the success or non-success of some candidate for the mayoralty. In my intent frame of mind, I had, as it were, imagined that all Broadway shared in my excitement, and were debating the same question with me. I passed on, very thankful that the uproar of the street screened my momentary absent-mindedness.

As I had intended, I was earlier than usual at my office door. I stood listening for a moment. All was still. He must be gone. I tried the knob. The door was locked. Yes, my procedure had worked to a charm; he indeed must be vanished. Yet a certain melancholy mixed with this: I was almost sorry for my brilliant success. I was fumbling under the door mat for the key, which Bartleby was to have left there for me, when accidentally my knee knocked against a panel, producing a summoning sound, and in response a voice came to me from within— 'Not yet; I am occupied.'

It was Bartleby.

I was thunderstruck. For an instant I stood like the man who, pipe in mouth, was killed one cloudless afternoon long ago in Virginia, by summer lightning; at his own warm open window he was killed, and remained leaning out there upon the dreamy afternoon, till someone touched him, when he fell.

'Not gone!' I murmured at last. But again obeying that wondrous ascendancy which the inscrutable scrivener had over me, and from which ascendancy, for all my chafing, I could not completely escape, I slowly went downstairs and out into the street, and while walking round the block, considered what I should next do in this unheard-of perplexity. Turn the man out by an actual thrusting I could not; to drive him away by calling him hard names would not do; calling in the police was an unpleasant idea; and yet, permit him to enjoy his cadaverous triumph over me—this, too, I could not think of. What was to be done? or, if nothing could be done, was there anything further that I could *assume* in the matter. Yes, as before I had prospectively assumed that Bartleby would depart, so now I might retrospectively assume that departed he was. In the legitimate carrying out of this assumption, I might enter my office in a great hurry, and pretending not to see Bartleby at all, walk straight against him as if he were air. Such a proceeding would in a singular degree have the appearance of a home-thrust. It was hardly possible that Bartleby could withstand such an application of the doctrine of assumptions. But upon second thoughts the success of the plan seemed rather dubious. I resolved to argue the matter over with him again.

'Bartleby,' said I, entering the office, with a quietly severe expression, 'I am seriously displeased. I am pained, Bartleby. I had thought better of you. I had imagined you of such a gentlemanly organization, that in any delicate dilemma a slight hint would suffice—in short, an assumption. But it appears I am deceived. Why,' I added, unaffectedly starting, 'you have not even touched that money yet,' pointing to it, just where I had left it the evening previous.

He answered nothing.

'Will you, or will you not, quit me?' I now demanded in a sudden passion, advancing close to him.

'I would prefer *not* to quit you,' he replied, gently emphasizing the *not*.

'What earthly right have you to stay here? Do you pay rent? Do you pay taxes? Or is this property yours?'

He answered nothing.

'Are you ready to go on and write now? Are your eyes recovered? Could you copy a small paper for me this morning? or help examine a few lines? or step round to the post office? In a word, will you do anything at all, to give a colouring to your refusal to depart the premises?'

He silently returned into his hermitage.

I was now in such a state of nervous resentment that I thought it but prudent to check myself at present from further demonstrations. Bartleby and I were alone.

I remembered the tragedy of the unfortunate Adams and the still more unfortunate Colt in the solitary office of the latter; and how poor Colt, being dreadfully incensed by Adams, and imprudently permitting himself to get wildly excited, was at unawares hurried into his fatal act—an act which certainly no man could possibly deplore more than the actor himself. Often it had occurred to me in my ponderings upon the subject that had that altercation taken place in the public street, or at a private residence, it would not have terminated as it did. It was the circumstances of being alone in a solitary office, upstairs, or a building entirely unhallowed by humanizing domestic associations—an uncarpeted office, doubtless, of a dusty, haggard sort of appearance—this it must have been, which greatly helped to enhance the irritable desperation of the harmless Colt.

But when this old Adam of resentment rose in me and tempted me concerning Bartleby, I grappled him and threw him. How? Why, simply by recalling the divine injunction: 'A new commandment give I unto you, that ye love one another.' Yes, this it was that saved me. Aside from higher considerations, charity often operates as a vastly wise and prudent principle—a great safeguard to its possessor. Men have committed murder for jealousy's sake, and anger's sake, and hatred's sake, and selfishness' sake, and spiritual pride's sake; but no man, that ever I heard of, ever committed a diabolical murder for sweet charity's sake. Mere self-interest, then, if no better motive can be enlisted, should, especially with high-tempered men, prompt all beings to charity and philanthropy. At any rate, upon the occasion in question, I strove to drown my exasperated feelings towards the scrivener by benevolently construing his conduct. Poor fellow, poor fellow! thought I, he don't mean anything; and besides, he has seen hard times, and ought to be indulged.

I endeavoured, also, immediately to occupy myself, and at the same time to comfort my despondency. I tried to fancy, that in the course of the morning, at such time as might prove agreeable to him, Bartleby, of his own free accord, would emerge from his hermitage and take up some decided line of march in the direction of the door. But no. Half-past twelve o'clock came; Turkey began to glow in the face, overturn his inkstand, and become generally obstreperous; Nippers abated down into quietude and courtesy; Ginger Nut munched his noon apple; and Bartleby remained standing at his window in one of his profoundest dead-wall reveries. Will it be credited? Ought I to acknowledge it? That afternoon I left the office without saying one further word to him.

Some days now passed, during which, at leisure intervals, I looked a little into 'Edwards on the Will', and 'Priestley on Necessity'. Under the circumstances, those books induced a salutary feeling. Gradually I slid into the persuasion that these troubles of mine, touching the scrivener, had been all predestinated from eternity, and Bartleby was billeted upon me for some mysterious purpose of an all-wise Providence, which it was not for a mere mortal like me to fathom. Yes, Bartleby, stay there behind your screen, thought I; I shall persecute you no more; you are harmless and noiseless as any of these old chairs; in short, I never feel so private as when I know you are here. At last I see it, I feel it; I penetrate to the predestinated purpose of my life. I am content. Others may have loftier parts to enact; but my mission in this world, Bartleby, is to furnish you with office-room for such period as you may see fit to remain.

I believe that this wise and blessed frame of mind would have continued with me, had it not been for the unsolicited and uncharitable remarks obtruded upon me by my professional friends who visited the rooms. But thus it often is, that the constant friction of illiberal minds wears out at last the best resolves of the more generous. Though to be sure, when I reflected upon it, it was not strange that people entering my office should be struck by the peculiar aspect of the unaccountable Bartleby, and so be tempted to throw out some sinister observations concerning him. Sometimes an attorney, having business with me, and calling at my office, and finding no one but the scrivener there, would undertake to obtain some sort of precise information from him touching my whereabouts; but without heeding his idle talk, Bartleby would remain standing immovable in the middle of the room. So after contemplating him in that position for a time, the attorney would depart, no wiser than he came.

Also, when a reference was going on, and the room full of lawyers and witnesses, and business driving fast, some deeply occupied legal gentleman present, seeing Bartleby wholly unemployed, would request him to run round to his (the legal gentleman's) office and fetch some papers for him. Thereupon, Bartleby would tranquilly decline, and yet remain idle as before. Then the lawyer would give a great stare, and turn to me. And what could I say? At last I was made aware that all through the circle of my professional acquaintance, a whisper of wonder was running round, having reference to the strange creature I kept at my office. This worried me very much. And as the idea came upon me of his possibly turning out a long-lived man, and keep occupying my chambers, and denying my authority; and perplexing my visitors; and scandalizing my professional reputation; and casting a general gloom over the premises; keeping soul and body together to the last upon his savings (for doubtless he spent but half a dime a day), and in the end perhaps outlive me, and claim possession of my office by right of his perpetual occupancy: as all these dark anticipations crowded upon me more and more, and my friends continually intruded their relentless remarks upon the apparition in my room; a great change was wrought in me. I resolved to gather all my faculties together, and forever rid me of this intolerable incubus.

Ere revolving any complicated project, however, adapted to this end, I first simply suggested to Bartleby the propriety of his permanent departure. In a calm and serious tone, I commended the idea to his careful and mature consideration. But, having taken three days to meditate upon it, he apprised me, that his original determination remained the same; in short, that he still preferred to abide with me.

What shall I do? I now said to myself, buttoning up my coat to the last button. What shall I do? what ought I to do? What does conscience say I *should* do with this man, or, rather, ghost. Rid myself of him, I must; go, he shall. But how? You will not thrust him, the poor, pale, passive mortal—you will not thrust such a helpless creature out of your door? you will not dishonour yourself by such cruelty? No, I will not, I cannot do that. Rather would I let him live and die here, and then mason up his remains in the wall. What, then, will you do? For all your coaxing, he will not budge. Bribes he leaves under your own paper-weight on your table; in short, it is quite plain that he prefers to cling to you.

Then something severe, something unusual must be done. What! surely you will not have him collared by a constable, and commit his innocent pallor to the common jail? And upon what ground could you procure such a thing to be done?—a vagrant, is he? What! he a vagrant, a wanderer, who refuses to budge? It is because he will *not* be a vagrant, then, that you seek to count him *as* a vagrant. That is too absurd. No visible means of support: there I have him. Wrong again: for indubitably he *does* support himself, and that is the only unanswerable proof that any man can show of his possessing the means so to do. No more then. Since he will not quit me, I must quit him. I will change my offices; I will move elsewhere, and give him fair notice, that if I find him on my new premises I will then proceed against him as a common trespasser.

Acting accordingly, next day I thus addressed him: 'I find these chambers too far from the City Hall; the air is unwholesome. In a word, I propose to remove my offices next week, and shall no longer require your services. I tell you this now, in order that you may seek another place.'

He made no reply, and nothing more was said.

On the appointed day I engaged carts and men, proceeded to my chambers, and, having but little furniture, everything was removed in a few hours. Throughout, the scrivener remained standing behind the screen, which I directed to be removed the last thing. It was withdrawn; and, being folded up like a huge folio, left him the motionless occupant of a naked room. I stood in the entry watching him a moment, while something from within me upbraided me.

I re-entered, with my hand in my pocket—and—and my heart in my mouth.

'Good-bye, Bartleby; I am going—good-bye, and God some way bless you; and take that,' slipping something in his hand. But it dropped upon the floor, and then—strange to say—I tore myself from him whom I had so longed to be rid of.

Established in my new quarters, for a day or two I kept the door locked, and started at every footfall in the passages. When I returned to my rooms, after any little absence, I would pause at the threshold for an instant, and attentively listen, ere applying my key. But these fears were needless. Bartleby never came nigh me.

I thought all was going well, when a perturbed-looking stranger visited me, inquiring whether I was the person who had recently occupied rooms at No. — Wall Street.

Full of forebodings, I replied that I was.

'Then, sir,' said the stranger, who proved a lawyer, 'you are responsible for the man you left there. He refuses to do any copying; he refuses to do anything; he says he prefers not to; and he refuses to quit the premises.'

'I am very sorry, sir,' said I, with assumed tranquility, but an inward tremor, 'but, really, the man you allude to is nothing to me—he is no relation or apprentice of mine, that you should hold me responsible for him.'

'In mercy's name, who is he?'

'I certainly cannot inform you. I know nothing about him. Formerly I employed him as a copyist; but he has done nothing for me now for some time past.'

'I shall settle him, then—good morning, sir.'

Several days passed, and I heard nothing more; and, though I often felt a charitable prompting to call at the place and see poor Bartleby, yet a certain squeamishness, of I know not what, withheld me.

All is over with him, by this time, thought I, at last, when, through another week, no further intelligence reached me. But, coming to my room the day after, I found several persons waiting at my door in a high state of nervous excitement.

'That's the man—here he comes,' cried the foremost one, whom I recognized as the lawyer who had previously called upon me alone.

'You must take him away, sir, at once,' cried a portly person among them, advancing upon me, and whom I knew to be the landlord of No. — Wall Street. 'These gentlemen, my tenants, cannot stand it any longer; Mr B——', pointing to the lawyer, 'has turned him out of his room, and he now persists in haunting the building generally, sitting upon the banisters of the stairs by day, and sleeping in the entry by night. Everybody is concerned; clients are leaving the offices; some fears are entertained of a mob; something you must do, and that without delay.'

Aghast at this torrent, I fell back before it, and would fain have locked myself in my new quarters. In vain I persisted that Bartleby was nothing to me—no more than to anyone else. In vain—I was the last person known to have anything to do with him, and they held me to the terrible account. Fearful, then, of being exposed in the papers (as one person present obscurely threatened), I considered the matter, and, at length, said, that if the lawyer would give me a confidential interview with the scrivener, in his (the lawyer's) own room, I would, that afternoon, strive my best to rid them of the nuisance they complained of.

Going upstairs to my old haunt, there was Bartleby silently sitting upon the banister at the landing.

'What are you doing here, Bartleby?' said I.

'Sitting upon the banister,' he mildly replied.

I motioned him into the lawyer's room, who then left us.

'Bartleby,' said I, 'are you aware that you are the cause of a great tribulation to me, by persisting in occupying the entry after being dismissed from the office?'

No answer.

'Now one of two things must take place. Either you must do something, or something must be done to you. Now what sort of business would you like to engage in? Would you like to re-engage in copying for someone?'

'No; I would prefer not to make any change.'

'Would you like a clerkship in a dry-goods store?'

'There is too much confinement about that. No, I would not like a clerkship; but I am not particular.'

'Too much confinement,' I cried, 'why, you keep yourself confined all the time!'

'I would prefer not to take a clerkship,' he rejoined, as if to settle that little item at once.

'How would a bartender's business suit you? There is no trying of the eyesight in that.'

'I would not like it at all; though, as I said before, I am not particular.'

His unwonted wordiness inspired me. I returned to the charge.

'Well, then, would you like to travel through the country collecting bills for the merchants? That would improve your health.'

'No, I would prefer to be doing something else.'

'How, then, would going as a companion to Europe, to entertain some young gentleman with your conversation—how would that suit you?'

'Not at all. It does not strike me that there is anything definite about that. I like to be stationary. But I am not particular.'

'Stationary you shall be, then,' I cried, now losing all patience, and, for the first time in all my exasperating connection with him, fairly flying into a passion. 'If you do not go away from these premises before night, I shall feel bound—indeed, I *am* bound—to—to—to quit the premises myself!' I rather absurdly concluded, knowing not with what possible threat to try to frighten his immobility into compliance. Despairing of all further efforts, I was precipitately leaving him, when a final thought occurred to me—one which had not been wholly unindulged before.

'Bartleby,' said I, in the kindest tone I could assume under such exciting circumstances, 'will you go home with me now—not to my office, but my dwelling—and remain there till we can conclude upon some convenient arrangement for you at our leisure? Come, let us start now, right away.'

'No: at present I would prefer not to make any change at all.'

I answered nothing; but, effectually dodging everyone by the suddenness and rapidity of my flight, rushed from the building, ran up Wall Street towards Broadway, and, jumping into the first omnibus, was soon removed from pursuit. As soon as tranquility returned, I distinctly perceived that I had now done all that I possibly could, both in respect to the demands of the landlord and his tenants, and with regard to my own desire and sense of duty, to benefit Bartleby, and shield him from rude persecution. I now strove to be entirely care-free and quiescent; and my conscience justified me in the attempt; though, indeed, it was not so successful as I could have wished. So fearful was I of being again hunted out by the incensed landlord and his exasperated tenants, that, surrendering my business to Nippers, for a few days, I drove about the upper part of the town and through the suburbs, in my rockaway; crossed over to Jersey City and Hoboken, and paid fugitive visits to Manhattanville and Astoria. In fact, I almost lived in my rockaway for the time.

When again I entered my office, lo, a note from the landlord lay upon the desk. I opened it with trembling hands. It informed me that the writer had sent to the police, and had Bartleby removed to the Tombs as a vagrant. Moreover, since I knew more about him than anyone else, he wished me to appear at that place, and make a suitable statement of the facts. These tidings had a conflicting effect upon me. At first I was indignant; but, at last, almost approved. The landlord's energetic, summary disposition, had led him to adopt a procedure which I do not think I would have decided upon myself; and yet, as a last resort, under such peculiar circumstances, it seemed the only plan.

As I afterwards learned, the poor scrivener, when told that he must be conducted to the Tombs, offered not the slightest obstacle, but, in his pale, unmoving way, silently acquiesced.

Some of the compassionate and curious bystanders joined the party; and headed by one of the constables arm-in-arm with Bartleby, the silent procession filed its way through all the noise, and heat, and joy of the roaring thoroughfares at noon.

The same day I received the note, I went to the Tombs, or, to speak more properly, the Halls of Justice. Seeking the right officer, I stated the purpose of my call, and was informed that the individual I described was, indeed, within. I then assured the functionary that Bartleby was a perfectly honest man, and greatly to be compassionated, however unaccountably eccentric. I narrated all I knew, and closed by suggesting the idea of letting him remain in as indulgent confinement as possible, till something less harsh might be done—though, indeed, I hardly knew what. At all events, if nothing else could be decided upon, the alms-house must receive him. I then begged to have an interview.

Being under no disgraceful charge, and quite serene and harmless in all his ways, they had permitted him freely to wander about the prison, and, especially, in the inclosed grass-platted yards thereof. And so I found him there, standing all alone in the quietest of the yards, his face towards a high wall, while all around, from the narrow slits of the jail windows, I thought I saw peering out upon him the eyes of murderers and thieves.

'Bartleby!'

'I know you,' he said, without looking round—'and I want nothing to say to you.'

'It was not I that brought you here, Bartleby,' said I, keenly pained at his implied suspicion. 'And to you, this should not be so vile a place. Nothing reproachful attaches to you by being here. And see, it is not so sad a place as one might think. Look, there is the sky, and here is the grass.'

'I know where I am,' he replied, but would say nothing more, and so I left him.

As I entered the corridor again, a broad meat-like man, in an apron accosted me, and, jerking his thumb over his shoulder, said—'Is that your friend?'

'Yes.'

'Does he want to starve? If he does, let him live on the prison fare, that's all.'

'Who are you?' asked I, not knowing what to make of such an unofficially speaking person in such a place.

'I am the grub-man. Such gentlemen as have friends here, hire me to provide them with something good to eat.'

'Is this so?' said I, turning to the turnkey.

He said it was.

'Well, then,' said I, slipping some silver into the grub-man's hand (for so they called him), 'I want you to give particular attention to my friend there; let him have the best dinner you can get. And you must be as polite to him as possible.'

'Introduce me, will you?' said the grub-man, looking at me with an expression which seemed to say he was all impatience for an opportunity to give a specimen of his breeding.

Thinking it would prove of benefit to the scrivener, I acquiesced; and, asking the grub-man his name, went up with him to Bartleby.

'Bartleby, this is a friend; you will find him very useful to you.'

'Your sarvant, sir, your sarvant,' said the grub-man, making a low salutation behind his apron. 'Hope you find it pleasant here, sir, nice grounds—cool apartments—hope you'll stay with us some time—try to make it agreeable. What will you have for dinner today?'

'I prefer not to dine today,' said Bartleby, turning away. 'It would disagree with me; I am unused to dinners.' So saying, he slowly moved to the other side of the enclosure, and took up a position fronting the dead-wall.

'How's this?' said the grub-man, addressing me with a stare of astonishment. 'He's odd, ain't he?'

'I think he is a little deranged,' said I, sadly.

'Deranged? deranged is it? Well, now, upon my word, I thought that friend of yourn was a gentleman forger; they are always pale and genteel-like, them forgers. I can't help pity 'em—can't help it, sir. Did you know Monroe Edwards?' he added, touchingly, and paused. Then, laying his hand piteously on my shoulder, sighed, 'He died of consumption at Sing-Sing. So you weren't acquainted with Monroe?'

'No, I was never socially acquainted with any forgers. But I can not stop longer. Look to my friend yonder. You will not lose by it. I will see you again.'

Some few days after this, I again obtained admission to the Tombs, and went through the corridors in quest of Bartleby; but without finding him.

'I saw him coming from his cell not long ago,' said a turnkey, 'maybe he's gone to loiter in the yards.'

So I went in that direction.

'Are you looking for the silent man?' said another turnkey, passing me. 'Yonder he lies—sleeping in the yard there. 'Tis not twenty minutes since I saw him lie down.'

The yard was entirely quiet. It was not accessible to the common prisoners. The surrounding walls, of amazing thickness, kept off all sounds behind them. The Egyptian character of the masonry weighed upon me with its gloom. But a soft imprisoned turf grew under foot. The heart of the eternal pyramids, it seemed, wherein, by some strange magic, through the clefts, grass-seed, dropped by birds, had sprung.

Strangely huddled at the base of the wall, his knees drawn up, and lying on his side, his head touching the cold stones, I saw the wasted Bartleby. But nothing stirred. I paused; then went close up to him; stooped over, and saw that his dim eyes were open; otherwise he seemed profoundly sleeping. Something prompted me to touch him. I felt his hand, when a tingling shiver ran up my arm and down my spine to my feet.

The round face of the grub-man peered upon me now. 'His dinner is ready. Won't he dine today, either? Or does he live without dining?'

'Lives without dining,' said I, and closed the eyes.

'Eh!—He's asleep, ain't he?'

'With kings and counsellors,' murmured I.

There would seem little need for proceeding further in this history. Imagination will readily supply the meagre recital of poor Bartleby's interment. But, ere parting with the reader, let me say, that if this little narrative has sufficiently interested him to awaken curiosity as to who Bartleby was, and what manner of life he led prior to the present narrator's making his acquaintance, I can only reply, that in such curiosity I fully share, but am wholly unable to gratify it. Yet here I hardly know whether I should divulge one little item of rumour, which came to my ear a few months after the scrivener's decease. Upon what basis it rested, I could never ascertain; and hence, how true it is I cannot tell. But, inasmuch as this vague report has not been without a certain suggestive interest to me, however sad, it may prove the same with some others, and so I will briefly mention it. The report was this: that Bartleby had been a subordinate clerk in the Dead Letter Office at Washington, from which he had been suddenly removed by a change in the administration. When I think over this rumour, hardly can I express the emotions which seize me. Dead letters! does it not sound like dead men? Conceive a man by nature and misfortune prone to a pallid hopelessness, can any business seem more fitted to heighten it than that of continually handling these dead letters, and assorting them for the flames? For by the cart-load they are annually burned. Sometimes from out of the folded paper the pale clerks take a ring—the finger it was meant for, perhaps, moulders in the grave; a bank-note sent in swiftest charity—he whom it would relieve, nor eats nor hungers anymore; pardon for those who died despairing; hope for those who died unhoping; good tidings for those who died stifled by unrelieved calamities. On errands of life, these letters speed to death.

Ah, Bartleby! Ah, humanity!

1856

# Kate Chopin

## 1851–1904

Kate O'Flaherty was born in St Louis, Missouri, to an Irish immigrant father and a French mother. She was educated in a Catholic convent school in St Louis, and married Oscar Chopin, a Louisiana banker, when she was 19. In Louisiana she had six children before her husband's death in 1882, after which she returned to St Louis and began writing to help support herself and her family. Her fine novel *The Awakening*, which has been called an American *Madame Bovary*, was published in 1899 and instantly became the target of attacks by reviewers. It was actually removed from the shelves of the Mercantile Library in St Louis, and Chopin was denied membership in the Fine Arts Club because the book was, as a local magazine said, 'too strong drink for moral babes and should be labelled "poison".' Like so many writers, Chopin began to get her due appreciation only after her death. Although the story reprinted here, which first appeared in *Vogue* (6 December 1894), is the shortest one of Chopin's works, it is, if not 'poison', strong medicine.

# The Story of an Hour

Knowing that Mrs Mallard was afflicted with a heart trouble, great care was taken to break to her as gently as possible the news of her husband's death.

It was her sister Josephine who told her, in broken sentences; veiled hints that revealed in half concealing. Her husband's friend Richards was there, too, near her. It was he who had been in the newspaper office when intelligence of the railroad disaster was received, with Brently Mallard's name leading the list of 'killed'. He had only taken the time to assure himself of its truth by a second telegram, and had hastened to forestall any less careful, less tender friend in bearing the sad message.

She did not hear the story as many have heard the same, with a paralyzed inability to accept its significance. She wept at once, with sudden, wild abandonment, in her sister's arms. When the storm of grief had spent itself she went away to her room alone. She would have no one follow her.

There stood, facing the open window, a comfortable, roomy armchair. Into this she sank, pressed down by a physical exhaustion that haunted her body and seemed to reach into her soul.

She could see in the open square before her house the tops of trees that were all aquiver with the new spring life. The delicious breath of rain in the air. In the street below a peddler was crying his wares. The notes of a distant song which someone was singing reached her faintly, and countless sparrows were twittering in the eaves.

There were patches of blue sky showing here and there through the clouds that had met and piled one above the other in the west facing her window.

She sat with her head thrown back upon the cushion of the chair, quite motionless, except when a sob came up into her throat and shook her, as a child who has cried itself to sleep continues to sob in its dreams.

She was young, with a fair, calm face, whose lines bespoke repression and even a certain strength. But now there was a dull stare in her eyes, whose gaze was fixed away off yonder on one of those patches of blue sky. It was not a glance of reflection, but rather indicated a suspension of intelligent thought.

There was something coming to her and she was waiting for it, fearfully. What was it? She did not know; it was too subtle and elusive to name. But she felt it, creeping out of the sky, reaching toward her through the sounds, the scents, the colour that filled the air.

Now her bosom rose and fell tumultuously. She was beginning to recognize this thing that was approaching to possess her, and she was striving to beat it back with her will—as powerless as her two white slender hands would have been.

When she abandoned herself a little whispered word escaped her slightly parted lips. She said it over and over under her breath: 'free, free, free!' The vacant stare and the look of terror that had followed it went from her eyes. They stayed keen and bright. Her pulses beat fast, and the coursing blood warmed and relaxed every inch of her body.

She did not stop to ask if it were or were not a monstrous joy that held her. A clear and exalted perception enabled her to dismiss the suggestion as trivial.

She knew that she would weep again when she saw the kind, tender hands folded in death; the face that had never looked save with love upon her, fixed and grey and dead. But she saw beyond that bitter moment a long procession of years to come that would belong to her absolutely. And she opened and spread her arms out to them in welcome.

There would be no one to live for her during those coming years; she would live for herself. There would be no powerful will bending hers in that blind persistence with which men and women believe they have a right to impose a private will upon a fellow creature. A kind intention or a cruel intention made the act seem no less a crime as she looked upon it in that brief moment of illumination.

And yet she had loved him—sometimes. Often she had not. What did it matter! What could love, the unsolved mystery, count for in face of this possession of self-assertion which she suddenly recognized as the strongest impulse of her being!

'Free! Body and soul free!' she kept whispering.

Josephine was kneeling before the closed door with her lips to the keyhole, imploring for admission. 'Louise, open the door! I beg; open the door—you will make yourself ill. What are you doing, Louise? For heaven's sake open the door.'

'Go away. I am not making myself ill.' No; she was drinking in a very elixir of life through that open window.

Her fancy was running riot along those days ahead of her. Spring days, and summer days, and all sorts of days that would be her own. She breathed a quick prayer that life might be long. It was only yesterday she had thought with a shudder that life might be long.

She arose at length and opened the door to her sister's importunities. There was a feverish triumph in her eyes, and she carried herself unwittingly like a goddess of Victory. She clasped her sister's waist, and together they descended the stairs. Richards stood waiting for them at the bottom.

Someone was opening the front door with a latchkey. It was Brently Mallard who entered, a little travel-stained, composedly carrying his grip-sack and umbrella. He had been far from the scene of accident, and did not even know there had been one. He stood amazed at Josephine's piercing cry; at Richards' quick motion to screen him from the view of his wife.

But Richards was too late.

When the doctors came they said she had died of heart disease—of joy that kills.

1894

# Charlotte Perkins Gilman

1860–1935

Born in Hartford, Connecticut, Charlotte Anna Perkins was the grandniece of Harriet Beecher Stowe, author of *Uncle Tom's Cabin*. She grew up in an unstable family environment that her father abandoned soon after her birth. She attended many different schools and ended her formal education when she was 15. Her first marriage ended in 1892, when she filed for divorce; she relinquished custody of her daughter, Katharine, to her husband and his new wife. In 1900 she married Houghton Gilman in a relationship founded on her beliefs in an equal partnership between the woman and the man.

In her autobiography Gilman wrote that her heredity included 'the Beecher urge to social service, the Beecher wit and gift of words, and such small sense of art as I have'. A journalist, she edited the monthly liberal journal *The Forerunner* and wrote and lectured on topics concerning women, social rights, and the labour movement. Her non-fiction works include *Women and Economics* (1898), which described the subordinate role of women and proposed social and labour reform. Later in her life she wrote novels, utopian in nature, that presented social evils and feminist remedies. A Gothic tale of a personal descent into insanity, 'The Yellow Wallpaper' is a semi-autobiographical story. Written after Gilman's institutionalization as a consequence of post-natal depression following Katharine's birth, it is a devastating indictment of the restricting bonds of marriage and motherhood.

## The Yellow Wallpaper

It is very seldom that mere ordinary people like John and myself secure ancestral halls for the summer.

A colonial mansion, a hereditary estate, I would say a haunted house, and reach the height of romantic felicity—but that would be asking too much of fate!

Still I will proudly declare that there is something queer about it.

Else, why should it be let so cheaply? And why have stood so long untenanted?

John laughs at me, of course, but one expects that in marriage.

John is practical in the extreme. He has no patience with faith, an intense horror of superstition, and he scoffs openly at any talk of things not to be felt and seen and put down in figures.

John is a physician, and *perhaps*—(I would not say it to a living soul, of course, but this is dead paper and a great relief to my mind—) *perhaps* that is one reason I do not get well faster.

You see he does not believe I am sick!

And what can one do?

If a physician of high standing, and one's own husband, assures friends and relatives that there is really nothing the matter with one but temporary nervous depression—a slight hysterical tendency—what is one to do?

My brother is also a physician, and also of high standing, and he says the same thing.

So I take phosphates or phosphites—whichever it is, and tonics, and journeys, and air, and exercise, and am absolutely forbidden to 'work' until I am well again.

Personally, I disagree with their ideas.

Personally, I believe that congenial work, with excitement and change, would do me good.

But what is one to do?

I did write for a while in spite of them; but it *does* exhaust me a good deal—having to be so sly about it, or else meet with heavy opposition.

I sometimes fancy that in my condition if I had less opposition and more society and stimulus—but John says the very worst thing I can do is think about my condition, and I confess it always makes me feel bad.

So I will let it alone and talk about the house.

The most beautiful place! It is quite alone, standing well back from the road, quite three miles from the village. It makes me think of English places that you read about, for there are hedges and walls and gates that lock, and lots of separate little houses for the gardeners and people.

There is a *delicious* garden! I never saw such a garden—large and shady, full of box-bordered paths, and lined with long grape-covered arbours with seats under them.

There were greenhouses, too, but they are all broken now.

There was some legal trouble, I believe, something about the heirs and co-heirs; anyhow, the place has been empty for years.

That spoils my ghostliness, I am afraid, but I don't care—there is something strange about the house—I can feel it.

I even said so to John one moonlight evening, but he said what I felt was a *draft*, and shut the window.

I get unreasonably angry with John sometimes. I'm sure I never used to be so sensitive. I think it is due to this nervous condition.

But John says if I feel so, I shall neglect proper self-control; so I take pains to control myself—before him, at least, and that makes me very tired.

I don't like our room a bit. I wanted one downstairs that opened on the piazza and had roses all over the window, and such pretty old-fashioned chintz hangings! but John would not hear of it.

He said there was only one window and not room for two beds, and no near room for him if he took another.

He is very careful and loving, and hardly lets me stir without special direction.

I have a schedule prescription for each hour in the day; he takes all care from me, and so I feel basely ungrateful not to value it more.

He said we came here solely on my account, that I was to have perfect rest and all the air I could get. 'Your exercise depends on your strength, my dear,' said he, 'and your food somewhat on your appetite; but air you can absorb all the time.' So we took the nursery at the top of the house.

It is a big, airy room, the whole floor nearly, with windows that look all ways, and air and sunshine galore. It was nursery first and then playroom and gymnasium,

I should judge; for the windows are barred for little children, and there are rings and things in the walls.

The paint and paper look as if a boys' school had used it. It is stripped off—the paper—in great patches all around the head of my bed, about as far as I can reach, and in a great place on the other side of the room low down. I never saw a worse paper in my life.

One of those sprawling flamboyant patterns committing every artistic sin.

It is dull enough to confuse the eye in following, pronounced enough to constantly irritate and provoke study, and when you follow the lame uncertain curves for a little distance they suddenly commit suicide—plunge off at outrageous angles, destroy themselves in unheard of contradictions.

The colour is repellant, almost revolting; a smouldering unclean yellow, strangely faded by the slow-turning sunlight.

It is a dull yet lurid orange in some places, a sickly sulphur tint in others.

No wonder the children hated it! I should hate it myself if I had to live in this room long.

There comes John, and I must put this away,—he hates to have me write a word.

We have been here two weeks, and I haven't felt like writing before, since that first day.

I am sitting by the window now, up in this atrocious nursery, and there is nothing to hinder my writing as much as I please, save lack of strength.

John is away all day, and even some nights when his cases are serious.

I am glad my case is not serious!

But these nervous troubles are dreadfully depressing.

John does not know how much I really suffer. He knows there is no *reason* to suffer, and that satisfies him.

Of course it is only nervousness. It does weigh on me so not to do my duty in any way!

I meant to be such a help to John, such a real rest and comfort, and here I am a comparative burden already!

Nobody would believe what an effort it is to do what little I am able,—to dress and entertain, and order things.

It is fortunate Mary is so good with the baby. Such a dear baby!

And yet I *cannot* be with him, it makes me so nervous.

I suppose John never was nervous in his life. He laughs at me so about this wallpaper!

At first he meant to repaper the room, but afterwards he said that I was letting it get the better of me, and that nothing was worse for a nervous patient than to give way to such fancies.

He said that after the wallpaper was changed it would be the heavy bedstead, and then the barred windows, and then that gate at the head of the stairs, and so on.

'You know the place is doing you good,' he said, 'and really, dear, I don't care to renovate the house just for a three months' rental.'

'Then do let us go downstairs,' I said, 'there are such pretty rooms there.'

Then he took me in his arms and called me a blessed little goose, and said he would go down cellar, if I wished, and have it whitewashed into the bargain.

But he is right enough about the beds and windows and things.

It is an airy and comfortable room as anyone need wish, and, of course, I would not be so silly as to make him uncomfortable just for a whim.

I'm really getting quite fond of the big room, all but that horrid paper.

Out of one window I can see the garden, those mysterious deep-shaded arbours, the riotous old-fashioned flowers, and bushes and gnarly trees.

Out of another I get a lovely view of the bay and a little private wharf belonging to the estate. There is a beautiful shaded lane that runs down there from the house. I always fancy I see people walking in these numerous paths and arbours, but John has cautioned me not to give way to fancy in the least. He says that with my imaginative power and habit of story-making, a nervous weakness like mine is sure to lead to all manner of excited fancies, and that I ought to use my will and good sense to check the tendency. So I try.

I think sometimes that if I were only well enough to write a little it would relieve the press of ideas and rest me.

But I find I get pretty tired when I try.

It is so discouraging not to have any advice and companionship about my work. When I get really well, John says he will ask Cousin Henry and Julia down for a long visit; but he says he would as soon put fireworks in my pillowcase as to let me have those stimulating people about now.

I wish I could get well faster.

But I must not think about that. This paper looks to me as if it *knew* what a vicious influence it had!

There is a recurrent spot where the pattern lolls like a broken neck and two bulbous eyes stare at you upside down.

I get positively angry with the impertinence of it and the everlastingness. Up and down and sideways they crawl, and those absurd, unblinking eyes are everywhere. There is one place where two breadths didn't match, and the eyes go all up and down the line, one a little higher than the other.

I never saw so much expression in an inanimate thing before, and we all know how much expression they have! I used to lie awake as a child and get more entertainment and terror out of blank walls and plain furniture than most children could find in a toy-store.

I remember what a kindly wink the knobs of our big, old bureau used to have, and there was one chair that always seemed like a strong friend.

I used to feel that if any of the other things looked too fierce I could always hop into that chair and be safe.

The furniture in this room is no worse than inharmonious, however, for we had to bring it all from downstairs. I suppose when this was used as a playroom they had to take the nursery things out, and no wonder! I never saw such ravages as the children have made here.

The wallpaper, as I said before, is torn off in spots, and it sticketh closer than a brother—they must have had perseverance as well as hatred.

Then the floor is scratched and gouged and splintered, the plaster itself is dug out here and there, and this great heavy bed which is all we found in the room, looks as if it had been through the wars.

But I don't mind a bit—only the paper.

There comes John's sister. Such a dear girl as she is, and so careful of me! I must not let her find me writing.

She is a perfect and enthusiastic housekeeper, and hopes for no better profession. I verily believe she thinks it is the writing which made me sick!

But I can write when she is out, and see her a long way off from these windows.

There is one that commands the road, a lovely shaded winding road, and one that just looks off over the country. A lovely country, too, full of great elms and velvet meadows.

This wallpaper has a kind of subpattern in a different shade, a particularly irritating one, for you can only see it in certain lights, and not clearly then.

But in the places where it isn't faded and where the sun is just so—I can see a strange, provoking, formless sort of figure, that seems to skulk about behind that silly conspicuous front design.

There's sister on the stairs!

Well, the Fourth of July is over! The people are all gone and I am tired out. John thought it might do me good to see a little company, so we just had mother and Nellie and the children down for a week.

Of course I didn't do a thing. Jennie sees to everything now.

But it tired me all the same.

John says if I don't pick up faster he shall send me to Weir Mitchell in the fall.

But I don't want to go there at all. I had a friend who was in his hands once, and she says he is just like John and my brother, only more so!

Besides, it is such an undertaking to go so far.

I don't feel as if it was worth while to turn my hand over for anything, and I'm getting dreadfully fretful and querulous.

I cry at nothing, and cry most of the time.

Of course, I don't when John is here, or anybody else, but when I am alone.

And I am alone a good deal just now. John is kept in town very often by serious cases, and Jennie is good and lets me alone when I want her to.

So I walk a little in the garden or down that lovely lane, sit on the porch under the roses, and lie down here a good deal.

I'm getting really fond of the room in spite of the wallpaper. Perhaps *because* of the wallpaper.

It dwells in my mind so!

I lie here on this great immovable bed—it is nailed down, I believe—and follow that pattern about by the hour. It is as good as gymnastics, I assure you. I start, we'll say, at the bottom, down in the corner over there where it has not been touched, and I determine for the thousandth time that I *will* follow that pointless pattern to some sort of conclusion.

I know a little of the principle of design, and I know this thing was not arranged on any laws of radiation, or alternation, or repetition, or symmetry, or anything else that I ever heard of.

It is repeated, of course, by the breadths, but not otherwise.

Looked at in one way each breadth stands alone, the bloated curves and flourishes—a kind of 'debased Romanesque' with *delirium tremens*—go waddling up and down in isolated columns of fatuity.

But, on the other hand, they connect diagonally, and the sprawling outlines run off in great slanting waves of optic horror, like a lot of wallowing seaweeds in full chase.

The whole thing goes horizontally, too, at least it seems so, and I exhaust myself in trying to distinguish the order of its going in that direction.

They have used a horizontal breadth for a frieze, and that adds wonderfully to the confusion.

There is one end of the room where it is almost intact, and there, when the crosslights fade and the low sun shines directly upon it, I can almost fancy radiation after all,—the interminable grotesques seem to form around a common centre and rush off in headlong plunges of equal distraction.

It makes me tired to follow it. I will take a nap I guess.

I don't know why I should write this.

I don't want to.

I don't feel able.

And I know John would think it absurd. But I *must* say what I feel and think in some way—it is such a relief!

But the effort is getting to be greater than the relief.

Half the time now I am awfully lazy, and lie down ever so much.

John says I mustn't lose my strength, and has me take cod liver oil and lots of tonics and things, to say nothing of ale and wine and rare meat.

Dear John! He loves me very dearly, and hates to have me sick. I tried to have a real earnest reasonable talk with him the other day, and tell him how I wish he would let me go and make a visit to Cousin Henry and Julia.

But he said I wasn't able to go, nor able to stand it after I got there; and I did not make out a very good case for myself, for I was crying before I had finished.

It is getting to be a great effort for me to think straight. Just this nervous weakness I suppose.

And dear John gathered me up in his arms, and just carried me upstairs and laid me on the bed, and sat by me and read to me till it tired my head.

He said I was his darling and his comfort and all he had, and that I must take care of myself for his sake, and keep well.

He says no one but myself can help me out of it, that I must use my will and self-control and not let any silly fancies run away with me.

There's one comfort, the baby is well and happy, and does not have to occupy this nursery with the horrid wallpaper.

If we had not used it, that blessed child would have! What a fortunate escape! Why, I wouldn't have a child of mine, an impressionable little thing, live in such a room for worlds.

I never thought of it before, but it is lucky that John kept me here after all, I can stand it so much easier than a baby, you see.

Of course I never mention it to them anymore—I am too wise,—but I keep watch of it all the same.

There are things in that paper that nobody knows but me, or ever will.

Behind that outside pattern the dim shapes get clearer every day.

It is always the same shape, only very numerous.

And it is like a woman stooping down and creeping about behind that pattern. I don't like it a bit. I wonder—I begin to think—I wish John would take me away from here!

It is so hard to talk with John about my case because he is so wise, and because he loves me so.

But I tried it last night.

It was moonlight. The moon shines in all around just as the sun does.

I hate to see it sometimes, it creeps so slowly, and always comes in by one window or another.

John was asleep and I hated to waken him, so I kept still and watched the moonlight on that undulating wallpaper till I felt creepy.

The faint figure behind seemed to shake the pattern, just as if she wanted to get out.

I got up softly and went to feel and see if the paper *did* move, and when I came back John was awake.

'What is it, little girl?' he said. 'Don't go walking about like that—you'll get cold.'

I thought it was a good time to talk, so I told him that I really was not gaining here, and that I wished he would take me away.

'Why, darling!' said he, 'our lease will be up in three weeks, and I can't see how to leave before.

'The repairs are not done at home, and I cannot possibly leave town just now. Of course if you were in any danger, I could and would, but you really are better, dear, whether you can see it or not. I am a doctor, dear, and I know. You are gaining flesh and colour, your appetite is better, I feel really much easier about you.'

'I don't weigh a bit more,' said I, 'nor as much; and my appetite may be better in the evening when you are here, but it is worse in the morning when you are away!'

'Bless her little heart!' said he with a big hug, 'she shall be as sick as she pleases! But now let's improve the shining hours by going to sleep, and talk about it in the morning!'

'And you won't go away?' I asked gloomily.

'Why, how can I, dear? It is only three weeks more and then we will take a nice little trip of a few days while Jennie is getting the house ready. Really dear you are better!'

'Better in body perhaps—' I began, and stopped short, for he sat up straight and looked at me with such a stern, reproachful look that I could not say another word.

'My darling,' said he, 'I beg of you, for my sake and for our child's sake, as well as for your own, that you will never for one instant let that idea enter your mind! There is nothing so dangerous, so fascinating, to a temperament like yours. It is a false and foolish fancy. Can you not trust me as a physician when I tell you so?'

So of course I said no more on that score, and we went to sleep before long. He thought I was asleep first, but I wasn't, and lay there for hours trying to decide whether that front pattern and the back pattern really did move together or separately.

On a pattern like this, by daylight, there is a lack of sequence, a defiance of law, that is a constant irritant to a normal mind.

The colour is hideous enough, and unreliable enough, and infuriating enough, but the pattern is torturing.

You think you have mastered it, but just as you get well underway in following, it turns a back-somersault and there you are. It slaps you in the face, knocks you down, and tramples upon you. It is like a bad dream.

The outside pattern is a florid arabesque, reminding one of a fungus. If you can imagine a toadstool in joints, an interminable string of toadstools, budding and sprouting in endless convolutions—why, that is something like it.

That is, sometimes!

There is one marked peculiarity about this paper, a thing nobody seems to notice but myself, and that is that it changes as the light changes.

When the sun shoots in through the east window—I always watch for that first long, straight ray—it changes so quickly that I never can quite believe it.

That is why I watch it always.

By moonlight—the moon shines in all night when there is a moon—I wouldn't know it was the same paper.

At night in any kind of light, in twilight, candlelight, lamplight, and worst of all by moonlight, it becomes bars! The outside pattern I mean, and the woman behind it is as plain as can be.

I didn't realize for a long time what the thing was that showed behind, that dim sub-pattern, but now I am quite sure it is a woman.

By daylight she is subdued, quiet. I fancy it is the pattern that keeps her so still. It is so puzzling. It keeps me quiet by the hour.

I lie down ever so much now. John says it is good for me, and to sleep all I can.

Indeed he started the habit by making me lie down for an hour after each meal.

It is a very bad habit I am convinced, for you see I don't sleep.

And that cultivates deceit, for I don't tell them I'm awake—O no!

The fact is I am getting a little afraid of John.

He seems very queer sometimes, and even Jennie has an inexplicable look.

It strikes me occasionally, just as a scientific hypothesis,—that perhaps it is the paper!

I have watched John when he did not know I was looking, and come into the room suddenly on the most innocent excuses, and I've caught him several times *looking at the paper*! And Jennie too. I caught Jennie with her hand on it once.

She didn't know I was in the room, and when I asked her in a quiet, a very quiet voice, with the most restrained manner possible, what she was doing with the paper—she turned around as if she had been caught stealing, and looked quite angry—asked me why I should frighten her so!

Then she said that the paper stained everything it touched, that she had found yellow smooches on all my clothes and John's, and she wished we would be more careful!

Did not that sound innocent? But I know she was studying that pattern, and I am determined that nobody shall find it out but myself!

Life is very much more exciting now than it used to be. You see I have something more to expect, to look forward to, to watch. I really do eat better, and am more quiet than I was.

John is so pleased to see me improve! He laughed a little the other day, and said I seemed to be flourishing in spite of my wallpaper.

I turned it off with a laugh. I had no intention of telling him it was *because* of the wallpaper—he would make fun of me. He might even want to take me away.

I don't want to leave now until I have found it out. There is a week more, and I think that will be enough.

I'm feeling ever so much better! I don't sleep much at night, for it is so interesting to watch developments; but I sleep a good deal in the daytime.

In the daytime it is tiresome and perplexing.

There are always new shoots on the fungus, and new shades of yellow all over it. I cannot keep count of them, though I have tried conscientiously.

It is the strangest yellow, that wallpaper! It makes me think of all the yellow things I ever saw—not beautiful ones like buttercups, but old foul, bad yellow things.

But there is something else about that paper—the smell! I noticed it the moment we came into the room, but with so much air and sun it was not bad. Now we have had a week of fog and rain, and whether the windows are open or not, the smell is here.

It creeps all over the house.

I find it hovering in the dining room, skulking in the parlour, hiding in the hall, lying in wait for me on the stairs.

It gets into my hair.

Even when I go to ride, if I turn my head suddenly and surprise it—there is that smell!

Such a peculiar odour, too! I have spent hours in trying to analyze it, to find what it smelled like.

It is not bad—at first, and very gentle, but quite the subtlest, most enduring odour I ever met.

In this damp weather it is awful, I wake up in the night and find it hanging over me.

It used to disturb me at first. I thought seriously of burning the house—to reach the smell.

But now I am used to it. The only thing I can think of that it is like is the *colour* of the paper! A yellow smell.

There is a very funny mark on this wall, low down, near the mopboard. A streak that runs around the room. It goes behind every piece of furniture, except the bed, a long, straight, even *smooch*, as if it had been rubbed over and over.

I wonder how it was done and who did it, and what they did it for. Round and round and round—round and round and round—it makes me dizzy!

I really have discovered something at last.

Through watching so much at night, when it changes so, I have finally found out.

The front pattern *does* move—and no wonder! The woman behind shakes it!

Sometimes I think there are a great many women behind, and sometimes only one, and she crawls around fast, and her crawling shakes it all over.

Then in the very bright spots she keeps still, and in the very shady spots she just takes hold of the bars and shakes them hard.

And she is all the time trying to climb through. But nobody could climb through that pattern—it strangles so; I think that is why it has so many heads.

They get through, and then the pattern strangles them off and turns them upside down, and makes their eyes white!

If those heads were covered or taken off it would not be half so bad.

I think that woman gets out in the daytime!

And I'll tell you why—privately—I've seen her!

I can see her out of every one of my windows!

It is the same woman, I know, for she is always creeping, and most women do not creep by daylight.

I see her in that long shaded lane, creeping up and down. I see her in those dark grape arbours, creeping all around the garden.

I see her on that long road under the trees, creeping along, and when a carriage comes she hides under the blackberry vines.

I don't blame her a bit. It must be very humiliating to be caught creeping by daylight!

I always lock the door when I creep by daylight. I can't do it at night, for I know John would suspect something at once.

And John is so queer now, that I don't want to irritate him. I wish he would take another room! Besides, I don't want anybody to get that woman out at night but myself.

I often wonder if I could see her out of all the windows at once.

But, turn as fast as I can, I can only see out of one at one time.

And though I always see her, she *may* be able to creep faster than I can turn!

I have watched her sometimes away off in the open country, creeping as fast as a cloud shadow in a high wind.

If only that top pattern could be gotten off from the under one! I mean to try it, little by little.

I have found out another funny thing, but I shan't tell it this time! It does not do to trust people too much.

There are only two more days to get this paper off, and I believe John is beginning to notice. I don't like the look in his eyes.

And I heard him ask Jennie a lot of professional questions about me. She had a very good report to give.

She said I slept a good deal in the daytime.

John knows I don't sleep well at night, for all I'm so quiet!

He asked me all sorts of questions, too, and pretended to be very loving and kind.

As if I couldn't see through him!

Still, I don't wonder he acts so, sleeping under this paper for three months.

It only interests me, but I feel sure John and Jennie are secretly affected by it.

Hurrah! This is the last day, but it is enough. John had to stay in town over night, and won't be out until this evening.

Jennie wanted to sleep with me—the sly thing! But I told her I should undoubtedly rest better for a night all alone.

That was clever, for really I wasn't alone a bit! As soon as it was moonlight and that poor thing began to crawl and shake the pattern, I got up and ran to help her.

I pulled and she shook, I shook and she pulled, and before morning we had peeled off yards of that paper.

A strip about as high as my head and half around the room.

And then when the sun came and that awful pattern began to laugh at me, I declared I would finish it today!

We go away tomorrow, and they are moving all my furniture down again to leave things as they were before.

Jennie looked at the wall in amazement, but I told her merrily that I did it out of pure spite at the vicious thing.

She laughed and said she wouldn't mind doing it herself, but I must not get tired.

How she betrayed herself that time!

But I am here, and no person touches this paper but me,—not *alive*!

She tried to get me out of the room—it was too patent! But I said it was so quiet and empty and clean now that I believed I would lie down again and sleep all I could; and not to wake me even for dinner—I would call when I woke.

So now she is gone, and the servants are gone, and the things are gone, and there is nothing left but that great bedstead nailed down, with the canvas mattress we found on it.

We shall sleep downstairs tonight, and take the boat home tomorrow.

I quite enjoy the room, now it is bare again.

How those children did tear about here!

This bedstead is fairly gnawed!

But I must get to work.

I have locked the door and thrown the key down into the front path.

I don't want to go out, and I don't want to have anybody come in, till John comes.

I want to astonish him.

I've got a rope up here that even Jennie did not find. If that woman does get out, and tries to get away, I can tie her!

But I forgot I could not reach far without anything to stand on!

This bed will *not* move!

I tried to lift and push it until I was lame, and then I got so angry I bit off a little piece at one corner—but it hurt my teeth.

Then I peeled off all the paper I could reach standing on the floor. It sticks horribly and the pattern just enjoys it! All those strangled heads and bulbous eyes and waddling fungus growths just shriek with derision!

I am getting angry enough to do something desperate. To jump out of the window would be admirable exercise, but the bars are too strong even to try.

Besides I wouldn't do it. Of course not. I know well enough that a step like that is improper and might be misconstrued.

I don't like to *look* out of the windows even—there are so many of those creeping women, and they creep so fast.

I wonder if they all come out of that wallpaper as I did?

But I am securely fastened now by my well-hidden rope—you don't get *me* out in the road there!

I suppose I shall have to get back behind the pattern when it comes night, and that is hard!

It is so pleasant to be out in this great room and creep around as I please!

I don't want to go outside. I won't, even if Jennie asks me to.

For outside you have to creep on the ground, and everything is green instead of yellow.

But here I can creep smoothly on the floor, and my shoulder just fits in that long smooch around the wall, so I cannot lose my way.

Why there's John at the door!

It is no use, young man, you can't open it!

How he does call and pound!

Now he's crying for an axe.

It would be a shame to break down that beautiful door!

'John dear!' said I in the gentlest voice, 'the key is down by the front steps, under a plantain leaf!'

That silenced him for a few moments.

Then he said—very quietly indeed, 'Open the door, my darling!'

'I can't,' said I. 'The key is down by the front door under a plantain leaf!'

And then I said it again, several times, very gently and slowly, and said it so often that he had to go and see, and he got it of course, and came in. He stopped short by the door.

'What is the matter?' he cried. 'For God's sake, what are you doing!'

I kept on creeping just the same, but I looked at him over my shoulder.

'I've got out at last,' said I, 'in spite of you and Jane! And I've pulled off most of the paper, so you can't put me back!'

Now why should that man have fainted? But he did, and right across my path by the wall, so that I had to creep over him every time!

1892

# Charles G.D. Roberts

## 1860–1935

Born in Douglas, New Brunswick, Charles G.D. Roberts was educated at the University of New Brunswick and taught English, French, and economics at King's College, Nova Scotia, from 1885 until 1895. It was during this time that he edited the literary journal *The Week* and wrote the poems that would establish his position as the father of Canadian poetry. He gave up his teaching career to devote himself to his writing and to promoting the literature of his own country. From 1896 until 1907 he worked as a freelance writer in New York, where he wrote some of his best-known fiction, including his animal stories. He then went abroad to live in Europe and to serve in the Great War before returning in 1925 to Canada, settling in Toronto.

Roberts's poetry is recognized as one of the first flowerings of the poetic voice in Canada, and his remarkable prose—in both short stories and novels—set the standard for his contemporaries and for future generations of writers. In 'Strayed', his first published short story, the animals are indeed animals, and the reader is invited to sympathize with them and their plight.

## Strayed

In the Cabineau Camp, of unlucky reputation, there was a young ox of splendid build, but of a wild and restless nature.

He was one of a yoke, of part Devon blood, large, dark-red, all muscle and nerve, and with wide, magnificent horns. His yoke-fellow was a docile steady worker, the pride of his owner's heart; but he himself seemed never to have been more than half broken in. The woods appeared to draw him by some spell. He wanted to get back to the pastures where he had roamed untrammelled of old with his fellow-steers. The remembrance was in his heart of the dewy mornings when the herd used to feed together on the sweet grassy hillocks, and of the clover-smelling heats of June when they would gather hock-deep in the pools under the green willow-shadows. He hated the yoke, he hated the winter; and he imagined that in the wild pastures he remembered it would be for ever summer. If only he could get back to those pastures!

One day there came the longed-for opportunity; and he seized it. He was standing unyoked beside his mate, and none of the teamsters were near. His head went up in the air, and with a snort of triumph he dashed away through the forest.

For a little while there was a vain pursuit. At last the lumbermen gave it up. 'Let him be!' said his owner, 'an' I rayther guess he'll turn up agin when he gits peckish. He kaint browse on spruce buds an' lung-wort.'

Plunging on with long gallop through the snow he was soon miles from camp. Growing weary he slackened his pace. He came down to a walk. As the lonely red of the winter sunset began to stream through the openings of the forest, flushing the snows of the tiny glades and swales, he grew hungry, and began to swallow unsatisfying mouthfuls of the long moss which roughened the tree-trunks. Ere the moon got up he had filled himself with this fodder, and then he lay down in a little thicket for the night.

But some miles back from his retreat a bear had chanced upon his foot-prints. A strayed steer! That would be an easy prey. The bear started straightway in pursuit. The moon was high in heaven when the crouched ox heard his pursuer's approach. He had no idea what was coming, but he rose to his feet and waited.

The bear plunged boldly into the thicket, never dreaming of resistance. With a muffled roar the ox charged upon him and bore him to the ground. Then he wheeled, and charged again, and the astonished bear was beaten at once. Gored by those keen horns he had no stomach for further encounter, and would fain have made his escape; but as he retreated the ox charged him again, dashing him against a huge trunk. The bear dragged himself up with difficulty, beyond his opponent's reach; and the ox turned scornfully back to his lair.

At the first yellow of dawn the restless creature was again upon the march. He pulled more mosses by the way, but he disliked them the more intensely now because he thought he must be nearing his ancient pastures with their tender grass and their streams. The snow was deeper about him, and his hatred of the winter grew apace. He came out upon a hill-side, partly open, whence the pine had years before been stripped, and where now grew young birches thick together. Here he browsed on the aromatic twigs, but for him it was harsh fare.

As his hunger increased he thought a little longingly of the camp he had deserted, but he dreamed not of turning back. He would keep on till he reached his pastures, and the glad herd of his comrades licking salt out of the trough beside the accustomed pool. He had some blind instinct as to his direction, and kept his course to the south very strictly, the desire in his heart continually leading him aright.

That afternoon he was attacked by a panther, which dropped out of a tree and tore his throat. He dashed under a low branch and scraped his assailant off, then, wheeling about savagely, put the brute to flight with his first mad charge. The panther sprang back into his tree, and the ox continued his quest.

Soon his steps grew weaker, for the panther's cruel claws had gone deep into his neck, and his path was marked with blood. Yet the dream in his great wild eyes was not dimmed as his strength ebbed away. His weakness he never noticed or heeded. The desire that was urging him absorbed all other thoughts—even, almost, his sense of hunger. This, however, it was easy for him to assuage, after a fashion, for the long, grey, unnourishing mosses were abundant.

By and by his path led him into the bed of a stream, whose waters could be heard faintly tinkling on thin pebbles beneath their coverlet of ice and snow. His slow steps conducted him far along this open course. Soon after he had disappeared, around a curve in the distance there came the panther, following stealthily upon his crimsoned trail. The crafty beast was waiting till the bleeding and the hunger should do its work, and the object of its inexorable pursuit should have no more heart left for resistance.

This was late in the afternoon. The ox was now possessed with his desire, and would not lie down for any rest. All night long, through the gleaming silver of the open spaces, through the weird and checkered gloom of the deep forest, heedless even of this hunger, or perhaps driven the mores by it as he thought of the wild clover bunches and tender timothy awaiting him, the solitary ox strove on. And all night, lagging far behind in his unabating caution, the panther followed him.

At sunrise the worn and stumbling animal came out upon the borders of the great lake, stretching its leagues of unshadowed snow away to the south before him. There was his path, and without hesitation he followed it. The wide and frost-bound water here and there had been swept clear of its snows by the wind, but for the most part its covering lay unruffled; and the pale dove-colours, and saffrons, and rose-lilacs of the dawn were sweetly reflected on its surface.

The doomed ox was now journeying very slowly, and with the greatest labour. He staggered at every step, and his beautiful head drooped almost to the snow. When he had got a great way out upon the lake, at the forest's edge appeared the pursuing panther, emerging cautiously from the coverts. The round tawny face and malignant green eyes were raised to peer out across the expanse. The labouring progress of the ox was promptly marked. Dropping its nose again to the ensanguined snow, the beast resumed his pursuit, first at a slow trot, and then at a long, elastic gallop. By this time the ox's quest was nearly done. He plunged forward upon his knees, rose again with difficulty, stood still, and looked around him. His eyes were clouding over, but he saw, dimly, the tawny brute that was now hard upon his steps. Back came a flash of the old courage, and he turned, horns lowered, to face the attack. With the last of his strength he charged, and the panther paused irresolutely; but the wanderer's knees gave way beneath his own impetus, and his horns ploughed the snow. With a deep bellowing groan he rolled over on his side, and the longing, and the dream of the pleasant pastures, faded from his eyes. With a great spring the panther was upon him, and the eager teeth were at his throat—but he knew nought of it. No wild beast, but his own desire, had conquered him.

When the panther had slaked his thirst for blood, he raised his head, and stood with his fore-paws resting on the dead ox's side, and gazed all about him.

To one watching from the lake shore, had there been anyone to watch in that solitude, the wild beast and his prey would have seemed but a speck of black on the gleaming waste. At the same hour league upon league back in the depth of the ancient forest, a lonely ox was lowing in his stanchions, restless, refusing to eat, grieving for the absence of his yoke-fellow.

1888

# Stephen Leacock

1869–1944

Humorist and humanist, professor and pundit, Stephen Leacock was born in the village of Swanmore, Hampshire, in England. His family emigrated in 1876 to a farm north of Toronto. Educated at the University of Toronto, he pursued graduate studies in economics at the University of Chicago, where he studied under Thorstein Veblen, author of *The Theory of the Leisure Class*. After completing his PhD in 1903, Leacock moved to McGill University to teach economics; he chaired the Department of Political Science and Economics from 1908 until his retirement in 1936. His most profitable work, the textbook *Elements of Political Science* (1906), was translated into 17 languages.

The author of 19 books and countless articles on economics, history, and political science, Leacock turned to writing humour as his beloved avocation. He approached it, like he approached his other writing, with professionalism and a shrewd business sense. His first collection of humorous stories, *Literary Lapses*, appeared in 1910, and from that time until his death he published a volume of humour almost every year. The two finest are the complementary volumes *Sunshine Sketches of a Little Town* (1912), with its now classic account of 'The Marine Excursion of the Knights of Pythias', and the urban satire *Arcadian Adventures with the Idle Rich* (1914). He also wrote popular biographies of his two favourite writers, *Mark Twain* (1932) and *Charles Dickens* (1933).

## The Marine Excursion of the Knights of Pythias

Half-past six on a July morning! The *Mariposa Belle* is at the wharf, decked in flags, with steam up ready to start.

Excursion day!

Half-past six on a July morning, and Lake Wissanotti lying in the sun as calm as glass. The opal colours of the morning light are shot from the surface of the water.

Out on the lake the last thin threads of the mist are clearing away like flecks of cotton wool.

The long call of the loon echoes over the lake. The air is cool and fresh. There is in it all the new life of the land of the silent pine and the moving waters. Lake Wissanotti in the morning sunlight! Don't talk to me of the Italian lakes, or the Tyrol or the Swiss Alps. Take them away. Move them somewhere else. I don't want them.

Excursion day, at half-past six of a summer morning! With the boat all decked in flags and all the people in Mariposa on the wharf, and the band in peaked caps with big cornets tied to their bodies ready to play at any minute! I say! Don't tell me about the Carnival of Venice and the Delhi Durbar. Don't! I wouldn't look at them. I'd shut my eyes! For light and colour give me every time an excursion out of Mariposa down the lake to the Indian's Island out of sight in the morning mist. Talk of your Papal Zouaves and your Buckingham Palace Guard! I want to see the Mariposa band in uniform and the Mariposa Knights of Pythias with their aprons and their insignia and their picnic baskets and their five-cent cigars!

Half-past six in the morning, and all the crowd on the wharf and the boat due to leave in half an hour. Notice it!—in half an hour. Already she's whistled twice (at six, and at six fifteen), and at any minute now, Christie Johnson will step into the pilot house and pull the string for the warning whistle that the boat will leave in half an hour. So keep ready. Don't think of running back to Smith's Hotel for the sandwiches. Don't be fool enough to try to go up to the Greek Store, next to Netley's, and buy fruit. You'll be left behind for sure if you do. Never mind the sandwiches and the fruit! Anyway, here comes Mr Smith himself with a huge basket of provender that would feed a factory. There must be sandwiches in that. I think I can hear them clinking. And behind Mr Smith is the German waiter from the caff with another basket—undubitably lager beer; and behind him, the bartender of the hotel, carrying nothing, as far as one can see. But of course if you know Mariposa you will understand that why he looks so nonchalant and empty-handed is because he has two bottles of rye whisky under his linen duster. You know, I think, the peculiar walk of a man with two bottles of whisky in the inside pockets of a linen coat. In Mariposa, you see, to bring beer to an excursion is quite in keeping with public opinion. But, whisky—well, one has to be a little careful.

Do I say that Mr Smith is here? Why, everybody's here. There's Hussell, the editor of the *Newspacket*, wearing a blue ribbon on his coat, for the Mariposa Knights of Pythias are, by their constitution, dedicated to temperance; and there's Henry Mullins, the manager of the Exchange Bank, also a Knight of Pythias, with a small flask of Pogram's Special in his hip pocket as a sort of amendment to the constitution. And there's Dean Drone, the Chaplain of the Order, with a fishing rod (you never saw such green bass as lie among the rocks at Indian's Island), and with a trolling line in case of maskinonge, and a landing-net in case of pickerel, and with his eldest daughter, Lilian Drone, in case of young men. There never was such a fisherman as the Rev. Rupert Drone.

Perhaps I ought to explain that when I speak of the excursion as being of the Knights of Pythias, the thing must not be understood in any narrow sense. In Mariposa practically everybody belongs to the Knights of Pythias just as they do to everything else. That's the great thing about the town and that's what makes it so different from the city. Everybody is in everything.

You should see them on the seventeenth of March, for example, when everybody wears a green ribbon and they're all laughing and glad—you know what the Celtic nature is—and talking about Home Rule.

On St Andrew's Day every man in town wears a thistle and shakes hands with everybody else, and you see the fine old Scotch honesty beaming out of their eyes.

And on St George's Day!—well, there's no heartiness like the good old English spirit, after all; why shouldn't a man feel glad that he's an Englishman?

Then on the Fourth of July there are stars and stripes flying over half the stores in town, and suddenly all the men are seen to smoke cigars, and to know all about Roosevelt and Bryan and the Philippine Islands. Then you learn for the first time that Jeff Thorpe's people came from Massachusetts and that his uncle fought at Bunker

Hill (anyway Jefferson will swear it was in Dakota all right enough); and you find that George Duff has a married sister in Rochester and that her husband is all right; in fact, George was down there as recently as eight years ago. Oh, it's the most American town imaginable is Mariposa—on the Fourth of July.

But wait, just wait, if you feel anxious about the solidity of the British connexion, till the twelfth of the month, when everybody is wearing an orange streamer in his coat and the Orangemen (every man in town) walk in the big procession. Allegiance! Well, perhaps you remember the address they gave to the Prince of Wales on the platform of the Mariposa station as he went through on his tour to the west. I think that pretty well settled that question.

So you will easily understand that of course everybody belongs to the Knights of Pythias and the Masons and Oddfellows, just as they all belong to the Snow Shoe Club and the Girls' Friendly Society.

And meanwhile the whistle of the steamer has blown again for a quarter to seven—loud and long this time, for anyone not here now is late for certain, unless he should happen to come down in the last fifteen minutes.

What a crowd upon the wharf and how they pile onto the steamer! It's a wonder that the boat can hold them all. But that's just the marvellous thing about the *Mariposa Belle.*

I don't know—I have never known—where the steamers like the *Mariposa Belle* come from. Whether they are built by Harland and Wolff of Belfast, or whether, on the other hand, they are not built by Harland and Wolff of Belfast, is more than one would like to say offhand.

The *Mariposa Belle* always seems to me to have some of those strange properties that distinguish Mariposa itself. I mean, her size seems to vary so. If you see her there in the winter, frozen in the ice beside the wharf with a snowdrift against the windows of the pilot house, she looks a pathetic little thing the size of a butternut. But in the summer time, especially after you've *been* in Mariposa for a month or two, and have paddled alongside of her in a canoe, she gets larger and taller, and with a great sweep of black sides, till you see no difference between the *Mariposa Belle* and the *Lusitania.* Each one is a big steamer and that's all you can say.

Nor do her measurements help you much. She draws about eighteen inches forward, and more than that—at least half an inch more, astern, and when she's loaded down with an excursion crowd she draws a good two inches more. And above the water—why, look at all the decks on her! There's the deck you walk onto, from the wharf, all shut in, with windows along it, and the after cabin with the long table, and above that the deck with all the chairs piled upon it, and the deck in front where the band stand round in a circle, and the pilot house is higher than that, and above the pilot house is the board with the gold name and the flag pole and the steel ropes and the flags; and fixed in somewhere on the different levels is the lunch counter where they sell the sandwiches, and the engine room, and down below the deck level, beneath the water line, is the place where the crew sleep. What with steps and stairs and passages and piles of cordwood for the engine—oh, no, I guess Harland and Wolff didn't build her. They couldn't have.

Yet even with a huge boat like the *Mariposa Belle,* it would be impossible for her to carry all of the crowd that you see in the boat and on the wharf. In reality, the crowd is made up of two classes—all of the people in Mariposa who are going on the excursion and all those who are not. Some come for the one reason and some for the other.

The two tellers of the Exchange Bank are both there standing side by side. But one of them—the one with the cameo pin and the long face like a horse—is going, and the other—with the other cameo pin and the face like another horse—is not. In the same way, Hussell of the *Newspacket* is going, but his brother, beside him, isn't. Lilian Drone is going, but her sister can't; and so on all through the crowd.

And to think that things should look like that on the morning of a steamboat accident.

How strange life is!

To think of all these people so eager and anxious to catch the steamer, and some of them running to catch it, and so fearful that they might miss it—the morning of a steamboat accident. And the captain blowing his whistle, and warning them so severely that he would leave them behind—leave them out of the accident! And everybody crowding so eagerly to be in the accident.

Perhaps life is like that all through.

Strangest of all to think, in a case like this, of the people who were left behind, or in some way or other prevented from going, and always afterwards told of how they had escaped being on board the *Mariposa Belle* that day!

Some of the instances were certainly extraordinary.

Nivens, the lawyer, escaped from being there merely by the fact that he was away in the city.

Towers, the tailor, only escaped owing to the fact that, not intending to go on the excursion he had stayed in bed till eight o'clock and so had not gone. He narrated afterwards that waking up that morning at half-past five, he had thought of the excursion and for some unaccountable reason had felt glad that he was not going.

The case of Yodel, the auctioneer, was even more inscrutable. He had been to the Oddfellows' excursion on the train the week before and to the Conservative picnic the week before that, and had decided not to go on this trip. In fact, he had not the least intention of going. He narrated afterwards how the night before someone had stopped him on the corner of Nippewa and Tecumseh Streets (he indicated the very spot) and asked: 'Are you going to take in the excursion tomorrow?' and he had said, just as simply as he was talking when narrating it: 'No.' And ten minutes after that, at the corner of Dalhousie and Brock Streets (he offered to lead a party of verification to the precise place) somebody else had stopped him and asked: 'Well, are you going on the steamer trip tomorrow?' Again he had answered: 'No,' apparently almost in the same tone as before.

He said afterwards that when he heard the rumour of the accident it seemed like the finger of Providence, and he fell on his knees in thankfulness.

There was the similar case of Morison (I mean the one in Glover's hardware store that married one of the Thompsons). He said afterwards that he had read so much in the papers about accidents lately—mining accidents, and aeroplanes and gasoline—that he had grown nervous. The night before his wife had asked him at supper: 'Are you going on the excursion?' He had answered: 'No, I don't think I feel like it,' and had added: 'Perhaps your mother might like to go.' And the next evening just at dusk, when the news ran through the town, he said the first thought that flashed through his head was: 'Mrs Thompson's on that boat.'

He told this right as I say it—without the least doubt or confusion. He never for a moment imagined she was on the *Lusitania* or the *Olympic* or any other boat. He knew she was on this one. He said you could have knocked him down where he stood. But no one had. Not even when he got halfway down—on his knees, and it would have been easier still to knock him down or kick him. People do miss a lot of chances.

Still, as I say, neither Yodel nor Morison nor anyone thought about there being an accident until just after sundown when they—

Well, have you ever heard the long booming whistle of a steamboat two miles out on the lake in the dusk, and while you listen and count and wonder, seen the crimson rockets going up against the sky and then heard the fire bell ringing right there beside you in the town, and seen the people running to the town wharf?

That's what the people of Mariposa saw and felt that summer evening as they watched the Mackinaw lifeboat go plunging out into the lake with seven sweeps to a side and the foam clear to the gunwale with the lifting stroke of fourteen men!

But, dear me, I am afraid that this is no way to tell a story. I suppose the true art would have been to have said nothing about the accident till it happened. But when you write about Mariposa, or hear of it, if you know the place, it's all so vivid and real, that a thing like the contrast between the excursion crowd in the morning and the scene at night leaps into your mind and you must think of it.

But never mind about the accident—let us turn back again to the morning.

The boat was due to leave at seven. There was no doubt about the hour—not only seven, but seven sharp. The notice in the *Newspacket* said: 'The boat will leave sharp at seven'; and the advertising posters on the telegraph poles on Missinaba Street that began, 'Ho, for Indian's Island!' ended up with the words: 'Boat leaves at seven sharp.' There was a big notice on the wharf that said: 'Boat leaves sharp on time.'

So at seven, right on the hour, the whistle blew loud and long, and then at seven-fifteen three short peremptory blasts, and at seven-thirty one quick angry call—just one—and very soon after that they cast off the last of the ropes and the *Mariposa Belle* sailed off in her cloud of flags, and the band of the Knights of Pythias, timing it to a nicety, broke into the 'Maple Leaf for Ever!'

I suppose that all excursions when they start are much the same. Anyway, on the *Mariposa Belle* everybody went running up and down all over the boat with deck chairs and camp stools and baskets, and found places, splendid places to sit, and then got scared that there might be better ones and chased off again. People hunted for places out of the sun and when they got them swore that they weren't going to freeze to please anybody; and the people in the sun said that they hadn't paid fifty cents to get roasted. Others said that they hadn't paid fifty cents to get covered with cinders, and there were still others who hadn't paid fifty cents to get shaken to death with the propeller.

Still, it was all right presently. The people seemed to get sorted out into the places on the boat where they belonged. The women, the older ones, all gravitated into the cabin on the lower deck and by getting round the table with needlework, and with all the windows shut, they soon had it, as they said themselves, just like being at home.

All the young boys and the toughs and the men in the band got down on the lower deck forward, where the boat was dirtiest and where the anchor was and the coils of rope.

And upstairs on the after deck there were Lilian Drone and Miss Lawson, the high-school teacher, with a book of German poetry—Gothey I think it was—and the bank teller and the young men.

In the centre, standing beside the rail, were Dean Drone and Dr Gallagher, looking through binocular glasses at the shore.

Up in front on the little deck forward of the pilot house was a group of the older men, Mullins and Duff and Mr Smith in a deck chair, and beside him Mr Golgotha Gingham, the undertaker of Mariposa, on a stool. It was part of Mr Gingham's principles to take in an outing of this sort, a business matter, more or less—for you never know what may happen at these water parties. At any rate, he was there in a neat suit of black, not, of course, his heavier or professional suit, but a soft clinging effect as of burnt paper that combined gaiety and decorum to a nicety.

'Yes,' said Mr Gingham, waving his black glove in a general way towards the shore, 'I know the lake well, very well. I've been pretty much all over it in my time.'

'Canoeing?' asked somebody.

'No,' said Mr Gingham, 'not in a canoe.' There seemed a peculiar and quiet meaning in his tone.

'Sailing, I suppose,' said somebody else.

'No,' said Mr Gingham. 'I don't understand it.'

'I never knowed that you went onto the water at all, Gol,' said Mr Smith, breaking in.

'Ah, not now,' explained Mr Gingham; 'it was years ago, the first summer I came to Mariposa. I was on the water practically all day. Nothing like it to give a man an appetite and keep him in shape.'

'Was you camping?' asked Mr Smith.

'We camped at night,' assented the undertaker, 'but we put in practically the whole day on the water. You see, we were after a party that had come up here from the city on his vacation and gone out in a sailing canoe. We were dragging. We were up every morning at sunrise, lit a fire on the beach and cooked breakfast, and then we'd light our pipes and be off with the net for a whole day. It's great life,' concluded Mr Gingham wistfully.

'Did you get him?' asked two or three together.

There was a pause before Mr Gingham answered.

'We did,' he said '—down in the reeds past Horseshoe Point. But it was no use. He turned blue on me right away.'

After which Mr Gingham fell into such a deep reverie that the boat had steamed another half-mile down the lake before anybody broke the silence again. Talk of this sort—and after all what more suitable for a day on the water?—beguiled the way.

Down the lake, mile by mile over the calm water, steamed the *Mariposa Belle.* They passed Poplar Point where the high sand-banks are with all the swallows' nests in them, and Dean Drone and Dr Gallagher looked at them alternately through the binocular glasses, and it was wonderful how plainly one could see the swallows and the banks and the shrubs—just as plainly as with the naked eye.

And a little farther down they passed the Shingle Beach, and Dr Gallagher, who knew Canadian history, said to Dean Drone that it was strange to think that Champlain had landed there with his French explorers three hundred years ago; and Dean Drone, who didn't know Canadian history, said it was stranger still to think that the hand of the Almighty had piled up the hills and rocks long before that; and Dr Gallagher said it was wonderful how the French had found their way through such a pathless wilderness; and Dean Drone said that it was wonderful also to think that the Almighty had placed even the smallest shrub in its appointed place. Dr Gallagher said it filled him with admiration. Dean Drone said it filled him with awe. Dr Gallagher said he'd been full of it every since he was a boy and Dean Drone said so had he.

Then a little further, as the *Mariposa Belle* steamed on down the lake, they passed the Old Indian Portage where the great grey rocks are; and Dr Gallagher drew Dean Drone's attention to the place where the narrow canoe track wound up from the shore to the woods, and Dean Drone said he could see it perfectly well without the glasses.

Dr Gallagher said that it was just here that a party of five hundred French had made their way with all their baggage and accoutrements across the rocks of the divide and down to the Great Bay. And Dean Drone said that it reminded him of Xenophon leading his ten thousand Greeks over the hill passes of Armenia down to the sea. Dr Gallagher said that he had often wished he could have seen and spoken to Champlain, and Dean Drone said how much he regretted to have never known Xenophon.

And then after that they fell to talking of relics and traces of the past, and Dr Gallagher said that if Dean Drone would come round to his house some night he would show him some Indian arrow heads that he had dug up in his garden. And Dean Drone said that if Dr Gallagher would come round to the rectory any afternoon he would show him a map of Xerxes' invasion of Greece. Only he must come some time between the Infant Class and the Mothers' Auxiliary.

So presently they both knew that they were blocked out of one another's houses for some time to come, and Dr Gallagher walked forward and told Mr Smith, who had never studied Greek, about Champlain crossing the rock divide.

Mr Smith turned his head and looked at the divide for half a second and then said he had crossed a worse one up north back of the Wahnipitae and that the flies were Hades—and then went on playing freezeout poker with the two juniors in Duff's bank.

So Dr Gallagher realized that that's always the way when you try to tell people things, and that as far as gratitude and appreciation goes one might as well never read books or travel anywhere or do anything.

In fact, it was at this very moment that he made up his mind to give the arrows to the Mariposa Mechanics' Institute—they afterwards became, as you know, the

Gallagher Collection. But, for the time being, the doctor was sick of them and wandered off round the boat and watched Henry Mullins showing George Duff how to make a John Collins without lemons, and finally went and sat down among the Mariposa band and wished that he hadn't come.

So the boat steamed on and the sun rose higher and higher, and the freshness of the morning changed into the full glare of noon, and pretty soon the *Mariposa Belle* had floated out onto the lake again and they went on to where the lake began to narrow in at its foot, just where the Indian's Island is—all grass and trees and with a log wharf running into the water. Below it the Lower Ossawippi runs out of the lake, and quite near are the rapids, and you can see down among the trees the red brick of the power house and hear the roar of the leaping water.

The Indian's Island itself is all covered with trees and tangled vines, and the water about it is so still that it's all reflected double and looks the same either way up. Then when the steamer's whistle blows as it comes into the wharf, you hear it echo among the trees of the island, and reverberate back from the shores of the lake.

The scene is all so quiet and still and unbroken, that Miss Cleghorn—the sallow girl in the telephone exchange, that I spoke of—said she'd like to be buried there. But all the people were so busy getting their baskets and gathering up their things that no one had time to attend to it.

I mustn't even try to describe the landing and the boat crunching against the wooden wharf and all the people running to the same side of the deck and Christie Johnson calling out to the crowd to keep to the starboard and nobody being able to find it. Everyone who has been on a Mariposa excursion knows all about that.

Nor can I describe the day itself and the picnic under the trees. There were speeches afterwards, and Judge Pepperleigh gave such offence by bringing in Conservative politics that a man called Patriotus Canadiensis wrote and asked for some of the invaluable space of the *Mariposa Times-Herald* and exposed it.

I should say that there were races too, on the grass on the open side of the island, graded mostly according to ages—races for boys under thirteen and girls over nineteen and all that sort of thing. Sports are generally conducted on that plan in Mariposa. It is realized that a woman of sixty has an unfair advantage over a mere child.

Dean Drone managed the races and decided the ages and gave out the prizes; the Wesleyan minister helped, and he and the young student, who was relieving in the Presbyterian Church, held the string at the winning point.

They had to get mostly clergymen for the races because all the men had wandered off, somehow, to where they were drinking lager beer out of two kegs stuck on pine logs among the trees.

But if you've ever been on a Mariposa excursion you know all about these details anyway.

So the day wore on and presently the sun came through the trees on a slant and the steamer whistle blew with a great puff of white steam and all the people came straggling down to the wharf and pretty soon the *Mariposa Belle* had floated out onto the lake again and headed for the town, twenty miles away.

I suppose you have often noticed the contrast there is between an excursion on its way out in the morning and what it looks like on the way home.

In the morning everybody is so restless and animated and moves to and from all over the boat and asks questions. But coming home, as the afternoon gets later and later and the sun sinks beyond the hills, all the people seem to get so still and quiet and drowsy.

So it was with the people on the *Mariposa Belle*. They sat there on the benches and the deck chairs in little clusters, and listened to the regular beat of the propeller and almost dozed off asleep as they sat. Then when the sun set and the dusk drew on, it grew almost dark on the deck and so still that you could hardly tell there was anyone on board.

And if you had looked at the steamer from the shore or from one of the islands, you'd have seen the row of lights from the cabin windows shining on the water and the red glare of the burning hemlock from the funnel, and you'd have heard the soft thud of the propeller miles away over the lake.

Now and then, too, you could have heard them singing on the steamer—the voices of the girls and the men blended into unison by the distance, rising and falling in long-drawn melody: '*O—Can-a-da—O—Can-a-da*.'

You may talk as you will about the intoning choirs of your European cathedrals, but the sound of '*O—Can-a-da*', borne across the waters of a silent lake at evening is good enough for those of us who know Mariposa.

I think that it was just as they were singing like this: '*O—Can-a-da*', that word went round that the boat was sinking.

If you have ever been in any sudden emergency on the water, you will understand the strange psychology of it—the way in which what is happening seems to become known all in a moment without a word being said. The news is transmitted from one to the other by some mysterious process.

At any rate, on the *Mariposa Belle* first one and then the other heard that the steamer was sinking. As far as I could ever learn the first of it was that George Duff, the bank manager, came very quietly to Dr Gallagher and asked him if he thought that the boat was sinking. The doctor said no, that he had thought so earlier in the day but that he didn't now think that she was.

After that Duff, according to his own account, had said to Macartney, the lawyer, that the boat was sinking, and Macartney said that he doubted it very much.

Then somebody came to Judge Pepperleigh and woke him up and said that there was six inches of water in the steamer and that she was sinking. And Pepperleigh said it was perfect scandal and passed the news on to his wife and she said that they had no business to allow it and that if the steamer sank that was the last excursion she'd go on.

So the news went all round the boat and everywhere the people gathered in groups and talked about it in the angry and excited way that people have when a steamer is sinking on one of the lakes like Lake Wissanotti.

Dean Drone, of course, and some others were quieter about it, and said that one must make allowances and that naturally there were two sides to everything. But most of them wouldn't listen to reason at all. I think, perhaps, that some of them were frightened. You see the last time but one that the steamer had sunk, there had been a man drowned and it made them nervous.

What? Hadn't I explained about the depth of Lake Wissanotti? I had taken it for granted that you knew; and in any case parts of it are deep enough, though I don't suppose in this stretch of it from the big reed beds up to within a mile of the town wharf, you could find six feet of water in it if you tried. Oh, pshaw! I was not talking about a steamer sinking in the ocean and carrying down its screaming crowds of people into the hideous depths of green water. Oh, dear me, no! That kind of thing never happens on Lake Wissanotti.

But what does happen is that the *Mariposa Belle* sinks every now and then, and sticks there on the bottom till they get things straightened up.

On the lakes round Mariposa, if a person arrives late anywhere and explains that the steamer sank, everybody understands the situation.

You see when Harland and Wolff built the *Mariposa Belle*, they left some cracks in between the timbers that you fill up with cotton waste every Sunday. If this is not attended to, the boat sinks. In fact, it is part of the law of the province that all the steamers like the *Mariposa Belle* must be properly corked—I think that is the word—every season. There are inspectors who visit all the hotels in the province to see that it is done.

So you can imagine now that I've explained it a little straighter, the indignation of the people when they knew that the boat had come uncorked and that they might be stuck out there on a shoal or a mud-bank half the night.

I don't say either that there wasn't any danger; anyway, it doesn't feel very safe when you realize that the boat is settling down with every hundred yards that she goes, and you look over the side and see only the black water in the gathering night.

Safe! I'm not sure now that I come to think of it that it isn't worse thank sinking in the Atlantic. After all, in the Atlantic there is wireless telegraphy, and a lot of trained sailors and stewards. But out on Lake Wissanotti—far out, so that you can only just see the lights of the town away off to the south—when the propeller comes to a stop—and you can hear the hiss of steam as they start to rake out the engine fires to prevent explosion—and when you turn from the red glare that comes from the furnace doors as they open them, to the black dark that is gathering over the lake—and there's a night wind beginning to run among the rushes—and you see the men going forward to the roof of the pilot house to send up the rockets to rouse the town—safe? Safe yourself, if you like; as for me, let me once get back to Mariposa again, under the night shadow of the maple trees, and this shall be the last, last time I'll go on Lake Wissanotti.

Safe! Oh, yes! Isn't it strange how safe other people's adventures seem after they happen? But you'd have been scared, too, if you'd been there just before the steamer sank, and seen them bringing up all the women onto the top deck.

I don't see how some of the people took it so calmly; how Mr Smith, for instance, could have gone on smoking and telling how he'd had a steamer 'sink on him' on Lake Nipissing and a still bigger one, a side-wheeler, sink on him in Lake Abbitibbi.

Then, quite suddenly, with a quiver, down she went. You could feel the boat sink, sink—down, down—would it never get to the bottom? The water came flush up to the lower deck, and then—thank heaven—the sinking stopped and there was the *Mariposa Belle* safe and tight on a reed bank.

Really, it made one positively laugh! It seemed so queer and, anyway, if a man has a sort of natural courage, danger makes him laugh. Danger? pshaw! fiddlesticks! everybody scouted the idea. Why, it is just the little things like this that give zest to a day on the water.

Within half a minute they were all running round looking for sandwiches and cracking jokes and talking of making coffee over the remains of the engine fires.

I don't need to tell at length how it all happened after that.

I suppose the people on the *Mariposa Belle* would have had to settle down there all night or till help came from the town, but some of the men who had gone forward and were peering out into the dark said that it couldn't be more than a mile across the water to Miller's Point. You could almost see it over there to the left—some of them, I think, said 'off on the port bow', because you know when you get mixed up in these marine disasters, you soon catch the atmosphere of the thing.

So pretty soon they had the davits swung out over the side and were lowering the old lifeboat from the top deck into the water.

There were men leaning out over the rail of the *Mariposa Belle* with lanterns that threw the light as they let her down, and the glare fell on the water and the reeds. But when they got the boat lowered, it looked such a frail, clumsy thing as one saw it from the rail above, that the cry was raised: 'Women and children first!' For what was the sense, if it should turn out that the boat wouldn't even hold women and children, of trying to jam a lot of heavy men into it?

So they put in mostly women and children and the boat pushed out into the darkness so freighted down it would hardly float.

In the bow of it was the Presbyterian student who was relieving the minister, and he called out that they were in the hands of Providence. But he was crouched and ready to spring out of them at the first moment.

So the boat went and was lost in the darkness except for the lantern in the bow that you could see bobbing on the water. Then presently it came back and they sent another load, till pretty soon the decks began to thin out and everybody got impatient to be gone.

It was about the time that the third boat-load put off that Mr Smith took a bet with Mullins for twenty-five dollars, that he'd be home in Mariposa before the people in the boats had walked round the shore.

No one knew just what he meant, but pretty soon they saw Mr Smith disappear down below the lowest part of the steamer with a mallet in one hand and a big bundle of marline in the other.

They might have wondered more about it, but it was just at this time that they heard the shouts from the rescue boat—the big Mackinaw lifeboat—that had put out from the town with fourteen men at the sweeps when they saw the first rockets go up.

I suppose there is always something inspiring about a rescue at sea, or on the water.

After all, the bravery of the lifeboat man is the true bravery—expended to save life, not to destroy it.

Certainly they told for months after of how the rescue boat came out to the *Mariposa Belle.*

I suppose that when they put her in the water the lifeboat touched it for the first time since the old Macdonald Government placed her on Lake Wissanotti.

Anyway, the water poured in at every seam. But not for a moment—even with two miles of water between them and the steamer—did the rowers pause for that.

By the time they were halfway there the water was almost up to the thwarts, but they drove her on. Panting and exhausted (for mind you, if you haven't been in a fool boat like that for years, rowing takes it out of you), the rowers stuck to their task. They threw the ballast over and chucked into the water the heavy cork jackets and lifebelts that encumbered their movements. There was no thought of turning back. They were nearer to the steamer than the shore.

'Hang to it, boys,' called the crowd from the steamer's deck, and hang they did.

They were almost exhausted when they got them; men leaning from the steamer threw them ropes and one by one every man was hauled aboard just as the lifeboat sank under their feet.

Saved! by heaven, saved by one of the smartest pieces of rescue work ever seen on the lake.

There's no use describing it; you need to see rescue work of this kind by lifeboats to understand it.

Nor were the lifeboat crew the only ones that distinguished themselves.

Boat after boat and canoe after canoe had put out from Mariposa to the help of the steamer. They got them all.

Pupkin, the other bank teller with a face like a horse, who hadn't gone on the excursion—as soon as he knew that the boat was signalling for help and that Miss Lawson was sending up rockets—rushed for a row boat, grabbed an oar (two would have hampered him)—and paddled madly out into the lake. He struck right out into the dark with the crazy skiff almost sinking beneath his feet. But they got him. They rescued him. They watched him, almost dead with exhaustion, make his way to the steamer, where he was hauled up with ropes. Saved! Saved!

They might have gone on that way half the night, picking up the rescuers, only, at the very moment when the tenth load of people left for the shore—just as suddenly and saucily as you please, up came the *Mariposa Belle* from the mud bottom and floated.

*Floated*?

Why, of course she did. If you take a hundred and fifty people off a steamer that has sunk, and if you get a man as shrewd as Mr Smith to plug the timber seams with mallet and marline, and if you turn ten bandsmen of the Mariposa band onto your hand pump on the bow of the lower decks—float? why, what else can she do?

Then, if you stuff in hemlock into the embers of the fire that you were raking out, till it hums and crackles under the boiler, it won't be long before you hear the propeller thud—thudding at the stern again, and before the long roar of the steam whistle echoes over to the town.

And so the *Mariposa Belle*, with all steam up again and with the long train of sparks careering from the funnel, is heading for the town.

But no Christie Johnson at the wheel in the pilot house this time.

'Smith! Get Smith!' is the cry.

Can he take her in? Well, now! Ask a man who has had steamers sink on him in half the lakes from Temiscaming to the Bay, if he can take her in? Ask a man who has run a York boat down the rapids of the Moose when the ice is moving, if he can grip the steering wheel of the *Mariposa Belle*? So there she steams safe and sound to the town wharf!

Look at the lights and the crowds! If only the federal census taker could count us now! Hear them calling and shouting back and forward from the deck to the shore! Listen! There is the rattle of the shore ropes as they get them ready, and there's the Mariposa band—actually forming in a circle on the upper deck just as she docks, and the leader with his baton—one—two—ready now—

'O CAN-A-DA!'

1912

# James Joyce

1882–1941

James Joyce was born near Dublin, Ireland, and educated at the Jesuit school Belvedere College and at University College, Dublin. He went into self-imposed exile in 1904, taking with him a young woman named Nora Barnacle. 'She'll never leave him,' said Joyce's father, and she did not. In Italy and in Switzerland Joyce earned a precarious living teaching English while trying to become a great writer. His short stories were all designed for a collection called *Dubliners*, 15 stories set in middle-class, Catholic Dublin, which waited 10 years before finally being published and then sold fewer than 500 copies in 1914; 'Araby', the third story, is the first-person account of a young boy's fascination with a girl down the street.

Joyce's autobiographical novel *A Portrait of the Artist as a Young Man* (1916) attracted the attention of T.S. Eliot and Ezra Pound, who helped him get support for his major project, *Ulysses* (1922), which took realism to its logical conclusion and beyond. *Finnegan's Wake* (1939) is all beyond—a book to keep the critics busy, as Joyce observed. Together these works had an immense influence on the form and structure of the modern novel and on the development of stream-of-consciousness narration. Just as remarkable, though less noticeable, as these technical breakthroughs are Joyce's comic spirit and humanity.

## Araby

North Richmond Street, being blind, was a quiet street except at the hour when the Christian Brothers' School set the boys free. An uninhabited house of two storeys stood at the blind end, detached from its neighbours in a square ground. The other houses of the street, conscious of decent lives within them, gazed at one another with brown imperturbable faces.

The former tenant of our house, a priest, had died in the back drawing room. Air, musty from having been long enclosed, hung in all the rooms, and the waste room behind the kitchen was littered with old useless papers. Among these I found a few paper-covered books, the pages of which were curled and damp: *The Abbot*, by Walter Scott, *The Devout Communicant*, and *The Memoirs of Vidocq*. I liked the last best because its leaves were yellow. The wild garden behind the house contained a central apple tree and a few straggling bushes under one of which I found the late tenant's rusty bicycle pump. He had been a very charitable priest; in his will he had left all his money to institutions and the furniture of his house to his sister.

When the short days of winter came dusk fell before we had well eaten our dinners. When we met in the street the houses had grown sombre. The space of the sky above us was the colour of ever-changing violet and towards it the lamps of the street lifted their feeble lanterns. The cold air stung us and we played till our bodies glowed. Our shouts echoed in the silent street. The career of our play brought us through the dark muddy lanes behind the houses where we ran the gauntlet of the rough tribes from the cottages, to the back doors of the dark dripping gardens where odours arose from the ashpits, to the dark odorous stables where a coachman smoothed and combed the horse or shook music from the buckled harness. When we returned to the street light from the kitchen windows had filled the areas. If my uncle was seen turning the corner we hid in the shadows until we had seen him safely housed. Or if Mangan's sister came out on the doorstep to call her brother in to his tea we watched her from our shadow peer up and down the street. We waited to see whether she would remain or go in and, if she remained, we left our shadow and walked up to Mangan's steps resignedly. She was waiting for us, her figure defined by the light from the half-opened door. Her brother always teased her before he obeyed and I stood by the railings looking at her. Her dress swung as she moved her body and the soft rope of her hair tossed from side to side.

Every morning I lay on the floor in the front parlour watching her door. The blind was pulled down to within an inch of the sash so that I could not be seen. When she came out on the doorstep my heart leaped. I ran to the hall, seized my books, and followed her. I kept her brown figure always in my eye and, when we came near the point at which our ways diverged, I quickened my pace and passed her. This happened morning after morning. I had never spoken to her, except for a few casual words, and yet her name was like a summons to all my foolish blood.

Her image accompanied me even in places the most hostile to romance. On Saturday evenings when my aunt went marketing I had to go to carry some of the parcels. We walked through the flaring streets, jostled by drunken men and bargaining women, amid the curse of labourers, the shrill litanies of shop-boys who stood on guard by the barrels of pigs' cheeks, the nasal chanting of street-singers, who sang a *come-all-you* about O'Donovan Rossa, or a ballad about the troubles in our native land. These noises converged in a single sensation of life for me: I imagined that I bore my chalice safely through a throng of foes. Her name sprang to my lips at moments in strange prayers and praises which I myself did not understand. My eyes were often full of tears (I could not tell why) and at times a flood from my heart seemed to pour itself out into my bosom. I thought little of the future. I did not know whether I would ever speak to her or not or, if I spoke to her, how I could tell her of my confused adoration. But my body was like a harp and her words and gestures were like fingers running upon the wires.

One evening I went into the back drawing room in which the priest had died. It was a dark rainy evening and there was no sound in the house. Through one of the broken panes I heard the rain impinge upon the earth, the fine incessant needles of water playing in the sodden beds. Some distant lamp or lighted window gleamed below me. I was thankful that I could see so little. All my senses seemed to desire to veil themselves and, feeling that I was about to slip from them, I pressed the palms of my hands together until they trembled, murmuring: '*O love! O love!*' many times.

At last she spoke to me. When she addressed the first words to me I was so confused that I did not know what to answer. She asked me was I going to *Araby*. I forgot whether I answered yes or no. It would be a splendid bazaar, she said she would love to go.

'And why can't you?' I asked.

While she spoke she turned a silver bracelet round and round her wrist. She could not go, she said, because there would be a retreat that week in her convent. Her brother and two other boys were fighting for their caps and I was alone at the railings. She held one of the spikes, bowing her head towards me. The light from the lamp opposite our door caught the white curve of her neck, lit up her hair that rested there and, falling, lit up the hand upon the railing. It fell over one side of her dress and caught the white border of a petticoat just visible as she stood at ease.

'It's well for you,' she said.

'If I go,' I said, 'I will bring you something.'

What innumerable follies laid waste my waking and sleeping thoughts after that evening! I wished to annihilate the tedious intervening days. I chafed against the work of school. At night in my bedroom and by day in the classroom her image came between me and the page I strove to read. The syllables of the word *Araby* were called to me through the silence in which my soul luxuriated and cast an Eastern enchantment over me. I asked for leave to go to the bazaar on Saturday night. My aunt was surprised and hoped it was not some Freemason affair. I answered few questions in class. I watched my master's face pass from amiability to sternness; he hoped I was not beginning to idle. I could not call my wandering thoughts together. I had hardly any patience with the serious work of life which, now that it stood between me and my desire, seemed to me child's play, ugly monotonous child's play.

On Saturday morning I reminded my uncle that I wished to go to the bazaar in the evening. He was fussing at the hallstand, looking for the hat-brush, and answered me curtly:

'Yes, boy, I know.'

As he was in the hall I could not go into the front parlour and lie at the window. I left the house in bad humour and walked slowly towards the school. The air was pitilessly raw and already my heart misgave me.

When I came home to dinner my uncle had not yet been home. Still it was early. I sat staring at the clock for some time and, when its ticking began to irritate me, I left the room. I mounted the staircase and gained the upper part of the house. The high cold empty gloomy rooms liberated me and I went from room to room singing. From the front window I saw my companions playing below in the street. Their cries reached me weakened and indistinct and, leaning my forehead against the cool glass, I looked over at the dark house where she lived. I may have stood there for an hour, seeing nothing but the brown-clad figure cast by my imagination, touched discreetly by the lamplight at the curved neck, at the hand upon the railings and at the border below the dress.

When I came downstairs again I found Mrs Mercer sitting at the fire. She was an old garrulous woman, a pawnbroker's widow, who collected used stamps for some pious purpose. I had to endure the gossip of the tea-table. The meal was prolonged beyond an hour and still my uncle did not come. Mrs Mercer stood up to go: she was very sorry she couldn't wait any longer, but it was after eight o'clock and she did not like to be out late, as the night air was bad for her. When she had gone I began to walk up and down the room, clenching my fists. My aunt said:

'I'm afraid you may put off your bazaar for this night of Our Lord.'

At nine o'clock I heard my uncle's latchkey in the halldoor. I heard him talking to himself and heard the hallstand rocking when it had received the weight of his overcoat. I could interpret these signs. When he was midway through his dinner I asked him to give me the money to go to the bazaar. He had forgotten.

'The people are in bed and after their first sleep now,' he said.

I did not smile. My aunt said to him energetically:

'Can't you give him the money and let him go? You've kept him late enough as it is.'

My uncle said he was very sorry he had forgotten. He said he believed in the old saying: 'All work and no play makes Jack a dull boy.' He asked me where I was going and, when I had told him a second time he asked me did I know *The Arab's Farewell to his Steed.* When I left the kitchen he was about to recite the opening lines of the piece to my aunt.

I held a florin tightly in my hand as I strode down Buckingham Street towards the station. The sight of the streets thronged with buyers and glaring with gas recalled to me the purpose of my journey. I took my seat in a third-class carriage of a deserted train. After an intolerable delay the train moved out of the station slowly. It crept onward among ruinous houses and over the twinkling river. At Westland Row Station a crowd of people pressed to the carriage doors; but the porters moved them back, saying that it was a special train for the bazaar. I remained alone in the bare carriage. In a few minutes the train drew up beside an improvised wooden platform. I passed out on to the road and saw by the lighted dial of a clock that it was ten minutes to ten. In front of me was a large building which displayed the magical name.

I could not find any sixpenny entrance and, fearing that the bazaar would be closed, I passed quickly through the turnstile, handing a shilling to a weary-looking man. I found myself in a big hall girdled at half its height by a gallery. Nearly all the stalls were closed and the greater part of the hall was in darkness. I recognized a silence like that which pervades a church after a service. I walked into the centre of the bazaar timidly. A few people were gathered about the stalls which were still open. Before a curtain, over which the words *Café Chantant* were written in coloured lamps, two men were counting money on a salver. I listened to the fall of the coins.

Remembering with difficulty why I had come I went over to one of the stalls and examined porcelain vases and flowered tea-sets. At the door of the stall a young lady was talking and laughing with two young gentlemen. I remarked their English accents and listened vaguely to their conversation.

'O, I never said such a thing!'

'O, but you did!'

'O, but I didn't!'

'Didn't she say that?'

'Yes. I heard her.'

'O, there's a . . . fib!'

Observing me the young lady came over and asked me did I wish to buy anything. The tone of her voice was not encouraging; she seemed to have spoken to me out of a sense of duty. I looked humbly at the great jars that stood like eastern guards at either side of the dark entrance to the stall and murmured:

'No, thank you.'

The young lady changed the position of one of the vases and went back to the two young men. They began to talk on the same subject. Once or twice the young lady glanced at me over her shoulder.

I lingered before her stall, though I knew my stay was useless, to make my interest in her wares seem the more real. Then I turned away slowly and walked down the middle of the bazaar. I allowed the two pennies to fall against the sixpence in my pocket. I heard a voice call from one end of the gallery that the light was out. The upper part of the hall was now completely dark.

Gazing up into the darkness I saw myself as a creature driven and derided by vanity; and my eyes burned with anguish and anger.

1914

# Katherine Mansfield

## 1888–1923

Born in Wellington, New Zealand, Kathleen Mansfield Beauchamp spent her early years in the nearby village of Karoi. In 1903 she went to Queen's College in London, where she studied to become a cellist. When she returned to New Zealand in 1906, she found the country oppressive and stifling and convinced her parents in 1908 to allow her to go back to London. She spent the rest of her life in Europe, always restlessly in search of a cure for the consumption that had first afflicted her a few years after her return to London. Her first book of stories, *In a German Pension*, was published in 1911 under the pseudonym Katherine Mansfield, and was followed by four more books of stories during her lifetime.

Although she made attempts at writing a novel, it was the short story that proved to be Mansfield's chosen form, accommodating her terse irony, her dissections of class, family, and relationships, and her evocations of natural settings. These features are evident in

'The Garden Party', in which the rituals of the upper-class family as they prepare for the afternoon's festivities seem to provide the context for the ironic presentation of Laura's responses to the workmen setting up the marquee. The story's complex perspective is reflected in the reactions of Laura and her family to the report of a fatal accident, particularly in Laura's inarticulate comments to her brother following her visit to the bereaved family.

## The Garden Party

And after all the weather was ideal. They could not have had a more perfect day for a garden party if they had ordered it. Windless, warm, the sky without a cloud. Only the blue was veiled with a haze of light gold, as it is sometimes in early summer. The gardener had been up since dawn, mowing the lawns and sweeping them, until the grass and the dark flat rosettes where the daisy plants had been seemed to shine. As for the roses, you could not help feeling they understood that roses are the only flowers that impress people at garden parties; the only flowers that everybody is certain of knowing. Hundreds, yes, literally hundreds, had come out in a single night; the green bushes bowed down as though they had been visited by archangels.

Breakfast was not yet over before the men came to put up the marquee.

'Where do you want the marquee put, mother?'

'My dear child, it's no use asking me. I'm determined to leave everything to you children this year. Forget I am your mother. Treat me as an honoured guest.'

But Meg could not possibly go and supervise the men. She had washed her hair before breakfast, and she sat drinking her coffee in a green turban, with a dark wet curl stamped on each cheek. Jose, the butterfly, always came down in a silk petticoat and a kimono jacket.

'You'll have to go, Laura, you're the artistic one.'

Away Laura flew, still holding her piece of bread-and-butter. It's so delicious to have an excuse for eating out of doors and, besides, she loved having to arrange things; she always felt she could do it so much better than anybody else.

Four men in their shirt-sleeves stood grouped together on the garden path. They carried staves covered with rolls of canvas, and they had big tool-bags slung on their backs. They looked impressive. Laura wished now that she was not holding that piece of bread-and-butter, but there was nowhere to put it, and she couldn't possibly throw it away. She blushed and tried to look severe and even a little bit short-sighted as she came up to them.

'Good morning,' she said, copying her mother's voice. But that sounded so fearfully affected that she was ashamed, and stammered like a little girl, 'Oh—er—have you come—is it about the marquee?'

'That's right, miss,' said the tallest of the men, a lanky, freckled fellow, and he shifted his tool-bag, knocked back his straw hat, and smiled down at her. 'That's about it.'

His smile was so easy, so friendly, that Laura recovered. What nice eyes he had, small, but such a dark blue! And now she looked at the others, they were smiling too. 'Cheer up, we won't bite,' their smile seemed to say. How very nice workmen were! And what a beautiful morning! She mustn't mention the morning; she must be business-like. The marquee.

'Well, what about the lily-lawn? Would that do?'

And she pointed to the lily-lawn with the hand that didn't hold the bread-and-butter. They turned, they stared in the direction. A little fat chap thrust out his underlip, and the tall fellow frowned.

'I don't fancy it,' said he. 'Not conspicuous enough. You see, with a thing like a marquee,' and he turned to Laura in his easy way, 'you want to put it somewhere where it'll give you a bang slap in the eye, if you follow me.'

Laura's upbringing made her wonder for a moment whether it was quite respectful of a workman to talk to her of bangs slap in the eye. But she did quite follow him.

'A corner of the tennis court,' she suggested. 'But the band's going to be in one corner.'

'H'm, going to have a band, are you?' said another of the workmen. He was pale. He had a haggard look as his dark eyes scanned the tennis court. What was he thinking?

'Only a very small band,' said Laura gently. Perhaps he wouldn't mind so much if the band was quite small. But the tall fellow interrupted.

'Look here, miss, that's the place. Against those trees. Over there. That'll do fine.'

Against the karakas. Then the karaka trees would be hidden. And they were so lovely, with their broad, gleaming leaves, and their clusters of yellow fruit. They were like trees you imagined growing up on a desert island, proud, solitary, lifting their leaves and fruits to the sun in a kind of silent splendour. Must they be hidden by a marquee?

They must. Already the men had shouldered their staves and were making for the place. Only the tall fellow was left. He bent down, pinched a sprig of lavender, put his thumb and forefinger to his nose and snuffed up the smell. When Laura saw that gesture she forgot all about the karakas in her wonder at him caring for things like that—caring for the smell of lavender. How many men that she knew would have done such a thing. *Oh, how extraordinarily nice workmen were,* she thought. Why couldn't she have workmen for friends rather than the silly boys she danced with and who came to Sunday night supper? She would get on much better with men like these.

It's all the fault, she decided, as the tall fellow drew something on the back of an envelope, something that was to be looped up or left to hang, of these absurd class distinctions. Well, for her part, she didn't feel them. Not a bit, not an atom. . . . And now there came the chock-chock of wooden hammers. Someone whistled, someone sang out, 'Are you right there, matey?' 'Matey!' The friendliness of it, the—the— Just to prove how happy she was, just to show the tall fellow how at home she felt, and how she despised stupid conventions, Laura took a big bite of her bread-and-butter as she stared at the little drawing. She felt just like a work-girl.

'Laura, Laura, where are you? Telephone, Laura!' a voice cried from the house.

'Coming!' Away she skimmed, over the lawn, up the path, up the steps, across the veranda, and into the porch. In the hall her father and Laurie were brushing their hats ready to go to the office.

'I say, Laura,' said Laurie very fast, 'you might just give a squiz at my coat before this afternoon. See if it wants pressing.'

'I will,' said she. Suddenly she couldn't stop herself. She ran at Laurie and gave him a small, quick squeeze. 'Oh, I do love parties, don't you?' gasped Laura.

'Ra-ther,' said Laurie's warm, boyish voice, and he squeezed his sister too, and gave her a gentle push. 'Dash off to the telephone, old girl.'

The telephone. 'Yes, yes; oh yes. Kitty? Good morning, dear. Come to lunch? Do, dear. Delighted of course. It will only be a very scratch meal—just the sandwich crusts and broken meringue-shells and what's left over. Yes, isn't it a perfect morning? Your white? Oh, I certainly should. One moment—hold the line. Mother's calling.' And Laura sat back. 'What, mother? Can't hear.'

Mrs Sheridan's voice floated down the stairs. 'Tell her to wear that sweet hat she had on last Sunday.'

'Mother says you're to wear that *sweet* hat you had on last Sunday. Good. One o'clock. Bye-bye.'

Laura put back the receiver, flung her arms over her head, took a deep breath, stretched, and let them fall. 'Huh,' she sighed, and the moment after the sigh she sat up quickly. She was still, listening. All the doors in the house seemed to be open. The house was alive with soft, quick steps and running voices. The green baize door that led to the kitchen regions swung open and shut with a muffled thud. And now there came a long, chuckling absurd sound. It was the heavy piano being moved on its stiff castors. But the air! If you stopped to notice, was the air always like this? Little faint winds were playing chase in at the tops of the windows, out at the doors. And there were two tiny spots of sun, one on the inkpot, one on a silver photograph frame, playing too. Darling little spots. Especially the one on the inkpot lid. It was quite warm. A warm little silver star. She could have kissed it.

The front door bell pealed, and there sounded the rustle of Sadie's print skirt on the stairs. A man's voice murmured; Sadie answered, careless, 'I'm sure I don't know. Wait. I'll ask Mrs Sheridan.'

'What is it, Sadie?' Laura came into the hall.

'It's the florist, Miss Laura.'

It was, indeed. There, just inside the door, stood a wide, shallow tray full of pots of pink lilies. No other kind. Nothing but lilies—canna lilies, big pink flowers, wide open, radiant, almost frighteningly alive on bright crimson stems.

'O-oh, Sadie!' said Laura, and the sound was like a little moan. She crouched down as if to warm herself at that blaze of lilies; she felt they were in her fingers, on her lips, growing in her breast.

'It's some mistake,' she said faintly. 'Nobody ever ordered so many. Sadie, go and find mother.'

But at that moment Mrs Sheridan joined them.

'It's quite right,' she said calmly. 'Yes, I ordered them. Aren't they lovely?' She pressed Laura's arm. 'I was passing the shop yesterday, and I saw them in the window, and I suddenly thought for once in my life I shall have enough canna lilies. The garden party will be a good excuse.'

'But I thought you said you didn't mean to interfere,' said Laura. Sadie had gone. The florist's man was still outside at his van. She put her arm round her mother's neck and gently, very gently, she bit her mother's ear.

'My darling child, you wouldn't like a logical mother, would you? Don't do that. Here's the man.'

He carried more lilies still, another whole tray.

'Bank them up, just inside the door, on both sides of the porch, please,' said Mrs Sheridan. 'Don't you agree, Laura?'

'Oh, I *do*, mother.'

In the drawing room Meg, Jose, and good little Hans had at last succeeded in moving the piano.

'Now, if we put this chesterfield against the wall and move everything out of the room except the chairs, don't you think?'

'Quite.'

'Hans, move these tables into the smoking room, and bring a sweeper to take these marks off the carpet and—one moment, Hans—' Jose loved giving orders to the servants, and they loved obeying her. She always made them feel they were taking part in some drama. 'Tell Mother and Miss Laura to come here at once.'

'Very good, Miss Jose.'

She turned to Meg. 'I want to hear what the piano sounds like, just in case I'm asked to sing this afternoon. Let's try over "This Life is Weary".'

*Pom!* Ta-ta-ta *Tee*-ta! The piano burst out so passionately that Jose's face changed. She clasped her hands. She looked mournfully and enigmatically at her mother and Laura as they came in.

This Life is *Wee*-ary,
A Tear—a Sigh.
A Love that *Chan*-ges,
This Life is *Wee*-ary,
A Tear—a Sigh.
A Love that *Chan*-ges,
And then . . . Good-bye!

But at the word 'Good-bye', and although the piano sounded more desperate than ever, her face broke into a brilliant, dreadfully unsympathetic smile.

'Aren't I in good voice, mummy?' she beamed.

This Life is *Wee*-ary,
Hope comes to Die,
A Dream—a *Wa*-kening.

But now Sadie interrupted them. 'What is it, Sadie?'

'If you please, m'm, cook says have you got the flags for the sandwiches?'

'The flags for the sandwiches, Sadie?' echoed Mrs Sheridan dreamily. And the children knew by her face that she hadn't got them. 'Let me see.' And she said to Sadie firmly, 'Tell cook I'll let her have them in ten minutes.'

Sadie went.

'Now, Laura,' said her mother quickly, 'come with me into the smoking room. I've got the names somewhere on the back of an envelope. You'll have to write them out for me. Meg, go upstairs this minute and take that wet thing off your head. Jose, run and finish dressing this instant. Do you hear me, children, or shall I have to tell your father when he comes home tonight? And—and, Jose, pacify cook if you do go into the kitchen, will you? I'm terrified of her this morning.'

The envelope was found at last behind the dining-room clock, though how it had got there Mrs Sheridan could not imagine.

'One of you children must have stolen it out of my bag, because I remember vividly—cream-cheese and lemon-curd. Have you done that?'

'Yes.'

'Egg and—' Mrs Sheridan held the envelope away from her. 'It looks like mice. It can't be mice, can it?'

'Olive, pet,' said Laura, looking over her shoulder.

'Yes, of course, olive. What a horrible combination it sounds. Egg and olive.'

They were finished at last, and Laura took them off to the kitchen. She found Jose there pacifying the cook, who did not look at all terrifying.

'I have never seen such exquisite sandwiches,' said Jose's rapturous voice. 'How many kinds did you say there were, cook? Fifteen?'

'Fifteen, Miss Jose.'

'Well, cook, I congratulate you.'

Cook swept up crusts with the long sandwich knife, and smiled broadly.

'Godber's has come,' announced Sadie, issuing out of the pantry. She had seen the man pass the window.

That meant that cream puffs had come. Godber's were famous for their cream puffs. Nobody ever thought of making them at home.

'Bring them in and put them on the table, my girl,' ordered cook.

Sadie brought them in and went back to the door. Of course Laura and Jose were far too grown-up to really care about such things. All the same, they couldn't help agreeing that the puffs looked very attractive. Very. Cook began arranging them, shaking off the extra icing sugar.

'Don't they carry one back to all one's parties?' said Laura.

'I suppose they do,' said practical Jose, who never liked to be carried back. 'They look beautifully light and feathery, I must say.'

'Have one each, my dears,' said cook in her comfortable voice. 'Yer ma won't know.'

Oh, impossible. Fancy cream puffs so soon after breakfast. The very idea made one shudder. All the same, two minutes later Jose and Laura were licking their fingers with that absorbed inward look that only comes from whipped cream.

'Let's go into the garden, out by the back way,' suggested Laura. 'I want to see how the men are getting on with the marquee. They're such awfully nice men.'

But the back door was blocked by cook, Sadie, Godber's man and Hans.

Something had happened.

'Tuk-tuk-tuk,' clucked cook like an agitated hen. Sadie had her hand clapped to her cheek as though she had a toothache. Hans's face was screwed up in the effort to understand. Only Godber's man seemed to be enjoying himself; it was his story.

'What's the matter? What happened?'

'There's been a horrible accident,' said cook. 'A man killed.'

'A man killed! Where? How? When?'

But Godber's man wasn't going to have his story snatched from under his very nose.

'Know those little cottages just below here, miss?' Know them? Of course, she knew them. 'Well, there's a young chap living there, name of *Scott*, a carter. His horse shied at a traction-engine, corner of Hawke Street this morning, and he was thrown out on the back of his head. Killed.'

'Dead!' Laura stared at Godber's man.

'Dead when they picked him up,' said Godber's man with relish. 'They were taking the body home as I come up here.' And he said to the cook, 'He's left a wife and five little ones.'

'Jose, come here.' Laura caught hold of her sister's sleeve and dragged her through the kitchen to the other side of the green baize door. There she paused and leaned against it. 'Jose!' she said, horrified, 'however are we going to stop everything?'

'Stop everything, Laura!' cried Jose in astonishment. 'What do you mean?'

'Stop the garden party, of course.' Why did Jose pretend?

But Jose was still more amazed. 'Stop the garden party? My dear Laura, don't be so absurd. Of course we can't do anything of the kind. Nobody expects us to. Don't be so extravagant.'

'But we can't possibly have a garden party with a man dead just outside the front gate.'

That really was extravagant, for the little cottages were in a lane to themselves at the very bottom of a steep rise that led up to the house. A broad road ran between. True, they were far too near. They were the greatest possible eyesore and they had no right to be in that neighbourhood at all. They were little mean dwellings painted a chocolate brown. In the garden patches there was nothing but cabbage stalks, sick hens and tomato cans. The very smoke coming out of their chimneys was poverty-stricken. Little rags and shreds of smoke, so unlike the great silvery plumes that uncurled from the Sheridans' chimneys. Washerwomen lived in the lane and sweeps and a cobbler and a man whose house-front was studded all over with minute bird-cages. Children swarmed. When the Sheridans were little they were forbidden to set foot there because of the revolting language and of what they might catch. But since they were grown up, Laura and Laurie on their prowls sometimes walked through. It was disgusting and sordid. They came out with a shudder. But still one must go everywhere; one must see everything. So through they went.

'And just think of what the band would sound like to that poor woman,' said Laura.

'Oh, Laura!' Jose began to be seriously annoyed. 'If you're going to stop a band playing every time someone has an accident, you'll lead a very strenuous life. I'm every bit as sorry about it as you. I feel just as sympathetic.' Her eyes hardened. She looked at her sister just as she used to when they were little and fighting together. 'You won't bring a drunken workman back to life by being sentimental,' she said softly.

'Drunk! Who said he was drunk?' Laura turned furiously on Jose. She said just as they had used to say on those occasions, 'I'm going straight up to tell mother.'

'Do, dear,' cooed Jose.

'Mother, can I come into your room?' Laura turned the big glass doorknob.

'Of course, child. Why, what's the matter? What's given you such a colour?' And Mrs Sheridan turned round from her dressing-table. She was trying on a new hat.

'Mother, a man's been killed,' began Laura.

'*Not* in the garden?' interrupted her mother.

'No, no!'

'Oh, what a fright you gave me!' Mrs Sheridan sighed with relief, and took off the big hat and held it on her knees.

'But listen, mother,' said Laura. Breathless, half-choking, she told the dreadful story. 'Of course, we can't have our party, can we?' she pleaded. 'The band and everybody arriving. They'd hear us, mother; they're nearly neighbours!'

To Laura's astonishment her mother behaved just like Jose; it was harder to bear because she seemed amused. She refused to take Laura seriously.

'But, my dear child, use your common sense. It's only by accident we've heard of it. If someone had died there normally—and I can't understand how they keep alive in those poky little holes—we should still be having our party, shouldn't we?'

Laura had to say 'yes' to that, but she felt it was all wrong. She sat down on her mother's sofa and pinched the cushion frill.

'Mother, isn't it really terribly heartless of us?' she asked.

'Darling!' Mrs Sheridan got up and came over to her, carrying the hat. Before Laura could stop her she had popped it on. 'My child!' said her mother, 'the hat is yours. It's made for you. It's much too young for me. I have never seen you look such a picture. Look at yourself!' And she held up her hand-mirror.

'But, mother,' Laura began again. She couldn't look at herself; she turned aside.

This time Mrs Sheridan lost patience just as Jose had done.

'You are being very absurd, Laura,' she said coldly. 'People like that don't expect sacrifices from us. And it's not very sympathetic to spoil everybody's enjoyment as you're doing now.'

'I don't understand,' said Laura, and she walked quickly out of the room into her own bedroom. There, quite by chance, the first thing she saw was this charming girl in the mirror, in her black hat trimmed with gold daisies and a long black velvet ribbon. Never had she imagined she could look like that. Is mother right? she thought. And now she hoped her mother was right. Am I being extravagant? Perhaps it was extravagant. Just for a moment she had another glimpse of that poor woman and those little children, and the body being carried into the house. But it all seemed blurred, unreal, like a picture in the newspaper. I'll remember it again after the party's over, she decided. And somehow that seemed quite the best plan. . . .

Lunch was over by half-past one. By half-past two they were all ready for the fray. The green-coated band had arrived and was established in a corner of the tennis court.

'My dear!' trilled Kitty Maitland, 'aren't they too like frogs for words? You ought to have arranged them round the pond with the conductor in the middle on a leaf.'

Laurie arrived and hailed them on his way to dress. At the sight of him Laura remembered the accident again. She wanted to tell him. If Laurie agreed with the others, then it was bound to be all right. And she followed him into the hall.

'Laurie!'

'Hallo!' He was halfway upstairs, but when he turned round and saw Laura he suddenly puffed out his cheeks and goggled his eyes at her. 'My word, Laura! You do look stunning,' said Laurie. 'What an absolutely topping hat!'

Laura said faintly 'Is it?' and smiled up at Laurie, and didn't tell him after all.

Soon after that people began coming in streams. The band struck up; the hired waiters ran from the house to the marquee. Wherever you looked there were couples strolling, bending to the flowers, greeting, moving on over the lawn. They were like bright birds that had alighted in the Sheridans' garden for this one afternoon, on their way to—where? Ah, what happiness it is to be with people who all are happy, to press hands, press cheeks, smile into eyes.

'Darling Laura, how well you look!'

'What a becoming hat, child!'

'Laura, you look quite Spanish. I've never seen you look so striking.'

And Laura, glowing, answered softly, 'Have you had tea? Won't you have an ice? The passion-fruit ices really are rather special.' She ran to her father and begged him: 'Daddy darling, can't the band have something to drink?'

And the perfect afternoon slowly ripened, slowly faded, slowly its petals closed.

'Never a more delightful garden party . . .' 'The greatest success . . .' 'Quite the most . . .'

Laura helped her mother with the good-byes. They stood side by side on the porch till it was all over.

'All over, all over, thank heaven,' said Mrs Sheridan. 'Round up the others, Laura. Let's go and have some fresh coffee. I'm exhausted. Yes, it's been very successful. But oh, these parties, these parties! Why will you children insist on giving parties!' And they all of them sat down in the deserted marquee.

'Have a sandwich, daddy dear. I wrote the flag.'

'Thanks.' Mr Sheridan took a bite and the sandwich was gone. He took another. 'I suppose you didn't hear of a beastly accident that happened today?' he said.

'My dear,' said Mrs Sheridan, holding up her hand, 'we did. It nearly ruined the party. Laura insisted we should put it off.'

'Oh, mother!' Laura didn't want to be teased about it.

'It was a horrible affair all the same,' said Mr Sheridan. 'The chap was married too. Lived just below in the lane, and leaves a wife and half a dozen kiddies, so they say.'

An awkward little silence fell. Mrs Sheridan fidgeted with her cup. Really, it was very tactless of father. . . .

Suddenly she looked up. There on the table were all those sandwiches, cakes, puffs, all uneaten, all going to be wasted. She had one of her brilliant ideas.

'I know,' she said. 'Let's make up a basket. Let's send that poor creature some of this perfectly good food. At any rate, it will be the greatest treat for the children. Don't you agree? And she's sure to have neighbours calling in and so on. What a point to have it all ready prepared. Laura!' She jumped up. 'Get me the big basket out of the stairs cupboard.'

'But, mother, do you really think it's a good idea?' said Laura.

Again, how curious, she seemed to be different from them all. To take scraps from their party. Would the poor woman really like that?

'Of course! What's the matter with you today? An hour or two ago you were insisting on us being sympathetic.'

Oh well! Laura ran for the basket. It was filled, it was now heaped by her mother.

'Take it yourself, darling,' said she. 'Run down just as you are. No, wait, take the arum lilies too. People of that class are so impressed by arum lilies.'

'The stems will ruin her lace frock,' said practical Jose.

So they would. Just in time. 'Only the basket, then. And, Laura!'—her mother followed her out of the marquee—'don't on any account—'

'What, mother?'

No, better not put such ideas into the child's head! 'Nothing! Run along.'

It was just growing dusky as Laura shut their garden gates. A big dog ran by like a shadow. The road gleamed white, and down below in the hollow the little cottages were in deep shade. How quiet it seemed after the afternoon. Here she was going down the hill to somewhere where a man lay dead, and she couldn't realize it. Why couldn't she? She stopped a minute. And it seemed to her that kisses, voices, tinkling spoons, laughter, the smell of crushed grass were somehow inside her. She had no room for anything else. How strange! She looked up at the pale sky, and all she thought was, 'Yes, it was the most successful party.'

Now the broad road was crossed. The lane began, smoky and dark. Women in shawls and men's tweed caps hurried by. Men hung over the palings; the children played in the doorways. A low hum came from the mean little cottages. In some of them there was a flicker of light, and a shadow, crab-like, moved across the window. Laura bent her head and hurried on. She wished now she had put on a coat. How her frock shone! And the big hat with the velvet streamer—if only it was another hat! Were the people looking at her? They must be. It was a mistake to have come; she knew all along it was a mistake. Should she go back even now?

No, too late. This was the house. It must be. A dark knot of people stood outside. Beside the gate an old, old woman with a crutch sat in a chair, watching. She had her feet on a newspaper. The voices stopped as Laura drew near. The group parted. It was as though she was expected, as though they had known she was coming here.

Laura was terribly nervous. Tossing the velvet ribbon over her shoulder, she said to a woman standing by, 'Is this Mrs Scott's house?' and the woman, smiling queerly, said, 'It is, my lass.'

Oh, to be away from this! She actually said, 'Help me, God,' as she walked up the tiny path and knocked. To be away from those staring eyes, or to be covered up in anything, one of those women's shawls even. I'll just leave the basket and go, she decided. I shan't even wait for it to be emptied.

Then the door opened. A little woman in black showed in the gloom.

Laura said, 'Are you Mrs Scott?' But to her horror the woman answered, 'Walk in, please, miss,' and she was shut in the passage.

'No,' said Laura, 'I don't want to come in. I only want to leave this basket. Mother sent—'

The little woman in the gloomy passage seemed not to have heard her. 'Step this way, please, miss,' she said in an oily voice, and Laura followed her.

She found herself in a wretched little low kitchen, lighted by a smoky lamp. There was a woman sitting before the fire.

'Em,' said the little creature who had let her in. 'Em! It's a young lady.' She turned to Laura. She said meaningly, 'I'm 'er sister, miss. You'll excuse 'er, won't you?'

'Oh, but of course!' said Laura. 'Please, please don't disturb her. I—I only want to leave—'

But at that moment the woman at the fire turned round. Her face, puffed up, red, with swollen eyes and swollen lips, looked terrible. She seemed as though she couldn't understand why Laura was there. What did it mean? Why was this stranger standing in the kitchen with a basket? What was it all about? And the poor face puckered up again.

'All right, my dear,' said the other. 'I'll thenk the young lady.'

And again she began, 'You'll excuse her, miss, I'm sure,' and her face, swollen too, tried an oily smile.

Laura only wanted to get out, to get away. She was back in the passage. The door opened. She walked straight through into the bedroom where the dead man was lying.

'You'd like a look at 'im, wouldn't you?' said Em's sister, and she brushed past Laura over to the bed. 'Don't be afraid, my lass,'—and now her voice sounded fond and sly, and fondly she drew down the sheet—' 'e looks a picture. There's nothing to show. Come along, my dear.'

Laura came.

There lay a young man, fast asleep—sleeping so soundly, so deeply, that he was far, far away from them both. Oh, so remote, so peaceful. He was dreaming. Never wake him up again. His head was sunk in the pillows, his eyes were closed; they were blind under the closed eyelids. He was given up to his dream. What did garden parties and baskets and lace frocks matter to him? He was far from all those things. He was wonderful, beautiful. While they were laughing and while the band was playing, this marvel had come to the lane. Happy . . . happy. . . . All is well, said that sleeping face. This is just as it should be. I am content.

But all the same you had to cry, and she couldn't go out of the room without saying something to him. Laura gave a loud childish sob.

'Forgive my hat,' she said.

And this time she didn't wait for Em's sister. She found her way out of the door, down the path, past all those dark people. At the corner of the lane she met Laurie.

He stepped out of the shadow. 'Is that you. Laura?'

'Yes.'

'Mother was getting anxious. Was it all right?'

'Yes, quite. Oh, Laurie!' She took his arm, she pressed up against him.

'I say, you're not crying, are you?' asked her brother.

Laura shook her head. She was.

Laurie put his arm round her shoulder. 'Don't cry,' he said in his warm, loving voice. 'Was it awful?'

'No,' sobbed Laura. 'It was simply marvellous. But, Laurie—' She stopped, she looked at her brother. 'Isn't life,' she stammered, 'isn't life—' But what life was she couldn't explain. No matter. He quite understood.

'*Isn't* it, darling?' said Laurie.

1922

# F. Scott Fitzgerald
## 1896–1940

Francis Scott Key Fitzgerald was born in St Paul, Minnesota, to a genteel but ineffectual father and a doting, eccentric mother. A delicate child, he was reluctant to go to school but finally went to a small Catholic school, then to St Paul Academy, to Newman, and finally to Princeton. He was unpopular at most of these places for most of the time, and unhappy as well, but his talent for writing and his remarkable good looks began to count for more as he grew up, so that at college he received much of the adulation for which he hungered so deeply. He was concerned to the point of obsession with social standing and prestige. Only his gift for writing and his capacity for ruthless self-criticism prevented him from sliding into a life of empty snobbery.

Shortly after the publication of his first novel, *This Side of Paradise* (1920), which brought him immediate fame, Fitzgerald married the strikingly beautiful Zelda Sayre, who shared his zest for high living. But Zelda's mental health was precarious, and the fame and riches garnered from his writing were more than he could handle. After a breakdown and painful recovery, which he described with a typical lack of self-protectiveness, he lived and worked in Hollywood, never quite recapturing the grace and beauty of his early work. He was the poet laureate of the Jazz Age, and in his finest novels (*The Great Gatsby*, 1925, and *Tender Is the Night*, 1934) and his remarkable short stories, we can find the best epitaph for that era as well as for Fitzgerald himself.

In the Depression-era story 'Babylon Revisited', Charlie Watts, now a widower, returns to Paris to reclaim his nine-year-old daughter Honoria. While some people, like his sister-in-law Marion Peters, cannot forget the past, Charlie, in the pain of the present, still hopes for a future that will bring him contentment.

# Babylon Revisited

## I

'And where's Mr Campbell?' Charlie asked.

'Gone to Switzerland. Mr Campbell's a pretty sick man, Mr Wales.'

'I'm sorry to hear that. And George Hardt?' Charlie inquired.

'Back in America, gone to work.'

'And where is the Snow Bird?'

'He was in here last week. Anyway, his friend, Mr Schaeffer, is in Paris.'

Two familiar names from the long list of a year and a half ago. Charlie scribbled an address in his notebook and tore out the page.

'If you see Mr Schaeffer, give him this,' he said. 'It's my brother-in-law's address. I haven't settled on a hotel yet.'

He was not really disappointed to find Paris was so empty. But the stillness in the Ritz bar was strange and portentous. It was not an American bar anymore—he felt polite in it, and not as if he owned it. It had gone back into France. He felt the stillness from the moment he got out of the taxi and saw the doorman, usually in a frenzy of activity at this hour, gossiping with a *chasseur* by the servants' entrance.

Passing through the corridor, he heard only a single, bored voice in the once clamorous women's room. When he turned into the bar he travelled the twenty feet of green carpet with his eyes fixed straight ahead by old habit; and then, with his foot firmly on the rail, he turned and surveyed the room, encountering only a single pair of eyes that fluttered up from a newspaper in the corner. Charlie asked for the head barman, Paul, who in the latter days of the bull market had come to work in his own custom-built car—disembarking, however, with due nicety at the nearest corner. But Paul was at his country house today and Alix giving him information.

'No, no more,' Charlie said, 'I'm going slow these days.'

Alix congratulated him: 'You were going pretty strong a couple of years ago.'

'I'll stick to it all right,' Charlie assured him. 'I've stuck to it for over a year and a half now.'

'How do you find conditions in America?'

'I haven't been to America for months. I'm in business in Prague, representing a couple of concerns there. They don't know about me down there.'

Alix smiled.

'Remember the night of George Hardt's bachelor dinner here?' said Charlie. 'By the way, what's become of Claude Fessenden?'

Alix lowered his voice confidentially: 'He's in Paris, but he doesn't come here anymore. Paul doesn't allow it. He ran up a bill of thirty thousand francs, charging all his drinks and his lunches, and usually his dinner, for more than a year. And when Paul finally told him he had to pay, he gave him a bad cheque.'

Alix shook his head sadly.

'I don't understand it, such a dandy fellow. Now he's all bloated up—' He made a plump apple of his hands.

Charlie watched a group of strident queens installing themselves in a corner.

'Nothing affects them,' he thought. 'Stocks rise and fall, people loaf or work, but they go on forever.' The place oppressed him. He called for the dice and shook with Alix for the drink.

'Here for long, Mr Wales?'

'I'm here for four or five days to see my little girl.'

'Oh-h! You have a little girl?'

Outside, the fire-red, gas-blue, ghost-green signs shone smokily through the tranquil rain. It was late afternoon and the streets were in movement; the *bistros* gleamed. At the corner of the Boulevard des Capucines he took a taxi. The Place de la Concorde moved by in pink majesty; they crossed the logical Seine, and Charlie felt the sudden provincial quality of the Left Bank.

Charlie directed his taxi to the Avenue de l'Opera, which was out of his way. But he wanted to see the blue hour spread over the magnificent façade, and imagine that the cab horns, playing endlessly the first few bars of *Le Plus que Lent*, were the trumpets of the Second Empire. They were closing the iron grille in front of Brentano's Book-store, and people were already at dinner behind the trim little bourgeois hedge of Duval's. He had never eaten at a really cheap restaurant in Paris. Five-course dinner, four francs fifty, eighteen cents, wine included. For some odd reason he wished that he had.

As they rolled on to the Left Bank and he felt its sudden provincialism, he thought, 'I spoiled this city for myself. I didn't realize it, but the days came along one after another, and then two years were gone, and everything was gone, and I was gone.'

He was thirty-five, and good to look at. The Irish mobility of his face was sobered by a deep wrinkle between his eyes. As he rang his brother-in-law's bell in the Rue Palatine, the wrinkle deepened till it pulled down his brows; he felt a cramping sensation in his belly. From behind the maid who opened the door darted a lovely little girl of nine who shrieked 'Daddy!' and flew up, struggling like a fish, into his arms. She pulled his head around by one ear and set her cheek against his.

'My old pie,' he said.

'Oh, daddy, daddy, daddy, daddy, dads, dads, dads!'

She drew him into the salon, where the family waited, a boy and a girl his daughter's age, his sister-in-law, and her husband. He greeted Marion with his voice pitched carefully to avoid either feigned enthusiasm or dislike, but the response was more frankly tepid, though she minimized her expression of unalterable distrust by directing her regard toward his child. The two men clasped hands in a friendly way and Lincoln Peters rested his for a moment on Charlie's shoulder.

The room was warm and comfortably American. The three children moved intimately about, playing through the yellow oblongs that led to other rooms; the cheer of six o'clock spoke in the eager smacks of the fire and the sounds of French activity in the kitchen. But Charlie did not relax; his heart sat up rigidly in his body and he drew confidence from his daughter, who from time to time came close to him, holding in her arms the doll he had brought.

'Really extremely well,' he declared in answer to Lincoln's question. 'There's a lot of business there that isn't moving at all, but we're doing even better than ever. In fact, damn well. I'm bringing my sister over from America next month to keep house for me. My income last year was bigger than it was when I had money. You see, the Czechs—'

His boasting was for a specific purpose; but after a moment, seeing a faint restiveness in Lincoln's eye, he changed the subject:

'Those are fine children of yours, well brought up, good manners.'

'We think Honoria's a great little girl too.'

Marion Peters came back from the kitchen. She was a tall woman with worried eyes, who had once possessed a fresh American loveliness. Charlie had never been sensitive to it and was always surprised when people spoke of how pretty she had been. From the first there had been an instinctive antipathy between them.

'Well, how do you find Honoria?' she asked.

'Wonderful. I was astonished how much she's grown in ten months. All the children are looking well.'

'We haven't had a doctor for a year. How do you like being back in Paris?'

'It seems very funny to see so few Americans around.'

'I'm delighted,' Marion said vehemently. 'Now at least you can go into a store without their assuming you're a millionaire. We've suffered like everybody, but on the whole it's a good deal pleasanter.'

'But it was nice while it lasted,' Charlie said. 'We were sort of royalty, almost infallible, with a sort of magic around us. In the bar this afternoon'—he stumbled, seeing his mistake—'there wasn't a man I knew.'

She looked at him keenly. 'I should think you'd have had enough of bars.'

'I only stayed a minute. I take one drink every afternoon, and no more.'

'Don't you want a cocktail before dinner?' Lincoln asked.

'I take only one drink every afternoon, and I've had that.'

'I hope you keep to it,' said Marion.

Her dislike was evident in the coldness with which she spoke, but Charlie only smiled; he had larger plans. Her very aggressiveness gave him an advantage, and he knew enough to wait. He wanted them to initiate the discussion of what they knew had brought him to Paris.

At dinner he couldn't decide whether Honoria was most like him or her mother. Fortunate if she didn't combine the traits of both that had brought them to disaster. A great wave of protectiveness went over him. He thought he knew what to do for her. He believed in character; he wanted to jump back a whole generation and trust in character again as the eternally valuable element. Everything else wore out.

He left soon after dinner, but not to go home. He was curious to see Paris by night with clearer and more judicious eyes than those of other days. He bought a *strapontin* for the Casino and watched Josephine Baker go through her chocolate arabesques.

After an hour he left and strolled toward Montmartre, up the Rue Pigalle into the Place Blanche. The rain had stopped and there were a few people in evening clothes disembarking from taxis in front of cabarets, and *cocottes* prowling singly or in pairs, and many Negroes. He passed a lighted door from which issued music, and stopped with the sense of familiarity; it was Bricktop's, where he had parted with so many hours and so much money. A few doors farther on he found another ancient rendezvous and incautiously put his head inside. Immediately an eager orchestra burst into sound, a pair of professional dancers leaped to their feet, and a maître d'hôtel swooped toward him, crying, 'Crowd just arriving, sir!' But he withdrew quickly.

'You have to be damn drunk,' he thought.

Zelli's was closed, the bleak and sinister cheap hotels surrounding it were dark; up the Rue Blanche there was more light and a local, colloquial French crowd. The Poet's Cave had disappeared, but the two great mouths of the Café of Heaven and the Café of Hell still yawned—even devoured, as he watched, the meagre contents of a tourist bus—a German, a Japanese, and an American couple who glanced at him with frightened eyes.

So much for the effort and ingenuity of Montmartre. All the catering to vice and waste was on an utterly childish scale, and he suddenly realized the meaning of the word 'dissipate'—to dissipate into thin air; to make nothing out of something. In the little hours of the night every move from place to place was an enormous human jump, an increase of paying for the privilege of slower and slower motion.

He remembered thousand-franc notes given to an orchestra for playing a single number, hundred-franc notes tossed to a doorman for calling a cab.

But it hadn't been given for nothing.

It had been given, even the most wildly squandered sum, as an offering to destiny that he might not remember the things most worth remembering, the things that now he would always remember—his child taken from his control, his wife escaped to a grave in Vermont.

In the glare of a *brasserie* a woman spoke to him. He bought her some eggs and coffee, and then, eluding her encouraging stare, gave her a twenty-franc note and took a taxi to his hotel.

**II**

He woke upon a fine fall day—football weather. The depression of yesterday was gone and he liked the people on the streets. At noon he sat opposite Honoria at Le Grand Vatel, the only restaurant he could think of not reminiscent of champagne dinners and long luncheons that began at two and ended in a blurred and vague twilight.

'Now, how about vegetables? Oughtn't you to have some vegetables?'

'Well, yes.'

'Here's *épinards* and *chou-fleur* and *carrots* and *haricots*.'

'I'd like *chou-fleur*.'

'Wouldn't you like to have two vegetables?'

'I usually only have one at lunch.'

The waiter was pretending to be inordinately fond of children. '*Qu'elle est mignonne la petite! Elle parle exactement comme une Française.*'

'How about dessert? Shall we wait and see?'

The waiter disappeared. Honoria looked at her father expectantly.

'What are we going to do?'

'First, we're going to that toy store in the Rue Saint-Honoré and buy you anything you like. And then we're going to the vaudeville at the Empire.'

She hesitated. 'I like it about the vaudeville, but not the toy store.'

'Why not?'

'Well, you brought me this doll.' She had it with her. 'And I've got lots of things. And we're not rich anymore, are we?'

'We never were. But today you are to have anything you want.'

'All right,' she agreed resignedly.

When there had been her mother and a French nurse he had been inclined to be strict; now he extended himself, reached out for a new tolerance; he must be both parents to her and not shut any of her out of communication.

'I want to get to know you,' he said gravely. 'First let me introduce myself. My name is Charles J. Wales, of Prague.'

'Oh, daddy!' her voice cracked with laughter.

'And who are you, please?' he persisted, and she accepted a rôle immediately: 'Honoria Wales, Rue Palatine, Paris.'

'Married or single?'

'No, not married. Single.'

He indicated the doll. 'But I see you have a child, madame.'

Unwilling to disinherit it, she took it to her heart and thought quickly: 'Yes, I've been married, but I'm not married now. My husband is dead.'

He went on quickly, 'And the child's name?'

'Simone. That's after my best friend at school.'

'I'm very pleased that you're doing so well at school.'

'I'm third this month,' she boasted. 'Elsie'—that was her cousin—'is only about eighteenth, and Richard is about at the bottom.'

'You like Richard and Elsie, don't you?'

'Oh, yes. I like Richard quite well and I like her all right.'

Cautiously and casually he asked: 'And Aunt Marion and Uncle Lincoln—which do you like best?'

'Oh, Uncle Lincoln, I guess.'

He was increasingly aware of her presence. As they came in, a murmur of '. . . adorable' followed them, and now the people at the next table bent all their silences upon her, staring as if she were something no more conscious than a flower.

'Why don't I live with you?' she asked suddenly. 'Because mamma's dead?'

'You must stay here and learn more French. It would have been hard for daddy to take care of you so well.'

'I don't really need much taking care of any more. I do everything for myself.'

Going out of the restaurant, a man and a woman unexpectedly hailed him.

'Well, the old Wales!'

'Hello there, Lorraine. . . . Dunc.'

Sudden ghosts out of the past: Duncan Schaeffer, a friend from college. Lorraine Quarrles, a lovely, pale blonde of thirty; one of a crowd who had helped them make months into days in the lavish times of three years ago.

'My husband couldn't come this year,' she said, in answer to his question. 'We're poor as hell. So he gave me two hundred a month and told me I could do my worst on that. . . . This your little girl?'

'What about coming back and sitting down?' Duncan asked.

'Can't do it.' He was glad for an excuse. As always, he felt Lorraine's passionate, provocative attraction, but his own rhythm was different now.

'Well, how about dinner?' she asked.

'I'm not free. Give me your address and let me call you.'

'Charlie, I believe you're sober,' she said judicially. 'I honestly believe he's sober, Dunc. Pinch him and see if he's sober.'

Charlie indicated Honoria with his head. They both laughed.

'What's your address?' said Duncan skeptically.

He hesitated, unwilling to give the name of his hotel.

'I'm not settled yet. I'd better call you. We're going to the vaudeville at the Empire.'

'There! That's what I want to do,' Lorraine said. 'I want to see some clowns and acrobats and jugglers. That's just what we'll do, Dunc.'

'We've got to do an errand first,' said Charlie. 'Perhaps we'll see you there.'

'All right, you snob. . . . Good-bye, beautiful little girl.'

'Good-bye.'

Honoria bobbed politely.

Somehow, an unwelcome encounter. They liked him because he was functioning, because he was serious; they wanted to see him, because he was stronger than they were now, because they wanted to draw a certain sustenance from his strength.

At the Empire, Honoria proudly refused to sit upon her father's folded coat. She was already an individual with a code of her own, and Charlie was more and more absorbed by the desire of putting a little of himself into her before she crystallized utterly. It was hopeless to try to know her in so short a time.

Between the acts they came upon Duncan and Lorraine in the lobby where the band was playing.

'Have a drink?'

'All right, but not up at the bar. We'll take a table.'

'The perfect father.'

Listening abstractedly to Lorraine, Charlie watched Honoria's eyes leave their table, and he followed them wistfully about the room, wondering what they saw. He met her glance and she smiled.

'I liked that lemonade,' she said.

What had she said? What had he expected? Going home in a taxi afterward, he pulled her over until her head rested against his chest.

'Darling, do you ever think about your mother?'

'Yes, sometimes,' she answered vaguely.

'I don't want you to forget her. Have you got a picture of her?'

'Yes, I think so. Anyhow, Aunt Marion has. Why don't you want me to forget her?'

'She loved you very much.'

'I loved her too.'

They were silent for a moment.

'Daddy, I want to come and live with you,' she said suddenly.

His heart leaped; he had wanted it to come like this.

'Aren't you perfectly happy?'

'Yes, but I love you better than anybody. And you love me better than anybody, don't you, now that mummy's dead?'

'Of course I do. But you won't always like me best, honey. You'll grow up and meet somebody your own age and go marry him and forget you ever had a daddy.'

'Yes, that's true,' she agreed tranquilly.

He didn't go in. He was coming back at nine o'clock and he wanted to keep himself fresh and new for the thing he must say then.

'When you're safe inside, just show yourself in that window.'

'All right. Good-bye, dads, dads, dads, dads.'

He waited in the dark street until she appeared, all warm and glowing, in the window above and kissed her fingers out into the night.

## III

They were waiting. Marion sat behind the coffee service in a dignified black dinner dress that just faintly suggested mourning. Lincoln was walking up and down with the animation of one who had already been talking. They were as anxious as he was to get into the question. He opened it almost immediately:

'I suppose you know what I want to see you about—why I really came to Paris.'

Marion played with the black stars on her necklace and frowned.

'I'm awfully anxious to have a home,' he continued. 'And I'm awfully anxious to have Honoria in it. I appreciate your taking in Honoria for her mother's sake, but things have changed now'—he hesitated and then continued more forcibly—'changed radically with me, and I want to ask you to reconsider the matter. It would be silly for me to deny that about three years ago I was acting badly—'

Marion looked up a him with hard eyes.

'—but all that's over. As I told you, I haven't had more than a drink a day for over a year, and I take that drink deliberately, so that the idea of alcohol won't get too big in my imagination. You see the idea?'

'No,' said Marion succinctly.

'It's a sort of stunt I set myself. It keeps the matter in proportion.'

'I get you,' said Lincoln. 'You don't want to admit it's got any attraction for you.'

'Something like that. Sometimes I forget and don't take it. But I try to take it. Anyway, I couldn't afford to drink in my position. The people I represent are more than satisfied with what I've done, and I'm bringing my sister over from Burlington to keep house for me, and I want awfully to have Honoria too. You know that even when her mother and I weren't getting along well we never let anything that happened touch Honoria. I know she's fond of me and I know I'm able to take care of her and—well, there you are. How do you feel about it?'

He knew that now he would have to take a beating. It would last an hour or two hours, and it would be difficult, but if he modulated his inevitable resentment to the chastened attitude of the reformed sinner, he might win his point in the end.

Keep your temper, he told himself. You don't want to be justified. You want Honoria.

Lincoln spoke first: 'We've been talking it over ever since we got your letter last month. We're happy to have Honoria here. She's a dear little thing, and we're glad to be able to help her, but of course that isn't the question—'

Marion interrupted suddenly. 'How long are you going to stay sober, Charlie?' she asked.

'Permanently, I hope.'

'How can anybody count on that?'

'You know I never did drink heavily until I gave up business and came over here with nothing to do. Then Helen and I began to run around with—'

'Please leave Helen out of it. I can't bear to hear you talk about her like that.'

He stared at her grimly; he had never been certain how fond of each other the sisters were in life.

'My drinking only lasted about a year and a half—from the time we came over until I—collapsed.'

'It was time enough.'

'It was time enough,' he agreed.

'My duty is entirely to Helen,' she said. 'I try to think what she would have wanted me to do. Frankly, from the night you did that terrible thing you haven't really existed for me. I can't help that. She was my sister.'

'Yes.'

'When she was dying she asked me to look out for Honoria. If you hadn't been in a sanitarium then, it might have helped matters.'

He had no answer.

'I'll never in my life be able to forget that morning when Helen knocked at my door, soaked to the skin and shivering and said you'd locked her out.'

Charlie gripped the sides of his chair. This was more difficult than he expected; he wanted to launch out into a long expostulation and explanation, but he only said: 'The night I locked her out—' and she interrupted, 'I don't feel up to going over that again.'

After a moment's silence Lincoln said: 'We're getting off the subject. You want Marion to set aside her legal guardianship and give you Honoria. I think the main point for her is whether she has confidence in you or not.'

'I don't blame Marion,' Charlie said slowly, 'but I think she can have entire confidence in me. I had a good record up to three years ago. Of course, it's within human possibilities I might go wrong any time. But if we wait much longer I'll lose Honoria's childhood and my chance for a home.' He shook his head, 'I'll simply lose her, don't you see?'

'Yes, I see,' said Lincoln.

'Why didn't you think of all this before?' Marion asked.

'I suppose I did, from time to time, but Helen and I were getting along badly. When I consented to the guardianship, I was flat on my back in a sanitarium and the market had cleaned me out. I knew I'd acted badly, and I thought if it would bring any peace to Helen, I'd agree to anything. But now it's different. I'm functioning, I'm behaving damn well, so far as—'

'Please don't swear at me,' Marion said.

He looked at her, startled. With each remark the force of her dislike became more and more apparent. She had built up all her fear of life into one wall and faced it toward him. This trivial reproof was possibly the result of some trouble with the cook several hours before. Charlie became increasingly alarmed at leaving Honoria in this atmosphere of hostility against himself; sooner or later it would come out, in a word here, a shake of the head there, and some of that distrust would be irrevocably implanted on Honoria. But he pulled his temper down out of his face and shut it up inside him; he had won a point, for Lincoln realized the absurdity of Marion's remark and asked her lightly since when she had objected to the word 'damn'.

'Another thing,' Charlie said: 'I'm able to give her certain advantages now. I'm going to take a French governess to Prague with me. I've got a lease on a new apartment—'

He stopped, realizing that he was blundering. They couldn't be expected to accept with equanimity the fact that his income was again twice as large as their own.

'I suppose you can give her more luxuries than we can,' said Marion. 'When you were throwing away money we were living along watching every ten francs. . . . I suppose you'll start doing it again.'

'Oh, no,' he said. 'I've learned. I worked hard for ten years, you know—until I got lucky in the market, like so many people. Terribly lucky. It won't happen again.'

There was a long silence. All of them felt their nerves straining, and for the first time in a year Charlie wanted a drink. He was sure now that Lincoln Peters wanted him to have his child.

Marion shuddered suddenly; part of her saw that Charlie's feet were planted on the earth now, and her own maternal feeling recognized the naturalness of his desire; but she had lived for a long time with a prejudice—a prejudice founded on a curious disbelief in her sister's happiness, and which, in the shock of one terrible night, had turned to hatred for him. It had all happened at a point in her life where the discouragement of ill health and adverse circumstances made it necessary for her to believe in tangible villainy and a tangible villain.

'I can't help what I think!' she cried out suddenly. 'How much you were responsible for Helen's death, I don't know. It's something you'll have to square with your own conscience.'

An electric current of agony surged through him; for a moment he was almost on his feet, an unuttered sound echoing from his throat. He hung on to himself for a moment, another moment.

'Hold on there,' said Lincoln uncomfortably. 'I never thought you were responsible for that.'

'Helen died of heart trouble,' Charlie said dully.

'Yes, heart trouble.' Marion spoke as if the phrase had another meaning for her.

Then, in the flatness that followed her outburst, she saw him plainly and she knew he had somehow arrived at control over the situation. Glancing at her husband, she found no help from him, and as abruptly as if it were a matter of no importance, she threw up the sponge.

'Do what you like!' she cried, springing up from her chair. 'She's your child. I'm not the person to stand in your way. I think if it were my child I'd rather see her—' She managed to check herself. 'You two decide it. I can't stand this. I'm sick. I'm going to bed.'

She hurried from the room; after a moment Lincoln said:

'This has been a hard day for her. You know how strongly she feels—' His voice was almost apologetic: 'When a woman gets an idea in her head.'

'Of course.'

'It's going to be all right. I think she sees now that you—can provide for the child, and so we can't very well stand in your way or Honoria's way.'

'Thank you, Lincoln.'

'I'd better go along and see how she is.'

'I'm going.'

He was still trembling when he reached the street, but a walk down the Rue Bonaparte to the *quais* set him up, and as he crossed the Seine, fresh and new by the *quai* lamps, he felt exultant. But back in his room he couldn't sleep. The image of Helen haunted him. Helen whom he had loved so until they had senselessly begun to abuse each other's love, tear it into shreds. On that terrible February night that Marion remembered so vividly, a slow quarrel had gone on for hours. There was a scene at the Florida, and then he attempted to take her home, and then she kissed young Webb at a table; after that there was what she had hysterically said. When he arrived home alone he turned the key in the lock in wild anger. How could he know she would arrive an hour later alone, that there would be a snowstorm in which she wandered about in slippers, too confused to find a taxi? Then the aftermath, her escaping pneumonia by a miracle, and all the attendant horror. They were 'reconciled', but that was the beginning of the end, and Marion, who had seen with her own eyes and who imagined it to be one of many scenes from her sister's martyrdom, never forgot.

Going over it again brought Helen nearer, and in the white, soft light that steals upon half sleep near morning he found himself talking to her again. She said that he was perfectly right about Honoria and that she wanted Honoria to be with him. She said she was glad he was being good and doing better. She said a lot of other things—very friendly things—but she was in a swing in a white dress, and swinging faster and faster all the time, so that at the end he could not hear clearly all that she said.

## IV

He woke up feeling happy. The door of the world was open again. He made plans, vistas, futures for Honoria and himself, but suddenly he grew sad, remembering all the plans he and Helen had made. She had not planned to die. The present was the thing—work to do and someone to love. But not to love too much, for he knew the injury that a father can do to a daughter or a mother to a son by attaching them too closely: afterward, out in the world, the child would seek in the marriage partner the same blind tenderness and, failing probably to find it, turn against love and life.

It was another bright, crisp day. He called Lincoln Peters at the bank where he worked and asked if he could count on taking Honoria when he left for Prague. Lincoln agreed that there was no reason for delay. One thing—the legal guardianship. Marion wanted to retain that a while longer. She was upset by the whole matter, and it would oil things if she felt that the situation was still in her control for another year. Charlie agreed, wanting only the tangible, visible child.

Then the question of a governess. Charlie sat in a gloomy agency and talked to a cross Béarnaise and to a buxom Breton peasant, neither of whom he could have endured. There were others whom he would see tomorrow.

He lunched with Lincoln Peters at Griffons, trying to keep down his exultation.

'There's nothing quite like your own child,' Lincoln said. 'But you understand how Marion feels too.'

'She's forgotten how hard I worked for seven years there,' Charlie said. 'She just remembers one night.'

'There's another thing.' Lincoln hesitated. 'While you and Helen were tearing around Europe throwing money away, we were just getting along. I didn't touch any of the prosperity because I never got ahead enough to carry anything but my insurance. I think Marion felt there was some kind of injustice in it—you not even working toward the end, and getting richer and richer.'

'It went just as quick as it came,' said Charlie.

'Yes, a lot of it stayed in the hands of *chasseurs* and saxophone players and maîtres d'hôtel—well, the big party's over now. I just said that to explain Marion's feelings about those crazy years. If you drop in about six o'clock tonight before Marion's too tired, we'll settle the details on the spot.'

Back at his hotel, Charlie found a *pneumatique*[1] that had been redirected from the Ritz bar where Charlie had left his address for the purpose of finding a certain man.

> DEAR CHARLIE: You were so strange when we saw you the other day that I wondered if I did something to offend you. If so, I'm not conscious of it. In fact, I have thought about you too much for the last year, and it's always been in the back of my mind that I might see you if I came over here. We *did* have such good times that crazy spring, like the night you and I stole the butcher's tricycle, and the time we tried to call on the president and you had the old derby rim and the wire cane. Everybody seems so old lately, but I don't feel old a bit. Couldn't we get together some time today for old time's sake? I've got a vile hangover for the moment, but will be feeling better this afternoon and will look for you about five in the sweatshop at the Ritz.
>
> Always devotedly,
>
> LORRAINE.

His first feeling was one of awe that he had actually, in his mature years, stolen a tricycle and pedalled Lorraine all over the étoile between the small hours and dawn. In retrospect it was a nightmare. Locking out Helen didn't fit in with any other act of his

1 a message conveyed by *pneumatique*, a system of sending mail along tubes by air pressure

life, but the tricycle incident did—it was one of many. How many weeks or months of dissipation to arrive at the condition of utter irresponsibility?

He tried to picture how Lorraine had appeared to him then—very attractive; Helen was unhappy about it, though she said nothing. Yesterday, in the restaurant, Lorraine had seemed trite, blurred, worn away. He emphatically did not want to see her, and he was glad Alix had not given away his hotel address. It was a relief to think, instead, of Honoria, to think of Sundays spent with her and of saying good morning to her and of knowing she was there in his house at night, drawing her breath in the darkness.

At five he took a taxi and bought presents for all the Peters—a piquant cloth doll, a box of Roman soldiers, flowers for Marion, big linen handkerchiefs for Lincoln.

He saw, when he arrived in the apartment, that Marion had accepted the inevitable. She greeted him now as though he were a recalcitrant member of the family, rather than a menacing outsider. Honoria had been told she was going; Charlie was glad to see that her tact made her conceal her excessive happiness. Only on his lap did she whisper her delight and the question 'When?' before she slipped away with the other children.

He and Marion were alone for a minute in the room, and on an impulse he spoke out boldly:

'Family quarrels are bitter things. They don't go according to any rules. They're not aches or wounds; they're more like splits in the skin that won't heal because there's not enough material. I wish you and I could be on better terms.'

'Some things are hard to forget,' she answered. 'It's a question of confidence.' There was no answer to this and presently she asked, 'When do you propose to take her?'

'As soon as I can get a governess. I hoped the day after tomorrow.'

'That's impossible. I've got to get her things in shape. Not before Saturday.'

He yielded. Coming back into the room, Lincoln offered him a drink.

'I'll take my daily whisky,' he said.

It was warm here, it was a home, people together by a fire. The children felt very safe and important; the mother and father were serious, watchful. They had things to do for the children more important than his visit here. A spoonful of medicine was, after all, more important than the strained relations between Marion and himself. They were not dull people, but they were very much in the grip of life and circumstances. He wondered if he couldn't do something to get Lincoln out of his rut at the bank.

A long peal at the doorbell; the *bonne à tout faire* passed through and went down the corridor. The door opened upon another long ring, and then voices, and the three in the salon looked up expectantly; Richard moved to bring the corridor within his range of vision, and Marion rose. Then the maid came back along the corridor, closely followed by the voices, which developed under the light into Duncan Schaeffer and Lorraine Quarrles.

They were gay, they were hilarious, they were roaring with laughter. For a moment Charlie was astounded; unable to understand how they ferreted out the Peters' address.

'Ah-h-h-!' Duncan wagged his finger roguishly at Charlie. 'Ah-h-h!'

They both slid down another cascade of laughter. Anxious and at a loss, Charlie shook hands with them quickly and presented them to Lincoln and Marion. Marion nodded, scarcely speaking. She had drawn back a step toward the fire; her little girl stood beside her, and Marion put an arm about her shoulder.

With growing annoyance at the intrusion, Charlie waited for them to explain themselves. After some concentration Duncan said:

'We came to invite you out to dinner. Lorraine and I insist that all this shishi, cagey business 'bout your address got to stop.'

Charlie came closer to them, as if to force them backward down the corridor.

'Sorry, but I can't. Tell me where you'll be and I'll phone you in half an hour.'

This made no impression. Lorraine sat down suddenly on the side of a chair, and focusing her eyes on Richard, cried, 'Oh, what a nice little boy! Come here, little boy.' Richard glanced at his mother, but did not move. With a perceptible shrug of her shoulders, Lorraine turned back to Charlie:

'Come and dine. Sure your cousins won' mine. See you so sel'om. Or solemn.'

'I can't,' said Charlie sharply. 'You two have dinner and I'll phone you.'

Her voice became suddenly unpleasant. 'All right, we'll go. But I remember once when you hammered on my door at four a.m. I was enough of a good sport to give you a drink. Come on, Dunc.'

Still in slow motion, with blurred, angry faces, with uncertain feet, they retired along the corridor.

'Good night,' Charlie said.

'Good night!' responded Lorraine emphatically.

When he went back into the salon Marion had not moved, only now her son was standing in the circle of her other arm. Lincoln was still swinging Honoria back and forth like a pendulum from side to side.

'What an outrage!' Charlie broke out. 'What an absolute outrage!'

Neither of them answered. Charlie dropped into an armchair, picked up his drink, set it down again and said:

'People I haven't seen for two years having the colossal nerve—'

He broke off. Marion had made the sound 'Oh!' in one swift, furious breath, turned her body from him with a jerk and left the room.

Lincoln set down Honoria carefully.

'You children go in and start your soup,' he said, and when they obeyed, he said to Charlie:

'Marion's not well and she can't stand shocks. That kind of people make her really physically sick.'

'I didn't tell them to come here. They wormed your name out of somebody. They deliberately—'

'Well, it's too bad. It doesn't help matters. Excuse me a minute.'

Left alone, Charlie sat tense in his chair. In the next room he could hear the children eating, talking in monosyllables, already oblivious to the scene between their elders. He heard a murmur of conversation from a farther room and then the ticking bell of a telephone receiver picked up, and in a panic he moved to the other side of the room and out of earshot.

In a minute Lincoln came back. 'Look here, Charlie. I think we'd better call off dinner for tonight. Marion's in bad shape.'

'Is she angry with me?'

'Sort of,' he said, almost roughly. 'She's not strong and—'

'You mean she's changed her mind about Honoria?'

'She's pretty bitter right now. I don't know. You phone me at the bank tomorrow.'

'I wish you'd explain to her I never dreamed these people would come here. I'm just as sore as you are.'

'I couldn't explain anything to her now.'

Charlie got up. He took his coat and hat and started down the corridor. Then he opened the door of the dining room and said in a strange voice, 'Good night, children.'

Honoria rose and ran around the table to hug him.

'Good night, sweetheart,' he said vaguely, and then trying to make his voice more tender, trying to conciliate something, 'Good night, dear children.'

## V

Charlie went directly to the Ritz bar with the furious idea of finding Lorraine and Duncan, but they were not there, and he realized that in any case there was nothing he could do. He had not touched his drink at the Peters', and now he ordered a whisky-and-soda. Paul came over to say hello.

'It's a great change,' he said sadly. 'We do about half the business we did. So many fellows I hear about back in the States lost everything, maybe not in the first crash, but then in the second. Your friend George Hardt lost every cent, I hear. Are you back in the States?'

'No, I'm in business in Prague.'

'I heard that you lost a lot in the crash.'

'I did,' and he added grimly, 'but I lost everything I wanted in the boom.'

'Selling short.'

'Something like that.'

Again the memory of those days swept over him like a nightmare—the people they met travelling; then people who couldn't add a row of figures or speak a coherent sentence. The little man Helen had consented to dance with at the ship's party, who had insulted her ten feet from the table; the women and girls carried screaming with drink or drugs out of public places—

—The men who locked their wives out in the snow, because the snow of twenty-nine wasn't real snow. If you didn't want it to be snow, you just paid some money.

He went to the phone and called the Peters' apartment; Lincoln answered.

'I called up because this thing is on my mind. Has Marion said anything definite?'

'Marion's sick,' Lincoln answered shortly. 'I know this thing isn't altogether your fault, but I can't have her go to pieces about it. I'm afraid we'll have to let it slide for six months; I can't take the chance of working her up to this state again.'

'I see.'

'I'm sorry, Charlie.'

He went back to his table. His whisky glass was empty, but he shook his head when Alix looked at it questioningly. There wasn't much he could do now except send

Honoria some things; he would send her a lot of things tomorrow. He thought rather angrily that this was just money—he had given so many people money. . . .

'No, no more,' he said to another waiter. 'What do I owe you?'

He would come back some day; they couldn't make him pay forever. But he wanted his child, and nothing was much good now, beside that fact. He wasn't young anymore, with a lot of nice thoughts and dreams to have by himself. He was absolutely sure Helen wouldn't have wanted him to be so alone.

1931

# Ernest Hemingway
## 1899–1961

Born in Oak Park, Illinois, the son of a doctor and music teacher, Ernest Hemingway spent his summer holidays in the upper peninsula of Michigan, where his father taught him early to hunt and fish. He was a physically active and popular boy, good at writing but bored with school. A couple of times he simply left and went on the road, but he worked on the school newspaper, graduated, and tried to enlist in the army for the First World War. A bad eye prevented this attempt, but he was able to enlist as an ambulance driver for the Red Cross in Italy, where he saw plenty of combat, was badly wounded, and showed genuine heroism under fire. When the war ended he returned to North America and did newspaper work in Chicago and in Toronto, where for four years he was employed as a staff writer and foreign correspondent for the *Toronto Star*.

In 1924 Hemingway moved to Europe, where he lived with his first wife, mostly in Paris. It was there that he met Ezra Pound and Gertrude Stein, who christened Hemingway and his young friends a 'lost generation'. There, too, Hemingway began to write the stories and novels that made his reputation, beginning with *In Our Time* (1925) and *The Sun Also Rises* (1926). In later years he became more of a public figure and less of a writer, as he hardened into a symbol of patriarchal machismo known as 'Papa'. But he had a fine success with *The Old Man and the Sea* (1952) and won the Nobel Prize for Literature in 1954. In 1961, in ill health and unable to write, he used his silver-inlaid, double-barrelled shotgun to end his life.

## A Clean, Well-Lighted Place

It was late and everyone had left the café except an old man who sat in the shadow the leaves of the tree made against the electric light. In the daytime the street was dusty, but at night the dew settled the dust and the old man liked to sit late because he was deaf and now at night it was quiet and he felt the difference. The two waiters inside the café knew the old man was a little drunk, and while he was a good client they knew that if he became too drunk he would leave without paying, so they kept watch on him.

'Last week he tried to commit suicide,' one waiter said.

'Why?'

'He was in despair.'

'What about?'

'Nothing.'

'How do you know it was nothing?'

'He has plenty of money.'

They sat together at a table that was close against the wall near the door of the café and looked at the terrace where the tables were all empty except where the old man sat in the shadow of the leaves of the tree that moved slightly in the wind. A girl and a soldier went by in the street. The street light shone on the brass number on his collar. The girl wore no head covering and hurried beside him.

'The guard will pick him up,' one waiter said.

'What does it matter if he gets what he's after?'

'He had better get off the street now. The guard will get him. They went by five minutes ago.'

The old man sitting in the shadow rapped on his saucer with his glass. The younger waiter went over to him.

'What do you want?'

The old man looked at him. 'Another brandy,' he said.

'You'll be drunk,' the waiter said. The old man looked at him. The waiter went away.

'He'll stay all night,' he said to his colleague. 'I'm sleepy now. I never get into bed before three o'clock. He should have killed himself last week.'

The waiter took the brandy bottle and another saucer from the counter inside the café and marched out to the old man's table. He put down the saucer and poured the glass full of brandy.

'You should have killed yourself last week,' he said to the deaf man. The old man motioned with his finger. 'A little more,' he said. The waiter poured on into the glass so that the brandy slopped over and ran down the stem into the top saucer of the pile. 'Thank you,' the old man said. The waiter took the bottle back inside the café. He sat down at the table with his colleague again.

'He's drunk now,' he said.

'He's drunk every night.'

'What did he want to kill himself for?'

'How should I know.'

'How did he do it?'

'He hung himself with a rope.'

'Who cut him down?'

'His niece.'

'Why did they do it?'

'Fear for his soul.'

'How much money has he got?'

'He's got plenty.'

'He must be eighty years old.'

'Anyway I should say he was eighty.'

'I wish he would go home. I never get to bed before three o'clock. What kind of hour is that to go to bed?'

'He stays up because he likes it.'

'He's lonely. I'm not lonely. I have a wife waiting in bed for me.'

'He had a wife once too.'

'A wife would be no good to him now.'

'You can't tell. He might be better with a wife.'

'His niece looks after him.'

'I know. You said she cut him down.'

'I wouldn't want to be that old. An old man is a nasty thing.'

'Not always. This old man is clean. He drinks without spilling. Even now, drunk. Look at him.'

'I don't want to look at him. I wish he would go home. He has no regard for those who must work.'

The old man looked from his glass across the square, then over at the waiters.

'Another brandy,' he said, pointing to his glass. The waiter who was in a hurry came over.

'Finished,' he said, speaking with that omission of syntax stupid people employ when talking to drunken people or foreigners. 'No more tonight. Close now.'

'Another,' said the old man.

'No. Finished.' The waiter wiped the edge of the table with a towel and shook his head.

The old man stood up, slowly counted the saucers, took a leather coin purse from his pocket and paid for the drinks, leaving half a peseta tip.

The waiter watched him go down the street, a very old man walking unsteadily but with dignity.

'Why didn't you let him stay and drink?' the unhurried waiter asked. They were putting up the shutters. 'It is half-past two.'

'I want to go home to bed.'

'What is an hour?'

'More to me than to him.'

'An hour is the same.'

'You talk like an old man yourself. He can buy a bottle and drink at home.'

'It's not the same.'

'No, it is not,' agreed the waiter with a wife. He did not wish to be unjust. He was only in a hurry.

'And you? You have no fear of going home before your usual hour?'

'Are you trying to insult me?'

'No, hombre, only to make a joke.'

'No,' the waiter who was in a hurry said, rising from pulling down the metal shutters. 'I have confidence. I am all confidence.'

'You have youth, confidence, and a job,' the older waiter said. 'You have everything.'

'And what do you lack?'

'Everything but work.'

'You have everything I have.'

'No. I have never had confidence and I am not young.'

'Come on. Stop talking nonsense and lock up.'

'I am of those who like to stay late at the café,' the older waiter said. 'With all those who do not want to go to bed. With all those who need a light for the night.'

'I want to go home and into bed.'

'We are of two different kinds,' the older waiter said. He was now dressed to go home. 'It is not only a question of youth and confidence although those things are very beautiful. Each night I am reluctant to close up because there may be someone who needs the café.'

'Hombre, there are bodegas open all night long.'

'You do not understand. This is a clean and pleasant café. It is well lighted. The light is very good and also, now, there are shadows of the leaves.'

'Good night,' said the younger waiter.

'Good night,' the other said. Turning off the electric light he continued the conversation with himself. It is the light of course but it is necessary that the place be clean and pleasant. You do not want music. Certainly you do not want music. Nor can you stand before a bar with dignity although that is all that is provided for these hours. What did he fear? It was not fear or dread. It was a nothing that he knew too well. It was all a nothing and a man was nothing too. It was only that and light was all it needed and a certain cleanness and order. Some lived in it and never felt it but he knew it all was nada y pues nada y nada y pues nada. Our nada who art in nada, nada be thy name thy kingdom nada thy will be nada in nada as it is in nada. Give us this nada our daily nada and nada us our nada as we nada our nadas and nada us not into nada but deliver us from nada; pues nada. Hail nothing full of nothing, nothing is with thee. He smiled and stood before a bar with a shining steam pressure coffee machine.

'What's yours?' asked the barman.

'Nada.'

'Otro loco mas,' said the barman and turned away.

'A little cup,' said the waiter.

The barman poured it for him.

'The light is very bright and pleasant but the bar is unpolished,' the waiter said.

The barman looked at him but did not answer. It was too late at night for conversation.

'You want another copita?' the barman asked.

'No, thank you,' said the waiter and went out. He disliked bars and bodegas. A clean, well-lighted café was a very different thing. Now, without thinking further, he would go home to his room. He would lie in the bed and finally, with daylight, he would go to sleep. After all, he said to himself, it is probably only insomnia. Many must have it.

1933

# Morley Callaghan

1903–1990

Canada's first professional writer, the first to devote his life to the vocation of writing, Toronto-born Morley Callaghan was a graduate of the University of Toronto and Osgoode Hall Law School. His first novel, *Strange Fugitive*, was published in 1928, the same year he was called to the bar. Fiction, however, commanded his complete attention, and he never practised law. In April 1929 he travelled with his wife to Paris, where their literary circle of friends included Ernest Hemingway—with whom Callaghan had already worked as a journalist at the *Toronto Star*—F. Scott Fitzgerald, James Joyce, and many others. The following autumn he returned to Toronto, which had been and which would remain his physical and literary home. His sojourn in Paris is the subject of his beautiful memoir, *That Summer in Paris* (1963).

The author of 20 novels and more than 100 shorter pieces of fiction, Callaghan focused his writing on individual lives, often exploring the moral courage and innate dignity of his characters as they confront adverse and demeaning social situations.

## A Cap for Steve

Dave Diamond, a poor man, a carpenter's assistant, was a small, wiry, quick-tempered individual who had learned how to make every dollar count in his home. His wife, Anna, had been sick a lot, and his twelve-year-old son, Steve, had to be kept in school. Steve, a big-eyed, shy kid, ought to have known the value of money as well as Dave did. It had been ground into him.

But the boy was crazy about baseball, and after school, when he could have been working as a delivery boy or selling papers, he played ball with the kids. His failure to appreciate that the family needed a few extra dollars disgusted Dave. Around the house he wouldn't let Steve talk about baseball, and he scowled when he saw him hurrying off with his glove after dinner.

When the Phillies came to town to play an exhibition game with the home team and Steve pleaded to be taken to the ballpark, Dave, of course, was outraged. Steve knew they couldn't afford it. But he had got his mother on his side. Finally Dave made a bargain with them. He said that if Steve came home after school and worked hard helping to make some kitchen shelves he would take him that night to the ballpark.

Steve worked hard, but Dave was still resentful. They had to coax him to put on his good suit. When they started out Steve held aloof, feeling guilty, and they walked down the street like strangers; then Dave glanced at Steve's face and, half-ashamed, took his arm more cheerfully.

As the game went on, Dave had to listen to Steve's recitation of the batting average of every Philly that stepped up to the plate; the time the boy must have wasted learning these averages began to appall him. He showed it so plainly that Steve felt guilty again and was silent.

After the game Dave let Steve drag him onto the field to keep him company while he tried to get some autographs from the Philly players, who were being hemmed in by gangs of kids blocking the way to the clubhouse. But Steve, who was shy, let the other kids block him off from the players. Steve would push his way in, get blocked out, and come back to stand mournfully beside Dave. And Dave grew impatient. He was wasting valuable time. He wanted to get home; Steve knew it and was worried.

Then the big, blond Philly outfielder, Eddie Condon, who had been held up by a gang of kids tugging at his arm and thrusting their scorecards at him, broke loose and made a run for the clubhouse. He was jostled, and his blue cap with the red peak, tilted far back on his head, fell off. It fell at Steve's feet, and Steve stooped quickly and grabbed it. 'Okay, son,' the outfielder called, turning back. But Steve, holding the hat in both hands, only stared at him.

'Give him his cap, Steve,' Dave said, smiling apologetically at the big outfielder who towered over them. But Steve drew the hat closer to his chest. In an awed trance he looked up at big Eddie Condon. It was an embarrassing moment. All the other kids were watching. Some shouted. 'Give him his cap.'

'My cap, son,' Eddie Condon said, his hand out.

'Hey, Steve,' Dave said, and he gave him a shake. But he had to jerk the cap out of Steve's hands.

'Here you are,' he said.

The outfielder, noticing Steve's white, worshipping face and pleading eyes, grinned and then shrugged. 'Aw, let him keep it,' he said.

'No, Mister Condon, you don't need to do that,' Steve protested.

'It's happened before. Forget it,' Eddie Condon said, and he trotted away to the clubhouse.

Dave handed the cap to Steve; envious kids circled around them and Steve said, 'He said I could keep it, Dad. You heard him, didn't you?'

'Yeah, I heard him,' Dave admitted. The wonder in Steve's face made him smile. He took the boy by the arm and they hurried off the field.

On the way home Dave couldn't get him to talk about the game; he couldn't get him to take his eyes off the cap. Steve could hardly believe in his own happiness. 'See,' he said suddenly, and he showed Dave that Eddie Condon's name was printed on the sweatband. Then he went on dreaming. Finally he put the cap on his head and turned to Dave with a slow, proud smile. The cap was too big for him; it fell down over his ears. 'Never mind,' Dave said. 'You can get your mother to take a tuck in the back.'

When they got home Dave was tired and his wife didn't understand the cap's importance, and they couldn't get Steve to go to bed. He swaggered around wearing the cap and looking in the mirror every ten minutes. He took the cap to bed with him.

Dave and his wife had a cup of coffee in the kitchen, and Dave told her again how they had got the cap. They agreed that their boy must have an attractive quality that showed in his face and that Eddie Condon must have been drawn to him—why else would he have singled Steve out from all the kids?

But Dave got tired of the fuss Steve made over that cap and of the way he wore it from the time he got up in the morning until the time he went to bed. Some kid was always coming in, wanting to try on the cap. It was childish, Dave said, for Steve to go around assuming that the cap made him important in the neighbourhood, and to keep telling them how he had become a leader in the park a few blocks away where he played ball in the evenings. And Dave wouldn't stand for Steve's keeping the cap on while he was eating. He was always scolding his wife for accepting Steve's explanation that he'd forgotten he had it on. Just the same, it was remarkable what a little thing like a ball cap could do for a kid, Dave admitted to his wife as he smiled to himself.

One night Steve was late coming home from the park. Dave didn't realize how late it was until he put down his newspaper and watched his wife at the window. Her restlessness got on his nerves. 'See what comes from encouraging the boy to hang around with those park loafers,' he said. 'I don't encourage him,' she protested. 'You do,' he insisted irritably, for he was really worried now. A gang hung around the park until midnight. It was a bad park. It was true that on one side there was a good district with fine, expensive apartment houses, but the kids from that neighbourhood left the park to the kids from the poorer homes. When his wife went out and walked down to the corner it was his turn to wait and worry and watch at the open window. Each waiting moment tortured him. At last he heard his wife's voice and Steve's voice, and he relaxed and sighed; then he remembered his duty and rushed angrily to meet them.

'I'll fix you, Steve, once and for all,' he said. 'I'll show you you can't start coming into the house at midnight.'

'Hold your horses, Dave,' his wife said. 'Can't you see the state he's in?' Steve looked utterly exhausted and beaten.

'What's the matter?' Dave asked quickly.

'I lost my cap,' Steve whispered; he walked past his father and threw himself on the couch in the living room and lay with his face hidden.

'Now, don't scold him, Dave,' his wife said.

'Scold him. Who's scolding him?' Dave asked, indignantly. 'It's his cap, not mine. If it's not worth his while to hang on to it, why should I scold him?' But he was implying resentfully that he alone recognized the cap's value.

'So you are scolding him,' his wife said. 'It's his cap. Not yours. What happened, Steve?'

Steve told them he had been playing ball and he found that when he ran the bases the cap fell off; it was still too big despite the tuck his mother had taken in the band. So the next time he came to bat he tucked the cap in his hip pocket. Someone had lifted it, he was sure.

'And he didn't even know whether it was still in his pocket,' Dave said sarcastically.

'I wasn't careless, Dad,' Steve said. For the last three hours he had been wandering around to the homes of the kids who had been in the park at the time; he wanted to go on, but he was too tired. Dave knew the boy was apologizing to him, but he didn't know why it made him angry.

'If he didn't hang on to it, it's not worth worrying about now,' he said, and he sounded offended.

After that night they knew that Steve didn't go to the park to play ball; he went to look for the cap. It irritated Dave to see him sit around listlessly, or walk in circles, trying to force his memory to find a particular incident which would suddenly recall to him the moment when the cap had been taken. It was no attitude for a growing, healthy boy to take, Dave complained. He told Steve firmly once and for all he didn't want to hear any more about the cap.

One night, two weeks later, Dave was walking home with Steve from the shoemaker's. It was a hot night. When they passed an ice-cream parlour Steve slowed down. 'I guess I couldn't have a soda, could I?' Steve said. 'Nothing doing,' Dave said firmly. 'Come on now,' he added as Steve hung back, looking in the window.

'Dad, look!' Steve cried suddenly, pointing at the window. 'My cap! There's my cap! He's coming out!'

A well-dressed boy was leaving the ice-cream parlour; he had on a blue ball cap with a red peak, just like Steve's cap. 'Hey, you!' Steve cried, and he rushed at the boy, his small face fierce and his eyes wild. Before the boy could back away Steve had snatched the cap from his head. 'That's my cap!' he shouted.

'What's this!' the bigger boy said. 'Hey, give me my cap or I'll give you a poke on the nose.'

Dave was surprised that his own shy boy did not back away. He watched him clutch the cap in his left hand, half crying with excitement as he put his head down and drew back his right fist: he was willing to fight. And Dave was proud of him.

'Wait, now,' Dave said. 'Take it easy, son,' he said to the other boy, who refused to back away.

'My boy says it's his cap,' Dave said.

'Well, he's crazy. It's my cap.'

'I was with him when he got this cap. When the Phillies played here. It's a Philly cap.'

'Eddie Condon gave it to me,' Steve said. 'And you stole it from me, you jerk.'

'Don't call me a jerk, you little squirt. I never saw you before in my life.'

'Look,' Steve said, pointing to the printing on the cap's sweatband. 'It's Eddie Condon's cap. See? See, Dad?'

'Yeah. You're right, son. Ever see this boy before, Steve?'

'No,' Steve said reluctantly.

The other boy realized he might lose the cap. 'I bought it from a guy,' he said. 'I paid him. My father knows I paid him.' He said he got the cap at the ballpark. He groped for some magically impressive words and suddenly found them. 'You'll have to speak to my father,' he said.

'Sure, I'll speak to your father,' Dave said. 'What's your name? Where do you live?'

'My name's Hudson. I live about ten minutes away on the other side of the park.' The boy appraised Dave, who wasn't any bigger than he was and who wore a faded blue windbreaker and no tie. 'My father is a lawyer,' he said boldly. 'He wouldn't let me keep the cap if he didn't think I should.'

'Is that a fact?' Dave asked belligerently. 'Well, we'll see. Come on. Let's go.' And he got between the two boys and they walked along the street. They didn't talk to each other. Dave knew the Hudson boy was waiting to get to the protection of his home, and Steve knew it, too, and he looked up apprehensively at Dave. Dave, reaching for his hand, squeezed it encouragingly and strode along, cocky and belligerent, knowing that Steve relied on him.

The Hudson boy lived in that row of fine apartment houses on the other side of the park. At the entrance to one of these houses Dave tried not to hang back and show he was impressed, because he could feel Steve hanging back. When they got into the small elevator Dave didn't know why he took off his hat. In the carpeted hall on the fourth floor the Hudson boy said, 'Just a minute,' and entered his own apartment. Dave and Steve were left alone in the corridor, knowing that the other boy was preparing his father for the encounter. Steve looked anxiously at his father, and Dave said, 'Don't worry, son,' and he added resolutely, 'No one's putting anything over on us.'

A tall, balding man in a brown velvet smoking-jacket suddenly opened the door. Dave had never seen a man wearing one of these jackets, although he had seen them in department-store windows. 'Good evening,' he said, making a deprecatory gesture at the cap Steve still clutched tightly in his left hand. 'My boy didn't get your name. My name is Hudson.'

'Mine's Diamond.'

'Come on in,' Mr Hudson said, putting out his hand and laughing good-naturedly. He led Dave and Steve into his living room. 'What's this about a cap?' he asked. 'The way kids can get excited about a cap. Well, it's understandable, isn't it?'

'So it is,' Dave said, moving closer to Steve, who was awed by the broadloom rug and the fine furniture. He wanted to show Steve he was at ease himself, and he wished Mr Hudson wouldn't be so polite. That meant Dave had to be polite and affable, too, and it was hard to manage when he was standing in the middle of the floor in his old windbreaker.

'Sit down, Mr Diamond,' Mr Hudson said. Dave took Steve's arm and sat him down beside him on the chesterfield. The Hudson boy watched his father. And Dave looked at Steve and saw that he wouldn't face Mr Hudson or the other boy; he kept looking up at Dave, putting all his faith in him.

'Well, Mr Diamond, from what I gathered from my boy, you're able to prove this cap belonged to your boy.'

'That's a fact,' Dave said.

'Mr Diamond, you'll have to believe my boy bought that cap from some kid in good faith.'

'I don't doubt it,' Dave said. 'But no kid can sell something that doesn't belong to him. You know that's a fact, Mr Hudson.'

'Yes, that's a fact,' Mr Hudson agreed. 'But that cap means a lot to my boy, Mr Diamond.'

'It means a lot to my boy, too, Mr Hudson.'

'Sure it does. But supposing we called in a policeman. You know what he'd say? He'd ask you if you were willing to pay my boy what he paid for the cap. That's usually the way it works out,' Mr Hudson said, friendly and smiling, as he eyed Dave shrewdly.

'But that's not right. It's not justice,' Dave protested. 'Not when it's my boy's cap.'

'I know it isn't right. But that's what they do.'

'All right. What did you say your boy paid for the cap?' Dave said reluctantly.

'Two dollars.'

'Two dollars!' Dave repeated. Mr Hudson's smile was still kindly, but his eyes were shrewd, and Dave knew that the lawyer was counting on his not having the two dollars; Mr Hudson thought he had Dave sized up; he had looked at him and decided he was broke. Dave's pride was hurt, and he turned to Steve. What he saw in Steve's face was more powerful than the hurt to his pride; it was the memory of how difficult it had been to get an extra nickel, the talk he heard about the cost of food, the worry on his mother's face as she tried to make ends meet, and the bewildered embarrassment that he was here in a rich man's home, forcing his father to confess that he couldn't afford to spend two dollars. Then Dave grew angry and reckless. 'I'll give you the two dollars,' he said.

Steve looked at the Hudson boy and grinned brightly. The Hudson boy watched his father.

'I suppose that's fair enough,' Mr Hudson said. 'A cap like this can be worth a lot to a kid. You know how it is. Your boy might want to sell—I mean be satisfied. Would he take five dollars for it?'

'Five dollars?' Dave repeated, 'Is it worth five dollars, Steve?' he asked uncertainly.

Steve shook his head and looked frightened.

'No thanks, Mr Hudson,' Dave said firmly.

'I'll tell you what I'll do,' Mr Hudson said. 'I'll give you ten dollars. The cap has a sentimental value for my boy, a Philly cap, a big-leaguer's cap. It's only worth about a buck and a half really,' he added. But Dave shook his head again. Mr Hudson frowned. He looked at his own boy with indulgent concern, but now he was embarrassed. 'I'll tell you what I'll do,' he said. 'This cap—well, it's worth as much as a day at the circus to my boy. Your boy should be recompensed. I want to be fair. Here's twenty dollars,' and he held out two ten-dollar bills to Dave.

That much money for a cap, Dave thought, and his eyes brightened. But he knew what the cap had meant to Steve; to deprive him of it now that it was within his reach would be unbearable. All the things he needed in his life gathered around him; his wife was there, saying he couldn't afford to reject the offer, he had no right to do it; and he turned to Steve to see if Steve thought it wonderful that the cap could bring them twenty dollars.

'What do you say, Steve?' he asked uneasily.

'I don't know,' Steve said. He was in a trance. When Dave smiled, Steve smiled too, and Dave believed that Steve was as impressed as he was, only more bewildered, and maybe even more aware that they could not possibly turn away that much money for a ball cap.

'Well, here you are,' Mr Hudson said, and he put the two bills in Steve's hand. 'It's a lot of money. But I guess you had a right to expect as much.'

With a dazed, fixed smile Steve handed the money slowly to his father, and his face was white.

Laughing jovially, Mr Hudson led them to the door. His own boy followed a few paces behind.

In the elevator Dave took the bills out of his pocket. 'See, Stevie,' he whispered eagerly. 'That windbreaker you wanted! And ten dollars for your bank! Won't Mother be surprised?'

'Yeah,' Steve whispered, the little smile still on his face. But Dave had to turn away quickly so their eyes wouldn't meet, for he saw it was a scared smile.

Outside, Dave said, 'Here, you carry the money home, Steve. You show it to your mother.'

'No, you keep it,' Steve said, and then there was nothing to say. They walked in silence.

'It's a lot of money,' Dave said finally. When Steve didn't answer him, he added angrily, 'I turned to you, Steve. I asked you, didn't I?'

'That man knew how much his boy wanted that cap,' Steve said.

'Sure. But he recognized how much it was worth to us.'

'No, you let him take it away from us,' Steve blurted.

'That's unfair,' Dave said. 'Don't dare say that to me.'

'I don't want to be like you,' Steve muttered, and he darted across the road and walked along on the other side of the street.

'It's unfair,' Dave said angrily, only now he didn't mean that Steve was unfair, he meant that what had happened in the prosperous Hudson home was unfair, and he didn't know quite why. He had been trapped, not just by Mr Hudson, but by his own life. Across the road Steve was hurrying along with his head down, wanting to be alone. They walked most of the way home on opposite sides of the street, until Dave could stand it no longer. 'Steve,' he called, crossing the street. 'It was very unfair. I mean, for you to say . . .' but Steve started to run. Dave walked as fast as he could and Steve was getting beyond him, and he felt enraged and suddenly yelled, 'Steve!' and he started to chase his son. He wanted to get hold of Steve and pound him, and he didn't know why. He gained on him, he gasped for breath and he almost got him by the shoulder. Turning, Steve saw his father's face in the street light and was terrified; he circled away, got to the house, and rushed in, yelling, 'Mother!'

'Son, son!' she cried, rushing from the kitchen. As soon as she threw her arms around Steve, shielding him, Dave's anger left him and he felt stupid. He walked past them into the kitchen.

'What happened?' she asked anxiously. 'Have you both gone crazy? What did you do, Steve?'

'Nothing,' he said sullenly.

'What did your father do?'

'We found the boy with my ball cap, and he let the boy's father take it from us.'

'No, no,' Dave protested. 'Nobody pushed us around. The man didn't put anything over us.' He felt tired and his face was burning. He told what had happened; then he slowly took the two ten-dollar bills out of his wallet and tossed them on the table and looked up guiltily at his wife.

It hurt him that she didn't pick up the money, and that she didn't rebuke him. 'It is a lot of money, son,' she said slowly. 'Your father was only trying to do what he knew was right, and it'll work out, and you'll understand.' She was soothing Steve, but Dave knew she felt that she needed to be gentle with him, too, and he was ashamed.

When she went with Steve to his bedroom, Dave sat by himself. His son had contempt for him, he thought. His son, for the first time, had seen how easy it was for another man to handle him, and he had judged him and had wanted to walk alone on the other side of the street. He looked at the money and he hated the sight of it.

His wife returned to the kitchen, made a cup of tea, talked soothingly, and said it was incredible that he had forced the Hudson man to pay him twenty dollars for the cap, but all Dave could think of was how scared Steve was of him.

Finally, he got up and went into Steve's room. The room was in darkness, but he could see the outlines of Steve's body on the bed, and he sat down beside him and whispered, 'Look, son, it was a mistake. I know why. People like us—in circumstances where money can scare us. No, no,' he said, feeling ashamed and shaking his head apologetically; he was taking the wrong way of showing the boy they were together; he was covering up his own failure. For the failure had been his, and it had come out of being so separated from his son that he had been blind to what was beyond the price in a boy's life. He longed now to show Steve he could be with him from day to day. His hand went out hesitantly to Steve's shoulder. 'Steve, look,' he said eagerly. 'The trouble was I didn't realize how much I enjoyed it that night at the ballpark. If I had watched you playing for your own team—the kids around here say you could be a great pitcher. We could take that money and buy a new pitcher's glove for you, and a catcher's mitt. Steve, Steve, are you listening? I could catch you, work with you in the lane. Maybe I could be your coach . . . watch you become a great pitcher.' In the half-darkness he could see the boy's pale face turn to him.

Steve, who had never heard his father talk like this, was shy and wondering. All he knew was that his father, for the first time, wanted to be with him in his hopes and adventures. He said, 'I guess you do know how important that cap was.' His hand went out to his father's arm. 'With that man the cap—well it was just something he could buy, eh Dad?' Dave gripped his son's hand hard. The wonderful generosity of childhood—the price a boy was willing to pay to be able to count on his father's admiration and approval—made him feel humble, then strangely exalted.

1952

## Sinclair Ross

1908–1996

Born on a homestead near Shellbrook in northern Saskatchewan, Sinclair Ross dropped out of school after grade 11 to work in a bank. His banking career took him to many small-town banks in Saskatchewan before he transferred to a bank in Winnipeg in 1933. Apart from wartime service with the Canadian army in London, England, he remained in banking until his retirement in 1968. In 1941 he published his first novel, *As for Me and My House*, with its stunning depiction of small-town prairie life during the Depression. The prairie is also the principal setting for his two collections of short fiction, *The Lamp at Noon and Other Stories* (1968) and *The Race and Other Stories* (1982), which explore the landscape's unique ability to sustain, to suffocate, or to challenge its inhabitants.

In 1984 the National Film Board of Canada made a faithful film adaptation of the selection reprinted here, 'The Painted Door'.

### The Painted Door

Straight across the hills it was five miles from John's farm to his father's. But in winter, with the roads impassable, a team had to make a wide detour and skirt the hills, so that from five the distance was more than trebled to seventeen.

'I think I'll walk,' John said at breakfast to his wife. 'The drifts in the hills wouldn't hold a horse, but they'll carry me all right. If I leave early I can spend a few hours helping him with his chores, and still be back by suppertime.'

Moodily she went to the window, and thawing a clear place in the frost with her breath, stood looking across the snowswept farmyard to the huddle of stables and sheds. 'There was a double wheel around the moon last night,' she countered presently. 'You said yourself we could expect a storm. It isn't right to leave me here alone. Surely I'm as important as your father.'

He glanced up uneasily, then drinking off his coffee tried to reassure her. 'But there's nothing to be afraid of—even supposing it does start to storm. You won't need to go near the stable. Everything's fed and watered now to last till night. I'll be back at the latest by seven or eight.'

She went on blowing against the frosted pane, carefully elongating the clear place until it was oval-shaped and symmetrical. He watched her a moment or two longer, then more insistently repeated, 'I say you won't need to go near the stable. Everything's fed and watered, and I'll see that there's plenty of wood in. That will be all right, won't it?'

'Yes—of course—I heard you—' It was a curiously cold voice now, as if the words were chilled by their contact with the frosted pane. 'Plenty to eat—plenty of wood to keep me warm—what more could a woman ask for?'

'But he's an old man—living there all alone. What is it, Ann? You're not like yourself this morning.'

She shook her head without turning. 'Pay no attention to me. Seven years a farmer's wife—it's time I was used to staying alone.'

Slowly the clear place on the glass enlarged: oval, then round, then oval again. The sun was risen above the frost mists now, so keen and hard a glitter on the snow that instead of warmth its rays seemed shedding cold. One of the two-year-old colts that had cantered away when John turned the horses out for water stood covered with rime at the stable door again, head down and body hunched, each breath a little plume of steam against the frosty air. She shivered, but did not turn. In the clear, bitter light the long white miles of prairie landscape seemed a region strangely alien to life. Even the distant farmsteads she could see served only to intensify a sense of isolation. Scattered across the face of so vast and bleak a wilderness it was difficult to conceive them as a testimony of human hardihood and endurance. Rather they seemed futile, lost. Rather they seemed to cower before the implacability of snow-swept earth and clear pale sun-chilled sky.

And when at last she turned from the window there was a brooding stillness in her face as if she had recognized this mastery of snow and cold. It troubled John. 'If you're really afraid,' he yielded, 'I won't go today. Lately it's been so cold, that's all. I just wanted to make sure he's all right in case we do have a storm.'

'I know—I'm not really afraid.' She was putting in a fire now, and he could no longer see her face. 'Pay no attention. It's ten miles there and back, so you'd better get started.'

'You ought to know by now I wouldn't stay away,' he tried to brighten her. 'No matter how it stormed. Twice a week before we were married I never missed—and there were bad blizzards that winter too.'

He was a slow, unambitious man, content with his farm and cattle, naively proud of Ann. He had been bewildered by it once, her caring for a dull-witted fellow like him; then assured at last of her affection he had relaxed against it gratefully, unsuspecting it might ever be less constant than his own. Even now, listening to the restless brooding in her voice, he felt only a quick, unformulated kind of pride that after seven years his absence for a day should still concern her. While she, his trust and earnestness controlling her again:

'I know. It's just that sometimes when you're away I get lonely. . . . There's a long cold tramp in front of you. You'll let me fix a scarf around your face.'

He nodded. 'And on my way I'll drop in at Steven's place. Maybe he'll come over tonight for a game of cards. You haven't seen anybody but me for the last two weeks.'

She glanced up sharply, then busied herself clearing the table. 'It will mean another two miles if you do. You're going to be cold and tired enough as it is. When you're gone I think I'll paint the kitchen woodwork. White this time—you remember we got the paint last fall. It's going to make the room a lot lighter. I'll be too busy to find the day long.'

'I will though,' he insisted, 'and if a storm gets up you'll feel safer, knowing that he's coming. That's what you need, Ann—someone to talk to besides me.'

She stood at the stove motionless a moment, then turned to him uneasily. 'Will you shave then, John—now—before you go?'

He glanced at her questioningly, and avoiding his eyes she tried to explain, 'I mean—he may be here before you're back—and you won't have a chance then.'

'But it's only Steven—he's seen me like this—'

'He'll be shaved, though—that's what I mean—and I'd like you too to spend a little time on yourself.'

He stood up, stroking the heavy stubble on his chin. 'Maybe I should all right, but it makes the skin too tender. Especially when I've got to face the wind.'

She nodded and began to help him dress, bringing heavy socks and a big woollen sweater from the bedroom, wrapping a scarf around his face and forehead. 'I'll tell Steven to come early,' he said, as he went out. 'In time for supper. Likely there'll be chores for me to do, so if I'm not back by six don't wait.'

From the bedroom window she watched him nearly a mile along the road. The fire had gone down when at last she turned away, and already through the house there was an encroaching chill. A blaze sprang up again when the drafts were opened, but as she went on clearing the table her movements were furtive and constrained. It was the silence weighing upon her—the frozen silence of the bitter fields and sun-chilled sky—lurking outside as if alive, relentlessly in wait, mile-deep between her now and John. She listened to it, suddenly tense, motionless. The fire crackled and the clock ticked. Always it was there. 'I'm a fool,' she whispered hoarsely, rattling the dishes in defiance, going back to the stove to put in another fire. 'Warm and safe—I'm a fool. It's a good chance when he's away to paint. The day will go quickly. I won't have time to brood.'

Since November now the paint had been waiting warmer weather. The frost in the walls on a day like this would crack and peel it as it dried, but she needed something to keep her hands occupied, something to stave off the gathering cold and loneliness. 'First of all,' she said aloud, opening the paint and mixing it with a little turpentine, 'I must get the house warmer. Fill up the stove and open the oven door so that all the heat comes out. Wad something along the window sills to keep out the drafts. Then I'll feel brighter. It's the cold that depresses.'

She moved briskly, performing each little task with careful and exaggerated absorption, binding her thoughts to it, making it a screen between herself and the surrounding snow and silence. But when the stove was filled and the windows sealed it was more difficult again. Above the quiet, steady swishing of her brush against the bedroom door the clock began to tick. Suddenly her movements became precise, deliberate, her posture self-conscious, as if someone had entered the room and were watching her. It was the silence again, aggressive, hovering. The fire spit and crackled at it. Still it was there. 'I'm a fool,' she repeated. 'All farmers' wives have to stay alone. I mustn't give in this way. I mustn't brood. A few hours now and they'll be here.'

The sound of her voice reassured her. She went on: 'I'll get them a good supper—and for coffee tonight after cards bake some of the little cakes with raisins that he likes. . . . Just three of us, so I'll watch, and let John play. It's better with four, but at least we can talk. That's all I need—someone to talk to. John never talks. He's stronger—he doesn't understand. But he likes Steven—no matter what the neighbours say. Maybe he'll have him come again, and some other young people too. It's what we need, both of us, to help keep young ourselves. . . . And then before we know it we'll be into March. It's cold still in March sometimes, but you never mind the same. At least you're beginning to think about spring.'

She began to think about it now. Thoughts that outstripped her words, that left her alone again with herself and the ever-lurking silence. Eager and hopeful first; then clenched, rebellious, lonely. Windows open, sun and thawing earth again, the urge of growing, living things. Then the days that began in the morning at half-past four and lasted till ten at night; the meals at which John gulped his food and scarcely spoke a word; the brute-tired stupid eyes he turned on her if ever she mentioned town or visiting.

For spring was drudgery again. John never hired a man to help him. He wanted a mortgage-free farm; then a new house and pretty clothes for her. Sometimes, because with the best of crops it was going to take so long to pay off anyway, she wondered whether they mightn't better let the mortgage wait a little. Before they were worn out, before their best years were gone. It was something of life she wanted, not just a house and furniture; something of John, not pretty clothes when she would be too old to wear them. But John of course couldn't understand. To him it seemed only right that she should have the clothes—only right that he, fit for nothing else, should slave away fifteen hours a day to give them to her. There was in his devotion a baffling, insurmountable humility that made him feel the need of sacrifice. And when his muscles ached, when his feet dragged stolidly with weariness, then it seemed that in some measure at least he was making amends for his big hulking body and simple mind. That by his sacrifice he succeeded only in the extinction of his personality never occurred to him. Year after year their lives went on in the same little groove. He drove his horses in the field; she milked cows and hoed potatoes. By dint of his drudgery he saved a few months' wages, added a few dollars more each fall to his payments on the mortgage; but the only real difference that it all made was to deprive her of his companionship, to make him a little duller, older, uglier than he might otherwise have been. He never saw their lives objectively. To him it was not what he actually accomplished by means of the sacrifice that mattered, but the sacrifice itself, the gesture—something done for her sake.

And she, understanding, kept her silence. In such a gesture, however futile, there was a graciousness not to be shattered lightly. 'John,' she would begin sometimes, 'you're doing too much. Get a man to help you—just for a month—' but smiling down at her he would answer simply, 'I don't mind. Look at the hands on me. They're made for work.' While in his voice there would be a stalwart ring to tell her that by her thoughtfulness she had made him only the more resolved to serve her, to prove his devotion and fidelity.

They were useless, such thoughts. She knew. It was his very devotion that made him useless, that forbade her to rebel. Yet over and over, sometimes hunched still before their bleakness, sometimes her brush making swift sharp strokes to pace the chafe and rancour that they brought, she persisted in them.

This now, the winter, was their slack season. She could sleep sometimes till eight, and John till seven. They could linger over their meals a little, read, play cards, go visiting the neighbours. It was the time to relax, to indulge and enjoy themselves; but instead, fretful and impatient, they kept on waiting for the spring. They were compelled now, not by labour, but by the spirit of labour. A spirit that pervaded their lives and brought with idleness a sense of guilt. Sometimes they did sleep late, sometimes they did play cards, but always uneasily, always reproached by the thought of more important things that might be done. When John got up at five to attend to the fire he wanted to stay up and go out to the stable. When he sat down to a meal he hurried his food and pushed his chair away again, from habit, from sheer work-instinct, even though it was only to put more wood on the stove, or go down cellar to cut up beets and turnips for the cows.

And anyway, sometimes she asked herself, why sit trying to talk with a man who never talked? Why talk when there was nothing to talk about but crops and cattle, the weather and the neighbours? The neighbours, too—why go visiting them when still it was the same—crops and cattle, the weather and the other neighbours? Why go to the dances in the schoolhouse to sit among the older women, one of them now, married seven years, or to waltz with the work-bent, tired old farmers to a squeaky fiddle tune? Once she had danced with Steven six or seven times in the evening, and they had talked about it for as many months. It was easier to stay home. John never danced or enjoyed himself. He was always uncomfortable in his good suit and shoes. He didn't like shaving in the cold weather oftener than once or twice a week. It was easier to stay at home, to stand at the window staring out across the bitter fields, to count the days and look forward to another spring.

But now, alone with herself in the winter silence, she saw the spring for what it really was. This spring—next spring—all the springs and summers to come. While they grew old, while their bodies warped, while their minds kept shrivelling dry and empty like their lives. 'I mustn't,' she said aloud again. 'I married him—and he's a good man. I mustn't keep on this way. It will be noon before long, and then time to think about supper. . . . Maybe he'll come early—and as soon as John is finished at the stable we can all play cards.'

It was getting cold again, and she left her painting to put in more wood. But this time the warmth spread slowly. She pushed a mat up to the outside door, and went back to the window to pat down the woollen shirt that was wadded along the sill. Then she paced a few times round the room, then poked the fire and rattled the stove lids, then paced again. The fire crackled, the clock ticked. The silence now seemed more intense than ever, seemed to have reached a pitch where it faintly moaned. She began to pace on tiptoe, listening, her shoulders drawn together, not realizing for a while that it was the wind she heard, thin-strained and whimpering through the eaves.

Then she wheeled to the window, and with quick short breaths thawed the frost to see again. The glitter was gone. Across the drifts sped swift and snakelike little tongues of snow. She could not follow them, where they sprang from, or where they disappeared. It was as if all across the yard the snow were shivering awake—roused by the warnings of the wind to hold itself in readiness for the impending storm. The sky had become sombre, whitish grey. It, too, as if in readiness, had shifted and lay close to earth. Before her as she watched a mane of powdery snow reared up breast-high against the darker background of the stable, tossed for a moment angrily, and then subsided again as if whipped down to obedience and restraint. But another followed, more reckless and impatient than the first. Another reeled and dashed itself against the window where she watched. Then ominously for a while there were only the angry little snakes of snow. The wind rose, creaking the troughs that were wired beneath the eaves. In the distance, sky and prairie now were merged into one another linelessly. All round her it was gathering; already in its press and whimpering there strummed a boding of eventual fury. Again she saw a mane of snow spring up, so dense and high this time that all the sheds and stables were obscured. Then others followed, whirling fiercely out of hand; and, when at last they cleared, the stables seemed in dimmer outline than before. It was the snow beginning, long lancet shafts of it, straight from the north, borne almost level by the straining wind. 'He'll be there soon,' she whispered, 'and coming home it will be in his back. He'll leave again right away. He saw the double wheel—he knows the kind of storm there'll be.'

She went back to her painting. For a while it was easier, all her thoughts half-anxious ones of John in the blizzard, struggling his way across the hills; but petulantly again she soon began, 'I knew we were going to have a storm—I told him so—but it doesn't matter what I say. Big stubborn fool—he goes his own way anyway. It doesn't matter what becomes of me. In a storm like this he'll never get home. He won't even try. And while he sits keeping his father company I can look after his stable for him, go ploughing through snowdrifts up to my knees—nearly frozen—'

Not that she meant or believed her words. It was just an effort to convince herself that she did have a grievance, to justify her rebellious thoughts, to prove John responsible for her unhappiness. She was young still, eager for excitement and distractions; and John's steadfastness rebuked her vanity, made her complaints seem weak and trivial. Fretfully she went on, 'If he'd listen to me sometimes and not be so stubborn we wouldn't still be living in a house like this. Seven years in two rooms—seven years and never a new stick of furniture. . . . There—as if another coat of paint could make it different anyway.'

She cleaned her brush, filled up the stove again, and went back to the window. There was a void white moment that she thought must be frost formed on the window pane; then, like a fitful shadow through the whirling snow, she recognized the stable roof. It was incredible. The sudden, maniac raging of the storm struck from her face all its pettishness. Her eyes glazed with fear a little; her lips blanched. 'If he starts for home now,' she whispered silently—'But he won't—he knows I'm safe—he knows Steven's coming. Across the hills he would never dare.'

She turned to the stove, holding out her hands to the warmth. Around her now there seemed a constant sway and tremor, as if the air were vibrating with the violent shudderings of the walls. She stood quite still, listening. Sometimes the wind struck with sharp, savage blows. Sometimes it bore down in a sustained, minute-long blast, silent with effort and intensity; then with a foiled shriek of threat wheeled away to gather and assault again. Always the eavestroughs creaked and sawed. She stared towards the window again, then detecting the morbid trend of her thoughts, prepared fresh coffee and forced herself to drink a few mouthfuls. 'He would never dare,' she whispered again. 'He wouldn't leave the old man anyway in such a storm. Safe in here—there's nothing for me to keep worrying about. It's after one already. I'll do my baking now, and then it will be time to get supper ready for Steven.'

Soon, however, she began to doubt whether Steven would come. In such a storm even a mile was enough to make a man hesitate. Especially Steven, who, for all his attractive qualities, was hardly the one to face a blizzard for the sake of someone else's chores. He had a stable of his own to look after anyway. It would be only natural for him to think that when the storm rose John had turned again for home. Another man would have—would have put his wife first.

But she felt little dread or uneasiness at the prospect of spending the night alone. It was the first time she had been left like this on her own resources, and her reaction, now that she could face and appraise her situation calmly, was gradually to feel it a kind of adventure and responsibility. It stimulated her. Before nightfall she must go to the stable and feed everything. Wrap up in some of John's clothes—take a ball of string in her hand, one end tied to the door, so that no matter how blinding the storm she could at least find her way back to the house. She had heard of people having to do that. It appealed to her now because suddenly it made life dramatic. She had not felt the storm yet, only watched it for a minute through the window.

It took nearly an hour to find enough string, to choose the right socks and sweaters. Long before it was time to start out she tried on John's clothes, changing and rechanging, striding around the room to make sure there would be play enough for pitching hay and struggling over snowdrifts; then she took them off again, and for a while busied herself baking the little cakes with raisins that he liked.

Night came early. Just for a moment on the doorstep she shrank back, uncertain. The slow dimming of the light clutched her with an illogical sense of abandonment. It was like the covert withdrawal of an ally, leaving the alien miles unleashed and unrestrained. Watching the hurricane of writhing snow rage past the little house she forced herself, 'They'll never stand the night unless I get them fed. It's nearly dark already, and I've work to last an hour.'

Timidly, unwinding a little of the string, she crept out from the shelter of the doorway. A gust of wind spun her forward a few yards, then plunged her headlong against a drift that in the dense white whirl lay invisible across her path. For nearly a minute she huddled still, breathless and dazed. The snow was in her mouth and nostrils, inside her scarf and up her sleeves. As she tried to straighten a smothering scud flung itself against her face, cutting off her breath a second time. The wind struck from all sides, blustering and furious. It was as if the storm had discovered her, as if all its forces were concentrated upon her extinction. Seized with panic suddenly she threshed out a moment with her arms, then stumbled back and sprawled her length across the drift.

But this time she regained her feet quickly, roused by the whip and batter of the storm to retaliative anger. For a moment her impulse was to face the wind and strike back blow for blow; then, as suddenly as it had come, her frantic strength gave way to limpness and exhaustion. Suddenly, a comprehension so clear and terrifying that it struck all thoughts of the stable from her mind, she realized in such a storm her puny insignificance. And the realization gave her new strength, stilled this time to a desperate persistence. Just for a moment the wind held her, numb and swaying in its vise; then slowly, buckled far forward, she groped her way again towards the house.

Inside, leaning against the door, she stood tense and still a while. It was almost dark now. The top of the stove glowed a deep, dull red. Heedless of the storm, self-absorbed and self-satisfied, the clock ticked on like a glib little idiot. 'He shouldn't have gone,' she whispered silently. 'He saw the double wheel—he knew. He shouldn't have left me here alone.'

For so fierce now, so insane and dominant did the blizzard seem, that she could not credit the safety of the house. The warmth and lull around her was not real yet, not to be relied upon. She was still at the mercy of the storm. Only her body pressing hard like this against the door was staving it off. She didn't dare move. She didn't dare ease the ache and strain. 'He shouldn't have gone,' she repeated, thinking of the stable again, reproached by her helplessness. 'They'll freeze in their stalls—and I can't reach them. He'll say it's all my fault. He won't believe I tried.'

Then Steven came. Quickly, startled to quietness and control, she let him in and lit the lamp. He stared at her a moment, then flinging off his cap crossed to where she stood by the table and seized her arms. 'You're so white—what's wrong? Look at me—' It was like him in such little situations to be masterful. 'You should have known better than to go out on a day like this. For a while I thought I wasn't going to make it here myself—'

'I was afraid you wouldn't come—John left early, and there was the stable—'

But the storm had unnerved her, and suddenly at the assurance of his touch and voice the fear that had been gripping her gave way to an hysteria of relief. Scarcely aware of herself she seized his arm and sobbed against it. He remained still a moment unyielding, then slipped his other arm around her shoulder. It was comforting and she relaxed against it, hushed by a sudden sense of lull and safety. Her shoulders trembled with the easing of the strain, then fell limp and still. 'You're shivering,'—he drew her gently towards the stove. 'There's nothing to be afraid of now, though. I'm going to do the chores for you.'

It was a quiet, sympathetic voice, yet with an undertone of insolence, a kind of mockery even, that made her draw away quickly and busy herself putting in a fire. With his lips drawn in a little smile he watched her till she looked at him again. The smile too was insolent, but at the same time companionable; Steven's smile, and therefore difficult to reprove. It lit up his lean, still-boyish face with a peculiar kind of arrogance; features and smile that were different from John's, from other men's—wilful and derisive, yet naively so—as if it were less the difference itself he was conscious of, than the long-accustomed privilege that thereby fell his due. He was erect, tall, square-shouldered. His hair was dark and trim, his lips curved soft and full. While John, she made the comparison swiftly, was thick-set, heavy-jowled, and stooped. He always stood before her helpless, a kind of humility and wonderment in his attitude. And Steven now smiled on her appraisingly with the worldly-wise assurance of one for whom a woman holds neither mystery nor illusion.

'It was good of you to come, Steven,' she responded, the words running into a sudden, empty laugh. 'Such a storm to face—I suppose I should feel flattered.'

For his presumption, his misunderstanding of what had been only a momentary weakness, instead of angering quickened her, roused from latency and long disuse all the instincts and resources of her femininity. She felt eager, challenged. Something was at hand that hitherto had always eluded her, even in the early days with John, something vital, beckoning, meaningful. She didn't understand, but she knew. The texture of the moment was satisfyingly dreamlike: an incredibility perceived as such, yet acquiesced in. She was John's wife—she knew—but also she knew that Steven standing here was different from John. There was no thought of motive, no understanding of herself as the knowledge persisted. Wary and poised round a sudden little core of blind excitement she evaded him, 'But it's nearly dark—hadn't you better hurry if you're going to do the chores? Don't trouble—I can get them off myself—'

An hour later when he returned from the stable she was in another dress, hair rearranged, a little flush of colour in her face. Pouring warm water for him from the kettle into the basin she said evenly, 'By the time you're washed supper will be ready. John said we weren't to wait for him.'

He looked at her a moment, 'But in a storm like this you're not expecting John?'

'Of course.' As she spoke she could feel the colour deepening in her face. 'We're going to play cards. He was the one that suggested it.'

He went on washing, and then as they took their places at the table, resumed, 'So John's coming. When are you expecting him?'

'He said it might be seven o'clock—or a little later.' Conversation with Steven at other times had always been brisk and natural, but now suddenly she found it strained. 'He may have work to do for his father. That's what he said when he left. Why do you ask, Steven?'

'I was just wondering—it's a rough night.'

'He always comes. There couldn't be a storm bad enough. It's easier to do the chores in the daylight, and I knew he'd be tired—that's why I started out for the stable.'

She glanced up again and he was smiling at her. The same insolence, the same little twist of mockery and appraisal. It made her flinch suddenly, and ask herself why she was pretending to expect John—why there should be this instinct of defence to force her. This time, instead of poise and excitement, it brought a reminder that she had changed her dress and rearranged her hair. It crushed in a sudden silence, through which she heard the whistling wind again, and the creaking saw of the eaves. Neither spoke now. There was something strange, almost terrifying, about this Steven and his quiet, unrelenting smile; but strangest of all was the familiarity: the Steven she had never seen or encountered, and yet had always known, always expected, always waited for. It was less Steven himself that she felt than his inevitability. Just as she had felt the snow, the silence and the storm. She kept her eyes lowered, on the window past his shoulder, on the stove, but his smile now seemed to exist apart from him, to merge and hover with the silence. She clinked a cup—listened to the whistle of the storm—always it was there. He began to speak, but her mind missed the meaning of his words. Swiftly she was making comparisons again; his face so different to John's, so handsome and young and clean-shaven. Swiftly, helplessly, feeling the imperceptible and relentless ascendancy that thereby he was gaining over her, sensing sudden menace in this new, more vital life, even as she felt drawn towards it.

The lamp between them flickered as an onslaught of the storm sent shudderings through the room. She rose to build up the fire again and he followed her. For a long time they stood close to the stove, their arms almost touching. Once as the blizzard creaked the house she spun around sharply, fancying it was John at the door; but quietly he intercepted her. 'Not tonight—you might as well make up your mind to it. Across the hills in a storm like this—it would be suicide to try.'

Her lips trembled suddenly in an effort to answer, to parry the certainty in his voice, then set thin and bloodless. She was afraid now. Afraid of his face so different from John's—of his smile, of her own helplessness to rebuke it. Afraid of the storm, isolating her here alone with him in its impenetrable fastness. They tried to play cards, but she kept starting up at every creak and shiver of the walls. 'It's too rough a night,' he repeated. 'Even for John. Just relax a few minutes—stop worrying and pay a little attention to me.'

But in his tone there was a contradiction to his words. For it implied that she was not worrying—that her only concern was lest it really might be John at the door.

And the implication persisted. He filled up the stove for her, shuffled the cards—won—shuffled—still it was there. She tried to respond to his conversation, to think of the game, but helplessly into her cards instead she began to ask, Was he right? Was that why he smiled? Why he seemed to wait, expectant and assured?

The clock ticked, the fire crackled. Always it was there. Furtively for a moment she watched him as he deliberated over his hand. John, even in the days before they were married, had never looked like that. Only this morning she had asked him to shave. Because Steven was coming—because she had been afraid to see them side by side—because deep within herself she had known even then. The same knowledge, furtive and forbidden, that was flaunted now in Steven's smile. 'You look cold,' he said at last, dropping his cards and rising from the table. 'We're not playing, anyway. Come over to the stove for a few minutes and get warm.'

'But first I think we'll hang blankets over the door. When there's a blizzard like this we always do.' It seemed that in sane, commonplace activity there might be release, a moment or two in which to recover herself. 'John has nails in to put them on. They keep out a little of the draft.'

He stood on a chair for her, and hung the blankets that she had carried from the bedroom. Then for a moment they stood silent, watching the blankets sway and tremble before the blade of wind that spurted around the jamb. 'I forgot', she said at last, 'that I painted the bedroom door. At the top there, see—I've smeared the blankets coming through.'

He glanced at her curiously, and went back to the stove. She followed him, trying to imagine the hills in such a storm, wondering whether John would come. 'A man couldn't live in it,' suddenly he answered her thoughts, lowering the oven door and drawing up their chairs one on each side of it. 'He knows you're safe. It isn't likely that he'd leave his father, anyway.'

'The wind will be in his back,' she persisted. 'The winter before we were married—all the blizzards that we had that year—and he never missed—'

'Blizzards like this one? Up in the hills he wouldn't be able to keep his direction for a hundred yards. Listen to it a minute and ask yourself.'

His voice seemed softer, kindlier now. She met his smile a moment, its assured little twist of appraisal, then for a long time sat silent, tense, careful again to avoid his eyes.

Everything now seemed to depend on this. It was the same as a few hours ago when she braced the door against the storm. He was watching her, smiling. She dared not move, unclench her hands, or raise her eyes. The flames crackled, the clock ticked. The storm wrenched the walls as if to make them buckle in. So rigid and desperate were all her muscles set, withstanding, that the room around her seemed to swim and reel. So rigid and strained that for relief at last, despite herself, she raised her head and met his eyes again.

Intending that it should be for only an instant, just to breathe again, to ease the tension that had grown unbearable—but in his smile now, instead of the insolent appraisal that she feared, there seemed a kind of warmth and sympathy. An understanding that quickened and encouraged her—that made her wonder why but a moment ago she had been afraid. It was as if the storm had lulled, as if she had suddenly found calm and shelter.

Or perhaps, the thought seized her, perhaps instead of his smile it was she that had changed. She who, in the long, wind-creaked silence, had emerged from the increment of codes and loyalties to her real, unfettered self. She who now felt his air of appraisal as nothing more than understanding of the unfulfilled woman that until this moment had lain within her brooding and unadmitted, reproved out of consciousness by the insistence of an outgrown, routine fidelity.

For there had always been Steven. She understood now. Seven years—almost as long as John—ever since the night they first danced together.

The lamp was burning dry, and through the dimming light, isolated in the fastness of silence and storm, they watched each other. Her face was white and struggling still. His was handsome, clean-shaven, young. Her eyes were fanatic, believing desperately, fixed upon him as if to exclude all else, as if to find justification. His were cool, bland, drooped a little with expectancy. The light kept dimming, gathering the shadows round them, hushed, conspiratorial. He was smiling still. Her hands again were clenched up white and hard.

'But he always came,' she persisted. 'The wildest, coldest nights—even such a night as this. There was never a storm—'

'Never a storm like this one.' There was a quietness in his smile now, a kind of simplicity almost, as if to reassure her. 'You were out in it yourself for a few minutes. He would have five miles, across the hills. . . . I'd think twice myself, on such a night, before risking even one.'

Long after he was asleep she lay listening to the storm. As a check on the draft up the chimney they had left one of the stovelids partly off, and through the open bedroom door she could see the flickerings of flame and shadow on the kitchen wall. They leaped and sank fantastically. The longer she watched the more alive they seemed to be. There was one great shadow that struggled towards her threateningly, massive and black and engulfing all the room. Again and again it advanced, about to spring, but each time a little whip of light subdued it to its place among the others on the wall. Yet though it never reached her still she cowered, feeling that gathered there was all the frozen wilderness, its heart of terror and invincibility.

Then she dozed a while, and the shadow was John. Interminably he advanced. The whips of light still flickered and coiled, but now suddenly they were the swift little snakes that this afternoon she had watched twist and shiver across the snow. And they too were advancing. They writhed and vanished and came again. She lay still, paralyzed. He was over her now, so close that she could have touched him. Already it seemed that a deadly tightening hand was on her throat. She tried to scream but her lips were locked. Steven beside her slept on heedlessly.

Until suddenly as she lay staring up at him a gleam of light revealed his face. And in it was not a trace of threat or anger—only calm, and stonelike hopelessness.

That was like John. He began to withdraw, and frantically she tried to call him back. 'It isn't true—not really true—listen, John—' but the words clung frozen to her lips. Already there was only the shriek of wind again, the sawing eaves, the leap and twist of shadow on the wall.

She sat up, startled now and awake. And so real had he seemed there, standing close to her, so vivid the sudden age and sorrow in his face, that at first she could not make herself understand she had been only dreaming. Against the conviction of his presence in the room it was necessary to insist over and over that he must still be with his father on the other side of the hills. Watching the shadows she had fallen asleep. It was only her mind, her imagination, distorted to a nightmare by the illogical and unadmitted dread of his return. But he wouldn't come. Steven was right. In such a storm he would never try. They were safe, alone. No one would ever know. It was only fear, morbid and irrational; only the sense of guilt that even her new-found and challenged womanhood could not entirely quell.

She knew now. She had not let herself understand or acknowledge it as guilt before, but gradually through the wind-torn silence of the night his face compelled her. The face that had watched her from the darkness with its stonelike sorrow—the face that was really John—John more than his features of mere flesh and bone could ever be.

She wept silently. The fitful gleam of light began to sink. On the ceiling and wall at last there was only a faint dull flickering glow. The little house shuddered and quailed, and a chill crept in again. Without wakening Steven she slipped out to build up the fire. It was burned to a few spent embers now, and the wood she put on seemed a long time catching light. The wind swirled through the blankets they had hung around the door, and struck her flesh like laps of molten ice. Then hollow and moaning it roared up the chimney again, as if against its will drawn back to serve still longer with the onrush of the storm.

For a long time she crouched over the stove, listening. Earlier in the evening, with the lamp lit and the fire crackling, the house had seemed a stand against the wilderness, against its frozen, blizzard-breathed implacability, a refuge of feeble walls wherein persisted the elements of human meaning and survival. Now, in the cold, creaking darkness, it was strangely extinct, looted by the storm and abandoned again. She lifted the stove lid and fanned the embers till at last a swift little tongue of flame began to lick around the wood. Then she replaced the lid, extending her hands, and as if frozen in that attitude stood waiting.

It was not long now. After a few minutes she closed the drafts, and as the flames whirled back upon each other, beating against the top of the stove and sending out flickers of light again, a warmth surged up to relax her stiffened limbs. But shivering and numb it had been easier. The bodily well-being that the warmth induced gave play again to an ever more insistent mental suffering. She remembered the shadow that was John. She saw him bent towards her, then retreating, his features pale and overcast with unaccusing grief. She re-lived their seven years together and, in retrospect, found them to be years of worth and dignity. Until crushed by it all at last, seized by a sudden need to suffer and atone, she crossed to where the draft was bitter, and for a long time stood unflinching on the icy floor.

The storm was close here. Even through the blankets she could feel a sift of snow against her face. The eaves sawed, the walls creaked. Above it all, like a wolf in howling flight, the wind shrilled lone and desolate.

And yet, suddenly she asked herself, hadn't there been other storms, other blizzards? And through the worst of them hadn't he always reached her?

Clutched by the thought she stood rooted a minute. It was hard now to understand how she could have so deceived herself—how a moment of passion could have quieted within her not only conscience, but reason and discretion too. John always came. There could never be a storm to stop him. He was strong, inured to the cold. He had crossed the hills since his boyhood, knew every creek-bed and gully. It was madness to go on like this—to wait. While there was still time she must waken Steven, and hurry him away.

But in the bedroom again, standing at Steven's side, she hesitated. In his detachment from it all, in his quiet, even breathing, there was such sanity, such realism. For him nothing had happened; nothing would. If she wakened him he would only laugh and tell her to listen to the storm. Already it was long past midnight; either John had lost his way or not set out at all. And she knew that in his devotion there was nothing foolhardy. He would never risk a storm beyond his endurance, never permit himself a sacrifice likely to endanger her lot or future. They were both safe. No one would ever know. She must control herself—be sane like Steven.

For comfort she let her hand rest a while on Steven's shoulder. It would be easier were he awake now, with her, sharing her guilt; but gradually as she watched his handsome face in the glimmering light she came to understand that for him no guilt existed. Just as there had been no passion, no conflict. Nothing but the sane appraisal of their situation, nothing but the expectant little smile, and the arrogance of features that were different from John's. She winced deeply, remembering how she had fixed her eyes on those features, how she had tried to believe that so handsome and young, so different from John's, they must in themselves be her justification.

In the flickering light they were still young, still handsome. No longer her justification—she knew now—John was the man—but wistfully still, wondering sharply at their power and tyranny, she touched them a moment with her fingertips again.

She could not blame him. There had been no passion, no guilt; therefore there could be no responsibility. Looking down at him as he slept, half-smiling still, his lips relaxed in the conscienceless complacency of his achievement, she understood that thus he was revealed in his entirety—all there ever was or ever could be. John was the man. With him lay all the future. For tonight, slowly and contritely through the day and years to come, she would try to make amends.

Then she stole back to the kitchen, and without thought, impelled by overwhelming need again, returned to the door where the draft was bitter still. Gradually towards morning the storm began to spend itself. Its terror blast became a feeble, worn-out moan. The leap of light and shadow sank, and a chill crept in again. Always the eaves creaked, tortured with wordless prophecy. Heedless of it all the clock ticked on in idiot content.

They found him the next day, less than a mile from home. Drifting with the storm he had run against his own pasture fence and overcome had frozen there, erect still, both hands clasping fast the wire.

'He was south of here,' they said wonderingly when she told them how he had come across the hills. 'Straight south—you'd wonder how he could have missed the buildings. It was the wind last night, coming every way at once. He shouldn't have tried. There was a double wheel around the moon.'

She looked past them a moment, then as if to herself said simply, 'If you knew him, though—John would try.'

It was later, when they had left her a while to be alone with him, that she knelt and touched his hand. Her eyes dimmed, still it was such a strong and patient hand; then, transfixed, they suddenly grew wide and clear. On the palm, white even against its frozen whiteness, was a little smear of paint.

1942

# Sheila Watson

## 1909–1998

Born in New Westminster, British Columbia, where her father was the superintendent of a mental hospital, Sheila Watson, the second of four children, lived with her family in one wing of the institution until her father died in 1920. After graduating from the University of British Columbia, she taught in elementary and secondary schools on the BC mainland and on Vancouver Island. Watson drew on her teaching experience in the Cariboo region of the British Columbia interior in writing her first novel, *Deep Hollow Creek*, which she did not publish until 1992. After World War II she moved east to undertake part-time graduate studies in English at the University of Toronto. In 1951 she began a two-year residence in Calgary, where she wrote much of *The Double Hook* (1959), the novel now regarded as the beginning of modern Canadian fiction. In the same decade she completed her graduate studies and began a doctoral dissertation on Wyndham Lewis. In 1961 she joined the Department of English at the University of Alberta, where she taught until her retirement in 1975.

In addition to her novel, Watson published six short stories. 'Antigone' (1959) employs classical myth to organize contemporary reality, to distance that reality, and to endow seemingly homely actions with the significance usually associated with myth.

# Antigone

My father ruled a kingdom on the right bank of the river. He ruled it with a firm hand and a stout heart though he was often more troubled than Moses, who was simply trying to bring a stubborn and moody people under God's yoke. My father ruled men who thought they were gods or the instruments of gods or, at very least, god-afflicted and god-pursued. He ruled Atlas who held up the sky, and Hermes who went on endless messages, and Helen who'd been hatched from an egg, and Pan the gardener, and Kallisto the bear, and too many others to mention by name. Yet my father had no thunderbolt, no trident, no helmet of darkness. His subjects were delivered bound into his hands. He merely watched over them as the hundred-handed ones watched over the dethroned Titans so that they wouldn't bother Hellas again.

Despite the care which my father took to maintain an atmosphere of sober common sense in his whole establishment, there were occasional outbursts of self-indulgence which he could not control. For instance, I have seen Helen walking naked down the narrow cement path under the chestnut trees for no better reason, I suppose, than that the day was hot and the white flowers themselves lay naked and expectant in the sunlight. And I have seen Atlas forget the sky while he sat eating the dirt which held him up. These were things which I was not supposed to see.

If my father had been as sensible through and through as he was thought to be, he would have packed me off to boarding school when I was old enough to be disciplined by men. Instead he kept me at home with my two cousins who, except for the accident of birth, might as well have been my sisters. Today I imagine people concerned with our welfare would take such an environment into account. At the time I speak of most people thought us fortunate—especially the girls whose father's affairs had come to an unhappy issue. I don't like to revive old scandal and I wouldn't except to deny it; but it takes only a few impertinent newcomers in any community to force open cupboards which have been decently sealed by time. However, my father was so busy setting his kingdom to rights that he let weeds grow up in his own garden.

As I said, if my father had had all his wits about him he would have sent me to boarding school—and Antigone and Ismene too. I might have fallen in love with the headmaster's daughter and Antigone might have learned that no human being can be right always. She might have found out besides that from the seeds of eternal justice grow madder flowers than any which Pan grew in the gardens of my father's kingdom.

Between the kingdom which my father ruled and the wilderness flows a river. It is this river which I am crossing now. Antigone is with me.

How often can we cross the same river, Antigone asks.

Her persistence annoys me. Besides, Heraklitos made nonsense of her question years ago. He saw a river too—the Inachos, the Kephissos, the Lethaios. The name doesn't matter. He said: See how quickly the water flows. However agile a man is, however nimbly he swims, or runs, or flies, the water slips away before him. See, even as he sets down his foot the water is displaced by the stream which crowds along in the shadow of its flight.

But after all, Antigone says, one must admit that it is the same kind of water. The oolichans run in it as they ran last year and the year before. The gulls cry above the same banks. Boats drift towards the Delta and circle back against the current to gather up the catch.

At any rate, I tell her, we're standing on a new bridge. We are standing so high that the smell of mud and river weeds passes under us out to the straits. The unbroken curve of the bridge protects the eye from details of river life. The bridge is foolproof as a clinic's passport to happiness.

The old bridge still spans the river, but the cat-walk with its cracks and knot-holes, with its gap between planking and handrail has been torn down. The centre arch still grinds open to let boats up and down the river, but a child can no longer be walked on it or swung out on it beyond the water-gauge at the very centre of the flood.

I've known men who scorned any kind of bridge, Antigone says. Men have walked into the water, she says, or, impatient, have jumped from the bridge into the river below.

But these, I say, didn't really want to cross the river. They went Persephone's way, cradled in the current's arms, down the long halls under the pink feet of the gulls, under the booms and towlines, under the soft bellies of the fish.

Antigone looks at me.

There's no coming back, she says, if one goes far enough.

I know she's going to speak of her own misery and I won't listen. Only a god has the right to say: Look what I suffer. Only a god should say: What more ought I to have done for you that I have not done?

Once in winter, she says, a man walked over the river.

Taking advantage of nature, I remind her, since the river had never frozen before.

Yet he escaped from the penitentiary, she says. He escaped from the guards walking round the walls or standing with their guns in the sentry-boxes at the four corners of the enclosure. He escaped.

Not without risk, I say. He had to test the strength of the ice himself. Yet safer perhaps than if he had crossed by the old bridge where he might have slipped through a knot-hole or tumbled out through the railing.

He did escape, she persists, and lived forever on the far side of the river in the Alaska tea and bulrushes. For where, she asks, can a man go farther than to the outermost edge of the world?

The habitable world, as I've said, is on the right bank of the river. Here is the market with its market stalls—the coops of hens, the long-tongued geese, the haltered calf, the bearded goat, the shoving pigs, and the empty bodies of cows and sheep and rabbits hanging on iron hooks. My father's kingdom provides asylum in the suburbs. Near it are the convent, the churches, and the penitentiary. Above these on the hill the cemetery looks down on the people and on the river itself.

It is a world spread flat, tipped up into the sky so that men and women bend forward, walking as men walk when they board a ship at high tide. This is the world I feel with my feet. It is the world I see with my eyes.

I remember standing once with Antigone and Ismene in the square just outside the gates of my father's kingdom. Here from a bust set high on a cairn the stone eyes of Simon Fraser look from his stone face over the river that he found.

It is the head that counts, Ismene said.

It's no better than an urn, Antigone said, one of the urns we see when we climb to the cemetery above.

And all I could think was that I didn't want an urn, only a flat green grave with a chain about it.

A chain won't keep out the dogs, Antigone said.

But his soul could swing on it, Ismene said, like a bird blown on a branch in the wind.

And I remembered Antigone's saying: The cat drags its belly on the ground and the rat sharpens its tooth in the ivy.

I should have loved Ismene, but I didn't. It was Antigone I loved. I should have loved Ismene because, although she walked the flat world with us, she managed somehow to see it round.

The earth is an oblate spheroid, she'd say. And I knew that she saw it there before her comprehensible and whole like a tangerine spiked through and held in place while it rotated on the axis of one of Nurse's steel sock needles. The earth was a tangerine and she saw the skin peeled off and the world parcelled out into neat segments, each segment sweet and fragrant in its own skin.

It's the head that counts, she said.

In her own head she made diagrams to live by, cut and fashioned after the eternal patterns spied out by Plato as he rummaged about in the sewing basket of the gods.

I should have loved Ismene. She would live now in some prefabricated and perfect chrysolite by some paradigm which made love round and whole. She would simply live and leave destruction in the purgatorial ditches outside her own walled paradise.

Antigone is different. She sees the world flat as I do and feels it tip beneath her feet. She has walked in the market and seen the living animals penned and the dead hanging stiff on their hooks. Yet she defies what she sees with a defiance which is almost denial. Like Atlas she tries to keep the vaulted sky from crushing the flat earth. Like Hermes she brings a message that there is life if one can escape to it in the brush and bulrushes in some dim Hades beyond the river. It is defiance not belief and I tell her that this time we walk the bridge to a walled cave where we can deny death no longer.

Yet she asks her question still. And standing there I tell her that Heraklitos has made nonsense of her question. I should have loved Ismene for she would have taught me what Plato meant when he said in all earnest that the union of the soul with the body is in no way better than dissolution. I expect that she understood things which Antigone is too proud to see.

I turn away from her and flatten my elbows on the high wall of the bridge. I look back at my father's kingdom. I see the terraces rolling down from the red-brick buildings with their barred windows. I remember hands shaking the bars and hear fingers tearing up paper and stuffing it through the meshes. Diktynna, mother of nets and high leaping fear. O Artemis, mistress of wild beasts and wild men.

The inmates are beginning to come out on the screened verandas. They pace up and down in straight lines or stand silent like figures which appear at the same time each day from some depths inside a clock.

On the upper terrace Pan the gardener is shifting sprinklers with a hooked stick. His face is shadowed by the brim of his hat. He moves as economically as an animal between the beds of lobelia and geranium. It is high noon.

Antigone has cut out a piece of sod and has scooped out a grave. The body lies in a coffin in the shade of the magnolia tree. Antigone and I are standing. Ismene is sitting between two low angled branches of the monkey puzzle tree. Her lap is filled with daisies. She slits the stem of one daisy and pulls the stem of another through it. She is making a chain for her neck and a crown for her hair.

Antigone reaches for a branch of the magnolia. It is almost beyond her grip. The buds flame above her. She stands on a small fire of daisies which smoulder in the roots of the grass.

I see the magnolia buds. They brood above me, whiteness feathered on whiteness. I see Antigone's face turned to the light. I hear the living birds call to the sun. I speak private poetry to myself: Between four trumpeting angels at the four corners of the earth a bride stands before the altar in a gown as white as snow.

Yet I must have been speaking aloud because Antigone challenges me: You're mistaken. It's the winds the angels hold, the four winds of the earth. After the just are taken to paradise the winds will destroy the earth. It's a funeral, she says, not a wedding.

She looks towards the building.

Someone is coming down the path from the matron's house, she says.

I notice that she has pulled one of the magnolia blossoms from the branch. I take it from her. It is streaked with brown where her hands have bruised it. The sparrow which she has decided to bury lies on its back. Its feet are clenched tight against the feathers of its breast. I put the flower in the box with it.

Someone is coming down the path. She is wearing a blue cotton dress. Her cropped head is bent. She walks slowly carrying something in a napkin.

It's Kallisto the bear, I say. Let's hurry. What will my father say if he sees us talking to one of his patients?

If we live here with him, Antigone says, what can he expect? If he spends his life trying to tame people he can't complain if you behave as if they were tame. What would your father think, she says, if he saw us digging in the Institution lawn?

Pan comes closer. I glower at him. There's no use speaking to him. He's deaf and dumb.

Listen, I say to Antigone, my father's not unreasonable. Kallisto thinks she's a bear and he thinks he's a bear tamer, that's all. As for the lawn, I say quoting my father without conviction, a man must have order among his own if he is to keep order in the state.

Kallisto has come up to see us. She is smiling and laughing to herself. She gives me her bundle.

Fish, she says.

I open the napkin.

Pink fish sandwiches, I say.

For the party, she says.

But it isn't a party, Antigone says. It's a funeral.

For the funeral breakfast, I say.

Ismene is twisting two chains of daisies into a rope. Pan has stopped pulling the sprinkler about. He is standing beside Ismene resting himself on his hooked stick. Kallisto squats down beside her. Ismene turns away, preoccupied, but she can't turn far because of Pan's legs.

*Father said we never should*
*Play with madmen in the wood.*

I look at Antigone.

It's my funeral, she says.

I go over to Ismene and gather up a handful of loose daisies from her lap. The sun reaches through the shadow of the magnolia tree.

It's my funeral, Antigone says. She moves possessively toward the body.

An ant is crawling into the bundle of sandwiches which I've put on the ground. A file of ants is marching on the sparrow's box.

I go over and drop daisies on the bird's stiff body. My voice speaks ritual words: Deliver me, O Lord, from everlasting death on this dreadful day. I tremble and am afraid.

The voice of a people comforts me. I look at Antigone. I look her in the eye.

It had better be a proper funeral then, I say.

Kallisto is crouched forward on her hands. Tears are running down her cheeks and she is licking them away with her tongue.

My voice rises again: I said in the midst of my days, I shall not see—

Antigone just stands there. She looks frightened, but her eyes defy me with their assertion.

It's my funeral, she says. It's my bird. I was the one who wanted to bury it.

She is looking for reason. She will say something which sounds eternally right.

Things have to be buried, she says. They can't be left lying around anyhow for people to see.

Birds shouldn't die, I tell her. They have wings. Cats and rats haven't wings.

Stop crying, she says to Kallisto. It's only a bird.

It has a bride's flower in its hand, Kallisto says.

We shall rise again, I mutter, but we shall not all be changed.

Antigone does not seem to hear me.

Behold, I say in a voice she must hear, in a moment, in the twinkling of an eye, the trumpet shall sound.

Ismene turns to Kallisto and throws the daisy chain about her neck.

Shall a virgin forget her adorning or a bride the ornament of her breast?

Kallisto is lifting her arms towards the tree.

The bridegroom has come, she says, white as a fall of snow. He stands above me in a great ring of fire.

Antigone looks at me now.

Let's cover the bird up, she says. Your father will punish us all for making a disturbance.

He has on his garment, Kallisto says, and on his thigh is written King of Kings.

I look at the tree. If I could see with Kallisto's eyes I wouldn't be afraid of death, or punishment, or the penitentiary guards. I wouldn't be afraid of my father's belt or his honing strap or his bedroom slipper. I wouldn't be afraid of falling into the river through a knot-hole in the bridge.

But, as I look, I see the buds falling like burning lamps and I hear the sparrow twittering in its box: Woe, woe, woe because of the three trumpets which are yet to sound.

Kallisto is on her knees. She is growling like a bear. She lumbers over to the sandwiches and mauls them with her paw.

Ismene stands alone for Pan the gardener has gone.

Antigone is fitting a turf in place above the coffin. I go over and press the edge of the turf with my feet. Ismene has caught me by the hand.

Go away, Antigone says.

I see my father coming down the path. He has an attendant with him. In front of them walks Pan holding the sprinkler hook like a spear.

What are you doing here? my father asks.

Burying a bird, Antigone says.

Here? my father asks again.

Where else could I bury it? Antigone says.

My father looks at her.

This ground is public property, he says. No single person has any right to an inch of it.

I've taken six inches, Antigone says. Will you dig up the bird again?

Some of his subjects my father restrained since they were moved to throw themselves from high places or to tear one another to bits from jealousy or rage. Others who disturbed the public peace he taught to walk in the airing courts or to work in the kitchen or the garden.

If men live at all, my father said, it is because discipline saves their life for them.

From Antigone he simply turned away.

1959

# Eudora Welty

## 1909–2001

Born in Jackson, Mississippi, where her father was president of an insurance company, Eudora Welty attended school in that city before going to the Mississippi College for Women. She left her home region to finish college at the University of Wisconsin in 1929, and she spent the next two years studying at the Columbia University School of Advertising. Returning to Mississippi, Welty worked for various radio stations and newspapers and took a job as a photographer documenting Depression-era life in her home state for the United States Works Progress Administration.

Welty began writing fiction in the 1930s, publishing her first collection, *A Curtain of Green*, in 1941. From that time until her death she led a quiet life in Mississippi, writing and publishing her uniquely perceptive and humorous stories and novels at regular intervals. In a masterful evocation of idiosyncratic southern speech, 'Why I Live at the P.O.' is an extended dramatic monologue in which Sister gives her account of the family confrontation that prompted her move to the local post office.

## Why I Live at the P.O.

I was getting along fine with Mama, Papa-Daddy, and Uncle Rondo until my sister Stella-Rondo just separated from her husband and came back home again. Mr Whitaker! Of course I went with Mr Whitaker first, when he first appeared here in China Grove, taking 'Pose Yourself' photos, and Stella-Rondo broke us up. Told him I was one-sided. Bigger on one side than the other, which is a deliberate, calculated falsehood: I'm the same. Stella-Rondo is exactly twelve months to the day younger than I am and for that reason she's spoiled.

She's always had anything in the world she wanted and then she'd throw it away. Papa-Daddy gave her this gorgeous Add-a-Pearl necklace when she was eight years old and she threw it away playing baseball when she was nine, with only two pearls.

So as soon as she got married and moved away from home the first thing she did was separate! From Mr Whitaker! This photographer with the popeyes she said she trusted. Came home from one of those towns up in Illinois and to our complete surprise brought this child of two.

Mama said she like to made her drop dead for a second. 'Here you had this marvellous blond child and never so much as wrote your mother a word about it,' says Mama. 'I'm thoroughly ashamed of you.' But of course she wasn't.

Stella-Rondo just calmly takes off this *hat*, I wish you could see it. She says, 'Why, Mama, Shirley-T.'s adopted, I can prove it.'

'How?' says Mama, but all I says was, 'H'm!' There I was over the hot stove, trying to stretch two chickens over five people and a completely unexpected child into the bargain, without one moment's notice.

'What do you mean—"H'm!"?' says Stella-Rondo, and Mama says, 'I heard that, Sister.'

I said that oh, I didn't mean a thing, only that whoever Shirley-T. was, she was the spit-image of Papa-Daddy if he'd cut off his beard, which of course he'd never do in the world. Papa-Daddy's Mamma's papa and sulks.

Stella-Rondo got furious! She said, 'Sister, I don't need to tell you you got a lot of nerve and always did have and I'll thank you to make no future reference to my adopted child whatsoever.'

'Very well,' I said. 'Very well, very well. Of course I noticed at once she looks like Mr Whitaker's side too. That frown. She looks like a cross between Mr Whitaker and Papa-Daddy.'

'Well, all I can say is she isn't.'

'She looks exactly like Shirley Temple to me,' says Mama, but Shirley-T. just ran away from her.

So the first thing Stella-Rondo did at the table was turn Papa-Daddy against me.

'Papa-Daddy,' she says. He was trying to cut up his meat. 'Papa-Daddy!' I was taken completely by surprise. Papa-Daddy is about a million years old and's got this long-long beard. 'Papa Daddy, Sister says she fails to understand why you don't cut off your beard.'

So Papa-Daddy l-a-y-s down his knife and fork! He's real rich. Mama says he is, he says he isn't. So he says, 'Have I heard correctly? You don't understand why I don't cut off my beard?'

'Why,' I says, 'Papa-Daddy, of course I understand, I did not say any such of a thing, the idea!'

He says, 'Hussy!'

I says, 'Papa-Daddy, you know I wouldn't any more want you to cut off your beard than the man in the moon. It was the farthest thing from my mind! Stella-Rondo sat there and made that up while she was eating breast of chicken.'

But he says, 'So the postmistress fails to understand why I don't cut off my beard. Which job I got you through my influence with the government. "Bird's nest"—is that what you call it?'

Not that it isn't the next to smallest P.O. in the entire state of Mississippi.

I says, 'Oh, Papa-Daddy,' I says, 'I didn't say any such of a thing, I never dreamed it was a bird's nest, I have always been grateful though this is the next to smallest P.O. in the state of Mississippi, and I do not enjoy being referred to as a hussy by my own grandfather.'

But Stella-Rondo says, 'Yes, you did say it too. Anybody in the world could of heard you, that had ears.'

'Stop right there,' says Mama, looking at *me*.

So I pulled my napkin straight back through the napkin ring and left the table.

As soon as I was out of the room Mama says, 'Call her back, or she'll starve to death,' but Papa-Daddy says, 'This is the beard I started growing on the Coast when I was fifteen years old.' He would of gone on till nightfall if Shirley-T. hadn't lost the Milky Way she ate in Cairo.

So Papa-Daddy says, 'I am going out and lie in the hammock, and you can all sit here and remember my words: I'll never cut off my beard as long as I live, even one inch, and I don't appreciate it in you at all.' Passed right by me in the hall and went straight out and got in the hammock.

It would be a holiday. It wasn't five minutes before Uncle Rondo suddenly appeared in the hall in one of Stella-Rondo's flesh-coloured kimonos, all cut on the bias, like something Mr Whitaker probably thought was gorgeous.

'Uncle Rondo!' I says. 'I didn't know who that was! Where are you going?'

'Sister,' he says, 'get out of my way, I'm poisoned.'

'If you're poisoned stay away from Papa-Daddy,' I says. 'Keep out of the hammock, Papa-Daddy will certainly beat you on the head if you come within forty miles of him. He thinks I deliberately said he ought to cut off his beard after he got me the P.O., and I've told him and told him and told him, and he acts like he just don't hear me. Papa-Daddy must of gone stone deaf.'

'He picked a fine day to do it then,' says Uncle Rondo, and before you could say 'Jack Robinson' flew out in the yard.

What he'd really done, he'd drunk another bottle of that prescription. He does it every single Fourth of July as sure as shooting, and it's horribly expensive. Then he falls over in the hammock and snores. So he insisted on zigzagging right on out to the hammock, looking like a half-wit.

Papa-Daddy woke up with this horrible yell and right there without moving an inch he tried to turn Uncle Rondo against me. I heard every word he said. Oh, he told Uncle Rondo I didn't learn to read till I was eight years old and he didn't see how in the world I ever got the mail put up at the P.O., much less read it all, and he said if Uncle Rondo could only fathom the lengths he had gone to to get me that job! And he said on the other hand he thought Stella-Rondo had a brilliant mind and deserved credit for getting out of town. All the time he was just lying there swinging as pretty as you please and looping out his beard, and poor Uncle Rondo was *pleading* with him to slow down the hammock, it was making him dizzy as a witch to watch it. But that's what Papa-Daddy likes about a hammock. So Uncle Rondo was too dizzy to get turned against me for the time being. He's Mama's only brother and is a good case of a one-track mind. Ask anybody. A certified pharmacist.

Just then I heard Stella-Rondo raising the upstairs window. While she was married she got this peculiar idea that it's cooler with the windows shut and locked. So she has to raise the window before she can make a soul hear her outdoors.

So she raises the window and says, '*Oh!*' You would have thought she was mortally wounded.

Uncle Rondo and Papa-Daddy didn't even look up, but kept right on with what they were doing. I had to laugh.

I flew up the stairs and threw the door open! I says, 'What in the wide world's the matter, Stella-Rondo? You mortally wounded?'

'No,' she says, 'I'm not mortally wounded but I wish you would do me the favour of looking out that window there and telling me what you see.'

So I shade my eyes and look out the window.

'I see the front yard,' I says.

'Don't you see any human beings?' she says.

'I see Uncle Rondo trying to run Papa-Daddy out of the hammock,' I says. 'Nothing more. Naturally, it's so suffocating-hot in the house, with all the windows shut and locked, everybody who cares to stay in their right mind will have to go out and get in the hammock before the Fourth of July is over.'

'Don't you notice anything different about Uncle Rondo?' asks Stella-Rondo.

'Why, no, except he's got on some terrible-looking flesh-coloured contraption I wouldn't be found dead in, is all I can see,' I says.

'Never mind, you won't be found dead in it, because it happens to be part of my trousseau, and Mr Whitaker took several dozen photographs of me in it,' says Stella-Rondo. 'What on earth could Uncle Rondo *mean* by wearing part of my trousseau out in the broad open daylight without saying so much as "Kiss my foot," *knowing* I only got home this morning after my separation and hung my negligee up on the bathroom door, just as nervous as I could be?'

'I'm sure I don't know, and what do you expect me to do about it?' I says. 'Jump out the window?'

'No, I expect nothing of the kind. I simply declare that Uncle Rondo looks like a fool in it, that's all,' she says. 'It makes me sick to my stomach.'

'Well, he looks as good as he can,' I says. 'As good as anybody in reason could.' I stood up for Uncle Rondo, please remember. And I said to Stella-Rondo, 'I think I would do well not to criticize so freely if I were you and came home with a two-year-old child I had never said a word about, and no explanation whatever about the separation.'

'I asked you the instant I entered this house not to refer one more time to my adopted child, and you gave me your word of honour you would not,' was all Stella-Rondo would say, and started pulling out every one of her eyebrows with some cheap Kress tweezers.

So I merely slammed the door behind me and went downstairs and made some green-tomato pickle. Somebody had to do it. Of course Mama had turned the both niggers loose; she always said no earthly power could hold one anyway on the Fourth of July, so she wouldn't even try. It turned out that Jaypan fell in the lake and came within a very narrow limit of drowning.

So Mama trots in. Lifts up the lid and says, 'H'm! Not very good for your Uncle Rondo in his precarious condition, I must say. Or poor little adopted Shirley-T. Shame on you!'

That made me tired. I says, 'Well, Stella-Rondo had better thank her lucky stars it was her instead of me came trotting in with that very peculiar-looking child. Now if it had been me that trotted in from Illinois and brought a peculiar-looking child of two, I shudder to think of the reception I'd of got, much less controlled the diet of an entire family.'

'But you must remember, Sister, that you were never married to Mr Whitaker in the first place and didn't go up to Illinois to live,' says Mama, shaking a spoon in my face. 'If you had I would of been just as overjoyed to see you and your little adopted girl as I was to see Stella-Rondo, when you wound up with your separation and came on back home.'

'You would not,' I says.

'Don't contradict me, I would,' says Mama.

But I said she couldn't convince me though she talked till she was blue in the face. Then I said, 'Besides, you know as well as I do that that child is not adopted.'

'She most certainly is adopted,' says Mama, stiff as a poker.

I says, 'Why Mama, Stella-Rondo had her just as sure as anything in this world, and just too stuck up to admit it.'

'Why, Sister,' said Mama. 'Here I thought we were going to have a pleasant Fourth of July, and you start right out not believing a word your own baby sister tells you!'

'Just like Cousin Annie Flo. Went to her grave denying the facts of life,' I remind Mama.

'I told you if you ever mentioned Annie Flo's name I'd slap your face,' says Mama, and slaps my face.

'All right, you wait and see,' I says.

'I,' says Mama, 'I prefer to take my children's word for anything when it's humanly possible.' You ought to see Mama, she weighs two hundred pounds and has real tiny feet.

Just then something perfectly horrible occurred to me.

'Mama,' I says, 'can that child talk?' I simply had to whisper! 'Mama, I wonder if that child can be—you know—in any way? Do you realize,' I says, 'that she hasn't spoken one single, solitary word to a human being up to this minute? This is the way she looks,' I says, and I looked like this.

Well, Mama and I just stood there and stared at each other. It was horrible!

'I remember well that Joe Whitaker frequently drank like a fish,' says Mama. 'I believed to my soul he drank *chemicals*.' And without another word she marches to the foot of the stairs and calls Stella-Rondo.

'Stella-Rondo? O-o-o-o-o! Stella-Rondo!'

'What?' says Stella-Rondo from upstairs. Not even the grace to get up off the bed.

'Can that child of yours talk?' asks Mama.

Stella-Rondo says, 'Can she what?'

'Talk! Talk!' says Mama. 'Burdyburdyburdyburdy!'

So Stella-Rondo yells back, 'Who says she can't talk?'

'Sister says so,' says Mama.

'You didn't have to tell me, I know whose word of honour don't mean a thing in this house,' says Stella-Rondo.

And in a minute the loudest Yankee voice I ever heard in my life yells out, 'OE'm Pop-OE the Sailor-r-r-r Ma-a-an!' and then somebody jumps up and down in the upstairs hall. In another second the house would of fallen down.

'Not only talks, she can tap-dance!' calls Stella-Rondo. 'Which is more than some people I won't name can do.'

'Why, the little precious darling thing!' Mama says, so surprised. 'Just as smart as she can be!' Starts talking baby talk right there. Then she turns on me. 'Sister, you ought to be thoroughly ashamed! Run upstairs this instant and apologize to Stella-Rondo and Shirley-T.'

'Apologize for what?' I says. 'I merely wondered if the child was normal, that's all. Now that she's proved she is, why, I have nothing further to say.'

But Mama just turned on her heels and flew out, furious. She ran right upstairs and hugged the baby. She believed it was adopted. Stella-Rondo hadn't done a thing but turn her against me from upstairs while I stood there helpless over the hot stove. So that made Mama, Papa-Daddy, and the baby all on Stella-Rondo's side.

Next, Uncle Rondo.

I must say that Uncle Rondo has been marvellous to me at various times in the past and I was completely unprepared to be made to jump out of my skin, the way it turned out. Once Stella-Rondo did something perfectly horrible to him—broke a chain letter from Flanders Field—and he took the radio back he had given her and gave it to me. Stella-Rondo was furious! For six months we all had to call her Stella instead of Stella-Rondo, or she wouldn't answer. I always thought Uncle Rondo had all the brains in the entire family. Another time he sent me to Mammoth Cave, with all expenses paid.

But this would be the day he was drinking that prescription, the Fourth of July.

So at supper Stella-Rondo speaks up and says she thinks Uncle Rondo ought to try to eat a little something. So finally Uncle Rondo said he would try a little cold biscuits and ketchup, but that was all. So *she* brought it to him.

'Do you think it wise to disport with ketchup in Stella-Rondo's flesh-coloured kimono?' I says. Trying to be considerate! If Stella-Rondo couldn't watch out for her trousseau, somebody had to.

'Any objections?' asks Uncle Rondo, just about to pour out all the ketchup.

'Don't mind what she says, Uncle Rondo,' says Stella-Rondo. 'Sister has been devoting this solid afternoon to sneering out my bedroom window at the way you look.'

'What's that?' says Uncle Rondo. Uncle Rondo has got the most terrible temper in the world. Anything is liable to make him tear the house down if it comes at the wrong time.

So Stella-Rondo says, 'Sister says, "Uncle Rondo certainly does look like a fool in that pink kimono!" '

Do you remember who really said that?

Uncle Rondo spills out all the ketchup and jumps out of his chair and tears off the kimono and throws it down on the dirty floor and puts his foot on it. It had to be sent all the way to Jackson to the cleaners and re-pleated.

'So that's your opinion of your Uncle Rondo, is it?' he says. 'I look like a fool, do I? Well, that's the last straw. A whole day in this house with nothing to do, and then to hear you come out with a remark like that behind my back!'

'I didn't say any such of a thing, Uncle Rondo,' I says, 'and I'm not saying who did, either. Why, I think you look all right. Just try to take care of yourself and not talk and eat at the same time,' I says. 'I think you better go lie down.'

'Lie down my foot,' says Uncle Rondo. I ought to of known by that he was fixing to do something perfectly horrible.

So he didn't do anything that night in the precarious state he was in—just played Casino with Mama and Stella-Rondo and Shirley T. and gave Shirley-T. a nickel with a head on both sides. It tickled her nearly to death, and she called him 'Papa'. But at 6:30 a.m. the next morning, he threw a whole five-cent package of some unsold one-inch firecrackers from the store as hard as he could into my bedroom, and they every one went off. Not one bad one in the string. Anybody else, there'd be one that wouldn't go off.

Well, I'm just terribly susceptible to noise of any kind, the doctor has always told me I was the most sensitive person he had ever seen in his whole life, and I was simply prostrated. I couldn't eat! People tell me they heard it as far as the cemetery, and old Aunt Jep Patterson, that had been holding her own so good, thought it was Judgment Day and she was going to meet her whole family. It's usually so quiet here.

And I'll tell you it didn't take me any longer than a minute to make up my mind what to do. There I was with the whole entire house on Stella-Rondo's side and turned against me. If I have anything at all I have pride.

So I just decided I'd go straight down to the P.O. There's plenty of room there in the back, I says to myself.

Well! I made no bones about letting the family catch on to what I was up to. I didn't try to conceal it.

The first thing they knew, I marched in where they were all playing Old Maid and pulled the electric oscillating fan out by the plug, and everything got real hot. Next I snatched the pillow I'd done the needlepoint on right off the davenport from behind Papa-Daddy. He went 'Ugh!' I beat Stella-Rondo up the stairs and finally found my charm bracelet in her bureau drawer under a picture of Nelson Eddy.

'So that's the way the land lies,' says Uncle Rondo. There he was, piecing on the ham. 'Well, Sister, I'll be glad to donate my army cot if you got any place to set it up, providing you'll leave right this minute and let me get some peace.' Uncle Rondo was in France.

'Thank you kindly for the cot and "peace" is hardly the word I would select if I had to resort to firecrackers at 6:30 a.m. in a young girl's bedroom,' I says back to him. 'And as to where I intend to go, you seem to forget my position as postmistress of China Grove, Mississippi,' I says. 'I've always got the P.O.'

Well, that made them all sit up and take notice.

I went out front and started digging up some four-o'clocks to plant around the P.O.

'Ah-ah-ah!' says Mama, raising the window. 'Those happen to be my four-o'clocks. Everything planted in that star is mine. I've never known you to make anything grow in your life.'

'Very well,' I says. 'But I take the fern. Even you, Mama, can't stand there and deny that I'm the one watered that fern. And I happen to know where I can send in a box top and get a packet of one thousand mixed seeds, no two the same kind, free.'

'Oh, where?' Mama wants to know.

But I says, 'Too late. You 'tend to your house, and I'll 'tend to mine. You hear things like that all the time if you know how to listen to the radio. Perfectly marvellous offers. Get anything you want free.'

So I hope to tell you I marched in and got that radio, and they could of all bit a nail in two, especially Stella-Rondo, that it used to belong to, and she well knew she couldn't get it back, I'd sue for it like a shot. And I very politely took the sewing-machine motor I helped pay the most on to give Mama for Christmas back in 1929, and a good big calendar, with the first-aid remedies on it. The thermometer and the Hawaiian ukulele certainly were rightfully mine, and I stood on the step-ladder and got all my watermelon-rind preserves and every fruit and vegetable I'd put up, every jar. Then I began to pull the tacks out of the bluebird wall vases on the archway to the dining room.

'Who told you you could have those, Miss Priss?' says Mama, fanning as hard as she could.

'I bought 'em and I'll keep track of 'em,' I says. 'I'll tack 'em up one on each side of the post-office window, and you can see 'em when you come to ask me for your mail, if you're so dead to see 'em.'

'Not I! I'll never darken the door to that post office again if I live to be a hundred,' Mama says. 'Ungrateful child! After all the money we spent on you at the Normal.'

'Me either,' says Stella-Rondo. 'You can just let my mail lie there and *rot*, for all I care. I'll never come and relieve you of a single, solitary piece.'

'I should worry,' I says. 'And who you think's going to sit down and write you all those big fat letters and postcards, by the way? Mr Whitaker? Just because he was the only man ever dropped down in China Grove and you got him—unfairly—is he going to sit down and write you a lengthy correspondence after you come home giving no rhyme nor reason whatsoever for your separation and no explanation for the presence of that child? I may not have your brilliant mind, but I fail to see it.'

So Mama says, 'Sister, I've told you a thousand times that Stella-Rondo simply got homesick, and this child is far too big to be hers,' and she says, 'Now, why don't you all just sit down and play Casino?'

Then Shirley-T. sticks out her tongue at me in this perfectly horrible way. She has no more manners than the man in the moon. I told her she was going to cross her eyes like that some day and they'd stick.

'It's too late to stop me now,' I says. 'You should have tried that yesterday. I'm going to the P.O. and the only way you can possibly see me is to visit me there.'

So Papa-Daddy says, 'You'll never catch me setting foot in that post office, even if I should take a notion into my head to write a letter some place.' He says, 'I won't have you reachin' out of that little old window with a pair of shears and cuttin' off any beard of mine. I'm too smart for you!'

'We all are,' says Stella-Rondo.

But I said, 'If you're so smart, where's Mr Whitaker?'

So then Uncle Rondo says, 'I'll thank you from now on to stop reading all the orders I get on postcards and telling everyone in China Grove what you think is the matter with them,' but I says, 'I draw my own conclusions and will continue in the future to draw them.' I says, 'If people want to write their inmost secrets on penny postcards, there's nothing in the wide world you can do about it, Uncle Rondo.'

'And if you think we'll ever *write* another postcard you're sadly mistaken,' says Mama.

'Cutting off your nose to spite your face then,' I says. 'But if you're all determined to have no more to do with the US mail, think of this: What will Stella-Rondo do now, if she wants to tell Mr Whitaker to come after her?'

'Wah!' says Stella-Rondo. I knew she'd cry. She had a conniption fit right there in the kitchen.

'It will be interesting to see how long she holds out,' I says. 'And now—I am leaving.'

'Good-bye,' says Uncle Rondo.

'Oh, I declare,' says Mama, 'to think that a family of mine should quarrel on the Fourth of July, or the day after, over Stella-Rondo leaving old Mr Whitaker and having the sweetest little adopted child! It looks like we'd all be glad!'

'Wah!' says Stella-Rondo, and has a fresh conniption fit.

'*He* left *her*—you mark my words,' I says. 'That's Mr Whitaker. I know Mr Whitaker. After all, I knew him first. I said from the beginning he'd up and leave her. I foretold every single thing that's happened.'

'Where did he go?' asks Mama.

'Probably to the North Pole, if he knows what's good for him,' I says.

But Stella-Rondo just bawled and wouldn't say another word. She flew to her room and slammed the door.

'Now look what you've gone and done, Sister,' says Mama. 'You go apologize.'

'I haven't got time, I'm leaving,' I says.

'Well, what are you waiting around for?' asks Uncle Rondo.

So I just picked up the kitchen clock and marched off, without saying 'Kiss my foot' or anything, and never did tell Stella-Rondo good-bye.

There was a nigger girl going along on a little wagon right in front.

'Nigger girl,' I says, 'come help me haul these things down the hill, I'm going to live in the post office.'

Took her nine trips in her express wagon. Uncle Rondo came out on the porch and threw her a nickel.

And that's the last I've laid eyes on any of my family or my family laid eyes on me for five solid days and nights. Stella-Rondo may be telling the most horrible tales in the world about Mr Whitaker, but I haven't heard them. As I tell everybody, I draw my own conclusions.

But oh, I like it here. It's ideal, as I've been saying. You see, I've got everything cater-cornered, the way I like it. Hear the radio? All the war news. Radio, sewing machine, book ends, ironing board, and that great big piano lamp—peace, that's what I like. Butter-bean vines planted all along the front where the strings are.

Of course, there's not much mail. My family are naturally the main people in China Grove, and if they prefer to vanish from the face of the earth, for all the mail they get or the mail they write, why, I'm not going to open my mouth. Some of the folks here in town are taking up for me and some turned against me. I know which is which. There are always people who will quit buying stamps just to get on the right side of Papa-Daddy.

But here I am, and here I'll stay. I want the world to know I'm happy. And if Stella-Rondo should come to me this minute, on bended knees, and *attempt* to explain the incidents of her life with Mr Whitaker, I'd simply put my fingers in both my ears and refuse to listen.

1941

# John Cheever

1912–1982

John Cheever was born in Quincy, Massachusetts, where his father owned a shoe factory until the economic disaster of 1929 wiped him out. After the crash his mother opened a gift shop that was quite successful. He went to school in Massachusetts until he was expelled from Thayer Academy for 'bad behaviour'—smoking. His first story, 'Expelled', appeared in the *New Republic* a few months later, in 1930.

Cheever was a writer from the beginning, living and working in Boston, New York, and the Yaddo writers' colony in Saratoga Springs, surviving with help from his brother and by doing odd jobs. He had published almost 40 stories when he joined the United States Army in the Second World War. His first collection of stories was published during the war, but his first real success came with the publication of his second collection, *The Enormous Radio*, in 1953. By then he was writing for the *New Yorker*, where he placed well over 100 stories following his first acceptance in 1940. His reputation as a writer grew steadily, so that the publication of his collected *Stories of John Cheever* in 1979 was a major literary event.

Although he also wrote novels, the short story was Cheever's form. With a mixture of realism and surrealism, 'The Swimmer' follows Neddy Merrill's quest to return home from a cocktail party by following the series of public and private swimming pools in his affluent neighbourhood. In its representation of all the neighbours he meets, the story is a commentary on the precarious relationship between personal wealth and genuine happiness.

## The Swimmer

It was one of those midsummer Sundays when everyone sits around saying, 'I *drank* too much last night.' You might have heard it whispered by the parishioners leaving church, heard it from the lips of the priest himself, struggling with his cassock in the *vestiarium*, heard it from the golf links and the tennis courts, heard it from the wildlife preserve where the leader of the Audubon group was suffering from a terrible hangover. 'I *drank* too much,' said Donald Westerhazy. 'We all *drank* too much,' said Lucinda Merrill. 'It must have been the wine,' said Helen Westerhazy. 'I *drank* too much of that claret.'

This was at the edge of the Westerhazys' pool. The pool, fed by an artesian well with a high iron content, was a pale shade of green. It was a fine day. In the west there was a massive stand of cumulus cloud so like a city seen from a distance—from the bow of an approaching ship—that it might have had a name. Lisbon. Hackensack. The sun was hot. Neddy Merrill sat by the green water, one hand in it, one around a glass of gin. He was a slender man—he seemed to have the especial slenderness of youth—and while he was far from young he had slid down his banister that morning and given the bronze backside of Aphrodite on the hall table a smack, as he jogged toward the smell of coffee in his dining room. He might have been compared to a summer's day, particularly the last hours of one, and while he lacked a tennis racket or a sail bag the impression was definitely one of youth, sport, and clement weather. He had been swimming and now he was breathing deeply, stertorously as if he could gulp into his lungs the components of that moment, the heat of the sun, the intenseness of his pleasure. It all seemed to flow into his chest. His own house stood in Bullet Park, eight miles to the south, where his four beautiful daughters would have had their lunch and might be playing tennis. Then it occurred to him that by taking a dogleg to the southwest he could reach his home by water.

His life was not confining and the delight he took in this observation could not be explained by its suggestion of escape. He seemed to see, with a cartographer's eye, that string of swimming pools, that quasi-subterranean stream that curved across the county. He had made a discovery, a contribution to modern geography; he would name the stream Lucinda after his wife. He was not a practical joker nor was he a fool but he was determinedly original and had a vague and modest idea of himself as a legendary figure. The day was beautiful and it seemed to him that a long swim might enlarge and celebrate its beauty.

He took off a sweater that was hung over his shoulders and dove in. He had an inexplicable contempt for men who did not hurl themselves into pools. He swam a choppy crawl, breathing either with every stroke or every fourth stroke and counting somewhere well in the back of his mind the one-two one-two of a flutter kick. It was not a serviceable stroke for long distances but the domestication of swimming had saddled the sport with some customs and in his part of the world a crawl was customary. To be embraced and sustained by the light green water was less a pleasure, it seemed, than the resumption of a natural condition, and he would have liked to swim without trunks, but this was not possible, considering his project. He hoisted himself up on the far curb—he never used the ladder—and started across the lawn. When Lucinda asked where he was going he said he was going to swim home.

The only maps and charts he had to go by were remembered or imaginary but these were clear enough. First there were the Grahams, the Hammers, the Lears, the Howlands, and the Crosscups. He would cross Ditmar Street to the Bunkers and come, after a short portage, to the Levys, the Welchers, and the public pool in Lancaster. Then there were the Hallorans, the Sachses, the Biswangers, Shirley Adams, the Gilmartins, and the Clydes. The day was lovely, and that he lived in a world so generously supplied with water seemed like a clemency, a beneficence. His heart was high and he ran across the grass. Making his way home by an uncommon route gave him the feeling that he was a pilgrim, an explorer, a man with a destiny, and he knew that he would find friends all along the way; friends would line the banks of the Lucinda River.

He went through a hedge that separated the Westerhazys' land from the Grahams', walked under some flowering apple trees, passed the shed that housed their pump and filter, and came out at the Grahams' pool. 'Why, Neddy,' Mrs Graham said, 'what a marvellous surprise. I've been trying to get you on the phone all morning. Here, let me get you a drink.' He saw then, like any explorer, that the hospitable customs and traditions of the natives would have to be handled with diplomacy if he was ever going to reach his destination. He did not want to mystify or seem rude to the Grahams nor did he have time to linger there. He swam the length of their pool and joined them in the sun and was rescued, a few minutes later, by the arrival of two carloads of friends from Connecticut. During the uproarious reunions he was able to slip away. He went down by the front of the Grahams' house, stepped over a thorny hedge, and crossed a vacant lot to the Hammers'. Mrs Hammer, looking up from her roses, saw him swim by although she wasn't quite sure who it was. The Lears heard him splashing past the open windows of their living room. The Howlands and the Crosscups were away. After leaving the Howlands' he crossed Ditmar Street and started for the Bunkers', where he could hear, even at that distance, the noise of a party.

The water refracted the sound of voices and laughter and seemed to suspend it in midair. The Bunkers' pool was on a rise and he climbed some stairs to a terrace where twenty-five or thirty men and women were drinking. The only person in the water was Rusty Towers, who floated there on a rubber raft. Oh, how bonny and lush were the banks of the Lucinda River! Prosperous men and women gathered by the sapphire-coloured waters while caterer's men in white coats passed them cold gin. Overhead a red de Havilland trainer was circling around and around and around in the sky with something like the glee of a child in a swing. Ned felt a passing affection for the scene, a tenderness for the gathering, as if it was something he might touch. In the distance he heard thunder. As soon as Enid Bunker saw him she began to scream. 'Oh, look who's here! What a marvellous surprise! When Lucinda said that you couldn't come I thought I'd *die*.' She made her way to him through the crowd, and when they had finished kissing she led him to the bar, a progress that was slowed by the fact that he stopped to kiss eight or ten other women and shake the hands of as many men. A smiling bartender he had seen at a hundred parties gave him a gin and tonic and he stood by the bar for a moment, anxious not to get stuck in any conversation that would delay his voyage. When he seemed about to be surrounded he dove in and swam close to the side to avoid colliding with Rusty's raft. At the far end of the pool he bypassed the Tomlinsons with a broad smile and jogged up the garden path. The gravel cut his feet but this was the only unpleasantness. The party was confined to the pool, and as he went toward the house he heard the brilliant, watery sound of voices fade, heard the noise of a radio from the Bunkers' kitchen, where someone was listening to a ball game. Sunday afternoon. He made his way through the parked cars and down the grassy border of their driveway to Alewives Lane. He did not want to be seen on the road in his bathing trunks but there was no traffic and he made the short distance to the Levys' driveway, marked with a PRIVATE PROPERTY sign and a green tube for the *New York*

*Times.* All the doors and windows of the big house were open but there were no signs of life; not even a dog barked. He went around the side of the house to the pool and saw that the Levys had only recently left. Glasses and bottles and dishes of nuts were on a table at the deep end, where there was a bathhouse or gazebo, hung with Japanese lanterns. After swimming the pool he got himself a glass and poured a drink. It was his fourth or fifth drink and he had swum nearly half the length of the Lucinda River. He felt tired, clean, and pleased at that moment to be alone; pleased with everything.

It would storm. The stand of cumulus cloud—that city—had risen and darkened, and while he sat there he heard the percussiveness of thunder again. The de Havilland trainer was still circling overhead and it seemed to Ned that he could almost hear the pilot laugh with pleasure in the afternoon; but when there was another peal of thunder he took off for home. A train whistle blew and he wondered what time it had gotten to be. Four? Five? He thought of the provincial station at that hour, where a waiter, his tuxedo concealed by a raincoat, a dwarf with some flowers wrapped in newspaper, and a woman who had been crying would be waiting for the local. It was suddenly growing dark; it was that moment when the pinheaded birds seemed to organize their song into some acute and knowledgeable recognition of the storm's approach. Then there was a fine noise of rushing water from the crown of an oak at his back, as if a spigot there had been turned. Then the noise of fountains came from the crowns of all the tall trees. Why did he love storms, what was the meaning of his excitement when the door sprang open and the rain wind fled rudely up the stairs, why had the simple task of shutting the windows of an old house seemed fitting and urgent, why did the first watery notes of a storm wind have for him the unmistakable sound of good news, cheer, glad tidings? Then there was an explosion, a smell of cordite, and rain lashed the Japanese lanterns that Mrs Levy had bought in Kyoto the year before last, or was it the year before that?

He stayed in the Levys' gazebo until the storm had passed. The rain had cooled the air and he shivered. The force of the wind had stripped a maple of its red and yellow leaves and scattered them over the grass and the water. Since it was midsummer the tree must be blighted, and yet he felt a peculiar sadness at this sign of autumn. He braced his shoulders, emptied his glass, and started for the Welchers' pool. This meant crossing the Lindleys' riding ring and he was surprised to find it overgrown with grass and all the jumps dismantled. He wondered if the Lindleys had sold their horses or gone away for the summer and put them out to board. He seemed to remember having heard something about the Lindleys and their horses but the memory was unclear. On he went, barefoot through the wet grass, to the Welchers', where he found their pool was dry.

This breach in his chain of water disappointed him absurdly, and he felt like some explorer who seeks a torrential headwater and finds a dead stream. He was disappointed and mystified. It was common enough to go away for the summer but no one ever drained his pool. The Welchers had definitely gone away. The pool furniture was folded, stacked, and covered with a tarpaulin. The bathhouse was locked. All the windows of the house were shut, and when he went around to the driveway in front he saw a FOR SALE sign nailed to a tree. When had he last heard from the Welchers—when, that is, had he and Lucinda last regretted an invitation to dine with them? It seemed only a week or so ago. Was his memory failing or had he so disciplined it in the repression of unpleasant facts that he had damaged his sense of truth? Then in the distance he heard the sound of a tennis game. This cheered him, cleared away all his apprehensions and let him regard the overcast sky and the cold air with indifference. This was the day that Neddy Merrill swam across the country. That was the day! He started off then for his most difficult portage.

Had you gone for a Sunday afternoon ride that day you might have seen him, close to naked, standing on the shoulders of Route 424, waiting for a chance to cross. You might have wondered if he was the victim of foul play, had his car broken down, or was he merely a fool. Standing barefoot in the deposits of the highway—beer cans, rags, and blowout patches—exposed to all kinds of ridicule, he seemed pitiful. He had known when he started that this was a part of his journey—it had been on his maps—but confronted with the lines of traffic, worming through the summery light, he found himself unprepared. He was laughed at, jeered at, a beer can was thrown at him, and he had no dignity or humour to bring to the situation. He could have gone back, back to the Westerhazys', where Lucinda would still be sitting in the sun. He had signed nothing, vowed nothing, pledged nothing, not even to himself. Why, believing as he did, that all human obduracy was susceptible to common sense, was he unable to turn back? Why was he determined to complete his journey even if it meant putting his life in danger? At what point had this prank, this joke, this piece of horseplay become serious? He could not go back, he could not even recall with any clearness the green water at the Westerhazys', the sense of inhaling the day's components, the friendly and relaxed voices saying that they had *drunk* too much. In the space of an hour, more or less, he had covered a distance that made his return impossible.

An old man, tooling down the highway at fifteen miles an hour, let him get to the middle of the road, where there was a grass divider. Here he was exposed to the ridicule of the northbound traffic, but after ten or fifteen minutes he was able to cross. From here he had only a short walk to the Recreation Centre at the edge of the village of Lancaster, where there were some handball courts and a public pool.

The effect of the water on voices, the illusion of brilliance and suspense, was the same here as it has been at the Bunkers' but the sounds here were louder, harsher, and more shrill, and as soon as he entered the crowded enclosure he was confronted with regimentation. 'ALL SWIMMERS MUST TAKE A SHOWER BEFORE USING THE POOL. ALL SWIMMERS MUST USE THE FOOTBATH. ALL SWIMMERS MUST WEAR THEIR IDENTIFICATION DISCS.' He took a shower, washed his feet in a cloudy and bitter solution, and made his way to the edge of the water. It stank of chlorine and looked to him like a sink. A pair of lifeguards in a pair of towers blew police whistles at what seemed to be regular intervals and abused the swimmers through a public address system. Neddy remembered the sapphire water at the Bunkers' with longing and thought that he might contaminate himself—damage his own prosperousness and charm—by swimming in this murk, but he reminded himself that he was an explorer, a pilgrim, and that this was merely a stagnant bend in the Lucinda River. He dove, scowling with distaste, into the chlorine and had to swim with his head above water to avoid collisions, but even so he was bumped into, splashed, and jostled. When he got to the shallow end both lifeguards were shouting at him: 'Hey, you, you without the identification disc, get outa the water.' He did, but they had no way of pursuing him and he went through the reek of suntan oil and chlorine out through the hurricane fence and passed the handball courts. By crossing the road he entered the wooded part of the Halloran estate. The woods were not cleared and the footing was treacherous and difficult until he reached the lawn and the clipped beech hedge that encircled their pool.

The Hallorans were friends, an elderly couple of enormous wealth who seemed to bask in the suspicion that they might be Communists. They were zealous reformers but they were not Communists, and yet when they were accused, as they sometimes were, of subversion, it seemed to gratify and excite them. Their beech hedge was yellow and he guessed this had been blighted like the Levys' maple. He called hullo, hullo, to warn the Hallorans of his approach, to palliate his invasion of their privacy. The Hallorans, for reasons that had never been explained to him, did not wear bathing suits. No explanations were in order, really. Their nakedness was a detail in their uncompromising zeal to reform and he stepped politely out of his trunks before he went through the opening in the hedge.

Mrs Halloran, a stout woman with white hair and a serene face, was reading the *Times*. Mr Halloran was taking beech leaves out of the water with a scoop. They seemed not surprised or displeased to see him. Their pool was perhaps the oldest in the country, a fieldstone rectangle, fed by a brook. It had no filter or pump and its waters were the opaque gold of the stream.

'I'm swimming across the county,' Ned said.

'Why, I didn't know one could,' exclaimed Mrs Halloran.

'Well, I've made it from the Westerhazys',' Ned said. 'That must be about four miles.'

He left his trunks at the deep end, walked to the shallow end, and swam this stretch. As he was pulling himself out of the water he heard Mrs Halloran say, 'We've been *terribly* sorry to hear about all your misfortunes, Neddy.'

'My misfortunes?' Ned asked. 'I don't know what you mean.'

'Why, we heard that you'd sold the house and that your poor children . . .'

'I don't recall having sold the house,' Ned said, 'and the girls are at home.'

'Yes,' Mrs Halloran sighed. 'Yes . . .' Her voice filled the air with an unseasonable melancholy and Ned spoke briskly. 'Thank you for the swim.'

'Well, have a nice trip,' said Mrs Halloran.

Beyond the hedge he pulled on his trunks and fastened them. They were loose and he wondered if, during the space of an afternoon, he could have lost some weight. He was cold and he was tired and the naked Hallorans and their dark water had depressed him. The swim was too much for his strength but how could he have guessed this, sliding down the banister that morning and sitting in the Westerhazys' sun? His arms were lame. His legs felt rubbery and ached at the joints. The worst of it was the cold in his bones and the feeling that he might never be warm again. Leaves were falling down around him and he smelled wood smoke on the wind. Who would be burning wood at this time of year?

He needed a drink. Whiskey would warm him, pick him up, carry him through the last of his journey, refresh his feeling that it was original and valorous to swim across the county. Channel swimmers took brandy. He needed a stimulant. He crossed the lawn in front of the Hallorans' house and went down a little path to where they had built a house for their only daughter, Helen, and her husband, Eric Sachs. The Sachses' pool was small and he found Helen and her husband there.

'Oh, *Neddy*,' Helen said. 'Did you lunch at Mother's?'

'Not *really*,' Ned said. 'I *did* stop to see your parents.' This seemed to be explanation enough. 'I'm terribly sorry to break in on you like this but I've taken a chill and I wonder if you'd give me a drink.'

'Why, I'd *love* to,' Helen said, 'but there hasn't been anything in this house to drink since Eric's operation. That was three years ago.'

Was he losing his memory, had his gift for concealing painful facts let him forget that he had sold his house, that his children were in trouble, and that his friend had been ill? His eyes slipped from Eric's face to his abdomen, where he saw three pale, sutured scars, two of them at least a foot long. Gone was his navel, and what, Neddy thought, would the roving hand, bed-checking one's gifts at 3 a.m., make of a belly with no navel, no link to birth, this breach in the succession?

'I'm sure you can get a drink at the Biswangers',' Helen said. 'They're having an enormous do. You can hear it from here. Listen!'

She raised her head and from across the road, the lawns, the gardens, the woods, the fields, he heard again the brilliant noise of voices over water. 'Well, I'll get wet,' he said, still feeling that he had no freedom of choice about his means of travel. He dove into the Sachses' cold water and, gasping, close to drowning, made his way from one end of the pool to the other. 'Lucinda and I want *terribly* to see you,' he said over his shoulder, his face set toward the Biswangers'. 'We're sorry it's been so long and we'll call you *very* soon.'

He crossed some fields to the Biswangers' and the sounds of revelry there. They would be honoured to give him a drink, they would be happy to give him a drink. The Biswangers invited him and Lucinda for dinner four times a year, six weeks in advance. They were always rebuffed and yet they continued to send out their invitations, unwilling to comprehend the rigid and undemocratic realities of their society. They were the sort of people who discussed the price of things at cocktails, exchanged market tips during dinner, and after dinner told dirty stories to mixed company. They did not belong to Neddy's set—they were not even on Lucinda's Christmas card list. He went toward the pool with feelings of indifference, charity, and some unease, since it seemed to be getting dark and these were the longest days of the year. The party when he joined it was noisy and large. Grace Biswanger was the kind of hostess who asked the optometrist, the veterinarian, the real-estate dealer, and the dentist. No one was swimming and the twilight, reflected on the water of the pool, had a wintry gleam. There was a bar and he started for this. When Grace Biswanger saw him she came toward him, not affectionately as he had every right to expect, but bellicosely.

'Why, this party has everything,' she said loudly, 'including a gate crasher.'

She could not deal him a social blow—there was no question about this and he did not flinch. 'As a gate crasher,' he asked politely, 'do I rate a drink?'

'Suit yourself,' she said. 'You don't seem to pay much attention to invitations.'

She turned her back on him and joined some guests, and he went to the bar and ordered a whiskey. The bartender served him but he served him rudely. His was a world in which the caterer's men kept the social score, and to be rebuffed by a part-time barkeep meant that he had suffered some loss of social esteem. Or perhaps the man was new and uninformed. Then he heard Grace at his back say: 'They went for broke overnight—nothing but income—and he showed up drunk one Sunday and asked us to loan him five thousand dollars. . . .' She was always talking about money. It was worse then eating your peas off a knife. He dove into the pool, swam its length and went away.

The next pool on his list, the last but two, belonged to his old mistress, Shirley Adams. If he had suffered any injuries at the Biswangers' they would be cured here. Love—sexual roughhouse in fact—was the supreme elixir, the pain killer, the brightly coloured pill that would put the spring back into his step, the joy of life in his heart. They had had an affair last week, last month, last year. He couldn't remember. It was he who had broken it off, his was the upper hand, and he stepped through the gate of the wall that surrounded her pool with nothing so considered as self-confidence. It seemed in a way to be his pool, as the lover, particularly the illicit lover, enjoys the possessions of his mistress with an authority unknown to holy matrimony. She was there, her hair the colour of brass, but her figure, at the edge of the lighted, cerulean water, excited in him no profound memories. It had been, he thought, a lighthearted affair, although she had wept when he broke it off. She seemed confused to see him and he wondered if she was still wounded. Would she, God forbid, weep again?

'What do you want?' she asked.

'I'm swimming across the county.'

'Good Christ. Will you ever grow up?'

'What's the matter?'

'If you've come here for money,' she said, 'I won't give you another cent.'

'You could give me a drink.'

'I could but I won't. I'm not alone.'

'Well, I'm on my way.'

He dove in and swam the pool, but when he tried to haul himself up onto the curb he found that the strength in his arms and shoulders had gone, and he paddled to the ladder and climbed out. Looking over his shoulder he saw, in the lighted bathhouse, a young man. Going out onto the dark lawn he smelled chrysanthemums or marigolds—some stubborn autumnal fragrance—on the night air, strong as gas. Looking overhead he saw that the stars had come out, but why should he seem to see Andromeda, Cepheus, and Cassiopeia? What had become of the constellations of midsummer? He began to cry.

It was probably the first time in his adult life that he had ever cried, certainly the first time in his life that he had ever felt so miserable, cold, tired, and bewildered. He could not understand the rudeness of the caterer's barkeep or the rudeness of a mistress who had come to him on her knees and showered his trousers with tears. He had swum too long, he had been immersed too long, and his nose and his throat were sore from the water. What he needed then was a drink, some company, and some clean, dry clothes, and while he could have cut directly across the road to his home he went on to the Gilmartins' pool. Here, for the first time in his life, he did not dive but went down the steps into the icy water and swam a hobbled side-stroke that he might have learned as a youth. He staggered with fatigue on his way to the Clydes' and paddled the length of their pool, stopping again and again with his hand on the curb to rest. He climbed up the ladder and wondered if he had the strength to get home. He had done what he wanted, he had swum the county, but he was so stupefied with exhaustion that his triumph seemed vague. Stooped, holding on to the gateposts for support, he turned up the driveway of his own house.

The place was dark. Was it so late that they had all gone to bed? Had Lucinda stayed at the Westerhazys' for supper? Had the girls joined her there or gone someplace else? Hadn't they agreed, as they usually did on Sunday, to regret all their invitations and stay at home? He tried the garage doors to see what cars were in but the doors were locked and rust came off the handles onto his hands. Going toward the house, he saw that the force of the thunderstorm had knocked one of the rain gutters loose. It hung down over the front door like an umbrella rib, but it could be fixed in the morning. The house was locked, and he thought that the stupid cook or the stupid maid must have locked the place up until he remembered that it had been some time since they had employed a maid or a cook. He shouted, pounded on the door, tried to force it with his shoulder, and then, looking in at the windows, saw that the place was empty.

1964

# Bernard Malamud

## 1914–1986

A city boy, the son of Russian Jewish immigrants, Bernard Malamud was born and raised in Brooklyn, New York. He went to City College for his BA and Columbia University for his MA, then taught night school for almost 10 years before taking a job at Oregon State University. His experiences in Oregon from 1949 to 1961 became the basis for his novel *A New Life* (1961). From 1961 he taught at Bennington College in Vermont. Among his most admired works are the novels *The Assistant* (1957) and *The Fixer* (1966) and the stories in *The Magic Barrel* (1958). A leader of the post–Second World War Jewish literary renaissance, Malamud introduced into American fiction Jewish immigrants and their urban locales, thus helping to ensure that marginal ethnic figures would become part of mainstream American fiction. In 'The Magic Barrel', Leo Finkle, a rabbinical student, learns the fundamental importance of his own humanity.

# The Magic Barrel

Not long ago there lived in uptown New York, in a small, almost meagre room, though crowded with books, Leo Finkle, a rabbinical student in the Yeshivah University. Finkle, after six years of study, was to be ordained in June and had been advised by an acquaintance that he might find it easier to win himself a congregation if he were married. Since he had no present prospects of marriage, after two tormented days of turning it over in his mind, he called in Pinye Salzman, a marriage broker whose two-line advertisement he had read in the *Forward*.

The matchmaker appeared one night out of the dark fourth-floor hallway of the greystone rooming house where Finkle lived, grasping a black, strapped portfolio that had been worn thin with use. Salzman, who had been long in the business, was of slight but dignified build, wearing an old hat, and an overcoat too short and tight for him. He smelled frankly of fish, which he loved to eat, and although he was missing a few teeth, his presence was not displeasing, because of an amiable manner curiously contrasted with mournful eyes. His voice, his lips, his wisp of beard, his bony fingers were animated, but give him a moment of repose and his mild blue eyes revealed a depth of sadness, a characteristic that put Leo a little at ease although the situation, for him, was inherently tense.

He at once informed Salzman why he had asked him to come, explaining that his home was in Cleveland, and that but for his parents, who had married comparatively late in life, he was alone in the world. He had for six years devoted himself almost entirely to his studies, as a result of which, understandably, he had found himself without time for a social life and the company of young women. Therefore he thought it the better part of trial and error—of embarrassing fumbling—to call in an experienced person to advise him on these matters. He remarked in passing that the function of the marriage broker was ancient and honourable, highly approved in the Jewish community, because it made practical the necessary without hindering joy. Moreover, his own parents had been brought together by a matchmaker. They had made, if not a financially profitable marriage—since neither had possessed any worldly goods to speak of—at least a successful one in the sense of their everlasting devotion to each other. Salzman listened in embarrassed surprise, sensing a sort of apology. Later, however, he experienced a glow of pride in his work, an emotion that had left him years ago, and he heartily approved of Finkle.

The two went to their business. Leo had led Salzman to the only clear place in the room, a table near a window that overlooked the lamp-lit city. He seated himself at the matchmaker's side but facing him, attempting by an act of will to suppress the unpleasant tickle in his throat. Salzman eagerly unstrapped his portfolio and removed a loose rubber band from a thin packet of much-handled cards. As he flipped through them, a gesture and sound that physically hurt Leo, the student pretended not to see and gazed steadfastly out the window. Although it was still February, winter was on its last legs, signs of which he had for the first time in years begun to notice. He now observed the round white moon, moving high in the sky through a cloud menagerie, and watched with half-open mouth as it penetrated a huge hen, and dropped out of her like an egg laying itself. Salzman, though pretending through eyeglasses he had just slipped on to be engaged in scanning the writing on the cards, stole occasional glances at the young man's distinguished face, noting with pleasure the long, severe scholar's nose, brown eyes heavy with learning, sensitive yet ascetic lips, and a certain, almost hollow quality of the dark cheeks. He gazed around at shelves upon shelves of books and let out a soft, contented sigh.

When Leo's eyes fell upon the cards, he counted six spread out in Salzman's hand.

'So few?' he asked in disappointment.

'You wouldn't believe me how much cards I got in my office,' Salzman replied. 'The drawers are already filled to the top, so I keep them now in a barrel, but is every girl good for a new rabbi?'

Leo blushed at this, regretting all he had revealed of himself in a curriculum vitae he had sent to Salzman. He had thought it best to acquaint him with his strict standards and specifications, but in having done so, felt he had told the marriage broker more than was absolutely necessary.

He hesitantly inquired, 'Do you keep photographs of your clients on file?'

'First comes family, amount of dowry, also what kind promises,' Salzman replied, unbuttoning his tight coat and settling himself in the chair. 'After comes pictures, rabbi.'

'Call me Mr Finkle. I'm not yet a rabbi.'

Salzman said he would, but instead called him doctor, which he changed to rabbi when Leo was not listening too attentively.

Salzman adjusted his horn-rimmed spectacles, gently cleared his throat, and read in an eager voice the contents of the top card:

'Sophie P. Twenty-four years. Widow one year. No children. Educated high school and two years college. Father promises eight thousand dollars. Has wonderful wholesale business. Also real estate. On the mother's side comes teachers, also one actor. Well known on Second Avenue.'

Leo gazed up in surprise. 'Did you say a widow?'

'A widow don't mean spoiled, rabbi. She lived with her husband maybe four months. He was a sick boy she made a mistake to marry him.'

'Marrying a widow has never entered my mind.'

'This is because you have no experience. A widow, especially if she is young and healthy like this girl, is a wonderful person to marry. She will be thankful to you the rest of her life. Believe me, if I was looking now for a bride, I would marry a widow.'

Leo reflected, then shook his head.

Salzman hunched his shoulders in an almost imperceptible gesture of disappointment. He placed the card down on the wooden table and began to read another.

'Lily H. High-school teacher. Regular. Not a substitute. Has savings and new Dodge car. Lived in Paris one year. Father is successful dentist thirty-five years. Interested in a professional man. Well Americanized family. Wonderful opportunity.

'I knew her personally,' said Salzman. 'I wish you could see this girl. She is a doll. Also very intelligent. All day you could talk to her about books and theyater and what not. She also knows current events.'

'I don't believe you mentioned her age?'

'Her age?' Salzman said, raising his brow. 'Her age is thirty-two years.'

Leo said after a while, 'I'm afraid that seems a little too old.'

Salzman let out a laugh. 'So how old are you, rabbi?'

'Twenty-seven.'

'So what is the difference, tell me, between twenty-seven and thirty-two? My own wife is seven years older than me. So what did I suffer?—Nothing. If Rothschild's daughter wants to marry you, would you say on account her age, no?'

'Yes,' Leo said dryly.

Salzman shook off the no in the yes. 'Five years don't mean a thing. I give you my word that when you will live with her for one week you will forget her age. What does it mean five years—that she lived more and knows more than somebody who is younger? On this girl, God bless her, years are not wasted. Each one that it comes makes better the bargain.'

'What subject does she teach in high school?'

'Languages. If you heard the way she speaks French, you will think it is music. I am in the business twenty-five years, and I recommend her with my whole heart. Believe me, I know what I'm talking, rabbi.'

'What's on the next card?' Leo said abruptly.

Salzman reluctantly turned up the third card:

'Ruth K. Nineteen years. Honour student. Father offers thirteen thousand cash to the right bridegroom. He is a medical doctor. Stomach specialist with marvellous practice. Brother-in-law owns own garment business. Particular people.'

Salzman looked as if he had read his trump card.

'Did you say nineteen?' Leo asked with interest.

'On the dot.'

'Is she attractive?' He blushed. 'Pretty?'

Salzman kissed his finger tips. 'A little doll. On this I give you my word. Let me call the father tonight and you will see what means pretty.'

But Leo was troubled. 'You're sure she's that young?'

'This I am positive. The father will show you the birth certificate.'

'Are you positive there isn't something wrong with her?' Leo insisted.

'Who says there is wrong?'

'I don't understand why an American girl her age should go to a marriage broker.'

A smile spread over Salzman's face.

'So for the same reason you went, she comes.'

Leo flushed. 'I am pressed for time.'

Salzman, realizing he had been tactless, quickly explained. 'The father came, not her. He wants she should have the best, so he looks around himself. When we will locate the right boy he will introduce him and encourage. This makes a better marriage than if a young girl without experience takes for herself. I don't have to tell you this.'

'But don't you think this young girl believes in love?' Leo spoke uneasily.

Salzman was about to guffaw but caught himself and said soberly, 'Love comes with the right person, not before.'

Leo parted dry lips but did not speak. Noticing that Salzman had snatched a glance at the next card, he cleverly asked, 'How is her health?'

'Perfect,' Salzman said, breathing with difficulty. 'Of course, she is a little lame on her right foot from an auto accident that it happened to her when she was twelve years, but nobody notices on account she is so brilliant and also beautiful.'

Leo got up heavily and went to the window. He felt curiously bitter and upbraided himself for having called in the marriage broker. Finally, he shook his head.

'Why not?' Salzman persisted, the pitch of his voice rising.

'Because I detest stomach specialists.'

'So what do you care what is his business? After you marry her do you need him? Who says he must come every Friday night in your house?'

Ashamed of the way the talk was going, Leo dismissed Salzman, who went home with heavy, melancholy eyes.

Though he had felt only relief at the marriage broker's departure, Leo was in low spirits the next day. He explained it as arising from Salzman's failure to produce a suitable bride for him. He did not care for his type of clientele. But when Leo found himself hesitating whether to seek out another matchmaker, one more polished than Pinye, he wondered if it could be—his protestations to the contrary, and although he honoured his father and mother—that he did not, in essence, care for the matchmaking institution? This thought he quickly put out of his mind yet found himself still upset. All day he ran around in the woods—missed an important appointment, forgot to give out his laundry, walked out of a Broadway cafeteria without paying and had to run back with the ticket in his hand; had even not recognized his landlady in the street when she passed with a friend and courteously called out, 'A good evening to you, Doctor Finkle.' By nightfall, however, he had regained sufficient calm to sink his nose into a book and there found peace from his thoughts.

Almost at once there came a knock on the door. Before Leo could say enter, Salzman, commercial cupid, was standing in the room. His face was grey and meagre, his expression hungry, and he looked as if he would expire on his feet. Yet the marriage broker managed, by some trick of the muscles, to display a broad smile.

'So good evening. I am invited?'

Leo nodded, disturbed to see him again, yet unwilling to ask the man to leave.

Beaming still, Salzman laid his portfolio on the table. 'Rabbi, I got for you tonight good news.'

'I've asked you not to call me rabbi. I'm still a student.'

'Your worries are finished. I have for you a first-class bride.'

'Leave me in peace concerning this subject.' Leo pretended lack of interest.

'The world will dance at your wedding.'

'Please, Mr Salzman, no more.'

'But first must come back my strength,' Salzman said weakly. He fumbled with the portfolio straps and took out of the leather case an oily paper bag, from which he extracted a hard, seeded roll and a small, smoked white fish. With a quick motion of his hand he stripped the fish out of its skin and began ravenously to chew. 'All day in a rush,' he muttered.

Leo watched him eat.

'A sliced tomato you have maybe?' Salzman hesitantly inquired.

'No.'

The marriage broker shut his eyes and ate. When he had finished he carefully cleaned up the crumbs and rolled up the remains of the fish, in the paper bag. His spectacled eyes roamed the room until he discovered, amid some piles of books, a one-burner gas stove. Lifting his hat he humbly asked, 'A glass tea you got, rabbi?'

Conscience-stricken, Leo rose and brewed the tea. He served it with a chunk of lemon and two cubes of lump sugar, delighting Salzman.

After he had drunk his tea, Salzman's strength and good spirits were restored.

'So tell me, rabbi,' he said amiably, 'you considered some more the three clients I mentioned yesterday?'

'There was no need to consider.'

'Why not?'

'None of them suits me.'

'What then suits you?'

Leo let it pass because he could give only a confused answer.

Without waiting for a reply, Salzman asked, 'You remember this girl I talked to you—the high school teacher?'

'Age thirty-two?'

But, surprisingly, Salzman's face lit in a smile. 'Age twenty-nine.'

Leo shot him a look. 'Reduced from thirty-two?'

'A mistake,' Salzman avowed. 'I talked today with the dentist. He took me to his safety deposit box and showed me the birth certificate. She was twenty-nine years last August. They made her a party in the mountains where she went for her vacation. When her father spoke to me the first time I forgot to write the age and I told you thirty-two, but now I remember this was a different client, a widow.'

'The same one you told me about? I thought she was twenty-four?'

'A different. Am I responsible that the world is filled with widows?'

'No, but I'm not interested in them, nor for that matter, in school teachers.'

Salzman pulled his clasped hands to his breast. Looking at the ceiling he devoutly exclaimed, 'Yiddishe kinder, what can I say to somebody that he is not interested in high-school teachers? So what then you are interested?'

Leo flushed but controlled himself.

'In what else will you be interested,' Salzman went on, 'if you not interested in this fine girl that she speaks four languages and has personally in the bank ten thousand dollars? Also her father guarantees further twelve thousand. Also she has a new car, wonderful clothes, talks on all subjects, and she will give you a first-class home and children. How near do we come in our life to paradise?'

'If she's so wonderful, why wasn't she married ten years ago?'

'Why?' said Salzman with a heavy laugh. '—Why? Because she is *partikiler.* This is why. She wants the *best.*'

Leo was silent, amused at how he had entangled himself. But Salzman had aroused his interest in Lily H., and he began seriously to consider calling on her. When the marriage broker observed how intently Leo's mind was at work on the facts he had supplied, he felt certain they would soon come to an agreement.

Late Saturday afternoon, conscious of Salzman, Leo Finkle walked with Lily Hirschorn along Riverside Drive. He walked briskly and erectly, wearing with distinction the black fedora he had that morning taken with trepidation out of the dusty hat box on his closet shelf, and the heavy black Saturday coat he had thoroughly whisked clean. Leo also owned a walking stick, a present from a distant relative, but quickly put temptation aside and did not use it. Lily, petite and not unpretty, had on something signifying the approach of spring. She was au courant, animatedly, with all sorts of subjects, and he weighed her words and found her surprisingly sound—score another for Salzman, whom he uneasily sensed to be somewhere around, hiding perhaps high in a tree along the street, flashing the lady signals with a pocket mirror; or perhaps a cloven-hoofed Pan, piping nuptial ditties as he danced his invisible way before them, strewing wild buds on the walk and purple grapes in their path, symbolizing fruit of a union, though there was of course still none.

Lily startled Leo by remarking, 'I was thinking of Mr Salzman, a curious figure, wouldn't you say?'

Not certain what to answer, he nodded.

She bravely went on, blushing, 'I for one am grateful for his introducing us. Aren't you?'

He courteously replied, 'I am.'

'I mean,' she said with a little laugh—and it was all in good taste, or at least gave the effect of being not in bad—'do you mind that we came together so?'

He was not displeased with her honesty, recognizing that she meant to set the relationship aright, and understanding that it took a certain amount of experience in life, and courage, to want to do it quite that way. One had to have some sort of past to make that kind of beginning.

He said that he did not mind. Salzman's function was traditional and honourable—valuable for what it might achieve, which, he pointed out, was frequently nothing.

Lily agreed with a sigh. They walked on for a while and she said after a long silence, again with a nervous laugh, 'Would you mind if I asked you something a little bit personal? Frankly, I find the subject fascinating.' Although Leo shrugged, she went on half embarrassedly, 'How was it that you came to your calling? I mean was it a sudden passionate inspiration?'

Leo after a time, slowly replied, 'I was always interested in the Law.'

'You saw revealed in it the presence of the Highest?'

He nodded and changed the subject. 'I understand that you spent a little time in Paris, Miss Hirschorn?'

'Oh, did Mr Salzman tell you, Rabbi Finkle?' Leo winced but she went on, 'It was ages ago and almost forgotten. I remember I had to return for my sister's wedding.'

And Lily would not be put off. 'When', she asked in a trembly voice, 'did you become enamoured of God?'

He stared at her. Then it came to him that she was talking not about Leo Finkle, but of a total stranger, some mystical figure, perhaps even passionate prophet that Salzman had dreamed up for her—no relation to the living or dead. Leo trembled with rage and weakness. The trickster had obviously sold her a bill of goods, just as he had him, who'd expected to become acquainted with a young lady of twenty-nine, only to behold, the moment he laid eyes upon her strained and anxious face, a woman past thirty-five and aging rapidly. Only his self-control had kept him this long in her presence.

'I am not', he said gravely, 'a talented religious person,' and in seeking words to go on, found himself possessed by shame and fear. 'I think', he said in a strained manner, 'that I came to God not because I loved Him, but because I did not.'

This confession he spoke harshly because its unexpectedness shook him.

Lily wilted. Leo saw a profusion of loaves of bread go flying like ducks high over his head, not unlike the winged loaves by which he had counted himself to sleep last night. Mercifully, then, it snowed, which he would not put past Salzman's machinations.

He was infuriated with the marriage broker and swore he would throw him out of the room the minute he reappeared. But Salzman did not come that night, and when Leo's anger had subsided, an unaccountable despair grew in its place. At first he thought this was caused by his disappointment in Lily, but before long it became evident that he had involved himself with Salzman without a true knowledge of his own intent. He gradually realized—with an emptiness that seized him with six hands—that he had called in the broker to find him a bride because he was incapable of doing it himself. This terrifying insight he had derived as a result of his meeting and conversation with Lily Hirschorn. Her probing questions had somehow irritated him into revealing—to himself more than her—the true nature of his relationship to God, and from that it had come upon him, with shocking force, that apart from his parents, he had never loved anyone. Or perhaps it went the other way, that he did not love God so well as he might, because he had not loved man. It seemed to Leo that his whole life stood starkly revealed and he saw himself for the first time as he truly was—unloved and loveless. This bitter but somehow not fully unexpected revelation brought him to a point of panic, controlled only by extraordinary effort. He covered his face with his hands and cried.

The week that followed was the worst of his life. He did not eat and lost weight. His beard darkened and grew ragged. He stopped attending seminars and almost never opened a book. He seriously considered leaving the Yeshivah, although he was deeply troubled at the thought of the loss of all his years of study—saw them like pages torn from a book, strewn over the city—and at the devastating effect of this decision upon his parents. But he had lived without knowledge of himself, and never in the Five Books and all the Commentaries—mea culpa—had the truth been revealed to him. He did not know where to turn, and in all this desolating loneliness there was no *to whom*, although he often thought of Lily but not once could bring himself to go downstairs and make the call. He became touchy and irritable, especially with his landlady, who asked him all manner of personal questions; on the other hand, sensing his own disagreeableness, he waylaid her on the stairs and apologized abjectly, until mortified, she ran from him.

Out of this, however, he drew the consolation that he was a Jew and that a Jew suffered. But gradually, as the long and terrible week drew to a close, he regained his composure and some idea of purpose in life: to go on as planned. Although he was imperfect, the ideal was not. As for his quest of a bride, the thought of continuing afflicted him with anxiety and heartburn, yet perhaps with this new knowledge of himself he would be more successful than in the past. Perhaps love would now come to him and a bride to that love. And for this sanctified seeking who needed a Salzman?

The marriage broker, a skeleton with haunted eyes, returned that very night. He looked, withal, the picture of frustrated expectancy—as if he had steadfastly waited the week at Miss Lily Hirschorn's side for a telephone call that never came.

Casually coughing, Salzman came immediately to the point: 'So how did you like her?'

Leo's anger rose and he could not refrain from chiding the matchmaker: 'Why did you lie to me, Salzman?'

Salzman's pale face went dead white, the world had snowed on him.

'Did you not state that she was twenty-nine?' Leo insisted.

'I give you my word—'

'She was thirty-five, if a day. At *least* thirty-five.'

'Of this don't be too sure. Her father told me—'

'Never mind. The worst of it was that you lied to her.'

'How did I lie to her, tell me?'

'You told her things about me that weren't true. You made me out to be more, consequently less than I am. She had in mind a totally different person, a sort of semi-mystical Wonder Rabbi.'

'All I said, you was a religious man.'

'I can imagine.'

Salzman sighed. 'This is my weakness that I have,' he confessed. 'My wife says to me I shouldn't be a salesman, but when I have two fine people that they would be wonderful to be married, I am so happy that I talk too much.' He smiled wanly. 'This is why Salzman is a poor man.'

Leo's anger left him. 'Well, Salzman, I'm afraid that's all.'

The marriage broker fastened hungry eyes on him.

'You don't want any more a bride?'

'I do,' said Leo, 'but I have decided to seek her in a different way. I am no longer interested in an arranged marriage. To be frank, I now admit the necessity of premarital love. That is, I want to be in love with the one I marry.'

'Love?' said Salzman, astounded. After a moment he remarked, 'For us, our love is our life, not for the ladies. In the ghetto they—'

'I know, I know,' said Leo. 'I've thought of it often. Love, I have said to myself, should be a by-product of living and worship rather than its own end. Yet for myself I find it necessary to establish the level of my need and fulfill it.'

Salzman shrugged but answered, 'Listen, rabbi, if you want love, this I can find for you also. I have such beautiful clients that you will love them the minute your eyes will see them.'

Leo smiled unhappily. 'I'm afraid you don't understand.'

But Salzman hastily unstrapped his portfolio and withdrew a manila packet from it.

'Pictures,' he said, quickly laying the envelope on the table.

Leo called after him to take the pictures away, but as if on the wings of the wind, Salzman had disappeared.

March came. Leo had returned to his regular routine. Although he felt not quite himself yet—lacked energy—he was making plans for a more active social life. Of course it would cost something, but he was an expert in cutting corners; and when there were no corners left he would make circles rounder. All the while Salzman's pictures had lain on the table, gathering dust. Occasionally as Leo sat studying, or enjoying a cup of tea, his eyes fell on the manila envelope, but he never opened it.

The days went by and no social life to speak of developed with a member of the opposite sex—it was difficult, given the circumstances of his situation. One morning Leo toiled up the stairs to his room and stared out the window at the city. Although the day was bright his view of it was dark. For some time he watched the people in the street below hurrying along and then turned with a heavy heart to his little room. On the table was the packet. With a sudden relentless gesture he tore it open. For a half-hour he stood by the table in a state of excitement, examining the photographs of the ladies Salzman had included. Finally, with a deep sigh he put them down. There were six, of varying degrees of attractiveness, but look at them long enough and they all became Lily Hirschorn: all past their prime, all starved behind bright smiles, not a true personality in the lot. Life, despite their frantic yoohooings, had passed them by; they were pictures in a brief case that stank of fish. After a while, however, as Leo attempted to return the photographs into the envelope, he found in it another, a snapshot of the type taken by a machine for a quarter. He gazed at it a moment and let out a cry.

Her face moved him. Why, he could at first not say. It gave him the impression of youth—spring flowers, yet age—a sense of having been used to the bone, wasted; this came from the eyes, which were hauntingly familiar, yet absolutely strange. He had a vivid impression that he had met her before, but try as he might he could not place her although he could almost recall her name, as if he had read it in her own handwriting. No, this couldn't be; he would have remembered her. It was not, he affirmed, that she had an extraordinary beauty—no, though her face was attractive enough; it was that *something* about her moved him. Feature for feature, even some of the ladies of the photographs could do better; but she leaped forth to his heart—had *lived*, or wanted to—more than just wanted, perhaps regretted how she had lived—had somehow deeply suffered: it could be seen in the depths of those reluctant eyes, and from the way the light enclosed and shone from her, and within her, opening realms of possibility: this was her own. Her he desired. His head ached and eyes narrowed with the intensity of his gazing, then as if an obscure fog had blown up in the mind, he experienced fear of her and was aware that he had received an impression, somehow, of evil. He shuddered, saying softly, it is thus with us all. Leo brewed some tea in a small pot and sat sipping it without sugar, to calm himself. But before he had finished drinking, again with excitement he examined the face and found it good: good for Leo Finkle. Only such a one could understand him and help him seek whatever he was seeking. She might, perhaps, love him. How she had happened to be among the discards in Salzman's barrel he could never guess, but he knew he must urgently go find her.

Leo rushed downstairs, grabbed up the Bronx telephone book, and searched for Salzman's home address. He was not listed, nor was his office. Neither was he in the Manhattan book. But Leo remembered having written down the address on a slip of paper after he had read Salzman's advertisement in the 'personals' column of the *Forward.* He ran up to his room and tore through his papers, without luck. It was exasperating. Just when he needed the matchmaker he was nowhere to be found. Fortunately Leo remembered to look in his wallet. There on a card he found his name written and a Bronx address. No phone number was listed, the reason—Leo now recalled—he had originally communicated with Salzman by letter. He got on his coat, put a hat on over his skull cap and hurried to the subway station. All the way to the far end of the Bronx he sat on the edge of his seat. He was more than once tempted to take out the picture and see if the girl's face was as he remembered it, but he refrained, allowing the snapshot to remain in his inside coat pocket, content to have her so close. When the train pulled into the station he was waiting at the door and bolted out. He quickly located the street Salzman had advertised.

The building he sought was less than a block from the subway, but it was not an office building, nor even a loft, nor a store in which one could rent office space. It was a very old tenement house. Leo found Salzman's name in pencil on a soiled tag under the bell and climbed three dark flights to his apartment. When he knocked, the door was opened by a thin, asthmatic, grey-haired woman, in felt slippers.

'Yes?' she said, expecting nothing. She listened without listening. He could have sworn he had seen her, too, before but knew it was an illusion.

'Salzman—does he live here? Pinye Salzman,' he said, 'the matchmaker?'

She stared at him a long minute. 'Of course.'

He felt embarrassed. 'Is he in?'

'No.' Her mouth, though left open, offered nothing more.

'The matter is urgent. Can you tell me where his office is?'

'In the air.' She pointed upward.

'You mean he has no office?' Leo asked.

'In his socks.'

He peered into the apartment. It was sunless and dingy, one large room divided by a half-open curtain, beyond which he could see a sagging metal bed. The near side of a room was crowded with rickety chairs, old bureaus, a three-legged table, racks of cooking utensils, and all the apparatus of a kitchen. But there was no sign of Salzman or his magic barrel, probably also a figment of the imagination. An odour of frying fish made Leo weak to the knees.

'Where is he?' he insisted. 'I've got to see your husband.'

At length she answered, 'So who knows where he is? Every time he thinks a new thought he runs to a different place. Go home, he will find you.'

'Tell him Leo Finkle.'

She gave no sign she had heard.

He walked downstairs, depressed.

But Salzman, breathless, stood waiting at his door.

Leo was astounded and overjoyed. 'How did you get here before me?'

'I rushed.'

'Come inside.'

They entered. Leo fixed tea, and a sardine sandwich for Salzman. As they were drinking he reached behind him for the packet of pictures and handed them to the marriage broker.

Salzman put down his glass and said expectantly, 'You found somebody you like?'

'Not among these.'

The marriage broker turned away.

'Here is the one I want.' Leo held forth the snapshot.

Salzman slipped on his glasses and took the picture into his trembling hand. He turned ghastly and let out a groan.

'What's the matter?' cried Leo.

'Excuse me. Was an accident this picture. She isn't for you.'

Salzman frantically shoved the manila packet into his portfolio. He thrust the snapshot into his pocket and fled down the stairs.

Leo, after momentary paralysis, gave chase and cornered the marriage broker in the vestibule. The landlady made hysterical outcries but neither of them listened.

'Give me back the picture, Salzman.'

'No.' The pain in his eyes was terrible.

'Tell me who she is then.'

'This I can't tell you. Excuse me.'

He made to depart, but Leo, forgetting himself, seized the matchmaker by his tight coat and shook him frenziedly.

'Please,' sighed Salzman. '*Please*.'

Leo ashamedly let him go. 'Tell me who she is,' he begged. 'It's very important for me to know.'

'She is not for you. She is a wild one—wild, without shame. This is not a bride for a rabbi.'

'What do you mean wild?'

'Like an animal. Like a dog. For her to be poor was a sin. This is why to me she is dead now.'

'In God's name, what do you mean?'

'Her I can't introduce to you,' Salzman cried.

'Why are you so excited?'

'Why, he asks,' Salzman said, bursting into tears. 'This is my baby, my Stella, she should burn in hell.'

Leo hurried up to bed and hid under the covers. Under the covers he thought his life through. Although he soon fell asleep he could not sleep her out of his mind. He woke, beating his breast. Though he prayed to be rid of her, his prayers went unanswered. Through days of torment he endlessly struggled not to love her; fearing success, he escaped it. He then concluded to convert her to goodness, himself to God. The idea alternately nauseated and exalted him.

He perhaps did not know that he had come to a final decision until he encountered Salzman in a Broadway cafeteria. He was sitting alone at a rear table, sucking the bony remains of a fish. The marriage broker appeared haggard, and transparent to the point of vanishing.

Salzman looked up at first without recognizing him. Leo had grown a pointed beard and his eyes were weighted with wisdom.

'Salzman,' he said, 'love has at last come to my heart.'

'Who can love from a picture?' mocked the marriage broker.

'It is not impossible.'

'If you can love her, than you can love anybody. Let me show you some new clients that they just sent me their photographs. One is a little doll.'

'Just her I want,' Leo murmured.

'Don't be a fool, doctor. Don't bother with her.'

'Put me in touch with her, Salzman,' Leo said humbly. 'Perhaps I can be of service.'

Salzman had stopped eating and Leo understood with emotion that it was now arranged.

Leaving the cafeteria, he was, however, afflicted by a tormenting suspicion that Salzman had planned it all to happen this way.

Leo was informed by letter that she would meet him on a certain corner, and she was there one spring night, waiting under a street lamp. He appeared, carrying a small bouquet of violets and rosebuds. Stella stood by the lamp post, smoking. She wore white with red shoes, which fitted his expectations, although in a troubled moment he had imagined the dress red, and only the shoes white. She waited uneasily and shyly. From afar he saw that her eyes—clearly her father's—were filled with desperate innocence. He pictured, in her, his own redemption. Violins and lit candles revolved in the sky. Leo ran forward with flowers outthrust.

Around the corner, Salzman, leaning against a wall, chanted prayers for the dead.

1954

# Doris Lessing

## 1919–2013

Doris Taylor was born in Kermanshah, Persia (now Iran), where her father held a managerial post in the Imperial Bank of Persia. He was an Englishman who had lost a leg in the Great War and married his nurse. In 1925 the family moved to southern Rhodesia (now Zimbabwe), where Alfred Taylor got a loan from the government land bank to buy 3,000 acres of land recently taken away from Africans, who had been put onto reservations. With cheap native labour the Taylors raised corn on the land but never made enough money to leave it. Doris Taylor went to a Catholic convent school and Girls' High School in the small city of Salisbury, leaving school at 14 and working as a nursemaid and then as a secretary. She was married twice (acquiring the name of Lessing), but left Rhodesia for England with her youngest child in 1949, after the breakup of her second marriage. She had been writing for some time, producing some stories and the manuscript for her first novel, *The Grass Is Singing* (1950). In England, she joined the Communist Party briefly and began her five-volume sequence of autobiographical novels, *Children of Violence.* Her most ambitious book, *The Golden Notebook* (1962), is considered one of the key texts of the feminist movement in the 1960s. Her concern with the future led her to write science fiction, including the ambitious series *Canopus in Argos: Archives* (1979–83). She completed two volumes of autobiography, *Under My Skin* (1994) and *Waiting in the Shade: 1949–1962* (1997), and won the Nobel Prize for Literature in 2007.

'A Sunrise on the Veld' recounts the joys of a 15-year-old boy as he awakens to the delights—and the horrors—of a new morning on the veld.

## A Sunrise on the Veld

Every night that winter he said aloud into the dark of the pillow: Half-past four! Half-past four! till he felt his brain had gripped the words and held them fast. Then he fell asleep at once, as if a shutter had fallen; and lay with his face turned to the clock so that he could see it first thing when he woke.

It was half-past four to the minute, every morning. Triumphantly pressing down the alarm-knob of the clock, which the dark of his mind had outwitted, remaining vigilant all night and counting the hours as he lay relaxed in sleep, he huddled down for a last warm moment under the clothes, playing with the idea of lying abed for this once only. But he played with it for the fun of knowing that it was a weakness he could defeat without effort; just as he set the alarm each night for the delight of the moment when he woke and stretched his limbs, feeling the muscles tighten, and thought: Even my brain—even that! I can control every part of myself.

Luxury of warm rested body, with the arms and legs and fingers waiting like soldiers for a word of command! Joy of knowing that the precious hours were given to sleep voluntarily!—for he had once stayed awake three nights running, to prove that he could, and then worked all day, refusing to admit that he was tired; and now sleep seemed to him a servant to be commanded and refused.

The boy stretched his frame full-length, touching the wall at his head with his hands, and the bedfoot with his toes; then he sprang out, like a fish leaping from water. And it was cold, cold.

He always dressed rapidly, so as to try and conserve his night-warmth till the sun rose two hours later; but by the time he had on his clothes his hands were numbed and he could scarcely hold his shoes. These he could not put on for fear of waking his parents, who never came to know how early he rose.

As soon as he stepped over the lintel, the flesh of his soles contracted on the chilled earth, and his legs began to ache with cold. It was night: the stars were glittering, the trees standing black and still. He looked for signs of day, for the greying of the edge of a stone, or a lightening in the sky where the sun would rise, but there was nothing yet. Alert as an animal he crept past the dangerous window, standing poised with his hand on the sill for one proudly fastidious moment, looking in at the stuffy blackness of the room where his parents lay.

Feeling for the grass-edge of the path with his toes, he reached inside another window further along the wall, where his gun had been set in readiness the night before. The steel was icy, and numbed fingers slipped along it, so that he had to hold it in the crook of his arm for safety. Then he tiptoed to the room where the dogs slept, and was fearful that they might have been tempted to go before him; but they were waiting, their haunches crouched in reluctance at the cold, but ears and swinging tails greeting the gun ecstatically. His warning undertone kept them secret and silent till the house was a hundred yards back: then they bolted off into the bush, yelping excitedly. The boy imagined his parents turning in their beds and muttering: Those dogs again! before they were dragged back in sleep; and he smiled scornfully. He always looked back over his shoulder at the house before he passed a wall of trees that shut it from sight. It looked so low and small, crouching there under a tall and brilliant sky. Then he turned his back on it, and on the frowsting sleepers, and forgot them.

He would have to hurry. Before the light grew strong he must be four miles away; and already a tint of green stood in the hollow of a leaf, and the air smelled of morning and the stars were dimming.

He slung the shoes over his shoulder, veld *skoen*[1] that were crinkled and hard with the dews of a hundred mornings. They would be necessary when the ground became too hot to bear. Now he felt the chilled dust push up between his toes, and he let the muscles of his feet spread and settle into the shapes of the earth; and he thought: I could walk a hundred miles on feet like these! I could walk all day, and never tire!

He was walking swiftly through the dark tunnel of foliage that in daytime was a road. The dogs were invisibly ranging the lower travelways of the bush, and he heard them panting. Sometimes he felt a cold muzzle on his leg before they were off again, scouting for a trail to follow. They were not trained, but free-running companions of the hunt, who often tired of the long stalk before the final shots, and went off on their own pleasure. Soon he could see them, small and wild-looking in a wild strange light,

1 Afrikaans for 'shoes'

now that the bush stood trembling on the verge of colour, waiting for the sun to paint earth and grass afresh.

The grass stood to his shoulders; and the trees were showering a faint silver rain. He was soaked; his whole body was clenched in a steady river.

Once he bent to the road that was newly scored with animal trails, and regretfully straightened, reminding himself that the pleasure of tracking must wait till another day.

He began to run along the edge of a field, noting jerkily how it was filmed over with fresh spiderweb, so that the long reaches of great black clods seemed netted in glistening grey. He was using the steady lope he had learned by watching the natives, the run that is a dropping of the weight of the body from one foot to the next in a slow balancing movement that never tires, nor shortens the breath; and he felt the blood pulsing down his legs and along his arms, and the exultation and pride of body mounted in him till he was shutting his teeth hard against a violent desire to shout his triumph.

Soon he had left the cultivated part of the farm. Behind him the bush was low and black. In front was a long *vlei,*[2] acres of long grass that sent back a hollowing gleam of light to a satiny sky. Near him thick swathes of grass were bent with the weight of water, and diamond drops sparkled on each frond.

The first bird woke at his feet and at once a flock of them sprang into the air calling shrilly that day had come; and suddenly, behind him, the bush woke into song, and he could hear the guinea fowl calling far ahead of him. That meant they would now be sailing down from their trees into thick grass, and it was for them he had come: he was too late. But he did not mind. He forgot he had come to shoot. He set his legs wide, and balanced from foot to foot, and swung his gun up and down in both hands horizontally, in kind of improvised exercise, and let his head sink back till it was pillowed in his neck muscles, and watched how above him small rosy clouds floated in a lake of gold.

Suddenly it all rose in him: it was unbearable. He leapt up into the air, shouting and yelling wild, unrecognizable noises. Then he began to run, not carefully, as he had before, but madly, like a wild thing. He was clean crazy, yelling mad with the joy of living and a superfluity of youth. He rushed down the *vlei* under a tumult of crimson and gold, while all the birds of the world sang about him. He ran in great leaping strides, and shouted as he ran, feeling his body rise into the crisp rushing air and fall back surely on to sure feet; and thought briefly, not believing that such a thing could happen to him, that he could break his ankle any moment, in this thick tangled grass. He cleared bushes like a *duiker,*[3] leapt over rocks; and finally came to a dead stop at a place where the ground fell abruptly away below him to the river. It had been a two-mile-long dash through waist-high growth, and he was breathing hoarsely and could no longer sing. But he poised on a rock and looked down at stretches of water that gleamed through stooping trees, and thought suddenly, I am fifteen! Fifteen! The words came new to him; so that he kept repeating them wonderingly, with swelling excitement; and he felt the years of his life with his hands, as if he were counting marbles, each one hard

2 a low-lying marshy ground, covered with water during the rainy season
3 a small antelope found in southern Africa

and separate and compact, each one a wonderful shining thing. That was what he was: fifteen years of this rich soil, and this slow-moving water, and air that smelt like a challenge whether it was warm and sultry at noon, or as brisk as cold water, like it was now.

There was nothing he couldn't do, nothing! A vision came to him, as he stood there, like when a child hears the word 'eternity' and tries to understand it, and time takes possession of the mind. He felt his life ahead of him as a great and wonderful thing, something that was his; and he said aloud, with the blood rising to his head: all the great men of the world have been as I am now, and there is nothing I can't become, nothing I can't do; there is no country in the world I cannot make part of myself, if I choose. I contain the world. I can make of it what I want. If I choose, I can change everything that is going to happen: it depends on me, and what I decide now.

The urgency, and the truth and the courage of what his voice was saying exulted him so that he began to sing again, at the top of his voice, and the sound went echoing down the river gorge. He stopped for the echo, and sang again: stopped and shouted. That was what he was!—he sang, if he chose; and the world had to answer him.

And for minutes he stood there, shouting and singing and waiting for the lovely eddying sound of the echo; so that his own new strong thoughts came back and washed round his head, as if someone were answering him and encouraging him; till the gorge was full of soft voices clashing back and forth from rock to rock over the river. And then it seemed as if there was a new voice. He listened, puzzled, for it was not his own. Soon he was leaning forward, all his nerves alert, quite still: somewhere close to him there was a noise that was no joyful bird, nor tinkle of falling water, nor ponderous movement of cattle.

There it was again. In the deep morning hush that held his future and his past, was a sound of pain, and repeated over and over: it was a kind of shortened scream, as if someone, something, had no breath to scream. He came to himself, looked about him, and called for the dogs. They did not appear: they had gone off on their own business, and he was alone. Now he was clean sober, all the madness gone. His heart beating fast, because of that frightened screaming, he stepped carefully off the rock and went towards a belt of trees. He was moving cautiously, for not so long ago he had seen a leopard in just this spot.

At the edge of the trees he stopped and peered, holding his gun ready; he advanced, looking steadily about him, his eyes narrowed. Then, all at once, in the middle of a step, he faltered, and his face was puzzled. He shook his head impatiently, as if he doubted his own sight.

There, between two trees, against a background of gaunt black rocks, was a figure from a dream, a strange beast that was horned and drunken-legged, but like something he had never even imagined. It seemed to be ragged. It looked like a small buck that had black ragged tufts of fur standing up irregularly all over it, with patches of raw flesh beneath . . . but the patches of rawness were disappearing under moving black and came again elsewhere; and all the time the creature screamed, in small gasping screams, and leaped drunkenly from side to side, as if it were blind.

Then the boy understood: it *was* a buck. He ran closer, and again stood still, stopped by a new fear. Around him the grass was whispering and alive. He looked wildly about, and then down. The ground was black with ants, great energetic ants that took no notice of him, but hurried and scurried towards the fighting shape, like glistening black water flowing through the grass.

And, as he drew in his breath and pity and terror seized him, the beast fell and the screaming stopped. Now he could hear nothing but one bird singing, and the sound of the rustling, whispering ants.

He peered over at the writhing blackness that jerked convulsively with the jerking nerves. It grew quieter. There were small twitches from the mass that still looked vaguely like the shape of a small animal.

It came into his mind that he should shoot it and end its pain; and he raised the gun. Then he lowered it again. The buck could no longer feel; its fighting was a mechanical protest of the nerves. But it was not that which made him put down the gun. It was a swelling feeling of rage and misery and protest that expressed itself in the thought: if I had not come it would have died like this: so why should I interfere? All over the bush things like this happen; they happen all the time; this is how life goes on, by living things dying in anguish. He gripped the gun between his knees and felt in his own limbs the myriad swarming pain of the twitching animal that could no longer feel, and set his teeth, and said over and over again under his breath: I can't stop it. I can't stop it. There is nothing I can do.

He was glad that the buck was unconscious and had gone past suffering so that he did not have to make a decision to kill it even when he was feeling with his whole body: this is what happens, this is how things work.

*It was right*—that was what he was feeling. *It was right and nothing could alter it.*

The knowledge of fatality, of what has to be, had gripped him and for the first time in his life; and he was left unable to make any movement of brain or body, except to say: 'Yes, yes. That is what living is.' It had entered his flesh and his bones and grown in to the furthest corners of his brain and would never leave him. And at that moment he could not have performed the smallest action of mercy, knowing as he did, having lived on it all his life, the vast unalterable, cruel veld, where at any moment one might stumble over a skull or crush the skeleton of some small creature.

Suffering, sick, and angry, but also grimly satisfied with his new stoicism, he stood there leaning on his rifle, and watched the seething black mound grow smaller. At his feet, now, were ants trickling back with pink fragments in their mouths, and there was a fresh acid smell in his nostrils. He sternly controlled the uselessly convulsing muscles of his empty stomach, and reminded himself: the ants must eat too! At the same time he found that the tears were streaming down his face, and his clothes were soaked with the sweat of that other creature's pain.

The shape had grown small. Now it looked like nothing recognizable. He did not know how long it was before he saw the blackness thin, and bits of white showed through, shining in the sun—yes, there was the sun, just up, glowing over the rocks. Why, the whole thing could not have taken longer than a few minutes.

He began to swear, as if the shortness of the time was in itself unbearable, using the words he had heard his father say. He strode forward, crushing ants with each step, and brushing them off his clothes, till he stood above the skeleton, which lay sprawled under a small bush. It was clean-picked. It might have been lying there years, save that on the white bone were pink fragments of gristle. About the bones ants were ebbing away, their pincers full of meat.

The boy looked at them, big black ugly insects. A few were standing and gazing up at him with small glittering eyes.

'Go away!' he said to the ants, very coldly. 'I am not for you—not just yet, at any rate. Go away.' And he fancied that the ants turned and went away.

He bent over the bones and touched the sockets in the skull; that was where the eyes were, he thought incredulously, remembering the liquid dark eyes of a buck. And then he bent the slim foreleg bone, swinging it horizontally in his palm.

That morning, perhaps an hour ago, this small creature had been stepping proud and free through the bush, feeling the chill on its hide even as he himself had done, exhilarated by it. Proudly stepping the earth, tossing its horns, frisking a pretty white tail, it had sniffed the cold morning air. Walking like kings and conquerors it had moved through this free-held bush, where each blade of grass grew for it alone, and where the river ran pure sparkling water for its slaking.

And then—what had happened? Such a swift surefooted thing could surely not be trapped by a swarm of ants?

The boy bent curiously to the skeleton. Then he saw that the back leg that lay uppermost and strained out in the tension of death was snapped midway in the thigh, so that broken bones jutted over each other uselessly. So that was it! Limping into the ant-masses it could not escape, once it had sensed danger. Yes, but how had the leg been broken? Had it fallen, perhaps? Impossible, a buck was too light and graceful. Had some jealous rival horned it?

What could possibly have happened? Perhaps some Africans had thrown stones at it, as they do, trying to kill it for meat, and had broken its leg. Yes, that must be it.

Even as he imagined the crowd of running, shouting natives, and the flying stones, and the leaping buck, another picture came into his mind. He saw himself, on any one of these bright ringing mornings, drunk with excitement, taking a snap shot at some half-seen buck. He saw himself with the gun lowered, wondering whether he had missed or not; and thinking at last that it was late, and he wanted his breakfast, and it was not worth while to track miles after an animal that would very likely get away from him in any case.

For a moment he would not face it. He was a small boy again, kicking sulkily at the skeleton, hanging his head, refusing to accept the responsibility.

Then he straightened up, and looked down at the bones with an odd expression of dismay, all the anger gone out of him. His mind went quite empty: all around him he could see trickles of ants disappearing into the grass. The whispering noise was faint and dry, like the rustling of a cast snakeskin.

At last he picked up his gun and walked homewards. He was telling himself half defiantly that he wanted his breakfast. He was telling himself that it was getting very hot, much too hot to be out roaming the bush.

Really, he was tired. He walked heavily, not looking where he put his feet. When he came within sight of his home he stopped, knitting his brows. There was something he had to think out. The death of that small animal was a thing that concerned him, and he was by no means finished with it. It lay at the back of his mind uncomfortably.

Soon, the very next morning, he would get clear of everybody and go to the bush and think about it.

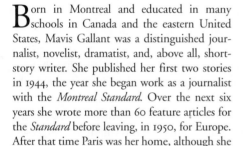

1951

# Mavis Gallant

1922–2014

Born in Montreal and educated in many schools in Canada and the eastern United States, Mavis Gallant was a distinguished journalist, novelist, dramatist, and, above all, short-story writer. She published her first two stories in 1944, the year she began work as a journalist with the *Montreal Standard*. Over the next six years she wrote more than 60 feature articles for the *Standard* before leaving, in 1950, for Europe. After that time Paris was her home, although she retained her Canadian citizenship.

Gallant devoted herself primarily to the writing of fiction. Her first collection of short stories, *The Other Paris* (1959), explores the lives of exiles and expatriates; here as elsewhere in her fiction, Gallant—an acute observer of social customs—examined men and women trapped in exiled lives that fail to satisfy them. She published two novels, *Green Water, Green Sky* (1959) and *A Fairly Good Time* (1970), seven more collections of short fiction, a play, *What Is to Be Done?* (1982), and a collection of essays and review articles, *Paris Notebooks* (1986). She was a frequent contributor to the *New Yorker*, where 'The Ice Wagon Going Down the Street' first appeared in 1963.

## The Ice Wagon Going Down the Street

Now that they are out of world affairs and back where they started, Peter Frazier's wife says, 'Everybody else did well in the international thing except us.'

'You have to be crooked,' he tells her.

'Or smart. Pity we weren't.'

It is Sunday morning. They sit in the kitchen, drinking their coffee, slowly, remembering the past. They say the names of people as if they were magic. Peter thinks, *Agnes Brusen*, but there are hundreds of other names. As a private married joke, Peter and Sheilah wear the silk dressing gowns they bought in Hong Kong. Each thinks the other a peacock, rather splendid, but they pretend the dressing gowns are silly and worn in fun.

Peter and Sheilah and their two daughters, Sandra and Jennifer, are visiting Peter's unmarried sister, Lucille. They have been Lucille's guests seventeen weeks, ever since they returned to Toronto from the Far East. Their big old steamer trunk blocks a corner of the kitchen, making a problem of the refrigerator door; but even Lucille says the trunk may as well stay where it is, for the present. The Fraziers' future is so unsettled; everything is still in the air.

Lucille has given her bedroom to her two nieces, and sleeps on a camp cot in the hall. The parents have the living-room divan. They have no privileges here; they sleep after Lucille has seen the last television show that interests her. In the hall closet their clothes are crushed by winter overcoats. They know they are being judged for the first time. Sandra and Jennifer are waiting for Sheilah and Peter to decide. They are waiting to learn where these exotic parents will fly to next. What sort of climate will Sheilah consider? What job will Peter consent to accept? When the parents are ready, the children will make a decision of their own. It is just possible that Sandra and Jennifer will choose to stay with their aunt.

The peacock parents are watched by wrens. Lucille and her nieces are much the same—sandy-coloured, proudly plain. Neither of the girls has the father's insouciance or the mother's appearance—her height, her carriage, her thick hair, and sky-blue eyes. The children are more cautious than their parents; more Canadian. When they saw their aunt's apartment they had been away from Canada nine years, ever since they were two and four; and Jennifer, the elder, said, 'Well, now we're home.' Her voice is nasal and flat. Where did she learn that voice? And why should this be home? Peter's answer to anything about his mystifying children is, 'It must be in the blood.'

On Sunday morning Lucille takes her nieces to church. It seems to be the only condition she imposes on her relations: the children must be decent. The girls go willingly, with their new hats and purses and gloves and coral bracelets and strings of pearls. The parents, ramshackle, sleepy, dim in the brain because it is Sunday, sit down to their coffee and privacy and talk of the past.

'We weren't crooked,' says Peter. 'We weren't even smart.'

Sheilah's head bobs up; she is no drowner. It is wrong to say they have nothing to show for time. Sheilah has the Balenciaga. It is a black afternoon dress, stiff and boned at the waist, long for the fashions of now, but neither Sheilah nor Peter would change a thread. The Balenciaga is their talisman, their treasure; and after they remember it they touch hands and think that the years are not behind them but hazy and marvellous and still to be lived.

The first place they went to was Paris. In the early 'fifties the pick of the international jobs was there. Peter had inherited the last scrap of money he knew he was ever likely to see, and it was enough to get them over: Sheilah and Peter and the babies and the steamer trunk. To their joy and astonishment they had money in the bank. They said to each other, 'It should last a year.' Peter was fastidious about the new job; he hadn't come all this distance to accept just anything. In Paris he met Hugh Taylor, who was earning enough smuggling gasoline to keep his wife in Paris and a girl in Rome. That impressed Peter, because he remembered Taylor as a sour scholarship student without the slightest talent for life. Taylor had a job, of course. He hadn't said to himself, I'll go over to Europe and smuggle gasoline. It gave Peter an idea; he saw the shape of things. First you catch your fish. Later, at an international party, he met Johnny Hertzberg, who told him Germany was the place. Hertzberg said that anyone who came out of Germany broke now was too stupid to be here, and deserved to be back home at a desk. Peter nodded, as if he had already thought of that. He began to think about Germany. Paris was fine for a holiday, but it had been picked clean. Yes, Germany. His money was running low. He thought about Germany quite a lot.

That winter was moist and delicate; so fragile that they daren't speak of it now. There seemed to be plenty of everything and plenty of time. They were living the dream of marriage, the fabric uncut, nothing slashed or spoiled. All winter they spent their money, and went to parties, and talked about Peter's future job. It lasted four months. They spent their money, lived in the future, and were never as happy again.

After four months they were suddenly moved away from Paris, but not to Germany—to Geneva. Peter thinks it was because of the incident at the Trudeau wedding at the Ritz. Paul Trudeau was a French-Canadian Peter had known at school and in the Navy. Trudeau had turned into a snob, proud of his career and his Paris connections. He tried to make the difference felt, but Peter thought the difference was only for strangers. At the wedding reception Peter lay down on the floor and said he was dead. He held a white azalea in a brass pot on his chest, and sang, 'Oh, hear us when we cry to Thee for those in peril on the sea.' Sheilah bent over him and said, 'Peter, darling, get up. Pete, listen, every single person who can do something for you is in this room. If you love me, you'll get up.'

'I do love you,' he said, ready to engage in a serious conversation. 'She's so beautiful,' he told a second face. 'She's nearly as tall as I am. She was a model in London. I met her over in London in the war. I met her there in the war.' He lay on his back with the azalea on his chest, explaining their history. A waiter took the brass pot away, and after Peter had been hauled to his feet he knocked the waiter down. Trudeau's bride, who was freshly out of an Ursuline[1] convent, became hysterical; and even though Paul Trudeau and Peter were old acquaintances, Trudeau never spoke to him again. Peter says now that French-Canadians always have that bit of spite. He says Trudeau asked the Embassy to interfere. Luckily, back home there were still a few people to whom the name 'Frazier' meant something, and it was to these people that Peter appealed. He wrote letters saying that a French-Canadian combine was preventing his getting a decent job, and could anything be done? No one answered directly, but it was clear that what they settled for was exile to Geneva: a season of meditation and remorse, as he explained to Sheilah, and it was managed tactfully, through Lucille. Lucille wrote that a friend of hers, May Fergus, now a secretary in Geneva, had heard about a job. The job was filing pictures in the information services of an international agency in the Palais des Nations. The pay was so-so, but Lucille thought Peter must be getting fed up doing nothing.

Peter often asks his sister now who put her up to it—what important person told her to write that letter suggesting Peter go to Geneva?

'Nobody,' says Lucille. 'I mean, nobody in the way *you* mean. I really did have this girlfriend working there, and I knew you must be running through your money pretty fast in Paris.'

'It must have been somebody pretty high up,' Peter says. He looks at his sister admiringly, as he has often looked at his wife.

1 The Ursuline Sisters are an order of Catholic nuns dedicated to the education of young girls.

Peter's wife had loved him in Paris. Whatever she wanted in marriage she found that winter, there. In Geneva, where Peter was a file clerk and they lived in a furnished flat, she pretended they were in Paris and life was still the same. Often, when the children were at supper, she changed as though she and Peter were dining out. She wore the Balenciaga, and put candles on the card table where she and Peter ate their meal. The neckline of the dress was soiled with make-up. Peter remembers her dabbing on the make-up with a wet sponge. He remembers her in the kitchen, in the soiled Balenciaga, patting on the make-up with a filthy sponge. Behind her, at the kitchen table, Sandra and Jennifer, in buttonless pajamas and bunny slippers, ate their supper of marmalade sandwiches and milk. When the children were asleep, the parents dined solemnly, ritually, Sheilah sitting straight as a queen.

It was a mysterious period of exile, and he had to wait for signs, or signals, to know when he was free to leave. He never saw the job any other way. He forgot he had applied for it. He thought he had been sent to Geneva because of a misdemeanour and had to wait to be released. Nobody pressed him at work. His immediate boss had resigned, and he was alone for months in a room with two desks. He read the *Herald-Tribune*, and tried to discover how things were here—how the others ran their lives on the pay they were officially getting. But it was a closed conspiracy. He was not dealing with adventurers now but civil servants waiting for pension day. No one ever answered his questions. They pretended to think his questions were a form of wit. His only solace in exile was the few happy weekends he had in the late spring and early summer. He had met another old acquaintance, Mike Burleigh. Mike was a serious liberal who had married a serious heiress. The Burleighs had two guest lists. The first was composed of stuffy people they felt obliged to entertain, while the second was made up of their real friends, the friends they wanted. The real friends strove hard to become stuffy and dull and thus achieve the first guest list, but few succeeded. Peter went on the first list straight away. Possibly Mike didn't understand, at the beginning, why Peter was pretending to be a file clerk. Peter had such an air—he might have been sent by a universal inspector to see how things in Geneva were being run.

Every Friday in May and June and part of July, the Fraziers rented a sky-blue Fiat and drove forty miles east of Geneva to the Burleighs' summer house. They brought the children, a suitcase, the childrens' tattered picture books, and a token bottle of gin. This, in memory, is a period of water and water birds; swans, roses, and singing birds. The children were small and still belonged to them. If they remember too much, their mouths water, their stomachs hurt. Peter says, 'It was fine while it lasted.' Enough. While it lasted Sheilah and Madge Burleigh were close. They abandoned their husbands and spent long summer afternoons comparing their mothers and praising each other's skin and hair. To Madge, and not to Peter, Sheilah opened her Liverpool childhood with the words 'rat poor'. Peter heard about it later, from Mike. The women's friendship seemed to Peter a bad beginning. He trusted women but not with each other. It lasted ten weeks. One Sunday, Madge said she needed the two bedrooms the Fraziers usually occupied for a party of sociologists from Pakistan, and that was the end. In November, the Fraziers heard that the summer house had been closed, and that the Burleighs were in Geneva, in their winter flat; they gave no sign. There was no help for it, and no appeal.

Now Peter began firing letters to anyone who had ever known his late father. He was living in a mild yellow autumn. Why does he remember the streets of the city dark, and the windows everywhere black with rain? He remembers being with Sheilah and the children as if they clung together while just outside their small shelter it rained and rained. The children slept in the bedroom of the flat because the window gave on the street and they could breathe air. Peter and Sheilah had the living-room couch. Their window was not a real window but a square on a wall of cement. The flat seemed damp as a cave. Peter remembers steam in the kitchen, pools under the sink, sweat on the pipes. Water streamed on him from the children's clothes, washed and dripping overhead. The trunk, upended in the children's room, was not quite unpacked. Sheilah had not signed her name to this life; she had not given in. Once Peter heard her drop her aitches. 'You kids are lucky,' she said to the girls. 'I never 'ad so much as a sit-down meal. I ate chips out of a paper or I 'ad a butty out on the stairs.' He never asked her what a butty was. He thinks it means bread and cheese.

The day he heard 'You kids are lucky' he understood they were becoming in fact something they had only *appeared* to be until now—the shabby civil servant and his brood. If he had been European he would have ridden to work on a bicycle, in the uniform of his class and condition. He would have worn a tight coat, a turned collar, and a dirty tie. He wondered then if coming here had been a mistake, and if he should not, after all, still be in a place where his name meant something. Surely Peter Frazier should live where 'Frazier' counts? In Ontario even now when he says 'Frazier' an absent look comes over his hearer's face, as if its owner were consulting an interior guide. What is Frazier? What does it mean? Oil? Power? Politics? Wheat? Real estate? The creditors had the house sealed when Peter's father died. His aunt collapsed with a heart attack in somebody's bachelor apartment, leaving three sons and a widower to surmise they had never known her. Her will was a disappointment. None of that generation left enough. One made it: the granite Presbyterian immigrants from Scotland. Their children, a generation of daunted women and maiden men, held still. Peter's father's crowd spent: they were not afraid of their fathers, and their grandfathers were old. Peter and his sister and his cousins lived on the remains. They were left the rinds of income, of notions, and the memories of ideas rather than ideas intact. If Peter can choose his reincarnation, let him be the oppressed son of a Scottish parson. Let Peter grow up on cuffs and iron principles. Let him make the fortune! Let him flee the manse! When he was small his patrimony was squandered under his nose. He remembers people dancing in his father's house. He remembers seeing and nearly understanding adultery in a guest room, among a pile of wraps. He thought he had seen a murder; he never told. He remembers licking glasses wherever he found them—on window sills, on stairs, in the pantry. In his room he listened while Lucille read Beatrix Potter. The bad rabbit stole the carrot from the good rabbit without saying please, and downstairs was the noise of the party—the roar of the crouched lion. When his father died he saw the chairs upside down and the bailiff's chalk marks. Then the doors were sealed.

He has often tried to tell Sheilah why he cannot be defeated. He remembers his father saying, 'Nothing can touch us,' and Peter believed it and still does. It has prevented his taking his troubles too seriously. 'Nothing can be as bad as this,' he will tell himself. 'It is happening to me.' Even in Geneva, where his status was file clerk, where he sank and stopped on the level of the men who never emigrated, the men on the bicycles—even there he had a manner of strolling to work as if his office were a pastime, and his real life a secret so splendid he could share it with no one except himself.

In Geneva Peter worked for a woman—a girl. She was a Norwegian from a small town in Saskatchewan. He supposed they had been put together because they were Canadian; but they were as strange to each other as if 'Canadian' meant any number of things, or had no real meaning. Soon after Agnes Brusen came to the office she hung her framed university degree on the wall. It was one of the gritty, prideful gestures that stand for push, toil, and family sacrifice. He thought, then, that she must be one of a family of immigrants for whom education is everything. Hugh Taylor had told him that in some families the older children never marry until the youngest have finished school. Sometimes every second child is sacrificed and made to work for the education of the next born. Those who finish college spend years paying back. They are white-hot Protestants, and they live with a load of work and debt and obligation. Peter placed his new colleague on scraps of information. He had never been in the West.

She came to the office on a Monday morning in October. The office was overheated and painted cream. It contained two desks, the filing cabinets, a map of the world as it had been in 1945, and the Charter of the United Nations left behind by Agnes Brusen's predecessor. (She took down the Charter without asking Peter if he minded, with the impudence of gesture you find in women who wouldn't say boo to a goose; and then she hung her college degree on the nail where the Charter had been.) Three people brought her in—a whole committee. One of them said, 'Agnes, this is Pete Frazier. Pete, Agnes Brusen. Pete's Canadian, too, Agnes. He knows all about the office, so ask him anything.'

Of course he knew all about the office: he knew the exact spot where the cord of the venetian blind was frayed, obliging one to give an extra tug to the right.

The girl might have been twenty-three: no more. She wore a brown tweed suit with bone buttons, and a new silk scarf and new shoes. She clutched an unscratched brown purse. She seemed dressed in going-away presents. She said, 'Oh, I never smoke,' with a convulsive movement of her hand, when Peter offered his case. He was courteous, hiding his disappointment. The people he worked with had told him a Scandinavian girl was arriving, and he had expected a stunner. Agnes was a mole: she was small and brown, and round-shouldered as if she had always carried parcels or younger children in her arms. A mole's profile was turned when she said goodbye to her committee. If she had been foreign, ill-favoured though she was, he might have flirted a little, just to show that he was friendly; but their being Canadian, and suddenly left together, was a sexual damper. He sat down and lit his own cigarette. She smiled at him, questioningly, he thought, and sat as if she had never seen a chair before. He wondered if his smoking was annoying her. He wondered if she was fidgety about drafts, or allergic to anything, and whether she would want the blind up or down. His social compass was out of order because the others couldn't tell Peter and Agnes apart. There was a world of difference between them, yet it was she who had been brought in to sit at the larger of the two desks.

While he was thinking this she got up and walked around the office, almost on tiptoe, opening the doors of closets and pulling out the filing trays. She looked inside everything except the drawers of Peter's desk. (In any case, Peter's desk was locked. His desk is locked wherever he works. In Geneva he went into Personnel one morning, early, and pinched his application form. He had stated on the form that he had seven years' experience in public relations and could speak French, German, Spanish, and Italian. He has always collected anything important about himself—anything useful. But he can never get on with the final act, which is getting rid of the information. He has kept papers about for years, a constant source of worry.)

'I know this looks funny, Mr Ferris,' said the girl. 'I'm not really snooping or anything. I just can't feel easy in a new place unless I know where everything is. In a new place everything seems so hidden.'

If she had called him 'Ferris' and pretended not to know he was Frazier, it could only be because they had sent her here to spy on him and see if he had repented and was fit for a better place in life. 'You'll be all right here,' he said. 'Nothing's hidden. Most of us haven't got brains enough to have secrets. This is Rainbow Valley.' Depressed by the thought that they were having him watched now, he passed his hand over his hair and looked outside to the lawn and the parking lot and the peacocks someone gave the Palais des Nations years ago. The peacocks love no one. They wander about the parked cars looking elderly, bad-tempered, mournful, and lost.

Agnes had settled down again. She folded her silk scarf and placed it just so, with her gloves beside it. She opened her new purse and took out a notebook and a shiny gold pencil. She may have written

Duster for desk
Kleenex
Glass jar for flowers
Air-Wick because he smokes
Paper for lining drawers

because the next day she brought each of these articles to work. She also brought a large black Bible, which she unwrapped lovingly and placed on the left-hand corner of her desk. The flower vase—empty—stood in the middle, and the Kleenex made a counterpoise for the Bible on the right.

When he saw the Bible he knew she had not been sent to spy on his work. The conspiracy was deeper. She might have been dispatched by ghosts. He knew everything about her, all in a moment: he saw the ambition, the terror, the dry pride. She was the true heir of the men from Scotland; she was at the start. She had been sent to tell him, 'You can begin, but not begin again.' She never opened the Bible, but she dusted it as she dusted her desk, her chair, and any surface the cleaning staff had overlooked. And Peter, the first days, watching her timid movements, her insignificant little face, felt, as you feel the approach of a storm, the charge of moral certainty round her, the belief in work, the faith in undertakings, the bread of the Black Sunday. He recognized and tasted all of it: ashes in the mouth.

After five days their working relations were settled. Of course, there was the Bible and all that went with it, but his tongue had never held the taste of ashes long. She was an inferior girl of poor quality. She had nothing in her favour except the degree on the wall. In the real world, he would not have invited her to his house except to mind the children. That was what he said to Sheilah. He said that Agnes was a mole, and a virgin, and that her tics and mannerisms were sending him round the bend. She had an infuriating habit of covering her mouth when she talked. Even at the telephone she put up her hand as if afraid of losing anything, even a word. Her voice was nasal and flat. She had two working costumes, both dull as the wall. One was the brown suit, the other a navy-blue dress with changeable collars. She dressed for no one; she dressed for her desk, her jar of flowers, her Bible, and her box of Kleenex. One day she crossed the space between the two desks and stood over Peter, who was reading a newspaper. She could have spoken to him from her desk, but she may have felt that being on her feet gave her authority. She had plenty of courage, but authority was something else.

'I thought—I mean, they told me you were the person . . .' She got on with it bravely: 'If you don't want to do the filing or any work, all right, Mr Frazier. I'm not saying anything about that. You might have poor health or your personal reasons. But it's got to be done, so if you'll kindly show me about the filing I'll do it. I've worked in Information before, but it was a different office, and every office is different.'

'My dear girl,' said Peter. He pushed back his chair and looked at her, astonished. 'You've been sitting there fretting, worrying. How insensitive of me. How trying for you. Usually I file on the last Wednesday of the month, so you see, you just haven't been around long enough to see a last Wednesday. Not another word, please. And let us not waste another moment.' He emptied the heaped baskets of photographs so swiftly, pushing 'Iran—Smallpox Control' into 'Irish Red Cross' (close enough), that the girl looked frightened, as if she had raised a whirlwind. She said slowly, 'If you'll only show me, Mr Frazier, instead of doing it so fast, I'll gladly look after it, because you might want to be doing other things, and I feel the filing should be done every day.' But Peter was too busy to answer, and so she sat down, holding the edge of her desk.

'There,' he said, beaming. 'All done.' His smile, his sunburst, was wasted, for the girl was staring round the room as if she feared she had not inspected everything the first day after all; some drawer, some cupboard, hid a monster. That evening Peter unlocked one of the drawers of his desk and took away the application form he had stolen from Personnel. The girl had not finished her search.

'How could you *not* know?' wailed Sheilah. 'You sit looking at her every day. You must talk about *something*. She must have told you.'

'She did tell me,' said Peter, 'and I've just told you.'

It was this: Agnes Brusen was on the Burleighs' guest list. How had the Burleighs met her? What did they see in her? Peter could not reply. He knew that Agnes lived in a bed-sitting room with a Swiss family and had her meals with them. She had been in Geneva three months, but no one had ever seen her outside the office. 'You *should* know,' said Sheilah. 'She must have something, more than you can see. Is she pretty? Is she brilliant? What is it?'

'We don't really talk,' Peter said. They talked in a way: Peter teased her and she took no notice. Agnes was not a sulker. She had taken her defeat like a sport. She did her work and a good deal of his. She sat behind her Bible, her flowers, and her Kleenex, and answered when Peter spoke. That was how he learned about the Burleighs—just by teasing and being bored. It was a January afternoon. He said, '*Miss* Brusen. Talk to me. Tell me everything. Pretend we have perfect rapport. Do you like Geneva?'

'It's a nice clean town,' she said. He can see to this day the red and blue anemones in the glass jar, and her bent head, and her small untended hands.

'Are you learning beautiful French with your Swiss family?'

'They speak English.'

'Why don't you take an apartment of your own?' he said. Peter was not usually impertinent. He was bored. 'You'd be independent then.'

'I am independent,' she said. 'I earn my living. I don't think it proves anything if you live by yourself. Mrs Burleigh wants me to live alone, too. She's looking for something for me. It mustn't be dear. I send money home.'

Here was the extraordinary thing about Agnes Brusen: she refused the use of Christian names and never spoke to Peter unless he spoke first, but she would tell anything, as if to say, 'Don't waste time fishing. Here it is.'

He learned all in one minute that she sent her salary home, and that she was a friend of the Burleighs. The first he had expected; the second knocked him flat.

'She's got to come to dinner.' Sheilah said. 'We should have had her right from the beginning. If only I'd known! But *you* were the one. You said she looked like—oh, I don't even remember. A Norwegian mole.'

She came to dinner one Saturday night in January, in her navy-blue dress, to which she had pinned an organdy gardenia. She sat upright on the edge of the sofa. Sheilah had ordered the meal from a restaurant. There was lobster, good wine, and a *pièce-montée* full of kirsch and cream. Agnes refused the lobster; she had never eaten anything from the sea unless it had been sterilized and tinned, and said so. She was afraid of skin poisoning. Someone in her family had skin poisoning after having eaten oysters. She touched her cheeks and neck to show where the poisoning had erupted. She sniffed her wine and put the glass down without tasting it. She could not eat the cake because of the alcohol it contained. She ate an egg, bread and butter, a sliced tomato, and drank a glass of ginger ale. She seemed unaware she was creating disaster and pain. She did not help clear away the dinner plates. She sat, adequately nourished, decently dressed, and waited to learn why she had been invited here—that was the feeling Peter had. He folded the card table on which they had dined, and opened the window to air the room.

'It's not the same cold as Canada, but you feel it more,' he said, for something to say.

'Your blood has gotten thin,' said Agnes.

Sheilah returned from the kitchen and let herself fall into an armchair. With her eyes closed she held out her hand for a cigarette. She was performing the haughty-lady act that was a family joke. She flung her head back and looked at Agnes through half-closed lids; then she suddenly brought her head forward, widening her eyes.

'Are you skiing madly?' she said.

'Well, in the first place there hasn't been any snow,' said Agnes. 'So nobody's doing any skiing so far as I know. All I hear is people complaining because there's no snow. Personally, I don't ski. There isn't much skiing in the part of Canada I come from. Besides, my family never had that kind of leisure.'

'Heavens,' said Sheilah, as if her family had every kind.

I'll bet they had, thought Peter. On the dole.

Sheilah was wasting her act. He had a suspicion that Agnes knew it was an act but did not know it was a joke. If so, it made Sheilah seem a fool, and he loved Sheilah too much to enjoy it.

'The Burleighs have been wonderful to me,' said Agnes. She seemed to have divined why she was here, and decided to give them all the information they wanted, so that she could put on her coat and go home to bed. 'They had me out to their place on the lake every weekend until the weather got cold and they moved back to town. They've rented a chalet for the winter, and they want me to come there, too. But I don't know if I will or not. I don't ski, and, oh, I don't know—I don't drink, either, and I don't always see the point. Their friends are too rich and I'm too Canadian.'

She had delivered everything Sheilah wanted and more: Agnes was on the first guest list and didn't care. No, Peter corrected; doesn't know. Doesn't care and doesn't know.

'I thought with you Norwegians it was in the blood, skiing. And drinking,' Sheilah murmured.

'Drinking, maybe,' said Agnes. She covered her mouth and said behind her spread fingers, 'In our family we were religious. We didn't drink or smoke. My brother was in Norway in the war. He saw some cousins. 'Oh,' she said, unexpectedly loud, 'Harry said it was just terrible. They were so poor. They had flies in their kitchen. They gave him something to eat a fly had been on. They didn't have a real toilet, and they'd been in the same house about two hundred years. We've only recently built our own home, and we have a bathroom and two toilets. I'm from Saskatchewan,' she said. 'I'm not from any other place.'

Surely one winter here had been punishment enough? In the spring they would remember him and free him. He wrote Lucille, who said he was lucky to have a job at all. The Burleighs had sent the Fraziers a second-guest-list Christmas card. It showed a Moslem refugee child weeping outside a tent. They treasured the card and left it standing long after the others had been given the children to cut up. Peter had discovered by now what had gone wrong in the friendship—Sheilah had charged a skirt at a dressmaker to Madge's account. Madge had told her she might, and then changed her mind. Poor Sheilah! She was new to this part of it—to the changing humours of independent friends. Paris was already a year in the past. At Mardi Gras, the Burleighs gave their annual party. They invited everyone, the damned and the dropped, with the prodigality of a child at prayers. The invitation said 'in costume', but the Fraziers were too happy to wear a disguise. They might not be recognized. Like many of the guests they expected to meet at the party, they had been disgraced, forgotten, and rehabilitated. They would be anxious to see one another as they were.

On the night of the party, the Fraziers rented a car they had never seen before and drove through the first snowstorm of the year. Peter had not driven since last summer's blissful trips in the Fiat. He could not find the switch for the windshield wiper in this car. He leaned over the wheel. 'Can you see on your side?' he asked. 'Can I make a left turn here? Does it look like a one-way?'

'I can't imagine why you took a car with a right-hand drive,' said Sheilah.

He had trouble finding a place to park; they crawled up and down unknown streets whose curbs were packed with snow-covered cars. When they stood at last on the pavement, safe and sound, Peter said, 'This is the first snow.'

'I can see that,' said Sheilah. 'Hurry, darling. My hair.'

'It's the first snow.'

'You're repeating yourself,' she said. 'Please hurry, darling. Think of my poor shoes. My *hair*.'

She was born in an ugly city, and so was Peter, but they have this difference: she does not know the importance of the first snow—the first clean thing in a dirty year. He would have told her that this storm, which was wetting her feet and destroying her hair, was like the first day of the English spring, but she made a frightened gesture, trying to shield her head. The gesture told him he did not understand her beauty.

'Let me,' she said. He was fumbling with the key, trying to lock the car. She took the key without impatience and locked the door on the driver's side; and then, to show Peter she treasured him and was not afraid of wasting her life or her beauty, she took his arm and they walked in the snow down a street and around a corner to the apartment house where the Burleighs lived. They were, and are, a united couple. They were afraid of the party, and each of them knew it. When they walk together, holding arms, they give each other whatever each can spare.

Only six people had arrived in costume. Madge Burleigh was disguised as Manet's 'Lola de Valence', which everyone mistook for Carmen. Mike was an Impressionist painter, with a straw hat and a glued-on beard. 'I am all of them,' he said. He would rather have dressed as a dentist, he said, welcoming the Fraziers as if he had parted from them the day before, but Madge wanted him to look as if he had created her. 'You know?' he said.

'Perfectly,' said Sheilah. Her shoes were stained and the snow had softened her lacquered hair. She was not wasted; she was the most beautiful woman here.

About an hour after their arrival, Peter found himself with no one to talk to. He had told about the Trudeau wedding in Paris and the pot of azaleas, and after he mislaid his audience he began to look around for Sheilah. She was on a window seat, partly concealed by a green velvet curtain. Facing her, so that their profiles were neat and perfect against the night, was a man. Their conversation was private and enclosed, as if they had in minutes covered leagues of time and arrived at a place where everything was implied, understood. Peter began working his way across the room, toward his wife, when he saw Agnes. He was granted the sight of her drowning face. She had dressed with comic intention, obviously with care, and now she was a ragged hobo, half tramp, half clown. Her hair was tucked up under a bowler hat. The six costumed guests who had made the same mistake—the ghost, the gypsy, the Athenian maiden, the geisha, the Martian, and the apache—were delighted to find a seventh; but Agnes was not amused; she was gasping for life. When a waiter passed with a crowded tray, she took a glass without seeing it; then a wave of the party took her away.

Sheilah's new friend was named Simpson. After Simpson said he thought perhaps he'd better circulate, Peter sat down where he had been. 'Now look, Sheilah,' he began. Their most intimate conversations have taken place at parties. Once at a party she told him she was leaving him; she didn't, of course. Smiling, blue-eyed, she gazed lovingly at Peter and said rapidly, 'Pete, shut up and listen. That man. The man you scared away. He's a big wheel in a company out in India or someplace like that. It's gorgeous out there. Pete, the *servants.* And it's warm. It never snows. He says there's heaps of jobs. You pick them off the trees like . . . orchids. He says it's even easier now than when we owned all those places, because now the poor pets can't run anything and they'll pay *fortunes.* Pete, he says it's warm, it's heaven, and Pete, they pay.'

A few minutes later, Peter was alone again and Sheilah part of a closed, laughing group. Holding her elbow was the man from the place where jobs grew like orchids. Peter edged into the group and laughed at a story he hadn't heard. He heard only the last line, which was, 'Here comes another tunnel.' Looking out from the tight laughing ring, he saw Agnes again, and he thought, I'd be like Agnes if I didn't have Sheilah. Agnes put her glass down on a table and lurched toward the doorway, head forward. Madge Burleigh, who never stopped moving around the room and smiling, was still smiling when she paused and said in Peter's ear, 'Go with Agnes, Pete. See that she gets home. People will notice if Mike leaves.'

'She probably just wants to walk around the block,' said Peter. 'She'll be back.'

'Oh, stop thinking about yourself, for once, and see that that poor girl gets home,' said Madge. 'You've still got your Fiat, haven't you?'

He turned away as if he had been pushed. Any command is a release, in a way. He may not want to go in that particular direction, but at least he is going somewhere. And now Sheilah, who had moved inches nearer to hear what Madge and Peter were murmuring, said, 'Yes, go, darling,' as if he were leaving the gates of Troy.

Peter was to find Agnes and see that she reached home: this he repeated to himself as he stood on the landing, outside the Burleighs' flat, ringing for the elevator. Bored with waiting for it, he ran down the stairs, four flights, and saw that Agnes had stalled the lift by leaving the door open. She was crouched on the floor, propped on her fingertips. Her eyes were closed.

'Agnes,' said Peter. '*Miss* Brusen, I mean. That's no way to leave a party. Don't you know you're supposed to curtsy and say thanks? My God, Agnes, anybody going by here just now might have seen you! Come on, be a good girl. Time to go home.'

She got up without his help and, moving between invisible crevasses, shut the elevator door. Then she left the building and Peter followed, remembering he was to see that she got home. They walked along the snowy pavement, Peter a few steps behind her. When she turned right for no reason, he turned, too. He had no clear idea where they were going. Perhaps she lived close by. He had forgotten where the hired car was parked, or what it looked like; he could not remember its make or its colour. In any case, Sheilah had the key. Agnes walked on steadily, as if she knew her destination, and he thought, Agnes Brusen is drunk in the street in Geneva and dressed like a tramp. He wanted to say, 'This is the best thing that ever happened to you, Agnes; it will help you understand how things are for some of the rest of us.' But she stopped and turned and, leaning over a low hedge, retched on a frozen lawn. He held her clammy forehead and rested his hand on her arched back, on muscles as tight as a fist. She straightened up and drew a breath but the cold air made her cough. 'Don't breath too deeply,' he said. 'It's the worst thing you can do. Have you got a handkerchief?' He passed his own handkerchief over her wet weeping face, upturned like the face of one of his little girls. 'I'm out without a coat,' he said, noticing it. 'We're a pair.'

'I never drink,' said Agnes. 'I'm just not used to it.' Her voice was sweet and quiet. He had never seen her so peaceful, so composed. He thought she must surely be all right, now, and perhaps he might leave her there. The trust in her tilted face had perplexed him. He wanted to get back to Sheilah and have her explain something. He had forgotten what it was, but Sheilah would know. 'Do you live around here?' he said. As he spoke, she let herself fall. He had wiped her face and now she trusted him to pick her up, set her on her feet, take her wherever she ought to be. He pulled her up and she stood, wordless, humble, as he brushed the snow from her tramp's clothes. Snow horizontally crossed the lamplight. The street was silent. Agnes had lost her hat. Snow, which he tasted, melted on her hands. His gesture of licking snow from her hands was formal as a handshake. He tasted snow on her hands and then they walked on.

'I never drink,' she said. They stood on the edge of a broad avenue. The wrong turning now could lead them anywhere; it was the changeable avenue at the edge of towns that loses its houses and becomes a highway. She held his arm and spoke in a gentle voice. She said, 'In our house we didn't smoke or drink. My mother was ambitious for me, more than for Harry and the others.' She said, 'I've never been alone before. When I was a kid I would get up in the summer before the others, and I'd see the ice wagon going down the street. I'm alone now. Mrs Burleigh's found me an apartment. It's only one room. She likes it because it's in an old part of town. I don't like old houses. Old houses are dirty. You don't know who was there before.'

'I should have a car somewhere,' Peter said. 'I'm not sure where we are.'

He remembers that on this avenue they climbed into a taxi, but nothing about the drive. Perhaps he fell asleep. He does remember that when he paid the driver Agnes clutched his arm, trying to stop him. She pressed extra coins into the driver's palm. The driver was paid twice.

'I'll tell you one thing about us,' said Peter. 'We pay everything twice.' This was part of a much longer theory concerning North American behaviour, and it was not Peter's own. Mike Burleigh had held forth about it on summer afternoons.

Agnes pushed open a door between a stationer's shop and a grocery, and led the way up a narrow inside stair. They climbed one flight, frightening beetles. She had to search every pocket for the latchkey. She was shaking with cold. Her apartment seemed little warmer than the street. Without speaking to Peter she turned on all the lights.

She looked inside the kitchen and the bathroom and then got down on her hands and knees and looked under the sofa. The room was neat and belonged to no one. She left him standing in this unclaimed room—she had forgotten him—and closed a door behind her. He looked for something to do—some useful action he could repeat to Madge. He turned on the electric radiator in the fireplace. Perhaps Agnes wouldn't thank him for it; perhaps she would rather undress in the cold. 'I'll be on my way,' he called to the bathroom door.

She had taken off the tramp's clothes and put on a dressing gown of orphanage wool. She came out of the bathroom and straight toward him. She pressed her face and rubbed her cheek on his shoulder as if hoping the contact would leave a scar. He saw her back and her profile and his own face in the mirror over the fireplace. He thought, This is how disasters happen. He saw floods of sea water moving with perfect punitive justice over reclaimed land; he saw lava covering vineyards and overtaking of dogs and stragglers. A bridge over an abyss snapped in two and the long express train, suddenly V-shaped, floated like snow. He thought amiably of every kind of disaster and thought, This is how they occur.

Her eyes were closed. She said, 'I shouldn't be over here. In my family we didn't drink or smoke. My mother wanted a lot from me, more than from Harry and the others.' But he knew that; he had known from the day of the Bible, and because once, at the beginning, she had made him afraid. He was not afraid of her now.

She said, 'It's no use staying here, is it?'

'If you mean what I think, no.'

'It wouldn't be better anywhere.'

She let him see full on her blotched face. He was not expected to do anything. He was not required to pick her up when she fell or wipe her tears. She was poor quality, really—he remembered having thought that once. She left him and went quietly in to the bathroom and locked the door. He heard taps running and supposed it was a hot bath. He was pretty certain there would be no more tears. He looked at his watch: Sheilah must be home, now, wondering what had become of him. He descended the beetle's staircase and for forty minutes crossed the city under a windless fall of snow.

The neighbour's child who had stayed with Peter's children was asleep on the living room sofa. Peter woke her and sent her, sleepwalking, to her own door. He sat down, wet to the bone, thinking. I'll call the Burleighs. In half an hour I'll call the police. He heard a car stop and the engine running and a confusion of two voices laughing and calling goodnight. Presently Sheilah let herself in, rosy-faced, smiling. She carried his trenchcoat over her arm. She said, 'How's Agnes?'

'Where were you?' he said. 'Whose car was that?'

Sheilah had gone into the children's room. He heard her shutting their window. She returned, undoing her dress, and said, 'Was Agnes all right?'

'Agnes is all right. Sheilah, this is about the worst . . .'

She stepped out of the Balcenciaga and threw it over a chair. She stopped and looked at him and said, 'Poor old Pete, are you in love with Agnes?' And then, as if the answer were of so little importance she hadn't time for it, she locked her arms around him and said, 'My love, we're going to Ceylon.'

Two days later, when Peter strolled into his office, Agnes was at her desk. She wore the blue dress, with a spotless collar. White and yellow freesias were symmetrically arranged in the glass jar. The room was hot, and the spring snow, glued for a second when it touched the window, blurred the view of parked cars.

'Quite a party,' Peter said.

She did not look up. He sighed, sat down, and thought if the snow held he would be skiing at the Burleighs' very soon. Impressed by his kindness to Agnes, Madge had invited the family for the first possible weekend.

Presently Agnes said, 'I'll never drink again or go to a house where people are drinking. And I'll never bother anyone the way I bothered you.'

'You didn't bother me,' he said. 'I took you home. You were alone and it was late. It's normal.'

'Normal for you, maybe, but I'm used to getting myself home by myself. Please never tell what happened.'

He stared at her. He can still remember the freesias and the Bible and the heat in the room. She looked as if the elements had no power. She felt neither heat nor cold. 'Nothing *happened*,' he said.

'I behaved in a silly way. I had no right to. I led you to think I might do something wrong.'

'I might have tried something,' he said gallantly. 'But that would be my fault and not yours.'

She put her knuckle to her mouth and he could scarcely hear. 'It was because of you. I was afraid you might be blamed, or else you'd blame yourself.'

'There's no question of any blame,' he said. 'Nothing happened. We'd both had a lot to drink. Forget about it. Nothing happened. You'd remember if it had.'

She put down her hand. There was an expression on her face. Now she sees me, he thought. She had never looked at him after the first day. (He has since tried to put a name to the look on her face; but how can he, now, after so many voyages, after Ceylon, and Hong Kong, and Sheilah's nearly leaving him, and all their difficulties—the money owed, the rows with hotel managers, the lost and found steamer trunk, the children throwing up the foreign food?) She sees me now, he thought. What does she see?

She said, 'I'm from a big family. I'm not used to being alone. I'm not a suicidal person, but I could have done something after that party, just not to see any more, or think or listen or expect anything. What can I think when I see these people? All my life I heard, Educated people don't do this, educated people don't do that. And now I'm here, and you're all educated people, and you're nothing but pigs. You're educated and you drink and do everything wrong and you know what you're doing, and that makes you worse than pigs. My family worked to make me an educated person, but they didn't know you. But what if I didn't see and hear and expect anything any more? It wouldn't change anything. You'd all be still the same. Only *you* might have thought it was your fault. You might have thought you were to blame. It could worry you all your life. It would have been wrong for me to worry you.'

He remembered that the rented car was still along a snowy curb somewhere in Geneva. He wondered if Sheilah had the key in her purse and if she remembered where they'd parked.

'I told you about the ice wagon,' Agnes said. 'I don't remember everything, so you're wrong about remembering. But I remember telling you that. That was the best. It's the best you can hope to have. In a big family, if you want to be alone, you have to get up before the rest of them. You get up early in the morning in the summer and it's you, you, once in your life alone in the universe. You think you know everything that can happen . . . Nothing is ever like that again.'

He looked at the smeared window and wondered if this day could end without disaster. In his mind he saw her falling in the snow wearing a tramp's costume, and he saw her coming to him in the orphanage dressing gown. He saw her drowning face at the party. He was afraid for himself. The story was still unfinished. It had to come to a climax, something threatening to him. But there was no climax. They talked that day, and afterward nothing else was said. They went on in the same office for a short time, until Peter left for Ceylon; until somebody read the right letter, passed it on for the right initials, and the Fraziers began the Oriental tour that should have made their fortune. Agnes and Peter were too tired to speak after that morning. They were like a married couple in danger, taking care.

But what were they talking about that day, so quietly, such old friends? They talked about dying, about being ambitious, about being religious, about different kinds of love. What did she see when she looked at him—taking her knuckle slowly from her mouth, bringing her hand down to the desk, letting it rest there? They were both Canadians, so they had this much together—the knowledge of the little you dare admit. Death, near-death, the best thing, the wrong thing—God knows what they were telling each other. Anyway, nothing happened.

When, on Sunday mornings, Sheilah and Peter talk about those times, they take on the glamour of something still to come. It is then he remembers Agnes Brusen. He never says her name. Sheilah wouldn't remember Agnes. Agnes is the only secret Peter has from his wife, the only puzzle he pieces together without her help. He thinks about families in the West as they were fifteen, twenty years ago—the iron-cold ambition, and every member pushing the next one on. He thinks of his father's parties. When he thinks of his father he imagines him with Sheilah, in a crowd. Actually, Sheilah and Peter's father never met, but they might have liked each other. His father admired good-looking women. Peter wonders what they were doing over there in Geneva—not Sheila and Peter, *Agnes* and Peter. It is almost as if they had once run away together, silly as children, irresponsible as lovers. Peter and Sheilah are back where they started. While they were out in world affairs picking up microbes and debts, always on the fringe of disaster, the fringe of a fortune, Agnes went on and did—what? They lost each other. He thinks of the ice wagon going down the street. He sees something he had never seen in his life—a Western town that belongs to Agnes. Here is Agnes—small, mole-faced, round-shouldered because she has always carried a younger child. She watches the ice wagon and the trail of ice water in a morning invented for her: hers. He sees the weak prairie trees and the shadows on the sidewalk. Nothing moves except the shadows and the ice wagon and the changing amber of the child's eyes. The child is Peter. He has seen the grain of the cement sidewalk and the grass in the cracks, and the dust, and the dandelions at the edge of the road. He is there. He has taken the morning that belongs to Agnes, he is up before the others, and he knows everything. There is nothing he doesn't know. He could keep the morning, if he wanted to, but what can Peter do with the start of a summer day? Sheilah is here, it is a true Sunday morning, with its dimness and headache and remorse and regrets and this is life. He says, 'We have the Balenciaga.' He touches Sheilah's hand. The children have their aunt now, and he and Sheilah have each other. Everything works out, somehow or other. Let Agnes have the start of the day. Let Agnes think it was invented for her. Who wants to be alone in the universe? No, begin at the beginning: Peter lost Agnes. Agnes says to herself somewhere, Peter is lost.

1963

# Flannery O'Connor

1925–1964

Mary Flannery O'Connor was born in Savannah, Georgia, to Roman Catholic parents whose families had lived in the South for generations. In Savannah she was educated at parochial schools. When she was 13 her father developed disseminated lupus, a fatal disease in which antibodies attack the blood vessels, joints, and internal organs. The family moved to Milledgeville, Georgia, to live with relatives, and Mary went to Peabody High School and then Georgia State College for Women. She edited the college's literary magazine and won a fellowship to the Writers' Workshop at the University of Iowa, where she received encouragement to publish her fiction. After earning her MFA she went to the writers' colony Yaddo, where she met people who supported her ambition to write and helped her arrange publication for more of her work.

In 1950 O'Connor was diagnosed with the disease that had killed her father nine years earlier. She moved to a farm near Milledgeville and continued writing there until her death in 1964, with her reputation growing steadily, even after her death. Most of her fiction can be found in *Collected Stories* (1971), which includes early versions of her two novels.

The setting for 'Everything That Rises Must Converge' is the recently integrated American South, where Julian, a university graduate, is escorting his mother to a weight loss class at the YWCA. The events that unfold on their bus ride expose their innate fears and prejudices.

## Everything That Rises Must Converge

Her doctor had told Julian's mother that she must lose twenty pounds on account of her blood pressure, so on Wednesday nights Julian had to take her downtown on the bus for a reducing class at the Y. The reducing class was designed for working girls over fifty, who weighed from 165 to 200 pounds. His mother was one of the slimmer ones, but she said ladies did not tell their age or weight. She would not ride the buses by herself at night since they had been integrated, and because the reducing class was one of her few pleasures, necessary for her health, and *free*, she said Julian could at least put himself out to take her, considering all she did for him. Julian did not like to consider all she did for him, but every Wednesday night he braced himself and took her.

She was almost ready to go, standing before the hall mirror, putting on her hat, while he, his hands behind him, appeared pinned to the door frame, waiting like Saint Sebastian for the arrows to begin piercing him. The hat was new and had cost her seven dollars and a half. She kept saying, 'Maybe I shouldn't have paid that for it. No, I shouldn't have. I'll take it off and return it tomorrow. I shouldn't have bought it.'

Julian raised his eyes to heaven. 'Yes, you should have bought it,' he said. 'Put it on and let's go.' It was a hideous hat. A purple velvet flap came down on one side of it and stood up on the other; the rest of it was green and looked like a cushion with the stuffing out. He decided it was less comical than jaunty and pathetic. Everything that gave her pleasure was small and depressed him.

She lifted the hat one more time and set it down slowly on top of her head. Two wings of grey protruded on either side of her florid face, but her eyes, sky-blue, were as innocent and untouched by experience as they must have been when she was ten. Were it not that she was a widow who had struggled fiercely to feed and clothe and put him through school and who was supporting him still, 'until he got on his feet', she might have been a little girl that he had to take to town.

'It's all right, it's all right,' he said. 'Let's go.' He opened the door himself and started down the walk to get her going. The sky was a dying violet and the houses stood out darkly against it, bulbous liver-coloured monstrosities of a uniform ugliness though no two were alike. Since this had been a fashionable neighbourhood forty years ago, his mother persisted in thinking they did well to have an apartment in it. Each house had a narrow collar of dirt around it in which sat, usually, a grubby child. Julian walked with his hands in his pockets, his head down and thrust forward, and his eyes glazed with the determination to make himself completely numb during the time he would be sacrificed to her pleasure.

The door closed and he turned to find the dumpy figure, surmounted by the atrocious hat, coming toward him. 'Well,' she said, 'you only live once and paying a little more for it, I at least won't meet myself coming and going.'

'Some day I'll start making money,' Julian said gloomily—he knew he never would—'and you can have one of those jokes whenever you take the fit.' But first they would move. He visualized a place where the nearest neighbours would be three miles away on either side.

'I think you're doing fine,' she said, drawing on her gloves. 'You've only been out of school a year. Rome wasn't built in a day.'

She was one of the few members of the Y reducing class who arrived in hat and gloves and who had a son who had been to college. 'It takes time,' she said, 'and the world is in such a mess. This hat looked better on me than any of the others, though when she brought it out I said, "Take that thing back. I wouldn't have it on my head," and she said,

"Now wait till you see it on," and when she put it on me, I said, "We-ull," and she said, "If you ask me, that hat does something for you and you do something for the hat, and besides," she said, "with that hat, you won't meet yourself coming and going." '

Julian thought he could have stood his lot better if she had been selfish, if she had been an old hag who drank and screamed at him. He walked along, saturated in depression, as if in the midst of his martyrdom he had lost his faith. Catching sight of his long, hopeless, irritated face, she stopped suddenly with a grief-stricken look, and pulled back on his arm. 'Wait on me,' she said. 'I'm going back to the house and take this thing off and tomorrow I'm going to return it. I was out of my head. I can pay the gas bill with the seven-fifty.'

He caught her arm in a vicious grip. 'You are not going to take it back,' he said. 'I like it.'

'Well,' she said, 'I don't think I ought . . .'

'Shut up and enjoy it,' he muttered, more depressed than ever.

'With the world in the mess it's in', she said, 'it's a wonder we can enjoy anything. I tell you, the bottom rail is on the top.'

Julian sighed.

'Of course,' she said, 'if you know who you are, you can go anywhere.' She said this every time he took her to the reducing class. 'Most of them in it are not our kind of people,' she said, 'but I can be gracious to anybody. I know who I am.'

'They don't give a damn for your graciousness,' Julian said savagely. 'Knowing who you are is good for one generation only. You haven't the foggiest idea where you stand now or who you are.'

She stopped and allowed her eyes to flash at him. 'I most certainly do know who I am,' she said, 'and if you don't know who you are, I'm ashamed of you.'

'Oh hell,' Julian said.

'Your great-grandfather was a former governor of this state,' she said. 'Your grandfather was a prosperous landowner. Your grandfather was a Godhigh.'

'Will you look around you,' he said tensely, 'and see where you are now?' and he swept his arm jerkily out to indicate the neighbourhood, which the growing darkness at least made less dingy.

'You remain what you are,' she said. 'Your great-grandfather had a plantation and two hundred slaves.'

'There are no more slaves,' he said irritably.

'They were better off when they were,' she said. He groaned to see that she was off on that topic. She rolled onto it every few days like a train on an open track. He knew every stop, every junction, every swamp along the way, and knew the exact point at which her conclusion would roll majestically into the station: 'It's ridiculous. It's simply not realistic. They should rise, yes, but on their own side of the fence.'

'Let's skip it,' Julian said.

'The ones I feel sorry for,' she said, 'are the ones that are half white. They're tragic.'

'Will you skip it?'

'Suppose we were half white. We would certainly have mixed feelings.'

'I have mixed feelings now,' he groaned.

'Well let's talk about something pleasant,' she said. 'I remember going to Grandpa's when I was a little girl. Then the house had double stairways that went up to what was really the second floor—all the cooking was done on the first. I used to like to stay down in the kitchen on account of the way the walls smelled. I would sit with my nose pressed against the plaster and take deep breaths. Actually the place belonged to the Godhighs but your grandfather Chestny paid the mortgage and saved it for them. They were in reduced circumstances,' she said, 'but reduced or not, they never forgot who they were.'

'Doubtless that decayed mansion reminded them,' Julian muttered. He never spoke of it without contempt or thought of it without longing. He had seen it once when he was a child before it had been sold. The double stairways had rotted and been torn down. Negroes were living in it. But it remained in his mind as his mother had known it. It appeared in his dreams regularly. He would stand on the wide porch, listening to the rustle of oak leaves, then wander through the high-ceilinged hall into the parlour that opened onto it and gaze at the worn rugs and faded draperies. It occurred to him that it was he, not she, who could have appreciated it. He preferred its threadbare elegance to anything he could name and it was because of it that all the neighbourhoods they had lived in had been a torment to him—whereas she had hardly known the difference. She called her insensitivity 'being adjustable'.

'And I remember the old darky who was my nurse, Caroline. There was no better person in the world. I've always had a great respect for my coloured friends,' she said. 'I'd do anything in the world for them and they'd . . .'

'Will you for God's sake get off that subject?' Julian said. When he got on a bus by himself, he made it a point to sit down beside a Negro, in reparation as it were for his mother's sins.

'You're mighty touchy tonight,' she said. 'Do you feel all right?'

'Yes I feel all right,' he said. 'Now lay off.'

She pursed her lips. 'Well, you certainly are in a vile humour,' she observed. 'I just won't speak to you at all.'

They had reached the bus stop. There was no bus in sight and Julian, his hands still jammed in his pockets and his head thrust forward, scowled down the empty street. The frustration of having to wait on the bus as well as ride on it began to creep up his neck like a hot hand. The presence of his mother was borne in upon him as she gave a pained sigh. He looked at her bleakly. She was holding herself very erect under the preposterous hat, wearing it like a banner of her imaginary dignity. There was in him an evil urge to break her spirit. He suddenly unloosened his tie and pulled it off and put it in his pocket.

She stiffened. 'Why must you look like that when you take me to town?' she said. 'Why must you deliberately embarrass me?'

'If you'll never learn where you are,' he said, 'you can at least learn where I am.'

'You look like a—thug,' she said.

'Then I must be one,' he murmured.

'I'll just go home,' she said. 'I will not bother you. If you can't do a little thing like that for me . . .'

Rolling his eyes upward, he put his tie back on. 'Restored to my class,' he muttered. He thrust his face toward her and hissed, 'True culture is in the mind, the *mind*,' he said, and tapped his head, 'the mind.'

'It's in the heart,' she said, 'and in how you do things and how you do things is because of who you *are*.'

'Nobody in the damn bus cares who you are.'

'I care who I am,' she said icily.

The lighted bus appeared on top of the next hill and as it approached, they moved out into the street to meet it. He put his hand under her elbow and hoisted her up on the creaking step. She entered with a little smile, as if she were going into a drawing room where everyone had been waiting for her. While he put in the tokens, she sat down in one of the broad front seats for three which faced the aisle. A thin woman with protruding teeth and long yellow hair was sitting on the end of it. His mother moved up beside her and left room for Julian beside herself. He sat down and looked at the floor across the aisle where a pair of thin feet in red and white canvas sandals were planted.

His mother immediately began a general conversation meant to attract anyone who felt like talking. 'Can it get any hotter?' she said and removed from her purse a folding fan, black with a Japanese scene on it, which she began to flutter before her.

'I reckon it might could,' the woman with the protruding teeth said, 'but I know for a fact my apartment couldn't get no hotter.'

'It must get the afternoon sun,' his mother said. She sat forward and looked up and down the bus. It was half filled. Everybody was white. 'I see we have the bus to ourselves,' she said. Julian cringed.

'For a change,' said the woman across the aisle, the owner of the red and white canvas sandals. 'I come on the other day and they were thick as fleas—up front and all through.'

'The world is in a mess everywhere,' his mother said. 'I don't know how we've let it get in this fix.'

'What gets my goat is all those boys from good families stealing automobile tires,' the woman with the protruding teeth said. 'I told my boy, I said you may not be rich but you been raised right and if I ever catch you in any such mess, they can send you on to the reformatory. Be exactly where you belong.'

'Training tells,' his mother said. 'Is your boy in high school?'

'Ninth grade,' the woman said.

'My son just finished college last year. He wants to write but he's selling typewriters until he gets started,' his mother said.

The woman leaned forward and peered at Julian. He threw her such a malevolent look that she subsided against the seat. On the floor across the aisle there was an abandoned newspaper. He got up and got it and opened it out in front of him. His mother discreetly continued the conversation in a lower tone but the woman across the aisle said in a loud voice, 'Well that's nice. Selling typewriters is close to writing. He can go right from one to the other.'

'I tell him', his mother said, 'that Rome wasn't built in a day.'

Behind the newspaper Julian was withdrawing into the inner compartment of his mind where he spent most of his time. This was a kind of mental bubble in which he established himself when he could not bear to be a part of what was going on around him. From it he could see out and judge but in it he was safe from any kind of penetration from without. It was the only place where he felt free of the general idiocy of his fellows. His mother had never entered it but from it he could see her with absolute clarity.

The old lady was clever enough and he thought that if she had started from any of the right premises, more might have been expected of her. She lived according to the laws of her own fantasy world, outside of which he had never seen her set foot. The law of it was to sacrifice herself for him after she had first created the necessity to do so by making a mess of things. If he had permitted her sacrifices, it was only because her lack of foresight had made them necessary. All of her life had been a struggle to act like a Chestny without the Chestny goods, and to give him everything she thought a Chestny ought to have; but since, said she, it was fun to struggle, why complain? And when you had won, as she had won, what fun to look back on the hard times! He could not forgive her that she had enjoyed the struggle and that she thought *she* had won.

What she meant when she said she had won was that she had brought him up successfully and had sent him to college and that he had turned out so well—good looking (her teeth had gone unfilled so that his could be straightened), intelligent (he realized he was too intelligent to be a success), and with a future ahead of him (there was of course no future ahead of him). She excused his gloominess on the grounds that he was still growing up and his radical ideas on his lack of practical experience. She said he didn't yet know a thing about 'life', that he hadn't even entered the real world—when already he was as disenchanted with it as a man of fifty.

The further irony of all this was that in spite of her, he had turned out so well. In spite of going to only a third-rate college, he had, on his own initiative, come out with a first-rate education; in spite of growing up dominated by a small mind, he had ended up with a large one; in spite of all her foolish views, he was free of prejudice and unafraid to face facts. Most miraculous of all, instead of being blinded by love for her as she was for him, he had cut himself emotionally free of her and could see her with complete objectivity. He was not dominated by his mother.

The bus stopped with a sudden jerk and shook him from his meditation. A woman from the back lurched forward with little steps and barely escaped falling in his newspaper as she righted herself. She got off and a large Negro got on. Julian kept his paper lowered to watch. It gave him a certain satisfaction to see injustice in daily operation. It confirmed his view that with a few exceptions there was no one worth knowing within a radius of three hundred miles. The Negro was well dressed and carried a briefcase. He looked around and then sat down on the other end of the seat where the woman with the red and white canvas sandals was sitting. He immediately unfolded a newspaper and obscured himself behind it. Julian's mother's elbow at once prodded insistently into his ribs. 'Now you see why I won't ride on these buses by myself,' she whispered.

The woman with the red and white canvas sandals had risen at the same time the Negro sat down and had gone further back in the bus and taken the seat of the woman who had got off. His mother leaned forward and cast her an approving look.

Julian rose, crossed the aisle, and sat down in the place of the woman with the canvas sandals. From this position, he looked serenely across at his mother. Her face had turned an angry red. He stared at her, making his eyes the eyes of a stranger. He felt the tension suddenly lift as if he had openly declared war on her.

He would have liked to get in conversation with the Negro and to talk with him about art or politics or any subject that would be above the comprehension of those around them, but the man remained entrenched behind his paper. He was either ignoring the change of seating or had never noticed it. There was no way for Julian to convey his sympathy.

His mother kept her eyes fixed reproachfully on his face. The woman with the protruding teeth was looking at him avidly as if he were a type of monster new to her.

'Do you have a light?' he asked the Negro.

Without looking away from his paper, the man reached in his pocket and handed him a packet of matches.

'Thanks,' Julian said. For a moment he held the matches foolishly. A NO SMOKING sign looked down upon him from over the door. This alone would not have deterred him; he had no cigarettes. He had quit smoking some months before because he could not afford it. 'Sorry,' he muttered and handed back the matches. The Negro lowered the paper and gave him an annoyed look. He took the matches and raised the paper again.

His mother continued to gaze at him but she did not take advantage of his momentary discomfort. Her eyes retained their battered look. Her face seemed to be unnaturally red, as if her blood pressure had risen. Julian allowed no glimmer of sympathy to show on his face. Having got the advantage, he wanted desperately to keep it and carry it through. He would have liked to teach her a lesson that would last her a while, but there seemed no way to continue to point. The Negro refused to come out from behind his paper.

Julian folded his arms and looked stolidly before him, facing her but as if he did not see her, as if he had ceased to recognize her existence. He visualized a scene in which, the bus having reached their stop, he would remain in his seat and when she said, 'Aren't you going to get off?' he would look at her as at a stranger who had rashly addressed him. The corner they got off on was usually deserted, but it was well lighted and it would not hurt her to walk by herself the four blocks to the Y. He decided to wait until the time came and then decide whether or not he would let her get off by herself. He would have to be at the Y at ten to bring her back, but he could leave her wondering if he was going to show up. There was no reason for her to think she could always depend on him.

He retired again into the high-ceilinged room sparsely settled with large pieces of antique furniture. His soul expanded momentarily but then he became aware of his mother across from him and the vision shrivelled. He studied her coldly. Her feet in little pumps dangled like a child's and did not quite reach the floor. She was training on him an exaggerated look of reproach. He felt completely detached from her. At that moment he could with pleasure have slapped her as he would have slapped a particularly obnoxious child in his charge.

He began to imagine various unlikely ways by which he could teach her a lesson. He might make friends with some distinguished Negro professor or lawyer and bring him home to spend the evening. He would be entirely justified but her blood pressure would rise to 300. He could not push her to the extent of making her have a stroke, and moreover, he had never been successful at making any Negro friends. He had tried to strike up an acquaintance on the bus with some of the better types, with ones that looked like professors or ministers or lawyers. One morning he had sat down next to a distinguished-looking dark brown man who had answered his questions with a sonorous solemnity but who had turned out to be an undertaker. Another day he had sat down beside a cigar-smoking Negro with a diamond ring on his finger, but after a few stilted pleasantries, the Negro had rung the buzzer and risen, slipping two lottery tickets into Julian's hand as he climbed over him to leave.

He imagined his mother lying desperately ill and his being able to secure only a Negro doctor for her. He toyed with that idea for a few minutes and then dropped it for a momentary vision of himself participating as a sympathizer in a sit-in demonstration. This was possible but he did not linger with it. Instead, he approached the ultimate horror. He brought home a beautiful suspiciously Negroid woman. Prepare yourself, he said. There is nothing you can do about it. This is the woman I've chosen. She's intelligent, dignified, even good, and she's suffered and she hasn't thought it *fun*. Now persecute us, go ahead and persecute us. Drive her out of here, but remember, you're driving me too. His eyes were narrowed and through the indignation he had generated, he saw his mother across the aisle, purple faced, shrunken to the dwarf-like proportions of her moral nature, sitting like a mummy beneath the ridiculous banner of her hat.

He was tilted out of his fantasy again as the bus stopped. The door opened with a sucking hiss and out of the dark a large, gaily dressed, sullen-looking coloured woman got on with a little boy. The child, who might have been four, had on a short plaid suit and a tyrolean hat with a blue feather in it. Julian hoped that he would sit down beside him and that the woman would push in beside his mother. He could think of no better arrangement.

As she waited for her tokens, the woman was surveying the seating possibilities—he hoped with the idea of sitting where she was least wanted. There was something familiar-looking about her but Julian could not place what it was. She was a giant of a woman. Her face was set not only to meet opposition but to seek it out. The downward tilt of her large lower lip was like a warning sign: DON'T TAMPER WITH ME. Her bulging figure was encased in a green crepe dress and her feet overflowed in red shoes. She had on a hideous hat. A purple velvet flap came down on one side of it and stood up on the other; the rest of it was green and looked like a cushion with the stuffing out. She carried a mammoth red pocketbook that bulged throughout as if it were stuffed with rocks.

To Julian's disappointment, the little boy climbed up on the empty seat beside his mother. His mother lumped all children, black and white, into a common category, 'cute', and she thought little Negroes were on the whole cuter than little white children. She smiled at the little boy as he climbed on the seat.

Meanwhile the woman was bearing down upon the empty seat beside Julian. To his annoyance, she squeezed herself into it. He saw his mother's face change as the woman settled herself next to him and he realized with satisfaction that this was more objectionable to her than it was to him. Her face seemed almost grey and there was a look of dull recognition in her eyes, as if suddenly she had sickened at some awful confrontation. Julian saw that it was because she and the woman had, in a sense, swapped sons. Though his mother would not realize the symbolic significance of this, she would feel it. His amusement showed plainly on his face.

The woman next to him muttered something unintelligible to herself. He was conscious of a kind of bristling next to him, muted growling like that of an angry cat. He could not see anything but the red pocketbook upright on the bulging green thighs. He visualized the woman as she had stood waiting for her tokens—the ponderous figure, rising from the red shoes upward over the solid hips, the mammoth bosom, the haughty face, to the green and purple hat.

His eyes widened.

The vision of the two hats, identical, broke upon him with the radiance of a brilliant sunrise. His face was suddenly lit with joy. He could not believe that Fate had thrust upon his mother such a lesson. He gave a loud chuckle so that she would look at him and see that he saw. She turned her eyes on him slowly. The blue in them seemed to have turned a bruised purple. For a moment he had an uncomfortable sense of her innocence, but it lasted only a second before principle rescued him. Justice entitled him to laugh. His grin hardened until it said to her as plainly as if he were saying aloud: Your punishment exactly fits your pettiness. This should teach you a permanent lesson.

Her eyes shifted to the woman. She seemed unable to bear looking at him and to find the woman preferable. He became conscious again of the bristling presence at his side. The woman was rumbling like a volcano about to become active. His mother's mouth began to twitch slightly at one corner. With a sinking heart, he saw incipient signs of recovery on her face and realized that this was going to strike her suddenly as funny and was going to be no lesson at all. She kept her eyes on the woman and an amused smile came over her face as if the woman were a monkey that had stolen her hat. The little Negro was looking up at her with large fascinated eyes. He had been trying to attract her attention for some time.

'Carver!' the woman said suddenly. 'Come heah!'

When he saw that the spotlight was on him at last, Carver drew his feet up and turned himself toward Julian's mother and giggled.

'Carver!' the woman said. 'You heah me? Come heah!'

Carver slid down from the seat but remained squatting with his back against the base of it, his head turned slyly around toward Julian's mother, who was smiling at him. The woman reached a hand across the aisle and snatched him to her. He righted himself and hung backwards on her knees, grinning at Julian's mother. 'Isn't he cute?' Julian's mother said to the woman with the protruding teeth.

'I reckon he is,' the woman said without conviction.

The Negress yanked him upright but he eased out of her grip and shot across the aisle and scrambled, giggling wildly, onto the seat beside his love.

'I think he likes me,' Julian's mother said, and smiled at the woman. It was the smile she used when she was being particularly gracious to an inferior. Julian saw everything lost. The lesson had rolled off her like rain on a roof.

The woman stood up and yanked the little boy off the seat as if she were snatching him from contagion. Julian could feel the rage in her at having no weapon like his mother's smile. She gave the child a sharp slap across his leg. He howled once and then thrust his head into her stomach and kicked his feet against her shins. 'Behave,' she said vehemently.

The bus stopped and the Negro who had been reading the newspaper got off. The woman moved over and set the little boy down with a thump between herself and Julian. She held him firmly by the knee. In a moment he put his hands in front of his face and peeped at Julian's mother through his fingers.

'I see yoooooooo!' she said and put her hand in front of her face and peeped at him.

The woman slapped his hand down. 'Quit yo' foolishness,' she said, 'before I knock the living Jesus out of you!'

Julian was thankful the next stop was theirs. He reached up and pulled the cord. The woman reached up and pulled it at the same time. Oh my God, he thought. He had the terrible intuition that when they got off the bus together, his mother would open her purse and give the little boy a nickel. The gesture would be as natural to her as breathing. The bus stopped and the woman got up and lunged to the front, dragging the child, who wished to stay on, after her. Julian and his mother got up and followed. As they neared the door, Julian tried to relieve her of her pocketbook.

'No,' she murmured, 'I want to give the little boy a nickel.'

'No!' Julian hissed. 'No!'

She smiled down at the child and opened her bag. The bus door opened and the woman picked him up by the arm and descended with him, hanging at her hip. Once in the street she set him down and shook him.

Julian's mother had to close her purse while she got down the bus step but as soon as her feet were on the ground, she opened it again and began to rummage inside. 'I can't find but a penny,' she whispered, 'but it looks like a new one.'

'Don't do it!' Julian said fiercely between his teeth. There was a streetlight on the corner and she hurried to get under it so that she could better see into her pocketbook. The woman was heading off rapidly down the street with the child still hanging backward on her hand.

'Oh little boy!' Julian's mother called and took a few quick steps and caught up with them just beyond the lamppost. 'Here's a bright new penny for you,' and she held out the coin, which shone bronze in the dim light.

The huge woman turned and for a moment stood, her shoulders lifted and her face frozen with frustrated rage, and stared at Julian's mother. Then all at once she seemed to explode like a piece of machinery that had been given one ounce of pressure too much. Julian saw the black fist swing out with the red pocketbook. He shut his eyes and cringed as he heard the woman shout, 'He don't take nobody's pennies!'

When he opened his eyes, the woman was disappearing down the street with the little boy staring wide-eyed over her shoulder. Julian's mother was sitting on the sidewalk.

'I told you not to do that,' Julian said angrily. 'I told you not to do that!'

He stood over her for a minute, gritting his teeth. Her legs were stretched out in front of her and her hat was on her lap. He squatted down and looked her in the face. It was totally expressionless. 'You got exactly what you deserved,' he said. 'Now get up.'

He picked up her pocketbook and put what had fallen out back in it. He picked the hat up off her lap. The penny caught his eye on the sidewalk and he picked that up and let it drop before her eyes into the purse. Then he stood up and leaned over and held his hands out to pull her up. She remained immobile. He sighed. Rising about them on either side were black apartment buildings, marked with irregular rectangles of light. At the end of the block a man came out of a door and walked off in the opposite direction. 'All right,' he said, 'suppose somebody happens by and wants to know why you're sitting on the sidewalk?'

She took the hand and, breathing hard, pulled heavily up on it and then stood for a moment, swaying slightly as if the spots of light in the darkness were circling around her. Her eyes, shadowed and confused, finally settled on his face. He did not try to conceal his irritation. 'I hope this teaches you a lesson,' he said. She leaned forward and her eyes raked his face. She seemed trying to determine his identity. Then, as if she found nothing familiar about him, started off with a headlong movement in the wrong direction.

'Aren't you going on to the Y'? he asked.

'Home,' she muttered.

'Well, are we walking?'

For answer she kept going. Julian followed along, his hands behind him. He saw no reason to let the lesson she had had go without backing it up with an explanation of its meaning. She might as well be made to understand what had happened to her. 'Don't think that was just an uppity Negro woman,' he said. 'That was the whole coloured race which will no longer take your condescending pennies. That was your black double. She can wear the same hat as you, and to be sure,' he added gratuitously (because he thought it was funny), 'it looked better on her than it did on you. What all this means', he said, 'is that the old world has gone. The old manners are obsolete and your graciousness is not worth a damn.' He thought bitterly of the house that had been lost for him. 'You aren't who you think you are,' he said.

She continued to plow ahead, paying no attention to him. Her hair had come undone on one side. She dropped her pocketbook and took no notice. He stooped and picked it up and handed it to her but she did not take it.

'You needn't act as if the world had come to an end,' he said, 'because it hasn't. From now on, you've got to live in a new world and face a few realities for a change. Buck up,' he said, 'it won't kill you.'

She was breathing fast.

'Let's wait on the bus,' he said.

'Home,' she said thickly.

'I hate to see you behave like this,' he said. 'Just like a child. I should be able to expect more of you.' He decided to stop where he was and make her stop and wait for a bus. 'I'm not going any farther,' he said, stopping. 'We're going on the bus.'

She continued to go on as if she had not heard him. He took a few steps and caught her arm and stopped her. He looked into her face and caught his breath. He was looking into a face he had never seen before. 'Tell Grandpa to come get me,' she said.

He stared, stricken.

'Tell Caroline to come get me,' she said.

Stunned, he let her go and she lurched forward again, walking as if one leg were shorter than the other. A tide of darkness seemed to be sweeping her from him. 'Mother!' he cried. 'Darling, sweetheart, wait!' Crumpling, she fell to the pavement. He dashed forward and fell at her side, crying, 'Mamma, Mamma!' He turned her over. Her face was fiercely distorted. One eye, large and staring, moved slightly on the left as if it had become unmoored. The other remained fixed on him, raked his face again, found nothing and closed.

'Wait here, wait here!' he cried and jumped up and began to run for help toward a cluster of lights he saw in the distance ahead of him. 'Help, help!' he shouted, but his voice was thin, scarcely a thread of sound. The lights drifted farther away the faster he ran and his feet moved numbly as if they carried him nowhere. The tide of darkness seemed to sweep him back to her, postponing from moment to moment his entry into the world of guilt and sorrow.

1961

# Margaret Laurence

1926–1987

The most distinguished Canadian novelist of her generation, Jean Margaret Wemys was born in the small prairie town of Neepawa, Manitoba, of Scottish Presbyterian ancestry. She attended United College in Winnipeg, now the University of Winnipeg, where she developed her interest in fiction writing. In 1947 she married Jack Laurence, a civil engineer. She spent the early 1950s with her husband in Africa, first in Somaliland (now Somalia) and later in the Gold Coast (now Ghana). Her stay in these countries introduced her to African culture and art, and she translated some Nigerian literature, wrote critical studies of African writings, and set her first novel, *This Side Jordan* (1960), and her first collection of short stories, *The Tomorrow-Tamer* (1963), in Africa. Even though she returned to Canada in 1957, she continued for five years to set her fiction in Africa. In 1962 Laurence moved to England, where she completed *The Stone Angel* (1964), her first novel set in the fictional prairie town of Manawaka. Three more novels, *A Jest of God* (1966), *The Fire-Dwellers* (1969), and *The Diviners* (1974), as well as the short-story sequence *A Bird in the House* (1970), continued Laurence's chronicling of Manawaka, each a close examination of the life of one woman in the town.

# A Bird in the House

The parade would be almost over by now, and I had not gone. My mother had said in a resigned voice, 'All right, Vanessa, if that's the way you feel,' making me suffer twice as many jabs of guilt as I would have done if she had lost her temper. She and Grandmother MacLeod had gone off, my mother pulling the low box-sleigh with Roddie all dolled up in his new red snowsuit, just the sort of little kid anyone would want people to see. I sat on the lowest branch of the birch tree in our yard, not minding the snowy wind, even welcoming its punishment. I went over my reasons for not going, trying to believe they were good and sufficient, but in my heart I felt I was betraying my father. This was the first time I had stayed away from the Remembrance Day parade. I wondered if he would notice that I was not there, standing on the sidewalk at the corner of River and Main while the parade passed, and then following to the Court House grounds where the service was held.

I could see the whole thing in my mind. It was the same every year. The Manawaka Civic Band always led the way. They had never been able to afford full uniforms, but they had peaked navy-blue caps and sky-blue chest ribbons. They were joined on Remembrance Day by the Salvation Army band, whose uniforms seemed too ordinary for a parade, for they were the same ones the bandsmen wore every Saturday night when they played 'Nearer My God to Thee' at the foot of River Street. The two bands never managed to practise quite enough together, so they did not keep in time too well. The Salvation Army band invariably played faster, and afterwards my father would say irritably, 'They play those marches just like they do hymns, blast them, as though they wouldn't get to heaven if they didn't hustle up.' And my mother, who had great respect for the Salvation Army because of the good work they did, would respond chidingly, 'Now, now, Ewen—' I vowed I would never say 'Now, now' to my husband or children, not that I ever intended having the latter, for I had been put off by my brother Roderick, who was now two years old with wavy hair, and everyone said what a beautiful child. I was twelve, and no one in their right mind would have said what a beautiful child, for I was big-boned like my Grandfather Connor and had straight lanky black hair like a Blackfoot or Cree.

After the bands would come the veterans. Even thinking of them at this distance, in the white and withdrawn quiet of the birch tree, gave me a sense of painful embarrassment. I might not have minded so much if my father had not been among them. How could he go? How could he not see how they all looked? It must have been a long time since they were soldiers, for they had forgotten how to march in step. They were old—that was the thing. My father was bad enough, being almost forty, but he wasn't a patch on Howard Tully from the drugstore, who was completely grey-haired and also fat, or Stewart MacMurchie, who was bald at the back of his head. They looked to me like imposters, plump or spindly caricatures of past warriors. I almost hated them for walking in that limping column down Main. At the Court House, everyone would sing *Lord God of Hosts, be with us yet, lest we forget, lest we forget.* Will Masterson would pick up his old Army bugle and blow the Last Post. Then it would be over and everyone could start gabbling once more and go home.

I jumped down from the birch bough and ran to the house, yelling, making as much noise as I could.

> I'm a poor lonesome cowboy
> An' a long way from home—

I stepped inside the front hall and kicked off my snow boots. I slammed the door behind me, making the dark ruby and emerald glass shake in the small leaded panes. I slid purposely on the hall rug, causing it to bunch and crinkle on the slippery polished oak of the floor. I seized the newel post, round as a head, and spun myself to and fro on the bottom stair.

> I ain't got no father
> To buy the clothes I wear,
> I'm a poor lonesome—

At this moment my shoulders were firmly seized and shaken by a pair of hands, white and delicate and old, but strong as talons.

'Just what do you think you're doing, young lady?' Grandmother MacLeod enquired, in a voice like frost on a windowpane, infinitely cold and clearly etched.

I went limp and in a moment she took her hands away. If you struggled, she would always hold on longer.

'Gee, I never knew you were home yet.'

'I would have thought that on a day like this you might have shown a little respect and consideration,' Grandmother MacLeod said, 'even if you couldn't make the effort to get cleaned up enough to go to the parade.'

I realized with surprise that she imagined this to be my reason for not going. I did not try to correct her impression. My real reason would have been even less acceptable.

'I'm sorry,' I said quickly.

In some families, *please* is described as the magic word. In our house, however, it was sorry.

'This isn't an easy day for any of us,' she said.

Her younger son, my Uncle Roderick, had been killed in the Great War. When my father marched, and when the hymn was sung, and when that unbearably lonely tune was sounded by the one bugle and everyone forced themselves to keep absolutely still, it would be that boy of whom she was thinking. I felt the enormity of my own offence.

'Grandmother—I'm sorry.'

'So you said.'

I could not tell her I had not really said it before at all. I went into the den and found my father there. He was sitting in the leather-cushioned armchair beside the fireplace. He was not doing anything, just sitting and smoking. I stood beside him, wanting to touch the light-brown hairs on his forearm, but thinking he might laugh at me or pull his arm away if I did.

'I'm sorry,' I said, meaning it.

'What for, honey?'

'For not going.'

'Oh—that. What was the matter?'

I did not want him to know, and yet I had to tell him, make him see.

'They look silly,' I blurted. 'Marching like that.'

For a minute I thought he was going to be angry. It would have been a relief to me if he had been. Instead, he drew his eyes away from mine and fixed them above the mantelpiece where the sword hung, the handsome and evil-looking crescent in its carved bronze sheath that some ancestor had once brought from the Northern Frontier of India.

'Is that the way it looks to you?' he said.

I felt in his voice some hurt, something that was my fault. I wanted to make everything all right between us, to convince him that I understood, even if I did not. I prayed that Grandmother MacLeod would stay put in her room, and that my mother would take a long time in the kitchen, giving Roddie his lunch. I wanted my father to myself, so I could prove to him that I cared more about him than any of the others did. I wanted to speak in some way that would be more poignant and comprehending than anything of which my mother could possibly be capable. But I did not know how.

'You were right there when Uncle Roderick got killed, weren't you?' I began uncertainly.

'Yes.'

'How old was he, Dad?'

'Eighteen,' my father said.

Unexpectedly, that day came into intense being for me. He had had to watch his own brother die, not in the antiseptic calm of some hospital, but out in the open, the stretches of mud I had seen in his snapshots. He would not have known what to do. He would just have had to stand there and look at it, whatever that might mean. I looked at my father with a kind of horrified awe, and then I began to cry. I had forgotten about impressing him with my perception. Now I needed him to console me for this unwanted glimpse of the pain he had once known.

'Hey, cut it out, honey,' he said, embarrassed. 'It was bad, but it wasn't all as bad as that part. There were a few other things.'

'Like what?' I said, not believing him.

'Oh—I don't know,' he replied evasively. 'Most of us were pretty young, you know, I and the boys I joined up with. None of us had ever been away from Manawaka before. Those of us who came back mostly came back here, or else went no further away from town than Winnipeg. So when we were overseas—that was the only time most of us were ever a long way from home.'

'Did you want to be?' I asked, shocked.

'Oh well—' my father said uncomfortably. 'It was kind of interesting to see a few other places for a change, that's all.'

Grandmother MacLeod was standing in the doorway.

'Beth's called you twice for lunch, Ewen. Are you deaf, you and Vanessa?'

'Sorry,' my father and I said simultaneously.

Then we went upstairs to wash our hands.

That winter my mother returned to her old job as nurse in my father's medical practice. She was able to do this only because of Noreen.

'Grandmother MacLeod says we're getting a maid,' I said to my father, accusingly, one morning. 'We're not, are we?'

'Believe you me, on what I'm going to be paying her,' my father growled, 'she couldn't be called anything as classy as a maid. Hired girl would be more like it.'

'Now, now, Ewen,' my mother put in, 'it's not as if we were cheating her or anything. You know she wants to live in town, and I can certainly see why, stuck out there on the farm, and her father hardly ever letting her come in. What kind of life is that for a girl?'

'I don't like the idea of your going back to work, Beth,' my father said. 'I know you're fine now, but you're not exactly the robust type.'

'You can't afford to hire a nurse any longer. It's all very well to say the Depression won't last forever—probably it won't, but what else can we do for now?'

'I'm damned if I know,' my father admitted. 'Beth—'

'Yes?'

They both seemed to have forgotten about me. It was at breakfast, which we always ate in the kitchen, and I sat rigidly on my chair, pretending to ignore and thus snub their withdrawal from me. I glared at the window, but it was so thickly plumed and scrolled with frost that I could not see out. I glanced back to my parents. My father had not replied, and my mother was looking at him in that anxious and half-frowning way she had recently developed.

'What is it, Ewen?' Her voice had the same nervous sharpness it bore sometimes when she would say to me, 'For mercy's sake, Vanessa, what is it *now*?' as though whatever was the matter, it was bound to be the last straw.

My father spun his sterling silver serviette ring, engraved with his initials, slowly around on the table.

'I never thought things would turn out like this, did you?'

'Please—' my mother said in a low strained voice, 'please, Ewen, let's not start all this again. I can't take it.'

'All right,' my father said. 'Only—'

'The MacLeods used to have money and now they don't,' my mother cried. 'Well, they're not alone. Do you think all that matters to me, Ewen? What I can't bear is to see you forever reproaching yourself. As if it were your fault.'

'I don't think it's the comedown,' my father said. 'If I were somewhere else, I don't suppose it would matter to me, either, except where you're concerned. But I suppose you'd work too hard wherever you were—it's bred into you. If you haven't got anything to slave away at, you'll sure as hell invent something.'

'What do you think I should do, let the house go to wrack and ruin? That would go over well with your mother, wouldn't it?'

'That's just it,' my father said. 'It's the damned house all the time. I haven't only taken on my father's house, I've taken on everything that goes with it, apparently. Sometimes I really wonder—'

'Well, it's a good thing I've inherited some practicality even if you haven't,' my mother said. 'I'll say that for the Connors—they aren't given to brooding, thank you Lord. Do you want your egg poached or scrambled?'

'Scrambled,' my father said. 'All I hope is that this Noreen doesn't get married straightaway, that's all.'

'She won't,' my mother said. 'Who's she going to meet who could afford to marry?'

'I marvel at you, Beth,' my father said. 'You look as though a puff of wind would blow you away. But underneath, by God, you're all hardwood.'

'Don't talk stupidly,' my mother said. 'All I hope is that she doesn't object to taking your mother's breakfast up on a tray.'

'That's right,' my father said angrily. 'Rub it in.'

'Oh Ewen, I'm sorry!' my mother cried, her face suddenly stricken. 'I don't know why I say these things. I didn't mean to.'

'I know,' my father said. 'Here, cut it out, honey. Just for God's sake please don't cry.'

'I'm sorry,' my mother repeated, blowing her nose.

'We're both sorry,' my father said. 'Not that that changes anything.'

After my father had gone, I got down from my chair and went to my mother.

'I don't want you to go back to the office. I don't want a hired girl here. I'll hate her.'

My mother sighed, making me feel that I was placing an intolerable burden on her, and yet making me resent having to feel this weight. She looked tired, as she often did these days. Her tiredness bored me, made me want to attack her for it.

'Catch me getting along with a dumb old hired girl,' I threatened.

'Do what you like,' my mother said abruptly. 'What can I do about it?'

And then, of course, I felt bereft, not knowing which way to turn.

My father need not have worried about Noreen getting married. She was, as it turned out, interested not in boys but in God. My mother was relieved about the boys but alarmed about God.

'It isn't natural,' she said, 'for a girl of seventeen. Do you think she's all right mentally, Ewen?'

When my parents, along with Grandmother MacLeod, went to the United Church every Sunday, I was made to go to Sunday school in the church basement, where there were small red chairs which humiliatingly resembled kindergarten furniture, and pictures of Jesus wearing a white sheet and surrounded by a whole lot of well-dressed kids whose mothers obviously had not suffered them to come unto Him until every face and ear was properly scrubbed. Our religious observances also included grace at meals, when my father would mumble 'For what we are about to receive the Lord make us truly thankful Amen,' running the words together as though they were one long word. My mother approved of these rituals, which seemed decent and moderate to her. Noreen's religion, however, was a different matter. Noreen belonged to the Tabernacle of the Risen and Reborn, and she had got up to testify no less than seven times in the past two years, she told us. My mother, who could not imagine anyone's voluntarily making a public spectacle of themselves, was profoundly shocked by this revelation.

'Don't worry,' my father soothed her. 'She's all right. She's just had kind of a dull life, that's all.'

My mother shrugged and went on worrying and trying to help Noreen without hurting her feelings, by tactful remarks about the advisability of modulating one's voice when singing hymns, and the fact that there was plenty of hot water so Noreen didn't need to hesitate about taking a bath. She even bought a razor and a packet of blades and whispered to Noreen that any girl who wore transparent blouses so much would probably like to shave under her arms. None of these suggestions had the slightest effect on Noreen. She did not cease belting out hymns at the top of her voice, she bathed once a fortnight, and the sorrel-coloured hair continued to bloom like a thicket of Indian paintbrush in her armpits.

Grandmother MacLeod refused to speak to Noreen. This caused Noreen a certain amount of bewilderment until she finally hit on an answer.

'Your poor grandma,' she said. 'She is deaf as a post. These things are sent to try us here on earth, Vanessa. But if she makes it into Heaven, I'll bet you anything she will hear clear as a bell.'

Noreen and I talked about Heaven quite a lot, and also Hell. Noreen had an intimate and detailed knowledge of both places. She not only knew what they looked like—she even knew how big they were. Heaven was seventy-seven thousand miles square and it had four gates, each one made out of a different kind of precious jewel. The Pearl Gate, the Topaz Gate, the Amethyst Gate, the Ruby Gate—Noreen would reel them off, all the gates of Heaven. I told Noreen they sounded like poetry, but she was puzzled by my reaction and said I shouldn't talk that way. If you said poetry, it sounded like it was just made up and not really so, Noreen said.

Hell was larger than Heaven, and when I asked why, thinking of it as something of a comedown for God, Noreen said naturally it had to be bigger because there were a darn sight more people there than in Heaven. Hell was one hundred and ninety million miles deep and was in perpetual darkness, like a cave or under the sea. Even the flames (this was the awful thing) *did not give off any light.*

I did not actually believe in Noreen's doctrines, but the images which they conjured up began to inhabit my imagination. Noreen's fund of exotic knowledge was not limited to religion, although in a way it all seemed related. She could do many things which had a spooky tinge to them. Once when she was making a cake, she found we had run out of eggs. She went outside and gathered a bowl of fresh snow and used it instead. The cake rose like a charm, and I stared at Noreen as though she were a sorceress. In fact, I began to think of her as a sorceress, someone not quite of this earth. There was nothing unearthly about her broad shoulders and hips and her forest of dark red hair, but even these features took on a slightly sinister significance to me. I no longer saw her through the eyes of the expressed opinions of my mother and father, as a girl who had quit school at grade eight and whose life on the farm had been endlessly drab. I knew the truth—Noreen's life had not been drab at all, for she dwelt in a world of violent splendours, a world filled with angels whose wings of delicate light bore real feathers, and saints shining like the dawn, and prophets who spoke in ancient tongues, and the ecstatic souls of the saved, as well as denizens of the lower regions—mean-eyed imps and crooked cloven-hoofed monsters and beasts with the bodies of swine and the human heads of murderers, and lovely depraved jezebels torn by dogs through all eternity. The middle layer of Creation, our earth, was equally full of grotesque presences, for Noreen believed strongly in the visitation of ghosts and the communication with spirits. She could prove this with her Ouija board. We would both place our fingers lightly on the indicator, and it would skim across the board and spell out answers to our questions. I did not believe wholeheartedly in the Ouija board, either, but I was cautious about the kind of question I asked, in case the answer would turn out unfavourable and I would be unable to forget it.

One day Noreen told me she could also make a table talk. We used the small table in my bedroom, and sure enough, it lifted very slightly under our fingertips and tapped once for *Yes*, twice for *No*. Noreen asked if her Aunt Ruthie would get better from the kidney operation, and the table replied No. I withdrew my hands.

'I don't want to do it any more.'

'Gee, what's the matter, Vanessa?' Noreen's plain placid face creased in a frown. 'We only just begun.'

'I have to do my homework.'

My heart lurched as I said this. I was certain Noreen would know I was lying, and that she would know not by any ordinary perception, either. But her attention had been caught by something else, and I was thankful, at least until I saw what it was.

My bedroom window was not opened in the coldest weather. The storm window, which was fitted outside as an extra wall against the winter, had three small circular holes in its frame so that some fresh air could seep into the house. The sparrow must have been floundering in the new snow on the roof, for it had crawled in through one of these holes and was now caught between the two layers of glass. I could not bear the panic of the trapped bird, and before I realized what I was doing, I had thrown open the bedroom window. I was not releasing the sparrow into any better a situation, I soon saw, for instead of remaining quiet and allowing us to catch it in order to free it, it began flying blindly around the room, hitting the lampshade, brushing against the walls, its wings seeming to spin faster and faster.

I was petrified. I thought I would pass out if those palpitating wings touched me. There was something in the bird's senseless movements that revolted me. I also thought it was going to damage itself, break one of those thin wing-bones, perhaps, and then it would be lying on the floor, dying, like the pimpled and horribly featherless baby birds we saw sometimes on the sidewalks in the spring when they had fallen out of their nests. I was not any longer worried about the sparrow. I wanted only to avoid the sight of it lying broken on the floor. Viciously, I thought that if Noreen said, *God sees the little sparrow fall*, I would kick her in the shins. She did not, however, say this.

'A bird in the house means a death in the house,' Noreen remarked.

Shaken, I pulled my glance away from the whirling wings and looked at Noreen. 'What?'

'That's what I've heard said, anyhow.'

The sparrow had exhausted itself. It lay on the floor, spent and trembling. I could not bring myself to touch it. Noreen bent and picked it up. She cradled it with great gentleness between her cupped hands. Then we took it downstairs, and when I had opened the back door, Noreen set the bird free.

'Poor little scrap,' she said, and I felt struck to the heart, knowing she had been concerned all along about the sparrow, while I, perfidiously, in the chaos of the moment, had been concerned only about myself.

'Wanna do some with the Ouija board, Vanessa?' Noreen asked.

I shivered a little, perhaps only because of the blast of cold air which had come into the kitchen when the door was opened.

'No thanks, Noreen. Like I said, I got my homework to do. But thanks all the same.'

'That's okay,' Noreen said in her guileless voice. 'Any time.'

But whenever she mentioned the Ouija board or the talking table, after that, I always found some excuse not to consult these oracles.

'Do you want to come to church with me this evening, Vanessa?' my father asked.

'How come you're going to the evening service?' I enquired.

'Well, we didn't go this morning. We went snowshoeing instead, remember? I think your grandmother was a little bit put out about it. She went alone this morning. I guess it wouldn't hurt you and me, to go now.'

We walked through the dark, along the white streets, the snow squeaking dryly under our feet. The streetlights were placed at long intervals along the sidewalks, and around each pole the circle of flimsy light created glistening points of blue and crystal on the crusted snow. I would have liked to take my father's hand, as I used to do, but I was too old for that now. I walked beside him, taking long steps so he would not have to walk more slowly on my account.

The sermon bored me, and I began leafing through the Hymnary for entertainment. I must have drowsed, for the next thing I knew, my father was prodding me and we were on our feet for the closing hymn.

Near the Cross, near the Cross,
  Be my glory ever,
Till my ransomed soul shall find
  Rest beyond the river.

I knew the tune well, so I sang loudly for the first verse. But the music to that hymn is sombre, and all at once the words themselves seemed too dreadful to be sung. I stopped singing, my throat knotted. I thought I was going to cry, but I did not know why, except that the song recalled to me my Grandmother Connor, who had been dead only a year now. I wondered why her soul needed to be ransomed. If God did not think she was good enough just as she was, then I did not have much use for His opinion. *Rest beyond the river*—was that what had happened to her? She had believed in Heaven, but I did not think that rest beyond the river was quite what she had in mind. To think of her in Noreen's flashy Heaven, though—that was even worse. Someplace where nobody ever got annoyed or had to be smoothed down and placated, someplace where there were never any family scenes—that would have suited my Grandmother Connor. Maybe she wouldn't have minded a certain amount of rest beyond the river, at that.

When we had the silent prayer, I looked at my father. He sat with his head bowed and his eyes closed. He was frowning deeply, and I could see the pulse in his temple. I wondered then what he believed. I did not have any real idea what it might be. When he raised his head, he did not look uplifted or anything like that. He merely looked tired. Then Reverend McKee pronounced the benediction, and we could go home.

'What do you think about all that stuff, Dad?' I asked hesitantly, as we walked.

'What stuff, honey?'

'Oh, Heaven and Hell, and like that.'

My father laughed. 'Have you been listening to Noreen too much? Well, I don't know. I don't think they're actual places. Maybe they stand for something that happens all the time here, or else doesn't happen. It's kind of hard to explain. I guess I'm not so good at explanations.'

Nothing seemed to have been made any clearer to me. I reached out and took his hand, not caring that he might think this a babyish gesture.

'I hate that hymn!'

'Good Lord,' my father said in astonishment. 'Why, Vanessa?'

But I did not know and so could not tell him.

Many people in Manawaka had flu that winter, so my father and Dr Cates were kept extremely busy. I had flu myself, and spent a week in bed, vomiting only the first day and after that enjoying poor health, as my mother put it, with Noreen bringing me ginger ale and orange juice, and each evening my father putting a wooden tongue-depressor into my mouth and peering down my throat, then smiling and saying he thought I might live after all.

Then my father got sick himself, and had to stay at home and go to bed. This was such an unusual occurrence that it amused me.

'Doctors shouldn't get sick,' I told him.

'You're right,' he said. 'That was pretty bad management.'

'Run along now, dear,' my mother said.

That night I woke and heard voices in the upstairs hall. When I went out, I found my mother and Grandmother MacLeod, both in their dressing gowns. With them was Dr Cates. I did not go immediately to my mother, as I would have done only a year before. I stood in the doorway of my room, squinting against the sudden light.

'Mother—what is it?'

She turned, and momentarily I saw the look on her face before she erased it and put on a contrived calm.

'It's all right,' she said. 'Dr Cates has just come to have a look at Daddy. You go on back to sleep.'

The wind was high that night, and I lay and listened to it rattling the storm windows and making the dry and winter-stiffened vines of the Virginia creeper scratch like small persistent claws against the red brick. In the morning, my mother told me that my father had developed pneumonia.

Dr Cates did not think it would be safe to move my father to the hospital. My mother began sleeping in the spare bedroom, and after she had been there for a few nights, I asked if I could sleep in there too. I thought she would be bound to ask me why, and I did not know what I would say, but she did not ask. She nodded, and in some way her easy agreement upset me.

That night Dr Cates came again, bringing with him one of the nurses from the hospital. My mother stayed upstairs with them. I sat with Grandmother MacLeod in the living room. That was the last place in the world I wanted to be, but I thought she would be offended if I went off. She sat as straight and rigid as a totem pole, and embroidered away at the needlepoint cushion cover she was doing. I perched on the edge of the chesterfield and kept my eyes fixed on *The White Company* by Conan Doyle, and from time to time I turned a page. I had already read it three times before, but luckily Grandmother MacLeod did not know that. At nine o'clock she looked at her gold brooch watch, which she always wore pinned to her dress, and told me to go to bed, so I did that.

I wakened in darkness. At first, it seemed to me that I was in my own bed, and everything was a usual, with my parents in their room, and Roddie curled up in the crib in his room, and Grandmother MacLeod sleeping with her mouth open in her enormous spool bed, surrounded by a half a dozen framed photos of Uncle Roderick and only one of my father, and Noreen snoring fitfully in the room next to mine, with the dark flames of her hair spreading out across the pillow, and the pink and silver motto cards from the Tabernacle stuck with adhesive tape onto the wall beside her bed—*Lean on Him, Emmanuel Is My Refuge, Rock of Ages Cleft for Me.*

Then in the total night around me, I heard a sound. It was my mother, and she was crying, not loudly at all, but from somewhere very deep inside her. I sat up in bed. Everything seemed to have stopped, not only time but my own heart and blood as well. Then my mother noticed that I was awake.

I did not ask her, and she did not tell me anything. There was no need. She held me in her arms, or I held her, I am not certain which. And after a while the first mourning stopped, too, as everything does sooner or later, for when the limits of endurance have been reached, then people must sleep.

In the days following my father's death, I stayed close beside my mother, and this was only partly for my own consoling. I also had the feeling that she needed my protection. I did not know from what, nor what I could possibly do, but something held me there. Reverend McKee called, and I sat with my grandmother and my mother in the living room. My mother told me I did not need to stay unless I wanted to, but I refused to go. What I thought chiefly was that he would speak of the healing power of prayer, and all that, and it would be bound to make my mother cry again. And in fact, it happened in just that way, but when it actually came, I could not protect her from this assault. I could only sit there and pray my own prayer, which was that he would go away quickly.

My mother tried not to cry unless she was alone or with me. I also tried, but neither of us was entirely successful. Grandmother MacLeod, on the other hand, was never seen crying, not even the day of my father's funeral. But that day, when we had returned to the house and she had taken off her black velvet overshoes and her heavy sealskin coat with its black fur that was the softest thing I had ever touched, she stood in the hallway and for the first time she looked unsteady. When I reached out instinctively towards her, she sighed.

'That's right,' she said. 'You might just take my arm while I go upstairs, Vanessa.'

That was the most my Grandmother MacLeod ever gave in, to anyone's sight. I left her in her bedroom, sitting on the straight chair beside her bed and looking at the picture of my father that had been taken when he graduated from medical college. Maybe she was sorry now that she had only the one photograph of him, but whatever she felt, she did not say.

I went down to the kitchen. I had scarcely spoken to Noreen since my father's death. This had not been done on purpose. I simply had not seen her. I had not really seen anyone except my mother. Looking at Noreen now, I suddenly recalled the sparrow. I felt physically sick, remembering the fearful darting and plunging of those wings, and the fact that it was I who had opened the window and let it in. Then an inexplicable fury took hold of me, some terrifying need to hurt, burn, destroy. Absolutely without warning, either to her or to myself, I hit Noreen as hard as I could. When she swung around, appalled, I hit out at her once more, my arms and legs flailing. Her hands snatched at my wrists, and she held me, but still I continued to struggle, fighting blindly, my eyes tightly closed, as though she were a prison all around me and I was battling to get out. Finally, too shocked at myself to go on, I went limp in her grasp and she let me drop to the floor.

'Vanessa! I never done one single solitary thing to you, and here you go hitting and scratching me like that! What in the world has got into you?'

I began to say I was sorry, which was certainly true, but I did not say it. I could not say anything.

'You're not yourself, what with your dad and everything,' she excused me. 'I been praying every night that your dad is with God, Vanessa. I know he wasn't actually saved in the regular way, but still and all—'

'Shut up,' I said.

Something in my voice made her stop talking. I rose from the floor and stood in the kitchen doorway.

'He didn't need to be saved,' I went on coldly, distinctly. 'And he is not in Heaven, because there is no Heaven. And it doesn't matter, see? *It doesn't matter!*'

Noreen's face looked peculiarly vulnerable now, her high wide cheekbones and puzzled childish eyes, and the thick russet tangle of her hair. I had not hurt her much before, when I hit her. But I had hurt her now, hurt her in some inexcusable way. Yet I sensed, too, that already she was gaining some satisfaction out of feeling sorrowful about my disbelief.

I went upstairs to my room. Momentarily I felt a sense of calm, almost of acceptance. *Rest beyond the river.* I knew now what that meant. It meant Nothing. It meant only silence, forever.

Then I lay down on my bed and spent the last of my tears, or what seemed then to be the last. Because, despite what I had said to Noreen, it did matter. It mattered, but there was no help for it.

Everything changed after my father's death. The MacLeod house could not be kept up any longer. My mother sold it to a local merchant who subsequently covered the deep red of the brick over with yellow stucco. Something about the house had always made me uneasy—that tower room where Grandmother MacLeod's potted plants drooped in a lethargic and lime-green confusion, those long stairways and hidden places, the attic which I had always imagined to be dwelt in by the spirits of the family dead, that gigantic portrait of the Duke of Wellington at the top of the stairs. It was never an endearing house. And yet when it was no longer ours, and when the Virginia creeper had been torn down and the dark walls turned to a light marigold, I went out of my way to avoid walking past, for it seemed to me that the house had lost the stern dignity that was its very heart.

Noreen went back to the farm. My mother and brother and myself moved into Grandmother Connor's house. Grandmother MacLeod went to live with Aunt Morag in Winnipeg. It was harder for her than for anyone, because so much of her life was bound up with the MacLeod house. She was fond of Aunt Morag, but that hardly counted. Her men were gone, her husband and her sons, and a family whose men are gone is no family at all. The day she left, my mother and I did not know what to say. Grandmother MacLeod looked even smaller than usual in her fur coat and her black velvet toque. She became extremely agitated about trivialities, and fussed about the possibility of the taxi not arriving on time. She had forbidden us to accompany her to the station. About my father, or the house, or anything important, she did not say a word. Then, when the taxi had finally arrived, she turned to my mother.

'Roddie will have Ewen's seal ring, of course, with the MacLeod crest on it,' she said. 'But there is another seal as well, don't forget, the larger one with the crest and motto. It's meant to be worn on a watch chain. I keep it in my jewel-box. It was Roderick's. Roddie's to have that, too, when I die. Don't let Morag talk you out of it.'

During the Second World War, when I was seventeen and in love with an airman who did not love me, and desperately anxious to get away from Manawaka and from my grandfather's house, I happened one day to be going through the old mahogany desk that had belonged to my father. It had a number of small drawers inside, and I accidentally pulled one of these all the way out. Behind it there was another drawer, one I had not known about. Curiously, I opened it. Inside there was a letter written on almost transparent paper in a cramped angular handwriting. It began—*Cher Monsieur Ewen*—That was all I could make out, for the writing was nearly impossible to read and my French was not good. It was dated 1919. With it, there was a picture of a girl, looking absurdly old-fashioned to my eyes, like the faces on long-discarded calendars or chocolate boxes. But beneath the dated quality of the photograph, she seemed neither expensive nor cheap. She looked like what she probably had been—an ordinary middle-class girl, but in another country. She wore her hair in long ringlets, and her mouth was shaped into a sweetly sad posed smile like Mary Pickford's. That was all. There was nothing else in the drawer.

I looked for a long time at the girl, and hoped she had meant some momentary and unexpected freedom. I remembered what he had said to me, after I hadn't gone to the Remembrance Day parade.

'What are you doing, Vanessa?' my mother called from the kitchen.

'Nothing,' I replied.

I took the letter and picture outside and burned them. That was all I could do for him. Now that we might have talked together, it was many years too late. Perhaps it would not have been possible anyway. I did not know.

As I watched the smile of the girl turn into scorched paper, I grieved for my father as though he had just died now.

1970

# Alice Munro
## *b.* 1931

Alice Laidlaw was born and raised in the rural community of Wingham in southwestern Ontario. After two years of study at the University of Western Ontario she moved to the West Coast, living first in Vancouver, where she worked as an assistant in the Vancouver Public Library, and then in Victoria, where she and her first husband, James Munro, opened a bookstore. She has generally set her 13 volumes of fiction in the rural area of southwestern Ontario where she was born and where she now resides. A prevailing theme of her stories is a young girl coming of age, searching for her identity as a woman. Her early short-story sequence *Lives of Girls and Women* (1971), which centres around a young heroine, Del Jordan, who must learn that true fiction is rooted in the factual and tactile world that surrounds her, is typical in this regard. In 'Child's Play', which comes from Munro's collection *Too Much Happiness* (2009), Marlene is reliving a terrifying event from her childhood; now an older woman, an anthropologist who never married, she remembers a scene from her young camp days when she and her childhood partner, Charlene, used to play together.

Acknowledging the fiction of Flannery O'Connor and Eudora Welty among the major influences on her own work, Munro writes out of the world she knows well, taking the ordinary, everyday reality around her and transforming it into fiction. Now regarded as one of the finest short-story writers in the English language, she won the Nobel Prize for Literature in 2013 as 'the master of the contemporary short story'.

# Child's Play

I suppose there was talk in our house, afterwards.

How sad, how *awful.* (My mother.)

There should have been supervision. Where were the counsellors? (My father.)

It is possible that if we ever passed the yellow house my mother said, 'Remember? Remember you used to be so scared of her? The poor thing.'

My mother had a habit of hanging on to—even treasuring—the foibles of my distant infantile state.

Every year, when you're a child, you become a different person. Generally it's in the fall, when you re-enter school, take your place in a higher grade, leave behind the muddle and lethargy of the summer vacation. That's when you register the change most sharply. Afterwards you are not sure of the month or year but the changes go on, just the same. For a long while the past drops away from you easily and it would seem automatically, properly. Its scenes don't vanish so much as become irrelevant. And then there's a switchback, what's been all over and done with sprouting up fresh, wanting attention, even wanting you to do something about it, though it's plain there is not on this earth a thing to be done.

Marlene and Charlene. People thought we must be twins. There was a fashion in those days for naming twins in rhyme. Bonnie and Connie. Ronald and Donald. And then of course we—Charlene and I—had matching hats. Coolie hats, they were called, wide shallow cones of woven straw with some sort of tie or elastic under the chin. They became familiar later on in the century, from television shots of the war in Vietnam. Men on bicycles riding along a street in Saigon would be wearing them, or women walking in the road against the background of a bombed village.

It was possible at that time—I mean the time when Charlene and I were at camp—to say *coolie*, without a thought of offence. Or *darkie*, or to talk about *jewing* a price down. I was in my teens, I think, before I ever related that verb to the noun.

So we had those names and those hats, and at the first roll call the counsellor—the jolly one we liked, Mavis, though we didn't like her as well as the pretty one, Pauline—pointed at us and called out, 'Hey. Twins,' and went on calling out other names before we had time to deny it.

Even before that we must have noticed the hats and approved of each other. Otherwise one or both of us would have pulled off those brand-new articles, and been ready to shove them under our cots, declaring that our mothers had made us wear them and we hated them, and so on.

I may have approved of Charlene, but I was not sure how to make friends with her. Girls nine or ten years old—that was the general range of this crop, though there were a few a bit older—do not pick friends or pair off as easily as girls do at six or seven. I simply followed some other girls from my town—none of them my particular friends—to one of the cabins where there were some unclaimed cots, and dumped my things on top of the brown blanket. Then I heard a voice behind me say, 'Could I please be next to my twin sister?'

It was Charlene, speaking to somebody I didn't know. The dormitory cabin held perhaps two dozen girls. The girl she had spoken to said, 'Sure,' and moved along.

Charlene had used a special voice. Ingratiating, teasing, self-mocking, and with a seductive merriment in it, like a trill of bells. It was evident right away that she had more confidence than I did. And not simply confidence that the other girl would move, and not say sturdily, 'I got here first.' (Or—if she was a roughly brought up sort of girl—and some were, having their way paid by the Lions Club or the church and not by their parents—she might have said, 'Go poop your pants, I'm not moving.') No. Charlene had confidence that anybody would *want* to do as she asked, not just agree to do it. With me too she had taken a chance, for could I not have said, 'I don't want to be twins,' and turned back to sort my things. But of course I didn't. I felt flattered, as she had expected, and I watched her dump out the contents of her suitcase with such an air of celebration that some things fell on the floor.

All I could think of to say was, 'You got a tan already.'

'I always tan easy,' she said.

The first of our differences. We applied ourselves to learning them. She tanned, I freckled. We both had brown hair but hers was darker. Hers was wavy, mine bushy. I was half an inch taller, she had thicker wrists and ankles. Her eyes had more green in them, mine more blue. We did not grow tired of inspecting and tabulating even the moles or notable freckles on our backs, length of our second toes (mine longer than the first toe, hers shorter). Or of recounting all the illnesses or accidents that had befallen us so far, as well as the repairs or removals performed on our bodies. Both of us had had our tonsils out—a usual precaution in those days—and both of us had had measles and whooping cough but not mumps. I had had an eyetooth pulled because it was growing in over my other teeth and she had a thumbnail with an imperfect half-moon, because her thumb had been slammed under a window.

And once we had the peculiarities and history of our bodies in place we went on to the stories—the dramas or near dramas or distinctions—of our families. She was the youngest and only girl in her family and I was an only child. I had an aunt who had died of polio in high school and she—Charlene—had an older brother who was in the navy. For it was wartime, and at the campfire singsong we would choose 'There'll Always Be an England' and 'Hearts of Oak,' and 'Rule Britannia,' and sometimes 'The Maple Leaf Forever.' Bombing raids and battles and sinking ships were the constant, though distant, backdrop of our lives. And once in a while there was a near strike, frightening but solemn and exhilarating, as when a boy from our town or our street would be killed, and the house where he had lived, without having any special wreath or black drapery on it seemed nevertheless to have a special weight inside it, a destiny fulfilled and dragging it down. Though there was nothing special inside it at all, maybe just a car that didn't belong there parked at the curb, showing that some relatives or a minister had come to sit with the bereaved family.

One of the camp counsellors had lost her fiancé in the war and wore his watch—we believed it was his watch—pinned to her blouse. We would like to have felt for her a mournful interest and concern, but she was sharp-voiced and bossy, and she even had an unpleasant name. Arva.

The other backdrop of our lives, which was supposed to be emphasized at camp, was religion. But since the United Church of Canada was officially in charge there was not so much harping on that subject as there would have been with the Baptists or the Bible Christians, or so much formal acknowledgment as the Roman Catholics or even the Anglicans would have provided. Most of us had parents who belonged to the United Church (though some of the girls who were having their way paid for them might not have belonged to any church at all), and being used to its hearty secular style, we did not even realize that we were getting off easy with just evening prayers and grace sung at meals and the half-hour special talk—it was called a Chat—after breakfast. Even the Chat was relatively free of references to God or Jesus and was more about honesty and loving-kindness and clean thoughts in our daily lives, and promising never to drink or smoke when we grew up. Nobody had any objection to this sort of thing or tried to get out of attending, because it was what we were used to and because it was pleasant to sit on the beach in the warming sun and a little too cold yet for us to long to jump into the water.

Grown-up women do the same sort of thing that Charlene and I did. Not counting the moles on each other's backs and comparing toe lengths, maybe. But when they meet and feel a particular sympathy with each other they also feel a need to set out the important information, the big events whether public or secret, and then go ahead to fill in all the blanks between. If they feel this warmth and eagerness it is quite impossible for them to bore each other. They will laugh at the very triviality and silliness of what they're telling, or at the revelation of some appalling selfishness, deception, meanness, sheer badness.

There has to be great trust, of course, but that trust can be established at once, in an instant.

I've observed this. It's supposed to have begun in those long periods of sitting around the campfire stirring the manioc porridge or whatever while the men were out in the bush deprived of conversation because it would warn off the wild animals. (I am an anthropologist by training, though a rather slack one.) I've observed but never taken part in these female exchanges. Not truly. Sometimes I've pretended because it seemed to be required, but the woman I was supposed to be making friends with always got wind of my pretense and became confused and cautious.

As a rule, I've felt less wary with men. They don't expect such transactions and are seldom really interested.

This intimacy I'm talking about—with women—is not erotic, or pre-erotic. I've experienced that as well, before puberty. Then too there would be confidences, probably lies, maybe leading to games. A certain hot temporary excitement, with or without genital teasing. Followed by ill feeling, denial, disgust.

Charlene did tell me about her brother, but with true repugnance. This was the brother now in the Navy. She went into his room looking for her cat and there he was doing it to his girlfriend. They never knew she saw them.

She said they slapped as he went up and down.

You mean they slapped on the bed, I said.

No, she said. It was his thing slapped when it was going in and out. It was gross. Sickening.

And his bare white bum had pimples on it. Sickening.

I told her about Verna.

Up until the time I was seven years old my parents had lived in what was called a double house. The word 'duplex' was perhaps not in use at that time, and anyway the house was not evenly divided. Verna's grandmother rented the rooms at the back and we rented the rooms at the front. The house was tall and bare and ugly, painted yellow. The town we lived in was too small to have residential divisions that amounted to anything, but I suppose that as far as there were divisions, that house was right on the boundary between decent and fairly dilapidated. I am speaking of the way things were just before the Second World War, at the end of the Depression. (That word, I believe, was unknown to us.)

My father being a teacher had a regular job but little money. The street petered out beyond us between the houses of those who had neither. Verna's grandmother must have had a little money because she spoke contemptuously of people who were On Relief. I believe my mother argued with her, unsuccessfully, that it was Not Their Fault. The two women were not particular friends but they were cordial about clothes-line arrangements.

The grandmother's name was Mrs Home. A man came to see her occasionally. My mother spoke of him as Mrs Home's friend.

You are not to speak to Mrs Home's friend.

In fact I was not even allowed to play outside when he came, so there was not much chance of my speaking to him. I don't even remember what he looked like, though I remember his car, which was dark blue, a Ford V-8. I took a special interest in cars, probably because we didn't have one.

Then Verna came.

Mrs Home spoke of her as her granddaughter and there is no reason to suppose that not to be true, but there was never any sign of a connecting generation. I don't know if Mrs Home went away and came back with her, or if she was delivered by the friend with the V-8. She appeared in the summer before I was to start school. I can't remember her telling me her name—she was not communicative in the ordinary way and I don't believe I would have asked her. From the very beginning I had an aversion to her unlike anything I had felt up to that time for any other person. I said that I hated her, and my mother said, How can you, what has she ever done to you?

The poor thing.

Children use that word 'hate' to mean various things. It may mean that they are frightened. Not that they feel in danger of being attacked—the way I did, for instance, by certain big boys on bicycles who liked to cut in front of you, yelling fearsomely, as you walked on the sidewalk. It is not physical harm that is feared—or that I feared in Verna's case—so much as some spell, or dark intention. It is a feeling you can have when you are very young even about certain house faces, or tree trunks, or very much about moldy cellars or deep closets.

She was a good deal taller than I was and I don't know how much older—two years, three years? She was skinny, indeed so narrowly built and with such a small head that she made me think of a snake. Fine black hair lay flat on this head, and fell over her forehead. The skin of her face seemed dull to me as the flap of our old canvas tent, and her cheeks puffed out the way the flap of that tent puffed in a wind. Her eyes were always squinting.

But I believe there was nothing remarkably unpleasant about her looks, as other people saw her. Indeed my mother spoke of her as pretty, or almost pretty (as in, *isn't it too bad, she could be pretty)*. Nothing to object to either, as far as my mother could see, in her behaviour. *She is young for her age.* A roundabout and inadequate way of saying that Verna had not learned to read or write or skip or play ball, and that her voice was hoarse and unmodulated, her words oddly separated, as if they were chunks of language caught in her throat.

Her way of interfering with me, spoiling my solitary games, was that of an older not a younger girl. But of an older girl who had no skill or rights, nothing but a strenuous determination and an inability to understand that she wasn't wanted.

Children of course are monstrously conventional, repelled at once by whatever is off-centre, out of whack, unmanageable. And being an only child I had been coddled a good deal (also scolded). I was awkward, precocious, timid, full of my private rituals and aversions. I hated even the celluloid barrette that kept slipping out of Verna's hair, and the peppermints with red or green stripes on them that she kept offering to me. In fact she did more than offer; she would try to catch me and push these candies into my mouth, chuckling all the time in her disconnected way. I dislike peppermint flavouring to this day. And the name Verna—I dislike that. It doesn't sound like spring to me, or like green grass or garlands of flowers or girls in flimsy dresses. It sounds more like a trail of obstinate peppermint, green slime.

I didn't believe my mother really liked Verna either. But because of some hypocrisy in her nature, as I saw it, because of a decision she had made, as it seemed to spite me, she pretended to be sorry for her. She told me to be kind. At first, she said that Verna would not be staying long and at the end of the summer holidays would go back to wherever she had been before. Then, when it became clear that there was nowhere for Verna to go back to, the placating message was that we ourselves would be moving soon. I had only to be kind for a little while longer. (As a matter of fact it was a whole year before we moved.) Finally, out of patience, she said that I was a disappointment to her and that she would never have thought I had so mean a nature.

'How can you blame a person for the way she was born? How is it her fault?'

That made no sense to me. If I had been more skilled at arguing I might have said that I didn't blame Verna, I just did not want her to come near me. But I certainly did blame her. I did not question that it was somehow her fault. And in this, whatever my mother might say, I was in tune to some degree with an unspoken verdict of the time and place I lived in. Even grown-ups smiled in a certain way, there was some irrepressible gratification and taken-for-granted superiority that I could see in the way they mentioned people who were *simple* or *a few bricks short of a load.* And I believed my mother must be really like this, underneath.

I started to school. Verna started to school. She was put into a special class in a special building in a corner of the school grounds. This was actually the original school building in the town, but nobody had any time for local history then, and a few years later it was pulled down. There was a fenced-off corner in which pupils housed in that building spent recess. They went to school a half-hour later than we did in the morning and got out a half-hour earlier in the afternoon. Nobody was supposed to harass them at recess but since they usually hung on the fence watching whatever went on in the regular school grounds there would be occasions when there was a rush, a whooping and brandishing of sticks, to scare them. I never went near that corner, hardly ever saw Verna. It was at home I still had to deal with her.

First she would stand at the corner of the yellow house, watching me, and I would pretend that I didn't know she was there. Then she would wander into the front yard, taking up a position on the front steps of the part of the house that was mine. If I wanted to go inside to the bathroom or because I was cold, I would have to go so close as to touch her and to risk her touching me.

She could stay in one place longer than anybody I ever knew, staring at just one thing. Usually me.

I had a swing hung from a maple tree, so that I either faced the house or the street. That is, I either had to face her or to know that she was staring at my back, and might come up to give me a push. After a while she would decide to do that. She always pushed me crooked, but that was not the worst thing. The worst was that her fingers had pressed my back. Through my coat, through my other clothing, her fingers like so many cold snouts. Another activity of mine was to build a leaf house. That is, I raked up and carried armloads of leaves fallen from the maple tree that held the swing, and I dumped and arranged these leaves into a house plan. Here was the living room, here was the kitchen, here was a big soft pile for the bed in the bedroom, and so on. I had not invented this occupation—leaf houses of a more expansive sort were laid out and, even in a way furnished, every recess in the girls' playground at school, until the janitor finally raked up all the leaves and burned them.

At first Verna just watched what I was doing, with her squinty-eyed expression of what seemed to me superior (how could she think herself superior?) puzzlement. Then the time came when she moved closer, lifted an armful of leaves that dripped all over because of her uncertainty or clumsiness. And these came not from the pile of spare leaves but from the very wall of my house. She picked them up and carried them a short distance and let them fall—dumped them—in the middle of one of my tidy rooms.

I yelled at her to stop, but she bent to pick up her scattered load again, and was unable to hang on to them, so she just flung them about and when they were all on the ground began to kick them foolishly here and there. I was still yelling at her to stop, but this had no effect, or else she took it for encouragement. So I lowered my head and ran at her and butted her in the stomach. I was not wearing a cap, so the hairs of my head came in contact with the woolly coat or jacket she had on, and it seemed to me that I had actually touched bristling hairs on the skin of a gross hard belly. I ran hollering with complaint up the steps of the house and when my mother heard the story she further maddened me by saying, 'She only wants to play. She doesn't know how to *play*.'

By the next fall we were in a new bungalow and I never had to go past the yellow house that reminded me so much of Verna, as if it had positively taken on her narrow slyness, her threatening squint. The yellow paint seemed to be the very colour of insult, and the front door, being off centre, added a touch of deformity.

The bungalow was only three blocks away from that house, close to the school. But my idea of the town's size and complexity was still such that it seemed I was escaping Verna altogether. I realized that this was not true, not altogether true, when a schoolmate and I came face-to-face with her one day on the main street. We must have been sent on some errand by one of our mothers. I did not look up but I believed I heard a chuckle of greeting or recognition as we passed.

The other girl said a horrifying thing to me.

She said, 'I used to think that was your sister.'

'What?'

'Well, I knew you lived in the same house so I thought you must be related. Like cousins, anyway. Aren't you? Cousins?'

'*No.*'

The old building where the Special Classes had been held was condemned, and its pupils were transferred to the Bible Chapel, now rented on weekdays by the town. The Bible Chapel happened to be across the street and around a corner from the bungalow where my mother and father and I now lived. There were a couple of ways that Verna could have walked to school, but the way she chose was past our house. And our house was only a few feet from the sidewalk, so this meant that her shadow could practically fall across our steps. If she wished she could kick pebbles onto our grass, and unless we kept the blinds down she could peer into our hall and front room.

The hours of the Special Classes had been changed to coincide with ordinary school hours, at least in the morning—the Specials still went home earlier in the afternoon. Once they were in the Bible Chapel it must have been felt that there was no need to keep them free of the rest of us on the way to school. This meant, now, that I had a chance of running into Verna on the sidewalk. I would always look in the direction from which she might be coming, and if I saw her I would duck back into the house with the excuse that I had forgotten something, or that one of my shoes was rubbing my heel and needed a plaster, or a ribbon was coming loose in my hair. I would never have been so foolish now as to mention Verna, and hear my mother say, 'What's the problem, what are you afraid of, do you think she's going to eat you?'

What was the problem? Contamination, infection? Verna was decently clean and healthy. And it was hardly likely that she was going to attack and pummel me or pull out my hair. But only adults would be so stupid as to believe she had no power. A power, moreover, that was specifically directed at me. I was the one she had her eye on. Or so I believed. As if we had an understanding between us that could not be described and was not to be disposed of. Something that clings, in the way of love, though on my side it felt absolutely like hate.

I suppose I hated her as some people hate snakes or caterpillars or mice or slugs. For no decent reason. Not for any certain harm she could do but for the way she could disturb your innards and make you sick of your life.

When I told Charlene about her we had got into the deeper reaches of our conversation—that conversation which seems to have been broken only when we swam or slept. Verna was not so solid an offering, not so vividly repulsive, as Charlene's brother's pumping pimpled bum, and I remember saying that she was awful in a way that I could not describe. But then I did describe her, and my feelings about her, and I must have done not too bad a job because one day toward the end of our two-week stay at camp Charlene came rushing into the dining hall at midday, her face lit up with horror and strange delight.

'She's here. She's here. That girl. That awful girl. Verna. She's *here*.'

Lunch was over. We were in the process of tidying up, putting our plates and mugs on the kitchen shelf to be grabbed away and washed by the girls on kitchen duty that day. Then we would line up to go to the Tuck Shop, which opened every day at one o'clock. Charlene had just run back to the dormitory to get some money. Being rich, with a father who was an undertaker, she was rather careless, keeping money in her pillowcase. Except when swimming I always had mine on my person. All of us who could in any way afford to went to the Tuck Shop after lunch, to get something to take away the taste of the desserts we hated but always tried, just to see if they were as disgusting as we expected. Tapioca pudding, mushy baked apples, slimy custard. When I first saw the look on Charlene's face I thought that her money had been stolen. But then I thought that such a calamity would not have made her look so transformed, the shock on her face so joyful.

Verna? How could Verna be here? Some mistake.

This must have been a Friday. Two more days at camp, two more days to go. And it turned out that a contingent of Specials—here too they were called Specials—had been brought in to enjoy with us the final weekend. Not many of them—maybe twenty altogether—and not all from my town but from other towns nearby. In fact as Charlene was trying to get the news through to me a whistle was being blown, and Counsellor Arva had jumped up on a bench to address us.

She said that she knew we would all do our best to make these visitors—these new campers—welcome, and that they had brought their own tents and their own counsellor with them. But they would eat and swim and play games and attend the Morning Chat with the rest of us. She was sure, she said, with that familiar warning or upbraiding note in her voice, that we would all treat this as an opportunity to make new friends.

It took some time to get the tents up and these newcomers and their possessions settled. Some apparently took no interest and wandered off and had to be yelled at and fetched back. Since it was our free time, or rest hour, we got our chocolate bars or licorice whips or sponge toffee from the Tuck Shop and went to lie on our bunks and enjoy them.

Charlene kept saying, 'Imagine. Imagine. She's here. I can't believe it. Do you think she followed you?'

'Probably,' I said.

'Do you think I can always hide you like that?'

When we were in the Tuck Shop lineup I had ducked my head and made Charlene get between me and the Specials as they were being herded by. I had taken one peek and recognized Verna from behind. Her drooping snaky head.

'We should think of some way to disguise you.'

From what I had said, Charlene seemed to have got the idea that Verna had actively harassed me. And I believed that was true, except that the harassment had been more subtle, more secret, than I had been able to describe. Now I let Charlene think as she liked because it was more exciting that way.

Verna did not spot me immediately, because of the elaborate dodges Charlene and I kept making, and perhaps because she was rather dazed, as most of the Specials appeared to be, trying to figure out what they were doing here. They were soon taken off to their own swimming class, at the far end of the beach.

At the supper table they were marched in while we sang.

*The more we get together, together, together,*
*The more we get together,*
*The happier we'll be.*

They were then deliberately separated, and distributed amongst the rest of us. They all wore name tags. Across from me there was one named Mary Ellen something, not from my town. But I had hardly time to be glad of that when I saw Verna at the next table, taller than those around her but thank God facing the same way I was so she could not see me during the meal.

She was the tallest of them, and yet not so tall, not so notable a presence, as I remembered her. The reason was probably that I had had a growing spurt during the last year, while she had perhaps stopped her growing altogether.

After the meal, when we stood up and, collected our dishes, I kept my head bowed, I never looked in her direction, and yet I knew when her eyes rested on me, when she recognized me, when she smiled her sagging little smile or made that odd chuckle in her throat.

'She's seen you,' said Charlene. 'Don't look. Don't look. I'll get between you and her. Move. Keep moving.'

'Is she coming this way?'

'No. She's just standing there. She's just looking at you.'

'Smiling?'

'Sort of.'

'I can't look at her. I'd be sick.'

How much did she persecute me in the remaining day and a half? Charlene and I used that word constantly, though in fact Verna never got near us. *Persecute.* It had an adult, legal sound. We were always on the lookout, as if we were being stalked, or I was. We tried to keep track of Verna's whereabouts, and Charlene reported on her attitude or expression. I did risk looking at her a couple of times, when Charlene had said, 'Okay. She won't notice now.'

At those times Verna appeared slightly downcast, or sullen, or bewildered, as if, like most of the Specials, she had been set adrift and did not completely understand where she was or what she was doing there. Some of them—though not she—had caused a commotion by wandering away into the pine and cedar and poplar woods on the bluff behind the beach, or along the sandy road that led to the highway. After that a meeting was called, and we were all asked to watch out for our new friends, who were not so familiar with the place as we were. Charlene poked me in the ribs at that. She of course was not aware of any change, any falling away of confidence or even a diminishing of physical size, in this Verna, and she continually reported on her sly and evil expression, her look of menace. And maybe she was right—maybe Verna saw in Charlene, this new friend or bodyguard of mine, this stranger, some sign of how everything was changed and uncertain here, and that made her scowl, though I didn't see it.

'You never told me about her hands,' said Charlene.

'What about them?'

'She's got the longest fingers I have ever seen. She could just twist them round your neck and strangle you. She could. Wouldn't it be awful to be in a tent with her at night?'

I said that it would be. Awful.

'But those others in her tent are too idiotic to notice.'

There was a change, that last weekend, a whole different feeling in the camp. Nothing drastic. The meals were announced by the dining room gong at the regular times, and the food served did not improve or deteriorate. Rest time arrived, game time and swimming time. The Tuck Shop operated as usual, and we were drawn together as always for the Chat. But there was an air of growing restlessness and inattention. You could detect it even in the counsellors, who might not have the same reprimands or words of encouragement on the tip of their tongues and would look at you for a second as if trying to recall what it was they usually said. And all this seemed to have begun with the arrival of the Specials. Their presence had changed the camp. There had been a real camp before, with all its rules and deprivations and enjoyments set up, inevitable as school or any part of a child's life, and then it had begun to crumple at the edges, to reveal itself as something provisional. Playacting.

Was it because we could look at the Specials and think that if they could be campers, then there was no such thing as real campers? Partly it was that. But it was partly that the time was coming very soon when all this would be over, the routines would be broken up, and we would be fetched by our parents to resume our old lives, and the counsellors would go back to being ordinary people, not even teachers. We were living in a stage set about to be dismantled, and with it all the friendships, enmities, rivalries that had flourished in the last two weeks. Who could believe it had been only two weeks?

Nobody knew how to speak of this, but a lassitude spread amongst us, a bored ill temper, and even the weather reflected this feeling. It was probably not true that every day during the past two weeks had been hot and sunny, but most of us would certainly go away with that impression. And now, on Sunday morning, there was a change. While we were having the Outdoor Devotions (that was what we had on Sundays instead of the Chat) the clouds darkened. There was no change in temperature—if anything, the heat of the day increased—but there was in the air what some people called the smell of a storm. And yet such stillness. The counsellors and even the minister, who drove out on Sundays from the nearest town, looked up occasionally and warily at the sky.

A few drops did fall, but no more. The service came to its end and no storm had broken. The clouds grew somewhat lighter, not so much as to promise sunshine, but enough so that our last swim would not have to be cancelled. After that there would be no lunch; the kitchen had been closed down after breakfast. The shutters on the Tuck Shop would not be opened. Our parents would begin arriving shortly after noon to take us home, and the bus would come for the Specials. Most of our things were already packed, the sheets were stripped, and the rough brown blankets, that always felt clammy, were folded across the foot of each cot.

Even when it was full of us, chattering and changing into our bathing suits, the inside of the dormitory cabin revealed itself as makeshift and gloomy.

It was the same with the beach. There appeared to be less sand than usual, more stones. And what sand there was seemed grey. The water looked as if it might be cold, though in fact it was quite warm. Nevertheless our enthusiasm for swimming had waned and most of us were wading about aimlessly. The swimming counsellors—Pauline and the middle-aged woman in charge of the Specials—had to clap their hands at us.

'Hurry up, what are you waiting for? Last chance this summer.'

There were good swimmers among us who usually struck out at once for the raft. And all who were even passably good swimmers—that included Charlene and me—were supposed to swim out to the raft at least once and turn around and swim back in order to prove that we could swim at least a couple of yards in water over our heads. Pauline would usually swim out there right away, and stay in the deeper water to watch out for anybody who got into trouble and also to make sure that everybody who was supposed to do the swim had done it. On this day, however, fewer swimmers than usual seemed to be going out there as they were supposed to, and Pauline herself after her first cries of encouragement or exasperation—required simply to get everybody into the water—was just bobbing around the raft laughing and teasing with the faithful expert swimmers. Most of us were still paddling around in the shallows, swimming a few feet or yards, then standing on the bottom and splashing each other or turning over and doing the dead man's float, as if swimming was something hardly anybody could be bothered with anymore. The woman in charge of the Specials was standing where the water came barely up to her waist—most of the Specials themselves went no farther than where the water came up to their knees—and the top part of her flowered, skirted bathing suit had not even got wet. She was bending over and making little hand splashes at her charges, laughing and telling them, Isn't this fun.

The water Charlene and I were in was probably up to our chests and no more. We were in the ranks of the silly swimmers, doing the dead man's, and flopping about backstroking or breaststroking, with nobody telling us to stop fooling around. We were trying to see how long we could keep our eyes open underwater, we were sneaking up and jumping on each other's backs. All around us were plenty of others yelling and screeching with laughter as they did the same things.

During this swim some parents or collectors of campers had arrived early and let it be known they had no time to waste, so the campers who belonged to them were being summoned from the water. This made for some extra calling and confusion.

'Look. Look,' said Charlene. Or sputtered, in fact, because I had pushed her underwater and she had just come up soaked and spitting.

I looked, and there was Verna making her way toward us, wearing a pale blue rubber bathing cap, slapping at the water with her long hands and smiling, as if her rights over me had suddenly been restored.

I have not kept up with Charlene. I don't even remember how we said goodbye. If we said goodbye. I have a notion that both sets of parents arrived at around the same time and that we scrambled into separate cars and gave ourselves over—what else could we do?—to our old lives. Charlene's parents would certainly have had a car not so shabby and noisy and unreliable as the one my parents now owned, but even if that had not been so we would never have thought of making the two sets of relatives acquainted with each other. Everybody, and we ourselves, would have been in a hurry to get off, to leave behind the pockets of uproar about lost property or who had or had not met their relatives or boarded the bus.

By chance, years later, I did see Charlene's wedding picture. This was at a time when wedding pictures were still published in the newspapers, not just in small towns but in the city papers as well. I saw it in a Toronto paper which I was looking through while I waited for a friend in a café on Bloor Street.

The wedding had taken place in Guelph. The groom was a native of Toronto and a graduate of Osgoode Hall. He was quite tall—or else Charlene had turned out to be quite short. She barely came up to his shoulder, even with her hair done up in the dense, polished helmet-style of the day. The hair made her face seem squashed and insignificant, but I got the impression her eyes were outlined heavily, Cleopatra fashion, her lips pale. This sounds grotesque but it was certainly the look admired at the time. All that reminded me of her child-self was the little humorous bump of her chin.

She—the bride, it said—had graduated from St Hilda's College in Toronto.

So she must have been here in Toronto, going to St Hilda's, while I was in the same city, going to University College. We had been walking around perhaps at the same time and on some of the same streets or paths on the campus. And never met. I did not think that she would have seen me and avoided speaking to me. I would not have avoided speaking to her. Of course I would have considered myself a more serious student, once I discovered she was going to St Hilda's. My friends and I regarded St Hilda's as a Ladies College.

Now I was a graduate student in anthropology. I had decided never to get married, though I did not rule out having lovers. I wore my hair long and straight—my friends and I were anticipating the style of the hippies. My memories of childhood were much more distant and faded and unimportant than they seem today.

I could have written to Charlene in care of her parents, whose Guelph address was in the paper. But I didn't do so. I would have thought it the height of hypocrisy to congratulate any woman on her marriage.

But she wrote to me, perhaps fifteen years later. She wrote in care of my publishers.

'My old pal Marlene,' she wrote. 'How excited and happy I was to see your name in *Maclean's* magazine. And how dazzled I am to think you have written a book. I have not picked it up yet because we had been away on holidays but I mean to do so—and read it too—as soon as I can. I was just going through the magazines that had accumulated in our absence and there I saw the striking picture of you and the interesting review. And I thought that I must write and congratulate you.

'Perhaps you are married but use your maiden name to write under? Perhaps you have a family? Do write and tell me all about yourself. Sadly, I am childless, but I keep busy with volunteer work, gardening, and sailing with Kit (my husband). There always seems to be plenty to do. I am presently serving on the Library Board and will twist their arms if they have not already ordered your book.

'Congratulations again. I must say I was surprised but not entirely because I always suspected you might do something special.'

I did not get in touch with her at that time either. There seemed to be no point to it. At first I took no notice of the word 'special' right at the end, but it gave me a small jolt when I thought of it later. However, I told myself, and still believe, that she meant nothing by it.

The book that she referred to was one that had grown out of a thesis I had been discouraged from writing. I went ahead and wrote another thesis but went back to the earlier one as a sort of hobby project when I had time. I have collaborated on a couple of books since then, as was duly expected of me, but that book I did on my own is the only one that got me a small flurry of attention in the outside world (and needless to say some disapproval from colleagues). It is out of print now. It was called *Idiots and Idols*—a title I would never get away with today and which even then made my publishers nervous, though it was admitted to be catchy.

What I was trying to explore was the attitude of people in various cultures—one does not dare say the word 'primitive' to describe such cultures—the attitude toward people who are mentally or physically unique. The words 'deficient,' 'handicapped,' 'retarded' being of course also consigned to the dustbin and probably for good reason—not simply because such words may indicate a superior attitude and habitual unkindness but because they are not truly descriptive. Those words push aside a good deal that is remarkable, even awesome—or at any rate peculiarly powerful, in such people. And what was interesting was to discover a certain amount of veneration as well as persecution, and the ascribing—not entirely inaccurately—of quite a range of abilities, seen as sacred, magical, dangerous, or valuable. I did the best I could with historical as well as contemporary research and took into account poetry and fiction and of course religious custom. Naturally I was criticized in my profession for being too literary and for getting all my information out of books, but I could not run around the world then; I had not been able to get a grant.

Of course I could see a connection, a connection that I thought it just possible Charlene might get to see too. It's strange how distant and unimportant that seemed, only a starting point. As anything in childhood appeared to me then. Because of the journey I had made since, the achievement of adulthood. Safety.

'Maiden name,' Charlene had written. That was an expression I had not heard for quite a while. It is next door to 'maiden lady,' which sounds so chaste and sad. And remarkably inappropriate in my case. Even when I looked at Charlene's wedding picture I was not a virgin—though I don't suppose she was either. Not that I have had a swarm of lovers—or would even want to call most of them lovers. Like most women in my age group who have not lived in monogamous marriage, I know the number. Sixteen. I'm sure that for many younger women that total would have been reached before they were out of their twenties or possibly out of their teens. (When I got Charlene's letter, of course, the total would have been less. I cannot—this is true—I cannot be bothered getting that straight now.) Three of them were important and all three of those in the chronological first half-dozen of the count. What I mean by 'important' is that with those three—no, only two, the third meaning a great deal more to me than I to him—with those two, then, the time would come when you want to split open, surrender far more than your body, dump your whole life safely into one basket with his.

I kept myself from doing so, but just barely.

So it seems I was not entirely convinced of that safety.

Not long ago I got another letter. This was forwarded from the university where I taught before I retired. I found it waiting when I returned from a trip to Patagonia. (I have become a hardy traveller.) It was over a month old.

A typed letter—a fact for which the writer immediately apologized.

'My handwriting is lamentable,' he wrote, and went on to introduce himself as the husband of 'your old childhood buddy, Charlene.' He said that he was sorry, very sorry, to send me bad news. Charlene was in Princess Margaret Hospital in Toronto. Her cancer had begun in the lungs and spread to the liver. She had, regrettably, been a lifelong smoker. She had only a short time left to live. She had not spoken of me very often, but when she did, over the years, it was always with delight in my remarkable accomplishments. He knew how much she valued me and now at the end of her life she seemed very keen to see me. She had asked him to get hold of me. It may be that childhood memories mean the most, he said. Childhood affections. Strength like no other.

Well, she is probably dead by now, I thought.

But if she was—this is how I worked things out—if she was, I would run no risk in going to the hospital and inquiring. Then my conscience or whatever you wanted to call it would be clear. I could write him a note saying that unfortunately I had been away, but had come as soon as I could.

No. Better not a note. He might show up in my life, thanking me. The word 'buddy' made me uncomfortable. So in a different way did 'remarkable accomplishments.'

Princess Margaret Hospital is only a few blocks away from my apartment building. On a sunny spring day I walked over there. I don't know why I didn't just phone. Perhaps I wanted to think I'd made as much effort as I could.

At the main desk I discovered that Charlene was still alive. When asked if I wanted to see her I could hardly say no.

I went up in the elevator still thinking that I might be able to turn away before I found the nurses' station on her floor. Or that I might make a simple U-turn, taking the next elevator down. The receptionist at the main desk downstairs would never notice my leaving. As a matter of fact she would not have noticed my leaving the moment she had turned her attention to the next person in line, and even if she had noticed, what would it have mattered?

I would have been ashamed, I suppose. Not ashamed at my lack of feeling so much as my lack of fortitude.

I stopped at the nurses' station and was given the number of the room.

It was a private room, quite a small room, with no impressive apparatus or flowers or balloons. At first I could not see Charlene. A nurse was bending over the bed in which there seemed to be a mound of bedclothes but no visible person. The enlarged liver, I thought, and wished I had run while I could.

The nurse straightened up, turned, and smiled at me. She was a plump brown woman who spoke in a soft, beguiling voice that might have meant she came from the West Indies.

'You are the Marlin,' she said.

Something in the word seemed to delight her.

'She was so wanting for you to come. You can come closer.'

I obeyed, and looked down at a bloated body and a sharp ruined face, a chicken's neck for which the hospital gown was a mile too wide. A frizz of hair—still brown—about a quarter of an inch long on her scalp. No sign of Charlene.

I had seen the faces of dying people before. The faces of my mother and father, even the face of the man I had been afraid to love. I was not surprised.

'She is sleeping now,' said the nurse. 'She was so hoping you would come.'

'She's not unconscious?'

'No. But she sleeps.'

Yes, I saw it now, there was a sign of Charlene. What was it? Maybe a twitch, that confident playful tucking away of a corner of her mouth.

The nurse was speaking to me in her soft happy voice. 'I don't know if she would recognize you,' she said. 'But she hoped you would come. There is something for you.'

'Will she wake up?'

A shrug. 'We have to give her injections often for the pain.'

She was opening the bedside table.

'Here. This. She told me to give it to you if it was too late for her. She did not want her husband to give it. Now you are here, she would be glad.'

A sealed envelope with my name on it, printed in shaky capital letters.

'Not her husband,' the nurse said, with a twinkle, then a broadening smile. Did she scent something illicit, a women's secret, an old love?

'Come back tomorrow,' she said. 'Who knows? I will tell her if it is possible.'

I read the note as soon as I got down to the lobby. Charlene had managed to write in an almost normal script, not wildly as in the sprawling letters on the envelope. Of course she might have written the note first and put it in the envelope, then sealed the envelope and put it by, thinking she would get to hand it to me herself. Only later would she see a need to put my name on it.

*Marlene. I am writing this in case I get too far gone to speak. Please do what I ask you. Please go to Guelph and go to the cathedral and ask for Father Hofstrader. Our Lady of Perpetual Help Cathedral. It is so big you don't need the name. Father Hofstrader. He will know what to do. This I cannot ask C. and do not want him ever to know. Father H. knows and I have asked him and he says it is possible to help me. Marlene please do this bless you. Nothing about you.*

C. That must be her husband. He doesn't know. Of course he doesn't.

Father Hofstrader.

Nothing about me.

I was free to crumple this up and throw it away once I got out into the street. And so I did, I threw the envelope away and let the wind sweep it into the gutter on University Avenue. Then I realized the note was not in the envelope; it was still in my pocket.

I would never go to the hospital again. And I would never go to Guelph.

Kit was her husband's name. Now I remembered. They went sailing. Christoper. Kit. Christopher. C.

When I got back to my apartment building I found myself taking the elevator down to the garage, not up to my apartment. Dressed just as I was I got into my car and drove out onto the street, and began to head toward the Gardiner Expressway.

The Gardiner Expressway, Highway 427, Highway 401. It was rush hour now, a bad time to get out of the city. I hate this sort of driving, I don't do it often enough to be confident. There was under half a tank of gas, and what was more, I had to go to the bathroom. Around Milton, I thought, I could pull off the highway and fill up on gas and use the toilet and reconsider. At present I could do nothing but what I was doing, heading north, then heading west.

I didn't get off. I passed the Mississauga exit, and the Milton exit. I saw a highway sign telling me how many kilometres to Guelph, and I translated that roughly into miles in my head, as I always have to do, and I figured the gas would hold out. The excuse I made to myself for not stopping was that the sun would be getting lower and more troublesome, now that we were leaving the haze that lies over the city even on the finest day.

At the first stop after I took the Guelph turnoff I got out and walked to the ladies' washroom with stiff trembling legs. Afterwards I filled the tank with gas and asked, when I paid, for directions to the cathedral. The directions were not very clear but I was told that it was on a big hill and I could find it from anywhere in the heart of town.

Of course that was not true, though I could see it from almost anywhere. A collection of delicate spires rising from four fine towers. A beautiful building where I had expected only a grand one. It was grand too, of course, a grand dominating cathedral for such a relatively small city (though someone told me later it was not actually a cathedral).

Could that have been where Charlene was married?

No. Of course not. She had been sent to a United Church camp, and there were no Catholic girls at that camp, though there was quite a variety of Protestants. And then there was the business about C. not knowing.

She might have converted secretly. Since.

I found my way in time to the cathedral parking lot, and sat there wondering what I should do. I was wearing slacks and a jacket. My idea of what was required in a Catholic church—a Catholic cathedral—was so antiquated that I was not even sure if my outfit would be all right. I tried to recall visits to great churches in Europe. Something about the arms being covered? Headscarves, skirts?

What a bright high silence there was up on this hill. April, not a leaf out yet on the trees, but the sun after all was still well up in the sky. There was one low bank of snow grey as the paving in the church lot.

The jacket I had on was too light for evening wear, or maybe it was colder here, the wind stronger, than in Toronto.

The building might well be locked at this time, locked and empty.

The grand front doors appeared to be so. I did not even bother to climb the steps to try them, because I decided to follow a couple of old women—old like me—who had just come up the long flight from the street and who bypassed those steps entirely, heading around to an easier entrance at the side of the building.

There were more people inside, maybe two or three dozen people, but there wasn't a sense that they were gathered for a service. They were scattered here and there in the pews, some kneeling and some chatting. The women ahead of me dipped their hands in a marble font without looking at what they were doing and said hello—hardly lowering their voices—to a man who was setting out baskets on a table.

'It looks a lot warmer out than it is,' said one of them, and the man said the wind would bite your nose off.

I recognized the confessionals. Like separate small cottages or large playhouses in a Gothic style, with a lot of dark wooden carving, dark brown curtains. Elsewhere all was glowing, dazzling. The high curved ceiling most celestially blue, the lower curves of the ceiling—those that joined the upright walls—decorated with holy images on gold-painted medallions. Stained-glass windows hit by the sun at this time of day were turned into columns of jewels. I made my way discreetly down one aisle, trying to get a look at the altar, but the chancel being in the western wall was too bright for me to look into. Above the windows, though, I saw that there were painted angels. Flocks of angels, all fresh and gauzy and pure as light.

It was a most insistent place but nobody seemed to be overwhelmed by all the insistence. The chatting ladies kept chatting softly but not in whispers. And other people after some proper nodding and crossing knelt down and went about their business.

As I ought to be going about mine. I looked around for a priest but there was not one in sight. Priests as well as other people must have a working day. They must drive home and go into their living rooms or offices or dens and turn on the television and loosen their collars. Fetch a drink and wonder if they were going to get anything decent for supper. When they did come into the church they would come officially. In their vestments, ready to perform some ceremony. Mass?

Or to hear confessions. But then you would never know when they were there. Didn't they enter and leave their grilled stalls by a private door?

I would have to ask somebody. The man who had distributed the baskets seemed to be here for reasons that were not purely private, though he was apparently not an usher. Nobody needed an usher. People chose where they wanted to sit—or kneel—and sometimes decided to get up and choose another spot, perhaps being bothered by the glare of the jewel-inflaming sun. When I spoke to him I whispered, out of old habit in a church—and he had to ask me to speak again. Puzzled or embarrassed, he nodded in a wobbly way toward one of the confessionals. I had to become very specific and convincing.

'No, no. I just want to talk to a priest. I've been sent to talk to a priest. A priest called Father Hofstrader.'

The basket man disappeared down the more distant side aisle and came back in a little while with a briskly moving stout young priest in ordinary black costume.

He motioned me into a room I had not noticed—not a room, actually, we went through an archway, not a doorway—at the back of the church.

'Give us a chance to talk, in here,' he said, and pulled out a chair for me.

'Father Hofstrader—'

'Oh no, I must tell you, I am not Father Hofstrader. Father Hofstrader is not here. He is on vacation.'

For a moment I did not know to proceed.

'I will do my best to help you.'

'There is a woman,' I said, 'a woman who is dying in Princess Margaret Hospital in Toronto—'

'Yes, yes. We know of Princess Margaret Hospital.'

'She asks me—I have a note from her here—She wants to see Father Hofstrader.'

'Is she a member of this parish?'

'I don't know. I don't know if she is a Catholic or not. She is from here. From Guelph. She is a friend I have not seen for a long time.'

'When did you talk with her?'

I had to explain that I hadn't talked with her, she had been asleep, but she had left the note for me.

'But you don't know if she is a Catholic?'

He had a cracked sore at the corner of his mouth. It must have been painful for him to talk.

'I think she is, but her husband isn't and he doesn't know she is. She doesn't want him to know.'

I said this in the hope of making things clearer, even though I didn't know for sure if it was true. I had an idea that this priest might shortly lose interest altogether. 'Father Hofstrader must have known all this,' I said.

'You didn't speak with her?'

I said that she had been under medication but that this was not the case all the time and I was sure she would have periods of lucidity. This too I stressed because I thought it necessary.

'If she wishes to make a confession, you know, there are priests available at Princess Margaret's.'

I could not think of what else to say. I got out the note, smoothed the paper, and handed it to him. I saw that the handwriting was not as good as I had thought. It was legible only in comparison with the letters on the envelope.

He made a troubled face.

'Who is this C.?'

'Her husband.' I was worried that he might ask for the husband's name, to get in touch with him, but instead he asked for Charlene's. This woman's name, he said.

'Charlene Sullivan.' It was a wonder that I even remembered the surname. And I was reassured for a moment, because it was a name that sounded Catholic. Of course that meant that it was the husband who could be Catholic. But the priest might conclude that the husband had lapsed, and that would surely make Charlene's secrecy more understandable, her message more urgent.

'Why does she need Father Hofstrader?'

'I think perhaps it's something special.'

'All confessions are special.'

He made a move to get up, but I stayed where I was. He sat down again.

'Father Hofstrader is on vacation, but he is not out of town. I could phone and ask him about this. If you insist.'

'Yes. Please.'

'I do not like to bother him. He has not been well.'

I said that if he was not well enough to drive himself to Toronto I could drive him.

'We can take care of his transportation if necessary.'

He looked around and did not see what he wanted, unclipped a pen from his pocket, and then decided that the blank side of the note would do to write on.

'If you'll just make sure I've got the name. Charlotte—'
'Charlene.'

Was I not tempted, during all this palaver? Not once? You'd think that I might break open, be wise to break open, glimpsing that vast though tricky forgiveness. But no. It's not for me. What's done is done. Flocks of angels, tears of blood, notwithstanding.

I sat in the car without thinking to turn the motor on, though it was freezing cold by now. I didn't know what to do next. That is, I knew what I could do. Find my way to the highway and join the bright everlasting flow of cars toward Toronto. Or find a place to stay overnight, if I did not think I had the strength to drive. Most places would provide you with a toothbrush, or direct you to a machine where you could get one. I knew what was necessary and possible but it was beyond my strength, for the moment, to do it.

—

The motorboats on the lake were supposed to stay a good distance out from the shore. And especially from our camping area, so that the waves they raised would not disturb our swimming. But on that last morning, that Sunday morning, a couple of them started a race and circled close in—not as close as the raft, of course, but close enough to raise waves. The raft was tossed around and Pauline's voice was lifted in a cry of reproach and dismay. The boats made far too much noise for their drivers to hear her, and anyway they had set a big wave rolling toward the shore, causing most of us in the shallows either to jump with it or be tumbled off our feet.

Charlene and I both lost our footing. We had our backs to the raft, because we were watching Verna come toward us. We were standing in water about up to our armpits, and we seemed to be lifted and tossed at the same moment that we heard Pauline's cry. We may have cried out as many others did, first in fear and then in delight as we regained our footing and that wave washed on ahead of us. The waves that followed proved to be not as strong, so that we could hold ourselves against them.

At the moment we tumbled, Verna had pitched toward us. When we came up, with our faces streaming, arms flailing, she was spread out under the surface of the water. There was a tumult of screaming and shouting all around, and this increased as the lesser waves arrived and people who had somehow missed the first attack pretended to be knocked over by the second. Verna's head did not break the surface, though now she was not inert, but turning in a leisurely way, light as a jellyfish in the water. Charlene and I had our hands on her, on her rubber cap.

This could have been an accident. As if we, in trying to get our balance, grabbed on to this nearby large rubbery object, hardly realizing what it was or what we were doing. I have thought it all out. I think we would have been forgiven. Young children. Terrified.

Yes, yes. Hardly knew what they were doing.

Is this in any way true? It is true in the sense that we did not decide anything, in the beginning. We did not look at each other and decide to do what we subsequently and consciously did. Consciously, because our eyes did meet as the head of Verna tried to rise up to the surface of the water. Her head was determined to rise, like a dumpling in a stew. The rest of her was making misguided feeble movements down in the water, but the head knew what it should do.

We might have lost our grip on the rubber head, the rubber cap, were it not for the raised pattern that made it less slippery. I can recall the colour perfectly, the pale insipid blue, but I never deciphered the pattern—a fish, a mermaid, a flower—whose ridges pushed into my palms.

Charlene and I kept our eyes on each other, rather than looking down at what our hands were doing. Her eyes were wide and gleeful, as I suppose mine were too. I don't think we felt wicked, triumphing in our wickedness. More as if we were doing just what was—amazingly—demanded of us, as if this was the absolute high point, the culmination, in our lives, of our being ourselves.

We had gone too far to turn back, you might say. We had no choice. But I swear that choice had not occurred, did not occur, to us.

The whole business probably took no more than two minutes. Three? Or a minute and a half?

It seems too much to say that the discouraging clouds cleared up just at that time, but at some point—perhaps at the trespass of the motorboats, or when Pauline screamed, or when the first wave hit, or when the rubber object under our palms ceased to have a will of its own—the sun burst out, and more parents popped up on the beach, and there were calls to all of us to stop horsing around and come out of the water. Swimming was over. Over for the summer, for those who lived out of reach of the lake or municipal swimming pools. Private pools were only in the movie magazines.

As I've said, my memory fails when it comes to parting from Charlene, getting into my parents' car. Because it didn't matter. At that age, things ended. You expected things to end.

I am sure we never said anything as banal, as insulting or unnecessary, as *Don't tell.*

I can imagine the unease starting, but not spreading quite so fast as it might have if there had not been competing dramas. A child has lost a sandal, one of the youngest children is screaming that she got sand in her eye from the waves. Almost certainly a child is throwing up, because of the excitement in the water or the excitement of families arriving or the too-swift consumption of contraband candy.

And soon but not right away the anxiety running through this, that someone is missing.

'Who?'

'One of the Specials.'

'Oh drat. Wouldn't you know.'

The woman in charge of the Specials running around, still in her flowered bathing suit, with the custard flesh wobbling on her thick arms and legs. Her voice wild and weepy.

Somebody go check in the woods, run up the trail, call her name.
'What is her name?'
'*Verna.*'
'Wait.'
'What?'
'Is that not something out there in the water?'

But I believe we were gone by then.

2012

# Alistair MacLeod

1936–2014

Born in North Battleford, Saskatchewan, Alistair MacLeod grew up in a coal-mining area of Alberta until he was 10, when his parents moved back to the family farm in Inverness County, Cape Breton. After obtaining his teacher's certificate from the Nova Scotia Teachers College, he took his BA and his BEd (1960) from Saint Francis Xavier University, his MA (1961) from the University of New Brunswick, and his PhD (1968) from the University of Notre Dame. He taught at Indiana University from 1966 until 1969, then moved to the University of Windsor, where he was a professor of English literature and creative writing until his retirement in 2000.

Most of the stories of MacLeod's two collections of short fiction, *The Lost Salt Gift of Blood* (1976) and *As Birds Bring Forth the Sun* (1986), are set on the usually rugged and turbulent terrain of Cape Breton, where characters tend to be stern individualists who make their living from the sea and find solace in their deep-rooted traditions. These collections, along with two additional stories, were gathered together in *Island: The Collected Stories* (2000). In 1999 MacLeod published a novel, *No Great Mischief*, which examines the pains and the endurance of the Cape Breton people; it won the International IMPAC Dublin Literary Award.

In 'The Boat', from *The Lost Salt Gift of Blood*, the narrator looks back on the winter when he was 15. As he reflects on his Cape Breton childhood, he comes to know and appreciate his feelings for his parents and to understand the emotional price he has paid for leaving the scene of his upbringing to pursue an advanced education.

## The Boat

There are times even now, when I awake at four o'clock in the morning with the terrible fear that I have overslept; when I imagine that my father is waiting for me in the room below the darkened stairs or that the shorebound men are tossing pebbles against my window while blowing their hands and stomping their feet impatiently on the frozen steadfast earth. There are times when I am half out of bed and fumbling for socks and mumbling for words before I realize that I am foolishly alone, that no one waits at the base of the stairs and no boat rides restlessly in the waters by the pier.

At such times only the grey corpses on the overflowing ashtray beside my bed bear witness to the extinction of the latest spark and silently await the crushing out of the most recent of their fellows. And then because I am afraid to be alone with death, I dress rapidly, make a great to-do about clearing my throat, turn on both faucets in the sink, and proceed to make loud splashing ineffectual noises. Later I go out and walk the mile to the all-night restaurant.

In the winter it is a very cold walk, and there are often tears in my eyes when I arrive. The waitress usually gives a sympathetic little shiver and says, 'Boy, it must be really cold out there; you got tears in your eyes.'

'Yes,' I say, 'it sure is; it really is.'

And then the three or four of us who are always in such places at such times make uninteresting little protective chit-chat until the dawn reluctantly arrives. Then I swallow the coffee, which is always bitter, and leave with a great busy rush because by that time I have to worry about being late and whether I have a clean shirt and whether my car will start and about all the other countless things one must worry about when one teaches at a great Midwestern university. And I know then that that day will go by as have all the days of the past ten years, for the call and the voices and the shapes and the boat were not really there in the early morning's darkness and I have all kinds of comforting reality to prove it. They are only shadows and echoes, the animals a child's hands make on the wall by lamplight, and the voices from the rain barrel; the cuttings from an old movie made in the black and white of long ago.

I first became conscious of the boat in the same way and at almost the same time that I became aware of the people it supported. My earliest recollection of my father is a view from the floor of gigantic rubber boots and then of being suddenly elevated and having my face pressed against the stubble of his cheek, and of how it tasted of salt and of how he smelled of salt from his red-soled rubber boots to the shaggy whiteness of his hair.

When I was very small, he took me for my first ride in the boat. I rode the half-mile from our house to the wharf on his shoulders and I remember the sound of his rubber boots galumphing along the gravel beach, the tune of the indecent little song he used to sing, and the odour of the salt.

The floor of the boat was permeated with the same odour and in its constancy I was not aware of change. In the harbour we made our little circle and returned. He tied the boat by its painter, fastened the stern to its permanent anchor, and lifted me high over his head to the solidity of the wharf. Then he climbed up the little iron ladder that led to the wharf's cap, placed me once more upon his shoulders, and galumphed off again.

When we returned to the house everyone made a great fuss over my precocious excursion and asked, 'How did you like the boat?' 'Were you afraid in the boat?' 'Did you cry in the boat?' They repeated 'the boat' at the end of all their questions and I knew it must be very important to everyone.

My earliest recollection of my mother is of being alone with her in the mornings while my father was away in the boat. She seemed to be always repairing clothes that were 'torn in the boat', preparing food 'to be eaten in the boat', or looking for 'the boat' through our kitchen window which faced upon the sea. When my father returned about noon, she would ask, 'Well, how did things go in the boat today?' It was the first question I remember asking: 'Well, how did things go in the boat today?' 'Well, how did things go in the boat today?'

The boat in our lives was registered at Port Hawkesbury. She was what Nova Scotians called a Cape Island boat and was designed for the small inshore fishermen who sought the lobsters of the spring and the mackerel of summer and later the cod and haddock and hake. She was thirty-two feet long and nine wide, and was powered by an engine from a Chevrolet truck. She had a marine clutch and a high-speed reverse gear and was painted light green with the name *Jenny Lynn* stencilled in black letters on her bow and painted on an oblong plate across her stern. Jenny Lynn had been my mother's maiden name and the boat was called after her as another link in the chain of tradition. Most of the boats that berthed at the wharf bore the names of some female member of their owner's household.

I say this now as if I knew it all then. All at once, all about boat dimensions and engines, and as if on the day of my first childish voyage I noticed the difference between a stencilled name and a painted name. But of course it was not that way at all, for I learned it all very slowly and there was not time enough.

I learned first about our house, which was one of about fifty that marched around the horseshoe of our harbour and the wharf that was its heart. Some of them were so close to the water that during a storm the sea spray splashed against their windows while others were built farther along the beach, as was the case with ours. The houses and their people, like those of the neighbouring towns and villages, were the result of Ireland's discontent and Scotland's Highland Clearances and America's War of Independence. Impulsive, emotional Catholic Celts who could not bear to live with England and shrewd, determined Protestant Puritans who, in the years after 1776, could not bear to live without.

The most important room in our house was one of those oblong old-fashioned kitchens heated by a wood- and coal-burning stove. Behind the stove was a box of kindlings and beside it a coal scuttle. A heavy wooden table with leaves that expanded or reduced its dimensions stood in the middle of the floor. There were five wooden homemade chairs which had been chipped and hacked by a variety of knives. Against the east wall, opposite the stove, there was a couch which sagged in the middle and had a cushion for a pillow, and above it a shelf which contained matches, tobacco, pencils, odd fish-hooks, bits of twine, and a tin can filled with bills and receipts. The south wall was dominated by a window which faced the sea and on the north there was a five-foot board which bore a variety of clothes hooks and the burdens of each. Beneath the board there was a jumble of odd footwear, mostly of rubber. There was also, on this wall, a barometer, a map of the marine area, and a shelf which held a tiny radio. The kitchen was shared by all of us and was a buffer zone between the immaculate order of ten other rooms and the disruptive chaos of the single room that was my father's.

My mother ran her house as her brothers ran their boats. Everything was clean and spotless and in order. She was tall and dark and powerfully energetic. In later years she reminded me of the women of Thomas Hardy, particularly Eustacia Vye, in a physical way. She fed and clothed a family of seven children, making all of the meals and most of the clothes. She grew miraculous gardens and magnificent flowers and raised broods of hens and ducks. She would walk miles on berry-picking expeditions and hoist her skirts to dig for clams when the tide was low. She was fourteen years younger then my father, whom she had married when she was twenty-six and had been a local beauty for a period of ten years. My mother was of the sea, as were all of her people, and her horizons were the very literal ones she scanned with her dark and fearless eyes.

Between the kitchen clothes rack and barometer, a door opened into my father's bedroom. It was a room of disorder and disarray. It was as if the wind which so often clamoured about the house succeeded in entering this single room and after whipping it into turmoil stole quietly away to renew its knowing laughter from without.

My father's bed was against the south wall. It always looked rumpled and unmade because he lay on top of it more than he slept within any folds it might have had. Beside it, there was a little brown table. An archaic goose-necked reading light, a battered table radio, a mound of wooden matches, one or two packages of tobacco, a deck of cigarette papers, and an overflowing ashtray cluttered its surface. The brown larvae of tobacco shreds and the grey flecks of ash covered both the table and the floor beneath it. The once-varnished surface of the table was disfigured by numerous black scars and gashes inflicted by the neglected burning cigarettes of many years. They had tumbled from the ashtray unnoticed and branded their statements permanently and quietly into the wood until the odour of their burning caused the snuffing out of their lives. At the bed's foot there was a single window which looked upon the sea.

Against the adjacent wall there was a battered bureau and beside it there was a closet which held his single ill-fitting serge suit, the two or three white shirts that strangled him and the square black shoes that pinched. When he took off his more friendly clothes, the heavy woollen sweaters, mitts, and socks which my mother knitted for him and the woollen and doeskin shirts, he dumped them unceremoniously on a single chair. If a visitor entered the room while he was lying on the bed, he would be told to throw the clothes on the floor and take their place upon the chair.

Magazines and books covered the bureau and competed with the clothes for domination of the chair. They further overburdened the heroic little table and lay on top of the radio. They filled a baffling and unknowable cave beneath the bed, and in the corner by the bureau they spilled from the walls and grew up from the floor.

The magazines were the most conventional: *Time*, *Newsweek*, *Life*, *Maclean's*, *The Family Herald*, *The Reader's Digest*. They were the result of various cut-rate subscriptions or of the gift subscriptions associated with Christmas, 'the two whole years for only $3.50'.

The books were more varied. There were a few hardcover magnificents and bygone Book-of-the-Month wonders and some were Christmas or birthday gifts. The majority of them, however, were used paperbacks which came from those second-hand bookstores that advertise in the backs of magazines: 'Miscellaneous Used Paperbacks 10¢

Each'. At first he sent for them himself, although my mother resented the expense, but in later years they came more and more often from my sisters who had moved to the cities. Especially at first they were very weird and varied. Mickey Spillane and Ernest Haycox vied with Dostoyevsky and Faulkner, and the Penguin Poets edition of Gerard Manley Hopkins arrived in the same box as a little book on sex technique called *Getting the Most Out of Love*. The former had been assiduously annotated by a very fine hand using a very blue-inked fountain pen while the latter had been studied by someone with very large thumbs, the prints of which were still visible in the margins. At the slightest provocation it would open almost automatically to particularly graphic and well-smudged pages.

When he was not in the boat, my father spent most of his time lying on the bed in his socks, the top two buttons of his trousers undone, his discarded shirt on the ever-ready chair and the sleeves of the woollen Stanfield underwear, which he wore both summer and winter, drawn half way up to his elbows. The pillows propped up the whiteness of his head and the goose-necked lamp illuminated the pages in his hands. The cigarettes smoked and smouldered on the ashtray and on the table and the radio played constantly, sometimes low and sometimes loud. At midnight and at one, two, three, and four, one could sometimes hear the radio, his occasional cough, the rustling thud of a completed book being tossed to the corner heap, or the movement necessitated by his sitting on the edge of the bed to roll the thousandth cigarette. He seemed never to sleep, only to doze, and the light shone constantly from his window to the sea.

My mother despised the room and all it stood for and she had stopped sleeping in it after I was born. She despised disorder in rooms and in houses and in hours and in lives, and she had not read a book since high school. There she had read *Ivanhoe* and considered it a colossal waste of time. Still the room remained, like a rock of opposition in the sparkling waters of clear deep harbour, opening off the kitchen where we really lived our lives, with its door always open and its contents visible to all.

The daughters of the room and of the house were very beautiful. They were tall and willowy like my mother and had her fine facial features set off by the reddish copper-coloured hair that had apparently once been my father's before it turned to white. All of them were very clever in school and helped my mother a great deal about the house. When they were young they sang and were very happy and very nice to me because I was the youngest, and the family's only boy.

My father never approved of their playing about the wharf like the other children, and they went there only when my mother sent them on a errand. At such times they almost always overstayed, playing screaming games of tag or hide-and-seek in and about the fishing shanties, the piled traps and tubs of trawl, shouting down to the perch that swam languidly about the wharf's algae-covered piles, or jumping in and out of the boats that tugged gently at their lines. My mother was never uneasy about them at such times, and when her husband criticized her she would say, 'Nothing will happen to them there,' or 'They could be doing worse things in worse places.'

By about the ninth or tenth grade my sisters one by one discovered my father's bedroom, and then the change would begin. Each would go into the room one morning when he was out. She would go with the ideal hope of imposing order or with the more practical objective of emptying the ashtray, and later she would be found spellbound by the volume in her hand. My mother's reaction was always abrupt, bordering on the angry. 'Take your nose out of that trash and come and do your work,' she would say, and once I saw her slap my youngest sister so hard that the print of her hand was scarletly emblazoned upon her daughter's cheek while the broken-spined paperback fluttered uselessly to the floor.

Thereafter my mother would launch a campaign against what she had discovered but could not understand. At times, although she was not overly religious, she would bring in God to bolster her arguments, saying, 'In the next world God will see to those who waste their lives reading useless books when they should be about their work.' Or without theological aid, 'I would like to know how books help anyone to live a life.' If my father were in, she would repeat the remarks louder than necessary, and her voice would carry into his room where he lay upon his bed. His usual reaction was to turn up the volume of the radio, although that action in itself betrayed the success of the initial thrust.

Shortly after my sisters began to read books, they grew restless and lost interest in darning socks and baking bread, and all of them eventually went to work as summer waitresses in the Sea Food Restaurant. The restaurant was run by a big American concern from Boston and catered to the tourists that flooded the area during July and August. My mother despised the whole operation. She said the restaurant was not run by 'our people', and 'our people' did not eat there, and that it was run by outsiders for outsiders.

'Who are these people anyway?' she would ask, tossing back her dark hair, 'and what do they, though they go about with their cameras for a hundred years, know about the way it is here, and what do they care about me and mine, and why should I care about them?'

She was angry that my sisters should even conceive of working in such a place, and more angry when my father made no move to prevent it, and she was worried about herself and about her family and about her life. Sometimes she would say softly to her sisters, 'I don't know what's the matter with my girls. It seems none of them are interested in any of the right things.' And sometimes there would be bitter savage arguments. One afternoon I was coming in with three mackerel I'd been given at the wharf when I heard her say, 'Well, I hope you'll be satisfied when they come home knocked up and you'll have had your way.'

It was the most savage thing I'd ever heard my mother say. Not just the words but the way she said them, and I stood there in the porch afraid to breathe for what seemed like the years from ten to fifteen, feeling the damp, moist mackerel with their silver glassy eyes growing clammy against my leg.

Through the angle in the screen door I saw my father, who had been walking into his room, wheel around on one of his rubber-booted heels and look at her with his blue eyes flashing like clearest ice beneath the snow that was his hair. His usually ruddy face was drawn and grey, reflecting the exhaustion of a man of sixty-five who had been working in those rubber boots for eleven hours on an August day, and for a fleeting moment I wondered what I would do if he killed my mother while I stood there in the porch with those three foolish mackerel in my hand. Then he turned and went into his room and the radio blared forth the next day's weather forecast and I retreated under the noise and returned again, stamping my feet and slamming the door too loudly to signal my approach. My mother was busy at the stove when I came in, and did not raise her head when I threw the mackerel in a pan. As I looked into my father's room, I said, 'Well, how did things go in the boat today?' and he replied, 'Oh, not too badly, all things considered.' He was lying on his back and lighting the first cigarette and the radio was talking about the Virginia coast.

All of my sisters made good money on tips. They bought my father an electric razor, which he tried to use for a while, and they took out even more magazine subscriptions. They bought my mother a great many clothes of the type she was very fond of, the wide-brimmed hats and the brocaded dresses, but she locked them all in trunks and refused to wear any of them.

On one August day my sisters prevailed upon my father to take some of their restaurant customers for an afternoon ride in the boat. The tourists with their expensive clothes and cameras and sun glasses awkwardly backed down the iron ladder at the wharf's side to where my father waited below, holding the rocking *Jenny Lynn* in snug against the wharf with one hand on the iron ladder and steadying his descending passengers with the other. They tried to look both prim and wind-blown like the girls in the Pepsi-Cola ads and did the best they could, sitting on the thwarts where the newspapers were spread to cover the splattered blood and fish entrails, crowding to one side so that they were in danger of capsizing the boat, taking the inevitable pictures or merely trailing their fingers through the water of their dreams.

All of them liked my father very much and, after he'd brought them back from their circles in the harbour, they invited him to their rented cabins which were located high on a hill overlooking the village to which they were so alien. He proceeded to get very drunk up there with the beautiful view and the strange company and the abundant liquor, and late in the afternoon he began to sing.

I was just approaching the wharf to deliver my mother's summons when he began, and the familiar yet unfamiliar voice that rolled down from the cabins made me feel as I had never felt before in my young life, or perhaps as I had always felt without really knowing it, and I was ashamed yet proud, younger yet old and saved yet forever lost, and there was nothing I could do to control my legs which trembled nor my eyes which wept, for what they could not tell.

The tourists were equipped with tape recorders and my father sang for more than three hours. His voice boomed down the hill and bounced off the surface of the harbour, which was an unearthly blue on that hot August day, and was then reflected to the wharf and the fishing shanties, where it was absorbed amidst the men who were baiting lines for the next day's haul.

He sang all the old sea chanteys that had come across from the old world and by which men like him had pulled ropes for generations, and he sang the East Coast sea songs that celebrated the sealing vessels of Northumberland Strait and the long liners of the Grand Banks, and of Anticosti, Sable Island, Grand Manan, Boston Harbor, Nantucket, and Block Island. Gradually he shifted to the seemingly unending Gaelic drinking songs with their twenty or more verses and inevitable refrains, and the men in the shanties smiled at the coarseness of some of the verses and at the thought that the singer's immediate audience did not know what they were applauding nor recording to take back to staid old Boston. Later as the sun was setting he switched to the laments and the wild and haunting Gaelic war songs of those spattered Highland ancestors he had never seen, and when his voice ceased, the savage melancholy of three hundred years seemed to hang over the peaceful harbour and the quiet boats and the men leaning in the doorways of their shanties with their cigarettes glowing in the dusk and the women looking to the sea from their open windows with their children in their arms.

When he came home he threw the money he had earned on the kitchen table as he did with all his earnings but my mother refused to touch it, and the next day he went with the rest of the men to bait his trawl in the shanties. The tourists came to the door that evening and my mother met them there and told them that her husband was not in, although he was lying on the bed only a few feet away, with the radio playing and the cigarette upon his lips. She stood in the doorway until they reluctantly went away.

In the winter they sent him a picture which had been taken on the day of the singing. On the back it said, 'To Our Ernest Hemingway' and the 'Our' was underlined. There was also an accompanying letter telling how much they had enjoyed themselves, how popular the tape was proving, and explaining who Ernest Hemingway was. In a way it almost did look like one of those unshaven, taken-in-Cuba pictures of Hemingway. My father looked both massive and incongruous in the setting. His bulky fisherman's clothes were too big for the green and white lawn chair in which he sat, and his rubber boots seemed to take up all of the well-clipped grass square. The beach umbrella jarred with his sunburned face and because he had already been singing for some time, his lips, which chapped in the winds of spring and burned in the water glare of summer, had already cracked in several places, producing tiny flecks of blood at their corners and on the whiteness of his teeth. The bracelets of brass chain which he wore to protect his wrists from chafing seemed abnormally large and his broad leather belt had been slackened and his heavy shirt and underwear were open at the throat, revealing an uncultivated wilderness of white chest hair bordering on the semi-controlled stubble of his neck and chin. His blue eyes had looked directly into the camera and his hair was whiter than the two tiny clouds that hung over his left shoulder. The sea was behind him and its immense blue flatness stretched out to touch the arching blueness of the sky. It seemed very far away from him or else he was so much in the foreground that he seemed too big for it.

Each year another of my sisters would read the books and work in the restaurant. Sometimes they would stay out quite late on the hot summer nights and when they came up the stairs my mother would ask them many long and involved questions which they resented and tried to avoid. Before ascending the stairs they would go into my father's room, and those of us who waited above could hear them throwing his clothes off the chair before sitting on it, or the squeak of the bed as they sat on its edge. Sometimes they would talk to him a long time, the murmur of their voices blending with the music of the radio into a mysterious vapour-like sound which floated softly up the stairs.

I say this again as if it all happened at once and as if all of my sisters were of identical ages and like so many lemmings going into another sea and, again, it was of course not that way at all. Yet go they did, to Boston, to Montreal, to New York with the young men they met during the summers and later married in those far-away cities. The young men were very articulate and handsome and wore fine clothes and drove expensive cars and my sisters, as I said, were very tall and beautiful with their copper-coloured hair, and were tired of darning socks and baking bread.

One by one they went. My mother had each of her daughters for fifteen years, then lost them for two and finally forever. None married a fisherman. My mother never accepted any of the young men, for in her eyes they seemed always a combination of the lazy, the effeminate, the dishonest, and the unknown. They never seemed to do any physical work and she could not comprehend their luxurious vacations and she did not know whence they came nor who they were. And in the end she did not really care, for they were not of her people and they were not of her sea.

I say this now with a sense of wonder at my own stupidity in thinking I was somehow free and would go on doing well in school and playing and helping in the boat and passing into my early teens while streaks of grey began to appear in my mother's dark hair and my father's rubber boots dragged sometimes on the pebbles of the beach as he trudged home from the wharf. And there were but three of us in the house that had at one time been so loud.

Then during the winter that I was fifteen he seemed to grow old and ill all at once. Most of January he lay upon the bed, smoking and reading and listening to the radio while the wind howled about the house and the needle-like snow blistered off the ice-covered harbour and the doors flew out of people's hands if they did not cling to them like death.

In February, when the men began overhauling their lobster traps, he still did not move, and my mother and I began to knit lobster trap headings in the evenings. The twine was as always very sharp and harsh, and blisters formed upon our thumbs and little paths of blood snaked quietly down between our fingers while the seals that had drifted down from distant Labrador wept and moaned like human children on the ice-floes of the Gulf.

In the daytime my mother's brother, who had been my father's partner as long as I could remember, also came to work upon the gear. He was a year older than my mother and was tall and dark and the father of twelve children.

By March we were very far behind and although I began to work very hard in the evenings I knew it was not hard enough and that there were but eight weeks left before the opening of the season on May first. And I knew that my mother worried and my uncle was uneasy and that all of our very lives depended on the boat being ready with her gear and two men, by the date of May the first. And I knew then that *David Copperfield* and *The Tempest* and all of those friends I had dearly come to love must really go forever. So I bade them all good-bye.

The night after my first full day at home and after my mother had gone upstairs he called me into his room, where I sat upon the chair beside his bed. 'You will go back tomorrow,' he said simply.

I refused then, saying I had made my decision and was satisfied.

'That is no way to make a decision,' he said, 'and if you are satisfied I am not. It is best that you go back.' I was almost angry then and told him as all children do that I wished he would leave me alone and stop telling me what to do.

He looked at me a long time then, lying there on the same bed on which he had fathered me those sixteen years before, fathered me his only son, out of who knew what emotions when he was already fifty-six and his hair had turned to snow. Then he swung his legs over the edge of the squeaking bed and sat facing me and looked into my own dark eyes with his of crystal blue and placed his hand upon my knee. 'I am not telling you to do anything,' he said softly, 'only asking you.'

The next morning I returned to school. As I left, my mother followed me to the porch and said, 'I never thought a son of mine would choose useless books over the parents that gave him life.'

In the weeks that followed he got up rather miraculously, and the gear was ready and the *Jenny Lynn* was freshly painted by the last two weeks of April when the ice began to break up and the lonely screaming gulls returned to haunt the silver herring as they flashed within the sea.

On the first day of May the boats raced out as they had always done, laden down almost to the gunwales with their heavy cargoes of traps. They were almost like living things as they plunged through the waters of the spring and manoeuvred between the still floating icebergs of crystal-white and emerald green on their way to the traditional grounds that they sought out every May. And those of us who sat that day in the high school on the hill, discussing the watery imagery of Tennyson, watched them as they passed back and forth beneath us until by afternoon the piles of traps which had been stacked upon the wharf were no longer visible but were spread about the bottoms of the sea. And the *Jenny Lynn* went too, all day, with my uncle tall and dark, like a latter-day Tashtego standing at the tiller with his legs wide apart and guiding her deftly between the floating pans of ice and my father in the stern standing in the same way with his hands upon the ropes that lashed the cargo to the deck. And at night my mother asked, 'Well, how did things go in the boat today?'

And the spring wore on and the summer came and school ended in the third week of June and the lobster season on July first and I wished that the two things I loved so dearly did not exclude each other in a manner that was so blunt and too clear.

At the conclusion of the lobster season my uncle said he had been offered a berth on a deep-sea dragger and had decided to accept. We all knew that he was leaving the *Jenny Lynn* forever and that before the next lobster season he would buy a boat of his own. He was expecting another child and would be supporting fifteen people by the next spring and could not chance my father against the family that he loved.

I joined my father then for the trawling season, and he made no protest and my mother was quite happy. Through the summer we baited the tubs of trawl in the afternoon and set them at sunset and revisited them in the darkness of the early morning. The men would come tramping by our house at four a.m. and we would join them and walk with them to the wharf and be on our way before the sun rose out of the ocean where it seemed to spend the night. If I was not up they would toss pebbles to my window and I would be very embarrassed and tumble downstairs to where my father lay fully clothed atop his bed, reading his book and listening to his radio and smoking his cigarette. When I appeared he would swing off his bed and put on his boots and be instantly ready and then we would take the lunches my mother had prepared the night before and walk off toward the sea. He would make no attempt to wake me himself.

It was in many ways a good summer. There were few storms and we went out almost every day and we lost a minimum of gear and seemed to land a maximum of fish and I tanned dark and brown after the manner of my uncles.

My father did not tan—he never tanned—because of his reddish complexion, and the salt water irritated his skin as it had for sixty years. He burned and reburned over and over again and his lips still cracked so that they bled when he smiled, and his arms, especially the left, still broke out into the oozing salt-water boils as they had ever since as a child I had first watched him soaking and bathing them in a variety of ineffectual solutions. The chafe-preventing bracelets of brass linked chain that all the men wore about their wrists in early spring were his the full season and he shaved but painfully and only once a week.

And I saw then, that summer, many things that I had seen all my life as if for the first time and I thought that perhaps my father had never been intended for a fisherman either physically or mentally. At least not in the manner of my uncles; he had never really loved it. And I remembered that, one evening in his room when we were talking about *David Copperfield*, he had said that he had always wanted to go to the university and I had dismissed it then in the way one dismisses one's father's saying he would like to be a tight-rope walker, and we had gone on to talk about the Peggottys and how they loved the sea.

And I thought then to myself that there were many things wrong with all of us and all our lives and I wondered why my father, who was himself an only son, had not married before he was forty and then I wondered why he had. I even thought that perhaps he had had to marry my mother and checked the dates on the flyleaf of the Bible where I learned that my oldest sister had been born a prosaic eleven months after the marriage, and I felt myself then very dirty and debased for my lack of faith and for what I had thought and done.

And then there came into my heart a very great love for my father and I thought it was very much braver to spend a life doing what you really do not want rather than selfishly following forever your own dreams and inclinations. And I knew then that I could never leave him alone to suffer the iron-tipped harpoons which my mother would forever hurl into his soul because he was a failure as a husband and a father who had retained none of his own. And I felt that I had been very small in a secret place within me and that even the completion of high school was for me a silly shallow selfish dream.

So I told him one night very resolutely and very powerfully that I would remain with him as long as he lived and we would fish the sea together. And he made no protest but only smiled through the cigarette smoke that wreathed his bed and replied, 'I hope you will remember what you've said.'

The room was now so filled with books as to be almost Dickensian, but he would not allow my mother to move or change them and he continued to read them, sometimes two or three a night. They came with great regularity now, and there were more hardcovers, sent by my sisters who had gone so long ago and now seemed so distant and so prosperous, and sent also pictures of small red-haired grandchildren with baseball bats and dolls, which he placed upon his bureau and which my mother gazed at wistfully when she thought no one would see. Red-haired grandchildren with baseball bats and dolls who would never know the sea in hatred or in love.

And so we fished through the heat of August and into the cooler days of September when the water was so clear we could almost see the bottom and the white mists rose like delicate ghosts in the early morning dawn. And one day my mother said to me, 'You have given added years to his life.'

And we fished on into October when it began to roughen and we could no longer risk night sets but took our gear out each morning and returned at the first sign of the squalls; and on into November when we lost three tubs of trawl and the clear blue water turned to a sullen grey and the trochoidal waves rolled rough and high and washed across our bows and decks as we ran within their troughs. We wore heavy sweaters now and the awkward rubber slickers and the heavy woollen mitts which soaked and froze into masses of ice that hung from our wrists like the limbs of gigantic monsters until we thawed them against the exhaust pipe's heat. And almost every day we would leave for home before noon, driven by the blasts of the northwest wind coating our eyebrows with ice and freezing our eyelids closed as we leaned into a visibility that was hardly there, charting our course from the compass and the sea, running the waves and between them but never confronting their towering might.

And I stood at the tiller now, on these homeward lunges, stood in the place and in the manner of my uncle, turning to look at my father and to shout over the roar of the engine and the slop of the sea to where he stood in the stern, drenched and dripping with the snow and the salt and the spray and his bushy eyebrows caked in ice. But on November twenty-first, when it seemed we might be making the final run of the season, I turned and he was not there and I knew even in that instant that he would never be again.

On November twenty-first the waves of the grey Atlantic are very high and the waters are very cold and there are no signposts on the surface of the sea. You cannot tell where you have been five minutes before and in the squalls of snow you cannot see. And it takes longer than you would believe to check a boat that has been running before a gale and turn her ever so carefully in a wide and stupid circle, with timbers creaking and straining, back into the face of storm. And you know that it is useless and that your voice does not carry the length of the boat and that even if you knew the original spot, the relentless waves would carry such burden perhaps a mile or so by the time you could return. And you know also, the final irony, that your father, like your uncles and all the men that form your past, cannot swim a stroke.

The lobster beds off the Cape Breton coast are still very rich and now, from May to July, their offerings are packed in crates of ice, and thundered by the gigantic transport trucks, day and night, through New Glasgow, Amherst, Saint John, and Bangor and Portland and into Boston where they are tossed still living into boiling pots of water, their final home.

And though the prices are higher and the competition tighter, the grounds to which the *Jenny Lynn* once went remain untouched and unfished as they have for the last ten years. For if there are no signposts on the sea in storm, there are certain ones in calm, and the lobster bottoms were disturbed in calm before any of us can remember, and the grounds my father fished were those his father fished before him and there were others before and before and before. Twice the big boats have come from forty and fifty miles, lured by the promise of the grounds, and strewn the bottom with their traps, and twice they have returned to find their buoys cut adrift and their gear lost and destroyed. Twice the Fisheries Officer and the Mounted Police have come and asked many long and involved questions, and twice they have received no answers from the men leaning in the doors of their shanties and the women standing at their windows with their children in their arms. Twice they have gone away saying: 'There are no legal boundaries in the Marine area'; 'No one can own the sea'; 'Those grounds don't wait for anyone.'

But the men and the women, with my mother dark among them, do not care for what they say, for to them the grounds are sacred and they think they wait for me.

It is not an easy thing to know that your mother lives alone on an inadequate insurance policy and that she is too proud to accept any other aid. And that she looks through her lonely window onto the ice of winter and the hot flat calm of summer and the rolling waves of fall. And that she lies awake in the early morning's darkness when the rubber boots of the men scrunch upon the gravel as they pass beside her house on their way down to the wharf. And she knows that the footsteps never stop, because no man goes from her house, and she alone of all the Lynns has neither son nor son-in-law who walks toward the boat that will take him to the sea. And it is not an easy thing to know that your mother looks upon the sea with love and on you with bitterness because the one has been so constant and the other so untrue.

But neither is it easy to know that your father was found on November twenty-eighth, ten miles to the north and wedged between two boulders at the base of the rock-strewn cliffs where he had been hurled and slammed so many many times. His hands were shredded ribbons, as were his feet which had lost their boots to the suction of the sea, and his shoulders came apart in our hands when we tried to move him from the rocks. And the fish had eaten his testicles and the gulls had pecked out his eyes and the white-green stubble of his whiskers had continued to grow in death, like the grass on graves, upon the purple, bloated mass that was his face. There was not much left of my father, physically, as he lay there with the brass chains on his wrists and the seaweed in his hair.

1968

# Bharati Mukherjee

## *b.* 1940

Indian-born Bharati Mukherjee received her BA (1959) from the University of Calcutta, her MA (1961) from the University of Baroda, and her MFA (1963) and PhD (1979) from the University of Iowa. She emigrated from the United States to Canada in 1966, and, after living in Montreal and Toronto, returned in 1980 to the United States, where she taught English at the University of California, Berkeley. Her fiction, like her life, is an exploration of cultural displacement, as her East Indian protagonists confront personal and social struggles both in India and in North America. In 'The Lady from Lucknow', Nafeesa Hafeez, a Muslim housewife, is carrying on an extramarital affair in Atlanta, Georgia; when the affair is revealed, her self-examination commences.

The author of several novels and collections of short stories, she also co-wrote, with her husband, the writer Clark Blaise, *Days and Nights in Calcutta* (1977), an autobiographical account of her return (with her husband) for a year to India. Her most recent book is *Miss New India* (2011).

## The Lady from Lucknow

When I was four, one of the girls next door fell in love with a Hindu. Her father intercepted a love note from the boy, and beat her with his leather sandals. She died soon after. I was in the room when my mother said to our neighbour, 'The Nawab-*sahib* had no choice, but Husseina's heart just broke, poor dear.' I was an army doctor's daughter, and I pictured the dead girl's heart—a rubbery squeezable organ with auricles and ventricles—first swelling, then bursting and coating the floor with thick, slippery blood.

We lived in Lucknow at the time, where the Muslim community was large. This was just before the British took the fat, diamond-shaped subcontinent and created two nations, a big one for the Hindus and a littler one for us. My father moved us to Rawalpindi in Pakistan two months after Husseina died. We were a family of soft, voluptuous children, and my father wanted to protect us from the Hindus' shameful lust.

I have fancied myself in love many times since, but never enough for the emotions to break through tissue and muscle. Husseina's torn heart remains the standard of perfect love.

At seventeen I married a good man, the fourth son of a famous poet-cum-lawyer in Islamabad. We have a daughter, seven, and a son, four. In the Muslim communities we have lived in, we are admired. Iqbal works for IBM, and because of his work we have made homes in Lebanon, Brazil, Zambia, and France. Now we live in Atlanta, Georgia, in a wide, new house with a deck and a backyard that runs into a golf course. IBM has been generous to us. We expect to pass on this good, decent life to our children. Our children are ashamed of the dingy cities where we got our start.

Some Sunday afternoons when Iqbal isn't at a conference halfway across the world, we sit together on the deck and drink gin and tonics as we have done on Sunday afternoons in a dozen exotic cities. But here, the light is different somehow. A gold haze comes off the golf course and settles on our bodies, our new house. When the light shines right in my eyes, I pull myself out of the canvas deck chair and lean against the railing that still smells of forests. Everything in Atlanta is so new!

'Sit,' Iqbal tells me. 'You'll distract the golfers. Americans are crazy for sex, you know that.'

He half rises out of his deck chair. He lunges for my breasts in mock passion. I slip out of his reach.

At the bottom of the backyard, the golfers, caddies, and carts are too minute to be bloated with lust.

But, who knows? One false thwock! of their golfing irons, and my little heart, like a golf ball, could slice through the warm air and vanish into the jonquil-yellow beyond.

It isn't trouble that I want, though I do have a lover. He's an older man, an immunologist with the Centers for Disease Control right here in town. He comes to see me when Iqbal is away at high-tech conferences in sunny, remote resorts. Just think, Beirut was once such a resort! Lately my lover comes to me on Wednesdays even if Iqbal's in town.

'I don't expect to live till ninety-five,' James teases on the phone. His father died at ninety-three in Savannah. 'But I don't want a bullet in the brain from a jealous husband right now.'

Iqbal owns no firearms. Jealously would inflame him.

Besides, Iqbal would never come home in the middle of the day. Not even for his blood-pressure pills. The two times he forgot them last month, I had to take the bottle downtown. One does not rise through the multinational hierarchy coming home in midday, arriving late, or leaving early. Especially, he says, if you're a 'not-quite' as we are. It is up to us to set the standards.

Wives who want to be found out will be found out. Indiscretions are deliberate. The woman caught in mid-shame is a woman who wants to get out. The rest of us carry on.

James flatters me indefatigably; he makes me feel beautiful, exotic, responsive. I am a creature he has immunized of contamination. When he is with me, the world seems a happy enough place.

Then he leaves. He slips back into his tweed suit and backs out of my driveway.

I met James Beamish at a reception for foreign students on the Emory University campus. Iqbal avoids these international receptions because he thinks of them as excuses for looking back when we should be looking forward. These evenings are almost always tedious, but I like to go; just in case there's someone new and fascinating. The last two years, I've volunteered as host in the 'hospitality program'. At Thanksgiving and Christmas, two lonely foreign students are sent to our table.

That first evening at Emory we stood with name tags on lapels, white ones for students and blue ones for hosts. James was by a long table, pouring Chablis into a plastic glass. I noticed him right off. He was dressed much like the other resolute, decent men in the room. But whereas the other men wore white or blue shirts under their dark wool suits, James's shirt was bright red.

His wife was with him that evening, a stoutish woman with slender ankles and expensive shoes.

'Darling,' she said to James. 'See if you can locate our Palestinian.' Then she turned to me, and smiling, peered into my name tag.

'I'm Nafeesa Hafeez,' I helped out.

'Na-fee-sa,' she read out. 'Did I get that right?'

'Yes, perfect,' I said.

'What a musical name,' she said. 'I hope you'll be very happy here. Is this your first time abroad?'

James came over with a glass of Chablis in each hand. 'Did we draw this lovely lady? Oops, I'm sorry, you're a *host*, of course.' A mocking blue light was in his eyes. 'Just when I thought we were getting lucky, dear.'

'Darling, ours is a Palestinian. I told you that in the car. This one is obviously not Palestinian, are you dear?' She took a bright orange notebook out of her purse and showed me the name.

I had to read it upside-down. Something Waheed. School of Dentistry.

'What are you drinking?' James asked. He kept a glass for himself and gave me the other one.

Maybe James Beamish said nothing fascinating that night, but he was attentive, even after the Beamishes' Palestinian joined us. Mrs Beamish was brave, she asked the dentist about his family and hometown. The dentist described West Beirut in detail. The shortage of bread and vegetables, the mortar poundings, the babies bleeding. I wonder when aphasia sets in. When does a dentist, even a Palestinian dentist, decide it's time to cut losses.

Then my own foreign student arrived. She was an Indian Muslim from Lucknow, a large, bold woman who this far from our common hometown claimed me as a countrywoman. India, Pakistan, she said, not letting go of my hand, what does it matter?

I'd rather have listened to James Beamish but I couldn't shut out the woman's voice. She gave us her opinions on Thanksgiving rituals. She said, 'It is very odd that the pumpkin vegetable should be used for dessert, no? We are using it as vegetable only. Chhi! Pumpkin as a sweet. The very idea is horrid.'

I promised that when she came to our house for Thanksgiving, I'd make sweetmeats out of ricotta cheese and syrup. When you live in as many countries as Iqbal had made me, you can't tell if you pity, or if you envy, the women who stayed back.

I didn't hear from James Beamish for two weeks. I thought about him. In fact I couldn't get him out of my mind. I went over the phrases and gestures, the mocking light in the eyes, but they didn't add up to much. After the first week, I called Amina and asked her to lunch. I didn't know her well but her husband worked at the Centers for Disease Control. Just talking to someone connected with the Centers made me feel good. I slipped his name into the small talk with Amina and her eyes popped open, 'Oh, he's famous!' she exclaimed, and I shrugged modestly. I stayed home in case he should call. I sat on the deck and in spite of the cold, pretended to read Barbara Pym novels. Lines from Donne and Urdu verses about love floated in my skull.

I wasn't sure Dr Beamish would call me. Not directly, that is. Perhaps he would play a subtler game, get his wife to invite Iqbal and me for drinks. Maybe she'd even include their Palestinian and my Indian and make an international evening out of it. It sounded plausible.

Finally James Beamish called me on a Tuesday afternoon, around four. The children were in the kitchen, and a batch of my special chocolate sludge cookies was in the oven.

'Hi,' he said, then nothing for a bit. Then he said, 'This is James Beamish from the CDC. I've been thinking of you.'

He was between meetings, he explained. Wednesday was the only flexible day in his week, his day for paperwork. Could we have lunch on Wednesday?

The cookies smelled gooey hot, not burned. My daughter had taken the cookie sheet out and put in a new one. She'd turned the cold water faucet on so she could let the water drip on a tiny rosebud burn on her arm.

I felt all the warm, familiar signs of lust and remorse. I dabbed the burn with an ice cube wrapped in paper towel and wondered if I'd have time to buy a new front-closing bra after Iqbal got home.

James I had lunch in a Dekalb County motel lounge.

He would be sixty-five in July, but not retire till sixty-eight. Then he would live in Tonga, in Fiji, see the world, travel across Europe and North America in a Winnebago. He wouldn't be tied down. He had five daughters and two grandsons, the younger one aged four, a month older than my son. He had been in the navy during the war (*his* war), and he had liked that.

I said, '"Goodbye, Mama, I'm off to Yokohama."' It was silly, but it was the only war footage I could come up with, and it made him laugh.

'You're special,' he said. He touched my knee under the table. 'You've already been everywhere.'

'Not because I've wanted to.'

He squeezed my knee again, then paid with his Mastercharge card.

As we were walking through the parking lot to his car (it was a Cougar or a Buick, and not German or British as I'd expected), James put his arm around my shoulders. I may have seen the world but I haven't gone through the American teenage rites of making out in parked cars and picnic grounds, so I walked briskly out of his embrace. He let his hand slide off my shoulder. The hand slid down my back. I counted three deft little pats to my bottom before he let his hand fall away.

Iqbal and I are sensual people, but secretive. The openness of James Beamish's advance surprised me.

I got in his car, wary, expectant.

'Do up the seatbelt,' he said.

He leaned into his seatbelt and kissed me lightly on the lips. I kissed him back, hard. 'You don't panic easily, do you?' he said. The mocking blue light was in his eyes again. His tongue made darting little thrusts and probes past my lips.

Yes, I do, I would have said if he'd let me.

We held hands on the drive to my house. In the driveway he parked behind my Honda. 'Shall I come in?'

I said nothing. Love and freedom drop into our lives. When we have to beg or even agree, it's already too late.

'Let's go in.' He said softly.

I didn't worry about the neighbours. In his grey wool slacks and tweed jacket, he looked too old, too respectable, for any sordid dalliance with a not-quite's wife.

Our house is not that different in size and shape from the ones on either side. Only the inside smells of heavy incense, and the walls are hung with rows of miniature paintings from the reign of Emperor Akbar. I took James's big wrinkled hand in mine. Adultery in my house is probably no different, no quieter, than in other houses in this neighbourhood.

Afterwards it wasn't guilt I felt (guilt comes with desire not acted), but wonder that while I'd dashed out Tuesday night and bought myself silky new underwear, James had worn an old T-shirt and lemon-pale boxer shorts. Perhaps he hadn't planned on seducing a Lucknow lady that afternoon. Adventure and freedom had come to him out of the blue, too. Or perhaps only younger men like Iqbal make a fetish of doing sit-ups and dieting and renewing their membership at the racquet club when they're on the prowl.

October through February our passion held. When we were together, I felt cherished. I only played at being helpless, hysterical, cruel. When James left, I'd spend the rest of the afternoon with a Barbara Pym novel. I kept the novels open at pages in which excellent British women recite lines from Marvell to themselves. I didn't read. I watched the golfers trudging over brown fairways instead. I let the tiny golfers—clumsy mummers—tell me stories of ambitions unfulfilled. Golf carts lurched into the golden vista. I felt safe.

In the first week of March we met in James's house for a change. His wife was in Madison to babysit a grandson while his parents flew to China for a three-week tour. It was a thrill to be in his house. I fingered the book spines, checked the colour of sheets and towels, the brand names of cereals and detergents. Jane Fonda's Workout record was on the VCR. He was a man who took exceptional care of himself, this immunologist. Real intimacy, at last. The lust of the winter months had been merely foreplay. I felt at home in his house, in spite of the albums of family photographs on the coffee table and the brutish metal vulvas sculpted by a daughter in art school and stashed in the den. James was more talkative in his own house. He showed me the photos he wanted me to see, named real lakes and mountains. His family was real, and not quite real. The daughters were hardy, outdoor types. I saw them hiking in Zermatt and bicycling through Europe. They had red cheeks and backpacks. Their faces were honest and marvellously ordinary. What would they say if they knew their father, at sixty-five, was in bed with a married woman from Lucknow? I feared and envied their jealousy more than any violence in my husband's heart.

Love on the decline is hard to tell from love on the rise. I have lived a life perched on the edge of ripeness and decay. The traveller feels at home everywhere, because she is never at home anywhere. I felt the hot red glow of blood rushing through capillaries.

His wife came back early, didn't call, caught a ride from Hartsfield International with a friend. She had been raised in Saskatchewan, and she'd remained thrifty.

We heard the car pull into the driveway, the loud 'thank yous' and 'no, I couldn'ts' and then her surprised shout, 'James? Are you ill? What're you doing home?' as she shut the front door.

We were in bed, sluggish cozy and still moist under the goosedown quilt that the daughter in Madison had sent them as a fortieth anniversary gift some years before. His clothes were on top of a long dresser; mine were on the floor, the stockings wrinkled and looking legless.

James didn't go to pieces. I had to admire that. He said. 'Get in the bathroom. Get dressed. I'll take care of this.'

I am submissive by training. To survive, the Asian wife will usually do as she is told. But this time I stayed in bed.

'How are you going to explain me away, James? Tell her I'm the new cleaning woman?' I laughed, and my laugh tinkled flirtatiously, at least to me.

'Get in the bathroom.' This was the fiercest I'd ever heard him.

'I don't think so,' I said. I jerked the quilt off my body but didn't move my legs.

So I was in bed with the quilt at my feet, and James was by the dresser buttoning his shirt when Kate Beamish stood at the door.

She didn't scream. She didn't leap for James's throat—or mine. I'd wanted passion, but Kate didn't come through. I pulled the quilt over me.

I tried insolence. 'Is your wife not the jealous kind?' I asked.

'Let's just get over this as quietly and quickly as we can, shall we?' she said. She walked to the window in her brown Wallabies. 'I don't see any unfamiliar cars, so I suppose you'll expect James to drive you home.'

'She's the jealous type,' James said. He moved towards his wife and tried to guide her out of the bedroom.

'I'm definitely the jealous kind,' Kate Beamish said. 'I might have stabbed you if I could take you seriously. But you are quite ludicrous lounging like a Goya nude on my bed.' She gave a funny little snort. I noticed straggly hairs in her nostrils and looked away.

James was running water in the bathroom sink. Only the panicky ones falls apart and call their lawyers from the bedroom.

She sat on my side of the bed. She stared at me. If that stare had made me feel secretive and loathsome, I might not have wept, later. She plucked the quilt from my breasts as an internist might, and snorted again. 'Yes,' she said, 'I don't deny a certain interest he might have had,' but she looked through my face to the pillow behind, and dropped the quilt as she stood. I was shadow without depth or colour, a shadow-temptress who would float back to a city of teeming millions when the affair with James had ended.

I had thought myself provocative and fascinating. What had begun as an adventure had become shabby and complex. I was just another involvement of a white man in a pokey little outpost, something that 'men do' and then come to their senses while the *memsahibs* drink gin and tonic and fan their faces. I didn't merit a stab wound through the heart.

It wasn't the end of the world. It was humorous, really. Still. I let James call me a cab. That half-hour wait for the cab, as Kate related tales of the grandson to her distracted husband was the most painful. It came closest to what Husseina must have felt. At least her father, the Nawab-*sahib*, had beaten her.

I have known all along that perfect love has to be fatal. I have survived on four of the five continents. I get by because I am at least moderately charming and open-minded. From time to time, James Beamish calls me. 'She's promised to file for divorce.' Or 'Let's go away for a weekend. Let's go to Bermuda. Have lunch with me this Wednesday.' Why do I hear a second voice? She has laughed at me. She has mocked my passion.

I want to say yes. I want to beg him to take me away to Hilton Head in his new, retirement Winnebago. The golden light from the vista is too yellow. Yes, *please*, let's run away, keep this new and simple.

I can hear the golfballs being thwocked home by clumsy mummers far away where my land dips. My arms are numb, my breathing loud and ugly from pressing hard against the cedar railing. The pain in my chest will not go away. I should be tasting blood in my throat by now.

1985

# Thomas King
## *b.* 1943

Born in Roseville, California, of Cherokee and Greek descent, Thomas King left university after one year to travel to Australia and New Zealand, where he worked as a photojournalist. In 1967 he returned to university in the US, obtaining his BA (1970) and his MA (1972) from Chico State University. He subsequently taught at the University of Minnesota, the University of Lethbridge, and the University of Guelph, interrupting his teaching to obtain his PhD (1986) from the University of Utah. An important voice in Aboriginal studies and an outspoken advocate for Native rights, he ran as a candidate for the New Democratic Party in the 2008 Canadian federal election. King won the 2014 BC National Award for Canadian Non-Fiction and the RBC Taylor Prize for *The Inconvenient Indian: A Curious Account of Native People in North America* (2012).

King has written for film, television, and radio, in addition to writing short stories and novels and, most recently, under the pseudonym Hartley GoodWeather, detective fiction. In his writings, he rejects the post-colonial approach to Aboriginal works as inappropriate, Aboriginal literature being a response not to colonialism but to Aboriginal traditions. 'Borders', from his short-story collection *One Good Story, That One* (1993), suggests that Canadians are more like Americans than they like to believe.

# Borders

When I was twelve, maybe thirteen, my mother announced that we were going to go to Salt Lake City to visit my sister who had left the reserve, moved across the line, and found a job. Laetitia had not left home with my mother's blessing, but over time my mother had come to be proud of the fact that Laetitia had done all of this on her own.

'She did real good,' my mother would say.

Then there were the fine points to Laetitia's going. She had not, as my mother liked to tell Mrs Manyfingers, gone floating after some man like a balloon on a string. She hadn't snuck out of the house, either, and gone to Vancouver or Edmonton or Toronto to chase rainbows down alleys. And she hadn't been pregnant.

'She did real good.'

I was seven or eight when Laetitia left home. She was seventeen. Our father was from Rocky Boy on the American side.

'Dad's American,' Laetitia told my mother, 'so I can go and come as I please.'

'Send us a postcard.'

Laetitia packed her things, and we headed for the border. Just outside of Milk River, Laetitia told us to watch for the water tower.

'Over the next rise. It's the first thing you see.'

'We got a water tower on the reserve,' my mother said. 'There's a big one in Lethbridge, too.'

'You'll be able to see the tops of the flagpole, too. That's where the border is.'

When we got to Coutts, my mother stopped at the convenience store and bought her and Laetitia a cup of coffee. I got an Orange Crush.

'This is real lousy coffee.'

'You're just angry because I want to see the world.'

'It's the water. From here on down, they got lousy water.'

'I can catch the bus from Sweetgrass. You don't have to lift a finger.'

'You're going to have to buy your water in bottles if you want good coffee.'

There was an old wooden building about a block away, with a tall sign in the yard that said 'Museum'. Most of the roof had been blown away. Mom told me to go and see when the place was open. There were boards over the windows and doors. You could tell that the place was closed, and I told Mom so, but she said to go and check anyway. Mom and Laetitia stayed by the car. Neither of them moved. I sat down on the steps of the museum and watched them, and I don't know that they ever said anything to each other. Finally, Laetitia got her bag out of the trunk and gave Mom a hug.

I wandered back to the car. The wind had come up, and it blew Laetitia's hair across her face. Mom reached out and pulled the strands out of Laetitia's eyes, and Laetitia let her.

'You can still see the mountain from here,' my mother told Laetitia in Blackfoot.

'Lots of mountains in Salt Lake,' Laetitia told her in English.

'The place is closed,' I said. 'Just like I told you.'

Laetitia tucked her hair into her jacket and dragged her bag down the road to the brick building with the American flag flapping on a pole. When she got to where the guards were waiting, she turned, put the bag down, and waved to us. We waved back. Then my mother turned the car around, and we came home.

We got postcards from Laetitia regular, and, if she wasn't spreading jelly on the truth, she was happy. She found a good job and rented an apartment with a pool.

'And she can't even swim,' my mother told Mrs Manyfingers.

Most of the postcards said we should come down and see the city, but whenever I mentioned this, my mother would stiffen up.

So I was surprised when she bought two new tires for the car and put on her blue dress with the green and yellow flowers. I had to dress up, too, for my mother did not want us crossing the border looking like Americans. We made sandwiches and put them in a big box with pop and potato chips and some apples and bananas and a big jar of water.

'But we can stop at one of those restaurants, too, right?'

'We maybe should take some blankets in case you get sleepy.'

'But we can stop at one of those restaurants, too, right?'

The border was actually two towns, though neither one was big enough to amount to anything. Coutts was on the Canadian side and consisted of the convenience store and gas station, the museum that was closed and boarded up, and a motel. Sweetgrass was on the American side, but all you could see was an overpass that arched across the highway and disappeared into the prairies. Just hearing the names of these towns, you would expect that Sweetgrass, which is a nice name and sounds like it is related to other places such as Medicine Hat and Moose Jaw and Kicking Horse Pass, would be on the Canadian side, and that Coutts, which sounds abrupt and rude, would be on the American side. But this was not the case.

Between the two borders was a duty-free shop where you could buy cigarettes and liquor and flags. Stuff like that.

We left the reserve in the morning and drove until we got to Coutts.

'Last time we stopped here', my mother said, 'you had an Orange Crush. You remember that?'

'Sure,' I said. 'That was when Laetitia took off.'

'You want another Orange Crush?'

'That means we're not going to stop at a restaurant, right?'

My mother got a coffee at the convenience store, and we stood around and watched the prairies move in the sunlight. Then we climbed back in the car. My mother straightened the dress across her thighs, leaned against the wheel, and drove all the way to the border in first gear, slowly, as if she were trying to see through a bad storm or riding high on black ice.

The border guard was an old guy. As he walked to the car, he swayed from side to side, his feet set wide apart, the holster on his hip pitching up and down. He leaned into the window, looked into the back seat, and looked at my mother and me.

'Morning, ma'am.'

'Good morning.'

'Where you heading?'

'Salt Lake City.'

'Purpose of your visit?'

'Visit my daughter.'

'Citizenship?'

'Blackfoot,' my mother told him.

'Ma'am?'

'Blackfoot,' my mother repeated.

'Canadian?'

'Blackfoot.'

It would have been easier if my mother had just said 'Canadian' and been done with it, but I could see she wasn't going to do that. The guard wasn't angry or anything. He smiled and looked towards the building. Then he turned back and nodded.

'Morning, ma'am.'

'Good morning.'

'Any firearms or tobacco?'

'No.'

'Citizenship?'

'Blackfoot.'

He told us to sit in the car and wait, and we did. In about five minutes, another guard came out with the first man. They were talking as they came, both men swaying back and forth like two cowboys headed for a bar or a gunfight.

'Morning, ma'am.'

'Good morning.'

'Cecil tells me you and the boy are Blackfoot.'

'That's right.'

'Now, I know that we got Blackfeet on the American side and the Canadians got Blackfeet on their side. Just so we can keep our records straight, what side do you come from?'

I knew exactly what my mother was going to say and I could have told them if they had asked me.

'Canadian side or American side?' asked the guard.

'Blackfoot side,' she said.

It didn't take them long to lose their sense of humour, I can tell you that. The one guard stopped smiling altogether and told us to park our car at the side of the building and come in.

We sat on a wood bench for about an hour before anyone came over to talk to us. This time it was a woman. She had a gun, too.

'Hi,' she said. 'I'm Inspector Pratt. I understand there is a little misunderstanding.'

'I'm going to visit my daughter in Salt Lake City,' my mother told her. 'We don't have any guns or beer.'

'It's a legal technicality, that's all.'

'My daughter's Blackfoot, too.'

The woman opened a briefcase and took out a couple of forms and began to write on one of them. 'Everyone who crosses our border has to declare their citizenship. Even Americans. It helps us keep track of the visitors we get from the various countries.'

She went on like that for maybe fifteen minutes, and a lot of the stuff she told us was interesting.

'I can understand how you feel about having to tell us your citizenship, and here's what I'll do. You tell me, and I won't put it down on the form. No-one will know but you and me.'

Her gun was silver. There were several chips in the wood handle and the name 'Stella' was scratched into the metal butt.

We were in the border office for about four hours, and we talked to almost everyone there. One of the men bought me a Coke. My mother brought a couple of sandwiches in from the car. I offered part of mine to Stella, but she said she wasn't hungry.

I told Stella that we were Blackfoot and Canadians, but she said that that didn't count because I was a minor. In the end, she told us that if my mother didn't declare her citizenship, we would have to go back to where we came from. My mother stood up and thanked Stella for her time. Then we got back in the car and drove to the Canadian border, which was only about a hundred yards away.

I was disappointed. I hadn't seen Laetitia for a long time, and I had never been to Salt Lake City. When she was still at home, Laetitia would go on and on about Salt Lake City. She had never been there, but her boyfriend Lester Tallbull had spent a year in Salt Lake at a technical school.

'It's a great place,' Lester would say. 'Nothing but blondes in the whole state.'

Whenever he said that, Laetitia would slug him on his shoulder hard enough to make him flinch. He had some brochures on Salt Lake and some maps, and every so often the two of them would spread them out on the table.

'That's the temple. It's right downtown. You got to have a pass to get in.'

'Charlotte says anyone can go in and look around.'

'When was Charlotte in Salt Lake? Just when the hell was Charlotte in Salt Lake?'

'Last year.'

'This is Liberty Park. It's got a zoo. There's good skiing in the mountains.'

'Got all the skiing we can use,' my mother would say. 'People come from all over the world to ski at Banff. Cardston's got a temple, if you like those kinds of things.'

'Oh, this one is real big,' Lester would say. 'They got armed guards and everything.'

'Not what Charlotte says.'

'What does she know?'

Lester and Laetitia broke up, but I guess the idea of Salt Lake stuck in her mind.

The Canadian border guard was a young woman, and she seemed happy to see us. 'Hi,' she said. 'You folks sure have a great day for a trip. Where are you coming from?'

'Standoff.'

'Is that in Montana?'

'No.'

'Where are you going?'

'Standoff.'

The woman's name was Carol and I don't guess she was any older than Laetitia. 'Wow, you both Canadians?'

'Blackfoot.'

'Really? I have a friend I went to school with who is Blackfoot. Do you know Mike Harley?'

'No.'

'He went to school in Lethbridge, but he's really from Browning.'

It was a nice conversation and there were no cars behind us, so there was no rush.

'You're not bringing any liquor back, are you?'

'No.'

'Any cigarettes or plants or stuff like that?'

'No.'

'Citizenship?'

'Blackfoot.'

'I know,' said the woman, 'and I'd be proud of being Blackfoot if I were Blackfoot. But you have to be American or Canadian.'

When Laetitia and Lester broke up, Lester took his brochures and maps with him, so Laetitia wrote to someone in Salt Lake City, and, about a month later, she got a big envelope of stuff. We sat at the table and opened up all the brochures, and Laetitia read each one out loud.

'Salt Lake City is the gateway to some of the world's most magnificent skiing.

'Salt Lake City is the home of one of the newest professional basketball franchises, the Utah Jazz.

'The Great Salt Lake is one of the natural wonders of the world.'

It was kind of exciting seeing all those colour brochures on the table and listening to Laetitia read all about how Salt Lake City was one of the best places in the entire world.

'That Salt Lake City place sounds too good to be true,' my mother told her.

'It has everything.'

'We got everything right here.'

'It's boring here.'

'People in Salt Lake City are probably sending away for brochures of Calgary and Lethbridge and Pincher Creek right now.'

In the end, my mother would say that maybe Laetitia should go to Salt Lake City, and Laetitia would say that maybe she would.

We parked the car to the side of the building and Carol led us into a small room on the second floor. I found a comfortable spot on the couch and flipped through some back issues of *Saturday Night* and *Alberta Report*.

When I woke up, my mother was just coming out of another office. She didn't say a word to me. I followed her down the stairs and out to the car. I thought we were going home, but she turned the car around and drove back towards the American border, which made me think we were going to visit Laetitia in Salt Lake City after all. Instead she pulled into the parking lot of the duty-free store and stopped.

'We going to see Laetitia?'

'No.'

'We going home?'

Pride is a good thing to have, you know. Laetitia had a lot of pride, and so did my mother. I figured that someday, I'd have it, too.

'So where are we going?'

Most of that day, we wandered around the duty-free store, which wasn't very large. The manager had a name tag with a tiny American flag on one side and a tiny Canadian flag on the other. His name was Mel. Towards evening, he began suggesting that we should be on our way. I told him we had nowhere to go, that neither the Americans nor the Canadians would let us in. He laughed at that and told us that we should buy something or leave.

The car was not very comfortable, but we did have all that food and it was April, so even if it did snow as it sometimes does on the prairies, we wouldn't freeze. The next morning my mother drove to the American border.

It was a different guard this time, but the questions were the same. We didn't spend as much time in the office as we had the day before. By noon, we were back at the Canadian border. By two we were back in the duty-free shop parking lot.

The second night in the car was not as much fun as the first, but my mother seemed in good spirits, and, all in all, it was as much an adventure as an inconvenience. There wasn't much food left and that was a problem, but we had lots of water as there was a faucet at the side of the duty-free shop.

One Sunday, Laetitia and I were watching television. Mom was over at Mrs Manyfingers's. Right in the middle of the program, Laetitia turned off the set and said she was going to Salt Lake City, that life around here was too boring. I had wanted to see the rest of the program and really didn't care if Laetitia went to Salt Lake City or not. When Mom got home, I told her what Laetitia had said.

What surprised me was how angry Laetitia got when she found out that I had told Mom.

'You got a big mouth.'

'That's what you said.'

'What I said is none of your business.'

'I didn't say anything.'

'Well, I'm going for sure, now.'

That weekend, Laetitia packed her bags, and we drove her to the border.

Mel turned out to be friendly. When he closed up for the night and found us still parked in the lot, he came over and asked us if our car was broken down or something. My mother thanked him for his concern and told him that we were fine, that things would get straightened out in the morning.

'You're kidding,' said Mel. 'You'd think they could handle the simplest things.'

'We got some apples and a banana,' I said, 'but we're all out of ham sandwiches.'

'You know, you read about these things, but you just don't believe it. You just don't believe it.'

'Hamburgers would be even better because they got more stuff for energy.'

My mother slept in the back seat. I slept in the front because I was smaller and could lie under the steering wheel. Late that night, I heard my mother open the car door. I found her sitting on her blanket leaning against the bumper of the car.

'You see all those stars,' she said. 'When I was a little girl, my grandmother used to take me and my sisters out on the prairies and tell us stories about all the stars.'

'Do you think Mel is going to bring us any hamburgers?'

'Every one of those stars has a story. You see that bunch of stars over there that look like a fish?'

'He didn't say no.'

'Coyote went fishing, one day. That's how it all started.' We sat out under the stars that night, and my mother told me all sorts of stories. She was serious about it, too. She'd tell them slow, repeating parts as she went, as if she expected me to remember each one.

Early the next morning, the television vans began to arrive, and guys in suits and women in dresses came trotting over to us, dragging microphones and cameras and lights behind them. One of the vans had a table set up with orange juice and sandwiches and fruit. It was for the crew, but when I told them we hadn't eaten for a while, a really skinny blonde woman told us we could eat as much as we wanted.

They mostly talked to my mother. Every so often one of the reporters would come over and ask me questions about how it felt to be an Indian without a country. I told them we had a nice house on the reserve and that my cousins had a couple of horses we rode when we went fishing. Some of the television people went over to the American border, and then they went to the Canadian border.

Around noon, a good-looking guy in a dark blue suit and an orange tie with little ducks on it drove up in a fancy car. He talked to my mother for a while, and, after they were done talking, my mother called me over, and we got into our car. Just as my mother started the engine, Mel came over and gave us a bag of peanut brittle and told us that justice was a damn hard thing to get, but that we shouldn't give up.

I would have preferred lemon drops, but it was nice of Mel anyway.

'Where are we going now?'

'Going to visit Laetitia.'

The guard who came out to our car was all smiles. The television lights were so bright they hurt my eyes, and, if you tried to look through the windshield in certain directions, you couldn't see a thing.

'Morning, ma'am.'

'Good morning.'

'Where you heading?'

'Salt Lake City.'

'Purpose of your visit?'
'Visit my daughter.'
'Any tobacco, liquor, or firearms?'
'Don't smoke.'
'Any plants or fruit?'
'Not any more.'
'Citizenship?'
'Blackfoot.

The guard rocked back on his heels and jammed his thumbs into his gun belt. 'Thank you,' he said, his fingers patting the butt of the revolver. 'Have a pleasant trip.'

My mother rolled the car forward, and the television people had to scramble out of the way. They ran alongside the car as we pulled away from the border, and, when they couldn't run any farther, they stood in the middle of the highway and waved and waved and waved.

We got to Salt Lake City the next day. Laetitia was happy to see us, and, that first night, she took us out to a restaurant that made really good soups. The list of pies took up a whole page. I had cherry. Mom had chocolate. Laetitia said that she saw us on television the night before and, during the meal, she had us tell her the story over and over again.

Laetitia took us everywhere. We went to a fancy ski resort. We went to the temple. We got to go shopping in a couple of large malls, but they weren't as large as the one in Edmonton, and Mom said so.

After a week or so, I got bored and wasn't at all sad when my mother said we should be heading back home. Laetitia wanted us to stay longer, but Mom said no, that she had things to do back home and that, next time, Laetitia should come up and visit. Laetitia said she was thinking about moving back, and Mom told her to do as she pleased, and Laetitia said that she would.

On the way home, we stopped at the duty-free shop, and my mother gave Mel a green hat that said 'Salt Lake' across the front. Mel was a funny guy. He took the hat and blew his nose and told my mother that she was an inspiration to us all. He gave us some more peanut brittle and came out into the parking lot and waved at us all the way to the Canadian border.

It was almost evening when we left Coutts. I watched the border through the rear window until all you could see were the tops of the flagpoles and the blue water tower, and then they rolled over a hill and disappeared.

1991

# Rohinton Mistry

*b.* 1952

Born in Bombay, India, Rohinton Mistry obtained his BA (1974) in mathematics and economics from the University of Bombay before immigrating in 1975 to Toronto, where he found employment as a clerk in the accounting department of a bank. He enrolled on a part-time basis at the University of Toronto, graduating with a second BA (1983) in English and history.

His first book, a collection of linked short stories titled *Tales from Firozsha Baag* (1987), from which 'The Collectors' is taken, examines the immediacy of daily life in a Bombay apartment building. Throughout the stories the worlds of the Parsi community evoke memories of Joyce's *Dubliners*. In his three novels, *Such a Long Journey* (1991), *A Fine Balance* (1995), and *Family Matters* (2002), the most vulnerable members of society follow the unending struggle, always through suffering, to affirm human dignity. Mistry won the Neustadt International Prize for Literature in 2012.

## The Collectors

I

When Dr Burjor Mody was transferred from Mysore to assume the principalship of the Bombay Veterinary College, he moved into Firozsha Baag with his wife and son Pesi. They occupied the vacant flat on the third floor of C Block, next to the Bulsara family.

Dr Mody did not know it then, but he would be seeing a lot of Jehangir, the Bulsara boy; the boy who sat silent and brooding, every evening, watching the others play, and called *chaarikhao* by them—quite unfairly, since he never tattled or told tales—(Dr Mody would call him, affectionately, the observer of C Block). And Dr Mody did not know this, either, at the time of moving, that Jehangir Bulsara's visits at ten a.m. every Sunday would become a source of profound joy for himself. Or that just when he would think he had found someone to share his hobby with, someone to mitigate the perpetual disappointment about his son Pesi, he would lose his precious Spanish dancing-lady stamp and renounce Jehangir's friendship, both in quick succession. And then two years later, he himself would—but *that* is never knowable.

Soon after moving in, Dr Burjor Mody became the pride of the Parsis in C Block. C Block, like the rest of Firozsha Baag, had a surfeit of low-paid bank clerks and bookkeepers, and the arrival of Dr Mody permitted them to feel a little better about themselves. More importantly, in A Block lived a prominent priest, and B Block boasted a chartered accountant. Now C Block had a voice in Baag matters as important as the others did.

While C Block went about its routine business, confirming and authenticating the sturdiness of the object of their pride, the doctor's big-boned son Pesi established himself as leader of the rowdier elements among the Baag's ten-to-sixteen population.

For Pesi, too, it was routine business; he was following a course he had mapped out for himself ever since the family began moving from city to city on the whims and megrims of his father's employer, the government.

To account for Pesi's success was the fact of his brutish strength. But he was also the practitioner of a number of minor talents which appealed to the crowd where he would be leader. The one no doubt complemented the other, the talents serving to dissemble the brutish qualifier of strength, and the brutish strength encouraging the crowd to perceive the appeal of his talents.

Hawking, for instance, was one of them. Pesi could summon up prodigious quantities of phlegm at will, accompanied by sounds such as the boys had seldom heard except in accomplished adults: deep, throaty, rasping, resonating rolls which culminated in a pthoo, with the impressive trophy landing in the dust at their feet, its size leaving them all slightly envious. Pesi could also break wind that sounded like questions, exclamations, fragments of the chromatic scale, and clarion calls, while the others sniffed and discussed the merits of pungency versus tonality. This ability earned him the appellation of Pesi *paadmaroo*, and he wore the sobriquet with pride.

Perhaps his single most important talent was his ability to improvise. The peculiarities of a locale were the raw material for his inventions. In Firozsha Baag, behind the three buildings, or blocks, as they were called, were spacious yards shared by all three blocks. These yards planted in Pesi's fecund mind the seed from which grew a new game: stoning-the-cats.

Till the arrival of the Mody family the yards were home for stray and happy felines, well fed on scraps and leftovers disgorged regularly as clockwork, after mealtimes, by the three blocks. The ground floors were the only ones who refrained. They voiced their protests in a periodic cycle of reasoning, pleading, and screaming of obscenities, because the garbage collected outside their windows where the cats took up permanent residency, miaowing, feasting, and caterwauling day and night. If the cascade of food was more than the cats could devour, the remainder fell to the fortune of the rats. Finally, flies and insects buzzed and hovered over the dregs, little pools of pulses and curries fermenting and frothing, till the *kuchrawalli* came next morning and swept it all away.

The backyards of Firozsha Baag constituted its squalid underbelly. And this would be the scenario for stoning-the-cats, Pesi decided. But there was one hitch: the backyards were off limits to the boys. The only way in was through the *kuchrawalli*'s little shack standing beyond A Block, where her huge ferocious dog, tied to the gate, kept the boys at bay. So Pesi decreed that the boys gather at the rear windows of their homes, preferably at a time of day when the adults were scarce, with the fathers away at work and the mothers not yet finished with their afternoon naps. Each boy brought a pile of small stones and took turns, chucking three stones each. The game could just as easily have been stoning-the-rats; but stoned rats quietly walked away to safety, whereas the yowls of cats provided primal satisfaction and verified direct hits: no yowl, no point.

The game added to Pesi's popularity—he called it a howling success. But the parents (except the ground floor) complained to Dr Mody about his son instigating their children to torment poor dumb and helpless creatures. For a veterinarian's son to harass animals was shameful, they said.

As might be supposed, Pesi was the despair of his parents. Over the years Dr Mody had become inured to the initial embarrassment in each new place they moved to. The routine was familiar: first, a spate of complaints from indignant parents claiming their sons *bugree nay dhoor thai gaya*—were corrupted to become useless as dust; next, the protestations giving way to sympathy when the neighbours saw that Pesi was the worm in the Modys' mango.

And so it was in Firozsha Baag. After the furor about stoning-the-cats had died down, the people of the Baag liked Dr Mody more than ever. He earned their respect for the initiative he took in Baag matters, dealing with the management for things like broken lifts, leaking water tanks, crumbling plaster, and faulty wiring. It was at his urging that the massive iron gate, set in the stone wall which ran all around the buildings, compound and backyards, was repaired, and a watchman installed to stop beggars and riff-raff. (And although Dr Mody would be dead by the time of the *Shiv Sena* riots, the tenants would remember him for the gate which would keep out the rampaging mobs.) When the Bombay Municipality tried to appropriate a section of Baag property for its road-widening scheme, Dr Mody was in the forefront of the battle, winning a compromise whereby the Baag only lost half the proposed area. But the Baag's esteem did nothing to lighten the despair for Pesi that hung around the doctor.

At the birth of his son, Dr Mody had deliberated long and hard about the naming. Peshotan, in the Persian epic *Shah-Nameh*, was the brother of the great Asfandyar, and a noble general, lover of art and learning, and man of wise counsel. Dr Mody had decided his son would play the violin, acquire the best from the cultures of East and West, thrill to the words of Tagore and Shakespeare, appreciate Mozart and Indian ragas; and one day, at the proper moment, he would introduce him to his dearest activity, stamp-collecting.

But the years passed in their own way. Fate denied fruition to all of Dr Mody's plans; and when he talked about stamps, Pesi laughed and mocked his beloved hobby. This was the point at which, hurt and confused, he surrendered his son to whatever destiny was in store. A perpetual grief entered to occupy the void left behind after the aspirations for his son were evicted.

The weight of grief was heaviest around Dr Mody when he returned from work in the evenings. As the car turned into the compound he usually saw Pesi before Pesi saw him, in scenes which made him despair, scenes in which his son was abusing someone, fighting, or making lewd gestures.

But Dr Mody was careful not to make a public spectacle of his despair. While the car made its way sluggishly over the uneven flagstones of the compound, the boys would stand back and wave him through. With his droll comments and jovial countenance he was welcome to disrupt their play, unlike two other car-owners of Firozsha Baag: the priest in A Block and the chartered accountant in B who habitually berated, from inside their vehicles, the sons of bank clerks and bookkeepers for blocking the driveway with their games. Their well-worn curses had become so predictable and ineffective that sometimes the boys chanted gleefully, in unison with their nemeses: 'Worse than *saala* animals!' or '*junglee* dogs-cats have more sense!' or 'you *sataans* ever have any lesson-*paani* to do or not!'

There was one boy who always stayed apart from his peers—the Bulsara boy, from the family next door to the Modys. Jehangir sat on the stone steps every evening while the gentle land breezes, drying and cooling the sweaty skins of the boys at play, blew out to sea. He sat alone through the long dusk, a source of discomfiture to the others. They resented his melancholy, watching presence.

Dr Mody noticed Jehangir, too, on the stone steps of C Block, the delicate boy with the build much too slight for his age. Next to a hulk like Pesi he was diminutive, but things other than size underlined his frail looks: he had slender hands, and forearms with fine downy hair. And while facial fuzz was incipient in most boys of his age (and Pesi was positively hirsute), Jehangir's chin and upper lip were smooth as a young woman's. But it pleased Dr Mody to see him evening after evening. The quiet contemplation of the boy on the steps and the noise and activity of the others at play came together in the kind of balance that Dr Mody was always looking for and was quick to appreciate.

Jehangir, in his turn, observed the burly Dr Mody closely as he walked past him each evening. When he approached the steps after parking his car, Jehangir would say *'Sahibji'* in greeting, and smile wanly. He saw that despite Dr Mody's constant jocularity there was something painfully empty about his eyes. He noticed the peculiar way he scratched the greyish-red patches of psoriasis on his elbows, both elbows simultaneously, by folding his arms across his chest. Sometimes Jehangir would arise from the stone steps and the two would go up together to the third floor. Dr Mody asked him once, 'You don't like playing with the other boys? You just sit and watch them?' The boy shook his head and blushed, and Dr Mody did not bring up the matter after that.

Gradually, a friendship of sorts grew between the two. Jehangir touched a chord inside the doctor which had lain silent for much too long. Now affection for the boy developed and started to linger around the region hitherto occupied by grief bearing Pesi's name.

## II

One evening, while Jehangir sat on the stone steps waiting for Dr Mody's car to arrive, Pesi was organizing a game of *naargolio.* He divided the boys into two teams, then discovered he was one short. He beckoned to Jehangir, who said he did not want to play. Scowling, Pesi handed the ball to one of the others and walked over to him. He grabbed his collar with both hands, jerking him to his feet. *'Arré choosya!'* he yelled, 'want a pasting?' and began dragging him by the collar to where the boys had piled up the seven flat stones for *naargolio.*

At that instant, Dr Mody's car turned into the compound, and he spied his son in one of those scenes which could provoke despair. But today the despair was swept aside by rage when he saw that Pesi's victim was the gentle and quiet Jehangir Bulsara. He left the car in the middle of the compound with the motor running. Anger glinted in his eyes. He kicked over the pile of seven flat stones as he walked blindly towards Pesi who, having seen his father, had released Jehangir. He had been caught by his father often enough to know that it was best to stand and wait. Jehangir, meanwhile, tried to keep back the tears.

Dr Mody stopped before his son and slapped him hard, once on each cheek, with the front and back of his right hand. He waited, as if debating whether that was enough, then put his arm around Jehangir and led him to the car.

He drove to his parking spot. By now, Jehangir had control of his tears, and they walked to the steps of C Block. The lift was out of order. They climbed the stairs to the third floor and knocked. He waited with Jehangir.

Jehangir's mother came to the door. '*Sahibji*, Dr Mody,' she said, a short, middle-aged woman, very prim, whose hair was always in a bun. Never without a *mathoobanoo*, she could do wonderful things with that square of fine white cloth which was tied and knotted to sit like a cap on her head, snugly packeting the bun. In the evenings, after the household chores were done, she removed the *mathoobanoo* and wore it in a more conventional manner, like a scarf.

'*Sahibji*,' she said, then noticed her son's tear-stained face. '*Arré*, Jehangoo, what happened, who made you cry?' Her hand flew automatically to the *mathoobanoo*, tugging and adjusting it as she did whenever she was concerned or agitated.

To save the boy embarrassment, Dr Mody intervened: 'Go, wash your face while I talk to your mother.' Jehangir went inside, and Dr Mody told her briefly about what had happened. 'Why does he not play with the other boys?' he asked finally.

'Dr Mody, what to say. The boy never wants even to go out. *Khoedai salaamat raakhé*, wants to sit at home all the time and read story books. Even this little time in the evening he goes because I force him and tell him he will not grow tall without fresh air. Every week he brings new-new story books from school. First, school library would allow only one book per week. But he went to Father Gonzalves who is in charge of library and got special permission for two books. God knows why he gave it.'

'But reading is good, Mrs Bulsara.'

'I know, I know, but a mania like this, all the time?'

'Some boys are outdoor types, some are indoor types. You shouldn't worry about Jehangir, he is a very good boy. Look at my Pesi, now there is a case for worry,' he said, meaning to reassure her.

'No, no. You mustn't say that. Be patient, *Khoedai* is great,' said Mrs Bulsara, consoling him instead. Jehangir returned, his eyes slightly red but dry. While washing his face he had wet a lock of his hair which hung down over his forehead.

'Ah, here comes my indoor champion,' smiled Dr Mody, and patted Jehangir's shoulder, brushing back the lock of hair. Jehangir did not understand, but grinned anyway; the doctor's joviality was infectious. Dr Mody turned again to the mother. 'Send him to my house on Sunday at ten o'clock. We will have a little talk.'

After Dr Mody left, Jehangir's mother told him how lucky he was that someone as important and learned as Burjor Uncle was taking an interest in him. Privately, she hoped he would encourage the boy towards a more all-round approach to life and to the things other boys did. And when Sunday came she sent Jehangir off to Dr Mody's promptly at ten.

Dr Mody was taking his bath, and Mrs Mody opened the door. She was a dour-faced woman, spare and lean—the opposite of her husband in appearance and disposition, yet retaining some quality from long ago which suggested that it had not always been so. Jehangir had never crossed her path save when she was exchanging civilities with his mother, while making purchases out by the stairs from the vegetablewalla or fruitwalla.

Not expecting Jehangir's visit, Mrs Mody stood blocking the doorway and said: 'Yes?' Meaning, what nuisance now?

'Burjor Uncle asked me to come at ten o'clock.'

'Asked you to come at ten o'clock? What for?'

'He just said to come at ten o'clock.'

Grudgingly, Mrs Mody stepped aside. 'Come in then. Sit down there.' And she indicated the specific chair she wanted him to occupy, muttering something about a *baap* who had time for strangers' children but not for his own son.

Jehangir sat in what must have been the most uncomfortable chair in the room. This was his first time inside the Modys' flat, and he looked around with curiosity. But his gaze was quickly restricted to the area of the floor directly in front of him when he realized that he was the object of Mrs Mody's watchfulness.

Minutes ticked by under her vigilant eye. Jehangir was grateful when Dr Mody emerged from the bedroom. Being Sunday, he had eschewed his usual khaki half-pants for loose and comfortable white pyjamas. His *sudra* hung out over it, and he strode vigorously, feet encased in a huge pair of *sapaat.* He smiled at Jehangir, who happily noted the crow's-feet appearing at the corners of his eyes. He was ushered into Dr Mody's room, and man and boy both seemed glad to escape the surveillance of the woman.

The chairs were more comfortable in Dr Mody's room. They sat at his desk and Dr Mody opened a drawer to take out a large book.

'This was the first stamp album I ever had,' said Dr Mody. 'It was given to me by my Nusserwanji Uncle when I was your age. All the pages were empty.' He began turning them. They were covered with stamps, each a feast of colour and design. He talked as he turned the pages, and Jehangir watched and listened, glancing at the stamps flying past, at Dr Mody's face, then at the stamps again.

Dr Mody spoke not in his usual booming, jovial tones but softly, in a low voice charged with inspiration. The stamps whizzed by, and his speech was gently underscored by the rustle of the heavily laden pages that seemed to turn of their own volition in the quiet room. (Jehangir would remember this peculiar rustle when one day, older, he'd stand alone in this very room, silent now forever, and turn the pages of Nusserwanji Uncle's album.) Jehangir watched and listened. It was as though a mask had descended over Dr Mody, a faraway look upon his face, and a shining in the eyes which heretofore Jehangir had only seen sad with despair or glinting with anger or just plain and empty, belying his constant drollery. Jehangir watched, and listened to the euphonious voice hinting at wondrous things and promises and dreams.

The album on the desk, able to produce such changes in Dr Mody, now worked its magic through him upon the boy. Jehangir, watching and listening, fascinated, tried to read the names of the countries at the top of the pages as they sped by: Antigua . . . Australia . . . Belgium . . . Bhutan . . . Bulgaria . . . and on through to Malta and Mauritius . . . Romania and Russia . . . Togo and Tonga . . . and a final blur through which he caught Yugoslavia and Zanzibar.

'Can I see it again?' he asked, and Dr Mody handed the album to him.

'So what do you think? Do you want to be a collector?'

Jehangir nodded eagerly and Dr Mody laughed. 'When Nusserwanji Uncle showed me his collection I felt just like that. I'll tell your mother what to buy for you to get you started. Bring it here next Sunday, same time!'

And next Sunday Jehangir was ready at nine. But he waited by his door with a Stamp Album For Beginners and a packet of 100 Assorted Stamps—All Countries. Going too early would mean sitting under the baleful eyes of Mrs Mody.

Ten o'clock struck and the clock's tenth bong was echoed by the Modys' door-chimes. Mrs Mody was expecting him this time and did not block the doorway. Wordlessly, she beckoned him in. Burjor Uncle was ready, too, and came out almost immediately to rescue him from her arena.

'Let's see what you've got there,' he said when they were in his room. They removed the cellophane wrapper, and while they worked Dr Mody enjoyed himself as much as the boy. His deepest wish appeared to be coming true: he had at last found someone to share his hobby with. He could not have hoped for a finer neophyte than Jehangir. His young recruit was so quick to learn how to identify and sort stamps by countries, learn the different currencies, spot watermarks. Already he was skilfully folding and moistening the little hinges and mounting the stamps as neatly as the teacher.

When it was almost time to leave, Jehangir asked if he could examine again Nusserwanji Uncle's album, the one he had seen last Sunday. But Burjor Uncle led him instead to a cupboard in the corner of the room. 'Since you enjoy looking at my stamps, let me show you what I have here.' He unlocked its doors.

Each of the cupboard's four shelves was piled with biscuit tins and sweet tins: round, oval, rectangular, square. It puzzled Jehangir: all this bore the unmistakable stamp of the worthless hoardings of senility, and did not seem at all like Burjor Uncle. But Burjor Uncle reached out for a box at random and showed him inside. It was chock-full of stamps! Jehangir's mouth fell open. Then he gaped at the shelves, and Burjor Uncle laughed. 'Yes, all these tins are full of stamps. And that big cardboard box at the bottom contains six new albums, all empty.'

Jehangir quickly tried to assign a number in his mind to the stamps in the containers of Maghanlal Bisuitwalla and Lokmanji Mithaiwalla, to all of the stamps in the round tins and the oval tins, the square ones and the oblong ones. He failed.

Once again Dr Mody laughed at the boy's wonderment. 'A lot of stamps. And they took me a lot of years to collect. Of course, I am lucky I have many contacts in foreign countries. Because of my job. I meet the experts from abroad who are invited by the Indian Government. When I tell them about my hobby they send me stamps from their countries. But no time to sort them, so I pack them in boxes. One day, after I retire, I will spend all my time with my stamps.' He paused, and shut the cupboard doors. 'So what you have to do now is start making lots of friends, tell them about your hobby. If they also collect, you can exchange duplicates with them. If they don't, you can still ask them for all the envelopes they may be throwing away with stamps on them. You do something for them, they will do something for you. Your collection will grow depending on how smart you are!'

He hesitated, and opened the cupboard again. Then he changed his mind and shut it—it wasn't yet time for the Spanish dancing-lady stamp.

## III

On the pavement outside St Xavier's Boys School, not far from the ornate iron gates, stood two variety stalls. They were the stalls of *Patla Babu* and *Jhaaria Babu*. Their real names were never known. Nor was known the exact source of the schoolboy inspiration that named them thus, many years ago, after their respective thinness and fatness.

Before the schoolboys arrived in the morning the two would unpack their cases and set up the displays, beating the beggars to the choice positions. Occasionally, there were disputes if someone's space was violated. The beggars did not harbour great hopes for alms from schoolboys but they stood there, nonetheless, like mute lessons in realism and the harshness of life. Their patience was rewarded when they raided the dustbins after breaks and lunches.

At the end of the school day the pavement community packed up. The beggars shuffled off into the approaching dark, *Patla Babu* went home with his cases, and *Jhaaria Babu* slept near the school gate under a large tree to whose trunk he chained his boxes during the night.

The two sold a variety of nondescript objects and comestibles, uninteresting to any save the eyes and stomachs of schoolboys: *supari*, A-1 chewing gum (which, in a most ungumlike manner, would, after a while, dissolve in one's mouth), *jeeragoli*, marbles, tops, *aampapud* during the mango season, pens, Camel Ink, pencils, rulers, and stamps in little cellophane packets.

*Patla Babu* and *Jhaaria Babu* lost some of their goods regularly due to theft. This was inevitable when doing business outside a large school like St Xavier's, with a population as varied as its was. The loss was an operating expense stoically accepted, like the success or failure of the monsoons, and they never complained to the school authorities or held it against the boys. Besides, business was good despite the losses: insignificant items like a packet of *jeeragoli* worth ten paise, or a marble of the kind that sold three for five paise. More often than not, the stealing went on for the excitement of it, out of bravado or on a dare. It was called 'flicking' and was done without any malice towards *Patla* and *Jhaaria*.

Foremost among the flickers was a boy in Jehangir's class called Eric D'Souza. A tall, lanky fellow who had been suspended a couple of times, he had had to repeat the year on two occasions, and held out the promise of more repetitions. Eric also had the reputation of doing things inside his half-pants under cover of his desk. In a class of fifty boys it was easy to go unobserved by the teacher, and only his immediate neighbours could see the ecstasy on his face and the vigorous back and forth movement of his hand. When he grinned at them they looked away, pretending not to have noticed anything.

Jehangir sat far from Eric and knew of his habits only by hearsay. He was oblivious to Eric's eye which had been on him for quite a while. In fact, Eric found Jehangir's delicate hands and fingers, his smooth legs and thighs very desirable. In class he gazed for hours, longingly, at the girlish face, curly hair, long eyelashes.

Jehangir and Eric finally got acquainted one day when the class filed out for games period. Eric had been made to kneel down by the door for coming in late and disturbing the class, and Jehangir found himself next to him as he stood in line. From his kneeling position Eric observed the smooth thighs emerging from the half-pants (half-pants was the school uniform requirement), winked at him, and unhindered by his underwear, inserted a pencil up the pant leg. He tickled Jehangir's genitals seductively with the eraser end, expertly, then withdrew it. Jehangir feigned a giggle, too shocked to say anything. The line started to move for the playground.

Shortly after this incident, Eric approached Jehangir during breaktime. He had heard that Jehangir was desperate to acquire stamps.

'*Arré* man, I can get you stamps, whatever kind you want,' he said.

Jehangir stopped. He had been slightly confused ever since the pass with the pencil; Eric frightened him a little with his curious habits and forbidden knowledge. But it had not been easy to accumulate stamps. Sundays with Burjor Uncle continued to be as fascinating as the first. He wished he had new stamps to show—the stasis of his collection might be misinterpreted as lack of interest. He asked Eric: 'Ya? You want to exchange?'

'No *yaar*, I don't collect. But I'll get them for you. As a favour, man.'

'Ya? What kind do you have?'

'I don't have, man. Come on with me to *Patla* and *Jhaaria*, just show me which ones you want. I'll flick them for you.'

Jehangir hesitated. Eric put his arm around him: 'C'mon man, what you scared for, I'll flick. You just show me and go away.' Jehangir pictured the stamps on display in cellophane wrappers: how well they would add to his collection. He imagined album pages bare no more but covered with exquisite stamps, each one mounted carefully and correctly, with a hinge, as Burjor Uncle had showed him to.

They went outside, Eric's arm still around him. Crowds of schoolboys were gathered around the two stalls. A multitude of groping, exploring hands handled the merchandise and browsed absorbedly, a multitude that was a prerequisite for flicking to begin. Jehangir showed Eric the individually wrapped stamps he wanted and moved away. In a few minutes Eric joined him triumphantly.

'Got them?'

'Ya ya. But come inside. He could be watching, man.'

Jehangir was thrilled. Eric asked, 'You want more or what?'

'Sure,' said Jehangir.

'But not today. On Friday. If you do me a favour in visual period on Thursday.'

Jehangir's pulse speeded slightly—visual period, with its darkened hall and projector, and the intimacy created by the teacher's policing abilities temporarily suspended. He remembered Eric's pencil. The cellophane-wrapped stamp packets rustled and crackled in his hand. And there was the promise of more. There had been nothing unpleasant about the pencil. In fact it had felt quite, well, exciting. He agreed to Eric's proposal.

On Thursday, the class lined up to go to the Visual Hall. Eric stood behind Jehangir to ensure their seats would be together.

When the room was dark he put his hand on Jehangir's thigh and began caressing it. He took Jehangir's hand and placed it on his crotch. It lay there inert. Impatient, he whispered, 'Do it, man, c'mon!' But Jehangir's lacklustre stroking was highly unsatisfactory. Eric arrested the hand, reached inside his pants and said, 'OK, hold it tight and rub it like this.' He encircled Jehangir's hand with his to show him how. When Jehangir had attained the right pressure and speed he released his own hand to lean back and sigh contentedly. Shortly Jehangir felt a warm stickiness fill his palm and fingers, and the hardness he held in his hand grew flaccid.

Eric shook off the hand. Jehangir wiped his palm with his hanky. Eric borrowed the hanky to wipe himself. 'Want me to do it for you?' he asked. But Jehangir declined. He was thinking of his hanky. The odour was interesting, not unpleasant at all, but he would have to find some way of cleaning it before his mother found it.

The following day, Eric presented him with more stamps. Next Thursday's assignation was also fixed.

And on Sunday Jehangir went to see Dr Mody at ten o'clock. The wife let him in, muttering something under her breath about being bothered by inconsiderate people on the one day that the family could be together.

Dr Mody's delight at the new stamps fulfilled Jehangir's every expectation: 'Wonderful, wonderful! Where did you get them all? No, no, forget it, don't tell me. You will think I'm trying to learn your tricks. I already have enough stamps to keep me busy in my retirement. Ha! ha!'

After the new stamps had been examined and sorted Dr Mody said, 'Today, as a reward for your enterprise, I'm going to show you a stamp you've never seen before.' From the cupboard of biscuit and sweet tins he took a small satin-covered box of the type in which rings or bracelets are kept. He opened it and, without removing the stamp from inside, placed it on the desk.

The stamp said España Correos at the bottom and its denomination was noted in the top left corner: 3 PTAS. The face of the stamp featured a flamenco dancer in the most exquisite detail and colour. But it was something in the woman's countenance, a look, an ineffable sparkle he saw in her eyes, which so captivated Jehangir.

Wordlessly, he studied the stamp. Dr Mody waited restlessly as the seconds ticked by. He kept fidgeting till the little satin-covered box was shut and back in his hands, then said, 'So you like the Spanish dancing-lady. Everyone who sees it likes it. Even my wife who is not interested in stamp-collecting thought it was beautiful. When I retire I can spend more time with the Spanish dancing-lady. And all my other stamps.' He relaxed once the stamp was locked again in the cupboard.

Jehangir left, carrying that vision of the Spanish dancer in his head. He tried to imagine the stamp inhabiting the pages of his album, to greet him every time he opened it, with the wonderful sparkle in her eyes. He shut the door behind him and immediately, as though to obliterate his covetous fantasy, loud voices rose inside the flat.

He heard Mrs Mody's, shrill in argument, and the doctor's, beseeching her not to yell lest the neighbours would hear. Pesi's name was mentioned several times in the quarrel that ensued, and accusations of neglect, and something about the terrible affliction on a son of an unloving father. The voices followed Jehangir as he hurried past the inquiring eyes of his mother, till he reached the bedroom at the other end of the flat and shut the door.

When the school week started, Jehangir found himself looking forward to Thursday. His pulse was racing with excitement when visual period came. To save his hanky this time he kept some paper at hand.

Eric did not have to provide much guidance. Jehangir discovered he could control Eric's reactions with variations in speed, pressure, and grip. When it was over and Eric offered to do it to him, he did not refuse.

The weeks sped by and Jehangir's collection continued to grow, visual period by visual period. Eric's and his masturbatory partnership was whispered about in class, earning the pair the title of *moothya-maroo.* He accompanied Eric on the flicking forays, helping to swell the milling crowd and add to the browsing hands. Then he grew bolder, studied Eric's methods, and flicked a few stamps himself.

But this smooth course of stamp-collecting was about to end. *Patla Babu* and *Jhaaria Babu* broke their long tradition of silence and complained to the school. Unlike marbles and *supari,* it was not a question of a few paise a day. When Eric and Jehangir struck, their haul could be totalled in rupees reaching double digits; the loss was serious enough to make the *Babus* worry about their survival.

The school assigned the case to the head prefect to investigate. He was an ambitious boy, always snooping around, and was also a member of the school debating team and the Road Safety Patrol. Shortly after the complaint was made he marched into Jehangir's class one afternoon just after lunch break, before the teacher returned, and made what sounded very much like one of his debating speeches: 'Two boys in this class have been stealing stamps from *Patla Babu* and *Jhaaria Babu* for the past several weeks. You may ask: who are those boys? No need for names. They know who they are and I know who they are, and I am asking them to return the stamps to me tomorrow. There will be no punishment if this is done. The *Babus* just want their stamps back. But if the missing stamps are not returned, the names will be reported to the principal and to the police. It is up to the two boys.'

Jehangir tried hard to appear normal. He was racked with trepidation, and looked to the unperturbed Eric for guidance. But Eric ignored him. The head prefect left amidst mock applause from the class.

After school, Eric turned surly. Gone was the tender, cajoling manner he reserved for Jehangir, and he said nastily: 'You better bring back all those fucking stamps tomorrow.' Jehangir, of course, agreed. There was no trouble with the prefect or the school after the stamps were returned.

But Jehangir's collection shrunk pitiably overnight. He slept badly the entire week, worried about explaining to Burjor Uncle the sudden disappearance of the bulk of his collection. His mother assumed the dark rings around his eyes were due to too much reading and not enough fresh air. The thought of stamps or of *Patla Babu* or *Jhaaria Babu* brought an emptiness to his stomach and a bitter taste to his mouth. A general sense of ill-being took possession of him.

He went to see Burjor Uncle on Sunday, leaving behind his stamp album. Mrs Mody opened the door and turned away silently. She appeared to be in a black rage, which exacerbated Jehangir's own feelings of guilt and shame.

He explained to Burjor Uncle that he had not bothered to bring his album because he had acquired no new stamps since last Sunday, and also, he was not well and would not stay for long.

Dr Mody was concerned about the boy, so nervous and uneasy; he put it down to his feeling unwell. They looked at some stamps Dr Mody had received last week from his colleagues abroad. Then Jehangir said he'd better leave.

'But you *must* see the Spanish dancing-lady before you go. Maybe she will help you feel better. Ha! ha!' and Dr Mody rose to go to the cupboard for the stamp. Its viewing at the end of each Sunday's session had acquired the significance of an esoteric ritual.

From the next room Mrs Mody screeched: 'Burjorji! Come here at once!' He made a wry face at Jehangir and hurried out.

In the next room, all the vehemence of Mrs Mody's black rage of that morning poured out upon Dr Mody: 'It has reached the limit now! No time for your own son and Sunday after Sunday sitting with some stranger! What does he have that your own son does not? Are you a *baap* or what? No wonder Pesi has become this way! How can I blame the boy when his own *baap* takes no interest . . .'

'Shh! The boy is in the next room! What do you want, that all the neighbours hear your screaming?'

'I don't care! Let them hear! You think they don't know already? You think you are . . .'

Mrs Bulsara next door listened intently. Suddenly, she realized that Jehangir was in there. Listening from one's own house was one thing—hearing a quarrel from inside the quarrellers' house was another. It made feigning ignorance very difficult.

She rang the Modys' doorbell and waited, adjusting her *mathoobanoo*. Dr Mody came to the door.

'Burjorji, forgive me for disturbing your stamping and collecting work with Jehangir. But I must take him away. Guests have arrived unexpectedly. Jehangir must go to the Irani, we need cold drinks.'

'That's okay, he can come next Sunday.' Then added, 'He *must* come next Sunday,' and noted with satisfaction the frustrated turning away of Mrs Mody who waited out of sight of the doorway. 'Jehangir! Your mother is calling.'

Jehangir was relieved at being rescued from the turbulent waters of the Mody household. They left without further conversation, his mother tugging in embarrassment at the knots of her *mathoobanoo*.

As a result of this unfortunate outburst, a period of awkwardness between the women was unavoidable. Mrs Mody, though far from garrulous, had never let her domestic sorrows and disappointments interfere with the civilities of neighbourly relations, which she respected and observed at all times. Now for the first time since the arrival of the Modys in Firozsha Baag these civilities experienced a hiatus.

When the *muchhiwalla* arrived next morning, instead of striking a joint deal with him as they usually did, Mrs Mody waited till Mrs Bulsara had finished. She stationed an eye at her peephole as he emphasized the freshness of his catch. 'Look *bai*, it is *saféd paani*,' he said, holding out the pomfret and squeezing it near the gills till white fluid oozed out. After Mrs Bulsara had paid and gone, Mrs Mody emerged, while the former took her turn at the peephole. And so it went for a few days till the awkwardness had run its course and things returned to normal.

But not so for Jehangir; on Sunday, he once again had to leave behind his sadly depleted album. To add to his uneasiness, Mrs Mody invited him in with a greeting of 'Come *bawa* come,' and there was something malignant about her smile.

Dr Mody sat at his desk, shoulders sagging, his hands dangling over the arms of the chair. The desk was bare—not a single stamp anywhere in sight, and the cupboard in the corner locked. The absence of his habitual, comfortable clutter made the room cold and cheerless. He was in low spirits; instead of the crow's-feet at the corners of his eyes were lines of distress and dejection.

'No album again?'

'No. Haven't got any new stamps yet,' Jehangir smiled nervously.

Dr Mody scratched the psoriasis on his elbows. He watched Jehangir carefully as he spoke. 'Something very bad has happened to the Spanish dancing-lady stamp. Look,' and he displayed the satin-covered box minus its treasure. 'It is missing.' Half-fearfully, he looked at Jehangir, afraid he would see what he did not want to. But it was inevitable. His last sentence evoked the head prefect's thundering debating-style speech of a few days ago, and the ugliness of the entire episode revisited Jehangir's features—a final ignominious postscript to Dr Mody's loss and disillusion.

Dr Mody shut the box. The boy's reaction, his silence, the absence of his album, confirmed his worst suspicions. More humiliatingly, it seemed his wife was right. With great sadness he rose from his chair. 'I have to leave now, something urgent at the College.' They parted without a word about next Sunday.

Jehangir never went back. He thought for a few days about the missing stamp and wondered what could have happened to it. Burjor Uncle was too careful to have misplaced it; besides, he never removed it from its special box. And the box was still there. But he did not resent him for concluding he had stolen it. His guilt about *Patla Babu* and *Jhaaria Babu*, about Eric and the stamps was so intense, and the punishment deriving from it so inconsequential, almost non-existent, that he did not mind this undeserved blame. In fact, it served to equilibrate his scales of justice.

His mother questioned him the first few Sundays he stayed home. Feeble excuses about homework, and Burjor Uncle not having new stamps, and it being boring to look at the same stuff every Sunday did not satisfy her. She finally attributed his abnegation of stamps to sensitivity and a regard for the unfortunate state of the Modys' domestic affairs. It pleased her that her son was capable of such concern. She did not press him after that.

## IV

Pesi was no longer to be seen in Firozsha Baag. His absence brought relief to most of the parents at first, and then curiosity. Gradually, it became known that he had been sent away to a boarding-school in Poona.

The boys of the Baag continued to play their games in the compound. For better or worse, the spark was lacking that lent unpredictability to those languid coastal evenings of Bombay; evenings which could so easily trap the unwary, adult or child, within a circle of lassitude and depression in which time hung heavy and suffocating.

Jehangir no longer sat on the stone steps of C Block in the evenings. He found it difficult to confront Dr Mody day after day. Besides, the boys he used to watch at play suspected some kind of connection between Pesi's being sent away to boarding-school, Jehangir's former friendship with Dr Mody, and the emerging of Dr Mody's constant sorrow and despair (which he had tried so hard to keep private all along, and had succeeded, but was now visible for all to see). And the boys resented Jehangir for whatever his part was in it—they bore him open antagonism.

Dr Mody was no more the jovial figure the boys had grown to love. When his car turned into the compound in the evenings, he still waved, but no crow's-feet appeared at his eyes, no smile, no jokes.

Two years passed since the Mody family's arrival in Firozsha Baag.

In school, Jehangir was as isolated as in the Baag. Most of his effeminateness had, of late, transformed into vigorous signs of impending manhood. Eric D'Souza had been expelled for attempting to sodomize a junior boy. Jehangir had not been involved in this affair, but most of his classmates related it to the furtive activities of their callow days and the stamp-flicking. *Patla Babu* and *Jhaaria Babu* had disappeared from the pavement outside St Xavier's. The Bombay police, in a misinterpretation of the nation's mandate: *garibi hatao*—eradicate poverty, conducted periodic round-ups of pavement dwellers, sweeping into their vans beggars and street-vendors, cripples and alcoholics, the homeless and the hungry, and dumped them somewhere outside the city limits; when the human detritus made its way back into the city, another clean-up was scheduled. *Patla* and *Jhaaria* were snared in one of these raids, and never found their way back. Eyewitnesses said their stalls were smashed up and *Patla Babu* received a *lathi* across his forehead for trying to salvage some of his inventory. They were not seen again.

Two years passed since Jehangir's visits to Dr Mody had ceased.

It was getting close to the time for another transfer for Dr Mody. When the inevitable orders were received, he went to Ahmedabad to make arrangements. Mrs Mody was to join her husband after a few days. Pesi was still in boarding-school, and would stay there.

So when the news arrived from Ahmedabad of Dr Mody's death of heart failure, Mrs Mody was alone in the flat. She went next door with the telegram and broke down.

The Bulsaras helped with all the arrangements. The body was brought to Bombay by car for a proper Parsi funeral. Pesi came from Poona for the funeral, then went back to boarding-school.

The events were talked about for days afterwards, the stories spreading first in C Block, then through A and B. Commiseration for Mrs Mody was general. The ordeal of the body during the two-day car journey from Ahmedabad was particularly horrifying, and was discussed endlessly. Embalming was not allowed according to Parsi rituals, and the body in the trunk, although packed with ice, had started to smell horribly in the heat of the Deccan Plateau which the car had had to traverse. Some hinted that this torment suffered by Dr Mody's earthly remains was the Almighty's punishment for neglecting his duties as a father and making Mrs Mody so unhappy. Poor Dr Mody, they said, who never went a day without a bath and talcum powder in life, to undergo this in death. Someone even had, on good authority, a count of the number of eau de cologne bottles used by Mrs Mody and the three occupants of the car over the course of the journey—it was the only way they could draw breath, through cologne-watered handkerchiefs. And it was also said that ever after, these four could never tolerate eau de cologne—opening a bottle was like opening the car trunk with Dr Mody's decomposing corpse.

A year after the funeral, Mrs Mody was still living in Firozsha Baag. Time and grief had softened her looks, and she was no longer the harsh and dour-faced woman Jehangir had seen during his first Sunday visit. She had decided to make the flat her permanent home now, and the trustees of the Baag granted her request 'in view of the unfortunate circumstances'.

There were some protests about this, particularly from those whose sons or daughters had been postponing marriages and families till flats became available. But the majority, out of respect for Dr Mody's memory, agreed with the trustee's decision. Pesi continued to attend boarding-school.

One day, shortly after her application had been approved by the trustees, Mrs Mody visited Mrs Bulsara. They sat and talked of old times, when they had first moved in, and about how pleased Dr Mody had been to live in a Parsi colony like Firozsha Baag after years of travelling, and then the disagreements she had had with her husband over Pesi and Pesi's future; tears came to her eyes, and also to Mrs Bulsara's, who tugged at the corner of her *mathoobanoo* to reach it to her eyes and dry them. Mrs Mody confessed how she had hated Jehangir's Sunday visits although he was such a fine boy, because she was worried about the way poor Burjorji was neglecting Pesi: 'But he could not help it. That was the way he was. Sometimes he would wish *Khoedai* had given him a daughter instead of a son. Pesi disappointed him in everything, in all his plans, and . . .' and here she burst into uncontrollable sobs.

Finally, after her tears subsided she asked, 'Is Jehangir home?' He wasn't. 'Would you ask him to come and see me this Sunday? At ten? Tell him I won't keep him long.'

Jehangir was a bit apprehensive when his mother gave him the message. He couldn't imagine why Mrs Mody would want to see him.

On Sunday, as he prepared to go next door, he was reminded of the Sundays with Dr Mody, the kindly man who had befriended him, opened up a new world for him, and then repudiated him for something he had not done. He remembered the way he would scratch the greyish-red patches of psoriasis on his elbows. He could still picture the sorrow on his face as, with the utmost reluctance, he had made his decision to end the friendship. Jehangir had not blamed Dr Mody then, and he still did not; he knew how overwhelmingly the evidence had been against him, and how much that stamp had meant to Dr Mody.

Mrs Mody led him in by his arm: 'Will you drink something?'

'No, thank you.'

'Not feeling shy, are you? You always were shy.' She asked him about his studies and what subjects he was taking in high school. She told him a little about Pesi, who was still in boarding-school and had twice repeated the same standard. She sighed. 'I asked you to come today because there is something I wanted to give you. Something of Burjor Uncle's. I thought about it for many days. Pesi is not interested, and I don't know anything about it. Will you take his collection?'

'The album in his drawer?' asked Jehangir, a little surprised.

'Everything. The album, all the boxes, everything in the cupboard. I know you will use it well. Burjor would have done the same.'

Jehangir was speechless. He had stopped collecting stamps, and they no longer held the fascination they once did. Nonetheless, he was familiar with the size of the collection, and the sheer magnitude of what he was now being offered had its effect. He remembered the awe with which he had looked inside the cupboard the first time its doors had been opened before him. So many sweet tins, cardboard boxes, biscuit tins . . .

'You will take it? As a favour to me, yes?' she asked a second time, and Jehangir nodded. 'You have some time today? Whenever you like, just take it.' He said he would ask his mother and come back.

There was a huge, old iron trunk which lay under Jehangir's bed. It was dented in several places and the lid would not shut properly. Undisturbed for years, it had rusted peacefully beneath the bed. His mother agreed that the rags it held could be thrown away and the stamps temporarily stored in it till Jehangir organized them into albums. He emptied the trunk, wiped it out, lined it with brown paper and went next door to bring back the stamps.

Several trips later, Dr Mody's cupboard stood empty. Jehangir looked around the room in which he had once spent so many happy hours. The desk was in exactly the same position, and the two chairs. He turned to go, almost forgetting, and went back to the desk. Yes, there it was in the drawer, Dr Mody's first album, given him by his Nusserwanji Uncle.

He started to turn the heavily laden pages. They rustled in a peculiar way—what was it about that sound? Then he remembered: that first Sunday, and he could almost hear Dr Mody again, the soft inspired tones speaking of promises and dreams, quite different from his usual booming jovial voice, and that faraway look in his eyes which had once glinted with rage when Pesi had tried to bully him . . .

Mrs Mody came into the room. He shut the album, startled: 'This is the last lot.' He stopped to thank her but she interrupted: 'No, no. What is the thank-you for? You are doing a favour to me by taking it, you are helping me to do what Burjor would like.' She took his arm. 'I wanted to tell you. From the collection one stamp is missing. With the picture of the dancing-lady.'

'I know!' said Jehangir. 'That's the one Burjor Uncle lost and thought that I . . .'

Mrs Mody squeezed his arm which she was still holding and he fell silent. She spoke softly, but without guilt: 'He did not lose it. I destroyed it.' Then her eyes went moist as she watched the disbelief on his face. She wanted to say more, to explain, but could not, and clung to his arm. Finally, her voice quavering pitiably, she managed to say, 'Forgive an old lady,' and patted his cheek. Jehangir left in silence, suddenly feeling very ashamed.

Over the next few days, he tried to impose some order on that greatly chaotic mass of stamps. He was hoping that sooner or later his interest in philately would be rekindled. But that did not happen; the task remained futile and dry and boring. The meaningless squares of paper refused to come to life as they used to for Dr Mody in his room every Sunday at ten o'clock. Jehangir shut the trunk and pushed it back under his bed where it had lain untroubled for so many years.

From time to time his mother reminded him about the stamps: 'Do something Jehangoo, do something with them.' He said he would when he felt like it and had the time; he wasn't interested for now.

Then, after several months, he pulled out the trunk again from under his bed. Mrs Bulsara watched eagerly from a distance, not daring to interrupt with any kind of advice or encouragement: her Jehangoo was at that difficult age, she knew, when boys automatically did the exact reverse of what their parents said.

But the night before Jehangir's sleep had been disturbed by a faint and peculiar rustling sound seeming to come from inside the trunk. His reasons for dragging it out into daylight soon became apparent to Mrs Bulsara.

The lid was thrown back to reveal clusters of cockroaches. They tried to scuttle to safety, and he killed a few with his slipper. His mother ran up now, adding a few blows of her own *chappal*, as the creatures began quickly to disperse. Some ran under the bed into hard-to-reach corners; others sought out the trunk's deeper recesses.

A cursory examination showed that besides cockroaches, the trunk was also infested with white ants. All the albums had been ravaged. Most of the stamps which had not been destroyed outright were damaged in one way or another. They bore haphazard perforations and brown stains of the type associated with insects and household pests.

Jehangir picked up an album at random and opened it. Almost immediately, the pages started to fall to pieces in his hands. He remembered what Dr Mody used to say: 'This is my retirement hobby. I will spend my retirement with my stamps.' He allowed the tattered remains of Burjor Uncle's beloved pastime to drop back slowly into the trunk.

He crouched beside the dented, rusted metal, curious that he felt no loss or pain. Why, he wondered. If anything, there was a slight sense of relief. He let his hands stray through the contents, through worthless paper scraps, through shreds of the work of so many Sunday mornings, stopping now and then to regard with detachment the bizarre patterns created by the mandibles of the insects who had feasted night after night under his bed, while he slept.

With an almost imperceptible shrug, he arose and closed the lid. It was doubtful if anything of value remained in the trunk.

1987

# Louise Erdrich

*b.* 1954

Born in Little Falls, Minnesota, of a Chippewa mother and a German-American father, Louise Erdrich obtained her BA from Dartmouth College (1976) and her MA from Johns Hopkins University (1979) and has taught creative writing at both places. A prolific and diverse author, she has written two volumes of poetry, *Jacklight* (1984) and *Baptism of Desire* (1989); collaborated with her now-deceased husband, anthropologist Michael Dorris, on *The Crown of Columbus* (1991), a novel based on their experience and understanding of contemporary Aboriginal life; authored Aboriginal novels for children; and written a series of adult novels that focus on her Chippewa ancestors in the fictional community of Argus, North Dakota, from 1912 to contemporary times. In her fiction she explores universal family life cycles while showing the losses suffered by Aboriginal communities and how these and other changes have affected contemporary Native experience. 'Fleur', which became a chapter in the novel *Tracks* (1988), examines the title character's youth and inexperience, though most honest readers are compelled at the end to admit that they, too, 'don't know anything'. The one fact that always holds true is the enduring power of stories.

## Fleur

The first time she drowned in the cold and glassy waters of Lake Turcot, Fleur Pillager was only a girl. Two men saw the boat tip, saw her struggle in the waves. They rowed over to the place she went down, and jumped in. When they dragged her over the gunwales, she was cold to the touch and stiff, so they slapped her face, shook her by the heels, worked her arms back and forth, and pounded her back until she coughed up lake water. She shivered all over like a dog, then took a breath. But it wasn't long afterward that those two men disappeared. The first wandered off, and the other, Jean Hat, got himself run over by a cart.

It went to show, my grandma said. It figured to her, all right. By saving Fleur Pillager, those two men had lost themselves.

The next time she fell in the lake, Fleur Pillager was twenty years old and no one touched her. She washed onshore, her skin a dull dead grey, but when George Many Women bent to look closer, he saw her chest move. Then her eyes spun open, sharp black riprock, and she looked at him. 'You'll take my place,' she hissed. Everybody scattered and left her there, so no one knows how she dragged herself home. Soon after that we noticed Many Women changed, grew afraid, wouldn't leave his house, and would not be forced to go near water. For his caution, he lived until the day that his sons brought him a new tin bathtub. Then the first time he used the tub he slipped, got knocked out, and breathed water while his wife stood in the other room frying breakfast.

Men stayed clear of Fleur Pillager after the second drowning. Even though she was good-looking, nobody dared to court her because it was clear that Misshepeshu, the waterman, the monster, wanted her for himself. He's a devil, that one, love-hungry with desire and maddened for the touch of young girls, the strong and daring especially, the ones like Fleur.

Our mothers warn us that we'll think he's handsome, for he appears with green eyes, copper skin, a mouth tender as a child's. But if you fall into his arms, he sprouts horns, fangs, claws, fins. His feet are joined as one and his skin, brass scales, rings to the touch. You're fascinated, cannot move. He casts a shell necklace at your feet, weeps gleaming chips that harden into mica on your breasts. He holds you under. Then he takes the body of a lion or a fat brown worm. He's made of gold. He's made of beach moss. He's a thing of dry foam, a thing of death by drowning, the death a Chippewa cannot survive.

Unless you are Fleur Pillager. We all knew she couldn't swim. After the first time, we thought she'd never go back to Lake Turcot. We thought she'd keep to herself, live quiet, stop killing men off by drowning in the lake. After the first time, we thought she'd keep the good ways. But then, after the second drowning, we knew that we were dealing with something much more serious. She was haywire, out of control. She messed with evil, laughed at the old women's advice, and dressed like a man. She got herself into some half-forgotten medicine, studied ways we shouldn't talk about. Some say she kept the finger of a child in her pocket and a powder of unborn rabbits in a leather thong around her neck. She laid the heart of an owl on her tongue so she could see at night, and went out, hunting, not even in her own body. We know for sure because the next morning, in the snow or dust, we followed the tracks of her bare feet and saw where they changed, where the claws sprang out, the pad broadened and pressed into the dirt. By night we heard her chuffing cough, the bear cough. By day her silence and the wide grin she threw to bring down our guard made us frightened. Some thought that Fleur Pillager should be driven off the reservation, but not a single person who spoke like this had the nerve. And finally, when people were just about to get together and throw her out, she left on her own and didn't come back all summer. That's what this story is about.

During that summer, when she lived a few miles south in Argus, things happened. She almost destroyed that town.

When she got down to Argus in the year of 1920, it was just a small grid of six streets on either side of the railroad depot. There were two elevators, one central, the other a few miles west. Two stores competed for the trade of the three hundred citizens, and three churches quarrelled with one another for their souls. There was a frame building for Lutherans, a heavy brick one for Episcopalians, and a long narrow shingled Catholic church. This last had a tall slender steeple, twice as high as any building or tree.

No doubt, across the low, flat wheat, watching from the road as she came near Argus on foot, Fleur saw that steeple rise, a shadow thin as a needle. Maybe in that raw space it drew her the way a lone tree draws lightning. Maybe, in the end, the Catholics are to blame. For if she hadn't seen that sign of pride, that slim prayer, that marker, maybe she would have kept walking.

But Fleur Pillager turned, and the first place she went once she came into town was to the back door of the priest's residence attached to the landmark church. She didn't go there for a handout, although she got that, but to ask for work. She got that too, or the town got her. It's hard to tell which came out worse, her or the men or the town, although the upshot of it all was that Fleur lived.

The four men who worked at the butcher's had carved up about a thousand carcasses between them, maybe half of that steers and the other half pigs, sheep, and game animals like deer, elk, and bear. That's not even mentioning the chickens, which were beyond counting. Pete Kozka owned the place, and employed Lily Veddar, Tor Grunewald, and my stepfather, Dutch James, who had brought my mother down from the reservation the year before she disappointed him by dying. Dutch took me out of school to take her place. I kept house half the time and worked the other in the butcher shop, sweeping floors, putting sawdust down, running a hambone across the street to a customer's bean pot or a package of sausage to the corner. I was a good one to have around because until they needed me, I was invisible. I blended into the stained brown wall, a skinny, big-nosed girl with staring eyes. Because I could fade into a corner or squeeze beneath a shelf, I knew everything, what the men said when no one was around, and what they did to Fleur.

Kozka's Meats served farmers for a fifty-mile area, both to slaughter, for it had a stock pen and chute, and to cure the meat by smoking it or spicing it in sausage. The storage locker was a marvel, made of many thicknesses of brick, earth insulation, and Minnesota timber, lined inside with sawdust and vast blocks of ice cut from Lake Turcot, hauled down from home each winter by horse and sledge.

A ramshackle board building, part slaughterhouse, part store, was fixed to the low, thick square of the lockers. That's where Fleur worked. Kozka hired her for her strength. She could lift a haunch or carry a pole of sausages without stumbling, and she soon learned cutting from Pete's wife, a string-thin blonde who chain-smoked and handled the razor-sharp knives with nerveless precision, slicing close to her stained fingers. Fleur and Fritzie Kozka worked afternoons, wrapping their cuts in paper, and Fleur hauled the packages to the lockers. The meat was left outside the heavy oak doors that were only opened at 5:00 each afternoon, before the men ate supper.

Sometimes Dutch, Tor, and Lily ate at the lockers, and when they did I stayed too, cleaned floors, restoked the fires in the front smokehouse, while the men sat around the squat cast-iron stove spearing slats of herring onto hardtack bread. They played long games of poker or cribbage on a board made from the planed end of a salt crate. They talked and I listened, although there wasn't much to hear since almost nothing ever happened in Argus. Tor was married, Dutch had lost my mother, and Lily read circulars. They mainly discussed about the auctions to come, equipment, or women.

Every so often, Pete Kozka came out front to make a whist, leaving Fritzie to smoke cigarettes and fry raised doughnuts in the back room. He sat and played a few rounds but kept his thoughts to himself. Fritzie did not tolerate him talking behind her back, and the one book he read was the New Testament. If he said something, it concerned weather or a surplus of sheep stomachs, a ham that smoked green or the markets for corn and wheat. He had a good-luck talisman, the opal-white lens of a cow's eye. Playing cards, he rubbed it between his fingers. That soft sound and the slap of cards was about the only conversation.

Fleur finally gave them a subject.

Her cheeks were wide and flat, her hands large, chapped, muscular. Fleur's shoulders were broad as beams, her hips fishlike, slippery, narrow. An old green dress clung to her waist, worn thin where she sat. Her braids were thick like the tails of animals, and swung against her when she moved, deliberately, slowly in her work, held in and half-tamed, but only half. I could tell, but the others never saw. They never looked into her sly brown eyes or noticed her teeth, strong and curved and very white. Her legs were bare, and since she padded around in beadwork moccasins they never saw that her fifth toes were missing. They never knew she'd drowned. They were blinded, they were stupid, they only saw her in the flesh.

And yet it wasn't just that she was a Chippewa, or even that she was a woman, it wasn't that she was good-looking or even that she was alone that made their brains hum. It was how she played cards.

Women didn't usually play with men, so the evening that Fleur drew a chair up to the men's table without being so much as asked, there was a shock of surprise.

'What's this,' said Lily. He was fat with a snake's cold pale eyes and precious skin, smooth and lily-white, which is how he got his name. Lily had a dog, a stumpy mean little bull of a thing with a belly drum-tight from eating pork rinds. The dog liked to play cards just like Lily, and straddled his barrel thighs through games of stud, rum poker, vingt-un. The dog snapped at Fleur's arm that first night, but cringed back, its snarl frozen, when she took her place.

'I thought', she said, her voice was soft and stroking, 'you might deal me in.'

There was a space between the heavy bin of spiced flour and the wall where I just fit. I hunkered down there, kept my eyes open, saw her black hair swing over the chair, her feet solid on the wood floor. I couldn't see up on the table where the cards slapped down, so after they were deep in their game I raised myself up in the shadows, and crouched on a sill of wood.

I watched Fleur's hands stack and ruffle, divide the cards, spill them to each player in a blur, rake them up and shuffle again. Tor, short and scrappy, shut one eye and squinted the other at Fleur. Dutch screwed his lips around a wet cigar.

'Gotta see a man,' he mumbled, getting up to go out back to the privy. The others broke, put their cards down, and Fleur sat alone in the lamplight that glowed in a sheen across the push of her breasts. I watched her closely, then she paid me a beam of notice for the first time. She turned, looked straight at me, and grinned the white wolf grin a Pillager turns on its victims, except that she wasn't after me.

'Pauline there,' she said, 'how much money you got?'

We'd all been paid for the week that day. Eight cents was in my pocket.

'Stake me,' she said, holding out her long fingers. I put the coins in her palm and then I melted back to nothing, part of the walls and tables. It was a long time before I understood that the men would not have seen me no matter what I did, how I moved. I wasn't anything like Fleur. My dress hung loose and my back was already curved, an old woman's. Work had roughened me, reading made my eyes sore, caring for my mother before she died had hardened my face. I was not much to look at, so they never saw me.

When the men came back and sat around the table, they had drawn together. They shot each other small glances, stuck their tongues in their cheeks, burst out laughing at odd moments, to rattle Fleur. But she never minded. They played their vingt-un, staying even as Fleur slowly gained. Those pennies I had given her drew nickels and attracted dimes until there was a small pile in front of her.

Then she hooked them with five-card draw, nothing wild. She dealt, discarded, drew, and then she sighed and her cards gave a little shiver. Tor's eye gleamed, and Dutch straightened in his seat.

'I'll pay to see that hand,' said Lily Veddar.

Fleur showed, and she had nothing there, nothing at all.

Tor's thin smile cracked open, and he threw his hand in too.

'Well, we know one thing,' he said, leaning back in his chair, 'the squaw can't bluff.'

With that I lowered myself into a mound of swept sawdust and slept. I woke up during the night, but none of them had moved yet, so I couldn't either. Still later, the men must have gone out again, or Fritzie come out to break the game, because I was lifted, soothed, cradled in a woman's arms and rocked so quiet that I kept my eyes shut while Fleur rolled me into a closet of grimy ledgers, oiled paper, balls of string, and thick files that fit beneath me like a mattress.

The game went on after work the next evening. I got my eight cents back five times over, and Fleur kept the rest of the dollar she'd won for a stake. This time they didn't play so late, but they played regular, and then kept going at it night after night. They played poker now, or variations, for one week straight, and each time Fleur won exactly one dollar, no more and no less, too consistent for luck.

By this time, Lily and the other men were so lit with suspense that they got Pete to join the game with them. They concentrated, the fat dog sitting tense in Lily Veddar's lap, Tor suspicious, Dutch stroking his huge square brow, Pete steady. It wasn't that Fleur won that hooked them in so, because she lost hands too. It was rather that she never had a freak hand or even anything above a straight. She only took on her low cards, which didn't sit right. By chance, Fleur should have gotten a full or flush by now. The irritating thing was she beat with pairs and never bluffed, because she couldn't, and still she ended up each night with exactly one dollar. Lily couldn't believe, first of all, that a woman could be smart enough to play cards, but even if she was, that she would then be stupid enough to cheat for a dollar at night. By day I watched him turn the problem over, his hard white face dull, small fingers probing at his knuckles, until he finally thought he had Fleur figured out as a bit-time player, caution her game. Raising the stakes would throw her.

More than anything now, he wanted Fleur to come away with something but a dollar. Two bits less or ten more, the sum didn't matter, just so he broke her streak.

Night after night she played, won her dollar, and left to stay in a place that just Fritzie and I knew about. Fleur bathed in the slaughtering tub, then slept in the unused brick smokehouse behind the lockers, a windowless place tarred on the inside with scorched fats. When I brushed against her skin I noticed that she smelled of the walls, rich and woody, slightly burnt. Since that night she put me in the closet I was no longer afraid of her, but followed her close, stayed with her, became her moving shadow that the men never noticed, the shadow that could have saved her.

August, the month that bears fruit, closed around the shop, and Pete and Fritzie left for Minnesota to escape the heat. Night by night, running, Fleur had won thirty dollars, and only Pete's presence had kept Lily at bay. But Pete was gone now, and one payday, with the heat so bad no one could move but Fleur, the men sat and played and waited while she finished work. The cards sweat, limp in their fingers, the table was slick with grease, and even the walls were warm to the touch. The air was motionless. Fleur was in the next room boiling heads.

Her green dress, drenched, wrapped her like a transparent sheet. A skin of lakeweed. Black snarls of veining clung to her arms. Her braids were loose, half-unravelled, tied behind her neck in a thick loop. She stood in steam, turning skulls through a vat with a wooden paddle. When scraps boiled to the surface, she bent with a round tin sieve and scooped them out. She'd filled two dishpans.

'Ain't that enough now?' called Lily. 'We're waiting.' The stump of a dog trembled in his lap, alive with rage. It never smelled me or noticed me above Fleur's smoky skin. The air was heavy in my corner, and pressed me down. Fleur sat with them.

'Now what do you say?' Lily asked the dog. It barked. That was the signal for the real game to start.

'Let's up the ante,' said Lily, who had been stalking this night all month. He had a roll of money in his pocket. Fleur had five bills in her dress. The men had each saved their full pay.

'Ante a dollar then,' said Fleur, and pitched hers in. She lost, but they let her scrape along, cent by cent. And then she won some. She played unevenly, as if chance was all she had. She reeled them in. The game went on. The dog was stiff now, poised on Lily's knees, a ball of vicious muscle with its yellow eyes slit in concentration. It gave advice, seemed to sniff the lay of Fleur's cards, twitched and nudged. Fleur was up, then down, saved by a scratch. Tor dealt seven cards, three down. The pot grew, round by round, until it held all the money. Nobody folded. Then it all rode on one last card and they went silent. Fleur picked hers up and blew a long breath. The heat lowered like a bell. Her card shook, but she stayed in.

Lily smiled and took the dog's head tenderly between his palms.

'Say, Fatso,' he said, crooning the words, 'you reckon that girl's bluffing?'

The dog whined and Lily laughed. 'Me too,' he said, 'let's show.' He swept his bills and coins into the pot and then they turned their cards over.

Lily looked once, looked again, then he squeezed the dog up like a fist of dough and slammed it on the table.

Fleur threw her arms out and drew the money over, grinning that same wolf grin that she'd used on me, the grin that had them. She jammed the bills in her dress, scooped the coins up in a waxed white paper that she tied with string.

'Let's go another round,' said Lily, his voice choked with burrs. But Fleur opened her mouth and yawned, then walked out back to gather slops for the one big hog that was waiting in the stock pen to be killed.

The men sat still as rocks, their hands spread on the oiled wood table. Dutch had chewed his cigar to damp shreds, Tor's eye was dull. Lily's gaze was the only one to follow Fleur. I didn't move. I felt them gathering, saw my stepfather's veins, the ones in his forehead that stood out in anger. The dog had rolled off the table and curled in a knot below the counter, where none of the men could touch it.

Lily rose and stepped out back to the closet of ledgers where Pete kept his private stock. He brought back a bottle, uncorked and tipped it between his fingers. The lump in his throat moved, then he passed it on. They drank, quickly felt the whisky's fire, and planned with their eyes things they couldn't say out loud.

When they left, I followed. I hid out back in the clutter of broken boards and chicken crates beside the stock pen, where they waited. Fleur could not be seen at first, and then the moon broke and showed her, slipping cautiously along the rough board chute with a bucket in her hand. Her hair fell, wild and coarse, to her waist, and her dress was a floating patch in the dark. She made a pig-calling sound, rang the tin pail lightly against the wood, froze suspiciously. But too late. In the sound of the ring Lily moved, fat and nimble, stepped right behind Fleur and put out his creamy hands. At his first touch, she whirled and doused him with the bucket of sour slops. He pushed her against the big fence and the package of coins split, went clinking and jumping, winked against the wood. Fleur rolled over once and vanished in the yard.

The moon fell behind a curtain of ragged clouds, and Lily followed into the dark muck. But he tripped, pitched over the huge flank of the pig, who lay mired to the snout, heavily snoring. I sprang out of the weeds and climbed the side of the pen, stuck like glue. I saw the sow rise to her neat, knobby knees, gain her balance, and sway, curious, as Lily stumbled forward. Fleur had backed into the angle of rough wood just beyond, and when Lily tried to jostle past, the sow tipped up on her hind legs and struck, quick and hard as a snake. She plunged her head into Lily's thick side and snatched a mouthful of his shirt. She lunged again, caught him lower, so that he grunted in pained surprise. He seemed to ponder, breathing deep. Then he launched his huge body in a swimmer's dive.

The sow screamed as his body smacked over hers. She rolled, striking out with her knife-sharp hooves, and Lily gathered himself upon her, took her foot-long face by the ears and scraped her snout and cheeks against the trestle of the pen. He hurled the sow's tight skull against an iron post, but instead of knocking her dead, he merely woke her from her dream.

She reared, shrieked, drew him with her so that they posed standing upright. They bowed jerkily to each other, as if to begin. Then his arms swung and flailed. She sank her black fangs into his shoulder, clasping him, dancing him forward and backward through the pen. Their steps picked up pace, went wild. The two dipped as one, box-stepped, tripped each other. She ran her split foot through his hair. He grabbed her kinked tail. They went down and came up, the same shape and then the same colour, until the men couldn't tell one from the other in that light and Fleur was able to launch herself over the gates, swing down, hit gravel.

The men saw, yelled, and chased her at a dead run to the smokehouse. And Lily too, once the sow gave up in disgust and freed him. That is where I should have gone to Fleur, saved her, thrown myself on Dutch. But I went stiff with fear and couldn't unlatch myself from the trestles or move at all. I closed my eyes and put my head in my arms, tried to hide, so there is nothing to describe but what I couldn't block out, Fleur's hoarse breath, so loud it filled me, her cry in the old language, and my name repeated over and over among the words.

The heat was still dense the next morning when I came back to work. Fleur was gone but the men were there, slack-faced, hungover. Lily was paler and softer than ever, as if his flesh had steamed on his bones. They smoked, took pulls off a bottle. It wasn't noon yet. I worked a while, waiting shop and sharpening steel. But I was sick, I was smothered, I was sweating so hard that my hands slipped on the knives, and I wiped my fingers clean of the greasy touch of the customers' coins. Lily opened his mouth and roared once, not in anger. There was no meaning to the sound. His boxer dog, sprawled limp beside his foot, never lifted its head. Nor did the other men.

They didn't notice when I stepped outside, hoping for a clear breath. And then I forgot them because I knew that we were all balanced, ready to tip, to fly, to be crushed as soon as the weather broke. The sky was so low that I felt the weight of it like a yoke. Clouds hung down, witch teats, a tornado's green-brown cones, and as I watched one flicked out and became a delicate probing thumb. Even as I picked up my heels and ran back inside, the wind blew suddenly, cold, and then came rain.

Inside, the men had disappeared already and the whole place was trembling as if a huge hand was pinched at the rafters, shaking it. I ran straight through, screaming for Dutch or for any of them, and then I stopped at the heavy doors of the lockers, where they had surely taken shelter. I stood there a moment. Everything went still. Then I heard a cry building in the wind, faint at first, a whistle and then a shrill scream that tore through the walls and gathered around me, spoke plain so I understood that I should move, put my arms out, and slam down the great iron bar that fit across the hasp and lock.

Outside, the wind was stronger, like a hand held against me. I struggled forward. The bushes tossed, the awnings flapped off storefronts, the rails of porches rattled. The odd cloud became a fat snout that nosed along the earth and sniffled, jabbed, picked at things, sucked them up, blew them apart, rooted around as if it was following a certain scent, then stopped behind me at the butcher shop and bored down like a drill.

I went flying, landed somewhere in a ball. When I opened my eyes and looked, stranger things were happening.

A herd of cattle flew through the air like giant birds, dropping their dung, their mouths open in stunned bellows. A candle, still lighted, blew past, and tables, napkins, garden tools, a whole school of drifting eyeglasses, jackets on hangers, hams, a checkerboard, a lampshade, and at last the sow from behind the lockers, on the run, her hooves a blur, set free, swooping, diving, screaming as everything in Argus fell apart and got turned upside down, smashed, and thoroughly wrecked.

Days passed before the town went looking for the men. They were bachelors, after all, except for Tor, whose wife had suffered a blow to the head that made her forgetful. Everyone was occupied with digging out, in high relief because even though the

Catholic steeple had been torn off like a peaked cap and sent across five fields, those huddled in the cellar were unhurt. Walls had fallen, windows were demolished, but the stores were intact and so were the bankers and shop owners who had taken refuge in their safes or beneath their cash registers. It was a fair-minded disaster, no one could be said to have suffered much more than the next, at least not until Fritzie and Pete came home.

Of all the businesses in Argus, Kozka's Meats had suffered worst. The boards of the front building had been split to kindling, piled in a huge pyramid, and the shop equipment was blasted far and wide. Pete paced off the distance the iron bathtub had been flung—a hundred feet. The glass candy case went fifty, and landed without so much as a cracked pane. There were other surprises as well, for the back rooms where Fritzie and Peter lived were undisturbed. Fritzie said the dust still coated her china figures, and upon her kitchen table, in the ashtray, perched the last cigarette she'd put out in haste. She lit it up and finished it, looking through the window. From there, she could see that the old smokehouse Fleur had slept in was crushed to a reddish sand and the stockpens were completely torn apart, the rails stacked helter-skelter. Fritzie asked for Fleur. People shrugged. Then she asked about the others and, suddenly, the town understood that three men were missing.

There was a rally of help, a gathering of shovels and volunteers. We passed boards from hand to hand, stacked them, uncovered what lay beneath the pile of jagged splinters. The lockers, full of the meat that was Pete and Fritzie's investment, slowly came into sight, still intact. When enough room was made for a man to stand on the roof, there were calls, a general urge to hack through and see what lay below. But Fritzie shouted that she wouldn't allow it because the meat would spoil. And so the work continued, board by board, until at last the heavy oak doors of the freezer were revealed and people pressed to the entry. Everyone wanted to be the first, but since it was my stepfather lost, I was let go in when Pete and Fritzie wedged through into the sudden icy air.

Pete scraped a match to his boot, lit the lamp Fritzie held, and then the three of us stood still in its circle. Light glared off the skinned and hanging carcasses, the crates of wrapped sausages, the bright and cloudy blocks of lake ice, pure as winter. The cold bit into us, pleasant at first, then numbing. We must have stood there a couple of minutes before we saw the men, or more rightly, the humps of fur, the iced and shaggy hides they wore, the bearskins they had taken down and wrapped around themselves. We stepped closer and tilted the lantern beneath the flaps of fur into their faces. The dog was there, perched among them, heavy as a doorstop. The three had hunched around a barrel where the game was still laid out, and a dead lantern and an empty bottle, too. But they had thrown down their last hands and hunkered tight, clutching one another, knuckles raw from beating at the door they had also attacked with hooks. Frost stars gleamed off their eyelashes and the stubble of their beards. Their faces were set in concentration, mouths open as if to speak some careful thought, some agreement they'd come to in each other's arms.

Power travels in the bloodlines, handed out before birth. It comes down through the hands, which in the Pillagers were strong and knotted, big, spidery, and rough, with sensitive fingertips good at dealing cards. It comes through the eyes, too, belligerent, darkest brown, the eyes of those in the bear clan, impolite as they gaze directly at a person.

In my dreams, I look straight back at Fleur, at the men. I am no longer the watcher on the dark sill, the skinny girl.

The blood draws us back, as if it runs through a vein of earth. I've come home and, except for talking to my cousins, live a quiet life. Fleur lives quiet too, down on Lake Turcot with her boat. Some say she's married to the waterman, Misshepeshu, or that she's living in shame with white men or windigos, or that she's killed them all. I'm about the only one here who ever goes to visit her. Last winter, I went to help out in her cabin when she bore a child, whose green eyes and skin the colour of an old penny made more talk, as no one could decide if the child was mixed blood or what, fathered in a smokehouse, or by a man with brass scales, or by the lake. The girl is bold, smiling in her sleep, as if she knows what people wonder, as if she hears the old men talk, turning the story over. It comes up different every time and has no ending, no beginning. They get the middle wrong too. They only know that they don't know anything.

1986

# Tamas Dobozy
## *b.* 1969

Born in Nanaimo, British Columbia, Tamas Dobozy, the son of Hungarian immigrants, obtained his BA/BFA (1991) from the University of Victoria, his MA (1993) from Concordia University, and his PhD (2000) from the University of British Columbia. After a time at Memorial University, he now teaches at Wilfrid Laurier University. His three volumes of short fiction, *When X Equals Marylou* (2002), *Last Notes and Other Stories* (2005), and *Siege 13: Stories* (2012), travel the spectrum from realistic narratives to surreal adventures. His fiction has increasingly studied the past, specifically the Second World War and its aftermath in Budapest. In 'The Ghosts of Budapest and Toronto' from *Siege 13: Stories*, which won the 2012 Rogers Writers' Trust Fiction Prize, he imagines war-torn Budapest, the time after the War, and the émigré experience in Toronto in more recent years.

## The Ghosts of Budapest and Toronto

Mária didn't die in the siege of Budapest. No, she suffered the fate of so many women—*millions of women*, according to historians—who were raped by the Red Army during their 'liberation' of eastern and central Europe. For the survivors of this ordeal—women and girls and grandmothers and sisters and any other kind of female the troops could get their hands on—there was a second ordeal once the first was over, and that was the look of shame and disgust in the eyes of the men—husbands, lovers, sons, nephews—who'd been powerless to help them, and for whom the women remained a continual reminder of how they'd failed. Of course, there was also the look of those men who *had* tried to do something, but this was even more haunting, for some of them had their brains bashed out with the butt ends of rifles, or were shot five or six times, or received so much in the way of injury that the look they gave you afterwards was, for the women, like gazing into a mirror.

Mária's husband, László, never did find out where the soldiers took her after they'd finished doing what they did, holding him down while they did it in such a way that he had the best view in the house, screaming and struggling so fiercely they finally had to knock him over the head. He returned to consciousness, Mária was gone, and no matter how he searched for her afterwards, paying visits to the Allied Control Commission offices, looking through lists of the wounded, the arrested, the dead, even wandering the neighbourhood where it happened and questioning every tenant or soldier or policeman he came upon, hopeful for just one witness, László got nothing but the same blank stare so many others received in the search for missing women after the war—all those families who eventually found peace by pretending that their wives or mothers or daughters had really died, burying them in proper ceremonies, their caskets and urns empty of bodies and ash; or that they were still alive, somewhere out there, emigrated to the west, enjoying happiness and prosperity; or that they'd never existed at all, removing their photos from walls and scrapbooks and family albums and tossing them into the fire. As the weeks and then months ticked by, László came to realize that what he feared the most was not Mária's disappearance but her return, that he would somehow have to find the words that would both console and still let him continue on beside her. So what László finally did, after a year had gone by, was mutter something to his father, Boldizsár—whose health was failing by then—about it being 1946 and the country in ruins and the Soviets not making any plans to leave, and the next day he gathered up his and Mária's son, Krisztián, and headed west, intending to write of his whereabouts to the family once he knew what it was. When he finally settled in Canada, he told everyone that Mária had died from the wounds inflicted upon her by the soldiers, and hoped he was right. As for Krisztián, then aged two, László waited a decade and then simply said, 'Your mother died in the war,' and let the kid's lack of memories do the rest.

The problems began three decades later, in 1975, by which point the rest of László's siblings—István, Adél and Anikó—had also left Hungary for Canada, and settled into low-paying jobs, and raised children who they hoped would do much better than they had. It was Adél, two years younger than László but still fifty-one at the time this all happened, who first caught a glimpse of Mária at the intersection of Yonge and King, where Adél worked as a janitor in an office building. The rule in the family was that Mária wasn't to be talked about, mainly for Krisztián's sake, but also for László's (though both Adél and Anikó sometimes wondered why they'd worked so hard to spare László, since it was Mária, not him, who'd truly suffered). Yet this sighting was so unnerving Adél just had to bring it up—'I saw the strangest thing the other day; I'm sure it was Mária . . . '—at which point István, older than László by a year, yelled out, 'This is great cake!' as if he could change the subject. But Adél caught his signal in time and went into a long phony coughing fit that made everyone jump up to help her and forget what she'd just said.

Adél, who was twenty-one at the time of the siege of Budapest, had seen what happened to women afterwards because she saw what had happened to Mária when she finally turned up, very much alive, six weeks after László and Krisztián left for Canada. She was in the care of Béla Kerepesi, a decorated war hero and communist, who sent word to Boldizsár that the family should come see her, also warning them that her memory had only recently returned, that she was 'still fragile, almost broken,' and needed to be treated gently. Boldizsár mulled it over for a few days, then called together István, Adél and Anikó to give them the news, insisting that the rest of the family should not know about this—Mária's survival—at least not yet, not until they'd gone and seen her and determined the extent of the damage, and under no circumstances should they tell her where László and Krisztián had gone. When they finally had gone to Béla's place, everyone acted toward Mária as if nothing had happened. It was easier to do this than try to imagine what sort of sympathy such a person might need. In fact, on that day three decades later, when Adél glimpsed Mária buying a hot dog from a vendor at Yonge and King, she saw that her sister-in-law was still wearing the look she'd worn back in 1946—like someone trying to catch a departing train. Immediately Adél stopped what she was doing, wiping dust off plastic ferns in the lobby of the Bingeman Building, and rushed outside and called to her, but Mária only looked around in bewilderment and then rushed on.

The second person in the family to see Mária was István. He was standing on a subway platform when the doors opened and she brushed by him with a plastic bag full of what looked like apples. István stepped into the car, waited as the doors closed, and then with a shudder realized who he'd just seen. As the subway pulled out of the station, his face was pressed to the glass, and his hands to either side of that, white and bloodless and mashed against the window as his eyes veered crazily from left to right searching the darkened platform for her face.

Finally, Anikó saw Mária in a Persian carpet store, or, more accurately, she heard her voice. It seemed like every time she peeled back the corner of a carpet to see the one underneath she caught Mária's low tone, speaking in Hungarian of course, haggling with a vendor over his prices, but when she dropped the carpet in surprise and looked around, there was nobody in the place other than the merchants and the other ladies who had no better way of spending a Thursday than by looking at things they couldn't afford.

The truth was, Mária was angry at the fact that the man behind the stall was charging five forints a kilo for what were clearly rotten apples, using the usual trick of displaying the ripe ones up front, but then filling your bag from the half-rotten pile under the counter. After a while, she began to shout and stamp her feet loud enough to scare off the other customers, at which point the vendor decided it wasn't worth it and gave the five forints back, waving her off with the usual curses about being a whore and her mother being a whore and her grandmother being a whore and all the rest. It was at this moment that Mária felt an inexplicable shame, not because of the vendor's language—she, like most of the women who frequented the market, was used to that—but because of the odd feeling that someone else, someone who knew her intimately, was watching. She hurried from the covered market, walked along the *körut*, down toward the Danube, where the breeze coming off the water streamed away the ghost that had suddenly latched onto her. After twenty minutes she felt armoured in the present again, protected not only against the ghost, but against the past, what she called 'the other Márias'—the one whose father had died in the First World War and whose mother had died in the second; the one with the torn thighs and face; the one who'd been taken away in a Russian military truck for more of the same but had escaped when they stopped at a checkpoint; the one who'd then wandered the city until she was discovered by Béla, a soldier who nursed her back to health, who provided medicine and doctors and therapists during the long year of her physical recovery, and who, despite having fallen in love with her, delivered news of Mária to the family patriarch, Boldizsár, when her memory returned, and then convinced her to stay with him when it became clear that the Kálmán family was not prepared to deal with the silences and weeping and raging violence, when it became clear that they did not want her. They crowded her, these Márias did, making claims on her body as if it was common property, but there was only room enough for one, and Mária, *this* Mária, was determined to make it her own. She was the wife of Béla Kerepesi, a decorated war hero, a wonderful man, and a member of Rákosi's inner circle, one who was spoken about in the Party as 'the future of communism in Hungary.'

But it was the *other* ghosts that Mária had the most trouble repressing—those people she'd once known, those gone or dead or escaped, especially Krisztián, her son. Unlike the Márias, these ghosts were not there to claim her, but to remind her, with their silences and empty gazes, that despite being ghosts they were more present, more real, than she was—that Mária was empty, that she'd become someone else too completely and too easily to say there had ever been a real Mária to begin with.

When László stepped through the door, Adél and István and Anikó would stop talking about how they'd seen her. They would stop talking altogether, as if they had nothing to talk about at all, and had been eagerly awaiting his arrival, the conversation-bringer. Naturally, László would be disconcerted by this, not being an especially talkative guy, and would wrack his brains for something with which to break the silence.

This often took the form of his retirement, since László was frightened by the time it had opened up for him, releasing odd impulses kept in check by the work he'd done for the last twenty-five years—collecting garbage for the city—impulses he hadn't even known were there. Now, it was all he could do to keep from drinking, from eating himself to death, all he could do to keep from looking at the magazines on the top rack in the corner store. Where had these appetites come from?

Of course he never told any of this to his brother and sisters, who wouldn't have understood. Instead, he asked them what hobbies he should pursue. But there was something odd—something suppressed—in their responses. For instance, he mentioned bowling, something he'd done as a teenager, heading down to the outdoor alleys with their hand-carved pins, the balls you had to hurl as hard as possible to make them go up the curved wall at the end and roll back along the trough. But when he mentioned that he was considering signing up at a place at Spadina and Eglinton that had a seniors' discount, István looked at Adél and back again. 'Spadina and Eglinton . . .' he began, 'subway stop there . . . uh, not a great place for an old man to be going to alone. I mean, it's, well . . . you never know who you might run into.'

László looked at him. He was used to István's halting manner, but this explanation was so cautious it was nonsensical.

The other thing László thought of doing was enrolling in a cooking course, something he'd only learned to do marginally well after leaving Hungary and having to raise Krisztián by himself. 'There's that place near where you work,' he said to Adél, 'that college. They have an adult cooking course Krisztián's been telling me about.'

'You cooked very well for Krisztián while he was growing up,' replied Adél frantically, 'and it's terribly ungrateful of him, after all that, to tell you to take a cooking course. If he has some bitterness over your cooking, why doesn't he just come out and say it?' she continued, glancing quickly from László to Anikó and back again.

László couldn't believe what he was hearing.

'And the other thing you don't want to do,' added Anikó without even waiting for László's next idea, 'is to shop for Persian carpets. There's no way they're going to match with the décor in your apartment.'

László didn't stick around after that, scratching his head, grabbing his jacket, and heading into the city, despite the combined efforts of István and Adél and Anikó to make him go straight home, or, better yet, if he was serious about needing a hobby, selling his place in Toronto and relocating, say, to Kitchener or Kingston or Guelph, where István had heard there was really good fly-fishing. 'Ever thought about doing more fly-fishing?' István said, to which László didn't even bother replying, except to shake his head and say, 'Maybe *you* need a hobby—all three of you.'

Anikó was convinced that the ghost of Mária was seeking out László in order to exact revenge. 'How do you know she's not looking for *us?*' István asked, angry that Anikó had never for a second thought of herself as sharing in László's guilt. 'Remember how we let Béla take her off our hands? We did nothing to help her. We never even told her we were planning on following László!'

'I don't remember that.'

'We did,' answered Adél. 'You wanted it kept from her more than any of us. You said she couldn't travel in the condition she was in. That's what you said.'

'I was trying to protect the family! What do you think would have happened if she'd had one of her hysterical fits at the border?'

'You said we should listen to Béla and let him take care of her.'

'That was Father's idea.'

'Your and Father's idea! And you were the one who talked Mária into it.'

'That's a lie! I remember she laughed and cried every time I visited her in Béla's apartment. You wouldn't believe the craziness. I visited her more than anyone else. It was the two of you who said there was no point in inviting her to come back to Mátyásföld because we were all leaving anyway.'

'Béla was a communist by then, and so was Mária! They could have given us away!' shouted Anikó, thrusting her face in front of Adél's.

'We left her no one to turn to but Béla,' whispered István.

After his sisters left, István sat in his chair and dreamed of the technology he might have had back then—Hungary in the mid-1940s—Polaroid cameras and photocopiers and tape recorders, so that he could have kept all the images and letters and conversations from that time not as they were remembered, but as they actually were. Because only he, of the three, would admit that they were guilty, that they had, each in his or her way—and however helpful or benign their motives now appeared—contributed to the distancing of Mária from the rest of the family—the slight, polite resistance they'd put up when Béla, sensing how there was no place for her at Mátyásföld, offered to keep Mária indefinitely; the regular bits of money put aside so that Anikó could go visit her with the food and clothing Mária no longer needed; the false admiration they showed on hearing that Béla was a rising star in the Communist Party; the pretence Boldizsár devised, and that they agreed upon, telling Mária that László and Krisztián had simply disappeared one day in 1946, whether they fled to the west or were arrested no one could say, so that she would stay with Béla knowing he had the best chance of finding them. The old man was hysterical when it came to Mária, forcing the three of them to swear on a Bible that they'd keep her whereabouts a secret from the rest of the family, 'from László and Krisztián and Jenö and Angyalka and Cornél and Tívadar and Margó and . . .' On and on he went, listing every relation near and far, as if the information would only be safe if the three of them heard and agreed to every single name, leaving not one crack, not one solitary leak, in the conspiracy—which, of course, was impossible. 'If any of them find out,' Boldizsár said, 'they might tell László and he'll be tortured the rest of his life out there in Canada, with no way to get back, no way to get her out. Or someone will want to bring Mária with us across the border, and you know we can't risk that with the condition she's in. Or they'll want us to stay because of her, and that's suicide with the way the ÁVÓ is coming after us, with the way that bastard, our *good friend*, Comrade Zoltán Erdész, is persecuting the family. We have to forget about her, there's no other way.'

It's true that she would regularly trash the room when they came to visit—tearing paintings from the wall, throwing glassware, even ripping the bedding into thin strips—and that it took all three of them to hold her down, and that only when Béla came back into the room did she seem neutralized, content, docile. But all of these were still excuses, ways of justifying the family's abandonment of her. They should have looked after Mária, should have made the sacrifice, instead of being so lazy, so eager to escape Hungary, that they convinced themselves that leaving her was the right thing to do.

For István knew that her trauma was only part of it. After the war she had a look to her that was terrifying, a hunger for solace so absolute it left you looking for ways to escape. She took to draping her hair over her eyes, whose glitter was not an emanation of light but its disappearance, vacuumed up, coalescing to two sparks before being swallowed. That was part of it, but there was also the family's inability—especially on the part of Boldizsár, whose dictates were absolute—to admit that in dumping Mária they were compromising their principles. Instead, they used Béla as a convenient excuse, as if it was Mária who wasn't living up to the things the family believed in—the glories of Austro-Hungarian monarchy, political conservatism, national autonomy. It was she who was consorting with a communist, the enemy, and was thus a disgrace and liability. In any case, István thought now, it was clear she'd seen Hungary's future better than anyone, and that in the absence of family she'd followed her intuition, surrounding herself with the sort of people who'd look after her, leaving no want unattended, for the next forty-five years.

It worked out better than, anyone (except Mária) could have imagined. Béla would wrap her in furs as he went out at night. The driver would bring the car around, whisking her off in a manner that was all too western, as if the Budapest she inhabited was not the city everyone else lived in, as if she, too, and not just the Kálmán family, had escaped to something better. Mária looked so good, in fact, that when Adél saw her next—as she was coming off a night shift, itchy with the disinfectants she used on toilets—it occurred to her that maybe she was not seeing a ghost at all. Mária looked radiant, what with her furs and jewellery, a face and hands untouched by work or worry.

Adél went home and phoned István and Anikó, asking them whether it was possible that Mária too had emigrated to Canada, and struck it rich, and was looking far better for the passage of years than anyone had a right to expect. 'You're crazy,' replied István; and Anikó said, 'You've been putting your nose too close to the disinfectant.'

Try as she might Adél couldn't convince them otherwise, even as she pointed out that traditionally ghosts only haunted those who had been responsible for their deaths, or who had caused them the greatest misery while they were alive, rarely appearing to those they hadn't known. Yet here was Mária holding sidewalk conversations with taxi drivers, and God knew whom else. 'No, no, no,' said István. 'What we've got to figure out is how we're going to get rid of her, exorcise her from our lives.'

Mária, for her part, would have liked to do what István, Adél and Anikó did—gone to a Catholic priest, who put them in touch with an exorcist, who in turn said the sighting of a ghost was highly unlikely, and a product of their guilt, and that what they needed was a solid hour each in the confessional. He added that he dealt with devils, and so wasn't qualified to help with ghosts, even if marrying a communist meant that Mária was most likely visiting them from hell. 'Try holy water,' he said. 'A crucifix above the door, and one around your necks.' He thought a moment more. 'And prayer, of course. As much as you can fit.' The three of them shook their heads and held a long argument about whether it was possible to follow the priest's advice.

For Mária, however, there was no such argument, she knew she couldn't observe any of the rituals. It would compromise Béla to put up a single crucifix, not to mention the risk of visiting a priest to obtain holy water. If the regime ever heard about it—if word reached Rákosi—Béla would be given a one-way ticket to Moscow, and from there who knows? House arrest. Siberian work camps. A starring role in a show trial. No, if she was going to keep the ghosts away it would have to be through some method other than the charms and totems of Christianity.

But there were so many ghosts! Anyone in her position would have had their hands full just beating back the past, but on top of it to be constantly running into the Kálmán family—to watch Adél in her janitor's apron staring after her on the street; and István in his dirty overalls on the way to tending the gardens of those who were as wealthy as he'd hoped to be after leaving Hungary; and Anikó in her Westminster Mall uniform as she went from table to table in the food court clearing away the trays and plastic cutlery and greasy plates left by those too lazy to clean up after themselves. Looking at them, Mária was amazed and terrified by her spectral knowledge, the realization that they'd been too frightened of communism to realize that the free market had its own forms of humiliation, of hardscrabble poverty.

She should have helped them while they were still in Hungary, Mária thought. She should have used Béla's connections. But the Kálmáns were so incapable of accepting her charity, so ashamed of dealing with her, that the gifts she provided would only have been further torture to them, especially Boldizsár, the grand patriarch, who'd already lost his wife and would die, just prior to the family's departure, from the thought that he was too weak to accompany them, defeated by his own anxiety over being defeated. They left the minute he was in the ground, starting out straight from the cemetery. All along, Boldizsár had kept piling on the reasons for why the family should let Béla keep her, why she should be abandoned—playing up his old age, his weakness, his need for sleep and peace and quiet, in order to prepare himself for the trek to the west. In fact, he was the reason she'd agreed to stay with Béla, the sight of Boldizsár as he looked away from her, the failure she reminded him of, his inability to protect a family he felt responsible for. She could shrink him with a glance, as if the sight of Mária's face stripped him of the beliefs that let him function in the world, and in a rush brought home his helplessness, his dependence on chance, his incapacity to even *know* his fate, much less influence it. In the end, Mária couldn't stand how sorry she felt for him.

Still, there was more she might have done, not just then, but later, once the communists came fully into power. She might have gotten Boldiszár medication for his heart and nerves, and maybe then everyone else would have stayed, because she'd shown Boldizsár the loyalty they'd been unable to show her. She could have left food for them on the doorstep, or had it delivered anonymously. She might have arranged it that they got better jobs. Or asked Béla to stop their harassment at the hands of the ÁVÓ—especially that bastard Zoltán Erdész, who wanted the villa for himself—for their past political allegiances, their Catholicism, their refusal to join the Party. But she'd never done any of this, and most of it was conjecture anyhow, things as they might have been. What she regretted most was that she'd felt too unprotected—from what had happened to her, from the past—and too busy getting that protection to realize that with the loss of the family she'd lost a far more crucial link, for they were her only point of contact with László and Krisztián. At night, as the driver guided Béla and her along streets, or when the two of them strolled down the *rakpart*, she wondered whether his arm around her waist, or holding her hand, was strong enough to keep her from one day wandering after those ghosts, just to see where they went. But she knew that to let go of Béla was to risk fragmentation, the falling apart of what she'd barely shored together, and which was held in place only because of him, a frame around her disintegration. Béla knew none of this, of course, only that it was possible to fall in love with someone because you could never replace what she lacked, and because of this feel a constant desire to fulfill her.

'We shall eat here tonight,' he said, taking his hand from Mária's eyes and leading her past the decaying exterior of a building into rooms of light and wine, walking backwards as he held her hands, allowing her one short glance at where she'd come from.

The family breathed a sigh of relief late in 1957 when Juliska sent Anikó a letter informing her of Mária's death, since it meant the lie they'd been telling Krisztián all those years had at last become the truth. Juliska had been caught trying to escape from the country two years prior and was rehabilitated, as best as was possible with someone who'd never been a Party member to begin with, and now shared a three-bedroom flat in Óbuda with three other families. Once in a while one of her letters would be missed by the censors in the post office and make it through to the west.

She wrote that Mária and Béla had not survived the revolution of 1956. Before the tanks had come rolling in—when it almost looked, miraculously, as if the partisans had succeeded in getting Moscow to capitulate—the two of them had been dragged from their mansion on Andrássy Boulevard and had guns put to their heads, or so the letter went, and reading it Anikó had no reason to doubt it, at least at the time.

But the night they went over to László's, she paused in the vestibule while István and Adél took off their coats and boots, and told them that while waiting for the College streetcar she'd seen Mária enter Chez Queux on the arm of a gentleman, and had decided to call out to her just as they reached the door.

'I wanted to see if you were right,' Anikó said, turning to Adél. 'I mean if Juliska got it wrong,' she continued in a hoarse whisper. 'And Mária turned! She saw me well enough, but then the gentleman she was with—he was so young and handsome *he looked like Béla!*—called to her. The look she gave me! As if I was hardly worth noticing. As if I was a beggar on the street. Then,' she hissed, 'the doorman opened the door for them. Both of them! He treated Mária as if she was as alive as you or I.'

'She's kept her looks, hasn't she?' asked Adél.

'Have you two gone insane?' murmured István. 'We're at László's!'

'It's hard to feel happy for her,' continued Adél, looking at her hands, lined with years of handling mop handles and cleanser. 'Getting to eat in places like that.'

'Are you coming inside or what?' asked László, coming out of the kitchen to greet them, holding aloft an uncorked bottle of Egri Bikavér.

It was the imploring figure of Anikó that Mária continued to see as Béla poured the wine and lifted his glass to the light and tilted it this way and that, pointing out how it coated the glass, how it flowed back. Mária was thinking she would have liked to invite Anikó inside the restaurant, that there was something in the pitiful way she'd stood holding her purse, hunched over with what looked like osteoporosis, as if her skeleton had had enough of holding up her body and decided to curl up and go to sleep inside her flesh. Life had not been kind to Anikó, and so why shouldn't Mária be kind to her, just this once, never mind that the old woman (she thought of her that way, though there was a time when they'd been the same age) was not dressed for Chez Queux? Béla, meanwhile, had stopped watching the splash and play of wine, set his glass aside, and followed Mária's look out the window, wondering what he could say that would complete her sense of loss, make her stop looking beyond him for what was missing.

After all, 1956 was still two years away, and Béla could not have known it, but they'd pack an incredible amount of life into the twenty-four months before they died, always appearing in public as the Party advised them to do, in solemn grey, clothing tailored from the finest materials but always made to look nondescript, so that no one would guess how well they were really living. In the next few weeks, it was in fact their clothing that would consume Mária's attention. He would come upon her frantically going through the closet as if there was something in there that would make her stand out even less than she already did, a disguise to throw off the pursuit of ghosts.

For they were pursuing her more than ever now. There wasn't a day Mária didn't turn a corner and find herself face to face with Anikó or István or Adél, their faces no longer betraying fear or aversion, but envy and lust. More often than not they would try to approach her, no longer content to remain on the periphery, as if they'd decided that Mária wasn't empty after all but full enough to fulfill everyone.

Anikó was the worst, the neediest, and more than once she called out, 'Mária, it's me, Anikó, remember me? Your sister-in-law. You look very fine in that overcoat. And what's that beautiful perfume you're wearing?'

At other times, the three ghosts appeared together, as if they were attempting to set themselves up in front of and behind her, cutting off all avenues of escape. But Mária knew that she would always be able to get by István, with his overwhelming guilt, since he always gave way in the last second, allowing her to jump into a car or bus or a restaurant too fine for them to follow her inside. He was the weak link, though even he attempted to get her favour, once offering a bouquet of red carnations, the official flower of Party bosses and apparatchiks, adorning every one of their corsages and buttonholes.

'What do you want?' she once asked Adél. 'How can I possibly help you?'

Adél stood there, finally put on the spot, stopped in seeking what she wanted by the fact that it had been offered to her. She hadn't considered how ashamed she'd be to ask for all the things Mária had—the clothes, the food, the luxuries—all the things Adél believed Mária could provide for them. But now, the only thing Adél could say was 'You should never forget your family; especially when they're in need.' And almost as soon as the words were spoken she looked up, afraid that clouds would close in, that buildings would shake, that the ground would open up. By the time the dizziness passed, and she wanted to beg forgiveness, Mária was gone, having fled, tears and all, down one of the streets of the fourteenth district, collapsing after an hour, sitting on the sidewalk and speaking to no one in particular about all the things that had been in her power to do for the Kálmán family in 1947. The things she hadn't done.

It was Béla who found her. He asked the driver to take him everywhere, and so he had, through the twisting alleys of districts seven, eight, nine; across the *körut*; and into district fourteen, where they found Mária crumpled into a ball under an art nouveau building, huddled there wondering why the February wind was no longer able to sweep everything behind her. Gathering her into his arms, Béla realized that the need to banish what Mária had been seeking was no longer a question of how much he wanted her to want him, but a question of keeping her alive. So for the next several days he listened to what she said in her sleep, in the fevers that overtook her sometimes for hours, and whose hallucinations played vividly across her face. Her intonation varied so much it sounded less like a monologue than a roomful of souls. Had Béla been even slightly religious, anything other than the atheist he was, he might even have thought there were ghosts massing inside her, that she was channelling voices from the other side.

Chief among these was István, who finally lost his temper with Anikó and Adél and their belief that Mária's death had been misreported, that she'd somehow immigrated to Canada and was among them. Their envy of her good life, and attempts to speak with her, to flatter her, to curry favour, sickened him, even after he'd agreed to help. 'She wants us to leave her alone,' he told them. 'She's made that very clear!'

'I don't know how she did it,' replied Anikó. 'She never had any more on the ball than any of us, but she came over here and got rich, and we came over here and we are lucky to have a roof over our heads!'

'C'mon,' István said. 'Heléna's in university. Krisztián's a professor. Maybe we didn't do so well, but our children have a future.'

'What about us?' yelled Adél. 'What about our future?'

'What makes you think you deserve one?' howled István. 'What makes you think any of us deserve one?'

The next day Anikó and Adél were back on the street, dressed in the best dresses they'd managed to find inside a box of clothing they'd long ago given up on wearing, dresses they cut along the seams and resewed to fit. Because this time there would be no fooling around with Mária—they were bringing Krisztián. They showed up at his office at the University of Toronto and put on the elderly aunt act, telling him they were out for a walk and decided to see where he worked, and wondered whether or not he was interested in treating them to lunch on his big university professor's salary. They chose Chez Queux, and marched him along, pretending to hold onto his elbows for support.

When they arrived they saw that a table had been reserved for them, and for Mária too, who was over by the window wearing a dress of the whitest silk, with the usual handsome man leaning across and holding her hand and placing a dossier between them.

After the waiter brought them to their table, Adél and Anikó turned to Krisztián and asked if he'd like to meet his mother, both their eyes swinging in the direction of the couple. Béla meanwhile had had enough of the voices and names issuing from Mária for the last two weeks, of watching her being torn apart, and decided that the only way to dispel them would be to find out what had happened to each and every one, her lost and absent relatives, even if it meant finding out, once and for all, that what Mária was missing would be missing forever, and that, because of this, he would only ever be what she loved second best.

'I searched everywhere,' he whispered consolingly, taking her face in his hands in the hope that his touch would make her eyes return from the distance she'd been staring into, tears streaming down her cheeks and along her jawbone and dripping off her chin. But she would not focus on him, and finally he had to stand, and pull the pictures from the file, and get between her and the gaze she was directing across the room at a young man and a couple of old ladies. 'They didn't make it,' he said. 'None of them.' She finally looked at him in panic. 'I'm sorry,' he said. 'There were a lot of people who didn't get across.' He wanted to say more but didn't know what, and instead he shifted his feet, holding the pictures he no longer knew what to do with, wondering for the first time if Mária's visions were not so much guilt but a way of wondering what life might have been like if she'd left, gone west instead of staying with him, spinning fantasies of the next forty-five years of the Kálmán family's existence.

'He didn't make it?' she asked, reaching for the picture of Krisztián as if he was there, as if she might with a curled finger again caress his face, even as she knew that what she was seeing, for the first time since Béla had found her huddled in the street, was not a ghost but an image. 'I wanted so much to know he was alive,' she said, 'to know he had a happy life.' Béla nodded, and said 'Yes,' and then slowly put the photographs back into the dossier as the curtains blew in through the window and what ghosts there were withdrew forever. Because Adél and Anikó *had* withdrawn, frantically apologizing—'She was there! A second ago! We saw her!'—trying to keep up to Krisztián as he stormed out of Chez Queux and away from them, wondering if either of his aunts had any idea how often he'd sat in bed as a boy, how often he still did, haunted by what wasn't there—the memory of a face, a touch, the voice you most wanted to hear—as if absence could live on in you like a ghost.

2012

# Madeleine Thien

*b.* 1974

Born in Vancouver, British Columbia, to Chinese-Malaysian parents after they and her older brother and sister emigrated from Malaysia, Madeleine Thien obtained her BA (1997) and her MFA (2001) from the University of British Columbia. She is the author of one collection of short stories, *Simple Recipes* (2001), and two novels, *Certainty* (2006), which has been translated into more than 15 languages, and *Dogs at the Perimeter* (2011), which has been translated into eight languages. She now lives in Montreal.

Although her stories are not autobiographical, she uses facts and details from the areas where she dwells. In 'Simple Recipes', the title story of her collection, a young woman searches her memories to locate that unique moment when her family and she herself lost faith in the family unit. She seeks to understand the earlier events that have shaped her life.

## Simple Recipes

There is a simple recipe for making rice. My father taught it to me when I was a child. Back then, I used to sit up on the kitchen counter watching him, how he sifted the grains in his hands, sure and quick, removing pieces of dirt or sand, tiny imperfections. He swirled his hands through the water and it turned cloudy. When he scrubbed the grains clean, the sound was as big as a field of insects. Over and over, my father rinsed the rice, drained the water, then filled the pot again.

The instructions are simple. Once the washing is done, you measure the water this way—by resting the tip of your index finger on the surface of the rice. The water should reach the bend of your first knuckle. My father did not need instructions or measuring cups. He closed his eyes and felt for the waterline.

Sometimes I still dream my father, his bare feet flat against the floor, standing in the middle of the kitchen. He wears old buttoned shirts and faded sweatpants drawn at the waist. Surrounded by the gloss of the kitchen counters, the sharp angles of the stove, the fridge, the shiny sink, he looks out of place. This memory of him is so strong, sometimes it stuns me, the detail with which I can see it.

Every night before dinner, my father would perform this ritual—rinsing and draining, then setting the pot in the cooker. When I was older, he passed this task on to me but I never did it with the same care. I went through the motions, splashing the water around, jabbing my finger down to measure the water level. Some nights the rice was a mushy gruel. I worried that I could not do so simple a task right. 'Sorry,' I would say to the table, my voice soft and embarrassed. In answer, my father would keep eating, pushing the rice into his mouth as if he never expected anything different, as if he noticed no difference between what he did so well and I so poorly. He would eat every last mouthful, his chopsticks walking quickly across the plate. Then he would rise, whistling, and clear the table, every motion so clean and sure, I would be convinced by him that all was well in the world.

*

My father is standing in the middle of the kitchen. In his right hand he holds a plastic bag filled with water. Caught inside the bag is a live fish.

The fish is barely breathing, though its mouth opens and closes. I reach up and touch it through the plastic bag, trailing my fingers along the gills, the soft, muscled body, pushing my finger overtop the eyeball. The fish looks straight at me, flopping sluggishly from side to side.

My father fills the kitchen sink. In one swift motion he overturns the bag and the fish comes sailing out with the water. It curls and jumps. We watch it closely, me on my tiptoes, chin propped up on the counter. The fish is the length of my arm from wrist to elbow. It floats in place, brushing up against the sides of the sink.

I keep watch over the fish while my father begins the preparations for dinner. The fish folds its body, trying to turn or swim, the water nudging overtop. Though I ripple tiny circles around it with my fingers, the fish stays still, bobbing side-to-side in the cold water.

For many hours at a time, it was just the two of us. While my mother worked and my older brother played outside, my father and I sat on the couch, flipping channels. He loved cooking shows. We watched *Wok with Yan*, my father passing judgement on Yan's methods. I was enthralled when Yan transformed orange peels into swans. My father sniffed. 'I can do that,' he said. 'You don't have to be a genius to do that.' He placed a sprig of green onion in water and showed me how it bloomed like a flower. 'I know many tricks like this,' he said. 'Much more than Yan.'

Still, my father made careful notes when Yan demonstrated Peking Duck. He chuckled heartily at Yan's punning. 'Take a wok on the wild side!' Yan said, pointing his spatula at the camera.

'Ha ha!' my father laughed, his shoulders shaking. '*Wok* on the wild side!'

In the mornings, my father took me to school. At three o'clock, when we came home again, I would rattle off everything I learned that day. 'The brachiosaurus,' I informed him, 'eats only soft vegetables.'

My father nodded. 'That is like me. Let me see your forehead.' We stopped and faced each other in the road. 'You have a high forehead,' he said, leaning down to take a closer look. 'All smart people do.'

I walked proudly, stretching my legs to match his steps. I was overjoyed when my feet kept time with his, right, then left, then right, and we walked like a single unit. My father was the man of tricks, who sat for an hour mining a watermelon with a circular spoon, who carved the rind into a castle.

My father was born in Malaysia and he and my mother immigrated to Canada several years before I was born, first settling in Montreal, then finally in Vancouver.

While I was born into the persistence of the Vancouver rain, my father was born in the wash of a monsoon country. When I was young, my parents tried to teach me their language but it never came easily to me. My father ran his thumb gently over my mouth, his face kind, as if trying to see what it was that made me different.

My brother was born in Malaysia but when he immigrated with my parents to Canada the language left him. Or he forgot it, or he refused it, which is also common, and this made my father angry. 'How can a child forget a language?' he would ask my mother. 'It is because the child is lazy. Because the child chooses not to remember.' When he was twelve years old, my brother stayed away in the afternoons. He drummed the soccer ball up and down the back alley, returning home only at dinner time. During the day, my mother worked as a sales clerk at the Woodward's store downtown, in the building with the red revolving W on top.

In our house, the ceilings were yellowed with grease. Even the air was heavy with it. I remember that I loved the weight of it, the air that was dense with the smell of countless meals cooked in a tiny kitchen, all those good smells jostling for space.

The fish in the sink is dying slowly. It has a glossy sheen to it, as if its skin is made of shining minerals. I want to prod it with both hands, its body tense against the pressure of my fingers. If I hold it tightly, I imagine I will be able to feel its fluttering heart. Instead, I lock eyes with the fish. *You're feeling verrrry sleepy*, I tell it. *You're getting verrrry tired.*

Beside me, my father chops green onions quickly. He uses a cleaver that he says is older than I am by many years. The blade of the knife rolls forward and backward, loops of green onion gathering in a pyramid beside my father's wrist. When he is done, he rolls his sleeve back from his right hand, reaches in through the water and pulls the plug.

The fish in the sink floats and we watch it in silence. The water level falls beneath its gills, beneath its belly. It drains and leaves the sink dry. The fish is lying on its side, mouth open and its body heaving. It leaps sideways and hits the sink. Then up again. It curls and snaps, lunging for its own tail. The fish sails into the air, dropping hard. It twitches violently.

My father reaches in with his bare hands. He lifts the fish out by the tail and lays it gently on the counter. While holding it steady with one hand, he hits the head with the flat of the cleaver. The fish falls still, and he begins to clean it.

*

In my apartment, I keep the walls scrubbed clean. I open the windows and turn the fan on whenever I prepare a meal. My father bought me a rice cooker when I first moved into my own apartment, but I use it so rarely it stays in the back of the cupboard, the cord wrapped neatly around its belly. I have no longing for the meals themselves, but I miss the way we sat down together, our bodies leaning hungrily forward while my father, the magician, unveiled plate after plate. We laughed and ate, white steam fogging my mother's glasses until she had to take them off and lay them on the table. Eyes closed, she would eat, crunchy vegetables gripped in her chopsticks, the most vivid green.

*

My brother comes into the kitchen and his body is covered with dirt. He leaves a thin trail of it behind as he walks. The soccer ball, muddy from outside, is encircled in one arm. Brushing past my father, his face is tense.

Beside me, my mother sprinkles garlic onto the fish. She lets me slide one hand underneath the fish's head, cradling it, then bending it backwards so that she can fill the fish's insides with ginger. Very carefully, I turn the fish over. It is firm and slippery, and beaded with tiny, sharp scales.

At the stove, my father picks up an old teapot. It is full of oil and he pours the oil into the wok. It falls in a thin ribbon. After a moment, when the oil begins crackling, he lifts the fish up and drops it down into the wok. He adds water and the smoke billows up. The sound of the fish frying is like tires on gravel, a sound so loud it drowns out all other noises. Then my father steps out from the smoke. 'Spoon out the rice,' he says as he lifts me down from the counter.

My brother comes back into the room, his hands muddy and his knees the colour of dusty brick. His soccer shorts flutter against the backs of his legs. Sitting down, he makes an angry face. My father ignores him.

Inside the cooker, the rice is flat like a pie. I push the spoon in, turning the rice over, and the steam shoots up in a hot mist and condenses on my skin. While my father moves his arms delicately over the stove, I begin dishing the rice out: first for my father, then my mother, then my brother, then myself. Behind me the fish is cooking quickly. In a crockery pot, my father steams cauliflower, stirring it round and round.

My brother kicks at a table leg.

'What's the matter?' my father asks.

He is quiet for a moment, then he says, 'Why do we have to eat fish?'

'You don't like it?'

My brother crosses his arms against his chest. I see the dirt lining his arms, dark and hardened. I imagine chipping it off his body with a small spoon.

'I don't like the eyeball there. It looks sick.'

My mother tuts. Her nametag is still clipped to her blouse. It says *Woodward's*, and then, *Sales Clerk*. 'Enough,' she says, hanging her purse on the back of the chair. 'Go wash your hands and get ready for supper.'

My brother glares, just for a moment. Then he begins picking at the dirt on his arms. I bring plates of rice to the table. The dirt flies off his skin, speckling the tablecloth. 'Stop it,' I say crossly.

'*Stop it*,' he says, mimicking me.

'Hey!' My father hits his spoon against the counter. It *pings*, high-pitched. He points at my brother. 'No fighting in this house.'

My brother looks at the floor, mumbles something, and then shuffles away from the table. As he moves farther away, he beings to stamp his feet.

Shaking her head, my mother takes her jacket off. It slides from her shoulders. She says something to my father in the language I can't understand. He merely shrugs his shoulders. And then he replies, and I think his words are so familiar, as if they are words I should know, as if maybe I did know them once but then I forgot them. The language that they speak is full of soft vowels, words running together so that I can't make out the gaps where they pause for breath.

My mother told me once about guilt. Her own guilt she held in the palm of her hands, like an offering. But your guilt is different, she said. You do not need to hold on to it. Imagine this, she said, her hands running along my forehead, then up into my hair. Imagine, she said. Picture it, and what do you see?

A bruise on the skin, wide and black.

A bruise, she said. Concentrate on it. Right now, it's a bruise. But if you concentrate, you can shrink it, compress it to the size of a pinpoint. And then, if you want to, if you see it, you can blow it off your body like a speck of dirt.

She moved her hands along my forehead.

I tried to picture what she said. I pictured blowing it away like so much nothing, just these little pieces that didn't mean anything, this complicity that I could magically walk away from. She made me believe in the strength of my own thoughts, as if I could make appear what had never existed. Or turn it around. Flip it over so many times you just lose sight of it, you lose the tail end and the whole thing disappears into smoke.

My father pushes at the fish with the edge of his spoon. Underneath, the meat is white and the juice runs down along the side. He lifts a piece and lowers it carefully onto my plate.

Once more, his spoon breaks skin. Gingerly, my father lifts another piece and moves it towards my brother.

'I don't want it,' my brother says.

My father's hand wavers. 'Try it,' he says, smiling. 'Take a wok on the wild side.'

'No.'

My father sighs and places the piece on my mother's plate. We eat in silence, scraping our spoons across the dishes. My parents use chopsticks, lifting their bowls and motioning the food into their mouths. The smell of food fills the room.

Savouring each mouthful, my father eats slowly, head tuned to the flavours in his mouth. My mother takes her glasses off, the lenses fogged, and lays them on the table. She eats with her head bowed down, as if in prayer.

Lifting a stem of cauliflower to his lips, my brother sighs deeply. He chews, and then his face changes. I have a sudden picture of him drowning, his hair waving like grass. He coughs, spitting the mouthful back onto his plate. Another cough. He reaches for his throat, choking.

My father slams his chopsticks down on the table. In a single movement, he reaches across, grabbing my brother by the shoulder. 'I have tried,' he is saying. 'I don't know what kind of son you are. To be so ungrateful.' His other hand sweeps by me and bruises into my brother's face.

My mother flinches. My brother's face is red and his mouth is open. His eyes are wet.

Still coughing, he grabs a fork, tines aimed at my father, and then in an unthinking moment, he heaves it at him. It strikes my father in the chest and drops.

'I hate you! You're just an asshole, you're just a fucking asshole chink!' My brother holds his plate in his hands. He smashes it down and his food scatters across the table. He is coughing and spitting. 'I wish you weren't my father! I wish you were dead.'

My father's hand falls again. This time pounding downwards. I close my eyes. All I can hear is someone screaming. There is a loud voice. I stand awkwardly, my hands covering my eyes.

'Go to your room,' my father says, his voice shaking.

And I think he is talking to me so I remove my hands.

But he is looking at my brother. And my brother is looking at him, his small chest heaving.

A few minutes later, my mother beings clearing the table, face weary as she scrapes the dishes one by one over the garbage.

I move away from my chair, past my mother, onto the carpet and up the stairs.

Outside my brother's bedroom, I crouch against the wall. When I step forward and look, I see my father holding the bamboo pole between his hands. The pole is smooth. The long grains, fine as hair, are pulled together, at intervals, jointed. My brother is lying on the floor, as if thrown down and dragged there. My father raises the pole into the air.

I want to cry out. I want to move into the room between them, but I can't.

It is like a tree falling, beginning to move, a slow arc through the air.

The bamboo drops silently. It rips the skin on my brother's back. I cannot hear any sound. A line of blood edges quickly across his body.

The pole rises and again comes down. I am afraid of bones breaking.

My father lifts his arms once more.

On the floor, my brother cries into the carpet, pawing at the ground. His knees folded into his chest, the crown of his head burrowing down. His back is hunched over and I can see his spine, little bumps on his skin.

The bamboo smashes into bone and the scene in my mind bursts into a million white pieces.

My mother picks me up off the floor, pulling me across the hall, into my bedroom, into bed. Everything is wet, the sheets, my hands, her body, my face, and she soothes me with words I cannot understand because all I can hear is screaming. She rubs her cool hands against my forehead. 'Stop,' she says. 'Please stop,' but I feel loose, deranged, as if everything in the known world is ending right there.

In the morning, I wake up to the sound of oil in the pan and the smell of French toast. I can hear my mother bustling around, putting dishes in the cupboards.

No one says anything when my brother doesn't come down for breakfast. My father piles French toast and syrup onto a plate and my mother pours a glass of milk. She takes everything upstairs to my brother's bedroom.

As always, I follow my father around the kitchen. I track his footprints, follow behind him and hide in the shadow of his body. Every so often, he reaches down and ruffles my hair with his hands. We cast a spell, I think. The way we move in circles, how he cooks without thinking because this is the task that comes to him effortlessly. He smiles down at me, but when he does this, it somehow breaks the spell. My father stands in place, hands dropping to his sides as if he has forgotten what he was doing mid-motion. On the walls, the paint is peeling and the floor, unswept in days, leaves little pieces of dirt stuck to our feet.

My persistence, I think, my unadulterated love, confuse him. With each passing day, he knows I will find it harder to ignore what I can't comprehend, that I will be unable to separate one part of him from another. The unconditional quality of my love for him will not last forever, just as my brother's did not. My father stands in the middle of the kitchen, unsure. Eventually, my mother comes downstairs again and puts her arms around him and holds him, whispering something to him, words that to me are meaningless and incomprehensible. But she offers them to him, sound after sound, in a language that was stolen from some other place, until he drops his head and remembers where he is.

Later on, I lean against the door frame upstairs and listen to the sound of a metal fork scraping against a dish. My mother is already there, her voice rising and falling. She is moving the fork across the plate, offering my brother pieces of French toast.

I move towards the bed, the carpet scratchy, until I can touch the wooden bed-frame with my hands. My mother is seated there, and I go to her, reaching my fingers out to the buttons on her cuff and twisting them over to catch the light.

'Are you eating?' I ask my brother.

He starts to cry. I look at him, his face half hidden in the blankets.

'Try and eat,' my mother says softly.

He only cries harder but there isn't any sound. The pattern of sunlight on his blanket moves with his body. His hair is pasted down with sweat and his head moves forward and backward like an old man's.

At some point I know my father is standing at the entrance of the room but I cannot turn to look at him. I want to stay where I am, facing the wall. I'm afraid that if I turn around and go to him, I will be complicit, accepting a portion of guilt, no matter how small that piece. I do not know how to prevent this from happening again, though now I know, in the end, it will break us apart. This violence will turn all my love to shame and grief. So I stand there, not looking at him or my brother. Even my father, the magician, who can make something beautiful out of nothing, he just stands and watches.

A face changes over time, it becomes clearer. In my father's face, I have seen everything pass. Anger that has stripped it of anything recognizable, so that it is only a face of bones and skin. And then, at other times, so much pain that it is unbearable, his face so full of grief it might dissolve. How to reconcile all that I know of him and still love him? For a long time, I thought it was not possible. When I was a child, I did not love my father because he was complicated, because he was human, because he needed me to. A child does not know yet how to love a person that way.

How simple it should be. Warm water running over, the feel of the grains between my hands, the sound of it like stones running along the pavement. My father would rinse the rice over and over, sifting it between his fingertips, searching for the impurities, pulling them out. A speck, barely visible, resting on the tip of his finger.

If there were some recourse, I would take it. A cupful of grains in my open hand, a smoothing out, finding the impurities, then removing them piece by piece. And then, to be satisfied with what remains.

Somewhere in my memory, a fish in the sink is dying slowly. My father and I watch as the water runs down.

2001

# POETRY

# The Elements of Poetry

## INTRODUCTION

### What Good Is Poetry?

If you ask a poet, 'What good is poetry?' you may get an answer like Marianne Moore's 'I, too, dislike it', or in A.M. Klein's phrasing, the poet 'simply does not count'. The modern poet is not likely to make grandiose claims for his or her craft, and we will try not to betray that honest and tough-minded attitude.

Poetry, with all its artificial rules, is essentially a game for two—a writer and a reader. The reader must be willing to play, or else the game will not work. Physical games have practical benefits. They promote physical fitness that is necessary to good health. A language game like poetry also has its uses, but they are by-products rather than its proper ends. Poetry exercises a valuable part of the mind: the imagination. Poetry can also help us learn to control and respond to language. But it is a game first of all, where, as Robert Frost said, 'the work is play for mortal stakes'.

A game can require great exertion, but it must reward that exertion with pleasure or there is no point playing it. Anyone who has ever responded to a nursery rhyme or to a well-crafted song lyric has experienced the fundamental pleasure of poetry. More complicated and sophisticated poems offer essentially the same kind of pleasure. We labour to understand the rules of the game so that we do not need to think about them when we are playing. We master technique to make our execution easier. When we are really proficient the work becomes play.

### The Qualities of Poetry

Part of the pleasure of poetry lies in its relation to music. It awakens in us a fundamental response to rhythmic repetitions of various kinds. Learning to read poetry is partly a matter of learning to respond to subtle and delicate rhythmic patterns as well as to the most obvious and persistent ones. But poetry is not just a kind of music. It is a special combination of musical and linguistic qualities—of sounds regarded both as pure sound and as meaningful speech. In particular, poetry is expressive language. It does for us what Samuel Beckett's character Watt wanted done for him:

> Not that Watt desired information, for he did not. But he desired words to be applied to his situation, to Mr Knott, to the house, to the grounds, to his duties, to the stairs, to his bedroom, to the kitchen, and in a general way to the conditions of being in which he found himself.

Poetry performs this function of applying words to our situations, to the conditions of being in which we find ourselves. By doing so, it gives us pleasure because it helps us articulate our states of mind. The poets we value are those who speak for us and help us learn to speak for ourselves. A revealing instance of a poet's learning to apply words to his own situation, and finding in their order and symmetry a soothing pleasure, is captured by James Joyce. Here we see a nine-year-old child making an important discovery about the nature and uses of poetry:

[*Bray: in the parlour of the house in Martello Terrace*]

MR VANCE (*comes in with a stick*) . . . O, you know, he'll have to apologise,
Mr Joyce.

MRS JOYCE O yes . . . Do you hear that, Jim?

MR VANCE Or else—if he doesn't—the eagles'll come and pull out his eyes.

MRS JOYCE O, but I'm sure he will apologise.

JOYCE (*under the table, to himself*)
—Pull out his eyes,
Apologise,
Apologise,
Pull out his eyes.
Apologise,
Pull out his eyes,
Pull out his eyes,
Apologise.

The coincidence of sound that links the four-word phrase 'Pull out his eyes' with the four-syllable word 'Apologise' offers the child a refuge from Mr Vance that is far more secure than the table under which he is hiding. In his novel *A Portrait of the Artist as a Young Man*, Joyce uses this moment from his own life to illustrate his protagonist's vocation for verbal art.

As a poem, the child's effort here is a simple one, but it achieves a real effect because of the contrast between the meaning of its two basic lines that sound so much alike. Gentle, conciliatory 'apologise' and fiercely vindictive 'pull out his eyes' should not fit together so neatly, the poem implies, and in doing so, it makes an ethical criticism of Mr Vance, who, after all, coupled them in the first place. Young Joyce's deliberate wit has made a poem from the old man's witless tirade.

Marianne Moore qualifies her dislike of poetry this way:

I, too, dislike it: there are things that are important beyond all this fiddle.
    Reading it, however, with a perfect contempt of it, one discovers in
    it after all, a place for the genuine.
        Hands that can grasp, eyes
        that can dilate, hair that can rise
            if it must, these things are important not because a

high-sounding interpretation can be put upon them but because they are
    useful. . . .

And Klein completes his evaluation of the poet thus:

> Therefore he seeds illusions. Look, he is
> the nth Adam taking a green inventory
> in world but scarcely uttered, naming, praising,
> the flowering fiats in the meadow, the
> syllabled fur, stars aspirate, the pollen
> whose sweet collusion sounds eternally.
> For to praise
>
> the world—he, solitary man—is breath
> to him. Until it has been praised, that part
> has not been. Item by exciting item—
> air to his lungs, and pressured blood to his heart—
> they are pulsated, and breathed, until they map,
> not the world's, but his own body's chart!
>
> And now in imagination he has climbed
> another planet, the better to look
> with single camera view upon this earth—
> its total scope, and each afflated tick,
> its talk, its trick, its tracklessness—and this,
> this, he would like to write down in a book!
>
> To find a new function for the *déclassé* craft
> archaic like the fletcher's; to make a new thing;
> to say the word that will become sixth sense;
> perhaps by necessity and indirection bring
> new forms to life, anonymously, new creeds—
> O, somehow pay back the daily larcenies of the lung!

Poetry, then, is a kind of musical word game that we value because of its expressive qualities. Not all poems are equally musical, or equally playful, or equally expressive. Nor are they necessarily musical, playful, or expressive in the same way. But we may consider these three qualities the basic constituents of poetry so that we may examine some of the various ways in which poets combine and modify them in making different kinds of poems. Recognizing various poetic possibilities is important to the study of poetry because the greatest single problem for the reader of a poem is the problem of tact.

## Tact

Tact acknowledges the diversity of poetry. A tactful approach to a poem is one that is appropriate to the special nature of the poem under consideration. Reading a poem for the first time ought to be a little like meeting a person for the first time. An initial conversation may lead to friendship, dislike, indifference, or any of dozens of other shades of attitude from love to hate. If the relationship progresses, it will gain in intimacy as surface politeness is replaced by exchange of ideas and feelings at a deeper level.

Of course, we need to speak the same language if we are to communicate in any meaningful way. So we generally make friends with people who speak the same language or languages we do, and we read poems written in those languages. But speaking the same language means more than just inheriting or acquiring the same linguistic patterns. Some poems, like some people, seem to talk to us not merely in our native language but in our own idiom as well. We understand them easily and naturally. Others speak to us in ways that seem strange and puzzling. With poems, as with people, our first response to the puzzling should be a polite effort to eliminate misunderstanding. We need not adopt any false reverence before a poem of an earlier age, but we should treat it with respect, paying attention to its words, trying to adjust to its idiom. This may turn out to be rewarding, or it may not. But only after we have made an honest attempt to understand a poem are we entitled to reject or accept it.

Since the English language has changed considerably over the centuries and continues to change, a greater effort is often required to understand an older poem than a modern one. Notions of what poetry is and should be have also changed over time and continue to change. The poetry game has not always been played by the same rules. The difference between a love lyric by an Elizabethan sonneteer and a contemporary poem of love may be as great as the difference between Elizabethan tennis and modern tennis. The Elizabethans played tennis indoors in an intricately walled court that required great finesse to master all its angles. The modern game is flat and open, all power serves and rushes to the net. Which ought to remind us that Robert Frost likened free verse (verse with unrhymed, irregular lines) to playing tennis with the net down. Such a game would make points easy to score but would not be much fun to play. Poetry, like tennis, depends on artificial rules and hindrances. These arbitrary restrictions are what give it its game-like quality.

Unlike the rules of tennis, the rules of poetry have never been written down. Although many critics over the years have tried to produce a 'poetics' that would operate like a code of rules, they have always failed because poetry is always changing. In fact poetic 'rules' are not really rules but conventions, which are always changing and which must change to prevent poems from being turned out on a mass scale according to formulas. All poets learn from their predecessors, but any poet who merely imitates them produces flat, stale poems. A poet is above all one who finds a unique idiom, a special voice for his or her own poetry. The tactful reader quickly picks up on the conventions operating in any particular poem and pays careful attention to the idiom of every poet, in order to understand and appreciate or criticize each separate poetic performance.

The following parts of this discussion are designed to help the reader of poetry acquire tact. They are arranged to present certain basic elements drawn from the whole system of poetic conventions. Tact itself cannot be 'learned' because it is of the spirit. But if the instinct for it is there, tact can be developed and refined through conscious effort.

## EXPRESSION

### Drama and Narration

Drama usually implies actors on a stage speaking to one another in a sequence of situations or scenes. A short poem with a single speaker is dramatic only in a limited sense. Yet *some* poems are very dramatic; the element of drama in them must be grasped if we are to understand them at all. And *all* poems are dramatic to some extent, however slight.

We can approach the dramatic element in poetry by assuming that every poem shares some qualities with a speech in a play: that it is spoken aloud by a 'speaker' who is a character in a situation that implies a certain relationship with other characters; and we assume that this speech is 'overheard' by an audience. We may have to modify these assumptions. For instance, the poem may be more like a soliloquy or unspoken thought than like a part of a dialogue. Or it may seem more like a letter or a song than a speech. Still, in approaching our poem we must make a tentative decision about who the speaker is, what the situation is, and whom the speaker seems to be addressing. In poems that are especially dramatic, the interest of the poem will depend on the interest of the character and situation presented. But because dramatic poems are short and compressed in comparison with plays, the reader must usually do a good deal of guessing or inferring in order to grasp the elements of character and situation. How well people read a poem will depend on how plausible their inferences are.

Consider the following lines from the beginning of a dramatic poem by Robert Bringhurst. This imaginary speech is attributed to Francesco Petrarca, the fourteenth-century Italian poet, scholar, and humanist, better known as Petrarch.

> I, Francesco, this April day . . .
> death stirs like a bud in the sunlight, and Urban
> has got off his French duff and re-entered Rome
> and for three years running has invited me to Rome . . .
> over the bright hills and down the Cassia,
> back through Arezzo one more time . . .
> my age sixty-five and my birthday approaching,
> the muggers on the streets in broad daylight in Rome,
> the hawks and the buzzards. . . .
>                                         Take this down.
>
> No one has thought too deeply of death.
> So few have left anything toward or against it.
> Peculiar, since thinking of death can never be
> wasted thinking, nor can it be come to
> too quickly. A man carries his death with him
> everywhere, waiting, but seldom thinking
> of waiting. Death is uncommonly like the soul.
> What I own other than that ought to fall

of its own weight and settle. But beggars and tycoons
and I are concerned with our possessions,
and a man with a reputation for truth
must have one also for precision.
                                        I leave
my soul to my saviour, my corpse to the earth.
And let it be done without any parades.
I don't care very much where I'm buried,
so it please God and whoever is digging.
Still, you will ask. You will badger me.
If I am dead you will badger each other.
But don't lug my bones through the public streets
in a box to be gabbled at and gawked at and followed.
Let it be done without any parades.

If I die here in Padova, bury me here
near the friend who is dead who invited me here.
If I die on my farm, you can use the chapel
I mean to build there, if I ever build it.
If not, try the village down the road.

If in Venezia, near the doorway.
If in Milano, next to the wall.
In Pavia, anywhere. Or if in Rome—
if in Rome, in the centre, of course, if there's room.
These are the places I think I might die in
in Italy.
          Or if I happen to be in Parma,
there is the cathedral, of which for some reason
I am the archdeacon. But I will avoid
going to Parma. It would scarcely be possible,
I suppose, in Parma, not to have a parade.

At any rate, put what flesh I have left
in a church. A Franciscan church if there is one.
I don't want it feeding a tree from which
rich people's children swipe apples.

Two hundred ducats go to the church in which
I am buried, with another hundred to be given
out in that parish to the poor, in small doses.
The money to the church, let it buy a piece of land
and the land be rented and the rental from the land
pay for an annual mass in my name.

I will be fitter company in that sanctuary
then, present in spirit and name only,
than this way, muttering to the blessed virgin
through my hemorrhoids and bad teeth. I should be glad
to be rid of this sagging carcass.
                                        Don't write that.

Now consider, in order, each of these questions:

1. What can we infer about the situation and its development?
2. To whom is Petrarch speaking in the opening lines?
3. What inferences could we make about Petrarch's attitude towards death?
4. In lines 26–7 the speaker addresses a different person. Whom is he addressing?
5. What kind of man do the details in these lines suggest is speaking?
6. How would you describe the progress of the situation? How might the events presented in these sixty lines be retold in the form of a story narrated by an observer of the action?

This series of questions—and their answers—should suggest the kind of inferential activity that many dramatic poems require of their readers. The words are points of departure, and the real poem is the one we create with our own imaginative but logical response to the poet's words. The poet offers us the pleasure of helping to create his poem, and also the pleasure of entering a world remote from our own in time and space. Dramatic poems like Bringhurst's do not so much apply words to our situations as take us out of ourselves into situations beyond our experience. When we speak Petrarch's words aloud or read them imaginatively, we are refreshed by this assumption of a strange role and this expression of a personality other than our own. Our minds are expanded, and we return to ourselves enriched by the experience. Yet even the strangest characters will often express ideas and attitudes we recognize as related to our own, related to certain moods or conditions of being in which we have found ourselves. Everyone who has ever considered his or her own death has something in common with Francesco Petrarca as he begins to speak.

The line between the dramatic and narrative elements in a poem is not always clear. But a narrative poem gives us a story as told by a narrator from a perspective outside the action, while a dramatic poem presents a fragment of an action (or story) through the voice, or point of view, of a character involved in that action. The principal speaker in a narrative poem addresses the audience directly, telling us about the situation and perhaps offering us introductions to characters who function as dramatic elements in the poem. In the days when long stories were recited aloud by bardic poets, verse was the natural form for narration, because it provided easily memorizable units of composition and a regular, flowing rhythm into which these units might be fitted. But now that printing has converted most of the audience for fiction from listeners to readers, stories today are typically told in prose. The only narrative verse form that is alive today is the ballad, which justifies its use of rhyme and rhythm by being set to music and sung. Verse meant to be sung has its own rules and conventions, which will be discussed later on. But here we can talk about the narrative element in ballads and other forms of fiction in verse, and how versified fiction differs from the kind of story we expect to find in prose.

If we think of a dramatic poem as something like a self-contained fragment torn from a play, which through its compression encourages us to fill out its dramatic frame by acts of inference and imagination, then we may think of a narrative poem as related to prose fiction in a similar way. In comparison to stories, narrative poems are compressed and elliptical, shifting their focus, concentrating on striking details, and leaving us to make appropriate connections and draw appropriate conclusions. In fact, there is a strong tendency toward the dramatic in short verse narratives—a tendency to present more dialogue or action in relation to description than we would expect to find in prose fiction dealing with the same subject matter.

We find poetic elements in much prose fiction and fictional elements in many poems. Here we are concerned mainly with the special problems posed by the compressed and elliptical form taken by fiction in short poems, where the compactness and brevity often move narration in the direction of drama. Consider the combination of drama and narration in the following poem by Michael Ondaatje:

## Bearhug

Griffin calls to come and kiss him goodnight
I yell ok. Finish something I'm doing,
then something else, walk slowly round
the corner to my son's room.
He is standing arms outstretched
waiting for a bearhug. Grinning.

Why do I give my emotion an animal's name,
give it that dark squeeze of death?
This is the hug which collects
all his small bones and his warm neck against me.
The thin tough body under the pyjamas
locks to me like a magnet of blood.

How long was he standing there
like that, before I came?

Here the speaker seems to be addressing us directly as a narrator. But he is describing a scene in which he is the central character, and describing it in the present tense as something in progress. Drama is always now; narrative is always then.

Because this is a poem, tightly compressed, it is possible for us to miss an essential aspect of the dramatic situation it presents. The narrator walks 'slowly round / the corner to my son's room.' But why is he hesitant to embrace his son? 'How long was he standing there / like that, before I came?' And why, too, does he give his emotion 'an animal's name'? In this short poem, there is so much we have to infer from the incident that stands behind the poem.

**Description and Meditation**

Description is the element in poetry closest to painting and sculpture. Poets like Edmund Spenser, John Keats, and Alfred Lord Tennyson have been sensitive to this relationship: Spenser maintained that the poet's wit 'passeth Painter farre', while Keats admitted that a painted piece of Greek pottery could 'express a flowery tale more sweetly than our rhyme'. In fact, portraying something with words has both advantages and disadvantages in comparison to plastic representation. Words are rich in meaning and suggestions but weak for rendering precise spatial relations and shades of colour. What descriptive words do best is convey an attitude or feeling through the objects that they describe.

Take a simple description from a short poem by William Carlos Williams:

A red wheel
barrow

glazed with rain
water

beside the white
chickens.

We sense a word game here in the arbitrary arrangement of the words in lines, as they lead us to consider a visual image dominated by contrasting colours and textures—feathery white and glazed red, living and inanimate things. But it is hard to sense distinctly any attitude conveyed by the description, which seems like a poor substitute for a painting.

Here is the entire poem:

so much depends
upon

a red wheel
barrow

glazed with rain
water

beside the white
chickens.

Now we can see how the description itself depends upon the assertion 'so much depends' for its animation. The assertion directs our search for meaning and conveys the speaker's attitude toward the objects described. We may wonder how anything can 'depend' on such insignificant objects, and yet this response is a response not just to a description but to a poem as well. The poem is created by the distance between this sweeping statement and the apparent insignificance of the objects it refers to. We understand, finally, that the poet is using this distance to make us feel his concern for trivial things, his sense that there is beauty in humble objects. Beyond that, he is encouraging us to share his alertness to the beautiful in things that are neither artful nor conventionally pretty. He is advising us to keep our eyes open, and he does it not with a direct admonition but with a description charged with the vigour of his own response to the visible world.

It is of the essence of poetic description that it comes to us charged with the poet's feelings and attitudes. Sometimes these will be made explicit by statement or commentary in the poem. Sometimes they will remain implicit, matters of tone, rhythm, and metaphor. Consider the opening four lines of a poem by Tennyson. What attitudes or emotions are conveyed by them, and how are they conveyed?

> The woods decay, the woods decay and fall,
> The vapours weep their burthen to the ground,
> Man comes and tills the field and lies beneath,
> And after many a summer dies the swan.

The topic is decay and death, presented in terms of generalized natural description. In the opening line the ongoing process of decay is emphasized by the exact repetition of a whole clause. In line 2 the vapours are presented as sentient creatures who weep. In line 3 the whole human adult life is compressed into just nine words, a few seconds, a patch of earth. In the climatic position, reserved by an inversion of normal syntax for the last place in the sentence, comes the death of the swan. Human life and death are thus surrounded by decay and death in other natural things, and in this way reduced, distanced. Death is not horrible but natural, and characterized by a melancholy beauty.

These lines of description serve in the poem as the beginning of a dramatic monologue. The nature of the speaker and that of his situation (as we come to understand them) help us to refine our grasp of the tone and the attitude these lines convey toward the objects they describe. Here is the opening verse-paragraph of the poem:

## Tithonus

> The woods decay, the woods decay and fall,
> The vapours weep their burthen to the ground,
> Man comes and tills the field and lies beneath,
> And after many a summer dies the swan.
> Me only cruel immortality
> Consumes: I wither slowly in thine arms,

Here at the quiet limit of the world,
A white-haired shadow roaming like a dream
The ever-silent spaces of the East,
Far-folded mists, and gleaming halls of morn.

The speaker is Tithonus, a mythological prince who became the lover of the dawn goddess; she made him immortal but could not prevent him from growing older throughout eternity. In the light of lines 5 and 6, the first four lines are enriched with the wistful envy of one who is unable to die. At the close of the poem (some seventy lines later) the speaker returns to the images of line 3 in speaking of 'happy men that have the power to die' and of 'the grassy barrows of the happier dead'. He asks for release so that he may become 'earth in earth' and forget his unhappy existence.

The melancholy beauty of the opening lines becomes more lovely and less sad as we move toward the conclusion of the poem with its powerful projection of one's return to earth as the most desirable of consummations. Behind the dramatic speaker in the poem—the mythological Tithonus—stands the poet, reminding us that death is natural and the appropriate end of life. In this poem, description and drama collaborate to suggest rather than state a meaning.

Serious English poetry has often embodied in particular poems a movement from description to overt meditation. This movement is frequently found in religious poetry, in which poets move from contemplation of created things to an awareness of their divine creator. William Wordsworth was a master—perhaps *the* master—of this kind of poetic movement in English. Thus, a selection from Wordsworth makes a fitting conclusion to this discussion of description and meditation. The poem is a sonnet, in which the first eight lines (the *octet*) are devoted to description of nature, and the last six (the *sestet*) take the form of a meditation on Wordsworth's daughter Caroline. 'Abraham's bosom' is a reference to the passage in the New Testament (Luke 16: 22) that proclaims that the righteous will join the patriarch Abraham in heaven after death. It is a reference to heaven.

It is a beauteous evening, calm and free,
The holy time is quiet as a Nun
Breathless with adoration; the broad sun
Is sinking down in its tranquility;
The gentleness of heaven broods o'er the Sea:
Listen! the mighty Being is awake,
And doth with his eternal motion make
A sound like thunder—everlastingly.
Dear Child! dear Girl! that walkest with me here,
If thou appear untouched by solemn thought,
Thy nature is not therefore less divine:
Thou liest in Abraham's bosom all the year;
And worshipp'st at the Temple's inner shrine,
God being with thee when we know it not.

## Word Games

Language can help us perceive connections between disparate things, or it can help us make discriminations that separate similar things. In poetry these two aspects of language take the form of metaphorical comparison and ironic contrast. Metaphor and irony are the twin bases of poetical language, and the reader of poetry must be especially alert and tactful in responding to metaphorical and ironic language. It is because poetry places such stress on these crucial aspects of language that it is of such great use in developing linguistic skills in its readers.

In the following sections on metaphoric and ironic language we have not tried to present an exhaustive list of poetical devices to be carefully noted and memorized. We have tried instead to examine some of the main varieties of metaphoric and ironic language, with a view to introducing these two crucial varieties of poetical wordplay.

## Some Varieties of Metaphorical Language

### *Simile*

Simile is the easiest form of metaphor to perceive because in it the images or ideas being joined are stated and explicitly linked by the word 'as' or 'like' or a similar linking word. Similes are often quite simple:

O my Love's like a red, red rose

But even a statement of resemblance as simple and direct as this one of Robert Burns's asks us to consider the ways in which his beloved is like a rose—and not a white or yellow rose, but a red rose. And not just a red rose but a 'red, red' rose. What the redness of the rose has to do with the qualities of the speaker's beloved is the first question this simile poses for us. In the poem, the simile is further complicated by a second line:

O my Love's like a red, red rose,
  That's newly sprung in June;

Here we are asked to associate the freshness of the flower and its early blooming with the qualities of the speaker's beloved. The next two lines add a second image, compounding the simile:

O my Love's like the melodie
  That's sweetly played in tune.

The first image emphasizes the spontaneous naturalness of the beloved, the second her harmonious composure. Both roses and sweet melodies are pleasing, so that, in a sense, the poet is using his similes to make the simple statement that the woman he loves is pleasing to behold. But the simile is also saying that she has a complicated kind of appeal: like the rose, to sight and smell; like the melody, to the sense of sound; like the rose, a natural, fresh quality; like the melody, a deliberate artfulness intended to please. The simile also conveys the strength of the poet's feeling; his choice of images tells us something about the qualities of his feeling for her because it is *he* who has found these words—which themselves have some of the qualities of spontaneous freshness and tuneful order.

A single simile can also be elaborated, as in the traditional epic simile, in which the image is often extensive enough to require the construction *as . . . so*, or *like . . . thus*. An extended simile, by multiplying possible points of contact between the thing presented and the illustrative image it is likened to, can often become very complicated, with the illustrative image itself becoming a thing to be illustrated or developed with other images still. Consider, for example, this epic simile from Book IV, Canto III, of Edmund Spenser's *Faerie Queene*:

**27**

Like as the tide that comes from th' Ocean main,
Flows up the Shanon with contrary force,
And overruling him in his own reign,
Drives back the current of his kindly course,
And makes it seem to have some other source:
But when the flood is spent, then back again
His borrowed waters forced to redisbourse,
He sends the sea his own with double gain,
And tribute eke withal, as to his Soveraine.

**28**

Thus did the battle vary to and fro . . .

#### *Metaphor*

The word 'metaphor' is used both as a general term for all kinds of poetic linking of images and ideas, and also as a specific term for such linking when the thing and image are not presented as a direct analogy (A *is like* B) but by discussing one in terms of the other (Albert *is* a dog or Albert *barked* at me). For example, within Spenser's epic simile we can find metaphor at work. Part of the simile describes hand-to-hand combat in terms of the ebb and flow of tides where the River Shannon meets the Atlantic Ocean. The ebb and flow of the waters illustrate the shifting tide of battle. But this basic simile in Spenser is enriched by the idea of Shannon and the Atlantic as hostile powers engaged in a struggle, with the ocean tide invading the river and 'overruling him in his own reign'.

The power struggle is itself further complicated by a financial metaphor. The phrase 'when the flood is spent' means literally when the incoming tide has expended its force and lost its momentum. But Spenser chooses to use the financial overtones in the word 'spent' to enrich his metaphor. From 'spent' he moves to 'borrowed' and 'redisburse', and to the concept of repayment with 100 per cent interest in the expression 'double gain'. This transaction between ocean and river can be seen as a combat or a loan. Finally, Spenser merges these two metaphors in the last line of the stanza by calling this double payment the 'tribute' of a lesser feudal power to a higher. And here Spenser turns his metaphor into a simile within the basic simile, with the expression 'as to his Soveraine'.

This interweaving of similes and metaphors is both playful and decorative. The metaphors seem to emerge naturally and blend easily with one another. But in fact they tell us nothing much about the course of the combat beyond suggesting that the fight ebbs and flows. The struggle is not so much described as dignified by this heroic comparison to two sovereign forces of nature.

In poems that depend heavily on metaphoric processes for their interest, the subtle interaction of images and ideas almost defies analysis, yet such poems may depend on our attempts to follow their metaphoric threads. For us to understand such a poem, to feel it, we must start our thoughts along the lines indicated by the metaphors. Consider Shakespeare's Sonnet 73 as an example of this kind of poem:

That time of year thou mayst in me behold
When yellow leaves, or none, or few, do hang
Upon those boughs which shake against the cold,
Bare ruined choirs where late the sweet birds sang.
In me thou seest the twilight of such day
As after sunset fadeth in the west,
Which by and by black night doth take away,
Death's second self, that seals up all in rest.
In me thou seest the glowing of such fire
That on the ashes of his youth doth lie
As the death-bed whereon it must expire,
Consumed with that which it was nourished by.
    This thou perceiv'st, which makes thy love more strong,
    To love all that well which thou must leave ere long.

The images of the first 12 lines are all elaborations of the simple notion that the speaker is getting old. The last two lines are a dramatic assertion, also rather simple. The speaker tells his listener that the listener will love him all the more precisely because old age and death threaten their relationship. We can infer that the speaker is older than the listener, and in terms of the dramatic situation we are entitled to wonder whether these self-assured words are merely wishful thinking or an honest appraisal of the listener's attitude. How, then, does the imagery of the first 12 lines contribute to our understanding of the situation? We have in these lines three separate but related metaphors, each developed for four lines. The speaker says, in effect, 'You see in me—autumn; you see in me—twilight; you see in me—embers.'

These three metaphors for aging have in common certain qualities: a growing coldness and darkness, suggestions of finality, and impending extinction. But each image generates its own attitude and emphasizes a different aspect of the aging process. The first four lines suggest an analogy between an aging person and trees whose leaves have fallen, leaving them exposed to cold winds. And the bare trees suggest, by a further reach of metaphor, a ruined and desolate church. Above all, this complex metaphor generates sympathy for the speaker, a sympathy based on our concern for lost beauty, for destruction of spiritual things, and for victims of the forces of nature.

The next four lines, focusing on the twilight after sunset, threaten coming darkness. By another extension of metaphor, 'black night' is called 'Death's second self'. The brevity of the time between sunset and night increases our sense of sympathetic urgency, and the introduction of 'Death' takes us full circle through the metaphors back to their object, an aging man. The next four lines also introduce a complex metaphor. The speaker compares himself to the glowing embers of a dying fire that lies upon 'the ashes of his youth'. The fire becomes human here and returns us again to the life of the speaker.

This final image is the most intense of the three because it likens the arrival of old age not merely to a seasonal change, worked by the passage of time, but to the consumption or destruction of matter that can never be restored to its original state. The ashes of the fire lying upon its deathbed are forcible reminders that the speaker's body will soon lie upon a deathbed, and will become ashes, to be returned to the ashes and dust of the grave. It is the emotional force of all 'This' that the speaker maintains, in the next-to-last line, the listener must perceive. And the confidence of the assertion is partly the confidence of a poet who still has his poetical power. He can still sing like a sweet bird and move his hearer with his poetry. The imagery justifies the dramatic situation, and the situation intensifies the significance of the imagery.

### *The Conceit*

It is useful to think of the conceit as an extension of the simile in which aspects of the basic analogy are developed with a kind of relentless ingenuity. The 'metaphysical' poets of the late sixteenth and the seventeenth centuries specialized in witty conceits. Here, for example, John Donne combines a dramatic situation with development of a conceit so that the images become an argument persuading his listener to give in to his romantic overtures.

## The Flea

Mark but this flea, and mark in this,
How little that which thou deny'st me is;
Me it sucked first, and now sucks thee,
And in this flea, our two bloods mingled be;
Confess it, this cannot be said
A sin, or shame, or loss of maidenhead,
    Yet this enjoys before it woo,
    And pampered swells with one blood made of two,
    And this, alas, is more than we would do.

Oh stay, three lives in one flea spare,
Where we almost, nay more than married are.
This flea is you and I, and this
Our marriage bed, and marriage temple is;
Though parents grudge, and you, we are met,
And cloistered in these living walls of jet.
Though use make you apt to kill me,
Let not to this, self-murder added be,
And sacrilege, three sins in killing three.

Cruel and sudden, hast thou since
Purpled thy nail, in blood of innocence?
In what could this flea guilty be,
Except in that drop which it sucked from thee?
Yet thou triumph'st, and say'st that thou
Find'st not thyself, nor me the weaker now;
'Tis true, then learn how false, fears be;
Just so much honour, when thou yield'st to me,
Will waste, as this flea's death took life from thee.

In the opening lines the speaker makes the basic analogy between the flea's having bitten both himself and the lady and the sexual dalliance he is attempting to initiate. In the rest of the poem he develops the analogy as an argument in a changing dramatic context. At the start of the second stanza the lady has threatened to kill the flea; by the third stanza she has done so. The speaker has imaginatively transformed the flea into a marriage bed, a temple, a cloister, and a figure of the Holy Trinity (Father, Son, and Holy Ghost), so that the flea's destruction can be hyperbolically described as murder, suicide, and sacrilege. All of this is in preparation for the turn of the argument in the last three lines of the poem. Donne's conceit is both ingenious and playful.

#### *The Symbol*

The symbol can be seen as an extension of the metaphor. In it, instead of saying that A is B-ish, or calling an A a B, the poet presents us with one half of the analogy only and requires us to supply the missing part. This invites the reader to be creative and imaginative in a situation controlled by the poet. The following is a symbolic poem by W.B. Yeats:

### The Dolls

A DOLL in the doll-maker's house
Looks at the cradle and balls:
'That is an insult to us.'
But the oldest of all the dolls
Who had seen, being kept for show,
Generations of his sort,
Out-screams the whole shelf: 'Although

There's not a man can report
Evil of this place,
The man and the woman bring
Hither, to our disgrace,
A noisy and filthy thing.'
Hearing him groan and stretch
The doll-maker's wife is aware
Her husband has heard the wretch,
And crouched by the arm of his chair,
She murmurs into his ear,
Head upon shoulder leant:
'My dear, my dear, oh dear,
It was an accident.'

This whole incident stands in a metaphoric relation to something else. In other words, the poem is only apparently about dolls and doll-makers. It is really about something symbolized by the incident narrated. Identifying the true subject of the poem requires us to work carefully from the situation toward possible analogies in the world of ideas and experience, first by exploring the situation and images in the poem. The situation derives from the doll-maker's two kinds of creation: his dolls and his child. The dolls in their lifeless perfection resent the noise and filth produced by the human child. The human baby is, in fact, as the doll-maker's wife apologetically points out, not 'made' in the same sense as dolls are made. Birth is an 'accident'; dolls are deliberately constructed. The situation leads us outward until we see it as an illustration of the opposition between art and life, between the ideal and the real. The doll-maker himself thus symbolizes any artist who is obliged to live in the real world but create idealized objects, or any person who faces the impossible problem of realizing his ideas—or idealizing reality.

Having got this far from the concrete situation of the poem, the reader is in a position to return and consider the ways in which Yeats has used language to control his tone and charge the scene with emotion. How should we react to the various characters in this drama? What, finally, should our attitude be toward the real/ideal conflict that the drama illustrates?

***The Pun***

Often disdained as a 'low' form of wit, the pun is essentially a kind of metaphor that can be used lightly and facetiously or for more serious purposes. Consider some verses by Thomas Hood (selected by William Empson to exemplify punning techniques):

How frail is our uncertain breath!
The laundress seems full hale, but death
Shall her 'last linen' bring;
The groom will die, like all his kind;
And even the stable boy will find
This life no stable thing. . . .

Cook, butler, Susan, Jonathan,
The girl that scours the pot and pan
And those that tend the steeds,
All, all shall have another sort
Of service after this—in short
The one the parson reads.

These puns on 'stable' and 'service' are playful but not funny. They use the basic device of the pun—dissimilar meanings for the same 'word', or rather the same sound—to convey an attitude toward an idea. That both the life of a servant and the servant's funeral are somehow included in that one piece of language—'service'—brings home to us the interconnection of life and death, which is the point of the poem.

Shakespeare was a master of the pun as of other metaphorical devices. Hamlet's bitter, punning responses to his uncle's smooth speeches are deadly serious and powerfully dramatic in their witty compression of his resentment.

KING . . . But now, my cousin Hamlet, and my son—
HAMLET [*Aside*] A little more than kin and less than kind!
KING How is it that the clouds still hang on you?
HAMLET Not so, my lord. I am too much i' the sun.

Hamlet and the King are more than *kin* (twice related: uncle/nephew and stepfather/son) but Hamlet feels they are not kindred spirits, not the same *kind*. And being called *son* by his father's murderer rouses all Hamlet's bitterness, causing him to return the King's metaphorical question about Hamlet's overcast mood with a pun that brings the metaphor back to the literal with a sarcastic bite: I am too much in the *son*.

## The Language of Animation and Personification

In addition to their playful or ingenious aspects, metaphorical devices help to generate the qualities of compression and intensity that we value in poetry. Similar qualities are often achieved by other means, such as animation and personification.

### *Animation*

Animation is a means of portraying objects or animals with a greater degree of awareness or purposefulness than we normally credit them with. When Tennyson writes, 'The vapours weep their burden to the ground,' he gives life to the vapours, animating them with an emotion, sadness, that only living creatures experience. Less lovely scenes can also be intensified by animation. Consider these lines from Samuel Johnson's 'Vanity of Human Wishes', which describe the treatment given the portraits of a statesman whose power has waned. Those who were once honoured to gaze upon his features, now that no more is to be gained from the man, suddenly find the likeness ugly:

From every room descends the painted face,
That hung the bright palladium of the place;

And, smoked in kitchens, or in auctions sold,
To better features yields the frame of gold;
For now no more we trace in every line
Heroic worth, benevolence divine;
The form distorted justifies the fall,
And detestation rids th' indignant wall.

In the last line Johnson intensifies his satire by animating the wall on which the picture hangs—even it is indignant and wishes to be rid of these odious features. The job of removing the portraits has been carried out by a person who has been transformed into an attitude—'detestation'.

***Personification***

In the example from Dr Johnson, we have a kind of reverse personification, in which a human being becomes an abstract idea. Personification usually works the other way, clothing abstractions with the attributes of personality. Love is the most common of all the ideas presented as sentient beings. In mythology, Love operates as the god Cupid or Eros, offering poets a ready-made personification that they have often used. The mechanical use of traditional personification can be dull and dreary. But observe Sir Philip Sidney as he personifies Love in this sonnet, and finds ways to make concrete a whole range of other abstractions such as reverence, fear, hope, will, memory, and desire. If Love is *personified* here, these other notions are *objectified*—turned into material objects.

I on my horse, and Love on me doth try
    Our horsemanships, while by strange work I prove
    A horseman to my horse, a horse to Love;
And now man's wrongs in me, poor beast, descry.

The reins wherewith my rider doth me tie,
    Are humbled thoughts, which bit of reverence move,
    Curb'd in with fear, but with gilt boss above
Of hope, which makes it seem fair to the eye.

The wand is will; thou, fancy, saddle art,
    Girt fast by memory, and while I spur
My horse, he spurs with sharp desire my heart:
He sits me fast, however I do stir:
    And now hath made me to his hand so right,
    That in the manage my self takes delight.

The dominant image of Love as horseman provides the subordinate imagery for making concrete the other abstractions that serve to amplify this picture of a love-ridden man. The effectiveness of the poem depends on the ingenuity with which the poet has matched the objects and ideas to one another, relating all to the dominant personification of Love. Like Spenser's epic simile, Sidney's personification seems to breed subordinate metaphors easily, gracefully, and naturally.

### The Anti-metaphorical Language of Irony

Verbal irony may be said to start with simple negation of resemblance in situations where resemblance is customarily insisted upon or expected, as in Shakespeare's sonnet 130, which begins

> My mistress' eyes are nothing like the sun;
> Coral is far more red than her lips' red.
> If snow be white, why then her breasts are dun;
> If hairs be wires, black wires grow on her head.

The 'anti-similes' of the first three lines serve the same function as the ugly metaphor in line 4. All four lines present attacks on what the speaker will name in the last line of the poem as 'false compare'—the misuse of metaphor in the language of poetry.

Usually irony is not so straightforward. We normally think of it as involving some deliberate misleading of the reader—some gap between what the words *seem* to be saying and what they *are* saying. In the same sonnet, after eight more lines of plain speaking about an ordinary human female, Shakespeare's speaker concludes

> And yet, by heaven, I think my love as rare
> As any she belied by false compare.

What we might have taken as criticism of the speaker's mistress turns out to be praise after all. She is not uglier than the others; she just has a lover who will not exaggerate her beauty with the usual clichés. The irony lies in the disparity between the apparent disparagement of the woman in the first part of the poem and the praise of her at the end. We can see, then, in those opening lines, a kind of understatement, which works in the end to convince us of the woman's beauty more effectively than a conventionally exaggerated simile of 'false compare' would have done.

Understatement and overstatement are two of the most frequently used kinds of verbal irony. When Jonathan Swift causes a character to observe (in prose), 'Last Week I saw a Woman *flay'd*, and you will hardly believe, how much it altered her Person for the worse'—the main thing that strikes us is the awful inadequacy of the sentiment for the event. Disparity, contrast, incongruity—these elements are at the heart of verbal irony.

Successful irony implicitly argues that all words are inadequate for the representation of things. The poet as maker of metaphors may be seen as a genuine magician, bringing new things into the world, or as a charlatan pretending with feeble words to unite things that are essentially separate. Metaphor celebrates the creative dimension of language, while irony exposes language's inadequacies. For example, in Marvell's 'To His Coy Mistress' the exaggerated declarations of the extent that the speaker's love would require 'Had we but world enough and time' are all based on the view that of course we do *not* have world enough and time. Even before we get there, we sense the presence of the 'But' on which the poem will make its turn:

> But at my back I always hear
> Time's wingèd chariot hurrying near:

The contrast between what the speaker *would* do:

> An hundred years should go to praise
> Thine eyes, and on thy forehead gaze;
> Two hundred to adore each breast,
> But thirty thousand to the rest;

And what he does urge:

> Now let us sport us while we may;

This last line is ironic, enhanced by the extreme distance in time between hundreds or thousands of years and 'Now'.

Irony can also take the form of metaphorical overstatement, as it does in Alexander Pope's description of coffee being poured into a China cup:

> From silver spouts the grateful liquors glide,
> While China's earth receives the smoking tide.

These lines are metaphorical in that they present one thing (pouring a cup of coffee) in terms of another image (a kind of burning flood pouring over the mainland of China), but they are ironic in that the equation is made mainly so that we will perceive the disparity between the two images and enjoy their incongruity. Something of this reverse, anti-metaphorical wit is present in many metaphors.

John Donne's 'The Flea' has a witty, ironic dimension derived from the inappropriateness of his basic image. To call a flea a temple is to establish a far-fetched metaphor. The conceits used by Donne and other 'metaphysical' poets of his time often have an ironic dimension. Samuel Johnson characterized the metaphysical poets precisely in terms of this dimension—a special and extreme form of 'wit' based on the 'discovery of occult resemblances in things apparently unlike', and resulting in poems in which 'the most heterogeneous ideas are yoked by violence together'. Johnson's description emphasizes ('yoked by violence') the tension between metaphoric comparison and ironic contrast in many metaphysical conceits. Conceits tend to be witty, cerebral, unnatural, while metaphors are serious, imaginative, and natural. The metaphors of Romantic poetry are perceptions of relationships felt to exist. Metaphysical conceits often establish powerful but artificial relationships where one would least expect to find them.

Linking incongruous things is a feature of most kinds of witty poetry. A simple list with one incongruous element can serve to indict a whole way of life, as when Alexander Pope surveys the debris on a young woman's dressing table:

> Puffs, powders, patches, bibles, billet-doux.

The inclusion of Bibles among love letters and cosmetics suggests a confusion between worldly and spiritual values—a failure to distinguish between true and false worth. The list is funny, but in an ironic and satiric way—as is this list of possible calamities from the same poem:

> Whether the nymph shall break Diana's law,
> Or some frail china jar receive a flaw,
> Or stain her honour, or her new brocade,
> Forget her prayers, or miss a masquerade,
> Or lose her heart, or necklace, at a ball; . . .

Here Pope mixes several serious matters of the spirit with trivial and worldly items. The breaking of 'Diana's law' of chastity is equated with damage to a jar. A single verb, 'stain', governs two objects—'honour' and 'brocade'—of different qualities and intensities. By this manipulation of grammar Pope makes us forcibly aware of the frivolousness of an attitude toward life that equates things that should have different values. He brings those two objects under that one verb so that we will feel a powerful urge to part them in our minds, resolving the incongruity by separating the elements he has brought together.

### Beyond Metaphor and Irony

Much of the best modern poetry presents combinations of images and ideas so stretched and disconnected that they go beyond metaphor, and yet so serious and appropriate they transcend irony also. The difficulty in understanding many modern poems stems from a profusion of images that seem ironically disconnected but nevertheless suggest genuine metaphorical connection. We can find a relatively simple illustration in a few lines from a ballad by W.H. Auden, 'As I Walked Out One Evening':

> The glacier knocks in the cupboard,
>     The desert sighs in the bed,
> And the crack in the tea-cup opens
>     A lane to the land of the dead.

Here Auden seems to be operating with ironic incongruities—the glacier in the cupboard and so on—but the sum of these incongruities is a coherent statement about the absurd and empty horror that threatens much of modern life. Such a collection of images seems to combine qualities of conceit and symbol with ironic incongruity, leaving us to resolve the problems of whether these assertions are ironic overstatements or powerful metaphors for our condition.

A poem composed of a number of these high-tension ironic metaphors can be immediately intelligible in a general way and still difficult to reduce to prose sense at every point. But we should make the effort to establish prose sense—or possible prose senses—for each image and situation, because even if we do not succeed entirely, we will be testing the ultimate intelligibility of the poem, the durability of its interest. As with certain kinds of modern art, it is sometimes hard to separate the fraudulent from the real in contemporary poetry. If we cannot discover intelligibility and coherence in a poem, if its images and situations do not enhance one another, we are confronted by either a flawed poem or a poem that is beyond us—one that we have not yet learned how to read. Differences in poetic quality cannot be demonstrated conclusively, yet they exist.

## MUSIC

The musical element in poetry is the hardest to talk about because it is non-verbal. Our responses to rhythm and pleasing combinations of sounds are in a sense too immediate, too fundamental to be understood in words. Yet music is important in all poetry, and for most poetry written before the last half-century it is crucial. It is important, then, to find words to grasp this poetical element, in order to do justice to most poetic achievement.

Students generally prefer discussing one aspect of poetry to another in an order something like this:

1. ideas
2. situations
3. language
4. metrics.

But if we are concerned about what makes poetry *poetry* rather than another kind of composition, we should probably reverse this order. If a piece of writing is neither especially rhythmical nor especially ironic nor metaphorical in its language, it is not poetry, regardless of its dramatic situations or the ideas it presents. The following sections introduce some of the fundamental aspects of versification.

### Metrics

Metrics has to do with all rhythmical effects in poetry. In English versification this means that it is largely a matter of accents and pauses. The pauses are determined by the usual grammatical principles that govern our speech and writing, and are indicated by the usual grammatical symbols—periods, commas, and so on—but one new factor is added. The end of a line of verse is itself a mark of punctuation. If a line ends with a regular mark of punctuation we call it *end-stopped*. If the last word of a line is followed by no punctuation and is part of a continuing grammatical unit like a prepositional phrase, we call the line *run-on* or *enjambed*. In end-stopped lines, the line-end works *with* punctuation and reinforces it, making each line a tight unit of thought. In enjambed lines the line-end works *against* the punctuation, throwing certain words into a prominence that they would not ordinarily have. The enjambed line adds a special kind of poetical punctuation to the language: something at once more and less than a comma. Poets who use free-verse forms with no regular rhythm are dependent on enjambment to give their words a special poetical quality.

Consider again the poem by Williams:

so much depends
upon

a red wheel
barrow

glazed with rain
water

beside the white
chickens.

If we write this out as prose we get, 'So much depends upon a red wheelbarrow, glazed with rainwater, beside the white chickens.' This is a simple, declarative prose sentence, with a couple of adjectival phrases tacked on, set off with commas. Has anything been lost by this rearrangement of the poem on the page? Decidedly so. The assertion being made is much less convincing in plain prose. The free-verse form of the sentence uses its line-endings to work against the prose movement, slowing it up, and providing a metrical equivalent for the visual highlighting of the images. Just where we would bring the words closest together in prose—making single words out of 'wheel' and 'barrow', 'rain' and 'water'—Williams has pulled them apart by breaking the line in mid-word.

The poem may or may not carry us to final agreement with its assertion, but in the free-verse form it certainly convinces us of the speaker's earnestness. We get a sense of how much he cares about what he is saying from the care with which he has spaced out his words. And when we read the poem aloud, with little pauses at line-ends, it carries us farther toward conviction than the same sentence in its prosaic form.

Williams's poem is a simple illustration of how poetry's special line-end punctuation can group words in a rhythm different from the natural rhythm of normal speech or prose. Here is a further illustration of how a poet can use the line-end to achieve an ironic effect that would be almost impossible to duplicate in prose. e.e. cummings begins a poem this way:

pity this busy monster, manunkind,
not.

The first word of the second line absolutely reverses the meaning of the first line. We pause, with a comma, at the end of line 1. We stop entirely, with a period, after the first word of line 2. We hover, thus, with the wrong meaning until we are given the word that changes it, whereupon we stop to contemplate the admonition offered us in the whole opening sentence. Consider it rearranged as plain prose:

Pity this monster, manunkind, not.

Or, more prosaically:

Do not pity this busy monster, manunkind.

By unravelling the poetical arrangement and combination of the words, we have destroyed the force of the admonition, taking away its suspense and eliminating the recoil in the original last word.

In verse that is not markedly rhythmical, unusual pauses and arrangements of words are the principal metrical device. Such is the case, for example, in the more experimental poetry of a poet like Christian Bök. In verse that is regularly rhythmical, however, the rhythm or metre itself is the crucial metrical element. Poetical arrangement does something to prosaic language, but not so much as does rhythm, which lifts an utterance and moves it in the direction of music. Just as the line-end pauses in a poem can work with or against the normal grammatical pauses of speech and prose, poetic rhythm can work both with and against our normal patterns of pronunciation.

In speech we begin with standard grammatical pronunciations for words. Take the word 'defence'. Normally we pronounce this word by accenting the first syllable lightly and the second syllable heavily. Indicating light accent by ∪ and heavy accent by —, we pronounce the word this way:

∪ —
defence.

That is grammatical accent or grammatical stress. But in certain situations we might change this pronunciation for purposes of emphasis, as in, 'Today's coaches preach *de*-fence first, *off*-ence second.' Here we pronounce the word

— ∪
defence.

This is not grammatical stress but rhetorical stress. We have altered the usual pattern of light and heavy accent in order to make a point. (Grammar, of course, keeps changing, and the repeated use of one particular rhetorical pattern can eventually alter standard pronunciation. Broadcasts of hockey and basketball games, for instance, are helping to make *de*-fence the standard way to accent this word.)

Both grammatical and rhetorical stress operate in poetry, where they are complicated by a third kind of accent, which we call poetical stress. Poetical stress is a regular system of accents that establishes the basic rhythm of a poem. There are only two fundamental systems of poetic stress in English verse, though they have many variations. Most frequently, English verse alternates light and heavy accents, giving every other syllable the same stress, like this:

> ∪ — ∪— ∪ — ∪— ∪ —
> The woods decay, the woods decay and fall

Less frequently, English verse uses two light syllables between each heavy stress, like this:

> ∪ ∪—∪ ∪ — ∪ ∪ — ∪ ∪ —
> The Assyrian came down like the wolf on the fold
>
> ∪ ∪ —∪ ∪ — ∪ ∪ —∪ ∪ —
> And his cohorts were gleaming in purple and gold

The rhythm of this second metrical pattern is more insistent than that of the first. The simple da-*dum*, da-*dum* of 'The woods decay' is more like the spoken language than the da-da-*dum*, da-da-*dum* of 'like the wolf on the fold'.

When discussing metrics, we use the term 'feet' for the units that are repeated to make a pattern. In the first example above, we have five repeated units in the line, five feet divided this way:

> ∪ — | ∪— | ∪ — | ∪— | ∪ —
> The woods | decay, | the woods | decay | and fall

In the second example each line has four feet, divided like this:

> ∪ ∪ —| ∪ ∪ — | ∪ ∪ — | ∪ ∪ —
> And his co | horts were gleam | ing in pur | ple and gold

In describing metrical patterns we usually state the number of feet in the basic line and name the standard foot in each line. The traditional name for the foot used in the first example (da-*dum*) is the *iamb*. The traditional name for the foot used in the second example (da-da-*dum*) is the *anapest*. In referring to the number of feet in the basic line of a poem, it is customary to use numerical prefixes derived from the Greek. Thus,

| | | | | | | | | |
|---|---|---|---|---|---|---|---|---|
| one-foot line | = | *mono* | + | *meter* | = | monometer |
| two-foot line | = | *di* | + | *meter* | = | dimeter |
| three-foot line | = | *tri* | + | *meter* | = | trimeter |
| four-foot line | = | *tetra* | + | *meter* | = | tetrameter |
| five-foot line | = | *penta* | + | *meter* | = | pentameter |
| six-foot line | = | *hexa* | + | *meter* | = | hexameter |

The iamb and the anapest have a variant foot that is made by placing the accented syllable at the beginning of each foot rather than at the end. These are called the *trochee* (*dum*-da) and the *dactyl* (*dum*-da-da). They are not used consistently for one good reason. Rhyme in poetry tends to be pleasing only if it includes the last accented syllable in a line and *all the unaccented syllables that follow it*. Thus, if you write

∪ — | ∪ — | ∪ — | ∪ —
Upon | a mid | night drear | y once

you need to find only a one-syllable rhyme for your rhyming line, such as

Upon a midnight dreary once
*I tried my hand at kicking punts.*

But if you use the trochee, and write

— ∪ | — ∪ | — ∪ | — ∪
Once u | pon a | midnight | dreary

then you must rhyme

Once upon a midnight dreary
*Of kicking punts my foot was weary.*

The trochaic foot can, in fact, grow wearisome if carried through to the rhyme word consistently, so we often get a variation that looks like this:

— ∪ — ∪ — ∪ —
Tiger, Tiger, burning bright

— ∪ — ∪ — ∪ —
In the forests of the night

These lines first appear trochaic (*dum*-da) and end by looking iambic (da-*dum*). The two lines could be made fully iambic by a slight change in each:

∪ — ∪ — ∪ — ∪ —
O, Tiger, Tiger burning bright

∪ — ∪ — ∪ — ∪ —
Within the forests of the night

Or we could make them fully trochaic by this kind of alteration:

— ∪ — ∪ — ∪ — ∪
Tiger, Tiger burning brightly,

— ∪ — ∪ — ∪ — ∪
Roaming through the forest nightly

In order to name the metrical pattern of 'Tiger, Tiger' we must supply an imaginary unaccented syllable at the start or end of the line, like this:

∪— | ∪ — | ∪ — | ∪ —
× Ti | ger, Ti | ger, burn | ing bright

or this:

—∪ |—∪ |— ∪ | — ∪
Tiger, | Tiger, | burning | bright ×

These manoeuvrings strongly suggest that the special terminology of metrical analysis is not important in itself, and that beyond the major distinction between the two-syllable foot and the three-syllable foot, we do not need to be too fussy in terms of how we classify them.

What, then, is the use of all these special terms? The art of metrics involves a poet's ability to generate and maintain a consistent metre without destroying normal patterns of grammar and syntax. To succeed metrically, a poet must make language dance without making it unnatural. A crucial aspect of this art is perceptible only when we have the terminology to recognize it. Any unvaryingly regular metre quickly becomes boring through repetition. But a totally irregular poem is wholly without the kind of interest and pleasure that rhythm provides.

All good poets who work in regular metres introduce metrical variations into their poems. The simplest way to understand this is to see the variations as substitutions of a different sort of foot for the one called for by the established metre of the poem. As an example of metrical variation, consider this stanza from 'The Railway Station', a sonnet by Archibald Lampman:

∪ — ∪ — ∪ —∪ — ∪ —
1 The darkness brings no quiet here, the light

— — ∪ —∪— ∪ — ∪ —
2 No waking: ever on my blinded brain

∪ — ∪ — ∪ — ∪ — ∪ —
3 The flare of lights, the rush, and cry, and strain,

∪ — ∪ — ∪ — ∪ —∪ —
4 The engines' scream, the hiss and thunder smite:

The metre is basically iambic, but there is variation. Both grammar and rhetoric urge us to accent and elongate the sound of the word 'No' at the beginning of the second line, giving this foot two accented syllables and no unaccented one. This is a kind of foot that is often used as a substitute but never as the metrical basis for a whole poem. Its technical name is a *spondee*. Lampman has used the spondee here for a slight variation of his rhythm.

Having noticed that substitution, we might notice also the word 'no' in the poem's opening line. Because of its position in the line we are not tempted to give it the emphasis we give to 'No' at the start of line 2, yet it can take a heavy accent. The basic terminology of metrical analysis establishes only the simple distinction between heavy and light, so it cannot take us too far into any metrical subtleties. In scansion, however, we need to consider subtleties and should probably be ready to use at least one more symbol to indicate a stress between heavy and light. Using a combination of the two stress marks we already have in operation to indicate an intermediate stress, we might re-scan the first line of the stanza this way:

∪ — ∪ — ∪̲ — ∪ — ∪ —
The darkness brings no quiet here, the light

Then we could point out that the intermediate accent on 'no' makes the middle foot of line 1 partly spondaic. Line 2 opens with a spondee, and lines 3 and 4 are strictly iambic.

Having established the fairly regular metre of the opening stanza, let us consider the second stanza of the poem:

∪ — ∪ — ∪ ∪ — ∪ — ∪ —
I see the hurrying crowds, the clasp, the flight,

— ∪ ∪ — — ∪ ∪ — ∪ —
Faces that touch, eyes that are dim with pain:

∪ — ∪ — — — ∪ ∪ — —
I see the hoarse wheels turn, and the great train

— — ∪ ∪ — ∪ — ∪ — ∪ —
Move labouring out into the bourneless night.

This stanza introduces quite a bit of variation to the iambic metre established in the opening four lines. The middle foot of line 5 has an extra unaccented syllable, making it an anapest rather than an iamb. This extra syllable quickens the tempo of the line. A similar effect occurs in line 6, where the substitution of trochees for iambs in the first and third feet results in consecutive unaccented syllables. The pace in lines 7 and 8 slows significantly with three spondees, two of which combine, in the final foot of line 7 and the first foot of line 8, to create four consecutive accented syllables.

The metre of the poem's closing stanza—a sestet—is once again fairly regular:

∪ — ∪ — ∪ — ∪ — ∪ — ∪
So many souls within its dim recesses,

∪ — ∪ — ∪ — ∪ — ∪ —
So many bright, so many mournful eyes:

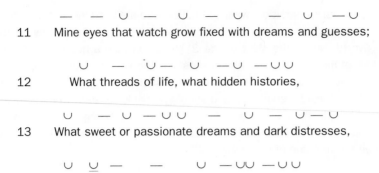

— — ∪ — ∪ — ∪ — ∪ — ∪
Mine eyes that watch grow fixed with dreams and guesses;

∪ — ∪ — ∪ — ∪ — ∪ ∪
What threads of life, what hidden histories,

∪ — ∪ — ∪ ∪ — ∪ — ∪ — ∪
What sweet or passionate dreams and dark distresses,

∪ ∪ — — ∪ — ∪∪ — ∪ ∪
What unknown thoughts, what various agonies!

The iambic metre is complicated by the extra syllable of feminine rhyme in lines 9, 11, and 13 ('re*cesses*', '*guesses*', 'dis*tresses*'—two-syllable rhymes are called *feminine*) and by the paired unaccented syllables that close lines 12 and 14 (each of these lines ends with a *pyrrhic* foot, consisting of two unaccented syllables). The second foot of line 14 is partly spondaic, for although the iambic metre calls for a stress on the second syllable ('un-'), the word 'unknown' is naturally stressed on its second syllable. These long syllables slow the first part of the final line, while the short ones in the second part speed it up.

Thus far we have considered the metrics of this poem only in terms of its pleasing variation within a firmly established pattern. We can see how the pattern is established in the first stanza and varied in the second stanza before it is reasserted in the closing six lines. Now we are in a position to deal with the question of the relation of the metrics to the meaning of the poem.

The railway station is the site of the speaker's contemplation about the diversity of human experience. His role as a passive observer is contrasted with the real joys and suffering of the people he watches in lines 10–11, where his eyes watch the 'bright' and 'mournful eyes' of others, trying to guess at their individual histories. The opening stanza is visual and aural. The speaker sets the scene of the railway station, describing the atmosphere with a series of sights and sounds in lines 3–4. These are frozen images, caught in the regular iambic metre of the opening stanza.

In the second stanza the speaker describes the activity of the railway station. As we read lines 5–6 we feel the tempo of the poem quickening, and this helps us imagine the hurrying crowds the speaker describes. In lines 7–8 the focus shifts to the train as it pulls out of the station. The longer accented syllables slow the pace of the poem, aptly reflecting the train as it labours to gather speed. By the end of the stanza the train has departed, and the poem has resumed its iambic metre.

The final stanza focuses on the speaker as he speculates on what he has been observing. His thoughts are carried along in fairly regular iambic lines, a pattern that contrasts with the variable metre that is used to describe the action in the second stanza. Metrics help reinforce the distinction between the speaker and the activity of the railway station. The speaker is not a participant in the events: he is an observer.

Before considering rhyme and other sound effects further, we need to look at one last important dimension of metrics. The standard line of English verse that is meant to be spoken rather than sung is a line of five iambic feet—iambic pentameter. This is the basic line of Chaucer's *Canterbury Tales*, of Spenser's *Faerie Queene*, of Shakespeare's plays, of Milton's *Paradise Lost*, of the satires of Dryden and Pope, of Byron's *Don Juan*, of Wordsworth's *The Prelude*, of Browning's *The Ring and the Book*. This line often appears unrhymed, as in Shakespeare's plays (for the most part), *Paradise Lost*, and *The Prelude*, or in pairs of rhymed lines. Technically, the unrhymed iambic pentameter line is called *blank verse*; the paired rhymes are called *couplets*. In both of these iambic pentameter forms, an important element is the mid-line pause, or *caesura*. Varying the location of the caesura is an important way of preventing monotony in blank verse and pentameter couplets. Consider, for example, these opening lines of Book II of *Paradise Lost*:

> High on a Throne of Royal State, which far
> Outshone the wealth of *Ormus* and of *Ind*,
> Or where the gorgeous East with riches hand
> Show'rs on her King's *Barbaric* Pearl and Gold,
> Satan exalted sat, by merit rais'd
> To that bad eminence; and from despair
> Thus high uplifted beyond hope, aspires
> Beyond thus high, insatiate to pursue
> Vain was with Heav'n, and by success untaught
> His proud imaginations thus display'd.

If we locate the obvious caesuras—those indicated by internal punctuation marks—we find this situation:

line 1 – end of 4th foot
line 2 – none
line 3 – none
line 4 – none
line 5 – end of 3rd foot
line 6 – end of 3rd foot
line 7 – end of 4th foot
line 8 – end of 2nd foot
line 9 – end of 2nd foot
line 10 – none

In reading a poem aloud, we will find ourselves pausing slightly at some point in nearly every line, whether a pause is indicated by punctuation or not. Thus, we can mark the whole passage this way, using a single slash for a slight pause, two for a noticeable one, and three for a full stop:

High on a throne of Royal State, // which far
Outshone / the wealth of Ormus / and of Ind,
Or where the gorgeous East / with riches hand
Show'rs on her kings / Barbaric Peal and Gold,
Satan exalted sat, // by merit rais'd
To that bad eminence; /// and from despair
Thus high uplifted beyond hope, // aspires
Beyond thus high, // insatiate to pursue
Vain war with Heav'n, // and by success untaught
His proud imaginations / thus display'd.

By varying end-stopped lines with enjambed, and deploying caesuras of varying strengths at different points in his line, Milton continually shifts his pauses to prevent the march of his lines from growing wearisome. He also uses substitute feet frequently—especially a trochee or spondee in the first foot of a line. There are three trochees and one spondee in the first feet of these 10 lines.

Now consider Alexander Pope's use of enjambment, caesura, and substitution of feet in the following lines. Pope uses a tight form, with punctuation coming nearly always at the end of each couplet. These closed couplets (as opposed to enjambed, or open, couplets) in iambic pentameter are called *heroic couplets* because they were the standard verse form of Restoration heroic drama (but they might better be called satiric, because they have been most successful in the satiric poems of John Dryden, Pope, and Samuel Johnson).

Using such a tight form as the heroic couplet requires great skill to avoid monotony. When we read only the real masters of such a form, we tend to take such skills for granted, but it is far from easy. In the following two passages, from his 'Essay on Criticism', we find Pope discussing poetic blunders and poetic skill, modulating his own verse deftly to illustrate the points he is making. (The *Alexandrine* referred to is an iambic hexameter line, occasionally used for variety in English iambic pentameter forms.)

These equal syllables alone require,
Though oft the ear the open vowels tire;
While expletives their feeble aid do join;
And ten low words oft creep in one dull line:
While they ring round the same unvaried chimes,
With sure returns of still expected rhymes;
Where'er you find 'the cooling western breeze',
In the next line, it 'whispers through the trees':
If crystal streams 'with pleasing murmurs creep',
The reader's threatened (not in vain) with 'sleep':
Then, at the last and only couplet fraught
With some unmeaning thing they call a thought,
A needless Alexandrine ends the song

That, like a wounded snake, drags its slow length along.
True ease in writing comes from art, not chance,
As those move easiest who have learned to dance.
'Tis not enough no harshness gives offence,
The sound must seem an Echo to the sense:
Soft is the strain when Zephyr gently blows,
And the smooth stream in smoother numbers flows;
But when loud surges lash the sounding shore,
The hoarse, rough verse should like the torrent roar:
When Ajax strives some rock's vast weight to throw,
The line too labours, and the words move slow;
Not so, when swift Camilla scours the plain,
Flies o'er th' unbending corn, and skims along the main.

Rhyme is an important element in musical poetry, but much less so in dramatic poetry—where it can be too artificial—or in meditative poetry. Associated with rhyme as elements designed to generate a pleasure in sound that is almost purely aesthetic are such devices as *alliteration* and *assonance*. Alliteration is the repetition of the same sound at the beginning of words in the same line or adjacent lines. Assonance is the repetition of vowel sounds in the same or adjacent lines. For full rhyme we require the same vowel sounds that end in the same consonantal sounds. 'Fight' and 'foot' are alliterative. 'Fight' and 'bike' are assonant, 'fight' and 'fire' are both assonant and alliterative but do not make a rhyme. 'Fight' and 'bite' make a rhyme. Consider the metrical and sonic effects in this stanza of a poem by Swinburne:

Till the slow sea rise and the sheer cliff crumble,
    Till terrace and meadow the deep gulfs drink,
Till the strength of the waves of the high tides humble
    The fields that lessen, the rocks that shrink,
Here now in his triumph where all things falter,
    Stretched out on the spoils that his own hand spread,
As a god self-slain on his own strange altar,
    Death lies dead.

The metre is mainly a mixture of anapests and spondees—an exotic combination of rapid and slow feet. When reading it, try to discern a pattern in the way the feet are combined. Is there variation in the pattern? Consider also what rhyme, assonance, and alliteration contribute to the pattern.

In addition to its purely aesthetic or decorative effect, designed to charm the reader out of a critical posture and into a receptive one, rhyme can be used for the opposite effect. In satiric or comic verse, strained rhymes are often used to awaken the reader's wits and give a comic kind of pleasure. In the following stanza from Byron's *Don Juan*, the poet uses feminine and even triple rhyme with deliberate clumsiness:

'Tis pity learnèd virgins ever wed
    With persons of no sort of education,
Or gentlemen, who, though well born and bred,
    Grow tired of scientific conversation:
I don't choose to say much upon this head,
    I'm a plain man, and in a single station,
But—Oh! ye lords of ladies intellectual,
Inform us truly, have they not hen-peck'd you all?

The last rhyme in particular is surprising, audacious, and deliberately strained—echoing in this way the sense of the stanza. Like imagery and metrics, rhyme can be used harmoniously or ironically to establish or to break a mood.

Before closing, we should note that it is customary to indicate the rhyme scheme of any given poetic selection by assigning letters of the alphabet to each rhyming sound, repeating each letter as the sound is repeated. The rhyme scheme of the Byron stanza we just considered would be designated this way: *abababcc*, with *a* standing for the sounds in *wed*, *bred*, and *head*; *b*, for . . . *ation*; and *c*, for . . . *ectual* and . . . *eck'd you all*.

## APPROACHING A POEM

Earlier we suggested that an initial reading of a poem is like meeting a person for the first time. We do not, if we are honest, keep in readiness a number of different approaches to poems or to people. We try to keep our integrity. But at the same time we must recognize and accept the otherness that we face. In getting to know a person or a poem we make the kind of accommodation that we have called tact. But we do not pretend, and we try not to let our prejudices govern the way we respond to superficial qualities. We do not judge people by the clothes they are wearing, and we do not judge a poem by words or ideas taken out of their full poetic context. We do not consider a statement in a poem without attention to its dramatic context, the overtones generated by its metaphors and ironies, the mood established by its metrics. And we try to give each element of every poem its proper weight.

Of course, there can be no single method for treating every poem with tact. What is required is a flexible procedure through which we can begin to understand the nature of any poem. The suggestions below are intended to facilitate such a procedure. Like everything else in this book they should serve as scaffolding only—a temporary structure inside of which the real building takes shape. Like any scaffolding, this one must be discarded as soon as it becomes constricting or loses its usefulness. This procedure is not designed to be memorized and applied mechanically. Like good manners learned by rote, it will have served its purpose once it has been replaced by naturally tactful behaviour.

1. Try to grasp the expressive dimension of the poem first. This means getting a clear sense of the nature and situation of the speaker. What are the circumstances under which he or she says, writes, or thinks these words? Who hears them? Are they part of an ongoing action that is implied by them?

2. Consider the relative importance of the narrative–dramatic dimension and the descriptive–meditative dimension in the poem. Is the main interest psychological or philosophical—in character or in idea? Or is the poem's verbal playfulness or music its main reason for being? How do the nature of the speaker and the situation in which the speaker talks colour the ideas and attitudes presented?

3. After you have a sense of the poem's larger, expressive dimension, re-read it with particular attention to the play of language. Consider the way that metaphor and irony colour the ideas and situations. How does the language work to characterize the speaker or to colour the ideas presented with shadings of attitude? How important is sheer wordplay or verbal wit in the poem? How well do the images and ideas fit together and reinforce one another in a metaphoric or ironic way?

4. Re-read the poem yet again, this time with special attention to its musical dimension. To the extent that it seems important, analyze the relation of rhythm and rhyme to the expressive dimension of the poem.

5. Throughout this process, reading the poem aloud can help you detect emphases and locate problems. Parts of a poem you haven't fully understood will prove troublesome in the reading. Questions of tone and attitude will become more insistent in oral performance. Thus, it is advisable to work toward a reading performance as a final check on the degree to which you have mastered situation, ideas, images, attitudes, and music. An expert may be able to read through a piece of piano music and hear in her mind a perfect performance of it. Most of us need to tap out the notes before we can grasp melodies, harmonies, and rhythms with any sureness. Reading poetry aloud helps us establish our grasp of it—especially if a patient and knowledgeable instructor is there to correct our performance and encourage us to try again.

# Geoffrey Chaucer

## 1342–1400

Geoffrey Chaucer was born in the early 1340s, the son of a prosperous merchant family. A member of diplomatic missions, a controller of customs, a justice of the peace, and a member of parliament, he moved in royal circles throughout his life. In his longest work—and an unfinished one—*The Canterbury Tales*, a group of pilgrims travelling together to Canterbury to worship at the shrine of Thomas à Becket decide to recount two tales each along the way. The 'General Prologue' introduces the pilgrims, and 'The Miller's Tale', the second tale in the series, is a fabliau, a comic account of the lower classes.

Chaucer is buried in Westminster Abbey because he was a member of the parish and a tenant of the Abbey. No one in England in 1400, the year of his death, could have imagined that Chaucer's tomb would be the beginning of Poets' Corner, nor that Chaucer himself would come to be acknowledged as the father of poetry in English.

## From *The Canterbury Tales*

### The Miller's Prologue and Tale

#### FROM THE GENERAL PROLOGUE

The MILLERE was a stout carl[1] for the nones;[2]
Ful byg[3] he was of brawn, and eek of bones.
That proved wel, for over al[4] ther he cam,
At wrastlynge he wolde have alwey the ram.[5]
He was short-sholdred,[6] brood, a thikke knarre;[7]
Ther was no dore that he nolde[8] heve of harre,[9]
Or breke it at a rennyng[10] with his heed.
His berd as any sowe or foxe was reed,
And therto brood, as though it were a spade.
Upon the cop[11] right of his nose he hade

1 fellow
2 indeed
3 strong
4 wherever
5 *have . . . ram*: always win the ram (given as a prize)
6 stoutly built (with a thick neck)
7 stout fellow
8 would not
9 lift off its hinges
10 by running up against it
11 top

A werte,[12] and theron stood a toft of herys,[13]
Reed as the brustles[14] of a sowes erys;[15]
His nosethirles[16] blake were and wyde.
A swerd and a bokeler bar he by his side.
His mouth as greet was as a greet forneys.[17]
He was a janglere[18] and a goliardeys,[19]
And that was moost of synne and harlotries.
Wel koude he stelen corn[20] and tollen thries;[21]
And yet he hadde a thombe of gold,[22] pardee.[23]
A whit cote and a blew hood wered he.
A baggepipe wel koude he blowe and sowne,[24]
And therwithal he broghte us out of towne.

## The Miller's Prologue

*Heere folwen the wordes bitwene the Hoost and the Millere.*

Whan that the knight had thus his tale ytoold,
In al the route nas ther yong ne oold
That he ne seyde it was a noble storie
And worthy for to drawen to memorie,[25]
And namely the gentils[26] everichon.
Oure Hooste lough and swoor, 'So moot I gon,
This gooth aright; unbokeled is the male.[27]
Lat se now who shal telle another tale;
For trewely the game is wel bigonne.
Now telleth ye, sir Monk, if that ye konne,[28]
Somwhat to quite with[29] the Knyghtes tale.'
The Millere, that for dronken[30] was al pale,

12 wart
13 tuft of hairs
14 bristles
15 sow's ears
16 nostrils
17 large cauldron
18 a teller of dirty stories
19 buffoon
20 steal grain
21 take toll (payment) three times
22 golden thumb; an ironic reference to a proverb, with the implication that there are no honest millers
23 indeed
24 play
25 *drawen . . . memorie*: remember
26 gentlefolk
27 *unbokeled . . . male*: the pouch is opened, i.e. the game is well begun
28 know
29 with which to repay, or match
30 because of being drunk

So that unnethe[31] upon his hors he sat,
He nolde avalen[32] neither hood ne hat,
Ne abyde no man for his curteisie,
But in Pilates voys[33] he gan to crie,
And swoor, 'By armes, and by blood and bones,
I kan a noble tale for the nones,
With which I wol now quite[34] the Knyghtes tale.'
Oure Hooste saugh that he was dronke of ale,
And seyde, 'Abyd,[35] Robyn, my leeve[36] brother;
Som better man shal telle us first another.
Abyd, and lat us werken thriftily.'[37]
'By Goddes soule,' Quod he, 'that wol nat I;
For I wol speke or elles go my wey.'
Oure Hoost answerde, 'Tel on, a devel wey![38]
Thou art a fool; thy wit is overcome.'
'Now herkneth', quod the Millere, 'alle and some![39]
But first I make a protestacioun
That I am dronke; I knowe it by my soun.
And therefore if that I mysspeke or seye,
Wyte it[40] the ale of Southwerk, I you preye.
For I wol telle a lengende and a lyf
Bothe of a carpenter and of his wyf,
How that a clerk hath set the wrightes cappe.'[41]
The Reve answerde and seyde, 'Stynt thy clappe![42]
Lat be thy lewed dronken harlotrye.
It is a synne and eek a greet folye
To apeyren[43] any man, or hym defame,
And eek to bryngen wyves in swich fame.
Thou mayst ynogh of othere thynges seyn.'
This dronke Millere spak ful soone ageyn[44]
And seyde, 'Leve brother Osewold,
Who hath no wyf, he is no cokewold.[45]

31 hardly
32 take off
33 a loud, ranting voice
34 pay back, requite
35 wait
36 dear
37 properly
38 in the Devil's name
39 one and all
40 blame it on
41 set . . . cappe: deceived, made a fool of the carpenter
42 stop your noisy talk, hold your tongue
43 injure
44 in reply
45 cuckold

But I sey nat therfore that thou art oon;
Ther been ful goode wyves many oon,
And evere a thousand goode ayeyns[46] oon badde.
That knowestow wel thyself, but if thou madde.[47]
Why artow angry with my tale now?
I have a wyf, pardee, as wel as thow;
Yet nolde I, for the oxen in my plogh,
Take upon me moore than ynogh,
As demen of[48] myself that I were oon;[49]
I wol bileve[50] wel that I am noon.
An housbonde shal nat been inquisityf
Of Goddes pryvetee,[51] nor of his wyf.
So he may fynde Goddes foyson[52] there,
Of the remenant nedeth nat enquere.'
What sholde I moore seyn, but this Millere
He nolde his wordes for no man forbere,
But tolde his cherles[53] tale in his manere.
M'athynketh[54] that I shal reherce[55] it here.
And therefore every gentil wight I preye,
For Goddes love, demeth nat that I seye
Of yvel entente, but for I moot reherce
Hir tales alle, be they bettre or werse,
Or elles falsen som of my mateere.
And therefore, whoso list it nat yheere,
Turne over the leef and chese[56] another tale;
For he shal fynde ynowe, grete and smale,[57]
Of storial[58] thyng that toucheth[59] gentillesse,
And eek moralitee and hoolynesse.
Blameth nat me if that ye chese amys.
The Millere is a cherl; ye knowe wel this.
So was the Reve eek and othere mo,
And harlotrie they tolden bothe two.

46 as opposed to
47 go mad
48 to judge, believe of
49 i.e. a cuckold
50 want to believe
51 secrets
52 God's plenty
53 low-born fellows'
54 it displeases me, I regret
55 repeat, narrate
56 choose
57 of every sort
58 historical, true
59 concerns

Avyseth yow,[60] and put me out of blame;
And eek men shal nat maken ernest of game.[61]

## The Miller's Tale

*Heere bigynneth the Millere his tale.*

Whilom ther was dwellynge at Oxenford
A riche gnof,[62] that gestes[63] heeld to bord,[64]
And of his craft he was a carpenter.
With hym ther was dwellynge a poure scoler,[65]
Hadde lerned art,[66] but al his fantasye[67]
Was turned for to lerne astrologye,
And koude[68] a certeyn of conclusiouns,[69]
To demen by interrogaciouns,[70]
If that men asked hym, in certain houres
Whan that men sholde have droghte or elles shoures,
Or if men asked hym what sholde bifalle
Of every thyng; I may nat rekene hem alle.
This clerk was cleped[71] hende[72] Nicholas.
Of deerne[73] love he koude and of solas;[74]
And therto he was sleigh[75] and ful privee,[76]
And lyk a mayden meke for to see.
A chamber hadde he in that hostelrye
Allone, withouten any compaignye,
Ful fetisly ydight with herbes swoote;[77]
And he hymself as sweete as is the roote
Of lycorys or any cetewale.[78]
His Almageste,[79] and bookes grete and smale,

60 consider, think about (this)
61 *make . . . game*: take a joke seriously
62 churl
63 lodgers
64 as boarders
65 impoverished student
66 the arts curriculum at university, esp. logic
67 fancy, desire
68 knew
69 *a . . . conclusions*: a certain number of astrological operations
70 *To . . . interrogaciouns*: to determine by scientific calculations
71 named
72 courteous
73 secret
74 pleasure, satisfaction (of sexual desires)
75 sly
76 discreet, secretive
77 *Ful . . . swoote*: very elegantly adorned with sweet-smelling herbs
78 zedoary (a spice resembling ginger, used as a condiment and stimulant)
79 ptolemy's treatise on astrology

His astrelabie,[80] longynge for[81] his art,
His augrym stones[82] layen faire apart,
On shelves couched[83] at his beddes heed;
His presse[84] ycovered with a faldyng reed;[85]
And al above ther lay a gay sautrie,[86]
On which he made a-nyghtes[87] melodie
So sweetly that all the chambre rong;
And Angelus ad virginem[88] he song;
And after that he song the Kynges Noote.[89]
Ful often blessed was his myrie throte.
And thus this sweete clerk his ryme spente
After his freendes fyndyng and his rente.[90]
This carpenter hadde wedded newe a wyf,
Which that he lovede moore than his lyf;
Of eighteteene yeer she was of age.
Jalous he was, and heeld hire narwe[91] in cage,
For she was wylde and yong, and he was old
And demed hymself been lik a cokewold.
He knew nat Catoun,[92] for his wit was rude,[93]
That bad man sholde wedde his simylitude.[94]
Men sholde wedden after hire estaat,
For youthe and elde[95] is often at debaat.
But sith that he was fallen in the snare,
He moste endure, as oother folk, his care.
Fair was this yonge wyf, and therwithal
As any wezel hir body gent[96] and smal.
A ceynt[97] she werede, barred[98] al of silk,
A barmclooth[99] as whit as morne milk

80 astrolabe
81 belonging to, necessary for (his art, astronomy)
82 counters, for use on an abacus
83 arranged
84 cupboard, linen press
85 coarse red woollen cloth
86 psaltry
87 at night
88 'The angel to the virgin [Mary]'
89 The King's Tune
90 After . . . rente: according to what his friends provided and his income
91 closely
92 cato, author of an elementary school text
93 ignorant, unlearned
94 equal, counterpart
95 old age
96 delicate
97 belt
98 with decorative strips
99 apron

Upon hir lendes,[1] ful of many a goore.[2]
Whit was hir smok,[3] and broyden[4] al bifoore
And eek bihynde, on hir coler[5] aboute,
Of col-blak silk, withinne and eek withoute.
The tapes[6] of hir white voluper[7]
Were of the same suyte of[8] hir coler;
Hir filet[9] brood of silk, and set ful hye.
And sikerly[10] she hadde a likerous[11] ye;
Ful smale ypulled[12] were hire browes two,
And tho were bent and blake as any sloo.[13]
She was ful moore blisful on to see
Than is the newe pere-jonette[14] tree,
And softer than the wolle[15] is of a wether.[16]
And by hir girdle[17] heeng a purs of lether,
Tasseled with silk and perled[18] with latoun.[19]
In al this world, to seken up and doun,
There nys no man so wys that koude thenche[20]
So gay a popelote[21] or swich a wenche.
Ful brighter was the shynyng of hir hewe
Than in the Tour[22] the noble[23] yforged newe.
But of hir song, it was as loude and yerne[24]
As any swalwe[25] sittynge on a berne.[26]
Therto she koude skippe and make game,
As any kyde or calf folwynge his dame.[27]

1 loins
2 flounce
3 shift, undergarment (over which aprons and more elaborate items of clothing are worn)
4 embroidered
5 collar
6 ribbons
7 cap
8 same colour as
9 headband
10 truly
11 flirtatious
12 plucked
13 sloe (a plum-like fruit)
14 early-ripe pear
15 wool
16 sheep (ram)
17 belt
18 adorned
19 a brass-like alloy
20 imagine
21 little doll
22 Tower of London (the mint)
23 a gold coin
24 eager, lively
25 swallow
26 barn
27 mother (dam)

Hir mouth was sweete as bragot[28] or the meeth,[29]
Or hoord of apples leyd in hey or heeth.
Wynsynge[30] she was, as is a joly[31] colt,
Long as a mast, and upright as a bolt.[32]
A brooch she baar upon hir lowe coler,
As brood as is the boos of a bokeler.[33]
Hir shoes were laced on hir legges hye.
She was a prymerole, a piggesnye,[34]
For any lord to leggen[35] in his bedde,
Or yet for any good yeman to wedde.
    Now, sire, and eft,[36] sire, so bifel the cas
That on a day this hende Nicholas
Fil with this yonge wyf to rage[37] and pleye,
Whil that hir housbonde was at Oseneye,
As clerkes ben ful subtile and ful queynte;[38]
And prively he caughte hire by the queynte,[39]
And seyde, 'Ywis,[40] but if ich have my wille,
For deerne[41] love of thee, lemman,[42] I spille.'[43]
And heeld hire harde by the haunchebones,[44]
And seyde, 'Lemman, love me al atones,[45]
Or I wol dyen, also[46] God me save!'
And she sproong[47] as a colt dooth in the trave,[48]
And with hir heed she wryed faste[49] awey,
And seyde, 'I wol nat kisse thee, by my fey!
Why, lat be!' quod she. 'Lat be, Nicholas,
Or I wol crie "out, harrow" and "allas"!
Do wey youre handes, for youre curteisye!'

28 country drink
29 mead
30 skittish
31 spirited
32 crossbow bolt
33 *boos . . . bokeler*: raised centre of a shield
34 primrose, 'pig's eye', names of flowers
35 lay
36 again
37 sport (sexually)
38 ingenious, clever
39 elegant, pleasing (thing), i.e. pudendum
40 truly, indeed
41 secret
42 my love, sweetheart
43 die
44 thighs
45 at once, immediately
46 as
47 sprang
48 frame for holding a horse to be shod
49 turned rapidly, twisted

This Nicholas gan mercy for to crye,
And spak so faire, and profred him[50] so faste,
That she hir love hym graunted atte laste,
And swoor hir ooth, by Seint Thomas of Kent,[51]
That she wol been at his comandement,
Whan that she may hir leyser[52] wel espie.
'Myn housbonde is so ful of jalousie
That but ye wayte[53] wel and been privee,[54]
I woot right wel I nam but deed,' quod she.
'Ye moste been ful deerne,[55] as in this cas.'
'Nay, therof care thee noght,' quod Nicholas.
'A clerk hadde litherly biset his whyle,[56]
But if he koude a carpenter bigyle.'
And thus they been accorded and ysworn
To wayte a tyme, as I have told biforn.
Whan Nicholas had doon thus everideel
And thakked[57] hire aboute the lendes[58] weel,
He kiste hire sweete and taketh his sawtrie,
And pleyeth faste, and maketh melodie.
Thanne fil it thus, that to the paryssh chirche,
Cristes owene wekes for to wirche,
This goode wyf went on an haliday.[59]
Hir forheed shoon as bright as any day,
So was it wasshen whan she leet[60] hir werk.
Now was ther of that chirche a parissh clerk,
The which that was ycleped Absolon.
Crul[61] was his heer, and as the gold it shoon,
And strouted as a fanne[62] large and brode;
Ful streight and evene lay his joly shode.[63]
His rode[64] was reed, his eyen greye as goos.
With Poules window[65] corven[66] on his shoos,

50 pressed his suit
51 Thomas Becket
52 opportunity
53 await, watch for (an opportunity)
54 discreet, secretive
55 secretive
56 *litherly . . . whyle*: wasted his time
57 patted
58 loins
59 holy day
60 left
61 curled
62 stretched out like a fan
63 parted hair
64 complexion
65 window of St Paul's
66 carved

In hoses rede he wente fetisly.[67]
Yclad he was ful smal[68] and properly
Al in a kirtel[69] of a light waget;[70]
Ful faire and thikke been the poyntes[71] set.
And thereupon he hadde a gay surplys[72]
As whit as is the blosme upon the rys.[73]
A myrie child[74] he was, so God me save.
Wel koude he laten blood,[75] and clippe[76] and shave,
  And maken a chartre[77] of lond or acquitaunce.[78]
In twenty manere[79] koude he trippe and daunce
After the scole[80] of Oxenforde tho,
And with his legges casten[81] to and fro,
And pleyen songes on a smal rubible;[82]
Therto he song som tyme a loud quynyble;[83]
And as wel koude he pleye on a giterne.[84]
In al the toun nas brewhous ne taverne
That he ne visited with his solas,[85]
Ther any gaylard tappestere[86] was.
But sooth so seyn, he was somdeel squaymous[87]
Of fartyng, and of speche daungerous.[88]
  This Absolon, that jolif[89] was and gay,
Gooth with a sencer[90] on the haliday,
Sensynge[91] the wyves of the parisshe faste;
And many a lovely look on hem he caste,
And namely on this carpenteris wyf.

67 elegantly
68 tightly, in close-fitting clothes
69 tunic
70 light blue
71 laces
72 surplice (ecclesiastical gown)
73 twig
74 young man
75 let blood (as a medical treatment)
76 cut hair
77 deed
78 quittance (legal release of property)
79 twenty ways
80 in the style, fashion
81 move quickly
82 rebeck, a kind of fiddle
83 high treble
84 cithern, a stringed instrument
85 entertainment
86 merry barmaid
87 somewhat squeamish
88 fastidious
89 pretty, lively
90 censer
91 censing

To looke on hire hym thoughte a myrie lyf,
She was so proper and sweete and likerous.
I dar wel seyn, if she hadde been a mous,
And he a cat, he wolde hire hente anon.
This parissh clerk, this joly Absolon,
Hath in his herte swich a love-longynge
That of no wyf took he noon offrynge;
For curteisie, he seyde, he wolde noon.
  The moone, whan it was nyght, ful brighte shoon,
And Absolon his gyterne hath ytake;
For paramours[92] he thoghte for to wake.
And forth he gooth, jolif and amorous,
Til he cam to the carpenteres hous
A litel after cokkes hadde ycrowe,
And dressed hym[93] up by a shot-wyndowe[94]
That was upon the carpenteris wal.
He syngeth in his voys gentil and smal,[95]
'Now, deere lady, if thy wille be,
I praye yow that ye wole rewe[96] on me,'
Ful wel acordaunt to[97] his gyternynge.[98]
This carpenter awook, and herde him synge,
And spak unto his wyf, and seyde anon,
'What! Alison! Herestow nat Absolon,
That chaunteth[99] thus under oure boures[1] wal?'
And she answerde hir housbonde therwithal,
'Yis, God woot, John, I here it every deel.'[2]
  This passeth forth; what wol ye bet than weel?[3]
Fro day to day this joly Absolon
So woweth hire that hym is wo bigon.
He waketh al the nyght and al the day;
He kembeth[4] his lokkes brode, and made hym gay;
He woweth hire by meenes[5] and brocage,[6]
And swoor he wolde been hir owene page;

92 for the sake of love
93 took his place
94 hinged window (one that opens and closes)
95 high
96 have mercy
97 in harmony with
98 playing on the cithern
99 sings
1 next to our bedchamber's
2 every bit
3 better than well (i.e. what more would you have?)
4 combs
5 go-betweens, intermediaries
6 use of an agent

He syngeth, brokkynge[7] as a nyghtyngale;
He sente hire pyment,[8] meeth, and spiced ale,
And wafres,[9] pipying hoot out of the gleede;[10]
And, for she was of town, he profred meede;[11]
For som folk wol ben wonnen for richesse,
And somme for strokes,[12] and somme for gentillesse.
  Somtyme, to shewe his lightnesse[13] and maistrye,[14]
He pleyeth Herodes[15] upon a scaffold hye.[16]
But what availleth hym as in this cas?
She loveth so this hende Nicholas
That Absolon may blowe the bukkes horn;[17]
He ne hadde for his labour but a scorn.
And thus she maketh Absolon hire ape,
And al his ernest turneth til a jape.[18]
Ful sooth is this proverbe, it is no lye,
Men seyn right thus: 'Alwey the nye slye[19]
Maketh the ferre leeve to be looth.'[20]
For though that Absolon be wood or wrooth,
By cause that he fer was from hire sight,
This nye Nicholas stood in his light.[21]
  Now ber thee wel, thou hende Nicholas,
For Absolon may waille and synge 'allas'.
And so bifel it on a Saterday,
This carpenter was goon til Osenay;
And hende Nicholas and Alisoun
Acorded been to this conclusioun,
That Nicholas shal shapen hym a wyle[22]
This sely[23] jalous housbonde to bigyle;
And if so be the game wente aright,
She sholde slepen in his arm al nyght.
For this was his desir and hire also.

7 trilling
8 spiced, sweetened wine
9 cakes
10 fire
11 offered money
12 i.e. by force
13 agility
14 skill
15 the part of Herod
16 stage
17 *blowe . . . horn*: go whistle
18 joke
19 nigh (at hand) sly one
20 *ferre . . . looth*: distant loved one to be disliked
21 in his way (i.e. prevented his being seen)
22 trick
23 innocent, simple, hapless

And right anon, witouten wordes mo,
This Nicholas no lenger wolde tarie,
But dooth ful softe unto his chamber carie
Bothe mete and drynke for a day or tweye,
And to hire housbonde bad hire for to seye,
If that he axed after Nicholas,
She sholde seye she nyste where he was;
Of al that day she saugh hym nat with ye;
She trowed[24] that he was in maladye,[25]
For, for no cry hir mayde koude hum calle,
He nolde answere for thyng that myghte falle.[26]
   This passeth forth al thilke Saterday,
That Nicholas stille in his chamber lay,
And eet and sleep, or dide what hym leste,
Til Sonday, that the sonne gooth to reste.
This sely carpenter hath greet merveyle
Of[27] Nicholas, or what thyng myghte hym eyle,[28]
And seyde, 'I am adrad, by Seint Thomas,
It stondeth nat aright with Nicholas.
God shilde[29] that he deyed sodeynly!
This world is now ful tikel,[30] sikerly.
I saugh today a cors[31] yborn to chirche
That now, on Monday last, I saugh hym[32] wirche.[33]
   'Go up,' quod he unto his knave[34] anoon,
'Clepe[35] at his dore, or knokke with a stoon.
Looke how it is, and tel me boldely.'
   This knave gooth hym up ful sturdily,[36]
And at the chambre dore whil that he stood,
He cride and knocked as that he were wood,
'What, how! What do ye, maister Nicholay?
How may ye slepen al the longe day?'
   But al for noght; he herde nat a word.
An hole he foond, ful lowe upon a bord,
Ther as the cat was wont in for to crepe,

24 believed
25 ill
26 befall, happen
27 *hath . . . Of*: wondered about
28 ail
29 God forbid
30 unstable, ticklish
31 corpse
32 *That . . . him*: whom
33 work
34 servant
35 call out
36 boldly

And at that hole he looked in ful depe,
And at the laste he hadde of hym a sight.
This Nicholas sat evere capyng upright,[37]
As he had kiked[38] on the newe moone.
Adoun he gooth, and tolde his maister soone[39]
In what array[40] he saugh this ilke man.
  This carpenter to blessen hym bigan,
And seyde, 'Help us, Seinte Frydeswyde![41]
A man woot litel what hym shal bityde.
This an is falle, with his astromye,[42]
In som woodnesse or in som agonye.[43]
I thoghte ay wel how that it sholde be!
Men sholde nat knowe of Goddes pryvetee.[44]
Ye, blessed be alwey a lewed man
That noght but oonly his bileve kan![45]
So ferde[46] another clerk with astromye;
He walked in the feeldes for to prye[47]
Upon the sterres, what ther sholde bifalle,
Til he was in a marle-pit[48] yfalle;
He saugh nat that. But yet, by Seint Thomas,
Me reweth soore of[49] hende Nicholas.
He shal be rated of[50] his studiyng,
If that I may, by Jhesus, hevene kyng!
Get me a staf, that I may underspore,[51]
Whil that thou, Robyn, hevest up the dore.
He shal[52] out of his studiyng, as I gesse.'
And to the chambre dore he gan hym dresse.
His knave was a strong carl for the nones,
And by the haspe he haaf it of[53] atones;[54]
Into the floor the dore fil anon.

37 gaping straight up
38 gazed
39 immediately
40 condition
41 St Frideswide, noted for her healing powers
42 astonomy
43 fit
44 God's secrets
45 *That . . . kan!*: who knows nothing but his creed
46 fared
47 gaze
48 clay pit
49 *Me . . . of*: I feel sorry for
50 scolded for
51 pry up from under
52 shall come (verb of motion is understood)
53 heaved it off
54 at once

This Nicholas sat ay as stille as stoon,
And evere caped[55] upward into the eir.
This carpenter wende he were[56] in despeir,
And hente hym by the sholdres myghtily,
And shook hym harde, and cride spitously,[57]
'What! Nicholay! What, how! What, looke adoun!
Awak, and thenk on Cristes passioun!
I crouche[58] thee from elves[59] and fro wightes.'[60]
Therwith the nyght-spel[61] seyde he anon-rightes[62]
On foure halves of the hous aboute,
And on the thresshfold of the dore withoute:
'Jhesu Crist and Seinte Benedight,
Blesse this hous from every wikked wight,[63]
For nyghtes verye,[64] the white *pater-noster*![65]
Where wentestow, Seinte Petres soster?'[66]
    And atte laste this hende Nicholas
Gan for to sik[67] soore, and seyde, 'Allas!
Shal al the world be lost eftsoones now?'[68]
    This carpenter answerde, 'What seystow?
What! Thynk on God, as we doon, men that swynke.'[69]
    This Nicholas answerde, 'Fecche me drynke,
And after wol I speke in pryvetee
Of certeyn thyng that toucheth[70] me and thee.
I wol telle it noon oother man, certeyn.'
    This carpenter goth doun, and comth ageyn,
And broghte of myghty ale a large quart;
And whan that ech of hem had dronke his part,
This Nicholas his dore faste shette,
And doun the carpenter by hym he sette.
    He sayde, 'John, myn hooste, lief[71] and deere,
Thou shalt upon thy trouthe swere me heere

55 gaped
56 supposed he was
57 vigorously, loudly
58 make the sign of the cross as a blessing over
59 evil spirits
60 (evil) creatures
61 a charm
62 straightaway
63 creature
64 *For . . . verye*: against evil spirits of the night (?)
65 a charm
66 *Where . . . soster?*: Where did you go, St Peter's sister?
67 sigh
68 right now
69 work
70 concerns
71 beloved

That to no wight thou shalt this conseil wreye[72]
For it is Cristes conseil that I seye,
And if thou telle it man, thou art forlore;[73]
For this vengeaunce thou shalt han therfore,
That if thou wreye[74] me, thou shalt be wood.'
'Nay, Crist forbade it, for his hooly blood!'
Quod tho this sely[75] man, 'I nam no labbe,[76]
Ne, though I seye, I nam nat lief to gabbe.[77]
Sey what thou wolt, I shal it nevere telle
To child ne wyf, by hym that harwed helle!'[78]
    'Now John,' quod Nicholas, 'I wol nat lye;
I have yfounde in my astrologye,
As I have looked in the moone bright,
That now a Monday next, at quarter nyght,[79]
Shal falle a reyn, and that so wilde and wood
That half so greet was nevere Noes[80] flood.
This world', he seyde, 'in lasse than an hour
Shal al be dreynt,[81] so hidous is the shour.
Thus shal mankynde drenche,[82] and lese hir lyf.'[83]
    This carpenter answerde, 'Allas, my wyf!
And shal she drenche? Allas, myn Alisoun!'
For sorwe of this he fil almoost adoun,
And seyde, 'Is ther no remedie in this cas?'
    'Why, yis, for Gode,' quod hende Nicholas,
'If thou wolt werken after loore[84] and reed.[85]
Thou mayst nat werken after thyn owene heed;[86]
For thus seith Salomon, that was ful trewe:
"Werk al by conseil, and thou shalt nat rewe." [87]
And if thou werken wolt by good conseil,
I undertake,[88] withouten mast and seyl,
Yet shal I saven hire and thee and me.

72 reveal
73 lost
74 betray
75 innocent, ignorant, hapless
76 blabbermouth
77 *I nam . . . gabbe*: I do not like to gab
78 *hym . . . helle*: Christ, who despoiled Hell of its captives
79 a quarter way through the night; in April, after midnight
80 Noah's
81 drowned
82 drown
83 their lives
84 learning
85 (good) advice
86 head (i.e. ideas)
87 be sorry
88 affirm, declare

Hastow nat herd hou saved was Noe,
Whan that oure Lord hadde warned hym biforn
That al the world with water sholde be lorn?'[89]
'Yis,' quod this Carpenter, 'ful yoore ago.'[90]
'Hastou nat herd', quod Nicholas, 'also
The sorwe of Noe[91] with his felaweshipe,
Er that he myghte gete his wyf to shipe?
Hym hadde be levere, I dar wel undertake,
At thilke tyme, than alle his wetheres blake
That she hadde had a ship hirself allone.[92]
And therfore, woostou what is best to doone?
This asketh haste, and of an hastif thyng
Men may nat preche or maken tariyng.
'Anon go gete us faste into this in[93]
A knedyng trogh,[94] or ellis a kymelyn,[95]
For ech of us, but looke that they be large,
In which we mowe swymme[96] as in a barge,
And han therinne vitaille suffisant[97]
But for a day—fy on the remenant!
The water shal aslake[98] and goon away
Aboute pryme[99] upon the nexte day.
But Robyn may nat wite of this, thy knave,
Ne eek thy mayde Gille I may nat save;
Axe nat why, for though thou aske me,
I wol nat tellen Goddes pryvetee.
Suffiseth thee, but if thy wittes madde,[1]
To han as greet a grace as Noe hadde.
Thy wyf shal I wel saven, out of doute.
Go now thy wey, and speed thee heer-aboute.[2]
'But whan thou hast, for hire and thee and me,
Ygeten us thise knedyng tubbes thre,
Thanne shaltow hange hem in the roof ful hye,

89 lost
90 long ago
91 Noah, here as a character in the popular mystery plays
92 *Hym hadde be levere . . . allone*: He would have preferred, I dare affirm, that she had a ship all to herself, than have all his black sheep; i.e. he would have given all his sheep for this.
93 house
94 a large trough for kneading dough
95 a large tub for brewing beer
96 float
97 enough food
98 subside
99 around 9 a.m.
1 go mad
2 about this matter

That no man of oure purveiaunce[3] espye.
And whan thou thus hast doon as I have seyd,
And hast oure vitaille faire in hem yleyd,
And eek an ax to smyte the corde atwo,[4]
Whan that the water comth, that we may go
And breke an hole an heigh, upon the gable,
Unto the gardyn-ward,[5] over the stable,
That we may frely passen forth oure way,
Whan that the grete shour is goon away.
Thanne shaltou swymme as myrie, I undertake,
As dooth the white doke after hire drake.
Thanne wol I clepe, "How, Alison! How, John!
Be myrie, for the flood wol passe anon."
And thou wolt seyn, "Hayl, maister Nicholay!
Good morwe, I se thee wel, for it is day."
And thanne shul we be lordes al oure lyf
Of al the world, as Noe and his wyf.
'But of o thyng I warne thee ful right:
Be wel avysed[6] on that ilke nyght
That we ben entred into shippes bord,
That noon of us ne speke nat a word,
Ne clepe, ne crie, but be in his preyere;
For it is Goddes owene heeste[7] deere.
'Thy wyf and thou moote hange fer atwynne;[8]
For that bitwixe yow shal be no synne,
Namoore in lookyng than ther shal in deede.
This ordinance is seyd. Go, God thee speede!
Tomorwe at nyght, whan men ben alle aslepe,
Into oure knedyng-tubbes wol we crepe,
And sitten there, abidyng Goddes grace.
Go now thy wey; I have no lenger space[9]
To make of this no lenger sermonyng.[10]
Men seyn thus, "sende the wise, and sey no thyng."
Thou art so wys, it needeth thee nat teche.
Go, save oure lyf, and that I the biseche.'
This sely carpenter goth forth his wey.
Ful ofte he seide, 'Allas and weylawey,'

3 preparations
4 in two
5 toward the garden
6 well warned
7 commandment
8 apart
9 time
10 talk

And to his wyf he tolde his pryvetee,
And she was war, and knew it bet[11] than he,
What al this queynte cast[12] was for to seye.[13]
But nathelees she ferde as she wolde deye,
And seyde, 'Allas! go forth thy wey anon,
Help us to scape, or we been dede echon![14]
I am thy trewe, verray wedded wyf;
Go, deere spouse, and help to save oure lyf.'
Lo, which a[15] greet thyng is affeccioun![16]
Men may dyen of ymaginacioun,[17]
So depe may impressioun be take.
This sely carpenter bigynneth quake;
Hym thynketh verraily that he may see
Noees flood come walwynge[18] as the see
To drenchen Alisoun, his hony deere.
He wepeth, weyleth, maketh sory cheere;[19]
He siketh with ful many a sory swogh;[20]
He gooth and geteth hym a knedyng trogh,
And after that a tubbe and a kymelyn,
And pryvely he sente hem to his in,
And heng him in the roof in pryvetee.
His owene hand[21] he made laddres thre,
To clymben by the ronges and the stalkes[22]
Unto the tubbes hangynge in the balkes,[23]
And hem vitailled,[24] bothe trogh and tubbe,
With breed, and chese, and good ale in a jubbe,[25]
Suffisynge right ynogh as for a day.
But er that he hadde maad al this array,[26]
He sente his knave and eek his wenche[27] also,
Upon his nede[28] to London for to go.

11 better
12 ingenious plot
13 mean
14 each one
15 what a
16 emotion
17 fantasy
18 surging
19 *maketh sory cheere*: looks sad, wretched
20 groan
21 *His owene hand*: by himself
22 uprights (of the ladder)
23 beams
24 stocked with provisions
25 large container, jug
26 preparation
27 servant girl
28 business

And on the Monday, whan it drow to nyght,
He shette his dore withoute candel-lyght,
And dressed[29] alle thynge as it sholde be.
And shortly, up they clomben alle thre;
They seten stille wel a furlong way.[30]
  'Now, *Pater-noster*, clom!'[31] seyde Nicholay,
And 'Clom!' quod John, and 'Clom!' seyde Alisoun.
This carpenter seyde his devocioun,
And stille he sit, and biddeth[32] his preyere,
Awaitynge on the reyn, if he it heere.
  The dede sleep, for wery bisynesse,[33]
Fil on this carpenter right, as I gesse,
Aboute corfew-tyme,[34] or litel moore;
For travaille of his goost[35] he groneth soore,
And eft[36] he routeth,[37] for his heed myslay.[38]
Doun of the laddre stalketh Nicholay,
And Alisoun ful softe adoun she spedde;
Withouten wordes mo they goon to bedde,
Ther as the carpenter is wont[39] to lye.
There was the revel and the melodye;
And thus lith Alison and Nicholas,
In bisyness of myrthe and of solas,
Til that the belle laudes[40] gan to rynge,
And frere in the cauncel gonne synge.
  This parissh clerk, this amorous Absolon,
That is for love alwey so wo bigon,
Upon the Monday was at Oseneye
With compaignye, hym to disporte and pley,
And axed upon cas[41] a cloisterer
Ful prively after John the carpenter;
And he drough[42] hym apart out of the chirche,
And seyde, 'I noot; I saugh hym heere nat wirche
Syn Saterday; I trowe that he be went

29 arranged
30 a couple of minutes
31 *Now . . . clom!*: now say a Paternoster (Lord's Prayer) and then hush!
32 prays
33 wearied by this work
34 dusk
35 suffering of his spirit, mental anguish
36 likewise
37 snores
38 lay wrong
39 accustomed
40 an early morning service, before daybreak
41 by chance
42 drew

For tymber, ther oure abbot hath hym sent;
For he is wont for tymber for to go
And dwellen at the grange[43] a day or two;
Or elles he is at his hous, certeyn.
Where that he be, I kan nat soothly seyn.'
  This Absolon ful joly was and light,[44]
And thoghte, 'Now is tyme to wake al nyght,
For sikirly I saugh hym nat stirynge
Aboute his dore, syn day bigan to sprynge.
  'So moot I thryve,[45] I shal, at cokkes crow,
Ful pryvely knokken at his wyndowe
That stant[46] ful lowe upon his boures wal.
To Alison now wol I tellen al
My love-longynge, for yet I shal nat mysse[47]
That at the leeste wey[48] I shal hire kisse.
Som maner confort shal I have, parfay.[49]
My mouth hath icched[50] al this longe day;
That is a signe of kissyng atte leeste.
Al nyght me mette[51] eek I was at a feeste.
Therfore I wol go slepe an houre or tweye,
And al the nyght thanne wol I wake and pleye.'
  Whan that the first cok hath crowe, anon
Up rist[52] this joly lovere Absolon,
And hym arraieth gay,[53] at poynt-devys.[54]
But first he cheweth greyn[55] and lycorys,
To smellen sweete, er he hadde kembd his heer.
Under his tonge a trewe-love[56] he beer,
For therby wende he to ben gracious.[57]
He rometh to the carpenteres hous,
And stille he stant under[58] the shot-wyndowe[59]—

43 outlying farm
44 happy
45 *So . . . thrive*: as I may prosper
46 stands
47 fail
48 at least
49 indeed, by my faith
50 itched
51 I dreamed
52 rises
53 *hym arraieth gay*: dresses himself handsomely
54 in every detail, completely
55 grain of Paradise, cardamom seed, a breath freshener
56 a four-leafed sprig of herb paris (Paris quadrifolia) in the shape of a fourfold true-love knot
57 attractive
58 next to
59 hinged window

Unto his brest it raughte,[60] it was so lowe—
And softe he cougheth with a semy soun:[61]
'What do ye, hony-comb, sweete Alisoun,
My faire bryd,[62] my sweete cynamome?[63]
Awaketh, lemman[64] myn, and speketh to me!
Wel litel thynken ye upon my wo,
That for youre love I swete ther I go.
No wonder is thogh that I swelte[65] and swete;[66]
I moorne[67] as dooth a lamb after the tete.
Ywis,[68] lemman, I have swich love-longynge
That lik a turtel[69] trewe is my moornynge.
I may nat ete na moore than a mayde.'
  'Go fro the wyndow, Jakke fool,'[70] she sayde;
'As help me God, it wol nat be "com pa me".[71]
I love another—and elles I were to blame—
Wel bet than thee, by Jhesu, Absolon.
Go forth thy wey, or I wol caste a ston,
And lat me slepe, a twenty devel wey!'[72]
  'Allas,' quod Absolon, 'and weylawey,
That trewe love was evere so yvel biset![73]
Thanne kysse me, syn it may be no bet,
For Jhesus love, and for the love of me.'
  'Wiltow thanne go thy wey therwith?' quod she.
  'Ye, certes, lemman,' quod this Absolon.
  'Thanne make thee redy,' quod she, 'I come anon.'
And unto Nicholas she seyde stille,
'Now hust,[74] and thou shalt laughen al thy fille.'
  This Absolon doun sette hym on his knees
And seyde, 'I am a lord at alle degrees;[75]
For after this I hope ther cometh moore.
Lemman, thy grace, and sweete bryd, thyn oore!'[76]

60 reached
61 small, gentle sound
62 bird (i.e. sweetheart)
63 cinnamon
64 sweetheart
65 grow faint
66 sweat
67 yearn
68 truly, indeed
69 turtledove
70 you idiot
71 come kiss me
72 in the name of twenty devils
73 *so yvel biset*: in such miserable circumstances
74 be quiet
75 in every way
76 mercy, grace

The wyndow she undoth,[77] and that in haste
'Have do,'[78] quod she, 'com of,[79] and speed the faste,[80]
Lest that oure neighebores thee espie.'
This Absolon gan wype his mouth ful drie.
Derk was the nyght as pich, or as the cole,
And at the wyndow out she putte hir hole,
And Absolon, hym fil no bet ne wers,
But with his mouth he kiste hir naked ers
Ful savourly, er he were war of this.
Abak he stirte, and thoughte it was amys,
For wel he wiste a womman hath no berd.
He felte a thyng al rough and long yherd,[81]
And seyde, 'Fy! allas! what have I do?'
'Tehee!' quod she, and clapte the wyndow to,
And Absolon gooth forth a sory pas.[82]
'A berd! A berd!'[83] quod hende Nicholas,
'By Goddes corpus,[84] this goth faire and weel.'
This sely Absolon herde every deel,[85]
And on his lippe he gan for anger byte,
And to hymself he seyde, 'I shal thee quyte.'[86]
Who rubbeth now, who froteth[87] now his lippes
With dust, with sond, with straw, with clooth, with chippes,
But Absolon, that seith ful ofte, 'Allas!'
'My soule bitake[88] I unto Sathanas,
But me were levere than al this toun,'[89] quod he,
'Of this despit[90] awroken[91] for to be.
Allas,' quod he, 'allas, I ne hadde ybleynt!'[92]
His hoote love was coold and al yqueynt;[93]
For fro that tyme that he hadde kist hir ers,
Of paramours he sette nat a kers,[94]
For he was heeled of his maladie.

77 opens
78 finish up
79 hurry up
80 be quick
81 long-haired
82 *a sory pas*: sadly
83 beard
84 body
85 every bit
86 pay back (revenge)
87 rubs
88 give
89 *But . . . toun*: if I would not rather than (own) all this town
90 insult
91 avenged
92 turned away
93 quenched
94 cress (i.e. something of no value)

Ful ofte paramours he gan deffie,[95]
And weep as dooth a child that is ybete.
A softe paas he wente over the strete
Until[96] a smyth men cleped daun[97] Gerveys,
That in his forge smythed plough harneys;[98]
He sharpeth[99] shaar[1] and kultour[2] bisily.
This Absolon knokketh al esily,[3]
And seyde, 'Undo,[4] Gerveys, and that anon.'
'What, who artow?' 'It am I, Absolon.'
'What, Absolon! for Cristes sweete tree,[5]
Why rise ye so rathe?[6] Ey, benedicitee!
What eyleth yow? Som gay gerl,[7] God it woot,
Hath broght yow thus upon the viritoot.[8]
By Seinte Note,[9] ye woot wel what I mene.'
This Absolon ne roghte nat a bene[10]
Of al his pley; no word agayn he yaf;
He hadde moore tow on his distaf[11]
Than Gerveys knew, and seyde, 'Freend so deere,
That hoote kultour in the chymenee[12] heere,
As lene[13] it me; I have therwith to doone,
And I wol brynge it thee agayn ful soone.'
Gerveys answerde, 'Certes, were it gold,
Or in a poke nobles alle untold,[14]
Thou sholdes have, as I am trewe smyth.
Ey, Cristes foo![15] What wol ye do therwith?'
'Therof', quod Absolon, 'be as be may.
I shal wel telle it thee to-morwe day'—
And caughte the kultour by the colde stele.[16]

95 repudiate
96 to
97 sir
98 ploughing equipment
99 sharpens
1 ploughshare
2 vertical blade at the front of the plough
3 gently
4 open up
5 dear cross
6 early
7 good-looking girl
8 *upon the virtroot*: astir (?)
9 St Neot
10 *roghte . . . bene*: cared not a bean
11 flax on his distaff (i.e. more business on hand)
12 hearth
13 lend
14 bag of countless gold coins
15 ah, by Christ's foe (i.e. the Devil)
16 handle

Ful softe out at the dore he gan to stele,
And wente unto the carpenteris wal.
He cogheth first, and knokketh therwithal
Upon the wyndowe, right as he dide er.
This Alison answerde, 'Who is ther
That knokketh so? I warante[17] it a theef.'
'Why, nay,' quod he, 'God woot, my sweete leef,[18]
I am thyn Absolon, my deerelyng.[19]
Of gold', quod he, 'I have thee broght a ryng.
My mooder yaf it me, so God me save;
Ful fyn it is, and therto wel ygrave.[20]
This wol I yeve thee, if thou me kisse.'
This Nicholas was risen for to pisse,
And thoughte he wolde amenden al the jape;[21]
He sholde kisse his ers er that he scape.
And up the wyndowe dide he hastily,
And out his ers he putteth pryvely
Over the buttok, to the haunche-bon;[22]
And therwith spak this clerk, this Absolon,
'Spek, sweete bryd, I noot nat where thou art.'
This Nicholas anon leet fle a fart
As greet as it had been a thonder-dent,[23]
That with the strook he was almoost yblent;[24]
And he was redy with his iren hoot,
And Nicholas amydde the ers he smoot.
Of[25] gooth the skyn an hande-brede aboute,[26]
The hoote kultour brende so his toute,[27]
And for the smert[28] he wende for to dye.[29]
As he were wood, for wo he gan to crye,
'Help! Water! Water! Help, for Goddes herte!'[30]
This carpenter out of his slomber sterte,
And herde oon crien 'Water!' as he were wood,

17 swear
18 beloved
19 darling
20 engraved
21 make the joke even better
22 thigh
23 thunder clap
24 blinded
25 off
26 a hand's width all around
27 rump
28 pain
29 thought he would die
30 heart

And thoughte, 'Allas, now comth Nowelis[31] flood!'
He sit hym up withouten wordes mo,
And with his ax he smoot the corde atwo,
And doun gooth al; he foond neither to selle,
Ne breed ne ale,[32] til he cam to the celle[33]
Upon the floor, and ther aswowne[34] he lay.
Up stirte hire Alison and Nicholay,
And criden 'Out' and 'Harrow' in the strete.
The neighebores, bothe smale and grete,[35]
In ronnen[36] for to gauren on[37] this man,
That yet aswowne lay, bothe pale and wan,
For with the fal he brosten[38] hadde his arm.
But stonde he moste unto his owene harm;[39]
For whan he spak, he was anon bore doun
With[40] hende Nicholas and Alisoun.
They tolden every man that he was wood;
He was agast[41] so of Nowelis flood
Thurgh fantasie that of his vanytee[42]
He hadde yboght hym knedyng tubbes thre,
And hadde hem hanged in the roof above;
And that he preyed hem, for Goddes love,
To sitten in the roof, par compaignye.[43]
The folk gan laughen at his fantasye;
Into the roof they kiken[44] and they cape,[45]
And turned al his harm unto a jape.
For what so that this carpenter answerde,
It was for noght; no man his reson herde.
With othes grete he was so sworn adoun[46]
That he was holde wood in al the toun;
For every clerk anonright[47] heeld[48] with oother.

31 Noah's
32 *he foond . . . ne ale*: he did not stop to sell bread or ale on the way (i.e. he wasted no time)
33 floor
34 in a faint
35 i.e. everyone
36 ran
37 stare at
38 broken
39 *But stonde . . . harm*: but he had to stand up, though it turned out badly for him
40 by
41 frightened
42 foolishness
43 for fellowship's sake, to keep him company
44 stare
45 gape
46 overcome by oaths
47 immediately
48 held, agreed

They seyde, 'The man is wood, my leeve brother';
And every wight gan laughen at this stryf.
Thus swyved[49] was this carpenteris wyf,
For al his kepyng[50] and his jalousye,
And Absolon hath kist hir nether ye,[51]
And Nicholas is scalded in the towte.
This tale is doon, and God save al the rowte!
*Heere endeth the Millere his tale.*

49 copulated with
50 guarding
51 lower eye

# William Shakespeare

1564–1616

William Shakespeare was born into a middle-class family in the Warwickshire market town of Stratford-on-Avon. His father, a glover by trade, was a leading citizen who held the office of bailiff, a position equivalent to mayor. As a boy, Shakespeare attended the very strict Stratford Grammar School, where the curriculum consisted of grammar, reading, writing, and recitation, done almost entirely in Latin. In 1582, when he was 18, Shakespeare married Anne Hathaway. Little else is known of him until 1592, by which time he had established himself as an author and playwright in the London theatre world. He turned to writing poetry when an outbreak of the plague closed the London theatres from the summer of 1592 until June 1594. Most of Shakespeare's 154 sonnets were written between 1593 and 1599, and about 10 were written between then and 1609, the year they were published. The sonnets were dedicated 'To the Onlie Begetter of these ensuing Sonnets Mr W.H.', who was probably Shakespeare's patron but whose identity is not known. Nor have scholars been able to establish identities for the characters found in the sonnets: the poet's young friend of high social position who is addressed in sonnets 1–126; the 'dark lady' of sonnets 127–54, who causes joy and pain for the poet; and a rival poet. Though the autobiographical mystery is tantalizing, it is probably wiser to read and enjoy the sonnets for the mastery of language and form that was to inspire so many other poets.

## Sonnets

### 18

Shall I compare thee to a summer's day?
Thou art more lovely and more temperate.
Rough winds do shake the darling buds of May,
And summer's lease hath all too short a date.
Sometime too hot the eye of heaven shines,

And often is his gold complexion dimmed,
And every fair from fair sometime declines,
By chance or nature's changing course untrimmed;
But thy eternal summer shall not fade
Nor lose possession of that fair thou ow'st,
Nor shall death brag thou wander'st in his shade
When in eternal lines to time thou grow'st.
So long as men can breathe or eyes can see,
So long lives this, and this gives life to thee.

## 29

When, in disgrace with fortune and men's eyes,
I all alone beweep my outcast state,
And trouble deaf heaven with my bootless cries,
And look upon myself and curse my fate,
Wishing me like to one more rich in hope,
Featured like him, like him with friends possessed,
Desiring this man's art and that man's scope,
With what I most enjoy contented least:
Yet in these thoughts myself almost despising,
Haply I think on thee, and then my state,
Like to the lark at break of day arising
From sullen earth, sings hymns at heaven's gate;
For thy sweet love remembered such wealth brings
That then I scorn to change my state with kings'.

## 35

No more be grieved at that which thou hast done:
Roses have thorns, and silver fountains mud.
Clouds and eclipses stain both moon and sun,
And loathsome canker lives in sweetest bud.
All men make faults, and even I in this,
Authorizing thy trespass with compare,
Myself corrupting salving thy amiss,
Excusing thy sins more than thy sins are;
For to thy sensual fault I bring in sense—
Thy adverse party is thy advocate—
And 'gainst myself a lawful plea commence.
Such civil war is in my love and hate
That I an accessory needs must be
To that sweet thief which sourly robs from me.

## 55

Not marble nor the gilded monuments
Of princes shall outlive this powerful rime,
But you shall shine more bright in these contents
Than unswept stone besmeared with sluttish time.
When wasteful war shall statues overturn,
And broils root out the work of masonry,
Nor Mars his sword nor war's quick fire shall burn
The living record of your memory.
'Gainst death and all oblivious enmity
Shall you pace forth; your praise shall still find room
Even in the eyes of all posterity
That wear this world out to the ending doom.
  So, till the judgement that yourself arise,
  You live in this, and dwell in lovers' eyes.

## 65

Since brass, nor stone, nor earth, nor boundless sea,
But sad mortality o'ersways their power,
How with this rage shall beauty hold a plea,
Whose action is no stronger than a flower?
O how shall summer's honey breath hold out
Against the wrackful siege of battering days
When rocks impregnable are not so stout,
Nor gates of steel so strong, but time decays?
O fearful meditation! Where, alack,
Shall time's best jewel from time's chest lie hid,
Or what strong hand can hold his swift foot back,
Or who his spoil of beauty can forbid?
  O none, unless this miracle have might:
  That in black ink my love may still shine bright.

## 73

That time of year thou mayst in me behold
When yellow leaves, or none, or few, do hang
Upon those boughs which shake against the cold,
Bare ruined choirs where late the sweet birds sang.
In me thou seest the twilight of such day
As after sunset fadeth in the west,
Which by and by black night doth take away,
Death's second self, that seals up all in rest.

In me thou seest the glowing of such fire
That on the ashes of his youth doth lie
As the death-bed whereon it must expire,
Consumed with that which it was nourished by.
This thou perceiv'st, which makes thy love more strong,
To love that well which thou must leave ere long.

### 130

My mistress' eyes are nothing like the sun;
Coral is far more red than her lips' red.
If snow be white, why then her breasts are dun;
If hairs be wires, black wires grow on her head.
I have seen roses damasked, red and white,
But no such roses see I in her cheeks;
And in some perfumes is there more delight
Than in the breath that from my mistress reeks.
I love to hear her speak, yet well I know
That music hath a far more pleasing sound.
I grant I never saw a goddess go:
My mistress when she walks treads on the ground.
And yet, by heaven, I think my love as rare
As any she belied with false compare.

1609

# John Donne

## 1572–1631

As a young man, John Donne appears to have pursued knowledge and women with equal passion—or so his earlier lyrics would lead us to believe. He may well have been more interested in flouting Elizabethan poetic conventions than in recounting his romantic adventures. Certainly he had his share of the latter, when as a young law student he was using his personal charm, wit, and learning to gain preferment in Elizabethan court circles. But his career in state affairs ended abruptly in 1601 when, working as a secretary to Sir Thomas Egerton, he eloped with Egerton's 16-year-old niece. Elopement was unlawful, and Donne had not the means to support a wife and family. Until 1615, when his fine sermons had made him well known, Donne lived on the edge of poverty. At the urging of King James he became an Anglican priest and was one of the greatest preachers of his time. But though he achieved material security, he was not a happy man. His poetry and devotional writing reveal a constant spiritual struggle that was worsened by frequent illness. During his lifetime, his eloquent devotional writing was widely read, but the genius of his love poetry, published after his death in 1633, with its stunningly unconventional metaphors and the strong, irregular rhythms of ordinary speech, was considered 'rough', and was not fully appreciated until Herbert Grierson's edition of his poems appeared in 1912.

## The Good Morrow

I wonder, by my troth, what thou and I
Did, till we loved? Were we not weaned till then,
But sucked on country pleasures, childishly?
Or snorted we in the seven sleepers' den?
'Twas so; but this, all pleasures fancies be.
If ever any beauty I did see,
Which I desired, and got, 'twas but a dream of thee.

And now good morrow to our waking souls,
Which watch not one another out of fear;
For love all love of other sights controls,
And makes one little room an everywhere.
Let sea-discoverers to new worlds have gone,
Let maps to other, worlds on worlds have shown,
Let us possess one world; each hath one, and is one.

My face in thine eye, thine in mine appears,
And true plain hearts do in the faces rest;
Where can we find two better hemispheres
Without sharp North, without declining West?
Whatever dies was not mixed equally;
If our two loves be one, or thou and I
Love so alike that none do slacken, none can die.

1633

## The Sun Rising

Busy old fool, unruly sun,
Why doest thou thus
Through windows and through curtains call on us?
Must to thy motions lovers' seasons run?
Saucy pedantic wretch, go chide
Late schoolboys and sour prentices,

Go tell court-huntsmen that the king will ride,
Call country ants to harvest offices;
Love, all alike, no season knows, nor clime,
Nor hours, days, months, which are the rags of time.

Thy beams, so reverend, and strong
Why shouldst thou think?
I could eclipse and cloud them with a wink,
But that I would not lose her sight so long;
If her eyes have not blinded thine,
Look, and tomorrow late tell me
Whether both the Indias of spice and mine
Be where thou left'st them, or lie here with me.
Ask for those kings whom thou saw'st yesterday,
And thou shalt hear, all here in one bed lay.

She is all states, and all princes I;
Nothing else is.
Princes do but play us; compared to this,
All honour's mimic, all wealth alchemy.
Thou, sun, art half as happy as we,
In that the world's contracted thus;
Thine age asks ease, and since thy duties be
To warm the world, that's done in warming us.
Shine here to us, and thou art everywhere;
This bed thy centre is, these walls thy sphere.

1633

## The Canonization

For God's sake hold your tongue and let me love;
Or chide my palsy or my gout,
My five grey hairs or ruined fortune flout,
With wealth your state, your mind with arts improve,
Take you a course, get you a place,
Observe His Honour, or His Grace,
Or the King's real, or his stamped face
Contemplate; what you will, approve,
So you will let me love.

Alas, alas, who's injured by my love?
What merchant's ships have my sighs drown'd?

Who says my tears have overflowed his ground?
When did my colds a forward spring remove?
When did the heats which my veins fill
Add one more to the plaguey bill?[1]
Soldiers find wars, and Lawyers find out still
Litigious men, which quarrels move,
Though she and I do love.

Call us what you will, we are made such by love;
Call her one, me another fly,
We are tapers too, and at our own cost die,
And we in us find the Eagle and the Dove.
The Phoenix[2] riddle hath more wit
By us: we two being one, are it.
So to one neutral thing both sexes fit;
We die and rise the same, and prove
Mysterious by this love.

We can die by it, if not live by love,
And if unfit for tombs and hearse
Our legend be, it will be fit for verse;
And if no piece of chronicle we prove,
We'll build in sonnets pretty rooms;
As well a well-wrought urn becomes
The greatest ashes, as half-acre tombs,
And by these hymns, all shall approve
Us *canonized* for Love;

And thus invoke us: You whom reverend love
Made one another's hermitage;
You, to whom love was peace, that now is rage;
Who did the whole world's soul contract, and drove
Into the glasses of your eyes
(So made such mirrors, and such spies,
That they did all to you epitomize);
Countries, towns, courts: Beg from above
A pattern of your love!

1633

1 a list of those who have died of the plague
2 a mythical bird of no sex that lived a thousand years, then burned itself and was reborn from the ashes

## The Flea

Mark but this flea, and mark in this,
How little that which thou deny'st me is;
Me it sucked first, and now sucks thee,
And in this flea, our two bloods mingled be;
Confess it, this cannot be said
A sin, or shame, or loss of maidenhead,
Yet this enjoys before it woo,
And pampered swells with one blood made of two,
And this, alas, is more than we would do.

Oh stay, three lives in one flea spare,
Where we almost, nay more than married are.
This flea is you and I, and this
Our marriage bed, and marriage temple is;
Though parents grudge, and you, we are met,
And cloistered in these living walls of jet.
Though use make you apt to kill me,
Let not to this, self-murder added be,
And sacrilege, three sins in killing three.

Cruel and sudden, hast thou since
Purpled thy nail, in blood of innocence?
In what could this flea guilty be,
Except in that drop which it sucked from thee?
Yet thou triumph'st, and say'st that thou
Find'st not thyself, nor me the weaker now;
'Tis true, then learn how false, fears be;
Just so much honour, when thou yield'st to me,
Will waste, as this flea's death took life from thee.

1633

## The Relic

When my grave is broke up again
Some second guest to entertain
(For graves have learned that womanhead
To be to more than one a bed)
And he that digs it spies
A bracelet of bright hair about the bone,
Will he not let us alone,
And think that there a loving couple lies,
Who thought that this device might be some way
To make their souls, at the last busy day,
Meet at this grave, and make a little stay?

If this fall in a time, or land,
Where mis-devotion doth command,
Then he that digs us up, will bring
Us to the Bishop and the King
To make us relics; then
Thou shalt be a Mary Magdalen,[1] and I
A something else thereby;
All women shall adore us, and some men;
And since at such time, miracles are sought,
I would have that age by this paper taught
What miracles we harmless lovers wrought.

First, we loved well and faithfully,
Yet knew not what we loved, nor why;
Difference of sex no more we knew
Than our guardian angels do;
Coming and going, we
Perchance might kiss, but not between those meals;
Our hands ne'er touched the seals
Which nature, injured by late law, sets free:
These miracles we did; but now, alas,
All measure and all language I should pass,
Should I tell what a miracle she was.

1633

1 In Christian tradition Mary Magdalene was a prostitute who reformed to follow Jesus—which suggests that the 'something else' in the next line refers to Christ.

## Holy Sonnets

### 10

Death, be not proud, though some have callèd thee
Mighty and dreadful, for thou are not so;
For those whom thou think'st thou dost overthrow
Die not, poor Death, nor yet canst thou kill me.
From rest and sleep, which but thy pictures be,
Much pleasure; then from thee much more must flow,
And soonest our best men with thee do go,
Rest of their bones, and soul's delivery.
Thou art slave to fate, chance, kings, and desperate men,
And dost with poison, war, and sickness dwell,
And poppy or charms can make us sleep as well
And better than thy stroke; why swell'st thou then?
One short sleep past, we wake eternally
And death shall be no more; Death, thou shalt die.

### 14

Batter my heart, three-personed God; for you
As yet but knock, breathe, shine, and seek to mend;
That I may rise and stand, o'erthrow me, and bend
Your force to break, blow, burn, and make me new.
I, like an usurped town, to another due,
Labour to admit you, but oh, to no end.
Reason, your viceroy in me, me should defend,
But is captived, and proves weak or untrue.
Yet dearly I love you, and would be loved fain,
But am betrothed unto your enemy:
Divorce me, untie or break that knot again,
Take me to you, imprison me, for I,
Except you enthrall me, never shall be free,
Nor ever chaste, except you ravish me.

1633

# John Milton
## 1608–1674

One of the most educated and learned of the major English poets, John Milton was born in Cheapside, London, and attended Saint Paul's School, where he studied Latin and Greek and mastered many modern European languages as well as Hebrew. In 1625 he entered Christ's College, Cambridge, where he received his BA (1629) and MA (1632). Rather than study with an aim to joining the ministry, he retired to his father's country home to read and to embark on a writing career. He wrote his elegy *Lycidas* in 1637 as a memorial to Edward King, his Cambridge classmate for six years, who had drowned that summer. He then travelled for two years on the continent. On his return to England, he became an apologist for Oliver Cromwell, defending the decision of Parliament to execute Charles I in 1649. Although he went blind in 1651, Milton continued to work as Latin secretary to Cromwell's Council of State. With the Restoration of the monarchy under Charles II in 1660, Milton found himself in political disfavour and was imprisoned. Through the intervention of friends his life was spared. During his last years he completed his epic *Paradise Lost* (1667), his shorter epic *Paradise Regained* (1671), and his tragedy *Samson Agonistes* (1671).

### On Shakespeare

What needs my Shakespeare for his honoured bones
The labour of an age in pilèd stones,
Or that his hallowed relics should be hid
Under a star-ypointing pyramid?
Dear son of memory, great heir of fame,
What need'st thou such weak witness of thy name?
Thou in our wonder and astonishment
Hast built thyself a live-long monument.
For whilst to th' shame of slow-endeavouring art,
Thy easy numbers flow, and that each heart
Hath from the leaves of thy unvalued book
Those Delphic lines with deep impression took;
Then thou, our fancy of itself bereaving,
Dost make us marble with too much conceiving;
And so sepùlchered in such pomp dost lie,
That kings for such a tomb would wish to die.

## Lycidas

*In this Monody*[1] *the Author bewails a learned Friend, unfortunately drowned in his passage from Chester on the Irish Sea, 1637; and, by occasion, foretells the ruin of our corrupted Clergy, then in their height.*

Yet once more, O ye laurels, and once more,
Ye myrtles brown, with ivy never sere,
I come to pluck your berries harsh and crude,
And with forced fingers rude
Shatter your leaves before the mellowing year.
Bitter constraint and sad occasion dear
Compels me to disturb your season due;
For Lycidas is dead, dead ere his prime,
Young Lycidas, and hath not left his peer.
Who would not sing for Lycidas? He knew
Himself to sing, and build the lofty rhyme.
He must not float upon his watery bier
Unwept, and welter to the parching wind,
Without the meed of some melodious tear.
Begin, then, Sisters of the sacred well[2]
That from beneath the seat of Jove doth spring;
Begin, and somewhat loudly sweep the string.
Hence with denial vain and coy excuse:
So may some gentle Muse
With lucky words favour my destined urn,
And as he passes turn,
And bid fair peace be to my sable shroud!
For we were nursed upon the self-same hill,
Fed the same flock, by fountain, shade, and rill;
Together both, ere the high lawns appeared
Under the opening eyelids of the Morn,
We drove afield, and both together heard
What time the grey-fly winds her sultry horn,
Batt'ning our flocks with the fresh dews of night,
Oft till the star that rose at evening bright
Toward heaven's descent had sloped his westering wheel.
Meanwhile the rural ditties were not mute,
Tempered to th' oaten flute;
Rough Satyrs danced, and Fauns with cloven heel

1 a dirge or elegy sung by a single voice. 'Lycidas' was first published in a volume of commemorative verse for Edward King, a friend of Milton's from his student days at Cambridge University.

2 *Sisters . . . well*: the muses, who dance at the altar of Jove at their sacred well, Aganippe, on Mt Helicon

From the glad sound would not be absent long;
And old Damaetas[3] loved to hear our song.
  But, oh! the heavy change, now thou art gone,
Now thou art gone, and never must return!
Thee, Shepherd, thee the woods, and desert caves,
With wild thyme and the gadding vine o'ergrown,
And all their echoes, mourn.
The willows, and the hazel copses green,
Shall now no more be seen,
Fanning their joyous leaves to thy soft lays.
As killing as the canker to the rose,
Or taint-worm to the weanling herds that graze,
Or frost to flowers, that their gay wardrobe wear,
When first the white-thorn blows;
Such, Lycidas, thy loss to shepherd's ear.
  Where were ye, Nymphs, when the remorseless deep
Closed o'er the head of your loved Lycidas?
For neither were ye playing on the steep,
Where your old bards, the famous Druids, lie,
Nor on the shaggy top on Mona[4] high,
Nor yet where Deva spreads her wizard stream.
Ay me! I fondly dream
Had ye been there, . . . for what could that have done?
What could the Muse[5] herself that Orpheus bore,
The Muse herself, for her enchanting son,
Whom universal nature did lament,
When, by the rout that made the hideous roar,
His gory visage down the stream was sent,
Down the swift Hebrus to the Lesbian shore?
  Alas! what boots it with incessant care
To tend the homely, slighted, shepherd's trade,
And strictly meditate the thankless Muse?
Were it not better done, as others use,
To sport with Amaryllis[6] in the shade,
Or with the tangles of Neaera's hair?
Fame is the spur that the clear spirit doth raise
(That last infirmity of noble mind)
To scorn delights, and live laborious days;
But the fair guerdon when we hope to find,
And think to burst out into sudden blaze,

3 a conventional pastoral name, referring probably to a Cambridge tutor
4 also known as Anglesey, an island off the northwest coast of Wales. King's ship apparently went down nearby.
5 Calliope the Muse of epic poetry and mother of Orpheus. Angry female votaries of Dionysus tore him to pieces and flung his head into the river Hebrus.
6 conventional female pastoral name

Comes the blind Fury[7] with th' abhorred shears,
And slits the thin-spun life. 'But not the praise,'
Phoebus[8] replied, and touched my trembling ears:
'Fame is no plant that grows on mortal soil,
Nor in the glistering foil
Set off to the world, nor in broad rumour lies,
But lives and spreads aloft by those pure eyes
And perfect witness of all-judging Jove;
As he pronounces lastly on each deed,
Of so much fame in heaven expect thy meed.'
O fountain Arethuse,[9] and thou honoured flood,
Smooth-sliding Mincius,[10] crowned with vocal reeds,
That strain I heard was of a higher mood.
But now my oat proceeds,
And listens to the Herald of the Sea
That came in Neptune's plea.
He asked the waves, and asked the felon winds,
What hard mishap hath doomed this gentle swain?
And questioned every gust of rugged wings
That blows from off each beaked promontory.
They knew not of his story;
And sage Hippotades[11] their answer brings,
That not a blast was from his dungeon strayed;
The air was calm, and on the level brine
Sleek Panope[12] with all her sisters played,
It was that fatal and perfidious bark,
Built in th' eclipse, and rigged with curses dark,
That sunk so low that sacred head of thine.
Next, Camus,[13] reverend sire, went footing slow,
His mantle hairy, and his bonnet sedge,
Inwrought with figures dim, and on the edge
Like to that sanguine flower inscribed with woe.
'Ah! who hath reft', quoth he, 'my dearest pledge?'
Last came, and last did go,
The Pilot of the Galilean Lake;[14]
Two massy keys he bore of metals twain
(The golden opes, the iron shuts amain).
He shook his mitred locks, and stern bespake:—

7 Atropos, third of the Fates, cuts the thread of life that is spun and measured by the other two.
8 Apollo, god of poetry
9 a fountain in Sicily, emblematic of early pastoral of Theocritus
10 the river on which Virgil was born
11 the god of winds
12 one of the Nereids or sea-nymphs
13 the god of the river Cam, representing Cambridge
14 St Peter

'How well could I have spared for thee, young swain,
Enow of such as, for their bellies' sake,
Creep, and intrude, and climb into the fold!
Of other care they little reck'ning make
Than how to scramble at the shearers' feast,
And shove away the worthy bidden guest.
Blind mouths! that scarce themselves know how to hold
A sheep-hook, or have learned aught else the least
That to the faithful herdman's art belongs!
What recks it them? What need they? They are sped;
And, when they list, their lean and flashy songs
Grate on their scrannel pipes of wretched straw;
The hungry sheep look up, and are not fed,
But, swoln with wind and the rank mist they draw,
Rot inwardly, and foul contagion spread:
Besides what the grim wolf with privy paw
Daily devours apace, and nothing said.
But that two-handed engine at the door
Stands ready to smite once, and smite no more.'
Return, Alpheus,[15] the dread voice is past
That shrunk thy streams; return, Sicilian Muse,[16]
And call the vales, and bid them hither cast
Their bells and flowers of a thousand hues.
Ye valleys low, where the mild whispers use
Of shades, and wanton winds, and gushing brooks,
On whose fresh lap the swart star[17] sparely looks,
Throw hither all your quaint enamelled eyes,
That on the green turf suck the honied showers,
And purple all the ground with vernal flowers.
Bring the rathe primrose that forsaken dies,
The tufted crow-toe, and pale jessamine,
The white pink, and the pansy freaked with jet,
The glowing violet,
The musk-rose, and the well-attired woodbine,
With cowslips wan that hang the pensive head,
And every flower that sad embroidery wears:
Bid amaranthus all his beauty shed,
And daffadillies fill their cups with tears,
To strew the laureate hearse where Lycid lies.
For so, to interpose a little ease,
Let our frail thoughts dally with false surmise.

15 a Greek river god
16 relates to Theocritan pastoral poetry
17 Sirius, the Dog Star

Ay me! whilst thee the shores and sounding seas
Wash far away, where'er thy bones are hurled;
Whether beyond the stormy Hebrides,
Where thou perhaps under the whelming tide
Visit'st the bottom of the monstrous world;
Or whether thou, to our moist vows denied,
Sleep'st by the fable of Bellerus old,
Where the great Vision of the guarded mount
Looks toward Namancos, and Bayona's hold;
Look homeward, Angel, now, and melt with ruth:
And, O ye dolphins, waft the hapless youth.
Weep no more, woeful shepherds, weep no more,
For Lycidas, your sorrow, is not dead,
Sunk though he be beneath the wat'ry floor.
So sinks the day-star in the ocean bed,
And yet anon repairs his drooping head,
And tricks his beams, and with new-spangled ore
Flames in the forehead of the morning sky:
So Lycidas sunk low, but mounted high,
Through the dear might of Him that walked the waves;
Where, other groves and other streams along,
With nectar pure his oozy locks he laves,
And hears the unexpressive nuptial song,
In the blest kingdoms meek of joy and love.
There entertain him all the Saints above,
In solemn troops, and sweet societies,
That sing, and singing in their glory move,
And wipe the tears forever from his eyes.
Now, Lycidas, the shepherds weep no more;
Henceforth thou art the Genius of the shore,
In thy large recompense, and shalt be good
To all that wander in that perilous flood.
Thus sang the uncouth swain to th' oaks and rills,
While the still morn went out with sandals grey:
He touched the tender stops of various quills,
With eager thought warbling his Doric[18] lay:
And now the sun had stretched out all the hills,
And now was dropped into the western bay;
At last he rose, and twitched his mantle blue:
Tomorrow to fresh woods, and pastures new.

1638

18 Greek dialect of the pastoral poets such as Theocritus

## How Soon Hath Time

How soon hath Time, the subtle thief of youth,
Stolen on his wing my three-and-twentieth year!
My hasting days fly on with full career,
But my late spring no bud or blossom show'th.
Perhaps my semblance might deceive the truth
That I to manhood am arrived so near;
And inward ripeness doth much less appear,
That some more timely-happy spirits indu'th.
Yet, be it less or more, or soon or slow,
It shall be still in strictest measure even
To that same lot, however mean or high,
Toward which Time leads me, and the will of Heaven.
All is, if I have grace to use it so,
As ever in my great Task-Master's eye.

1645

## When I Consider How My Light Is Spent

When I consider how my light is spent,
Ere half my days in this dark world and wide,
And that one talent which is death to hide
Lodged with me useless, though my soul more bent
To serve therewith my Maker, and present
My true account, lest he returning chide;
'Doth God exact day-labour, light denied?'
I fondly ask; but Patience, to prevent
That murmur, soon replies, 'God doth not need
Either man's work or his own gifts. Who best
Bear his mild yoke, they serve him best: his state
Is kingly: thousands at his bidding speed,
And post o'er land and ocean without rest;
They also serve who only stand and wait.'

1673

# Andrew Marvell

## 1621–1678

Andrew Marvell is an elusive figure whose life presents as many paradoxes as his poetry does. During his lifetime he was known as a public servant and a politician, and not as a poet. But during this public career he was writing a private kind of poetry, extolling pastoral solitude and the inner life of the mind. He was a Puritan, yet he wrote one of the most erotic proposals of all time, 'To His Coy Mistress'.

Marvell was born in Winestead, England, near Hull, where his father was rector of the parish church. He went to Trinity College, Cambridge, at the age of 12 and mastered six ancient languages. After his father died in 1641, he worked as a clerk in a Hull business house. He later travelled to Europe for four years before becoming a tutor to the 12-year-old daughter of Lord Fairfax, whose garden at Nun Appleton House probably inspired the 'green thoughts' of Marvell's lyrics, for he wrote prolifically during this period. In 1657, Marvell was an assistant to the blind poet John Milton, then Cromwell's Latin secretary, and in 1659 he was elected to Parliament, where he represented Hull for the rest of his life. When his poems were published in 1681—three years after his death—they were considered out of date and were ignored. Though his work was appreciated by later poets such as Blake, Wordsworth, and Tennyson, Marvell did not receive full critical attention until the twentieth century.

### To His Coy Mistress

Had we but world enough, and time,
This coyness, lady, were no crime.
We would sit down, and think which way
To walk, and pass our long love's day.
Thou by the Indian Ganges' side
Should'st rubies find: I by the tide
Of Humber would complain. I would
Love you ten years before the Flood,
And you should, if you please, refuse
Till the conversion of the Jews.
My vegetable love should grow
Vaster than empires, and more slow;
An hundred years should go to praise
Thine eyes, and on thy forehead gaze;
Two hundred to adore each breast,
But thirty thousand to the rest;
An age at least to every part,
And the last age should show your heart.
For, lady, you deserve this state,

Nor would I love at lower rate.
    But at my back I always hear
Time's wingèd chariot hurrying near:
And yonder all before us lie
Deserts of vast eternity.
Thy beauty shall no more be found;
Nor, in thy marble vault, shall sound
My echoing song: then worms shall try
That long-preserved virginity.
And your quaint honour turn to dust,
And into ashes all my lust.
The grave's a fine and private place,
But none, I think, do there embrace.
    Now, therefore, while the youthful hue
Sits on thy skin like morning dew,
And while thy willing soul transpires
At every pore with instant fires,
Now let us sport us while we may;
And now, like amorous birds of prey,
Rather at once our Time devour,
Than languish in his slow-chapt power.
Let us roll all our strength and all
Our sweetness up into one ball,
And tear our pleasures with rough strife
Thorough the iron gates of life.
Thus, though we cannot make our sun
Stand still, yet we will make him run.

1681

## The Garden

How vainly men themselves amaze
To win the palm, the oak, or bays;
And their incessant labours see
Crowned from some single herb, or tree,
Whose short and narrow-vergèd shade
Does prudently their toils upbraid;
While all flowers and all trees do close
To weave the garlands of repose!

Fair Quiet, have I found thee here,
And Innocence, thy sister dear!
Mistaken long, I sought you then

In busy companies of men.
Your sacred plants, if here below,
Only among the plants will grow;
Society is all but rude
To this delicious solitude.

No white nor red was ever seen
So amorous as this lovely green.
Fond lovers, cruel as their flame,
Cut in these trees their mistress' name:
Little, alas! they know or heed
How far these beauties hers exceed!
Fair trees! wheres'e'er your barks I wound
No name shall but your own be found.

When we have run our passion's heat,
Love hither makes his best retreat.
The gods, that mortal beauty chase,
Still in a tree did end their race;
Apollo hunted Daphne so,
Only that she might laurel grow;
And Pan did after Syrinx speed,
Not as a nymph, but for a reed.

What wondrous life is this I lead!
Ripe apples drop about my head;
The luscious clusters of the vine
Upon my mouth do crush their wine;
The nectarine, and curious peach,
Into my hands themselves do reach;
Stumbling on melons, as I pass,
Ensnared with flowers, I fall on grass.

Meanwhile, the mind, from pleasure less,
Withdraws into its happiness:
The mind, that ocean where each kind
Does straight its own resemblance find;
Yet it creates, transcending these,
Far other worlds, and other seas;
Annihilating all that's made
To a green thought in a green shade.

Here at the fountain's sliding foot,
Or at some fruit-tree's mossy root,

Casting the body's vest aside,
My soul into the boughs does glide:
There like a bird it sits, and sings,
Then whets and combs its silver wings;
And, till prepared for longer flight,
Waves in its plumes the various light.

Such was that happy garden-state,
While man there walked without a mate:
After a place so pure and sweet,
What other help could yet be meet?
But 'twas beyond a mortal's share
To wander solitary there:
Two paradises 'twere in one,
To live in paradise alone.

How well the skilful gardener drew
Of flowers, and herbs, this dial new;
Where, from above, the milder sun
Does through a fragrant zodiac run;
And, as it works, the industrious bee
Computes its time as well as we.
How could such sweet and wholesome hours
Be reckoned but with herbs and flowers!

1681

## The Fair Singer

To make a final conquest of all me,
Love did compose so sweet an enemy,
In whom both beauties to my death agree,
Joining themselves in fatal harmony;
That while she with her eyes my heart does bind,
She with her voice might captivate my mind.

I could have fled from one but singly fair:
My disentangled soul itself might save,
Breaking the curlèd trammels of her hair;
But how should I avoid to be her slave,
Whose subtle art invisibly can wreath
My fetters of the very air I breathe?

It had been easy fighting in some plain,
Where victory might hang in equal choice.
But all resistance against her is vain,
Who has th' advantage both of eyes and voice.
And all my forces needs must be undone,
She having gainèd both the wind and sun.

1681

## The Coronet

When for the thorns with which I long, too long,
With many a piercing wound,
My Saviour's head have crown'd
I seek with garlands to redress that wrong:
Through every garden, every mead,
I gather flow'rs (my fruits are only flow'rs)
Dismantling all the fragrant tow'rs
That once adorn'd my shepherdess's head.
And now when I have summed up all my store,
Thinking (so I myself deceive)
So rich a chaplet thence to weave
As never yet the King of glory wore:
Alas I find the serpent old
That, twining in his speckled breast,
About the flow'rs disguised does fold,
With wreaths of fame and interest.
Ah, foolish man, that would'st debase with them,
And mortal glory, heaven's diadem!
But Thou who only could'st the serpent tame
Either his slippery knots at once untie,
And disentangle all his winding snare:
Or shatter too with him my curious frame:
And let these wither, so that he may die,
Though set with skill and chosen out with care.
That they, while Thou on both their spoils dost tread,
May crown Thy feet, that could not crown Thy head.

1681

# Alexander Pope

1688–1744

Alexander Pope was born in London, the son of a linen merchant, and was privately educated. As a Roman Catholic, he could not attend university, hold public office, or vote. Deformed by tuberculosis of the spine, he was left with a hunched, crooked frame and was just four-and-a-half feet tall. He taught himself Greek, learned French and Italian, and read extensively in English and Latin poetry. In his verse *Essay on Criticism* (1711), he outlined the ideals of the neoclassical tradition in criticism. With some of his friends and fellow writers, including Jonathan Swift and John Gay—both Tories like himself—he formed the Scriblerus Club to satirize all forms of false learning and pedantry.

Pope established his reputation as a poet with his translation of Homer's *Iliad* (1715–20) and attacked his literary and personal enemies—those who had maligned him for his religion or his deformity—with his mock epic *The Dunciad* (1728). He often used the epistles of Horace as models for his own verse epistles on the cultural, moral, and political malaise of his time. Translator, editor, and critic, he was a superb poet whose mastery of the heroic couplet confirmed the form as the standard for the time.

## The Rape of the Lock

### AN HEROI-COMICAL POEM

**CANTO I**

What dire offence from am'rous causes springs,
What mighty contests rise from trivial things,
I sing—This verse to *Caryll*, Muse! is due;
This, ev'n Belinda may vouchsafe to view:
Slight is the subject, but not so the praise,
If she inspire, and he approve my lays.
Say what strange motive, Goddess! could compel
A well-bred Lord t'assault a gentle Belle?
Oh say what stranger cause, yet unexplored,
Could make a gentle Belle reject a Lord?
In tasks so bold, can little men engage,
And in soft bosoms dwells such mighty rage?
*Sol* through white curtains shot a tim'rous ray,
And op'd those eyes that must eclipse the day;
Now lapdogs give themselves the rousing shake,
And sleepless lovers, just at twelve, awake:

Thrice rung the bell, the slipper knocked the ground,
And the pressed watch returned a silver sound.
Belinda still her downy pillow pressed,
Her guardian Sylph prolonged the balmy rest.
'Twas he had summoned to her silent bed
The morning dream that hovered o'er her head.
A youth more glitt'ring than a birth-night Beau,
(That ev'n in slumber caused her cheek to glow)
Seemed to her ear his winning lips to lay,
And thus in whispers said, or seemed to say:
'Fairest of mortals, thou distinguished care
Of thousand bright inhabitants of air!
If e'er one vision touched thy infant thought,
Of all the nurse and all the priest have taught,
Of airy elves by moonlight shadows seen,
The silver token, and the circled green,
Or virgins visited by angel-pow'rs,
With golden crowns and wreaths of heav'nly flow'rs,
Hear and believe! thy own importance know,
Nor bound thy narrow views to things below.
Some secret truths from learned pride concealed,
To maids alone and children are revealed:
What though no credit doubting wits may give?
The fair and innocent shall still believe.
Know, then, unnumbered spirits round thee fly,
The light militia of the lower sky;
These, though unseen, are ever on the wing,
Hang o'er the box, and hover round the ring.
Think what an equipage thou hast in air,
And view with scorn two pages and a chair.
As now your own, our beings were of old,
And once enclosed in woman's beauteous mould;
Thence, by a soft transition, we repair
From earthly vehicles to these of air.
Think not, when woman's transient breath is fled,
That all her vanities at once are dead:
Succeeding vanities she still regards,
And though she plays no more, o'erlooks the cards.
Her joy in gilded chariots, when alive,
And love of ombre, after death survive.
For when the fair in all their pride expire,
To their first elements their souls retire:
The sprites of fiery termagants in flame

Mount up, and take a salamander's name.
Soft yielding minds to water glide away,
And sip, with nymphs, their elemental tea.
The graver prude sinks downward to a gnome,
In search of mischief still on earth to roam.
The light coquettes in sylphs aloft repair,
And sport and flutter in the fields of air.
'Know farther yet; Whoever fair and chaste
Rejects mankind, is by some sylph embraced:
For spirits, freed from mortal laws, with ease
Assume what sexes and what shapes they please.
What guards the purity of melting maids,
In courtly balls, and midnight masquerades,
Safe from the treach'rous friend, and daring spark,
The glance by day, the whisper in the dark;
When kind occasion prompts their warm desires,
When music softens, and when dancing fires?
'Tis but their sylph, the wise celestials know,
Though honour is the word with men below.
'Some nymphs there are, too conscious of their face,
For life predestined to the gnomes' embrace.
These swell their prospects and exalt their pride,
When offers are disdained, and love denied.
Then gay ideas crowd the vacant brain;
While peers and dukes, and all their sweeping train,
And garters, stars, and coronets appear,
And in soft sounds, Your Grace salutes their ear.
'Tis these that early taint the female soul,
Instruct the eyes of young coquettes to roll,
Teach infant cheeks a bidden blush to know,
And little hearts to flutter at a beau.
'Oft when the world imagine women stray,
The sylphs through mystic mazes guide their way,
Through all the giddy circle they pursue,
And old impertinence expel by new.
What tender maid but must a victim fall
To one man's treat, but for another's ball?
When Florio speaks, what virgin could withstand,
If gentle Damon did not squeeze her hand?
With varying vanities, from ev'ry part,
They shift the moving toyshop of their heart;
Where wigs with wigs, with sword-knots sword-knots strive,
Beaus banish beaus, and coaches coaches drive.

This erring mortals levity may call,
Oh blind to truth! The sylphs contrive it all.
    'Of these am I, who thy protection claim,
A watchful sprite, and Ariel is my name.
Late, as I ranged the crystal wilds of air,
In the clear mirror of thy ruling star
I saw, alas! some dread event impend,
Ere to the main this morning sun descend.
But Heav'n reveals not what, or how, or where:
Warned by thy sylph, oh pious maid, beware!
This to disclose is all thy guardian can.
Beware of all, but most beware of man!'
    He said; when Shock, who thought she slept too long,
Leapt up, and waked his mistress with his tongue.
'Twas then Belinda! if report say true,
Thy eyes first opened on a billet-doux;
Wounds, charms, and ardours, were no sooner read,
But all the vision vanished from thy head.
    And now, unveiled, the toilet stands displayed,
Each silver vase in mystic order laid.
First, robed in white, the nymph intent adores
With head uncovered, the cosmetic pow'rs.
A heav'nly image in the glass appears,
To that she bends, to that her eyes she rears;
Th' inferior priestess, at her altar's side,
Trembling, begins the sacred rites of pride.
Unnumbered treasures ope at once, and here
The various off'rings of the world appear;
From each she nicely culls with curious toil,
And decks the goddess with the glitt'ring spoil.
This casket India's glowing gems unlocks,
And all Arabia breathes from yonder box.
The tortoise here and elephant unite,
Transformed to combs, the speckled and the white.
Here files of pins extend their shining rows,
Puffs, powders, patches, bibles, billet-doux.
Now awful beauty puts on all its arms;
The fair each moment rises in her charms,
Repairs her smiles, awakens ev'ry grace,
And calls forth all the wonders of her face;
Sees by degrees a purer blush arise,
And keener lightnings quicken in her eyes.
The busy sylphs surround their darling care;
These set the head, and those divide the hair,

Some fold the sleeve, while others plait the gown;
And Betty's praised for labours not her own.

**CANTO II**

Not with more glories, in th' Ethereal Plain,
The sun first rises o'er the purpled main,
Than issuing forth, the rival of his beams
Launched on the bosom of the silver Thames.
Fair nymphs, and well-dressed youths around her shone,
But ev'ry eye was fixed on her alone.
On her white breast a sparkling cross she wore,
Which Jews might kiss, and infidels adore.
Her lively looks a sprightly mind disclose,
Quick as her eyes, and as unfixed as those:
Favours to none, to all she smiles extends,
Oft she rejects, but never once offends.
Bright as the sun, her eyes the gazers strike,
And, like the sun, they shine on all alike.
Yet graceful ease, and sweetness void of pride,
Might hide her faults, if Belles had faults to hide:
If to her share some female errors fall,
Look on her face, and you'll forget 'em all.
    This nymph, to the destruction of mankind,
Nourished two locks, which graceful hung behind
In equal curls, and well conspired to deck
With shining ringlets her smooth ivory neck.
Love in these labyrinths his slaves detains,
And mighty hearts are held in slender chains.
With hairy sprindges we the birds betray,
Slight lines of hair surprise the finny prey,
Fair tresses man's imperial race ensnare,
And beauty draws us with a single hair.
    Th' adventurous Baron the bright locks admired,
He saw, he wished, and to the prize aspired:
Resolved to win, he meditates the way,
By force to ravish, or by fraud betray;
For when success a lover's toil attends,
Few ask, if fraud or force attained his ends.
    For this, ere Phoebus rose, he had implored
Propitious Heav'n, and ev'ry pow'r adored,
But chiefly Love—to Love an altar built,
Of twelve vast French romances, neatly gilt.
There lay three garters, half a pair of gloves;

And all the trophies of his former loves.
With tender billet-doux he lights the pyre,
And breathes three am'rous sighs to raise the fire.
Then prostrate falls, and begs with ardent eyes
Soon to obtain, and long possess the prize:
The pow'rs gave ear, and granted half his prayer,
The rest, the winds dispersed in empty air.

But now secure the painted vessel glides,
The sunbeams trembling on the floating tides,
While melting music steals upon the sky,
And softened sounds along the waters die.
Smooth flow the waves, the zephyrs gently play,
Belinda smiled, and all the world was gay.
All but the sylph—With careful thoughts oppressed,
Th' impending woe sat heavy on his breast.
He summons strait his denizens of air;
The lucid squadrons round the sails repair:
Soft o'er the shrouds Aerial whispers breathe,
That seemed but zephyrs to the train beneath.
Some to the sun their insect-wings unfold,
Waft on the breeze, or sink in clouds of gold.
Transparent forms, too fine for mortal sight,
Their fluid bodies half dissolved in light.
Loose to the wind their airy garments flew,
Thin glitt'ring textures of the filmy dew;
Dipped in the richest tincture of the skies,
Where light disports in ever-mingling dyes,
While ev'ry beam new transient colours flings,
Colours that change whene'er they wave their wings.
Amid the circle, on the gilded mast,
Superior by the head, was Ariel placed;
His purple pinions opening to the sun,
He raised his azure wand, and thus begun.

'Ye Sylphs and Sylphids, to your chief give ear,
Fays, Fairies, Genii, Elves, and Daemons hear!
Ye know the spheres and various tasks assigned,
By laws eternal to th' aerial kind.
Some in the fields of purest aether play,
And bask and whiten in the blaze of day.
Some guide the course of wand'ring orbs on high,
Or roll the planets through the boundless sky.
Some less refined, beneath the moon's pale light
Pursue the stars that shoot athwart the night,
Or suck the mists in grosser air below,

Or dip their pinions in the painted bow,
Or brew fierce tempests on the wintry main,
Or o'er the glebe distill the kindly rain.
Others on earth o'er human race preside,
Watch all their ways, and all their actions guide:
Of these the chief the care of nations own,
And guard with arms divine the British Throne.
'Our humbler province is to tend the fair,
Not a less pleasing, though less glorious care.
To save the powder from too rude a gale,
Nor let th' imprisoned essences exhale,
To draw fresh colours from the vernal flow'rs,
To steal from rainbows e'er they drop in show'rs
A brighter wash; to curl their waving hairs,
Assist their blushes, and inspire their airs;
Nay oft, in dreams, invention we bestow,
To change a flounce, or add a furbelow.
'This day, black omens threat the brightest fair
That e'er deserved a watchful spirit's care;
Some dire disaster, or by force, or sleight,
But what, or where, the fates have wrapped in night.
Whether the nymph shall break Diana's law,
Or some frail china jar receive a flaw,
Or stain her honour, or her new brocade,
Forget her prayers, or miss a masquerade,
Or lose her heart, or necklace, at a ball;
Or whether Heav'n has doomed that Shock must fall.
Haste then, ye spirits! to your charge repair:
The flutt'ring fan be Zephyretta's care;
The drops to thee, Brillante, we consign;
And, Momentilla, let the watch be thine;
Do thou, Crispissa, tend her fav'rite lock;
Ariel himself shall be the guard of Shock.
'To fifty chosen sylphs, of special note,
We trust th' important charge, the petticoat:
Oft have we known that sev'nfold fence to fail,
Though stiff with hoops, and armed with ribs of whale.
Form a strong line about the silver bound,
And guard the wide circumference around.
'Whatever spirit, careless of his charge,
His post neglects, or leaves the fair at large,
Shall feel sharp vengeance soon o'ertake his sins,
Be stopped in vials, or transfixed with pins;
Or plunged in lakes of bitter washes lie,

Or wedged whole ages in a bodkin's eye:
Gums and pomatums shall his flight restrain,
While clogged he beats his silken wings in vain;
Or alum styptics with contracting power
Shrink his thin essence like a rivelled flower.
Or as Ixion fixed, the wretch shall feel
The giddy motion of the whirling mill,
In fumes of burning chocolate shall glow,
And tremble at the sea that froths below!'
He spoke; the spirits from the sails descend;
Some, orb in orb, around the nymph extend,
Some thrid the mazy ringlets of her hair,
Some hang upon the pendants of her ear;
With beating hearts the dire event they wait,
Anxious, and trembling for the birth of fate.

## CANTO III

Close by those meads forever crowned with flow'rs,
Where Thames with pride surveys his rising tow'rs,
There stands a structure of majestic frame,
Which from the neighb'ring Hampton takes its name.
Here Britain's statesmen oft the fall foredoom
Of foreign tyrants, and of nymphs at home;
Here thou, great Anna! whom three realms obey,
Dost sometimes counsel take—and sometimes tea.
Hither the heroes and the nymphs resort,
To taste awhile the pleasures of a court;
In various talk th' instructive hours they past,
Who gave the ball, or paid the visit last:
One speaks the glory of the British Queen,
And one describes a charming Indian screen;
A third interprets motions, looks, and eyes;
At ev'ry word a reputation dies.
Snuff, or the fan, supply each pause of chat,
With singing, laughing, ogling, and all that.
Mean while declining from the noon of day,
The sun obliquely shoots his burning ray;
The hungry judges soon the sentence sign,
And wretches hang that jurymen may dine;
The merchant from th' Exchange returns in peace,
And the long labours of the toilette cease—
Belinda now, whom thirst of fame invites,
Burns to encounter two adventurous knights,

At ombre singly to decide their doom;
And swells her breast with conquests yet to come.
Strait the three bands prepare in arms to join,
Each band the number of the Sacred Nine.
Soon as she spreads her hand, th' aerial guard
Descend, and sit on each important card:
First Ariel perched upon a Matadore,
Then each, according to the rank they bore;
For sylphs, yet mindful of their ancient race,
Are, as when women, wondrous fond of place.
    Behold, four Kings in majesty revered,
With hoary whiskers and a forky beard;
And four fair Queens whose hands sustain a flow'r,
Th' expressive emblem of their softer pow'r;
Four Knaves in garbs succinct, a trusty band,
Caps on their heads, and halberds in their hand;
And particoloured troops, a shining train,
Draw forth to combat on the velvet plain.
    The skilful nymph reviews her force with care;
'Let spades be trumps!' she said, and trumps they were.
    Now move to war her sable Matadores,
In show like leaders of the swarthy Moors.
Spadillio first, unconquerable lord!
Let off two captive trumps, and swept the board.
As many more Manillio forced to yield,
And marched a victor from the verdant field.
Him Basto followed, but his fate more hard
Gained but one trump and one plebeian card.
With his broad sabre next, a chief in years,
The hoary Majesty of Spades appears,
Puts forth one manly leg, to sight revealed;
The rest, his many-coloured robe concealed.
The rebel-Knave, who dares his prince engage,
Proves the just victim of his royal rage.
Ev'n mighty Pam, that kings and queens o'erthrew,
And mowed down armies in the fights of Lu,
Sad chance of war! now, destitute of aid,
Falls undistinguished by the victor spade!
    Thus far both armies to Belinda yield;
Now to the Baron Fate inclines the field.
His warlike Amazon her host invades,
Th' imperial consort of the crown of spades.
The club's black tyrant first her victim died,

Spite of his haughty mien, and barb'rous pride:
What boots the regal circle on his head,
His giant limbs in state unwieldy spread?
That long behind he trails his pompous robe,
And of all monarchs only grasps the globe?
    The Baron now his diamonds pours apace;
Th' embroidered King who shows but half his face,
And his refulgent Queen, with pow'rs combined,
Of broken troops an easy conquest find.
Clubs, diamonds, hearts, in wild disorder seen,
With throngs promiscuous strew the level green.
Thus when dispersed a routed army runs,
Of Asia's troops, and Afric's sable sons,
With like confusion different nations fly,
Of various habit and of various dye,
The pierced battalions disunited fall,
In heaps on heaps; one fate o'erwhelms them all.
    The Knave of diamonds tries his wily arts,
And wins (oh shameful Chance!) the Queen of hearts.
At this, the blood the virgin's cheek forsook,
A livid paleness spreads o'er all her look;
She sees, and trembles at th' approaching ill,
Just in the jaws of ruin, and Codille.
And now, (as oft in some distempered state)
On one nice trick depends the gen'ral fate.
An Ace of hearts steps forth: the King unseen
Lurked in her hand, and mourned his captive Queen.
He springs to vengeance with an eager pace,
And falls like thunder on the prostrate Ace.
The nymph exulting fills with shouts the sky,
The walls, the woods, and long canals reply.
    Oh thoughtless mortals! ever blind to Fate,
Too soon dejected, and too soon elate!
Sudden these honours shall be snatched away,
And cursed for ever this victorious day.
    For lo! the board with cups and spoons is crowned,
The berries crackle, and the mill turns round.
On shining altars of Japan they raise
The silver lamp; the fiery spirits blaze.
From silver spouts the grateful liquors glide,
While China's earth receives the smoking tide.
At once they gratify their scent and taste,
And frequent cups prolong the rich repast.

Strait hover round the fair her airy band;
Some, as she sipped, the fuming liquor fanned,
Some o'er her lap their careful plumes displayed,
Trembling, and conscious of the rich brocade.
Coffee, (which makes the politician wise,
And see through all things with his half-shut eyes)
Sent up in vapours to the Baron's brain
New stratagems, the radiant lock to gain.
Ah cease, rash youth! desist ere 'tis too late,
Fear the just gods, and think of Scylla's fate!
Changed to a bird, and sent to flit in air,
She dearly pays for Nisus' injured hair!
But when to mischief mortals bend their will,
How soon they find fit instruments of ill!
Just then, Clarissa drew with tempting grace
A two-edged weapon from her shining case;
So ladies in romance assist their knight,
Present the spear, and arm him for the fight.
He takes the gift with rev'rence, and extends
The little engine on his fingers' ends,
This just behind Belinda's neck he spread,
As o'er the fragrant steams she bends her head:
Swift to the lock a thousand sprites repair,
A thousand wings, by turns, blow back the hair,
And thrice they twitched the diamond in her ear,
Thrice she looked back, and thrice the foe drew near.
Just in that instant, anxious Ariel sought
The close recesses of the virgin's thought;
As on the nosegay in her breast reclined,
He watched th' ideas rising in her mind,
Sudden he viewed, in spite of all her art,
An earthly lover lurking at her heart.
Amazed, confused, he found his pow'r expired,
Resigned to Fate, and with a sigh retired.
The peer now spreads the glittering forfex wide,
T' enclose the lock; now joins it, to divide.
Ev'n then, before the fatal engine closed,
A wretched sylph too fondly interposed;
Fate urged the shears, and cut the sylph in twain,
(But airy substance soon unites again),
The meeting points the sacred hair dissever
From the fair head, forever and forever!
Then flashed the living lightning from her eyes,
And screams of horror rend th' affrighted skies.

Not louder shrieks to pitying Heav'n are cast,
When husbands or when lapdogs breathe their last,
Or when rich China vessels, fallen from high,
In glitt'ring dust and painted fragments lie!
'Let wreaths of triumph now my temples twine,'
(The victor cried) 'the glorious prize is mine!
While fish in streams, or birds delight in air,
Or in a coach and six the British fair,
As long as Atalantis shall be read,
Or the small pillow grace a lady's bed,
While visits shall be paid on solemn days,
When numerous wax-lights in bright order blaze,
While nymphs take treats, or assignations give,
So long my honour, name, and praise shall live!'
What time would spare, from steel receives its date,
And monuments, like men, submit to Fate!
Steel could the labour of the gods destroy,
And strike to dust th' imperial tow'rs of Troy;
Steel could the works of mortal pride confound,
And hew triumphal arches to the ground.
What wonder then, fair nymph! thy hairs should feel
The conqu'ring force of unresisted steel?

## CANTO IV

But anxious cares the pensive nymph oppressed,
And secret passions laboured in her breast.
Not youthful kings in battle seized alive,
Not scornful virgins who their charms survive,
Not ardent lovers robbed of all their bliss,
Not ancient ladies when refused a kiss,
Not tyrants fierce that unrepenting die,
Not Cynthia when her manteau's pinned awry,
E'er felt such rage, resentment and despair,
As thou, sad virgin! for thy ravished hair.
For, that sad moment, when the sylphs withdrew,
And Ariel weeping from Belinda flew,
Umbriel, a dusky melancholy sprite,
As ever sullied the fair face of light,
Down to the central earth, his proper scene,
Repaired to search the gloomy Cave of Spleen.
Swift on his sooty pinions flits the Gnome,
And in a vapour reached the dismal dome.
No cheerful breeze this sullen region knows,

The dreaded East is all the wind that blows.
Here, in a grotto, sheltered close from air,
And screened in shades from day's detested glare,
She sighs for ever on her pensive bed,
Pain at her side, and megrim at her head.
    Two handmaids wait the throne: alike in place,
But diff'ring far in figure and in face.
Here stood Ill Nature like an ancient maid,
Her wrinkled form in black and white arrayed;
With store of prayers, for mornings, nights, and noons,
Her hand is filled; her bosom with lampoons.
    There Affectation with a sickly mien
Shows in her cheek the roses of eighteen,
Practised to lisp, and hang the head aside,
Faints into airs, and languishes with pride;
On the rich quilt sinks with becoming woe,
Wrapped in a gown, for sickness, and for show.
The Fair Ones feel such maladies as these,
When each new nightdress gives a new disease.
    A constant vapour o'er the palace flies;
Strange phantoms rising as the mists arise;
Dreadful, as hermit's dreams in haunted shades,
Or bright as visions of expiring maids.
Now glaring fiends, and snakes on rolling spires,
Pale spectres, gaping tombs, and purple fires:
Now lakes of liquid gold, Elysian scenes,
And crystal domes, and angels in machines.
    Unnumbered throngs on ev'ry side are seen
Of bodies changed to various forms by spleen.
Here living teapots stand, one arm held out,
One bent; the handle this, and that the spout:
A pipkin there like Homer's tripod walks;
Here sighs a jar, and there a goose pie talks;
Men prove with child, as pow'rful fancy works,
And maids turned bottles, call aloud for corks.
    Safe past the gnome through this fantastic band,
A branch of healing spleenwort in his hand.
Then thus addressed the power—'Hail wayward Queen!
Who rule the sex to fifty from fifteen,
Parent of vapors and of female wit,
Who give th' hysteric, or poetic fit,
On various tempers act by various ways,
Make some take physic, others scribble plays;
Who cause the proud their visits to delay,

And send the godly in a pet to pray.
A nymph there is, that all thy pow'r disdains,
And thousands more in equal mirth maintains.
But oh! if e'er thy Gnome could spoil a grace,
Or raise a pimple on a beauteous face,
Like citron-waters matrons' cheeks inflame,
Or change complexions at a losing game;
If e'er with airy horns I planted heads,
Or rumpled petticoats, or tumbled beds,
Or caused suspicion when no soul was rude,
Or discomposed the headdress of a prude,
Or e'er to costive lapdog gave disease,
Which not the tears of brightest eyes could ease:
Hear me, and touch Belinda with chagrin;
That single act gives half the world the spleen.'
    The goddess with a discontented air
Seems to reject him, though she grants his prayer.
A wondrous bag with both her hands she binds,
Like that where once Ulysses held the winds;
There she collects the force of female lungs,
Sighs, sobs, and passions, and the war of tongues.
A vial next she fills with fainting fears,
Soft sorrows, melting griefs, and flowing tears.
The gnome rejoicing bears her gift away,
Spreads his black wings, and slowly mounts to day.
    Sunk in Thalestris' arms the nymph he found,
Her eyes dejected and her hair unbound.
Full o'er their heads the swelling bag he rent,
And all the Furies issued at the vent.
Belinda burns with more than mortal ire,
And fierce Thalestris fans the rising fire.
'O wretched maid!' she spread her hands, and cried,
(While Hampton's echoes, 'Wretched maid!' replied)
'Was it for this you took such constant care
The bodkin, comb, and essence to prepare;
For this your locks in paper-durance bound,
For this with torturing irons wreathed around?
For this with fillets strained your tender head,
And bravely bore the double loads of lead?
Gods! shall the ravisher display your hair,
While the fops envy, and the ladies stare!
Honour forbid! at whose unrivalled shrine
Ease, pleasure, virtue, all, our sex resign.
Methinks already I your tears survey,

Already hear the horrid things they say,
Already see you a degraded toast,
And all your honour in a whisper lost!
How shall I, then, your helpless fame defend?
'Twill then be infamy to seem your friend!
And shall this prize, th' inestimable prize,
Exposed thro' crystal to the gazing eyes,
And heightened by the diamond's circling rays,
On that rapacious hand for ever blaze?
Sooner shall grass in Hyde Park Circus grow,
And wits take lodgings in the sound of Bow;
Sooner let Earth, Air, Sea, to Chaos fall,
Men, monkeys, lapdogs, parrots, perish all!'
 She said; then raging to Sir Plume repairs,
And bids her beau demand the precious hairs:
(Sir Plume, of amber snuffbox justly vain,
And the nice conduct of a clouded cane)
With earnest eyes, and round unthinking face,
He first the snuffbox opened, then the case,
And thus broke out—'My lord, why, what the devil?
Z——ds! damn the lock! 'fore Gad, you must be civil!
Plague on't! 'tis past a jest—nay prithee, pox!
Give her the hair'—he spoke, and rapped his box.
 'It grieves me much' (replied the peer again)
'Who speaks so well should ever speak in vain.
But by this lock, this sacred lock I swear,
(Which never more shall join its parted hair,
Which never more its honours shall renew,
Clipped from the lovely head where late it grew)
That while my nostrils draw the vital air,
This hand, which won it, shall for ever wear.'
He spoke, and speaking, in proud triumph spread
The long-contended honours of her head.
 But Umbriel, hateful gnome! forbears not so;
He breaks the vial whence the sorrows flow.
Then see! the nymph in beauteous grief appears,
Her eyes half languishing, half drowned in tears;
On her heaved bosom hung her drooping head,
Which, with a sigh, she raised; and thus she said:
 'Forever cursed be this detested day,
Which snatched my best, my fav'rite curl away!
Happy! ah ten times happy, had I been,
If Hampton Court these eyes had never seen!
Yet am not I the first mistaken maid,
By love of courts to num'rous ills betrayed.

Oh had I rather un-admired remained
In some lone isle, or distant northern land;
Where the gilt chariot never marks the way,
Where none learn ombre, none e'er taste bohea!
There kept my charms concealed from mortal eye,
Like roses that in deserts bloom and die.
What moved my mind with youthful lords to roam?
O had I stayed, and said my prayers at home!
'Twas this, the morning omens seemed to tell;
Thrice from my trembling hand the patch-box fell;
The tott'ring china shook without a wind,
Nay, Poll sat mute, and Shock was most unkind!
A sylph too warned me of the threats of fate,
In mystic visions, now believed too late!
See the poor remnants of these slighted hairs!
My hands shall rend what ev'n thy rapine spares:
These, in two sable ringlets taught to break,
Once gave new beauties to the snowy neck.
The sister-lock now sits uncouth, alone,
And in its fellow's fate foresees its own;
Uncurled it hangs, the fatal sheers demands;
And tempts once more thy sacrilegious hands.
Oh hadst thou, cruel! been content to seize
Hairs less in sight, or any hairs but these!'

## CANTO V

She said: the pitying audience melt in tears,
But Fate and Jove had stopped the Baron's ears.
In vain Thalestris with reproach assails,
For who can move when fair Belinda fails?
Not half so fixed the Trojan could remain,
While Anna begged and Dido raged in vain.
Then grave Clarissa graceful waved her fan;
Silence ensued, and thus the nymph began.
'Say, why are beauties praised and honoured most,
The wise man's passion, and the vain man's toast?
Why decked with all that land and sea afford,
Why angels called, and angel-like adored?
Why round our coaches crowd the white-gloved beaus,
Why bows the side-box from its inmost rows?
How vain are all these glories, all our pains,
Unless good sense preserve what beauty gains:
That men may say, when we the front-box grace,

"Behold the first in virtue, as in face!"
Oh! if to dance all night, and dress all day,
Charmed the smallpox, or chased old age away,
Who would not scorn what housewife's cares produce,
Or who would learn one earthly thing of use?
To patch, nay ogle, might become a saint,
Nor could it sure be such a sin to paint.
But since, alas! frail beauty must decay,
Curled or uncurled, since locks will turn to grey,
Since painted or not painted, all shall fade,
And she who scorns a man, must die a maid;
What then remains, but well our pow'r to use,
And keep good humour still whate'er we lose?
And trust me, Dear! good humour can prevail,
When airs, and flights, and screams, and scolding fail.
Beauties in vain their pretty eyes may roll;
Charms strike the sight, but merit wins the soul.'
    So spoke the dame, but no applause ensued;
Belinda frowned, Thalestris called her prude.
'To arms, to arms!' the fierce virago cries,
And swift as lightning to the combat flies.
All side in parties, and begin th' attack;
Fans clap, silks rustle, and tough whalebones crack;
Heroes' and heroines' shouts confus'dly rise,
And bass, and treble voices strike the skies.
No common weapons in their hands are found;
Like gods they fight, nor dread a mortal wound.
    So when bold Homer makes the gods engage,
And heav'nly breasts with human passions rage;
'Gainst Pallas, Mars; Latona, Hermes arms;
And all Olympus rings with loud alarms.
Jove's thunder roars, Heav'n trembles all around;
Blue Neptune storms, the bellowing deeps resound;
Earth shakes her nodding tow'rs, the ground gives way;
And the pale ghosts start at the flash of day!
    Triumphant Umbriel on a sconce's height
Clapped his glad wings, and sat to view the fight:
Propped on their bodkin spears, the sprites survey
The growing combat, or assist the fray.
    While through the press enraged Thalestris flies,
And scatters death around from both her eyes,
A beau and witling perished in the throng;
One died in metaphor, and one in song.
'O cruel nymph! a living death I bear,'
Cried Dapperwit, and sunk beside his chair.

A mournful glance Sir Fopling upwards cast,
'Those eyes are made so killing'—was his last:
Thus on Maeander's flow'ry margin lies
Th' expiring swan, and as he sings he dies.
　When bold Sir Plume had drawn Clarissa down,
Chloe stepped in, and killed him with a frown;
She smiled to see the doughty hero slain,
But at her smile, the beau revived again.
　Now Jove suspends his golden scales in air,
Weighs the men's wits against the lady's hair;
The doubtful beam long nods from side to side;
At length the wits mount up, the hairs subside.
　See fierce Belinda on the Baron flies,
With more than usual lightning in her eyes;
Nor feared the Chief th' unequal fight to try,
Who sought no more than on his foe to die.
But this bold lord, with manly strength endued,
She with one finger and a thumb subdued:
Just where the breath of life his nostrils drew,
A charge of snuff the wily virgin threw;
The gnomes direct, to ev'ry atom just,
The pungent grains of titillating dust.
Sudden, with starting tears each eye o'erflows,
And the high dome re-echoes to his nose.
　'Now meet thy fate,' incensed Belinda cried,
And drew a deadly bodkin from her side.
(The same, his ancient personage to deck,
Her great great grandsire wore about his neck
In three seal rings; which after, melted down,
Formed a vast buckle for his widow's gown:
Her infant grandame's whistle next it grew,
The bells she jingled, and the whistle blew;
Then in a bodkin graced her mother's hairs,
Which long she wore, and now Belinda wears.)
　'Boast not my fall' (he cried) 'insulting foe!
Thou by some other shalt be laid as low.
Nor think, to die dejects my lofty mind;
All that I dread is leaving you behind!
Rather than so, ah let me still survive,
And burn in Cupid's flames—but burn alive.'
　'Restore the lock!' she cries; and all around
'Restore the lock!' the vaulted roofs rebound.
Not fierce Othello in so loud a strain
Roared for the handkerchief that caused his pain.
But see how oft ambitious aims are crossed,

And chiefs contend till all the prize is lost!
The lock, obtained with guilt, and kept with pain,
In ev'ry place is sought, but sought in vain:
With such a prize no mortal must be blest,
So Heav'n decrees! with Heav'n who can contest?
Some thought it mounted to the lunar sphere,
Since all things lost on earth, are treasured there.
There heroes' wits are kept in pond'rous vases,
And beaus' in snuffboxes and tweezer cases.
There broken vows, and deathbed alms are found,
And lovers' hearts with ends of riband bound;
The courtier's promises, and sick man's prayers,
The smiles of harlots, and the tears of heirs,
Cages for gnats, and chains to yoke a flea,
Dried butterflies, and tomes of casuistry.
But trust the Muse—she saw it upward rise,
Though marked by none but quick poetic eyes:
(So Rome's great founder to the Heav'ns withdrew,
To Proculus alone confessed in view.)
A sudden star, it shot through liquid air,
And drew behind a radiant trail of hair.
Not Berenice's locks first rose so bright,
The heavens bespangling with dishevelled light.
The sylphs behold it kindling as it flies,
And pleased pursue its progress through the skies.
This the beau monde shall from the Mall survey,
And hail with music its propitious ray.
This, the blest lover shall for Venus take,
And send up vows from Rosamonda's lake.
This Partridge soon shall view in cloudless skies,
When next he looks through Galileo's eyes;
And hence th' egregious wizard shall foredoom
The fate of Louis, and the fall of Rome.
Then cease, bright nymph! to mourn the ravished hair
Which adds new glory to the shining sphere!
Not all the tresses that fair head can boast
Shall draw such envy as the lock you lost.
For, after all the murders of your eye,
When, after millions slain, yourself shall die;
When those fair suns shall set, as set they must,
And all those tresses shall be laid in dust;
This lock, the Muse shall consecrate to fame,
And midst the stars inscribe Belinda's Name!

1712–14

# Epistle IV
# To Richard Boyle, Earl of Burlington

**The Argument:**
***Of the Use of* Riches**

*The Vanity of Expence in People of Wealth and Quality. The abuse of the word* Taste, v. 13. *That the first principle and foundation, in this as in everything else, is* Good Sense, v. 40. *The chief proof of it is to* follow Nature, *even in works of mere Luxury and Elegance. Instanced in* Architecture *and* Gardening, *where all must be adapted to the* Genius *and* Use *of the Place, and the Beauties not forced into it, but resulting from it,* v. 50. *How men are disappointed in their most expensive undertakings, for want of this true Foundation, without which nothing can please* long, *if* at all; *and the best* Examples *and* Rules *will but be perverted into something* burdensome *or ridiculous,* v. 65, &c. to 92. *A description of the* false Taste *of* Magnificence; *the first grand Error of which is to imagine that* Greatness *consists in the* Size *and* Dimension, *instead of the* Proportion *and* Harmony *of the whole,* v. 97, *and the second, either in joining together* Parts incoherent, *or too* minutely resembling, *or in the* Repetition *of the* same *too frequently,* v. 105, &c. *A word or two of false Taste in* Books, *in* Music, *in* Painting, *even in* Preaching *and* Prayer, *and lastly in* Entertainments, v. 133, &c. *Yet* PROVIDENCE *is justified in giving Wealth to be squandered in this manner, since it is dispersed to the Poor and Laborious part of mankind,* v. 169. [*Recurring to what is laid down in the first book, Ep.ii. and in the Epistle preceding this,* v. 159, &c.] *What are the* proper Objects *of Magnificence, and a proper field for the Expence of* Great Men, v. 177, &c. *and finally, the Great and Public Works which become a* Prince, v. 191, to the end.

MY LORD,

*The Clamour raised about this Epistle could not give me so much pain, as I received pleasure in seeing the general Zeal of the World in the cause of a Great Man who is Beneficent, and the particular Warmth of your Lordship in that of a private Man who is innocent.*

*It was not the* Poem *that deserved this from you; for as I had the Honour to be your friend, I cou'd not treat you quite like a Poet: but sure the* Writer *deserved more Candor even from those who knew him not, that to promote a Report which in regard to that Noble Person, was* Impertinent; *in regard to me,* Villainous. *Yet I had no great Cause to wonder, that a Character belonging to* twenty *shou'd be applied to one*; *since, by that means,* nineteen *wou'd escape the Ridicule.*

*I was too well content with my Knowledge of that Noble Person's Opinion in this Affair, to trouble the publick about it. But since Malice and Mistake are so long a dying, I take the opportunity of this third Edition to declare* His Belief, *not only of* My Innocence, *but of* Their Malignity, *of the former of which my own Heart is as conscious, as I fear of theirs must be of the latter. His Humanity feels a Concern for the Injury done to* Me, *while His Greatness of Mind can bear with Indifference the Insult offered to* Himself.

*However,* my Lord, *I own, that Critics of* this Sort *can intimidate me, nay half incline me to write no more: It wou'd be making the Town a Compliment which I think it deserves, and which some, I am sure, wou'd take very kindly. This way of Satire is dangerous, as long as Slander raised by Fools of the lowest Rank, can find any Countenance from those of a Higher. Even from the Conduct shewn on this occasion, I have learnt there are some who wou'd rather be* wicked *than* ridiculous; *and therefore it may be safer to attack* Vices *than* Follies. *I will leave my Betters in the quiet Possession of their* Idols, *their* Groves, *and their* High-Places; *and change my Subject from their* Pride *to their* Meanness, *from their* Vanities *to their* Miseries: *And as the only certain way to avoid Misconstruction, to lessen Offence, and not to multiply ill-natured Applications, I may probably in my next make use of* Real *Names and not of Fictitious Ones.*

I am,

My Lord,

Your Faithful,
Affectionate Servant,
A. POPE.

'Tis strange, the Miser should his Cares employ,
To gain those Riches he can ne'er enjoy:
Is it less strange, the Prodigal should waste
His wealth, to purchase what he ne'er can taste?
Not for himself he sees, or hears, or eats;
Artists must chuse his Pictures, Music, Meats:
He buys for Topham,[1] Drawings and Designs,
For Pembroke[2] Statues, dirty Gods, and Coins;
Rare monkish Manuscripts for Hearne[3] alone,
And Books for Mead, and Butterflies for Sloane.[4]
Think we all these are for himself? no more
Than his fine Wife, alas! or finer Whore.
For what has Virro painted, built, and planted?
Only to show, how many Tastes he wanted.
What brought Sir Visto's ill got wealth to waste?
Some Daemon whispered, 'Visto! have a Taste.'
Heav'n visits with a Taste the wealthy fool,
And needs no Rod but Ripley[5] with a Rule.
See! sportive fate, to punish aukward pride,

1 'A Gentleman famous for judicious collection of Drawings' [Pope's note]: Richard Topham (d. 1735), Keeper of the Records in the Tower of London
2 Thomas Herbert (*c.* 1656–1733), eighth Earl of Pembroke and a Whig politician
3 Thomas Hearne (1678–1735), a famous medievalist and medical scholar
4 'Two eminent Physicians: the one [Richard Mead 1673–1754] had an excellent Library, the other [Sir Hans Sloane 1660–1753] the finest collection in Europe of natural curiosities; both men of great learning and humanity' [Pope's note].
5 'This man was a carpenter, employed by a first Minister [Sir Robert Walpole], who raised him to an Architect, without any genius in the art; and after some wretched proofs of his insufficiency in public Buildings, made him Comptroller of the Board of works' [Pope's note].

Bids Bubo[6] build, and sends him such a Guide:
A standing sermon, at each year's expence,
That never Coxcomb reached Magnificence!
    You show us, Rome was glorious, not profuse,[7]
And pompous buildings once were things of Use.
Yet shall (my Lord) your just, your noble rules
Fill half the land with Imitating-Fools;
Who random drawings from your sheets shall take,
And of one beauty many blunders make;
Load some vain Church with old Theatric state,
Turn Arcs of triumph to a Garden-gate;
Reverse your Ornaments, and hang them all
On some patched dog-hole eked with ends of wall,
Then clap four slices of Pilaster on't,
That, laced with bits of rustic, makes a Front:
Or call the winds thro' long arcades to roar,
Proud to catch cold at a Venetian[8] door;
Conscious they act a true Palladian part,
And if they starve, they starve by rules of art.
    Oft have you hinted to your brother Peer,
A certain truth, which many buy too dear:
Something there is, more needful than Expence,
And something previous ev'n to Taste—'tis Sense:
Good Sense, which only is the gift of Heav'n,
And tho' no Science, fairly worth the seven:
A Light, which in yourself you must perceive;
Jones and Le Nôtre have it not to give.[9]
    To build, to plant, whatever you intend,
To rear the Column, or the Arch to bend,
To swell the Terras, or to sink the Grot;
In all, let Nature never be forgot.
But treat the Goddess like a modest fair,
Nor over-dress, nor leave her wholly bare;
Let not each beauty ev'ry where be spy'd,
Where half the skill is decently to hide.
He gains all points, who pleasingly confounds,
Surprizes, varies, and conceals the Bounds.
    Consult the Genius of the Place in all;

6 George Bubb (1691–1762), a Whig politician and literary patron

7 'The Earl of Burlington was then publishing the Designs of Inigo Jones, and the Antiquities of Rome by Palladio' [Pope's note].

8 'A Door or Window, so called, from being much practised at Venice, by Palladio and others' [Pope's note].

9 '*Inigo Jones* the celebrated Architect, and M. Le Nôtre [1613–1700], the designer of the best Gardens of France' [Pope's note].

That tells the Waters or to rise, or fall,
Or helps th'ambitious Hill the heav'ns to scale,
Or scoops in circling theatres the Vale;
Calls in the Country, catches op'ning glades,
Joins willing woods, and varies shades from shades;
Now breaks, or now directs, th'intending Lines,
Paints as you plant, and as you work, designs.
Still follow Sense, of ev'ry Art the Soul,
Parts answ'ring parts shall slide into a whole,
Spontaneous beauties all around advance,
Start ev'n from Difficulty, strike from Chance;
Nature shall join you; Time shall make it grow
A Work to wonder at—perhaps a STOW.[10]
Without it, proud Versailles! thy glory falls,
And Nero's Terraces desert their walls:
The vast Parterres a thousand hands shall make,
Lo! COBHAM comes, and floats them with a Lake:
Or cut wide views thro' Mountains to the Plain,
You'll wish your hill or sheltered seat again.
Ev'n in an ornament its place remark,
Nor in an Hermitage set Dr Clarke.[11]
Behold Villario's ten-years toil compleat;
His Arbours darken, his Espaliers meet;
The Wood supports the Plain, the parts unite,
And strength of Shade contends with strength of light:
A waving Glow the bloomy beds display,
Blushing in bright diversities of day,
With silver-quiv'ring rills maeandered o'er—
Enjoy them, you! Villario can no more;
Tired of the scene Parterres and Fountains yield,
He finds at last he better likes a Field.
Thro' his young Woods how pleased Sabinus strayed
Or sat delighted in the thick'ning shade,
With annual joy the red'ning shoots to greet,
Or see the stretching branches long to meet.
His Son's fine Taste an op'ner Vista loves,
Foe to the Dryads of his Father's groves,
One boundless Green, or flourished Carpet views,[12]

10 'The seat and gardens of the Lord Viscount Cobham in Buckinghamshire' [Pope's note].

11 'Dr S. Clarke's busto placed by the Queen in the Hermitage, while the Dr duely frequented the Court' [Pope's note]; Samuel Clarke (1675–1729), a philosopher and divine.

12 'The two extremes in parterres, which are equally faulty; a *boundless Green*, large and naked as a field, or a *flourished Carpet*, where the greatness and nobleness of the piece is lessened by being divided into too many parts, with scrolled works and beds, of which the examples are frequent' [Pope's note].

With all the mournful family of Yews;[13]
The thriving plants ignoble broomsticks made,
Now sweep those Alleys they were born to shade.
At Timon's Villa[14] let us pass a day,
Where all cry out, 'What sums are thrown away!'
So proud, so grand, of that stupendous air,
Soft and Agreeable come never there.
Greatness, with Timon, dwells in such a draught
As brings all Brobdignag before your thought.
To compass this, his building is a Town,
His pond an Ocean, his parterre a Down:
Who but must laugh, the Master when he sees?
A puny insect, shiv'ring at a breeze.
Lo! What huge heaps of littleness around!
The whole, a laboured Quarry above ground.
Two Cupids squirt before: a Lake behind
Improves the keenness of the Northern wind.
His Gardens next your admiration call,
On ev'ry side you look, behold the Wall!
No pleasing Intricacies intervene,
No artful wildness to perplex the scene;
Grove nods at grove, each Alley has a brother,
And half the platform just reflects the other.
The suff'ring eye inverted Nature sees,
Trees cut to Statues, Statues thick as trees,
With here a Fountain, never to be played,
And there a Summer-house, that knows no shade.
Here Amphitrite sails thro' myrtle bow'rs;
There Gladiators fight, or die, in flow'rs;[15]
Un-watered see the drooping sea-horse mourn,
And swallows roost in Nilus' dusty Urn.
My Lord advances with majestic mien,
Smit with the mighty pleasure, to be seen:
But soft—by regular approach—not yet—
First thro' the length of yon hot Terrace sweat,[16]
And when up ten steep slopes you've dragged your thighs,
Just at his Study-door he'll bless your eyes.

13 'Touches upon the ill taste of those who are so fond of Ever-greens (particularly Yews, which are the most tonsile) as to destroy the nobler Forest-trees, to make way for such little ornaments as Pyramids of dark-green, continually repeated, not unlike a Funeral procession' [Pope's note].

14 'This description is intended to comprize the principles of a false Taste of Magnificence, and to exemplify what was said before, that nothing but Good Sense can obtain it' [Pope's note].

15 'The two statues of the *Gladiator pugnans* and *Gladiator moriens*' [Pope's note].

16 'The *Approaches and Communications* of house with garden, or of one part with another, ill judged and inconvenient' [Pope's note].

His Study! with what Authors is it stored?[17]
In Books, not Authors, curious is my Lord;
To all their dated Backs he turns you round:
These Aldus[18] printed, those Du Suëil[19] has bound.
Lo some are Vellom, and the rest as good
For all his Lordship knows, but they are Wood.
For Locke or Milton 'tis in vain to look,
These shelves admit not any modern book.
And now the Chapel's silver bell you hear,
That summons you to all the Pride of Pray'r:
Light quirks of Music, broken and uneven,[20]
Make the soul dance upon a Jig to Heav'n.
On painted Cielings you devoutly stare,[21]
Where sprawl the Saints of Verrio or Laguerre,
On gilded clouds in fair expansion lie,
And bring all Paradise before your eye.
To rest, the Cushion and soft Dean invite,
Who never mentions Hell to ears polite.[22]
But hark! the chiming Clocks to dinner call;
A hundred footsteps scrape the marble Hall:
The rich Buffet well-coloured Serpents grace,[23]
And gaping Tritons spew to wash your face.
Is this a dinner? this a Genial room?[24]
No, 'tis a Temple, and a Hecatomb,
A solemn Sacrifice, performed in state,
You drink by measure, and to minutes eat.
So quick retires each flying course, you'd swear
Sancho's dread Doctor and his Wand were there.[25]
Between each Act the trembling salvers ring,

17 'The false Taste in Books; a satyr on the vanity in collecting them, more frequent in men of Fortune than the study to understand them. Many delight chiefly in the elegance of the print, or of the binding; some have carried it so far, as to cause the upper shelves to be filled with painted books of wood; others pique themselves so much upon books in a language they do not understand as to exclude the most useful in one they do' [Pope's note].
18 Aldus Manutio (1450–1515), the Venetian printer who introduced italic type
19 Abbé Du Suëil (1673–1746), a well-known Paris bookbinder
20 'The false Taste in Music, improper to the subjects, as of light airs in Churches, often practised by the organists, &c.' [Pope's note].
21 'Verrio [1639–1707] painted many cielings, &c. at Windsor, Hamptoncourt, &c., and Laguerre [1663–1721] at Blenheim-castle, and other Places' [Pope's note].
22 'This is a fact; a reverend Dean [Knightly Chetwood (1650–1720), Dean of Gloucester] preaching at Court, threatened the sinner with punishment in "a place which he thought it not decent to name in so polite assembly"' [Pope's note].
23 'Taxes the incongruity of *Ornaments* (tho' sometimes practised by the ancients) where an open mouth ejects the water into a fountain, or where the shocking images of serpents, &c. are introduced in Grottos or Buffets' [Pope's note].
24 'The proud Festivals of some men are here set forth to ridicule, where pride destroys the ease, and formal regularity all the pleasurable enjoyment of the entertainment' [Pope's note].
25 'See Don Quixote, chap. xlvii' [Pope's note].

From soup to sweet-wine, and God bless the King.
In plenty starving, tantalized in state,
And complaisantly helped to all I hate,
Treated, caressed, and tired, I take my leave,
Sick of his civil Pride from Morn to Eve;
I curse such lavish cost, and little skill,
And swear no Day was ever past so ill.
  Yet[26] hence the Poor are cloathed, the Hungry fed;
Health to himself, and to his Infants bread
The Lab'rer bears: What his hard Heart denies,
His charitable Vanity supplies.
  Another age shall see the golden Ear
Imbrown the Slope, and nod on the Parterre,
Deep Harvests bury all his pride has planned,
And laughing Ceres re-assume the land.
  Who then shall grace, or who improve the Soil?
Who plants like BATHURST,[27] or who builds like BOYLE.[28]
'Tis Use alone that sanctifies Expence,
And Splendor borrows all her rays from Sense.
  His Father's Acres who enjoys in peace,
Or makes his Neighbours glad, if he encrease;
Whose chearful Tenants bless their yearly toil,
Yet to their Lord owe more than to the soil;
Whose ample Lawns are not ashamed to feed
The milky heifer and deserving steed;
Whose rising Forests, not for pride or show,
But future Buildings, future Navies grow:
Let his plantation stretch from down to down,
First shade a Country, and then raise a Town.
  You too proceed! make falling Arts your care,
Erect new wonders, and the old repair;
Jones and Palladio to themselves restore,
And be whate'er Vitruvius[29] was before:
Till Kings call forth th' Ideas of your mind,
(Proud to accomplish what such hands designed,)
Bid Harbours open, public Ways extend,
Bid Temples, worthier of the God, ascend,
Bid the broad Arch the dang'rous Flood contain,

26 'The *Moral* of the whole, where PROVIDENCE is justified in giving Wealth to those who squander it in this manner. A bad Taste employs more hands, and diffuses Expence more than a good one' [Pope's note].

27 Allan, Lord Bathurst (1684–1775), a landscape architect, to whom Pope addressed a later essay on the use of riches

28 Boyle is the family name of the Earl of Burlington, to whom this poem is dedicated.

29 M. Vitruvius Pollio (b. 88 BCE), a Roman architect and engineer

The Mole projected break the roaring Main;
Back to his bounds their subject Sea command,
And roll obedient Rivers thro' the Land:
These Honours, Peace to happy Britain brings,
These are Imperial Works, and worthy Kings.

1731

# William Blake
## 1757–1827

William Blake's wife once said, 'I have very little of Mr Blake's company. He is always in Paradise.' Living with a visionary and literary genius was probably not easy, especially for a woman who had been illiterate until her marriage, when her husband taught her to read and write. Blake, the son of a tradesman and interested in the mystical ideas of Swedenborg and Jacob Boehme, was mostly self-taught, and formally schooled only in drawing. At the age of 14 he was apprenticed for seven years to an engraver, and he later supported himself with engraving and printing work. He lived most of his life in London, whose dull and ugly streets infused him with the sense of social injustice so poignantly expressed in such poems as 'The Chimney-Sweeper' and 'London'. For Blake, the world of senses was full of symbols and a source of the metaphors in his poetry. In his earlier poems he turned to forms such as the ballad as inspiration for new forms and techniques. Utterly unorthodox in his religious and moral beliefs, he developed a complete mythology of his own, a radically spiritual interpretation of the Bible. He sought a vision that would transfigure the natural, or fallen, world, revealing its correspondence with an eternal form (see 'Auguries of Innocence', below). Much of his poetry was printed with his engravings, for he made little distinction between these two expressive forms. In his art, he refused to cater to popular taste, and his work was largely ignored by the public. Like many geniuses, he seemed not to belong to his time or place, and though he battled with poverty for much of his life, he died serene and full of joy.

## From *Songs of Innocence*

### The Lamb

Little lamb who made thee
Dost thou know who made thee
Gave thee life & bid thee feed
By the stream & o'er the mead;
Gave thee clothing of delight,
Softest clothing wooly bright;
Gave thee such a tender voice,

Making all the vales rejoice!
Little Lamb who made thee
Dost thou know who made thee

Little Lamb I'll tell thee,
Little Lamb I'll tell thee!
He is callèd by thy name,
For he calls himself a Lamb:
He is meek & he is mild,
He became a little child:
I a child & thou a lamb,
We are callèd by his name.
Little Lamb God bless thee.
Little Lamb God bless thee.

1789

## From *Songs of Experience*

### The Clod and the Pebble

'Love seeketh not itself to please,
Nor for itself hath any care,
But for another gives its ease,
And builds a heaven in hell's despair.'

So sung a little clod of clay,
Trodden with the cattle's feet,
But a pebble of the brook
Warbled out these metres meet:

'Love seeketh only self to please,
To bind another to its delight,
Joys in another's loss of ease,
And builds a hell in heaven's despite.'

### The Chimney-Sweeper

A little black thing among the snow,
Crying ''weep, 'weep' in notes of woe!
'Where are thy father and mother, say?'—
'They are both gone up to church to pray.

'Because I was happy upon the heath,
And smiled among the winter's snow,
They clothed me in the clothes of death,
And taught me to sing the notes of woe.

'And because I am happy, and dance and sing,
They think they have done me no injury,
And are gone to praise God and his Priest and King,
Who make up a heaven of our misery.'

## The Sick Rose

O Rose, thou art sick:
The invisible worm,
That flies in the night,
In the howling storm,

Has found out thy bed
Of crimson joy;
And his dark secret love
Does thy life destroy.

## The Tyger

Tyger! Tyger! burning bright
In the forests of the night,
What immortal hand or eye
Could frame thy fearful symmetry?

In what distant deeps or skies
Burnt the fire of thine eyes?
On what wings dare he aspire?
What the hand dare seize the fire?

And what shoulder, and what art,
Could twist the sinews of thy heart?
And when thy heart began to beat,
What dread hand? and what dread feet?

What the hammer? what the chain?
In what furnace was thy brain?
What the anvil? what dread grasp
Dare its deadly terrors clasp?

When the stars threw down their spears,
And water'd heaven with their tears,
Did he smile his work to see?
Did he who made the Lamb make thee?

Tyger! Tyger! burning bright
In the forests of the night,
What immortal hand or eye,
Dare frame thy fearful symmetry?

## London

I wander through each charter'd[1] street,
Near where the charter'd Thames does flow,
And mark in every face I meet
Marks of weakness, marks of woe.

In every cry of every man,
In every infant's cry of fear,
In every voice in every ban,
The mind-forg'd manacles I hear.

How the chimney-sweeper's cry
Every blackening church appalls;
And the hapless soldier's sigh
Runs in blood down palace walls.

But most through midnight streets I hear
How the youthful harlot's curse
Blasts the new born infant's tear,
And blights with plagues the marriage hearse.

1794

1 pre-empted and rented out

## Auguries of Innocence

To see a world in a grain of sand
And a heaven in a wild flower,
Hold infinity in the palm of your hand,
And eternity in an hour.

A robin redbreast in a cage
Puts all heaven in a rage.
A dove-house filled with doves and pigeons
Shudders hell through all its regions.
A dog starved at his master's gate
Predicts the ruin of the state.
A horse misused upon the road
Calls to heaven for human blood.
Each outcry of the hunted hare
A fibre from the brain does tear.
A skylark wounded in the wing,
A cherubim does cease to sing;
The game cock clipped and armed for fight
Does the rising sun affright.
Every wolf's and lion's howl
Raises from hell a human soul.
The wild deer wandering here and there,
Keeps the human soul from care.
The lamb misused breeds public strife
And yet forgives the butcher's knife.
The bat that flits at close of eve
Has left the brain that won't believe.
The owl that calls upon the night
Speaks the unbeliever's fright.
He who shall hurt the little wren
Shall never be beloved by men.
He who the ox to wrath has moved
Shall never be by woman loved.
The wanton boy that kills the fly
Shall feel the spider's enmity.
He who torments the chafer's sprite
Weaves a bower in endless night.
The caterpillar on the leaf
Repeats to thee thy mother's grief.
Kill not the moth nor butterfly,
For the last judgment draweth nigh.
He who shall train the horse to war

Shall never pass the polar bar.
The beggar's dog and widow's cat,
Feed them and thou wilt grow fat.
The gnat that sings his summer's song
Poison gets from slander's tongue.
The poison of the snake and newt
Is the sweat of envy's foot.
The poison of the honey bee
Is the artist's jealousy.
The prince's robes and beggar's rags
Are toadstools on the miser's bags.
A truth that's told with bad intent
Beats all the lies you can invent.
It is right it should be so;
Man was made for joy and woe;
And when this we rightly know,
Through the world we safely go.
Joy and woe are woven fine,
A clothing for the soul divine;
Under every grief and pine
Runs a joy with silken twine.
The babe is more than swadling bands,
Throughout all these human lands;
Tools were made, and born were hands,
Every farmer understands.
Every tear from every eye
Becomes a babe in eternity;
This is caught by females bright,
And returned to its own delight.
The bleat, the bark, bellow, and roar
Are waves that beat on heaven's shore.
The babe that weeps the rod beneath
Writes revenge in realms of death.
The beggar's rags, fluttering in air,
Does to rags the heavens tear.
The soldier, armed with sword and gun,
Palsied strikes the summer's sun.
The poor man's farthing is worth more
Than all the gold on Afric's shore.
One mite wrung from the lab'rer's hands
Shall buy and sell the miser's lands;
Or, if protected from on high,
Does that whole nation sell and buy.
He who mocks the infant's faith

Shall be mocked in age and death.
He who shall teach the child to doubt
The rotting grave shall never get out.
He who respects the infant's faith
Triumphs over hell and death.
The child's toys and the old man's reasons
Are the fruits of the two seasons.
The questioner, who sits so sly
Shall never know how to reply.
He who replies to words of doubt
Doth put the light of knowledge out.
The strongest poison ever known
Came from Caesar's laurel crown.
Naught can deform the human race
Like to the armour's iron brace.
When gold and gems adorn the plow
To peaceful arts shall envy bow.
A riddle, or the cricket's cry,
Is to doubt a fit reply.
The emmet's inch and eagle's mile
Make lame philosophy to smile.
He who doubts from what he sees
Will ne'er believe, do what you please.
If the sun and moon should doubt,
They'd immediately go out.
To be in a passion you good may do,
But no good if a passion is in you.
The whore and gambler, by the state
Licensed, build that nation's fate.
The harlot's cry from street to street
Shall weave Old England's winding sheet.
The winner's shout, the loser's curse,
Dance before dead England's hearse.
Every night and every morn
Some to misery are born.
Every morn and every night
Some are born to sweet delight.
Some are born to sweet delight,
Some are born to endless night.
We are led to believe a lie
When we see not through the eye,
Which is born in a night to perish in a night,
When the soul slept in beams of light.
God appears, and God is light,

To those poor souls who dwell in night,
But does a human form display
To those who dwell in realms of day.

1863

# William Wordsworth

1770–1850

William Wordsworth was born and educated at the edge of the Lake District in Cumberland, England, where he spent his youth roaming the countryside, absorbing the sights and sounds that would inspire his greatest poems. The headmaster of his boarding school encouraged Wordsworth's early interest in poetry, an interest that deepened when he attended St John's College, Cambridge. In 1791, after graduation, he travelled to the continent, excited by the possibilities of the French Revolution. In France he met Annette Vallon, with whom he had a child. But after financial problems forced him to return to England, the outbreak of war prevented Wordsworth from getting back to France. His ardour for Vallon eventually cooled, and they never married. Wordsworth settled with his sister Dorothy in a cottage at Racedown, and then moved to Alfoxden, Somerset, to be near Samuel Taylor Coleridge, with whom he wrote the *Lyrical Ballads*. The *Ballads* signalled a new trend in poetry, and a break with the neoclassical tradition. Subjects for poetry, according to Wordsworth, should be 'incidents and situations from common life', and they should be written in language 'really used by men', rather than in the elevated diction typical of eighteenth-century poetry.

Wordsworth and Dorothy eventually moved back to the Lake District, settling in Grasmere in a little house called Dove Cottage. Wordsworth married a woman he had known since childhood and steadily acquired a reputation as an outstanding poet, as well as financial security. For the young Wordsworth, nature was invested with an almost divine radiance, but such vision was lost as he grew older, and in the *Immortality Ode*, Wordsworth mourns this loss and tries to take comfort 'In years that bring the philosophic mind'. It is generally agreed that Wordsworth's best poetry was written before 1807 when his youthful experience was the source of his poetry. Much of his later poetry is prosaic, reflecting an orthodoxy that replaced his earlier revolutionary fervour. He was named poet laureate of England in 1843.

## Lines

*Composed a Few Miles above Tintern Abbey*
*on Revisiting the Banks of the Wye during a Tour.*
*July 13, 1798*

Five years have passed; five summers, with the length
Of five long winters! and again I hear

These waters, rolling from their mountain-springs
With a soft inland murmur. Once again
Do I behold these steep and lofty cliffs,
That on a wild secluded scene impress
Thoughts of more deep seclusion; and connect
The landscape with the quiet of the sky.
The day is come when I again repose
Here, under this dark sycamore, and view
These plots of cottage ground, these orchard tufts,
Which at this season, with their unripe fruits,
Are clad in one green hue, and lose themselves
'Mid groves and copses. Once again I see
These hedgerows, hardly hedgerows, little lines
Of sportive wood run wild; these pastoral farms,
Green to the very door; and wreaths of smoke
Sent up, in silence, from among the trees!
With some uncertain notice, as might seem
Of vagrant dwellers in the houseless woods,
Or of some Hermit's cave, where by his fire
The Hermit sits alone.

These beauteous forms,
Through a long absence, have not been to me
As is a landscape to a blind man's eye;
But oft, in lonely rooms, and 'mid the din
Of towns and cities, I have owed to them,
In hours of weariness, sensations sweet,
Felt in the blood, and felt along the heart;
And passing even into my purer mind,
With tranquil restoration—feelings too
Of unremembered pleasures; such, perhaps,
As have no slight or trivial influence
On that best portion of a good man's life,
His little, nameless, unremembered, acts
Of kindness and of love. Nor less, I trust,
To them I may have owed another gift,
Of aspect more sublime; that blessed mood,
In which the burthen of the mystery,
In which the heavy and the weary weight
Of all this unintelligble world,
Is lightened—that serene and blessed mood,
In which the affections greatly lead us on—
Until, the breath of this corporeal frame
And even the motion of our human blood

Almost suspended, we are laid asleep
In body, and become a living soul;
While with an eye made quiet by the power
Of harmony, and the deep power of joy,
We see into the life of things.

If this
Be but a vain belief, yet, oh! how oft—
In darkness and amid the many shapes
Of joyless daylight; when the fretful stir
Unprofitable, and the fever of the world,
Have hung upon the beatings of my heart—
How oft, in spirit, have I turned to thee,
O sylvan Wye! thou wanderer through the woods,
How often has my spirit turned to thee!

And now, with gleams of half-extinguished thought,
With many recognitions dim and faint,
And somewhat of a sad perplexity,
The picture of the mind revives again;
While here I stand, not only with the sense
Of present pleasure, but with pleasing thoughts
That in this moment there is life and food
For future years. And so I dare to hope,
Though changed, no doubt, from what I was when first
I came among these hills; when like a roe
I bounded o'er the mountains, by the sides
Of the deep rivers, and the lonely streams,
Wherever nature led—more like a man
Flying from something that he dreads than one
Who sought the thing he loved. For nature then
(The coarser pleasures of my boyish days,
And their glad animal movements all gone by)
To me was all in all.—I cannot paint
What then I was. The sounding cataract
Haunted me like a passion; the tall rock,
The mountain, and the deep and gloomy wood,
Their colours and their forms, were then to me
An appetite; a feeling and a love,
That had no need of a remoter charm,
By thought supplied, nor any interest
Unborrowed from the eye.—That time is past,
And all its aching joys are now no more,
And all its dizzy raptures. Not for this

Faint I, nor mourn nor murmur; other gifts
Have followed; for such loss, I would believe,
Abundant recompense. For I have learned
To look on nature, not as in the hour
Of thoughtless youth; but hearing oftentimes
The still, sad music of humanity,
Nor harsh nor grating, though of ample power
To chasten and subdue. And I have felt
A presence that disturbs me with the joy
Of elevated thoughts; a sense sublime
Of something far more deeply interfused,
Whose dwelling is the light of setting suns,
And the round ocean and the living air,
And the blue sky, and in the mind of man:
A motion and a spirit, that impels
All thinking things, all objects of all thought,
And rolls through all things. Therefore am I still
A lover of the meadows and the woods,
And mountains; and of all that we behold
From this green earth; of all the mighty world
Of eye, and ear—both what they half create,
And what perceive; well pleased to recognize
In nature and the language of the sense
The anchor of my purest thoughts, the nurse,
The guide, the guardian of my heart, and soul
Of all my moral being.

Nor perchance,
If I were not thus taught, should I the more
Suffer my genial spirits to decay:
For thou art with me here upon the banks
Of this fair river; thou my dearest Friend,
My dear, dear Friend; and in thy voice I catch
The language of my former heart, and read
My former pleasures in the shooting lights
Of thy wild eyes. Oh! yet a little while
May I behold in thee what I was once,
My dear, dear Sister! and this prayer I make,
Knowing that Nature never did betray
The heart that loved her; 'tis her privilege,
Through all the years of this our life, to lead
From joy to joy: for she can so inform
The mind that is within us, so impress
With quietness and beauty, and so feed

With lofty thoughts, that neither evil tongues,
Rash judgments, nor the sneers of selfish men,
Nor greetings where no kindness is, nor all
The dreary intercourse of daily life,
Shall e'er prevail against us, or disturb
Our cheerful faith, that all which we behold
Is full of blessings. Therefore let the moon
Shine on thee in thy solitary walk;
And let the misty mountain winds be free
To blow against thee: and, in after years,
When these wild ecstasies shall be matured
Into a sober pleasure; when thy mind
Shall be a mansion for all lovely forms,
Thy memory be as a dwelling place
For all sweet sounds and harmonies; oh! then,
If solitude, or fear, or pain, or grief
Should be thy portion, with what healing thoughts
Of tender joy wilt thou remember me,
And these my exhortations! Nor, perchance—
If I should be where I no more can hear
Thy voice, nor catch from thy wild eyes these gleams
Of past existence—wilt thou then forget
That on the banks of this delightful stream
We stood together; and that I, so long
A worshiper of Nature, hither came
Unwearied in that service; rather say
With warmer love—oh! with far deeper zeal
Of holier love. Nor wilt thou then forget,
That after many wanderings, many years
Of absence, these steep woods and lofty cliffs,
And this green pastoral landscape, were to me
More dear, both for themselves and for thy sake!

1798

## I Wandered Lonely as a Cloud

I wandered lonely as a cloud
That floats on high o'er vales and hills,
When all at once I saw a crowd,
A host, of golden daffodils;
Beside the lake, beneath the trees,
Fluttering and dancing in the breeze.

Continuous as the stars that shine
And twinkle on the milky way,
They stretched in never-ending line
Along the margin of a bay:
Ten thousand saw I at a glance,
Tossing their heads in sprightly dance.

The waves beside them danced; but they
Outdid the sparkling waves in glee:
A poet could not but be gay,
In such a jocund company:
I gazed—and gazed—but little thought
What wealth the show to me had brought:

For oft, when on my couch I lie
In vacant or in pensive mood,
They flash upon that inward eye
Which is the bliss of solitude;
And then my heart with pleasure fills,
And dances with the daffodils.

1807

## Ode

*Intimations of Immortality*
*from Recollections of Early Childhood*

The Child is father of the Man;
And I could wish my days to be
Bound each to each by natural piety.

I

There was a time when meadow, grove, and stream,
The earth, and every common sight,
To me did seem
Apparelled in celestial light,
The glory and the freshness of a dream.
It is not now as it hath been of yore;—
Turn whereso'er I may,
By night or day,
The things which I have seen I now can see no more.

II

The Rainbow comes and goes
And lovely is the Rose,
The Moon doth with delight
Look round her when the heavens are bare,
Waters on a starry night
Are beautiful and fair;
The sunshine is a glorious birth;
But yet I know, where'er I go,
That there hath past away a glory from the earth.

III

Now, while the birds thus sing a joyous song,
And while the young lambs bound
As to the tabor's sound,
To me alone there came a thought of grief:
A timely utterance gave that thought relief,
And I again am strong:
The cataracts blow their trumpets from the steep;
No more shall grief of mine the season wrong;
I hear the Echoes through the mountains throng,
The Winds come to me from the fields of sleep,
And all the earth is gay;
Land and sea
Give themselves up to jollity.
And with the heart of May
Doth every Beast keep holiday;—
Thou Child of Joy,
Shout round me, let me hear thy shouts, thou happy Shepherd-boy!

IV

Ye blessèd Creatures, I have heard the call
Ye to each other make; I see
The heavens laugh with you in your jubilee;
My heart is at your festival,
My head hath its coronal,
The fulness of your bliss, I feel—I feel it all.
Oh evil day! if I were sullen
While Earth herself is adorning,
This sweet May-morning,
And the Children are culling
On every side,

In a thousand valleys far and wide,
Fresh flowers; while the sun shines warm,
And the Babe leaps up on his Mother's arm:—
I hear, I hear, with joy I hear!
—But there's a Tree, of many, one,
A single Field which I have looked upon,
Both of them speak of something that is gone:
The Pansy at my feet
Doth the same repeat:
Whither is fled the visionary gleam?
Where is it now, the glory and the dream?

V

Our birth is but a sleep and a forgetting:
The Soul that rises with us, our life's Star,
Hath had elsewhere its setting,
And cometh from afar:
Not in entire forgetfulness,
And not in utter nakedness,
But trailing clouds of glory do we come
From God, who is our home:
Heaven lies about us in our infancy!
Shades of the prison-house begin to close
Upon the growing Boy,
But He beholds the light, and whence it flows,
He sees it in his joy;
The Youth, who daily farther from the east
Must travel, still is Nature's Priest,
And by the vision splendid
Is on his way attended;
At length the Man perceives it die away,
And fade into the light of common day.

VI

Earth fills her lap with pleasures of her own;
Yearnings she hath in her own natural kind,
And, even with something of a Mother's mind,
And no unworthy aim,
The homely Nurse doth all she can
To make her Foster-child, her Inmate Man,
Forget the glories he hath known,
And that imperial palace whence he came.

VII

Behold the Child among his new-born blisses,
A six years' Darling of a pigmy size!
See, where 'mid work of his own hand he lies,
Fretted by sallies of his mother's kisses,
With light upon him from his father's eyes!
See, at his feet, some little plan or chart,
Some fragment from his dream of human life,
Shaped by himself with newly-learned art;
A wedding or a festival,
A mourning or a funeral;
And this hath now his heart,
And unto this he frames his song.
Then will he fit his tongue
To dialogues of business, love, or strife;
But it will not be long
Ere this be thrown aside,
And with new joy and pride
The little Actor cons another part;
Filling from time to time his 'humorous stage'
With all the Persons, down to palsied Age,
That Life brings with her in her equipage;
As if his whole vocation
Were endless imitation.

VIII

Thou, whose exterior semblance doth belie
Thy Soul's immensity;
Thou best Philosopher, who yet dost keep
Thy heritage, thou Eye among the blind,
That, deaf and silent, read'st the eternal deep,
Haunted for ever by the eternal mind,—
Mighty Prophet! Seer blest!
On whom those truths do rest,
Which we are toiling all our lives to find,
In darkness lost, the darkness of the grave,
Thou, over whom thy Immortality
Broods like the Day, a Master o'er a Slave,
A Presence which is not to be put by;
Thou little Child, yet glorious in the might
Of heaven-born freedom on thy being's height,
Why with such earnest pains dost thou provoke
The years to bring the inevitable yoke,

Thus blindly with thy blessedness at strife?
Full soon thy Soul shall have her earthly freight,
And custom lie upon thee with a weight,
Heavy as frost, and deep almost as life!

IX

O joy! that in our embers
Is something that doth live
That nature yet remembers
What was so fugitive!
The thought of our past years in me doth breed
Perpetual benediction: not indeed
For that which is most worthy to be blest;
Delight and liberty, the simple creed
Of Childhood, whether busy or at rest,
With new-fledged hope still fluttering in his breast:—
Not for these I raise
The song of thanks and praise:
But for those obstinate questionings
Of sense and outward things,
Fallings from us, vanishings;
Blank misgivings of a Creature
Moving about in worlds not realised,
High instincts before which our mortal Nature
Did tremble like a guilty Thing surprised:
But for those first affections,
Those shadowy recollections,
Which, be they what they may,
Are yet the fountain-light of all our day,
Are yet a master-light of all our seeing;
Uphold us, cherish, and have power to make
Our noisy years seem moments in the being
Of the eternal Silence: truths that wake,
To perish never:
Which neither listlessness, nor mad endeavour,
Nor Man nor Boy,
Nor all that is at enmity with joy,
Can utterly abolish or destroy!
Hence in a season of calm weather
Though inland far we be,
Our Souls have sight of that immortal sea
Which brought us hither,
Can in a moment travel thither,

And see the Children sport upon the shore,
And hear the mighty waters rolling evermore.

X

Then sing, ye Birds, sing, sing a joyous song!
And let the young Lambs bound
As to the tabor's sound!
We in thought will join your throng,
Ye that pipe and ye that play,
Ye that through your hearts today
Feel the gladness of the May!
What though the radiance which was once so bright
Be now for ever taken from my sight,
Though nothing can bring back the hour
Of splendour in the grass, of glory in the flower;
We will grieve not, rather find
Strength in what remains behind;
In the primal sympathy
Which having been must ever be;
In the soothing thoughts that spring
Out of human suffering;
In the faith that looks through death,
In years that bring the philosophic mind.

XI

And O, ye Fountains, Meadows, Hills, and Groves,
Forebode not any severing of our loves!
Yet in my heart of hearts I feel your might;
I only have relinquished one delight
To live beneath your more habitual sway.
I love the Brooks which down their channels fret,
Even more than when I tripped lightly as they;
The innocent brightness of a new-born Day
Is lovely yet;
The Clouds that gather round the setting sun
Do take a sober colouring from an eye
That hath kept watch o'er man's mortality;
Another race hath been, and other palms are won.
Thanks to the human heart by which we live,
Thanks to its tenderness, its joys, and fears,
To me the meanest flower that blows can give
Thoughts that do often lie too deep for tears.

1807

## Sonnets

### 4

*Composed upon Westminster Bridge,*
*September 3, 1802*

Earth has not anything to show more fair:
Dull would he be of soul who could pass by
A sight so touching in its majesty:
This City now doth, like a garment, wear
The beauty of the morning; silent, bare,
Ships, towers, domes, theatres, and temples lie
Open unto the fields, and to the sky;
All bright and glittering in the smokeless air.
Never did sun more beautifully steep
In his first splendour, valley, rock, or hill;
Ne'er saw I, never felt, a calm so deep!
The river glideth at his own sweet will:
Dear God! the very houses seem asleep;
And all that mighty heart is lying still!

### 14

The world is too much with us; late and soon,
Getting and spending, we lay waste our powers:
Little we see in Nature that is ours;
We have given our hearts away, a sordid boon!
This Sea that bares her bosom to the moon;
The winds that will be howling at all hours,
And are up-gathered now like sleeping flowers;
For this, for everything, we are out of tune;
It moves us not.—Great God! I'd rather be
A Pagan suckled in a creed outworn;
So might I, standing on this pleasant lea,
Have glimpses that would make me less forlorn;
Have sight of Proteus rising from the sea;
Or hear old Triton blow his wreathèd horn.

1807

# John Keats

## 1795–1821

'Here lies one whose name was writ in water.' This is the epitaph John Keats chose for his gravestone. Though his life was pitifully brief, his name survives as one of the greatest of English poets. Perhaps his creative fire burned the more intensely because he knew he would be doomed by the tuberculosis that had killed other members of his family. His father had died when Keats was nine, his mother when he was fifteen, and at that time his formal schooling came to an end. At his school in Enfield, the handsome, small but tough boy was well liked by his classmates, and it was during this period that he became fascinated with the classical mythology that was to structure much of his poetry. He was apprenticed to an apothecary-surgeon and then continued his medical studies and was licensed to practise. But his love for literature made him give up medicine for poetry and what was to be a difficult life. Yet during the most difficult period of his life—when he was deeply in love with Fanny Brawne but too poor to marry her, when his brother Tom had just died of tuberculosis, and when the symptoms of that awful disease appeared in him—he produced some of his finest poetry: the Odes and his verse romances. He died at the age of 25 in Rome, where he had gone in a desperate search for health in a warmer climate.

### Ode to a Nightingale

1

My heart aches, and a drowsy numbness pains
  My sense, as though of hemlock I had drunk,
Or emptied some dull opiate to the drains
  One minute past, and Lethe-wards[1] had sunk:
'Tis not through envy of thy happy lot,
  But being too happy in thine happiness,—
    That thou, light-wingèd Dryad[2] of the trees,
      In some melodious plot
Of beechen green, and shadows numberless,
  Singest of summer in full-throated ease.

2

O, for a draught of vintage! that hath been
  Cool'd a long age in the deep-delved earth,

1 toward Lethe, the river of Hades whose waters cause forgetfulness
2 a wood nymph

Tasting of Flora[3] and the country green,
Dance, and Provençal song, and sunburnt mirth!
O for a beaker full of the warm South,
Full of the true, the blushful Hippocrene,[4]
With beaded bubbles winking at the brim,
And purple-stained mouth;
That I might drink, and leave the world unseen,
And with thee fade away into the forest dim:

3

Fade far away, dissolve, and quite forget
What thou among the leaves hast never known,
The weariness, the fever, and the fret
Here, where men sit and hear each other groan;
Where palsy shakes a few, sad, last grey hairs,
Where youth grows pale, and spectre-thin, and dies;
Where but to think is to be full of sorrow
And leaden-eyed despairs,
Where Beauty cannot keep her lustrous eyes,
Or new Love pine at them beyond tomorrow.

4

Away! away! for I will fly to thee,
Not charioted by Bacchus[5] and his pards,
But on the viewless wings of Poesy,
Though the dull brain perplexes and retards:
Already with thee! tender is the night,
And haply the Queen-Moon is on her throne,
Cluster'd around by all her starry fays;
But here there is no light,
Save what from heaven is with the breezes blown
Through verdurous glooms and winding mossy ways.

5

I cannot see what flowers are at my feet,
Nor what soft incense hangs upon the boughs,
But, in embalmèd darkness, guess each sweet
Wherewith the seasonable month endows

3 a goddess of flowers, here personifying flowers
4 fountain of the Muses on Mt Helicon
5 god of wine, whose chariot is drawn by leopards

The grass, the thicket, and the fruit-tree wild;
White hawthorn, and the pastoral eglantine;
Fast fading violets cover'd up in leaves;
And mid-May's eldest child.
The coming musk-rose, full of dewy wine,
The murmurous haunt of flies on summer eves.

6

Darkling I listen; and, for many a time
I have been half in love with easeful Death,
Call'd him soft names in many a musèd rhyme,
To take into the air my quiet breath;
Now more than ever seems it rich to die,
To cease upon the midnight with no pain,
While thou art pouring forth thy soul abroad
In such an ecstasy!
Still wouldst thou sing, and I have ears in vain—
To thy high requiem become a sod.

7

Thou wast not born for death, immortal Bird!
No hungry generations tread thee down;
The voice I hear this passing night was heard
In ancient days by emperor and clown:
Perhaps the self-same song that found a path
Through the sad heart of Ruth,[6] when, sick for home,
She stood in tears amid the alien corn;
The same that oft-times hath
Charm'd magic casements, opening on the foam
Of perilous seas, in faery lands forlorn.

8

Forlorn! the very word is like a bell
To toll me back from thee to my sole self!
Adieu! the fancy cannot cheat so well
As she is fam'd to do, deceiving elf.
Adieu! adieu! thy plaintive anthem fades
Past the near meadows, over the still stream,

6 In the Bible, Ruth forsook her native land to live in Israel with Naomi, her mother-in-law.

Up the hill-side; and now 'tis buried deep
In the next valley-glades:
Was it a vision, or a waking dream?
Fled is that music:—Do I wake or sleep?

1819

## Ode on a Grecian Urn

1

Thou still unravish'd bride of quietness,
Thou foster-child of silence and slow time,
Sylvan historian, who canst thus express
A flowery tale more sweetly than our rhyme:
What leaf-fring'd legend haunts about thy shape
Of deities or mortals, or of both,
In Tempe or the dales of Arcady?[1]
What men or gods are these? What maidens loth?
What mad pursuit? What struggle to escape?
What pipes and timbrels?[2] What wild ecstasy?

2

Heard melodies are sweet, but those unheard
Are sweeter; therefore, ye soft pipes, play on;
Not to the sensual ear, but, more endear'd,
Pipe to the spirit ditties of no tone;
Fair youth, beneath the trees, thou canst not leave
Thy song, nor ever can those trees be bare;
Bold lover, never, never canst thou kiss,
Though winning near the goal—yet, do not grieve;
She cannot fade, though thou hast not thy bliss,
For ever wilt thou love, and she be fair!

1 In Greek poetry, Tempe and Arcady are symbols of pastoral beauty.
2 tambourines

3

Ah, happy, happy boughs! that cannot shed
Your leaves, nor ever bid the Spring adieu;
And, happy melodist, unwearièd,
For ever piping songs for ever new;
More happy love! more happy, happy love!
For ever warm and still to be enjoy'd,
For ever panting, and for ever young;
All breathing human passion far above,
That leaves a heart high-sorrowed and cloy'd,
A burning forehead, and a parching tongue.

4

Who are these coming to the sacrifice?
To what green altar, O mysterious priest,
Lead'st thou that heifer lowing at the skies,
And all her silken flanks with garlands drest?
What little town by river or sea shore,
Or mountain-built with peaceful citadel,
Is emptied of this folk, this pious morn?
And, little town, thy streets for evermore
Will silent be; and not a soul to tell
Why thou art desolate, can e'er return.

5

O Attic shape! Fair attitude! with brede
Of marble men and maidens overwrought,
With forest branches and the trodden weed;
Thou, silent form, dost tease us out of thought
As doth eternity: Cold Pastoral!
When old age shall this generation waste,
Thou shalt remain, in midst of other woe
Than ours, a friend to man, to whom thou say'st,
'Beauty is truth, truth beauty,'—that is all
Ye know on earth, and all ye need to know.

1820

## Ode to Autumn

I

Season of mists and mellow fruitfulness!
Close bosom-friend of the maturing sun;
Conspiring with him how to load and bless
With fruit the vines that round the thatch-eaves run;
To bend with apples the moss'd cottage-trees,
And fill all fruit with ripeness to the core;
To swell the gourd, and plump the hazel shells
With a sweet kernel; to set budding more
And still more, later flowers for the bees,
Until they think warm days will never cease;
For summer has o'er-brimm'd their clammy cells.

2

Who hath not seen thee oft amid thy store?
Sometimes whoever seeks abroad may find
Thee sitting careless on a granary floor,
Thy hair soft-lifted by the winnowing wind;
Or on a half-reap'd furrow sound asleep,
Drowsed with the fume of poppies, while thy hook
Spares the next swath and all its twinèd flowers;
And sometimes like a gleaner thou dost keep
Steady thy laden head across a brook;
Or by a cider-press, with patient look,
Thou watchest the last oozings, hours by hours.

3

Where are the songs of Spring? Aye, where are they?
Think not of them,—thou hast thy music too,
While barred clouds bloom the soft-dying day
And touch the stubble-plains with rosy hue;
Then in a wailful choir the small gnats mourn
Among the river-sallows, borne aloft
Or sinking as the light wind lives or dies;
And full-grown lambs loud bleat from hilly bourn;
Hedge-crickets sing, and now with treble soft
The redbreast whistles from a garden-croft:
And gathering swallows twitter in the skies.

1820

## La Belle Dame sans Merci: A Ballad

I

O what can ail thee, knight at arms,
    Alone and palely loitering?
The sedge has wither'd from the lake,
    And no birds sing.

II

O what can ail thee, knight at arms,
    So haggard and so woe-begone?
The squirrel's granary is full,
    And the harvest's done.

III

I see a lily on thy brow
    With anguish moist and fever dew,
And on thy cheeks a fading rose
    Fast withereth too.

IV

I met a lady in the meads,
    Full beautiful, a faery's child;
Her hair was long, her foot was light,
    And her eyes were wild.

V

I made a garland for her head
    And bracelets too, and fragrant zone;
She look'd at me as she did love,
    And made sweet moan.

VI

I set her on my pacing steed,
And nothing else saw all day long,
For sidelong would she bend, and sing
A faery's song.

VII

She found me roots of relish sweet,
And honey wild, and manna dew,
And sure in language strange she said—
I love thee true.

VIII

She took me to her elfin grot,
And there she wept, and sigh'd full sore,
And there I shut her wild wild eyes
With kisses four.

IX

And there she lulled me asleep,
And there I dream'd—Ah! woe betide!
The latest dream I ever dream'd
On the cold hill's side.

X

I saw pale kings, and princes too,
Pale warriors, death pale were they all;
They cried—'La belle dame sans merci
Hath thee in thrall!'

XI

I saw their starv'd lips in the gloam
With horrid warning gaped wide,
And I awoke and found me here
On the cold hill's side.

XII

And this is why I sojourn here,
Alone and palely loitering,
Though the sedge is wither'd from the lake,
And no birds sing.

1820

## Bright Star

Bright Star! would I were steadfast as thou art—
Not in lone splendour hung aloft the night
And watching, with eternal lids apart
Like Nature's patient sleepless Eremite,[1]
The moving waters at their priestlike task
Of pure ablution round earth's human shores,
Or gazing on the new soft fallen mask
Of snow upon the mountains and the moors—
No—yet still steadfast, still unchangeable,
Pillowed upon my fair love's ripening breast,
To feel forever its soft fall and swell,
Awake forever in a sweet unrest,
Still, still to hear her tender-taken breath,
And so live ever—or else swoon to death.

1838

1 religious hermit

## On the Sonnet

If by dull rhymes our English must be chained,
And, like Andromeda,[1] the Sonnet sweet
Fettered, in spite of pained loveliness;
Let us find out, if we must be constrained,
Sandals more interwoven and complete
To fit the naked foot of poesy;
Let us inspect the lyre, and weigh the stress
Of every chord, and see what may be gained
By ear industrious, and attention meet;
Misers of sound and syllable, no less
Than Midas of his coinage, let us be
Jealous of dead leaves in the bay-wreath crown;
So, if we may not let the Muse be free,
She will be bound with garlands of her own.

1848

1 Ethiopian princess chained as prey for a monster and rescued by Perseus, who then married her

# Alfred Lord Tennyson

1809–1892

Alfred Tennyson was the fourth son born into an eccentric but loving family in Lincolnshire, England. Eleven children and many pets, including an owl and a monkey, filled Somersby Rectory, which was presided over by George Clayton Tennyson, a clergyman of erratic moods, and his wife Elizabeth, a gentle and beautiful woman who was so casual a housekeeper that she often forgot to order food for family meals. The house was full of books; both parents loved poetry and often read it to their children, who at very early ages started composing their own.

Tennyson spent four miserable years at Louth Grammar School, an institution that featured thrashing as an incentive to learning. At the age of 11 he returned home to be tutored by his father. Because George Tennyson was frequently ill, Alfred often escaped to roam the countryside, composing and reciting his poetry aloud, a habit he kept for the rest of his life. He went to Trinity College, Cambridge, where he became close friends with Arthur Henry Hallam, whose lively wit complemented Tennyson's shyness and melancholy humour. Hallam's sudden death at the age of 22 was a shock from which Tennyson never fully recovered. Some of his greatest poetry, including 'Ulysses' and *In Memoriam*, resulted from his struggle with grief, faith, and doubt.

After leaving Cambridge, Tennyson, who never wanted to be anything but a poet, assumed a sort of nomadic existence, inviting himself to the homes of friends in London and in the countryside. He would stay for weeks or months at a time, filling the rooms with pungent pipesmoke, composing aloud, and consuming large amounts of port. By 1850, when *In Memoriam* was published to great acclaim and when he became poet laureate, he finally felt himself financially secure enough to marry Emily Sellwood after a 14-year courtship. When he died he was the most popular poet in Victorian England and North America, and he was buried with his head crowned with laurel from Virgil's tomb, and a copy of Shakespeare's *Cymbeline*, the last thing he read, in his hand.

## The Lady of Shalott

PART I

On either side the river lie
Long fields of barley and of rye,
That clothe the wold and meet the sky;
And through the field the road runs by
        To many-towered Camelot;
And up and down the people go,
Gazing where the lilies blow
Round an island there below,
        The island of Shalott.

Willows whiten, aspens quiver
Little breezes dusk and shiver
Through the wave that runs for ever
By the island in the river
        Flowing down to Camelot.
Four grey walls, and four grey towers,
Overlook a space of flowers
And the silent isle imbowers
        The Lady of Shalott.

By the margin, willow-veiled,
Slide the heavy barges trailed
By slow horses; and unhailed
The shallop flitteth silken-sailed
        Skimming down to Camelot;
But who hath seen her wave her hand?
Or at the casement seen her stand?
Or is she known in all the land,
        The Lady of Shalott?

Only reapers, reaping early
In among the bearded barley,
Hear a song that echoes cheerly
From the river winding clearly,
          Down to towered Camelot:
And by the moon the reaper weary,
Piling sheaves in uplands airy,
Listening, whispers ''Tis the fairy
          Lady of Shalott.'

PART II

There she weaves by night and day
A magic web with colours gay.
She has heard a whisper say,
A curse is on her if she stay
          To look down to Camelot.
She knows not what the curse may be,
And so she weaveth steadily,
And little other care hath she,
          The Lady of Shalott.

And moving through a mirror clear
That hangs before her all the year,
Shadows of the world appear.
There she sees the highway near
          Winding down to Camelot;
There the river eddy whirls,
And there the surly village-churls,
And the red cloaks of market girls,
          Pass onward from Shalott.

Sometimes a troop of damsels glad,
An abbot on an ambling pad,
Sometimes a curly shepherd-lad,
Or long-haired page in crimson clad,
          Goes by to towered Camelot;
And sometimes through the mirror blue
The knights come riding two and two:
She hath no loyal knight and true,
          The Lady of Shalott.

But in her web she still delights
To weave the mirror's magic sights,
For often through the silent nights
A funeral, with plumes and lights
And music, went to Camelot;
Or when the moon was overhead,
Came two young lovers lately wed:
'I am half sick of shadows,' said
The Lady of Shalott.

PART III

A bow-shot from her bower-eaves,
He rode between the barley-sheaves,
The sun came dazzling through the leaves,
And flamed upon the brazen greaves
Of bold Sir Lancelot.
A red-cross knight for ever kneeled
To a lady in his shield,
That sparkled on the yellow field,
Beside remote Shalott.

The gemmy bridle glittered free,
Like to some branch of stars we see
Hung in the golden Galaxy.
The bridle bells rang merrily
As he rode down to Camelot;
And from his blazoned baldric slung
A mighty silver bugle hung,
And as he rode his armour rung,
Beside remote Shalott.

All in the blue unclouded weather
Thick-jewelled shone the saddle-leather,
The helmet and the helmet-feather
Burned like one burning flame together,
As he rode down to Camelot.
As often through the purple night,
Below the starry clusters bright,
Some bearded meteor, trailing light,
Moves over still Shalott.

His broad clear brow in sunlight glowed;
On burnished hooves his war-horse trode;
From underneath his helmet flowed
His coal-black curls as on he rode,
As he rode down to Camelot.
From the bank and from the river
He flashed into the crystal mirror,
'Tirra lirra,' by the river
Sang Sir Lancelot.

She left the web, she left the loom,
She made three paces through the room,
She saw the water-lily bloom,
She saw the helmet and the plume,
She looked down to Camelot.
Out flew the web and floated wide;
The mirror cracked from side to side;
'The curse is come upon me,' cried
The Lady of Shalott.

PART IV

In the stormy east-wind straining,
The pale yellow woods were waning,
The broad stream in his banks complaining.
Heavily the low sky raining
Over towered Camelot;
Down she came and found a boat
Beneath a willow left afloat,
And round about the prow she wrote
*The Lady of Shalott.*

And down the river's dim expanse
Like some bold seer in a trance,
Seeing all his own mischance—
With a glassy countenance
Did she look to Camelot.
And at the closing of the day
She loosened the chain, and down she lay;
The broad stream bore her far away,
The Lady of Shalott.

Lying, robed in snowy white
That loosely flew to left and right—
The leaves upon her falling light—
Through the noises of the night
        She floated down to Camelot;
And as the boat-head wound along
The willowy hills and fields among,
They heard her singing her last song,
        The Lady of Shalott.

Heard a carol, mournful, holy,
Chanted loudly, chanted lowly,
Till her blood was frozen slowly,
And her eyes were darkened wholly,
        Turned to towered Camelot.
For ere she reached upon the tide
The first house by the water-side,
Singing in her song she died,
        The Lady of Shalott.

Under tower and balcony,
By garden-wall and gallery,
A gleaming shape she floated by,
Dead-pale between the houses high,
        Silent into Camelot.
Out upon the wharfs they came,
Knight and burgher, lord and dame,
And round the prow they read her name,
        *The Lady of Shalott.*

Who is this? and what is here?
And in the lightened palace near
Died the sound of royal cheer;
And they crossed themselves for fear,
        All the knights at Camelot;
But Lancelot mused a little space;
He said, 'She has a lovely face;
God in his mercy lend her grace,
        The Lady of Shalott.'

1832

## Ulysses

It little profits that an idle king,
By this still hearth, among these barren crags,
Matched with an aged wife, I mete and dole
Unequal laws unto a savage race,
That hoard, and sleep, and feed, and know not me.

I cannot rest from travel: I will drink
Life to the lees: all times I have enjoyed
Greatly, have suffered greatly, both with those
That loved me, and alone; on shore, and when
Thro' scudding drifts the rainy Hyades
Vext the dim sea: I am become a name;
For always roaming with a hungry heart
Much have I seen and known: cities of men,
And manners, climates, councils, governments,
Myself not least, but honoured of them all;
And drunk delight of battle with my peers,
Far on the ringing plains of windy Troy.
I am a part of all that I have met;
Yet all experience is an arch wherethro'
Gleams that untravelled world, whose margin fades
For ever and for ever when I move.
How dull it is to pause, to make an end,
To rust unburnished, not to shine in use!
As tho' to breathe were life. Life piled on life
Were all too little, and of one to me
Little remains: but every hour is saved
From that eternal silence, something more,
A bringer of new things; and vile it were
For some three suns to store and hoard myself,
And this grey spirit yearning in desire
To follow knowledge like a sinking star,
Beyond the utmost bound of human thought.

This is my son, mine own Telemachus,
To whom I leave the sceptre and the isle—
Well-loved of me, discerning to fulfill
This labour, by slow prudence to make mild
A rugged people, and thro' soft degrees
Subdue them to the useful and the good.
Most blameless is he, centred in the sphere

Of common duties, decent not to fail
In offices of tenderness, and pay
Meet adoration to my household gods
When I am gone. He works his work, I mine.

There lies the port; the vessel puffs her sail:
There gloom the dark broad seas. My mariners,
Souls that have toiled, and wrought, and thought with me—
That ever with a frolic welcome took
The thunder and the sunshine, and opposed
Free hearts, free foreheads—you and I are old;
Old age hath yet his honour and his toil;
Death closes all: but something ere the end,
Some work of noble note, may yet be done,
Not unbecoming men that strove with Gods.
The lights begin to twinkle from the rocks:
The long day wanes: the slow moon climbs: the deep
Moans round with many voices. Come, my friends,
'Tis not too late to seek a newer world.
Push off, and sitting well in order smite
The sounding furrows; for my purpose holds
To sail beyond the sunset, and the baths
Of all the western stars, until I die.
It may be that the gulfs will wash us down:
It may be we shall touch the Happy Isles,
And see the great Achilles, whom we knew.
Tho' much is taken, much abides; and tho'
We are not now that strength which in old days
Moved earth and heaven; that which we are, we are;
One equal temper of heroic hearts,
Made weak by time and fate, but strong in will
To strive, to seek, to find, and not to yield.

1842

## Tears, Idle Tears

Tears, idle tears, I know not what they mean,
Tears from the depth of some divine despair
Rise in the heart, and gather to the eyes,
In looking on the happy Autumn-fields,
And thinking of the days that are no more.

Fresh as the first beam glittering on a sail,
That brings our friends up from the underworld,
Sad as the last which reddens over one
That sinks with all we love below the verge;
So sad, so fresh, the days that are no more.

Ah, sad and strange as in dark summer dawns
The earliest pipe of half-awakened birds
To dying ears, when unto dying eyes
The casement slowly grows a glimmering square;
So sad, so strange, the days that are no more.

Dear as remembered kisses after death,
And sweet as those by hopeless fancy feigned
On lips that are for others; deep as love,
Deep as first love, and wild with all regret;
O Death in Life, the days that are no more.

1847

## From *In Memoriam*

### 7

Dark house, by which once more I stand
Here in the long unlovely street,
Doors, where my heart was used to beat
So quickly, waiting for a hand,

A hand that can be clasped no more—
Behold me, for I cannot sleep,
And like a guilty thing I creep
At earliest morning to the door.

He[1] is not here; but far away
The noise of life begins again,
And ghastly thro' the drizzling rain
On the bald street breaks the blank day.

1 Arthur Henry Hallam, Tennyson's friend, whose death inspired the sequence of poems entitled *In Memoriam A.H.H.*

## 8

A happy lover who has come
    To look on her that loves him well,
    Who 'lights and rings the gateway bell,
And learns her gone and far from home;

He saddens, all the magic light
    Dies off at once from bower and hall,
    And all the place is dark, and all
The chambers emptied of delight:

So find I every pleasant spot
    In which we two were wont to meet,
    The field, the chamber and the street,
For all is dark where thou are not.

Yet as that other, wandering there
    In those deserted walks, may find
    A flower beat with rain and wind,
Which once she fostered up with care;

So seems it in my deep regret,
    O my forsaken heart, with thee
    And this poor flower of poesy
Which little cared for fades not yet.

But since it pleased a vanished eye,
    I go to plant it on his tomb,
    That if it can it there may bloom,
Or dying, there at least may die.

## 115

Now fades the last long streak of snow,
    Now burgeons every maze of quick
    About the flowering squares, and thick
By ashen roots the violets blow.

Now rings the woodland loud and long,
    The distance takes a lovelier hue,
    And drowned in yonder living blue
The lark becomes a sightless song.

Now dance the lights on lawn and lea,
The flocks are whiter down the vale,
And milkier every milky sail
On winding stream or distant sea;

Where now the seamew pipes, or dives
In yonder greening gleam, and fly
The happy birds, that change their sky
To build and brood; that live their lives

From land to land; and in my breast
Spring wakens too; and my regret
Becomes an April violet,
And buds and blossoms like the rest.

1850

# Robert Browning
## 1812–1889

Robert Browning is a poet of masks. While we know a lot about his life, we seldom feel that we really know him. He hides behind the faces of the rogues' gallery in his dramatic monologues, allowing his characters to present psychological portraits of themselves, but not of him. His greatest work, *The Ring and the Book*, is a seventeenth-century Roman murder mystery featuring the despicable Count Guido Franceschini. It is recounted through dramatic monologues in which each character presents a contrasting point of view. Browning's interest in things Italian started when he was a boy living in the London suburb of Camberwell. Largely educated at home by tutors, he all but devoured his father's 6,000-volume library, from which he acquired much of his wide knowledge of Italian history, art, and literature. He lived happily with his parents until the age of 34, when he eloped to Italy with the poet Elizabeth Barrett, rescuing her from her jealous, tyrannical father. This love affair was the great romance of its time, and continued for 15 idyllic years, mostly in Italy, until Elizabeth's death in 1861.

Like Tennyson, Browning was enormously productive, and also like Tennyson, he was an extremely popular poet. Shortly before his death, the first Browning Society was formed. These literary groups blossomed throughout the English-speaking world, revering Browning as the great affirmative voice of the age, a voice that, they sincerely believed, would refute Tennysonian doubt.

## Porphyria's Lover

The rain set early in tonight
The sullen wind was soon awake,
It tore the elm-tops down for spite,
And did its worst to vex the lake:
I listen'd with heart fit to break.
When glided in Porphyria; straight
She shut the cold out and the storm,
And kneel'd and made the cheerless grate
Blaze up, and all the cottage warm;
Which done, she rose, and from her form
Withdrew the dripping cloak and shawl,
And laid her soil'd gloves by, untied
Her hat and let the damp hair fall,
And, last, she sat down by my side
And call'd me. When no voice replied,
She put my arm about her waist,
And made her smooth white shoulder bare,
And all her yellow hair displaced,
And, stooping, made my cheek lie there,
And spread, o'er all, her yellow hair,
Murmuring how she loved me—she
Too weak, for all her heart's endeavour,
To set its struggling passion free
From pride, and vainer ties dissever,
And give herself to me for ever.
But passion sometimes would prevail,
Nor could tonight's gay feast restrain
A sudden thought of one so pale
For love of her, and all in vain:
So, she was come through wind and rain.
Be sure I look'd up at her eyes
Happy and proud; at last I knew
Porphyria worshipp'd me; surprise
Made my heart swell, and still it grew
While I debated what to do.
That moment she was mine, mine, fair,
Perfectly pure and good: I found
A thing to do, and all her hair
In one long yellow string I wound
Three times her little throat around,
And strangled her. No pain felt she;
I am quite sure she felt no pain.

As a shut bud that holds a bee,
  I warily oped her lids: again
  Laugh'd the blue eyes without a stain.
And I untighten'd next the tress,
  About her neck; her cheek once more
Blush'd bright beneath my burning kiss:
  I propp'd her head up as before,
  Only, this time my shoulder bore
Her head, which droops upon it still:
  The smiling rosy little head,
So glad it has its utmost will,
  That all it scorn'd at once is fled,
  And I, its love, am gain'd instead!
Porphyria's love: she guess'd not how
  Her darling one wish would be heard.
And thus we sit together now,
  And all night long we have not stirr'd,
And yet God has not said a word!

1836

## Soliloquy of the Spanish Cloister

Gr-r-r—there go, my heart's abhorrence!
  Water your damned flower-pots, do!
If hate killed men, Brother Lawrence,
  God's blood, would not mine kill you!
What? your myrtle-bush wants trimming?
  Oh, that rose has prior claims—
Needs its leaden vase filled brimming?
  Hell dry you up with its flames!

At the meal we sit together;
  *Salve tibi!*[1] I must hear
Wise talk of the kind weather,
  Sort of season, time of year:
*Not a plenteous cork-crop: scarcely*
  *Dare we hope oak-galls, I doubt;*
*What's the Latin name for 'parsley'?*
  What's the Greek name for Swine's Snout?

1 Greeting to you!

Whew! We'll have our platter burnished,
  Laid with care on our own shelf!
With a fire-new spoon we're furnished,
  And a goblet for ourself,
Rinsed like something sacrificial
  Ere 'tis fit to touch our chaps—
Marked with L. for our initial!
  (He-he! There his lily snaps!)

*Saint*, forsooth! while brown Dolores
  Squats outside the Convent bank
With Sanchicha, telling stories,
  Steeping tresses in the tank,
Blue-black, lustrous, thick like horsehairs,
  —Can't I see his dead eye glow,
Bright as 'twere a Barbary corsair's?
  (That is, if he'd let it show!)

When he finishes refection,
  Knife and fork he never lays
Cross-wise, to my recollection,
  As do I, in Jesu's praise.
I, the Trinity illustrate,
  Drinking watered orange-pulp—
In three sips the Arian[2] frustrate;
  While he drains his at one gulp!

Oh, those melons! if he's able
  We're to have a feast; so nice!
One goes to the Abbot's table,
  All of us get each a slice.
How go on your flowers? None double?
  Not one fruit-sort can you spy?
Strange!—And I, too, at such trouble,
  Keep them close-nipped on the sly!

There's a great text in Galatians,[3]
  Once you trip on it, entails
Twenty-nine distinct damnations,
  One sure, if another fails;
If I trip him just a-dying,
  Sure of heaven as sure can be,

2 a follower of the heretic Arius, who denied the Trinity
3 one of St Paul's Epistles

Spin him round and send him flying
    Off to hell, a Manichee?[4]

Or, my scrofulous French novel
    On grey paper with blunt type!
Simply glance at it, you grovel
    Hand and foot in Belial's[5] gripe;
If I double down its pages
    At the woeful sixteenth print,
When he gathers his greengages,
    Ope a sieve and slip it in't?

Or, there's Satan!—one might venture
    Pledge one's soul to him, yet leave
Such a flaw in the indenture
    As he'd miss till, past retrieve,
Blasted lay that rose-acacia
    We're so proud of! *Hy, Zy, Hine. . . .*
'St, there's Vespers![6] *Plena Gratia*
    *Ave, Virgo!* Gr-r-r—you swine!

1842

4 a follower of the heretic Mani
5 a devil
6 evening prayers. The speaker intones 'Hail Virgin, full of grace.'

## My Last Duchess

*Ferrara*

That's my last Duchess painted on the wall,
Looking as if she were alive. I call
That piece a wonder, now: Frà Pandolf's hands
Worked busily a day, and there she stands.
Will't please you sit and look at her? I said
'Frà Pandolf' by design, for never read
Strangers like you that pictured countenance,
The depth and passion of its earnest glance,
But to myself they turned (since none puts by
The curtain I have drawn for you, but I)
And seemed as they would ask me, if they durst,
How such a glance came there; so, not the first
Are you to turn and ask thus. Sir, 'twas not
Her husband's presence only, called that spot

Of joy into the Duchess' cheek; perhaps
Frà Pandolf chanced to say, 'Her mantle laps
Over my lady's wrist too much,' or 'Paint
Must never hope to reproduce the faint
Half-flush that dies along her throat': such stuff
Was courtesy, she thought, and cause enough
For calling up that spot of joy. She had
At heart—how shall I say?—too soon made glad,
Too easily impressed: she liked whate'er
She looked on, and her looks went everywhere.
Sir, 'twas all one! My favour at her breast,
The dropping of the daylight in the West,
The bough of cherries some officious fool
Broke in the orchard for her, the white mule
She rode with around the terrace—all and each
Would draw from her alike the approving speech.
Or blush, at least. She thanked men,—good! but thanked
Somehow—I know not how—as if she ranked
My gift of a nine-hundred-years-old name
With anybody's gift. Who'd stoop to blame
This sort of trifling? Even had you skill
In speech—(which I have not)—to make your will
Quite clear to such an one, and say, 'Just this
Or that in you disgusts me; here you miss,
Or there exceed the mark'—and if she let
Herself be lessoned so, nor plainly set
Her wits to yours, forsooth, and made excuse,
—E'en then would be some stooping; and I choose
Never to stoop. Oh sir, she smiled, no doubt,
Whene'er I passed her; but who passed without
Much the same smile? This grew; I gave commands;
Then all smiles stopped together. There she stands
As if alive. Will't please you rise? We'll meet
The company below, then. I repeat,
The Count your master's known munificence
Is ample warrant that no just pretence
Of mine for dowry will be disallowed;
Though his fair daughter's self, as I avowed
At starting, is my object. Nay, we'll go
Together down, sir. Notice Neptune, though,
Taming a sea-horse, thought a rarity,
Which Claus of Innsbruck cast in bronze for me!

1842

## The Bishop Orders His Tomb at Saint Praxed's Church

*Rome, 15—*

Vanity, saith the preacher, vanity!
Draw round my bed: is Anselm keeping back?
Nephews—sons mine . . . ah God, I know not! Well—
She, men would have to be your mother once,
Old Gandolf envied me, so fair she was!
What's done is done, and she is dead beside,
Dead long ago, and I am Bishop since,
And as she died so must we die ourselves,
And thence ye may perceive the world's a dream.
Life, how and what is it? As here I lie
In this state-chamber, dying by degrees,
Hours and long hours in the dead night, I ask,
'Do I live, am I dead?' Peace, peace seems all.
Saint Praxed's ever was the church for peace;
And so, about this tomb of mine. I fought
With tooth and nail to save my niche, ye know:
—Old Gandolf cozened me, despite my care;
Shrewd was that snatch from out the corner South
He graced his carrion with, God curse the same!
Yet still my niche is not so cramped but thence
One sees the pulpit o' the epistle-side,
And somewhat of the choir, those silent seats,
And up into the aery dome where live
The angels, and a sunbeam's sure to lurk:
And I shall fill my slab of basalt there,
And 'neath my tabernacle take my rest,
With those nine columns round me, two and two,
The odd one at my feet where Anselm stands:
Peach-blossom marble all, the rare, the ripe
As fresh-poured red wine of a mighty pulse.
—Old Gandolf with his paltry onion-stone,
Put me where I may look at him! True peach,
Rosy and flawless: how I earned the prize!
Draw close: that conflagration of my church
—What then? So much was saved if aught were missed!
My sons, ye would not be my death? Go dig
The white-grape vineyard where the oil-press stood,
Drop water gently till the surface sink,
And if ye find . . . Ah God, I know not, I! . . .
Bedded in store of rotten fig-leaves soft,

And corded up in a tight olive-frail,
Some lump, ah God, of *lapis lazuli*,
Big as a Jew's head cut off at the nape,
Blue as a vein o'er the Madonna's breast . . .
Sons, all have I bequeathed you, villas, all,
That brave Frascati villa with its bath,
So, let the blue lump poise between my knees,
Like God the Father's globe on both his hands
Ye worship in the Jesus Church so gay,
For Gandolf shall not choose but see and burst!
Swift as a weaver's shuttle fleet our years:
Man goeth to the grave, and where is he?
Did I say basalt for my slab, sons? Black—
'Twas ever antique-black I meant! How else
Shall ye contrast my frieze to come beneath?
The bas-relief in bronze ye promised me,
Those Pans and Nymphs ye wot of, and perchance
Some tripod, thyrsus, with a vase or so,
The Saviour at his sermon on the mount,
Saint Praxed in a glory, and one Pan
Ready to twitch the Nymph's last garment off,
And Moses with the tables . . . but I know
Ye mark me not! What do they whisper thee,
Child of my bowels, Anselm? Ah, ye hope
To revel down my villas while I gasp
Bricked o'er with beggar's mouldy travertine
Which Gandolf from his tomb-top chuckles at!
Nay, boys, ye love me—all of jasper, then!
'Tis jasper ye stand pledged to, lest I grieve.
My bath must needs be left behind, alas!
One block, pure green as a pistachio-nut,
There's plenty jasper somewhere in the world—
And have I not Saint Praxed's ear to pray
Horses for ye, and brown Greek manuscripts,
And mistresses with great smooth marbly limbs?
—That's if ye carve my epitaph aright,
Choice Latin, picked phrase, Tully's every word,
No gaudy ware like Gandolf's second line—
Tully, my masters? Ulpian serves his need!
And then how I shall lie through centuries,
And hear the blessed mutter of the mass,
And see God made and eaten all day long,
And feel the steady candle-flame, and taste
Good, strong, thick, stupefying incense-smoke!

For as I lie here, hours of the dead night,
Dying in state and by such slow degrees,
I fold my arms as if they clasped a crook,
And stretch my feet forth straight as stone can point,
And let the bedclothes, for a mortcloth, drop
Into great laps and folds of sculptor's-work:
And as yon tapers dwindle, and strange thoughts
Grow, with a certain humming in my ears,
About the life before I lived this life,
And this life too, popes, cardinals and priests,
Saint Praxed at his sermon on the mount,
Your tall pale mother with her talking eyes,
And new-found agate urns as fresh as day,
And marble's language, Latin pure, discreet,
—Aha, ELUCESCEBAT[1] quoth our friend?
No Tully, said I, Ulpian at the best!
Evil and brief hath been my pilgrimage.
All *lapis*, all, sons! Else I give the Pope
My villas! Will ye ever eat my heart?
Ever your eyes were as a lizard's quick,
They glitter like your mother's for my soul,
Or ye would heighten my impoverished frieze,
Piece out its starved design, and fill my vase
With grapes, and add a visor and a Term,
And to the tripod ye would tie a lynx
That in his struggle throws the thyrsus down,
To comfort me on my entablature
Whereon I am to lie till I must ask,
'Do I live, am I dead?' There, leave me, there!
For ye have stabbed me with ingratitude
To death—ye wish it—God, ye wish it! Stone—
Gritstone, a-crumble! Clammy squares which sweat
As if the corpse they keep were oozing through—
And no more *lapis* to delight the world!
Well, go! I bless ye. Fewer tapers there,
But in a row: and, going, turn your backs
—Aye, like departing altar-ministrants,
And leave me in my church, the church for peace,
That I may watch at leisure if he leers—
Old Gandolf—at me, from his onion-stone,
As still he envied me, so fair she was!

1845

1 He was famous: not in the pure Latin of Cicero (Tully) but in the debased style of Ulpian.

# Walt Whitman

## 1819–1892

In 1844 Ralph Waldo Emerson called for a truly American poet who would see that 'America is a poem in our eyes'. Eleven years later Walt Whitman's 'barbaric yawp', as he himself called it, gave answer to Emerson's request. The voice was distinctly American, and the form broke away from conventional metrical regularity, its line swelling and undulating with oceanic rhythm, echoing the biblical psalmists, or declaiming oratorically in the best American political tradition. It was an expansive voice for an expanding nation, and Whitman saw himself as prophet and seer celebrating individualism and democratic idealism as it manifested itself in all experience. Though Emerson was impressed with the first edition of *Leaves of Grass,* he was shocked at some of Whitman's subject matter. The book initially was not considered respectable, and each new edition was inevitably pronounced 'obscene'.

Whitman was born on Long Island, New York, and grew up in Brooklyn, though he returned frequently to Long Island and his beloved ocean. Mostly self-educated, he attended school for only six years and then worked variously as an office boy, schoolteacher, newspaper editor, and carpenter. During the Civil War he was a wound dresser in a Washington army hospital, and after the war he lost his job in the Office of Indian Affairs when it was discovered he had written an 'indecent' book. Never financially secure, Whitman supported himself as he could, continuing to expand and rearrange the poetry of *Leaves of Grass,* which began to gain acceptance and recognition only toward the end of his life.

### Crossing Brooklyn Ferry

1

Flood-tide below me! I see you face to face!
Clouds of the west—sun there half an hour high—I see you also face to face.

Crowds of men and women attired in the usual costumes, how curious you are to me!
On the ferry-boats the hundreds and hundreds that cross, returning home, are more curious to me than you suppose,
And you that shall cross from shore to shore years hence are more to me, and more in my meditations, than you might suppose.

2

The impalpable sustenance of me from all things at all hours of the day,
The simple, compact, well-join'd scheme, myself disintegrated, every one disintegrated yet part of the scheme,

The similitudes of the past and those of the future,
The glories strung like beads on my smallest sights and hearings, on the walk in the street and the passage over the river,
The current rushing so swiftly and swimming with me far away,
The others that are to follow me, the ties between me and them,
The certainty of others, the life, love, sight, hearing of others.
Others will enter the gates of the ferry and cross from shore to shore,
Others will watch the run of the flood-tide,
Others will see the shipping of Manhattan north and west, and the heights of Brooklyn to the south and east,
Others will see the islands large and small;
Fifty years hence, others will see them as they cross, the sun half an hour high,
A hundred years hence, or ever so many hundred years hence, others will see them,
Will enjoy the sunset, the pouring-in of the flood-tide, the falling-back to the sea of the ebb-tide.

3

It avails not, time nor place Crossing Brooklyn Ferry distance avails not,
I am with you, you men and women of a generation, or ever so many generations hence,
Just as you feel when you look on the river and sky, so I felt,
Just as any of you is one of a living crowd, I was one of a crowd,
Just as you are refresh'd by the gladness of the river and the bright flow, I was refresh'd,
Just as you stand and lean on the rail, yet hurry with the swift current, I stood yet was hurried,
Just as you look on the numberless masts of ships and the thick-stemm'd pipes of steamboats, I look'd.

I too many and many a time cross'd the river of old,
Watched the Twelfth-month sea-gulls, saw them high in the air floating with motionless wings, oscillating their bodies,
Saw how the glistening yellow lit up parts of their bodies and left the rest in strong shadow,
Saw the slow-wheeling circles and the gradual edging toward the south,
Saw the reflection of the summer sky in the water,
Had my eyes dazzled by the shimmering track of beams,
Look'd at the fine centrifugal spokes of light round the shape of my head in the sunlit water,
Look'd on the haze on the hills southward and south-westward,
Look'd on the vapour as it flew in fleeces tinged with violet,

Look'd toward the lower bay to notice the vessels arriving,
Saw their approach, saw aboard those that were near me,
Saw the white sails of schooners and sloops, saw the ships at anchor,
The sailors at work in the rigging or out astride the spars,
The round masts, the swinging motion of the hulls, the slender serpentine pennants,
The large and small steamers in motion, the pilots in their pilot-houses,
The white wake left by the passage, the quick tremulous whirl of the wheels,
The flags of all nations, the falling of them at sunset,
The scallop-edged waves in the twilight, the ladled cups, the frolicsome crests and glistening,
The stretch afar growing dimmer and dimmer, the grey walls of the granite storehouses by the docks,
On the river the shadowy group, the big steam-tug closely flank'd on each side by the barges, the hay-boat, the belated lighter,
On the neighbouring shore the fires from the foundry chimneys burning high and glaringly into the night,
Casting their flicker of black contrasted with wild red and yellow light over the tops of houses and down into the clefts of streets.

4

These and all else were to me the same as they are to you,
I loved well those cities, loved well the stately and rapid river,
The men and women I saw were all near to me,
Others the same—others who look back on me because I look'd forward to them,
(The time will come, though I stop here to-day and to-night.)

5

What is it then between us?
What is the count of the scores or hundreds of years between us?

Whatever it is, it avails not—distance avails not, and place avails not,
I too lived, Brooklyn of ample hills was mine,
I too walk'd the streets of Manhattan island, and bathed in the waters around it,
I too felt the curious abrupt questionings stir within me,
In the day among crowds of people sometimes they came upon me,
In my walks home late at night or as I lay in my bed they came upon me,
I too had been struck from the float forever held in solution,

I too had receiv'd identity by my body,
That I was I knew was of my body, and what I should be I knew I should be of my body.

6

It is not upon you alone the dark patches fall,
The dark threw its patches down upon me also,
The best I had done seem'd to me blank and suspicious,
My great thoughts as I supposed them, were they not in reality meagre?
Nor is it you alone who knows what it is to be evil,
I am he who knew what it was to be evil,
I too knitted the old knot of contrariety,
Blabb'd, blush'd, resented, lied, stole, grudg'd,
Had guile, anger, lust, hot wishes I dared not speak,
Was wayward, vain, greedy, shallow, sly, cowardly, malignant,
The wolf, the snake, the hog, not wanting in me,
The cheating look, the frivolous word, the adulterous wish, not wanting,
Refusals, hates, postponements, meanness, laziness, none of these wanting,
Was one with the rest, the days and haps of the rest,
Was call'd by my nighest name by clear loud voices of young men as they saw me approaching or passing,
Felt their arms on my neck as I stood, or the negligent leaning of their flesh against me as I sat,
Saw many I loved in the street or ferry-boat or public assembly, yet never told them a word,
Lived the same life with the rest, the same old laughing, gnawing, sleeping,
Play'd the part that still looks back on the actor or actress,
The same old role, the role that is what we make it, as great as we like,
Or as small as we like, or both great and small.

7

Closer yet I approach you,
What thought you have of me now, I had as much of you—I laid in my stores in advance,
I consider'd long and seriously of you before you were born.

Who was to know what should come home to me?
Who knows but I am enjoying this?
Who knows, for all the distance, but I am as good as looking at you now, for all you cannot see me?

8

Ah, what can ever be more stately and admirable to me than mast-hemm'd Manhattan?
River and sunset and scallop-edg'd waves of flood-tide?
The sea-gulls oscillating their bodies, the hay-boat in the twilight, and the belated lighter?
What gods can exceed these that clasp me by the hand, and with voices I love call me promptly and loudly by my nighest name as I approach?
What is more subtle than this which ties me to the woman or man that looks in my face?
Which fuses me into you now, and pours my meaning into you?
We understand then do we not?
What I promis'd without mentioning it, have you not accepted?
What the study could not teach—what the preaching could not accomplish is accomplish'd, is it not?

9

Flow on, river! flow with the flood-tide, and ebb with the ebb-tide!
Frolic on, crested and scallop-edg'd waves!
Gorgeous clouds of the sunset! drench with your splendour me, or the men and women generations after me!
Cross from shore to shore, countless crowds of passengers!
Stand up, tall masts of Mannahatta! stand up, beautiful hills of Brooklyn!
Throb, baffled and curious brain! throw out questions and answers!
Suspend here and everywhere, eternal float of solution!
Gaze, loving and thirsty eyes, in the house or street or public assembly!
Sound out, voices of young men! loudly and musically call me by my nighest name!
Live, old life! play the part that looks back on the actor or actress!
Play the old role, the role that is great or small according as one makes it!
Consider, you who peruse me, whether I may not in unknown ways be looking upon you;
Be firm, rail over the river, to support those who lean idly, yet haste with the hasting current;
Fly on, sea-birds! fly sideways, or wheel in large circles high in the air;
Receive the summer sky, you water, and faithfully hold it till all downcast eyes have time to take it from you!
Diverge, fine spokes of light, from the shape of my head, or any one's head, in the sunlit water!
Come on, ships from the lower bay! pass up or down, white-sail'd schooners, sloops, lighters!

Flaunt away, flags of all nations! be duly lower'd at sunset!
Burn high your fires, foundry chimneys! cast black shadows at nightfall! cast red and yellow light over the tops of the houses!
Appearances, now or henceforth, indicate what you are,
You necessary film, continue to envelop the soul,
About my body for me, and your body for you, be hung out divinest aromas,
Thrive, cities—bring your freight, bring your shows, ample and sufficient rivers,
Expand, being than which none else is perhaps more spiritual,
Keep your places, objects than which none else is more lasting.

You have waited, you always wait, you dumb, beautiful ministers,
We receive you with free sense at last, and are insatiate henceforward,
Not you any more shall be able to foil us, or withhold yourselves from us,
We use you, and do not cast you aside—we plant you permanently within us,
We fathom you not—we love you—there is perfection in you also,
You furnish your parts toward eternity,
Great or small, you furnish your parts toward the soul.

1856

## I Hear America Singing

I hear America singing, the varied carols I hear,
Those of mechanics, each one singing his as it should be blithe and strong,
The carpenter singing his as he measures his plank or beam,
The mason singing his as he makes ready for work, or leaves off work.
The boatman singing what belongs to him in his boat, the deckhand singing on the steamboat deck,
The shoemaker singing as he sits on his bench, the hatter singing as he stands,
The wood-cutter's song, the ploughboy's on his way in the morning, or at noon intermission or at sundown,
The delicious singing of the mother, or of the young wife at work, or of the girl sewing or washing,
Each singing what belongs to him or her and to none else,
The day what belongs to the day—at night the party of young fellows, robust, friendly,
Singing with open mouths their strong melodious songs.

1860

## A Sight in Camp in the Daybreak Grey and Dim

A sight in camp in the daybreak grey and dim,
As from my tent I emerge so early sleepless,
As slow I walk in the cool fresh air the path near by the hospital tent,
Three forms I see on stretchers lying, brought out there untended lying,
Over each the blanket spread, ample brownish woolen blanket,
Grey and heavy blanket, folding, covering all.

Curious I halt and silent stand,
Then with light fingers I from the face of the nearest the first just lift the blanket;
Who are you elderly man so gaunt and grim, with well-grey'd hair, and flesh all sunken about the eyes?
Who are you my dear comrade?
Then to the second I step—and who are you my child and darling?
Who are you sweet boy with cheeks yet blooming?

Then to the third—a face nor child nor old, very calm, as of beautiful yellow-white ivory;
Young man I think I know you—I think this face is the face of the Christ himself,
Dead and divine and brother of all, and here again he lies.

1865

## The Ox-Tamer

In a far-away northern county in the placid pastoral region,
Lives my farmer friend, the theme of my recitative, a famous tamer of oxen,
There they bring him the three-year-olds and the four-year-olds to break them,
He will take the wildest steer in the world and break him and tame him,
He will go fearless without any whip where the young bullock chafes up and down the yard,
The bullock's head tosses restless high in the air with raging eyes,
Yet see you! how soon his rage subsides—how soon this tamer tames him;
See you! on the farms hereabout a hundred oxen young and old, and he is the man who has tamed them,
They all know him, all are affectionate to him;
See you! some are such beautiful animals, so lofty looking;
Some are buff-colour'd, some mottled, one has a white line running along his back, some are brindled,
Some have wide flaring horns (a good sign)—see you! the bright hides,

See, the two with stars on their foreheads—see, the round bodies and broad backs,
How straight and square they stand on their legs—what fine sagacious eyes!
How they watch their tamer—they wish him near them—how they turn to look after him!
What yearning expression! how uneasy they are when he moves away from them;
Now I marvel what it can be he appears to them, (books, politics, poems, depart—all else departs,)
I confess I envy only his fascination—my silent, illiterate friend,
Whom a hundred oxen love there in his life on farms,
In the northern county far, in the placid pastoral region.

1874

## The Dalliance of the Eagles

Skirting the river road, (my forenoon walk, my rest,)
Skyward in air a sudden muffled sound, the dalliance of the eagles,
The rushing amorous contact high in space together,
The clinching interlocking claws, a living, fierce, gyrating wheel,
Four beating wings, two beaks, a swirling mass tight grappling,
In tumbling turning clustering loops, straight downward falling,
Till o'er the river pois'd, the twain yet one, a moment's lull,
A motionless still balance in the air, then parting, talons loosing,
Upward again on slow-firm pinions slanting, their separate diverse flight,
She hers, he his, pursuing.

1880

# Emily Dickinson
## 1830–1886

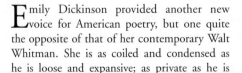

Emily Dickinson provided another new voice for American poetry, but one quite the opposite of that of her contemporary Walt Whitman. She is as coiled and condensed as he is loose and expansive; as private as he is public. She was born and raised in Amherst, Massachusetts, studying at Amherst Academy before entering nearby Mount Holyoke Female Seminary. But less than a year later she returned home because she could not accept the Seminary's rigid brand of Christianity, and because she was homesick. She lived the rest of her life in her father's house, rarely leaving Amherst, and eventually becoming a recluse, seeing only a few visitors a year. Though some biographers have characterized Dickinson as a frail, highly eccentric spinster, hiding from the world and frustrated in life and in love, the power of her poetry and the sheer amount of her literary output belie such a picture. Instead, we might consider her withdrawal from society a choice for the freedom to pursue the career of a poet. She produced over 1,700 poems, of which only 7 were published during her lifetime. Though the form of her poetry looks simple, with its patterns of metre and rhyme suggesting her use of nineteenth-century hymnals as models of prosody, there is nothing simplistic in what she says, and her unconventional punctuation forces us to pause with her thoughts as she examines faith and doubt, death, nature, and varieties of love.

## [Success Is Counted Sweetest]

Success is counted sweetest
By those who ne'er succeed.
To comprehend a nectar
Requires sorest need.

Not one of all the purple Host
Who took the Flag today
Can tell the definition
So clear of Victory

As he defeated—dying—
On whose forbidden ear
The distant strains of triumph
Burst agonized and clear!

1878

## [I'm 'Wife'—I've Finished That]

I'm 'wife'—I've finished that—
That other state—
I'm Czar—I'm 'Woman' now—
It's safer so—

How odd the Girl's life looks
Behind this soft Eclipse—
I think that Earth feels so
To folks in Heaven—now—

This being comfort—then
That other kind—was pain—
But why compare?
I'm 'Wife'! Stop there!

1890

## [The Heart Asks Pleasure—First]

The Heart asks Pleasure—first—
And then—Excuse from Pain—
And then—those little Anodynes
That deaden suffering—
And then—to go to sleep—
And then—if it should be
The will of its Inquisitor
The privilege to die—

1890

## [Because I Could Not Stop for Death]

Because I could not stop for Death—
He kindly stopped for me—
The Carriage held but just Ourselves—
And Immortality.

We slowly drove—He knew no haste
And I had put away
My labour and my leisure too,
For His Civility—

We passed the School, where Children strove
At Recess—in the Ring—
We passed the Fields of Gazing Grain—
We passed the Setting Sun—

Or rather—He passed Us—
The Dews drew quivering and chill—
For only Gossamer, my Gown—
My Tippet—only Tulle—

We paused before a House that seemed
A Swelling of the Ground—
The Roof was scarcely visible—
The Cornice—in the Ground—

Since then—'tis Centuries—and yet
Feels shorter than the Day
I first surmised the Horses' Heads
Were toward Eternity—

1890

## [What Is—'Paradise']

What is—'Paradise'—
Who live there—
Are they 'Farmers'—
Do they 'hoe'—
Do they know that this is 'Amherst'—
And that I—am coming—too—
Do they wear 'new shoes'—in 'Eden'—
Is it always pleasant—there—
Won't they scold us—when we're hungry—
Or tell God—how cross we are—
You are sure there's such a person
As 'a Father'—in the sky—
So if I get lost—there—ever—
Or do what the nurse calls 'die'—
I shan't walk the 'Jasper'—barefoot—
Ransomed folks—won't laugh at me—
Maybe—'Eden' a'nt so lonesome
As New England used to be!

1891

## [I Never Hear the Word]

I never hear the word 'escape'
Without a quicker blood,
A sudden expectation,
A flying attitude!

I never hear of prisons broad
By soldiers battered down,
But I tug childish at my bars
Only to fail again!

1891

## [I Heard a Fly Buzz]

I heard a Fly buzz—when I died—
The Stillness in the Room
Was like the Stillness in the Air—
Between the Heaves of Storm—

The Eyes around—had wrung them dry—
And Breaths were gathering firm
For that last Onset—when the King
Be witnessed—in the Room—

I willed my Keepsakes—Signed away
What portion of me be
Assignable—and then it was
There interposed a Fly—

With Blue—uncertain stumbling Buzz—
Between the light—and me—
And then the Windows failed—and then
I could not see to see—

1896

# Thomas Hardy

1840–1928

One of the great novelists of English literature, Thomas Hardy pursued a writing career in fiction, poetry, and drama that spanned more than six decades. Born near Dorchester in southwestern England, the area that would become Wessex in his writings, he was apprenticed to an architect at the age of 15. In 1861 he moved to London to continue his architectural work. At the same time he began to write poetry and fiction; his first novel, *Desperate Remedies*, appeared in 1871. His commitment to fiction led him to abandon a career in architecture, freeing him to publish 15 novels, including *The Mayor of Casterbridge* (1885) and *Tess of the D'Urbervilles* (1891), as well as several collections of short fiction. Hardy's poetry, like his fiction, explores in naturalistic terms the hapless condition of humankind, caught in a world without design, providence, or God. Unable to return to the religious faith of his Victorian upbringing, he shares with many modern poets a belief in the futility and waste of human existence.

## Hap

If but some vengeful god would call to me
From up the sky, and laugh: 'Thou suffering thing,
Know that thy sorrow is my ecstasy,
That thy love's loss is my hate's profiting!'

Then would I bear it, clench myself, and die,
Steeled by the sense of ire unmerited;
Half-eased in that a Powerfuller than I
Had willed and meted me the tears I shed.

But not so. How arrives it joy lies slain,
And why unblooms the best hope ever sown!
—Crass Casualty obstructs the sun and rain,
And dicing Time for gladness casts a moan. . . .
These purblind Doomsters had as readily strown
Blisses about my pilgrimage as pain.

1898

## The Darkling Thrush

I leant upon a coppice gate
When Frost was spectre-grey
And Winter's dregs made desolate
The weakening eye of day.
The tangled bine-stems scored the sky
Like strings of broken lyres,
And all mankind that haunted nigh
Had sought their household fires.

The land's sharp features seemed to be
The Century's corpse outleant,
His crypt the cloudy canopy,
The wind his death-lament.
The ancient pulse of germ and birth
Was shrunken hard and dry,
And every spirit upon earth
Seemed fervourless as I.

At once a voice arose among
The bleak twigs overhead
In a full-hearted evensong
Of joy illimited;
An aged thrush, frail, gaunt, and small,
In blast-beruffled plume,
Had chosen thus to fling his soul
Upon the growing gloom.

So little cause for carolings
Of such ecstatic sound
Was written on terrestrial things
Afar or nigh around,
That I could think there trembled through
His happy good-night air
Some blessed Hope, whereof he knew
And I was unaware.

1901

## The Convergence of the Twain

(Lines on the loss of the *Titanic*)

I

In a solitude of the sea
Deep from human vanity,
And the Pride of Life that planned her, stilly couches she.

II

Steel chambers, late the pyres
Of her salamandrine fires,
Cold currents thrid, and turn to rhythmic tidal lyres.

III

Over the mirrors meant
To glass the opulent
The sea-worm crawls—grotesque, slimed, dumb, indifferent.

IV

Jewels in joy designed
To ravish the sensuous mind
Lie lightless, all their sparkles bleared and black and blind.

V

Dim moon-eyed fishes near
Gaze at the gilded gear
And query: 'What does this vaingloriousness down here?' . . .

VI

Well: while was fashioning
This creature of cleaving wing,
The Immanent Will that stirs and urges everything

VII

Prepared a sinister mate
For her—so gaily great—
A Shape of Ice, for the time far and dissociate.

VIII

And as the smart ship grew
In stature, grace, and hue,
In shadowy silent distance grew the Iceberg too.

IX

Alien they seemed to be:
No mortal eye could see
The intimate welding of their later history.

X

Or sign that they were bent
By paths coincident
On being anon twin halves of one august event,

XI

Till the Spinner of the Years
Said 'Now!' And each one hears,
And consummation comes, and jars two hemispheres.

1912

## In Time of 'The Breaking of Nations'

I

Only a man harrowing clods
In a slow silent walk
With an old horse that stumbles and nods
Half asleep as they stalk.

II

Only thin smoke without flame
From the heaps of couch-grass;
Yet this will go onward the same
Though Dynasties pass.

III

Yonder a maid and her wight
   Come whispering by:
War's annals will fade into night
   Ere their story die.

1916

## The Oxen

Christmas Eve, and twelve of the clock.
   'Now they are all on their knees.'
An elder said as we sat in a flock
   By the embers in hearthside ease.

We pictured the meek mild creatures where
   They dwelt in their strawy pen,
Nor did it occur to one of us there
   To doubt they were kneeling then.

So fair a fancy few would weave
   In these years! Yet, I feel,
If someone said on Christmas Eve,
   'Come; see the oxen kneel,

In the lonely barton by yonder coomb
   Our childhood used to know,'
I should go with him in the gloom,
   Hoping it might be so.

1917

## During Wind and Rain

They sing their dearest songs—
He, she, all of them—yea,
Treble and tenor and bass,
    And one to play;
With the candles mooning each face. . . .
    Ah, no; the years O!
How the sick leaves reel down in throngs!

They clear the creeping moss—
Elders and juniors—aye,
Making the pathways neat
    And the garden gay;
And they build a shady seat. . . .
    Ah, no; the years, the years;
See, the white storm-birds wing across!

They are blithely breakfasting all—
Men and maidens—yea,
Under the summer tree,
    With a glimpse of the bay,
While pet fowl come to the knee. . . .
    Ah, no; the years O!
And the rotten rose is ript from the wall.

They change to a high new house,
He, she, all of them—aye,
Clocks and carpets and chairs
    On the lawn all day,
And brightest things that are theirs. . . .
    Ah, no; the years, the years;
Down their carved names the rain-drop ploughs.

1917

# Gerard Manley Hopkins

1844–1889

Born in Stratford, Essex, Gerard Manley Hopkins showed an early interest in poetry, winning a prize for his work at Highgate School in London. As he entered Balliol College in Oxford, he aspired to become a painter. Caught up in the Oxford Movement, a revival of ritualistic Christianity, he converted to Catholicism in 1866. Two years later he joined the Jesuits; he was ordained as a priest in 1877, and served as a missionary in the squalid slums of Liverpool. Hopkins later took a church at Oxford, and near the end of his life was a professor of Greek at University College, Dublin.

While studying for the priesthood, Hopkins had burned all his poetry, but in 1875, still struggling with the demands of his faith and with his aesthetic interests, he began writing again, exploring this struggle in his poetry. An intense observer of the natural world, Hopkins saw patterns, which he called 'inscapes', in natural phenomena, and his poetry attempts to convey the complex unity of his sensual observation. Yet his is primarily a poetry for the ear. Experimenting in prosody, he drew on rhythms of early English poetry, modelling his 'sprung rhythm' on ordinary speech. Wrenching and straining syntax into original and startling forms, he presents us with an inspired vision of the beauty of nature infused with the glory of God. During his lifetime Hopkins's poems were little known outside his small circle of friends. The first volume of his work was not published until 1918, 30 years after his death, when it was widely read and admired by many of the younger modern poets.

## God's Grandeur

The world is charged with the grandeur of God.
    It will flame out, like shining from shook foil;
    It gathers to a greatness, like the ooze of oil
Crushed. Why do men then now not reck his rod?
Generations have trod, have trod, have trod;
    And all is seared with trade; bleared, smeared with toil;
    And wears man's smudge and shares man's small: the soil
Is bare now, nor can foot feel, being shod.

And for all this, nature is never spent;
    There lives the dearest freshness deep down things;
And though the last lights off the black West went
    Oh, morning, at the brown brink eastward, springs—
Because the Holy Ghost over the bent
    World broods with warm breast and with ah! bright wings.

1918

## The Windhover

*To Christ Our Lord*

I caught this morning morning's minion, king-
  dom of daylight's dauphin, dapple-dawn-drawn Falcon, in his riding
  Of the rolling level underneath him steady air, and striding
High there, how he rung upon the rein of a wimpling wing
In his ecstasy! then off, off forth on swing,
  As a skate's heel sweeps smooth on a bow-bend: the hurl and gliding
  Rebuffed the big wind. My heart in hiding
Stirred for a bird,—the achieve of, the mastery of the thing!

Brute beauty and valour and act, oh, air, pride, plume, here
  Buckle! AND the fire that breaks from thee then, a billion
Times told lovelier, more dangerous, O my chevalier!

  No wonder of it: shéer plód makes plough down sillion
Shine, and blue-bleak embers, ah my dear,
  Fall, gall themselves, and gash gold-vermilion.

1918

## Pied Beauty

Glory be to God for dappled things—
  For skies of couple-colour as a brinded cow;
    For rose-moles all in stipple upon trout that swim;
Fresh-firecoal chestnut-falls; finches' wings;
  Landscape plotted and pieced—fold, fallow, and plough;
    And áll trádes, their gear and tackle and trim.
All things counter, original, spare, strange;
  Whatever is fickle, freckled (who knows how?)
    With swift, slow; sweet, sour; adazzle, dim;
He fathers-forth whose beauty is past change:
                Praise him.

1918

## Spring and Fall: To a Young Child

Márgarét, are you gríeving
Over Goldengrove unleaving?
Leáves, líke the things of man, you
With your fresh thoughts care for, can you?
Áh! ás the heart grows older
It will come to such sights colder
By and by, nor spare a sigh
Though worlds of wanwood leafmeal lie;
And yet you *will* weep and know why.
Now no matter, child, the name:
Sórrow's spríngs áre the same.
Nor mouth had, no nor mind, expressed
What heart heard of, ghost guessed:
It ís the blight man was born for,
It is Margaret you mourn for.

1918

## [Though Art Indeed Just, Lord]

*Justus quidem tu es, Domine, si disputem tecum: verumtamen Justa loquar ad te: Quare via impiorum prosperatur? &c.*[1]

Thou art indeed just, Lord, if I contend
With thee; but, sir, so what I plead is just.
Why do sinners' ways prosper? and why must
Disappointment all I endeavour end?

Wert thou my enemy, O thou my friend,
How wouldst thou worse, I wonder, than thou dost
Defeat, thwart me? Oh, the sots and thralls of lust
Do in spare hours more thrive than I that spend,

Sir, life upon thy cause. See, banks and brakes
Now, leavèd how thick! lacèd they are again
With fretty chervil, look, and fresh wind shakes

Them; birds build—but not I build; no, but strain,
Time's eunuch, and not breed one work that wakes.
Mine, O thou lord of life, send my roots rain.

1918

1 quoted from the biblical prophet Jeremiah, and translated in the first three lines of the poem

# Archibald Lampman

1861–1899

Archibald Lampman was born in Morpeth, Ontario, of United Empire Loyalist stock. A case of rheumatic fever when he was seven left him lame for four years and probably weakened his health permanently. His early education had to take place at home, although by the age of nine he was able to attend a private school. He graduated from the University of Toronto in 1882. After teaching high school for four months, he resigned and joined the Post Office Department in Ottawa, where he worked until his death from pneumonia.

A nature poet, Lampman took comfort and poetic delight in the changing seasons and their dramatic effect on natural life. Yet his verse, unlike that of many of his Canadian contemporaries, also ventures into social commentary. 'The City of the End of Things', published in 1899, is a startling apocalyptic vision, a denunciation of commercial society. In 1942 the critic E.K. Brown discovered among Lampman's scribblers and notebooks 'At the Long Sault: May 1660', a stirring lyrical evocation of a great moment in Canadian history and an indication of new directions that his poetry might have followed had death not cut short his career.

## The Railway Station

The darkness brings no quiet here, the light
No waking: ever on my blinded brain
The flare of lights, the rush, and cry, and strain,
The engines' scream, the hiss and thunder smite:

I see the hurrying crowds, the clasp, the flight,
Faces that touch, eyes that are dim with pain:
I see the hoarse wheels turn, and the great train
Move labouring out into the bourneless night.

So many souls within its dim recesses,
So many bright, so many mournful eyes:
Mine eyes that watch grow fixed with dreams and guesses;
What threads of life, what hidden histories,
What sweet or passionate dreams and dark distresses,
What unknown thoughts, what various agonies!

1888

## The Death of Tennyson

They tell that when his final hour drew near,
He whose fair praise the ages shall rehearse,
Whom now the living and the dead hold dear;
Our grey-haired master of immortal verse,
Called for his Shakespeare, and with touch of rue
Turned to that page in stormy Cymbeline
That bears the dirge. Whether he read none knew,
But on the book he laid his hand serene,
And kept it there unshaken, till there fell
The last grey change, and from before his eyes,
This glorious world that Shakespeare loved so well,
Slowly, as at a beck, without surprise—
Its woe, its pride, its passion, and its play—
Like mists and melting shadows passed away.

1892

## The City of the End of Things

Beside the pounding cataracts
Of midnight streams unknown to us
'Tis builded in the leafless tracts
And valleys huge of Tartarus.[1]
Lurid and lofty and vast it seems;
It hath no rounded name that rings,
But I have heard it called in dreams
The City of the End of Things.

Its roofs and iron towers have grown
None knoweth how high within the night,
But in its murky streets far down
A flaming terrible and bright
Shakes all the stalking shadows there,
Across the walls, across the floors,
And shifts upon the upper air
From out a thousand furnace doors;
And all the while an awful sound
Keeps roaring on continually,

1 the infernal abyss below Hades: true hell where Zeus threw rebel Titans

And crashes in the ceaseless round
Of a gigantic harmony.

Through its grim depths re-echoing
And all its weary height of walls,
With measured roar and iron ring,
The inhuman music lifts and falls.
Where no thing rests and no man is,
And only fire and night hold sway;
The beat, the thunder and the hiss
Cease not, and change not, night nor day.

And moving at unheard commands,
The abysses and vast fires between,
Flit figures that with clanking hands
Obey a hideous routine;
They are not flesh, they are not bone,
They see not with the human eye,
And from their iron lips is blown
A dreadful and monotonous cry;
And whoso of our mortal race
Should find that city unaware,
Lean Death would smite him face to face,
And blanch him with its venomed air:
Or caught by the terrific spell,
Each thread of memory snapt and cut,
His soul would shrivel and its shell
Go rattling like an empty nut.

It was not always so, but once,
In days that no man thinks upon,
Fair voices echoed from its stones,
The light above it leaped and shone:
Once there were multitudes of men,
That built that city in their pride,
Until its might was made, and then
They withered age by age and died.
But now of that prodigious race,
Three only in an iron tower,
Set like carved idols face to face,
Remain the masters of its power;
And at the city gate a fourth,
Gigantic and with dreadful eyes,
Sits looking toward the lightless north,

Beyond the reach of memories;
Fast rooted to the lurid floor,
A bulk that never moves a jot,
In his pale body dwells no more,
Or mind or soul,—an idiot!
But sometimes in the end those three
Shall perish and their hands be still,
And with the master's touch shall flee
Their incommunicable skill.
A stillness absolute as death
Along the slacking wheels shall lie,
And, flagging at a single breath,
The fires shall moulder out and die.
The roar shall vanish at its height,
And over that tremendous town
The silence of eternal night
Shall gather close and settle down.
All its grim grandeur, tower and hall,
Shall be abandoned utterly,
And into rust and dust shall fall
From century to century;
Nor ever living thing shall grow,
Nor trunk of tree, nor blade of grass;
No drop shall fall, no wind shall blow,
Nor sound of any foot shall pass:
Alone of its accursèd state,
One thing the hand of Time shall spare,
For the grim Idiot at the gate
Is deathless and eternal there.

1895

## Winter-Solitude

I saw the city's towers on a luminous pale-grey sky;
Beyond them a hill of the softest mistiest green,
With naught but frost and the coming of night between,
And a long thin cloud above it the colour of August rye.

I sat in the midst of a plain on my snowshoes with bended knee
Where the thin wind stung my cheeks,
And the hard snow ran in little ripples and peaks,
Like the fretted floor of a white and petrified sea.

And a strange peace gathered about my soul and shone,
As I sat reflecting there,
In a world so mystically fair,
So deathly silent—I so utterly alone.

*February, 1893*

1943

## At the Long Sault: May 1660[1]

Under the day-long sun there is life and mirth
In the working earth,
And the wonderful moon shines bright
Through the soft spring night,
The innocent flowers in the limitless woods are springing
Far and away
With the sound and the perfume of May,
And ever up from the south the happy birds are winging,
The waters glitter and leap and play
While the grey hawk soars.

But far in an open glade of the forest set
Where the rapid plunges and roars,
Is a ruined fort with a name that men forget,—
A shelterless pen
With its broken palisade,
Behind it, musket in hand,
Beyond message or aid
In this savage heart of the wild,
Mere youngsters, grown in a moment to men,
Grim and alert arrayed,
The comrades of Daulac stand.
Ever before them, night and day,
The rush and skulk and cry
Of foes, not men but devils, panting for prey;
Behind them the sleepless dream
Or the little frail-walled town,[2] far away by the plunging stream.
Of maiden and matron and child,
With ruin and murder impending, and none but they
To beat back the gathering horror

1 On 1 May 1660 Adam Dollard des Ormeaux (sometimes called Daulac), with sixteen companions and forty-four Hurons and Algonkins, laid an ambush for some Iroquois at an abandoned fort on the Ottawa River. The Iroquois were joined by a reinforcement of 500, but it took them ten days to vanquish the French and their allies. Until fairly recently this event was considered to have saved the colony of Montreal from Iroquois attack, and the French were considered martyrs for the faith.

2 Montreal

Deal death while they may,
  And then die.

Day and night they have watched while the little plain
Grew dark with the rush of the foe, but their host
Broke ever and melted away, with no boast
But to number their slain;
And now as the days renew
Hunger and thirst and care
Were they never so stout, so true,
Press at their hearts; but none
Falters or shrinks or utters a coward word,
Though each setting sun
Brings from the pitiless wild new hands to the Iroquois horde,
And only to them despair.

Silent, white-faced, again and again
Charged and hemmed round by furious hands,
Each for a moment faces them all and stands
In his little desperate ring; like a tired bull moose
Whom scores of sleepless wolves, a ravening pack,
Have chased all night, all day
Through the snow-laden woods, like famine let loose;
And he turns at last in his track
Against a wall of rock and stands at bay;
Round him with terrible sinews and teeth of steel
They charge and recharge; but with many a furious plunge and wheel,
Hither and thither over the trampled snow,
He tosses them bleeding and torn;
Till, driven, and ever to and fro
Harried, wounded, and weary grown,
His mighty strength gives way
And all together they fasten upon him and drag him down.

So Daulac turned him anew
With a ringing cry to his men
In the little raging forest glen,
And his terrible sword in the twilight whistled and slew.
And all his comrades stood
With their backs to the pales,[3] and fought
Till their strength was done;

3 a row of spiked wooden poles, here the walls of the fort

The thews that were only mortal flagged and broke
Each struck his last wild stroke,
And they fell one by one,
And the world that had seemed so good
Passed like a dream and was naught.

And then the great night came
With the triumph-songs of the foe and the flame
Of the camp-fires.
Out of the dark the soft wind woke,
The song of the rapid rose alway
And came to the spot where the comrades lay,
Beyond help or care,
With none but the red men round them
To gnash their teeth and stare.

All night by the foot of the mountain
   The little town lieth at rest,
The sentries are peacefully pacing;
   And neither from East nor from West
Is there rumour of death and danger;
   None dreameth tonight in his bed
That ruin was near and the heroes
   That met it and stemmed it are dead.

But afar in the ring of the forest,
   Where the air is so tender with May
And the waters are wild in the moonlight
   They lie in their silence of clay.

The numberless stars out of heaven
   Look down with a pitiful glance;
And the lilies asleep in the forest
   Are closed like the lilies of France.[4]

1943

4 that is, the fleur-de-lis, the emblematic flower of France, often appearing as a heraldic emblem on the shields of warriors

# William Butler Yeats

## 1865–1939

William Butler Yeats was born at Sandymount, near Dublin, Ireland. His father, John Butler Yeats, was a well-known artist. Educated at schools in London and Dublin, Yeats was never an outstanding scholar, and after attending art school for two years, he left to devote himself to poetry. As a boy, he had loved to roam the countryside of County Sligo, listening to folk tales told around peat fires and absorbing the 'symbols, popular beliefs, and old scraps of verse that made Ireland romantic to herself'. His early poems are full of Irish mythology, with the poet striking a romantic pose and musically intoning in archaic diction.

Yeats grew out of this phase, influenced by the movement for Irish nationalism, and he turned to actual events and real people to speak for 'the new Ireland, overwhelmed by responsibility, [which] begins to long for psychological truth.' In 1899, with the help of Lady Gregory, herself a writer and promoter of Irish literature, he founded the Irish National Theater. He went on to become a public figure, serving from 1922 until 1928 as a senator of the Irish Free State, at the same time as he was achieving worldwide recognition as a great poet. In 1917 he married Georgie Hyde-Lees, who claimed to have powers as a spiritualist medium. She would fall into trances, and through automatic writing she produced many of the symbols Yeats used in *A Vision,* a work that presents his theories of the cyclical patterns of history, human psychology, and the soul's migrations after death. After his death, he was buried as he requested in County Sligo, near the mountain that had figured so much both in Irish legend and in Yeats's poetry: 'Under bare Ben bulben's head / In Drumcliff churchyard Yeats is laid.'

### The Lake Isle of Innisfree

I will arise and go now, and go to Innisfree,
And a small cabin build there, of clay and wattles made:
Nine bean-rows will I have there, a hive for the honeybee,
And live alone in the bee-loud glade.

And I shall have some peace there, for peace comes dropping slow,
Dropping from the veils of the morning to where the cricket sings;
There midnight's all a glimmer, and noon a purple glow,
And evening full of the linnet's wings.

I will arise and go now, for always night and day
I hear lake water lapping with low sounds by the shore;
While I stand on the roadway, or on the pavements grey,
I hear it in the deep heart's core.

1890

## The Dolls

A DOLL in the doll-maker's house
Looks at the cradle and balls:
'That is an insult to us.'
But the oldest of all the dolls
Who had seen, being kept for show,
Generations of his sort,
Out-screams the whole shelf: 'Although
There's not a man can report
Evil of this place,
The man and the woman bring
Hither to our disgrace,
A noisy and filthy thing.'
Hearing him groan and stretch
The doll-maker's wife is aware
Her husband has heard the wretch,
And crouched by the arm of his chair,
She murmurs into his ear,
Head upon shoulder leant:
'My dear, my dear, oh dear,
It was an accident.'

1916

## Easter, 1916

I have met them at close of day
Coming with vivid faces
From counter or desk among grey
Eighteenth-century houses.
I have passed with a nod of the head
Or polite meaningless words,
Or have lingered awhile and said
Polite meaningless words,
And thought before I had done
Of a mocking tale or a gibe
To please a companion
Around the fire at the club,
Being certain that they and I
But lived where motley is worn:
All changed, changed utterly:
A terrible beauty is born.

That woman's days were spent
In ignorant good will,
Her nights in argument
Until her voice grew shrill.
What voice more sweet than hers
When young and beautiful,
She rode to harriers?
This man had kept a school
And rode our winged horse;
This other his helper and friend
Was coming into his force;
He might have won fame in the end,
So sensitive his nature seemed,
So daring and sweet his thought.
This other man I had dreamed
A drunken, vain-glorious lout.
He had done most bitter wrong
To some who are near my heart,
Yet I number him in the song;
He, too, has resigned his part
In the casual comedy;
He, too, has been changed in his turn,
Transformed utterly:
A terrible beauty is born.

Hearts with one purpose alone
Through summer and winter seem
Enchanted to a stone
To trouble the living stream.
The horse that comes from the road,
The rider, the birds that range
From cloud to tumbling cloud,
Minute by minute change;
A shadow of cloud on the stream
Changes minute by minute;
A horse-hoof slides on the brim,
And a horse plashes within it
Where long-legged moor-hens dive,
And hens to moor-cocks call.
Minute by minute they live:
The stone's in the midst of all.

Too long a sacrifice
Can make a stone of the heart.

O when may it suffice?
That is Heaven's part, our part
To murmur name upon name,
As a mother names her child
When sleep at last has come
On limbs that had run wild.
What is it but nightfall?
No, no, not night but death;
Was it needless death after all?
For England may keep faith
For all that is done and said.
We know their dream; enough
To know they dreamed and are dead.
And what if excess of love
Bewildered them till they died?
I write it out in a verse—
MacDonagh and MacBride
And Connolly and Pearse
Now and in time to be,
Wherever green is worn,
Are changed, changed utterly:
A terrible beauty is born.

1916

## The Wild Swans at Coole

The trees are in their autumn beauty,
The woodland paths are dry,
Under the October twilight the water
Mirrors a still sky;
Upon the brimming water among the stones
Are nine-and-fifty swans.

The nineteenth autumn has come upon me
Since I first made my count;
I saw, before I had well finished,
All suddenly mount
And scatter wheeling in great broken rings
Upon their clamorous wings.

I have looked upon those brilliant creatures,
And now my heart is sore.

All's changed since I, hearing at twilight,
The first time on this shore,
The bell-beat of their wings above my head,
Trod with a lighter tread.

Unwearied still, lover by lover,
They paddle in the cold
Companionable streams or climb the air;
Their hearts have not grown old;
Passion or conquest, wander where they will,
Attend upon them still.

But now they drift on the still water,
Mysterious, beautiful;
Among what rushes will they build,
By what lake's edge or pool
Delight men's eyes when I awake some day
To find they have flown away?

1917

## The Second Coming

Turning and turning in the widening gyre
The falcon cannot hear the falconer;
Things fall apart; the centre cannot hold;
Mere anarchy is loosed upon the world
The blood-dimmed tide is loosed, and everywhere
The ceremony of innocence is drowned;
The best lack all conviction, while the worst
Are full of passionate intensity.

Surely some revelation is at hand;
Surely the Second Coming is at hand.
The Second Coming! Hardly are those words out
When a vast image out of *Spiritus Mundi*
Troubles my sight: somewhere in sands of the desert
A shape with lion body and the head of a man,
A gaze blank and pitiless as the sun,
Is moving its slow thighs, while all about it
Reel shadows of the indignant desert birds.
The darkness drops again; but now I know
That twenty centuries of stony sleep

Were vexed to nightmare by a rocking cradle,
And what rough beast, its hour come round at last,
Slouches towards Bethlehem to be born?

1920

## Leda and the Swan[1]

A sudden blow: the great wings beating still
Above the staggering girl, her thighs caressed
By the dark webs, her nape caught in his bill
He holds her helpless breast upon his breast.

How can those terrified vague fingers push
The feathered glory from her loosening thighs?
And how can body, laid in that white rush,
But feel the strange heart beating where it lies?

A shudder in the loins engenders there
The broken wall, the burning roof and tower
And Agamemnon dead.
Being so caught up,
So mastered by the brute blood of the air,
Did she put on his knowledge with his power
Before the indifferent beak could let her drop?

1924

1 Zeus, in the form of a swan, ravished Leda, who gave birth to Helen, whose desertion of her husband, King Menelaus, caused the Trojan War. Another of Leda's daughters, Clytemnestra, murdered her husband Agamemnon.

## Among School Children

I

I walk through the long schoolroom questioning;
A kind old nun in a white hood replies;
The children learn to cipher and to sing,
To study reading-books and history,

To cut and sew, be neat in everything
In the best modern way—the children's eyes
In momentary wonder stare upon
A sixty-year-old smiling public man.

II

I dream of a Ledaean body, bent
Above a sinking fire, a tale that she
Told of a harsh reproof, or trivial event
That changed some childish day to tragedy—
Told, and it seemed that our two natures blent
Into a sphere from youthful sympathy,
Or else, to alter Plato's parable,
Into the yolk and white of the one shell.

III

And thinking of that fit of grief or rage
I look upon one child or t'other there
And wonder if she stood so at that age—
For even daughters of the swan can share
Something of every paddler's heritage—
And had that colour upon cheek or hair,
And thereupon my heart is driven wild:
She stands before me as a living child.

IV

Her present image floats into the mind—
Did Quattrocento finger fashion it
Hollow of cheek as though it drank the wind
And took a mess of shadows for its meat?
And I though never of Ledaean kind
Had pretty plumage once—enough of that,
Better to smile on all that smile, and show
There is a comfortable kind of old scarecrow.

V

What youthful mother, a shape upon her lap
Honey of generation had betrayed,
And that must sleep, shriek, struggle to escape

As recollection or the drug decide,
Would think her son, did she but see that shape
With sixty or more winters on its head,
A compensation for the pang of his birth,
Or the uncertainty of his setting forth?

VI

Plato thought nature but a spume that plays
Upon a ghostly paradigm of things;
Solider Aristotle played the taws
Upon the bottom of the king of kings;
World-famous golden-thighed Pythagoras
Fingered upon a fiddle-stick or strings
What a star sang and careless Muses heard:
Old clothes upon old sticks to scare a bird.

VII

Both nuns and mothers worship images,
But those the candles light are not as those
That animate a mother's reveries,
But keep a marble or a bronze repose.
And yet they too break hearts—O Presences
That passion, piety or affection knows,
And that all heavenly glory symbolise—
O self-born mockers of man's enterprise;

VIII

Labour is blossoming or dancing where
The body is not bruised to pleasure soul,
Nor beauty born out of its own despair,
Nor blear-eyed wisdom out of midnight oil.
O chestnut tree, great rooted blossomer,
Are you the leaf, the blossom or the bole?
O body swayed to music, O brightening glance,
How can we know the dancer from the dance?

1927

## Sailing to Byzantium[1]

That is no country for old men. The young
In one another's arms, birds in the trees
—Those dying generations—at their song,
The salmon-falls, the mackerel-crowded seas,
Fish, flesh, or fowl, commend all summer long
Whatever is begotten, born, and dies.
Caught in that sensual music all neglect
Monuments of unaging intellect.

An aged man is but a paltry thing,
A tattered coat upon a stick, unless
Soul clap its hands and sing, and louder sing
For every tatter in its mortal dress,
Nor is there singing school but studying
Monuments of its own magnificence;
And therefore I have sailed the seas and come
To the holy city of Byzantium.

O sages standing in God's holy fire
As in the gold mosaic of a wall,
Come from the holy fire, perne in a gyre,[2]
And be the singing-masters of my soul.
Consume my heart away; sick with desire
And fastened to a dying animal
It knows not what it is; and gather me
Into the artifice of eternity.

Once out of nature I shall never take
My bodily form from any natural thing,
But such a form as Grecian goldsmiths make
Of hammered gold and gold enamelling
To keep a drowsy emperor awake;
Or set upon a golden bough to sing
To lords and ladies of Byzantium
Of what is past, or passing, or to come.

1927

1 now Istanbul
2 revolve in a spiral

## The Circus Animals' Desertion

I

I sought a theme and sought for it in vain,
I sought it daily for six weeks or so.
Maybe at last, being but a broken man,
I must be satisfied with my heart, although
Winter and summer till old age began
My circus animals[1] were all on show,
Those stilted boys, that burnished chariot,
Lion and woman and the Lord knows what.

II

What can I but enumerate old themes?
First that sea-rider Oisin led by the nose
Through three enchanted islands, allegorical dreams,
Vain gaiety, vain battle, vain repose,
Themes of the embittered heart, or so it seems,
That might adorn old songs or courtly shows;
But what cared I that set him on to ride,
I, starved for the bosom of his faery bride?

And then a counter-truth filled out its play,
*The Countess Cathleen* was the name I gave it;
She, pity-crazed, had given her soul away,
But masterful Heaven had intervened to save it.
I thought my dear must her own soul destroy,
So did fanaticism and hate enslave it,
And this brought forth a dream and soon enough
This dream itself had all my thought and love.

And when the Fool and Blind Man stole the bread
Cuchulain fought the ungovernable sea;
Heart-mysteries there, and yet when all is said
It was the dream itself enchanted me:
Character isolated by a deed

1 In the course of the poem, Yeats alludes to much of his previous work, especially his mythological and symbolic figures.

To engross the present and dominate memory.
Players and painted stage took all my love,
And not those things that they were emblems of.

III

Those masterful images because complete
Grew in pure mind, but out of what began?
A mound of refuse or the sweeping of a street,
Old kettles, old bottles, and a broken can,
Old iron, old bones, old rags, that raving slut
Who keeps the till. Now that my ladder's gone,
I must lie down where all the ladders start,
In the foul rag-and-bone shop of the heart.

1939

# Robert Frost

1874–1963

Robert Frost was born in San Francisco, where his father was a journalist and an aspiring politician. Frost's mother wrote poetry and introduced her son to Scottish poetry and to such poets as Wordsworth, Bryant, and Emerson, whose use of nature in their work undoubtedly influenced Frost. After his father died, Frost's family moved to New England, where his mother taught school. After graduating from high school in Lawrence, Massachusetts, where he was class poet and where he shared the post of valedictorian with Elinor White, whom he later married, Frost attended Dartmouth and Harvard. He did not graduate, but returned home to marry Elinor. They moved to a farm in Derry, New Hampshire, where Frost taught school, wrote poetry, and tried to run a farm. These were years of hardship for the growing family, and discouraged by his inability to interest American publishers in his poetry, Frost sold the farm, and the family moved to England. Shortly after his arrival, his first collection of poetry, *A Boy's Will*, was accepted for publication; *North of Boston* followed soon after. Frost met Ezra Pound, who introduced Frost's poetry to American publishers, and three years later, when the family returned to the United States at the outbreak of the First World War, Frost had achieved recognition as a major poetic talent.

Frost has always had a wide audience of readers; there are those who read him as a New England nature poet who extols the values of rural America and its work ethic, and those who read him as one who sees nature as other, as a sometimes barren landscape against which human dramas are played out, as they so effectively are in Frost's dramatic narratives. Frost described poetry as 'a momentary stay against confusion', but he also said: 'The figure a poem makes. It begins in delight and ends in wisdom. The figure is the same as for love.'

## Mending Wall

Something there is that doesn't love a wall,
That sends the frozen-ground-swell under it
And spills the upper boulders in the sun,
And makes gaps even two can pass abreast.
The work of hunters is another thing:
I have come after them and made repair
Where they have left not one stone on a stone,
But they would have the rabbit out of hiding,
To please the yelping dogs. The gaps I mean,
No one has seen them made or heard them made,
But at spring mending-time we find them there.
I let my neighbour know beyond the hill;
And on a day we meet to walk the line
And set the wall between us once again.
We keep the wall between us as we go.
To each the boulders that have fallen to each.
And some are loaves and some so nearly balls
We have to use a spell to make them balance:
'Stay where you are until our backs are turned!'
We wear our fingers rough with handling them.
Oh, just another kind of outdoor game,
One on a side. It comes to little more:
There where it is we do not need the wall:
He is all pine and I am apple orchard.
My apple trees will never get across
And eat the cones under his pines, I tell him.
He only says, 'Good fences make good neighbours.'
Spring is the mischief in me, and I wonder
If I could put a notion in his head:
'*Why* do they make good neighbours? Isn't it
Where there are cows? But here there are no cows.
Before I built a wall I'd ask to know
What I was walling in or walling out,
And to whom I was like to give offence.
Something there is that doesn't love a wall,
That wants it down.' I could say 'Elves' to him,
But it's not elves exactly, and I'd rather
He said it for himself. I see him there
Bringing a stone grasped firmly by the top
In each hand, like an old-stone savage armed.
He moves in darkness as it seems to me,
Not of woods only and the shade of trees.

He will not go behind his father's saying,
And he likes having thought of it so well
He says again, 'Good fences make good neighbours.'

1914

## After Apple-Picking

My long two-pointed ladder's sticking through a tree
Toward heaven still,
And there's a barrel that I didn't fill
Beside it, and there may be two or three
Apples I didn't pick upon some bough.
But I am done with apple-picking now.
Essence of winter sleep is on the night,
The scent of apples: I am drowsing off.
I cannot rub the strangeness from my sight
I got from looking through a pane of glass
I skimmed this morning from the drinking trough
And held against the world of hoary grass.
It melted, and I let it fall and break.
But I was well
Upon my way to sleep before it fell,
And I could tell
What form my dreaming was about to take.
Magnified apples appear and disappear,
Stem end and blossom end,
And every fleck of russet showing clear.
My instep arch not only keeps the ache,
It keeps the pressure of a ladder-round.
I feel the ladder sway as the boughs bend.
And I keep hearing from the cellar bin
The rumbling sound
Of load on load of apples coming in.
For I have had too much
Of apple-picking: I am overtired
Of the great harvest I myself desired.
There were ten thousand thousand fruit to touch,
Cherish in hand, lift down, and not let fall.
For all
That struck the earth,
No matter if not bruised or spiked with stubble,
Went surely to the cider-apple heap
As of no worth.

One can see what will trouble
This sleep of mine, whatever sleep it is.
Were he not gone,
The woodchuck could say whether it's like his
Long sleep, as I describe its coming on,
Or just some human sleep.

1916

## Birches

When I see birches bend to left and right
Across the lines of straighter darker trees,
I like to think some boy's been swinging them.
But swinging doesn't bend them down to stay
As ice-storms do. Often you must have seen them
Loaded with ice a sunny winter morning
After a rain. They click upon themselves
As the breeze rises, and turn many-coloured
As the stir cracks and crazes their enamel.
Soon the sun's warmth makes them shed crystal shells
Shattering and avalanching on the snow-crust—
Such heaps of broken glass to sweep away
You'd think the inner dome of heaven had fallen.
They are dragged to the withered bracken by the load,
And they seem not to break; though once they are bowed
So low for long, they never right themselves:
You may see their trunks arching in the woods
Years afterwards, trailing their leaves on the ground
Like girls on hands and knees that throw their hair
Before them over their heads to dry in the sun.
But I was going to say when Truth broke in
With all her matter-of-fact about the ice-storm
I should prefer to have some boy bend them
As he went out and in to fetch the cows—
Some boy too far from town to learn baseball,
Whose only play was what he found himself,
Summer or winter, and could play alone.
One by one he subdued his father's trees
By riding them down over and over again
Until he took the stiffness out of them,
And not one but hung limp, not one was left
For him to conquer. He learned all there was

To learn about not launching out too soon
And so not carrying the tree away
Clear to the ground. He always kept his poise
To the top branches, climbing carefully
With the same pains you use to fill a cup
Up to the brim, and even above the brim.
Then he flung outward, feet first, with a swish,
Kicking his way down through the air to the ground.
So was I once myself a swinger of birches.
And so I dream of going back to be.
It's when I'm weary of considerations,
And life is too much like a pathless wood
Where your face burns and tickles with the cobwebs
Broken across it, and one eye is weeping
From a twig's having lashed across it open.
I'd like to get away from earth awhile
And then come back to it and begin over.
May no fate wilfully misunderstand me
And half grant what I wish and snatch me away
Not to return. Earth's the right place for love:
I don't know where it's likely to go better.
I'd like to go by climbing a birch tree,
And climb black branches up a snow-white trunk
*Toward* heaven, till the tree could bear no more,
But dipped its top and set me down again.
That would be good both going and coming back.
One could do worse than be a swinger of birches.

1916

## Design

I found a dimpled spider, fat and white,
On a white heal-all, holding up a moth
Like a white piece of rigid satin cloth—
Assorted characters of death and blight
Mixed ready to begin the morning right,
Like the ingredients of a witches' broth—
A snow-drop spider, a flower like a froth,
And dead wings carried like a paper kite.

What had that flower to do with being white,
The wayside blue and innocent heal-all?

What brought the kindred spider to that height,
Then steered the white moth thither in the night?
What but design of darkness to appall?—
If design govern in a thing so small.

1922

## Stopping by Woods on a Snowy Evening

Whose woods these are I think I know.
His house is in the village, though;
He will not see me stopping here
To watch his woods fill up with snow.

My little horse must think it queer
To stop without a farmhouse near
Between the woods and frozen lake
The darkest evening of the year.

He gives his harness bells a shake
To ask if there is some mistake.
The only other sound's the sweep
Of easy wind and downy flake.

The woods are lovely, dark, and deep,
But I have promises to keep,
And miles to go before I sleep,
And miles to go before I sleep.

1923

## Provide, Provide

The witch that came (the withered hag)
To wash the steps with pail and rag,
Was once the beauty Abishag,[1]

The picture pride of Hollywood
Too many fall from great and good
For you to doubt the likelihood.

1 a biblical beauty brought in to warm dying King David

Die early and avoid the fate.
Or if predestined to die late,
Make up your mind to die in state.

Make the whole stock exchange your own!
If need be occupy a throne,
Where nobody can call you crone.

Some have relied on what they knew;
Others on simply being true.
What worked for them might work for you.

No memory of having starred
Atones for later disregard,
Or keeps the end from being hard.

Better to go down dignified
With boughten friendship at your side
Than none at all. Provide, provide!

1934

# Wallace Stevens

1879–1955

Wallace Stevens was born in Reading, Pennsylvania, where his father was an attorney and a schoolteacher with an interest in poetry. After graduating from high school, Stevens attended Harvard for three years. He was writing poetry at this time, some of which was published in the *Harvard Advocate*, and when he left Harvard, he intended to pursue a literary career in New York City. He became a reporter for the *Herald Tribune*, but did not like the job. He entered law school and was admitted to the bar, but was unsuccessful in private practice. He then joined the legal staff of a bonding company, and feeling himself sufficiently settled, he married Elsie Moll, a young woman from his home town. Seven years later, he joined the Hartford Accident and Insurance Company and, in 1916, moved to Connecticut, where he lived the rest of his life.

Stevens wrote his poetry during his spare time, and though he had some literary friends such as William Carlos Williams and Marianne Moore, his business activities kept him at some remove from literary circles. *Harmonium*, his first volume of poems, appeared in 1923, and though Stevens began to acquire a reputation as one of the outstanding poets of the twentieth century, his co-workers at the insurance company were not aware of this until he won the Bollingen Prize in 1950. This was partly because of Stevens's natural reticence about himself, and partly because he doubtless felt they would not understand. Certainly, it is difficult to reconcile the pragmatics of Stevens's business activities with the gaiety of language and the celebration of the imagination in his poetry.

## Sunday Morning

I

Complacencies of the peignoir, and late
Coffee and oranges in a sunny chair,
And the green freedom of a cockatoo
Upon a rug mingle to dissipate
The holy hush of ancient sacrifice.
She dreams a little, and she feels the dark
Encroachment of that old catastrophe,
As a calm darkens among water-lights.
The pungent oranges and bright, green wings
Seem things in some procession of the dead,
Winding across wide water, without sound.
The day is like wide water, without sound,
Stilled for the passing of her dreaming feet
Over the seas, to silent Palestine,
Dominion of the blood and sepulchre.

II

Why should she give her bounty to the dead?
What is divinity if it can come
Only in silent shadows and in dreams?
Shall she not find in comforts of the sun,
In pungent fruit and bright, green wings, or else
In any balm or beauty of the earth,
Things to be cherished like the thought of heaven?
Divinity must live within herself:
Passions of rain, or moods in falling snow;
Grievings in loneliness, or unsubdued
Elations when the forest blooms; gusty
Emotions on wet roads on autumn nights;
All pleasures and all pains, remembering
The bough of summer and the winter branch.
These are the measures destined for her soul.

III

Jove in the clouds had his inhuman birth.
No mother suckled him, no sweet land gave

Large-mannered motions to his mythy mind.
He moved among us, as a muttering king,
Magnificent, would move among his hinds,
Until our blood, commingling, virginal,
With heaven, brought such requital to desire
The very hinds discerned it, in a star.
Shall our blood fail? Or shall it come to be
The blood of paradise? And shall the earth
Seem all paradise that we shall know?
The sky will be much friendlier then than now,
A part of labour and a part of pain,
And next in glory to enduring love,
Not this dividing and indifferent blue.

IV

She says, 'I am content when wakened birds,
Before they fly, test the reality
Of misty fields, by their sweet questionings;
But when the birds are gone, and their warm fields
Return no more, where, then, is paradise?'
There is not any haunt of prophecy,
Nor any old chimera of the grave,
Neither the golden underground, nor isle
Melodious, where spirits gat them home,
Nor visionary south, nor cloudy palm
Remote on heaven's hill, that has endured
As April's green endures; or will endure
Like her remembrance of awakened birds,
Or her desire for June and evening, tipped
By the consummation of the swallow's wings.

V

She says, 'But in contentment I still feel
The need of some imperishable bliss.'
Death is the mother of beauty; hence from her,
Alone, shall come fulfillment to our dreams
And our desires. Although she strews the leaves
Of sure obliteration on our paths,
The path sick sorrow took, the many paths
Where triumph rang its brassy phrase, or love

Whispered a little out of tenderness,
She makes the willow shiver in the sun
For maidens who were wont to sit and gaze
Upon the grass, relinquished to their feet.
She causes boys to pile new plums and pears
On disregarded plate. The maidens taste
And stray impassioned in the littering leaves.

## VI

Is there no change of death in paradise?
Does ripe fruit never fall? Or do the boughs
Hang always heavy in that perfect sky,
Unchanging, yet so like our perishing earth,
With rivers like our own that seek for seas
They never find, the same receding shores
That never touch with inarticulate pang?
Why set the pear upon those river banks
Or spice the shores with odours of the plum?
Alas, that they should wear our colours there,
The silken weavings of our afternoons,
And pick the strings of our insipid lutes!
Death is the mother of beauty, mystical,
Within whose burning bosom we devise
Our earthly mothers waiting, sleeplessly.

## VII

Supple and turbulent, a ring of men
Shall chant in orgy on a summer morn
Their boisterous devotion to the sun,
Not as a god, but as a god might be,
Naked among them, like a savage source.
Their chant shall be a chant of paradise,
Out of their blood, returning to the sky;
And in their chant shall enter, voice by voice,
The windy lake wherein their lord delights,
The trees, like serafin, and echoing hills,
That choir among themselves long afterward.
They shall know well the heavenly fellowship
Of men that perish and of summer morn.

And whence they came and whither they shall go
The dew upon their feet shall manifest.

VIII

She hears, upon that water without sound,
A voice that cries, 'The tomb in Palestine
Is not the porch of spirits lingering.
It is the grave of Jesus, where he lay.'
We live in an old chaos of the sun,
Or old dependency of day and night,
Or island solitude, unsponsored, free,
Of that wide water, inescapable.
Deer walk upon our mountains, and the quail
Whistle about us their spontaneous cries;
Sweet berries ripen in the wilderness;
And, in the isolation of the sky,
At evening, casual flocks of pigeons make
Ambiguous undulations as they sink,
Downward to darkness, on extended wings.

1915

## Anecdote of the Jar

I placed a jar in Tennessee,
And round it was, upon a hill.
It made the slovenly wilderness
Surround that hill.

The wilderness rose up to it,
And sprawled around, no longer wild.
The jar was round upon the ground
And tall and of a port in air.

It took dominion everywhere.
The jar was grey and bare.
It did not give of bird or bush,
Like nothing else in Tennessee.

1923

## A High-Toned Old Christian Woman

Poetry is the supreme fiction, madame.
Take the moral law and make a nave of it
And from the nave build haunted heaven. Thus,
The conscience is converted into palms,
Like windy citherns hankering for hymns.
We agree in principle. That's clear. But take
The opposing law and make a peristyle,
And from the peristyle project a masque
Beyond the planets. Thus, our bawdiness,
Unpurged by epitaph, indulged at last,
Is equally converted into palms,
Squiggling like saxophones. And palm for palm,
Madame, we are where we began. Allow,
Therefore, that in the planetary scene
Your disaffected flagellants, well-stuffed,
Smacking their muzzy bellies in parade,
Proud of such novelties of the sublime,
Such tink and tank and tunk-a-tunk-tunk,
May, merely may, madame, whip from themselves
A jovial hullabaloo among the spheres.
This will make widows wince. But fictive things
Wink as they will. Wink most when widows wince.

1923

## Thirteen Ways of Looking at a Blackbird

I

Among twenty snowy mountains,
The only moving thing
Was the eye of the blackbird.

II

I was of three minds,
Like a tree
In which there are three blackbirds.

III

The blackbird whirled in the autumn winds.
It was a small part of the pantomime.

IV

A man and a woman
Are one.
A man and a woman and a blackbird
Are one.

V

I do not know which to prefer,
The beauty of inflections
Or the beauty of innuendoes,
The blackbird whistling
Or just after.

VI

Icicles filled the long window
With barbaric glass.
The shadow of the blackbird
Crossed it, to and fro.
The mood
Traced in the shadow
An indecipherable cause.

VII

O thin men of Haddam,
Why do you imagine golden birds?
Do you not see how the blackbird
Walks around the feet
Of the women about you?

VIII

I know noble accents
And lucid, inescapable rhythms;

But I know, too,
That the blackbird is involved
In what I know.

IX

When the blackbird flew out of sight,
It marked the edge
Of one of many circles.

X

At the sight of blackbirds
Flying in a green light,
Even the bawds of euphony
Would cry out sharply.

XI

He rode over Connecticut
In a glass coach.
Once, a fear pierced him,
In that he mistook
The shadow of his equipage
For blackbirds.

XII

The river is moving.
The blackbird must be flying.

XIII

It was evening all afternoon.
It was snowing
And it was going to snow.
The blackbird sat
In the cedar-limbs.

1931

## The Snow Man

One must have a mind of winter
To regard the frost and the boughs
Of the pine-trees crusted with snow;

And have been cold a long time
To behold the junipers shagged with ice,
The spruces rough in the distant glitter

Of the January sun; and not to think
Of any misery in the sound of the wind,
In the sound of a few leaves,

Which is the sound of the land
Full of the same wind
That is blowing in the same bare place

For the listener, who listens in the snow,
And, nothing himself, beholds
Nothing that is not there and the nothing that is.

1931

## Of Modern Poetry

The poem of the mind in the act of finding
What will suffice. It has not always had
To find: the scene was set; it repeated what
Was in the script.
Then the theatre was changed
To something else. Its past was a souvenir.
It has to be living, to learn the speech of the place.
It has to face the men of the time and to meet
The women of the time. It has to think about war
And it has to find what will suffice. It has
To construct a new stage. It has to be on that stage
And, like an insatiable actor, slowly and
With meditation, speak words that in the ear,
In the delicatest ear of the mind, repeat,
Exactly, that which it wants to hear, at the sound

Of which, an invisible audience listens,
Not to the play, but to itself, expressed
In an emotion as of two people, as of two
Emotions becoming one. The actor is
A metaphysician in the dark, twanging
An instrument, twanging a wiry string that gives
Sounds passing through sudden rightness, wholly
Containing the mind, below which it cannot descend,
Beyond which it has no will to rise.
                                                    It must
Be the finding of a satisfaction, and may
Be of a man skating, a woman dancing, a woman
Combing. The poem of the act of the mind.

1942

## William Carlos Williams
1883–1963

Born in Rutherford, New Jersey, to an English father and a Puerto Rican mother, William Carlos Williams attended preparatory schools in Switzerland and Paris, and after graduating from Horace Mann High School in New York went to medical school at the University of Pennsylvania. There he was friendly with poets Ezra Pound and Hilda Doolittle, and over a dish of prunes in a Philadelphia boarding house, he met painter Charles Demuth, with whom he shared a keen interest in modernist painting. Williams did further pediatric study in Leipzig, Germany, and in 1912 he began his medical practice in Rutherford, a practice in which he was fully active until he suffered a stroke in 1952.

Williams wrote his poetry at night and between professional appointments, for while he was 'determined to be a poet', he was convinced that 'only medicine, a job I enjoyed, would make it possible for me to live and write as I wanted to.' And write he did: in addition to numerous volumes of poetry, he published short stories, essays, novels, and an autobiography. Energetic and feisty, he railed against T.S. Eliot's poetry of literary allusion, stressing that American poets should break with traditional conventions and use the diction and rhythms of American speech. Like Whitman, he celebrated the 'vitality of the body' as he saw and felt it in his everyday life as a physician. His most ambitious work, *Paterson*, is an epic that gives metaphoric expression to an American city and its people, past and present, while presenting new poetic forms that greatly influenced other American poets.

## The Widow's Lament in Springtime

Sorrow is my own yard
where the new grass
flames as it has flamed
often before but not
with the cold fire
that closes round me this year.
Thirtyfive years
I lived with my husband.
The plumtree is white today
with masses of flowers.
Masses of flowers
load the cherry branches
and colour some bushes
yellow and some red
but the grief in my heart
is stronger than they
for though they were my joy
formerly, today I notice them
and turn away forgetting.
Today my son told me
that in the meadows
at the edge of the heavy woods
in the distance, he saw
trees of white flowers.
I feel that I would like
to go there
and fall into those flowers
and sink into the marsh near them.

1921

## Spring and All

By the road to the contagious hospital
under the surge of the blue
mottled clouds driven from the
northeast—a cold wind. Beyond, the
waste of broad, muddy fields

brown with dried weeds, standing and fallen
patches of standing water
the scattering of tall trees
All along the road the reddish

purplish, forked, upstanding, twiggy
stuff of bushes and small trees
with dead, brown leaves under them
leafless vines—

Lifeless in appearance, sluggish
dazed spring approaches—

They enter the new world naked,
cold, uncertain of all
save that they enter. All about them
the cold, familiar wind—

Now the grass, tomorrow
the stiff curl of wildcarrot leaf
One by one objects are defined—
It quickens: clarity, outline of leaf

But now the stark dignity of
entrance—Still, the profound change
has come upon them: rooted, they
grip down and begin to awaken

1923

## The Red Wheelbarrow

so much depends
upon

a red wheel
barrow

glazed with rain
water

beside the white
chickens.

1923

## Flowers by the Sea

When over the flowery, sharp pasture's
edge, unseen, the salt ocean

lifts its form—chicory and daisies
tied, released, seem hardly flowers alone

but colour and the movement—or the shape
perhaps—of restlessness, whereas

the sea is circled and sways
peacefully upon its plantlike stem

1923

## The Last Words of My English Grandmother

There were some dirty plates
and a glass of milk
beside her on a small table
near the rank, dishevelled bed—

Wrinkled and nearly blind
she lay and snored
rousing with anger in her tones
to cry for food,

Gimme something to eat—
They're starving me—
I'm all right I won't go
to the hospital. No, no, no

Give me something to eat
Let me take you
to the hospital, I said
and after you are well

you can do as you please.
She smiled, Yes
you do what you please first
then I can do what I please—

Oh, oh, oh! she cried
as the ambulance men lifted
her to the stretcher—
Is this what you call

making me comfortable?
By now her mind was clear—
Oh you think you're smart
you young people,

she said, but I'll tell you
you don't know anything.
Then we started.
On the way

we passed a long row
of elms. She looked at them
awhile out of
the ambulance window and said,

What are all those
fuzzy-looking things out there?
Trees? Well, I'm tired
of them and rolled her head away.

1924

## The Yachts

contend in a sea which the land partly encloses
shielding them from the too-heavy blows
of an ungoverned ocean which when it chooses

tortures the biggest hulls, the best man knows
to pit against its beatings, and sinks them pitilessly.
Mothlike in mists, scintillant in the minute

brilliance of cloudless days, with broad bellying sails
they glide to the wind tossing green water
from their sharp prows while over them the crew crawls

ant-like, solicitously grooming them, releasing,
making fast as they turn, lean far over and having
caught the wind again, side by side, head for the mark.

In a well guarded arena of open water surrounded by
lesser and greater craft which, sycophant, lumbering
and flittering follow them, they appear youthful, rare

as the light of a happy eye, live with the grace
of all that in the mind is fleckless, free and
naturally to be desired. Now the sea which holds them

is moody, lapping their glossy sides, as if feeling
for some slightest flaw but fails completely.
Today no race. Then the wind comes again. The yachts

move, jockeying for a start, the signal is set and they
are off. Now the waves strike at them but they are too
well made, they slip through, though they take in canvas.

Arms with hands grasping seek to clutch at the prows.
Bodies thrown recklessly in the way are cut aside.
It is a sea of faces about them in agony, in despair

until the horror of the race dawns staggering the mind,
the whole sea become an entanglement of watery bodies
lost to the world bearing what they cannot hold. Broken,

beaten, desolate, reaching from the dead to be taken up
they cry out, failing, failing! their cries rising
in waves still as the skillful yachts pass over.

1935

## Landscape with the Fall of Icarus[1]

According to Brueghel
when Icarus fell
it was spring

1 This is the second poem of a series based on the paintings of the Flemish artist Pieter Brueghel. This painting shows the mythical youth Icarus, son of Daedalus, falling into the sea after the wings made for him by his father had melted. W.H. Auden also based a poem on this painting (see p. 575).

a farmer was ploughing
his field
the whole pageantry

of the year was
awake tingling
near

the edge of the sea
concerned
with itself

sweating in the sun
that melted
the wings' wax

unsignificantly
off the coast
there was

a splash quite unnoticed
this was
Icarus drowning

1962

# Marianne Moore
1887–1972

Marianne Moore was born in Kirkwood, Missouri, to a very devout Presbyterian family. After her father abandoned the family following a mental breakdown and the collapse of his business, Moore and her mother moved to Carlisle, Pennsylvania. Moore attended Metzger Institute, where her mother taught, and went on to Bryn Mawr College. Though she was getting better grades in biology than in literature, she aspired to write poetry. After her graduation in 1909, she taught at the United States Indian School in Carlisle, and starting in 1915, her poetry began to be accepted by literary journals.

The Moores were a close family, and when her brother, a Presbyterian minister, took a position in Brooklyn, she and her mother joined him. Moore worked as a tutor and secretary in a girls' school, and as an assistant in a branch library. She was at this time enjoying the company of artists and writers, as well as writing and publishing her poetry. For three years she edited *The Dial*, a literary magazine. After that, she concentrated solely on her writing. In later years Moore was renowned as probably the most literate baseball fan the Brooklyn Dodgers ever had.

## Poetry

I, too, dislike it: there are things that are important beyond all this fiddle.
Reading it, however, with a perfect contempt of it, one discovers in
it after all, a place for the genuine.
Hands that can grasp, eyes
that can dilate, hair that can rise
if it must, these things are important not because a

high-sounding interpretation can be put upon them but because they are
useful. When they become so derivative as to become unintelligible,
the same thing may be said for all of us, that we
do not admire what
we cannot understand: the bat
holding on upside down or in quest of something to

eat, elephants pushing, a wild horse taking a roll, a tireless wolf under
a tree, the immovable critic twitching his skin like a horse that feels a flea,
the base-
ball fan, the statistician—
nor is it valid
to discriminate against 'business documents and

school-books';[1] all these phenomena are important. One must make a distinction
however: when dragged into prominence by half poets, the result is not poetry,
nor till the poets among us can be
'literalists of
the imagination'[2]—above
insolence and triviality and can present

for inspection, imaginary gardens with real toads in them, shall we have
it. In the meantime, if you demand on the one hand,
the raw material of poetry in
all its rawness and
that which is on the other hand
genuine, then you are interested in poetry.

1921

1 Tolstoy in his *Diary* writes: 'Where the boundary between prose and poetry lies, I shall never be able to understand. . . . Poetry is verse: prose is not verse. Or else poetry is everything with the exception of business documents and school books' [Marianne Moore's note].

2 W.B. Yeats in his essay 'William Blake and the Imagination' speaks of Blake as a 'too literal realist of the imagination, as others are of nature' [Marianne Moore's note].

## The Fish

wade
through black jade.
Of the crow-blue mussel-shells, one keeps
adjusting the ash-heaps;
Opening and shutting itself like

an
injured fan.
The barnacles which encrust the side
of the wave, cannot hide
there for the submerged shafts of the

sun,
split like spun
glass, move themselves with spotlight swiftness
into crevices—
in and out, illuminating

the
turquoise sea
of bodies. The water drives a wedge
of iron through the iron edge
of the cliff; whereupon the stars,

pink
rice-grains, ink-
bespattered jelly-fish, crabs like green
lilies, and submarine
toadstools, slide each on the other.

All
external
marks of abuse are present on this
defiant edifice—
all the physical features of

ac-
cident—lack
of cornice, dynamite grooves, burns, and
hatchet strokes, these things stand
out on it; the chasm-side is

dead.
Repeated
evidence has proved that it can live
on what can not revive
its youth. The sea grows old in it.

1921

## Nevertheless

you've seen a strawberry
that's had a struggle; yet
was, where the fragments met

a hedgehog or a star-
fish for the multitude
of seeds. What better food

than apple-seeds—the fruit
within the fruit—locked in
like counter-curved twin

hazel-nuts? Frost that kills
the little rubber-plant-
leaves of *kok-saghyz* stalks, can't

harm the roots; they still grow
in frozen ground. Once where
there was a prickly-pear-

leaf clinging to barbed wire,
a root shot down to grow
in earth two feet below;

as carrots form mandrakes
or a ram's-horn root sometimes. Victory won't come

to me unless I go
to it; a grape-tendril
ties a knot in knots till

knotted thirty times,—so
the bound twig that's undergone and over-gone, can't stir.

The weak overcomes its
  menace, the strong over-
  Comes itself. What is there

like fortitude! What sap
  went through that little thread
  to make the cherry red!

1944

## A Jellyfish

Visible, invisible,
  a fluctuating charm
an amber-tinctured amethyst
  inhabits it, your arm
approaches and it opens
  and it closes; you had meant
to catch it and it quivers;
  you abandon your intent.

1959

# T.S. Eliot

## 1888–1965

Thomas Stearns Eliot was born in St Louis, Missouri, the youngest of seven children of a well-to-do family with deep roots in New England. Both parents were cultured and well read, and Eliot showed an early interest in literature; his first published poem, an imitation of Ben Jonson, appeared in Smith Academy's literary journal when Eliot was 15. Eliot went on to Harvard for his undergraduate and graduate work, absorbing Dante and Donne and discovering the French symbolist poets who would have a strong influence on his early work. He went on to Oxford to do further studies in Greek and philosophy, finally completing his dissertation on philosopher F.H. Bradley in 1916. But by then he wished to pursue a literary rather than an academic career, and he was already achieving a reputation in literary circles with the publication of his 'Preludes' and 'J. Alfred Prufrock'.

In 1915, Eliot had entered into what was to prove a disastrous marriage, and was supporting himself and his wife by working in Lloyd's Bank, writing book reviews, and editing journals. Somehow he found time to write, and in 1922, after a struggle with a mental breakdown, and with the editorial help of Ezra Pound, *The Waste Land* was published. This was the most influential poem of its time, partly because of its innovative fragmented structure, and partly because to many it symbolized the enervation and spiritual emptiness of the post–World War I period. The poetry Eliot wrote after *The Waste Land* is generated from a spiritual struggle that culminated in his joining the Anglican Church. He considered the meditative poetry of *Four Quartets* his finest work, though some critics feel that his Christian orthodoxy dulled his poetic edge. Nevertheless, he was considered the major poet of his generation, and won the Nobel Prize for Literature in 1948.

## The Love Song of J. Alfred Prufrock

*S'io credessi che mia risposta fosse*
*A persona che mai tornasse al mondo,*
*Questa fiamma staria senza più scosse.*
*Ma per ciò che giammai de questo fondo*
*Non tornò vivo alcun, s'i'odo il vero*
*Senza tema d'infamia ti rispondo.*[1]

Let us go then, you and I,
When the evening is spread out against the sky
Like a patient etherized upon a table;
Let us go, through certain half-deserted streets,
The muttering retreats
Of restless nights in one-night cheap hotels
And sawdust restaurants with oyster-shells:
Streets that follow like a tedious argument
Of insidious intent
To lead you to an overwhelming question. . . .
Oh, do not ask, 'What is it?'
Let us go and make our visit.

In the room the women come and go
Talking of Michelangelo.

The yellow fog that rubs its back upon the window-panes,
The yellow smoke that rubs its muzzle on the window-panes,
Licked its tongue into the corners of the evening,
Lingered upon the pools that stand in drains,
Let fall upon its back the soot that falls from chimneys,

1 'If I believed that my answer were to a person who should ever return to the world, this flame would stand without further movement; but since never one returns alive from this deep, if I hear true, I answer you without fear of infamy' (*Inferno*, xxvii, 61–6). These words are the response a damned soul in Hell makes when a question is put to him.

Slipped by the terrace, made a sudden leap,
And seeing that it was a soft October night,
Curled once about the house, and fell asleep.

And indeed there will be time
For the yellow smoke that slides along the street
Rubbing its back upon the window-panes;
There will be time, there will be time
To prepare a face to meet the faces that you meet;
There will be time to murder and create,
And time for all the works and days of hands
That lift and drop a question on your plate;
Time for you and time for me,
And time yet for a hundred indecisions,
And for a hundred visions and revisions,
Before the taking of a toast and tea.

In the room the women come and go
Talking of Michelangelo.

And indeed there will be time
To wonder, 'Do I dare?' and, 'Do I dare?'
Time to turn back and descend the stair,
With a bald spot in the middle of my hair—
(They will say: 'How his hair is growing thin!')
My morning coat, my collar mounting firmly to the chin,
My necktie rich and modest, but asserted by a simple pin—
(They will say: 'But how his arms and legs are thin!')
Do I dare
Disturb the universe?
In a minute there is time
For decisions and revisions which a minute will reverse.

For I have known them all already, known them all—
Have known the evenings, mornings, afternoons,
I have measured out my life with coffee spoons;
I know the voices dying with a dying fall
Beneath the music from a farther room.
So how should I presume?

And I have known the eyes already, known them all—
The eyes that fix you in a formulated phrase,
And when I am formulated, sprawling on a pin,
When I am pinned and wriggling on the wall,

Then how should I begin
To spit out all the butt-ends of my days and ways?
And how should I presume?

And I have known the arms already, known them all—
Arms that are braceleted and white and bare
(But in the lamplight, downed with light brown hair!)
Is it perfume from a dress
That makes me so digress?
Arms that lie along a table, or wrap about a shawl.
And should I then presume?
And how should I begin?

* * *

Shall I say, I have gone at dusk through narrow streets
And watched the smoke that rises from the pipes
Of lonely men in shirt-sleeves, leaning out of windows? . . .

I should have been a pair of ragged claws
Scuttling across the floors of silent seas.

* * *

And the afternoon, the evening, sleeps so peacefully!
Smoothed by long fingers,
Asleep . . . tired . . . or it malingers,
Stretched on the floor, here beside you and me.
Should I, after tea and cakes and ices,
Have the strength to force the moment to its crisis?
But though I have wept and fasted, wept and prayed,
Though I have seen my head (grown slightly bald) brought in upon a platter,[2]
I am no prophet—and here's no great matter;
I have seen the moment of my greatness flicker,
And I have seen the eternal Footman hold my coat, and snicker,
And in short, I was afraid.

And would it have been worth it, after all,
After the cups, the marmalade, the tea,
Among the porcelain, among some talk of you and me,

2 The head of John the Baptist was 'brought in upon a platter' at the request of Salome as a reward for her dancing before Herod.

Would it have been worth while,
To have bitten off the matter with a smile,
To have squeezed the universe into a ball
To roll it toward some overwhelming question,
To say: 'I am Lazarus, come from the dead,
Come back to tell you all, I shall tell you all'—
If one, settling a pillow by her head,
    Should say: 'That is not what I meant at all.
    That is not it, at all.'

    And would it have been worth it, after all,
Would it have been worth while,
After the sunsets and the dooryards and the sprinkled streets,
After the novels, after the teacups, after the skirts that trail along
        the floor—
And this, and so much more?—
It is impossible to say just what I mean!
But as if a magic lantern threw the nerves in patterns on a screen:
Would it have been worth while
If one, settling a pillow or throwing off a shawl,
And turning toward the window, should say:
    'That is not it at all,
    That is not what I meant, at all.'

* * *

No! I am not Prince Hamlet, nor was meant to be;
Am an attendant lord, one that will do
To swell a progress,[3] start a scene or two,
Advise the prince; no doubt, an easy tool,
Deferential, glad to be of use,
Politic, cautious, and meticulous;
Full of high sentence, but a bit obtuse;
At times, indeed, almost ridiculous—
Almost, at times, the Fool.

    I grow old. . . . I grow old. . . .
I shall wear the bottoms of my trousers rolled.

    Shall I part my hair behind? Do I dare to eat a peach?
I shall wear white flannel trousers, and walk upon the beach.
I have heard the mermaids singing, each to each.

3 a ceremonial procession at a royal court

I do not think that they will sing to me.

I have seen them riding seaward on the waves
Combing the white hair of the waves blown back
When the wind blows the water white and black.

We have lingered in the chambers of the sea
By sea-girls wreathed with seaweed red and brown
Till human voices wake us, and we drown.

1915

## The Hollow Men

*Mistah Kurtz—he dead.*
*A penny for the Old Guy*

I

We are the hollow men
We are the stuffed men
Leaning together
Headpiece filled with straw. Alas!
Our dried voices, when
We whisper together
Are quiet and meaningless
As wind in dry grass
Or rats' feet over broken glass
In our dry cellar

Shape without form, shade without colour,
Paralyzed force, gesture without motion;

Those who have crossed
With direct eyes, to death's other Kingdom
Remember us—if at all—not as lost
Violent souls, but only
As the hollow men
The stuffed men.

II

Eyes I dare not meet in dreams
In death's dream kingdom
These do not appear:
There, the eyes are
Sunlight on a broken column
There, is a tree swinging
And voices are
In the wind's singing
More distant and more solemn
Than a fading star.

Let me be no nearer
In death's dream kingdom
Such deliberate disguises
Let me also wear
Rat's coat, crowskin, crossed staves
In a field
Behaving as the wind behaves
No nearer—

Not that final meeting
In the twilight kingdom

III

This is the dead land
This is cactus land
Here the stone images
Are raised, here they receive
The supplication of a dead man's hand
Under the twinkle of a fading star.

Is it like this
In death's other kingdom
Waking alone
At the hour when we are
Trembling with tenderness
Lips that would kiss
Form prayers to broken stone.

IV

The eyes are not here
There are no eyes here
In this valley of dying stars
In this hollow valley
This broken jaw of our lost kingdoms

In this last of meeting places
We grope together
And avoid speech
Gathered on this beach of the tumid river

Sightless, unless
The eyes reappear
As the perpetual star
Multifoliate rose
Of death's twilight kingdom
The hope only
Of empty men.

V

*Here we go round the prickly pear*
*Prickly pear prickly pear*
*Here we go round the prickly pear*
*At five o'clock in the morning.*

Between the idea
And the reality
Between the motion
And the act
Falls the Shadow
*For Thine is the Kingdom*

Between the conception
And the creation
Between the emotion
And the response
Falls the Shadow
*Life is very long*

Between the desire
And the spasm
Between the potency
And the existence
Between the essence
And the descent
Falls the Shadow
*For Thine is the Kingdom*

For Thine is
Life is
For Thine is the

*This is the way the world ends*
*This is the way the world ends*
*This is the way the world ends*
*Not with a bang but a whimper.*

1925

## Journey of the Magi

'A cold coming we had of it,
Just the worst time of the year
For a journey, and such a long journey:
The ways deep and the weather sharp,
The very dead of winter.'
And the camels galled, sore-footed, refractory,
Lying down in the melting snow.
There were times we regretted
The summer palaces on slopes, the terraces,
And the silken girls bringing sherbet.
Then the camel men cursing and grumbling
And running away, and wanting their liquor and women,
And the night-fires going out, and the lack of shelters,
And the cities hostile and the towns unfriendly
And the villages dirty and charging high prices:
A hard time we had of it.
At the end we preferred to travel all night,
Sleeping in snatches,
With the voices singing in our ears, saying
That this was all folly.

Then at dawn we came down to temperate valley,
Wet, below the snow line, smelling of vegetation;
With a running stream and a water-mill beating the darkness,
And three trees on the low sky,
And an old white horse galloped away in the meadow.
Then we came to a tavern with vine-leaves over the lintel,
Six hands at an open door dicing for pieces of silver,
And feet kicking the empty wine-skins.
But there was no information, and so we continued
And arrived at evening, not a moment too soon
Finding the place; it was (you may say) satisfactory.

All this was a long time ago, I remember,
And I would do it again, but set down
This set down
This: were we led all that way for
Birth or Death? There was a Birth, certainly,
We had evidence and no doubt. I had seen birth and death,
But had thought they were different; this Birth was
Hard and bitter agony for us, like Death, our death.
We returned to our places, these Kingdoms,
But no longer at ease here, in the old dispensation,
With an alien people clutching their gods.
I should be glad of another death.

1927

## Marina

*Quis hic locus, quae*
*regio, quae mundi plaga?*[1]

What seas what shores what grey rocks and what islands
What water lapping the bow
And scent of pine and the woodthrush singing through the fog
What images return
O my daughter.

Those who sharpen the tooth of the dog, meaning
Death
Those who glitter with the glory of the hummingbird, meaning
Death

1 'What place is this, what kingdom, what part of the world?' (Seneca, *Hercules Furens*)

Those who sit in the sty of contentment, meaning
Death
Those who suffer the ecstasy of the animals, meaning
Death

Are become unsubstantial, reduced by a wind,
A breath of pine, and the woodsong fog
By this grace dissolved in place

What is this face, less clear and clearer
The pulse in the arm, less strong and stronger—
Given or lent? more distant than stars and nearer than the eye

Whispers and small laughter between leaves and hurrying feet
Under sleep, where all the waters meet.

Bowsprit cracked with ice and paint cracked with heat.
I made this, I have forgotten
And remember.
The rigging weak and the canvas rotten
Between one June and another September.
Made this unknowing, half conscious, unknown, my own.
The garboard strake leaks, the seams need caulking.
This form, this face, this life
Living to live in a world of time beyond me; let me
Resign my life for this life, my speech for that unspoken,
The awakened, lips parted, the hope, the new ships.

What seas what shores what granite islands towards my timbers
And woodthrush calling through the fog
My daughter.

1930

# e.e. cummings
## 1894–1962

He was born Edward Estlin Cummings, the son of a Harvard English professor who was later pastor of the Old South Church in Boston. cummings took his BA and MA at Harvard, and then joined the Norton Harjes Ambulance Corps in France during World War I. Because of the wrong-headed suspicions of a censor regarding 'unpatriotic' letters, cummings was imprisoned in a French concentration camp for three months, a period that is memorably evoked in his novel *The Enormous Room*, which made him famous. After the war he lived in Paris and studied painting before settling in New York's Greenwich Village with other writers and artists, where he continued to paint and to write poetry. He developed an innovative, playful poetic style, flaunting the rules of syntax, grammar, and punctuation in order to make the reader see words and their relationships in a new way. In the form of his poetry and in his themes, he strikes out against conformity and celebrates the vitality of human love. He was not a poet of ideas but was one of the most joyful singers of the traditional themes of love and spring, as well as one of the sharpest satirists in modern poetry.

### Buffalo Bill 's

Buffalo Bill 's
defunct
            who used to
            ride a watersmooth-silver
                                                stallion
and break onetwothreefourfive pigeonsjustlikethat
                                                                        Jesus

he was a handsome man
                                        and what i want to know is
how do you like your blueeyed boy
Mister Death

1920

### Spring is like a perhaps hand

Spring is like a perhaps hand
(which comes carefully
out of Nowhere)arranging
a window,into which people look(while

people stare
arranging and changing placing
carefully there a strange
thing and a known thing here)and

changing everything carefully

spring is like a perhaps
Hand in a window
(carefully to
and fro moving New and
Old things,while
people stare carefully
moving perhaps
fraction of flower here placing
an inch of air there)and

without breaking anything.

1925

## somewhere i have never travelled

somewhere i have never travelled,gladly beyond
any experience,your eyes have their silence:
in your most frail gesture are things which enclose me,
or which i cannot touch because they are too near

your slightest look easily will unclose me
though i have closed myself as fingers,
you open always petal by petal myself as Spring opens
(touching skilfully,mysteriously)her first rose

or if your wish be to close me,i and
my life will shut very beautifully,suddenly,
as when the heart of this flower imagines
the snow carefully everywhere descending;

nothing which we are to perceive in this world equals
the power of your intense fragility:whose texture
compels me with the colour of its countries,
rendering death and forever with each breathing

(i do not know what it is about you that closes
and opens;only something in me understands
the voice of your eyes is deeper than all roses)
nobody,not even the rain,has such small hands

1931

## my father moved through dooms of love

my father moved through dooms of love
through sames of am through haves of give,
singing each morning out of each night
my father moved through depths of height

this motionless forgetful where
turned at his glance to shining here;
that if(so timid air is firm)
under his eyes would stir and squirm

newly as from unburied which
floats the first who,his april touch
drove sleeping selves to swarm their fates
woke dreamers to their ghostly roots

and should some why completely weep
my father's fingers brought her sleep:
vainly no smallest voice might cry
for he could feel the mountains grow.

Lifting the valleys of the sea
my father moved through griefs of joy;
praising a forehead called the moon
singing desire into begin

joy was his song and joy so pure
a heart of star by him could steer
and pure so now and now so yes
the wrists of twilight would rejoice

keen as midsummer's keen beyond
conceiving mind of sun will stand,
so strictly(over utmost him
so hugely)stood my father's dream

his flesh was flesh his blood was blood:
no hungry man but wished him food;
no cripple wouldn't creep one mile
uphill to only see him smile.

Scorning the pomp of must and shall
my father moved through dooms of feel;
his anger was as right as rain
his pity was as green as grain

septembering arms of year extend
less humbly wealth to foe and friend
than he to foolish and to wise
offered immeasurable is

proudly and(by octobering flame
beckoned)as earth will downward climb,
so naked for immortal work
his shoulders marched against the dark

his sorrow was as true as bread:
no liar looked him in the head;
if every friend became his foe
he'd laugh and build a world with snow.

My father moved through theys of we,
singing each new leaf out of each tree
(and every child was sure that spring
danced when she heard my father sing)

then let men kill which cannot share,
let blood and flesh be mud and mire,
scheming imagine,passion willed,
freedom a drug that's bought and sold

giving to steal and cruel kind,
a heart to fear,to doubt a mind,
to differ a disease of same,
conform the pinnacle of am

though dull were all we taste as bright,
bitter all utterly things sweet,
maggoty minus and dumb death
all we inherit,all bequeath

and nothing quite so least as truth
—i say though hate were why men breathe—
because my father lived his soul
love is the whole and more than all

1940

## pity this busy monster

pity this busy monster,manunkind,

not. Progress is a comfortable disease:
your victim(death and life safely beyond)

plays with the bigness of his littleness
—electrons deify one razorblade
into a mountainrange;lenses extend

unwish through curving wherewhen till unwish
returns on its unself.
                                        A world of made
is not a world of born—pity poor flesh

and trees,poor stars and stones,but never this
fine specimen of hypermagical

ultraomnipotence. We doctors know

a hopeless case if—listen:there's a hell
of a good universe next door;let's go

1944

# W.H. Auden

## 1907–1973

Wystan Hugh Auden was born in York, England, and developed an early interest in geology during family outings on the limestone moors of Yorkshire; evocations of those barren, simple landscapes can be found in much of his poetry. These outings took him also to Hadrian's Wall, and to investigations of pre-Norman churches and crosses. It seems natural that when he was at Oxford he should study Anglo-Saxon poetry, whose rhythms and alliteration he later emulated. He experimented with many other forms, including the folk ballad, and was an extremely talented versifier. His first book of poetry appeared in 1928; this was followed by *September Poems*, and in 1932, *The Orators*.

Auden became well known as one of the major voices of the 1930s, an 'age of anxiety' resulting from worldwide depression and growing threat of another war. Influenced by Freud, Auden wrote of the guilt and fears of the human heart, but he wrote just as strongly of the power of love as the only force that could overcome anxiety. He came to the United States in 1939 and taught at a number of colleges and universities, becoming an American citizen in 1946. A prolific writer, he produced a large number of reviews and essays in addition to his poetry. He also wrote plays with Christopher Isherwood and opera librettos with Chester Kallmann. In 1957 he bought a farmhouse in Kirchstetten, Austria, where he spent springs and summers until his death there in 1973.

### Who's Who

A shilling life will give you all the facts:
How Father beat him, how he ran away,
What were the struggles of his youth, what acts
Made him the greatest figure of his day:

Of how he fought, fished, hunted, worked all night,
Though giddy, climbed new mountains; named a sea:
Some of the last researchers even write
Love made him weep his pints like you and me.

With all his honours on, he sighed for one
Who, say astonished critics, lived at home;
Did little jobs about the house with skill
And nothing else; could whistle; would sit still
Or potter round the garden; answered some
Of his long marvellous letters but kept none.

1936

## As I Walked Out One Evening

As I walked out one evening,
Walking down Bristol Street,
The crowds upon the pavement
Were fields of harvest wheat.

And down by the brimming river
I heard a lover sing
Under an arch of the railway:
'Love has no ending.

'I'll love you, dear, I'll love you
Till China and Africa meet,
And the river jumps over the mountain
And the salmon sing in the street,

'I'll love you till the ocean
Is folded and hung up to dry
And the seven stars go squawking
Like geese about the sky.

'The years shall run like rabbits,
For in my arms I hold
The Flower of the Ages,
And the first love of the world.'

But all the clocks in the city
Began to whirr and chime:
'O let not Time deceive you,
You cannot conquer Time.

'In the burrows of the Nightmare
Where Justice naked is,
Time watches from the shadow
And coughs when you would kiss.

'In headaches and in worry
Vaguely life leaks away,
And Time will have his fancy
Tomorrow or today.

'Into many a green valley
Drifts the appalling snow;
Time breaks the threaded dances
And the diver's brilliant bow.

'O plunge your hands in water,
Plunge them in up to the wrist;
Stare, stare in the basin
And wonder what you've missed.

'The glacier knocks in the cupboard,
The desert sighs in the bed,
And the crack in the tea-cup opens
A lane to the land of the dead.

'Where the beggars raffle the banknotes
And the Giant is enchanting to Jack,
And the Lily-white Boy is a Roarer,
And Jill goes down on her back.

'O look, look in the mirror,
O look in your distress;
Life remains a blessing
Although you cannot bless.

'O stand, stand at the window
As the tears scald and start;
You shall love your crooked neighbour
With your crooked heart.'

It was late, late in the evening,
The lovers they were gone;
The clocks had ceased their chiming,
And the deep river ran on.

1940

## Lullaby

Lay your sleeping head, my love,
Human on my faithless arm;
Time and fevers burn away
Individual beauty from
Thoughtful children, and the grave
Proves the child ephemeral:
But in my arms till break of day
Let the living creature lie,
Mortal, guilty, but to me
The entirely beautiful.

Soul and body have no bounds:
To lovers as they lie upon
Her tolerant enchanted slope
In their ordinary swoon,
Grave the vision Venus sends
Of supernatural sympathy,
Universal love and hope;
While an abstract insight wakes
Among the glaciers and the rocks
The hermit's carnal ecstasy.

Certainty, fidelity
On the stroke of midnight pass
Like vibrations of a bell
And fashionable madmen raise
Their pedantic boring cry:
Every farthing of the cost,
All the dreaded cards foretell,
Shall be paid, but from this night
Not a whisper, not a thought,
Not a kiss nor look be lost.

Beauty, midnight, vision dies:
Let the winds of dawn that blow
Softly round your dreaming head
Such a day of welcome show
Eye and knocking heart may bless,
Find our mortal world enough;
Noons of dryness find you fed
By the involuntary powers,
Nights of insult let you pass
Watched by every human love.

1940

## Musée des Beaux Arts[1]

About suffering they were never wrong,
The Old Masters: how well they understood
Its human position; how it takes place
While someone else is eating or opening a window or just walking dully along;

1 Museum of Fine Arts. See the note to William Carlos Williams's 'Landscape with the Fall of Icarus', p. 553.

How, when the aged are reverently, passionately waiting
For the miraculous birth, there always must be
Children who did not specially want it to happen, skating
On a pond at the edge of the wood:
They never forgot
That even the dreadful martyrdom must run its course
Anyhow in a corner, some untidy spot
Where the dogs go on with their doggy life and the torturer's horse
Scratches its innocent behind on a tree.

In Brueghel's *Icarus,* for instance: how everything turns away
Quite leisurely from the disaster; the ploughman may
Have heard the splash, the forsaken cry,
But for him it was not an important failure; the sun shone
As it had to on the white legs disappearing into the green
Water; and the expensive delicate ship that must have seen
Something amazing, a boy falling out of the sky,
Had somewhere to get to and sailed calmly on.

1940

## In Memory of W.B. Yeats

(d. Jan. 1939)

I

He disappeared in the dead of winter:
The brooks were frozen, the airports almost deserted,
And snow disfigured the public statues;
The mercury sank in the mouth of the dying day.
What instruments we have agree
The day of his death was a dark cold day.

Far from his illness
The wolves ran on through the evergreen forests,
The pleasant river was untempted by the fashionable quays;
By mourning tongues
The death of the poet was kept from his poems.

But for him it was his last afternoon as himself,
An afternoon of nurses and rumours;
The provinces of his body revolted,

The squares of his mind were empty,
Silence invaded the suburbs,
The current of his feeling failed; he became his admirers.

Now he is scattered among a hundred cities
And wholly given over to unfamiliar affections,
To find his happiness in another kind of wood
And be punished under a foreign code of conscience.
The words of a dead man
Are modified in the guts of the living.

But in the importance and noise of to-morrow
When the brokers are roaring like beasts on the floor of the Bourse,
And the poor have the sufferings to which they are fairly accustomed,
And each in the cell of himself is almost convinced of his freedom,
A few thousand will think of this day
As one thinks of a day when one did something slightly unusual.
What instruments we have agree
The day of his death was a dark cold day.

II

You were silly like us; your gifts survived it all:
The parish of rich women, physical decay,
Yourself. Mad Ireland hurt you into poetry.
Now Ireland has her madness and her weather still,
For poetry makes nothing happen: it survives
In the valley of its making where executives
Would never want to tamper, flows on south
From ranches of isolation and the busy griefs,
Raw towns that we believe and die in; it survives,
A way of happening, a mouth.

III

Earth, receive an honoured guest:
William Yeats is laid to rest.
Let the Irish vessel lie
Emptied of its poetry.

In the nightmare of the dark
All the dogs of Europe bark,

And the living nations wait,
Each sequestered in its hate;

Intellectual disgrace
Stares from every human face,
And the seas of pity lie
Locked and frozen in each eye.

Follow, poet, follow right
To the bottom of the night,
With your unconstraining voice
Still persuade us to rejoice;

With the farming of a verse
Make a vineyard of the curse,
Sing of human unsuccess
In a rapture of distress;

In the deserts of the heart
Let the healing fountain start,
In the prison of his days
Teach the free man how to praise.

1940

## The Unknown Citizen

To JS/07/M/378
This Marble Monument
Is Erected by the State

He was found by the Bureau of Statistics to be
One against whom there was no official complaint,
And all the reports on his conduct agree
That, in the modern sense of an old-fashioned word, he was a saint,
For in everything he did he served the Greater Community.
Except for the War till the day he retired
He worked in a factory and never got fired,
But satisfied his employers, Fudge Motors Inc.
Yet he wasn't a scab or odd in his views,
For his Union reports that he paid his dues,
(Our report on his Union shows it was sound)

And our Social Psychology workers found
That he was popular with his mates and liked a drink.
The Press are convinced that he bought a paper every day
And that his reactions to advertisements were normal in every way.
Policies taken out in his name prove that he was fully insured,
And his Health-card shows he was once in hospital but left it cured.
Both Producers Research and High-Grade Living declare
He was fully sensible to the advantages of the Instalment Plan
And had everything necessary to the Modern Man,
A phonograph, a radio, a car and a frigidaire.
Our researchers into Public Opinion are content
That he held the proper opinions for the time of year;
When there was peace, he was for peace; when there was war, he went.
He was married and added five children to the population,
Which our Eugenist says was the right number for a parent of his generation,
And our teachers report that he never interfered with their education.
Was he free? Was he happy? The question is absurd:
Had anything been wrong, we should certainly have heard.

1940

# A.M. Klein
## 1909–1972

Abraham Moses Klein was born in Ratno, Ukraine. His family emigrated in 1910 to Montreal, where he spent the rest of his life. Though he was raised in an Orthodox Jewish family, he abandoned his strict orthodoxy during his high-school years and embarked on a passionate and lifelong dedication to Zionism. He graduated from McGill University in 1930 and from the law school of the University of Montreal in 1933. But the practice of law never satisfied him, for writing consumed his attention. He published five volumes of poetry, the novel *The Second Scroll* (1951), several short stories, and numerous literary essays and reviews.

Klein's early poetry explores the humour, pathos, and richness of his Jewish heritage. The influence of T.S. Eliot and the symbolist poets is evident in his later colloquial and ironic poems of social commentary, where he decries the absence of human dignity in a commercial world. His final volume of poetry, *The Rocking Chair and Other Poems* (1948), a beautiful evocation of Canada and its traditions, concludes with 'Portrait of the Poet as Landscape', which examines the poet's tragic isolation in the secular world. He was deeply distressed by the events of the Second World War and its aftermath, and as a result he suffered prolonged psychological anxiety in the early 1950s. For the last two decades of his life, he lived in virtual seclusion, relinquishing any commitment to his writing.

## Soirée of Velvel Kleinburger

In back-room dens of delicatessen stores,
In curtained parlours of garrulous barber shops,
While the rest of the world most comfortably snores
On mattresses, or on more fleshly props,
My brother Velvel vigils in the night,
Not as he did last night with two French whores,
But with a deck of cards that once were white.

He sees three wan ghosts, as the thick smoke fades,
Dealing him clubs, and diamonds, hearts and spades.

His fingers, pricked with a tailor's needle, draw
The well-thumbed cards; while Hope weighs down his jaw.

O for the ten spade in its proper place,
Followed by knave in linen lace,
The queen with her gaunt face,
The king and mace,
The ace!

Then Velvel adds a footnote to his hoax:
I will not have your wherefores and your buts;
For I am for the Joker and his jokes;
I laugh at your alases and tut-tuts,
My days, they vanish into circular smokes,
My life lies on a tray of cigarette butts.

For it is easy to send pulpit wind
From bellies sumptuously lined;
Easy to praise the sleep of the righteous, when
The righteous sleep on cushions ten,
And having risen from a well-fed wife
Easy it is to give advice on life.

But you who upon sated palates clack a moral,
And pick a sermon from between your teeth,
Tell me with what bay, tell me with what laurel
Shall I entwine the heaven-praising wreath,
I, with whom Deity sets out to quarrel?

*But, prithee, wherefore these thumbed cards?*

O do not make a pack of cards your thesis
And frame no lesson on a house of cards
Where diamonds go lustreless, and hearts go broken
And clubs do batter the skull to little shards,
And where, because the spade is trump
One must perforce kiss Satan's rump.

For I have heard these things from teachers
With dirty beards and hungry features.

Now, after days in dusty factories,
Among machines that manufacture madness
I have no stomach for these subtleties
About rewards and everlasting gladness;
And having met your over-rated dawns,
Together with milkmen watering their milk,
And having trickled sweat, according to a scale of wages,
Sewing buttons to warm the navels of your business sages,
I have brought home at dusk,
My several bones, my much-flailed husk.

My meals are grand,
When supper comes
I feed on canned
Aquariums.

The salmon dies.
The evening waits
As I catch flies
From unwashed plates.

And my true love,
She combs and combs,
The lice from off
My children's domes.

Such is the idyll of my life.
But I will yet achieve
An easier living and less scrawny wife
And not forever will the foreman have
The aces up his sleeve,
But some day I will place the lucky bet.
(Ho! Ho! the social revolutions on a table of roulette!)

Alas, that Velvel's sigh makes eddies in the smoke.
For what's the use?
While the pale faces grin, his brow is hot;
He grasps a deuce . . .

*A nicotined hand beyond the smoke sweeps off the pot.*

O good my brother, should one come to you
And knock upon the door at mid of night
And show you, writ in scripture, black on white,
That this is no way for a man to do?—
What a pale laughter from these ghosts, and 'Who
Are you, my saint, to show us what is right?
Make a fifth hand, and we will be contrite;
Shuffle the cards, be sociable, Reb. Jew.'

My brother's gesture snaps; *I spoke.*
His cheeks seek refuge in his mouth.
His nostrils puff superior smoke.
His lips are brown with drouth.

Hum a hymn of sixpence,
A tableful of cards
Fingers slowly shuffling
Ambiguous rewards.
When the deck is opened
The pauper once more gave
His foes the kings and aces
And took himself the knave.

Once more he cuts the cards, and dreams his dream;
A rolls-Royce hums within his brain;
Before it stands a chauffeur, tipping his hat,
'You say that it will rain, Sir; it will rain!'
Upon his fingers diamonds gleam,
His wife wears gowns of ultra-Paris fashion,
And she boasts jewels as large as wondrous eyes
The eyes of Og, the giant-king of Bashan.

So Velvel dreams; dreaming, he rises, and
Buttons his coat, coughs in his raised lapel,
Gropes his way home; he rings a raucous bell.

1932

## The Rocking Chair

It seconds the crickets of the province. Heard
in the clean lamplit farmhouses of Quebec,—
wooden,—it is no less a national bird;
and rivals, in its cage, the mere stuttering clock.
To its time, the evenings are rolled away;
and in its peace the pensive mother knits
contentment to be worn by her family,
grown-up, but still cradled by the chair in which she sits.

It is also the old man's pet, pair to his pipe,
the two aids of his arithmetic and plans,
plans rocking and puffing into market-shape;
and it is the toddler's game and dangerous dance.
Moved to the verandah, on summer Sundays, it is,
among the hanging plants, the girls, the boyfriends,
sabbatical and clumsy, like the white haloes
dangling above the blue serge suits of the young men.

It has a personality of its own;
is a character (like that old drunk Lacoste,
exhaling amber,[1] and toppling on his pins);
it is alive; individual; and no less
an identity than those about it. And
it is tradition. Centuries have been flicked
from its arcs, alternately flicked and pinned.
It rolls with the gait of St Malo.[2] It is act

and symbol, symbol of this static folk
which moves in segments, and returns to base,—
a sunken pendulum: *invoke, revoke*;
loosed yon, leashed hither, motion on no space.
O, like some Anjou ballad, all refrain,[3]
which turns about its longing, and seems to move
to make a pleasure out of repeated pain,
its music moves, as if always back to a first love.

1948

1 perfume (perhaps from having drunk bay rum or cologne)
2 with the walk of sailors (St Malo is a town on the coast of France.)
3 Anjou is a former province of western France. What Klein seems to have in mind is the repetitive quality of those French-Canadian songs that had their root in medieval France. About these, Edith Fowke quotes an early traveller in Canada: '[the song] seems endless. After each short line comes the refrain, and the story twines itself along like a slender creeping plant' (*The Penguin Book of Canadian Folk Songs*, 1973).

## Portrait of the Poet as Landscape

I

Not an editorial-writer, bereaved with bartlett,[1]
mourns him, the shelved Lycidas.[2]
No actress squeezes a glycerine tear for him.
The radio broadcast lets his passing pass.
And with the police, no record. Nobody, it appears,
either under his real name or his alias,
missed him enough to report.

It is possible that he is dead, and not discovered.
It is possible that he can be found some place
in a narrow closet, like the corpse in a detective story,
standing, his eyes staring, and ready to fall on his face.
It is also possible that he is alive
and amnesiac, or mad, or in retired disgrace,
or beyond recognition lost in love.

We are sure only that from our real society
he has disappeared; he simply does not count,
except in the pullulation[3] of vital statistics—
somebody's vote, perhaps, an anonymous taunt
of the Gallup poll, a dot in a government table—
but not felt, and certainly far from eminent—
in a shouting mob, somebody's sigh.

O, he who unrolled our culture from his scroll—
the prince's quote, the rostrum-rounding roar—
who under one name made articulate
heaven, and under another the seven-circled air,[4]
is, if he is at all, a number, an x,
a Mr Smith in a hotel register,—
incognito, lost, lacunal.[5]

1 Bartlett's *Familiar Quotations*
2 Klein is referring here to Milton's pastoral elegy mourning the death by drowning of the young poet Edward King (see p. 411).
3 rapid breeding; teeming
4 According to the pre-Copernican versions of the universe, the earth was surrounded by seven concentric spheres (the sun, the moon, and the five known planets).
5 i.e. of a lacuna or empty space

II

The truth is he's not dead, but only ignored—
like the mirroring lenses forgotten on a brow
that shine with the guilt of their unnoticed world.
The truth is he lives among neighbours, who, though they will allow
him a passable fellow, think him eccentric, not solid,
a type that one can forgive, and for that matter, forgo.

Himself he has his moods, just like a poet.
Sometimes, depressed to nadir, he will think all lost,
will see himself as throwback, relict,[6] freak,
his mother's miscarriage, his great-grandfather's ghost,
and he will curse his quintuplet senses, and their tutors
in whom he put, as he should not have put, his trust.

Then he will remember his travels over that body—
the torso verb, the beautiful face of the noun,
and all those shaped and warm auxiliaries!
A first love it was, the recognition of his own.
Dear limbs adverbial, complexion of adjective,
dimple and dip of conjugation!

And then remember how this made a change in him
affecting for always the glow and growth of his being;
how suddenly was aware of the air, like shaken tinfoil,[7]
of the patents of nature, the shock of belated seeing,
the loneliness peering from the eyes of crowds;
the integers of thought; the cube-roots of feeling.

Thus, zoomed to zenith, sometimes he hopes again,
and sees himself as a character, with a rehearsed role:
the Count of Monte Cristo,[8] come for his revenges;
the unsuspecting heir, with papers; the risen soul;
or the chloroformed prince awakening from his flowers;
or—deflated again—the convict on parole.

6 an organism from a previous age surviving in a changed environment
7 This is an echo of the opening lines of Hopkins' 'God's Grandeur' (see p. 513).
8 In the novel *The Count of Monte Cristo* (1844–5), by Alexandre Dumas père, an innocent man, imprisoned on trumped-up charges, escapes to the Island of Monte Cristo, where he finds fabulous riches. He returns to Paris a powerful man, and under various guises, takes revenge on those responsible for his ill treatment.

III

He is alone; yet not completely alone.
Pins on a map of a colour similar to his,
each city has one, sometimes more than one;
here, caretakers of art, in colleges;
in offices, there, with arm-bands, and green-shaded;
and there, pounding their catalogued beats in libraries,—

everywhere menial, a shadow's shadow.
And always for their egos—their outmoded art.
Thus, having lost the bevel[9] in the ear,
they know neither up nor down, mistake the part
for the whole, curl themselves in a comma,
talk technics, make a colon their eyes. They distort—

such is the pain of their frustration—truth
to something convolute and cerebral.
How they do fear the slap of the flat of the platitude!
Now Pavlov's victims, their mouths water at bell,
the platter empty.
See they set twenty-one jewels
into their watches; the time they do not tell!

Some, patagonian[10] in their own esteem,
and longing for the multiplying word,
join party and wear pins, now have a message,
and ear, and the convention-hall's regard.
Upon the knees of ventriloquists, they own,
of their dandled[11] brightness, only the paint and board.

And some go mystical, and some go mad.
One stares at a mirror all day long, as if
to recognize himself; another courts
angels,—for here he does not fear rebuff;
and a third, alone, and sick with sex, and rapt,
doodles him symbols convex and concave.

O schizoid solitudes! O purities
curdling upon themselves! Who live for themselves,
or for each other, but for nobody else;

9 a tool for ascertaining angles
10 gigantic (because the Patagonian Indians of South America are said to be the tallest human beings)
11 moved lightly up and down on the knee

desire affection, private and public loves;
are friendly, and then quarrel and surmise
the secret perversions of each other's lives.

IV

He suspects that something has happened, a law
been passed, a nightmare ordered. Set apart,
he finds himself, with special haircut and dress,
as on a reservation. Introvert.
He does not understand this; sad conjecture
muscles and palls thrombotic on his heart.

He thinks an impostor, having studied his personal biography,
his gestures, his moods, now has come forward to pose
in the shivering vacuums his absence leaves.
Wigged with his laurel, that other, and faked with his face,
he pats the heads of his children, pecks his wife,
and is at home, and slippered, in his house.

So he guesses at the impertinent silhouette
that talks to his phone-piece and slits open his mail.
Is it the local tycoon who for a hobby
plays poet, he so epical in steel?
The orator, making a pause? Or is that man
he who blows his flash of brass in the jittering hall?

Or is he cuckolded by the troubadour
rich and successful out of celluloid?
Or by the don who unrhymes atoms? Or
the chemist death built up? Pride, lost impostor'd pride,
it is another, another, whoever he is,
who rides where he should ride.

V

*Fame*, the adrenalin: to be talked about;
to be a verb; to be introduced as *The*:
to smile with endorsement from slick paper; make
caprices anecdotal; to nod to the world; to see
one's name like a song upon the marquees played;
to be forgotten with embarrassment; to be—
to be.

It has its attractions, but is not the thing;
nor is it the ape mimesis[12] who speaks from the tree
ancestral; nor the merkin joy[13] . . .
Rather it is stark infelicity
which stirs him from his sleep, undressed, asleep
to walk upon roofs and window-sills and defy
the gape of gravity.

## VI

Therefore he seeds illusions. Look, he is
the nth Adam taking a green inventory
in world but scarcely uttered, naming, praising,
the flowering fiats in the meadow, the
syllabled fur, stars aspirate, the pollen
whose sweet collusion sounds eternally.
For to praise

the world—he, solitary man—is breath
to him. Until it has been praised, that part
has not been. Item by exciting item—
air to his lungs, and pressured blood to his heart—
they are pulsated, and breathed, until they map,
not the world's, but his own body's chart!

And now in imagination he has climbed
another planet, the better to look
with single camera view upon this earth—
its total scope, and each afflated[14] tick,
its talk, its trick, its tracklessness—and this,
this, he would like to write down in a book!

To find a new function for the *déclassé* craft
archaic like the fletcher's;[15] to make a new thing;
to say the word that will become sixth sense;
perhaps by necessity and indirection bring
new forms to life, anonymously, new creeds—
O, somehow pay back the daily larcenies of the lung!

12 imitation (perhaps in reference to the Aristotelian concept of poetry as an imitation of an action)
13 a deceptive joy; 'merkin': a wig for the female pubic area
14 breathed upon, inspired
15 arrow-maker

These are not mean ambitions. It is already something
merely to entertain them. Meanwhile, he
makes of his status as zero a rich garland,
a halo of his anonymity,
and lives alone, and in his secret shines
like phosphorus. At the bottom of the sea.

1948

# Elizabeth Bishop

1911–1979

Though born in Worcester, Massachusetts, Elizabeth Bishop considered herself a Canadian by upbringing, if not by birth. She spent her early years in Great Village, Nova Scotia, and many later summers in the Maritimes. In 1930 she entered Vassar College, where, as a senior, she was introduced to Marianne Moore, destined to become a close friend and a formative influence on her career. Their friendship may well have been the cause of her decision to pursue writing rather than medicine. Throughout her life Bishop was passionately fond of travelling. After graduating from Vassar in 1934 she moved to New York City and, the following year, to Europe. France and Florida, Mexico and Brazil—these were her homes for extended periods. In 1970 she settled in Boston, where she taught at Harvard University and later at the Massachusetts Institute of Technology. One of the finest lyric poets of the twentieth century, she does not reveal in her writings any exhaustive philosophy or approach to life. Rather, she shows the rich texture and variety of the world with its joys and pains, injustices and confusions.

## The Map

Land lies in water; it is shadowed green.
Shadows, or are they shallows, at its edges
showing the line of long sea-weeded ledges
where weeds hang to the simple blue from green.
Or does the land lean down to lift the sea from under,
drawing it unperturbed around itself?
Along the fine tan sandy shelf
is the land tugging at the sea from under?

The shadow of Newfoundland lies flat and still.
Labrador's yellow, where the moony Eskimo
has oiled it. We can stroke these lovely bays,

under a glass as if they were expected to blossom,
or as if to provide a clean cage for invisible fish.
The names of seashore towns run out to sea,
the names of cities cross the neighbouring mountains
—the printer here experiencing the same excitement
as when emotion too far exceeds its cause.
These peninsulas take the water between thumb and finger
like women feeling for the smoothness of yard-goods.

Mapped waters are more quiet than the land is,
lending the land their waves' own conformation:
and Norway's hare runs south in agitation,
profiles investigate the sea, where land is.
Are they assigned, or can the countries pick their colours?
—What suits the character or the native waters best.
Topography displays no favourites; North's as near as West.
More delicate than the historians' are the map-makers' colours.

1955

## First Death in Nova Scotia

In the cold, cold parlour
my mother laid out Arthur
beneath the chromographs:
Edward, Prince of Wales,
with Princess Alexandra,
and King George with Queen Mary.
Below them on the table
stood a stuffed loon
shot and stuffed by Uncle
Arthur, Arthur's father.

Since Uncle Arthur fired
a bullet into him,
he hadn't said a word.
He kept his own counsel
on his white, frozen lake,
the marble-topped table.
His breast was deep and white,
cold and caressable;
his eyes were red glass,
much to be desired.

'Come,' said my mother,
'Come and say goodbye
to your little cousin Arthur.'
I was lifted up and given
one lily of the valley
to put in Arthur's hand.
Arthur's coffin was
a little frosted cake,
and the red-eyed loon eyed it
from his white, frozen lake.

Arthur was very small.
He was all white, like a doll
that hadn't been painted yet.
Jack Frost had started to paint him
the way he always painted
the Maple Leaf (Forever).
He had just begun on his hair,
a few red strokes, and then
Jack Frost had dropped the brush
and left him white, forever.

The gracious royal couples
were warm in red and ermine;
their feet were well wrapped up
in the ladies' ermine trains.
They invited Arthur to be
the smallest page at court.
But how could Arthur go,
clutching his tiny lily,
with his eyes shut up so tight
and the roads deep in snow?

1965

## In the Waiting Room

In Worcester, Massachusetts,
I went with Aunt Consuelo
to keep her dentist's appointment
and sat and waited for her
in the dentist's waiting room.
It was winter. It got dark

early. The waiting room
was full of grown-up people,
arctics and overcoats,
lamps and magazines.
My aunt was inside
what seemed like a long time
and while I waited I read
the *National Geographic*
(I could read) and carefully
studied the photographs:
The inside of a volcano,
black, and full of ashes;
then it was spilling over
in rivulets of fire.
Osa and Martin Johnson
dressed in riding breeches,
laced boots, and pith helmets.
A dead man slung on a pole
—'Long Pig,' the caption said.
Babies with pointed heads
wound round and round with string;
black, naked women with necks
wound round and round with wire
like the necks of light bulbs.
Their breasts were horrifying.
I read it right straight through.
I was too shy to stop.
And then I looked at the cover:
the yellow margins, the date.

Suddenly, from inside,
came an *oh!* of pain
—Aunt Consuelo's voice—
not very loud or long.
I wasn't at all surprised;
even then I knew she was
a foolish, timid woman.
I might have been embarrassed,
but wasn't. What took me
completely by surprise
was that it was me:
my voice, in my mouth.
Without thinking at all
I was my foolish aunt,

I—we—were falling, falling,
our eyes glued to the cover
of the *National Geographic*,
February, 1918.

I said to myself: three days
and you'll be seven years old.
I was saying it to stop
the sensation of falling off
the round, turning world
into cold, blue-black space.
But I felt: you are an *I*,
you are an *Elizabeth*,
you are one of *them*.
*Why* should you be one, too?
I scarcely dared to look
to see what it was I was.
I gave a sidelong glance
—I couldn't look any higher—
at shadowy grey knees,
trousers and skirts and boots
and different pairs of hands
lying under the lamps.
I knew that nothing stranger
had ever happened, that nothing
stranger could ever happen.
Why should I be my aunt,
or me, or anyone?
What similarities—
boots, hands, the family voice
I felt in my throat, or even
the *National Geographic*
and those awful hanging breasts—
held us all together
or made us all just one?
How—I didn't know any
word for it—how 'unlikely' . . .
How had I come to be here,
like them, and overhear
a cry of pain that could have
got loud and worse but hadn't?

The waiting room was bright
and too hot. It was sliding

beneath a big black wave,
another, and another.

Then I was back in it.
The War was on. Outside
in Worcester, Massachusetts,
were night and slush and cold,
and it was still the fifth
of February, 1918.

1976

## One Art

The art of losing isn't hard to master;
so many things seem filled with the intent
to be lost that their loss is no disaster.

Lose something every day. Accept the fluster
of lost door keys, the hour badly spent.
The art of losing isn't hard to master.

Then practice losing farther, losing faster:
places, and names, and where it was you meant
to travel. None of these will bring disaster.

I lost my mother's watch. And look! my last, or
next-to-last, of three loved houses went.
The art of losing isn't hard to master.

I lost two cities, lovely ones. And, vaster,
some realms I owned, two rivers, a continent.
I miss them, but it wasn't a disaster.

—Even losing you (the joking voice, a gesture
I love) I shan't have lied. It's evident
the art of losing's not too hard to master
though it may look like (*Write* it!) like disaster.

1976

# Dylan Thomas

1914–1953

Born in Swansea, Wales, Dylan Thomas attended the Swansea Grammar School where his father was senior English master. Never much of a scholar, Thomas did well only in English, and loved to act in school plays and small theatre productions. When he left school in 1931, he worked for two newspapers, writing on books and theatre, and his explorations of the pubs and streets of his seaport town provided him with material for the short stories he was writing at the time. He was also writing poems in penny exercise books, composing much of his carefully crafted syllabic verse in pubs, with a glass of beer by his notebook. Much of his finest poetry was written before he was 20, and from 1933 on he was published regularly. Thomas enjoyed playing the role of poet and became known as an extraordinarily fine reader of poetry, doing regular poetry readings for BBC radio. Though he was popular and making a good income, he was always in debt and incapable of managing money. On his tours to the United States, he was renowned not just for his readings but for his wild drinking bouts. He died suddenly and prematurely in New York after downing 18 straight whiskies.

## The Force That through the Green Fuse Drives the Flower

The force that through the green fuse drives the flower
Drives my green age; that blasts the roots of trees
Is my destroyer.
And I am dumb to tell the crooked rose
My youth is bent by the same wintry fever.

The force that drives the water through the rocks
Drives my red blood; that dries the mouthing streams
Turns mine to wax.
And I am dumb to mouth unto my veins
How at the mountain spring the same mouth sucks.

The hand that whirls the water in the pool
Stirs the quicksand; that ropes the blowing wind
Hauls my shroud sail.
And I am dumb to tell the hanging man
How of my clay is made the hangman's lime.

The lips of time leech to the fountain head;
Love drips and gathers, but the fallen blood
Shall calm her sores.

And I am dumb to tell a weather's wind
How time has ticked a heaven round the stars.

And I am dumb to tell the lover's tomb
How at my sheet goes the same crooked worm.

1933

## A Refusal to Mourn the Death, by Fire, of a Child in London

Never until the mankind making
Bird beast and flower
Fathering and all humbling darkness
Tells with silence the last light breaking
And the still hour
Is come of the sea tumbling in harness

And I must enter again the round
Zion of the water bead
And the synagogue of the ear of corn
Shall I let pray the shadow of a sound
Or sow my salt seed
In the least valley of sackcloth to mourn

The majesty and burning of the child's death.
I shall not murder
The mankind of her going with a grave truth
Nor blaspheme down the stations of the breath
With any further
Elegy of innocence and youth.

Deep with the first dead lies London's daughter,
Robed in the long friends,
The grains beyond age, the dark veins of her mother,
Secret by the unmourning water
Of the riding Thames.
After the first death, there is no other.

1946

## Fern Hill

Now as I was young and easy under the apple boughs
About the lilting house and happy as the grass was green,
The night above the dingle starry,
Time let me hail and climb
Golden in the heydays of his eyes,
And honoured among wagons I was prince of the apple towns
And once below a time I lordly had the trees and leaves
Trail with daisies and barley
Down the rivers of the windfall light.

And as I was green and carefree, famous among the barns
About the happy yard and singing as the farm was home,
In the sun that is young once only,
Time let me play and be
Golden in the mercy of his means,
And green and golden I was huntsman and herdsman, the calves
Sang to my horn, the foxes on the hills barked clear and cold,
And the sabbath rang slowly
In the pebbles of the holy streams.

All the sun long it was running, it was lovely, the hay
Fields high as the house, the tunes from the chimneys, it was air
And playing, lovely and watery
And fire green as grass.
And nightly under the simple stars
As I rode to sleep the owls were bearing the farm away,
All the moon long I heard, blessed among stables, the night-jars
Flying with the ricks, and the horses
Flashing into the dark

And then to awake, and the farm, like a wanderer white
With the dew, come back, the cock on his shoulder: it was all
Shining, it was Adam and maiden,
The sky gathered again
And the sun grew round that very day.
So it must have been after the birth of the simple light
In the first, spinning place, the spellbound horses walking warm
Out of te whinnying green stable
On to the fields of praise.

And honoured among foxes and pheasants by the gay house
Under the new made clouds and happy as the heart was long,
        In the sun born over and over,
                I ran my heedless ways,
        My wishes raced through the house high hay
And nothing I cared, at my sky blue trades, that time allows
In all his tuneful turning so few and such morning songs
        Before the children green and golden
                Follow him out of grace,

Nothing I cared, in the lamb white days, that time would take me
Up to the swallow thronged loft by the shadow of my hand,
        In the moon that is always rising,
                Nor that riding to sleep
        I should hear him fly with the high fields
And wake to the farm forever fled from the childless land.
Oh as I was young and easy in the mercy of his means,
                Time held me green and dying
        Though I sang in my chains like the sea.

1946

## Do Not Go Gentle into That Good Night

Do not go gentle into that good night,
Old age should burn and rave at close of day;
Rage, rage against the dying of the light.

Though wise men at their end know dark is right,
Because their words had forked no lightning they
Do not go gentle into that good night.

Good men, the last wave by, crying how bright
Their frail deeds might have danced in a green bay,
Rage, rage against the dying of the light.

Wild men who caught and sang the sun in flight,
And learn, too late, they grieved it on its way,
Do not go gentle into that good night.

Grave men, near death, who see with blinding sight
Blind eyes could blaze like meteors and be gay,

Rage, rage against the dying of the light.

And you, my father, there on the sad height,
Curse, bless, me now with your fierce tears, I pray.
Do not go gentle into that good night.
Rage, rage against the dying of the light.

1951

# P.K. Page
## 1916–2010

Born in Swanage, Dorset, England, Patricia Kathleen Page emigrated with her family to Alberta in 1919. She lived in many areas of Canada before settling in 1941 in Montreal, where she edited, along with Patrick Anderson and F.R. Scott, *Preview* magazine, a literary journal designed to 'preview', or try out, new poetry written in a cosmopolitan mode. She engaged in many occupations, including radio actor, research assistant, and scriptwriter for the National Film Board. In 1950 she married W.A. Irwin, commissioner for the film board, who later became Canadian high commissioner to Australia and then ambassador to Brazil and to Mexico.

Page published her first poems as well as a novel, *The Sun and the Moon*, in 1944. In addition to several short stories, she published numerous collections of poetry, including *Planet Earth: Poems Selected and New* (2002). Under her married name, P.K. Irwin, she also achieved eminence as a painter. 'In all essential particulars writing and painting are interchangeable', she observed. Like the painter that she was, she explored in her poetry an image or a scene by gathering together precise details and impressions in a rich tapestry.

### The Stenographers

After the brief bivouac of Sunday,
their eyes, in the forced march of Monday to Saturday,
hoist the white flag, flutter in the snow-storm of paper,
haul it down and crack in the mid-sun of temper.

In the pause between the first draft and the carbon
they glimpse the smooth hours when they were children—
the ride in the ice-cart, the ice-man's name,
the end of the route and the long walk home;

remember the sea where floats at high tide
were sea marrows growing on the scatter-green vine
or spools of grey toffee, or wasps' nests on water;
remember the sand and the leaves of the country.

Bell rings and they go and the voice draws their pencil
like a sled across snow; when its runners are frozen
rope snaps and the voice then is pulling no burden
but runs like a dog on the winter of paper.

Their climates are winter and summer—no wind
for the kites of their hearts—no wind for a flight;
a breeze at the most, to tumble them over
and leave them like rubbish—the boy-friends of blood.

In the inch of the noon as they move they are stagnant.
The terrible calm of the noon is their anguish;
the lip of the counter, the shapes of the straws
like icicles breaking their tongues, are invaders.

Their beds are their oceans—salt water of weeping
the waves that they know—the tide before sleep;
and fighting to drown they assemble their sheep
in columns and watch them leap desks for their fences
and stare at them with their own mirror-worn faces.

In the felt of the morning the calico-minded,
sufficiently starched, insert papers, hit keys,
efficient and sure as their adding machines;
yet they weep in the vault, they are taut as net curtains
stretched upon frames. In their eyes I have seen
the pin men[1] of madness in marathon trim
race round the track of the stadium pupil.

1946

1 'stick figures, such as children draw' [Page's note]

## Photos of a Salt Mine

How innocent their lives look,
how like a child's
dream of caves and winter, both combined;
the steep descent to whiteness
and the stope[1]
with its striated walls
their folds all leaning as if pointing to
the greater whiteness still,
that great white bank

with its decisive front,
that seam upon a slope,
salt's lovely ice.

And wonderful underfoot the snow of salt
the fine
particles a broom could sweep,
one thinks
muckers might make angels in its drifts
as children do in snow,
lovers in sheets,
lie down and leave imprinted where they lay
a feathered creature holier than they.

And in the outworked stopes
with lamps and ropes
up miniature matterhorns
the miners climb
probe with their lights
the ancient folds of rock—
syncline[2] and anticline—
and scoop from darkness an Aladdin's cave:
rubies and opals glitter from its walls.

But hoses douse the brilliance of these jewels,
melt fire to brine.
Salt's bitter water trickles thin and forms,
slow fathoms down,

1 an excavation in the form of steps made as ore is mined from vertical or steeply inclined veins
2 a low, troughlike fold in stratified rock, the opposite of 'anticline': a fold with strata sloping downwards on both sides away from a common crest

a lake within a cave,
lacquered with jet—
white's opposite.
There grey on black the boating miners float
to mend the stays and struts of that old stope
and deeply underground
their words resound,
are multiplied by echo, swell and grow
and make a climate of a miner's voice.

So all the photographs like children's wishes
are filled with caves or winter,
innocence
has acted as a filter,
selected only beauty from the mine.
Except in the last picture,
it is shot
from an acute high angle. In a pit
figures the size of pins are strangely lit
and might be dancing but you know they're not.
Like Dante's vision of the nether hell[3]
men struggle with the bright cold fires of salt,
locked in the black inferno of the rock:
the filter here, not innocence but guilt.

1954

3 In *The Inferno*, which forms the first part of Dante's fourteenth-century poem *The Divine Comedy*, hell is divided into three parts. The lowest part contains both fire and ice.

## Arras[1]

Consider a new habit—classical,
and trees espaliered on the wall like candelabra.
How still upon that lawn our sandalled feet.

But a peacock rattling his rattan tail and screaming
has found a point of entry. Through whose eye
did it insinuate in furled disguise
to shake its jewels and silk upon that grass?

1 a wall hanging, particularly a tapestry

The peaches hang like lanterns. No one joins
those figures on the arras.
Who am I
or who am I become that walking here
I am observer, other, Gemini,
starred for a green garden of cinema?

I ask, what did they deal me in this pack?
The cards, all suits, are royal when I look.
My fingers slipping on a monarch's face
twitch and grow slack.
I want a hand to clutch, a heart to crack.

No one is moving now, the stillness is
infinite. If I should make a break. . . .
take to my springy heels. . . . ? But nothing moves.
The spinning world is stuck upon its poles,
the stillness points a bone[2] at me. I fear
the future on this arras.
I confess:

It was my eye.
Voluptuous it came.
Its head the ferrule[3] and its lovely tail
folded so sweetly; it was strangely slim
to fit the retina. And then it shook
and was a peacock—living patina,
eye-bright, maculate!
Does no one care?

I thought their hands might hold me if I spoke.
I dreamed the bite of fingers in my flesh,
their poke smashed by an image, but they stand
as if with a treacle,[4] motionless,
folding slow eyes on nothing. While they stare
another line has trolled the encircling air,
another bird assumes its furled disguise.

1967

2 'Aboriginal projective magic. A prepared human or kangaroo bone is pointed by a sorcerer at an intended victim (who may be miles away) to bring about his death' [from Page's glossary of Australian terms in *Cry Ararat!*].
3 a metal cap used to reinforce or secure the end of a pole or handle—here belonging to an umbrella
4 molasses or sweet syrup, used here as the kind that entraps the insects it attracts

## The New Bicycle

All the molecules in the house
re-adjust on its arrival,
make way for its shining presence
its bright dials,
and after it has settled
and the light
has explored its surfaces
—and the night—
they compose themselves again
in another order.

One senses the change at once
without knowing what one senses.
Has somebody cleaned the windows
used different soap
or is there a bowl of flowers
on the mantelpiece?—
for the air makes another shape
it is thinner or denser,
a new design
is invisibly stamped upon it.

How we all adapt ourselves
to the bicycle
aglow in the furnace room,
turquoise where turquoise
has never before been seen,
its chrome gleaming
on gears and pedals,
its spokes glistening.
Lightly resting on the incised
rubber of its airy tires
it has changed us all.

1985

## Deaf-Mute in the Pear Tree

His clumsy body is a golden fruit
pendulous in the pear tree

Blunt fingers among the multitudinous buds

Adriatic blue the sky above and through
the forking twigs

Sun ruddying tree's trunk, his trunk
his massive head thick-nobbed with burnished curls
tight-clenched in bud

(Painting by Generalić. Primitive.)

I watch him prune with silent secateurs

Boots in the crotch of branches shift their weight
heavily as oxen in a stall

Hear small inarticulate mews from his locked mouth
a kitten in a box

Pear clippings fall
                    soundlessly on the ground
Spring finches sing
                      soundlessly in the leaves

A stone. A stone in ears and on his tongue

Through palm and fingertip he knows the tree's
quick springtime pulse

Smells in its sap the sweet incipient pears

Pale sunlight's choppy water glistens on
his mutely snipping blades

and flags and scraps of blue
above him make regatta of the day

But when he sees his wife's foreshortened shape
sudden and silent in the grass below
uptilt its face to him

then air is kisses, kisses

stone dissolves

his locked throat finds a little door

and through it feathered joy
flies screaming like a jay

1985

# Robert Lowell

1917–1977

Robert Lowell's poetry is primarily autobiographical, revealing his deep interest in his family's New England history, as well as his reactions to his lineage. He was born in Boston and attended St Mark's School (founded by his grandfather). Then, as was proper for young men of good family in Boston, he went on to Harvard. But after two years he left and went to study with poet and critic John Crowe Ransom at Kenyon College. He converted to Catholicism in 1940, and during World War II he tried unsuccessfully to enlist in the navy. He refused to be drafted into the army, and as a conscientious objector, was jailed for six months.

Lowell's first book of poetry was published in 1944, and in 1947 he won the Pulitzer Prize for *Lord Weary's Castle*, and became consultant in poetry to the Library of Congress. *Life Studies* (1959) reveals some influence of the self-revelatory mode of the Beat poets, and of William Carlos Williams's colloquial American diction. Lowell's form is highly controlled as he strives for a tone of 'heightened conversation' in these complex and personal portraits that many consider his finest poetry. During his career, Lowell taught at several universities, including Harvard, wrote for the theatre, and translated European poetry. In his last book, *Day by Day*, he returned to an exploration of his childhood.

## 'To Speak of Woe That Is in Marriage'

*'It is the future generation that presses into being by means of these exuberant feelings and supersensible soap bubbles of ours.'*

—Schopenhauer

'The hot night makes us keep our bedroom windows open.
Our magnolia blossoms. Life begins to happen.
My hopped up husband drops his home disputes,

and hits the streets to cruise for prostitutes,
free-lancing out along the razor's edge.
This screwball might kill his wife, then take the pledge.
Oh the monotonous meanness of his lust. . . .
It's the injustice . . . he is so unjust—
whiskey-blind, swaggering home at five.
My only thought is how to keep alive.
What makes him tick? Each night now I tie
ten dollars and his car key to my thigh. . . .
Gored by the climacteric of his want,
he stalls above me like an elephant.'

1959

## Skunk Hour

*for Elizabeth Bishop*

Nautilus Island's hermit
heiress still lives through winter in her Spartan cottage;
her sheep still graze above the sea.
Her son's a bishop. Her farmer
is first selectman in our village;
she's in her dotage.

Thirsting for
the hierarchic privacy
of Queen Victoria's century,
she buys up all
the eyesores facing her shore,
and lets them fall.

The season's ill—
we've lost our summer millionaire,
who seemed to leap from an L.L. Bean
catalogue. His nine-knot yawl
was auctioned off to lobstermen.
A red fox stain covers Blue Hill.

And now our fairy
decorator brightens his shop for fall;
his fishnet's filled with orange cork,

orange, his cobbler's bench and awl;
there is no money in his work,
he'd rather marry.

One dark night,
my Tudor Ford climbed the hill's skull;
I watched for love-cars. Lights turned down,
they lay together, hull to hull,
where the graveyard shelves on the town. . . .
My mind's not right.

A car radio bleats,
'Love, O careless Love. . . .' I hear
my ill-spirit sob in each blood cell,
as if my hand were at its throat. . . .
I myself am hell;
nobody's here—

only skunks, that search
in the moonlight for a bite to eat.
They march on their soles up Main Street:
white stripes, moonstruck eyes' red fire
under the chalk-dry and spar spire
of the Trinitarian Church.

I stand on top
of our back steps and breathe the rich air—
a mother skunk with her column of kittens swills the garbage pail.
She jabs her wedge-head in a cup
of sour cream, drops her ostrich tail,
and will not scare.

1959

## Water

It was a Maine lobster town—
each morning boatloads of hands
pushed off for granite
quarries on the islands,

and left dozens of bleak
white frame houses stuck
like oyster shells
on a hill of rock,

and below us, the sea lapped
the raw little match-stick
mazes of a weir,
where the fish for bait were trapped.

Remember? We sat on a slab of rock.
From this distance in time,
it seems the colour
of iris, rotting and turning purpler,

but it was only
the usual grey rock
turning the usual green
when drenched by the sea.

The sea drenched the rock
at our feet all day,
and kept tearing away
flake after flake.

One night you dreamed
you were a mermaid clinging to a wharf-pile,
and trying to pull
off the barnacles with your hands.

We wished our two souls
might return like gulls
to the rock. In the end,
the water was too cold for us.

1959

## For the Union Dead

*'Relinquunt Omnia Servare Rem Publicam.'*[1]

The old South Boston Aquarium stands
in a Sahara of snow now. Its broken windows are boarded.
The bronze weathervane cod has lost half its scales.
The airy tanks are dry.

Once my nose crawled like a snail on the glass;
my hand tingled
to burst the bubbles
drifting from the noses of the cowed, compliant fish.

My hand draws back. I often sigh still
for the dark downward and vegetating kingdom
of the fish and reptile. One morning last March,
I pressed against the new barbed and galvanized

fence on the Boston Common. Behind their cage,
yellow dinosaur steamshovels were grunting
as they cropped up tons of mush and grass
to gouge their underworld garage.

Parking spaces luxuriate like civic
sandpiles in the heart of Boston.
A girdle of orange, Puritan-pumpkin coloured girders
braces the tingling Statehouse,

shaking over the excavations, as it faces Colonel Shaw[2]
and his bell-cheeked Negro infantry
on St Gaudens' shaking Civil War relief,
propped by a plank splint against the garage's earthquake.

Two months after marching through Boston,
half the regiment was dead;
at the dedication,
William James could almost hear the bronze Negroes breathe.

Their monument sticks like a fishbone
in the city's throat.
Its Colonel is as lean
as a compass-needle.

1 'They give up everything to serve the republic.'
2 Robert Gould Shaw led the first northern black regiment, the Massachusetts 54th. He and many of his men were killed leading an attack on Fort Wagner, South Carolina.

He has an angry wrenlike vigilance,
a greyhound's gentle tautness;
he seems to wince at pleasure,
and suffocate for privacy.

He is out of bounds now. He rejoices in man's lovely,
peculiar power to choose life and die—
when he leads his black soldiers to death,
he cannot bend his back.

On a thousand small town New England greens,
the old white churches hold their air
of sparse, sincere rebellion; frayed flags
quilt the graveyards of the Grand Army of the Republic.

The stone statues of the abstract Union Soldier
grow slimmer and younger each year—
wasp-waisted, they doze over muskets
and muse through their sideburns . . .

Shaw's father wanted no monument
except the ditch,
where his son's body was thrown
and lost with his 'niggers'.

The ditch is nearer.
There are no statues for the last war here;
on Boylston Street, a commercial photograph
shows Hiroshima boiling

over a Mosler Safe, the 'Rock of Ages'
that survived the blast. Space is nearer.
When I crouch to my television set,
the drained faces of Negro school-children rise like balloons.

Colonel Shaw
is riding on his bubble,
he waits
for the blessèd break.

The Aquarium is gone. Everywhere,
giant finned cars nose forward like fish;
a savage servility
slides by on grease.

1959

# Margaret Avison
## 1918–2007

Born in Galt (now Cambridge), Ontario, Margaret Avison graduated in English from Victoria College, University of Toronto, in 1940. She also studied at Indiana University (1955) and, on a Guggenheim Fellowship, at the University of Chicago (1956–7). Her first collection of poetry, *Winter Sun* (1960), won the Governor General's Award, as did her later collection *No Time* (1989). During the 1960s she returned to the University of Toronto to pursue graduate studies. She was a librarian, a lecturer at University of Toronto Scarborough, and a social worker for the Presbyterian Church Mission in Toronto. Her poems are often careful and close observations of physical landscapes, and, like Gerard Manley Hopkins, she delights in the natural world's ability to shadow forth spiritual realities. In 2003 *Concrete and Wild Carrot* won the Griffin Poetry Prize.

### Snow

Nobody stuffs the world in at your eyes.
The optic heart must venture: a jail-break
And re-creation. Sedges and wild rice
Chase rivery pewter. The astonished cinders quake
With rhizomes. All ways through the electric air
Trundle candy-bright disks; they are desolate
Toys if the soul's gates seal, and cannot bear,
Must shudder under, creation's unseen freight.
But soft, there is snow's legend: colour of mourning
Along the yellow Yangtze where the wheel
Spins an indifferent stasis that's death's warning.
Asters of tumbled quietness reveal
Their petals. Suffering this starry blur
The rest may ring your change, sad listener.

1960

### New Year's Poem

The Christmas twigs crispen and needles rattle
Along the windowledge.
                    A solitary pearl
Shed from the necklace spilled at last week's party
Lies in the suety, snow-luminous plainness

Of morning, on the windowledge beside them.
And all the furniture that circled stately
And hospitable when these rooms were brimmed
With perfumes, furs, and black-and-silver
Crisscross of seasonal conversation, lapses
Into its previous largeness.
                    I remember
Anne's rose-sweet gravity, and the stiff grave
Where cold so little can contain;
I mark the queer delightful skull and crossbones
Starlings and sparrows left, taking the crust,
And the long loop of winter wind
Smoothing its arc from dark Arcturus down
To the bricked corner of the drifted courtyard,
And the still windowledge.
                    Gentle and just pleasure
It is, being human, to have won from space
This unchill, habitable interior
Which mirrors quietly the light
Of the snow, and the new year.

1960

## The Swimmer's Moment

For everyone
The swimmer's moment at the whirlpool comes,
But many at that moment will not say
'This is the whirlpool, then.'
By their refusal they are saved
From the black pit, and also from contesting
The deadly rapids, and emerging in
The mysterious, and more ample, further waters.
And so their bland-blank faces turn and turn
Pale and forever on the rim of suction
They will not recognize.
Of those who dare the knowledge
Many are whirled into the ominous centre
That, gaping vertical, seals up
For them an eternal boon of privacy,
So that we turn away from their defeat
With a despair, not for their deaths, but for
Ourselves, who cannot penetrate their secret

Nor even guess at the anonymous breadth
Where one or two have won:
(The silver reaches of the estuary).

1960

## Butterfly Bones; or Sonnet against Sonnets

The cyanide jar seals life, as sonnets move
towards final stiffness. Cased in a white glare
these specimens stare for peering boys, to prove
strange certainties. Plane dogsled and safari
assure continuing range. The sweep-net skill,
the patience, learning, leave all living stranger.
Insect—or poem—waits for the fix, the frill
precision can effect, brilliant with danger.
What law and wonder the museum spectres
bespeak is cryptic for the shivery wings,
the world cut-diamond-eyed, those eyes' reflectors,
or herbal grass, sunned motes, fierce listening.
Might sheened and rigid trophies strike men blind
like Adam's lexicon locked in the mind?

1960

## In a Season of Unemployment

These green painted park benches are
all new. The Park Commissioner had them
planted.
Sparrows go on
having dust baths at the edge of
the park maple's shadow, just where
the bench is cemented down, planted
and then cemented.

Not a breath moves
this newspaper.
I'd rather read it by the Lapland sun at midnight. Here we're
bricked in early by a
stifling dark.

On that bench a man in a
pencil-striped white shirt
keeps his head up and steady.

The newspaper-astronaut says
'I feel excellent under the condition of weightlessness.'
And from his bench a
scatter of black bands in the hollow air
ray out—too quick for the eye—
and cease.

'Ground observers watching him on a TV circuit said
At the time of this report he
was smiling,' Moscow ra-
dio reported.
I glance across at him, and mark that
he is feeling
excellent too, I guess, and
weightless and
'smiling'.

1966

## We the Poor Who Are Always with Us

The cumbering hungry
and the uncaring ill
become too many
try as we will.

Try on and on, still?
In fury, fly
out, smash shards (and quail
at tomorrow's new supply,
and fail anew to find and smash the why?)

It is not hopeless.
One can crawling move
in useless recognition
there, still free to love
past use, where none survive.

And there is reason in
the hope that then can shine
when other hope is none.

1978

# Robert Kroetsch

1927–2011

Born in Heisler, Alberta, Robert Kroetsch obtained his BA (1948) from the University of Alberta, his MA (1955) from Middlebury College, and his PhD (1961) from the University of Iowa. He taught in the Department of English of the State University of New York in Binghamton before returning to Canada to teach at the University of Manitoba. He turned to poetry in the midst of a distinguished career as a novelist and critic. In his short lyrics, which he began to write in the early 1970s, he fashioned a complex archaeological metaphor out of autobiography, gathering up the fragments of his many stories to dig up his own being as a poet. His poetry became an ongoing set of field notes, signposts of where the poet has been. In marking out the landscapes that are filled with past stories waiting to be unearthed, he created poetry in the state of becoming, always aware of what can be and still is not. His *Hornbooks of Rita K* (2001) watches an 'archivist' working his way through the writings of a prairie poet whose initials are the same as the book's real author.

## The Poet's Mother

I

In the death of my mother
I read the empty sky.

In the death of my mother
I learn to bite the wind.

In the death of my mother
I hear the clarinet.

In the death of my mother
I say goodbye to myself.

In the death of my mother
I speak to the grass.

In the death of my mother
I enter the cave.

In the death of my mother
I recite my name.

2

I have sought my mother
on the shores of a dozen islands.

I have sought my mother
inside the covers
of ten thousand books.

I have sought my mother
in the bars of a hundred cities.

I have sought my mother
on the head of a pin.

I have sought my mother
in the arms of younger women.

I have sought my mother
in the spaces between
the clouds.

I have sought my mother
under the typewriter keys.

3

In the fall of snow
I hear my mother.
I know she is there.
In the weight of the snow
I hear her silence.

I count white stones
in October moonlight.

I break dry bread
with a flock of gulls.

I tear sheep's wool
from barbed wire fences

The visible,
the visible—

where are you?

4

These are the scars
that make us whole.

These are the scars
that empty us
into our lives.

Hold your horses.
It was a nice trip
to heaven. Let us
now visit the

earth.
The scarred earth
is our only
home.

Mother, where are you?

1989

## From *The Hornbooks of Rita K*

### [HORNBOOK #43]

Rita thought of calling her book *Chance of Flurries.* That
she elected not to is fortunate, since I would surely
propose other titles for her unfinished magnum opus.

We write as a way of inviting love. Each text is a request
that says, please, love me a little.

Rita Kleinhart was an admirer of snow. Snow, she remarks,
is the caress of impossible meanings. Snow is closure
without ending. Snow is the veil that lets us see the shape
of the dream.

Rita left two solitary lines that seem to belong nowhere:

> A skiff of snow, this morning, rides the stubble sun.
> The gosling, holding madly still, accounts the gun.

I, too, have walked in the ribald dark, asking forgiveness. In
the absence of the gun, snow suffices.

### [HORNBOOK #45]

What is the heart but the muscular, thick skin of an
abiding secret?

She referred to me as the intrigued lover.

Broken, she said, and wrote these lines after that solitary
word, as if she had put down a title:

> He is the intrigued lover who loves first
> his own hands. His hands betray my nipples.
> His hands are scissors that break rocks.
> And yet he is the intrigued lover who asks,
> Where do you go when you close your eyes?

There is a break on the page. Then she continues:

> You of the stalled orgasm, fearing an end—
> I give you nothing. Die by your own hand.
> Love is a pleasure of the mouth. Eat your words.

Surely she intends these final lines for me. She is nothing
if not direct. I see in these lines intimations of her
disappearance; what is love but a disappearing act that
leaves the beholder staggering in blind pursuit? I find Rita
nowhere, and yet I am in her arms when I awaken. She ties
me to her bed.

Her restless words begin, like the lick of snow, their
incisions.

2001

# Phyllis Webb
## *b.* 1927

Born in Victoria, British Columbia, Phyllis Webb graduated from the University of British Columbia in 1949. After running unsuccessfully as a CCF candidate for the provincial legislature in 1949 she moved to Montreal, where she pursued graduate studies at McGill University and came into contact with many of the city's writers, including F.R. Scott. During the 1960s she lived in Toronto, where she conceived the CBC radio program *Ideas*; from 1966 until 1969 she served as its executive producer. At the end of the decade she returned to the West Coast and settled on Saltspring Island, which remains her home.

Webb's seamless verses are intense lyrical examinations, often of human loneliness and despair, and the perfect shape of her poems brings an order to the seeming shapelessness of the human condition. Just as love offers some meaning to the chaos of life, so, too, poetry offers some order to the chaos. Webb has taught at the University of British Columbia and the University of Victoria.

### Marvell's Garden[1]

Marvell's garden, that place of solitude,
is not where I'd choose to live
yet is the fixed sundial
that turns me round
unwillingly
in a hot glade
as closer, closer I come to contradiction
to the shade green within the green shade.

1 This is a reply to Andrew Marvell's poem 'The Garden' (see p. 418).

The garden where Marvell scorned love's solicitude—
that dream—and played instead an arcane solitaire,
shuffling his thoughts like shadowy chance
across the shrubs of ecstasy,
and cast the myths away to flowering hours
as yes, his mind, that sea, caught at green
thoughts shadowing a green infinity.

And yet Marvell's garden was not Plato's
garden—and yet—he did care more for the form
of things than for the thing itself—
ideas and visions,
resemblances and echoes,
things seeming and being
not quite what they were.

That was his garden, a kind of attitude
struck out of an earth too carefully attended,
wanting to be left alone.
And I don't blame him for that.
God knows, too many fences fence us out
and his garden closed in on Paradise.

On Paradise! When I think of his hymning
Puritans in the Bermudas, the bright oranges
lighting up that night! When I recall
his rustling tinsel hopes
beneath the cold decree of steel.
Oh, I have wept for some new convulsion
to tear together this world and his.

But then I saw his luminous plumèd Wings
prepared for flight,
and then I heard him singing glory
in a green tree,
and then I caught the vest he'd laid aside
all blest with fire.

And I have gone walking slowly in
his garden of necessity
leaving brothers, lovers, Christ
outside my walls
where they have wept without
and I within.

1956

## Lament

Knowing that everything was wrong,
how can we go on giving birth
either to poems or the troublesome lie,
to children, most of all, who sense
the stress in our distracted wonder
the instant of their entry with their cry?

For every building in this world
receives our benediction of disease.
Knowing that everything is wrong
means only that we all know where we're going.

But I, how can I, I
craving the resolution of my earth,
take up my little gang of sweet pretence
and saunter day-dreary down the alleys, or pursue
the half-disastrous night? Where is that virtue
I would claim with tense impersonal unworth,
where does it dwell, that virtuous land
where one can die without a second birth?

It is not here, neither in the petulance
of my cries, nor in the tracers of my active fear,
not in my suicide of love, my dear.
That place of perfect animals and men
is simply the circle we would charm our children in
and why we frame our lonely poems in
the shape of a frugal sadness.

1962

## To Friends Who Have Also Considered Suicide

It's still a good idea.
Its exercise is discipline;
to remember to cross the street without looking,
to remember not to jump when the cars side-swipe,
to remember not to bother to have clothes cleaned,
to remember not to eat or want to eat,
to consider the numerous methods of killing oneself,

that is surely the finest exercise of the imagination:
death by drowning, sleeping pills, slashed wrists,
kitchen fumes, bullets through the brain or through
the stomach, hanging by the neck in attic or basement,
a clean frozen death—the ways are endless.
And consider the drama! It's better than a whole season
at Stratford when you think of the emotion of your
family on hearing the news and when you imagine
how embarrassed some will be when the body is found.
One could furnish a whole chorus in a Greek play
with expletives and feel sneaky and omniscient
at the same time. But there's no shame
in this concept of suicide.
It has concerned our best philosophers
and inspired some of the most popular
of our politicians and financiers.
Some people swim lakes, others climb flagpoles,
some join monasteries, but we, my friends,
who have considered suicide take our daily walk
with death and are not lonely.
In the end it brings more honesty and care
than all the democratic parliaments of tricks.
It is the 'sickness unto death'[1]; it is death;
it is not death; it is the sand from the beaches
of a hundred civilizations, the sand in the teeth
of death and barnacles our singing tongue:
and this is 'life' and we owe at least this much
contemplation to our western fact: to Rise,
Decline, Fall, to futility and larks,
to the bright crustaceans of the oversky.

1962

1 The phrase is taken from *The Sickness Unto Death* (1849) by Danish philosopher and theologian Sören Kierkegaard (1813–55); for Kierkegaard, the 'sickness unto death' is despair.

## The Days of the Unicorns

I remember when the unicorns
roved in herds through the meadow
behind the cabin, and how they would
lately pause, tilting their jewelled

horns to the falling sun as we shared
the tensions of private property
and the need to be alone.

Or as we walked along the beach
a solitary delicate beast
might follow on his soft paws
until we turned and spoke the words
to console him.

It seemed they were always near
ready to show their eyes and stare
us down, standing in their creamy
skins, pink tongues out
for our benevolence.

As if they knew that always beyond
and beyond the ladies were weaving them
into their spider looms.

I knew where they slept
and how the grass was bent
by their own wilderness
and I pitied them.

It was only yesterday, or seems
like only yesterday when we could
touch and turn and they came
perfectly real into our fictions.
But they moved on with the courtly sun
grazing peacefully beyond the story
horns lowering and lifting and
lowering.

I know this is scarcely credible now
as we cabin ourselves in cold
and the motions of panic
and our cells destroy each other
performing music and extinction
and the great dreams pass on
to the common good.

1984

# Adrienne Rich

## 1929–2012

Adrienne Rich was born in Baltimore, Maryland, and completed her first book of poetry, *A Change of World* (1952), while still an undergraduate at Radcliffe College in Cambridge, Massachusetts. W.H. Auden, who had chosen her book for publication in the Yale Series of Younger Poets, described her poems as 'neatly and modestly dressed', as poems that 'respect their elders but are not cowed by them'. Rich's work quickly evolved from closed forms to a poetics of change, rooted in a radical imagination and politics. Apparent in her poetry is her maturation from 'the girl who wrote poems, who defined herself in writing poems, and the girl who was to define herself by her relationship with men', to the poet who was 'able to write for the first time, directly about experiencing myself as a woman'. Much of her poetry deals with the separation between men and women, between self and others, though her later poetry emphasized the possibility of a 'common language' which would transcend such separation.

Rich taught at a number of colleges and universities, including Stanford University. She was the recipient of the Dorothea Tanning Prize of the Academy of American Poets 'for mastery in the art of poetry', the Lannan Foundation Lifetime Achievement Award, and the National Book Foundation's award for Distinguished Contribution to American Letters.

### Moving in Winter

Their life, collapsed like unplayed cards,
is carried piecemeal through the snow:
Headboard and footboard now, the bed
where she has lain desiring him
where overhead his sleep will build
its canopy to smother her once more;
their table, by four elbows worn
evening after evening while the wax runs down;
mirrors grey with reflecting them,
bureaus coffining from the cold
things that can shuffle in a drawer,
carpets rolled up around those echoes
which, shaken out, take wing and breed
new altercations, the old silences.

1957

## The Afterwake

Nursing your nerves
to rest, I've roused my own; well,
now for a few bad hours!
Sleep sees you behind closed doors.
Alone, I slump in his front parlour.
You're safe inside. Good. But I'm
like a midwife who at dawn
has all in order: bloodstains
washed up, teapot on the stove,
and starts her five miles home
walking, the birthyell still
exploding in her head.

Yes, I'm with her now: here's
the streaked, livid road
edged with shut houses
breathing night out and in.
Legs tight with fatigue,
we move under morning's coal-blue star,
colossal as this load
of unexpired purpose, which drains
slowly, till scissors of cockcrow snip the air.

1963

## Novella

Two people in a room, speaking harshly.
One gets up, goes out to walk.
(That is the man.)
The other goes into the next room
and washes the dishes, cracking one.
(That is the woman.)
It gets dark outside.
The children quarrel in the attic.
She has no blood left in her heart.
The man comes back to a dark house.
The only light is in the attic.
He has forgotten his key.
He rings at his own door
and hears sobbing on the stairs.

The lights go on in the house.
The door closes behind him.
Outside, separate as minds,
the stars too come alight.

1963

## Night-Pieces: For a Child

### *1. The Crib*

You sleeping I bend to cover.
Your eyelids work. I see
your dream, cloudy as a negative,
swimming underneath.
You blurt a cry. Your eyes
spring open, still filmed in dream.
Wider, they fix me—
—death's head, sphinx, medusa?
You scream.
Tears lick my cheeks, my knees
droop at your fear.
Mother I no more am,
but woman, and nightmare.

### *2. Her Waking*

Tonight I jerk astart in a dark
hourless as Hiroshima,
almost hearing you breathe
in a cot three doors away.

You still breathe, yes—
and my dream with its gift of knives,
its murderous hider and seeker,
ebbs away, recoils

back into the egg of dreams,
the vanishing point of mind.
All gone.

But you and I—
swaddled in a dumb dark
old as sickheartedness,

modern as pure annihilation—

we drift in ignorance.
If I could hear you now
mutter some gentle animal sound!
If milk flowed from my breast again. . . .

1966

## Rape

There is a cop who is both prowler and father:
he comes from your block, grew up with your brothers,
had certain ideals.
You hardly know him in his boots and silver badge,
on horseback, one hand touching his gun.

You hardly know him but you have to get to know him:
he has access to machinery that could kill you.
He and his stallion clop like warlords among the trash,
his ideals stand in the air, a frozen cloud
from between his unsmiling lips.

And so, when the time comes, you have to turn to him,
the maniac's sperm still greasing your thighs,
your mind whirling like crazy. You have to confess
to him, you are guilty of the crime
of having been forced.

And you see his blue eyes, the blue eyes of all the family
whom you used to know, grow narrow and glisten,
his hand types out the details
and he wants them all
but the hysteria in your voice pleases him best.

You hardly know him but now he thinks he knows you:
he has taken down your worst moment
on a machine and filed it in a file.
He knows, or thinks he knows, how much you imagined;
he knows, or thinks he knows, what you secretly wanted.

He has access to machinery that could get you put away;
and if, in the sickening light of the precinct,
and if, in the sickening light of the precinct,
your details sound like a portrait of your confessor,
will you swallow, will you deny them, will you lie your way home?

1973

# Sylvia Plath

1932–1963

Sylvia Plath was the daughter of a high-school teacher of Austrian parentage, and a professor of biology at Boston University, who had emigrated to the United States from Prussia at the age of 16 and who was an authority on bees. After her father's death in 1940, Plath and her family moved to Wellesley, where her mother taught high school and encouraged her children in their literary pursuits. By the time Plath entered Smith College, she was beginning to have her poems and short stories published. She graduated from Smith in 1955 and won a Fulbright Scholarship to Newnham College, Cambridge. There she met, and in 1956 married, British poet Ted Hughes. Except for a year during which Plath taught freshman English at Smith College, the couple lived in England. In 1960, Plath published her first book of poems, *Colossus*, and her first child was born. After the birth of a second child in 1962, Plath and Hughes separated. Plath was frequently ill, working to support herself and her children, and waking before daybreak to write her poetry, turning out two to three poems a day. The strain proved too great, and she took her life in February 1963.

## Sheep in Fog

The hills step off into whiteness.
People or stars
Regard me sadly, I disappoint them.

The train leaves a line of breath.
O slow
Horse the colour of rust,

Hooves, dolorous bells—
All morning the
Morning has been blackening,

A flower left out.
My bones hold a stillness, the far
Fields melt my heart.

They threaten
To let me through to a heaven
Starless and fatherless, a dark water.

1966

## Daddy

You do not do, you do not do
Any more, black shoe
In which I have lived like a foot
For thirty years, poor and white,
Barely daring to breathe or Achoo.

Daddy, I have had to kill you.
You died before I had time—
Marble-heavy, a bag full of God,
Ghastly statue with one grey toe
Big as a Frisco seal

And a head in the freakish Atlantic
Where it pours bean green over blue
In the waters off beautiful Nauset.
I used to pray to recover you.
Ach, du.

In the German tongue, in the Polish town
Scraped flat by the roller
Of wars, wars, wars.
But the name of the town is common.
My Polack friend

Says there are a dozen or two.
So I never could tell where you
Put your foot, your root,

I never could talk to you.
The tongue stuck in my jaw.

It stuck in a barb wire snare.
Ich, ich, ich, ich,
I could hardly speak.
I thought every German was you.
And the language obscene

An engine, an engine
Chuffing me off like a Jew.
A Jew to Dachau, Auschwitz, Belsen.
I began to talk like a Jew.
I think I may well be a Jew.

The snows of the Tyrol, the clear beer of Vienna
Are not very pure or true.
With my gypsy ancestress and my weird luck
And my Taroc pack and my Taroc pack
I may be a bit of a Jew.

I have always been scared of *you*.
With your Luftwaffe, your gobbledygoo.
And your neat mustache
And your Aryan eye, bright blue.
Panzer-man, panzer-man, O You—

Not God but a swastika
So black no sky could squeak through.
Every woman adores a Fascist,
The boot in the face, the brute
Brute heart of a brute like you.

You stand at the blackboard, daddy,
In the picture I have of you,
A cleft in your chin instead of your foot
But no less a devil for that, no not
Any less the black man who

Bit my pretty red heart in two.
I was ten when they buried you.
At twenty I tried to die
And get back, back, back to you.
I thought even the bones would do.

But they pulled me out of the sack,
And they stuck me together with glue.
And then I knew what to do.
I made a model of you,
A man black with a Meinkampf look

And a love of the rack and the screw.
And I said I do, I do.
So daddy, I'm finally through.
The black telephone's off at the root,
The voices just can't worm through.

If I've killed one man, I've killed two—
The vampire who said he was you
And drank my blood for a year,
Seven years, if you want to know.
Daddy, you can lie back now.

There's a stake in your fat black heart
And the villagers never liked you.
They are dancing and stamping on you.
They always *knew* it was you.
Daddy, daddy, you bastard, I'm through.

1966

## Kindness

Kindness glides about my house.
Dame Kindness, she is so nice!
The blue and red jewels of her rings smoke
In the windows, the mirrors
Are filling with smiles.

What is so real as the cry of a child?
A rabbit's cry may be wilder
But it has no soul.
Sugar can cure everything, so Kindness says.
Sugar is a necessary fluid,

Its crystals a little poultice.
O kindness, kindness
Sweetly picking up pieces!
My Japanese silks, desperate butterflies,
May be pinned any minute, anaesthetized.

And here you come, with a cup of tea
Wreathed in steam.
The blood jet is poetry,
There is no stopping it.
You hand me two children, two roses.

1966

## Edge

The woman is perfected.
Her dead

Body wears the smile of accomplishment,
The illusion of a Greek necessity

Flows in the scrolls of her toga,
Her bare

Feet seem to be saying:
We have come so far, it is over.

Each dead child coiled, a white serpent,
One at each little

Pitcher of milk, now empty.
She has folded

Them back into her body as petals
Of a rose close when the garden

Stiffens and odours bleed
From the sweet, deep throats of the night flower.

The moon has nothing to be sad about,
Staring from her hood of bone.

She is used to this sort of thing.
Her blacks crackle and drag.

1966

## Words

Axes
After whose stroke the wood rings,
And the echoes!
Echoes travelling
Off from the centre like horses.

The sap
Wells like tears, like the
Water striving
To re-establish its mirror
Over the rock

That drops and turns,
A white skull,
Eaten by weedy greens.
Years later I
Encounter them on the road—

Words dry and riderless,
The indefatigable hooftaps.
While
From the bottom of the pool, fixed stars
Govern a life.

1966

# Leonard Cohen

*b.* 1934

Born into a traditional Jewish family in Montreal, Leonard Cohen received his BA (1955) from McGill University. The following year, he published his first collection of poetry, *Let Us Compare Mythologies*, where he attempts to reconcile his Jewish beliefs with those of other cultures and religions; in this volume, and in his later poetry, he subverts religious dogmas by synthesizing systems of faith. He received the Governor General's Award for Poetry in 1968, which he declined. He has also published two novels, *The Favourite Game* (1963) and *Beautiful Losers* (1966). In addition to his writing, he pursues a distinguished career as a singer and songwriter; he has won Juno awards for Male Vocalist of the Year (1993), Songwriter of the Year (1994), and Artist of the Year (2013). His most recent volume of poetry is *Book of Longing* (2006). He now lives in Los Angeles with frequent trips back to the city of his birth.

## Prayer for Messiah

His blood on my arm is warm as a bird
his heart in my hand is heavy as lead
his eyes through my eyes shine brighter than love
O send out the raven ahead of the dove

His life in my mouth is less than a man
his death on my breast is harder than stone
his eyes through my eyes shine brighter than love
O send out the raven ahead of the dove

O send out the raven ahead of the dove
O sing from your chains where you're chained in a cave
your eyes through my eyes shine brighter than love
your blood in my ballad collapses the grave

O sing from your chains where you're chained in a cave
your eyes through my eyes shine brighter than love
your heart in my hand is heavy as lead
your blood on my arm is warm as a bird

O break from your branches a green branch of love
after the raven has died for the dove

1956

## Snow Is Falling

Snow is falling.
There is a nude in my room.
She surveys the wine-coloured carpet.

She is eighteen.
She has straight hair.
She speaks no Montreal language.

She doesn't feel like sitting down.
She shows no gooseflesh.
We can hear the storm.

She is lighting a cigarette
from the gas range.
She holds back her long hair.

1958

## A Kite Is a Victim

A kite is a victim you are sure of.
You love it because it pulls
gentle enough to call you master,
strong enough to call you fool;
because it lives
like a desperate trained falcon
in the high sweet air,
and you can always haul it down
to tame it in your drawer.

A kite is a fish you have already caught
in a pool where no fish come,
so you play him carefully and long,
and hope he won't give up,
or the wind die down.

A kite is the last poem you've written,
so you give it to the wind,
but you don't let it go
until someone finds you
something else to do.

A kite is a contract of glory
that must be made with the sun,
so you make friends with the field
the river and the wind,
then you pray the whole cold night before,
under the travelling cordless moon,
to make you worthy and lyric and pure.

1961

## What I'm Doing Here

I do not know if the world has lied
I have lied
I do not know if the world has conspired against love
I have conspired against love
The atmosphere of torture is no comfort
I have tortured
Even without the mushroom cloud
still I would have hated
Listen
I would have done the same things
even if there were no death
I will not be held like a drunkard
under the cold tap of facts
I refuse the universal alibi

Like an empty telephone booth passed at night
and remembered
like mirrors in a movie palace lobby consulted
only on the way out
like a nymphomaniac who binds a thousand
into strange brotherhood
I wait
for each one of you to confess

1964

## I Threw Open the Shutters

I threw open the shutters:
light fell on these lines
(which are incomplete)
It fell on two words
which I must erase:
name of a man
tortured on a terrace
above a well-known street
I swore by the sunlight
to take his advice:
remove all evidence from my verse
forget about his punctured feet

1972

## Never Mind

The war was lost
The treaty signed
I was not caught
I crossed the line

I had to leave
My life behind
I had a name
But never mind

Your victory
Was so complete
That some among you
Thought to keep

A record of
Our little truth
The cloth we wove
The tools we used

The games of luck
Our soldiers played
The stones we cut
The songs we made

Our law of peace
Which understands
A husband leads
A wife commands

And all of this
Expressions of
The Sweet Indifference
Some call Love

The Sweet Indifference
Some call Fate
But we had Names
More intimate

Names so deep
and Names so true
They're lost to me
And dead to you

There is no need
That this survive
There's truth that lives
And truth that dies

There's truth that lives
And truth that dies
I don't know which
So never mind

I could not kill
The way you kill
I could not hate
I tried I failed

No man can see
The vast design
Or who will be
Last of his kind

The story's told
With facts and lies
You own the world
So never mind

2006

# Seamus Heaney

1939–2013

Born in Castledawson, Northern Ireland, Seamus Heaney received his BA (1961) from Queen's University Belfast. He then pursued a career in teaching while exploring his own poetic talents. In 1966 he brought out his first major collection, *Death of a Naturalist*; in his life he published more than a dozen major collections as well as countless translations, including his award-winning translation of *Beowulf*.

Although he maintained his Irish residence, first in Belfast and then from 1972 in Dublin, he taught at Harvard University from 1981 until 2006 and served as professor of poetry at Oxford University from 1989 until 1994. 'With his wonderful gift of eye and ear', Robert Pinsky has remarked, 'Heaney has the gift of the story-teller'. In 1995 he received the Nobel Prize for Literature for 'works of lyrical beauty and ethical depth, which exalt everyday miracles and the living past'. Heaney won the Griffin Lifetime Recognition Award in 2012.

## Requiem for the Croppies

The pockets of our greatcoats full of barley—
No kitchens on the run, no striking camp—
We moved quick and sudden in our own country.
The priest lay behind ditches with the tramp.
A people, hardly marching—on the hike—
We found new tactics happening each day:
We'd cut through reins and rider with the pike
And stampede cattle into infantry,
Then retreat through hedges where cavalry must be
thrown.
Until, on Vinegar Hill, the fatal conclave.
Terraced thousands died, shaking scythes at cannon.
The hillside blushed, soaked in our broken wave.
They buried us without shroud or coffin
And in August the barley grew up out of the grave.

1969

# Traditions

*for Tom Flanagan*

I

Our guttural muse
was bulled long ago
by the alliterative tradition,
her uvula grows

vestigial, forgotten
like the coccyx
or a Brigid's Cross
yellowing in some outhouse

while custom, that 'most
sovereign mistress',
beds us down into
the British isles.

II

We are to be proud
of our Elizabethan English:
'varsity', for example,
is grass-roots stuff with us;

we 'deem' or we 'allow'
when we suppose
and some cherished archaisms
are correct Shakespearean.

Not to speak of the furled
consonants of lowlanders
shuttling obstinately
between bawn and mossland.

III

MacMorris, gallivanting
round the Globe, whinged
to courtier and groundling
who had heard tell of us

as going very bare
of learning, as wild hares,
as anatomies of death:
'What ish my nation?'

And sensibly, though so much
later, the wandering Bloom
replied, 'Ireland,' said Bloom,
'I was born here. Ireland.'

1972

## Seeing Things

I

Inishbofin on a Sunday morning.
Sunlight, turfsmoke, seagulls, boatslip, diesel.
One by one we were being handed down
Into a boat that dipped and shilly-shallied
Scaresomely every time. We sat tight
On short cross-benches, in nervous twos and threes,
Obedient, newly close, nobody speaking
Except the boatmen, as the gunwales sank
And seemed they might ship water any minute.
The sea was very calm but even so,
When the engine kicked and our ferryman
Swayed for balance, reaching for the tiller,
I panicked at the shiftiness and heft
Of the craft itself. What guaranteed us—
That quick response and buoyancy and swim—
Kept me in agony. All the time
As we went sailing evenly across
The deep, still, seeable-down-into water,
It was as if I looked from another boat
Sailing through air, far up, and could see
How riskily we fared into the morning,
And loved in vain our bare, bowed, numbered heads.

II

*Claritas.* The dry-eyed Latin word
Is perfect for the carved stone of the water
Where Jesus stands up to his unwet knees
And John the Baptist pours out more water
Over his head: all this in bright sunlight
On the façade of a cathedral. Lines
Hard and thin and sinuous represent
The flowing river. Down between the lines
Little antic fish are all go. Nothing else.
And yet in that utter visibility
The stone's alive with what's invisible:
Waterweed, stirred sand-grains hurrying off,
The shadowy, unshadowed stream itself.
All afternoon, heat wavered on the steps
And the air we stood up to our eyes in wavered
Like the zig-zag hieroglyph for life itself.

III

Once upon a time my undrowned father
Walked into our yard. He had gone to spray
Potatoes in a field on the riverbank
And wouldn't bring me with him. The horse-
 sprayer
Was too big and new-fangled, bluestone might
Burn me in the eyes, the horse was fresh, I
Might scare the horse, and so on. I threw stones
At a bird on the shed roof, as much for
The clatter of the stones as anything,
But when he came back, I was inside the house
And saw him out the window, scatter-eyed
And daunted, strange without his hat,
His step unguided, his ghosthood immanent.
When he was turning on the riverbank,
The horse had rusted and reared up and pitched
Cart and sprayer and everything off balance
So the whole rig went over into a deep
Whirlpool, hoofs, chains, shafts, cartwheels, barrel
And tackle, all tumbling off the world,
And the hat already merrily swept along

The quieter reaches. That afternoon
I saw him face to face, he came to me
With his damp footprints out of the river,
And there was nothing between us there
That might not still be happily ever after.

1991

## The Schoolbag

*In Memoriam John Hewitt*

My handsewn leather schoolbag. Forty years.
Poet, you were *nel mezzo del cammin*
When I shouldered it, half-full of blue-lined jotters,
And saw the classroom charts, the displayed bean,

The wallmap with its spray of shipping lanes
Describing arcs across the blue North Channel . . .
And in the middle of the road to school,
Ox-eye daisies and wild dandelions.

*Learning's easy carried!* The bag is light,
Scuffed and supple and unemptiable
As an itinerant school conjuror's hat.
So take it, for a word-hoard and a handsel,

As you step out trig and look back all at once
Like a child on his first morning leaving parents.

1991

## The Crossing

(*Inferno*, Canto III, Lines 82–129)

And there in a boat that came heading towards us
Was an old man, his hair snow-white with age,
Raging and bawling, 'Woe to you, wicked spirits!

O never hope to see the heavenly skies!
I come to bring you to the other shore,
To eternal darkness, to the fire and ice.

And you there, you, the living soul, separate
Yourself from these others who are dead.'
But when he saw that I did not stand aside

He said, 'By another way, by other harbours
You shall reach a different shore and pass over.
A lighter boat must be your carrier.'

And my guide said, 'Quiet your anger, Charon.
There where all can be done that has been willed
This has been willed; so there can be no question.'

Then straightaway he shut his grizzled jaws,
The ferryman of that livid marsh,
Who had wheels of fire flaming round his eyes.

But as soon as they had heard the cruel words,
Those lost souls, all naked and exhausted,
Changed their colour and their teeth chattered;

They blasphemed God and their parents on the earth,
The human race, the place and date and seedbed
Of their own begetting and of their birth,

Then all together, bitterly weeping, made
Their way towards the accursed shore that waits
For every man who does not fear his God.

The demon Charon's eyes are like hot coals fanned.
He beckons them and herds all of them in
And beats with his oar whoever drops behind:

As one by one the leaves fall off in autumn
Until at last the branch is bare and sees
All that was looted from it on the ground,

So the bad seed of Adam, at a signal
Pitch themselves off that shore one by one,
Each like a falcon answering its call.

They go away like this over the brown waters
And before they have landed on the other side
Upon this side once more a new crowd gathers.

'My son,' the courteous master said to me,
'All those who die under the wrath of God
Come together here from every country

And they are eager to go across the river
Because Divine Justice goads them with its spur
So that their fear is turned into desire.

No good spirits ever pass this way
And therefore, if Charon objects to you,
You should understand well what his words imply.'

1991

# Margaret Atwood
## *b.* 1939

The most prolific writer of her generation in Canada, Margaret Atwood is the author and editor of more than 30 books of poetry, short fiction, and literary criticism, as well as novels. Born in Ottawa, she spent her early years in the bush country of Quebec and northern Ontario; when she was seven years old, her family settled in Toronto. Atwood graduated from the University of Toronto in 1961, obtained her MA from Radcliffe College, and pursued doctoral studies in Victorian literature at Harvard University. Her first volume of poetry, *Double Persephone*, appeared in 1961; her first novel, *The Edible Woman*, appeared in 1967. She sees her work, poetry and fiction, as an artistic lens focused carefully and caringly on contemporary society. Her poetry, which may seem almost prosaic in its stark verse patterns, captures with clinical precision the subjects of her sensitive explorations. An ardent nationalist, she is a frequent and articulate speaker for Canada on both the national and international stages.

### At the Tourist Centre in Boston

There is my country under glass,
a white relief-
map with red dots for the cities,
reduced to the size of a wall

and beside it 10 blownup snapshots
one for each province,
in purple-browns and odd reds,
the green of the trees dulled;
all blues however
of an assertive purity.

Mountains and lakes and more lakes
(though Quebec is a restaurant and Ontario the empty
interior of the parliament buildings),
with nobody climbing the trails and hauling out
the fish and splashing in the water

but arrangements of grinning tourists—
look here, Saskatchewan
is a flat lake, some convenient rocks
where two children pose with a father
and the mother is cooking something
in immaculate slacks by a smokeless fire,
her teeth white as detergent.

Whose dream is this, I would like to know:
is this a manufactured
hallucination, a cynical fiction, a lure
for export only?

I seem to remember people,
at least in the cities, also slush,
machines and assorted garbage. Perhaps
that was my private mirage
which will just evaporate
when I go back. Or the citizens will be gone,
run off to the peculiarly-
green forests
to wait among the brownish mountains
for the platoons of tourists
and plan their old red massacres.

1968

## Progressive Insanities of a Pioneer

I

He stood, a point
on a sheet of green paper
proclaiming himself the centre,

with no walls, no borders
anywhere; the sky no height
above him, totally un-
enclosed
and shouted:

Let me out!

II

He dug the soil in rows,
imposed himself with shovels.
He asserted
into the furrows, I
am not random.

The ground
replied with aphorisms:

a tree-sprout, a nameless
weed, words
he couldn't understand.

III

The house pitched
the plot staked
in the middle of nowhere.

At night the mind
inside, in the middle
of nowhere.

The idea of an animal
patters across the roof.

In the darkness the fields
defend themselves with fences
in vain:
        everything
        is getting in.

IV

By daylight he resisted.
Be said, disgusted
with the swamp's clamourings and the outbursts
of rocks,
        This is not order
        but the absence
        of order.

He was wrong, the unanswering
forest implied:

        It was
        an ordered absence

V

For many years
he fished for a great vision,
dangling the hooks of sown
roots under the surface
the shallow earth.

It was like
enticing whales with a bent
pin. Besides he thought

in that country
only the worms were biting.

VI

If he had known unstructured
space is a deluge
and stocked his log house-
boat with all the animals

even the wolves,

he might have floated.

But obstinate he
stated, The land is solid
and stamped,

watching his foot sink
down through stone
up to the knee.

VII

Things
refused to name themselves; refused
to let him name them.

The wolves hunted
outside.

On his beaches, his clearings,
by the surf of under-
growth breaking
at his feet, he foresaw
disintegration
                    and in the end
through eyes
made ragged by his
effort, the tension
between subject and object,

the green
vision, the unnamed
whale invaded.

1968

## Variations on the Word *Love*

This is a word we use to plug
holes with. It's the right size for those warm
blanks in speech, for those red heart-
shaped vacancies on the page that look nothing
like real hearts. Add lace
and you can sell
it. We insert it also in the one empty
space on the printed form
that comes with no instructions. There are whole
magazines with not much in them
but the word *love*, you can
rub it all over your body and you
can cook with it too. How do we know
it isn't what goes on at the cool
debaucheries of slugs under damp
pieces of cardboard? As for the weed-
seedlings nosing their tough snouts up
among the lettuces, they shout it.
Love! Love! sing the soldiers, raising
their glittering knives in salute.

Then there's the two
of us. This word
is far too short for us, it has only
four letters, too sparse
to fill those deep bare
vacuums between the stars
that press on us with their deafness.
It's not love we don't wish
to fall into, but that fear.
This word is not enough but it will
have to do. It's a single
vowel in this metallic
silence, a mouth that says
O again and again in wonder
and pain, a breath, a finger-
grip on a cliffside. You can
hold on or let go.

1981

## Variation on the Word *Sleep*

I would like to watch you sleeping,
which may not happen.
I would like to watch you,
sleeping. I would like to sleep
with you, to enter
your sleep as its smooth dark wave
slides over my head

and walk with you through that lucent
wavering forest of bluegreen leaves
with its watery sun & three moons
towards the cave where you must descend,
towards your worst fear
I would like to give you the silver
branch, the small white flower, the one
word that will protect you
from the grief at the centre
of your dream, from the grief
at the centre. I would like to follow
you up the long stairway
again & become
the boat that would row you back
carefully, a flame
in two cupped hands
to where your body lies
beside me, and you enter
it as easily as breathing in

I would like to be the air
that inhabits you for a moment
only. I would like to be that unnoticed
& that necessary.

1981

## Interlunar

Darkness waits apart from any occasion for it;
like sorrow it is always available.
This is only one kind,

the kind in which there are stars
above the leaves, brilliant as steel nails
and countless and without regard.

We are walking together
on dead wet leaves in the intermoon
among the looming nocturnal rocks
which would be pinkish grey
in daylight, gnawed and softened
by moss and ferns, which would be green,
in the musty fresh yeast smell
of trees rotting, each returning
itself to itself

and I take your hand, which is the shape a hand
would be if you existed truly.
I wish to show you the darkness
you are so afraid of.

Trust me. This darkness
is a place you can enter and be
as safe in as you are anywhere;
you can put one foot in front of the other
and believe the sides of your eyes.
Memorize it. You will know it
again in your own time.
When the appearances of things have left you,
you will still have this darkness.
Something of your own you can carry with you.

We have come to the edge:
the lake gives off its hush;
in the outer night there is a barred owl
calling, like a moth
against the ear, from the far shore
which is invisible.
The lake, vast and dimensionless,
doubles everything, the stars,
the boulders, itself, even the darkness
that you can walk so long in
it becomes light.

1984

## The Door

The door swings open,
you look in.
It's dark in there,
most likely spiders:
nothing you want.
You feel scared.
The door swings closed.

The full moon shines,
it's full of delicious juice;
you buy a purse,
the dance is nice.
The door opens
and swings closed so quickly
you don't notice.

The sun comes out,
you have swift breakfasts
with your husband, who is still thin;
you wash the dishes,
you love your children,
you read a book,
you go to the movies.
It rains moderately.

The door swings open,
you look in:
why does this keep happening now?
Is there a secret?
The door swings closed.

The snow falls,
you clear the walk while breathing heavily;
it's not as easy as once.
Your children telephone sometimes.
The roof needs fixing.
You keep yourself busy.
The spring arrives.

The door swings open:
it's dark in there,
with many steps going down.

But what is that shining?
Is it water?
The door swings closed.

The dog has died.
This happened before.
You got another;
not this time though.
Where is your husband?
You gave up the garden.
It became too much.
At night there are blankets;
nonetheless you are wakeful.

The door swings open:
O god of hinges,
god of long voyages,
you have kept faith.
It's dark in there.
You confide yourself to the darkness.
You step in.
The door swings closed.

2007

# Robert Pinsky

## *b.* 1940

Born in Long Branch, New Jersey, Robert Pinsky received his BA from Rutgers University and his MA and PhD from Stanford University. Currently professor in the writing program at Boston University, he is a careful, erudite poet who seeks full engagement with his equally careful readers. Observing that 'the kind of poetry I write emphasizes the physical qualities of the words', he sees poetry as a vocal art; the most significant aspect of poetry for Pinsky is the rhythm of the words. In 1997 he became the poet laureate consultant in poetry to the Library of Congress, the first poet to hold this position for three terms. He is the founder of the Favourite Poem Project—a project that emerged from Pinsky's belief that poetry plays a major role in American culture—which films Americans of various ages and backgrounds reciting their favourite poems.

## The Figured Wheel

The figured wheel rolls through shopping malls and prisons,
Over farms, small and immense, and the rotten little downtowns.
Covered with symbols, it mills everything alive and grinds
The remains of the dead in the cemeteries, in unmarked graves and oceans.

Sluiced by salt water and fresh, by pure and contaminated rivers,
By snow and sand, it separates and recombines all droplets and grains,
Even the infinite sub-atomic particles crushed under the illustrated,
Varying treads of its wide circumferential track.

Spraying flecks of tar and molten rock it rumbles
Through the Antarctic station of American sailors and technicians,
And shakes the floors and windows of whorehouses for diggers and smelters
From Bethany, Pennsylvania to a practically nameless, semi-penal New Town

In the mineral-rich tundra of the Soviet northernmost settlements.
Artists illuminate it with pictures and incised mottoes
Taken from the Ten Thousand Stories and the Register of True Dramas.
They hang it with colored ribbons and with bells of many pitches.

With paints and chisels and moving lights they record
On its rotating surface the elegant and terrifying doings
Of the inhabitants of the Hundred Pantheons of major Gods
Disposed in iconographic stations at hub, spoke and concentric bands,

And also the grotesque demi-Gods, Hopi gargoyles and Ibo dryads.
They cover it with wind-chimes and electronic instruments
That vibrate as it rolls to make an all-but-unthinkable music,
So that the wheel hums and rings as it turns through the births of stars

And through the dead-world of bomb, fireblast and fallout
Where only a few doomed races of insects fumble in the smoking grasses.
It is Jesus oblivious to hurt turning to give words to the unrighteous,
And is also Gogol's feeding pig that without knowing it eats a baby chick

And goes on feeding. It is the empty armor of My Cid, clattering
Into the arrows of the credulous unbelievers, a metal suit
Like the lost astronaut revolving with his useless umbilicus
Through the cold streams, neither energy nor matter, that agitate

The cold, cyclical dark, turning and returning.
Even in the scorched and frozen world of the dead after the holocaust

The wheel as it turns goes on accreting ornaments.
Scientists and artists festoon it from the grave with brilliant

Toys and messages, jokes and zodiacs, tragedies conceived
From among the dreams of the unemployed and the pampered,
The listless and the tortured. It is hung with devices
By dead masters who have survived by reducing themselves magically

To tiny organisms, to wisps of matter, crumbs of soil,
Bits of dry skin, microscopic flakes, which is why they are called 'great',
In their humility that goes on celebrating the turning
Of the wheel as it rolls unrelentingly over

A cow plodding through car-traffic on a street in Iasi,
And over the haunts of Robert Pinsky's mother and father
And wife and children and his sweet self
Which he hereby unwillingly and inexpertly gives up, because it is

There, figured and pre-figured in the nothing-transfiguring wheel.

1984

## From the Childhood of Jesus

One Saturday morning he went to the river to play.
He modeled twelve sparrows out of the river clay

And scooped a clear pond, with a dam of twigs and mud.
Around the pond he set the birds he had made,

Evenly as the hours. Jesus was five. He smiled,
As a child would who had made a little world

Of clear still water and clay beside a river.
But a certain Jew came by, a friend of his father,

And he scolded the child and ran at once to Joseph,
Saying, 'Come see how your child has profaned the Sabbath,

Making images at the river on the Day of Rest.'
So Joseph came to the place and took his wrist

And told him, 'Child, you have offended the Word.'
Then Jesus freed the hand that Joseph held

And clapped his hands and shouted to the birds
To go away. They raised their beaks at his words

And breathed and stirred their feathers and flew away.
The people were frightened. Meanwhile, another boy,

The son of Annas the scribe, had idly taken
A branch of driftwood and leaning against it had broken

The dam and muddied the little pond and scattered
The twigs and stones. Then Jesus was angry and shouted,

'Unrighteous, impious, ignorant, what did the water
Do to harm you? Now you are going to wither

The way a tree does, you shall bear no fruit
And no leaves, you shall wither down to the root.'

At once, the boy was all withered. His parents moaned,
The Jews gasped, Jesus began to leave, then turned

And prophesied, his child's face wet with tears:
'Twelve times twelve times twelve thousands of years

Before these heavens and this earth were made,
The Creator set a jewel in the throne of God

With Hell on the left and Heaven to the right,
The Sanctuary in front, and behind, an endless night

Endlessly fleeing a Torah written in flame.
And on that jewel in the throne, God wrote my name.'

Then Jesus left and went into Joseph's house.
The family of the withered one also left the place,

Carrying him home. The Sabbath was nearly over.
By dusk, the Jews were all gone from the river.

Small creatures came from the undergrowth to drink
And foraged in the shadows along the bank.

Alone in his cot in Joseph's house, the Son
Of Man was crying himself to sleep. The moon

Rose higher, the Jews put out their lights and slept,
And all was calm and as it had been, except

In the agitated household of the scribe Annas,
And high in the dark, where unknown even to Jesus

The twelve new sparrows flew aimlessly through the night,
Not blinking or resting, as if never to alight.

1990

## Shirt

The back, the yoke, the yardage. Lapped seams,
The nearly invisible stitches along the collar
Turned in a sweatshop by Koreans or Malaysians

Gossiping over tea and noodles on their break
Or talking money or politics while one fitted
This armpiece with its overseam to the band

Of cuff I button at my wrist. The presser, the cutter,
The wringer, the mangle. The needle, the union,
The treadle, the bobbin. The code. The infamous blaze

At the Triangle Factory in nineteen-eleven.
One hundred and forty-six died in the flames
On the ninth floor, no hydrants, no fire escapes—

The witness in a building across the street
Who watched how a young man helped a girl to step
up to the windowsill, then held her out

Away from the masonry wall and let her drop.
And then another. As if he were helping them up
To enter a streetcar, and not eternity.

A third before he dropped her put her arms
Around his neck and kissed him. Then he held
Her into space, and dropped her. Almost at once

He stepped to the sill himself, his jacket flared
And fluttered up from his shirt as he came down,
Air filling up the legs of his gray trousers—

Like Hart Crane's Bedlamite, 'shrill shirt ballooning'
Wonderful how the pattern matches perfectly
Across the placket and over the twin bar-tacked

Corners of both pockets, like a strict rhyme
Or a major chord. Prints, plaids, checks,
Houndstooth, Tattersall, Madras. The clan tartans

Invented by mill-owners inspired by the hoax of Ossian,
To control their savage Scottish workers, tamed
By a fabricated heraldry: MacGregor,

Bailey, MacMartin. The kilt, devised for workers
To wear among the dusty clattering looms.
Weavers, carders, spinners. The loader,

The docker, the navvy. The planter, the picker, the sorter
Sweating at her machine in a litter of cotton
As slaves in calico headrags sweated in fields:

George Herbert, your descendant is a Black
Lady in South Carolina, her name is Irma
And she inspected my shirt. Its color and fit

And feel and its clean smell have satisfied
Both her and me. We have culled its cost and quality
Down to the buttons of simulated bone,

The buttonholes, the sizing, the facing, the characters
Printed in black on neckband and tail. The shape,
The label, the labor, the color, the shade. The shirt.

1990

## At Pleasure Bay

In the willows along the river at Pleasure Bay
A catbird singing, never the same phrase twice.
Here under the pines a little off the road
In 1927 the Chief of Police
And Mrs W. killed themselves together,
Sitting in a roadster. Ancient unshaken pilings
And underwater chunks of still-mortared brick
In shapes like bits of puzzle strew the bottom
Where the landing was for Price's Hotel and Theater.
And here's where boats blew two blasts for the keeper
To shunt the iron swing-bridge. He leaned on the gears
Like a skipper in the hut that housed the works
And the bridge moaned and turned on its middle pier
To let them through. In the middle of the summer
Two or three cars might wait for the iron trusswork
Winching aside, with maybe a child to notice
A name on the stern in black-and-gold on white,
*Sandpiper, Patsy Ann, Do Not Disturb,*
*The Idler.* If a boat was running whiskey,
The bridge clanged shut behind it as it passed
And opened up again for the Coast Guard cutter
Slowly as a sundial, and always jammed halfway.
The roadbed whole, but opened like a switch,
The river pulling and coursing between the piers.
Never the same phrase twice, the catbird filling
The humid August evening near the inlet
With borrowed music that he melds and changes.
Dragonflies and sandflies, frogs in the rushes, two bodies
Not moving in the open car among the pines,
A sliver of story. The tenor at Price's Hotel,
In clown costume, unfurls the sorrow gathered
In ruffles at his throat and cuffs, high quavers
That hold like splashes of light on the dark water,
The aria's closing phrases, changed and fading.
And after a gap of quiet, cheers and applause
Audible in the houses across the river,
Some in the audience weeping as if they had melted
Inside the music. Never the same. In Berlin
The daughter of an English lord, in love
With Adolf Hitler, whom she has met. She is taking
Possession of the apartment of a couple,

Elderly well-off Jews. They survive the war
To settle here in the Bay, the old lady
Teaches piano, but the whole world swivels
And gapes at their feet as the girl and a high-up Nazi
Examine the furniture, the glass, the pictures,
The elegant story that was theirs and now
Is a part of hers. A few months later the English
Enter the war and she shoots herself in a park,
An addled, upper-class girl, her life that passes
Into the lives of others or into a place.
The taking of lives—the Chief and Mrs W.
Took theirs to stay together, as local ghosts.
Last flurries of kisses, the revolver's barrel,
Shivers of a story that a child might hear
And half remember, voices in the rushes,
A singing in the willows. From across the river,
Faint quavers of music, the same phrase twice and again,
Ranging and building. Over the high new bridge
The flashing of traffic homeward from the racetrack,
With one boat chugging under the arches, outward
Unnoticed through Pleasure Bay to the open sea.
Here's where the people stood to watch the theater
Burn on the water. All that night the fireboats
Kept playing their spouts of water into the blaze.
In the morning, smoking pilasters and beams.
Black smell of char for weeks, the ruin already
Soaking back into the river. After you die
You hover near the ceiling above your body
And watch the mourners awhile. A few days more
You float above the heads of the ones you knew
And watch them through a twilight. As it grows darker
You wander off and find your way to the river
And wade across. On the other side, night air,
Willows, the smell of the river, and a mass
Of sleeping bodies all along the bank,
A kind of singing from among the rushes
Calling you further forward in the dark.
You lie down and embrace one body, the limbs
Heavy with sleep reach eagerly up around you
And you make love until your soul brims up
And burns free out of you and shifts and spills
Down over into that other body, and you
Forget the life you had and begin again
On the same crossing—maybe as a child who passes

Through the same place. But never the same way twice.
Here in the daylight, the catbird in the willows,
The new café, with a terrace and a landing,
Frogs in the cattails where the swing-bridge was—
Here's where you might have slipped across the water
When you were only a presence, at Pleasure Bay.

1990

# Michael Ondaatje

*b.* 1943

Born in Sri Lanka (then Ceylon), Michael Ondaatje moved to England in 1954 before settling in Canada in 1963. He obtained his BA from the University of Toronto and his MA from Queen's University. He taught English at the University of Western Ontario before joining the Department of English at Glendon College, York University, in 1971. Poet and novelist, critic and editor, he constantly questions the dimension between poetry and prose and between fact and fiction in writing that challenges his readers' perception and understanding of reality. *The Collected Works of Billy the Kid* (1970), a collage of poetry, prose, and photographs, is a discontinuous narrative of Billy the Kid and Pat Garrett that explores the traditional interpretation of this duo as insane outlaw-renegade and sane representative of law and order. *Running in the Family* (1982), also a collage, is the story of Ondaatje's own family, transformed into fiction. Always intensely visual, his poetry eschews formal structures in order to capture with vivid immediacy the dramatic dimensions of a particular character or moment. He has won international acclaim for both his poetry and his novels, including *The English Patient*, which was awarded the prestigious Booker Prize and made into a successful Hollywood film.

## Letters & Other Worlds

*'for there was no more darkness for him and, no doubt like
Adam before the fall, he could see in the dark'* [1]

My father's body was a globe of fear
His body was a town we never knew
He hid that he had been where we were going
His letters were a room he seldom lived in
In them the logic of his love could grow

1 translation from Alfred Jarry's *La Dragonne* (1943), cited in *The Banquet Years* by Roger Shattuck (1955)

My father's body was a town of fear
He was the only witness to its fear dance
He hid where he had been that we might lose him
His letters were a room his body scared

He came to death with his mind drowning.
On the last day he enclosed himself
in a room with two bottles of gin, later
fell the length of his body
so that brain blood moved
to new compartments
that never knew the wash of fluid
and he died in minutes of a new equilibrium.

His early life was a terrifying comedy
and my mother divorced him again and again.
He would rush into tunnels magnetized
by the white eye of trains
and once, gaining instant fame,
managed to stop a Perahara[2] in Ceylon
—the whole procession of elephants dancers
local dignitaries—by falling
dead drunk into the street.

As a semi-official, and semi-white at that,
the act was seen as a crucial
turning point in the Home Rule Movement
and led to Ceylon's independence in 1948.
(My mother had done her share too—
her driving so bad
she was stoned by villagers
whenever her car was recognized)

For 14 years of marriage
each of them claimed he or she
was the injured party.
Once on the Colombo docks
saying goodbye to a recently married couple
my father, jealous
at my mother's articulate emotion,
dove into the waters of the harbour
and swam after the ship waving farewell.

2 religious ceremony celebrated by a parade

My mother pretending no affiliation
mingled with the crowd back to the hotel.

Once again he made the papers
though this time my mother
with a note to the editor
corrected the report—saying he was drunk
rather than broken hearted at the parting of friends.
The married couple received both editions
of *The Ceylon Times* when their ship reached Aden.[3]

And then in his last years
he was a silent drinker,
the man who once a week
disappeared into his room with bottles
and stayed there until he was drunk
and until he was sober.

There speeches, head dreams, apologies,
the gentle letters, were composed.
With the clarity of architects
he would write of the row of blue flowers
his new wife had planted,
the plans for electricity in the house,
how my half-sister fell near a snake
and it had awakened and not touched her.
Letters in a clear hand of the most complete empathy
his heart widening and widening and widening
to all manner of change in his children and friends
while he himself edged
into the terrible acute hatred
of his own privacy
till he balanced and fell
the length of his body
the blood screaming in
the empty reservoir of bones
the blood searching in his head without metaphor

1973

3 capital of the British colony of the same name (Aden is now the capital of Southern Yemen)

## Bearhug

Griffin calls to come and kiss him goodnight
I yell ok. Finish something I'm doing,
then something else, walk slowly round
the corner to my son's room.
He is standing arms outstretched
waiting for a bearhug. Grinning.

Why do I give my emotion an animal's name,
give it that dark squeeze of death?
This is the hug which collects
all his small bones and his warm neck against me.
The thin tough body under the pyjamas
locks to me like a magnet of blood.

How long was he standing there
like that, before I came?

1979

## Elizabeth

Catch, my Uncle Jack said
and oh I caught this huge apple
red as Mrs Kelly's bum.
It's red as Mrs Kelly's bum, I said
and Daddy roared
and swung me on his stomach with a heave.
Then I hid the apple in my room
till it shrunk like a face
growing eyes and teeth ribs.

Then Daddy took me to the zoo
he knew a man there
they put a snake around my neck
and it crawled down the front of my dress.
I felt its flicking tongue
dripping onto me like a shower.
Daddy laughed and said Smart Snake
and Mrs Kelly with us scowled.

In the pond where they kept the goldfish
Philip and I broke the ice with spades
and tried to spear the fishes;

we killed one and Phillip ate it,
then he kissed me
with raw saltless fish in his mouth.

My sister Mary's got bad teeth
and said I was lucky, then she said
I had big teeth, but Philip said I was pretty.
He had big hands that smelled.

I would speak of Tom, soft laughing,
who danced in the mornings round the sundial
teaching me the steps from France, turning
with the rhythm of the sun on the warped branches,
who'd hold my breast and watch it move like a snail
leaving his quick urgent love in my palm.
And I kept his love in my palm till it blistered.

When they axed his shoulders and neck
the blood moved like a branch into the crowd.
And he staggered with his hanging shoulder
cursing their thrilled cry, wheeling,
waltzing in the French style to his knees
holding his head with the ground,
blood settling on his clothes like a blush;
this way
when they aimed the thud into his back.

And I find cool entertainment now
with white young Essex, and my nimble rhymes.[1]

1979

1 The 'Elizabeth' of this poem is Elizabeth I (1533–1603), who assumed the throne of England in 1558 following the reigns of her father, Henry VIII (1491–1547), her brother Edward VI (1537–53), and her sister Mary Tudor (1515–58). 'Philip' is Philip II of Spain (1527–98), who married Mary Tudor in 1554; 'Tom' is Lord Thomas Seymour of Sudeley (1508?–49), whose repeated attempts to compromise and marry the adolescent Elizabeth, as well as to overthrow his brother Edward Seymour, the protector of Edward VI, led to his execution; 'Essex' is the second Earl of Essex, Robert Devereux (1566–1601), soldier and favourite of Elizabeth, who was executed for attempting to incite an uprising against the court. 'Uncle Jack' and 'Mrs Kelly' are characters invented by Ondaatje.

## The Cinnamon Peeler

If I were a cinnamon peeler[1]
I would ride your bed
and leave the yellow bark dust
on your pillow.

Your breasts and shoulders would reek
you could never walk through markets
without the profession of my fingers
floating over you. The blind would
stumble certain of whom they approached
though you might bathe
under rain gutters, monsoon.

Here on the upper thigh
at this smooth pasture
neighbour to your hair
or the crease
that cuts your back. This ankle.
You will be known among strangers
as the cinnamon peeler's wife.

I could hardly glance at you
before marriage
never touch you
—your keen nosed mother, your rough brothers.
I buried my hands
in saffron, disguised them
over smoking tar,
helped the honey gatherers . . .

When we swam once
I touched you in water
and our bodies remained free,
you could hold me and be blind of smell.
You climbed on the bank and said

this is how you touch other women
the grass cutter's wife, the lime burner's daughter.
And you searched your arms
for the missing perfume
and knew

what good is it
to be the lime burner's daughter
left with no trace
as if not spoken to in the act of love
as if wounded without the pleasure of a scar.

1 one who peels the cinnamon bark, the source of the spice, from the trees

You touched
your belly to my hands
in the dry air and said
I am the cinnamon
peeler's wife. Smell me.

1982

# Robert Bringhurst

*b.* 1946

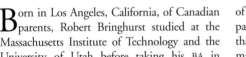

Born in Los Angeles, California, of Canadian parents, Robert Bringhurst studied at the Massachusetts Institute of Technology and the University of Utah before taking his BA in comparative literature from Indiana University (1973) and his MFA in creative writing from the University of British Columbia (1975). A restlessly intellectual poet who is never sentimental or confessional, he broke away from the modernist techniques of Pound and Eliot to create his own unique way of regarding the world around him. Showing little support for the crass materialism of the present age, he captures the beauty of the past and the wisdom of the ages in austere poetry that is often rich with allusions. 'I wanted—no matter how preposterous and impossible it might be—to learn all the words and grammars in the world', he affirms. 'Poetry nevertheless precedes them all and can make its way, if it must, with the help of none.' It is the importance Bringhurst places on the past that makes him a tireless researcher into North American cultural history, seeking an understanding of the diverse cultures and their oral literatures.

## Essay on Adam

There are five possibilities. One: Adam fell.
Two: he was pushed. Three: he jumped. Four:
he only looked over the edge, and one look silenced him.
Five: nothing worth mentioning happened to Adam.

The first, that he fell, is too simple. The fourth,
fear, we have tried. It is useless. The fifth,
nothing happened, is dull. The choices are these:
he jumped or was pushed. And the difference between them

is only an issue of whether the demons
work from the inside out or from the outside
in: the one
theological question.

1975

## The Stonecutter's Horses

*Sepe de eo mecum cogitans de quo nemo nimis pauci satis cogitant. . . .*[1]

§ Pavia, 4 April 1370:

Francesco Petrarca (1304–1374)[2]

[Francesca], *his illegitimate daughter*

Franceschino da Brossano, *in law Petrarca's adopted son, but in actuality his son-in-law*

I, Francesco, this April day . . .
death stirs like a bud in the sunlight, and Urban
has got off his French duff and re-entered Rome[3]
and for three years running has invited me to Rome . . .
over the bright hills and down the Cassia,
back through Arezzo one more time . . .
my age sixty-five and my birthday approaching,
the muggers on the streets in broad daylight in Rome,
the hawks and the buzzards. . . .
Take this down.

No one has thought too deeply of death.
So few have left anything toward or against it.
Peculiar, since thinking of death can never be
wasted thinking, nor can it be come to
too quickly. A man carries his death with him
everywhere, waiting, but seldom thinking
of waiting. Death is uncommonly like the soul.

What I own other than that ought to fall
of its own weight and settle. But beggars and tycoons
and I are concerned with our possessions,
and a man with a reputation for truth
must have one also for precision.
I leave
my soul to my saviour, my corpse to the earth.

1 'Thinking often about what no one considers very much and few enough. . . .'
2 the Italian poet, scholar, and humanist best known as Petrarch (the Latinized form of his name)
3 With the appointment of a French pope, Clement V, in 1305, the seat of the papacy was moved to Avignon and fell under the control of the French monarchy until 1378. Pope Urban V made an unsuccessful attempt to bring the papacy from Avignon to Rome (1367–70), a move Petrarch had long supported.

And let it be done without any parades.
I don't care very much where I'm buried,
so it please God and whoever is digging.
Still, you will ask. You will badger me.
If I am dead you will badger each other.
But don't lug my bones through the public streets
in a box to be gabbled at and gawked at and followed.
Let it be done without any parades.

If I die here in Padova, bury me here
near the friend who is dead who invited me here.
If I die on my farm, you can use the chapel
I mean to build there, if I ever build it.
If not, try the village down the road.

If in Venezia, near the doorway.
If in Milano, next to the wall.
In Pavia, anywhere. Or if in Rome—
if in Rome, in the centre, of course, if there's room.
These are the places I think I might die in
in Italy.
Or if I happen to be in Parma,
there is the cathedral, of which for some reason
I am the archdeacon. But I will avoid
going to Parma. It would scarcely be possible,
I suppose, in Parma, not to have a parade.

At any rate, put what flesh I have left
in a church. A Franciscan church if there is one.
I don't want it feeding a tree from which
rich people's children swipe apples.

Two hundred ducats go to the church in which
I am buried, with another hundred to be given
out in that parish to the poor, in small doses.
The money to the church, let it buy a piece of land
and the land be rented and the rental from the land
pay for an annual mass in my name.
I will be fitter company in that sanctuary
then, present in spirit and name only,
than this way, muttering to the blessed virgin
through my hemorrhoids and bad teeth. I should be glad
to be rid of this sagging carcass.
Don't write that.

I have cleared no fields of their stones. I have built
no barns and no castles. I have built a name
out of other men's voices by banging my own
like a kitchen pan. My name to the Church
with the money it takes to have it embalmed.

Very few other things. My Giotto[4] to the Duke.
Most men cannot fathom its beauty. Those
who know painting are stunned by it. The Duke
does not need another Giotto, but the Duke knows painting.

To Dondi,[5] money for a plain ring to remind him
to read me.
To Donato—what? I forgive him
the loan of whatever he owes me. And I
myself am in debt to della Seta. Pay
that, if I haven't paid it. And give him
my silver cup. Della Seta drinks
water. Damned metal ruins the wine.

To Boccaccio,[6] I am unworthy to leave
anything, and have nothing worthy to leave.
Money then, for a coat to keep himself warm
when he works after dark, as he frequently does,
while the river wind stutters and bleats at his window,
and his hand-me-down cordwood fizzles and steams.

My lute to Tommaso.[7] I hope he will play it
for God and himself and not to gain fame
for his playing.
These are such trivial legacies.

Money to Pancaldo,[8] but not for the card table.
Money to Zilio—at least his back salary.
Money to the other servants. Money to the cook.
Money to their heirs if they die before I do.

4 that is, a work by innovative Florentine painter Giotto di Bondone (*c.* 1267–1337)
5 Giovanni Dondi (*c.* 1318–1389), a noted humanist and friend of Petrarch's, a professor of medicine, mathematics, and philosophy. 'Donato' is Donato degli Albanzani da Pratovecchio, who translated Petrarch's *De viris illustribus*—a series of biographies of figures from Antiquity (begun *c.* 1338)—into Italian. Lombardo della Seta assisted Petrarch in the writing of this work.
6 Giovanni Boccaccio (1313–74), the famous Italian poet and storyteller best known for *The Decameron* (1351–3); his work was influenced by Petrarch, and they were lifelong friends from the time of their initial meeting in 1350. His old age was troubled by poverty and ill health.
7 The poet Tommaso Caloiro, also known as Tomasso da Messina, was a friend and correspondent of Petrarch's.
8 'Pancaldo': Like Zilio, one of Petrarch's servants.

Give my Bible back to the Church.
                                        And my horses . . .
my horses.
            Let a few of my friends, if they wish to,
draw lots for my horses. Horses
are horses. They cannot be given away.

The rest to my heir and executor, Brossano,
who knows he is to split it, and how he is to split it,
and the names I prefer not to put into this
instrument. Names of no other importance.
Care for them. Care for them here in this house
if you can. And don't sell off the land to get money
in any case. Selling the earth without cause
from the soul is simony, Brossano. Real-estate
hucksters are worse than funeral parades.
I have lived long enough in quite enough
cities, notwithstanding the gifts
of free lodging in some of them, long enough, Brossano,
to know the breath moves underfoot in the clay.
The stone quarried and cut and reset
in the earth is a lover's embrace, not an overlay.

The heart splits like a chinquapin pod,
spilling its angular seed on the ground.

Though we ride to Rome and back aboard animals,
nothing ever takes root on the move.
I have seen houses and fields bartered
like cargo on shipboard. But nothing takes root
without light in the eye and earth in the hand.

The land is our solitude and our silence.
A man should hoard what little silence
he is given and what little solitude he can get.

Just the one piece over the mountains
ought, I think, to be given away. Everything
I have ever done that has lasted began there.
And I think my heir will have no need to go there.

If Brossano die before I do,
look to della Seta. And for his part, let him
look into that cup. He will know my mind.

A man who can write as I can ought not
to talk of such things at such length. Keep this
back if you can. Let the gifts speak
for themselves if you can, small though they are.
But I don't like the thought of what little there is
spilling into the hands of lawyers through lawsuits.
The law is no ritual meant to be practised
in private by scavengers. Law is the celebration
of duty and the ceremony of vengeance. The Duke's
law has nothing to do with my death
or with horses.
                    Done.
                              Ask the notary to come over
precisely at noon. I will rewrite it
and have it to sign by the time he arrives.

1979

## Leda and the Swan[1]

*for George Faludy*

Before the black beak reappeared
like a grin from in back of a drained cup,
letting her drop,
she fed at the sideboard of his thighs,
the lank air tightening in the sunrise,
yes. But no, she put on no knowledge
with his power. And it was his power alone
that she saved of him for her daughter.
Not his knowledge.
No.
He was the one who put on knowledge.
He was the one who looked down out of heaven
with a dark croak, knowing more
than he had ever known before,
and knowing he knew it:

knowing the xylophone of her bones,
the lute of her back and the harp of her belly,
the flute of her throat,

1 Compare with Yeats's poem, p. 526

woodwinds and drums of her muscles,
knowing the organ pipes of her veins;

knowing her as a man knows mountains he has hunted
naked and alone in—
knowing the fruits, the roots and the grasses,
the tastes of the streams
and the depths of the mosses,
knowing as he moves in the darkness he is also
resting at noon in the shade of her blood—
leaving behind him in the sheltered places
glyphs meaning mineral and moonlight and mind
and possession and memory,
leaving on the outcrops signs meaning mountain
and sunlight and lust and rest and forgetting.

Yes. And the beak that opened to croak
of his knowing that morning creaked like a rehung
door and said nothing, felt nothing. The past
is past. What is known is as lean
as the day's edge and runs
one direction. The truth floats
down, out of fuel,
indigestible, like a feather. The lady
herself, though—whether
or not she was truth or untruth, or both, or was neither—
she dropped through the air like a looped rope,
a necklace of meaning, remembering
everything forward and backward—
the middle, the end, the beginning—
and lit like a fishing skiff gliding aground.

That evening, of course, while her husband, to whom
she told nothing, strode like the king
of Lakonia through the orchestra
pit of her body, touching
this key and that string in his passing,
she lay like so much
green kindling,
fouled tackle and horse harness under his hands
and said nothing, felt
nothing, but only
lay thinking
not flutes, lutes and xylophones,

no: thinking soldiers
and soldiers and soldiers and soldiers
and daughters,
the rustle of knives in his motionless wings.

1982

# Dionne Brand

## *b.* 1953

Dionne Brand was born in Guayaguayare, Trinidad, and emigrated in 1970 to Canada, where she 'joined the civil rights, feminist and socialist movements. I was only 17 but I already knew that to live freely in the world as a Black woman I would have to involve myself in political action as well as writing.' She obtained her BA (1975) in English and philosophy from the University of Toronto, later completing her MA (1988) in educational studies. As an editor and essayist as well as a poet and fiction writer, she concerns herself with the damage and tragedy brought about by sexism and racism, especially with the repression that continues to exist in Canada. From her own experiences as an immigrant in a supposedly tolerant new land, as someone from a racial minority, and as a lesbian, she writes cogently of dislocation. In *Land to Light On* (1997), which won the Governor General's Award for Poetry and the Trillium Award for Literature, she studies immigrant exile, voicing despair in a world brutalized by global politics and oppressed by its failure to achieve equality for women and racialized people. The immigrant condition is central also to *Thirsty* (2002), a long poem that presents the modern city of Toronto with a murky, indeed tragic underside. Brand won the Griffin Poetry Prize for *Ossuaries* (2010) in 2011.

## Islands Vanish

### XIII

In this country where islands vanish, bodies submerge,
the heart of darkness is these white roads, snow
at our throats, and at the windshield a thick white cop
in a blue steel windbreaker peering into our car, suspiciously,
even in the blow and freeze of a snowstorm, or perhaps
not suspicious but as a man looking at aliens.
Three Blacks in a car on a road blowing eighty miles an hour
in the wind between a gas station and Chatham. We stumble
on our antiquity. The snow-blue laser of a cop's eyes fixes us
in this unbearable archaeology.

How quickly the planet can take itself back. I saw this
once in the summer in daylight, corn dangling bronze, flat
farm land growing flatter, eaten up in highways, tonight,
big and rolling it is storming in its sleep. A cop is standing at its
lip.

Coca-Cola can light, the car shakes, trembles along as in a
gutter, a bellow of wind rushes into my face breathless
checking the snowbank, I might have seen something
out there, every two minutes the imagination conjures
an exact bridge, the mind insists on solidity, we lose
the light of the car ahead, in the jagged beam of the cop's
blistering eye we lose the names of things, the three of us,
two women who love women, one man with so many demons
already his left foot is cold, still, making our way to Chatham,
Buxton, waiting as they once waited for Black travellers like us,
blanketed, tracked in this cold shimmering.

Out there I see nothing . . . not one thing out there
just the indifference of a cop. It takes us six hours
to travel three. I coil myself up into a nerve and quarrel
with the woman, lover, and the man for landing me in
this white hell.

We have been in this icy science only a short time. What
we are doing here is not immediately understandable
and no one is more aware of it than we, she from Uganda
via Kenya running from arranged marriages, he from Sri
Lanka via Colombo English-style boarding school to make him
the minister of the interior, me hunting for slave castles with a
pencil for explosives, what did we know that our pan-colonial
flights would end up among people who ask stupid questions
like, where are you from . . . and now here we are on their road,
in their snow, faced with their childishness.

How are we to say that these paths are involuntary and
the line of trees we are looking for will exist when we
find it, that this snow is just a cipher for our feverishness.

Only Sarah Vaughan thank god sings in this snow, Sarah
and her big band . . . gotta right to sing the blues . . .

I desert the others to her voice, fanning fire, then, even Sarah
cannot take me away but she moves the car and we live
on whatever she's given to this song, each dive of her voice,
each swoop, her vibrato holds us to the road, the outcome
of this white depends on Sarah's entries and exits from a
note. We cannot turn back, ahead Buxton must hear this so we
can arrive, up ahead Sarah singing she can see the midnight sun.

Only this much sound, only this much breath, only this much
grace, only how long, only how much road can take us away.

That cop's face has it. 'They had been in this vast and dark
country only a short time.'[1] Something there, written as
wilderness, wood, nickel, water, coal, rock, prairie, erased
as Athabasca, Algonquin, Salish, Inuit . . . hooded in Buxton
fugitive, Preston Black Loyalist, railroaded to gold mountain,
swimming in *Komagata Maru* . . . Are we still moving?
Each body submerged in its awful history. When will we arrive?
In a motel room later, we laugh, lie that we are not harmed,
play poker and fall asleep, he on the floor with his demons,
she, legs wrapped around me.

How can we say that when we sign our names in letters
home no one can read them, when we send photographs
they vanish. Black heart, blackheart . . . can't take it tonight
across this old road . . . take me home some other way.

1997

1 from Joseph Conrad's 'An Outpost of Progress'

## From *thirsty*

### I

This city is beauty
unbreakable and amorous as eyelids,
in the streets, pressed with fierce departures,
submerged landings,
I am innocent as thresholds
and smashed night birds, lovesick,
as empty elevators

let me declare doorways,
corners, pursuit, let me say
standing here in eyelashes, in
invisible breasts, in the shrinking lake
in the tiny shops of untrue recollections,
the brittle, gnawed life we live,
I am held, and held

the touch of everything blushes me,
pigeons and wrecked boys,
half-dead hours, blind musicians,
inconclusive women in bruised dresses
even the habitual grey-suited men with terrible
briefcases, how come, how come
I anticipate nothing as intimate as history

would I have had a different life
failing this embrace with broken things,
iridescent veins, ecstatic bullets, small cracks
in the brain, would I know these particular facts,
how a phrase scars a cheek, how water
dries love out, this, a thought as casual
as any second eviscerates a breath
and this, we meet in careless intervals,
in coffee bars, gas stations, in prosthetic
conversations, lotteries, untranslatable
mouths, in versions of what we may be,
a tremor of the hand in the realization
of endings, a glancing blow of tears
on skin, the keen dismissal in speed

## II

There was a Sunday morning scent,
an early morning air, then the unarranged light
that hovers on a street before a city wakes
unrelieved to the war fumes of fuel exhaust

The city was empty, except for the three,
they seemed therefore poised, as when you are alone
anywhere all movement is arrested, light, dun,
except, their hearts, scintillant as darkness

clothy blooms of magnolia, bedraggled shrubs,
wept over a past winter, a car sped by,
scatterling from sleep, their mirage disquiets,
the subway, tumescent, expectant like a grave

They had hoped without salvation for a trolley,
they arrived at the corner impious, then,
wracked on the psalmody of the crossroad,
they felt, the absences of a morning

They circled sovereign thoughts, taking
for granted the morning, the solidity of things,
the bank to one corner, the driving school on another,
the milk store and the church

each her own separate weight,
each carried it in some drenched region of flesh,
the calculus of silence, its chaos,
the wraith and rate of absence pierced them

Chloe bathed in black, then the youngest,
leather bag strapped to a still school
girlish back, the last a precise look to her yet,
a violet lace, a hackle from forehead to neck

captured in individual doubt, a hesitation,
and what they could not put into words,
indevotion, on this eighteenth Sunday
every cool black-dressed year since 1980

This slender lacuna beguiles them,
a man frothing a biblical lexis at Christie
Pits, the small barren incline where his mad sermons
cursed bewildered subway riders, his faith unstrained

then nothing of him but his parched body's declension
a curved caesura, mangled with clippers, and
clematis cirrhosa and a budding grape vine he was still
to plant when he could, saying when he had fallen, '. . . thirsty . . .'

## III

That north burnt country ran me down
to the city, mordant as it is, the whole

terror of nights with yourself and what
will happen, animus, loose like that, sweeps
you to embrace its urban meter,
the caustic piss of streets,
you surrender your heart to a numb symmetry
of procedures, you study the metaphysics of
corporate instructions and not just,
besieged by now, the ragged, serrated theories
of dreams walking by, banked in sleep

that wild waiting at traffic lights off
the end of the world, where nothing is simple,
nothing, in the city there is no simple love
or simple fidelity, the heart is slippery,
the body convulsive with disguises
abandonments, everything is emptied,
wrappers, coffee cups, discarded shoes,
trucks, street corners, shop windows, cigarette
ends, lungs, ribs, eyes, love,
the exquisite rush of nothing,
the damaged horizon of skyscraping walls,
nights insomniac with pinholes of light

2002

# George Elliott Clarke

*b.* 1960

Born in Windsor Plains, Nova Scotia, George Elliott Clarke obtained his BA (1984) from the University of Waterloo, his MA (1986) from Dalhousie University, and his PhD (1993) from Queen's University. Activist, poet, playwright, and professor of literature at the University of Toronto, he hails from 'Africadia', a word he coined to suggest that he was formed by the combined inheritances of Africa and Acadia, regarding himself as a fusion of Black and Canadian. He is committed to the expansion of the traditions of Nova Scotia to include the contributions of the Black community. In his powerful verse novel *Whylah Falls* (1990) he recounts as fiction the true story of the 1985 death in Weymouth Falls of Graham Jarvis, whose killer was ultimately acquitted by an all-white jury; the poems celebrate both the enduring vitality and the tragedy of this small community. His most recent collection of poetry is *I & I* (2009).

## From *Whylah Falls*

### Look Homeward, Exile

I can still see that soil crimsoned by butchered
Hog and imbrued with rye, lye, and homely
Spirituals everybody must know,
Still dream of folks who broke or cracked like shale:
Pushkin, who twisted his hands in boxing,
Marrocco, who ran girls like dogs and got stabbed,
Lavinia, her teeth decayed to black stumps,
Her lovemaking still in demand, spitting
Black phlegm—her pension after twenty towns,
And Toof, suckled on anger that no Baptist
Church could contain, who let wrinkled Eely
Seed her moist womb when she was just thirteen.
    And the tyrant sun that reared from barbed-wire
Spewed flame that charred the idiot crops
To Depression, and hurt my granddaddy
To bottle after bottle of sweet death,
His dreams beaten to one, tremendous pulp,
Until his heart seized, choked; his love gave out.
    But Beauty survived, secreted
In freight trains snorting in their pens, in babes
Whose faces were coal-black mirrors, in strange
Strummers who plucked Ghanaian banjos, hummed
Blind blues—precise, ornate, rich needlepoint,
In sermons scorched with sulphur and brimstone,
And in my love's dark, orient skin that smelled
Like orange peels and tasted like rum, good God!
    I remember my Creator in the old ways:
I sit in taverns and stare at my fists;
I knead earth into bread, spell water into wine.
Still, nothing warms my wintry exile—neither
Prayers nor fine love, neither votes nor hard drink:
For nothing heals those saints felled in green beds,
Whose loves are smashed by just one word or glance
Or pain—a screw jammed in thick, straining wood.

## Bees' Wings

This washed-out morning, April rain descants,
Weeps over gravity, the broken bones
Of gravel and graveyards, and Cora puts
Away gold dandelions to sugar
And skew into gold wine, then discloses
That Pablo gutted his engine last night
Speeding to Beulah Beach under a moon
As pocked and yellowed as aged newsprint.
Now, Othello, famed guitarist, heated
By rain-clear rum, voices transparent notes
Of sad, anonymous heroes who hooked
Mackerel and slept in love-pried-open thighs
And gave out booze in vain crusades to end
Twenty centuries of Christianity.
  His voice is simple, sung air; without notes,
There's nothing. His unknown, imminent death
(The feel of iambs ending as trochees
In a slow, decasyllabic death-waltz;
His vertebrae trellised on his stripped spine
Like a xylophone or keyboard of nerves)
Will also be nothing: the sun pours gold
Upon Shelley, his sis', light as bees' wings,
Who roams a garden sprung from rotten wood
And words, picking green nouns and fresh, bright verbs,
For there's nothing I will not force language
To do to make us one—whether water
Hurts like whisky or the sun burns like oil
Or love declines to weathered names on stone.

## Blank Sonnet

The air smells of rhubarb, occasional
Roses, or first birth of blossoms, a fresh,
Undulant hurt, so body snaps and curls
Like flower. I step through snow as thin as script,
Watch white stars spin dizzy as drunks, and yearn
To sleep beneath a patchwork quilt of rum,
I want the slow, sure collapse of language

Washed out by alcohol. Lovely Shelley,
I have no use for measured, cadenced verse
If you won't read. Icarus-like, I'll fall
Against this page of snow, tumble blackly
Across vision to drown in the white sea
That closes every poem—the white reverse
That cancels the blackness of each image.

1990

## Le Tombeau de Bishop

*for Sandra Barry*

Cruel scrutiny is your furious power:
It orders light—orcharded, hoarded fast
In your dark poems: miniature Bibles
Monstrous with agonies of pneumonia
Or cranky Bedlams, shelving sick mothers
Like just-hooked fish, their eyes jumpy with shock.
To dredge your poems is to grapple nightmares—
Offal of Presbyterian-depressed
Nouvelle-Écosse (its poverty of love,
Its raw, tubercular winters)—and snag
Images smelling of hookrust and flesh,
Death-randy.
Photographic, spiky, rank,
Your gospels dramatize the malicious,
Narrow cold that cankers our compassion
And blisters our dreams, freezing us into
This penal colony peninsula.
Peeling back our pitched ensembles of blossoms,
You expose a snow-riled landscape, our warped
Shacks, our nicest incests, our plums slumped in dirt.
Your metaphors pierce us like frigid spears
Or hot, Botticellian syphilis.
Accurate as aches, you chill and scald us.
Dread Elizabeth Bishop, seize our lives,
Anatomize them—like a liar's diary.
Your lyrics still inflict wounds choice eyes brave—
Their lines slash icy, incendiary.

2001

## Paris Annapolis

There is a light in Paris—Baudelaire's
Or Rimbaud's—that cuts like grey *Pernod*
Drizzling misery in the brain. You pick
It up in smeared glasses, blurry with tears—
The glycerine light of memory, pale,
Unstable, unholy water, panicked
As paeans and elegies to how *Love*
Perishes in a thousand sins, famous
And rehearsed, the way it always must die.
Once I floated along the Seine, my brain
Pickled wicked on Belgian beer that's ten
Per cent alcohol, and I wrote of her,
And the river cried out to me to drown.
All my years have been mere dodges of death.
I came here to this valley, to forget—
To lush pastures, to forget a parched love.
But that spectacular, parrhesian light—
The Parisian light of the Annapolis
Valley, that frosty brightness lilting
Over Gothic orchards, gargoyle apple trees
Reaped by apocalyptic autumn,
A thousand white, clapboard Notre Dames
Pastelling the Annapolis as the Seine,
That river, queasy like the Quai d'Orsay—
Shines her image upon my welling heart
That brims at Heaven like a word-swamped page,
Brooking a delirium that banks clouds
(Their liquid palimpsests), and asks that soul
Steep under unadulterate Beauty.
And I sink, eyeing Gallic moonlight sculpt
An Arc de Triomphe from frank, conjuncting trees,
From this flaming stream, a Champs Elysées—
Or an ash-white Napoleonic tomb.

2001

## Burning Poems

A pen burns paper. A black *Blitzkrieg*
Blazes, leaving the glinting odour of charred
Diction, a vocabulary in ashes: Detritus.
The word-scorched paper smells darkly.

How oblivion buckles. Or suffers arrest.
The chancy arson that parades as poetry
Smells of paper yellowed and time-seared,
Mottled, reeking of always-flaming news.

Walcott's holocaust. Pound's inferno.
Layton's *Fornalutx*. My own slavish suttee.
Every poem is its own pyre, flamboyant,
The smoking words laying waste to *Time*.

2001

# Christian Bök
## *b.* 1966

Born in Toronto, Christian Bök received his BA (1989) and his MA (1990) from Carleton University, returning to Toronto to complete his PhD (2008) from York University. His first collection of poetry, *Crystallography* (1994), revealed his interest in finding poetry in the language of geology. His second collection, *Eunoia* (2001), meaning 'beautiful thinking', as well as being the shortest word in English that uses all five vowels, took him seven years to complete, each chapter using only a single vowel; this book proves, he avers, 'that each vowel has its own personality, and demonstrates the flexibility of the English language.' *Eunoia* won the Griffin Poetry Prize in 2002. A fiercely experimental poet, Bök teaches at the University of Calgary.

## From *Eunoia*

### Chapter I

*for Dick Higgins*

Writing is inhibiting. Sighing, I sit, scribbling in ink this pidgin script. I sing with nihilistic witticism, disciplining signs with trifling gimmicks—impish hijinks which highlight stick sigils. Isn't it glib? Isn't it chic? I fit childish insights within rigid limits, writing shtick which might instill priggish misgivings in critics blind with hindsight. I dismiss nitpicking criticism which flirts with philistinism. I bitch; I kibitz—griping whilst criticizing dimwits, sniping whilst indicting nitwits, dismissing simplistic thinking, in which philippic wit is still illicit.

Pilgrims, digging in shifts, dig till midnight in mining pits, chipping flint with picks, drilling schist with drills, striking it rich mining zinc. Irish firms, hiring micks whilst firing Brits, bring in smiths with mining skills: kilnwrights grilling brick in brickkilns, millwrights grinding grist in gristmills. Irish tinsmiths, fiddling with widgits, fix this rig, driving its drills which spin whirring drillbits. I pitch in, fixing things. I rig this winch with its wiring; I fit this drill with its piping. I dig this ditch, filling bins with dirt, piling it high, sifting it, till I find bright prisms twinkling with glitz.

Hiking in British districts, I picnic in virgin firths, grinning in mirth with misfit whims, smiling if I find birch twigs, smirking if I find mint sprigs. Midspring brings with it singing birds, six kinds (finch, siskin, ibis, tit, pipit, swift), whistling shrill chirps, trilling *chirr chirr* in high pitch. Kingbirds flit in gliding flight, skimming limpid springs, dipping wingtips in rills which brim with living things: krill, shrimp, brill—fish with gilt fins, which swim in flitting zigs. Might Virgil find bliss implicit in this primitivism? Might I mimic him in print if I find his writings inspiring?

Fishing till twilight, I sit, drifting in this birch skiff,
jigging kingfish with jigs, bringing in fish which nip
this bright string (its vivid glint bristling with stick
pins). Whilst I slit this fish in its gills, knifing it, slicing
it, killing it with skill, shipwrights might trim this jib,
swinging it right, hitching it tight, riding brisk winds
which pitch this skiff, tipping it, tilting it, till this ship
in crisis flips. Rigging rips. Christ, this ship is sinking. Diving in, I swim, fighting this frigid swirl, kicking, kicking, swimming in it till I sight high cliffs,
rising, indistinct in thick mists, lit with lightning.

Lightning blinks, striking things in its midst with
blinding light. Whirlwinds whirl; driftwinds drift.
Spindrift is spinning in thrilling whirligigs. Which
blind spirit is whining in this whistling din? Is it
this grim lich, which is writhing in its pit, lifting its
lid with whitish limbs, rising, vivific, with ill will in
its mind, victimizing kids timid with fright? If it is—
which blind witch is midwifing its misbirth, binding
this hissing djinni with witching spiritism? Is it this
thin, sickish girl, twitching in fits, whilst writing
things in spirit-writing? If it isn't—it is I; it is I . . .

Lightning flicks its riding whip, blitzing this night
with bright schisms. Sick with phthisis in this drizzling mist, I limp, sniffling, spitting bilic spit, itching
livid skin (skin which is tingling with stinging pin-
pricks). I find this frigid drisk dispiriting; still, I fight
its chilling windchill. I climb cliffs, flinching with
skittish instincts. I might slip. I might twist this infirm wrist, crippling it, wincing whilst I bind it in its
splint, cringing whilst I gird it in its sling; still, I risk
climbing, sticking with it, striving till I find this rift,
in which I might fit, hiding in it till winds diminish.

Minds grim with nihilism still find first light inspiring. Mild pink in tint, its shining twilight brings bright
tidings which lift sinking spirits. With firm will, I finish
climbing, hiking till I find this inviting inn, in which

I might sit, dining. I thirst. I bid girls bring stiff drinks —gin fizz which I might sip whilst finishing this rich dish, nibbling its tidbits: ribs with wings in chili, figs with kiwis in icing. I swig citric drinks with vim, tippling kirsch, imbibing it till, giggling, I flirt with girlish virgins in miniskirts: *wink, wink.* I miss living in sin, pinching thighs, kissing lips pink with lipstick.

Slick pimps, bribing civic kingpins, distill gin in stills, spiking drinks with illicit pills which might bring bliss. Whiz kids in silk-knit shirts script films in which slim girls might strip, jiggling tits, wiggling hips, inciting wild shindigs. Twin siblings in bikinis might kiss rich bigwigs, giving this prim prig his wish, whipping him, tickling him, licking his limp dick till, rigid, his prick spills its jism. Shit! This ticklish victim is trifling with kink. Sick minds, thriving in kinship with pigs, might find insipid thrills in this filth. This flick irks critics. It is swinish; it is piggish. It stinks.

Thinking within strict limits is stifling. Whilst Viking knights fight griffins, I skirmish with this riddling sphinx (this sigil—I). I print lists, filing things (kin with kin, ilk with ilk), inscribing this distinct sign, listing things in which its imprint is intrinsic. I find its missing links, divining its implicit tricks. I find it whilst skindiving in Fiji; I find it whilst picnicking in Linz. I find it in Inniskillin; I find it in Mississippi. I find it whilst skiing in Minsk. (Is this intimism civilizing if Klimt limns it, if Liszt lilts it?) I sigh; I lisp. I finish writing this writ, signing it, kind sir: NIHIL DICIT, FINI.

2009

## Vowels

A black, E white, I red, U green, O blue: the vowels.
I will tell thee, one day, of thy newborn portents:
A, the black velvet cuirass of flies whose essence
commingles, abuzz, around the cruellest of smells,

Wells of shadow; E, the whitewash of mists and tents,
glaives of icebergs, albino kings, frostbit fennels;
I, the bruises, the blood spat from lips of damsels
who must laugh in scorn or shame, both intoxicants;

U, the waves, divine vibratos of verdant seas,
pleasant meadows rich with venery, grins of ease
which alchemy grants the visages of the wise;

O, the supreme Trumpeter of our strange sonnet—
quietudes crossed by another [World and Spirit]:
O, the Omega!—the violet raygun of [Her] Eyes . . .

2009

# DRAMA

# The Elements of Drama

## CONTEXTS OF DRAMA

### Drama, Literature, and Representational Art

The essence of drama is imitative action. When actors appear on stage, they make believe they are people other than themselves, much as children do, and in doing so create a world apart—a world modelled on ours, resembling ours, yet separate.

Drama, of course, is not child's play, but it does share with it the essential quality of *enactment*. This quality should remind us that drama is not solely a form of literature. It is at once literary art *and* representational art. As literary art a play is a fiction, made of words. It has a plot, characters, and dialogue. But it is a special kind of fiction—a fiction *acted out* rather than narrated. In a novel or short story, we learn about characters and events through the words of a narrator who stands between us and them. But in a play nothing stands between us and the total makeup of its world. Characters appear and events happen without any intermediate comment or explanation. Drama, then, offers us a *direct* presentation of its imaginative reality. In this sense it is representational art.

In studying drama we are faced with a paradox. Because it is literature, a play can be read. But because it is representational art, a play is meant to be witnessed. Viewed another way, the text of a play is something like the score of a symphony—a finished work, yet only a potentiality until it is performed. Most plays, after all, are written to be performed. (Those that are written only to be read are usually referred to as *closet dramas*.) For most of us, however, the experience of drama is usually confined to plays in print, and this means that we have to be unusually resourceful in our study of drama. Careful reading is not enough. We have to be creative in order to imagine drama on the stage. This means that we must not only attend to the meanings and implications of words but also envision those words in performance. By doing so, we can begin to experience the understanding and pleasure that spectators gain when they attend a play in a theatre. This is where our study begins.

### Drama and Theatrical Performance

The magic of theatre, its ability to conjure up such incredible characters as the Ghost in *Hamlet* or the Witches in *Macbeth*, depends on the power of spectacle. By spectacle we mean all the sights and sounds of performance—the slightest twitch or the boldest thrust of a sword, the faintest whisper or the loudest cry. Spectacle, in short, is the means by which the fictional world of a play is brought to life in the theatre. When we witness a play, our thoughts and feelings may be stirred as much by the spectacle as by the words themselves. Thus in reading the text of a play, we should continually try to imagine its spectacle. This requires us to adopt a special approach to reading.

The text of a play is a script for performance, and we should read it as if we were directors and actors involved in staging the play. Once we begin to interpret it as a script, we can see that the text contains innumerable cues from which we can construct the spectacle in our mind's eye. These cues, if we are attentive to them, will tell us about the various elements that make up the total spectacle: *setting, costuming, props, blocking* (the arrangement of characters on the stage), *movement, gestures, intonation*, and *pacing* (the tempo and coordination of performance). By keeping those elements continuously in mind, we can imagine what the play looks and sounds like on stage. We can enter the world of the play, and by doing so not only understand, but also experience, its meaning.

Some dramatists, such as Ibsen, Shaw, and Beckett, provide extensive and explicit directions for performance in parenthetical remarks preceding the dialogue and interspersed with it. But no matter how extensive their remarks may be, they are never complete guides to production. They still require us to infer elements of the spectacle from the dialogue itself. Other dramatists such as Sophocles and Shakespeare provide little, if any, explicit guidance about staging. When we read their plays, we must gather our cues almost entirely from the dialogue, just as directors staging their plays must do.

It is important to bear in mind that the *King Lear* we see in a modern theatre is not the spectacle Shakespeare's seventeenth-century audiences would have seen when they witnessed the play. The Globe Theatre, where Shakespeare's plays were originally produced, was an open-air structure without sets or lights of any kind. The spectators of Shakespeare's time could not have witnessed the 'realistic' illusion of a storm such as the one in Act III of *King Lear*. They would have seen the action take place in broad daylight on a bare stage without a backdrop. Thus they would have depended wholly upon the language and the actors to evoke the setting. Even so, they would have had a more intimate involvement with the characters and the action, for the Globe stage, rather than being set behind an arch, extended out into the audience itself. Their experience of the scene would thus have been quite different from the experience offered by a modern stage version. In light of that difference, we might ask which version is valid. Both, in fact, are valid, but for different reasons. The modern version is valid because it is true to the theatrical conditions of our own time. Most modern theatres, after all, are not designed like the Globe, and if we attend a performance of *King Lear* we should not expect it to duplicate the scene as produced in Shakespeare's day. But when we are reading the play, we can imagine how it would have been produced in the Globe and thus be true to the theatrical conditions for which Shakespeare created it.

Imagining a play in the context of the theatre for which it was written will give us an understanding that we may bring to any production of the play we may happen to witness. We can compare our imagined production with the production on stage, and in this way we can recognize how the director and actors have adapted the original context of the play to their own theatrical circumstances. If, for example, we were to attend a production of *King Lear*, we might see the storm scene performed on a bare stage, without sets or props of any kind. Having imagined the play in its original theatrical context, we would then not be surprised or puzzled by that bare stage, but would recognize that the director was attempting to incorporate an important element of seventeenth-century theatre in a contemporary production. Thus, by being historically informed play-readers, we can also become critically enlightened play-goers.

## Drama and Other Literary Forms

When we consider drama as a representational art—a theatrical event to be performed and witnessed—we are concerned with the uniquely dramatic experience created by a play in performance. But any performance is an *interpretation* of how the lines should be acted and delivered. Thus every production of a play stresses some words and minimizes others, includes some meanings and excludes others. No single production can convey all the implications in the language of a play. This should remind us that drama is also a form of literary art and should be understood in relation not just to the theatre but also to other forms of literature—story, poem, and essay.

Each literary form has a unique way of using words and communicating them to the reader. Drama in its pure form uses words to create action through the dialogue of characters talking to one another rather than to the reader: its essential quality is interaction. But different forms, though they may be unique, also share similarities. Drama resembles a story in its concern with plot and character. Like a poem, it is overheard by, rather than addressed to, the reader. Like an essay, it is capable of being used to explore issues and propose ideas. Using these relationships as points of departure, we can examine some of the ways in which drama takes on the characteristics and devices of the other literary forms.

### *Drama and Narration*

A play is at its most dramatic when it uses dialogue to create interaction. But the interaction always takes place within a specific context—a background in time and place without which it cannot be properly understood. To bring about this understanding, drama turns to the narrative techniques of the story. This is not to say we should expect to find storytellers addressing us directly in plays, though occasionally they do turn up. More often the characters become storytellers in their dialogue with one another. This kind of storytelling typically occurs at the beginning of a play, and it is called the *exposition* because it sets forth and explains in a manner typical of narrative.

Exposition is important not only because it establishes the mood of a play but also because it conveys information about the world of that play. Through expository dialogue the dramatist may reveal information about the public state of affairs, as Sophocles does in the opening lines of *Oedipus Rex*, or disclose information about the past deeds and private relations of the characters. This information often comes in snatches of dialogue that, as in life itself, we must piece together on our own. Once we have done so, we have a framework for understanding the action that takes place during the play.

Related to exposition is another narrative device called *retrospection*. Characters, during the action, often look back on significant events that have taken place before the time of the play. This 'looking back' is retrospection, and it is an important element of narration. Sometimes retrospection may lead to major revelations about the characters and the motivations for their behaviour. In some cases, it may be the principal activity of the play, as in *Oedipus Rex*, where the chief character becomes preoccupied with piecing together elements from the past, and the climax occurs when his retrospection leads him to discoveries about the past that totally reverse his view of himself and his world.

Exposition and retrospection are narrative elements that refer to pre-play action, but there are occasions when narration is used to convey the action of the play itself—when narration replaces character interaction to advance the plot. Narration is used when offstage action is reported rather than represented—for even when characters are offstage they are still doing things that we must know about in order to have a full understanding of the action. When offstage action is reported, a play takes on elements of a story. Words are being used to develop a view of character and situation rather than to create action through dialogue. This process can be seen operating in *Oedipus Rex* when the Second Messenger tells the Choragus about the death of Iocastê and the self-blinding of Oedipus. The interaction on stage ceases entirely for the length of almost fifty lines, and what we get instead has all the features of a miniature story. The Messenger first establishes his narrative authority and then moves into his tale, supplying detailed information, offering explanations for facts he cannot provide, reporting dialogue, and concluding with a general reflection on the fate of Oedipus and Iocastê, whose experience he sees as epitomizing the 'misery of mankind'. One reason that Sophocles has these events reported instead of presented on stage is that they are too gruesome to be displayed. But it is true also that through the Messenger's report, Sophocles is able to provide a comment on the meaning of the events.

The Messenger's commentary brings us to the last important element of narration in drama: *choric commentary*. When the narrator of a story wishes to comment on characters and events, he or she can do so at will. But the dramatist, of course, cannot suddenly appear in the play—or on stage—to provide a point of view on the action. The dramatist's alternative is the *chorus*, or *choric characters*—that is, characters who are relatively detached from the action and can thus stand off from it, somewhat like a narrator, to reflect on the significance of events. In Greek drama the chorus performed this function.

The existence of a chorus, however, is no guarantee that its opinions are always to be trusted. Sometimes the chorus can be as wrongheaded as any of the more involved characters. Sometimes it is completely reliable, as it is in *Oedipus Rex*, where it comments, in its concluding remarks, about the frailty of the human condition. Choric commentary, then, provides a point of view, but not necessarily an authoritative one, or one to be associated necessarily with the dramatist. In each case it has to be judged in the context of the entire play. But whether it is valid, or partially reliable, or completely invalid, the chorus does provoke us to reflect on the meaning of events by providing commentary for us to assess.

After the classical Greek period, the formal chorus disappeared almost entirely from drama, though remnants of the chorus can be found in later plays—even in modern drama. It is important to recognize that despite the absence of a formally designated chorus, choric characters persist in drama. Minor characters such as messengers, servants, clowns, whether or not they are directly involved in the action, can carry out the functions of a chorus, as the Fool does in *King Lear*. Ultimately, any character is capable of becoming a commentator of a sort, simply by standing off from the action and viewing it as a spectator rather than as a participant. The reflections of these characters should be taken no less seriously than those of a chorus.

### *Drama and Meditation*

When we recall that interaction through dialogue is the basis of drama, we can readily see that a play is committed by its nature to showing us the public side of its characters. Realizing this, we can see as well the artistic problem a dramatist faces when trying to reveal the private side of the same characters. The narrator of a story can manage this problem by telling us the innermost thoughts of the characters. But a dramatist must turn to the conventions of the poem, using words addressed by a speaker talking or thinking to himself or herself.

When we read a purely lyric poem, we tend to assume that the situation is private rather than public and that we can overhear the words even though they might never be spoken aloud. When we read or watch a play, we must make a similar effort of the imagination. To assist our efforts, dramatists have traditionally organized their plays in order to make sure that characters thinking to themselves are seen in private. That special situation is captured by the term 'soliloquy', which means, literally, 'to speak alone'. But it is true also that we have private thoughts even in the presence of others, and this has been recognized by dramatists such as Aphra Behn, whose characters may often be seen thinking to themselves in the most public situations. Whatever the circumstances, private or public, the soliloquy makes unusual demands on both actors and audience.

As readers, we should be aware that the soliloquy can perform a variety of functions, and, since it is so unusual an element in drama, it achieves its purposes with great effectiveness. Customarily, the soliloquy is a means of giving expression to a complex state of mind and feeling, and in most cases the speaker is seen struggling with problems of the utmost consequence. This accounts for the intensity we often find in the soliloquy. We are all familiar, for example, with Hamlet's predicaments—to be or not to be, to kill or not to kill the king—and these are typical of the weighty issues that usually burden the speaker of a soliloquy. In soliloquy, then, the interaction among characters is replaced by the interaction of a mind with itself.

When a play shifts from dramatic interaction to meditation, its process of events is temporarily suspended, and the soliloquizing character necessarily becomes a spectator of his or her world. In this way the soliloquy, like choric commentary, offers the dramatist a means of providing a point of view on the action of the play. In reading a soliloquy, then, we should examine it not only as the private revelation of a character but also as a significant form of commentary on other characters and events.

In considering the soliloquy, we have been examining only one element of meditation in drama. It is possible for plays to become primarily or even exclusively meditative, though this may sound like a contradiction of dramatic form. If drama depends on the interaction of characters through dialogue, how is it possible for internalized thought and feeling to be the principal subject of a play? This can happen in a number of ways. One way—a traditional way—is to create a cast of characters who represent not persons but abstractions—who embody aspects, or qualities, or thoughts, or feelings of a single mind. This is a common device in morality plays, which were popular in the fifteenth and early sixteenth centuries. These religious dramas portrayed personified virtues in an attempt to instill Christian values. So, in *Everyman* (*c.* 1515), one of the best known of the morality plays, the title character is shown in conversation with characters named Beauty, Strength, Discretion, and Five Wits. Interaction among characters of this sort is meant to represent the interaction of a mind with itself, and so it constitutes the dramatization of a meditative experience achieved through what we might call an allegory of the mind.

We can also recognize plays dramatizing mental processes through methods other than allegory. Many modern plays, such as Sharon Pollock's *Doc* or Michel Tremblay's *For the Pleasure of Seeing Her Again*, include not only soliloquies and other kinds of monologue but also imaginary sequences depicting dreams and fantasies. And some modern plays, such as *Krapp's Last Tape*, consist exclusively of a single character talking to himself. Plays such as these reflect the influence of modern psychological theories about the behaviour of the mind. Writing in 1932, the playwright Eugene O'Neill defined the 'modern dramatist's problem' as discovering how to 'express those profound hidden conflicts of the mind which the probings of psychology continue to disclose to us'. Almost fifty years earlier, in 1888, the Swedish dramatist Johan Strindberg anticipated the same idea, writing, 'I have noticed that what interests people most nowadays is the psychological action.' Looking at their statements side by side, we can see that they share the same concern: O'Neill speaks of 'hidden conflicts of the mind', and Strindberg of 'psychological action'. We might also call it *meditative drama*.

Whatever form a meditative drama may take, we as readers must be alert to the 'hidden conflicts' it aims to dramatize. To recognize such conflicts we must be attentive to not just the external but also the 'internal' action. We should examine both plot and dialogue for what they can tell us about the mental life of the characters. And rather than looking for a clearly defined sequence of events, we should expect to find a kind of movement as irregular and hazy as the workings of the mind itself.

### *Drama and Persuasion*

A play could be exclusively a piece of persuasion only if it consisted of a single character—the dramatist—presenting ideas directly to the audience. Of course, such a performance would be difficult to distinguish from a lecture. This extreme case should remind us that drama is rarely, if ever, simply an exposition or assertion of ideas. Ideas can be found throughout the dialogue of almost any play, but as we have seen in the preceding sections, it is best to assume that those ideas are sentiments of the characters rather than the opinions of the dramatist. A character is a character, the dramatist is the dramatist, and dramatists are never present to speak for themselves, except in prefaces, prologues, epilogues, stage directions—and other statements outside the framework of the play.

Although dramatists cannot speak for themselves, their plays can. The essential quality of drama—interaction—may be made to serve the purposes of an essay. Dialogue, plot, and character may be used to expound ideas and sway the opinions of an audience. The desire to persuade usually implies the existence of conflicting ideas, and plays with a persuasive intention are customarily designed to demonstrate the superiority of one idea, or a set of attitudes, over another. Thus, characters may become spokespersons for ideas, dialogue a way of debating ideas, and action a means of testing ideas. Plays of this kind inevitably force audiences and readers to examine the merits of each position and align themselves with one side or the other. In reading such plays, we must be attentive not only to the motives and personalities of characters but also to the ideas they espouse. Similarly, we must be interested not only in the fate of the characters but also in the success or failure of their ideas. Ultimately, then, these plays do not allow us the pleasure of simply witnessing the interaction of characters. Like essays, they are intended to challenge our ideas and change our minds.

Because they focus on conflicting beliefs and ideas, plays with a persuasive purpose often embody elements similar to a formal argument or debate. Like *Pygmalion*, they usually set up opposing values in their opening scenes. Thus Shaw establishes a conflict between the 'Professor of Phonetics' Henry Higgins and the Cockney flower-seller Eliza Doolittle, whose speech qualifies her for the group Shaw describes in his preface as 'people with troubled accents that cut them off from all high employment'. In defending their ideas, these characters behave so much like contestants in a debate that their dialogue sounds like disputation rather than conversation. And in the process of reading or witnessing the debate, we are clearly invited to take a stand ourselves, to side with one view or the other. The choice, of course, is not an easy one, and the play is designed to keep us from making a simple choice.

## MODES OF DRAMA

### Drama, the World, and Imitation

Drama, as we said at the start, creates a world modelled on our own: its essence is imitative action. But drama is not imitative in the ordinary sense of the word. It does not offer us a literal copy of reality, for the truth of drama does not depend on reproducing the world exactly as it is. Drama is true to life by being false to our conventional notions of reality.

The coincidences discovered at the end of *The Importance of Being Earnest* are unimaginable. The scheming and contrivance of the characters in *The Rover* are outrageous. The Bingo scene in *The Rez Sisters* is surreal. And yet each of these plays creates a world that we recognize as being in some sense like our own. Our problem, then, is to define the special sense in which drama is imitative. We can begin by recognizing that its mode of imitation must be selective rather than all-inclusive, intensive rather than extensive. It has to be, since time is short and space is limited in the theatre. Faced with limitations in stage size and performance time, the dramatist obviously cannot hope to reproduce the world exactly as it is. By selecting and intensifying things, however, the dramatist can emphasize the dominant patterns and essential qualities of human experience. Thus, our understanding of any play requires that we define the principles of emphasis that determine the makeup of its world and the experience of its characters.

In defining the emphasis of a play, we can ask ourselves whether the dramatist has focused on the beautiful or the ugly, on the orderly or the chaotic, on what is best or what is worst in the world. A play that emphasizes the beautiful and the orderly tends toward an idealized vision of the world, which is the mode we call *romance*. A play focusing on the ugly and chaotic tends toward a debased view of the world; we call this mode *satire*. Both of these emphases depend for their effect on extreme views of human nature and existence.

In contrast to the extreme conditions of romance and satire, another pair of dramatic processes takes place in a world neither as beautiful as that of romance nor as ugly as that of satire—in a world more nearly like our own. Rather than focusing on essential qualities in the world, these processes—*comedy* and *tragedy*—emphasize the dominant patterns of experience that characters undergo in the world. In comedy the principal characters typically begin in a state of opposition either to one another or to their world—often to both. By the end of the play, their opposition is replaced by harmony. In this way the characters are integrated with one another and with their world. In tragedy, however, the hero and the hero's world begin in a condition of harmony that subsequently disintegrates, leaving the character by the end of the play completely isolated or destroyed.

With these four possibilities in mind, we might draw a simple diagram such as this:

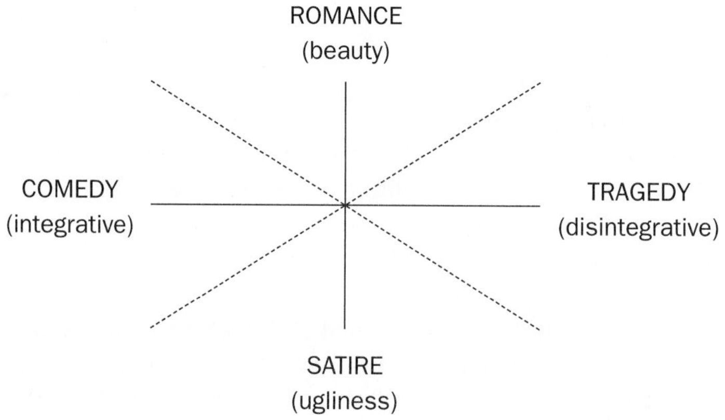

The vertical axis emphasizes the essential qualities in the world; the horizontal axis emphasizes the dominant patterns of human experience; the point of intersection—which represents the absence of any emphasis—represents the world as it is. In this way we can immediately visualize each of the four points of emphasis, its distinguishing characteristics, and its relation to each of the others. Once we have recognized these possibilities, we might be tempted to categorize plays in terms of the characteristics we have identified with each emphasis. Yet it is important to recognize that each emphasis is at best an abstraction—a definition formulated in order to generalize about a number of plays, not an explanation of any one play in particular. Thus, when we turn to individual plays we should not necessarily expect that they can be accurately described and understood simply by labelling them comedy or tragedy, satire or romance.

As a way of anticipating some of the complexities, we can see in the diagram that each emphasis borders on two others. Comedy, for example, tends toward romance on the one hand, and satire on the other. The same is true of tragedy, and the others. Even the antithetical possibilities, as we see, can interact. This should hardly surprise us, for if the world can incorporate both the beautiful and the ugly, then so can a play. These categories will serve us best if we use them tactfully as guides to understanding rather than as a rigid system of classification. But before they can serve us as guides, we must familiarize ourselves with their characteristics in greater detail.

## Tragedy and Comedy

Tragedies typically end in death and mourning, comedies in marriage and dancing. That difference accounts for the two familiar masks of drama, one expressing sorrow, the other joy, one provoking tears, the other laughter. That difference also accounts for the commonly held notion that tragedy is serious and comedy frivolous. But when we consider that both modes are probably descended from primitive fertility rites—tragedy from ritual sacrifice, comedy from ritual feasting—we can recognize that they dramatize equally important dimensions of human experience. Tragedy embodies the inevitability of individual death, comedy the irrepressibility of social rebirth. So, like autumn and spring, tragedy and comedy are equally significant phases in a natural cycle of dramatic possibilities. Indeed, like the seasons of the year and the nature of human experience, they are inextricably bound up with one another.

Every comedy contains a potential tragedy—the faint possibility that harmony may not be achieved, that the lovers may not come together to form a new society. And every tragedy contains a potential comedy—the faint possibility that disaster may be averted, that the hero or heroine may survive. This in turn should remind us that we must be concerned not only with the distinctive endings of tragedy and of comedy, but also with the means by which each of those ends is reached. Catastrophe in and of itself does not constitute tragedy, nor does marriage alone (or any other favourable outcome) make for comedy. The unique experience of each mode is produced by the design of its plot and the nature of the characters who take part in it. We can see this most clearly by looking first at the elements of tragedy, then at the elements of comedy.

Tragedy was first defined by the Greek philosopher Aristotle (384–322 BCE), who inferred its essential elements from witnessing the plays of his own time. His observations, which he set down in his *Poetics*, cannot be expected to explain all the tragedies that have ever been written; no single theory could do so. But Aristotle's theory has influenced more dramatists—and critics—than any other propounded since his time, and thus it remains the best guide we have to the nature of tragedy.

Aristotle considered plot to be the most important element of tragedy, because he believed that 'all human happiness or misery takes the form of action', that 'it is in our actions—what we do—that we are happy or the reverse'. In discussing tragedy, he emphasized the design of the plot and set out several important qualities that contribute to its effect. First, he stressed the *unity* of a tragic plot. By unity he meant that the plot represents a single action, or story, with a definite beginning, middle, and end, and further that all its incidents are 'so closely connected that the transposal or withdrawal of any one of them will disjoin or dislocate the whole'. By close connection he meant that the incidents are causally related to one another so that their sequence is probable and necessary. Ultimately, then, we can see that, in emphasizing the unity of a tragic plot, Aristotle was calling attention to the quality of the inevitable that we associate with tragedy. Thus in reading a tragedy we should try to define the chain of cause and effect that links each incident in the plot. In this way we will understand the process that makes its catastrophe inevitable, and in this way we will gain insight into the meaning of the catastrophe.

In examining the plot of a tragedy such as *Oedipus Rex*, we may be tempted to look at its catastrophe as not only inevitable but also inescapable. Aristotle, however, did not see the inevitable change in the fortunes of the tragic hero as being the result of chance, of coincidence, of fate, or even of some profound flaw in the character of the hero. Rather, he saw the change of fortune as being caused by 'some error of judgment', a 'great error' on the part of the hero. In defining this element of tragedy, Aristotle clearly regarded the hero, and not some condition beyond human control, as responsible for initiating the chain of events leading to his or her change in fortune. Even a profound flaw in character is, after all, beyond human control. Accordingly, Aristotle described the tragic hero as an 'intermediate kind of personage' in moral character, neither 'preeminently virtuous and just' nor afflicted 'by vice and depravity'. Simply put, the tragic hero is someone morally 'like ourselves', in whom we can engage our emotional concern. Thus, according to Aristotle's theory, we should not regard tragic protagonists such as Oedipus or King Lear as victims of absurd circumstances, but should try to identify the sense in which they are agents of their own undoing.

Even as we attempt to understand the nature of their errors, we should not forget that most tragic heroes are admirable characters—people, as Aristotle tells us, who deservedly enjoy 'great reputation and prosperity'. The reputation of a tragic hero is a function not simply of social rank but also of his or her commitment to noble purposes. Oedipus is not just a king but also a man committed to discovering the truth and ridding his city of the plague. King Lear is not only a king but a father who loves and trusts his children. Our response to these characters should therefore combine judgment with sympathy and admiration.

Once we make the effort to discover their error, we should find that we undergo an experience that parallels that of the protagonists themselves. We should find that we are compelled by the process of events—by the turn of the plot—to recognize how they have undone themselves. The protagonist's act of recognition is defined by Aristotle as the *discovery* because it entails 'a change from ignorance to knowledge'. And the discovery, as Aristotle recognized, is caused inevitably by a *reversal*, an incident or sequence of incidents that goes contrary to the protagonist's expectations. Reversal and discovery are crucial elements of the tragic experience because they crystallize its meaning for the protagonist—and for us. When events go contrary to their expectations, when the irony of their situation becomes evident, they—and we—have no choice but to recognize exactly how the noblest intentions can bring about the direst consequences. Thus, in its discovery, as in its entire plot, tragedy affirms both the dignity and the frailty of human existence.

Discovery scenes take place in comedy as well, but rather than accounting for an inevitable disaster, comic discoveries reveal information that enables characters to avoid a probable catastrophe. Lost wills may be found, or mistaken identities corrected, or some other fortuitous circumstance may be revealed. Somehow comedy always manages to bring about a happy turn of events for its heroes—and those heroes are rarely the sole or primary agents of their success. Usually, in fact, they get a large helping hand from chance, or coincidence, or some other lucky state of affairs. Comedy thrives on improbability. And in doing so it defies the mortal imperatives of tragedy.

In this sense comedy embodies the spirit of spring, with its eternal promise of rebirth and renewal; it embodies, too, the festive air and festive activities we associate with spring. The term 'comedy', in fact, is derived from a Greek word, *komoidia*, that means 'revel-song', and revelry always finds its way into comedy, whether in the form of feasts and dancing, tricks and joking, sex and loving—or all of them combined. The perils that develop in the world of comedy rarely seem perilous to us. Although the characters themselves may feel temporarily threatened, the festive air makes us sense that ultimately no permanent damage will be done.

Though comedy avoids the experience of death, it does not ignore the significance of life. Comic plots usually arise out of conflicts that embody opposing values and beliefs. These conflicts inevitably pit one set of attitudes against another, one kind of social vision against another. In reading comedies, therefore, we should try to identify the attitudes that bring characters into conflict. In *Pygmalion*, Henry Higgins is committed to social structure and etiquette, Eliza Doolittle to social freedom. Once we have identified those conflicting values, we will discover that they can help us to understand the meaning of a comic plot.

Comedy usually begins with a state of affairs dominated by one kind of social idea, and so the resolution of a comic plot—achieved through its scenes of discovery—embodies the triumph of a new social order. Whoever wins out in comedy is invariably on the right side, no matter how improbable the victory may seem. Thus it is that the characters who oppose the new order of things—the 'blocking figures'—are usually subjected to comic ridicule throughout the play. Comedy, after all, expresses an irreverent attitude toward old and inflexible ideas, toward any idea that stifles natural and reasonable impulses in the human spirit. But comedy, as we said earlier, also embodies the generous and abundant spirit of spring. Its heroes and heroines—the proponents of the new society—always seek to include their opponents in the final comic festivities. Comedy seeks not to destroy the old, but rather to reclaim it. And in this may be seen the ultimate expression of its exuberant faith in life.

### Tragicomedy, Naturalism, and Absurdist Drama

Tragedy, comedy, satire, and romance—each of these primary modes embodies its own unique pattern of dramatic experience. Each incorporates distinctly different kinds of plots and characters, distinctly different kinds of conflicts and discovery scenes, and each achieves a distinctly different view of human existence. Thus, when we read or witness a tragedy or comedy, a satire or romance, we undergo an experience that is more or less clear-cut. We feel sorrow or joy, scorn or admiration. We know, in short, exactly how we feel, exactly what we think.

But some plays—many modern ones, especially—do not arouse such clear-cut responses. As we read or watch them, our feelings and judgments may be confused, or ambiguous, or mixed in one way or another. When we read a play such as *The Rez Sisters* we may feel torn between sorrow and joy, scorn and admiration. Indeed, we may not know exactly how we feel, or exactly what we think. When we find ourselves experiencing such mixed feelings, we will probably discover that the play has been designed to leave us in an unresolved state of mind—that it does not embody a clear-cut pattern of catastrophe or rebirth (as in tragedy or comedy) or present clear-cut images of good or evil (as in romance or satire). Many plays, rather than being dominated by a single mode, combine differing or opposing modes of dramatic experience. In characterizing such works we use the term 'tragicomedy' as a means of defining the ambiguous experience that we witness in the play and feel within ourselves. Tragicomedy leaves us with a complex reaction, similar to the uncertainty we often feel in response to life itself.

Uncertainty about the nature of human existence is a fundamental source of the tragicomic quality we find in many modern and contemporary plays. In some, that quality is produced by a *naturalistic* view of human nature and experience—a view of men and women as influenced by psychological, social, and economic forces so complex that the behaviour of individuals cannot be easily judged or explained. That view of human nature led Johan Strindberg, for example, to create characters whom he describes as being 'somewhat "characterless"'—characters, that is, who are influenced by 'a whole series of motives', rather than by any single, or simple, purpose. Like other naturalistic dramatists, Strindberg is unwilling to offer us simple explanations to account for human behaviour:

> A suicide is committed. Business troubles, says the man of affairs. Unrequited love, say the women. Sickness, says the invalid. Despair, says the down-and-out. But it is possible that the motive lay in all or none of these directions, or that the dead man concealed his actual motive by revealing quite another, likely to reflect more to his glory.

Just as we cannot definitely account for their actions, the characters in a realistic drama cannot themselves perceive, much less control, all the forces influencing their behaviour. Typically, then, the protagonists of naturalistic drama, such as the central characters in *The Rez Sisters*, are placed in dramatic situations portraying them as being in some sense victims of their environment. They may attempt to alter their circumstances, or they may wilfully deceive themselves about the nature of them, or they may acquiesce in them, or they may sit in judgment upon them; but whatever action they take, it does not lead to a clear-cut resolution of the kind we associate with tragedy and comedy. Nor does their situation allow us to make the clear-cut moral judgment that we do of characters in satire and romance. For this reason naturalistic drama leaves us with a problematic view of human experience, and the most we can hope for is to understand, to the degree that we humanly can, the psychological, social, and economic circumstances that are contributing to the problematic situations of its characters.

In some modern plays the problematic situation is produced by conditions that transcend even naturalistic explanations. In these plays we sense the presence of some profound situation that afflicts the characters but is in the end indefinable. In *Krapp's Last Tape*, we are faced with a single character whose existence is defined almost exclusively by an insatiable appetite for bananas, an unquenchable thirst for soda water, and an obsessive fixation on his tape-recorded diary. These mysterious, even ridiculous, circumstances lead us to wonder whether there is any ultimate source of meaning *at all* in the world of such plays, or for that matter whether there is *any* rational source of explanation *at all* for the experience of the characters. For this reason, such plays are known as *absurdist* drama.

The 'absurdity' of absurdist drama is usually evident not only in its plot but in its dialogue. Often, for example, the conversation of characters does not make perfect sense, either because they are talking at cross purposes or because their language has no clear point of reference to anything in their world. Yet even as we read the dialogue we will find it to be at once laughably out of joint and terrifyingly uncommunicative. In much the same way we may be puzzled by the resolution of these plays. We may be left wondering whether the characters' situation at the end is in any significant respect different from what it was at the beginning, wondering whether the play is tragic or comic, wondering even whether there is any single word or concept—like 'tragicomedy'—that can adequately express the possibility that human existence may be meaningless. Ultimately, then, absurdist drama, like the other modes, does embody a view of human existence, but rather than perceiving existence as dominated by one pattern or another, one quality or another, the view implies that existence may have no pattern or meaning at all.

## ELEMENTS OF DRAMA

### Contexts, Modes, and the Elements of Drama

*Characters, dialogue, plot*—these are the indispensable elements of drama. Together they make possible the imitative world of every play, for characters are like people, dialogue and plot like the things people say and do. But *likeness* does not mean *identicalness*. As we indicated in our discussion of dramatic modes, the 'truth' of drama does not depend on reproducing the world exactly as it is. For this reason, we should not expect to find characters who talk and act in just the same way that we do, nor should we expect to find plots that develop in just the same way that ordinary events do. The characters who populate the worlds of romance and satire, for example, are modelled less on specific people than on human potentialities. Similarly, the plots elaborated in comedy and tragedy are based less on real occurrences than on basic patterns of human experience. The elements of drama, then, are highly specialized versions of the elements that make up the world as it is. The particular version we encounter in any single play will be determined by a variety of circumstances—by the mode of the play, the purpose of the play, the literary form of the play, and the design of the theatre for which it was written. We should always keep these circumstances in mind when we study the elements of drama.

## Dialogue

The dialogue of a play is a specialized form of conversation. Designed as it is to serve the needs created by the various contexts and modes of drama, it can hardly be expected to sound exactly like our customary patterns of speech. In ordinary conversation, for example, we adjust our style to meet the needs of the people we are talking with, and we reinforce our words with a wide range of facial expressions, bodily gestures, and vocal inflections, many of which we use unconsciously. If we recognize that we are not being understood, we may stammer momentarily while trying to rephrase our feelings and ideas. Before we have managed to get the words out, someone may have interrupted us and completely changed the topic of conversation. Whatever the case, we find ourselves continuously adjusting to circumstances that are as random as our thoughts and the thoughts of those we are speaking with. If we were to transcribe and then listen to the tape of an ordinary conversation, even one that we considered coherent and orderly, we would probably find it far more erratic and incoherent than we had imagined.

Drama cannot afford to reproduce conversation as faithfully as though it were recorded. To begin with, the limitations of performance time require that characters express their ideas and feelings much more economically than we do in the leisurely course of ordinary conversation. The conditions of theatrical performance demand also that dialogue be formulated so that it can not only be heard by characters talking to one another but also be overheard and understood by the audience in the theatre. Thus, the continuity of dialogue must be clearly marked out at every point. On the basis of what is overheard, the audience—or the reader—must be able to develop a full understanding of the characters and the plot.

Dialogue, then, is an extraordinarily significant form of conversation, for it is the means by which every play conveys the total makeup of its imaginative world. And this is not all. Dialogue must convey clues about this imaginative world that will help the director, the set designer, and the actors perform their roles. This means that the dialogue must serve as a script for all the elements of production and performance—in short, for the entire theatrical realization of a play.

Because it has to serve so many purposes all at once, dialogue is necessarily a more artificial form of discourse than ordinary conversation. Thus, in reading any segment of dialogue, we should always keep in mind its special purposes. It is a script for theatrical production, and that means that we should see what it can tell us about the total spectacle: the setting, the arrangement of characters on the stage, their physical movements, gestures, facial expressions, and inflections. It is also a text for conveying the imaginative world of the play, which means that we should see what it can tell us about the character speaking, the character listening, and the other characters not present; about the public and private relations among the characters, and the quality of the world they inhabit; about the events that have taken place prior to the play, the events that have taken place offstage during the play, the events that have caused the interaction of the characters during the dialogue itself, and the events that are likely to follow from their interaction. If we read the dialogue with all these concerns in mind, we will find in the end that it takes us out of ourselves and leads us into the imaginative experience of the play.

### Plot

Plot is a specialized form of experience. We can see just how specialized it is if we consider for a moment what happens to us in the course of our everyday lives. Between waking and sleeping we perform a variety of actions and probably converse with a number of people. But most of these events have little to do with one another, and they are usually not part of any single purpose. In general, the events that take place in our daily existence do not embody a significant pattern or process. If they have any pattern at all, it is merely the product of habit and routine.

On the other hand, in drama every event is part of a carefully designed pattern and process. This process is what we call plot. Plot, then, is not at all like the routine, and often random, course of our daily existence. Rather, it is a wholly interconnected system of events, deliberately selected and arranged for the purpose of fulfilling a complex set of imaginative and theatrical purposes. Plot is really an extremely artificial element, and it has to be so. Within the limits of a few hours the interest of spectators—and readers—has to be deeply engaged and continuously sustained; that requires a system of events that quickly develops complications and suspense, and leads in turn to a climax and resolution. Interest must also be aroused by events that make up a process capable of being represented on stage. And the totality of events must create a coherent imitation of the world.

In order to understand how plot fulfills these multiple purposes, we should first recognize that plot comprises *everything* that takes place in the imaginative world of a play. In other words, it is not confined to what takes place on stage (the *scenario*): it includes offstage action as well. Thus, if we wish to identify the plot of a play, we have to distinguish it from the scenario. The scenario embodies the plot and presents it to us, but it is not itself the plot. Here is another way to understand this distinction: in a plot all the events are necessarily arranged *chronologically*, whereas in a scenario events are arranged *dramatically*—that is, in an order that will create the greatest impact on the audience. In some cases that order may be non-chronological. We may reach the end of a scenario before we learn about events that took place years before. For this reason, in studying the plot of a play, we must consider not only the events of which it consists but also the order in which those events are presented by the scenario.

The ordering of events can best be understood if we think of the scenario as being constructed of a series of dramatic units: each time a character enters or leaves the stage, a new dramatic unit begins. The appearance or departure of a character or group of characters is almost like a form of punctuation that we should note carefully whenever we are reading or witnessing a play. As one grouping of characters gives way to another, the dramatic situation necessarily changes—sometimes slightly, sometimes very perceptibly—to carry the play forward in the evolution of its process and the fulfillment of its plot. It is important to examine each unit individually in order to discover not only what onstage action takes place within it but also what offstage action is revealed within it. Then we should determine how the offstage action that is reported affects the onstage action, as well as how it shapes our own understanding of the characters and the plot.

Consider, for example, the opening dramatic unit of *Oedipus Rex*. Here we witness a conversation between Oedipus and a priest, in which the priest pleads with Oedipus to rid Thebes of the plague, while Oedipus assures him that he is eager to cure the city of its sickness. During that conversation we also learn from the priest that, in years past, Oedipus had through his wisdom and knowledge liberated the city from the domination of the Sphinx, and we learn from Oedipus that he has recently sent his brother-in-law, Kreon, to seek advice from the oracle at Delphi. These two reports of offstage action establish the heroic stature of Oedipus, revealing him to be an exceptionally effective and responsible leader. The dramatic unit leads the priest and Oedipus—and us as spectators—to expect that he will be equally successful in this crisis. In this way we see that the unit not only identifies the motivating problem of the plot but also establishes Oedipus as the hero of the play, and that, moreover, it creates a set of positive expectations about his ability to overcome the problem. (He does, of course, overcome the problem but not without undoing himself in the process.) The unit, then, is crucial in creating a complicated mixture of true and false expectations within both the characters and us.

In addition to examining dramatic units individually, we should examine them in relation to one another—in other words, in context. Context is one of the dramatist's most useful techniques for influencing our perception and understanding of characters and plot. Dramatists usually arrange events so as to produce significant parallels or contrasts between them. Thus, if we look at the units in context, we will be able to perceive those relationships and their implications.

Finally, of course, we must move beyond pairs and series of units to an overview of all the units together. By doing this we will be able to recognize the dominant process of the play. That is, we will be able to perceive how it sets up the complications and works toward the discoveries and resolution of tragedy, comedy, satire, romance, or tragicomedy. By examining the overall design of the plot, we can recognize the dominant view of experience represented in the play.

It should be apparent that plot is an extremely complicated element, one that can best be understood through a detailed analysis of dramatic units. Here, then, are some reminders and suggestions to follow in analyzing the plot of any play. Identify all the events that take place within the plot and the chronological order in which they occur. In order to do this, examine the scenario closely, paying attention to instances of implied and reported action. Once you have established the details and makeup of the plot, examine how the plot is presented by the scenario. In order to do this, examine each dramatic unit in detail, beginning with the first and proceeding consecutively through the play. Remember that a single dramatic unit can serve a variety of purposes. Remember, too, that every unit exists within a context of units—within the context of units that immediately precede and follow it, and within the context of all the units of the play.

### Character

Although characters in a play are like real people in some respects, they are by no means identical to people in real life. Real people, after all, exist in the world as it is, whereas characters exist in an imaginative world shaped by the theatrical contexts and imitative purposes of drama. In the classical Greek theatre, for example, a character was defined visually by the fixed expression of his or her mask. Clearly, it would have been impossible for spectators to regard such characters as identical to complex human personalities. And if we look at Oedipus, we can see that he is conceived in terms of a few dominant traits that could be projected through the bold acting required by the enormous size of the ancient Greek theatre.

Because of its sustained interest in psychological behaviour, modern drama tends to put a great deal of emphasis on character. Yet even plays—such as *Hedda Gabler* or *For the Pleasure of Seeing Her Again*—that are concerned specifically with the workings of the human mind do not embody characters who can be taken as identical to real people. It would be misleading to think of Ibsen's Hedda, for example, or Michel Tremblay's Nana as a fully developed personality. Although each represents a complex study in human psychology, they are conceived to dramatize specific ideas about the impact of the family and society upon the individual. In other words, they exhibit patterns of behaviour that are *typical* rather than *actual*.

Although dramatic characters are not real people, they are endowed with human capacities. They talk and act and interact with one another. They experience pleasure and endure pain. They feel, and they act on their feelings. They believe, and they behave according to their beliefs. It would be inhuman of us not to respond to their humanity. But we can respond appropriately only if we know what we are responding to: we have to consider all of the ways in which characters are revealed and defined by dialogue and plot.

The most immediate way to understand a character is to examine in detail everything the character says in order to identify the important attitudes, beliefs, and feelings of that character. It is important to examine not only the content but also the style of such utterances. Look, for example, at the kinds of words and images and sentence structures that mark the character's dialogue, for often these elements of style provide insight into subtle aspects of character. A further source of information is what others in the play say about the character. Since characters, like real people, are repeatedly talking about one another—to their faces and behind their backs—what they have to say will often provide valuable insights into the character.

The things a character does may reveal as much as what the character says and what others have to say. In examining actions, pay careful attention to context, for characters are likely to behave differently in different situations. The challenge in such a case is to determine whether the character has actually changed, for what appears to be a change in character may simply be the result of our knowing the character more fully. Another important key to understanding is to compare and contrast a character with others in the play. A study of this kind often sharpens the perceptions we have gained from examining the character in isolation.

Character analysis can be a source of pleasure and understanding in its own right, but it should ultimately lead us more deeply into the play as a whole. For that reason, when we analyze characters, we should always keep in mind the theatrical contexts and imaginative purposes that shape their being. In this way we shall be able to appreciate the dramatic imitation of a world created by the wedding of literary and of representational art.

## A GUIDE TO OUR PLAYS

Theatre, as we have come to understand it, originates in the Greek tragedies of the fifth century BCE. Tragedy was an important part of annual spring festivals honouring Dionysus, the god of agriculture and fertility. During the proceedings, an actor would come on stage to carry on a conversation with the chorus. Together, they would recite the triumphs and failures of the major character. It became customary at the festivals to have each competing poet write three tragedies and a satyr play of a burlesque nature.

Aeschylus, the creator of tragedy, introduced a second actor/character. Although his plays still centred on the chorus, they began to take on a new life. Of approximately seventy plays that he wrote, only seven have survived, and we know that he made a dramatic whole of the three tragedies he wrote for the festivals by using the three dramas to treat a single story over an extended period of time. His plays present human actions in relation to the overriding will of the gods.

Sophocles, Aeschylus's successor, put aside the practice of composing his tragedies in groups of three. He also introduced a third actor/character to the stage, reducing considerably the significance of the chorus, and he showed a vital interest in character. Of more than 110 plays that he wrote, only 7 have survived.

No longer focusing on the gods themselves, Sophocles shifts his focus to the human beings who populate our world, and his plays reveal a strong sense of tragic moments in the lives of men and women who are both heroic and deeply human. Though he wrote his plays well over 2000 years ago, many of his insights into human experience are enduring and timeless. He wrote, for example, of Antigone and her sister Ismene, an account that Sheila Watson reworked in a contemporary setting in her story 'Antigone'. Oedipus Rex, the most renowned of all Greek tragedies, has influenced literatures from its time to the present; it is here presented in the well-known modern English translation by Dudley Fitts and Robert Fitzgerald. In the festival in which it was first performed, held around the year 425 BCE, however, the play gained only second prize; first prize in that year's contest went to Philocles, a nephew of Aeschylus, of whom little else—including his work—is known.

At the start of the play, Oedipus's kingdom, the city of Thebes, is suffering from a plague, and in the opening scene a crowd of suppliants appeal to the great king to find them some relief from their woe. Sixteen years have passed since Oedipus freed Thebes from the tyranny of King Laïos by solving a riddle posed by the Sphinx; his act of heroism earned him the hand of the queen and the crown of the king. An intelligent and determined ruler, he is also a man of strong temper and too sure of himself. The chain of events that leads to his downfall has already begun in the early scenes when the strengths and weaknesses of his character are evident. What befalls him is part of the complex web of human life.

In *King Lear*, which was first performed in 1605, Shakespeare, who had already written histories, comedies, and some tragedies, reached the zenith of his art with the retelling of the story of a fabled king and his three daughters. Going back to native English sources, he fashioned the tale into a play that Alfred Lord Tennyson considered 'too titanic'. It presents a state of society where people's passions are, as Tennyson commented, 'savage and uncurbed. No play like this anywhere—not even the *Agamemnon* [by Aeschylus]—is so terrifically human.'

The Lear tale goes back as far as Geoffrey of Monmouth's *History of the Kings of Britain* (1137), which tells of how the monarch divides his kingdom in half, forsaking his fair-speaking daughter Cordelia. Shakespeare may have read this in the original Latin (no Elizabethan translation exists), or he may have taken details from more recent writers who were directly or indirectly influenced by Geoffrey—writers such as Holinshed, Sir Philip Sidney, or even Edmund Spenser. Whatever his sources were, Shakespeare chose to dramatize his story in pre-Roman, pre-Christian Britain, making *King Lear* his first and earliest English history play.

To the basic plot of the Lear story Shakespeare added the subplot of Gloucester and his two sons, which parallels that of Lear and his three daughters. Thus, the play's opening scene shows Cordelia's rebellion against her father's wishes, just as the second scene reveals the duplicity of Edmund's rebellion against his father. Lear, in the opening scene, wishes to divide his kingdom among his three daughters, exacting as his price their declarations of love for him: 'Which of you shall we say doth love us most?' At this moment, he wishes to abdicate his kingly responsibilities, though not necessarily his kingly position. The play traces his abdication and the subsequent assaults to his human dignity. At the end of the play, we can only agree with the last speaker: 'The oldest hath borne most: we that are young / Shall never see so much, nor live so long.'

In magnificent poetry *King Lear* explores both one man's folly in abdicating his position and the dire consequences of his decision. People are blinded; people are murdered; people die. The tragedy ends with Edgar, Lear's godson, whom Lear himself named, inheriting the throne of England.

Like tragedy, comedy arose, though 50 years later than tragedy, in the same festivals honouring Dionysus. The Greek comedies were originally filled with abuse and obscenity, and they were intended primarily to ward off evil spirits. Later, Aristophanes wrote strikingly original plays that were ripe with moral invective and political criticism. Comedies, as we have noted, always bring their characters together at the end, unlike tragedies, which lead to the outcast condition or death of one or more people in the play.

Our two classic comedies come respectively from the seventeenth and nineteenth centuries. First produced on or before 24 March 1677 by the King's Company at Dorset Garden with King Charles II in attendance, Aphra Behn's *The Rover. Or, The Banish't Cavaliers* proved to be Behn's most popular play. Centring on love and marriage from a female perspective, the play follows the tribulations of two sisters, Florinda and Hellena, in their determination not to be governed by men. More than two centuries later, on 14 February 1895, Oscar Wilde premiered *The Importance of Being Earnest* at London's St James's Theatre. Subtitled 'A Trivial Comedy for Serious People', Wilde's masterpiece revolves around the dalliances, scheming, and social commentary of Algernon 'Algy' Moncrieff and John 'Jack' Worthing. The result is a perfect comedy filled with mistaken identities, would-be lovers, and a happy revelation and reunion at the conclusion.

Across the sea from Wilde and his theatrical escapades, the Norwegian playwright Henrik Ibsen was creating plays that mark the beginning of modern naturalistic drama. His work typically reveals a conflict between the world of human imagination and its personal aspirations and an oppressive society that restricts or destroys such flights of fancy. The death of an individual may be tragic, but it is also liberating, because it frees the isolated individual from the constrictions of society.

In a fine translation by Jens Arup, *Hedda Gabler* centres around one woman's battle with her social environment. Positioned in her claustrophobic reception room, Hedda seeks some higher form of life than her society offers. Men often have outlets for their aspirations; women have almost none. Hedda looks longingly for some kind of perspective on her world, remaining finally isolated and alone in her thoughts.

George Bernard Shaw proposed ways of improving society, often by amalgamating the stage and the lectern. He wrote lengthy prefaces and sequels to his plays to make certain that the issues raised were being fully and properly treated. Through another reworking of a Greek myth, *Pygmalion*, his romance, as he calls the play, casts the mythical Greek sculptor as a professor of phonetics and the Galatea figure—his creation brought to life—as a young Cockney girl. 'His relation to her is too godlike to be altogether agreeable', Shaw states in his sequel, and, as a consequence, she marries not the professor but a young, infatuated lover. Delightful as *Pygmalion* is, we often wonder about the propriety of the ending. Is it satisfactory to readers and playgoers? Consider the musical adaptation, *My Fair Lady*, and notice how Alan Jay Lerner altered the play's conclusion to give his work a romantic ending.

The 'Theatre of the Absurd', a category encompassing dramatists of the 1950s and 1960s who view the world as essentially mysterious and unknowable, often presents actions and events filled with purposelessness and loss. The leading figure of absurdist drama, Samuel Beckett, places his characters in situations that are frequently meaningless. Krapp switches on his tape, switches it off, switches it on again, then off, then on, all the time listening intently to the personal relationship he knew 30 years ago. Edward Albee's *The Zoo Story* portrays strangers in New York City prattling aimlessly in rambling, and frequently puzzling, conversation; then one of them meets his death. *The Zoo Story* had its American debut on a double bill with *Krapp's Last Tape*.

Three plays in this collection showcase the variety and depth of contemporary Canadian theatre.

Sharon Pollock's *Doc*, which premiered in 1984 at Theatre Calgary, is a semi-autobiographical work that explores a woman's relationship with her successful father, a Maritime doctor, whose wife, like Pollock's own mother, has died tragically. The detailed time sequences underscore and emphasize the theme of female identity.

In *The Rez Sisters* (1986), Tomson Highway brings his Aboriginal roots to the surface in this celebratory, award-winning play that reflects the dramatist's deep commitment to preserving his First Nations heritage. Electrifying in its initial and subsequent successes on stages throughout Canada, the play marked the arrival on the Canadian scene of Aboriginal theatre.

The dean of Canadian playwrights, Michel Tremblay, wrote the hauntingly beautiful *For the Pleasure of Seeing Her Again* (1998) to dramatize the loving relationship he shared with his mother, who has died. It is joyous and fantastical, funny and touching.

All of the plays in our anthology repay reading and re-reading. Each one highlights specific features of the drama of its time. Whether you are reading the plays, or seeing them, or even acting in them, you will be startled by their undeniable lustre.

# Sophocles

## 496–406 BCE

Born in Greece, where his father was a wealthy and influential businessman, Sophocles became a very influential and admired public figure in Athens during the remarkable century of its rise and fall as a great city-state. During his lifetime he served his country as an ambassador, general, and treasurer; he served its religion as a priest of the god of healing; and he served its culture as a pre-eminent tragic dramatist. His plays, like those of his Greek contemporaries, were written and produced for an extraordinary drama competition that was held in Athens each spring as the major event in a festival celebrating Dionysus, the Greek god who embodied the power and fertility of nature. Each tragic dramatist who chose to compete submitted a set of either three or four plays (*trilogies* or *tetralogies*), and Sophocles won the contest 24 times. He reportedly wrote more than 120 plays, but only 7 of them have survived, all of them showing him to have been a master in the conception and elaboration of tragically compelling plots and characters. His best known plays—*Antigone* (*c.* 440), *Oedipus Rex* (*c.* 425), and *Oedipus at Colonus* (406)—though written more than 30 years apart, all deal with related characters and themes from the haunting myth of Oedipus and Thebes.

## Oedipus Rex[1]

### *CHARACTERS*

| | |
|---|---|
| OEDIPUS | MESSENGER |
| A PRIEST | SHEPHERD OF LAÏOS |
| KREON | SECOND MESSENGER |
| TEIRESIAS | CHORUS OF THEBAN ELDERS |
| IOKASTÊ | |

*The scene: Before the palace of Oedipus, King of Thebes. A central door and two lateral doors open onto a platform which runs the length of the façade. On the platform, right and left, are altars; and three steps lead down into the 'orchêstra', or chorus-ground. At the beginning of the action these steps are crowded by suppliants who have bought branches and chaplets of olive leaves and who sit in various attitudes of despair.*

*Oedipus enters.*

1 an English version by Dudley Fitts and Robert Fitzgerald

## PROLOGUE

OEDIPUS: My children, generations of the living
In the line of Kadmos, nursed at his ancient hearth:
Why have you strewn yourselves before these altars
In supplication, with your boughs and garlands?

The breath of incense rises from the city
With a sound of prayer and lamentation.
Children,
I would not have you speak through messengers,
And therefore I have come myself to hear you—
I, Oedipus, who bear the famous name.

*To a Priest*

You, there, since you are eldest in the company,
Speak for them all, tell me what preys upon you,
Whether you come in dread, or crave some blessing:
Tell me, and never doubt that I will help you
In every way I can; I should be heartless
Were I not moved to find you suppliant here.
PRIEST: Great Oedipus, O powerful King of Thebes!
You see how all the ages of our people
Cling to your altar steps: here are boys
Who can barely stand alone, and here are priests
By weight of age, as I am a priest of God,
And young men chosen from those yet unmarried;
As for the others, all that multitude,
They wait with olive chaplets in the squares,
At the two shrines of Pallas, and where Apollo
Speaks in the glowing embers.
Your own eyes
Must tell you: Thebes is tossed on a murdering sea
And can not lift her head from the death surge.
A rust consumes the buds and fruits of the earth;
The herds are sick; children die unborn,
And labour is vain. The god of plague and pyre
Raids like detestable lightning through the city,
And all the house of Kadmos is laid waste,
All emptied, and all darkened: Death alone
Battens upon the misery of Thebes.

You are not one of the immortal gods, we know;
Yet we have come to you to make our prayer

As to the man surest in mortal ways
And wisest in the ways of God. You saved us
From the Sphinx, that flinty singer, and the tribute
We paid to her so long; yet you were never
Better informed than we, nor could we teach you:
A god's touch, it seems, enabled you to help us.

Therefore, O mighty power, we turn to you:
Find us our safety, find us a remedy,
Whether by counsel of the gods or of men.
A king of wisdom tested in the past
Can act in a time of troubles, and act well.
Noblest of men, restore
Life to your city! Think how all men call you
Liberator for your boldness long ago;
Ah, when your years of kingship are remembered,
Let them not say *We rose, but later fell*—
Keep the State from going down in the storm!
Once, years ago, with happy augury,
You brought us fortune; be the same again!
No man questions your power to rule the land:
But rule over men, not over a dead city!
Ships are only hulls, high walls are nothing,
When no life moves in the empty passageways.

OEDIPUS: Poor children! You may be sure I know
All that you longed for in your coming here.
I know that you are deathly sick; and yet,
Sick as you are, not one is as sick as I.
Each of you suffers in himself alone
His anguish, not another's; but my spirit
Groans for the city, for myself, for you.

I was not sleeping, you are not waking me.
No, I have been in tears for a long while
And in my restless thought walked many ways.
In all my search I found one remedy,
And I have adopted it: I have sent Kreon,
Son of Menoikeus, brother of the Queen,
To Delphi, Apollo's place of revelation,
To learn there, if he can,
What act or pledge of mine may save the city.
I have counted the days, and now, this very day,
I am troubled, for he has overstayed his time.
What is he doing? He has been gone too long.

Yet whenever he comes back, I should do ill
Not to take any action the god orders.
PRIEST: It is a timely promise. At this instant
They tell me Kreon is here.
OEDIPUS: O Lord Apollo!
May his news be fair as his face is radiant!
PRIEST: Good news, I gather: he is crowned with bay,
The chaplet is thick with berries.
OEDIPUS: We shall soon know;
He is near enough to hear us now.

*Enter Kreon.*

O Prince:
Brother: son of Menoikeus:
What answer do you bring us from the God?
KREON: A strong one. I can tell you, great afflictions
Will turn out well, if they are taken well.
OEDIPUS: What was the oracle? These vague words
Leave me still hanging between hope and fear.
KREON: Is it your pleasure to hear me with all these
Gathered around us? I am prepared to speak,
But should we not go in?
OEDIPUS: Speak to them all.
It is for them I suffer, more than for myself.
KREON: Then I will tell you what I heard at Delphi.
In plain words
The god commands us to expel from the land of Thebes
An old defilement we are sheltering.
It is a deadly thing, beyond cure;
We must not let it feed upon us longer.
OEDIPUS: What defilement? How shall we rid ourselves of it?
KREON: By exile or death, blood for blood. It was
Murder that brought the plague-wind on the city.
OEDIPUS: Murder of whom? Surely the god has named him?
KREON: My lord: Laïos once ruled this land,
Before you came to govern us.
OEDIPUS: I know:
I learned of him from others; I never saw him.
KREON: He was murdered; and Apollo commands us now
To take revenge upon whoever killed him.
OEDIPUS: Upon whom? Where are they? Where shall we find a clue
To solve that crime, after so many years?
KREON: Here in this land, he said. Search reveals

Things that escape an inattentive man.
OEDIPUS: Tell me: Was Laïos murdered in his house,
Or in the fields, or in some foreign country?
KREON: He said he planned to make a pilgrimage.
He did not come home again.
OEDIPUS: And was there no one,
No witness, no companion, to tell what happened?
KREON: They were all killed but one, and he got away
So frightened that he could remember one thing only.
OEDIPUS: What was that one thing? One may be the key
To everything, if we resolve to use it.
KREON: He said that a band of highwaymen attacked them,
Outnumbered them, and overwhelmed the King.
OEDIPUS: Strange, that a highwayman should be so daring—
Unless some faction here bribed him to do it.
KREON: We though of that. But after Laïos' death
New troubles arose and we had no avenger.
OEDIPUS: What troubles could prevent your hunting down the killers?
KREON: The riddling Sphinx's song
Made us deaf to all mysteries but her own.
OEDIPUS: Then once more I must bring what is dark to light.
It is most fitting that Apollo shows,
As you do, this compunction for the dead.
You shall see how I stand by you, as I should,
Avenging this country and the god as well,
And not as though it were for some distant friend,
But for my own sake, to be rid of evil.
Whoever killed King Laïos might—who knows?—
Lay violent hands even on me—and soon.
I act for the murdered king in my own interest.

Come, then, my children: leave the altar steps,
Lift up your olive boughs!
One of you go
And summon the people of Kadmos to gather here.
I will do all that I can; you may tell them that.

*Exit a Page.*

So, with the help of God.
We shall be saved—or else indeed we are lost.
PRIEST: Let us rise, children. It was for this we came,
And now the King has promised it.

Phoibos has sent us an oracle; may he descend
Himself to save us and drive out the plague.

*Exeunt Oedipus and Kreon into the palace by the central door. The Priest and the Suppliants disperse right and left. After a short pause the Chorus enters the* orchêstra.

## PÁRODOS

CHORUS: What is God singing in his profound **Strophe 1**
Delphi of gold and shadow?
What oracle for Thebes, the sunwhipped city?

Fear unjoints me, the roots of my heart tremble.

Now I remember, O Healer, your power and wonder:
Will you send doom like a sudden cloud, or weave it
Like nightfall of the past?

Speak, speak to us, issue of holy sound;
Dearest to our Expectancy: be tender!

Let me pray to Athenê, the immortal daughter of Zeus, **Antistrophe 1**
And to Artemis her sister
Who keeps her famous throne in the market ring,
And to Apollo, archer from distant heaven—

O gods, descend! Like three streams leap against
The fires of our grief, the fires of darkness;
Be swift to bring us rest!

As in the old time from the brilliant house
Of air you stepped to save us, come again!

Now our afflictions have no end **Strophe 2**
Now all our stricken host lies down
And no man fights off death with his mind;

The noble plowland bears no grain,
And groaning mothers can not bear—

See, how our lives like birds take wing,

Like sparks that fly when a fire soars,
To the shore of the god of evening.

**Antistrophe 2**

The plague burns on, it is pitiless,
Though pallid children laden with death
Lie unwept in the stony ways,

And old grey women by every path
Flock to the strand about the altars

There to strike their breasts and cry
Worship of Phoibos in wailing prayers:
Be kind, God's golden child!

**Strophe 3**

There are no swords in this attack by fire,
No shields, but we are ringed with cries.

Send the besieger plunging from our homes
Into the vast sea-room of the Atlantic
Or into the waves that foam eastward of Thrace—
For the day ravages what the night spares—

Destroy our enemy, lord of the thunder!
Let him be riven by lightning from heaven!

**Antistrophe 3**

Phoibos Apollo, stretch the sun's bowstring,
That golden cord, until it sing for us,
Flashing arrows in heaven!
Artemis, Huntress,
Race with flaring lights upon our mountains!

O scarlet god, O golden-banded brow,
O Theban Bacchos in a storm of Maenads,

*Enter Oedipus, centre.*

Whirl upon Death, that all the Undying hate!
Come with blinding torches, come in joy!

## SCENE I

OEDIPUS: Is this your prayer? It may be answered. Come,
Listen to me, act as the crisis demands,
And you shall have relief from all these evils.

Until now I was a stranger to this tale,
As I had been a stranger to the crime.
Could I track down the murderer without a clue?
But how, friends,
As one who became a citizen after the murder,
I make this proclamation to all Thebans:

If any man knows by whose hand Laïos, son of Labdakos,
Met his death, I direct that man to tell me everything,
No matter what he fears for having so long withheld it.
Let it stand as promised that no further trouble
Will come to him, but he may leave the land in safety.

Moreover: If anyone knows the murderer to be foreign,
Let him not keep silent: he shall have his reward from me.
However, if he does conceal it; if any man
Fearing for his friend or for himself disobeys this edict,
Hear what I propose to do:

I solemnly forbid the people of this country,
Where power and throne are mine, ever to receive that man
Or speak to him, no matter who he is, or let him
Join in sacrifice, lustration, or in prayer.
I decree that he be driven from every house,
Being, as he is, corruption itself to us: the Delphic
Voice of Apollo has pronounced this revelation.
Thus I associate myself with the oracle
And take the side of the murdered king.

As for the criminal, I pray to God—
Whether, it be a lurking thief, or one of a number—
I pray that the man's life be consumed in evil and wretchedness.
And as for me, this curse applies no less
If it should turn out that the culprit is my guest here,
Sharing my hearth.
You have heard the penalty.

I lay it on you now to attend to this
For my sake, for Apollo's, for the sick
Sterile city that heaven has abandoned.
Suppose the oracle had given you no command:
Should this defilement go uncleansed for ever?

You should have found the murderer: your king,
A noble king, had been destroyed!
Now I,
Having the power that he held before me,
Having this bed, begetting children there
Upon his wife, as he would have, had he lived—
Their son would have been my children's brother,
If Laïos had had luck in fatherhood!
(And now his bad fortune has struck him down)—
I say I take the son's part, just as though
I were his son, to press the fight for him
And see it won! I'll find the hand that brought
Death to Labdakos' and Polydoros' child,
Heir of Kadmos' and Agenor's line.
And as for those who fail me,
May the gods deny them the fruit of the earth,
Fruit of the womb, and may they rot utterly!
Let them be wretched as we are wretched, and worse!
For you, for loyal Thebans, and for all
Who find my actions right, I pray the favour
Of justice, and of all the immortal gods.

CHORAGOS: Since I am under oath, my lord, I swear
I did not do this murder, I can not name
The murderer. Phoibos ordained the search;
Why did he not say who the culprit was?

OEDIPUS: An honest question. But no man in the world
Can make the gods do more than the gods will.

CHORAGOS: There is an alternative, I think—

OEDIPUS: Tell me.
Any or all, you must not fail to tell me.

CHORAGOS: A lord clairvoyant to the lord Apollo,
As we all know, is the skilled Teiresias.
One might learn much about this from him, Oedipus.

OEDIPUS: I am not wasting time:
Kreon spoke of this, and I have sent for him—
Twice, in fact; it is strange that he is not here.

CHORAGOS: The other matter—that old report—seems useless.

OEDIPUS: What was that? I am interested in all reports.

CHORAGOS: The King was said to have been killed by highwaymen.
OEDIPUS: I know. But we have no witnesses to that.
CHORAGOS: If the killer can feel a particle of dread,
Your curse will bring him out of hiding!
OEDIPUS: No.
The man who dared that act will fear no curse.

*Enter the blind seer Teiresias, led by a Page.*

CHORAGOS: But there is one man who may detect the criminal.
This is Teiresias, this is the holy prophet
In whom, alone of all men, truth was born.
OEDIPUS: Teiresias: seer: student of mysteries,
Of all that's taught and all that no man tells,
Secrets of Heaven and secrets of the earth:
Blind though you are, you know the city lies
Sick with plague; and from this plague, my lord,
We find that you alone can guard or save us.

Possibly you did not hear the messengers?
Apollo, when we sent to him,
Sent us back word that this great pestilence
Would lift, but only if we established clearly
The identity of those who murdered Laïos.
They must be killed or exiled.
Can you use
Birdflight or any art of divination
To purify yourself, and Thebes, and me
From this contagion? We are in your hands.
There is no fairer duty
Than that of helping others in distress.
TEIRESIAS: How dreadful knowledge of the truth can be
When there's no help in truth! I knew this well
But did not act on it: else I should not have come.
OEDIPUS: What is troubling you? Why are you eyes so cold?
TEIRESIAS: Let me go home. Bear your own fate, and I'll
Bear mine. It is better so: trust what I say.
OEDIPUS: What you say is ungracious and unhelpful
To your native country. Do not refuse to speak.
TEIRESIAS: When it comes to speech, your own is neither temperate
Nor opportune. I wish to be more prudent.
OEDIPUS: In God's name, we all beg you—
TEIRESIAS: You are all ignorant.
No; I will never tell you what I know.
Now it is my mystery; then, it would be yours.

OEDIPUS: What! You do know something, and will not tell us?
You would betray us all and wreck the State?
TEIRESIAS: I do not intend to torture myself, or you.
Why persist in asking? You will not persuade me.
OEDIPUS: What a wicked old man you are! You'd try a stone's
Patience! Out with it! Have you no feeling at all?
TEIRESIAS: You call me unfeeling. If you could only see
The nature of your own feelings . . .
OEDIPUS: Why,
Who would not feel as I do? Who could endure
Your arrogance toward the city?
TEIRESIAS: What does it matter?
Whether I speak or not, it is bound to come.
OEDIPUS: Then, if 'it' is bound to come, you are bound to tell me.
TEIRESIAS: No, I will not go on. Rage as you please.
OEDIPUS: Rage? Why not!
And I'll tell you what I think:
You planned it, you had it done, you all but
Killed him with your own hands: if you had eyes,
I'd say the crime was yours, and yours alone.
TEIRESIAS: So? I charge you, then,
Abide by the proclamation you have made:
From this day forth
Never speak again to these men or to me;
You yourself are the pollution of this country.
OEDIPUS: You dare say that! Can you possibly think you have
Some way of going free, after such insolence?
TEIRESIAS: I have gone free. It is the truth sustains me.
OEDIPUS: Who taught you shamelessness? It was not your craft.
TEIRESIAS: You did. You made me speak. I did not want to.
OEDIPUS: Speak what? Let me hear it again more clearly.
TEIRESIAS: Was it not clear before? Are you tempting me?
OEDIPUS: I did not understand it. Say it again.
TEIRESIAS: I say that you are the murderer whom you seek.
OEDIPUS: Now twice you have spat out infamy. You'll pay for it!
TEIRESIAS: Would you care for more? Do you wish to be really angry?
OEDIPUS: Say what you will. Whatever you say is worthless.
TEIRESIAS: I say you live in hideous shame with those
Most dear to you. You can not see the evil.
OEDIPUS: Can you go on babbling like this for ever?
TEIRESIAS: I can, if there is power in truth.
OEDIPUS: There is:
But not for you, not for you,
You sightless, witless, senseless, mad old man!

TEIRESIAS: You are the madman. There is no one here
Who will not curse you soon, as you curse me.
OEDIPUS: You child of total night! I would not touch you;
Neither would any man who sees the sun.
TEIRESIAS: True: it is not from you my fate will come.
That lies within Apollo's competence,
As it is his concern.
OEDIPUS: Tell me, who made
These fine discoveries? Kreon? or someone else?
TEIRESIAS: Kreon is no threat. You weave your own doom.
OEDIPUS: Wealth, power, craft of statesmanship!
Kingly position, everywhere admired!
What savage envy is stored up against these,
If Kreon, whom I trusted, Kreon my friend,
For this great office which the city once
Put in my hands unsought—if for this power
Kreon desires in secret to destroy me!

He has bought this decrepit fortune-teller, this
Collector of dirty pennies, this prophet fraud—
Why, he is no more clairvoyant than I am!
Tell us:
Has your mystic mummery ever approached the truth?
When that hellcat the Sphinx was performing here,
What help were you to these people?
Her magic was not for the first man who came along:
It demanded a real exorcist. Your birds—
What good were they? or the gods, for the matter of that?
But I came by,
Oedipus, the simple man, who knows nothing—
I thought it out for myself, no birds helped me!
And this is the man you think you can destroy.
That you may be close to Kreon when he's king!
Well, you and your friend Kreon, it seems to me,
Will suffer most. If you were not an old man,
You would have paid already for your plot.
CHORAGOS: We can not see that his words or yours
Have been spoken except in anger, Oedipus,
And of anger we have no need. How to accomplish
The god's will best: that is what most concerns us.
TEIRESIAS: You are a king. But where argument's concerned
I am your man, as much a king as you.
I am not your servant, but Apollo's;
I have no need of Kreon's name.

Listen to me. You mock my blindness, do you?
But I say that you, with both your eyes, are blind:
You can not see the wretchedness of your life,
Nor in whose house you live, no, nor with whom.
Who are your father and mother? Can you tell me?
You do not even know the blind wrongs
That you have done them, on earth and in the world below.
But the double lash of your parents' curse will whip you
Out of this land some day, with only night
Upon your precious eyes.
Your cries then—where will they not be heard?
What fastness of Kithairon will not echo them?
And that bridal-descant of yours—you'll know it then,
The song they sang when you came here to Thebes
And found your misguided berthing.
All this, and more, that you can not guess at now,
Will bring you to yourself among your children.

Be angry, then. Curse Kreon. Curse my words.
I tell you, no man that walks upon the earth
Shall be rooted out more horribly than you.

OEDIPUS: Am I to bear this from him?—Damnation
Take you! Out of this place! Out of my sight!
TEIRESIAS: I would not have come at all if you had not asked me.
OEDIPUS: Could I have told that you'd talk nonsense, that
You'd come here to make a fool of yourself, and of me?
TEIRESIAS: A fool? Your parents thought me sane enough.
OEDIPUS: My parents again!—Wait: who were my parents?
TEIRESIAS: This day will give you a father, and break your heart.
OEDIPUS: Your infantile riddles! Your damned abracadabra!
TEIRESIAS: You were a great man once at solving riddles.
OEDIPUS: Mock me with that if you like; you will find it true.
TEIRESIAS: It was true enough. It brought about your ruin.
OEDIPUS: But if it saved this town?
TEIRESIAS: [*To the Page*] Boy, give me your hand.
OEDIPUS: Yes, boy; lead him away.
—While you are here
We can do nothing. Go; leave us in peace.
TEIRESIAS: I will go when I have said what I have to say.
How can you hurt me? And I tell you again:
The man you have been looking for all this time,
The damned man, the murderer of Laïos,
That man is in Thebes. To your mind he is foreign-born,
But it will soon be shown that he is a Theban,

A revelation that will fail to please.
A blind man,
Who has his eyes now; a penniless man, who is rich now;
And he will go tapping the strange earth with his staff.
To the children with whom he lives now he will be
Brother and father—the very same; to her
Who bore him, son and husband—the very same
Who came to his father's bed, wet with his father's blood.

Enough. Go think that over.
If later you find error in what I have said,
You may say that I have no skill in prophecy.

*Exit Teiresias, led by his Page. Oedipus goes into the palace.*

## ODE I

CHORUS: The Delphic stone of prophecies **Strophe 1**
Remembers ancient regicide
And a still bloody hand.

That killer's hour of flight has come.
He must be stronger than riderless
Coursers of untiring wind,
For the son of Zeus armed with his father's thunder
Leaps in lightning after him;
And the Furies hold his track, the sad Furies.

Holy Parnassos' peak of snow **Antistrophe 1**
Flashes and blinds that secret man,
That all shall hunt him down:
Though he may roam the forest shade
Like a bull gone wild from pasture
To rage through glooms of stone.
Doom comes down on him; flight will not avail him;
For the world's heart calls him desolate,
And the immortal voices follow, for ever follow.

But now a wilder thing is heard **Strophe 2**
From the old man skilled at hearing Fate in the wing-beat of a bird.
Bewildered as a blown bird, my soul hovers and can not find
Foothold in this debate, or any reason or rest of mind.
But no man ever brought—none can bring

Proof of strife between Thebes' royal house,
Labdakos' line, and the son of Polybos;
And never until now has any brought word
Of Laïos' dark death staining Oedipus the King.

Divine Zeus and Apollo hold **Antistrophe 2**
Perfect intelligence alone of all tales ever told;
And well though this diviner works, he works in his own night;
No man can judge that rough unknown or trust in second sight,
For wisdom changes hands among the wise.
Shall I believe my great lord criminal
At a raging word that a blind old man let fall?
I saw him, when the carrion woman faced him of old,
Prove his heroic mind. These evil words are lies.

## SCENE II

KREON: Men of Thebes:
I am told that heavy accusations
Have been brought against me by King Oedipus.
I am not the kind of man to bear this tamely.

If in these present difficulties
He holds me accountable for any harm to him
Through anything I have said or done—why, then,
I do not value life in this dishonour.

It is not as though this rumour touched upon
Some private indiscretion. The matter is grave.
The fact is that I am being called disloyal
To the State, to my fellow citizens, to my friends.
CHORAGOS: He may have spoken in anger, not from his mind.
KREON: But did you not hear him say I was the one
Who seduced the old prophet into lying?
CHORAGOS: The thing was said; I do not know how seriously.
KREON: But you were watching him! Were his eyes steady?
Did he look like a man in his right mind?
CHORAGOS: I do not know.
I can not judge the behaviour of great men.
But here is the King himself.

*Enter Oedipus.*

OEDIPUS: So you dared come back.
Why? How brazen of you to come to my house,
You murderer!
Do you think I do not know
That you plotted to kill me, plotted to steal my throne?
Tell me, in God's name: am I coward, a fool,
That you should dream you could accomplish this?
A fool who could not see your slippery game?
A coward, not to fight back when I saw it?
You are the fool, Kreon, are you not? hoping
With support or friends to get a throne?
Thrones may be won or bought: you could do neither.

KREON: Now listen to me. You have talked; let me talk, too.
You can not judge unless you know the facts.

OEDIPUS: You speak well: there is one fact; but I find it hard
To learn from the deadliest enemy I have.

KREON: That above all I must dispute with you.

OEDIPUS: That above all I will not hear you deny.

KREON: If you think there is anything good in being stubborn
Against all reason, then I say you are wrong.

OEDIPUS: If you think a man can sin against his own kind
And not be punished for it, I say you are mad.

KREON: I agree. But tell me: what have I done to you?

OEDIPUS: You advised me to send for that wizard, did you not?

KREON: I did. I should do it again.

OEDIPUS: Very well. Now tell me:
How long has it been since Laïos—

KREON: What of Laïos?

OEDIPUS: Since he vanished in that onset by the road?

KREON: It was long ago, a long time.

OEDIPUS: And this prophet,
Was he practicing here then?

KREON: He was; and with honour, as now.

OEDIPUS: Did he speak of me at that time?

KREON: He never did;
At least, not when I was present.

OEDIPUS: But . . . the inquiry?
I suppose you held one?

KREON: We did, but we learned nothing.

OEDIPUS: Why did the prophet not speak against me then?

KREON: I do not know; and I am the kind of man
Who holds his tongue when he has no facts to go on.

OEDIPUS: There's one fact that you know, and you could tell it.

KREON: What fact is that? If I know it, you shall have it.

OEDIPUS: If he were not involved with you, he could not say
That it was I who murdered Laïos.
KREON: If he says that, you are the one that knows it!—
But now it is my turn to question you.
OEDIPUS: Put your questions. I am no murderer.
KREON: First, then: You married my sister?
OEDIPUS: I married your sister.
KREON: And you rule the kingdom equally with her?
OEDIPUS: Everything that she wants she has from me.
KREON: And I am the third, equal to both of you?
OEDIPUS: That is why I call you a bad friend.
KREON: No. Reason it out, as I have done.
Think of this first: Would any sane man prefer
Power, with all a king's anxieties,
To that same power and the grace of sleep?
Certainly not I.
I have never longed for the king's power—only his rights.
Would any wise man differ from me in this?
As matters stand, I have my way in everything
With your consent, and no responsibilities.
If I were king, I should be a slave to policy.
How could I desire a sceptre more
Than what is now mine—untroubled influence?
No, I have not gone mad; I need no honours,
Except those with the perquisites I have now.
I am welcome everywhere; every man salutes me,
And those who want your favour seek my ear,
Since I know how to manage what they ask.
Should I exchange this ease for that anxiety?
Besides, no sober mind is treasonable.
I hate anarchy
And never would deal with any man who likes it.

Test what I have said. Go to the priestess
At Delphi, ask if I quoted her correctly.
And as for this other thing: if I am found
Guilty of treason with Teiresias,
Then sentence me to death. You have my word
It is a sentence I should cast my vote for—
But not without evidence!
You do wrong
When you take good men for bad, bad men for good.
A true friend thrown aside—why, life itself

Is not more precious!
In time you will know this well:
For time, and time alone, will show the just man,
Though scoundrels are discovered in a day.

CHORAGOS: This is well said, and a prudent man would ponder it.
Judgments too quickly formed are dangerous.

OEDIPUS: But is he not quick in his duplicity?
And shall I not be quick to parry him?
Would you have me stand still, holding my peace, and let
This man win everything, through my inaction?

KREON: And you want—what is it, then? To banish me?

OEDIPUS: No, not exile. It is your death I want,
So that all the world may see what treason means.

KREON: You will persist, then? You will not believe me?

OEDIPUS: How can I believe you?

KREON: Then you are a fool.

OEDIPUS: To save myself?

KREON: In justice, think of me.

OEDIPUS: You are evil incarnate.

KREON: But suppose that you are wrong?

OEDIPUS: Still I must rule.

KREON: But not if you rule badly.

OEDIPUS: O city, city!

KREON: It is my city, too!

CHORAGOS: Now, my lords, be still. I see the Queen,
Iokastê, coming from her palace chambers;
And it is time she came, for the sake of you both.
This dreadful quarrel can be resolved through her.

*Enter Iokastê.*

IOKASTÊ: Poor foolish men, what wicked din is this?
With Thebes sick to death, is it not shameful
That you should rake some private quarrel up?
[*To Oedipus*]
Come into the house
—And you, Kreon, go now:
Let us have no more of this tumult over nothing.

KREON: Nothing? No, sister: what your husband plans for me
Is one of two great evils: exile or death.

OEDIPUS: He is right.
Why, woman I have caught him squarely
Plotting against my life.

KREON: No! Let me die
Accurst if ever I have wished you harm!
IOKASTÊ: Ah, believe it, Oedipus!
In the name of the gods, respect this oath of his
For my sake, for the sake of these people here!
CHORAGOS: **Strophe 1**
Open your mind to her, my lord. Be ruled by her, I beg you!
OEDIPUS: What would you have me do?
CHORAGOS: Respect Kreon's word. He has never spoken like a fool,
And now he has sworn an oath.
OEDIPUS: You know what you ask?
CHORAGOS: I do.
OEDIPUS: Speak on, then.
CHORAGOS: A friend so sworn should not be baited so,
In blind malice, and without final proof.
OEDIPUS: You are aware, I hope, that what you say
Means death for me, or exile at the least.
CHORAGOS: **Strophe 2**
No, I swear by Helios, first in Heaven!
May I die friendless and accurst,
The worst of deaths, if ever I meant that!
It is the withering fields
That hurt my sick heart:
Must we bear all these ills,
and now you bad blood as well?
OEDIPUS: Then let him go. And let me die, if I must,
Or be driven by him in shame from the land of Thebes.
It is your unhappiness, and not his talk,
That touches me.
As for him—
Wherever he goes, hatred will follow him.
KREON: Ugly in yielding, as you were ugly in rage!
Natures like yours chiefly torment themselves.
OEDIPUS: Can you not go? Can you not leave me?
KREON: I can.
You do not know me; but the city knows me,
And in its eyes I am just, if not in yours.

*Exit Kreon.*

CHORAGOS: **Antistrophe 1**
Lady Iokastê, did you not ask the King to go to his chambers?
IOKASTÊ: First tell me what has happened.
CHORAGOS: There was suspicion without evidence; yet it rankled
As even false charges will.

IOKASTÊ: On both sides?
CHORAGOS: On both.
IOKASTÊ: But what was said?
CHORAGOS: Oh let it rest, let it be done with!
Have we not suffered enough?
OEDIPUS: You see to what your decency has brought you:
You have made difficulties where my heart saw none.

CHORAGOS: **Antistrophe 2**

Oedipus, it is not once only I have told you—
You must know I should count myself unwise
To the point of madness, should I now forsake you—
You, under whose hand,
In the storm of another time,
Our dear land sailed out free.
But now stand fast at the helm!

IOKASTÊ: In God's name, Oedipus, inform your wife as well:
Why are you so set in this hard anger?
OEDIPUS: I will tell you, for none of these men deserves
My confidence as you do. It is Kreon's work,
His treachery, his plotting against me.
IOKASTÊ: Go on, if you can make this clear to me.
OEDIPUS: He charges me with the murder of Laïos.
IOKASTÊ: Has he some knowledge? Or does he speak from hearsay?
OEDIPUS: He would not commit himself to such a charge,
But he has brought in that damnable soothsayer
To tell his story.
IOKASTÊ: Set your mind at rest.
If it is a question of soothsayers, I tell you
That you will find no man whose craft gives knowledge
Of the unknowable.
Here is my proof:
An oracle was reported to Laïos once
(I will not say from Phoibos himself, but from
His appointed ministers, at any rate)
That his doom would be death at the hands of his own son—
His son, born of his flesh and of mine!

Now, you remember the story: Laïos was killed
By marauding strangers where three highways meet;
But his child had not been three days in this world
Before the King had pierced the baby's ankles
And left him to die on a lonely mountainside.

Thus, Apollo never caused that child
To kill his father, and it was not Laïos' fate
To die at the hands of his son, as he had feared.
This is what prophets and prophecies are worth!
Have no dread of them.
It is God himself
Who can show us what he wills, in his own way.

OEDIPUS: How strange a shadowy memory crossed my mind,
Just now while you were speaking; it chilled my heart.

IOKASTÊ: What do you mean? What memory do you speak of?

OEDIPUS: If I understand you, Laïos was killed
At a place where three roads meet.

IOKASTÊ: So it was said:
We have no later story.

OEDIPUS: Where did it happen?

IOKASTÊ: Phokis, it is called: at a place where the Theban Way
Divides into the roads toward Delphi and Daulia.

OEDIPUS: When?

IOKASTÊ: We had the news not long before you came
And proved the right to your succession here.

OEDIPUS: Ah, what net has God been weaving for me?

IOKASTÊ: Oedipus! Why does this trouble you?

OEDIPUS: Do not ask me yet.
First, tell me how Laïos looked, and tell me
How old he was.

IOKASTÊ: He was tall, his hair just touched
With white; his form was not unlike your own.

OEDIPUS: I think that I myself may be accurst
By my own ignorant edict.

IOKASTÊ: You speak strangely.
It makes me tremble to look at you, my King.

OEDIPUS: I am not sure that the blind man can not see.
But I should know better if you were to tell me—

IOKASTÊ: Anything—though I dread to hear you ask it.

OEDIPUS: Was the King lightly escorted, or did he ride
With a large company, as a ruler should?

IOKASTÊ: There were five men with him in all: one was a herald;
And a single chariot, which he was driving.

OEDIPUS: Alas, that makes it plain enough!
But who—
Who told you how it happened?

IOKASTÊ: A household servant,
The only one to escape.

OEDIPUS: And is he still
A servant of ours?
IOKASTÊ: No; for when he came back at last
And found you enthroned in the place of the dead king,
He came to me, touched my hand with his, and begged
That I would send him away to the frontier district
Where only the shepherds go—
As far away from the city as I could send him.
I granted his prayer; for although the man was a slave,
He had earned more than this favour at my hands.
OEDIPUS: Can he be called back quickly?
IOKASTÊ: Easily.
But why?
OEDIPUS: I have taken too much upon myself
Without enquiry; therefore I wish to consult him.
IOKASTÊ: Then he shall come.
But am I not one also
To whom you might confide these fears of yours?
OEDIPUS: That is your right; it will not be denied you,
Now least of all; for I have reached a pitch
Of wild foreboding. Is there anyone
To whom I should sooner speak?

Polybos of Corinth is my father.
My mother is a Dorian: Meropê.
I grew up chief among the men of Corinth
Until a strange thing happened—
Not worth my passion, it may be, but strange.

At a feast, a drunken man maundering in his cups
Cries out that I am not my father's son!
I contained myself that night, though I felt anger
And a sinking heart. The next day I visited
My father and mother, and questioned them. They stormed,
Calling it all the slanderous rant of a fool;
And this relieved me. Yet the suspicion
Remained always aching in my mind;
I knew there was talk; I could not rest;
And finally, saying nothing to my parents,
I went to the shrine at Delphi.

The god dismissed my question without reply;
He spoke of other things.
Some were clear,

Full of wretchedness, dreadful, unbearable:
As that I should lie with my own mother, breed
Children from whom all men would turn their eyes;
And that I should be my father's murderer.

I heard all this, and fled. And from that day
Corinth to me was only in the stars
Descending in that quarter of the sky,
As I wandered farther and farther on my way
To a land where I should never see the evil
Sung by the oracle. And I came to this country
Where, so you say, King Laïos was killed.
I will tell you all that happened there, my lady.

There were three highways
Coming together at a place I passed;
And there a herald came towards me, and a chariot
Drawn by horses, with a man such as you describe
Seated in it. The groom leading the horses
Forced me off the road at his lord's command;
But as this charioteer lurched over towards me
I struck him in my rage. The old man saw me
And brought his double goad down upon my head
As I came abreast.
He was paid back, and more!
Swinging my club in this right hand I knocked him
Out of his car, and he rolled on the ground.
I killed him.
I killed them all.
Now if that stranger and Laïos were—kin,
Where is a man more miserable than I?
More hated by the gods? Citizen and alien alike
Must never shelter me or speak to me—
I must be shunned by all.
And I myself
Pronounced this malediction upon myself!

Think of it: I have touched you with these hands,
These hands that killed your husband. What defilement!

Am I all evil, then? It must be so,
Since I must flee from Thebes, yet never again
See my own countrymen, my own country,
For fear of joining my mother in marriage

And killing Polybos, my father.
Ah,
If I was created so, born to this fate,
Who could deny the savagery of God?

O holy majesty of heavenly powers!
May I never see that day! Never!
Rather let me vanish from the race of men
Than know the abomination destined me!

CHORAGOS: We too, my lord, have felt dismay at this.
But there is hope: you have yet to hear the shepherd.

OEDIPUS: Indeed, I fear no other hope is left me.

IOKASTÊ: What do you hope from him when he comes?

OEDIPUS: This much:
If his account of the murder tallies with yours,
Then I am cleared.

IOKASTÊ: What was it that I said
Of such importance?

OEDIPUS: Why, 'marauders', you said,
Killed the King, according to this man's story.
If he maintains that still, if there were several,
Clearly the guilt is not mine: I was alone.
But if he says one man, singlehanded, did it,
Then the evidence all points to me.

IOKASTÊ: You may be sure that he said there were several;
And can he call back that story now? He can not.
The whole city heard it as plainly as I.
But suppose he alters some detail of it:
He can not ever show that Laïos' death
Fulfilled the oracle: for Apollo said
My child was doomed to kill him; and my child—
Poor baby!—it was my child that died first.

No. From now on, where oracles are concerned,
I would not waste a second thought on any.

OEDIPUS: You may be right.
But come: let someone go
For the shepherd at once. This matter must be settled.

IOKASTÊ: I will send for him.
I would not wish to cross you in anything.
And surely not in this.—Let us go in.

*Exeunt into the palace.*

## ODE II

CHORUS: Let me be reverent in the ways of right, **Strophe 1**
Lowly the paths I journey on;
Let all my words and actions keep
The laws of the pure universe
From highest Heaven handed down.
For Heaven is their bright nurse,
Those generations of the realms of light;
Ah, never of mortal kind were they begot,
Nor are they slaves of memory, lost in sleep:
Their Father is greater than Time, and ages not.

The tyrant is a child of Pride **Antistrophe 1**
Who drinks from his great sickening cup
Recklessness and vanity,
Until from his high crest headlong
He plummets to the dust of hope.
That strong man is not strong.
But let no fair ambition be denied;
May God protect the wrestler for the State
In government, in comely policy,
Who will fear God, and on His ordinance wait.

Haughtiness and the high hand of disdain **Strophe 2**
Tempt and outrage God's holy law;
And any mortal who dares hold
No immortal Power in awe
Will be caught up in a net of pain:
The price for which his levity is sold.
Let each man take due earnings, then,
And keep his hands from holy things,
And from blasphemy stand apart—
Else the crackling blast of heaven
Blows on his head, and on his desperate heart.
Though fools will honour impious men,
In their cities no tragic poet sings.

Shall we lose faith in Delphi's obscurities, **Antistrophe 2**
We have heard the world's core
Discredited, and the sacred wood
Of Zeus at Elis praised no more?
The deeds and the strange prophecies
Must make a pattern yet to be understood.

Zeus, if indeed you are lord of all,
Throned in light over night and day,
Mirror this in your endless mind:
Our masters call the oracle
Words on the wind, and the Delphic vision blind!
Their hearts no longer know Apollo,
And reverence for the gods has died away.

## SCENE III

*Enter Iokastê.*

IOKASTÊ: Princess of Thebes, it has occurred to me
To visit the altars of the gods, bearing
These branches as a suppliant, and this incense.
Our King is not himself: his noble soul
Is overwrought with fantasies of dread,
Else he would consider
The new prophecies in the light of the old.
He will listen to any voice that speaks disaster,
And my advice goes for nothing.

*She approaches the altar, right.*

To you, then, Apollo,
Lycéan lord, since you are nearest, I turn in prayer.

Receive these offerings, and grant us deliverance
From defilement. Our hearts are heavy with fear
When we see our leader distracted, as helpless sailors
Are terrified by the confusion of their helmsman.

*Enter Messenger.*

MESSENGER: Friends, no doubt you can direct me:
Where shall I find the house of Oedipus,
Or, better still, where is the King himself?
CHORAGOS: It is this very place, stranger; he is inside.
This is his wife and mother of his children.
MESSENGER: I wish her happiness in a happy house,
Blest in all the fulfillment of her marriage.
IOKASTÊ: I wish as much for you: your courtesy
Deserves a like good fortune. But now, tell me:
Why have you come? What have you to say to us?
MESSENGER: Good news, my lady, for your house and your husband.

IOKASTÊ: What news? Who sent you here?
MESSENGER: I am from Corinth.
The news I bring ought to mean joy for you,
Though it may be you will find some grief in it.
IOKASTÊ: What is it? How can it touch us in both ways?
MESSENGER: The word is that the people of the Isthmus
Intend to call Oedipus to be their king.
IOKASTÊ: But old King Polybos—is he not reigning still?
MESSENGER: No. Death holds him in his sepulchre.
IOKASTÊ: What are you saying? Polybos is dead?
MESSENGER: If I am not telling the truth, may I die myself.
IOKASTÊ: [*To a Maidservant*]
Go in, go quickly; tell this to your master.

O riddlers of God's will, where are you now!
This was the man whom Oedipus, long ago,
Feared so, fled so, in dread of destroying him—
But it was another fate by which he died.

*Enter Oedipus, centre.*

OEDIPUS: Dearest Iokastê, why have you sent for me?
IOKASTÊ: Listen to what this man says, and then tell me
What has become of the solemn prophecies.
OEDIPUS: Who is this man? What is his news for me?
IOKASTÊ: He has come from Corinth to announce your father's death!
OEDIPUS: Is it true, stranger? Tell me in your own words.
MESSENGER: I can not say it more clearly: the King is dead.
OEDIPUS: Was it by treason? Or by an attack of illness?
MESSENGER: A little thing brings old men to their rest.
OEDIPUS: It was sickness, then?
MESSENGER: Yes, and his many years.
OEDIPUS: Ah!
Why should a man respect the Pythian hearth, or
Give heed to the birds that jangle above his head?
They prophesied that I should kill Polybos,
Kill my own father; but he is dead and buried,
And I am here—I never touched him, never,
Unless he died of grief for my departure,
And thus, in a sense, through me. No. Polybos
Has packed the oracles off with him underground.
They are empty words.
IOKASTÊ: Had I not told you so?
OEDIPUS: You had; it was my faint heart that betrayed me.

IOKASTÊ: From now on never think of those things again.
OEDIPUS: And yet—must I not fear my mother's bed?
IOKASTÊ: Why should anyone in this world be afraid,
Since Fate rules us and nothing can be foreseen?
A man should live only for the present day.
Have no more fear of sleeping with your mother:
How many men, in dreams, have lain with their mothers!
No reasonable man is troubled by such things.
OEDIPUS: That is true; only—
If only my mother were not still alive!
But she is alive. I can not help my dread.
IOKASTÊ: Yet this news of your father's death is wonderful.
OEDIPUS: Wonderful. But I fear the living woman.
MESSENGER: Tell me, who is this woman that you fear?
OEDIPUS: It is Meropê, man; the wife of King Polybos.
MESSENGER: Meropê? Why should you be afraid of her?
OEDIPUS: An oracle of the gods, a dreadful saying.
MESSENGER: Can you tell me about it or are you sworn to silence?
OEDIPUS: I can tell you, and I will.
Apollo said through his prophet that I was the man
Who should marry his own mother, shed his father's blood
With his own hands. And so, for all these years
I have kept clear of Corinth, and no harm has come—
Though it would have been sweet to see my parents again.
MESSENGER: And is this the fear that drove you out of Corinth?
OEDIPUS: Would you have me kill my father?
MESSENGER: As for that
You must be reassured by the news I gave you.
OEDIPUS: If you could reassure me, I would reward you.
MESSENGER: I had that in mind, I will confess: I thought
I could count on you when you returned to Corinth.
OEDIPUS: No: I will never go near my parents again.
MESSENGER: Ah, son, you still do not know what you are doing—
OEDIPUS: What do you mean? In the name of God tell me!
MESSENGER: —If these are your reasons for not going home.
OEDIPUS: I tell you, I fear the oracle may come true.
MESSENGER: And guilt may come upon you through your parents?
OEDIPUS: That is the dread that is always in my heart.
MESSENGER: Can you not see that all your fears are groundless?
OEDIPUS: Groundless? Am I not my parents' son?
MESSENGER: Polybos was not your father.
OEDIPUS: Not my father?
MESSENGER: No more your father than the man speaking to you.
OEDIPUS: But you are nothing to me!

MESSENGER: Neither was he.
OEDIPUS: Then why did he call me son?
MESSENGER: I will tell you:
Long ago he had you from my hands, as a gift.
OEDIPUS: Then how could he love me so, if I was not his?
MESSENGER: He had no children, and his heart turned to you.
OEDIPUS: What of you? Did you buy me? Did you find me by chance?
MESSENGER: I came upon you in the woody vales of Kithairon.
OEDIPUS: And what were you doing there?
MESSENGER: Tending my flocks.
OEDIPUS: A wandering shepherd?
MESSENGER: But your saviour, son, that day.
OEDIPUS: From what did you save me?
MESSENGER: Your ankles should tell you that.
OEDIPUS: Ah, stranger, why do you speak of that childhood pain?
MESSENGER: I pulled the skewer that pinned your feet together.
OEDIPUS: I have had the mark as long as I can remember.
MESSENGER: That was why you were given the name you bear.
OEDIPUS: God! Was it my father or my mother who did it? Tell me!
MESSENGER: I do not know. The man who gave you to me
Can tell you better than I.
OEDIPUS: It was not you that found me, but another?
MESSENGER: It was another shepherd gave you to me.
OEDIPUS: Who was he? Can you tell me who he was?
MESSENGER: I think he was said to be one of Laïos' people.
OEDIPUS: You mean the Laïos who was king here years ago?
MESSENGER: Yes; King Laïos; and the man was one of his herdsmen.
OEDIPUS: Is he still alive? Can I see him?
MESSENGER: These men here
Know best about such things.
OEDIPUS: Does anyone here
Know this shepherd that he is talking about?
Have you seen him in the fields, or in the town?
If you have, tell me. It is time things were made plain.
CHORAGOS: I think the man he means is that same shepherd
You have already asked to see. Iokastê perhaps
Could tell you something.
OEDIPUS: Do you know anything
About him, Lady? Is he the man we have summoned?
Is that the man this shepherd means?
IOKASTÊ: Why think of him?
Forget this herdsman. Forget it all.
This talk is a waste of time.
OEDIPUS: How can you say that,

When the clues to my true birth are in my hands?
IOKASTÊ: For God's love, let us have no more questioning!
Is your life nothing to you?
My own is pain enough for me to bear.
OEDIPUS: You need not worry. Suppose my mother a slave,
And born of slaves: no baseness can touch you.
IOKASTÊ: Listen to me, I beg you: do not do this thing!
OEDIPUS: I will not listen; the truth must be made known.
IOKASTÊ: Everything that I say is for your own good!
OEDIPUS: My own good
Snaps my patience, then; I want none of it.
IOKASTÊ: You are fatally wrong! May you never learn who you are!
OEDIPUS: Go, one of you, and bring the shepherd here.
Let us leave this woman to brag of her royal name.
IOKASTÊ: Ah, miserable!
That is the only word I have for you now.
That is the only word I can ever have.

*Exit into the Palace.*

CHORAGOS: Why has she left us, Oedipus? Why has she gone
In such a passion of sorrow? I fear this silence:
Something dreadful may come of it.
OEDIPUS: Let it come!
However base my birth, I must know about it.
The Queen, like a woman, is perhaps ashamed
To think of my low origin. But I
Am a child of Luck; I can not be dishonoured.
Luck is my mother; the passing months, my brothers,
Have seen me rich and poor.
If this is so,
How could I wish that I were someone else?
How could I not be glad to know my birth?

## ODE III

CHORUS: If ever the coming time were known **Strophe**
To my heart's pondering,
Kithairon, now by Heaven I see the torches
At the festival of the next full moon,
And see the dance, and hear the choir sing
A grace to your gentle shade:

Mountain where Oedipus was found,
O mountain guard of a noble race!
May the god who heals us lend his aid,
And let that glory come to pass
For our king's cradling-ground.
Of the nymphs that flower beyond the years, **Antistrophe**
Who bore you, royal child,
To Pan of the hills or the timberline Apollo,
Cold in delight where the upland clears,
Or Hermês for whom Kyllenê's heights are piled?
Or flushed as evening cloud,
Great Dionysos, roamer of mountains,
He—was it he who found you there,
And caught you up in his own proud
Arms from the sweet god-ravisher
Who laughed by the Muses' fountains?

## SCENE IV

OEDIPUS: Sirs: though I do not know the man,
I think I see him coming, this shepherd we want:
He is old, like our friend here, and the men
Bringing him seem to be servants of my house.
But you can tell, if you have ever seen him.

*Enter Shepherd escorted by servants.*

CHORAGOS: I know him, he was Laïos' man. You can trust him.
OEDIPUS: Tell me first, you from Corinth: is this the shepherd
We were discussing?
MESSENGER: This is the very man.
OEDIPUS: [*To Shepherd*]
Come here. No, look at me. You must answer
Everything I ask.—You belonged to Laïos?
SHEPHERD: Yes: born his slave, brought up in his house.
OEDIPUS: Tell me: what kind of work did you do for him?
SHEPHERD: I was a shepherd of his, most of my life.
OEDIPUS: Where mainly did you go for pasturage?
SHEPHERD: Sometimes Kithairon, sometimes the hills nearby.
OEDIPUS: Do you remember ever seeing this man out there?
SHEPHERD: What would he be doing there? This man?
OEDIPUS: This man standing here. Have you ever seen him before?
SHEPHERD: No. At least, not to my recollection.

MESSENGER: And that is not strange, my lord. But I'll refresh
His memory: he must remember when we two
Spent three whole seasons together, March to September,
On Kithairon or thereabouts. He had two flocks;
I had one. Each autumn I'd drive mine home
And he would go back with his to Laïos' sheepfold.—
Is this not true, just as I have described it?
SHEPHERD: True, yes; but it was all so long ago.
MESSENGER: Well, then: do you remember, back in those days,
That you gave me a baby boy to bring up as my own?
SHEPHERD: What if I did? What are you trying to say?
MESSENGER: King Oedipus was once that little child.
SHEPHERD: Damn you, hold your tongue!
OEDIPUS: No more of that!
It is your tongue needs watching, not this man's.
SHEPHERD: My King, my Master, what is it I have done wrong?
OEDIPUS: You have not answered his question about the boy.
SHEPHERD: He does not know . . . He is only making trouble . . .
OEDIPUS: Come, speak plainly, or it will go hard with you.
SHEPHERD: In God's name, do not torture an old man!
OEDIPUS: Come here, one of you; bind his arms behind him.
SHEPHERD: Unhappy king! What more do you wish to learn?
OEDIPUS: Did you give this man the child he speaks of?
SHEPHERD: I did.
And I would to God I had died that very day.
OEDIPUS: You will die now unless you speak the truth.
SHEPHERD: Yet if I speak the truth, I am worse than dead.
OEDIPUS: [*To Attendant*]
He intends to draw it out, apparently—
SHEPHERD: No! I have told you already that I gave him the boy.
OEDIPUS: Where did you get him? From your house? From somewhere else?
SHEPHERD: Not from mine, no. A man gave him to me.
OEDIPUS: Is that man here? Whose house did he belong to?
SHEPHERD: For God's love, my King, do not ask me any more!
OEDIPUS: You are a dead man if I have to ask you again.
SHEPHERD: Then . . . Then the child was from the palace of Laïos.
OEDIPUS: A slave child? or a child of his own line?
SHEPHERD: Ah, I am on the brink of dreadful speech!
OEDIPUS: And I of dreadful hearing. Yet I must hear.
SHEPHERD: If you must be told, then . . .
They said it was Laïos' child:
But it is your wife who can tell you about that.
OEDIPUS: My wife!—Did she give it to you?
SHEPHERD: My Lord, she did.

OEDIPUS: Do you know why?
SHEPHERD: I was told to get rid of it.
OEDIPUS: Oh heartless mother!
SHEPHERD: But in dread of prophecies . . .
OEDIPUS: Tell me.
SHEPHERD: It was said that the boy would kill his own father.
OEDIPUS: Then why did you give him over to this old man?
SHEPHERD: I pitied the baby, my King,
And I thought that this man would take him far away
To his own country.
He saved him—but for what a fate!
For if you are what this man says you are,
No man living is more wretched than Oedipus.
OEDIPUS: Ah God!
It was true!
All the prophecies!
—Now,
O Light, may I look on you for the last time!
I, Oedipus,
Oedipus, damned in his birth, in his marriage damned,
Damned in the blood he shed with his own hand!

*He rushes into the palace.*

## ODE IV

CHORUS: Alas for the seed of men. **Strophe 1**
What measure shall I give these generations
That breathe on the void and are void
And exist and do not exist?

Who bears more weight of joy
Than mass of sunlight shifting in images,
Or who shall make his thought stay on
That down time drifts away?

Your splendour is all fallen.

O naked brow of wrath and tears,
O change of Oedipus!
I who saw your days call no man blest—
Your great days like ghósts góne.

That mind was a strong bow. **Antistrophe 1**

Deep, how deep you drew it then, hard archer,
At a dim fearful range,
And brought dear glory down!

You overcame the stranger—
The virgin with her hooking lion claws—
And though death sang, stood like a tower
To make pale Thebes take heart.
Fortress against our sorrow!

True king, giver of laws,
Majestic Oedipus!
No prince in Thebes had ever such renown,
No prince won such grace of power.

**Strophe 2**

And now of all men ever known
Most pitiful is this man's story:
His fortunes are most changed, his state
Fallen to a low slave's
Ground under bitter fate.

O Oedipus, most royal one!
The great door that expelled you to the light
Gave at night—ah, gave night to your glory:
As to the father, to the fathering son.

All understood too late.

How could that queen whom Laïos won,
The garden that he harrowed at his height,
Be silent when the act was done?

**Antistrophe 2**

But all eyes fail before time's eye,
All actions come to justice there.
Though never willed, though far down the deep past,
Your bed, your dread sirings,
Are brought to book at last.

Child by Laïos doomed to die,
Then doomed to lose that fortunate little death,
Would God you never took breath in this air
That with my wailing lips I take to cry:

For I weep the world's outcast.

I was blind, and now I can tell why:
Asleep, for you had given ease of breath
To Thebes, while the false years went by.

## ÉXODOS

*Enter, from the palace, Second Messenger.*

SECOND MESSENGER: Elders of Thebes, most honoured in this land,
What horrors are yours to see and hear, what weight
Of sorrows to be endured, if, true to your birth,
You venerate the line of Labdakos!
I think neither Istros nor Phasis, those great rivers,
Could purify this place of all the evil
It shelters now, or soon must bring to light—
Evil not done unconsciously, but willed.

The greatest griefs are those we cause ourselves.
CHORAGOS: Surely, friend, we have grief enough already;
What new sorrow do you mean?
SECOND MESSENGER: The Queen is dead.
CHORAGOS: O miserable Queen! But at whose hand?
SECOND MESSENGER: Her own.
The full horror of what happened you can not know,
For you did not see it; but I, who did, will tell you
As clearly as I can how she met her death.

When she had left us,
In passionate silence, passing through the court,
She ran to her apartment in the house,
Her hair clutched by the fingers of both hands.
She closed the doors behind her; then, by that bed
Where long ago the fatal son was conceived—
That son who should bring about his father's death—
We heard her call upon Laïos, dead so many years,
And heard her wail for the double fruit of her marriage,
A husband by her husband, children by her child.
Exactly how she died I do not know:
For Oedipus burst in moaning and would not let us
Keep vigil to the end: it was by him
As he stormed about the room that our eyes were caught.

From one to another of us he went, begging a sword,
Hunting the wife who was not his wife, the mother
Whose womb had carried his own children and himself.
I do not know: it was none of us aided him,
But surely one of the gods was in control!
For with a dreadful cry
He hurled his weight, as though wrenched out of himself,
At the twin doors: the bolts gave, and he rushed in.
And there we saw her hanging, her body swaying
From the cruel cord she had noosed about her neck.
A great sob broke from him, heartbreaking to hear,
As he loosed the rope and lowered her to the ground.

I would blot out from my mind what happened next!
For the King ripped from her gown the golden brooches
That were her ornament, and raised them, and plunged them down
Straight into his own eyeballs, crying, 'No more,
No more shall you look on the misery about me,
The horrors of my own doing! Too long you have known
The faces of those whom I should never have seen,
Too long been blind to those for whom I was searching!
From this hour, go in darkness!' And as he spoke,
He struck at his eyes—not once, but many times;
And the blood spattered his beard,
Bursting from his ruined sockets like red hail.

So from the unhappiness of two this evil has sprung,
A curse on the man and woman alike. The old
Happiness of the house of Labdakos
Was happiness enough: where is it today?
It is all wailing and ruin, disgrace, death—all
The misery of mankind that has a name—
And it is wholly and for ever theirs.

CHORAGOS: Is he in agony still? Is there no rest for him?

SECOND MESSENGER: He is calling for someone to open the doors wide
So that all the children of Kadmos may look upon
His father's murderer, his mother's—no,
I can not say it!
And then he will leave Thebes,
Self-exiled, in order that the curse
Which he himself pronounced may depart from the house.
He is weak, and there is none to lead him,
So terrible is his suffering.
But you will see:

Look, the doors are opening; in a moment
You will see a thing that would crush a heart of stone.

*The central door is opened; Oedipus, blinded, is led in.*

CHORAGOS: Dreadful indeed for men to see.
Never have my own eyes
Looked on a sight so full of fear.
Oedipus!
What madness came upon you, what daemon
Leaped on your life with heavier
Punishment than a mortal man can bear?
No: I can not even
Look at you, poor ruined one.
And I would speak, question, ponder,
If I were able. No.
You make me shudder.
OEDIPUS: God. God.
Is there a sorrow greater?
Where shall I find harbour in this world?
My voice is hurled far on a dark wind.
What has God done to me?
CHORAGOS: Too terrible to think of, or to see.

**Strophe 1**

OEDIPUS: O cloud of night,
Never to be turned away: night coming on,
I can not tell how: night like a shroud!
My fair winds brought me here.
O God. Again
The pain of the spikes where I had sight,
The flooding pain
Of memory, never to be gouged out.

CHORAGOS: This is not strange.
You suffer it all twice over, remorse in pain,
Pain in remorse.

**Antistrophe 1**

OEDIPUS: Ah dear friend
Are you faithful even yet, you alone?
Are you still standing near me, will you stay here,
Patient, to care for the blind?
The blind man!
Yet even blind I know who it is attends me,
By the voice's tone—
Though my new darkness hide the comforter.

CHORAGOS: Oh fearful act!
What god was it drove you to rake black
Night across your eyes?

OEDIPUS: Apollo. Apollo. Dear **Strophe 2**
Children, the god was Apollo.
He brought my sick, sick fate upon me.
But the blinding hand was my own!
How could I bear to see
When all my sight was horror everywhere?

CHORAGOS: Everywhere; that is true.
OEDIPUS: And now what is left?
Images? Love? A greeting even,
Sweet to the senses? Is there anything?
Ah, no, friends: lead me away.
Lead me away from Thebes.
Lead the great wreck
And hell of Oedipus, whom the gods hate.

CHORAGOS: Your misery, you are not blind to that.
Would God you had never found it out!

OEDIPUS: Death take the man who unbound **Antistrophe 2**
My feet on that hillside
And delivered me from death to life! What life?
If only I had died,
This weight of monstrous doom
Could not have dragged me and my darlings down.

CHORAGOS: I would have wished the same.
OEDIPUS: Oh never to have come here
With my father's blood upon me! Never
To have been the man they call his mother's husband!
Oh accurst! Oh child of evil,
To have entered that wretched bed—
the selfsame one!
More primal than sin itself, this fell to me.

CHORAGOS: I do not know what words to offer you.
You were better dead than alive and blind.

OEDIPUS: Do not counsel me any more. This punishment
That I have laid upon myself is just.
If I had eyes,

I do not know how I could bear the sight
Of my father, when I came to the house of Death,
Or my mother; for I have sinned against them both
So vilely that I could not make my peace
By strangling my own life.
                    Or do you think my children,
Born as they were born, would be sweet to my eyes?
Ah never, never! Nor this town with its high walls,
Nor the holy images of the gods.
                    For I,
Thrice miserable!—Oedipus, noblest of all the line
Of Kadmos, have condemned myself to enjoy
These things no more, by my own malediction
Expelling that man whom the gods declared
To be a defilement in the house of Laïos.
After exposing the rankness of my own guilt,
How could I look men frankly in the eyes?
No, I swear it,
If I could have stifled my hearing at its source,
I would have done it and made all this body
A tight cell of misery, blank to light and sound:
So I should have been safe in my dark mind
Beyond external evil.
                    Ah Kithairon!
Why did you shelter me? When I was cast upon you,
Why did I not die? Then I should never
Have shown the world my execrable birth.

Ah Polybos! Corinth, city that I believed
The ancient seat of my ancestors: how fair
I seemed, your child! And all the while this evil
Was cancerous within me!
                    For I am sick
In my own being, sick in my origin.

O three roads, dark ravine, woodland and way
Where three roads met: you, drinking my father's blood,
My own blood, spilled by my own hand: can you remember
The unspeakable things I did there, and the things
I went on from there to do?
                    O marriage, marriage!
The act that engendered me, and again the act
Performed by the son in the same bed—
                    Ah, the net

Of incest, mingling fathers, brothers, sons,
With brides, wives, mothers: the last evil
That can be known by men: no tongue can say
How evil!
No. For the love of God, conceal me.
Somewhere far from Thebes; or kill me; or hurl me
Into the sea, away from men's eyes for ever.
Come, lead me. You need not fear to touch me.
Of all men, I alone can bear this guilt.

*Enter Kreon.*

CHORAGOS: Kreon is here now. As to what you ask,
He may decide the course to take. He only
Is left to protect the city in your place.
OEDIPUS: Alas, how can I speak to him? What right have I
To beg his courtesy whom I have deeply wronged?
KREON: I have not come to mock you, Oedipus,
Or to reproach you, either.
[*To Attendants*] —You standing there:
If you have lost all respect for man's dignity,
At least respect the flame of Lord Helios:
Do not allow this pollution to show itself
Openly here, an affront to the earth
And Heaven's rain and the light of day. No, take him
Into the house as quickly as you can.
For it is proper
That only the close kindred see his grief.
OEDIPUS: I pray you in God's name, since your courtesy
Ignores my dark expectation, visiting
With mercy this man of all men most execrable:
Give me what I ask—for your good, not for mine.
KREON: And what is it that you turn to me begging for?
OEDIPUS: Drive me out of this country as quickly as may be
To a place where no human voice can ever greet me.
KREON: I should have done that before now—only,
God's will had not been wholly revealed to me.
OEDIPUS: But his command is plain: the parricide
Must be destroyed. I am that evil man.
KREON: That is the sense of it, yes; but as things are,
We had best discover clearly what is to be done.
OEDIPUS: You would learn more about a man like me?
KREON: You are ready now to listen to the god.
OEDIPUS: I will listen. But it is to you
That I must turn for help. I beg you, hear me.

The woman in there—
Give her whatever funeral you think proper:
She is your sister.
—But let me go, Kreon!
Let me purge my father's Thebes of the pollution
Of my living here, and go out to the wild hills,
To Kithairon, that has won such fame with me,
The tomb my mother and father appointed for me,
And let me die there, as they willed I should.
And yet I know
Death will not ever come to me through sickness
Or in any natural way: I have been preserved
For some unthinkable fate. But let that be.

As for my sons, you need not care for them.
They are men, they will find some way to live.
But my poor daughters, who have shared my table,
Who never before have been parted from their father—
Take care of them, Kreon; do this for me.
And will you let me touch them with my hands
A last time, and let us weep together?
Be kind, my lord,
Great prince, be kind!
Could I but touch them,
They would be mine again, as when I had my eyes.

*Enter Antigone and Ismene, attended.*

Ah, God!
Is it my dearest children I hear weeping?
Has Kreon pitied me and sent my daughters?
KREON: Yes, Oedipus: I knew that they were dear to you
In the old days, and know you must love them still.
OEDIPUS: May God bless you for this—and be friendlier
Guardian to you than he has been to me!

Children, where are you?
Come quickly to my hands: they are your brother's—
Hands that have brought your father's once clear eyes
To this way of seeing—
Ah dearest ones,
I had neither sight nor knowledge then, your father
By the woman who was the source of his own life!
And I weep for you—having no strength to see you—
I weep for you when I think of the bitterness

That men will visit upon you all your lives.
What homes, what festivals can you attend
Without being forced to depart again in tears?
And when you come to marriageable age,
Where is the man, my daughters, who would dare
Risk the bane that lies on all my children?
Is there any evil wanting? Your father killed
His father; sowed the womb of her who bore him;
Engendered you at the fount of his own existence!
That is what they will say of you.
Then, whom
Can you ever marry? There are no bridegrooms for you,
And your lives must wither away in sterile dreaming.

O Kreon, son of Menoikeus!
You are the only father my daughters have,
Since we, their parents, are both of us gone for ever.
They are your own blood: you will not let them
Fall into beggary and loneliness;
You will keep them from the miseries that are mine!
Take pity on them; see, they are only children,
Friendless except for you. Promise me this,
Great Prince, and give me your hand in token of it.

*Kreon clasps his right hand.*

Children:
I could say much, if you could understand me,
But as it is, I have only this prayer for you:
Live where you can, be as happy as you can—
Happier, please God, than God has made your father.
KREON: Enough. You have wept enough. Now go within.
OEDIPUS: I must; but it is hard.
KREON: Time eases all things.
OEDIPUS: You know my mind, then?
KREON: Say what you desire.
OEDIPUS: Send me from Thebes!
KREON: God grant that I may!
OEDIPUS: But since God hates me . . .
KREON: No, he will grant your wish.
OEDIPUS: You promise?
KREON: I can not speak beyond my knowledge.
OEDIPUS: Then lead me in.
KREON: Come now, and leave your children.

OEDIPUS: No! Do not take them from me!

KREON: Think no longer
That you are in command here, but rather think
How, when you were, you served your own destruction.

*Exeunt into the house all but the Chorus; the Choragos chants directly to the audience.*

CHORAGOS: Men of Thebes: look upon Oedipus.

This is the king who solved the famous riddle
And towered up, most powerful of men.
No mortal eyes but looked on him with envy.
Yet in the end ruin swept over him.

Let every man in mankind's frailty
Consider his last day; and let none
Presume on his good fortune until he find
Life, at his death, a memory without pain.

*c.* 425 BCE

# William Shakespeare

## 1564–1616

William Shakespeare was born and raised in Stratford-upon-Avon, where his father was a glover, tanner, and dealer in hides. He was educated locally at the King's New School, where he acquired some familiarity with the classics, particularly Latin grammar and literature. He did not go on to attend one of the universities, however. Instead, he went off to London, probably attracted by the touring theatrical companies of the period, to make a career for himself as an actor and dramatist. He made his way to London sometime in the late 1580s, when public theatre was just beginning to become a popular enterprise in the city, and he likely started out as an actor with one of the local companies. By 1590 his earliest plays were being produced, and during his remaining 23 years of involvement with the theatre he wrote 37 plays, while becoming a leading actor and shareholder in one of the major theatrical companies of the period. His plays cover a broad range of dramatic modes, extending from the comedies and history plays that figured largely in his early career, through the problem plays, tragedies, and romances that predominated in his later career. His plays reflect an equally broad range of experience, extending from the English battle scenes and tavern life of *1 Henry IV*, to the Roman and Egyptian court scenes of *Antony and Cleopatra*, and to the fantastic island world of *The Tempest*. Like most of his contemporaries he borrowed ideas for many of his works from classical, continental, or—as in the case of *King Lear*—native sources.

**A Note on This Version**

No single authoritative edition of *King Lear* exists. The play comes to modern readers through two early printed versions of the text: the First Quarto, published in 1608 during Shakespeare's life, and the First Folio, published in 1623 after his death. Although the two initial versions of Shakespeare's play are verbally identical at many points, several differences exist between them. Each contains words, lines, and even entire passages not found in the other version. The play printed here is based on the version included in the *Oxford Shakespeare* (edited by J.W. Craig). It generally follows the text of the Folio edition, but also includes several of the lines and passages found only in the Quarto.

# King Lear

## *CHARACTERS*

LEAR, King of Britain
KING OF FRANCE
DUKE OF BURGUNDY
DUKE OF CORNWALL
DUKE OF ALBANY
EARL OF KENT
EARL OF GLOUCESTER
EDGAR, Son to Gloucester
EDMUND, Bastard Son to Gloucester
CURAN, a Courtier
OSWALD, Steward to Goneril
OLD MAN, Tenant to Gloucester
DOCTOR
FOOL
AN OFFICER, Employed by Edmund
A GENTLEMAN, Attendant on Cordelia
A HERALD
SERVANTS, to Cornwall
GONERIL, REGAN, CORDELIA, } Daughters to Lear
KNIGHTS OF LEAR'S TRAIN, OFFICERS, MESSENGERS, SOLDIERS, ATTENDANTS

---

*The scene: Britain*

## ACT I

### SCENE 1

*A Room of State in King Lear's Palace.*

*Enter Kent, Gloucester, and Edmund.*

KENT: I thought the king had more affected[1] the Duke of Albany than Cornwall.

GLOUCESTER: It did always seem so to us; but now, in the division of the kingdom, it appears not which of the dukes he values most; for equalities are so weighed[2] that curiosity[3] in neither can make choice of either's moiety.[4]

KENT: Is not this your son, my lord?

1 *had . . . affected*: was more partial to, preferred
2 *equalities . . . weighed*: shares are so carefully equalized. ll. 3–5 i.e. neither duke can find ground for preferring the other's share to his own
3 careful examination
4 part, share (not necessarily half)

GLOUCESTER: His breeding,[5] sir, hath been at my charge: I have so often blushed to acknowledge him, that now I am brazed[6] to it.

KENT: I cannot conceive[7] you.

GLOUCESTER: Sir, this young fellow's mother could; whereupon she grew round-wombed, and had, indeed, sir, a son for her cradle ere she had a husband for her bed. Do you smell a fault?

KENT: I cannot wish the fault undone, the issue[8] of it being so proper.[9]

GLOUCESTER: But I have a son, sir, by order of law,[10] some year[11] elder than this, who yet is no dearer in my account:[12] though this knave came something[13] saucily into the world before he was sent for, yet was his mother fair; there was good sport at his making, and the whoreson[14] must be acknowledged. Do you know this noble gentleman, Edmund?

EDMUND: No, my lord.

GLOUCESTER: My Lord of Kent: remember him hereafter as my honourable friend.

EDMUND: My services to your lordship.

KENT: I must love you, and sue[15] to know you better.

EDMUND: Sir, I shall study deserving.[16]

GLOUCESTER: He hath been out[17] nine years, and away he shall again. The king is coming.

*Sennet.[18] Enter Lear, Cornwall, Albany, Goneril, Regan, Cordelia, and Attendants.*

LEAR: Attend[19] the Lords of France and Burgundy, Gloucester.

GLOUCESTER: I shall, my leige. [*Exeunt Gloucester and Edmund.*]

LEAR: Meantime we shall express[20] our darker[21] purpose.
Give me the map there. Know that we have divided
In three our kingdom; and 'tis our fast[22] intent
To shake all cares and business from our age,
Conferring them on younger strengths, while we
Unburden'd crawl toward death. Our son[23] of Cornwall,

5 upbringing
6 hardened (as in one slang sense of 'brass')
7 understand
8 *both* (1) result *and* (2) offspring
9 handsome
10 *son . . . law*: legitimate, born in wedlock
11 about a year
12 reckoning
13 somewhat
14 rascal (literally 'son of a whore' but often used playfully, like 'knave' above)
15 beg
16 try to be worth (the effort you make)
17 away from home, abroad
18 a set of notes on a trumpet heralding a procession
19 wait upon (and bring in)
20 expound, show
21 hitherto unrevealed (i.e. the details of the division)
22 firm, fixed
23 (-in-law), Duke of Cornwall

And you, our no less loving son of Albany,
We have this hour a constant[24] will to publish
Our daughters' several dowers,[25] that future strife
May be prevented now. The princes, France and Burgundy,
Great rivals in our youngest daughter's love,
Long in our court have made their amorous sojourn,[26]
And here are to be answer'd.[27] Tell me, my daughters,—
Since now we will divest us both of rule,
Interest[28] of territory, cares of state,—
Which of you shall we say doth love us most?
That we our largest bounty may extend
Where nature[29] doth with merit challenge.[30] Goneril,
Our eldest-born, speak first.

GONERIL: Sir, I love you more than words can wield the matter;
Dearer than eye-sight, space,[31] and liberty;
Beyond what can be valu'd, rich or rare;
No less than life, with[32] grace, health, beauty, honour;
As much as child e'er lov'd, or father found;[33]
A love that makes breath poor and speech unable;[34]
Beyond all manner of so much[35] I love you.

CORDELIA [*Aside*]: What shall Cordelia do? Love, and be silent.

LEAR: Of all these bounds, even from this line to this,
With shadowy[36] forests and with champains[37] rich'd,
With plenteous rivers and wide-skirted meads,
We make thee lady: to thine and Albany's issue
Be this perpetual. What says our second daughter,
Our dearest Regan, wife to Cornwall? Speak.

REGAN: I am made of that self[38] metal[39] as my sister,
And prize me at her worth.[40] In my true heart[41]
I find she names my very deed of love;[42]

24 firm
25 respective dowries
26 stay for purposes of love (to woo Cordelia)
27 *are . . . answer'd*: await a decision
28 right, title to (and so possession of)
29 *affection*
30 claim (it)
31 the world (unless the word simply expands the notion of 'liberty')
32 *combined with*
33 experienced (love)
34 unequal to expressing it
35 *all . . . much*: all degree of such comparisons
36 shady
37 meadows, open country
38 same
39 (1) material, (2) temperament (in this sense now spelt *mettle*)
40 *prize . . . worth*: I count myself equal to her (in my affection for you)
41 *In . . . heart*: in all sincerity
42 *names . . . love*: exactly describes my love

Only she comes too short: that[43] I profess
Myself an enemy to all other joys
Which the most precious square of sense[44] possesses
And find I am alone felicitate[45]
In your dear highness' love.

CORDELIA [*Aside*]: Then, poor Cordelia!
And yet not so; since, I am sure, my love's
More richer than my tongue.

LEAR: To thee and thine, hereditary ever,[46]
Remain this ample third of our fair kingdom,
No less in space, validity,[47] and pleasure,
Than that conferr'd on Goneril. Now, our joy,
Although our last, not least; to whose young love
The vines of France and milk of Burgundy[48]
Strive to be interess'd;[49] what can you say to draw
A third more opulent than your sisters? Speak.

CORDELIA: Nothing, my lord.

LEAR: Nothing?

CORDELIA: Nothing.

LEAR: Nothing will come of nothing: speak again.

CORDELIA: Unhappy that I am, I cannot heave
My heart into my mouth: I love your majesty
According to my bond;[50] nor more nor less.

LEAR: How, how, Cordelia! mend your speech a little,
Lest you may mar your fortunes.

CORDELIA: Good my lord,
You have begot me, bred me, lov'd me: I
Return those duties back as are right fit,[51]
Obey you, love you, and most honour you.
Why have my sisters husbands, if they say
They love you all?[52] Haply, when I shall wed,
That lord whose hand must take my plight[53] shall carry
Half my love with him, half my care and duty:
Sure I shall never marry like my sisters,
To love my father all.

LEAR: But goes thy heart with this?

43 in that
44 *most . . . sense*: most delicate sense
45 made happy
46 and to your heirs for ever
47 value
48 i.e. the King of F., rich in vineyards, and the Duke of B., rich in pastures
49 concerned, bound up with (interess is an old form of interest, Lat. *interesse*)
50 obligation (cf. 'bounden duty and service' of *Prayer Book*)
51 duties right and fit to be returned
52 entirely
53 plighted troth, vows

CORDELIA: Ay, good my lord.
LEAR: So young, and so untender?
CORDELIA: So young, my lord, and true.
LEAR: Let it be so; thy truth then be thy dower:[54]
For, by the sacred radiance of the sun,
The mysteries of Hecate[55] and the night,
By all the operation[56] of the orbs[57]
From whom we do exist and cease to be,
Here I disclaim all my paternal care,
Propinquity[58] and property of blood,[59]
And as a stranger to my heart and me
Hold thee from this for ever. The barbarous Scythian,
Or he that makes his generation[60] messes[61]
To gorge his appetite, shall to my bosom
Be as well neighbour'd,[62] pitied, and reliev'd,
As thou my sometime daughter.
KENT: Good my liege,—
LEAR: Peace, Kent!
Come not between the dragon and his wrath[63]
I lov'd her most, and thought to set my rest[64]
On her kind nursery.[65] Hence, and avoid my sight!
So be my grave my peace, as here I give
Her father's heart from[66] her! Call France. Who stirs?[67]
Call Burgundy. Cornwall and Albany,
With my two daughters' dowers digest the third;
Let pride, which she calls plainness, marry her.[68]
I do invest you jointly with my power,
Pre-eminence, and all the large effects[69]
That troop with[70] majesty. Ourself by monthly course,[71]
With reservation of[72] a hundred knights,

54 dowry
55 Hécate (here two syllables)
56 work, influence
57 *heavenly bodies*
58 *lit.* nearness, so kinship
59 ownership of your blood
60 children
61 dishes
62 *as . . . neighbour'd*: held as near
63 *Come . . . wrath*: i.e. don't try to stop my (natural) wrath (cf. l. 165 below)
64 *set . . . rest*: stake my all (a gaming metaphor, but also involving the ordinary sense of 'rest')
65 nursing
66 away from
67 *Who stirs?*: make haste
68 *Let . . . her*: let her pride find her a husband, i.e. let her find one for herself without a dowry
69 *manifestations of splendour*
70 *troop with*: accompany
71 *by . . . course*: for a month in turn
72 *With . . . of*: i.e. reserving to ourselves (properly a legal word for an exception)

By you to be sustain'd, shall our abode
Make with you by due turn. Only we shall retain
The name and all th' addition[73] to a king;
The sway, revenue, execution of the rest,
Beloved sons, be yours: which to confirm,
This coronet part between you.

KENT: Royal Lear,
Whom I have ever honour'd as my king,
Lov'd as my father, as my master follow'd,
As my great patron thought on in my prayers,—

LEAR: The bow is bent and drawn; make from[74] the shaft.

KENT: Let it fall rather, though the fork[75] invade
The region of my heart: be Kent unmannerly
When Lear is mad. What wouldst thou do, old man?
Think'st thou that duty shall have dread to speak
When power to flattery bows? To plainness[76] honour's bound
When majesty falls to folly. Reserve thy state;[77]
And, in thy best consideration,[78] check
This hideous rashness: answer my life my judgment,[79]
Thy youngest daughter does not love thee least;
Nor are those empty-hearted whose low sound
Reverbs[80] no hollowness.

LEAR: Kent, on thy life,[81] no more.

KENT: My life I never held[82] but as a pawn
To wage[83] against thine enemies; nor fear to lose it,
Thy safety being the motive.

LEAR: Out of my sight!

KENT: See better, Lear; and let me still remain
The true blank of thine eye.[84]

LEAR: Now, by Apollo,—

KENT: Now, by Apollo, king,
Thou swear'st thy gods in vain.

LEAR: O vassal! miscreant![85]

[*Laying his hand on his sword.*]

73 title
74 *make from*: avoid
75 head, barb
76 plain-speaking
77 regal power
78 *best consideration*: considering the matter more carefully
79 *answer . . . judgment*: let my life answer for (the correctness of) my judgment
80 echoes back
81 *on . . . life*: as you value your life
82 accounted
83 *pawn to wage*: stake to wager, risk
84 *let . . . eye*: keep me always in view, always with you (*blank* = *white* centre of a target)
85 *vassal! miscreant!* and *recreant!* (160): all used loosely as terms of abuse, 'villain'

ALBANY:
CORNWALL: } Dear sir, forbear.

KENT: Do;[86]
Kill thy physician, and the fee bestow
Upon the foul disease.[87] Revoke thy gift;[88]
Or, whilst I can vent clamour from my throat,
I'll tell thee thou dost evil.

LEAR: Hear me, recreant!
On thine allegiance, hear me!
Since thou hast sought to make us break our vow,—
Which we durst never yet,—and, with strain'd[89] pride
To come betwixt our sentence and our power,—[90]
Which nor our nature nor our place can bear,—
Our potency made good,[91] take thy reward,
Five days we do allot thee for provision
To shield thee from diseases[92] of the world;
And, on the sixth, to turn[93] thy hated back
Upon our kingdom: if, on the tenth day following
Thy banish'd trunk[94] be found in our dominions,
The moment is thy death. Away! By Jupiter,
This shall not be revok'd.

KENT: Fare thee well, king; sith[95] thus thou wilt appear,[96]
Freedom lives hence, and banishment is here.
[*To Cordelia.*] The gods to their dear shelter take thee, maid,
That justly think'st and hast most rightly said!
[*To Regan and Goneril.*] And your large[97] speeches may your deeds approve,[98]
That good effects may spring from words of love.
Thus Kent, O princes! bids you all adieu;
He'll shape his old course[99] in a country new. [*Exit.*]

*Flourish.*[100] *Re-enter Gloucester, with France, Burgundy, and Attendants.*

86 execute your will
87 *the fee . . . disease*: i.e. make things worse for yourself
88 i.e. of Cordelia's share
89 exaggerated
90 *our power*: the execution of it
91 *potency . . . good*: power shown to be (still) valid
92 discomforts (consequent on lack of preparation for exile)
93 we sentence thee to turn
94 body
95 since
96 show thyself
97 grand
98 make good
99 *shape . . . course*: make his way, old as he is, *or* continues his old habits (of plain-speaking etc.)
100 a blast of trumpets or horns

GLOUCESTER: Here's France and Burgundy, my noble lord.
LEAR: My Lord of Burgundy,
We first address toward[101] you, who with this king
Hath rivall'd for[102] our daughter. What, in the least,
Will you require in present dower with her,
Or cease your quest of love?
BURGUNDY: Most royal majesty,
I crave no more than hath your highness offer'd,
Nor will you tender[103] less.
LEAR: Right noble Burgundy,
When she was dear to us we did hold her so.[104]
But now her price is fall'n. Sir, there she stands:
If aught within that little-seeming substance,[105]
Or all of it, with our displeasure piec'd,[106]
And nothing more, may fitly like[107] your Grace,
She's there, and she is yours.
BURGUNDY: I know no answer.
LEAR: Will you, with those infirmities she owes,[108]
Unfriended, new-adopted to our hate,
Dower'd with our curse, and stranger'd with[109] our oath,
Take her, or leave her?
BURGUNDY: Pardon me, royal sir;
Election makes not up[110] on such conditions.
LEAR: Then leave her, sir; for, by the power that made me,
I tell you all her wealth.—[*To France.*] For you,[111] great king,
I would not from your love make such a stray[112]
To[113] match you where I hate; therefore, beseech you
To avert[114] your liking a more worthier way[115]
Than on a wretch whom nature is asham'd
Almost to acknowledge hers.
FRANCE: This is most strange,
That she, who even but now was your best[116] object,

101 *address* (ourselves) *toward*: speak to
102 entered into rivalry for
103 offer
104 dear (in value), worth a good dowry
105 *little-seeming substance*: person of few pretensions (sarcastic)
106 pieced out (with), added (to it)
107 please
108 owns
109 made a stranger (to us) by (cf. l. 108)
110 *Election . . . up*: choice does not decide, will not choose
111 as for you
112 *make . . . stray*: depart from, i.e. offend against
113 as to
114 turn aside
115 *a . . . way*: in a worthier direction
116 favourite

The argument[117] of your praise, balm of your age,[118]
The best, the dearest, should in this trice[119] of time
Commit a thing so monstrous, to dismantle[120]
So many folds of favour. Sure, her offence
Must be of such unnatural degree
That monsters[121] it, or your fore-vouch'd affection
Fall into taint;[122] which to believe of her,
Must be a faith that reason without miracle
Could never plant in me.

CORDELIA: I yet beseech your majesty—
If for[123] I want that glib and oily art
To speak and purpose not;[124] since what I well intend,
I'll do't before I speak—that you make known
It is no vicious blot nor other foulness,[125]
No unchaste action, or dishonour'd[126] step,
That hath depriv'd me of your grace and favour,
But even for want of[127] that for which I am richer,
A still-soliciting[128] eye, and such a tongue
That I am glad I have not, though not to have it
Hath lost me in your liking.

LEAR: Better thou
Hadst not been born than not to have pleas'd me better.

FRANCE: Is it but this? A tardiness in nature[129]
Which often leaves the history[130] unspoke
That it intends to do? My Lord of Burgundy,
What say you to the lady?[131] Love is not love
When it is mingled with regards[132] that stand
Aloof from the entire[133] point. Will you have her?
She is herself a dowry.

BURGUNDY: Royal Lear,
Give but that portion which yourself propos'd,

117 subject
118 *balm . . . age*: see ll. 116–17
119 moment (Spanish)
120 shed off
121 makes it monstrous
122 *your . . . taint*: your previously affirmed affection must be discredited
123 If (you are disowning me) because
124 *purpose not:* not intend to carry out
125 i.e. no wickedness, such as murder or fornication
126 dishonourable
127 *even . . . of*: it is just because I lack
128 always begging (for something)
129 *tardiness in nature*: natural slowness (to speak)
130 verbal record
131 *What . . . lady?*: How do you like the lady?
132 considerations (so *respects*, l. 242)
133 whole

And here I take Cordelia by the hand,
Duchess of Burgundy.
LEAR: Nothing: I have sworn; I am firm.
BURGUNDY: I am sorry, then, you have so lost a father
That you must lose a husband.
CORDELIA: Peace be with[134] Burgundy!
Since that respects of fortune are his love,
I shall not be his wife.
FRANCE: Fairest Cordelia, that art most rich, being poor;
Most choice, forsaken; and most lov'd, despis'd!
Thee and thy virtues here I seize upon:
Be it lawful I take up what's cast away.
Gods, gods! 'tis strange that from their cold'st neglect
My love should kindle to inflam'd respect.[135]
Thy dowerless daughter, king, thrown to my chance,[136]
Is queen of us, of ours, and our fair France:
Not all the dukes of waterish[137] Burgundy
Shall buy this unpriz'd[138] precious maid of me.
Bid them farewell, Cordelia, though unkind:[139]
Thou losest here, a better where[140] to find.
LEAR: Thou hast her, France; let her be thine, for we
Have no such daughter, nor shall ever see
That face of hers again, therefore be gone
Without our grace, our love, our benison.[141]
Come, noble Burgundy.

*Flourish. Exeunt Lear, Burgundy, Cornwall, Albany, Gloucester, and Attendants.*

FRANCE: Bid farewell to your sisters.
CORDELIA: The jewels[142] of our father, with wash'd eyes
Cordelia leaves you: I know you what you are;
And like a sister am most loath to call
Your faults as they are nam'd.[143] Use well our father:
To your professed bosoms[144] I commit him:
But yet, alas! stood I within his grace,

134 *Peace be with*: good-bye to
135 *inflam'd respect*: ardent esteem
136 lot
137 perhaps literally 'well-watered', but certainly implying that the man is as thin-blooded as his country is inferior in wines to France (cf. l. 77)
138 *either* not (properly) valued *or* priceless
139 see III. iv. 58
140 place (to parallel 'here')
141 blessing
142 *The jewels*: vocative case
143 *as . . . nam'd*: by their true names
144 *love*

I would prefer[145] him to a better place.
So farewell to you both.
REGAN: Prescribe not us our duties.
GONERIL: Let your study
Be to content your lord, who hath receiv'd you
At fortune's alms;[146] you have obedience scanted,
And well are worth the want that you have wanted.[147]
CORDELIA: Time shall unfold what plighted[148] cunning hides;
Who[149] covers faults, at last shame them derides.
Well may you prosper!
FRANCE: Come, my fair Cordelia.

[*Exeunt France and Cordelia.*]

GONERIL: Sister, it is not little I have to say of what most nearly appertains to us both. I think our father will hence[150] to-night.

REGAN: That's most certain, and with you; next month with us.

GONERIL: You see how full of changes his age is;[151] the observation we have made of it hath not been little: he always loved our sister most; and with what poor judgment he hath now cast her off appears too grossly.[152]

REGAN: 'Tis the infirmity of his age; yet he hath ever but slenderly known himself.

GONERIL: The best and soundest of his time hath been but rash;[153] then, must we look to receive from his age, not alone the imperfections of long-engraffed condition,[154] but, therewithal the unruly waywardness that infirm and choleric years[155] bring with them.

REGAN: Such unconstant starts[156] are we like[157] to have from him as this of Kent's banishment.

GONERIL: There is further compliment[158] of leave-taking between France and him. Pray you, let us hit together:[159] if our father carry[160] authority with such dispositions[161] as he bears, this last surrender[162] of his will but offend[163] us.

145 advance, recommend
146 *At . . . alms*: as a humble gift of fortune; cf. l. 251
147 *are . . . wanted*: deserve the destitution that has befallen you
148 folded
149 those who (antecedent to *them*)
150 *will* go *hence*
151 *full . . . is*: changeable he is now he is old
152 obviously
153 hot-headed
154 *long-engraffed condition*: a temperament that has become firmly fixed (ingrafted) by habit
155 *infirm . . . years*: years of physical weakness and proneness to anger
156 *unconstant starts*: fits of waywardness
157 likely
158 formal civility
159 *hit together*: strike a bargain, i.e. make joint plans
160 i.e. still wields
161 moods
162 harm (stronger than nowadays)
163 i.e. of the crown

REGAN: We shall further think on 't.
GONERIL: We must do something, and i' the heat.[164] [*Exeunt.*]

164 *i' . . . heat*: at once (cf. 'strike while the iron is hot')

## SCENE 2

*A Hall in the Earl of Gloucester's Castle.*

*Enter Edmund, with a letter.*

EDMUND: Thou, Nature, art my goddess; to thy law
My services are bound. Wherefore should I
Stand in the plague of custom,[1] and permit
The curiosity[2] of nations to deprive me,[3]
For that I am some twelve or fourteen moonshines
Lag of[4] a brother? Why bastard? wherefore base?
When my dimensions[5] are as well compact,[6]
My mind as generous,[7] and my shape as true,
As honest madam's[8] issue? Why brand they us
With base? with baseness? bastardy? base, base?
Who in the lusty stealth[9] of nature[10] take
More composition and fierce quality
Than doth, within a dull, stale, tired bed,
Go to the creating a whole tribe of fops,[11]
Got[12] 'tween asleep and wake? Well then,
Legitimate Edgar, I must have your land:
Our fathers' love is to the bastard Edmund
As[13] to the legitimate. Fine word, 'legitimate!'
Well, my legitimate, if this letter speed,

1 *stand . . . custom*: suffer from the inferior position custom assigns to bastards
2 scrupulousness, squeamishness
3 keep me out of my rights
4 *lag of*: behind (in coming into the world)
5 *my dimensions*: the proportions of my body
6 made
7 high-spirited
8 *honest madam's*: the true wife
9 secret act
10 (sexual) desire
11 fools
12 begotten
13 as much as

And my invention thrive, Edmund the base
Shall top[14] the legitimate:—I grow, I prosper;
Now, gods, stand up for bastards!

*Enter Gloucester.*

GLOUCESTER: Kent banished thus! And France in choler[15] parted![16]
And the king gone to-night![17] subscrib'd[18] his power!
Confin'd to exhibition![19] All this done
Upon the gad![20] Edmund, how now! what news?

EDMUND: So please you lordship, none. [*Putting up the letter.*]

GLOUCESTER: Why so earnestly seek you to put up[21] that letter?

EDMUND: I know no news, my lord.

GLOUCESTER: What paper were you reading?

EDMUND: Nothing, my lord.

GLOUCESTER: No? What needed then that terrible[22] dispatch[23] of it into your pocket? the quality of nothing hath not such need to hide itself. Let's see; come; if it be nothing, I shall not need spectacles.

EDMUND: I beseech you, sir, pardon me;[24] it is a letter from my brother that I have not all o'er-read, and for[25] so much as I have perused, I find it not fit for your o'er-looking.[26]

GLOUCESTER: Give me the letter, sir.

EDMUND: I shall offend, either to detain or give it. The contents, as in part I understand them, are to blame.

GLOUCESTER: Let's see, let's see.

EDMUND: I hope, for my brother's justification, he wrote this but as an essay[27] or taste of my virtue.

GLOUCESTER: 'This policy and reverence of age[28] makes the world bitter to the best of our times;[29] keeps our fortunes from us till our oldness cannot relish them. I begin to find an idle and fond[30] bondage in the oppression of

14 get the better of
15 anger
16 departed
17 last night
18 surrendered
19 an allowance (cf. university use)
20 *upon the gad*: suddenly (as if pricked by a gad, = goad)
21 put away
22 frightened (*not* our slang use)
23 haste in putting away
24 excuse me from showing it you
25 as for
26 examination
27 trial
28 *policy . . . age*: policy of reverence for old age
29 *the best . . . times*: our best days, i.e. men in their prime
30 foolish

aged tyranny,[31] who sways,[32] not as it hath power, but as it is suffered. Come to me, that of this I may speak more. If our father would sleep till I waked him, you should enjoy half his revenue for ever, and live the beloved of your brother, EDGAR.'—Hum! Conspiracy! 'Sleep till I waked him, you should enjoy half his revenue.'—My son Edgar! Had he a hand to write this? a heart and brain to breed it in? When came this to you? Who brought it?

EDMUND: It was not brought me, my lord; there's the cunning of it; I found it thrown in at the casement[33] of my closet.

GLOUCESTER: You know the character[34] to be your brother's?

EDMUND: If the matter were good, my lord, I durst swear it were his; but, in respect of that,[35] I would fain think it were not.

GLOUCESTER: It is his.

EDMUND: It is his hand, my lord; but I hope his heart is not in the contents.

GLOUCESTER: Hath he never heretofore sounded you in this business?

EDMUND: Never, my lord: but I have often heard him maintain it to be fit that, sons at perfect age,[36] and fathers declined,[37] the father should be as ward to the son, and the son manage his revenue.

GLOUCESTER: O villain, villain! His very opinion in the letter! Abhorred villain! Unnatural, detested, brutish villain! worse than brutish! Go, sirrah, seek him; I'll apprehend him. Abominable villain! Where is he?

EDMUND: I do not well know, my lord. If it shall please you to suspend your indignation against my brother till you can derive from him better testimony of his intent, you shall run a certain course;[38] where,[39] if you violently proceed against him, mistaking his purpose, it would make a great gap[40] in your own honour, and shake in pieces the heart of his obedience. I dare pawn[41] down my life for him, that he hath writ this to feel[42] my affection to your honour, and to no other pretence of danger.[43]

GLOUCESTER: Think you so?

EDMUND: If your honour judge it meet, I will place you where you shall hear us confer on this, and by an auricular[44] assurance have your satisfaction; and that without any further delay than this very evening.

31 *aged tyranny*: my aged father (abstract for concrete, as often)
32 rules
33 (open) window
34 handwriting
35 its goodness or lack of it, i.e. (in this case) its badness
36 *perfect age*: the prime of life
37 in years
38 *run . . . course*: act safely
39 whereas
40 breach
41 see I. i. 148
42 try
43 *to no . . . danger*: not with a view to any (other) dangerous design
44 through the ear

GLOUCESTER: He cannot be such a monster—

EDMUND: Nor is not, sure.

GLOUCESTER: —to his father, that so tenderly and entirely loves him. Heaven and earth! Edmund, seek him out; wind me into him,[45] I pray you; frame the business after your own wisdom. I would unstate myself[46] to be in a due resolution.[47]

EDMUND: I will seek him, sir, presently;[48] convey[49] the business as I shall find means, and acquaint you withal.[50]

GLOUCESTER: These late eclipses in the sun and moon portend no good to us: though the wisdom of nature can reason it thus and thus,[51] yet nature finds itself scourged by the sequent effects.[52] Love cools, friendship falls off, brothers divide: in cities, mutinies;[53] in countries, discord; in palaces, treason; and the bond cracked between son and father. This villain of mine comes under the prediction; there's son against father: the king falls from bias of nature;[54] there's father against child. We have seen the best of our time: machinations,[55] hollowness,[56] treachery, and all ruinous disorders, follow us disquietly to our graves. Find out this villain, Edmund; it shall lose thee nothing: do it carefully. And the noble and true-hearted Kent banished! his offence, honesty! 'Tis strange! [*Exit.*]

EDMUND: This is the excellent foppery[57] of the world, that, when we are sick in fortune,—often the surfeit[58] of our own behaviour,—we make guilty of our disasters the sun, the moon, and the stars; as if we were villains by necessity, fools by heavenly compulsion, knaves, thieves, and treachers[59] by spherical predominance,[60] drunkards, liars, and adulterers by an enforced obedience of planetary influence; and all that we are evil in, by a divine thrusting on: an admirable evasion[61] of whoremaster[62] man, to lay his goatish[63] disposition to the charge of a star! My father compounded with

45 *wind . . . him*: insinuate yourself, get into familiar talk with him, please (*me* is not the object of 'wind' but the so-called ethic dative)
46 *unstate myself*: give up my position
47 *to be . . . resolution*: to have my doubts resolved
48 immediately
49 carry out
50 *acquaint you withal*: inform you of it
51 *the wisdom . . . and thus*: natural philosophy can give good explanations
52 *sequent effects*: effects that follow (eclipses)
53 disturbances
54 *from . . . nature*: away from natural inclination (i.e. of affection towards Cordelia)
55 plots
56 insincerity
57 folly
58 evil result
59 traitors
60 *spherical predominance*: dominance of some special star
61 of responsibility
62 *lecherous*
63 lascivious

my mother under the dragon's tail,[64] and my nativity was under *Ursa Major*;[65] so that it follows I am rough and lecherous. 'Sfoot! I should have been that I am had the maidenliest star in the firmament twinkled on my bastardizing.[66] Edgar—

*Enter Edgar.*

and pat[67] he comes, like the catastrophe of the old[68] comedy: my cue[69] is villanous melancholy, with a sigh like Tom o' Bedlam.[70] O, these eclipses do portend these divisions! *Fa, sol, la, mi.*[71]

EDGAR: How now, brother Edmund! What serious contemplation are you in?

EDMUND: I am thinking, brother, of a prediction I read this other day, what[72] should follow these eclipses.

EDGAR: Do you busy yourself with that?

EDMUND: I promise you the effects he writes of succeed[73] unhappily; as of unnaturalness between the child and the parent; death, dearth, dissolutions of ancient amities; divisions in state; menaces and maledictions against king and nobles; needless diffidences,[74] banishment of friends, dissipation of cohorts,[75] nuptial breaches, and I know not what.

EDGAR: How long have you been a sectary astronomical?[76]

EDMUND: Come, come; when saw you my father last?

EDGAR: The night gone by.

EDMUND: Spake you with him?

EDGAR: Ay, two hours together.

EDMUND: Parted you in good terms? Found you no displeasure in him by word or countenance?

EDGAR: None at all.

EDMUND: Bethink yourself wherein you may have offended him; and at my entreaty forbear[77] his presence till some little time hath qualified[78] the heat of his displeasure, which at this instant so rageth in him that with the mischief of your person it would scarcely allay.[79]

EDGAR: Some villain hath done me wrong.

64 *dragon's tail*: in astronomy, 'the descending node of the moon's orbit with the ecliptic' (*Shorter OED*)
65 *Ursa Major*: the Great Bear
66 unlawful begetting
67 just at the right moment
68 any old
69 part
70 *Tom o' Bedlam*: beggar feigning madness
71 *Fa . . . mi*: Edmund sings or hums a series of musical notes
72 (as to) *what*
73 turn out
74 distrust (of others)
75 *dissipation of cohorts*: just possibly 'troops deserting'
76 *sectary astronomical*: follower of, believer in astrology
77 avoid
78 reduced
79 subside

EDMUND: That's my fear. I pray you have a continent forbearance[80] till the speed of his rage goes slower, and, as I say, retire with me to my lodging, from whence I will fitly[81] bring you to hear my lord speak. Pray you, go; there's my key. If you do stir abroad, go armed.

EDGAR: Armed, brother!

EDMUND: Brother, I advise you to the best; go armed; I am no honest man if there be any good meaning[82] toward you; I have told you what I have seen and heard; but faintly, nothing like the image and horror[83] of it; pray you, away.

EDGAR: Shall I hear from you anon?

EDMUND: I do serve you in this business. [*Exit Edgar.*]
A credulous father, and a brother noble,
Whose nature is so far from doing harms
That he suspects none; on whose foolish honesty
My practices[84] ride easy! I see the business.
Let me, if not by birth, have lands by wit:
All with me's meet that I can fashion fit.[85] [*Exit.*]

80 *a . . . forbearance*: the restraint to keep away
81 at a suitable time
82 intentions
83 *image . . . horror*: horrible reality
84 plots
85 to my purpose

## SCENE 3

*A Room in the Duke of Albany's Palace.*

*Enter Goneril and Oswald her Steward.*

GONERIL: Did my father strike my gentleman for chiding of his fool?

OSWALD: Ay, madam.

GONERIL: By day and night[1] he wrongs me; every hour
He flashes into[2] one gross crime[3] or other,
That sets us all at odds:[4] I'll not endure it:
His knights grow riotous, and himself upbraids us
On every trifle. When he returns from hunting
I will not speak with him; say I am sick:
If you come slack of former services,
You shall do well; the fault of it I'll answer.[5]

OSWALD: He's coming, madam; I hear him. [*Horns within.*]

1 *By . . . night*: probably 'continually', rather than an oath
2 *flashes into*: breaks out into
3 offence
4 *sets . . . odds*: upsets
5 (for), be responsible for

GONERIL: Put on what weary negligence you please,
You and your fellows; I'd have it come to question:[6]
If he distaste[7] it, let him to my sister,
Whose mind and mine, I know, in that are one,
Not to be over-rul'd. Idle[8] old man,
That still would manage those authorities[9]
That he hath given away! Now, by my life,
Old fools are babes again, and must be us'd
With checks as flatteries, when they are seen abus'd.[10]
Remember what I have said.

OSWALD: Well, madam.

GONERIL: And let his knights have colder looks among you;
What grows of it,[11] no matter; advise your fellows so:
I would breed from hence occasions,[12] and I shall,
That I may speak: I'll write straight to my sister
To hold my very course.[13] Prepare for dinner. [*Exeunt.*]

6 *I'd . . . question*: I want it discussed
7 dislike (as Q reads)
8 foolish
9 *manage . . . authorities*: exercise the powers
10 *us'd . . . abus'd*: rebuked as well as flattered when they are seen to be misled (by their followers) *or* deluded
11 *grows of it*: results from it
12 opportunities
13 *my . . . course*: exactly my course

## SCENE 4

*A Hall in the Same.*

*Enter Kent, disguised.*

KENT: If but as well I other accents borrow,
That can my speech defuse,[1] my good intent
May carry through itself to that full issue[2]
For which I raz'd[3] my likeness. Now, banish'd Kent
If thou canst serve where thou dost stand condemn'd,
So may it come, thy master, whom thou lov'st,
Shall find thee full of labours.

*Horns within. Enter Lear, Knights, and Attendants.*

1 confuse, disguise
2 *my . . . issue*: I may be able to bring off the purpose
3 erased

LEAR: Let me not stay a jot[4] for dinner: go, get it ready. [*Exit an Attendant.*] How now! what art thou?

KENT: A man, sir.

LEAR: What dost thou profess?[5] What wouldst thou with us?

KENT: I do profess to be no less than I seem; to serve him truly that will put me in trust; to love him that is honest; to converse[6] with him that is wise, and says a little; to fear judgment;[7] to fight when I cannot choose; and to eat no fish.[8]

LEAR: What art thou?

KENT: A very honest-hearted fellow, and as poor as the king.

LEAR: If thou be as poor for a subject as he is for a king, thou art poor enough. What wouldst thou?

KENT: Service.

LEAR: Whom wouldst thou serve?

KENT: You.

LEAR: Dost thou know me, fellow?

KENT: No, sir; but you have that in your countenance[9] which I would fain call master.

LEAR: What's that?

KENT: Authority.

LEAR: What services canst thou do?

KENT: I can keep honest counsel,[10] ride, run, mar a curious[11] tale in telling it, and deliver a plain message bluntly; that which ordinary men are fit for, I am qualified in, and the best of me is diligence.

LEAR: How old art thou?

KENT: Not so young, sir, to love[12] a woman for singing, nor so old to dote on her for any thing; I have years on my back forty-eight.

LEAR: Follow me; thou shalt serve me: if I like thee no worse after dinner I will not part from thee yet. Dinner, ho! dinner! Where's my knave?[13] my fool? Go you and call my fool hither. [*Exit an Attendant.*]

*Enter Oswald.*

You, you, sirrah, where's my daughter?

OSWALD: So please you,[14]— [*Exit.*]

4 *stay a jot*: wait a moment
5 *What . . . profess?*: what is your business, job? (But Kent takes the word in the sense of 'claim'.)
6 have to do with (Lat. *conversari*)
7 here *or* hereafter
8 *eat no fish*: be a loyal subject (not fast like a Papist)
9 bearing
10 *honest counsel*: an honourable secret
11 elaborate, difficult (Kent is only a plain man.)
12 (as) *to love*
13 boy (as in a pack of cards)
14 *So . . . you*: excuse me (as he goes out)

LEAR: What says the fellow there? Call the clotpoll[15] back. [*Exit a Knight.*] Where's my fool, ho? I think the world's asleep. How now! where's that mongrel?[16]

*Re-enter Knight.*

KNIGHT: He says, my lord, your daughter is not well.

LEAR: Why came not the slave back to me when I called him?

KNIGHT: Sir, he answered me in the roundest[17] manner, he would not.

LEAR: He would not!

KNIGHT: My lord, I know not what the matter is; but, to my judgment, your highness is not entertained with that ceremonious affection as you were wont; there's a great abatement of kindness as well in the general dependants as in the duke also and your daughter.

LEAR: Ha! sayest thou so?

KNIGHT: I beseech you, pardon me, my lord, if I be mistaken; for my duty cannot be[18] silent when I think your highness wronged.

LEAR: Thou but rememberest me of mine own conception: I have perceived a most faint[19] neglect of late; which I have rather blamed as mine own jealous curiosity[20] than as a very pretence[21] and purpose of unkindness: I will look further into 't. But where's my fool? I have not seen him this two days.

KNIGHT: Since my young lady's going into France, sir, the fool hath much pined him away.

LEAR: No more of that; I have noted it well. Go you and tell my daughter I would speak with her. [*Exit an Attendant.*]
Go you, call hither my fool. [*Exit an Attendant.*]

*Re-enter Oswald.*

O! you sir, come you hither, sir. Who am I, sir?

OSWALD: My lady's father.

LEAR: 'My lady's father!' my lord's knave: you whoreson dog! you slave! you cur!

OSWALD: I am none of these, my lord; I beseech your pardon.

LEAR: Do you bandy[22] looks with me, you rascal? [*Striking him.*]

OSWALD: I'll not be struck, my lord.

15 clodpate, blockhead
16 i.e. Oswald
17 plainest
18 *my . . . be*: my sense of duty forbids me to be
19 slight *or* (possibly) cold
20 watchfulness, suspicion
21 *very pretence*: real intention
22 exchange (originally in tennis)

KENT: Nor tripped neither, you base football player. [*Tripping up his heels.*]

LEAR: I thank thee, fellow; thou servest me, and I'll love thee.

KENT: Come, sir, arise, away! I'll teach you differences:[23] away, away! If you will measure your lubber's length again, tarry; but away! Go to;[24] have you wisdom?[25] So.[26] [*Pushes Oswald out.*]

LEAR: Now, my friendly knave, I thank thee: there's earnest[27] of thy service. [*Gives Kent money.*]

*Enter Fool.*

FOOL: Let me hire him too: here's my coxcomb.[28] [*Offers Kent his cap.*]

LEAR: How now, my pretty knave! how dost thou?

FOOL: Sirrah, you were best[29] take my coxcomb.

KENT: Why, fool?

FOOL: Why? for taking one's part that's out of favour. Nay, an[30] thou canst not smile as the wind sits,[31] thou'lt catch cold shortly: there, take my coxcomb. Why, this fellow has banished two on 's[32] daughters, and did the third a blessing against his will: if thou follow him thou must needs wear my coxcomb. How now, nuncle![33] Would I had two coxcombs and two daughters!

LEAR: Why, my boy?

FOOL: If I gave them all my living, I'd keep my coxcombs myself. There's mine; beg another of thy daughters.

LEAR: Take heed, sirrah; the whip.

FOOL: Truth's a dog must to kennel; he must be whipped out when Lady the brach[34] may stand by the fire and stink.

LEAR: A pestilent gall[35] to me!

FOOL [*To Kent.*]: Sirrah, I'll teach thee a speech.

LEAR: Do.

FOOL: Mark it nuncle:—

Have more than thou showest,
Speak less than thou knowest,
Lend less than thou owest,[36]

23 i.e. of rank (between you and a king)
24 *Go to*: Pshaw! (expression of impatience)
25 *have . . . wisdom?*: are you in your senses?
26 good (as Oswald goes out)
27 a pledge (of further reward)
28 fool's cap
29 *you . . . best*: you had better (*literally* it were, i.e. would be, best for you)
30 if
31 *smile . . . sits*: see which way things are going, trim your sail to the breeze
32 of his
33 contracted for 'mine uncle', a regular address of fools to their master
34 bitch
35 irritant *or* bitterness
36 ownest

Ride more than thou goest,[37]
Learn more than thou trowest,[38]
Set less than thou throwest;[39]
Leave thy drink and thy whore,
And keep in-a-door,[40]
And thou shalt have more
Than two tens to a score.[41]

KENT: This is nothing, fool.

FOOL: Then 'tis like the breath of an unfree'd lawyer, you gave me nothing for't. Can you make no use of nothing, nuncle?

LEAR: Why, no, boy; nothing can be made out of nothing.

FOOL [*To Kent.*]: Prithee, tell him, so much the rent of his land comes to: he will not believe a fool.

LEAR: A bitter fool!

FOOL: Dost thou know the difference, my boy, between a bitter fool and a sweet fool?

LEAR: No, lad; teach me.

FOOL:
That lord that counsell'd thee
  To give away thy land,
Come place him here by me,
  Do thou for him stand:
The sweet and bitter fool
  Will presently appear;
The one in motley[42] here,
  The other found out there.

LEAR: Dost thou call me fool, boy?

FOOL: All thy other titles thou hast given away; that thou wast born with.

KENT: This is not altogether fool, my lord.

FOOL: No, faith, lords and great men will not let me;[43] if I had a monopoly out,[44] they would have part on 't, and ladies too: they will not let me have all fool to myself; they'll be snatching. Nuncle, give me an egg, and I'll give thee two crowns.

LEAR: What two crowns shall they be?

FOOL: Why, after I have cut the egg i' the middle and eat up the meat, the two crowns[45] of the egg. When you clovest thy crown i' the middle, and gavest away both parts, thou borest thine ass on thy back o'er the dirt:[46] thou hadst

37 walkest
38 i.e. (probably) don't believe all you hear
39 i.e. stake less than you win (at a throw)
40 indoors
41 *And . . . score*: i.e. you'll do well
42 fool's dress (as I am)
43 *let me*: (be the complete fool)
44 taken out, granted (as often by Stuart kings)
45 i.e. half shells
46 *borest . . . dirt*: reversed the proper order of things (from a fable of Aesop)

little wit in thy bald crown when thou gavest thy golden one away. If I speak like myself[47] in this, let him be whipped that first finds it so.

Fools had ne'er less grace[48] in a year;
For wise men are grown foppish,[49]
And know not how their wits to wear,[50]
Their manners are so apish.

LEAR: When were you wont to be so full of songs, sirrah?

FOOL: I have used it,[51] nuncle, ever since thou madest thy daughters thy mothers; for when thou gavest them the rod and puttest down thine own breeches,

Then they for sudden joy did weep,
And I for sorrow sung,
That such a king should play bo-peep,[52]
And go the fools among.

Prithee, nuncle, keep a schoolmaster that can teach thy fool to lie: I would fain learn to lie.

LEAR: An you lie, sirrah, we'll have you whipped.

FOOL: I marvel what kin thou and thy daughters are: they'll have me whipped for speaking true, thou'lt have me whipped for lying; and sometimes I am whipped for holding my peace. I had rather be any kind o' thing than a fool; and yet I would not be thee, nuncle; thou hast pared thy wit o' both sides, and left nothing i' the middle:[53] here comes one o' the parings.

*Enter Goneril.*

LEAR: How now, daughter! what makes[54] that frontlet[55] on? Methinks you are too much of late i' the frown.

FOOL: Thou wast a pretty fellow when thou hadst no need to care for her frowning; now thou art an O without a figure.[56] I am better than thou art now; I am a fool, thou art nothing. [*To Goneril.*] Yes, forsooth, I will hold my tongue; so your face bids me, though you say nothing.

47 *like myself*: foolishly
48 *had . . . grace*: were never less in favour
49 foolish
50 *their . . . wear*: show their wisdom
51 *used it*: made it my habit
52 *play bo-peep*: behave like a child
53 *pared . . . middle*: i.e. by giving away both halves of thy kingdom
54 means
55 i.e. frown (*lit.* cloth worn on forehead)
56 *an . . . figure*: a mere cipher, thing of nought

Mum, mum;
He that keeps nor crust nor crumb,
Weary of all, shall want some.

That's a shealed peascod.[57] [*Pointing to Lear.*]

GONERIL: Not only, sir, this your all-licens'd fool,
But other of your insolent retinue
Do hourly carp and quarrel, breaking forth
In rank[58] and not-to-be-endured riots. Sir,
I had thought, by making this well known unto you,
To have found a safe redress;[59] but now grow fearful,
By what yourself too late have spoke and done,
That you protect this course, and put it on[60]
By your allowance; which if you should, the fault
Would not 'scape censure, nor the redresses sleep,
Which, in the tender of a wholesome weal,[61]
Might in their working do you that offence,
Which else was shame,[62] that then necessity
Will call discreet proceeding.[63]

FOOL: For you trow, nuncle.
The hedge-sparrow fed the cuckoo so long,
That it had its head bit off by its young.[64]
So out went the candle, and we were left darkling.[65]

LEAR: Are you our daughter?

GONERIL: I would you would make use of your good wisdom,
Whereof I know you are fraught;[66] and put away
These dispositions[67] which of late transform you
From what you rightly are.

FOOL: May not an ass know when the cart draws the horse?[68] Whoop, Jug! I love thee.

LEAR: Does any here know me? This is not Lear:
Does Lear walk thus? speak thus? Where are his eyes?

57 *shealed peascod*: pod without peas (provincial form of 'shelled')
58 gross
59 *safe redress*: sure remedy
60 *put it on*: encourage it
61 *in . . . weal*: in their regard for a healthy state of affairs
62 *Which . . . shame*: which would be disgraceful if the motive (behind my remedial action) were not good
63 *that . . . proceeding*: i.e. although, considering the need, people would approve my conduct ('that' = 'which' again—an awkward construction)
64 its (as often) apparent young, i.e. the young cuckoo (corresponding to Goneril)
65 in the dark
66 stored
67 moods
68 cf. l. 134

Either his notion[69] weakens, his discernings[70]
Are lethargied.[71] Ha! waking?[72] 'tis not so.
Who is it that can tell me who I am?

FOOL: Lear's shadow.

LEAR: I would[73] learn that; for, by the marks of sovereignty, knowledge and reason, I should be false[74] persuaded I had daughters.

FOOL: Which[75] they will make an obedient father.

LEAR: Your name, fair gentlewoman?

GONERIL: This admiration,[76] sir, is much o' the favour[77]
Of other your[78] new pranks. I do beseech you
To understand my purposes aright:
As you are old and reverend, should[79] be wise.
Here do you keep a hundred knights and squires;
Men so disorder'd,[80] so debosh'd,[81] and bold,
That this our court, infected with their manners,
Shows like a riotous inn: epicurism[82] and lust
Make it more like a tavern or a brothel
Than a grac'd[83] palace. The shame itself doth speak
For[84] instant remedy; be then desir'd[85]
By her that else will take the thing she begs,
A little to disquantity[86] your train;
And the remainder, that shall still depend,[87]
To be[88] such men as may besort[89] your age,
Which know themselves and you.

LEAR: Darkness and devils!
Saddle my horses; call my train together.
Degenerate bastard! I'll not trouble thee:
Yet have I left a daughter.

69 understanding
70 powers of discernment
71 dulled
72 am I awake?
73 I must
74 falsely
75 whom (Lear's shadow)
76 (feigned) surprise
77 nature
78 *other* (of) *your*
79 (you) *should*
80 disorderly
81 debauched
82 epicureanism, luxury
83 honourable
84 *speak for*: demand
85 *be . . . desir'd*: let yourself be requested
86 reduce the number of
87 serve you
88 *the remainder . . . be*: allow the remainder to be
89 suit

GONERIL: You strike my people, and your disorder'd rabble
Make servants of their betters.

*Enter Albany.*

LEAR: Woe, that[90] too late repents;
[*To Albany.*] O! sir, are you come?
Is it your will? Speak, sir. Prepare my horses.
Ingratitude, thou marble-hearted fiend,
More hideous, when thou show'st thee in a child
Than the[91] sea-monster.
ALBANY: Pray, sir, be patient.
LEAR [*To Goneril.*]: Detested kite! thou liest:
My train are men of choice and rarest parts,
That all particulars of duty know,
And in the most exact regard[92] support
The worships[93] of their name. O most small fault,[94]
How ugly didst thou in Cordelia show!
Which, like an engine,[95] wrench'd my frame of nature[96]
From the fix'd place, drew from my heart all love,
And added to the gall. O Lear, Lear, Lear!
Beat at this gate, that let thy folly in, [*Striking his head.*]
And thy dear[97] judgment out! Go, go, my people.
ALBANY: My lord, I am guiltless, as I am ignorant
Of what hath mov'd you.
LEAR: It may be so, my lord.
Hear, Nature, hear! dear goddess, hear!
Suspend thy purpose, if thou didst intend
To make this creature fruitful!
Into her womb convey sterility!
Dry up in her the organs of increase,
And from her derogate[98] body never spring
A babe to honour her! If she must teem,[99]
Create her child of spleen, that it may live
And be a thwart[100] disnatur'd[101] torment to her!

90 *Woe, that*: Woe to him who
91 a (generic use, cf. I. ii. 109)
92 *in . . . regard*: with scrupulous care
93 honour (plural sometimes used when a plurality of persons is concerned)
94 *O . . . fault*: i.e. Cordelia's obstinacy
95 the rack (a torture, wrenching the body apart)
96 *frame of nature*: system of natural affection
97 precious
98 debased
99 bear children
100 cross, perverse
101 unnatural

Let it stamp wrinkles in her brow of youth,
With cadent[102] tears fret[103] channels in her cheeks,
Turn all her mother's pains and benefits[104]
To laughter and contempt, that she may feel
How sharper than a serpent's tooth it is
To have a thankless child! Away, away! [*Exit.*]

ALBANY: Now, gods that we adore, whereof comes this?

GONERIL: Never afflict yourself to know the cause;
But let his disposition have that scope[105]
That dotage gives it.

*Re-enter Lear.*

LEAR: What! fifty of my followers at a clap,[106]
Within a fortnight?

ALBANY: What's the matter, sir?

LEAR: I'll tell thee. [*To Goneril.*] Life and death! I am asham'd
That thou hast power to shake my manhood thus,
That these hot tears, which break from me perforce,
Should make thee worth them. Blasts and fogs upon thee!
Th' untented[107] woundings of a father's curse
Pierce every sense about thee! Old fond[108] eyes,
Beweep[109] this cause again, I'll pluck ye out,
And cast you, with the waters that you lose,[110]
To temper[111] clay. Yea, is it come to this?
Let it be so: I have another daughter,
Who, I am sure, is kind and comfortable:[112]
When she shall hear this of thee, with her nails
She'll flay thy wolvish visage. Thou shalt find
That I'll resume the shape which thou dost think
I have cast off for ever; thou shalt, I warrant thee.

[*Exeunt Lear, Kent, and Attendants.*]

GONERIL: Do you mark that?

ALBANY: I cannot be so partial, Goneril,
To the great love I bear you.[113]—

102 falling
103 wear away
104 kindness done to the child
105 disposition: cf. l. 188
106 *at a clap*: at a stroke, all at once
107 unexplored, deep, and so incurable (a surgeon probed a wound with a 'tent' or roll of lint)
108 foolish
109 if you weep for
110 waste
111 moisten
112 comforting
113 *I cannot . . . you*: i.e. so prejudiced by my love for you (as to approve your conduct now)

GONERIL: Pray you, content.[114] What, Oswald, ho! [*To the Fool*.]: You, sir, more knave than fool, after your master.

FOOL: Nuncle Lear, nuncle Lear! tarry, and take the fool with thee.

A fox, when one has caught her,
And such a daughter,
Should sure[115] to the slaughter,
If my cap would buy a halter;
So the fool follows after. [*Exit.*]

GONERIL: This man[116] hath had good counsel. A hundred knights!
'Tis politic and safe to let him keep
At point[117] a hundred knights; yes, that on every dream,
Each buzz,[118] each fancy, each complaint, dislike,
He may enguard[119] his dotage with their powers,
And hold our lives in mercy.[120] Oswald, I say!

ALBANY: Well, you may fear too far.

GONERIL: Safer than trust too far.
Let me still[121] take away the harms I fear,
Not fear still to be taken:[122] I know his heart.[123]
What he hath utter'd I have writ my sister;
If she sustain him and his hundred knights,
When I have show'd the unfitness,—

*Re-enter Oswald.*

How now, Oswald!
What![124] have you writ that letter to my sister?

OSWALD: Ay, madam.

GONERIL: Take you some company, and away to horse:
Inform her full[125] of my particular[126] fear;
And thereto add such reasons of your own
As may compact[127] it more. Get you gone,
And hasten your return. [*Exit Oswald.*]
No, no, my lord,
This milky gentleness and course[128] of yours

114 (be) *content*: calm, almost 'shut up!'
115 should surely go
116 *This man*: Lear (the whole speech is ironical)
117 *At point: armed and ready*
118 rumour
119 guard
120 *in mercy*: at his mercy
121 always
122 overtaken by harm
123 *his heart*: i.e. (perhaps) that he is plotting to recover his throne
124 Well!
125 fully
126 personal
127 strengthen
128 *gentleness . . . course*: gentleness of your course (hendiadys)

Though I condemn not, yet, under pardon,
You are much more attask'd[129] for want of wisdom
Than prais'd for harmful mildness.[130]

ALBANY: How far your eyes may pierce I cannot tell:
Striving to better, oft we mar what's well.

GONERIL: Nay, then—

ALBANY: Well, well; the event.[131] [*Exeunt.*]

129 blamed, held to account
130 *harmful mildness*: a mildness which can only prove harmful to us
131 *the event*: (let us see) what turns out

## SCENE 5

*Court before the Same.*

*Enter Lear, Kent, and Fool.*

LEAR: Go you before to Gloucester[1] with these letters.[2] Acquaint my daughter no further with any thing you know than comes from her demand out of[3] the letter. If your diligence be not speedy I shall be there before you.

KENT: I will not sleep, my lord, till I have delivered your letter. [*Exit.*]

FOOL: If a man's brains were in 's heels, were 't[4] not in danger of kibes?[5]

LEAR: Ay, boy.

FOOL: Then, I prithee, be merry; thy wit shall not go slip-shod.[6]

LEAR: Ha, ha, ha!

FOOL: Shalt see thy other daughter will use thee kindly;[7] for though she's as like this[8] as a crab[9] is like an apple, yet I can tell what I can tell.

LEAR: What canst tell, boy?

FOOL: She will taste as like this as a crab does to a crab. Thou canst tell why one's nose stands i' the middle on 's face?

LEAR: No.

FOOL: Why, to keep one's eyes of either side 's[10] nose, that what a man cannot smell out, he may spy into.

LEAR: I did her wrong,—

FOOL: Canst tell how an oyster makes his shell?

LEAR: No.

1 the town, not the Earl
2 this letter (Latin *litterae*)
3 *demand out of*: questions arising out of
4 it, his brain(s)
5 chaps or chilblains
6 in slippers (to ease chilblains on the heel)
7 (1) affectionately, (2) after her kind, or nature (the Fool foresees the second)
8 Goneril
9 (apple)
10 *'s nose*: of one's nose

FOOL: Nor I neither; but I can tell why a snail has a house.

LEAR: Why?

FOOL: Why, to put his head in; not to give it away to his daughters, and leave his horns without a case.

LEAR: I will forget my nature.[11] So kind a father! Be my horses ready?

FOOL: Thy asses[12] are gone about 'em. The reason why the seven stars[13] are no more than seven is a pretty reason.

LEAR: Because they are not eight?

FOOL: Yes, indeed: thou wouldst make a good fool.

LEAR: To take it again perforce! Monster ingratitude![14]

FOOL: If thou wert my fool, nuncle, I'd have thee beaten for being old before thy time.

LEAR: How's that?

FOOL: Thou shouldst not have been old before thou hadst been wise.

LEAR: O! let me not be mad, not mad, sweet heaven;
Keep me in temper; I would not be mad!

*Enter Gentleman.*

How now! Are those horses ready!

GENTLEMAN: Ready, my lord.

LEAR: Come, boy.

FOOL: She that's a maid now, and laughs at my departure,
Shall not be a maid long, unless things be cut shorter.[15] [*Exeunt.*]

11 *my nature*: my natural affection (for my daughters)
12 *Thy asses*: those who are fools enough to serve you still
13 *the . . . stars*: the Pleiades
14 *Either* Lear contemplates trying to resume his royal power by force, *or* he is thinking of Goneril's withdrawing the privileges he had been allowed
15 *She . . . shorter*: i.e. 'The maid who sees only the funny side of the Fool's gibes and does not realize that Lear is going on a tragic journey is such a simpleton that she won't know how to preserve her virginity' (K. Muir)

## ACT II

### SCENE 1

*A Court within the Castle of the Earl of Gloucester.*

*Enter Edmund and Curan, meeting.*

EDMUND: Save thee,[1] Curan.

CURAN: And you, sir. I have been with your father, and given him notice that the Duke of Cornwall and Regan his duchess will be here with him to-night.

EDMUND: How comes that?

1 (God) *save thee*

CURAN: Nay, I know not. You have heard of the news abroad? I mean the whispered ones,[2] for they are yet but ear-kissing arguments?[3]

EDMUND: Not I: pray you, what are they?

CURAN: Have you heard of no likely wars toward,[4] 'twixt the Dukes of Cornwall and Albany?

EDMUND: Not a word.

CURAN: You may do then, in time. Fare you well, sir. [*Exit.*]

EDMUND: The duke be here tonight! The better![5] best!
This weaves itself perforce into my business.
My father hath set guard to take my brother;
And I have one thing, of a queasy question,[6]
Which I must act. Briefness[7] and fortune, work!
Brother, a word; descend:[8] brother, I say!

*Enter Edgar.*

My father watches: O sir! fly this place;
Intelligence is given where you are hid;
You have now the good advantage of the night.
Have you not spoken 'gainst the Duke of Cornwall?
He's coming hither, now, i' the night, i' the haste,[9]
And Regan with him; have you nothing said
Upon his party 'gainst[10] the Duke of Albany?
Advise yourself.

EDGAR: I am sure on 't, not a word.

EDMUND: I hear my father coming; pardon me;
In cunning[11] I must draw my sword upon you;
Draw; seem to defend yourself; now 'quit you well.
Yield;[12]—come before my father. Light, ho! here!
Fly, brother. Torches! torches! So, farewell. [*Exit Edgar.*]
Some blood drawn on me would beget opinion [*Wounds his arm.*]
Of my more fierce endeavour:[13] I have seen drunkards
Do more than this in sport. Father! father!
Stop, stop! No help?

2 news
3 *ear-kissing arguments*: subjects of secret conversation (as with the mouth close to the hearer's ear)
4 in view
5 (all) *the better*
6 *of . . . question*: awkward, ticklish to handle
7 swift action
8 Edgar would have entered on the upper stage
9 *i' the haste*: in haste
10 *Upon . . . 'gainst*: about the party formed by him against
11 in pretence (as if we were enemies)
12 said louder, for Gloucester to hear
13 *beget . . . endeavour*: make men think that I have really been fighting seriously

*Enter Gloucester, and Servants with torches.*

GLOUCESTER: Now, Edmund, where's the villain?
EDMUND: Here stood he in the dark, his sharp sword out,
Mumbling of wicked charms, conjuring the moon
To stand auspicious mistress.[14]
GLOUCESTER: But where is he?
EDMUND: Look, sir, I bleed.
GLOUCESTER: Where is the villain, Edmund?
EDMUND: Fled this way, sir. When by no means he could—
GLOUCESTER: Pursue him, ho! Go after. [*Exeunt some Servants.*] 'By no means' what?
EDMUND: Persuade me to the murder of your lordship;
But that I told him,[15] the revenging gods
'Gainst parricides did all their thunders bend;
Spoke with how manifold and strong a bond
The child was bound to the father; sir, in fine,
Seeing how loathly opposite[16] I stood
To his unnatural purpose, in fell motion,[17]
With his prepared sword he charges home[18]
My unprovided[19] body, lanc'd mine arm:
But when he saw my best alarum'd spirits[20]
Bold in quarrel's right, rous'd to the encounter,
Or whether gasted[21] by the noise I made,
Full suddenly he fled.
GLOUCESTER: Let him fly far:
Not in this land shall he remain uncaught;
And found—dispatch.[22] The noble duke my master,
My worthy arch[23] and patron, comes to-night:
By his authority I will proclaim it,
That he which finds him shall deserve our thanks,
Bringing the murderous coward to the stake;
He that conceals him, death.

14 *stand . . . mistress*: favour him as if she were his mistress (as she was of Endymion in classical mythology)
15 *But . . . him*: without my telling him (in reply) that
16 *loathly opposite*: opposed, with loathing, to
17 *fell motion*: fierce thrust
18 *charges home*: makes a home (effective) thrust at
19 unprotected
20 *best . . . spirits*: my best spirits stirred up
21 frightened
22 when he is found, the order will be 'dispatch him!'
23 chief

EDMUND: When I dissuaded him from his intent,
And found him pight[24] to do it, with curst speech
I threaten'd to discover him: he replied,
'Thou unpossessing[25] bastard! dost thou think,
If I would[26] stand against thee, would the reposal
Of any trust, virtue, or worth, in thee
Make the words faith'd? No: what I should deny,—
As this I would; ay, though thou didst produce
My very character,[27]—I'd turn it all
To thy suggestion,[28] plot, and damned practice:[29]
And thou must make a dullard of the world,[30]
If they not thought[31] the profits of my death
Were very pregnant[32] and potential spurs[33]
To make thee seek it.'

GLOUCESTER: Strong and fasten'd[34] villain!
Would he deny his letter? I never got[35] him. [*Tucket within.*]
Hark! the duke's trumpets. I know not why he comes.
All ports I'll bar; the villain shall not 'scape;
The duke must grant me that: besides, his picture
I will send far and near, that all the kingdom
May have due note of him; and of my land,
Loyal and natural[36] boy, I'll work the means
To make thee capable.[37]

*Enter Cornwall, Regan, and Attendants.*

CORNWALL: How now, my noble friend! since I came hither,—
Which I can call but now,—I have heard strange news.

REGAN: If it be true, all vengeance comes too short
Which can pursue the offender. How dost, my lord?

GLOUCESTER: O! madam, my old heart is crack'd, it's crack'd.

REGAN: What! did my father's godson seek your life?
He whom my father name'd?[38] your Edgar!

24 determined
25 as unable to inherit
26 should
27 handwriting
28 temptation
29 treachery
30 *make . . . world*: suppose people very stupid
31 *not thought*: should not think
32 clear, obvious (of different derivation from the word meaning 'with child')
33 *potential spurs*: powerful inducements
34 confirmed
35 begot
36 true, affectionate (with a glance at the meaning of 'born out of wedlock')
37 legally able to inherit (cf. l. 67)
38 in baptism

GLOUCESTER: O! lady, lady, shame would have it hid.
REGAN: Was he not companion with the riotous knights
That tend upon my father?
GLOUCESTER: I know not, madam; 'tis too bad, too bad.
EDMUND: Yes, madam, he was of that consort.[39]
REGAN: No marvel then though he were ill affected;
'Tis they have put him on[40] the old man's death,
To have the expense and waste of[41] his revenues.
I have this present evening from my sister
Been well-inform'd of them, and with such cautions
That if they come to sojourn at my house,
I'll not be there.
CORNWALL: Nor I, assure thee, Regan.
Edmund, I hear that you have shown your father
A child-like[42] office.
EDMUND: 'Twas my duty, sir.
GLOUCESTER: He did bewray[43] his practice;[44] and receiv'd
This hurt you see, striving to apprehend him.
CORNWALL: Is he pursu'd?
GLOUCESTER: Ay, my good lord.
CORNWALL: If he be taken he shall never more
Be fear'd of doing[45] harm; make your own purpose,
How in my strength you please.[46] For you, Edmund,
Whose virtue and obedience[47] doth this instant
So much commend itself, you shall be ours:
Natures of such deep trust we shall much need;
You we first seize on.
EDMUND: I shall serve you, sir,
Truly, however else.[48]
GLOUCESTER: For him I thank your Grace.
CORNWALL: You know now why we came to visit you,—
REGAN: Thus out of season, threading dark-ey'd[49] night:
Occasions, noble Gloucester, of some prize,[50]
Wherein we must have use of your advice.
Our father he hath writ, so hath our sister,

39 (accent consórt) company
40 *put him on*: egged him on to (attempt)
41 *To . . . of*: that he might be able to spend wastefully
42 truly filial
43 reveal
44 plot
45 *of doing*: lest he should do
46 *make . . . please*: use my authority and resources as you like in carrying out your purpose
47 *virtue and obedience*: virtuous obedience (hence verb in singular)
48 successfully or not
49 *threading dark-ey'd*: (with a pun on the eye of a needle)
50 *Occasions . . . prize*: incidents of some importance have occurred

Of differences, which I best thought it fit
To answer from[51] our home; the several messengers
From hence attend dispatch.[52] Our good old friend,
Lay comforts to your bosom, and bestow
Your needful counsel to our businesses,
Which craves the instant use.[53]

GLOUCESTER: I serve you, madam.
Your Graces are right welcome. [*Exeunt.*]

51 away from
52 *attend dispatch*: wait to be sent out
53 *craves . . . use*: demands immediate execution

## SCENE 2

*Before Gloucester's Castle.*

*Enter Kent and Oswald, severally.*

OSWALD: Good dawning to thee, friend: art of this house?[1]

KENT: Ay.

OSWALD: Where may we set our horses?

KENT: I' the mire.

OSWALD: Prithee, if thou lovest me, tell me.

KENT: I love thee not.

OSWALD: Why, then I care not for thee.

KENT: If I had thee in Lipsbury pinfold,[2] I would make thee care for me.

OSWALD: Why dost thou use me thus? I know thee not.

KENT: Fellow, I know thee.

OSWALD: What dost thou know me for?

KENT: A knave, a rascal, an eater of broken meats;[3] a base, proud, shallow, beggarly, three suited,[4] hundred-pound,[5] filthy, worsted-stocking[6] knave; a lily-liver'd,[7] action-taking[8] knave; a whoreson, glass-gazing,[9] super-serviceable,[10] finical[11] rogue; one-trunk-inheriting[12] slave; one that wouldst be a

1 *of this house*: a dependant, servant
2 *in Lipsbury pinfold*: possibly 'in my jaws'
3 *eater . . . meats*: finisher up of scraps
4 the allowance of some servants
5 owning only a hundred pounds (the qualification for a jury then)
6 woollen (as opposed to silk)
7 see IV. ii. 50
8 resorting to legal protection (instead of defending himself)
9 vain
10 *either* above his work, *or* over officious
11 affected
12 whose possessions would all go in one chest

bawd, in way of[13] good service, and art nothing but the composition[14] of a knave, beggar, coward, pandar, and the son and heir of a mongrel bitch: one whom I will beat into clamorous whining if thou deniest the least syllable of thy addition.[15]

OSWALD: Why, what a monstrous fellow art thou, thus to rail on one that is neither known of thee nor knows thee!

KENT: What a brazen-faced varlet art thou, to deny thou knowest me! Is it two days since I tripped up thy heels and beat thee before the king? Draw, you rogue; for, though it be night, yet the moon shines: I'll make a sop o' the moonshine of you. [*Drawing his sword.*] Draw, you whoreson, cullionly,[16] barber-monger,[17] draw.

OSWALD: Away! I have nothing to do with thee.

KENT: Draw, you rascal; you come with letters against the king, and take vanity the puppet's[18] part against the royalty of her father. Draw, you rogue, or I'll so carbonado[19] your shanks: draw, you rascal; come your ways.[20]

OSWALD: Help, ho! murder! help!

KENT: Strike, you slave; stand, rogue, stand; you neat[21] slave, strike. [*Beating him.*]

OSWALD: Help, oh! murder! murder!

*Enter Edmund with his rapier drawn.*

EDMUND: How now! What's the matter? [*Parting them.*]

KENT: With you,[22] goodman boy, if you please: come, I'll flesh[23] ye; come on, young master.

*Enter Cornwall, Regan, Gloucester, and Servants.*

GLOUCESTER: Weapons! arms! What's the matter here?

CORNWALL: Keep peace, upon your lives:
He dies that strikes again. What is the matter?

REGAN: The messengers from our sister and the king.

CORNWALL: What is your difference?[24] speak.

OSWALD: I am scarce in breath, my lord.

13 *in way of*: in order to perform
14 mixture
15 *thy addition*: these titles
16 rascally
17 frequenter of barbers, fop
18 *vanity the puppet's*: i.e. Goneril's
19 slice, slash
20 *come . . . ways*: come on
21 dandified *or* utter
22 *With you*: my matter, quarrel is with you *or* I'm your man (for a fight)
23 initiate (into bloodshed)
24 (ground of) quarrel

KENT: No marvel, you have so bestirred your valour. You cowardly rascal, nature disclaims[25] in thee: a tailor made thee.

CORNWALL: Thou art a strange fellow; a tailor make a man?

KENT: Ay, a tailor, sir: a stone-cutter[26] or a painter could not have made him so ill, though they had been but two hours o' the trade.

CORNWALL: Speak yet, how grew your quarrel?

OSWALD: This ancient ruffian, sir, whose life I have spar'd at suit of his grey beard,—

KENT: Thou whoreson zed! thou unnecessary letter! My lord, if you will give me leave, I will tread this unbolted[27] villain into mortar, and daub the wall of a jakes[28] with him. Spare my grey beard, you wagtail?[29]

CORNWALL: Peace, sirrah!
You beastly knave, know you no reverence?

KENT: Yes, sir; but anger hath a privilege.

CORNWALL: Why art thou angry?

KENT: That such a slave as this should wear a sword,
Who wears no honesty. Such smiling rogues as these,
Like rats, oft bite the holy cords[30] a-twain
Which are too intrinse[31] t' unloose; smooth[32] every passion
That in the natures of their lords rebel;
Bring oil to fire, snow to their colder moods;
Renege,[33] affirm, and turn their halcyon beaks
With every gale and vary[34] of their masters,
Knowing nought, like dogs, but following.
A plague upon your epileptic[35] visage!
Smile you[36] my speeches, as I were a fool?
Goose, if I had you upon Sarum[37] plain,
I'd drive ye cackling home to Camelot.[38]

CORNWALL: What! art thou mad, old fellow?

GLOUCESTER: How fell you out? say that.

KENT: No contraries hold more antipathy
Than I and such a knave.

25 disown (any share)
26 sculptor
27 perhaps 'unmitigated' (bolt = sift flour)
28 privy
29 probably 'obsequious', from its bouncing or bobbing
30 *the holy cords*: of intimate relationship
31 intricate, tight
32 flatter, fall in with
33 deny
34 *gale and vary*: varying breeze
35 distorted and pale, as in an epileptic fit
36 *Smile you*: do you smile at?
37 Salisbury
38 supposed to be near Winchester

CORNWALL: Why dost thou call him knave? What is his fault?
KENT: His countenance likes[39] me not.
CORNWALL: No more, perchance, does mine, nor his, nor hers.
KENT: Sir, 'tis my occupation[40] to be plain:
I have seen better faces in my time
Than stands on any shoulder that I see
Before me at this instant.
CORNWALL: This is some fellow,
Who, having been prais'd for bluntness, doth affect
A saucy roughness, and constrains the garb
Quite from his nature:[41] he cannot flatter, he
An honest mind and plain, he must speak truth:
An they will take it, so;[42] if not, he's plain.
These kind of knaves I know, which in this plainness
Harbour more craft and more corrupter[43] ends
Than twenty silly-ducking observants,[44]
That stretch their duties nicely.[45]
KENT: Sir, in good sooth, in sincere verity,
Under the allowance of your grand aspect,[46]
Whose influence, like the wreath of radiant fire
On flickering Phoebus' front,—
CORNWALL: What mean'st by this?
KENT: To go out of my dialect, which you discommend so much. I know, sir, I am no flatterer: he that[47] beguiled you in a plain accent was a plain knave;[48] which for my part I will not be, though I should win your displeasure[49] to entreat me to 't.[50]
CORNWALL: What was the offence you gave him?
OSWALD: I never gave him any:
It pleas'd the king his master very late
To strike at me, upon his misconstruction;[51]
When he, conjunct,[52] and flattering his displeasure,

39 pleases
40 business, habit
41 *constrains . . . nature*: is behaving in a manner quite unnatural to him (garb = fashion, manner, but not of *dress* in Shakespeare)
42 well and good
43 *more corrupter*: double comparative, not uncommon in Shakespeare
44 *silly-ducking observants*: obsequious attendants foolishly bowing and scraping (observe = pay court to)
45 *stretch . . . nicely*: are over-particular in the performance of
46 power, influence (astrological)
47 *he that*: i.e. the 'kind of knaves' referred to in l. 87
48 *a plain knave*: a real knave (which I am not)
49 you, in your displeasure
50 *to 't*: to flatter you
51 *upon his misconstruction*: misunderstanding me; see I. iv. 68
52 joining in with (Lear)

Tripp'd me behind; being down, insulted, rail'd,
And put upon him such a deal of man,
That worthied him,[53] got praises of the king
For him attempting[54] who was self-subdu'd;
And, in the fleshment[55] of this dread exploit,
Drew on me here again.

KENT: None of these rogues and cowards
But Ajax is their fool.[56]

CORNWALL: Fetch forth the stocks!
You stubborn ancient knave, you reverend[57] braggart,
We'll teach you.

KENT: Sir, I am too old to learn,
Call not your stocks for me; I serve the king,
On whose employment I was sent to you;
You shall do small respect, show too bold malice
Against the grace and person of my master,
Stocking[58] his messenger.

CORNWALL: Fetch forth the stocks! As I have life and honour,
There shall he sit till noon.

REGAN: Till noon! Till night, my lord; and all night too.

KENT: Why, madam, if I were your father's dog,
You should not use me so.

REGAN: Sir, being his knave, I will.

CORNWALL: This is a fellow of the same colour[59]
Our sister speaks of. Come, bring away[60] the stocks. [*Stocks brought out.*]

GLOUCESTER: Let me beseech your Grace not to do so.
His fault is much, and the good king his master
Will check him for't: your purpos'd low correction
Is such as basest and contemned'st[61] wretches
For pilferings and most common trespasses
Are punish'd with: the king must take it ill,
That he, so slightly valu'd in his messenger,
Should have him thus restrain'd.

CORNWALL: I'll answer[62] that.

53 *put . . . worthied him*: made such a show of valour as to win the reputation of honour
54 *him attempting*: attacking a man
55 excitement resulting from first success, see l. 35
56 *their fool*: a fool compared to them
57 grey-headed, old enough to know better
58 putting in stocks
59 complexion, kind
60 bring in
61 most despicable
62 take responsibility for

REGAN: My sister may receive it much more worse
To have her gentleman abus'd, assaulted,
For following her affairs. Put in his legs. [*Kent is put in the stocks.*]
Come, my good lord, away. [*Exeunt all but Gloucester and Kent.*]
GLOUCESTER: I am sorry for thee, friend; 'tis the duke's pleasure,
Whose disposition, all the world well knows,
Will not be rubb'd[63] nor stopp'd: I'll entreat for thee.
KENT: Pray, do not, sir. I have watch'd[64] and travell'd hard;
Some time I shall sleep out, the rest I'll whistle.
A good man's fortune may grow out at heels:[65]
Give you good morrow!
GLOUCESTER: The duke's to blame in this; 'twill be ill taken. [*Exit.*]
KENT: Good king, that must approve[66] the common saw,[67]
Thou out of heaven's benediction comest
To the warm sun.[68]
Approach, thou beacon[69] to this under globe,[70]
That by thy comfortable beams I may
Peruse this letter. Nothing almost sees miracles
But misery:[71] I know 'tis from Cordelia,
Who hath most fortunately been inform'd
Of my obscured course;[72] and shall find time
From this enormous state, seeking to give
Losses their remedies.[73] All weary and o'er-watch'd,
Take vantage,[74] heavy eyes, not to behold
This shameful lodging.
Fortune, good night, smile once more; turn thy wheel! [*He sleeps.*]

63 hindered (a 'rub' is an obstacle in bowls)
64 lain awake at night
65 *out at heels*: a metaphor for 'in a bad way', like 'out at elbow' or 'down at heel'
66 prove (the truth of)
67 proverb
68 *Thou . . . sun*: i.e. from better to worse (a surprising sense, but proved by other examples)
69 *thou beacon*: the sun
70 *this . . . globe*: our world, as opposed to heaven (l. 147)
71 the wretched
72 *my . . . course*: what has happened to me who appears to have disappeared
73 *and shall . . . remedies*: and who will find the opportunity to deliver us from this unnatural state of affairs, putting right what is wrong
74 advantage (of the opportunity)

## SCENE 3

*A Part of the Heath.*

*Enter Edgar.*

EDGAR: I heard myself proclaim'd;[1]
And by the happy[2] hollow of a tree
Escap'd the hunt. No port is free; no place,
That[3] guard, and most unusual vigilance,
Does not attend my taking.[4] While I may 'scape
I will preserve myself; and am bethought
To take[5] the basest and most poorest shape
That ever penury, in contempt of man,
Brought near to beast; my face I'll grime with filth,
Blanket my loins, elf[6] all my hair in knots,
And with presented[7] nakedness outface
The winds and persecutions of the sky.
The country gives me proof and precedent
Of Bedlam[8] beggars, who with roaring voices,
Strike[9] in their numb'd and mortified bare arms
Pins, wooden pricks,[10] nails, sprigs of rosemary;
And with this horrible object,[11] from low farms,
Poor pelting[12] villages, sheep-cotes, and mills,
Sometime with lunatic bans,[13] sometime with prayers,
Enforce their charity. Poor Turlygood![14] poor Tom!
That's something yet: Edgar I nothing am.[15] [*Exit.*]

1 see II. i. 60 ff.
2 luckily found
3 i.e. where
4 *attend my taking*: wait to arrest me
5 *am . . . take*: have bethought myself of taking
6 tangle (as an elf might)
7 *either* assumed *or* exposed to view
8 cf. I. ii. 110
9 drive
10 skewers
11 appearance
12 petty
13 curses
14 no certain explanation
15 *Edgar . . . am*: either I am Edgar no more, *or* As Edgar I no longer exist

## SCENE 4

*Before Gloucester's Castle.*

*Kent in the stocks.*

*Enter Lear, Fool, and Gentleman.*

LEAR: 'Tis strange that they[1] should so depart from home,
And not send back my messenger.
GENTLEMAN: As I learn'd,
The night before there was no purpose in them
Of this remove.[2]
KENT: Hail to thee, noble master!
LEAR: Ha!
Mak'st thou this shame thy pastime?
KENT: No, my lord.
FOOL: Ha, ha! he wears cruel[3] garters. Horses are tied by the head, dogs and bears by the neck, monkeys by the loins, and men by the legs: when a man is over-lusty at legs, then he wears wooden nether-stocks.[4]
LEAR: What's he that hath so much thy place[5] mistook
To set thee here?
KENT: It is both he and she,
Your son and daughter.
LEAR: No.
KENT: Yes.
LEAR: No, I say.
KENT: I say, yea.
LEAR: No, no; they would not.
KENT: Yes, they have.
LEAR: By Jupiter, I swear, no.
KENT: By Juno, I swear, ay.
LEAR: They durst not do 't;
They could not, would not do 't; 'tis worse than murder,
To do upon respect[6] such violent outrage.
Resolve me,[7] with all modest[8] haste, which way
Thou mightst deserve, or they impose, this usage,
Coming from us.[9]

1 Cornwall and Regan
2 change of residence
3 with a pun on 'crewel' = worsted yarn
4 stockings (as opposed to 'upper stocks' = breeches)
5 rank, status as my envoy
6 *upon respect*: deliberately
7 *Resolve me*: explain to me
8 becoming
9 *Coming . . . us*: seeing that you came from me

KENT: My lord, when at their home
I did commend your highness' letters to them,
Ere I was risen from the place that show'd
My duty kneeling, there came a reeking post,[10]
Stew'd[11] in his haste, half breathless, panting forth
From Goneril his mistress salutations;
Deliver'd letters, spite of intermission,[12]
Which presently[13] they read: on whose contents
They summon'd up their meiny,[14] straight took horse;
Commanded me to follow, and attend
The leisure of their answer; gave me cold looks:
And meeting[15] here the other messenger,
Whose welcome, I perceiv'd, had poison'd mine,—
Being the very fellow which of late
Display'd[16] so saucily against your highness,—
Having more man[17] than wit about me,—drew:
He rais'd the house with loud and coward cries.
You son and daughter found this trespass worth
The shame which here it suffers.

FOOL: Winter's not gone yet,[18] if the wild geese fly that way.
Fathers that wear rags
Do make their children blind,[19]
But fathers that bear bags[20]
Shall see their children kind.
Fortune, that arrant whore,
Ne'er turns the key[21] to the poor.
But for all this thou shalt have as many dolours[22] for[23] thy daughters as thou canst tell[24] in a year.

LEAR: O! how this mother[25] swells up toward my heart;
*Hysterica passio!*[26] down, thou climbing sorrow!
Thy element's below. Where is this daughter?

10 messenger
11 sweating
12 *spite of intermission*: in spite of the fact he was interrupting me
13 immediately
14 household, company
15 And I, meeting
16 showed off
17 courage (cf. II. ii. 105)
18 i.e. We are not out of trouble
19 to filial duty
20 of money
21 *turns the key*: to admit
22 griefs (with pun on 'dollars' = money)
23 from, because of
24 (1) recount griefs, (2) count money
25 hysteria
26 *Hysterica passio!*: suffering in the 'mother' (archaic for womb, Gk *hystera*), so-called as commoner in women

KENT: With the earl, sir: here within.

LEAR: Follow me not; stay here. [*Exit.*]

GENTLEMAN: Made you no more offence than what you speak of?

KENT: None.
How chance the king comes with so small a number?

FOOL: An thou hadst been set i' the stocks for that question, thou hadst well deserved it.[27]

KENT: Why fool?

FOOL: We'll set thee to school to an ant, to teach thee there's no labouring i' the winter. All that follow their noses are led by their eyes but blind men; and there's not a nose among twenty but can smell him that's stinking.[28] Let go thy hold when a great wheel runs down a hill, lest it break thy neck with following it; but the great one that goes up the hill, let him draw thee after. When a wise man gives thee better counsel, give me mine again: I would have none but knaves follow it, since a fool gives it.

That sir[29] which serves and seeks for gain,
And follows but for form,
Will pack[30] when it begins to rain,
And leave thee in the storm.
But I will tarry; the fool will stay,
And let the wise[31] man fly:
The knave turns fool[32] that runs away;
The fool[33] no knave, perdy.[34]

KENT: Where learn'd you this, fool?

FOOL: Not i' the stocks, fool.

*Re-enter Lear, with Gloucester.*

LEAR: Deny[35] to speak with me! They are sick! they are weary!
They have travell'd hard to-night! Mere fetches,[36]
The images[37] of revolt and flying off.[38]
Fetch me a better answer.

27 *And thou . . . it*: i.e. you should know that people desert a losing cause
28 *there's . . . stinking*: i.e. it does not take the keen smell of a blind man to smell out the poor state of Lear's fortunes
29 gentleman
30 clear off
31 i.e. worldly wise
32 *turns fool*: i.e. judged from a higher, less self-interested point of view
33 *The fool*: the Fool, I
34 par Dieu
35 refuse
36 tricks, excuses (with pun in l. 84)
37 tokens *or* embodiment (cf. IV. vi. 149)
38 *flying off*: desertion

GLOUCESTER: My dear lord,
You know the fiery quality[39] of the duke;
How unremovable and fix'd he is
In his own course.
LEAR: Vengeance! plague! death! confusion!
Fiery! what quality? Why, Gloucester, Gloucester,
I'd speak with the Duke of Cornwall and his wife.
GLOUCESTER: Well, my good lord, I have inform'd them so.
LEAR: Inform'd them! Dost thou understand me, man?
GLOUCESTER: Ay, my good lord.
LEAR: The king would speak with Cornwall; the dear father
Would with his daughter speak, commands her service:
Are they inform'd of this? My breath and blood!
Fiery! the fiery duke! Tell the hot[40] duke that—
No, but not yet; may be he is not well:
Infirmity[41] doth still neglect all office[42]
Whereto our health is bound;[43] we are not ourselves
When nature, being oppress'd, commands the mind
To suffer with the body. I'll forbear;
And am fall'n out with my more headier will,[44]
To take the indispos'd and sickly fit
For the sound man. Death on my state! [*Looking on Kent.*] Wherefore
Should he sit here? This act persuades me
That this remotion[45] of the duke and her
Is practice[46] only. Give me my servant forth.
Go, tell the duke and 's wife I'd speak with them
Now, presently: bid them come forth and hear me,
Or at their chamber-door I'll beat the drum
Till it cry sleep to death.[47]
GLOUCESTER: I would have all well betwixt you. [*Exit.*]
LEAR: O, me! my heart, my rising heart! but, down!
FOOL: Cry to it, nuncle, as the cockney[48] did to the eels when she put 'em i' the paste alive; she knapped[49] 'em o' the coxcombs[50] with a stick, and cried,

39 nature
40 hot-tempered
41 a sick man
42 duty
43 *Whereto . . . bound*: which, if well, we should feel bound to perform
44 *And . . . will*: i.e. I turn back from my overhasty determination
45 removal (from their home)
46 a trick
47 *cry . . . death*: drown sleep with its noise (as Macbeth heard a voice 'murder' sleep, Macbeth II. ii. 36–7)
48 (probably) an affected woman
49 rapped, struck
50 heads

'Down, wantons,[51] down!' 'Twas her brother that, in pure kindness to his horse, buttered his hay.[52]

*Enter Cornwall, Regan, Gloucester, and Servants.*

LEAR: Good morrow to you both.
CORNWALL: Hail to your Grace! [*Kent is set at liberty.*]
REGAN: I am glad to see your highness.
LEAR: Regan, I think you are; I know what reason
I have to think so: if thou shouldst not be glad,
I would divorce me from thy mother's tomb,
Sepulchring[53] and adultress.—[*To Kent.*] O! are you free?
Some other time for that. Beloved Regan,
Thy sister's naught: O Regan! she hath tied
Sharp-tooth'd unkindness, like a vulture, here: [*Points to his heart.*]
I can scarce speak to thee; thou'lt not believe
With how deprav'd a quality[54]—O Regan!
REGAN: I pray you, sir, take patience. I have hope
You less know how to value her desert[55]
Than she to scant[56] her duty.
LEAR: Say, how is that?
REGAN: I cannot think my sister in the least
Would fail her obligation: if, sir, perchance
She have restrain'd the riots of your followers,
'Tis on such ground, and to such wholesome end,
As clears her from all blame.
LEAR: My curses on her.
REGAN: O, sir! you are old;
Nature in you stands on the very verge
Of her confine:[57] you should be rul'd and led
By some discretion[58] that discerns your state
Better than you yourself. Therefore I pray you
That to our sister you do make return;[59]
Say, you have wrong'd her, sir.
LEAR: Ask her forgiveness?
Do you but mark how this becomes the house:[60]

51 pert, cheeky creatures
52 *buttered his hay*: i.e. did something equally silly
53 (as it would then be) the tomb of
54 manner (she treated me)
55 merits
56 *Than she* (know how) *to scant*: is capable of falling short of
57 boundary, utmost limit
58 discreet people
59 *make return*: return
60 *the house*: our family relationship *or* the royal house

'Dear daughter, I confess that I am old;
Age is unnecessary:[61] on my knees I beg [*Kneeling.*]
That you'll vouchsafe me raiment, bed, and food.'
REGAN: Good sir, no more; these are unsightly tricks:
Return you to my sister.
LEAR: [*Rising.*] Never, Regan.
She hath abated[62] me of half my train;
Look'd black upon me; struck me with her tongue,
Most serpent-like, upon the very heart.
All the stor'd vengeances of heaven fall
On her ingrateful top![63] Strike her young bones,
You taking[64] airs, with lameness!
CORNWALL: Fie, sir, fie!
LEAR: You nimble lightnings, dart your blinding flames
Into her scornful eyes! Infect her beauty,
You fen-suck'd fogs, drawn by the powerful sun,
To fall and blast her pride!
REGAN: O the blest gods! So will you wish on me,
When the rash mood[65] is on.
LEAR: No, Regan, thou shalt never have my curse:
Thy tender-hefted[66] nature shall not give
Thee o'er to harshness: her eyes are fierce, but thine
Do comfort and not burn. 'Tis not in thee
To grudge my pleasures, to cut off my train,
To bandy hasty words, to scant my sizes,[67]
And, in conclusion, to oppose the bolt[68]
Against my coming in: thou better know'st
The offices of nature, bond of childhood,
Effects[69] of courtesy, dues of gratitude;
Thy half o' the kingdom hast thou not forgot,
Wherein I thee endow'd.
REGAN: Good sir, to the purpose.[70]
LEAR: Who put my man i' the stocks? [*Tucket within.*]
CORNWALL: What trumpet's that?

61 useless, has no right to exist
62 curtailed
63 head
64 infecting, infectious
65 *the . . . mood*: cf. I. i. 285
66 (probably) set in a delicate bodily frame (heft = haft = handle), womanly
67 allowances (cf. sizar = exhibitioner, sometimes at Cambridge)
68 *oppose the bolt*: bar the door
69 manifestations
70 *to the purpose*: come to the point

REGAN: I know 't, my sister's; this approves[71] her letter,
That she would soon be here. Is your lady come?

*Enter Oswald.*

LEAR: This is a slave, whose easy-borrow'd[72] pride
Dwells in the fickle[73] grace of her he follows.
Out, varlet, from my sight!
CORNWALL: What means your Grace?

*Enter Goneril.*

LEAR: Who stock'd my servant? Regan, I have good hope
Thou didst not know on 't. Who comes here? O heavens,
If you do love old men, if your sweet sway
Allow[74] obedience, if yourselves are old,
Make it your cause;[75] send down and take my part!
[*To Goneril.*] Art not asham'd to look upon this beard?
O Regan, wilt thou take her by the hand?
GONERIL: Why not by the hand, sir? How have I offended?
All's not offence that indiscretion[76] finds[77]
And dotage terms so.
LEAR: O sides! you are too tough;
Will you yet hold? How came my man i' the stocks?
CORNWALL: I set him there, sir: but his own disorders
Deserv'd much less advancement.[78]
LEAR: You! did you?
REGAN: I pray you, father, being weak, seem so.[79]
If, till the expiration of your month,
You will return and sojourn with my sister,
Dismissing half your train, come then to me:
I am now from[80] home, and out of that provision
Which shall be needful for your entertainment.
LEAR: Return to her? and fifty men dismiss'd!
No, rather I abjure all roofs, and choose
To wage against[81] the enmity o' the air;

71 confirms
72 assumed without justification
73 unreliable (as not given for merit)
74 approve
75 *Make . . . cause*: identify yourselves with my side
76 cf. l. 141
77 holds
78 *much . . . advancement*: greater disgrace
79 *seem so*: admit it, behave accordingly
80 away from
81 *wage* (war) *against*: contend with

To be a comrade with the wolf and owl,
Necessity's sharp pinch![82] Return with her!
Why, the hot-blooded France, that dowerless took
Our youngest born, I could as well be brought
To knee[83] his throne, and squire-like, pension beg
To keep base life afoot. Return with her!
Persuade me rather to be slave and sumpter[84]
To this detested groom. [*Pointing to Oswald.*]

GONERIL: At your choice, sir.

LEAR: I prithee, daughter, do not make me mad:
I will not trouble thee, my child; farewell.
We'll no more meet, no more see one another;
But yet thou art my flesh, my blood, my daughter;
Or rather a disease that's in my flesh,
Which I must needs call mine: thou art a boil,
A plague-sore, an embossed[85] carbuncle,
In my corrupted blood. But I'll not chide thee;
Let shame come when it will, I do not call it:
I do not bid the thunder-bearer[86] shoot,[87]
Nor tell tales of thee to high-judging[88] Jove.
Mend when thou canst; be better at thy leisure:
I can be patient; I can stay with Regan,
I and my hundred knights.

REGAN: Not altogether so:
I look'd not for you yet, nor am provided
For your fit welcome. Give ear, sir, to my sister;
For those that mingle reason with your passion[89]
Must be content to think you old, and so[90]—
But she knows what she does.

LEAR: Is this well spoken?

REGAN: I dare avouch it, sir: what! fifty followers?
Is it not well? What should you need of more?
Yea, or so many, sith[91] that both charge[92] and danger[93]

82 *Necessity's . . . pinch*: straits to which need will reduce me (cf. 'Necessitie must first pinch you by the throat' in Florio's *Montaîgne*)
83 kneel before
84 beast of burden
85 swollen
86 *the thunder-bearer*: the god Jupiter
87 strike with lightning
88 supreme judge *or* judge in heaven
89 *mingle . . . passion*: examine your passionate utterances in the light of reason (but the figure is probably from mixing drinks)
90 *and so—*: *sc.* not take you seriously (or something similar)
91 since
92 the expense
93 i.e. of disturbance

Speak 'gainst so great a number? How, in one house,
Should many people, under two commands,
Hold amity?[94] 'Tis hard; almost impossible.

GONERIL: Why might not you, my lord, receive attendance
From those that she calls servants, or from mine?

REGAN: Why not, my lord? If then they chanc'd to slack you[95]
We could control them. If you will come to me,
For now I spy a danger, I entreat you
To bring but five-and-twenty; to no more
Will I give place or notice.[96]

LEAR: I gave you all—

REGAN: And in good time you gave it.

LEAR: Made you my guardians, my depositaries,[97]
But kept a reservation[98] to be follow'd
With such a number. What! must I come to you
With five-and-twenty? Regan, said you so?

REGAN: And speak 't again, my lord; no more with me.

LEAR: Those wicked creatures[99] yet do look well-favour'd,
When others are more wicked; not being the worst
Stands in some rank of praise. [*To Goneril.*] I'll go with thee:
Thy fifty yet doth double five-and-twenty,
And thou art twice her love.[100]

GONERIL: Hear me, my lord.
What need you five-and-twenty, ten, or five,
To follow in a house, where twice so many
Have a command to tend you?

REGAN: What need one?

LEAR: O! reason not[101] the need; our basest beggars
Are in the poorest thing superfluous:[102]
Allow not nature[103] more than nature needs,
Man's life is cheap as[104] beast's. Thou art a lady;
If only to go warm were gorgeous,
Why, nature needs not what thou gorgeous wear'st,

94 friendship
95 *slack you*: be negligent in serving you
96 recognition
97 trustees
98 *kept a reservation*: made a saving clause or exception (see I. i. 126)
99 *Those . . . creatures*: i.e. Goneril
100 *art . . . love*: show me twice as much love
101 *reason not*: don't argue about
102 possessing more than they actually need
103 *Allow not nature*: if you don't allow men to possess
104 *cheap as*: of as little value as

Which scarcely keeps thee warm.[105] But, for true need,[106]—
You heavens, give me that[107] patience, patience I need!
You see me here, you gods, a poor old man,
As full of grief as age; wretched in both!
If it be you that stir these daughters' hearts
Against their father, fool me not so much
To[108] bear it tamely; touch me with noble anger,
And let not women's weapons, water-drops,
Stain my man's cheeks! No, you unnatural hags,
I will have such revenges on you both
That all the world shall—I will do such things,—
What they are yet I know not,—but they shall be
The terrors of the earth. You think I'll weep;
No, I'll not weep:
I have full cause of weeping, but this heart
Shall break into a hundred thousand flaws[109]
Or ere[110] I'll weep. O fool! I shall go mad.

[*Exeunt Lear, Gloucester, Kent, and Fool.*]

CORNWALL: Let us withdraw; 'twill be a storm. [*Storm heard at a distance.*]
REGAN: This house is little: the old man and his people
Cannot be well bestow'd.[111]
GONERIL: 'Tis his own blame; hath[112] put himself from[113] rest,
And must needs taste his folly.
REGAN: For his particular,[114] I'll receive him gladly,
But not one follower.
GONERIL: So am I purpos'd.
Where is my Lord of Gloucester?
CORNWALL: Follow'd the old man forth. He is return'd.

*Re-enter Gloucester.*

GLOUCESTER: The king is in high rage.
CORNWALL: Whither is he going?
GLOUCESTER: He calls to horse; but will I know not whither.

105 *if only . . . need*: i.e. If the need for warmth were the only purpose of wearing (fine) clothes, well, your body does not need the fine clothes you wear—which incidentally hardly do keep you warm. (The first 'gorgeous' is not the logical word but is effective.)
106 *for . . . need*: as for what I really need most
107 the omission of this word would improve sense and metre
108 *fool . . . To*: do not make me such a fool as to (perhaps with reference to a Fool who has to endure what his master does to him)
109 cracks *and/or* fragments
110 *Or ere*: before (which each word means)
111 accommodated
112 he hath
113 out of
114 *his particular*: himself alone

CORNWALL: 'Tis best to give him way;[115] he leads himself.[116]
GONERIL: My lord, entreat him by no means to stay.
GLOUCESTER: Alack! the night comes on, and the bleak winds
Do sorely ruffle;[117] for many miles about
There's scarce a bush.
REGAN: O! sir, to wilful men,
The injuries that they themselves procure
Must be their schoolmasters. Shut up your doors;
He is attended with[118] a desperate train,
And what they may incense him to, being apt
to have his ear abus'd,[119] wisdom bids fear.
CORNWALL: Shut up your doors, my lord; 'tis a wild night:
My Regan counsels well: come out o' the storm. [*Exeunt.*]

115 *give him way*: let him be
116 *leads himself*: insists on his own way
117 bluster
118 by
119 misled

## ACT III

### SCENE 1

*A Heath.*

*A storm, with thunder and lightning. Enter Kent and a Gentleman, meeting.*

KENT: Who's here, beside foul weather?
GENTLEMAN: One minded like the weather, most unquietly.
KENT: I know you. Where's the king?
GENTLEMAN: Contending with the fretful elements;
Bids the wind blow the earth into the sea,
Or swell the curled waters 'bove the main,[1]
That things[2] might change or cease; tears his white hair,
Which the impetuous blasts, with eyeless[3] rage,
Catch in their fury, and make nothing of;[4]
Strives in his little world of man to out-scorn
The to-and-fro-conflicting wind and rain.
This night, wherein the cub-drawn[5] bear would couch,[6]

1 mainland (as in 'Spanish main')
2 the order of the world *natura rerum*
3 blind
4 *make . . . of*: show no respect for
5 drained by her cubs (and so ravenous)
6 lie down

The lion and the belly-pinched wolf
Keep their fur dry, unbonneted[7] he runs,
And bids what will take all.[8]
KENT: But who is with him?
GENTLEMAN: None but the fool, who labours to out-jest[9]
His heart-struck[10] injuries.
KENT: Sir, I do know you;
And dare, upon the warrant of my note,[11]
Commend a dear[12] thing to you. There is division,
Although as yet the face of it be cover'd
With mutual cunning, 'twixt Albany and Cornwall;
Who have—as who have not, that their great stars
Thron'd and set high—servants, who seem no less,[13]
Which are to France the spies and speculations[14]
Intelligent of[15] our state; what hath been seen,
Either in snuffs[16] and packings[17] of the dukes,
Or the hard rein[18] which both of them have borne
Against the old kind king; or something deeper,
Whereof perchance these are but furnishings;[19]
But, true it is, from France there comes a power[20]
Into this scatter'd[21] kingdom; who already,
Wise in our negligence, have secret feet[22]
In some of our best ports, and are at point[23]
To show their open banner. Now to you:[24]
If on my credit you dare build[25] so far
To make your speed to Dover, you shall find
Some that will thank you, making[26] just report
Of how unnatural and bemadding sorrow

7 bare-headed (reminding us also of the *crown* he has given up)
8 *what . . . all*: everything go hang (a gesture of despair)
9 jest him out of
10 which have struck him to the heart (cf. II. iv. 152–3)
11 *upon . . . note*: on the strength of my knowledge
12 important
13 *seem no less*: at any rate appear to be servants
14 observers, spies (abstract for concrete, as often)
15 *Intelligent of*: giving information about
16 resentments, quarrels
17 plots
18 *hard rein*: metaphor from curbing a horse severely
19 the trimmings
20 army
21 divided
22 *secret feet*: landed secretly
23 *at point*: ready
24 *Now to you*: to come to your part
25 *on . . . build*: trust me
26 when you make

The king hath cause to plain.[27]
I am a gentleman of blood and breeding,
And from some knowledge and assurance[28] offer
This office to you.

GENTLEMAN: I will talk further with you.

KENT: No, do not.
For confirmation that I am much more
Than my out-wall,[29] open this purse, and take
What it contains. If you shall see Cordelia,—
As doubt not but you shall,—show her this ring,
And she will tell you who your fellow[30] is
That yet you do not know. Fie on this storm!
I will go seek the king.

GENTLEMAN: Give me your hand. Have you no more to say?

KENT: Few words, but, to effect,[31] more than all yet;
That, when we have found the king,—in which your pain
That way, I'll this,[32]—he that first lights on him
Holla the other. [*Exeunt severally.*]

27 complain of
28 *knowledge and assurance*: sure knowledge
29 exterior (suggests)
30 (present) companion
31 *to effect*: in importance
32 *your . . . this*: let it be your task to go that way while I go this way

**SCENE 2**

*Another Part of the Heath. Storm still.*

*Enter Lear and Fool.*

LEAR: Blow winds, and crack your cheeks! rage! blow!
You cataracts[1] and hurricanoes,[2] spout
Till you have drench'd our steeples, drown'd the cocks![3]
You sulphurous and thought-executing[4] fires,
Vaunt-couriers[5] to oak-cleaving thunderbolts,
Singe my white head! And thou, all-shaking thunder,
Strike flat the thick rotundity o' the world!

1 waterspouts (from heaven)
2 emphatic form of 'hurricanes'
3 weathercocks
4 *either* swift as thought *or* executing Jove's wishes
5 precusors

Crack nature's moulds,[6] all germens[7] spill[8] at once
That make ingrateful man!

FOOL: O nuncle, court holy-water[9] in a dry house is better than this rain-water out o' door. Good nuncle, in, and ask thy daughters' blessing;[10] here's a night pities neither wise man nor fool.

LEAR: Rumble thy bellyful! Spit, fire! spout, rain!
Nor rain, wind, thunder, fire, are my daughters:
I tax[11] not you, you elements, with unkindness;
I never gave you kingdom, call'd you children,
You owe me no subscription:[12] then, let fall
Your horrible pleasure; here I stand, your slave,
A poor, infirm, weak, and despis'd old man.
But yet I call you servile ministers,[13]
That have with two pernicious daughters join'd
Your high-engender'd battles[14] gainst a head
So old and white as this. O! O! 'tis foul.

FOOL: He that has a house to put his head in has a good head-piece.[15]

The cod-piece[16] that will house
Before the head has any.[17]
The head and he shall louse;[18]
So beggars marry many.[19]
The man that makes his toe
What he his heart should make,
Shall of a corn cry woe,
And turn his sleep to wake.[20]

For there was never yet fair woman but she made mouths[21] in a glass.

*Enter Kent.*

LEAR: No, I will be the pattern of all patience;
I will say nothing.

6 *nature's moulds*: the moulds in which things are made
7 seeds
8 destroy
9 *court holy-water*: flattery (a common phrase at the time)
10 *ask . . . blessing*: apologize to and make peace with
11 charge (cf. I. iv. 310)
12 submission
13 agents
14 *high-engender'd battles*: battalions bred in the sky
15 *both* headcovering *and* brain
16 covering worn by men between legs under close-fitting hose
17 house
18 be lousy, infected with lice
19 *So . . . many*: (perhaps) in that condition many beggars marry
20 *The cod-piece . . . wake*: i.e. the man who prefers a meaner part of his body to the more honourable will get himself into trouble
21 *made mouths*: made faces, preened herself

KENT: Who's there?
FOOL: Marry, here's grace[22] and a cod-piece;[23] that's a wise man and a fool.
KENT: Alas! sir, are you here? things that love night
Love not such sights as these; the wrathful skies
Gallow[24] the very wanderers of the dark,
And make them keep their caves.[25] Since I was man
Such sheets of fire, such bursts of horrid thunder,
Such groans of roaring wind and rain, I never
Remember to have heard; man's nature cannot carry[26]
The affliction nor the fear.
LEAR: Let the great gods,
That keep this dreadful pother[27] o'er our heads,
Find out their enemies now. Tremble, thou wretch,
That hast within thee undivulged crimes,
Unwhipp'd of[28] justice; hide thee, thou bloody hand;
Thou perjur'd,[29] and thou simular of[30] virtue
That art incestuous; caitiff,[31] to pieces shake,[32]
That under covert[33] and convenient seeming[34]
Hast practis'd on[35] man's life; close[36] pent-up guilts,[37]
Rive your concealing continents,[38] and cry
These dreadful summoners[39] grace.[40] I am a man
More sinn'd against than sinning.
KENT: Alack! bare-headed!
Gracious my lord, hard by here is a hovel;
Some friendship will it lend[41] you 'gainst the tempest;
Repose you there while I to this hard[42] house,—
More harder than the stone whereof 'tis rais'd,[43]—

22 the king's grace
23 *a cod-piece*: something comparatively worthless
24 frighten (now only in dialect)
25 *keep . . . caves*: cf. III. i. 12–14
26 bear
27 disturbance, commotion
28 by
29 *perjur'd* (man)
30 *simular of*: pretender to
31 wretch
32 *to . . . shake*: i.e. with fear and trembling
33 secret
34 pretence, hypocrisy
35 *practis'd on*: plotted against
36 (adjective)
37 crimes (for criminals)
38 *Rive . . . continents*: burst open the receptacles that hide you
39 officers who summon to justice
40 *cry . . . grace*: beg mercy from
41 afford
42 cruel
43 built

Which even but now, demanding after you,
Denied me to come in,[44] return and force
Their scanted courtesy.

LEAR: My wits begin to turn
Come on, my boy. How dost, my boy? Art cold?
I am cold myself. Where is this straw, my fellow?
The art of our necessities[45] is strange,
That can make vile[46] things precious. Come, your hovel.
Poor fool and knave, I have one part in my heart
That's sorry yet for thee.

FOOL: He that has a little tiny wit,
With hey, ho, the wind and the rain,
Must make content with his fortunes fit,[47]
Though the rain it raineth every day.

LEAR: True, my good boy. Come, bring us to this hovel.

[*Exeunt Lear and Kent.*]

FOOL: This is a brave[48] night to cool a courtezan.
I'll speak a prophecy ere I go:

When priests are more in word than matter;[49]
When brewers mar their malt with water;
When nobles are their tailors' tutors;[50]
No heretics burn'd, but wenches' suitors;[51]
When every case in law is right;
No squire in debt, nor no poor knight;[52]
When slanders do not live in tongues;
Nor cutpurses come not to throngs;
When usurers tell[53] their gold i' the field;
And bawds and whores do churches build;
Then shall the realm of Albion[54]
Come to great confusion:
Then comes the time, who lives[55] to see't,
That going shall be us'd with feet.[56]

This prophecy Merlin shall make; for I live before his time. [*Exit.*]

44 *Denied . . . in*: refused me admittance
45 *The art . . . necessities*: necessity is an art, like alchemy, which can change the nature of things
46 worthless
47 *make . . . fit*: make content fit his fortunes, make the best of what he has
48 fine
49 *more . . . matter*: preach more than they practise
50 *are . . . tutors*: teach their tailors the latest fashions
51 *wenches' suitors*: i.e. lovers burn with lust and its results
52 *no . . . knight*: no knight poor
53 count out
54 England
55 *who lives*: for whoever lives
56 *going . . . feet*: feet shall be used to walk on (the lame conclusion is intentional)

**SCENE 3**

*A room in Gloucester's Castle.*

*Enter Gloucester and Edmund.*

GLOUCESTER: Alack, alack! Edmund, I like not this unnatural dealing. When I desired their leave that I might pity[1] him, they took from me the use of mine own house; charged me, on pain of their perpetual displeasure, neither to speak of him, entreat for him, nor any way sustain him.

EDMUND: Most savage, and unnatural!

GLOUCESTER: Go to;[2] say you nothing. There is division between the dukes, and a worse matter[3] than that. I have received a letter this night; 'tis dangerous to be spoken; I have locked the letter in my closet. These injuries the king now bears will be revenged home;[4] there's part of a power[5] already footed;[6] we must incline to[7] the king. I will seek him and privily relieve him; go you and maintain talk with the duke, that my charity be not of him perceived. If he ask for me, I am ill and gone to bed. If I die for it, as no less is threatened me, the king, my old master, must be relieved. There is some strange thing toward,[8] Edmund; pray you, be careful. [*Exit.*]

EDMUND: This courtesy, forbid thee,[9] shall the duke
Instantly know; and of that letter too:
This seems a fair deserving,[10] and must draw me
That which my father loses; no less than all:
The younger rises when the old doth fall. [*Exit.*]

1 show pity, i.e. relieve (cf. l. 4 'sustain')
2 *Go to*: come!
3 *a worse matter*: the French landing
4 fully (cf. II. i. 51)
5 force
6 see III. i. 32
7 *incline to*: side with
8 imminent
9 *courtesy . . . thee*: (bit of) kindness which was forbidden you
10 that for which one deserves well, service

## SCENE 4

*The Heath. Before a Hovel.*

*Enter Lear, Kent, and Fool.*

KENT: Here[1] is the place, my lord; good my lord, enter:
The tyranny of the open night's[2] too rough
For nature[3] to endure. [*Storm still.*]
LEAR: Let me alone.
KENT: Good my lord, enter here.
LEAR: Wilt break my heart?[4]
KENT: I'd rather break mine own. Good my lord, enter.
LEAR: Thou think'st 'tis much that this contentious[5] storm
Invades us to the skin: so 'tis to thee;
But where the greater malady is fix'd,
The lesser is scarce felt. Thou'dst shun a bear;
But if thy flight lay toward the roaring sea,
Thou'dst meet the bear i' the mouth. When the mind's free[6]
The body's delicate;[7] the tempest in my mind
Doth from my senses take all feeling else
Save what beats there.[8] Filial ingratitude!
Is it not as[9] this mouth should tear his hand
For lifting food to 't? But I will punish home:
No, I will weep no more. In such a night
To shut me out! Pour on; I will endure.
In such a night as this! O Regan, Goneril!
Your old kind father, whose frank heart gave all,
O! that way madness lies; let me shun that;
No more of that.
KENT: Good, my lord, enter here.
LEAR: Prithee, go in thyself; seek thine own ease:
This tempest will not give me leave[10] to ponder
On things would hurt me more. But I'll go in.
[*To the Fool.*] In, boy; go first. You houseless poverty,[11]—
Nay, get thee in. I'll pray, and then I'll sleep. [*Fool goes in.*]

1 see III. ii. 57
2 *The open night*: night in the open
3 human nature, man
4 *Wilt . . . heart*: explained by 23–5
5 quarrelsome, contending with us
6 at ease
7 fastidious (about its comfort)
8 i.e. in the mind (when the thought that throbs is 'Filial ingratitude')
9 as if
10 *will . . . leave*: does not leave me free
11 (abstract for concrete)

Poor naked wretches, whereso'er you are,
That bide[12] the pelting of this pitiless storm,
How shall your houseless heads and unfed sides,
Your loop'd and window'd raggedness,[13] defend you
From seasons such as these? O! I have ta'en
Too little care of this. Take physic, pomp;
Expose thyself to feel what wretches feel,
That thou mayst shake the superflux[14] to them,
And show the heavens more just.

EDGAR [*Within.*]: Fathom and half,[15] fathom and half! Poor Tom![16]

[*The Fool runs out from the hovel.*]

FOOL: Come not in here, nuncle; here's a spirit.
Help me! help me!

KENT: Give me thy hand. Who's there?

FOOL: A spirit, a spirit: he says his name's poor Tom.

KENT: What art thou that dost grumble here i' the straw?
Come forth.

*Enter Edgar disguised as a madman.*

EDGAR: Away! the foul fiend follows me!
Through the sharp hawthorn blow the winds.
Hum! go to thy cold bed and warm thee.

LEAR: Didst thou give all to thy two daughters?
And art thou come to this?

EDGAR: Who gives anything to poor Tom? whom the foul fiend hath led through fire and through flame, through ford and whirlpool, o'er bog and quagmire; that hath laid knives under his pillow, and halters in his pew: set ratsbane by his porridge; made him proud of heart, to ride on a bay trotting-horse over four-inched[17] bridges, to course[18] his own shadow for a traitor. Bless thy five wits! Tom's a-cold. O! do de, do de, do de.[19] Bless thee from whirlwinds, star-blasting,[20] and taking![21] Do poor Tom some charity, whom the foul fiend vexes. There[22] could I have him now, and there, and there again, and there. [*Storm still.*]

12 endure
13 *loop'd . . . raggedness*: clothes full of holes (loop = hole)
14 *the superflux*: your superfluity (metaphor from an overladen tree)
15 *Fathom and half*: suggested by the heavy rain
16 *Poor Tom*: cf. II. iii. 20
17 four inches wide
18 pursue
19 *do . . . de*: represents chattering teeth and shivering
20 being struck by the evil influence of stars
21 infection (cf. II. iv. 156)
22 as he pretends to feel the devil biting some part of his body, perhaps in the form of vermin (see 137)

LEAR: What! have his daughters brought him to this pass?
Couldst thou save nothing? Didst thou give them all?
FOOL: Nay, he reserved a blanket, else we had been all shamed.
LEAR: Now all the plagues that in the pendulous[23] air
Hang fated[24] o'er men's faults light on thy daughters!
KENT: He hath no daughters, sir.
LEAR: Death, traitor! nothing could have subdu'd nature
To such a lowness, but his unkind[25] daughters.
Is it the fashion that discarded fathers
Should have thus little mercy on their flesh?
Judicious punishment! 'twas this flesh begot
Those pelican daughters.[26]
EDGAR: Pillicock[27] sat on Pillicock-hill:
Halloo, halloo, loo, loo![28]
FOOL: This cold night will turn us all to fools and madmen.
EDGAR: Take heed o' the foul fiend. Obey thy parents; keep thy word justly; swear not; commit[29] not with man's sworn spouse; set not thy sweet heart on proud array. Tom's a-cold.
LEAR: What hast thou been?
EDGAR: A servingman,[30] proud in heart and mind; that curled my hair, wore gloves[31] in my cap, served the lust of my mistress's heart, and did the act of darkness with her; swore as many oaths as I spake words, and broke them in the sweet face of heaven; one that slept in the contriving of lust, and waked to do it. Wine loved I deeply, dice dearly, and in woman out-paramoured the Turk:[32] false of heart, light of ear,[33] bloody of hand; hog in sloth, fox in stealth, wolf in greediness, dog in madness, lion in prey. Let not the creaking of shoes nor the rustling of silks betray thy poor heart to woman: keep thy foot out of brothels, thy hand out of plackets,[34] thy pen from lenders'[35] books, and defy the foul fiend. Still through the hawthorn blows the cold wind; says suum, mun ha no nonny.[36] Dolphin[37] my boy, my boy; sessa![38] let him trot by. [*Storm still.*]

23 hanging over us
24 full of fate
25 unnatural (also suggesting 'cruel')
26 pelicans were supposed to feed their young on their life-blood
27 darling, pretty knave (the line, adapted from an old one, was suggested by the word 'pelican')
28 properly a cry to encourage hounds
29 sin
30 *either* lover *or* servant
31 as a favour
32 *the Turk*: the Sultan with his many wives
33 *light of ear*: quick to believe evil
34 openings in petticoats or skirts
35 money lenders
36 *suum . . . nonny*: the refrain of a song
37 perhaps addressing an imaginary horse (but Dolphin = Dauphin of France)
38 an interjection of uncertain meaning (perhaps = *cessez*, stop!, perhaps 'off with you')

LEAR: Why, thou wert better in thy grave than to answer[39] with thy uncovered body this extremity of the skies. Is man no more than this? Consider him well. Thou[40] owest the worm no silk, the beast no hide, the sheep no wool, the cat no perfume. Ha! here's three on 's are sophisticated;[41] thou art the thing itself; unaccommodated[42] man is no more but such a poor, bare, forked animal as thou art. Off, off, you lendings![43] Come; unbutton here.

[*Tearing off his clothes.*]

FOOL: Prithee, nuncle, be contented; 'tis a naughty[44] night to swim in. Now a little fire in a wide field were like an old lecher's heart; a small spark, all the rest on 's body cold. Look! here comes a walking fire.

*Enter Gloucester with a torch.*

EDGAR: This is the foul fiend Flibbertigibbet: he begins at curfew, and walks till the first cock;[45] he gives the web and the pin,[46] squinies[47] the eye, and makes the harelip; mildews the white[48] wheat, and hurts the poor creature of earth.[49]

Swithold[50] footed thrice the old;[51]
He met the night-mare,[52] and her nine-fold;[53]
Bid her alight,
And her troth plight,[54]
And aroint thee, witch, aroint[55] thee!

KENT: How fares your Grace?

LEAR: What's he?[56]

KENT: Who's there? What is't you seek?

GLOUCESTER: What are you there? Your names?

39 expose yourself to
40 man (in Edgar's state)
41 adulterated, unnatural
42 without the advantages (*Lat.* commoda) of civilization
43 borrowed articles, things not man's own
44 bad
45 *first cock*: cockcrow.
46 *the web . . . pin*: cataract, an eye disease
47 makes it squint
48 ripening
49 *the . . . earth*: mankind
50 St Withold
51 wold
52 incubus, demon (*not* female horse)
53 brood
54 *her . . . plight*: give her pledge (not to vex men)
55 begone
56 i.e. Gloucester

EDGAR: Poor Tom; that eats the swimming frog; the toad, the tadpole, the wall-newt,[57] and the water;[58] that in the fury of his heart, when the foul rages, eats cow-dung for sallets;[59] swallows the old rat and the fiend ditch-dog; drinks the green mantle[60] of the standing pool; who is whipped from tithing[61] to tithing, and stock-punished,[62] and imprisoned; who hath had three suits to his back, six shirts to his body, horse to ride, and weapon to wear;

But mice and rats and such small deer[63]
Have been Tom's food for seven long year.

Beware my follower.[64] Peace, Smulkin! peace, thou fiend.
GLOUCESTER: What! hath your Grace no better company?
EDGAR: The prince of darkness is a gentleman; Modo he's call'd, and Mahu.
GLOUCESTER: Our flesh and blood,[65] my lord, is grown so vile,
That it doth hate what gets[66] it.
EDGAR: Poor Tom's a-cold.
GLOUCESTER: Go in with me. My duty cannot suffer[67]
To obey in all[68] your daughters' hard commands:
Though their injunction be to bar my doors,
And let this tyrannous night take hold upon you,
Yet have I ventur'd to come seek you out
And bring you where both fire and food is ready.
LEAR: First let me talk with this philosopher.
What is the cause of thunder?
KENT: Good my lord, take his offer; go into the house.
LEAR: I'll take a word with this same learned Theban.
What is your study?[69]
EDGAR: How to prevent[70] the fiend, and to kill vermin.
LEAR: Let me ask you one word in private.
KENT: Importune him once more to go, my lord;
His wits begin to unsettle.
GLOUCESTER: Canst thou blame him? [*Storm still.*]

57 lizard
58 newt
59 salads
60 covering, screen
61 hamlet (originally holding *ten* families)
62 punished by being put in the stocks
63 beasts
64 familiar spirit
65 *Our . . . blood*: our children
66 begets
67 submit, agree
68 *in all*: in everything
69 pursuit, brand of learning
70 anticipate, so defeat

His daughters seek his death. Ah! that good Kent;
He said it would be thus, poor banish'd man!
Thou sayst the king grows mad; I'll tell thee, friend,
I am almost mad myself. I had a son,
Now outlaw'd from my blood;[71] he sought my life,
But lately, very late; I lov'd him, friend,
No father his son dearer; true to tell thee, [*Storm continues.*]
The grief hath craz'd my wits. What a night's this!
I beseech your Grace,—

LEAR: O! cry you mercy,[72] sir.
Noble philosopher, your company.

EDGAR: Tom's a-cold.

GLOUCESTER: In, fellow, there, into the hovel: keep thee warm.

LEAR: Come, let's in all.

KENT: This way, my lord.

LEAR: With him;
I will keep still with my philosopher.

KENT: Good my lord, soothe[73] him; let him take the fellow.

GLOUCESTER: Take him you on.

KENT: Sirrah, come on; go along with us.

LEAR: Come, good Athenian.

GLOUCESTER: No words, no words: hush.

EDGAR: Child[74] Rowland[75] to the dark tower came,
His[76] word was still, Fie, foh, and fum,
I smell the blood of a British man. [*Exeunt.*]

71 *outlaw'd . . . blood*: disinherited
72 *cry you mercy*: (I) beg your pardon
73 humour
74 Sir (title of a young knight)
75 Roland (Charlemagne's hero)
76 the giant's

## SCENE 5

*A Room in Gloucester's Castle.*

*Enter Cornwall and Edmund.*

CORNWALL: I will have my revenge ere I depart his house.

EDMUND: How, my lord, I may be censured, that nature thus gives way to loyalty, something fears me to think of.[1]

CORNWALL: I now perceive it was not altogether your brother's evil disposition made him seek his[2] death; but a provoking merit, set a-work by a reproveable badness in himself.[3]

EDMUND: How malicious is my fortune, that I must repent to be just![4] This is the letter[5] he spoke of, which approves[6] him an intelligent party[7] to the advantages of France. O heavens! that this treason were not, or not I the detector!

CORNWALL: Go with me to the duchess.

EDMUND: If the matter of this paper be certain, you have mighty business in hand.

CORNWALL: True, or false, it hath made thee Earl of Gloucester. Seek out where thy father is, that he may be ready for our apprehension.[8]

EDMUND [*Aside*]: If I find him comforting[9] the king, it will stuff his suspicion more fully.[10] I will persever[11] in my course of loyalty, though the conflict be sore between that and my blood.[12]

CORNWALL: I will lay trust upon thee; and thou shalt find a dearer father in my love. [*Exeunt.*]

1 *How . . . of*: i.e. I am rather afraid what people will think of me for allowing my natural affection to give way to my sense of duty
2 Gloucester's
3 *a provoking . . . himself*: i.e. (probably) Gloucester's deserts inviting punishment, which, however, was only brought into action by Edgar's own wickedness
4 *to be just*: of being loyal
5 *the letter*: see III. iii. 7
6 proves
7 *intelligent party*: person giving intelligence, informer
8 arrest
9 supporting, strengthening
10 *stuff . . . fully*: make our suspicion of him more justified
11 persevere
12 natural temperament

### SCENE 6

*A Chamber in a Farmhouse adjoining the Castle.*

*Enter Gloucester, Lear, Kent, Fool, and Edgar.*

GLOUCESTER: Here is better than the open air; take it thankfully. I will piece out[1] the comfort with what addition I can: I will not be long from you.

KENT: All the power of his wits has given way to his impatience. The gods reward your kindness! [*Exit Gloucester.*]

EDGAR: Frateretto[2] calls me, and tells me Nero is an angler in the lake of darkness. Pray, innocent,[3] and beware the foul fiend.

FOOL: Prithee, nuncle, tell me whether a madman be a gentleman or a yeoman!

LEAR: A king, a king!

FOOL: No; he's a yeoman that has a gentleman to his son;[4] for he's a mad yeoman that sees his son a gentleman before him.

LEAR: To have a thousand with red burning spits[5]
Come hizzing[6] in upon 'em,—

EDGAR: The foul fiend bites my back.

FOOL: He's mad that trusts in the tameness of a wolf, a horse's health,[7] a boy's love, or a whore's oath.

LEAR: It shall be done; I will arraign them straight.
[*To Edgar.*] Come, sit thou here, most learned justicer;[8]
[*To the Fool.*] Thou, sapient sir, sit here. Now, you she foxes!

EDGAR: Look, where he[9] stands and glares! wantest thou eyes[10] at trial, madam?[11] Come o'er the bourn,[12] Bessy, to me,—

FOOL: Her boat hath a leak,
And she must not speak
Why she dares not come over to thee.

EDGAR: The foul fiend haunts poor Tom in the voice of a nightingale. Hop-dance cries in Tom's belly for two white[13] herring. Croak[14] not, black angel; I have no food for thee.

KENT: How do you, sir? Stand you not so amaz'd:[15]
Will you lie down and rest upon the cushions?

1 *piece out*: increase
2 an imaginary familiar spirit; so Hop-dance (24–5) (both from Harsnett)
3 simple man
4 *has . . . son*: has his son a gentleman (i.e. a reversal of nature, like your daughters' conduct)
5 Lear is brooding over the very course he would like to see the Furies take on his daughters
6 a variant of 'hissing', perhaps in order to sound like 'whizzing'
7 *a . . . health*: perhaps as described by the vendor; or simply as horses are delicate animals
8 judge
9 a fiend *or* (possibly) Lear
10 *wantest . . . eyes*: do you want people to look at you? *or* can't you see him?
11 Goneril or Regan (present on trial in imagination)
12 stream (the line is a fragment of an old song)
13 (probably) fresh
14 in the stomach, from hunger
15 dumbfounded

LEAR: I'll see their trial first. Bring in their evidence.[16]
[*To Edgar.*] Thou robed man of justice, take thy place;
[*To the Fool.*] And thou, his yoke-fellow of equity,
Bench by his side. [*To Kent.*] You are o' the commission,[17]
Sit you too.
EDGAR: Let us deal justly.

Sleepest or wakest thou, jolly shepherd?
Thy sheep be in the corn;
And for one blast of thy minikin[18] mouth,[19]
Thy sheep shall take no harm.[20]

Purr! The cat[21] is grey.
LEAR: Arraign her first; 'tis Goneril. I here take my oath before this honourable assembly, she kicked the poor king her father.
FOOL: Come hither, mistress. Is your name Goneril?
LEAR: She cannot deny it.
FOOL: Cry you mercy, I took you for a joint-stool.[22]
LEAR: And here's another,[23] whose warp'd[24] looks proclaim
What store[25] her heart is made on. Stop her there!
Arms, arms, sword, fire! Corruption in the place!
False justicer, why hast thou let her 'scape?
EDGAR: Bless thy five wits!
KENT: O pity! Sir, where is the patience now
That you so oft have boasted to retain?
EDGAR [*Aside*]: My tears begin to take his part so much,
They'll mar my counterfeiting.
LEAR: The little dogs and all,
Tray, Blanch, and Sweet-heart, see, they bark at me.
EDGAR: Tom will throw his head at them. Avaunt, you curs!

Be thy mouth or black or[26] white,
Tooth that poisons if it bite;
Mastiff, greyhound, mongrel grim,
Hound or spaniel, brach or lym;[27]

16 *their evidence*: the witnesses against them
17 *o' the commission*: commissioned, appointed a justice of the peace
18 dainty
19 i.e. while you turn aside to play us a tune
20 perhaps ironical, as the sheep would harm the corn more than the corn them
21 *the cat*: a 'familiar' again, called 'Purr' (in Harsnett), or Purr may be only the sound
22 stool made carefully by a 'joiner' or carpenter (in fact Lear took the stool for Goneril)
23 i.e. Regan
24 crooked, perverse
25 material (but probably a corruption, perhaps for 'stone', since 'store' can hardly mean stuff)
26 *or . . . or*: either . . . or
27 a kind of bloodhound

Or bobtail tike or trundle-tail;[28]
Tom will make them weep and wail:
For, with throwing thus my head,
Dogs leap the hatch,[29] and all are fled.

Do de, de, de. Sessa![30] Come, march to wakes and fairs and market-towns. Poor Tom, thy horn[31] is dry.

LEAR: Then let them anatomize[32] Regan, see what breeds about her heart. Is there any cause in nature that makes these hard hearts? [*To Edgar.*] You, sir, I entertain[33] you for one of my hundred; only I do not like the fashion of your garments: you will say, they are Persian[34] attire; but let them be changed.

KENT: Now, good my lord, lie here and rest awhile.

LEAR: Make no noise, make no noise; draw the curtains:[35] so, so, so. We'll go to supper i' the morning: so, so, so.

FOOL: And I'll go to bed at noon.

*Re-enter Gloucester.*

GLOUCESTER: Come hither, friend: where is the king thy master?

KENT: Here, sir; but trouble him not, his wits are gone.

GLOUCESTER: Good friend, I prithee, take him in thy arms;
I have o'erheard a plot of death upon[36] him.
There is a litter ready; lay him in 't,
And drive toward Dover, friend, where thou shalt meet
Both welcome and protection. Take up thy master:
If thou shouldst dally half an hour, his life,
With thine, and all that offer[37] to defend him,
Stand in assured loss.[38] Take up, take up;
And follow me, that will to some provision[39]
Give thee quick conduct.[40]

28 long-tailed
29 *leap the hatch*: make a hurried exit
30 *Do de . . . Sessa*: see III. iv. 54 and 88
31 the Bedlam beggar's drinking flask
32 dissect
33 take on
34 proverbial for 'luxurious' (here ironical)
35 of old-fashioned beds
36 against
37 presume, dare
38 *Stand . . . loss*: are certain to be lost
39 *some provision*: something provided (l. 80)
40 guidance

KENT: Oppress'd nature sleeps:
This rest might yet have balm'd[41] thy broken sinews,[42]
Which, if convenience will not allow,[43]
Stand in hard cure.[44]—[*To the Fool.*] Come, help to bear thy master;
Thou must not stay behind.

GLOUCESTER: Come, come, away.

[*Exeunt Kent, Gloucester, and the Fool, bearing away Lear.*]

EDGAR: When we our betters see bearing our woes,[45]
We scarcely think our miseries our foes.
Who alone[46] suffers suffers most i' the mind,
Leaving free[47] things and happy shows[48] behind;
But then the mind much sufferance doth o'erskip,
When grief hath mates, and bearing[49] fellowship.
How light and portable[50] my pain seems now,
When that which makes me bend makes the king bow;
He childed as I father'd:[51] Tom, away!
Mark the high noises,[52] and thyself bewray[53]
When false opinion,[54] whose wrong thought defiles thee,
In thy just proof[55] repeals[56] and reconciles[57] thee.
What will hap[58] more to-night, safe 'scape the king!
Lurk, lurk.[59] [*Exit.*]

41 healed like a balm
42 *broken sinews*: racked nerves
43 *if . . . allow*: unless circumstances are favourable
44 *Stand . . . cure*: are hardly likely to be cured
45 *our woes*: the same trouble as we have
46 emphasize *alone*
47 carefree, free from distress
48 sights
49 when suffering (has)
50 easy to bear
51 *childed . . . father'd*: treated by his children as I by my father
52 *high noises*: disturbances in the state, in high quarters
53 *thyself bewray*: only reveal who you really are
54 *false opinion*: wrong suspicions (felt about you)
55 *In . . . proof*: when your character is vindicated
56 recalls you (from banishment)
57 restores you to your position and reconciles you to your father
58 *What . . . hap*: whatever happens
59 hide yourself, lie low

**SCENE 7**

*A Room in Gloucester's Castle.*

*Enter Cornwall, Regan, Goneril, Edmund, and Servants.*

CORNWALL: Post speedily to my lord your husband; show him this letter: the army of France is landed. Seek out the traitor Gloucester.

[*Exeunt some of the Servants.*]

REGAN: Hang him instantly.
GONERIL: Pluck out his eyes.
CORNWALL: Leave him to my displeasure. Edmund, keep you our sister company: the revenges we are bound to take upon your traitorous father are not fit for your beholding. Advise the duke, where you are going, to a most festinate[1] preparation: we are bound to[2] the like. Our posts[3] shall be swift and intelligent[4] betwixt us. Farewell, dear sister: farewell, my Lord of Gloucester.[5]

*Enter Oswald.*

How now? Where's the king?
OSWALD: My Lord of Gloucester hath convey'd him hence:
Some five or six and thirty of his knights,
Hot questrists[6] after him, met him at gate;
Who, with some other of the lord's dependants,
Are gone with him toward Dover, where they boast
To have well-armed friends.
CORNWALL: Get horses for your mistress.
GONERIL: Farewell, sweet lord, and sister.
CORNWALL: Edmund, farewell. [*Exeunt Goneril, Edmund, and Oswald.*]
Go seek the traitor Gloucester,
Pinion him like a thief, bring him before us. [*Exeunt other Servants.*]
Though well we may not pass upon[7] his life
Without the form of justice, yet our power
Shall do a courtesy to[8] our wrath, which men
May blame but not control. Who's there? The traitor?

*Re-enter Servants, with Gloucester.*

1 speedy
2 *bound to*: purposed to, proposing (so also, probably in 6)
3 messengers
4 bringing good information
5 see III. v. 14–15
6 seekers (*Lat.* quaero)
7 *pass* (sentence) *upon*
8 *do . . . to*: bow before, give way to

REGAN: Ingrateful fox! 'tis he.
CORNWALL: Bind fast his corky[9] arms.
GLOUCESTER: What mean your Graces? Good my friends, consider
You are my guests: do me no foul play, friends.
CORNWALL: Bind him, I say. [*Servants bind him.*]
REGAN: Hard, hard. O filthy[10] traitor!
GLOUCESTER: Unmerciful lady as you are, I'm none.
CORNWALL: To this chair bind him. Villain, thou shalt find—

[*Regan plucks his beard.*]

GLOUCESTER: By the kind gods, 'tis most ignobly done
To pluck me by the beard.
REGAN: So white, and such a traitor!
GLOUCESTER: Naughty[11] lady,
These hairs, which thou dost ravish from my chin,
Will quicken,[12] and accuse thee: I am your host:
With robbers' hands my hospitable favours[13]
You should not ruffle[14] thus. What will you do?
CORNWALL: Come, sir, what letters had you late[15] from France?
REGAN: Be simple-answer'd,[16] for we know the truth.
CORNWALL: And what confederacy have you with the traitors
Late footed[17] in the kingdom?
REGAN: To whose hands have you sent the lunatic king?
Speak.
GLOUCESTER: I have a letter guessingly set down,[18]
Which came from one that's of a neutral heart,
And not from one oppos'd.
CORNWALL: Cunning.
REGAN: And false.
CORNWALL: Where hast thou sent the king?
GLOUCESTER: To Dover.
REGAN: Wherefore to Dover? Wast thou not charg'd at peril—
CORNWALL: Wherefore to Dover? Let him answer that.
GLOUCESTER: I am tied to the stake, and I must stand the course.[19]
REGAN: Wherefore to Dover?

9 dry (as he is old)
10 beastly, disgraceful
11 wicked (not then a childish word)
12 come to life
13 *my . . . favours*: the features of me, your host
14 disturb, violate (cf. II. iv. 294, where, however, it was intransitive)
15 lately
16 *Be simple-answer'd*: answer straightforwardly
17 see III. i. 32
18 *guessingly set down*: written from conjecture, not knowledge
19 attack of the dogs in bear-baiting

GLOUCESTER: Because I would not see thy cruel nails
Pluck out his poor old eyes; nor thy fierce sister
In his anointed[20] flesh stick boarish fangs.
The sea, with such a storm as his bare head
In hell-black night endur'd, would have bouy'd up,[21]
And quench'd the stelled[22] fires;
Yet, poor old heart, he holp[23] the heavens to rain.
If wolves had at thy gate howl'd that dern[24] time,
Thou shouldst have said, 'Good porter, turn the key,'[25]
All cruels else[26] subscrib'd:[27] but I shall see
The winged vengeance[28] overtake such children.
CORNWALL: See 't shalt thou never. Fellows, hold the chair.
Upon these eyes of thine I'll set my foot.
GLOUCESTER: He that will think to live till he be old,
Give me some help! O cruel! O ye gods! [*Gloucester's eye put out.*]
REGAN: One side will mock another; the other too.[29]
CORNWALL: If you see vengeance—
FIRST SERVANT: Hold your hand, my lord:
I have serv'd you ever since I was a child,
But better service have I never done you
Than now to bid you hold.
REGAN: How now, you dog!
FIRST SERVANT: If you did wear a beard upon your chin,
I'd shake it[30] on this quarrel.
REGAN: What do you mean?
CORNWALL: My villain![31] [*Draws.*]
FIRST SERVANT: Nay then, come on, and take the chance of anger.[32]

[*Draws. They fight. Cornwall is wounded.*]

REGAN: Give me thy sword. A peasant stand up thus!

[*Takes a sword and runs at him behind.*]

FIRST SERVANT: O! I am slain. My lord, you have one eye left
To see some mischief on him.[33] O! [*Dies.*]

20 royal
21 risen up, like a buoy
22 *either* starry *or* (more probably) fixed (Middle Eng. stellen = fix), or part of both
23 encouraged (lit. helped)
24 dreary, dread
25 *turn the key*: i.e. admit them
26 *All . . . else*: all other cruel things (except the storm)
27 being admitted
28 *winged vengeance*: vengeance of heaven (as in Jove's arrows)
29 *the other* (eye) *too*
30 *shake it*: i.e. challenge you to fight
31 serf (perhaps also in modern sense as in l. 93)
32 *take . . . anger*: take the chance result where anger, not skill, directs the weapons
33 Cornwall

CORNWALL: Lest it see more, prevent it.[34] Out, vile jelly!
Where is thy lustre now?
GLOUCESTER: All dark and comfortless. Where's my son Edmund?
Edmund, enkindle all the sparks of nature
To quit[35] this horrid act.
REGAN: Out, treacherous villain!
Thou call'st on him that hates thee; it was he
That made the overture[36] of thy treasons to us,
Who is too good to pity thee.
GLOUCESTER: O my follies! Then Edgar was abus'd.[37]
Kind gods, forgive me that, and prosper him!
REGAN: Go thrust him out at gates, and let him smell
His way to Dover. [*Exit one with Gloucester.*]
How is't, my lord? How look you?[38]
CORNWALL: I have receiv'd a hurt. Follow me, lady.
Turn out that eyeless villain; throw this slave
Upon the dunghill. Regan, I bleed apace:
Untimely comes this hurt. Give me your arm.

[*Exit Cornwall led by Regan.*]

SECOND SERVANT: I'll never care what wickedness I do
If this man come to good.
THIRD SERVANT: If she live long,
And, in the end, meet the old[39] course of death,
Women will all turn monsters.
SECOND SERVANT: Let's follow the old earl, and get the Bedlam
To lead him where he would:[40] his roguish madness
Allows itself to any thing.[41]
THIRD SERVANT: Go thou; I'll fetch some flax, and whites of eggs,
To apply to his bleeding face. Now, heaven help him! [*Exeunt severally.*]

34 *Lest . . . prevent it*: prevent it from seeing more
35 requite, avenge
36 disclosure
37 deceived
38 *How look you?*: What do you appear like (almost) How do you feel?
39 usual, ordinary
40 like to be led
41 *his . . . any thing*: as he (the Bedlamite, Edgar) is a mad vagrant he will lend himself to anything, go anywhere he is asked, *or* his madness affords him licence to do what he likes

## ACT IV

### SCENE 1

*The Heath.*

*Enter Edgar.*

EDGAR: Yet better thus,[1] and known to be contemn'd,[2]
Than still[3] contemn'd and flatter'd. To be worst,
The lowest and most dejected thing of fortune,[4]
Stands still in esperance,[5] lives not in fear:
The lamentable change is from the best;
The worst returns to laughter.[6] Welcome, then,
Thou unsubstantial air that I embrace:
The wretch that thou hast blown unto the worst
Owes nothing to[7] thy blasts. But who comes here?

*Enter Gloucester, led by an Old Man.*

My father, poorly led?[8] World, world, O world!
But that[9] thy strange mutations make us hate thee,
Life would not yield to age.[10]
OLD MAN: O my good lord!
I have been your tenant, and your father's tenant,
These fourscore years.
GLOUCESTER: Away, get thee away; good friend, be gone;
Thy comforts can do me no good at all;
Thee they may hurt.
OLD MAN: You cannot see your way.
GLOUCESTER: I have no way, and therefore want no eyes;
I stumbled when I saw. Full oft 'tis seen,
Our means secure us[11] and our mere defects
Prove our commodities.[12] Ah! dear son Edgar,
The food[13] of thy abused[14] father's wrath;

1 *Yet* (it is better to be) *thus*
2 *known . . . contemn'd*: known to yourself to be, conscious of being despised
3 all the same
4 *most . . . fortune*: the thing (i.e. creature) cast down lowest by fortune
5 *stands . . . esperance*: puts you in a situation of permanent hopefulness
6 *returns to laughter*: may yet see you happy again
7 *Owes . . . to*: has paid his full debt to, and has therefore nothing more to fear from
8 *poorly led*: led by a poor man
9 *But that*: if it were not that
10 *Life . . . age*: we should not be reconciled to old age and death
11 *Our . . . us*: our resources make us careless (*Lat.* securus)
12 *our mere . . . commodities*: it is precisely our weaknesses that turn out to our advantage
13 object
14 misled

Might I but live to see thee in my touch,
I'd say I had eyes again.[15]
OLD MAN: How now! Who's there?
EDGAR [*Aside*]: O gods! Who is't can say, 'I am at the worst?'
I am worse than e'er I was.
OLD MAN: 'Tis poor mad Tom.
EDGAR [*Aside*]: And worse I may be yet; the worst is not,
So long as we can say, 'This is the worst.'
OLD MAN: Fellow, where goest?
GLOUCESTER: Is it a beggar-man?
OLD MAN: Madman and beggar too.
GLOUCESTER: He has some reason,[16] else he could not beg.
I' the last night's storm I such a fellow saw,
Which made me think a man a worm: my son[17]
Came then into my mind; and yet my mind
Was then scarce friends with him: I have heard more[18] since.
As flies to wanton[19] boys, are we to the gods;
They kill us for their sport.
EDGAR [*Aside*]: How should this be?[20]
Bad is the trade that must play fool to sorrow,[21]
Angering itself and others.—[*To Gloucester.*] Bless thee, master!
GLOUCESTER: Is that the naked fellow?
OLD MAN: Ay, my lord.
GLOUCESTER: Then, prithee, get thee gone. If, for my sake,
Thou wilt o'ertake us, hence a mile or twain,
I' the way toward Dover, do it for ancient love;
And bring some covering for this naked soul
Who I'll entreat to lead me.
OLD MAN: Alack, sir! he is mad.
GLOUCESTER: 'Tis the times' plague,[22] when madmen lead the blind.
Do as I bid thee, or rather do thy pleasure;
Above the rest,[23] be gone.
OLD MAN: I'll bring him the best 'parel[24] that I have,
Come on 't[25] what will. [*Exit.*]

15 *I'd . . . again*: i.e. it would be as good as recovering my sight
16 *He . . . reason*: he's not quite mad
17 *my son*: see III. iv. 144
18 viz. III. vii. 85–7
19 playful
20 *How . . . be?*: probably refers to second half of 35
21 i.e. it's a bad job when we have to pretend to folly in the presence of sorrow (as I am now doing)
22 *'Tis . . . plague*: the world's in a bad way
23 *Above the rest*: above all things
24 apparel
25 *on 't*: of it

GLOUCESTER: Sirrah, naked fellow,—
EDGAR: Poor Tom's a-cold. [*Aside*] I cannot daub it[26] further.
GLOUCESTER: Come hither, fellow.
EDGAR [*Aside*]: And yet I must. Bless thy sweet eyes, they bleed.
GLOUCESTER: Know'st thou the way to Dover?

EDGAR: Both stile and gate, horse-way and footpath. Poor Tom hath been scared out of his good wits: bless thee, good man's son, from[27] the foul fiend! Five fiends have been in poor Tom at once; of lust, as Obidicut; Hobbididance, prince of dumbness; Mahu, of stealing; Modo, of murder; and Flibbertigibbet, of mopping and mowing;[28] who since possesses chambermaids and waiting-women. So, bless thee, master!

GLOUCESTER: Here, take this purse, thou whom the heavens' plagues
Have humbled to[29] all strokes: that I am wretched
Makes thee the happier: heavens, deal so still!
Let the superfluous[30] and lust-dieted[31] man,
That slaves your ordinance,[32] that will not see
Because he doth not feel,[33] feel your power quickly;
So distribution should undo excess,
And each man have enough. Dost thou know Dover?
EDGAR: Ay, master.
GLOUCESTER: There is a cliff, whose high and bending[34] head
Looks fearfully[35] in[36] the confined[37] deep;
Bring me but to the very brim of it,
And I'll repair the misery thou dost bear
With something rich about me; from that place
I shall no leading need.
EDGAR: Give me thy arm:
Poor Tom shall lead thee. [*Exeunt.*]

26 *daub it*: dissemble, pretend (lit. cover up with plaster)
27 *bless . . . from*: God preserve thee from
28 *mopping and mowing*: grimacing, making faces (Fr. *moue*)
29 *humbled to*: humbled into bearing
30 having more than he needs (cf. II. iv. 258), spoilt
31 gluttonous or (perhaps) indulgent to his sexual appetite (cf. III. iv. 81–3)
32 *slaves . . . ordinance*: makes your commands his slaves, enslaves them (esp. the command to charity)
33 (sympathy for others)
34 overhanging
35 frighteningly
36 into
37 bounded by it

## SCENE 2

*Before the Duke of Albany's Palace.*

*Enter Goneril and Edmund.*

GONERIL: Welcome,[1] my lord; I marvel our mild[2] husband
Not met[3] us on the way. [*Enter Oswald.*] Now, where's your master?
OSWALD: Madam, within; but never man so chang'd.
I told him of the army that was landed;
He smil'd at it: I told him you were coming;
His answer was, 'The worse': of Gloucester's treachery
And of the loyal service of his son,
When I inform'd him, then he call'd me sot,[4]
And told me I had turn'd the wrong side out:[5]
What most he should dislike seems pleasant to him;
What like, offensive.[6]
GONERIL [*To Edmund.*]: Then, shall you go no further.
It is the cowish[7] terror of his spirit
That dares not undertake;[8] he'll not feel wrongs
Which tie him to[9] an answer. Our wishes on the way
May prove effects.[10] Back, Edmund, to my brother;[11]
Hasten his musters and conduct his powers:[12]
I must change arms[13] at home, and give the distaff
Into my husband's hands. This trusty servant
Shall pass between us; ere long you are like to hear,
If you dare venture in your own behalf,
A mistress's command. Wear this; spare speech; [*Giving a favour.*]
Decline[14] your head: this kiss, if it durst speak,
Would stretch thy spirits up into the air.
Conceive,[15] and fare thee well.

1 to our house (see III. vii. 1–10 for their journey together)
2 sarcastic, cf. l. 12
3 *Not met*: did not meet (so in l. 53)
4 fool (not drunkard)
5 *turn'd . . . out*: got things inside out, inverted right and wrong
6 *What* (he should like, seem) *offensive*
7 cowardly (cf. 50 below and I. iv. 308 'milky gentleness')
8 venture take up enterprises
9 *tie him to*: demand, require
10 *Our . . . effects*: What we wished for may be realized (i.e. that you should replace him)
11 (-in-law) Cornwall
12 *conduct his powers*: lead his forces
13 *change arms*: i.e. take in exchange (for the distaff) his warlike weapons
14 put down (for a kiss)
15 take my meaning

EDMUND: Yours in the ranks of death.
GONERIL: My most dear Gloucester!

[*Exit Edmund.*]

O! the difference of man and man!
To thee a woman's services are due:
My fool[16] usurps my bed.
OSWALD: Madam, here comes my lord. [*Exit.*]

*Enter Albany.*

GONERIL: I have been worth the whistle.[17]
ALBANY: O Goneril!
You are not worth the dust which the rude wind
Blows in your face. I fear[18] your disposition:
That nature, which contemns its origin,
Cannot be border'd certain[19] in itself;
She that herself will sliver[20] and disbranch
From her material[21] sap, perforce must wither
And come to deadly use.[22]
GONERIL: No more; the text[23] is foolish.
ALBANY: Wisdom and goodness to the vile seem vile;
Filths savour but themselves.[24] What have you done?
Tigers, not daughters, what have you perform'd?
A father, and a gracious aged man,
Whose reverence the head-lugg'd[25] bear would lick,[26]
Most barbarous, most degenerate! have you madded.[27]
Could my good brother suffer you to do it?
A man, a prince, by him[28] so benefited!
If that the heavens do not their visible[29] spirits
Send quickly down to tame these vile offences,[30]
It[31] will come,
Humanity must perforce prey on itself,
Like monsters of the deep.

16 *My fool*: My husband who is a fool
17 *worth the whistle*: worth something to you (cf. proverb 'It's a poor dog that is not worth the whistling')
18 fear for (what it may lead to)
19 *border'd certain*: contained within fixed bounds, trusted not to break the limits (of right)
20 tear off (as a twig from a branch)
21 forming the substance of a thing, essential
22 *deadly use*: come to a bad end, the only use for dead wood is burning
23 subject of your moral (cf. l. 58) discourse, sermons
24 *Filths . . . themselves*: filthy creatures enjoy only things that are filthy
25 tugged about by the head ('by the nose' in Harsnett!)
26 *Whose . . . lick*: i.e. whose grey hairs even a beast would respect
27 maddened
28 Lear
29 in visible form
30 offenders
31 punishment

GONERIL: Milk-liver'd[32] man!
That bear'st a cheek for blows, a head for wrongs;[33]
Who hast not in thy brows an eye discerning
Thine honour from thy suffering;[34] that not know'st
Fools do those villains[35] pity who are punish'd
Ere they have done their mischief. Where's thy drum?
France spreads his banners in our noiseless[36] land,
With plumed helm thy state begins to threat,[37]
Whilst thou, a moral[38] fool, sitt'st still, and criest
'Alack! why does he so?'

ALBANY: See thyself, devil!
Proper[39] deformity seems not in the fiend
So horrid as in woman.

GONERIL: O vain fool!

ALBANY: Thou changed and self-cover'd[40] thing, for shame,
Be-monster not thy feature.[41] Were 't my fitness[42]
To let these hands obey my blood,[43]
They are apt[44] enough to dislocate and tear
Thy flesh and bones; howe'er[45] thou art a fiend,
A woman's shape doth shield thee.

GONERIL: Marry, your manhood.—Mew![46]

*Enter a Messenger.*

ALBANY: What news?

MESSENGER: O! my good lord, the Duke of Cornwall's dead;
Slain by his servant, going to put out
The other eye of Gloucester.

ALBANY: Gloucester's eyes!

32 cowardly (cf. 'the liver white and pale, which is the badge of pusillanimity and cowardice,' 2 *Henry IV*, IV. iii. 103)
33 *That . . . wrongs*: i.e. you are the sort of man to 'turn the other cheek' (Matthew v. 39)
34 *discerning . . . suffering*: able to distinguish between what your honour can let you endure and what it cannot
35 *those villains*: in this case (probably) Lear
36 with no sound of drums or other preparations for war
37 *state . . . threat*: begins to threaten thy power, position
38 moralizing
39 which belongs to him (rightly)
40 veiling thy true (devilish) self
41 appearance
42 *my fitness:* befitting me
43 *my blood*: my instinct
44 ready
45 although
46 pooh! A fig for it

MESSENGER: A servant that he bred, thrill'd[47] with remorse,[48]
Oppos'd against the act, bending[49] his sword
To[50] his great master; who, thereat enrag'd,
Flew on him, and amongst them[51] fell'd him dead;
But not without that harmful stroke, which since
Hath pluck'd him after.[52]
ALBANY: This shows you are above,
You justicers,[53] that these our nether[54] crimes
So speedily can venge! But, O poor Gloucester!
Lost he his other eye?
MESSENGER: Both, both, my lord.
This letter, madam, craves a speedy answer;
'Tis from your sister.
GONERIL [*Aside*]: One way I like this well;
But being widow, and my Gloucester with her,[55]
May all the building in my fancy pluck
Upon my hateful life;[56] another way,[57]
This news is not so tart.[58] [*To Messenger.*] I'll read and answer. [*Exit.*]
ALBANY: Where was his son when they did take his eyes?
MESSENGER: Come with my lady hither.
ALBANY: He is not here.
MESSENGER: No, my good lord; I met him back[59] again.
ALBANY: Knows he the wickedness?
MESSENGER: Ay, my good lord; 'twas he inform'd against him,
And quit the house on purpose that their punishment
Might have the freer course.
ALBANY: Gloucester, I live
To thank thee for the love thou show'dst the king,
And to revenge thine eyes. Come hither, friend:
Tell me what more thou knowest. [*Exeunt.*]

47 excited
48 pity (as often)
49 directing
50 against
51 *amongst them*: between them they (he and Regan)
52 *pluck'd him after*: snatched away him too (to death)
53 judges (as in III. vi. 17, where it was a conjecture)
54 committee on earth (the *lower* world as opposed to heaven)
55 *But . . . her*: i.e. the fact that Regan is a widow and Gloucester, whom I desire, is with her
56 *May . . . life*: i.e. may pull down all my fine schemes and so make my life hateful to me
57 *another way*: the 'one way' cf. l. 84. Goneril sees a chance of the whole kingdom
58 bitter
59 going back (Edmund had only escorted Goneril home)

## SCENE 3

*The French Camp, near Dover.*

*Enter Kent and a Gentleman.*

KENT: Why the King of France is so suddenly gone back know you the reason?

GENTLEMAN: Something he left imperfect in the state, which since his coming forth is thought of; which imports[1] to the kingdom so much fear and danger, that his personal return was most required and necessary.

KENT: Who hath he left behind him general?

GENTLEMAN: The Marshal of France, Monsieur la Far.

KENT: Did your letters pierce[2] the queen to any demonstration of grief?

GENTLEMAN: Ay, sir; she took them, read them in my presence;
And now and then an ample tear trill'd down
Her delicate cheek; it seem'd she was a queen
Over her passion;[3] who,[4] most rebel-like,
Sought to be king o'er her.

KENT: O! then it mov'd her.

GENTLEMAN: Not to a rage; patience and sorrow strove
Who should express her goodliest.[5] You have seen
Sunshine and rain at once; her smiles and tears
Were like a better way;[6] those happy smilets
That play'd on her ripe lip seem'd not to know
What guests were in her eyes; which[7] parted thence.
As pearls from diamonds[8] dropp'd. In brief,
Sorrow would be a rarity most belov'd
If all could so become[9] it.

KENT: Made she no verbal question?[10]

GENTLEMAN: Faith, once or twice she heav'd the name of 'father'
Pantingly forth, as if it press'd her heart;
Cried, 'Sisters! sisters! Shame of ladies! sisters!
Kent! father! sisters! What, i' the storm? i' the night?
Let pity not be believed!'[11] There she shook
The holy water from her heavenly eyes,

1 involves, carries with it
2 wound, excite
3 motion (*not* anger)
4 which
5 *Who . . . goodliest*: as to which should become her best
6 *like . . . way*: like that (sunshine and rain together), only better (a comma could be inserted after 'like')
7 the guest, i.e. tears
8 her eyes
9 suit
10 *Made . . . question?*: Didn't she say anything?
11 to exist, if people can do such things (but 'not believe it' is a likely reading)

And clamour-moisten'd,[12] then away she started
To deal with grief alone.

KENT: It is the stars,
The stars above us, govern our conditions;[13]
Else one self mate and make[14] could not beget
Such different issues. You spoke not with her since?

GENTLEMAN: No.

KENT: Was this before the king[15] return'd?

GENTLEMAN: No, since.

KENT: Well, sir, the poor distress'd Lear 's i' the town,
Who sometime,[16] in his better tune,[17] remembers
What we are come about, and by no means
Will yield[18] to see his daughter.

GENTLEMAN: Why, good sir?

KENT: A sovereign[19] shame so elbows him:[20] his own unkindness,
That stripp'd her from his benediction, turn'd her
To foreign casualties,[21] gave her dear rights
To his dog-hearted daughters,—these things sting
His mind so venomously that burning shame
Detains him from Cordelia.

GENTLEMAN: Alack! poor gentleman.

KENT: Of Albany's and Cornwall's powers[22] you heard not?

GENTLEMAN: 'Tis so,[23] they are afoot.

KENT: Well, sir, I'll bring you to our master Lear,
And leave you to attend him. Some dear cause[24]
Will in concealment wrap me up awhile;
When I am known aright, you shall not grieve
Lending me this acquaintance.[25] I pray you, go
Along with me. [*Exeunt.*]

12 having her outburst, emotion, calmed by a flood of tears
13 character
14 *one . . . make*: the same husband and wife ('make' comes from a root meaning 'equal')
15 *the king* (of France)
16 *sometime(s)*
17 *better tune*: saner moments
18 agree
19 (1) all-powerful, *but also* (2) worthy of a king
20 *elbows him*: pushes him away (from her)
21 *foreign casualties*: the chances of life abroad
22 forces
23 *'Tis so*: it is true that
24 *dear cause*: important reason (cf. III. i. 19)
25 *Lending . . . acquaintance*: for having got to know me

## SCENE 4

*The Same. A Tent.*

*Enter with drum and colours, Cordelia, Doctor, and Soldiers.*

CORDELIA: Alack! 'tis he: why, he was met even now
As mad as the vex'd[1] sea; singing aloud;
Crown'd with rank[2] fumiter[3] and furrow weeds,[4]
With burdocks, hemlock, nettles, cuckoo-flowers,[5]
Darnel, and all the idle weeds that grow
In our sustaining[6] corn. A century[7] send forth;
Search every acre in the high-grown field.
And bring him to our eye. [*Exit an Officer.*]
What can[8] man's wisdom
In the restoring his bereaved[9] sense?
He that helps[10] him take all my outward worth.[11]
DOCTOR: There is means, madam;
Our foster-nurse of nature[12] is repose,
The which he lacks; that to provoke[13] in him,
Are many simples operative,[14] whose power
Will close the eye of anguish.
CORDELIA: All bless'd secrets,
All you unpublish'd virtues[15] of the earth,
Spring with[16] my tears! be aidant and remediate[17]
In the good man's distress! Seek, seek for him,
Lest his ungovern'd rage dissolve the life
That wants the means to lead it.[18]

*Enter a Messenger.*

1 stirred up (by winds)
2 luxuriant
3 fumitory
4 *furrow weeds*: weeds that grow in ploughed land
5 (uncertain)
6 life-giving
7 a hundred men
8 knows, can do
9 lost
10 heals
11 *outward worth*: possessions
12 *Our . . . nature*: the foster-nurse of our nature
13 induce
14 *simples operative*: effective (medicinal) plants
15 properties, (healing) powers
16 *Spring with*: spring up watered by
17 remedial
18 *That . . . it*: i.e. which lacks the power (sanity) to control it(self)

MESSENGER: News, madam;
The British powers are marching hitherward.
CORDELIA: 'Tis known before; our preparation stands
In expectation of them. O dear father!
It is thy business that I go about;
Therefore great France[19]
My mourning and important[20] tears hath pitied,
No blown[21] ambition doth our arms incite,
But love, dear love, and our ag'd father's right,
Soon may I hear and see him! [*Exeunt.*]

19 the king of France
20 importunate, urgent
21 proud

## SCENE 5

*A Room in Gloucester's Castle.*

*Enter Regan and Oswald.*

REGAN: But are my brother's[1] powers set forth?
OSWALD: Ay, madam.
REGAN: Himself in person there?
OSWALD: Madam, with much ado:[2]
Your sister is the better soldier.
REGAN: Lord Edmund spake not with your lord at home?
OSWALD: No, madam.
REGAN: What might import[3] my sister's letter to him?
OSWALD: I know not, lady.
REGAN: Faith, he is posted hence on serious matter.
It was great ignorance,[4] Gloucester's eyes being out,
To let him live; where he arrives he moves
All hearts against us. Edmund, I think, is gone,
In pity of his misery, to dispatch
His nighted[5] life; moreover, to descry
The strength o' the enemy.
OSWALD: I must needs after him, madam, with my letter.
REGAN: Our troops set forth to-morrow; stay with us,
The ways are dangerous.

1 *brother*(-in-law)'s
2 *with much ado*: i.e. Goneril had great difficulty in getting Albany to take up arms in a bad cause
3 signify
4 folly
5 darkened, blinded

OSWALD: I may not, madam;
My lady charg'd my duty[6] in this business.
REGAN: Why should she write to Edmund? Might not you
Transport her purposes by word? Belike,[7]
Something—I know not what. I'll love thee much,
Let me unseal the letter.
OSWALD: Madam, I had rather—[8]
REGAN: I know your lady does not love her husband;
I am sure of that: and at her late being here
She gave strange oeilliades[9] and most speaking[10] looks
To noble Edmund. I know you are of her bosom.[11]
OSWALD: I, madam!
REGAN: I speak in understanding; you are, I know't:
Therefore I do advise you, take this note:[12]
My lord is dead; Edmund and I have talk'd,[13]
And more convenient is he for my hand
Than for your lady's. You may gather[14] more.
If you do find him, pray you, give him this,[15]
And when your mistress hears thus much from you,
I pray desire her call her wisdom to her:[16]
So, fare you well.
If you do chance to hear of that blind traitor,
Preferment falls on him that cuts him off.[17]
OSWALD: Would I could meet him, madam: I would show
What party I do follow.
REGAN: Fare thee well. [*Exeunt.*]

6 *charg'd my duty*: invoked my sense of duty to her (to deliver this letter at once)
7 probably
8 *I had rather—*: s.d. refusing the letter (Johnson)
9 glad eyes
10 eloquent of her wishes
11 *of her bosom*: trusted by her
12 *take this note*: (probably) take note of this
13 come to an understanding
14 infer
15 a token *or* letter
16 *call her . . . her*: show some sense (remember she has a husband)
17 *Preferment . . . off*: i.e. you will be promoted if you kill him

## SCENE 6

*The Country near Dover.*

*Enter Gloucester, and Edgar dressed like a peasant.*

GLOUCESTER: When shall I come to the top of that same hill?[1]
EDGAR: You do climb up it now; look how we labour.
GLOUCESTER: Methinks the ground is even.
EDGAR: Horrible steep:
Hark! do you hear the sea?
GLOUCESTER: No, truly.
EDGAR: Why, then your other senses grow imperfect
By your eyes' anguish.
GLOUCESTER: So may it be, indeed.
Methinks thy voice is alter'd, and thou speak'st
In better phrase and matter than thou didst.
EDGAR: Y'are much deceiv'd; in nothing am I chang'd
But in my garments.
GLOUCESTER: Methinks you're better spoken.
EDGAR: Come on, sir; here's the place: stand still.
How fearful
And dizzy 'tis to cast one's eyes so low!
The crows and choughs[2] that wing the midway air
Show scarce so gross[3] as beetles; half way down
Hangs one that gathers samphire,[4] dreadful trade!
Methinks he seems no bigger than his head.
The fishermen that walk upon the beach
Appear like mice, and yond tall anchoring bark
Diminish'd to her cock,[5] her cock a buoy
Almost too small for sight. The murmuring surge,
That on the unnumber'd[6] idle[7] pebbles[8] chafes,
Cannot be heard so high. I'll look no more,
Lest my brain turn, and the deficient sight[9]
Topple down headlong.
GLOUCESTER: Set me where you stand.

1 *that same hill*: see IV. i. 71
2 still a cliff bird in Cornwall
3 large
4 a herb used for pickles
5 cock-boat, ship's boat
6 innumerable
7 moved to no purpose
8 (used as plural)
9 *the . . . sight*: I, through failing sight

EDGAR: Give me your hand; you are now within a foot
Of the extreme verge: for all beneath the moon
Would I not leap upright.[10]
GLOUCESTER: Let go my hand.
Here, friend, 's another purse;[11] in it a jewel
Well worth a poor man's taking: fairies and gods
Prosper it with thee![12] Go thou further off;
Bid me farewell, and let me hear thee going.
EDGAR: Now fare you well, good sir.
GLOUCESTER: With all my heart.
EDGAR: Why I do trifle thus with his despair
Is done to cure it.[13]
GLOUCESTER: O you mighty gods!
This world I do renounce, and, in your sights,
Shake patiently my great affliction off;
If I could bear it longer, and not fall
To quarrel with[14] your great opposeless[15] wills,
My snuff and loathed part of nature should
Burn itself out.[16] If Edgar live, O, bless him!
Now, fellow, fare thee well.
EDGAR: Gone, sir:[17] farewell. [*Gloucester falls forward.*]
[*Aside*] And yet I know not how[18] conceit[19] may rob
The treasury of life when life itself
Yields to the theft;[20] had he been where he thought
By this had thought been past. Alive or dead?
[*To Gloucester.*] Ho, you sir! friend! Hear you, sir? speak![21]
Thus might he pass indeed; yet he revives.[22]
What are you, sir?
GLOUCESTER: Away and let me die.
EDGAR: Hadst thou been aught but gossamer, feathers, air,
So many fathom down precipitating,[23]
Thou'dst shiver'd like an egg; but thou dost breathe,
Hast heavy substance, bleed'st not, speak'st, art sound.

10 *leap upright*: he is so near the edge that even such a movement would be fatal
11 *another purse*: see IV. i. 62
12 *Prosper . . . thee*: make the purse lucky for you (perhaps a reference to a belief that fairies multiplied treasure trove)
13 *Why . . . it*: i.e. The object of my trifling . . . is to cure it (a mixture of constructions)
14 *quarrel with*: rebel against
15 irresistible
16 *My . . . out*: i.e. I would let the miserable remnant of my life expire naturally, instead of seeking my own death (snuff = the half-burnt wick)
17 *Gone, sir*: answer to l. 31
18 *I . . . how*: I don't know how it is that
19 imagination
20 *when . . . theft*: when there is no longer the will to live
21 is spoken in a different voice as if by a stranger who has found Gloucester at the foot of the cliff
22 (an aside)
23 falling headlong

Ten masts at each[24] make not the altitude
Which thou hast perpendicularly fell:
Thy life's a miracle. Speak yet again.
GLOUCESTER: But have I fallen or no?
EDGAR: From the dread summit of this chalky bourn.[25]
Look up a-height;[26] the shrill-gorg'd[27] lark so far
Cannot be seen or heard: do but look up.
GLOUCESTER: Alack! I have no eyes.
Is wretchedness depriv'd that benefit
To end itself by death? 'Twas yet some comfort,
When misery could beguile[28] the tyrant's rage,
And frustrate his proud will.
EDGAR: Give me your arm:
Up: so. How is't? Feel you your legs? You stand.
GLOUCESTER: Too well, too well.
EDGAR: This is above all strangeness.
Upon the crown o' the cliff, what thing was that
Which parted from you?
GLOUCESTER: A poor unfortunate beggar.
EDGAR: As I stood here below methought his eyes
Were two full moons; he had a thousand noses,
Horns whelk'd[29] and wav'd like the enridged[30] sea:
It was some fiend; therefore, thou happy father,[31]
Think that the clearest[32] gods, who make them honours
Of men's impossibilities, have preserv'd thee.
GLOUCESTER: I do remember now; henceforth I'll bear
Affliction till it do cry out itself
'Enough, enough,' and die. That thing you speak of
I took it for a man; often 'twould say
'The fiend, the fiend': he led me to that place.
EDGAR: Bear free[33] and patient[34] thoughts. But who comes here?

*Enter Lear, fantastically dressed with flowers.*[35]

The safer sense will ne'er accommodate
His master thus.[36]

24 *at each*: on end
25 the limit of the sea (cf. IV. i. 72)
26 on high
27 shrill-throated, high-voiced
28 cheat (by death)
29 (probably) twisted
30 ridged, furrowed
31 ambiguous, since it could be addressed to any old man
32 purest, open and righteous
33 free from fear, happy (and so not inclined to suicide) *or* generous towards men and (34) patient towards God
35 based on IV. iv. 3–6
36 *The . . . thus*: i.e. a man in his right senses would not get himself up like this ('safer' = saner)

LEAR: No, they cannot touch[37] me for coining;
I am the king himself.
EDGAR: O thou side-piercing[38] sight!
LEAR: Nature's above art[39]in that respect. There's your press-money.[40] That fellow handles his bow like a crow-keeper:[41] draw me[42] a clothier's yard.[43] Look, look! a mouse. Peace, peace! this piece of toasted cheese will do 't. There's my gauntlet;[44] I'll prove it on a giant. Bring up the brown bills.[45] O! well flown, bird;[46] i' the clout,[47] hewgh![48] Give the word.[49]
EDGAR: Sweet marjoram.[50]
LEAR: Pass.
GLOUCESTER: I know that voice.
LEAR: Ha! Goneril, with a white beard! They flatter'd me like a dog,[51] and told me I had white hairs[52] in my beard ere the black ones were there. To say 'ay' and 'no' to everything I said! 'Ay' and 'no' too was no good divinity.[53] When the rain came to wet me once and the wind to make me chatter, when the thunder would not peace at my bidding, there I found 'em, there I smelt 'em out. Go to, they are not men o' their words: they told me I was everything; 'tis a lie, I am not ague-proof.
GLOUCESTER: The trick[54] of that voice I do well remember:
Is 't not the king?
LEAR: Ay, every inch the king:
When I do stare, see how the subject quakes.
I pardon that man's life. What was thy cause?[55]
Adultery?
Thou shalt not die: die for adultery! No:
The wren goes to 't, and the small gilded fly
Does lecher in my sight.

37 get at, punish
38 heart-rending
39 *Nature's . . . art*: (probably) a king's above a coiner (issuer of false money)
40 payment given a man forced into the services (cf. press-gang)
41 scarer of birds
42 for me to see
43 *clothier's yard*: long arrow
44 mailed glove as a challenge
45 *brown bills*: halberds painted brown *or* the bearers of them
46 here used for arrow
47 mark, target
48 the whistling sound of the arrow in the air
49 password
50 used as a remedy for madness
51 *like a dog*: as a dog fawns on people
52 *white hairs*: i.e. the wisdom of age
53 *no . . . divinity*: not sound theologically (in view of St Paul's words 'For the Son of God, Jesus Christ . . . was not yea and nay, but in him was yea,' 2 Cor. i. 19)
54 accent
55 crime, subject of accusation

Let copulation thrive; for Gloucester's bastard son
Was kinder to his father than my daughters
Got 'tween the lawful sheets.
To 't luxury,[56] pell-mell![57] for I lack soldiers.
Behold yond simpering dame,
Whose face between her forks presageth snow;[58]
That minces[59] virtue, and does shake the head
To hear of pleasure's name;
The fitchew[60] nor the soiled[61] horse goes to 't
With a more riotous appetite.
Down from the waist they are Centaurs,[62]
Though women all above:
But to[63] the girdle do the gods inherit,[64]
Beneath is all the fiends':
There's hell, there's darkness, there is the sulphurous pit, burning, scalding, stench, consumption; fie, fie, fie! pah, pah! Give me an ounce of civet,[65] good apothecary, to sweeten my imagination: there's money for thee.

GLOUCESTER: O! let me kiss that hand!

LEAR: Let me wipe it first; it smells of mortality.[66]

GLOUCESTER: O ruin'd piece[67] of nature! This great world
Shall so[68] wear out to nought. Dost thou know me?

LEAR: I remember thine eyes well enough. Dost thou squiny[69] at me? No, do thy worst, blind Cupid;[70] I'll not love. Read thou this challenge; mark but the penning of it.

GLOUCESTER: Were all the letters suns, I could not see.

EDGAR [*Aside*]: I would not take this from report; it is,
And my heart breaks at it.

LEAR: Read.

GLOUCESTER: What! with the case[71] of eyes?

56 lust
57 promiscuously
58 *Whose . . . snow*: i.e. Whose face would make you think she had little sexual desire
59 affects
60 (1) pole-cat, *and* (2) harlot
61 overfed
62 half men, half horses, in Greek mythology
63 *But to*: only as far as
64 own
65 scent
66 (1) humanity, *and perhaps also* (2) death
67 (perhaps) masterpiece
68 as you have done
69 squint
70 *blind Cupid*: the sign over brothels (may recall Gloucester's sin)
71 sockets

LEAR: O, ho! are you there with me?[72] No eyes in your head, nor no money in your purse? Your eyes are in a heavy case,[73] your purse in a light: yet you see how this world goes.

GLOUCESTER: I see it feelingly.[74]

LEAR: What! art mad? A man may see how this world goes with no eyes. Look with thine ears: see how yond justice rails upon yon simple[75] thief. Hark, in thine ear: change places; and, handy-dandy,[76] which is the justice, which is the thief? Thou hast seen a farmer's dog bark at a beggar?

GLOUCESTER: Ay, sir.

LEAR: And the creature[77]run from the cur? There thou mightst behold the great image[78] of authority; a dog's[79] obey'd in office.[80]
Thou rascal beadle,[81] hold thy bloody hand!
Why dost thou lash that whore? Strip thine own back;
Thou hotly lusts to use her in that kind[82]
For which thou whipp'st her. The usurer hangs the cozener.[83]
Through tatter'd clothes small vices do appear;
Robes and furr'd gowns[84] hide all. Plate sin with gold,[85]
And the strong lance of justice hurtless[86] breaks;
Arm it in rags, a pigmy's straw doth pierce it.
None does offend, none, I say none; I'll able[87] 'em:
Take that of me, my friend, who have the power
To seal the accuser's lips. Get thee glass eyes;
And, like a scurvy politician,[88] seem[89]
To see the things thou dost not. Now, now, now, now;
Pull off my boots; harder, harder; so.

EDGAR [*Aside*]: O! matter[90] and impertinency[91] mix'd;
Reason in madness!

72 *are . . . me?*: Is that what you mean?
73 *in . . . case*: because in a bad way
74 by my sense of feeling (perhaps also suggests 'I feel it deeply')
75 humble
76 take which you like (from a children's game)
77 human being
78 type, example
79 even a dog
80 *in office*: in a position of authority
81 parish constable
82 *in that kind*: i.e. lustfully
83 *The . . . cozener*: i.e. a magistrate who has a man hanged for a petty theft may himself lend money for interest (condemned by medieval church)
84 *furr'd gowns*: worn by judges and aldermen
85 *Plate . . . gold*: give the sinner the armour of riches
86 inflicting no wound
87 vouch for, protect
88 *scurvy politician*: rascally schemer
89 pretend
90 good sense
91 irrelevance, nonsense

LEAR: If thou wilt weep my fortunes, take my eyes;
I know thee well enough; thy name is Gloucester:[92]
Thou must be patient; we came crying hither:
Thou know'st the first time that we smell the air
We waul[93] and cry. I will preach to thee: mark.
GLOUCESTER: Alack! alack the day!
LEAR: When we are born, we cry that we are come
To this great stage of fools. This'[94] a good block![95]
It were a delicate stratagem to shoe
A troop of horse with felt; I'll put it in proof,[96]
And when I have stol'n upon these sons-in-law,
Then, kill, kill, kill, kill, kill, kill!

*Enter Gentleman, with Attendants.*

GENTLEMAN: O! here he is; lay hand upon him. Sir,
Your most dear daughter—
LEAR: No rescue? What! a prisoner? I am even[97]
The natural fool of[98] fortune. Use me well;
You shall have ransom. Let me have surgeons;
I am cut to the brains.[99]
GENTLEMAN: You shall have any thing.
LEAR: No seconds?[100] All myself?
Why this would make a man a man of salt,[101]
To use his eyes for garden water-pots,
Ay, and laying autumn's dust.
GENTLEMAN: Good sir,—
LEAR: I will die bravely as a bridegroom.[102] What!
I will be jovial: come, come; I am a king,
My masters, know you that?
GENTLEMAN: You are a royal one, and we obey you.
LEAR: Then there's life in it.[103] Nay, an you get it, you shall get it by running.
Sa, sa, sa, sa.[104] [*Exit. Attendants follow.*]

92 see l. 130
93 wail (cf. caterwaul)
94 This is
95 (perhaps) a felt hat
96 *in proof*: on trial
97 Lear has been found by Cordelia's attendants whom he imagines to be enemies
98 *The . . . of*: born to be the sport, victim of (bad) fortune
99 *cut . . . brains*: cf. 'cut to the heart'
100 supporters
101 *a . . . salt*: all tears (but cf. Lot's wife in Genesis xix. 26)
102 *as a bridegroom*: meeting death like a bride
103 *there's . . . it*: there's still hope for me
104 *Sa, sa*: a cry inciting to action, as to hunting dogs

GENTLEMAN: A sight most pitiful in the meanest wretch,
Past speaking of in a king! Thou hast one daughter,
Who redeems nature[105] from the general curse
Which twain have brought her to.
EDGAR: Hail, gentle sir!
GENTLEMAN: Sir, speed you:[106] what's your will?
EDGAR: Do you hear aught, sir, of a battle toward?[107]
GENTLEMAN: Most sure and vulgar;[108] every one hears that,
Which can distinguish sound.
EDGAR: But, by your favour,
How near's the other army?
GENTLEMAN: Near, and on speedy foot; the main descry
Stands on the hourly thought.[109]
EDGAR: I thank you, sir: that's all.
GENTLEMAN: Though that the queen on special cause is here,
Her army is mov'd on.
EDGAR: I thank you, sir.

[*Exit Gentleman.*]

GLOUCESTER: You ever-gentle gods, take my breath from me:[110]
Let not my worser spirit[111] tempt me again
To die before you please!
EDGAR: Well pray you, father.[112]
GLOUCESTER: Now, good sir, what are you?
EDGAR: A most poor man, made tame to fortune's blows;
Who, by the art of[113] known and feeling[114] sorrows,
Am pregnant to[115] good pity. Give me your hand,
I'll lead you to some biding.[116]
GLOUCESTER: Hearty thanks:
The bounty and the benison[117] of heaven
To boot, and boot![118]

*Enter Oswald.*

105 human nature, disgraced by Goneril and Regan
106 (God) *speed you*
107 imminent
108 commonly known
109 *the main . . . thought*: the sight of the main body is expected every hour
110 i.e. let me die in heaven's good time
111 *my . . . spirit*: the worse part of me, my evil genius (a phrase used in Sonnet 144)
112 see l. 73, and cf. l. 242 &c.
113 *by . . . of*: taught by
114 heart-felt
115 *pregnant to*: disposed to show
116 abode, resting place
117 blessing
118 *To boot, and boot*: in addition, and may it help you (two meanings of 'boot')

OSWALD: A proclaim'd prize![119] Most happy!
That eyeless head of thine was first fram'd[120] flesh
To raise my fortunes. Thou old unhappy traitor,
Briefly thyself remember:[121] the sword is out[122]
That must destroy thee.

GLOUCESTER: Now let thy friendly[123] hand
Put strength enough to 't. [*Edgar interposes.*]

OSWALD: Wherefore, bold peasant,
Dar'st thou support a publish'd traitor? Hence;
Lest that infection of his fortune take
Like hold on thee.[124] Let go his arm.

EDGAR: Chill[125] not let go, zur, without vurther 'casion.[126]

OSWALD: Let go, slave, or thou diest.

EDGAR: Good gentleman, go your gait,[127] and let poor volk pass. An chud ha' bin zwaggered[128] out of my life, 'twould not ha' ben zo long as 'tis by a vortnight. Nay, come not near th' old man; keep out, che vor ye,[129] or ise[130] try whether your costard[131] or my ballow[132] be the harder. Chill be plain with you.

OSWALD: Out, dunghill!

EDGAR: Chill pick your teeth,[133] zur. Come; no matter vor your foins.[134]

[*They fight and Edgar knocks him down.*]

OSWALD: Slave, thou hast slain me. Villain,[135] take my purse.
If ever thou wilt thrive, bury my body;
And give the letters which thou find'st about me
To Edmund Earl of Gloucester; seek him out
Upon[136] the English party:[137] O! untimely death. [*Dies.*]

119 *A . . . prize*: a publish'd traitor (l. 222) for whose arrest a reward had been offered
120 made
121 *thyself remember*: remember your sins, prepare for death
122 unsheathed
123 Gloucester desires to die
124 *Lest . . . thee*: lest the same fate overtake you
125 I will
126 reason
127 way
128 *An . . . zwaggered*: If I could have been bullied
129 *che vor ye*: I warrant you
130 I shall
131 head (lit. a kind of apple)
132 cudgel
133 *pick . . . teeth*: i.e. fight you
134 thrusts
135 serf
136 on, among
137 *party*: side

EDGAR: I know thee well: a serviceable villain;[138]
As duteous to the vices of thy mistress
As badness would desire.
GLOUCESTER: What! is he dead?
EDGAR: Sit you down, father; rest you.
Let's see his pockets: these letters that he speaks of
May be my friends. He's dead; I am only sorry
He hath no other deaths-man. Let us see:
Leave,[139] gentle wax; and, manners, blame us not:
To know our enemies' minds, we'd rip their hearts;
Their papers, is more lawful.

'Let our reciprocal vows be remembered. You have many opportunities to cut him[140] off; if your will want not,[141] time and place will be fruitfully offered. There is nothing done if he return the conqueror; then am I the prisoner, and his bed my gaol; from the loathed warmth whereof deliver me, and supply the place for[142] your labour.

'Your—wife, so I would say—

'Affectionate servant,

'GONERIL.'

O undistinguish'd[143] space[144] of woman's will![145]
A plot upon her virtuous husband's life,
And the exchange my brother! Here, in the sands,
Thee I'll rake up,[146] the post[147] unsanctified
Of murderous lechers; and in the mature time[148]
With this ungracious[149] paper strike the sight
Of the death-practis'd[150] duke. For him 'tis well
That of thy death and business I can tell.
GLOUCESTER: The king is mad: how stiff[151] is my vile sense,
That I stand up, and have ingenious[152] feeling
Of my huge sorrows! Better I were distract:[153]

138 rascal
139 by your leave
140 Albany
141 *want not*: is not deficient
142 as a reward for
143 indistinguishable, illimitable
144 range
145 desire, lust (cf. IV. ii. 32–3 with this whole line)
146 *rake up*: bury
147 messenger, postman
148 *in . . . time*: at the right moment
149 disgraceful
150 whose death has been plotted
151 unbending, unfeeling
152 intelligent, conscious
153 *distract*(ed): mad

So should my thoughts be sever'd from my griefs,[154]
And woes by wrong imaginations[155] lose
The knowledge of themselves. [*Drums afar off.*]

EDGAR: Give me your hand:
Far off, methinks, I hear the beaten drum.
Come, father, I'll bestow[156] you with a friend. [*Exeunt.*]

154 *So . . . grief*: i.e. I should not realize my miseries
155 *wrong imaginations*: illusions
156 lodge

## SCENE 7

*A Tent in the French Camp.*

*Enter Cordelia, Kent, Doctor, and Gentleman.*

CORDELIA: O thou good Kent! how shall I live and work
To match[1] thy goodness? My life will be too short,
And every measure[2] fail me.

KENT: To be acknowledg'd, madam, is o'erpaid.
All my reports[3] go with the modest truth,
Nor more nor clipp'd, but so.[4]

CORDELIA: Be better suited:[5]
These weeds[6] are memories of those worser hours:
I prithee, put them off.

KENT: Pardon me, dear madam;
Yet[7] to be known shortens my made intent;[8]
My boon I make it[9] that you know me not
Till time and I think meet.[10]

CORDELIA: Then be 't so, my good lord.—[*To the Doctor.*] How does the king?

DOCTOR: Madam, sleeps still.

CORDELIA: O you kind gods,
Cure this great breach in his abused nature!
The untun'd and jarring senses, O! wind up[11]
Of this child-changed[12] father!

1 come up to, in recompensing it
2 degree (of gratitude, compared with Kent's services)
3 *my reports*: the reports I have given you
4 *Nor more . . . so*: neither exaggerated nor understated but accurate
5 *suited*: dressed
6 clothes
7 at present
8 *my . . . intent*: the plan I have made
9 *My . . . it*: the favour I ask is
10 *Till . . . meet*: i.e. Till I think the time ripe
11 *wind up*: tune
12 *child-changed*: (1) changed into a child (in mind), (2) changed by (the cruelty of) his children—very probably *both*

DOCTOR: So please[13] your majesty
That we may wake the king? he hath slept long.
CORDELIA: Be govern'd by your knowledge, and proceed
I' the sway of your own will.[14] Is he array'd?

*Enter Lear in his chair, carried by Servants.*

GENTLEMAN: Ay, madam; in the heaviness of sleep,
We put fresh garments on him.
DOCTOR: Be by, good madam, when we do awake him;
I doubt not of his temperance.[15]
CORDELIA: Very well. [*Music.*]
DOCTOR: Please you, draw near. Louder the music there.
CORDELIA: O my dear father! Restoration,[16] hang
Thy medicine on my lips, and let this kiss
Repair those violent harms that my two sisters
Have in thy reverence made!
KENT: Kind and dear princess!
CORDELIA: Had you not been their father, these white flakes[17]
Had challeng'd pity of[18] them. Was this a face
To be expos'd against the warring winds?
To stand against the deep[19] dread-bolted[20] thunder?
In the most terrible and nimble stroke
Of quick cross[21] lightning? to watch[22]—poor perdu!—
With this thin helm?[23] Mine enemy's dog,
Though he had bit me, should have stood that night
Against[24] my fire. And wast thou fain, poor father,
To hovel thee with swine and rogues forlorn,
In short[25] and musty straw? Alack, alack!
'Tis wonder that thy life and wits at once
Had not concluded all.[26] He wakes; speak to him.
DOCTOR: Madam, do you; 'tis fittest.
CORDELIA: How does my royal lord? How fares your majesty?

13 may it please
14 *I' . . . will*: as you think best
15 sanity
16 the power of restoring the senses (personified)
17 *white flakes*: his *snowy* hair and beard
18 from
19 deep-voiced
20 armed with the dreaded thunderbolt
21 forked
22 stand exposed
23 *thin helm*: unprotected head
24 in front of
25 cut short (and therefore uncomfortable), and/or scanty
26 *concluded all*: entirely ended

LEAR: You do me wrong to take me out o' the grave;
Thou art a soul in bliss; but I am bound
Upon a wheel of fire, that[27] mine own tears
Do scald[28] like molten lead.
CORDELIA: Sir, do you know me?
LEAR: You are a spirit, I know; when did you die?
CORDELIA: Still, still, far wide.[29]
DOCTOR: He's scarce awake; let him alone awhile.
LEAR: Where have I been? Where am I? Fair daylight?
I am mightily abus'd.[30] I should even die with pity
To see another thus. I know not what to say.
I will not swear these are my hands: let's see;
I feel this pin prick. Would I were assur'd
Of my condition!
CORDELIA: O! look upon me, sir,
And hold your hands in benediction o'er me.
No, sir, you must not kneel.
LEAR: Pray, do not mock me:
I am a very foolish fond[31] old man,
Fourscore and upward, not an hour more or less;
And, to deal plainly,
I fear I am not in my perfect mind.
Methinks I should know you and know this man;
Yet I am doubtful: for I am mainly[32] ignorant
What place this is, and all the skill I have
Remembers not these garments; nor I know not
Where I did lodge last night. Do not laugh at me;
For, as I am a man, I think this lady
To be my child Cordelia.
CORDELIA: And so I am, I am.
LEAR: Be your tears wet? Yes, faith. I pray, weep not:
If you have poison for me, I will drink it.
I know you do not love me; for your sisters
Have, as I do remember, done me wrong:
You have some cause, they have not.
CORDELIA: No cause, no cause.
LEAR: Am I in France?
KENT: In your own kingdom, sir.

27 so that
28 scald me
29 astray (in mind)
30 deceived, deluded (cf. l. 77 below)
31 simple, foolish
32 completely

LEAR: Do not abuse me.
DOCTOR: Be comforted, good madam; the great rage,[33]
You see, is kill'd in him; and yet it is danger
To make him even o'er[34] the time he has lost.
Desire him to go in; trouble him no more
Till further settling.[35]
CORDELIA: Will 't please your highness walk?[36]
LEAR: You must bear with me.
Pray you now, forget and forgive: I am old and foolish.

[*Exeunt Lear, Cordelia, Doctor, and Attendants.*]

GENTLEMAN: Holds it true, sir, that the Duke of Cornwall was so slain?

KENT: Most certain, sir.

GENTLEMAN: Who is conductor of his people?

KENT: As 'tis said, the bastard son of Gloucester.

GENTLEMAN: They say Edgar, his banished son, is with the Earl of Kent in Germany.

KENT: Report is changeable. 'Tis time to look about; the powers of the kingdom approach apace.

GENTLEMAN: The arbitrement[37] is like to be bloody. Fare you well, sir. [*Exit.*]

KENT: My point and period[38] will be throughly wrought,
Or well or ill, as this day's battle's fought. [*Exit.*]

33 frenzy, madness
34 *even o'er*: smooth over, straighten out, make the recollection continuous
35 *Till . . . settling*: till his mind has had more time to settle down again
36 withdraw
37 decision (of the war)
38 *point and period*: object and end

## ACT V

### SCENE 1

*The British Camp near Dover.*

*Enter, with drum and colours, Edmund, Regan, Officers, Soldiers, and Others.*

EDMUND: Know[1] of the duke if his last purpose hold,[2]
Or whether since[3] he is advis'd[4] by aught
To change the course; he's full of alteration
And self-reproving; bring his constant pleasure.[5]

[*To an Officer, who goes out.*]

REGAN: Our sister's man[6] is certainly miscarried.
EDMUND: 'Tis to be doubted,[7] madam.
REGAN: Now, sweet lord,
You know the goodness I intend upon you:[8]
Tell me, but truly, but then[9] speak the truth,
Do you not love my sister?
EDMUND: In honour'd[10] love.
REGAN: But have you never found my brother's way
To the forefended[11] place?
EDMUND: That thought abuses[12] you.
REGAN: I am doubtful that you have been conjunct
And bosom'd with her, as far as we call hers.[13]
EDMUND: No, by mine honour, madam.
REGAN: I never shall endure her:[14] dear my lord,
Be not familiar with her.
EDMUND: Fear[15] me not.
She and the duke her husband!

*Enter with drums and colours, Albany, Goneril, and Soldiers.*

1 find out
2 still holds good
3 since then
4 induced
5 *constant pleasure*: firm decision
6 *Our . . . man*: Oswald (see IV. vi. 238)
7 feared (so 'doubtful' in l. 12 = afraid)
8 *goodness I intend* (to confer) *upon you*: i.e. my hand
9 even if it is what I fear
10 honourable, not adulterous
11 forbidden
12 deceives
13 i.e. intimate with her to the fullest degree
14 *endure her*: i.e. bear to see her separate us
15 distrust

GONERIL [*Aside*]: I had rather lose the battle than that sister
Should loosen him and me.
ALBANY: Our very loving sister, well be-met.[16]
Sir, this I heard, the king is come to his daughter,
With others; whom the rigour of our state[17]
Forc'd to cry out.[18] Where I could not be honest
I never yet was valiant: for this business,
It toucheth us, as[19] France invades our land,
Not bolds[20] the king, with others, whom, I fear,
Most just and heavy causes make oppose.[21]
EDMUND: Sir, you speak nobly.
REGAN: Why is this reason'd?[22]
GONERIL: Combine together 'gainst the enemy;
for these domestic and particular[23] broils
Are not the question here.
ALBANY: Let's then determine
With the ancient of war[24] on our proceeding.
EDMUND: I shall attend you presently[25] at your tent.
REGAN: Sister, you'll go with us?
GONERIL: No.
REGAN: 'Tis most convenient; pray you, go with us.
GONERIL [*Aside*]: O, ho! I know the riddle.[26] [*Aloud.*] I will go.

*Enter Edgar, disguised.*

EDGAR: If e'er your Grace had speech with man so poor,
Hear me one word.
ALBANY: I'll overtake you. Speak.

[*Exeunt Edmund, Regan, Goneril, Officers, Soldiers, and Attendants.*]

EDGAR: Before you fight the battle, ope this letter.
If you have victory, let the trumpet sound
For him that brought it: wretched though I seem,
I can produce a champion that will prove
What is avouched[27] there. If you miscarry,

16 met
17 *our state*: our rule
18 *cry out*: protest, rebel
19 *toucheth us, as*: concerns me in so far as
20 *Not bolds*: not in so far as the king of France emboldens (supports)
21 *whom . . . oppose*: who, I fear, have good and weighty reasons for taking up arms against us
22 *Why . . . reason'd?*: Why all this argument (about the cause of rebellion)?
23 private
24 *the . . . war*: veteran soldiers
25 at once
26 *the riddle*: i.e. what you are after
27 asserted

Your business of the world[28] hath so an end,
And machination[29] ceases. Fortune love you!
ALBANY: Stay till I have read the letter.
EDGAR: I was forbid it.
When time shall serve, let but the herald cry,
And I'll appear again.
ALBANY: Why, fare thee well: I will o'erlook[30] thy paper. [*Exit Edgar.*]

*Re-enter Edmund.*

EDMUND: The enemy's in view; draw up your powers.
Here is the guess[31] of their true strength and forces
By diligent discovery;[32] but your haste
Is now urg'd on you.
ALBANY: We will greet the time.[33] [*Exit.*]
EDMUND: To both sisters have I sworn my love;
Each jealous[34] of the other, as the stung
Are of the adder. Which of them shall I take?
Both? one? or neither? Neither can be enjoy'd
If both remain alive: to take the widow
Exasperates, makes mad her sister Goneril;
And hardly shall I carry out my side,[35]
Her husband being alive. Now then, we'll use
His countenance[36] for the battle; which being done
Let her who would be rid of him devise
His speedy taking off.[37] As for the mercy
Which he intends to Lear, and to Cordelia,
The battle done, and they within our power,
Shall[38] never see his pardon; for my state[39]
Stands on me[40] to defend, not to debate. [*Exit.*]

28 *Your . . . world*: your worldly concerns, your life
29 plotting, i.e. Edmund's
30 look over, peruse
31 estimate
32 inquiry, spying
33 *greet the time*: go to meet the occasion, emergency
34 suspicious
35 *carry . . . side*: attain my object, i.e. the throne
36 authority, prestige
37 *taking off*: murder (a euphemism like 'liquidation' today)
38 they shall (grammatical confusion)
39 position
40 *Stands on me*: (it) concerns me, it is up to me

## SCENE 2

*A Field between the two Camps.*

*Alarum within. Enter, with drum and colours, Lear, Cordelia, and their Forces; and exeunt. Enter Edgar and Gloucester.*

EDGAR: Here, father, take the shadow of this tree
for your good host;[1] pray that the right may thrive.
If ever I return to you again,
I'll bring you comfort.
GLOUCESTER: Grace go with you, sir! [*Exit Edgar.*]

*Alarum; afterwards a retreat. Re-enter Edgar.*

EDGAR: Away, old man! give me thy hand: away!
King Lear hath lost, he and his daughter ta'en.
Give me thy hand; come on.
GLOUCESTER: No further, sir; a man may rot even here.
EDGAR: What! in ill thoughts again? Men must endure[2]
Their going hence, even as their coming hither:
Ripeness is all.[3] Come on.
GLOUCESTER: And that's true too. [*Exeunt.*]

1 shelterer, protection
2 wait for, live patiently until
3 *Ripeness is all*: the important thing is to be ready for death when it does come

## SCENE 3

*The British Camp, near Dover.*

*Enter, in conquest, with drum and colours, Edmund; Lear and Cordelia, prisoners; Officers, Soldiers, &c.*

EDMUND: Some officers take them away: good guard,[1]
Until their greater pleasures first be known
That[2] are to censure[3] them.
CORDELIA: We are not the first
Who, with best meaning,[4] have incurr'd the worst.
For thee, oppress'd king, am I cast down;

1 *good guard*: keep good guard over them
2 *their . . . That*: the pleasure (decision as to their fate) of those higher authorities (Albany &c.) who
3 judge
4 *with . . . meaning*: trying to act for the best

Myself could else out-frown false Fortune's frown.[5]
Shall we not see these daughters and these sisters?
LEAR: No, no, no, no! Come, let's away to prison;
We two alone will sing like birds i' the cage:[6]
When thou dost ask me blessing, I'll kneel down,
And ask of thee forgiveness: so we'll live,
And pray, and sing, and tell old tales, and laugh
At gilded butterflies,[7] and hear poor rogues
Talk of court news; and we'll talk with them too,
Who loses and who wins; who's in, who's out;
And take upon 's the mystery of things
As if we were God's spies:[8] and we'll wear out,[9]
In a wall'd prison, packs and sets of great ones
That ebb and flow by the moon.[10]
EDMUND: Take them away.
LEAR: Upon such sacrifices,[11] my Cordelia,
The gods themselves throw incense. Have I caught thee?
He that parts us shall bring a brand from heaven,[12]
And fire us hence like foxes.[13] Wipe thine eyes;
The good years[14] shall devour them, flesh and fell,[15]
Ere they shall make us weep: we'll see 'em starve first.
Come. [*Exeunt Lear and Cordelia, guarded.*]
EDMUND: Come hither, captain; hark,
Take thou this note; [*Giving a paper.*] go follow them to prison:
One step I have advan'd thee; if thou dost
As this instructs thee, thou dost make the way
To noble fortunes; know thou this, that men
Are as the time is; to be tender-minded
Does not become a sword;[16] thy great employment
Will not bear question;[17] either say thou'lt do't,
Or thrive by other means.
OFFICER: I'll do't, my lord.

5 *out-frown . . . frown*: defy misfortune
6 *also* meant a prison
7 *gilded butterflies*: court gallants (cf. l. 85)
8 *And . . . spies*: i.e. imagine we understand the ways of God in the world as if we were His agents or saw with His eyes
9 *wear out*: outlast
10 *packs . . . moon*: sets and parties at court who go in and out of favour like the changes of the moon
11 *such sacrifices*: as our imprisonment
12 *He . . . heaven*: i.e. no power on earth shall separate us
13 *like foxes*: as foxes are smoked out of their holes
14 *The good years*: the Devil
15 skin
16 *a sword*: i.e. a soldier
17 investigation, discussion

EDMUND: About it; and write happy[18] when thou hast done.
Mark,—I say, instantly, and carry it[19] so
As I have set it down.
OFFICER: I cannot draw a cart nor eat dried oats;
If it be man's work I will do it. [*Exit.*]

*Flourish. Enter Albany, Goneril, Regan, Officers, and Attendants.*

ALBANY: Sir, you have show'd to-day your valiant strain,[20]
And fortune led you well; you have the captives
Who were the opposites of[21] this day's strife;
We do require them of you, so to use them
As we[22] shall find their merits[23] and our safety
May equally determine.
EDMUND: Sir, I thought it fit
To send the old and miserable king
To some retention, and appointed guard;
Whose[24] age has charms in it, whose title more,
To pluck the common bosom[25] on his side,
And turn our impress'd lances[26] in our eyes[27]
Which do command them. With him I sent the queen;
My reason all the same; and they are ready
To-morrow, or at further space, to appear
Where you shall hold your session. At this time
We sweat and bleed; the friend hath lost his friend,
And the best quarrels,[28] in the heat,[29] are curs'd
By those that feel their sharpness;
The question of Cordelia and her father
Requires a fitter place.
ALBANY: Sir, by your patience,[30]
I hold you but a subject of this war,
Not as a brother.
REGAN: That's as we list[31] to grace him:
Methinks our pleasure might have been demanded,

18 *write happy*: count yourself happy
19 *carry it* (out)
20 lineage
21 *the opposites of*: our opponents in
22 I and my counsellors
23 deserts, deeds
24 refers back to 'king'
25 *the . . . bosom*: the affections of the common people
26 *our . . . lances*: the soldiers we had conscripted
27 *in our eyes*: against ourselves
28 *the . . . quarrels*: battles in the best causes
29 *in the heat (of the moment)*: before passions have cooled
30 *by . . . patience*: if you will excuse me saying so
31 choose

Ere you had spoke so far. He led our powers,
Bore the commission of my place[32] and person;
The which immediacy[33] may well stand up,[34]
And call itself your brother.

GONERIL: Not so hot;[35]
In his own grace he doth exalt himself
More than in your addition.[36]

REGAN: In my rights,
By me invested, he compeers the best.

GONERIL: That were the most, if[37] he should husband you.

REGAN: Jesters do oft prove prophets.

GONERIL: Holla, holla!
That eye that told you so look'd but a-squint.

REGAN: Lady, I am not well; else I should answer
From a full-flowing stomach.[38] General,
Take thou my soldiers, prisoners, patrimony;
Dispose of them, of me; the walls[39] are thine;
Witness the world, that I create thee here
My lord and master.

GONERIL: Mean you to enjoy him?

ALBANY: The let-alone[40] lies not in your good will.

EDMUND: Nor in thine, lord.

ALBANY: Half-blooded[41] fellow, yes.

REGAN [*To Edmund*.]: Let the drum strike, and prove my title thine.

ALBANY: Stay yet; hear reason. Edmund, I arrest thee
On capital treason; and, in thy attaint,[42]
This gilded[43] serpent. [*Pointing to Goneril.*] For your claim, fair sister,
I bar it in the interest of my wife;
'Tis she is sub-contracted[44] to this lord,
And I, her husband, contradict your bans.
If you will marry, make your love to me,
My lady is bespoke.

GONERIL: An interlude![45]

32 rank
33 closeness to me
34 *well . . . up*: i.e. justify him in standing up, &c.
35 *Not so hot*: Don't be in such a hurry
36 *your addition*: the position you have claimed for him
37 *the most* (he could do, even) *if*
38 *full-flowing stomach*: the eloquence of passion
39 *the walls*: of my fortress (metaphorically), i.e. I myself
40 power to forbid it
41 bastard
42 impeachment
43 gilded-over, fair-seeming
44 betrothed for the second time
45 *An interlude*: (This is as good as) a play

ALBANY: Thou art arm'd, Gloucester; let the trumpet sound:
If none appear to prove upon thy person
Thy heinous, manifest, and many treasons,
There is my pledge; [*Throws down a glove.*] I'll prove it on thy heart,
Ere I taste bread, thou art in nothing less
Than I have here proclaim'd thee.
REGAN: Sick! O sick!
GONERIL [*Aside*]: If not, I'll ne'er trust medicine.[46]
EDMUND: There's my exchange: [*Throws down a glove.*] what in the world he is
That names me traitor, villain-like he lies.
Call by thy trumpet: he that dares approach,
On him, on you, who not? I will maintain
My truth and honour firmly.
ALBANY: A herald, ho!
EDMUND: A herald, ho! a herald!
ALBANY: Trust to thy single virtue;[47] for thy soldiers,
All levied in my name, have in my name
Took their discharge.
REGAN: My sickness grows upon me.
ALBANY: She is not well; convey her to my tent. [*Exit Regan, led.*]
Come hither, herald,—

*Enter a Herald.*

Let the trumpet sound,—
And read out this.
OFFICER: Sound, trumpet! [*A trumpet sounds.*]
HERALD: 'If any man of quality or degree within the lists[48] of the army will maintain upon Edmund, supposed Earl of Gloucester, that he is a manifold traitor, let him appear at the third sound of the trumpet. He is bold in his defence.'
EDMUND: Sound! [*First Trumpet.*]
HERALD: Again! [*Second Trumpet.*]
HERALD: Again! [*Third Trumpet.*]
[*Trumpet answers within.*]

*Enter Edgar, armed, with a Trumpet before him.*[49]

ALBANY: Ask him his purposes, why he appears
Upon this call o' the trumpet.
HERALD: What are you?
Your name? your quality?[50] and why you answer
This present summons?

46 euphemism for 'poison'
47 valour (*virtus*)
48 role, muster
49 *with . . . him*: preceded by a trumpeter
50 rank

EDGAR: Know, my name is lost;
By treason's tooth bare-gnawn[51] and canker-bit:[52]
Yet am I noble as the adversary
I come to cope.[53]
ALBANY: Which is that adversary?
EDGAR: What's he that speaks for Edmund Earl of Gloucester?
EDMUND: Himself: what sayst thou to him?
EDGAR: Draw thy sword,
That, if my speech offend a noble heart,
Thy arm may do thee justice; here is mine:
Behold, it[54] is the privilege of mine honours,
My oath, and my profession:[55] I protest,
Maugre[56] thy strength, youth, place, and eminence,
Despite thy victor[57] sword and fire-new[58] fortune,
Thy valour and thy heart,[59] thou art a traitor,
False to thy gods, thy brother, and thy father,
Conspirant[60] 'gainst this high illustrious prince,
And, from the extremest upward[61] of thy head
To the descent[62] and dust below thy foot,
A most toad-spotted[63] traitor. Say thou 'No',
This sword, this arm, and my best spirits are bent
To prove upon thy heart, whereto I speak,
Thou liest.
EDMUND: In wisdom I should ask thy name;
But since thy outside looks so fair and war-like,
And that thy tongue some say[64] of breeding breathes,
What[65] safe[66] and nicely[67] I might well delay
By rule of knighthood, I disdain and spurn;[68]
Back do I toss these treasons to thy head,[69]

51 gnawed bare
52 devoured, as by the canker worm
53 engage
54 to fight, to maintain the truth of my assertion
55 *my profession*: of knighthood
56 in spite of
57 (lately) victorious
58 fresh like coins from the mint. Edmund is a *novus homo*, a *parvenu*
59 courage
60 conspiring *or* a conspirer
61 top
62 lowest part, sole of the feet
63 covered with shame as a toad with spots
64 suggestion, trace
65 i.e. the combat
66 safely (from the point of view of honour)
67 by insisting on the exact code of honour (which only requires me to answer an equal; see l. 152 below)
68 *I . . . spurn*: viz. to insist on my rights (change of construction)
69 *to thy head*: in thy teeth

With the hell-hated[70] lie o'erwhelm thy heart,
Which,[71] for[72] they yet glance by and scarcely bruise,
This sword of mine shall give them instant way,[73]
Where they shall rest for ever. Trumpets, speak!

[*Alarums. They fight. Edmund falls.*]

ALBANY: Save him, save him!
GONERIL: This is practice,[74] Gloucester:
By the law of arms thou wast not bound to answer
An unknown opposite; thou art not vanquish'd,
But cozen'd[75] and beguil'd.
ALBANY: Shut your mouth, dame,
Or with this paper[76] shall I stop it. Hold, sir;[77]
Thou[78] worse than any name, read thine own evil:
No tearing, lady; I perceive you know it. [*Gives the letter to Edmund.*]
GONERIL: Say, if I do, the laws are mine, not thine:
Who can arraign me for 't. [*Exit.*]
ALBANY: Most monstrous!
Know'st thou this paper?
EDMUND: Ask me not what I know.
ALBANY: Go after her: she's desperate; govern her.[79] [*Exit an Officer.*]
EDMUND: What you have charg'd me with, that have I done,
And more, much more; the time will bring it out:
'Tis past, and so am I. But what art thou
That hast this fortune on me?[80] If thou'rt noble,
I do forgive thee.
EDGAR: Let's exchange charity.[81]
I am no less in blood than thou art, Edmund;
If more, the more thou hast wrong'd me.
My name is Edgar, and thy father's son.
The gods are just, and of our pleasant vices
Make instruments to plague us:
The dark and vicious place where thee he got[82]
Cost him his eyes.

70 hated like hell
71 treasons
72 because
73 *give . . . way*: press them urgently back (upon you)
74 treachery
75 tricked
76 *this paper*: the love-letter of Goneril to Edmund (see IV. vi. 262)
77 *Hold, sir*: wait a moment (to Edmund)
78 Goneril
79 *govern her*: control her, e.g. prevent her suicide
80 *fortune on me*: advantage given thee by fortune over me
81 including forgiveness
82 *The . . . got*: i.e. the act of adultery which led to your birth

EDMUND: Thou hast spoken right, 'tis true;
The wheel is come full circle; I am here.
ALBANY: Methought thy very gait did prophesy
A royal nobleness; I must embrace thee:
Let sorrow split my heart, if ever I
Did hate thee or thy father.
EDGAR: Worthy prince, I know 't.
ALBANY: Where have you hid yourself?
How have you known the miseries of your father?
EDGAR: By nursing them, my lord. List a brief tale;
And, when 'tis told, O that my heart would burst!
The bloody proclamation to escape[83]
That follow'd me so near,—O! our lives' sweetness,[84]
That we the pain of death would hourly die
Rather than die at once!—taught me to shift[85]
Into a madman's rags, to assume a semblance
That very dogs disdain'd: and in this habit
Met I my father with his bleeding rings,[86]
Their precious stones new lost; became his guide,
Led him, begg'd for him, sav'd him from despair;
Never,—O fault!—reveal'd myself unto him,
Until some half hour past, when I was arm'd;
Not sure, though hoping, of this good success,
I ask'd his blessing, and from first to last
Told him my pilgrimage: but his flaw'd[87] heart,—
Alack! too weak the conflict to support;
'Twixt two extremes of passion, joy and grief,
Burst smilingly.
EDMUND: This speech of yours hath mov'd me,
And shall perchance do good; but speak you on;
You look as you had something more to say.
ALBANY: If there be more, more woeful, hold it in;
For I am almost ready to dissolve,[88]
Hearing of this.
EDGAR: This would have seem'd a period[89]
To such as love not sorrow; but another,[90]

83 *to escape*: governs 'the bloody proclamation'
84 *our . . . sweetness*: how highly we value our lives!
85 change
86 eye-sockets
87 cracked, worn out
88 in tears, melt away
89 limit, ending
90 sorrow *or* tale

To amplify too much,[91] would make much more,
And top extremity.[92]
Whilst I was big[93] in clamour came there a man,
Who, having seen me in my worst estate,[94]
Shunn'd my abhorr'd society; but then, finding
Who 'twas that so endur'd, with his strong arms
He fasten'd on my neck, and bellow'd out
As[95] he'd burst heaven; threw him on my father;
Told the most piteous tale of Lear and him
That ever ear receiv'd; which in recounting
His grief grew puissant,[96] and the strings of life
Began to crack: twice then the trumpet sounded,
And there I left him tranc'd.[97]
ALBANY: But who was this?
EDGAR: Kent, sir, the banish'd Kent; who in disguise
Follow'd his enemy[98] king, and did him service
Improper for[99] a slave.

*Enter a Gentleman, with a bloody knife.*

GENTLEMAN: Help, help! O help!
EDGAR: What kind of help?
ALBANY: Speak, man.
EDGAR: What means that bloody knife?
GENTLEMAN: 'Tis hot, it smokes;
It came even from the heart of—O! she's dead.
ALBANY: Who dead? speak, man.
GENTLEMAN: Your lady, sir, your lady: and her sister
By her is poison'd; she confesses it.
EDMUND: I was contracted[100] to them both: all three
Now marry in an instant.
EDGAR: Here comes Kent.
ALBANY: Produce the bodies, be they alive or dead:
This judgment of the heavens, that makes us tremble,
Touches us not with pity. [*Exit Gentleman.*]

*Enter Kent.*

91 *To . . . much*: (probably) by increasing what is already excessive
92 *top extremity*: pass the (due) limit
93 loud
94 state
95 as if
96 (too) powerful
97 insensible
98 (turned) hostile
99 *Improper for*: too humble even for
100 engaged, promised

O! is this he?
The time will not allow the compliment[101]
Which very manners urges.

KENT: I am come
To bid my king and master aye good-night;
Is he not here?

ALBANY: Great thing of us forgot!
Speak, Edmund, where's the king? and where's Cordelia?
Seest thou this object,[102] Kent?

[*The bodies of Goneril and Regan are brought in.*]

KENT: Alack! why thus?

EDMUND: Yet Edmund was belov'd:
The one the other poison'd for my sake,
And after[103] slew herself.

ALBANY: Even so. Cover their faces.

EDMUND: I pant for life:[104] some good I mean to do
Despite of mine own nature. Quickly send,
Be brief in it, to the castle; for my writ[105]
Is on the life of Lear and on Cordelia.
Nay, send in time.

ALBANY: Run, run! O run!

EDGAR: To whom, my lord? who has the office? send
Thy token of reprieve.

EDMUND: Well thought on: take my sword,
Give it the captain.

ALBANY: Haste thee, for thy life. [*Exit Edgar.*]

EDMUND: He hath commission from thy wife and me
To hang Cordelia in the prison, and
To lay the blame upon her own despair,
That she fordid[106] herself.

ALBANY: The gods defend her! Bear him hence awhile. [*Edmund is borne off.*]

*Enter Lear, with Cordelia dead in his arms; Edgar, Officer, and Others.*

LEAR: Howl, howl, howl, howl! O! you are men of stones:[107]
Had I your tongues and eyes, I'd use them so
That heaven's vaults should crack. She's gone for ever.

101 formal courtesy (as in I. i. 291)
102 sight, something thrown in the way (Lat. *obicio*)
103 *after*(wards)
104 *pant for life*: struggle to live a little longer
105 writing, the order given (ll. 28 above)
106 destroyed
107 *men of stones*: unfeeling

I know when one is dead, and when one lives;
She's dead as earth. Lend me a looking-glass;
If that her breath will mist or stain the stone,[108]
Why, then she lives.
KENT: Is this the promis'd end?[109]
EDGAR: Or image[110] of that horror?
ALBANY: Fall and cease![111]
LEAR: This feather stirs; she lives! if it be so,
It is a chance which does redeem all sorrows
That ever I have felt.
KENT [*Kneeling.*]: O, my good master!
LEAR: Prithee, away.
EDGAR: 'Tis noble Kent, your friend.
LEAR: A plague upon you, murderers, traitors all!
I might have sav'd her; now, she's gone for ever!
Cordelia, Cordelia! stay a little. Ha!
What is 't thou sayst? Her voice was ever soft,
Gentle and low, an excellent thing in woman.
I kill'd the slave[112] that was a-hanging thee.
OFFICER: 'Tis true, my lord, he did.
LEAR: Did I not, fellow?
I have seen the day, with my good biting falchion[113]
I would have made them skip: I am old now,
And these same crosses[114] spoil me.[115] Who are you?
Mine eyes are not o' the best: I'll tell you straight.[116]
KENT: If fortune brag of two she lov'd and hated,[117]
One of them[118] we behold.
LEAR: This is a dull[119] sight. Are you not Kent?
KENT: The same,
Your servant Kent. Where is your servant Caius?[120]
LEAR: He's a good fellow, I can tell you that;
He'll strike,[121] and quickly too. He's dead and rotten.
KENT: No, my good lord; I am the very man—

108 a mirror of polished stone
109 *the . . . end*: the end of the world foretold (in biblical prophecy)
110 copy, reproduction (cf. 'great doom's image', Macbeth II. iii. 61)
111 *Fall and cease!*: (probably) let the heavens fall and all things come to an end!
112 *the slave*: not literal, but abusive
113 a kind of light sword
114 troubles
115 *spoil me*: destroy me (as a fighter)
116 straightaway, in a moment
117 *two . . . hated*: one whom she raised up (to the highest) and one whom she put down (to the lowest)
118 *One of them*: in Lear
119 melancholy
120 *Where . . . Caius?*: probably Kent is inviting Lear to recognize in him the former Caius
121 as he did Oswald (I. iv. 68)

LEAR: I'll see that straight.[122]
KENT: That, from your first of difference[123] and decay,
Have followed your sad steps.
LEAR: You are welcome hither.
KENT: Nor no man else;[124] all's cheerless, dark, and deadly:
Your eldest daughters have fordone themselves,
And desperately[125] are dead.
LEAR: Ay, so I think.
ALBANY: He knows not what he says, and vain it is
That we present us[126] to him.
EDGAR: Very bootless.[127]

*Enter an Officer.*

OFFICER: Edmund is dead, my lord.
ALBANY: That's but a trifle here.
Your lords and noble friends, know our[128] intent;
What comfort to this great decay[129] may come
Shall be applied: for us, we will resign,
During the life of this old majesty,
To him our absolute power:—[*To Edgar and Kent.*] You, to your rights;[130]
With boot and such addition[131] as your honours[132]
Have more than merited. All friends shall taste
The wages[133] of their virtue, and all foes
The cup of their deservings. O! see, see!
LEAR: And my poor fool[134] is hang'd! No, no, no life!
Why should a dog, a horse, a rat, have life,
And thou no breath at all? Thou'lt come no more,
Never, never, never, never, never!
Pray you, undo this button: thank you, sir.
Do you see this? Look on her, look, her lips,
Look there, look there! [*Dies.*]
EDGAR: He faints!—my lord, my lord!

122 cf. l. 278. But Lear is only half conscious of what is going on
123 *your . . . difference*: the commencement of your change of fortunes
124 *Nor . . . else*: *either* neither I nor anyone else can be very welcome (well come?) to this scene (which suits what follows), *or* a continuation of his words at l. 285
125 in despair
126 ourselves
127 useless
128 the royal plural, since Albany represents those to whom Lear surrendered power
129 *great decay*: ruin of greatness (Lear)
130 *to . . . rights*: betake you to, enjoy your rights
131 *boot . . . addition*: the profit of such additions
132 honourable deeds
133 rewards
134 *poor fool*: (term of endearment) Cordelia

KENT: Break, heart;[135] I prithee, break.
EDGAR: Look up, my lord.
KENT: Vex not his ghost:[136] O! let him pass; he hates him
That would upon the rack[137] of this tough world
Stretch him out longer.
EDGAR: He is gone, indeed.
KENT: The wonder is he hath endur'd so long:
He but usurp'd[138] his life.
ALBANY: Bear them from hence. Our present business
Is general woe. [*To Kent and Edgar.*] Friends of my soul, you twain
Rule in this realm,[139] and the gor'd[140] state sustain.
KENT: I have a journey, sir, shortly to go;
My master calls me, I must not say no.
ALBANY: The weight of this sad time we must obey;
Speak what we feel, not what we ought to say.[141]
The oldest[142] hath borne most: we that are young,
Shall never see so much, nor live so long.[143] [*Exeunt, with a dead march.*]

1608

135 *Break, heart*: *either* to his own heart *or* of Lear's
136 spirit
137 metaphor from an instrument of torture ('racking' the limbs)
138 kept what was due to death
139 *this realm*: (probably) that half of Britain which had been Regan's share
140 maimed, injured
141 *Speak . . . say*: i.e. (probably) at present we can only speak from the heart, not prudently as after reflection
142 *The oldest*: especially Lear
143 In the quarto text of *Lear* the final speech is attributed to Albany; in the folio text this speech is attributed to Edgar.

# Aphra Behn

## c. 1640–1689

Born in southeast England during the preparations for the English Civil War, Aphra Behn intentionally obscured details of her life, giving her the reputation, in the words of Germaine Greer, as 'a palimpsest; she has scratched herself out.' She married Johan Behn, who may have been a merchant of possibly Dutch or German background. He died, or else the couple separated after 1664. A devoted monarchist, she supported the restored King Charles II, for whom she served as a political spy in Antwerp. When she returned to England, she embarked on her writing career. A prolific playwright in the 1670s and 1680s— the author of 19 plays—she was the first professional female playwright in England, exploring in her plays questions of gender and sexual involvements. *The Rover*, generally regarded as her masterpiece, premiered in 1677. She is buried in the East Cloister of Westminster Abbey.

# The Rover
# Or, The Banish't Cavaliers

## *CHARACTERS*

| | |
|---|---|
| DON ANTONIO | The Vice-Roy's Son |
| DON PEDRO | A Noble *Spaniard*, his Friend |
| BELVILE | An *English* Colonel in Love with *Florinda* |
| WILLMORE | The *ROVER* |
| FREDERICK | An *English* Gentleman, and Friend to *Bel.* and *Fred.* |
| BLUNT | An *English* Country Gentleman |
| STEPHANO | Servant to *Don Pedro* |
| PHILIPPO | *Lucetta's* Gallant |
| SANCHO | Pimp to *Lucetta* |
| BISKEY and SEBASTIAN | *Two Bravo's to* Angellica |
| Officers and Souldiers | |
| Page [DIEGO] | To *Don Antonio* |
| [SERVANT | To *Blunt*] |
| [PAGE | To *Belvile* and *Willmore*] |
| FLORINDA | Sister to *Don Pedro* |
| HELLENA | A gay Young Woman design'd for a Nun, and Sister to *Florinda* |
| VALERIA | A Kinswoman to *Florinda* |
| ANGELLICA BIANCA | A Famous Courtizan |
| MORETTA | Her Woman |
| CALLIS | Governess to *Florinda* and *Hellena* |
| LUCETTA | A Jilting Wench |
| [PAGE | To *Hellena*] |

Servants, Other *Masqueraders* Men and Women

**SCENE**

*NAPLES, in Carnival time*

## PROLOGUE

*Scene: Naples, in Carnival time*

*Witts, like Physitians never can agree,*
*When of a different Societie.*

*And* Rabel's *Drops were never more cry'd down*
*By all the Learned Doctors of the Town,*
*Than a New* Play *whose Author is unknown.*
*Nor can those Doctors with more Malice sue*
*(And powerful Purses) the discenting Few,*
*Than those with an Insulting Pride, do raile*
*At all who are not of their own Caball:*
*If a Young Poet hitt your Humour right,*
*You judg him then out of Revenge and Spight.*
*So amongst men there are Ridiculous Elves,*
*Who Monkeys hate for being too like themselves.*
*So that the reason of the grand debate,*
*Why Witt so oft is damn'd, when good* Plays *take,*
*Is, that you Censure as you love, or hate.*
*Thus like a Learned Conclave Poets sit,*
*Catholique Judges both of Sense and Wit,*
*And Damn or Save, as they themselves think fit.*
*Yet those who to others' faults are so severe,*
*Are not so perfect but themselves may Erre.*
*Some write Coract indeed, but then the whole*
*(Bating their own Dull stuff i'th'* Play*) is stole:*
*As Bees do suck from Flowers their Honey dew,*
*So they rob others, striving to please you.*
*Some write their Characters Gentiele and fine,*
*But then they do so Toyl for every line,*
*That what to you does Easie seem, and Plain,*
*Is the hard Issue of their labouring Brain.*
*And some th' Effects of all their pains we see,*
*Is but to Mimick good Extemporie.*
*Others by long Converse about the Town,*
*Have Witt enough to write a Lew'd* Lampoon,
*But their chief skill lyes in a Bawdy Song.*
*In short, the only Witt that's now in Fashon,*
*Is but the gleenings of good Conversation.*
*As for the Author of this Coming* Play,
*I ask't him what he thought fit I shou'd say*
*In thanks for your good Company to day:*
*He call'd me Fool, and said it was well known,*
*You came not here for our sakes, but your own.*
*New* Plays *are stuff'd with Witts, and with Deboches,*
*That Crowd and sweat like* Citts, *in* May-Day *Coaches.*

WRITTEN BY A PERSON OF QUALITY.

## ACT I

### SCENE 1

*A Chamber*

*Enter* FLORINDA *and* HELLENA

FLORINDA: What an Impertinent thing is a Young Girl bred in a Nunnery? How full of Questions? Prithee no more *Hellena,* I have told thee more than thou understand'st already.

HELLENA: The more's my grief, I wou'd fain know as much as you, which makes me so Inquisitive; nor is't enough I know you'r a Lover, unless you tell me too, who 'tis you sigh for.

FLORINDA: When you'r a Lover, I'le think you fit for a Secret of that Nature.

HELLENA: 'Tis true, I never was a Lover yet—but I begin to have a shrew'd guess, what 'tis to be so, and fancy it very pretty to sigh, and sing, and blush, and wish, and dream and wish, and long and wish to see the Man; and when I do look pale and tremble; just as you did when my Brother brought home the fine English Colonel to see you—what do you call him *Don Belvile.*

FLORINDA: Fye *Hellena.*

HELLENA: That blush betrays you.—I am sure 'tis so—or is it *Don Antonio* the Vice-Roy's Son?—or perhaps the Rich Old *Don Vincentio* whom my Father designs you for a Husband?—why do you blush again?

FLORINDA: With Indignation, and how near soever my Father thinks I am to Marrying that hated Object, I shall let him see, I understand better, what's due to my Beauty, Birth and Fortune, and more to my Soul, than to obey those unjust Commands.

HELLENA: Now hang me, if I don't love thee for that dear disobedience. I love mischief strangely, as most of our Sex do, who are come to Love nothing else—but tell me dear *Florinda,* don't you love that fine *Anglese*?—for I vow next to loving him my self, 'twill please me most that you do so, for he is so gay and so handsome.

FLORINDA: *Hellena,* a Maid design'd for a Nun, ought not to be so Curious in a discourse of Love.

HELLENA: And dost thou think that ever I'le be a Nun? or at least till I'm so Old, I'm fit for nothing else—Faith no Sister; and that which makes me long to know whether you love *Belvile,* is because I hope he has some mad Companion or other, that will spoil my devotion, nay I'm resolv'd to provide my self this Carnival, if there be ere a handsome proper fellow of my humour above ground, tho I ask first.

FLORINDA: Prithee be not so wild.

HELLENA: Now you have provided yourself of a Man, you take no care for poor me—prithee tell me, what dost thou see about me that is unfit for Love—have I not a World of Youth? a humour gay? a Beauty passable? a Vigour desirable? Well Shap't? clean limb'd? sweet breath'd? and sense enough to know how all these ought to be employ'd to the best advantage; yes I do and will, therefore lay aside your hopes of my Fortune, by my being a Devote, and tell me how you came acquainted with this *Belvile?* for I perceive you knew him before he came to *Naples.*

FLORINDA: Yes, I knew him at the Siege of *Pamplona*, he was then a Colonel of *French* Horse, who when the Town was Ransack't, Nobly treated my Brother and my self, preserving us from all Insolences; and I must own, (besides great Obligations) I have I know not what, that pleads kindly for him about my Heart, and will suffer no other to enter.—But see my Brother.

*Enter* DON PEDRO, STEPHANO *with a Masquing habit and* CALLIS

PEDRO: Good morrow Sister.—Pray when saw you your Lover *Don Vincentio*?

FLORINDA: I know not Sir—*Callis* when was he here? for I consider it so little, I know not when it was.

PEDRO: I have a Command from my Father here to tell you, you ought not to despise him, a Man of so vast a Fortune, and such a Passion for you—*Stephano* my things.

*Puts on his Masquing habit*

FLORINDA: A Passion for me, 'tis more than e're I saw, or he had a desire should be known—I hate *Vincentio*, Sir, and I wou'd not have a Man so dear to me as my Brother, follow the ill Customes of our Countrey, and make a slave of his Sister—and Sir, my Father's will, I'm sure you may divert.

PEDRO: I know not how dear I am to you, but I wish only to be ranckt in your esteem, equal with the English Coll. *Belvile*—why do you frown and blush? is there any guilt belongs to the Name of that Cavalier.

FLORINDA: I'le not deny I value *Belvile*, when I was expos'd to such dangers as the Licenc'd Lust of common Souldiers threatned, when Rage and Conquest flew through the City—then *Belvile* this Criminal for my sake, threw himself into all dangers to save my Honour and will you not allow him my esteem?

PEDRO: Yes, pay him what you will in Honour—but you must consider *Don Vincentio's* Fortune, and the Joynture he'l make you.

FLORINDA: Let him consider my Youth, Beauty and Fortune; which ought not to be thrown away on his Age and Joynture.

PEDRO: 'Tis true, he's not so young and fine a Gentleman, as that *Belvile*,—but what Jewels will that Cavalier present you with? those of his Eyes and Heart?

HELLENA: And are not those better than any *Don Vincentio* has brought from the *Indies*.

PEDRO: Why how now! has your Nunnery breeding taught you to understand the value of Hearts and Eyes?

HELLENA: Better than to believe *Vincentio's* deserve value from any Woman—he may perhaps encrease her Baggs, but not her Family.

PEDRO: This is fine—go—up to your Devotion, you are not design'd for the conversation of Lovers.

HELLENA: Nor Saints, yet awhile I hope. *Aside*

I'st not enough you make a Nun of me, but you must cast my Sister away too? exposing her to a worse confinement than a Religious life.

PEDRO: The Girl's mad—it is a confinement to be carry'd into the Countrey, to an Antient Villa belonging to the Family of the *Vincentio's* these five hundred Years, and have no other Prospect than that pleasing one of seeing all her own that meets her Eyes—a fine Ayr, large Fields and Gardens, where she may walk and gather Flowers.

HELLENA: When by Moon Light? For I am sure she dares not encounter with the heat of the Sun, that were a task only for *Don Vincentio* and his Indian breeding, who loves it in the Dog dayes.—and if these be her daily divertisements, what are those of the Night, to lye in a wide Motheaten Bed Chamber, with furniture in Fashion in the Reign of King *Sancho* the First; The Bed, that which his Fore-fathers liv'd and dy'd in.

PEDRO: Very well.

HELLENA: This Appartment (now furbrusht and fitted out for the young Wife) he (out of freedom) makes his dressing Room, and being a Frugal and a Jealus Coxcomb, instead of a Valet to uncase his feeble Carcass, he desires you to do that Office—signs of favour I'll assure you, and such as you must not hope for, unless your Woman be out of the way.

PEDRO: Have you done yet?

HELLENA: That Honour being past, the Gyant stretches it self; yawns and sighs a Belch or two, loud as a Musket, throws himself into Bed, and expects you in his foul sheets, and e're you can get yourself undrest, call's you with a snore or Two—and are not these fine Blessings to a young Lady?

PEDRO: Have you done yet?

HELLENA: And this Man you must kiss, nay you must kiss none but him too—and nuzel through his Beard to find his Lips.—And this you must submit to for Threescore years, and all for a Joynture.

PEDRO: For all your Character of *Don Vincentio*, she is as like to Marry him, as she was before.

HELLENA: Marry *Don Vincentio*! hang me such a Wedlock would be worse than Adultery with another Man. I had rather see her in the *Hostel de Dieu*, to wast her Youth there in Vowes, and be a hand-Maid to Lazers and Cripples, than to lose it in such a Marriage.

PEDRO: You have consider'd Sister, that *Belvile* has no Fortune to bring you to, banisht his Countrey, despis'd at home, and pitty'd abroad.

HELLENA: What then, the Vice-Roy's Son is better than that Old Sir Fifty, *Don Vicentio*! *Don Indian*! he thinks he's trading to *Gambo* still, and wou'd *Barter* himself (that Bell and Bawble) for your Youth and Fortune.

PEDRO: *Callis* take her hence, and lock her up all this Carnival, and at Lent she shall begin her everlasting Pennance in a Monastery.

HELLENA: I care not, I had rather be a Nun, than be oblig'd to Marry as you wou'd have me, if I were design'd for't.

PEDRO: Do not fear the blessing of that choice—you shall be a Nun.

HELLENA: Shall I so? you may chance to be mistaken in my way of devotion:—a Nun! yes I am like to make a fine Nun! I have an excellent humour for a Grate: no, I'le have a *Saint* of my own to pray to shortly, if I like any that dares venture on me. *Aside*

PEDRO: *Callis*, make it your business to watch this Wild Cat.

As for you *Florinda*, I've only try'd you all this while and urg'd my Father's will; but mine is, that you wou'd love *Antonio*, he is Brave and young, and all that can compleat the happiness of a Gallant Maid—this absence of my Father will give us opportunity, to free you from *Vincentio*, by Marrying here, which you must do to Morrow.

FLORINDA: To Morrow!

PEDRO: To Morrow, or 'twill be too late—tis not my Friendship to *Antonio*, which makes me urge this, but Love to thee, and hatred to *Vincentio*—therefore resolve upon to Morrow.

FLORINDA: Sir, I shall strive to do, as shall become your Sister.

PEDRO: I'le both believe and trust you—Adieu. *Exeunt Pedro and Stephano*

HELLENA: As becomes his Sister!—that is to be as resolv'd your way,
as he is his— *Hellena goes to Callis*

FLORINDA: I ne're till now perceiv'd my Ruine near,
I've no defence against *Antonio*'s Love,
For he has all the Advantages of Nature,
The moving Arguments of Youth and Fortune.

HELLENA: But heark you *Callis*, you will not be so cruel to lock me up indeed, will you.

CALLIS: I must obey the Commands I have—besides, do you consider what a life you are going to lead?

HELLENA: Yes, *Callis*, that of a Nun: and till then I'll be indebted a world of Prayers to you, if you'll let me now see, what I never did, the Divertisements of a *Carnival.*

CALLIS: What, go in Masquerade? 'twill be a fine farewel to the World I take it—pray what wou'd you do there?

HELLENA: That which all the World does, as I am told, be as mad as the rest, and take all Innocent freedomes—Sister you'll go too, will you not? come prithee be not sad. —We'll out-wit Twenty Brothers, if you'll be rul'd by me—come put off this dull humour with your Cloths, and Assume one as gay, and as fantastick, as the Dress my Couzen *Valeria*, and I have provided, and let's Ramble.

FLORINDA: *Callis,* will you give us leave to go?

CALLIS: I have a Youthful itch of going myself *Aside*
—Madam, if I thought your Brother might not know it, and I might wait on you; for by my troth I'll not trust Young Girles alone.

FLORINDA: Thou see'st my Brother's gone already, and thou shalt attend, and watch us.

*Enter* STEPHANO

STEPHANO: Madam? the Habits are come, and your Couzen *Valeria* is drest, and stayes for you.

FLORINDA: 'Tis well.—I'll write a Note, and if I chance to see *Belvile*, and want an opportunity to speak to him, that shall let him know, what I've resolv'd in favour of him.

HELLENA: Come, let's in and dress us. *Exeunt*

## ACT I

### SCENE 2

*A Long Street*

*Enter* BELVILE *Melancholy,* BLUNT *and* FREDERICK

FREDERICK: Whe what the devil ails the Colonel? In a time when all the World is gay, to look like meer *Lent* thus? Had'st thou been long enough in *Naples* to have been in Love, I shou'd have sworn some such Judgment had befall'n thee.

BELVILE: No, I have made no new Amours since I came to *Naples*?

FREDERICK: You have left none behind you in *Paris*?

BELVILE: Neither.

FREDERICK: I cannot divine the Cause then, unless the Old Cause, the want of Money.

BLUNT: And another Old Cause, the want of a Wench—Wou'd not that revive you?

BELVILE: You are mistaken, *Ned.*

BLUNT: Nay, 'Sheartlikins, then thou'rt past Cure.

FREDERICK: I have found it out; thou hast renew'd thy acquaintance with the Lady that cost thee so many sighs at the Siege of *Pamplona*—Pox on't, what d'e you call her—her Brother's a Noble *Spaniard*—Nephew to the Dead General—*Florinda*—Ay *Florinda*—and will nothing serve thy turn but that damn'd virtuous Woman? whom on my Conscience thou lovest inspight too, because thou seest little or no possibility of gaining her.

BELVILE: Thou art mistaken, I have Int'rest enough in that lovely Virgins heart, to make me proud and vain, were it not abated by the severity of a Brother, who perceiving my happiness—

FREDERICK: Has civily forbid thee the House?

BELVILE: 'Tis so, to make way for a Pow'rful Rival, the Vice-Roy's Son, who has the advantage of me, in being a Man of Fortune, a *Spaniard,* and her Brother's Friend, which gives him Liberty to make his Court, whilst I have recourse only to Letters, and distant looks from her Window, which are as soft and kind as those which Heav'n sends down on Penitents.

BLUNT: Heyday! 'Sheartlikins, simile! by this Light the Man is quite spoild. —*Fred.* What the Devil are we made of, that we cannot be thus concern'd for a Wench—'Sheartlikins our Cupids are like the Cooks of the Camp, they can Roast or Boil a Woman, but they have none of the fine tricks to set 'em off, no Hogoes to make the Sawce pleasant and the Stomach sharp.

FREDERICK: I dare swear I have had a hundred as young kind and handsom as this *Florinda*; and Dogs eat me, if they were not as troublesom to me i'th Morning, as they were welcome o're Night.

BLUNT: And yet I warrant, he wou'd not touch another Woman, if he might have her for nothing.

BELVILE: That's thy joy, a cheap Whore.

BLUNT: Why Ay 'Sheartlikins I love a Franck Soul—when did you ever hear of an honest Woman that took a Man's Money? I warrant 'em good ones—but

Gentlemen, You may be free, you have been kept so poor with Parliaments and Protectors, that the little Stock you have is not worth preserving—but I thank my Stars, I had more Grace than to forfeit my Estate by Cavaliering.

BELVILE: Methinks only following the Court, shou'd be sufficient to entitle 'em to that.

BLUNT: 'Sheartlikins, they know I follow it to do it no good, unless they pick a hole in my Coat for lending you Money now and then, which is a greater Crime to my Conscience, Gentlemen, than to the Common-Wealth.

*Enter* WILLMORE

WILLMORE: Ha! dear *Belvile*! noble Colonel!

BELVILE: *Willmore*! welcom ashore, my dear Rover!—what happy wind blew us this good Fortune?

WILLMORE: Let me salute my dear *Fred*, and then Command me.—How is't honest Lad?

FREDERICK: Faith, Sir, the Old Complement, infinitely the better to see my dear mad *Willmore* again.— Prithee why camest thou ashore? and where's the Prince?

WILLMORE: He's well, and Reigns still Lord of the watry Element.—I must abord again within a day or two, and my business ashore was only to enjoy myself a little this Carnival.

BELVILE: Pray know our new Friend, Sir, he's but bashful, a raw Traveller, but honest, stout, and one of us.

WILLMORE: That you esteem him, gives him an Intr'est here. *Embraces Blunt*

BLUNT: Your Servant, Sir.

WILLMORE: But well,—Faith I'm glad to meet you again in a warm Climate, where the kind Sun has its God-like Pow'r still over the Wine and Women—Love and Mirth! are my bus'ness in *Naples*, and if I mistake not the place, here's an Excellent Market for Chapmen of my humour.

BELVILE: See, here be those kind Merchants of Love you look for.

*Enter several* MEN *in Masquing Habits, some playing on Musique, others dancing after,* WOMEN *drest like Courtizans, with Papers pinn'd on their Breasts, and Baskets of Flowers in their Hands*

BLUNT: 'Sheartlikins, what have we here?

FREDERICK: Now the Game begins.

WILLMORE: Fine pretty Creatures! may a stranger have leave to look and love?—What's here—*Roses for every Month?* *Reads the Papers*

BLUNT: Roses for every Month? what means that?

BELVILE: They are, or wou'd have you think they're Courtizans, who here in *Naples*, are to be hir'd by the Moneth.

WILLMORE: Kind, and obliging to inform us—Pray where do these Roses grow? I wou'd fain plant some of 'em in a Bed of mine.

WOMAN: Beware such Roses, Sir.

WILLMORE: A Pox of Fear: I'll be bak't with thee between a pair of Sheets, and that's thy proper Still; so I might but strew such Roses over me, and under me—Fair one, Wou'd you wou'd give me leave to gather at your Bush this idle Moneth; I wou'd go near to make some Body smell of it all the year after.

BELVILE: And thou hast need of such a Remedy, for thou stink'st of Tar and Ropes Ends, like a Dock or Pest-house.

*The Woman puts herself into the Hands of a Man, and Exeunt*

WILLMORE: Nay, nay, you shall not leave me so.

BELVILE: By all means use no violence here.

WILLMORE: Death! Just as I was going to be damnably in Love, to have her led off! I could pluck that Rose out of his Hand, and even kiss the Bed, the Bush grew in.

FREDERICK: No Friend to Love, like a long Voyage at Sea.

BLUNT: Except a Nunnery, *Fred.*

WILLMORE: Death! But will they not be kind? quickly be kind? Thou know'st I'm no tame sigher, but a Rampant Lion of the Forrest.

*Advances from the farther end of the Scenes, two* MEN *drest all over with Horns of several sorts, making Grimasses at one another, with Papers pinn'd on their Backs*

BELVILE: Oh the fantastical Rogues, how they'r drest! 'Tis a Satyre against the whole Sex.

WILLMORE: Is this a Fruit that grows in this warm Countrey?

BELVILE: Yes: 'Tis pretty to see these *Italians* start, swell and stab, at the word Cuckold, and yet stumble at Horns on every Threshold.

WILLMORE: See what's on their Back—*Flowers of every Night.* *Reads*
—Ah Rogue! and more sweet than Roses of ev'ry Moneth! This is a Gardiner of *Adam's* own breeding. *They dance [and Exeunt]*

BELVILE: What think you of these Grave People?—is a Wake in *Essex* half so mad or Extravagant?

WILLMORE: I like their sober grave way, 'tis a kind of Legal Authoriz'd Fornication, where the Men are not chid for't, nor the Women despis'd as amongst our dull English, even the Monsieurs want that part of good Manners.

BELVILE: But here in *Italy*, a Monsieur is the humblest best bred Gentleman—Duels are so bafled by *Bravo's* that an Age shews not one but between a *French-man*, and a hang-man, who is as much too hard for him on the *Piaza*, as they are for a *Dutch-man* on the New Bridge—but see another Crew.

*Enter* FLORINDA, HELLENA *and* VALERIA, *drest like Gipsies;* CALLIS *and* STEPHANO, LUCETTA, PHILIPPO *and* SANCHO *in Masquerade*

HELLENA: Sister, there's your *English Man,* and with him a handsome proper Fellow—I'le to him, and instead of telling him his Fortune, try my own.

WILLMORE: *Gipsies* on my life—sure these will prattle if a Man crosse their hands. *Goes to Hellena*
—dear, pretty, (and I hope) young Devil, will you tell an Amorous stranger, what luck he's like to have?

HELLENA: Have a care how you venture with me Sir, least I pick your Pocket, which will more vex your *English* humour, than an *Italian* Fortune will please you.

WILLMORE: How the Devil cam'st thou to know my Countrey and Humour?

HELLENA: The First I guess by a certain forward Impudence, which does not displease me at this time, and the loss of your Money will vex you, because I hope you have but very little to lose.

WILLMORE: Egad Child thou'rt i'th' right, it is so little, I dare not offer it thee for a kindness—but cannot you divine what other things of more value I have about me, that I wou'd more willingly part with.

HELLENA: Indeed no, that's the bus'ness of a Witch, and I am but a Gipsie yet.—Yet without looking in your hand, I have a parlous guess, 'tis some Foolish heart you mean, an Inconstant *English* heart, as little worth stealing as your Purse.

WILLMORE: Nay, then thou dost deal with the Devil, that's certain.—thou hast guest as right, as if thou had'st been one of that number it has languisht for.—I find you'l be better acquainted with it, nor can you take it in a better time; for I am come from Sea, Child, and *Venus* not being propitious to me in her own Element: I have a world of Love in store—wou'd you wou'd be good natur'd and take some on't off my hands.

HELLENA: Whe—I cou'd be inclin'd that way—but for a Foolish Vow I am going to make—to dye a Maid.

WILLMORE: Then thou art damn'd without redemption, and as I am a good Christian, I ought in Charity to divert so wicked a design—therefore prithee dear Creature to let me know quickly when, and where I shall begin to set a helping hand to so good a Work.

HELLENA: If you shou'd prevail with my tender heart (as I begin to fear you will, for you have horrible loving Eyes) there will be difficulty in't, that you'l hardly undergo for my sake.

WILLMORE: Faith Child I have been bred in dangers, and wear a Sword, that has been employ'd in a worse Cause, than for a handsome kind Woman—name the danger—let it be any thing but a long Siege—and I'le undertake it.

HELLENA: Can you storm?

WILLMORE: Oh most furiously.

HELLENA: What think you of a Nunnery Wall? for he that wins me, must gain that first.

WILLMORE: A Nun! Oh how I love thee for't! there's no sinner like a young Saint—nay now there's no denying me, the Old Law had no Curse (to a Woman) like dying a Maid; witness *Jeptha's* Daughter.

HELLENA: A very good Text this, if well handled, and I perceive Father Captain, you wou'd impose no severe penance on her who were inclin'd to Console her self, before she took Orders.

WILLMORE: If she be Young and Handsome.

HELLENA: Ay there's it—but if she be not—

WILLMORE: By this hand, Child, I have an Implicit Faith, and dare venture on thee with all Faults—besides, 'tis more meritorious to leave the World, when thou hast tasted and prov'd the pleasure on't. Then 'twill be a virtue in thee, which now will be pure Ignorance.

HELLENA: I perceive good Father Captain, you design only to make me fit for Heaven—but if on the contrary, you shou'd quite divert me from it, and bring me back to the World again, I shou'd have a new Man to seek I find; and what a grief that will be—for when I begin, I fancy I shall love like any thing, I never try'd yet.

WILLMORE: Egad and that's kind—prithee dear Creature, give me credit for a Heart, for faith I'm a very honest Fellow—Oh, I long to come first to the Banquet of Love! and such a swinging Appetite I bring—Oh I'm impatient.—thy Lodging sweetheart, thy Lodging! or I'm a dead Man!

HELLENA: Why must we be either guilty of Fornication or Murder if we converse with you Men—and is there no difference between leave to love me, and leave to lye with me?

WILLMORE: Faith Child they were made to go together.

LUCETTA: Are you sure this is the Man? *Pointing to Blunt*

SANCHO: When did I mistake your Game?

LUCETTA: This is a Stranger, I know by his gazing; if he be brisk, he'l venture to follow me; and then if I understand my Trade, he's mine, he's English too; and they say that's a sort of good natur'd loving People, and have generally so kind an opinion of themselves, that a Woman with any Wit may Flatter 'em into any sort of Fool she pleases.

*She often passes by Blunt, and gazes on him, he struts and Cocks, and walks and gazes on her*

BLUNT: 'Tis so—she is taken—I have Beauties which my false Glass at home did not discover.

FLORINDA: This Woman watches me so, I shall get no opportunity to discover my self to him, and so miss the intent of my coming—but as I was saying, Sir,—by this Line you shou'd be a Lover.

*Looking in his hand*

BELVILE: I thought how right you guest, all Men are in Love, or pretend to be so—come let me go, I'm weary of this fooling.

*Walks away. She holds him, he strives to get from her*

FLORINDA: I will not, till you have confest whether the Passion that you have vow'd *Florinda*, be true or false?

BELVILE: *Florinda*! *Turns quick towards her*

FLORINDA: Softly.

BELVILE: Thou hast nam'd one will fix me here for ever.

FLORINDA: She'll be disappointed then, who expects you this Night at the Garden-gate, and if you fail not—as let me see the other hand—you will go near to do—she vows to dye or make you happy.

*Looks on Callis who observes 'em*

BELVILE: What canst thou mean?

FLORINDA: That which I say—Farewel. *Offers to go*

BELVILE: Oh charming Sybil stay, complete that joy which as it is will turn into destraction!—where must I be? at the Garden-gate? I know it—at Night you say?—I'll sooner forfeit Heav'n than disobey.

*Enter* DON PEDRO *and other* MASQUERS, *and pass over the Stage*

CALLIS: Madam, your Brother's here.

FLORINDA: Take this to instruct you farther. *Gives him a Letter, and goes off*

FREDERICK: Have a care, Sir, what you promise; this may be a Trap laid by her Brother to ruine you.

BELVILE: Do not disturb my happiness with doubts. *Opens the Letter*

WILLMORE: My dear pretty Creature, a Thousand Blessings on thee! still in this habit you say? —and after Dinner at this place.

HELLENA: Yes, if you will swear to keep your heart, and not bestow it between this and that.

WILLMORE: By all the little Gods of Love I swear, I'l leave it with you, and if you run away with it, those Deities of Justice will revenge me. *Exeunt all the Women*

FREDERICK: Do you know the hand?

BELVILE: 'Tis *Florinda*'s.
All Blessings fall upon the virtuous Maid.

FREDERICK: Nay, no Idolatry, a sober Sacrifice I'l allow you.

BELVILE: Oh Friends, the welcom'st News! the softest Letter!—nay you shall all see it! and cou'd you now be serious, I might be made the happiest Man the Sun shines on!

WILLMORE: The reason of this mighty joy?

BELVILE: See how kindly she invites me to deliver her from the threatned violence of her Brother—will you not assist me?

WILLMORE: I know not what thou mean'st, but I'll make one at any mischief where a Woman's concerned—but she'l be grateful to us for the favour, will she not?

BELVILE: How mean you?

WILLMORE: How shou'd I mean? thou know'st there's but one way for a Woman to oblige me.

BELVILE: Do not prophane—the Maid is nicely virtuous.

WILLMORE: Who Pox, then she's fit for nothing but a husband, let her e'n go, Colonel.

FREDERICK: Peace, she's the Colonel's Mistris, Sir.

WILLMORE: Let her be the Devil, if she be thy Mistris, I'l serve her—name the way.

BELVILE: Read here this Postscript. *Gives him a Letter*

WILLMORE (*Reads*): *At Ten at night—at the Garden-Gate—of which, if I cannot get the Key, I will contrive a way over the Wall—come attended with a Friend or Two.*— Kind Heart, if we Three cannot weave a string to let her down a Garden-Wall, 'twere pity but the Hang-man wove one for us all.

FREDERICK: Let her alone for that, your Womans wit! your fair kind Woman! will out-trick a Broker or a Jew: and contrive like a Jesuit in Chains—but see, *Ned Blunt* is stolne out after the Lure of a Damsel. *Exeunt Blunt and Lucetta*

BELVILE: So, he'll scarce find his way home again, unless we get him cry'd by the Bell-man in the Market-place, and 'twou'd sound prettily—a lost English Boy of Thirty.

FREDERICK: I hope 'tis some Common crafty Sinner, one that will fit him; it may be she'll sell him for *Perue*, the Rogue's sturdy, and wou'd work well in a Mine; at least I hope she'll dress him for our Mirth, cheat him of all, then have him well-favourd'ly bang'd, and turn'd out Naked at Midnight.

WILLMORE: Prithee what humour is he of, that you wish him so well?

BELVILE: Why of an *English* Elder Brother's humour, Educated in a Nursery, with a Maid to tend him till Fifteen, and lyes with his Grand-Mother till he's of Age: one that knowes no pleasure beyond riding to the next Fair, or going up to *London* with his right Worshipful Father in Parliament-time; wearing gay Cloths, or making honourable Love to his Lady Mothers Landry-Maid: gets drunk at a Hunting-Match, and ten to one then gives some proofs of his Prowess.—A Pox upon him, he's our *Banker*, and has all our Cash about him, and if he fail, we are all Broke.

FREDERICK: Oh let him alone for that matter, he's of a damn'd stingey quality, that will secure our stock; I know not in what danger it were indeed if the Jilt shou'd pretend she's in Love with him, for 'tis a kind believing Coxcomb; otherwise if he part with more than a piece of Eight—gueld him: for which offer he may chance to be beaten, if she be a Whore of the First Rank.

BELVILE: Nay the Rogue will not be easily beaten, he's stout enough; perhaps if they talk beyond his capacity, he may chance to exercise his Courage upon some of them, else I'm sure they'll find it as difficult to beat as to please him.

WILLMORE: 'Tis a luckey Devil to light upon so kind a Wench!

FREDERICK: Thou had'st a great deal of talk with thy little Gipsie, coud'st thou do no good upon her? for mine was hard-hearted:

WILLMORE: Hang her, she was some damn'd honest Person of Quality I'm sure, she was so very free and witty. If her face be but answerable to her Witt, and humour, I wou'd be bound to Constancy this Moneth to gain her—in the mean time, have you made no kind acquaintance since you came to Town?—you do not use to be honest so long, Gentlemen.

FREDERICK: Faith Love has kept us honest, we have been all fir'd with a Beauty newly come to Town, the Famous *Paduana Angellica Bianca.*

WILLMORE: What the Mistris of the dead *Spanish* General?

BELVILE: Yes, she's now the only ador'd Beauty of all the Youth in *Naples*, who put on all their Charms to appear lovely in her sight, their Coaches, Liveries, and themselves, all gay, as on a Monarch's Birth-Day, to attract the Eyes of this fair Charmer, while she has the pleasure to behold all languish for her that see her.

FREDERICK: 'Tis pretty to see with how much Love the Men regard her, and how much Envy the Women.

WILLMORE: What Gallant has she?

BELVILE: None, she's expos'd to Sale, and Four days in the Week she's yours—for so much a Month.

WILLMORE: The very thought of it quenches all manner of Fire in me—yet prithee let's see her.

BELVILE: Let's first to Dinner, and after that wee'l pass the day as you please—but at Night yee must all be at my Devotion.

WILLMORE: I will not fail you.

*The End of the First Act*

## ACT II

### SCENE 1

*The Long Street*

*Enter* BELVILE *and* FREDERICK *in Masquing Habits, and* WILLMORE *in his own Cloaths, with a Vizard in his Hand*

WILLMORE: But why thus disguis'd and muzzel'd?

BELVILE: Because whatever Extravagances we commit in these Faces, our own may not be oblig'd to answer 'em.

WILLMORE: I shou'd have chang'd my Eternal Buffe too; but no matter, my little Gipsie wou'd not have found me out then; for if she shou'd change hers, it is impossible I should know her, unless I should hear her prattle.—A Pox on't, I cannot get her out of my Head: Pray Heaven, if ever I do see her again, she prove damnably ugly, that I may fortifie my self against her Tongue.

BELVILE: Have a care of Love; for o' my conscience she was not of a quality to give thee any hopes.

WILLMORE: Pox on 'em, why do they draw a Man in then? She has play'd with my Heart so, that 'twill never lye still, till I have met with some kind Wench, that will play the Game out with me—Oh for my Arms full of soft, white, kind—Woman! such as I fancy *Angellica.*

BELVILE: This is her House, if you were but in stock to get admittance; they have not din'd yet; I perceive the Picture is not out.

*Enter* BLUNT

WILLMORE: I long to see the Shadow of the fair Substance; a Man may gaze on that for nothing.

BLUNT: Colonel, Thy Hand—and thine *Fred.* I have been an Ass, a deluded Fool, a very Coxcomb from my Birth till this hour, and heartily repent my little Faith.

BELVILE: What the Devil's the matter with thee *Ned*?

[BLUNT]: —Oh such a Mistris, *Fred.* such a Girl!

WILLMORE: Ha! where.

FREDERICK: Ay where!

[BLUNT]: So fond, so amorous, so toying and so fine! and all for sheer Love ye Rogue! Oh how she lookt and kist! and sooth'd my Heart from my Bosom—I cannot think I was awake, and yet methinks I see and feel her charms still—*Fred.*—Try if she have not left the taste of her Balmey Kisses upon my Lips— *Kisses him*

BELVILE: Ha! Ha! Ha!

WILLMORE: Death Man where is she?

[BLUNT]: —What a Dog was I to stay in dull *England* so long,—How have I laught at the Colonel, when he sigh'd for Love! but now the little Archer has reveng'd him! and by this one Dart, I can guess at all his joys, which then I took for Fancies, meer Dreams and Fables.—Well, I'm resolv'd to sell all in *Essex*, and plant here for ever.

BELVILE: What a Blessing 'tis, thou hast a Mistris thou dar'st boast of; for I know thy Humour is, rather to have a proclaim'd Clap, than a secret Amour.

WILLMORE: Dost know her Name?

BLUNT: Her Name? No, 'sheartlikins what care I for Names.—She's fair! young! brisk and kind! even to ravishment! and what a Pox care I for knowing her by any other Title.

WILLMORE: Didst give her any thing?

BLUNT: Give her! —Ha, ha, ha! whe she's a Person of Quality; —that's a good one, give her! 'sheartlikins dost think such Creatures are to be bought? Or are we provided for such a Purchase? give her quoth ye? Why she presented me with this Bracelet, for the Toy of a Diamond I us'd to wear: No, Gentlemen, *Ned Blunt* is not every Body—She expects me again to Night.

WILLMORE: Egad that's well; we'll all go.

BLUNT: Not a Soul: No, Gentlemen, you are Wits; I am a dull Countrey Rogue, I.

FREDERICK: Well, Sir, for all your Person of Quality, I shall be very glad to understand your Purse be secure; 'tis our whole Estate at present, which we are loth to hazard in one Bottom; come, Sir, unlade.

BLUNT: Take the necessary Trifle useless now to me, that am belov'd by such a Gentlewoman—'sheartlikins Money! Here take mine too.

FREDERICK: No, keep that to be couzen'd, that we may laugh.

WILLMORE: Couzen'd!—Death! wou'd I cou'd meet with one, that wou'd couzen me of all the Love I cou'd spare to Night.

FREDERICK: Pox, 'tis some common Whore upon my life.

BLUNT: A Whore!—yes with such Cloths! such Jewels! such a House! such Furniture, and so Attended! a Whore!

BELVILE: Why yes Sir, they are Whores, tho' they'll neither entertain you with Drinking, Swearing, or Bawdry; are Whores in all those gay Cloths, and right Jewels, are Whores with those great Houses richly furnisht with Velvet Beds, Store of Plate, handsome Attendance, and fine Coaches, are Whores and Errant ones.

WILLMORE: Pox on't, where do these fine Whores live?

BELVILE: Where no Rogues in Office Eclipsed Constables, dare give 'em Laws, nor the Wine Inspir'd Bullies of the Town, break their Windows; yet they are Whores tho this *Essex* Calf believe 'em Persons of Quality.

BLUNT: 'Sheartlikins, y'are all Fools, there are things about this *Essex* Calf, that shall take with the Ladies, beyond all your Witt and Parts—this Shape and Size Gentlemen are not to be despis'd—my Waist too tolerably long, with other inviting signs, that shall be nameless.

WILLMORE: Egad I believe he may have met with some Person of Quality that may be kind to him.

BELVILE: Dost thou perceive any such tempting things about him, that shou'd make a fine Woman, and of Quality, pick him out from all Mankind, to throw away her Youth and Beauty upon, nay and her dear heart too!—no, no, *Angellica* has rais'd the Price too high.

WILLMORE: May she languish for Mankind till she dye, and be damn'd for that one sin alone.

*Enter* TWO BRAVO's, *and hang up a great Picture of Angellica's, against the Balcone, and Two little ones at each side of the Door*

BELVILE: See there the fair Sign to the Inn where a Man may Lodg that's Fool enough to give her price. *Willmore gazes on the Picture*

BLUNT: 'Sheartlikins, Gentlemen, what's this!

BELVILE: A Famous *Courtizan*, that's to be sold.

BLUNT: How? to be sold! nay then I have nothing to say to her—sold! what Impudence is practic'd in this Countrey?—with what Order and decency Whoring's Establisht here by Virtue of the Inquisition—come let's begone, I'm sure wee're no Chapmen for this Commodity.

FREDERICK: Thou art none I'm sure, unless thou coud'st have her in thy Bed at a price of a Coach in the Street.

WILLMORE: How wondrous fair she is—a Thousand Crowns a Month—by Heaven as many Kingdoms were too little, a plague of this Poverty—of which I ne're complain, but when it hinders my approach to Beauty: which Virtue ne're cou'd purchase. *Turns from the Picture*

BLUNT: What's this?—(*Reads*) *A Thousand Crowns a Month!*
—'Sheartlikins here's a Sum! sure 'tis a mistake.
—Heark you Friend, does she take or give so much by the Month?

FREDERICK: A Thousand Crowns! why 'tis a Portion for the *Infanta.*

BLUNT: Heark ye Friends, won't she trust?

BRAVO: This is a Trade, Sir, that cannot live by Credit.

*Enter* DON PEDRO *in Masquerade, follow'd by* STEPHANO

BELVILE: See, here's more Company, let's walk off a while.

*Exeunt English. Pedro Reads*

*Enter* ANGELLICA *and* MORETTA *in the Balcone, and draw a Silk Curtain*

PEDRO: Fetch me a thousand Crowns, I never wisht to buy this beauty at an easier rate. *passes off*

ANGELLICA: Prithee what said those Fellows to thee?

BRAVO: Madam, the first were admirers of Beauty only, but no purchasers, they were merry with your Price and Picture, laught at the Sum, and so past off.

ANGELLICA: No Matter, I'm not displeas'd with their rallying; their wonder feeds my vanity, and he that wishes but to buy, gives me more Pride, than he that gives my Price, can make my pleasure.

BRAVO: Madam, the last I knew through all his disguises to be *Don Pedro*, Nephew to the General, and who was with him in *Pamplona.*

ANGELLICA: *Don Pedro*! my old Gallant's Nephew, when his Uncle dy'd he left him a vast Sum of Money; it is he who was so in love with me at *Padua*, and who us'd to make the General so Jealous.

MORETTA: Is this he that us'd to prance before our Window, and take such care to shew himself an Amorous Ass? If I am not mistaken he is the likeliest Man to give your price.

ANGELLICA: The Man is brave and generous, but of an humour so uneasie and inconstant, that the victory over his heart is as soon lost as won, a Slave that can add little to the Triumph of the Conquerour, but Inconstancy's the sin of all Mankind, therefore I'm resolv'd that nothing but Gold, shall charm my heart.

MORETTA: I'm glad on't; 'tis only Interest that Women of our profession ought to consider: tho' I wonder what has kept you from that general Disease of our Sex so long, I mean that of being in Love.

ANGELLICA: A kind, but sullen Star under which I had the happiness to be born; yet I have had no time for Love; the bravest and noblest of Mankind have purchast my favours at so dear a rate, as if no Coin but Gold were currant with our Trade—but here's *Don Pedro* again, fetch me my Lute—for 'tis for him or *Don Antonio* the Vice-Roys Son, that I have spread my Nets.

*Enter at one Door* DON PEDRO, STEPHANO*;* DON ANTONIO *and* DIEGO *at the other Door with People following him in Masquerade, antickly attir'd, some with Musick, they both go up to the Picture*

ANTONIO: A Thousand Crowns! had not the Painter flatter'd her, I shou'd not think it dear.

PEDRO: Flatter'd her! by Heav'n he cannot, I have seen the Original, nor is there one Charm here more than Adorns her Face and Eyes; all this soft and sweet, with a certain languishing Air, that no Artist can represent.

ANTONIO: What I heard of her Beauty before had fir'd my Soul, but this confirmation of it has blown it to a flame.

PEDRO: Ha!

[DIEGO]: Sir, I have known you throw away a Thousand Crowns on a worse face, and tho y'are near your Marriage, you may venture a little Love here; *Florinda* will not miss it.

PEDRO: Ha! *Florinda*!—sure 'tis *Antonio.* *Aside*

ANTONIO: *Florinda*! name not those distant joyes, there's not one thought of her will check my Passion here.

PEDRO: *Florinda* scorn'd! and all my hopes defeated, of the Possession of *Angellica.* Her Injuries! by Heaven he shall not boast of. [*Aside*]

*A noise of a Lute above. Antonio gazes up.*

*Song to a Lute above*

SONG

*When* Damon *first began to Love*
*He languisht in a soft desire,*
*And knew not how the Gods to move,*
*To lessen or increase his Fire.*
*For* Cælia *in her charming Eyes*
*Wore all Love's sweets, and all his cruelties.*

II

*But as beneath a Shade he lay,*
*Weaving of Flow'rs for* Cælia*'s hair,*
*She chanc't to lead her Flock that way,*
*And saw the Am'rous Shepherd there.*
*She gaz'd around upon the place,*
*And saw the Grove (resembling Night)*
*To all the joys of Love invite,*
*Whilst guilty smiles and blushes drest her Face.*
*At this the bashful Youth all Transport grew,*
*And with kind force he taught the Virgin how*
*To yield what all his sighs cou'd never do.*

ANGELLICA *throws open the Curtains, and bows to Antonio, who pulls off his Vizard and bows and blows up kisses. Pedro unseen looks in's face*

ANTONIO: By Heav'n she's charming fair!
PEDRO: 'Tis he; the false *Antonio*! [*Aside*]
ANTONIO: Friend, where must I pay my Offring of Love? *To the Bravo*
My Thousand Crowns I mean.
PEDRO: That Offring I have design'd to make.
And yours will come too late.
ANTONIO: Prithee begone, I shall grow angry else.
And then thou art not safe.
PEDRO: My Anger may be fatal, Sir, as yours;
And he that enters here may prove this truth.
ANTONIO: I know that who thou art, but I am sure thou'rt worth my killing, for aiming at *Angelica*.

*They draw and fight*

*Enter* WILLMORE *and* BLUNT, *who draw and part 'em*

BLUNT: 'Sheartlikins here's fine doings.
WILLMORE: Tilting for the Wench I'm sure—nay gad, if that wou'd win her, I have as good a Sword as the best of ye.—Put up,—put up, and take another time and place, for this is design'd for Lovers only. *They all put up*

PEDRO: We are prevented; dare you meet me to Morrow on the *Molo*?
For I've a Title to a better quarrel,
That of *Florinda* in whose credulous heart
Thou'st, made an Int'rest, and destroyd my hopes.

ANTONIO: Dare!
I'll meet thee there as early as the day.

PEDRO: We will come thus disguis'd, that whosoever chance to get the better, he may escape unk[n]own.

ANTONIO: It shall be so. *Exeunt Pedro and Stephano*
Who shou'd this Rival be? unless the *English* Colonel, of whom I've often heard *Don Pedro* speak; it must be he, and time he were remov'd, who lays a claim to all my happiness.

*Willmore having gaz'd all this while on the Picture, pulls down a little one*

WILLMORE: This Posture's loose and negligent,
The sight on't wou'd beget a warm desire,
In Souls whom Impotence and Age had chill'd.
—This must along with me.

BRAVO: What means this rudeness, Sir? —restore the Picture.

ANTONIO: Ha! Rudeness committed to the fair *Angellica*!
—Restore the Picture, Sir—

WILLMORE: Indeed I will not, Sir.

ANTONIO: By Heav'n but you shall.

WILLMORE: Nay, do not shew your Sword, if you do, by this dear Beauty—I will shew mine too.

ANTONIO: What right can you pretend to't?

WILLMORE: That of Possession which I will maintain—you perhaps have a 1000 Crowns to give for the Original.

ANTONIO: No matter, Sir, you shall restore the Picture.

ANGELLICA: Oh *Moretta*! what's the matter? *Angellica and Moretta above*

ANTONIO: Or leave your life behind,

WILLMORE: Death! you lye—I will do neither.

ANGELLICA: Hold, I command you, if for me you Fight.

*They Fight, the Spaniards joyn with Antonio, Blunt [joins with Willmore] laying on like mad. They leave off and bow*

WILLMORE: How Heavenly fair she is!—ah Plague of her price.

ANGELLICA: You Sir in Buffe, you that appear a Souldier, that first began this Insolence—

WILLMORE: 'Tis true, I did so, if you call it Insolence for a Man to preserve himself; I saw your Charming Picture and was wounded; quite through my Soul each pointed Beauty ran; and wanting a Thousand Crowns to procure my remedy—I laid this little Picture to my Bosom—which if you cannot allow me, I'll resign.

ANGELLICA: No you may keep the Trifle.

ANTONIO: You shall first ask me leave, and this. *Fight again as before.*

*Enter* BELVILE *and* FREDERICK *who joyn with the English*

ANGELLICA: Hold! will you ruine me!—*Biskey—Sebastian*—part' em.

*The Spaniards are beaten off. [Exeunt men]*

MORETTA: Oh Madam, we're undone, a pox upon that rude Fellow, he's set on to ruine us: we shall never see good days, till all these fighting poor are sent to the Gallies.

*Enter* BELVILE, BLUNT, FREDERICK *and* WILLMORE *with's shirt bloody*

BLUNT: 'Sheartlikins, beat me at this sport, and I'le ne're wear Sword more.

BELVILE: The Devil's in thee for a mad Fellow, thou art always one, at an unluckey Adventure—come let's begon whil'st wee're safe, and remember these are *Spaniards*, a sort of People that know how to revenge an Affront.

FREDERICK: You bleed! I hope you are not wounded. *To Willmore*

WILLMORE: Not much:—a plague on your *Dons*, if they fight no better they'l ne're recover *Flanders*.—what the Devil was't to them that I took down the Picture?

BLUNT: Took it! 'Sheartlikins we'll have the great one too; 'tis ours by Conquest.—prithee help me up and I'll pull it down—

ANGELLICA: Stay Sir, and e're you Affront me farther, let me know how you durst commit this out-rage—to you I speak Sir, for you appear a Gentleman.

WILLMORE: To me, Madam—Gentlemen your Servant.

BELVILE: Is the Devil in thee? do'st know the danger of entring the house of an incens'd *Courtizan*? *Belvile stays him*

WILLMORE: I thank you for your care—but there are other matters in hand, there are, tho we have no great Temptation—Death! let me go.

FREDERICK: Yes to your Lodging if you will, but not in here.—Damn these Gay Harlots—by this hand I'll have as sound and handsome a Whore, for a Patacoone, —death Man, she'll Murder thee.

WILLMORE: Oh! fear me not, shall I not venture where a Beauty calls? a lovely Charming Beauty! for fear of danger! when by Heav'n there's none so great, as to long for her, whil'st I want Mo[ney] to purchase her.

FREDERICK: Therefore 'tis loss of time unless you had the Thousand Crowns to pay.

WILLMORE: It may be she may give a Favour, at least I shall have the pleasure of Saluting her when I enter, and when I depart.

BELVILE: Pox, she'll as soon lye with thee, as kiss thee, and sooner stab than do either—you shall not go.

ANGELLICA: Fear not Sir, all I have to wound with is my Eyes.

BLUNT: Let him go, 'Sheartlikins, I believe the Gentlewoman means well.

BELVILE: Well take thy Fortune, we'll expect you in the next Street—farewell Fool—Farewell—

WILLMORE: 'Bye Colonel— *Goes in*

FREDERICK: The Rogue's stark mad for a Wench. *Exeunt*

## SCENE 2

*A fine Chamber*

*Enter* WILLMORE, ANGELLICA *and* MORETTA

ANGELLICA: Insolent Sir, how durst you pull down my Picture?

WILLMORE: Rather, how durst you set it up, to tempt poor Am'rous Mortals with so much excellence? which I find you have but too well consulted by the unmerciful price you set upon't.—Is all this Heaven of Beauty shewn to move despair in those that cannot buy? and can you think th' effects of that despair, shou'd be less extravagant than I have shewn?

ANGELLICA: I sent for you to ask my Pardon Sir, not to Aggravate your Crime—I thought I shou'd have seen you at my Feet imploring it.

WILLMORE: You are deceiv'd, I came to rail at you, and rail such truths too, as shall let you see, the vanity of that Pride, which taught you how, to set such Price on Sin. For such it is, whilst that which is Love's due is meanly barter'd for.

ANGELLICA: Ha! ha! ha! alas good Captain, what pitty 'tis your edifying Doctrine will do no good upon me—*Moretta*! fetch the Gentleman a Glass, and let him surveigh himself. To see what Charms he has—and guess my business. *Aside, in a soft tone*

MORETTA: He knows himself of Old, I believe those Breeches and he have been acquainted ever since he was beaten at *Worcester*.

ANGELLICA: Nay do not abuse the poor Creature—

MORETTA: Good Weather beaten Corporal, will you march off? we have no need of your Doctrine, tho' you have of our Charity, but at present we have no scraps, we can afford no kindness for God's sake; in fine Sirrah, the price is too high i'th'Mouth for you, therefore Troop I say.

WILLMORE: Here good Fore-Woman of the Shop serve me, and I'll be gone.

MORETTA: Keep it to pay your La[u]ndress, your Linnen stinks of the Gun Room; for here's no selling by Retail.

WILLMORE: Thou hast sold plenty of thy Stale Ware at a Cheap rate.

MORETTA: Ay the more Silly kind Heart I, but this is an Age wherein Beauty is at higher rates—In fine you know the price of this.

WILLMORE: I grant you 'tis here—set down a Thousand Crowns a Month—pray how much may come to my Share for a Pistol.—Bawd take your black Lead and Sum it up, that I may have a Pistols worth of this vain gay thing, and I'll trouble you no more.

MORETTA: Pox on him he'll fret me to death:—abominable Fellow, I tell thee, wee only sell by the whole piece.

WILLMORE: 'Tis very hard, the whole Cargo or nothing—Faith Madam, my Stock will not reach it, I cannot be your Chapman—Yet I have Country Men in Town, Merchants of Love like me; I'll see if they'll put in for a Share, we cannot lose much by it, and what we have no use for, we'll sell upon the *Frydays* Mart at—*Who gives more*? I am studying Madam how to purchase you, tho' at present I am unprovided of Money.

ANGELLICA: Sure this from any other Man would anger me—nor shall he know the Conquest he has made [*Aside*]—poor angry Man, how I despise this railing.

WILLMORE: Yes, I am poor—but I'm a Gentleman,
And one that Scornes this baseness which you practice;
Poor as I am, I wou'd not sell my self,
No not to gain your Charming high priz'd Person.
Tho' I admire you strangely for your Beauty,
Yet I contemn your mind.
—And yet I wou'd at any rate enjoy you,
At your own rate—but cannot—see here
The only Sum I can command on Earth;
I know not where to eat when this is gon.
Yet such a Slave I am to Love and Beauty
This last reserve I'll sacrifice to enjoy you.
—Nay do not frown, I know you're to be bought,
And wou'd be bought by me, by me,
For a mean triffling sum if I cou'd pay it down
Which happy knowledge I will still repeat,
And lay it to my Heart, it has a Virtue in't,
And soon will cure those Wounds your Eyes have made.
—And yet—there's something so Divinely powerful there—
Nay I will gaze—to let you see my strength.
*Holds her, looks on her, and pawses and sighs*
—By Heav'n bright Creature—I would not for the World
Thy Fame were half so fair, as is thy Face. *Turns her away from him*

ANGELLICA: His words go through me to the very Soul. *Aside*
—If you have nothing else to say to me—

WILLMORE: Yes, you shall hear how Infamous you are—
For which I do not hate thee—
But that secures my heart, and all the Flames it feels
Are but so many Lusts—
I know it by their sudden bold Intrusion.
The Fire's impatient and betrays, 'tis false—
For had it been the purer flame of Love,
I shou'd have pin'd and languisht at your feet,
E're found the impudence to have discover'd it.
I now dare stand your scorn, and your denyal.

MORETTA: Sure she's bewitch, that she can stand thus tamely and hear his sawcy railing [*Aside*]—Sirrah, will you be gon?

ANGELLICA: How dare you take this Liberty?—withdraw. *To Moretta*
—Pray tell me, Sir, are not you guilty of the same Mercenary Crime, When a Lady is propos'd to you for a Wife, you never ask, how fair—discreet—or virtuous she is; but what's her Fortune—which if but small, you cry—she will not

do my business—and basely leave her, thou she languish for you—say, is not this as poor?

WILLMORE: It is a Barbarous Custome, which I will scorn to defend in our Sex, and do despise in yours.

ANGELLICA: Thou'rt a brave Fellow! put up thy Gold, and know,
That were thy Fortune large as is thy Soul,
Thou shoud'st not buy my Love,
Coudst thou forget those mean effects of vanity
Which set me out to sale, and, as a Lover, prize my yielding joys.
Canst thou believe they'l be intirely thine,
Without considering they were Mercenary?

WILLMORE: I cannot tell, I must bethink me first—ha—death I'm going to believe her. *Aside*

ANGELLICA: Prithee confirm that faith—or if thou canst not—flatter me a little, 'twill please me from thy mouth.

WILLMORE: Curse on thy charming Tongue! dost thou return
My feign'd contempt with so much subtilty? *Aside*
Thou'st found the easiest way into my heart,
Tho I yet know, that all thou say'st is false. *Turning from her in Rage*

ANGELLICA: By all that's good 'tis real,
I never lov'd before, tho oft a Mistress.
—Shall my first Vows be slighted?

WILLMORE: What can she mean? *Aside*

ANGELLICA: I find you cannot credit me.— *In an angry tone*

WILLMORE: I know you take me for an errant Ass,
An Ass that may be sooth'd into belief,
And then be us'd at pleasure;
—But, Madam, I have been so often cheated
By perjur'd soft deluding Hypocrites,
That I've no faith left for the couzening Sex;
Especially for Women of your Trade.

ANGELLICA: The low esteem you have of me, perhaps
May bring my heart again:
For I have pride, that yet surmounts my Love.

*She turns with pride*[:] *he holds her*

WILLMORE: Throw off this Pride, this Enemy to Bliss,
And shew the Pow'r of Love: 'tis with those Arms
I can be only vanquisht, made a Slave.

ANGELLICA: Is all my mighty expectation vanisht?
—No, I will not hear thee talk—thou hast a Charm
In every word that draws my heart away.
And all the Thousand Trophies I design'd
Thou hast undone—Why art thou soft?

Thy looks are bravely rough, and meant for War.
Coud'st thou not storm on still?
I then perhaps had been as free as thou.

WILLMORE: Death, how she throws her Fire about my Soul! *Aside*
—Take heed, fair Creature, how you raise my hopes,
Which once assum'd pretends to all dominion.
There's not a joy thou hast in store,
I shall not then Command.
—For which I'll pay thee back my Soul! my Life!
—Come, let's begin th' account this happy minute!

ANGELLICA: And will you pay me then the price I ask?

WILLMORE: Oh why dost thou draw me from an awful Worship,
By shewing thou art no Divinity.
Conceal the Fiend, and shew me all the Angel!
Keep me but ignorant, and I'll be devout
And pay my Vows for ever at this shrine. *Kneels and kisses her hand*

ANGELLICA: The pay, I mean, is but thy Love for mine.
—Can you give that?

WILLMORE: Intirely—come, let's withdraw! where I'll renew my Vows—and breath 'em with such Ardour thou shalt not doubt my zeal.

ANGELLICA: Thou hast a Pow'r too strong to be resisted.

*Exeunt Willmore and Angellica*

MORETTA: Now my Curse go with you—is all our Project fallen to this? to love the only Enemy to our Trade? nay, to love such a Shameroone, a very Beggar, nay a Pyrate Beggar, whose business is to rifle, and be gone, a no Purchase, no Pay Taterdemalion, and *English* Piccaroon.
A Rogue that fights for daily drink, and takes a Pride in being Loyally Lousie—Oh I cou'd curse now, if I durst.—This is the Fate of most Whores.

*Trophies, which from believing Fops we win,*
*Are Spoils to those who couzen us agen.*

*The End of the Second Act*

## ACT III

### SCENE 1

*A Street*

*Enter* FLORINDA, VALERIA, HELLENA, *in Antick different Dresses, from what they were in before.* CALLIS *attending*

FLORINDA: I wonder what shou'd make my Brother in so ill a humour? I hope he has not found out our Ramble this Morning.

HELLENA: No, if he had, we shou'd have heard on't at both Ears, and have been Mew'd up this Afternoon; which I wou'd not for the World shou'd have hapned—hey ho, I'm as sad as a Lover's Lute.—

VALERIA: Well, methinks we have learnt this Trade of Gipsies as readily, as if we had been bred upon the Road to *Loretta*: and yet I did so fumble, when I told the stranger his Fortune, that I was afraid I should have told my own and yours by mistake—but, methinks *Hellena* has been very serious ever since.

FLORINDA: I wou'd give my Garters she were in Love, to be reveng'd upon her, for abusing me—how is't, *Hellena*?

HELLENA: Ah—wou'd I had never seen my mad Monsieur—and yet for all your laughing, I am not in Love—and yet this small acquaintance o' my Conscience will never out of my head.

VALERIA: Ha, ha, ha—I laugh to think how thou art fitted with a Lover, a fellow that I warrant loves every new Face he sees.

HELLENA: Hum—he has not kept his word with me here—and may be taken up—that thought is not very pleasant to me—what the Deuce shou'd this be now, that I feel?

VALERIA: What is't like?

HELLENA: Nay, the Lord knows—but if I shou'd be hang'd, I cannot choose, but be angry and afraid, when I think, that mad Fellow shou'd be in Love with any Body but me—what to think of my self, I know not—wou'd I cou'd meet with some true damn'd Gipsie, that I might know my Fortune.

VALERIA: Know it! why there's nothing so easie, thou wilt love this wandring Inconstant, till thou findst thy self hang'd about his Neck, and then be as mad to get free again.

FLORINDA: Yes, *Valeria*, we shall see her bestride his Baggage Horse, and follow him to the Campaigne.

HELLENA: So, so, now you are provided for, there's no care taken of poor me—but since you have set my heart a wishing—I am resolv'd to know for what, I will not dye of the Pip, so I will not.

FLORINDA: Art thou mad to talk so? who will like thee well enough to have thee, that hears what a mad Wench thou art?

HELLENA: Like me! I don't intend every he that likes me shall have me, but he that I like; I shou'd have staid in the Nunnery still, if I had lik'd my Lady *Abbesse* as well as she lik'd me—no, I came thence not (as my wise Brother imagines) to take an Eternal Farewel of the World, but to Love, and to be belov'd, and I will be belov'd, or I'll get one of your Men, so I will.

VALERIA: Am I put into the number of Lovers?

HELLENA: You? why Couz, I know thou'rt too good natur'd to leave us in any design: thou wou't venture a Cast, tho thou comest off a loser, especially with such a Gamester.—I observe[d] your Man, and your willing Ear incline that way; and if you are not a Lover, 'tis an Art soon learnt—that I find. *Sighs*

FLORINDA: I wonder how you learnt to Love so easily, I had a 1000 Charms to meet my Eyes and Ears, e're I cou'd yield, and 'twas the knowledge of *Belvile*'s merit, not the surprizing Person took my Soul—thou art too rash to give a heart at first sight.

HELLENA: Hang your considering Lover; I never thought beyond the fancy that 'twas a very pretty, idle, silly, kind of pleasure to pass ones time with, to write little soft Nonsensical Billiets, and with great difficulty and danger receive Answers; in which I shall have my Beauty prais'd, my Wit admir'd, (tho little or none) and have the vanity and pow'r to know I am desirable; then I have the more inclination that way, because I am to be a Nun, and so shall not be suspected to have any such Earthly thoughts about me—but when I walk thus—and sigh thus—they'l think my mind's upon my Monastery, and cry how happy 'tis she's so resolv'd. —But not word of Man.

FLORINDA: What a mad Creature's this?

HELLENA: I'll warrant, if my Brother hears either of you sigh, he cryes (*gravely*)—I fear you have the indiscretion to be in Love, but take heed of the Honour of our House, and your own unspotted Fame, and so he Conjures on till he has laid the soft wing'd God in your Hearts, or broke the Birds Nest—but see here comes your Lover, but where's my Inconstant? let's step aside, and wee may learn something. *Go aside*

*Enter* BELVILE, FREDERICK *and* BLUNT

BELVILE: What means this! the Picture's taken in.

BLUNT: It may be the Wench is good Natur'd, and will be kind Gratis. Your Friend's a proper handsome Fellow.

BELVILE: I rather think she has cut his Throat and is fled: I am mad he shou'd throw himself into dangers—pox on't I shall want him too at Night—let's knock and ask for him.

HELLENA: My Heart goes a pit, a pat, for fear 'tis my Man they talk of.

*Knock, Moretta above*

MORETTA: What wou'd you have!

BELVILE: Tell the stranger that enter'd here about two hours agoe, that his Friends stay here for him.

MORETTA: A Curse upon him for *Moretta*, wou'd he were at the Devil—but he's coming to you.

HELLENA: Ay, Ay, 'tis he! Oh how this vexes me.

BELVILE: And how and how dear Lad, has Fortune smil'd! are we to break her Windows! or raise up Alters to her. Hah!

WILLMORE: Does not my Fortune sit Triumphant on my Brow! dost not see the little wanton God there all gay and smiling. Have I not an Air about my Face and Eyes, that distinguish me from the Crow'd of common Lovers! By Heav'n *Cupids* Quiver has not half so many Darts as her Eyes!—Oh such a Bona Roba! to sleep in her Arms is lying in Fresco, all perfum'd Air about me.

HELLENA: Here's fine encouragement for me to fool on. *Aside*

WILLMORE: Hark'ey where didst thou purchase that rich Canary we drank to day! tell me that I may Adore the Spigot, and Sacrifice to the Butt! the Juice was Divine!

into which I must dip my Rosary, and then bless all things that I would have bold or Fortunate.

BELVILE: Well Sir, let's go take a Bottle, and hear the story of your Success.

FREDERICK: Wou'd not *French* Wine do better.

WILLMORE: Damn the hungry Balderdash, chearful Sack has a generous Virtue in't inspiring a successful confidence, gives Eloquence to the Tongue! and vigour to the Soul! and has in a few hours compleated all my hopes and wishes! There's nothing left to raise a new desire in me—come let's be gay and wanton—and Gentlemen study, study what you want, for here are Friends,—that will supply Gentlemen,—heark! what a Charming sound they make—'tis he and she Gold whil'st here, and shall beget new pleasures every Moment.

BLUNT: But heark'ey Sir, you are not Marryed are you?

WILLMORE: All the honey of Matrimony, but none of the sting Friend.

BLUNT: 'Sheartlikins thou'rt a Fortunate Rogue!

WILLMORE: I am so Sir, let these—inform you!—ha how sweetly they Chime!—pox of Poverty it makes a Man a slave, makes Wit and Honour sneak, my Soul grew lean and rusty for want of credit.

BLUNT: 'Sheartlikins this I like well, it looks like my lucky Bargain! Oh how I long for the approach of my Squire, that is to conduct me to her House again whe— here's two provided for.

FREDERICK: By this light y'are happy Men.

BLUNT: Fortune is pleas'd to smile on us Gentlemen—to smile on us.

*Enter* SANCHO *and pulls down Blunt by the sleeve. They go aside*

SANCHO: Sir my Lady expects you—she has remov'd all that might oppose your will and pleasure—and is impatient till you come.

BLUNT: Sir I'll attend you—oh the happiest Rogue! I'll take no leave, least they either dog me, or stay me. *Exit with Sancho*

BELVILE: But then the little Gipsie is forgot?

WILLMORE: A mischief on thee for putting her into my thoughts, I had quite forgot her else, and this Nights debauch had drunk her quite down.

HELLENA: Had it so good Captain! *Claps him on the Back*

WILLMORE: Hah! I hope she did not hear me. *Aside*

HELLENA: What, afraid of such a Champion?

WILLMORE: Oh! you're a fine Lady of your word, are you not? to make a Man languish a whole day—

HELLENA: In tedious search of me.

WILLMORE: Egad Child thou'rt in the right, had'st thou seen what a Melancholy Dog I have been ever since I was a Lover, how I have walkt the streets like a *Capuchin* with my Hands in my Sleeves—Faith sweet Heart thou would'st pitty me.

HELLENA: Now if I shou'd be hang'd I can't be angry with him he dissembles so Heartily [*Aside*]—alas good Captain what pains you have taken—now were I ungrateful not to reward so true a Servant.

WILLMORE: Poor Soul! that's kindly said, I see thou barest a Conscience—come then for a beginning shew me thy dear Face.

HELLENA: I'm afraid, my small acquaintance, you have been staying that swinging Stomach you boasted of this Morning; I then remember my little Collation wou'd have gone down with you, without the Sauce of a handsome Face—is your Stomach so queasiy now?

WILLMORE: Faith long fasting Child, spoils a Mans Appetite—yet if you durst treat, I cou'd so lay about me still—

HELLENA: And wou'd you fall to, before a Priest says Grace?

WILLMORE: Oh fie, fie, what an Old out of fashion'd thing hast thou nam'd? thou cou'st not dash me more out of Countenance shoud'st thou shew me an an ugly Face.

*Whilst he is seemingly Courting Hellena enter* ANGELLICA[,] MORETTA[,] BISKEY *and* SEBASTIAN *all in Masquerade, Angellica sees Willmore and stares*

ANGELLICA: Heavens 't[i]s he! and passionately fond to see another Woman.

MORETTA: What cou'd you less expect from such a swaggerer?

ANGELLICA: Expect! as much as I paid him, a Heart intire
Which I had Pride enough to think when 'ere I gave,
It would have rais'd the Man above the Vulgar
Made him all Soul! and that all soft and constant.

HELLENA: You see Captain, how willing I am to be Friends with you, till time and ill luck make us Lovers, and ask you the Question first, rather than put your Modesty to the blush, by asking me (for alas!) I know you Captains are such strict Men, and such severe observers of your Vows to Chastity, that 'twill be hard to prevail with your tender Conscience to Marry a young willing Maid.

WILLMORE: Do not abuse me, for fear I shou'd take thee at thy word, and Marry thee indeed, which I'm sure will be revenge sufficient.

HELLENA: O' my Conscience, that will be our Destiny, because we are both of one humour; I am as inconstant as you, for I have consider'd, Captain, that a handsome Woman has a great deal to do whilst her Face is good, for then is our Harvest-time to gather Friends; and should I in these dayes of my Youth, catch a fit of foolish Constancy, I were undone; 'tis loitering by day-light in our great Journey: therefore I declare, I'll allow but one year for Love, one year for indifference, and one year for hate—and then—go hang yourself—for I profess my self the gay, the kind, and the Inconstant—the Devil's in't if this won't please you.

WILLMORE: Oh most damnably—I have a heart with a hole quite through it too, no Prison mine to keep a Mistress in.

ANGELLICA: Perjur'd Man! how I believe thee now. *Aside*

HELLENA: Well, I see our business as well as humours are alike, yours to couzen as many Maids as will trust you, and I as many Men as have Faith—see if I have not as desperate a lying look, as you can have for the heart of you.

*Pulls off her Vizard: he starts*

—How do you like it Captain?

WILLMORE: Like it! by Heav'n, I never saw so much beauty! Oh the Charms of those sprightly black Eyes! that strangely fair Face! full of smiles and dimples! those soft round melting Cherry Lips! and small even white Teeth! not to be exprest, but silently ador'd!—oh one look more! and strike me dumb, or I shall repeat nothing else till I'm mad.

*He seems to Court her to pull off her Vizar: she refuses*

ANGELLICA: I can endure no more—nor is it fit to interrupt him, for if I do, my Jealousie has so destroy'd my Reason,—I shall undo him—therefore I'l retire—and you, *Sebastian*, *To one of her Bravo's* follow that Woman, and learn who 'tis; while you tell the Fugitive, I wou'd speak to him instantly. *To the other Bravo*

*Exit [Angellica]. This while Florinda is talking to Belvile, who stands sullenly. Frederick courting Valeria*

VALERIA: Prithee, dear stranger, be not so sullen, for tho you have lost your Love, you see my Friend franckly offers you hers to play with in the mean time.

BELVILE: Faith Madam, I am sorry I can't play at her Game.

FREDERICK: Pray leave your Intercession, and mind your own Affair, they'l better agree apart; he's a modest sigher in Company, but alone no Woman scapes him.

FLORINDA: Sure he does but rally—yet if it shou'd be true—I'll tempt him farther—believe me, Noble Stranger, I'm no common Mistris—and for a little proof on't—wear this Jewel—nay, take it, Sir, 'tis right, and Bills of Exchange may sometimes miscarry.

BELVILE: Madam, why am I chose out of all Mankind to be the Object of your Bounty?

VALERIA: There's another civil Question askt.

FREDERICK: Pox of's Modesty, it spoils his own Markets & hinders mine. [*Aside*]

FLORINDA: Sir, from my Window I have often seen you, and Women of my Quality have so few opportunities for Love, that we ought to loose none.

FREDERICK: Ay, this is something! here's a Woman!—when shall I be blest with so much kindness from your fair Mouth?—take the Jewel, Fool. *Aside to Belvile*

BELVILE: You tempt me strangely Madam every way—

FLORINDA: So, if I find him false, my whole Repose is gone. *Aside*

BELVILE: And but for a Vow I've made to a very fair Lady, this goodness had subdu'd me.

FREDERICK: Pox on't be kind, in pitty to me be kind, for I am to thrive here but as you treat her Friend.

HELLENA: Tell me what you did in yonder House, and I'll unmasque.

WILLMORE: Yonder House—oh—I went to—a—to—why there's a Friend of mine lives there.

HELLENA: What a Shee, or a Hee Friend?

WILLMORE: A Man upon Honour! a Man—a Shee Friend—no, no Madam you have done my business I thank you.

HELLENA: And wast your Man Friend, that had more Darts in's Eyes, than *Cupid* carries in's whole Budget of Arrowes.

WILLMORE: So—

HELLENA: Ah such a *Bona Roba*! to be in her Arms is lying in *Fresco*, all perfum'd Air about me—was this your Man Friend too?

WILLMORE: So—

HELLENA: That gave you the He, and the She Gold, that begets young pleasures?

WILLMORE: Well, well Madam, then you see there are Ladies in the World, that will not be cruel—there are Madam there are—

HELLENA: And there be Men too, as fine, wild Inconstant Fellowes as yourself, there be Captain there be, if you go to that now—therefore I'm resolv'd—

WILLMORE: Oh!—

HELLENA: To see your Face no more—

WILLMORE: Oh!

HELLENA: Till to morrow.

WILLMORE: Egad you frighted me.

HELLENA: Nor then neither, unless you'll swear never to see that Lady more.

WILLMORE: See her!—whe never to think of Woman kind again.

HELLENA: Kneel,—and swear— *Kneels, she gives him her hand*

WILLMORE: I do never to think—to see—to Love—nor Lye—with any but thyself.

HELLENA: Kiss the Book.

WILLMORE: Oh most Religiously. *Kisses her hand*

HELLENA: Now what a wicked Creature am I, to damn a proper Fellow.

CALLIS: Madam, I'll stay no longer, 'tis e'ne dark. *To Florinda*

FLORINDA: How ever Sir, I'll leave this with you—that when I'm gone, you may repent the opportunity you have lost, by your Modesty.

*Gives him the Jewel which is her Picture, and Exit. He gazes after her*

WILLMORE: 'Twill be an Age till to Morrow,—and till then I will most impatiently expect you—Adieu my Dear pretty *Angell*. *Exeunt all the Women*

BELVILE: Ha! *Florinda's* Picture—'twas she her self—what a dull Dog was I? I wou'd have given the World for one minuts discourse with her—

FREDERICK: This comes of your modesty!—ah pox o' your vow, 'twas ten to one, but we had lost the Jewel by't.

BELVILE: *Willmore*! the blessed'st opportunity lost! *Florinda*! Friends! *Florinda*!

WILLMORE: Ah Rogue! such black Eyes! such a Face! such a Mouth! such Teeth—and so much Witt!—

BELVILE: All, all, and a Thousand Charmes besides.

WILLMORE: Why dost thou know her?

BELVILE: Know her! Ay, Ay, and a pox take me with all my Heart for being Modest.

WILLMORE: But hearkey Friend of mine, are you my Rival? and have I been only beating the Bush all this while?

BELVILE: I understand thee not—I'm mad—see here— *Shews the Picture*

WILLMORE: Ha! whose Picture's this!—'tis a fine Wench!

FREDERICK: The Colonels Mistris Sir.

WILLMORE: Oh oh here—I thought 'thad been another prize—come, come, a Bottle will set thee right again. *Gives the Picture back*

BELVILE: I am content to try, and by that time 'twill be late enough for our design.

WILLMORE: Agreed.

*Love does all day the Soules great Empire keep,*
*But Wine at night Lulls the soft God asleep.*

*Exeunt*

## ACT III

### SCENE 2

*Lucetta's House*

*Enter* BLUNT *and* LUCETTA *with a Light*

LUCETTA: Now we are safe and free; no fears of the coming home of my Old Jealous Husband, which made me a little thoughtful when you came in first—but now Love is all the business of my Soul.

BLUNT: I am transported!—pox on't, that I had but some fine things to say to her, such as Lovers use,—I was a Fool not to learn of *Fred.* a little by heart before I came—something I must say— *Aside*

'Sheartlikins sweet Soul! I am not us'd to Complement, but I'm an honest Gentleman, and thy humble Servant.

LUCETTA: I have nothing to pay for so great a Favour, but such a Love as cannot but be great, since at first sight of that sweet Face and Shape, it made me your absolute Captive.

BLUNT: Kind heart! how prettily she talks! Egad I'll shew her Husband a *Spanish* trick; send him out of the World and Marry her: she's damnably in Love with me, and will ne're mind Settlements, and so there's that sav' d. *Aside*

LUCETTA: Well Sir, I'll go and undress me, and be with you instantly.

BLUNT: Make hast then, for adsheartlikins dear Soul thou canst not guess at the pain of a longing Lover; when his joys are drawn within the compass of a few Minutes.

LUCETTA: You speak my sense, and I'l make hast to prove it. *Exit*

BLUNT: 'Tis a rare Girl! and this one Nights enjoyment with her, will be worth all the days I ever past in Essex.—wou'd she wou'd go with me into *England*; tho' to say truth there's plenty of Whores already.—But a Pox on 'em they are such Mercenary—Prodigal Whores, that they want such a one as this, that's Free and Generous to give 'em good Examples—Whe what a house she has, how rich and fine!

*Enter* SANCHO

SANCHO: Sir, my Lady has sent me to conduct you to her Chamber.

BLUNT: Sir, I shall be proud to follow—here's one of her Servants too! 'Sheartlikins by this garb and gravity, he might be a Justice of Peace in *Essex*, and is but a Pimp here. *Exeunt*

**SCENE 3**

*Changes to a Chamber with an Alcove Bed in't, a Table, &c.* LUCETTA *in Bed. Enter* SANCHO *and* BLUNT, *who takes the Candle of Sancho at the Door*

SANCHO: Sir, my Commission reaches no farther.

BLUNT: Sir I'll excuse your Complement—what in Bed my sweet Mistress.

LUCETTA: You see, I still out-do you in kindness.

BLUNT: And thou shalt see what haste I'l make to quit scores—oh the luckiest Rogue! *He undresses himself*

LUCETTA: Shou'd you be false or cruel now!—

BLUNT: False! 'Sheartlikins, what dost thou take me for? A *Jew*? an insensible heathen—a Pox of thy Old Jealous Husband, an he were dead, Egad, sweet Soul, it shou'd be none of my fault, if I did not Marry thee.

LUCETTA: It never shou'd be mine.

BLUNT: Good Soul! I'm the fortunate Dog!

LUCETTA: Are you not undrest yet?

BLUNT: As much as my impatience will permit.

*Goes towards the Bed in his shirt, Drawers, &c*

LUCETTA: Hold, Sir, put out the Light, it may betray us else.

BLUNT: Any thing, I need no other Light, but that of thine Eyes!—Sheartlikins, there I think I had it. *Puts out the Candle, the Bed descends, he groaps about to find it* —Whe—whe—where am I got? what not yet?—where are you sweetest?—ah, the Rogue's silent now—a pretty Love-trick this—how she'l laugh at me anon!—you need not, my dear Rogue! you need not!—I'm all on fire already—come, come, now call me in pity.—Sure I'm Enchanted! I have been round the Chamber, and can find neither Woman, nor Bed—I lockt the Door, I'm sure she cannot go that way—or if she cou'd, the Bed cou'd not.—Enough, enough, my pretty wanton, do not carry the jest too far—ha, Betraid! Dogs! Rogues! Pimps!—help! help! *Lights on a Trap, and is let down*

*Enter* LUCETTA, PHILIPPO *and* SANCHO *with a Light*

PHILIPPO: Ha, ha, ha, he's dispatcht finely.

LUCETTA: Now, Sir, had I been Coy, we had mist of this Booty.

PHILIPPO: Nay, when I saw 'twas a substantial Fool, I was mollified; but when you doat upon a Serenading Coxcomb, upon a Face, fine Cloaths, and a Lute, it makes me rage.

LUCETTA: You know I was never guilty of that Folly, my dear *Philippo*, but with yourself—but come, let's see what we have got by this.

PHILIPPO: A rich Coat!—Sword and Hat—these Breeches too—are well lin'd!—see here, a Gold Watch!—a Purse—ha!—Gold!—at least Two Hundred Pistols!—a bunch of Diamond Rings! and one with the Family Arms!—a Gold Box!—with a Medal of his King! and his Lady Mother's Picture!—these were Sacred Reliques, believe me!—see, the Wasteband of his Breeches have a Mine of Gold!—Old Queen *Besse*'s, we have a quarrel to her ever since *Eighty Eight*, and may therefore justifie the Theft, the Inquisition might have committed it.

LUCETTA: —See, a Bracelet of bowd Gold! these his Sisters ty'd about his Arms at parting—but well—for all this, I fear his being a Stranger, may make a noise and hinder our Trade with them hereafter.

PHILIPPO: That's our security; he is not only a Stranger to us, but to the Countrey too—the Common Shoar into which he is descended, thou knowst conducts him into another Street, which this Light will hinder him from ever finding again—he knows neither your Name, nor that of the Street where your House is, nay nor the way to his own Lodgings.

LUCETTA: And art not thou an unmerciful Rogue! not to afford him one Night for all this?—I shou'd not have been such a *Jew*.

PHILIPPO: Blame me not, *Lucetta*, to keep as much of thee as I can to my self—come, that thought makes me wanton!—let's to Bed!—*Sancho*, lock up these.

*This is the Fleece which Fools do bear,*
*Design'd for witty Men to sheere.*

*Exeunt*

**SCENE 4**

*Changes, and discovers* BLUNT, *creeping out of a Common-Shoar, his Face, &c. all dirty*

BLUNT: Oh Lord! *Climbing up*

I am got out at last, and (which is a Miracle) without a Clue—and now to Damning and Cursing!—but if that wou'd ease me, where shall I begin? with my Fortune, my self, or the Quean that couzen'd me—what a Dog was I to believe in Woman? oh Coxcomb!—Ignorant conceited Coxcomb! to fancy she cou'd be enamour'd with my Person! at first sight enamour'd!—oh, I'm a cursed Puppy! 'tis plain, Fool was writ upon my Forehead! she perceiv'd it!—saw the *Essex*-Calf there—for what Allurements cou'd there be in this Countenance? which I can indure, because I'm acquainted with it—oh, dull silly Dog! to be thus sooth'd into a Couzening! had I been drunk, I might fondly have credited the young Quean!—but as I was in my right Wits, to be thus cheated, confirms it I am a dull believing *English* Country Fop—but my Camrades! death and the Devil! there's the worst of all—then a Ballad will be Sung to Morrow on the *Prado*, to a Lousie Tune of the Enchanted 'Squire, and the Annihilated Damsel—but *Fred.* that Rogue! and the Colonel, will abuse me beyond all Christian patience—had she left me my Clothes, I have a Bill of Exchange at home, wou'd have sav'd my

Credit—but now all hope is taken from me—well, I'l home (if I can find the way) with this Consolation, that I am not the first kind believing Coxcomb; but there are Gallants many such good Natures amongst ye.

*And tho you've better Arts to hide your Follies,*
*Adsheartlikins y'are all as errant Cullies.*

[*Exit*]

**SCENE 5**

*The Garden in the Night*

*Enter* FLORINDA *in an undress, with a Key and a little Box*

FLORINDA: Well, thus far I'm in my way to happiness; I have got my self free from *Callis*; my Brother too I find by yonder light is got into his Cabinet, and thinks not of me; I have by good Fortune, got the Key of the Garden back-door.—I'l open it to prevent *Belvile's* knocking—a little noise will now Allarm my Brother. Now am I as fearful as a young Thief. *Unlocks the door* —heark—what noise is that—oh, 'twas the Wind that plaid amongst the Boughs—*Belvile* stays long, methinks—it's time—stay—for fear of a surprise—I'l hide these Jewels in yonder Jessamin.

*She goes to lay down the Box. Enter* WILLMORE *drunk*

WILLMORE: What the Devil is become of these fellows, *Belvile* and *Frederick* they promiss'd to stay at the next Corner for me, but who the Devil knows the Corner of a Full Moon—now—whereabouts am I!—hah—what have we here a Garden!—a very convenient place to sleep in—hah—what has God sent us here!—a Female!—by this Light a Woman!—I'm a Dog if it be not a very Wench!—

FLORINDA: He's come!—hah—who's there?

WILLMORE: Sweet Soul! let me salute thy Shoe-string.

FLORINDA: 'Tis not my *Belvile.*—good Heavens! I know him not—who are you, and from whence come you?

WILLMORE: Prithee—prithee Child—not so many hard questions—let it suffice I am here Child—come, come kiss me.

FLORINDA: Good Gods! what luck is mine?

WILLMORE: Only good luck Child, parlous good luck—come hither,—'tis a delicate shining Wench—by this hand she's perfum'd, and smells like any Nosegay—prithee dear Soul, let's not play the Fool, and lose time—precious time—for as Gad shall save me I'm as honest a Fellow as breathes, tho' I'm a little disguis'd at present—come I say—whe thou may'st be free with me, I'll be very secret. I'll not boast who 'twas oblig'd me, not I—for hang me if I know thy name.

FLORINDA: Heavens! what a filthy Beast is this?

WILLMORE: I am so, and thou ought'st the sooner to lye with me for that reason—for look you Child, there will be no sin in't, because 'twas neither design'd nor premeditated. 'Tis pure Accident on both sides—that's a certain thing now—indeed shou'd I make Love to you, and vow you fidelity—and swear and lye till you believ'd and yielded—that were to make it wilful Fornication—the crying Sin of the Nation—thou art therefore (as thou art a good Christian) oblig'd in Conscience to deny me nothing. Now—come be kind without any more idle prating.

FLORINDA: Oh I am ruin'd—Wicked Man unhand me.

WILLMORE: Wicked!—Egad Child a Judge were he young and vigorous, and saw those Eyes of thine, wou'd know 'twas they gave the first blow—the first provocation—come prithee let's lose no time, I say—this is a fine convenient place.

FLORINDA: Sir, let me go, I conjure you, or I'll call out.

WILLMORE: Ay, Ay, you were best to call Witness to see how finely you treat me—do—

FLORINDA: I'll cry Murder! Rape! or any thing! if you do not instantly let me go.

WILLMORE: A Rape! Come, come, you lye you Baggage, you lye, what, I'll warrant you wou'd fain have the World believe now that you are not so forward as I. No, not you—why at this time of Night was your Cobweb Door set open dear Spider—but to catch Flyes?—Hah—come—or I shall be damnably angry.—Whe what a Coyl is here—

FLORINDA: Sir, can you think—

WILLMORE: That you wou'd do't for nothing—oh, oh I find what you wou'd be at—look here, here's a Pistol for you—here's a work indeed—here—take it I say—

FLORINDA: For Heavn's sake Sir, as you're a Gentleman—

WILLMORE: So—now—now—she wou'd be wheadling me for more—what you will not take it then—you are resolv'd you will not—come—come take it, or I'll put it up again—for look ye, I never give more—whe how now Mistris, are you so high i'th' Mouth a *Pistol* won't down with you—hah—whe what a works here—in good time—come, no struggling to be gone—but an y'are good at a dumb Wrestle I'm for ye—look ye—I'm for yee—

*She struggles with him. Enter* BELVILE *and* FREDERICK

BELVILE: The Door is open, a pox of this mad Fellow, I'm angry that wee've lost him, I durst have sworn he had followed us.

FREDERICK: But you were so hasty Colonel to be gone.

FLORINDA: Help! help!—Murder!—help—oh I am ruin'd.

BELVILE: Ha! sure that's *Florindas* voyce. *Comes up to them*
—A Man! Villain let go that Lady.

*A Noise. Willmore turns and draws, Frederick interposes*

FLORINDA: *Belvile*! Heavens! my Brother too is coming, and 'twill be impossible to escape—*Belvile* I conjure you to walk under my Chamber Window, from whence I'll give you some Instructions what to do—this rude Man has undone us. *Exit*

WILLMORE: *Belvile*!

*Enter* PEDRO, STEPHANO, *and other* SERVANTS *with Lights*

PEDRO: I'm betray'd! run *Stephano* and see if *Florinda* be safe?

*Exit Stephano. They Fight, and Pedro's Party beats 'em out*

So, who e're they be, all is not well, I'll to *Florindas* Chamber.

*Going out, meets Stephano*

STEPHANO: You need not Sir, the poor Lady's fast asleep and thinks no harm. I wou'd not awake her Sir, for fear of frighting her with your danger.

PEDRO: I'm glad she's there—Rascals how came the Garden Door open?

STEPHANO: That Question comes too late Sir, some of my Fellow Servants Masquerading I'le warrant.

PEDRO: Masquerading! a lewd Custome to debauch our youth,—there's something more in this than I imagine. *Exeunt*

## SCENE 6

*Changes to the Street*

*Enter* BELVILE *in Rage.* FREDERICK *holding him, and* WILLMORE *Melancholy*

WILLMORE: Whe how the Devil shou'd I know *Florinda*?

BELVILE: Ah plague of your Ignorance! if it had not been *Florinda*, must you be a Beast?—a Brute? a Senseless Swine.

WILLMORE: Well Sir, you see I am endu'd with patience—I can bear—tho Egad y'are very free with me, methinks.—I was in good hopes the Quarrel wou'd have been on my side, for so uncivilly interrupting me.

BELVILE: Peace Brute! whilst thou'rt safe—oh I'm distracted.

WILLMORE: Nay, nay, I'm an unlucky Dogg, that's certain.

BELVILE: Ah Curse upon the Star that Rul'd my Birth! or whatsoever other Influence that makes me still so wretched.

WILLMORE: Thou break'st my Heart with these complaints; there is no Star in fault, no Influence, but Sack, the cursed Sack I drunk.

FREDERICK: Whe how the Devil came you so drunk?

WILLMORE: Whe how the Devil came you so sober?

BELVILE: A Curse upon his thin Skull, he was always before-hand that way.

FREDERICK: Prithee Dear Colonel forgive him, he's sorry for his Fault.

BELVILE: He's always so after he has done a mischief—a plague on all such Brutes.

WILLMORE: By this Light I took her for an Errant Harlot.

BELVILE: Damn your debaucht opinion! tell me Sot had'st thou so much sense and light about thee to distinguish her Woman, and coudst not see something about her Face and Person, to strike an awful Reverence into thy Soul?

WILLMORE: Faith no, I consider'd her as meer a Woman as I cou'd wish.

BELVILE: 'Sdeath, I have no patience—draw, or I'll kill you.

WILLMORE: Let that alone till to Morrow, and if I set not all right again, use your pleasure.

BELVILE: To Morrow! damn it
The Spightful Light will lead me to no happiness.
To Morrow is *Antonio*'s, and perhaps
Guides him to my undoing;—oh that I cou'd meet
This Rival! this pow'rfull Fortunate!

WILLMORE: What then?

BELVILE: Let thy own Reason, or my Rage instruct thee.

WILLMORE: I shall be finely inform'd then, no doubt; hear me Colonel—hear me—shew me the Man and I'le do his Business.

BELVILE: I know him no more than thou, or if I did I shou'd not need thy Aid.

WILLMORE: This you say is *Angellicas* House, I promis'd the kind Baggage to lye with her to Night. *Offers to go in*

*Enter* ANTONIO *and his* PAGE. *Antonio knock on the Hilt of's Sword*

ANTONIO: You paid the Thousand Crowns I directed?

PAGE: To the Ladies Old Woman, Sir I did.

WILLMORE: Who the Devil have we here!

BELVILE: I'll now plant my self under *Florinda*'s Window, and if I find no comfort there, I'll dye. *Exeunt Belvile and Frederick*

*Enter* MORETTA

MORETTA: Page!

PAGE: Here's my Lord.

WILLMORE: How is this! a Pickroone going to board my Fregate! here's one Chase Gun for you.

*Drawing his Sword, justles Antonio who turns and draws. They fight, Antonio falls*

MORETTA: Oh bless us! we're all undone! *Runs in and shuts the Door*

PAGE: Help! Murder!

BELVILE *returns at the noise of fighting*

BELVILE: Ha! the mad Rogue's engag'd in some unlucky Adventure again.

*Enter two or three* MASQUERADERS

MASQUERADER: Ha! a Man kill'd!

WILLMORE: How! a Man kill'd! then I'l go home to sleep.

*Puts up and reels out. Exeunt Masqueraders another way*

BELVILE: Who shou'd it be! pray Heaven the Rogue is safe for all my Quarrel to him.

*As Belvile is groping about, Enter an Officer and six Soldiers*

SOLDIER: Who's there?

OFFICER: So, here's one dispatcht—secure the Murderer.

BELVILE: Do not mistake my Charity for Murder!
I came to his Assistance. *Soldiers seize on Belvile*

OFFICER: That shall be try'd, Sir—St *Jago*, Swords drawn in the Carnival time!

*Goes to Antonio*

ANTONIO: Thy hand prithee.

OFFICER: Ha! *Don Antonioz*! look well to the Villain there.—How is it, Sir?

ANTONIO: I'm hurt.

BELVILE: Has my humanity made me a Criminal?

OFFICER: Away with him.

BELVILE: What a curst chance is this? *Exeunt Soldiers with Belvile*

ANTONIO: This is the Man, that has set upon me twice—carry him to my Appartment, till you have farther Orders from me.

*To the Officer. Exeunt, Antonio led*

*The End of the Third Act*

## ACT IV

### SCENE 1

*A fine Room*

*Discovers* BELVILE *as by dark alone*

BELVILE: When shall I be weary of railing on Fortune, who is resolv'd never to turn with smiles upon me—Two such defeats in one Night—none but the Devil, and that mad Rogue cou'd have contriv'd to have plagu'd me with—I am here a Prisoner—but where—Heav'n knows—and if there be Murder done, I can soon decide the Fate of a Stranger in a Nation without mercy—yet this is nothing to the Torture my Soul bows with, when I think of losing my fair, my dear *Florinda*—heark—my door opens—a Light—a Man—and seems of Quality—arm'd too!—now shall I dye like a Dog without defence.

*Enter* ANTONIO *in a Night-Gown, with a Light; his Arm in a Scarf, and a Sword under his Arm: he sets the Candle on the Table*

ANTONIO: Sir, I come to know what Injuries I have done you, that cou'd provoke you to so mean an Action, as to Attack me basely, without allowing time for my defence?

BELVILE: Sir, for a Man in my circumstances to plead Innocence, wou'd look like fear—but view me well, and you will find no marks of Coward on me; nor any thing that betrays that Brutality you accuse me with.

ANTONIO: In vain, Sir, you impose upon my sense.
You are not only he who drew on me last Night,
But yesterday before the same house, that of *Angellica*.
Yet there is something in your Face and Meine
That makes me wish I were mistaken.

BELVILE: I own I fought to day in the defence of a Friend of mine, with whom you (if you're the same) and your Party were first engag'd. Perhaps you think this Crime enough to kill me, But if you do; I cannot fear you'l do it basely.

ANTONIO: No, Sir, I'l make you fit for a defence with this.

*Gives him the Sword*

BELVILE: This Gallantry surprizes me—nor know I how to use this Present, Sir, against a Man so brave.

ANTONIO: You shall not need;
For know, I come to snatch you from a danger
That is decreed against you:
Perhaps your Life, or long Imprisonment;
And 'twas with so much Courage you offended,
I cannot see you punisht.

BELVILE: How shall I pay this Generosity?

ANTONIO: It had been safer to have kill'd another.
Than have attempted me:
To shew your danger, Sir, I'l let you know my Quality;
And 'tis the Vice-Roy's Son, whom you have wounded.

BELVILE: The Vice-Roy's Son!
Death and Confusion! was the Plague reserv'd
To compleat all the rest—oblig'd by him!
The Man of all the World I wou'd destroy. *Aside*

ANTONIO: You seem disorder'd, Sir.

BELVILE: Yes, trust me, Sir, I am, and 'tis with pain
That Man receives such Bounties,
who wants the Pow'r to pay 'em back again.

ANTONIO: To gallant Spirits 'tis indeed uneasie;
—But you may quickly overpay me, Sir.

BELVILE: Then I am well—kind Heav'n! but set us even,
That I may fight with him and keep my Honour safe. *Aside*
—Oh, I'm impatient, Sir, to be discounting
The mighty Debt I owe you, Command me quickly—

ANTONIO: I have a Quarrel with a Rival, Sir,
About the Maid we love.

BELVILE: Death, 'tis *Florinda* he means— *Aside*
That thought destroys my Reason,
And I shall kill him—

ANTONIO: My Rival, Sir,
Is one has all the Virtues Man can boast of—

BELVILE: Death! who shou'd this be? *Aside*

[ANTONIO]: He challeng'd me to meet him on the *Molo*,
As soon as day appear'd, but last Nights quarrel,
Has made my Arm unfit to guide a Sword.

BELVILE: I apprehend you, Sir, you'd have me kill the Man,
That lays a Claim to the Maid you speak of.
—I'l do't—I'l fly to do't!
ANTONIO: Sir, do you know her?
BELVILE: —No, Sir, but 'tis enough she is admir'd by you.
ANTONIO: Sir, I shall rob you of the Glory on't,
For you must fight under my Name and Dress.
BELVILE: That Opinion must be strangely obliging that makes
You think I can personate the brave *Antonio*,
Whom I can but strive to imitate.
ANTONIO: You say too much to my Advantage;
—Come, Sir, the day appears that calls you forth.
—Within, Sir, is the habit. *Exit Antonio*
BELVILE: Fantastick Fortune, thou deceitful Light,
That Cheats the wearied Traveller by Night,
Tho on a Precipice each step you tread,
I am resolv'd to follow where you lead. *Exit*

**SCENE 2**

*The Molo*

*Enter* FLORINDA *and* CALLIS *in Masques with* STEPHANO

FLORINDA: I'm dying with my fears, *Belvile*'s not coming *Aside*
as I expected under my Window,
Makes me believe that all those fears are true.
—Canst thou not tell with whom my Brother fights?

STEPHANO: No, Madam, they were both in Masquerade, I was by when they challeng'd one another, and they had decided the Quarrel then, but were prevented by some Cavaliers; which made' em put it off till now—but I am sure 'tis about you they fight.

FLORINDA: Nay, then 'tis with *Belvile*, for what other Lover *Aside* have I that dares fight for me, except *Antonio*? and he is too much in favour with my Brother—if it be he, for whom shall I direct my Prayers to Heav'n?

STEPHANO: Madam, I must leave you, for if my Master see me, I shall be hang'd for being your Conductor—[I] escapt narrowly for the excuse I made for you last Night i'th' Garden.

FLORINDA: And I'l reward thee for't—prithee no more. *Exit Stephano*

*Enter* DON PEDRO *in his Masquing Habit*

PEDRO: *Antonio*'s late to day, the place will fill, and we may be prevented. *Walks about*

FLORINDA: *Antonio* sure I heard amiss. *Aside*

PEDRO: But who will not excuse a happy Lover
When soft fair Arms confine the yielding Neck;
And the kind whisper languishingly breathes.
—Must you begone so soon?—
Sure I had dwelt for ever on her Bosome.
—But stay, he's here.

*Enter* BELVILE *drest in Antonio's Clothes*

FLORINDA: 'Tis not *Belvile*, half my fears are vanisht. *[Aside]*
PEDRO: *Antonio*!
BELVILE: This must be he.
You're early, Sir—I do not use to be out-done this way.
PEDRO: The wretched, Sir, are watchful, and 'tis enough
You've the advantage of me in *Angellica.*
BELVILE: *Angellica*! or I've mistook my Man! or else *Antonio.* *Aside*
—Can he forget his Intrest in *Florinda*,
And fight for common Prize?
PEDRO: Come, Sir, you know our terms—
BELVILE: By Heav'n not I. *Aside*
—No talking, I am ready, Sir. *Offers to fight, Florinda runs in*
FLORINDA: Oh hold! who e're you be, I do conjure you hold!
If you strike here—I dye— *To Belvile*
PEDRO: *Florinda*!
BELVILE: *Florinda* imploring for my Rival!
PEDRO: Away, this kindness is unseasonable.
*Puts her by, they fight; she runs in just as Belvile disarms Pedro*
FLORINDA: Who are you, Sir, that dares deny my Prayers?
BELVILE: Thy Prayers destroy him, if thou wouldst preserve him,
Do that thou'rt unacquainted with and Curse him. *She holds him*
FLORINDA: By all you hold most dear, by her you love,
I do conjure you, touch him not.
BELVILE: By her I love!
See—I obey—and at your feet resign
The useless Trophy of my Victory. *Lays his Sword at her feet*
PEDRO: *Antonio*, you've done enough to prove you love *Florinda.*
BELVILE: Love *Florinda*!
Does Heav'n love Adoration! Pray'r! or Penitence! Love her! here, Sir,—your Sword again. *Snatches up the Sword and gives it him*
Upon this truth I'l fight my life away.
PEDRO: No, you've redeem'd my Sister, and my Friendship!
*He gives him Florinda and pulls off his Vizard to shew his Face and puts it on again*
BELVILE: *Don Pedro*!
PEDRO: Can you resign your Claims to other Women,
And give your heart intirely to *Florinda*?

BELVILE: Intire! as dying Saints Confessions are!
I can delay my happiness no longer.
This Minute! let me make *Florinda* mine.
PEDRO: This Minute let it be—no time so proper,
This Night my Father will arrive from *Rome*,
And possibly may hinder what wee purpose!
FLORINDA: Oh Heavens! this Minute.
*Enter Masqueraders and pass over*
BELVILE: Oh, do not ruine me!
PEDRO: The place begins to fill, and that we may not be observ'd, do you walk off to St *Peters* Church, where I will meet you, and conclude your happiness.
BELVILE: I'll meet you there.—If there be no more Saints Churches in *Naples*. *Aside*
FLORINDA: Oh stay Sir, and recal your hasty doom!
alas I have not yet prepar'd my Heart
To entertain so strange a Guest.
PEDRO: Away this silly modesty is Assum'd too late.
BELVILE: Heaven Madam! what do you do?
FLORINDA: Do! despise the Man that lays a Tyrant's Claim
To what he ought to Conquer by submission.
BELVILE: You do not know me—move a little this way. *Draws her aside*
FLORINDA: Yes, you may force me even to the Alter,
But not the holy Man that offers there
Shall force me to be thine. *Pedro talks to Callis this while*
BELVILE: Oh do not loose so blest an opportunity!
—See—'tis your *Belvile—not Antonio*,
Whom your mistaken Scorn & Anger ruines. *Pulls off his Vizard*
FLORINDA: *Belvile*.
Where was my Soul it cou'd not meet thy Voyce!
And take this knowledge in.

*As they are talking, Enter* WILLMORE *finely drest, and* FREDERICK

WILLMORE: No Intelligence! no News of *Belvile* yet—well I am the most unlucky Rascal in Nature—ha—am I deceiv'd—or is it he—look *Fred*.—'tis he—my dear *Belvile*.

*Runs and Embraces him. Belvile[’s] Vizard falls out on's Hand*

BELVILE: Hell and confusion seize thee!
PEDRO: Ha! *Belvile*! I beg your Pardon Sir. *Takes Florinda from him*
BELVILE: Nay touch her not, she's mine by Conquest Sir,
I won her by my Sword.
WILLMORE: Did'st thou so—and Egad Child wee'l keep her by the Sword.
*Draws on Pedro. Belvile goes between*
BELVILE: Stand off
Thou'rt so profanely Lewd, so curst by Heaven,
All quarrels thou espousest must be Fatal.

WILLMORE: Nay an you be so hot, my Valour's Coy, and shall be Courted when you want it next. *Puts up his Sword*

BELVILE: You know I ought to Claim a Victors right. *To Pedro*
But you're the Brother to Divine *Florinda*,
To whom I'm such a Slave—to purchase her,
I durst not hurt the Man she holds so dear.

PEDRO: 'Twas by *Antonio*'s, not by *Belvile*'s Sword
This question should have been decided Sir;
I must confess much to your Bravery's due,
Both now, and when I met you last in Arms.
But I am nicely punctual in my word,
As Men of Honour ought, and beg your Pardon.
—For this mistake another time shall dear.
—This was some Plot between you and *Belvile*.
But I'll prevent you.

*Aside to Florinda as they are going out. Belvile looks after her and begins to walk up and down in Rage*

WILLMORE: Do not be Modest now and loose the Woman, but if wee shall fetch her back so—

BELVILE: Do not speak to me—

WILLMORE: Not speak to you—Egad I'll speak to you, and will be answer'd too.

BELVILE: Will you Sir—

WILLMORE: I know I've done some mischief, but I'm so dull a Puppey, that I'm the Son of a Whore, if I know how, or where—prithee inform my understanding—

BELVILE: Leave me I say, and leave me instantly.

WILLMORE: I will not leave you in this humour, nor till I know my Crime.

BELVILE: Death I'll tell you Sir—

*Draws and runs at Willmore, he runs out, Belvile after him, Frederick interposes*
*Enter* ANGELLICA, MORETTA *and* SEBASTIAN

ANGELLICA: Ha—*Sebastian*—
Is not that *Willmore*?—hast—hast and bring him back.

FREDERICK: The Colonel's mad—I never saw him thus before, I'l after 'em least he do some mischief, for I am sure *Willmore* will not draw on him. *Exit*

ANGELLICA: I am all Rage! my first desires defeated!
For one for ought he knows that has no
Other Merit than her Quality
—Her being *Don Pedro*'s Sister—he loves her!
I know 'tis so—dull, dull, Insensible—
He will not see me now tho oft invited;
And broke his word last Night—false perjur'd Man!
—He that but Yesterday fought for my Favours,
And wou'd have made his Life a Sacrifice

To've gain'd one Night with me,
Must now be hir'd and Courted to my Arms.

MORETTA: I told you what wou'd come on't, but *Moretta*'s an old doating Fool—why did you give him five Hundred Crowns, but to set himself out for other Lovers! you shou'd have kept him Poor, if you had meant to have had any good from him.

ANGELLICA: Oh, name not such mean trifles;—had I given him all
My Youth has earn'd from Sin,
I had not lost a thought, nor sigh upon't.
But I have given him my Eternal rest,
My whole repose, my future joys, my Heart!
My Virgin heart *Moretta*; Oh 'tis gone!

MORETTA: Curse on him here he comes;
How fine she has made him too.

*Enter* WILLMORE *and* SEBASTIAN. *Angellica turns and walks away*

WILLMORE: How now turn'd shaddow!
Fly when I pursue! and follow when I fly!
*Stay gentle shadow of my Dove* *Sings*
*And tell me e're I go,*
*Whether the substance may not prove*
*A Fleeting thing like you.*
There's a soft kind look remaining yet. *As she turns she looks on him*

ANGELLICA: Well Sir, you may be gay, all happiness, all joyes pursue you still, Fortune's your Slave, and gives you every hour choyce of new hearts and Beauties, till you are cloy'd with the repeated Bliss, which others vainly languish for.——But know false Man that I shall be reveng'd. *Turns away in Rage*

WILLMORE: So gad there are of those faint-hearted Lovers, whom such a sharp Lesson next their hearts, wou'd make as Impotent as Fourscore—pox o' this whining.—My bus'ness is to laugh and love—a pox on't, I hate your sullen Lover, a Man shall lose as much time to put you in humour now, as wou'd serve to gain a new Woman.

ANGELLICA: I scorn to cool that Fire I cannot raise,
Or do the Drudgery of your virtuous Mistris.

WILLMORE: A virtuous Mistress! death, what a thjing thou hast found out for me! why what the Devil, shou'd I do with a virtuous Woman?—a sort of ill-natur'd Creatures, that take a Pride to torment a Lover, Virtue is but an infirmity in Woman; a Disease that renders even the handsome ungrateful; whilst the ill-favour'd for want of Solicitations and Address, only fancy themselves so.—I have layn with a Woman of Quality, who has all the while been railing at Whores.

ANGELLICA: I will not answer for your Mistress's Virtue,
Though she be Young enough to know no Guilt;
And I cou'd wish you wou'd perswade my heart
'Twas the Two hundred Thousand Crowns you Courted.

WILLMORE: Two Hundred Thousand Crowns! what Story's this?—what Trick?—what Woman?—ha!

ANGELLICA: How strange you make it, have you forgot the Creature you entertain'd on the *Piazo* last Night?

WILLMORE: Ha! my Gipsie worth Two Hundred Thousand Crowns!—oh how I long to be with her—pox, I knew she was of Quality. *Aside*

ANGELLICA: False Man! I see my ruine in thy face.
How many Vows you breath'd upon my Bosome,
Never to be unjust—have you forgot so soon?

WILLMORE: Faith no, I was just coming to repeat 'em—but here's a humour indeed—wou'd make a Man a Saint—wou'd she wou'd be angry enough to leave me, and Command me not to wait on her. *Aside*

*Enter* HELLENA *drest in Man's Cloths*

HELLENA: This must be *Angellica*! I know it by her mumping Matron here—Ay, ay, 'tis she! my Mad Captain's with her too, for all his swearing—how this unconstant humour makes me love him! [*Aside*]—Pray good grave Gentlewoman is not this *Angellica*?

MORETTA: My too young Sir, it is—[*Aside*] I hope 'tis one from *Don Antonio.*
*Goes to Angellica*

HELLENA: Well, something I'l do to vex him for this. *Aside*

ANGELLICA: I will not speak with him; am I in humour to receive a Lover.

WILLMORE: Not speak with him! whe I'l begon—and wait your idler Minutes—can I shew less obedience to the thing I love so fondly? *Offers to go*

ANGELLICA: A fine excuse, this!—stay—

WILLMORE: And hinder your advantage! shou'd I repay your Bounties so ungratefully?

ANGELLICA: Come hither, Boy—that I may let you see
How much above the advantages you name
I prize one Minutes joy with you.

WILLMORE: Oh, you destroy me with this indearment. *Impatient to be gone*
—Death! how shall I get away—Madam, 'twill not be fit I shou'd be seen with you—besides, it will not be convenient—and I've a Friend—that's dangerously sick.

ANGELLICA: I see you're impatient—yet you shall stay.

WILLMORE: And miss my Assignation with my Gipsie.
*Aside, and walks about impatiently*
*Moretta brings Hellena, who addresses her self to Angellica*

HELLENA: Madam,
You'l hardly pardon my Intrusion,
When you shall know my business!
And I'm too young to tell my Tale with Art;
But there must be a wondrous store of goodness,
Where so much Beauty dwells.

ANGELLICA: A pretty Advocate whoever sent thee.
—Prithee proceed—Nay, Sir, you shall not go. *To Willmore who is stealing off*

WILLMORE: Then I shall lose my dear Gipsie for ever *Aside*
—Pox on't, she stays me out of spight.
HELLENA: I am related to a Lady, Madam,
Young, Rich, and nobly born, but has the Fate
To be in Love with a young *English* Gentleman.
Strangely she loves him, at first sight she lov'd him,
But did Adore him when she heard him speak;
For he, she said, had Charms in every word,
That faild not to surprize, to Wound and Conquer.
WILLMORE: Ha! Egad I hope this concerns me. *Aside*
ANGELLICA: 'Tis my false man, he means—wou'd he were gone.
This Praise will raise his Pride, and ruin me [*Aside*]—well
Since you are so impatient to be gon
I will release you, Sir. *To Willmore*
WILLMORE: Nay, then I'm sure 'twas me he spoke off, *Aside*
this cannot be the effects of kindness in her.
—No, Madam, I've consider'd better on't,
And will not give you Cause of Jealousie.
ANGELLICA: But, Sir, I've—bus'ness, that—
WILLMORE: This shall not do, I know 'tis but to try me.
ANGELLICA: Well, to your story, Boy,—tho 'twill undo me. *Aside*
HELLENA: With this addition to his other Beauties,
He won her unresisting tender heart,
He vow'd, and sigh't, and swore he lov'd her dearly;
And she believ'd the cunning flatterer,
And thought her self the happiest Maid alive,
To day was the appointed time by both
To consummate their Bliss,
The Virgin, Altar, and the Priest were drest,
And whilst she languisht for th' expected Bridegroom,
She heard, he paid his broken Vows to you.
WILLMORE: So, this is some dear Rogue that's in Love with me,
And this way lets me know it; or if it be not me, she means some one whose
place I may supply. [*Aside*]
ANGELLICA: Now I perceive
The cause of thy impatience to be gone,
And all the business of this Glorious Dress.
WILLMORE: Damn the young Prater, I know not what he means.
HELLENA: Madam,
In your fair Eyes I read too much concern,
To tell my farther business.
ANGELLICA: Prithee, sweet Youth, talk on, thou maist perhaps
Raise here a storm that may undo my passion,
And then I'l grant thee any thing.

HELLENA: Madam, 'tis to intreat you, (oh unreasonable)
You wou'd not see this stranger;
For if you do, she Vows you are undone,
Tho Nature never made a Man so Excellent,
And sure he'ad been a God, but for inconstancy.
WILLMORE: Ah, Rogue, how finely he's instructed! *Aside*
'Tis plain; some woman that has seen me en passant.
ANGELLICA: Oh, I shall burst with Jealousie! do you know the Man you speak off?—
HELLENA: Yes, Madam, he us'd to be in Buff and Scarlet.
ANGELLICA: Thou, false as Hell, what canst thou say to this? *To Willmore*
WILLMORE: By Heaven—
ANGELLICA: Hold, do not Damn thy self—
HELLENA: Nor hope to be believ'd.— *He walks about, they follow*
ANGELLICA: Oh perjur'd Man!
Is't thus you pay my generous Passion back?
HELLENA: Why wou'd you, Sir, abuse my Lady's Faith?—
ANGELLICA: And use me so unhumanely.
HELLENA: A Maid so young, so innocent—
WILLMORE: Ah, young Divel.
ANGELLICA: Dost thou not know thy life is [in] my pow'r?
HELLENA: Or think my Lady cannot be reveng'd.
WILLMORE: So, so, the storm comes finely on. *Aside*
ANGELLICA: Now thou art silent, guilt has struck thee dumb.
Oh, hadst thou still been so, I'd liv'd in safety. *She turns away and weeps*
WILLMORE: Sweet heart, the Lady's Name and House,—quickly: I'm impatient to be with her.—

*Aside to Hellena, looks towards Angellica to watch her turning, and as she comes towards them he meets her*

HELLENA: So, now is he for another Woman. *Aside*
WILLMORE: The impudents young thing in nature;
I cannot perswade him out of his Error, Madam.
ANGELLICA: I know he's in the right,—yet thou'st a tongue
That wou'd perswade him to deny his Faith. *In rage walks away*
WILLMORE: Her Name, her Name, dear Boy.— *Said softly to Hellena*
HELLENA: Have you forgot it, Sir?
WILLMORE: Oh, I perceive he's not to know I am a stranger to his Lady. *Aside*
—Yes, yes I do know—but—I have forgot the— *Angellica turns*
—By Heaven such early confidence I never saw.
ANGELLICA: Did I not charge you with this Mistris, Sir?
Which you deny'd, tho' I beheld your Perjury.
This little generosity of thine, has render'd back my heart. *Walks away*
WILLMORE: So, you have made sweet work here, my little mischief;

Look your Lady be kind and good natur'd now, or
I shall have but a Cursed Bargain on't. *Angellica turns towards them*
—The Rogue's bred up to mischief,
Art thou so great a Fool to credit him?

ANGELLICA: Yes, I do, and you in vain impose upon me.
—Come hither, Boy,—is not this he you spake of.

HELLENA: I think—it is, I cannot swear, but I vow he has just such another lying Lovers look. *Hellena looks in his face, he gazes on her*

WILLMORE: Hah! do not I know that face—
By Heaven my little Gipsie, what a dull Dog was I, *Aside*
Had I but lookt that way I'd known her.
Are all my hopes of a new Woman banisht?
—Egad if I do not fit thee for this, hang me.
—Madam, I have found out the Plot.

HELLENA: Oh Lord, what does he say? am I discover'd now? [*Aside*]

WILLMORE: Do you see this young Spark here?—

HELLENA: He'l tell her who I am. [*Aside*]

WILLMORE: —Who do you think this is?

HELLENA: Ay, ay, he does know me—Nay, dear Captain! I am undone if you discover me.

WILLMORE: Nay, nay, no cogging, she shall know what a pretious Mistris I have.

HELLENA: Will you be such a Devil?

WILLMORE: Nay, nay, I'l teach you to spoil sport you will not make.—this small Ambassador comes not from a Person of Quality as you Imagine, and he says: but from a very Errant Gipsie, the talking'st, prating'st, canting'st little Animal thou ever saw'st.

ANGELLICA: What news you tell me, that's the thing I mean.

HELLENA: Wou'd I were well off the place, if ever I go a Captain Hunting again— *Aside*

WILLMORE: Mean that thing? that Gipsie thing, thou mayst as well be Jealous of thy Monkey or Parrot, as of her, a *Geman* Motion were worth a duzen of her, and a Dream were a better enjoyment, a Creature of a Constitution fitter for Heaven then Man.

HELLENA: Tho I'm sure he lyes, yet this vexes me. *Aside*

ANGELLICA: You are mistaken, she's a *Spanish* Woman
Made up of no such dull Materials.

WILLMORE: Materials, Egad an shee be made of any that will either dispence or admit of Love, I'le be bound to continence.

HELLENA: Unreasonable Man, do you think so? *Aside to him*

[WILLMORE]: —you may return my little Brazen Head, and tell your Lady, that till she be handsom enough to be belov'd, or I dull enough to be Religious, there will be small hopes of me.

ANGELLICA: Did you not promise then to marry her?

WILLMORE: Not I by Heaven.

ANGELLICA: You cannot undeceive my fears and torments, till you have vow'd you will not marry her.

HELLENA: If he Swears that, he'le be reveng'd on me indeed for all my Rogueries. *Aside*

ANGELLICA: I know what Arguments you'll bring against me, Fortune, and Honour.—

WILLMORE: Honour, I tell you, I hate it in your Sex, and those that fancy themselves possest of that Foppery, are the most impertinently troublesome of all Woman kind, and will transgress Nine Commandments to keep one, and to satisfie your Jealousie I swear.—

HELLENA: Oh, no swearing dear Captain.— *Aside to him*

WILLMORE: If it were possible, I should ever be inclin'd to marry, it shou'd be some kind young Sinner, one that has generosity, enough to give a favour hansomely to one that can ask it discreetly, one that has Witt enough to Manage an intrigue of Love—oh, how civil such a Wench is, to a Man that does her the Honour to marry her.

ANGELLICA: By Heaven there's no Faith in any thing he says. [*Aside*]

*Enter* SEBASTIAN

SEBASTIAN: Madam, *Don Antonio*—

ANGELLICA: Come hither.

HELLENA: Ha! *Antonio,* he may be coming hither and he'l certainly discover me, I'le therefore retire without a Ceremony. [*Aside*] *Exit Hellena*

ANGELLICA: I'le see him, get my Coach ready.

SEBASTIAN: It waits you Madam, [*Exit Sebastian*]

WILLMORE: This is luckey: what Madam, now I may be gone and leave you to the injoyment of my Rival?

ANGELLICA: Dull man, that can'st not see how Ill, how poor,
That false dissimulation looks—begon
And never let me see thy Couzening Face again,
Least I relaps and kill thee.

WILLMORE: Yes, you can spare me now,—farewel, till you're in better
Humour— [*Aside*] I'm glad of this release—
Now for my Gipsie:
For tho' to worse we change, yet still we find
New Joys, new Charms, in a New Miss that's kind. *Exit Willmore*

ANGELLICA: He's gone, and in this Ague of my Soul
The Shivering fit returns;
Oh with what willing haste, he took his leave,
As if the long'd-for Minute, were arriv'd
Of some [b]lest assignation.
In vain *I* have Consulted all my Charms,
In vain this Beauty priz'd, in vain believ'd,
My Eyes cou'd kindle any lasting fires;
I had forgot my Name, my Infamie,

And the reproach that Honour lays on those
That dare pretend a sober passion here.
    Nice reputation, tho' it leave behind
More Vertues than inhabit where that dwells;
Yet that once gone, those Vertues shine no more.
—Then since I am not fit to be belov'd,
I am resolv'd to think on a revenge
On him that sooth'd me thus to my undoing. *Exit*

## SCENE 3

*A Street*

*Enter* FLORINDA *and* VALERIA *in Habits different from what they have been seen in*

FLORINDA: We're happily Escap't, and yet I tremble still.

VALERIA: A Lover and fear! whe I am but half an one, and yet I have Courage for any attempt, wou'd *Hellena* were here, I wou'd fain have had her as deep in this Mischief as we, she'le fare but ill else I doubt.

FLORINDA: She pretended a Visit to the *Augustine* Nuns, but I believe some other design carried her out, pray Heaven we light on her.—Prithee what did'st do with *Callis*?

VALERIA: When I saw no reason wou'd do good on her, I follow'd her into the Wardrobe, and as she was looking for something in a great Chest, I topled her in by the heels, snatch't the Key of the Appartment where you were confin'd, lock't her in, and left her bawling for help.

FLORINDA: 'Tis well you resolve to follow my Fortunes, for thou darest never appear at home again after such an action.

VALERIA: That's according as the young Stranger and I shall agree.—but to our bus'ness—I deliver'd your Letter, your Note to *Belvile*, when I got out under pretence of going to Mass, I found him at his Lodging, and believe me it came seasonably; for never was Man in so desperate a Condition, I told him of your resolution of making your Escape to day, if your Brother would be absent long enough to permit you; if not, to die rather than be *Antonio*'s.

FLORINDA: Thou should'st have told him I was confined to my Chamber upon my Brothers suspition, that the bus'ness on the *Molo* was a Plott laid between him and I.

VALERIA: I said all this, and told him your Brother was now gone to his Devotion, and he resolves to visit every Church till he find him; and not only undeceive him in that, but carress him so as shall delay his return home.

FLORINDA: Oh Heavens! he's here, and *Belvile* with him too.

*They put on their Vizards. Enter* DON PEDRO, BELVILE, WILLMORE. *Belvile and Don Pedro seeming in serious discourse*

VALERIA: Walk boldly by them, and I'le come at distance, least he suspect us.

*[Florinda] walks by them, and looks back on them*

WILLMORE: Hah! a Woman, and of an Excellent Mien.

PEDRO: She throws a kind look back on you.

WILLMORE: Death, 'tis a likely Wench, and that kind look shall not be cast away—I'le follow her.

BELVILE: Prithee do not.

WILLMORE: Do not, by Heavens to the Antipodies, with such an invitation.

*She goes out, and Willmore follows her [Exit Valeria]*

BELVILE: 'Tis a mad Fellow for a Wench.

*Enter* FREDERICK

FREDERICK: Oh Colonel such News!

BELVILE: Prithee what?

FREDERICK: News that will make you laugh in spight of Fortune.

BELVILE: What, *Blunt* has had some Damn'd Trick put upon him, Cheated, Bang'd or Clapt.

FREDERICK: Cheated Sir, rarely Cheated of all but his Shirt & Drawers, the unconscionable Whore too turn'd him out before Consummation, so that traversing the Streets at Midnight, the Watch found him in this *Fresco*, and conducted him home: By Heaven 'tis such a sight, and yet I durst as well been hang'd as laught at him, or pity him; he beats all that do but ask him a question, and is in such an Humour.

PEDRO: Who is't has met with this Ill usage, Sir?

BELVILE: A Friend of ours whom you must see for mirths-sake: I'l imploy him to give *Florinda* time for an escape. *Aside*

PEDRO: What is he?

BELVILE: A Young Countryman of ours, one that has been Educated at so plentiful a rate, he yet ne're knew the want of Money, and 'twill be a great Jeast to see how simply he'le look without it, for my part I'le lend him none, an the Rogue know not how to put on a Borrowing face, and ask first, I'le let him see how good 'tis to play our parts whilst I play his—prithee *Fred.* do you go home and keep him in that posture till we come. *Exeunt*

*Enter* FLORINDA *from the farther end of the Scene, looking behind her*

FLORINDA: I am follow'd still—hah—my Brother too advancing this way, good Heavens defend me from being seen by him. *She goes off*

*Enter* WILLMORE, *and after him* VALERIA, *at a little distance*

WILLMORE: Ah! There she sailes, she looks back as she were willing to be boarded, I'le warrant her Prize. w*He goes out, Valeria following*

*Enter* HELLENA, *just as he goes out, with a* PAGE

HELLENA: Hah, is not that my Captain that has a Woman in chase?—'tis not *Angellica*; Boy, follow those people at a distance, and bring me an account where they go in,—I'le find his haunts, and plague him every where,—ha—my Brother—

*Exit Page.* BELVILE, WILLMORE, PEDRO *cross the Stage: Hellena runs off*

**SCENE 4**

*Changes to another Street*

*Enter* FLORINDA

FLORINDA: What shall I do, my Brother now pursues me,
Will no kind Pow'r protect me from his tyranny?
—hah, here's a door open, I'le venture in, since nothing can be worse than to fall into his hands, my life and honour are at stake, and my Necessity has no choyce. *She goes in*

*Enter* VALERIA *and Hellena's* PAGE *peeping after Florinda*

PAGE: Here she went in, I shall remember this house. *Exit* [*Page*]

VALERIA: This is *Belvil's* Lodging; she's gone in as readily as if she knew it,—hah— here's that Mad Fellow again, I dare not venture in,—I'le watch my opportunity. *Goes aside*

*Enter* WILLMORE, *gazing about him*

WILLMORE: I have lost her hereabouts—Pox on't she must not scape me so. *Goes out*

**SCENE 5**

*Changes to* BLUNTS *Chamber, discovers him sitting on a Couch in his Shirt and Drawers, reading*

BLUNT: So, now my mind's a little at peace, since I have resolv'd revenge—a Pox on this Tayler tho, for not bringing home the Clothes I bespoke; and a Pox of all poor Cavaliers, a Man can never keep a spare Suit for 'em; and I shall have these Rogues come in and find me naked, and then I'm undone; but I'm resolv'd to arm my self—the Rascals shall not insult over me too much. *Puts on an old rusty Sword, and Buff Belt*

—Now, how like a Morrice-Dancer I am Equipt—a fine Lady-like Whore to Cheat me thus, without affording me a kindness for my Money, a Pox light on her, I shall never be reconcil'd to the Sex more, she has made me as faithless as a Phisitian, as uncharitable as a Church-man, and as ill natur'd as a Poet. Oh how I'l use all woman-kind hereafter! what wou'd I give to have one of 'em within my reach now! any Mortal thing in Petticoats, kind Fortune, send me! and I'l forgive thy last nights Malice—here's a Cursed Book too, (a warning to all young Travellers) that can instruct me how to prevent such Mischiefs now 'tis too late, well 'tis a rare convenient thing to read a little now and then, as well as Hawk and Hunt.

*Sits down again and Reads. Enter to him* FLORINDA

FLORINDA: This House is haunted sure, 'tis well furnisht and no living thing inhabits it—hah—a Man, Heavens how he's attir'd! sure 'tis some Rope-dancer, or Fencing-master; I tremble now for fear, and yet I must venture now to speak to him—Sir, if I may not interrupt your Meditations— *He starts up and gazes*

BLUNT: Hah—what's here! are my wishes granted? and is not that a she Creature? ads heartlikins 'tis! what wretched thing art thou—hah!

FLORINDA: Charitable Sir, you've told yourself already what I am; a very wretched Maid, forc't by a strange unlucky accident, to seek a safety here, And must be ruin'd, if you do not grant it.

BLUNT: Ruin'd! is there any ruin so inevitable as that which now threatens thee? dost thou know, miserable Woman! into what Den of Mischiefs thou art fall'n? what abiss of Confusion—hah!—dost not see something in my looks that frights thy guilty Soul, and makes thee wish to change that shape of Woman for any humble Animal, or Devil? for those were safer for thee, and less mischievous.

FLORINDA: Alas, what mean you, Sir? I must confess, your looks have something in 'em, makes me fear, but I beseech you, as you seem a Gentleman, pity a harmless Virgin, that takes your house for Sanctuary.

BLUNT: Talk on, talk on, and weep too, till my Faith return. Do, flatter me out of my Senses again—a harmless Virgin with a Pox, as much one as 'tother, adsheartlikins. Whe what the Devil can I not be safe in my House for you, not in my Chamber, nay, even being naked too cannot secure me: this is an Impudence greater than has invaded me yet—Come, no resistance. *Pulls her rudely*

FLORINDA: Dare you be so cruel?

BLUNT: Cruel, adsheartlikins as a Galley-slave, or a *Spanish*-Whore: Cruel, yes, I will kiss and beat thee all over; kiss, and see thee all over; thou shalt lye with me too, not that I care for the injoyment, but to let thee see I have tain deliberated Malice to thee, and will be reveng'd on one Whore for the sins of another; I will smile and deceive thee, flatter thee, and beat thee, kiss and swear, and lye to thee, imbrace thee and rob thee, as she did me, fawn on thee, and strip thee stark naked, then hang thee out at my window by the heels, with a Paper of scruvy Verses fasten'd to thy breast, in praise of damnable women—Come, come along.

FLORINDA: Alas, Sir, must I be sacrific'd for the Crimes of the most infamous of my Sex, I never understood the sins you name.

BLUNT: Do, perswade the Fool you Love him, or that one of you can be just or honest, tell me I was not an easie Coxcomb, or any strange impossible tale: it will be believ'd sooner than thy false Showres or Protestations. A generation of damn'd Hypocrites! to flatter my very Clothes from my Back! dissembling Witches! are these the returns you make an honest Gentleman, that trusts, believes, and loves you—but if I be not even with you—Come along—or I shall—

*Pulls her again. Enter* FREDERICK

FREDERICK: Hah! what's here to do?

BLUNT: Adsheartlikins, *Fred.* I am glad thou art come, to be a witness of my dire revenge.

FREDERICK: What's this, a Person of Quality too, who is upon the ramble to supply the defects of some grave impotent Husband?

BLUNT: No, this has another pretence, some very unfortunate accident, brought her hither, to save a life pursu'd by I know not who, or why, and forc't to take sanctuary here at Fools Haven. Adsheartlikins to me of all Mankind for protection? is the Ass to be Cajold again, think ye? No, young one, no Prayers or Tears shall mitigate my rage; therefore prepare for both my pleasures of injoyment and revenge, for I am resolv'd to make up my loss here on thy body, I'l take it out in kindness and in beating.

FREDERICK: Now Mistress of mine, what do you think of this?

FLORINDA: I think he will not—dares not be so barbarous.

FREDERICK: Have a care, *Blunt*, she fetch't a deep sigh, she is inamour'd with thy Shirt and Drawers, she'l strip thee even of that, there are of her calling such unconscionable Baggages, and such dexterous Thieves, they'l flay a man and he shall ne're miss his skin, till he feels the cold. There was a Country-man of ours Rob'd of a Row of Teeth whilst he was a sleeping, which the Jilt made him buy again when he wak't—you see Lady how little reason we have to trust you.

BLUNT: 'Dsheartlikins, whe this is most abominable.

FLORINDA: Some such Devils there may be, but by all that's Holy, I am none such, I enter'd here to save a Life in danger.

BLUNT: For no goodness, I'l warrant her.

FREDERICK: Faith, Damsel, you had e'en confest the plain truth, for we are fellows not to be caught twice in the same Trap: look on that Wreck, a tite Vessel when he set out of Haven, well Trim'd and Laden, and see how a Female Piccaroon of this Island of Rogues has shatter'd him, and canst thou hope for any Mercy?

BLUNT: No, no, Gentlewoman, come along, adsheartlikins we must be better acquainted—we'l both lye with her, and then let me alone to bang her.

FREDERICK: I'm ready to serve you in matters of Revenge that has a double pleasure in't.

BLUNT: Well said. You hear, little one, how you are condemn'd by publick Vote to the Bed within, there's no resisting your Destiny, sweet heart. *Pulls her*

FLORINDA: Stay, Sir, I have seen you with *Belvile*, an *English* Cavalier, for his sake use me kindly; you know him, Sir.

BLUNT: *Belvile*, whe yes, sweeting, we do know *Belvile*, and wish he were with us now, he's a Cormorant at Whore and Bacon, he'd have a Limb or two of thee my Virgin Pullet, but 'tis no matter, we'l leave him the bones to pick.

FLORINDA: Sir, if you have any Esteem for that *Belvile*, I conjure you to treat me with more gentleness; he'l thank you for the justice.

FREDERICK: Harkey, *Blunt*, I doubt we are mistaken in this Matter.

FLORINDA: Sir, if you find me not worth *Belvile*'s care, use me as you please, and that you may think I merit better treatment than you threaten—pray take this present— *Gives him a Ring: he looks on it*

BLUNT: Hum—a Diamond! whe 'tis a wonderful Virtue now that lies in this Ring, a mollifying Virtue; adsheartlikins there's more perswasive Rhetorick in't, than all her Sex can utter.

FREDERICK: I begin to suspect something; and 'twould anger us vilely to be trust up for a rape upon a Maid of quality, when we only believe we ruffle a Harlot.

BLUNT: Thou art a credulous Fellow, but adsheartlikins I have no Faith yet, whe my Saint prattled as parlously as this does, she gave me a Bracelet too, a Devil on her, but I sent my Man to sell it to day for Necessaries, and it prov'd as counterfeit as her Vows of Love.

FREDERICK: However let it reprieve her till we see *Belvile.*

BLUNT: That's hard, yet I will grant it.

*Enter a* SERVANT

SERVANT: Oh, Sir, the Colonel is just come in with his new Friend and a *Spaniard* of Quality, and talks of having you to Dinner with 'em.

BLUNT: 'Dsheartlikins, I'm undone—I would not see 'em for the World. Harkey, *Fred.* lock up the Wench in your Chamber.

FREDERICK: Fear nothing, Madam, what e're he threatens, you are safe whilst in my hands. *Exeunt Frederick and Florinda*

BLUNT: And, Sirrah—upon your life, say—I am not at home,—or that I am asleep—or—or any thing—away—I'l prevent their coming this way. *Locks the Door, and Exeunt*

*The End of the Fourth ACT*

## ACT V

### SCENE 1

BLUNT'S *Chamber*

*After a great knocking as at his Chamber Door, Enter* BLUNT *softly crossing the Stage, in his Shirt and Drawers as before*

[VOICES]: Ned, Ned Blunt, Ned Blunt. *Call within*

BLUNT: The Rogues are up in Arms, 'Sheartlikins this Villainous *Frederick* has betray'd me, they have heard of my blessed Fortune, [*Aside*]

[VOICES]: Ned *Blunt,* Ned, Ned— *And knocking within*

BELVILE: Whe he's dead Sir, without dispute dead, he has not been seen to day, let's break open the door—here—Boy— [*Within*]

BLUNT: Ha, break open the door. D'sheartlikins that mad Fellow will be as good as his word. [*Aside*]

BELVILE: Boy bring something to force the door. [*Within*]

*A great noise within, at the door again*

BLUNT: So, now must I speak, in my own defence, I'l try what Rhetorick will do [*Aside*]—hold—hold what do you mean Gentlemen, what do you mean?

BELVILE: Oh Rogue art alive, prithee open the door and convince us. *Within*

BLUNT: Yes, I am alive Gentlemen,—but at present a little busie.

BELVILE: How, *Blunt* grown a Man of business, come, come, open and let's see this Miracle. *Within*

BLUNT: No, no, no, no, Gentlemen 'tis no great business—but—I am—at—my Devotion—d'sheartlikins will you not alow a Man time to Pray.

BELVILE: Turn'd Religious! a greater wonder than the first, therefore open quickly, or we shall unhinge, we shall. *Within*

BLUNT: This won't do—whe hearkey Colonel to tell you the plain truth, I am about a necessary affair of life—I have a wench with me—you apprehend me? the Devils in't if they be so uncivil as to disturb me now,

WILLMORE: How a Wench! Nay then we must enter and partake no resistance—unless it be your Lady of Quality, and then we'l keep our distance,

BLUNT: So, the bus'ness is out.

WILLMORE: Come, come lends more hands to the Door—now heave altogether—so well done my Boyes— *Breaks open the Door*

*Enter* BELVILE, WILLMORE, FREDERICK, PEDRO [*and* BOY]. BLUNT *looks simply, they all laugh at him, he lays his hand on his Sword, and comes up to Willmore*

BLUNT: Hearkey Sir, laugh out your laugh quickly, de ye hear, and begone. I shall spoil your sport else, 'adsheartlikins Sir, I shall—the jeast has been carryed on too long—a plague upon my Tayler.— *Aside*

WILLMORE: 'Sdeath, how the Whore has drest him, Faith Sir I'm sorry.

BLUNT: Are you so Sir, keep't to your self then Sir, I advise you, de'ye hear, for I can as little endure your pitty as his Mirth. *Lays his hand on's Sword*

BELVILE: Indeed *Willmore*, thou wer't a little too rough with *Ned Blunts* Mistress, call a Person of Quality whore? and one so young, so handsome, and so Eloquent—ha, ha, he.—

BLUNT: Harkey Sir, you know me, and know I can be angry, have a care—for 'adsheartlikins I can fight too—I can Sir,—do you mark me—no more—

BELVILE: Why so peevish good *Ned*, some disappointments I'le warrant—what? did the Jealous Count her Husband return just in the nick?

BLUNT: Or the Devil Sir—de'ye laugh— *They laugh*
Look ye settle me a good sober countenance, and that quickly too, or you shall know *Ned Blunt* is not—

BELVILE: Not every Body, we know that.

BLUNT: Not an Ass to be laught at Sir,

WILLMORE: Unconscionable sinner, to bring a Lover so neer his happiness, a vigorous passionate Lover, and then not only cheat him of his moveables, but his very desires to.

BELVILE: Ah! Sir a Mistress, is a trifle with *Blunt.* he'l have a duzen the next time he looks abroad, his Eyes have Charms, not to be resisted, there needs no more than to expose that taking Person, to the view of the Fair, and he leads 'em all in Triumph.

PEDRO: Sir, tho' I'me a stranger to you, I am asham'd at the rudeness of my Nation; and cou'd you learn who did it, wou'd assist you to make an Example of 'em.

BLUNT: Whe aye, there's one speaks Sense now, and han'somly; and let me tell you Gentlemen, I shou'd not have shew'd my self like a Jack Puding, thus to have made you Mirth, but that I have revenge within my power, for know, I have got into my possession a Femal, who had better have fallen under any Curse, than the ruine I design her: 'adsheartlikins she assaulted me here in my own Lodgings, and had doubtless committed a Rape upon me, had not this Sword defended me.

FREDERICK: I know not that, but O my conscience thou had Ravisht her, had shee not redeem'd herself with a Ring—let's see't *Blunt.* *Blunt shews the Ring*

BELVILE: Hah!—the Ring I gave *Florinda,* when we Exchange[d] our Vows—harkey *Blunt,*— *Goes to whisper to him*

WILLMORE: No whispering good Colonel there's a Woman in the case, no whispering.

BELVILE: Harkey Fool, be advis'd, and conceal both the Ring and the story for your Reputations sake, do not let people know what despis'd Cullies we *English* are, to be cheated and abus'd by one Whore, and another rather bribe thee than be kind to thee is an Infamy to our Nation.

WILLMORE: Come, come where's the Wench, we'l see her, let her be what she will, wee'l see her.

PEDRO: Ay, ay, let us see her, I can soon discover whether she be of quality, or for your diversion.

BLUNT: She's in *Freds* Custody.

WILLMORE: Come, come the Key, *To Frederick who gives him the Key, they are going*

BELVILE: Death, what shall I do—

Stay Gentleman—yet if I hinder em I shall discover all,—hold—lets go one at once—give me the Key.

WILLMORE: Nay hold there Colonel I'le go first.

FREDERICK: Nay no dispute, *Ned* and I have the propriety of her.

WILLMORE: Damn propriety—then we'l draw cuts,

*Belvile goes to whisper [to] Willmore*

—nay no corruption good Colonel come the longest Sword carries her—

*They all draw forgetting Don Pedro being as a Spaniard had the longest*

BLUNT: I yield up my int'rest to you Gentlemen, and that will be; revenge sufficient.

WILLMORE: The Wench is yours—(*to Pedro*). Pox of his *Tolledo,* I had forgot that. [*Aside*]

FREDERICK: Come Sir, I'le Conduct you to the Lady. *Exeunt Frederick & Pedro*

BELVILE: To hinder him will certainly discover her— *Aside*

Do'st know Dull beast what mischief thou hast done?

*Willmore walking up and down out of Humour*

WILLMORE: Aye, Aye, to trust our Fortune to Lotts, a Devil on't, 'twas madness that's the truth on't.

BELVILE: Oh intollerable Sott—

*Enter* FLORINDA *running mask't,* PEDRO *after her:* WILLMORE *gazing round her*

FLORINDA: Good Heaven defend me from discovery. *Aside*

PEDRO: 'Tis but in vain to fly me, you're fallen to my Lot.

BELVILE: Sure she's undiscovered yet, but now I fear there is no way to bring her off:

WILLMORE: Whe what a Pox is not this my woman, the same I follow'd but now?

*Pedro talking to Florinda, who walks up and down*

PEDRO: As if I did not know yee, and your business here.

FLORINDA: Good Heaven, I fear he does indeed— *Aside*

PEDRO: Come, pray be kind, I know you meant to be so when you enter'd here, for these are proper Gentlemen.

WILLMORE: But Sir—perhaps the Lady will not be impos'd upon, She'l chuse her Man.

PEDRO: I am better bred, than not to leave her choice free.

*Enter* VALERIA *and is surpriz'd at sight of Don Pedro*

VALERIA: *Don Pedro* here! there's no avoiding him. *Aside*

FLORINDA: *Valeria*! then I'm undone,— *Aside*

VALERIA: Oh! have I found you Sir— *To Pedro running to him*
—the strangest accident—if I had breath—to tell it.

PEDRO: Speak—is *Florinda* safe? *Hellena* well?

VALERIA: Ay, Ay Sir—*Florinda*—is safe—from any fears of you.

PEDRO: Why where's *Florinda*?—speak—

VALERIA: Aye, where indeed Sir, I wish I cou'd inform you,
—but to hold you no longer in doubt—

FLORINDA: Oh what will she say— *Aside*

VALERIA: She's fled away in the habit—of one of her Pages Sir—but *Callis* thinks you may retrieve her yet, if you make haste away, she'l tell you, Sir, the rest—if you can find her out. *Aside*

PEDRO: Dishonourable Girle, she has undone my Aime—Sir—you see my necessity of leaving you, and hope you'l Pardon it; my Sister I know will make her flight to you; and if she do, I shall Expect she shou'd be render'd back.

BELVILE: I shall consult my Love and Honour Sir. *Exit Pedro*

FLORINDA: My dear Preserver, let me imbrace thee. [*Unmasking*] *to Valeria*

WILLMORE: What the Devil's all this?

BLUNT: Mysterie by this light.

VALERIA: Come, come, make haste and get your selves married quickly, for your Brother will return again.

BELVILE: I'm so surpriz'd with fears and joyes, so amaz'd to find you here in safety. I can scarce perswade my heart into a faith of what I see—

WILLMORE: Harkey Colonel, is this that Mistress who has cost you so many sighs, and me so many quarrels with you?

BELVILE: It is—pray give him the honour of your hand. *To Florinda*

WILLMORE: Thus it must be receiv'd then
And with it give your Pardon too. *Kneels and kisses her hand*

FLORINDA: The Friend to *Belvile* may command me any thing.

WILLMORE: Death, wou'd I might, 'tis a surprizing Beauty. *Aside*

BELVILE: Boy run and fetch a Father instantly. *Exit Boy*

FREDERICK: So, now do I stand like a Dog, and have not a syllable to plead my own Cause with: by this hand, Madam, I was never throughly confounded before, nor shall I ever more dare look up with confidence, till you are pleas'd to Pardon me.

FLORINDA: Sir, I'le be reconcil'd to you on one condition, that you'l follow the Example of your Friend, in Marrying a Maid that does not hate you, and whose fortune (I believe) will not be unwelcome to you.

FREDERICK: Madam, had I not Inclinations that way, I shou'd obey your kind Commands.

BELVILE: Who *Fred.* marry, he has so few inclinations for Woman kind, that had he been possest of Paradice, he might have continu'd there to this day, if no Crime but Love cou'd have disinherited him.

FREDERICK: Oh I do not use to boast of my intregues.

BELVILE: Boast, whe thou dost nothing but boast; and I dare swear, wer't thou as Innocent from the sin of the Grape, as thou art from the Apple, thou might'st yet claim that right in *Eden* which our first parents lost by too much Loving.

FREDERICK: I wish this Lady would think me so modest a man.

VALERIA: She wou'd be sorry then, and not like you half so well, and I should be loath to break my word with you, which was, That if your Friend and mine agreed, it shou'd be a Match between you and I. *She gives him her hand*

FREDERICK: Bear witness, Colonel, 'tis a Bargain. *Kisses her hand*

BLUNT: I have a Pardon to beg too, but adsheartlikins I am so out of Countenance, that I'm a Dog if I can say any thing to Purpose. *To Florinda*

FLORINDA: Sir, I heartily forgive you all.

BLUNT: That's nobly said, sweet Lady,—*Belvile*, prithee present her her Ring again; for I find I have not Courage to approach her my self.

*Gives him the Ring, he gives* [*it*] *to Florinda. Enter* BOY

BOY: Sir, I have brought the Father that you sent for.

BELVILE: 'Tis well, and now my dear *Florinda*, let's fly to compleat that mighty joy we have so long wish't and sigh't for:
—Come *Fred.*—you'l follow?

FREDERICK: Your Example Sir, 'twas ever my ambition in War, and must be so in Love.

WILLMORE: And must not I see this juggling knot ty'd?

BELVILE: No, thou shalt do us better service, and be our guard, least *Don Pedro*'s suddain return interrupt the Ceremony.

WILLMORE: Content—I'l secure this pass.

*Exeunt Belvile, Florinda, Frederick and Valeria*

*Enter* BOY

BOY: Sir, there's a Lady without wou'd speak to you. *To Willmore*

WILLMORE: Conduct her in, I dare not quit my Post.

BOY: And Sir, your Taylor waits you in your Chamber. [*To Blunt*]

BLUNT: Some comfort yet, I shall not dance naked at the Wedding.

*Exeunt Blunt and Boy. Enter again the* BOY, *conducting in* ANGELLICA *in a Masquing Habit and a Vizard. Willmore runs to her.* [*Exit Boy*]

WILLMORE: This can be none but my pretty Gipsie—Oh, I see you can follow as well as fly—Come, confess thy self the most malicious Devil in Nature, you think you have done my bus'ness with *Angellica.*—

ANGELLICA: Stand off, base Villain— *She draws a Pistol, and holds to his Brest*

WILLMORE: Hah, 'tis not she, who art thou? and what's thy business?

ANGELLICA: One thou hast injur'd, and who comes to kill thee for't.

WILLMORE: What the Devil canst thou mean?

ANGELLICA: By all my hopes to kill thee—

*Holds still the Pistol to his Brest, he going back, she following still*

WILLMORE: Prithee on, what acquaintance? for I know thee not.

ANGELLICA: Behold this face!—so lost to thy remembrance,
And then call all thy sins about thy Soul,
And let 'em dye with thee. *Pulls off her Vizard*

WILLMORE: *Angellica*!

ANGELLICA: Yes, Traitor,
Does not thy guilty blood run shivering through thy Veins?
Hast thou no horrour at this sight, that tells thee,
Thou hast not long to boast thy shameful Conquest?

WILLMORE: Faith, no Child, my blood keeps its old Ebbs and Flows still, and that usual heat too, that cou'd oblige thee with a kindness, had I but opportunity.

ANGELLICA: Devil! dost wanton with my pain—have at thy heart.

WILLMORE: Hold, dear Virago! hold thy hand a little,
I am not now at leasure to be kill'd—hold and hear me—
—Death, I think she's in earnest. *Aside*

ANGELLICA: Oh if I take not heed.
My coward heart will leave me to his mercy. *Aside, turning from him*
—What have you, Sir, to say?—but shou'd I hear thee,
Thoud'st talk away all that is brave about me:
*Follows him with the Pistol to his Brest*
And I have vow'd thy death, by all that's Sacred.

WILLMORE: Whe then there's an end of a proper handsome Fellow,
That might a liv'd to have done good service yet;
—That's all I can say to't.

ANGELLICA: Yet—I wou'd give thee—time for—penitence. *Pausingly*

WILLMORE: Faith Child, I thank God, I have ever took
Care to lead a good sober, hopeful Life, and am of a Religion
That teaches me to believe, I shall depart in peace.

ANGELLICA: So will the Devil! tell me,
How many poor believing Fools thou hast undone?

How many hearts thou hast betray'd to ruin?
—Yet these are little mischiefs to the Ills
Thoust taught mine to commit: thoust taught it Love?

WILLMORE: Egad 'twas shrewdly hurt the while.

ANGELLICA: —Love, that has rob'd it of its unconcern
Of all that Pride that taught me how to value it.
And in its room
A mean submissive Passion was convey'd,
That made me humbly bow, which I nere did
To any thing but Heaven.
—Thou, Perjur'd Man, didst this, and with thy Oaths,
Which on thy Knees, thou didst devoutly make,
Soften'd my yielding heart—And then, I was a slave—
—Yet still had been content to've worn my Chains:
Worn 'em with vanity and joy for ever,
Hadst thou not broke those Vows that put them on.
—'Twas then I was undone.

*All this while follows him with the Pistol to his Breast*

WILLMORE: Broke my Vows! whe where hast thou liv'd?
Amongst the Gods? for I never heard of mortal Man,
That has not broke a thousand Vows.

ANGELLICA: Oh Impudence!

WILLMORE: *Angellica*! that Beauty has been too long tempting,
Not to have made a thousand Lovers languish,
Who in the Amorous Fever, no doubt have Sworn
Like me: did they all dye in that Faith? still Adoring?
I do not think they did.

ANGELLICA: No, faithless Man: had I repaid their Vows, as I did thine, I wou'd have kill'd the ingrateful that had abandon'd me.

WILLMORE: This Old General has quite spoil'd thee, nothing makes a Woman so vain, as being flatter'd; your old Lover ever supplies the defects of Age, with intollerable Dotage, vast Charge, and that which you call Constancy; and attributing all this to your own Merits, you domineer, and throw your Favours in's Teeth, upbraiding him still with the defects of Age, and Cuckold him as often as he deceives your Expectations. But the Gay, Young, Brisk Lover, that brings his equal Fires, and can give you dart for dart, he'll be as nice as you sometimes.

ANGELLICA: All this thou'st made me know, for which I hate thee.
Had I remain'd in innocent security,
I shou'd have thought all men were born my slaves,
And worn my pow'r like lightening in my Eyes,
To have destroy'd at pleasure when offended:
—But when Love held the Mirror, the undeceiving Glass
Reflected all the weakness of my Soul, and made me know
My richest treasure being lost, my Honour,
All the remaining spoil cou'd not be worth

The Conqueror's Care or Value.
—Oh how I fell like a long worship't Idol
Discovering all the Cheat.
Wou'd not the Insence and rich Sacrifice,
Which blind Devotion offer'd at my Alters,
Have fall'n to thee?
Why wou'dst thou then destroy my fancy'd pow'r.

WILLMORE: By Heaven thou'rt brave, and I admire thee strangely,
I wish I were that dull, that constant thing
Which thou wou'dst have, and Nature never meant me:
I must, like cheerful Birds, sing in all Groves,
And perch on every Bough,
Billing the next kind she that flies to meet me;
Yet after all cou'd build my Nest with thee,
Thither repairing when I'd lov'd my round,
And still reserve a tributary Flame.
—To gain your credit, I'l pay you back your Charity,
And be oblig'd for nothing but for Love. *Offers her a Purse of Gold*

ANGELLICA: Oh that thou wert in earnest!
So mean a thought of me,
Wou'd turn my rage to scorn, and I shou'd pity thee,
And give thee leave to live;
Which for the publick safety of our Sex,
And my own private Injuries, I dare not do.
Prepare— *Follows still, as before*
—I will no more be tempted with replies.

WILLMORE: Sure—

ANGELLICA: Another word will damn thee! I've heard thee talk too long.

*She follows him with the Pistol ready to shoot; he retires still amaz'd. Enter* DON ANTONIO, *his Arm in a Scarf, and layes hold on the Pistol*

ANTONIO: Hah! *Angellica*!

ANGELLICA: *Antonio*! what Devil brought thee hither?

ANTONIO: Love and Curiosity, seeing your Coach at door.
Let me disarm you of this unbecoming intrument of death—
*Takes away the Pistol*
amongst the Number of your slaves, was there not one, worthy the Honour to have fought your quarrel?
—Who are you Sir, that are so very wretched
To merit death from her?

WILLMORE: One Sir, that cou'd have made a better End of an Amorous quarrel without you, than with you.

ANTONIO: Sure 'tis some Rival,—hah—the very Man took down her Picture yesterday—the very same that set on me last night—blest opportunity—
*Offers to shoot him*

ANGELLICA: Hold, you're mistaken Sir.
ANTONIO: By Heaven the very same!
—Sir, what pretensions have you to this Lady?
WILLMORE: Sir, I do not use to be Examin'd, and am Ill at all disputes but this—
*Draws: Antonio offers to shoot*
ANGELLICA: Oh hold! you see he's Arm'd with certain death; *To Willmore*
—And you *Antonio,* I command you hold,
By all the Passion you've so lately vow'd me.

*Enter* DON PEDRO, *sees Antonio, and stays*

PEDRO: Hah, *Antonio*! and *Angellica*! *Aside*
ANTONIO: When I refuse obedience to your Will,
May you destroy me with your Mortal hate.
By all that's Holy I Adore you so,
That even my Rival, who has Charms enough
To make him fall a Victim to my jealousie
Shall live, nay and have leave to love on still.
PEDRO: What's this I hear? *Aside*
ANGELLICA: Ah thus! 'twas thus! he talkt, and I believ'd *Pointing to Willmore*
—Antonio yesterday,
I'd not have sold my Intrest in his heart,
For all the Sword has won and lost in Battail.
—But now to show my utmost of contempt,
I give thee Life—which if thou wou'dst preserve,
Live where my Eyes may never see thee more,
Live to undo some one, whose Soul may prove,
So bravely constant to revenge my Love.

*Goes out, Antonio follows, but Pedro pulls him back*

PEDRO: *Antonio*—stay.
ANTONIO: *Don Pedro*—
PEDRO: What Coward fear was that prevented thee
From meeting me this morning on the *Molo*?
ANTONIO: Meet thee?
PEDRO: Yes me; I was the Man that dar'd thee to't.
ANTONIO: Hast thou so often seen me fight in War,
To find no better Cause to excuse my absence?
—I sent my Sword and one to do thee right,
Finding my self uncapable to use a Sword.
PEDRO: But 'twas *Florinda*'s Quarrel that we fought,
And you to shew how little you esteem'd her,
Sent me your Rival, giving him your Intrest.
—But I have found the cause of this affont,
And when I meet you fit for the dispute,
—I'l tell you my resentment.

ANTONIO: I shall be ready, Sir, e're long to do you reason. *Exit Antonio*

PEDRO: If I cou'd find *Florinda*, now whilst my angers high,
I think I shou'd be kind, and give her to *Belvile* in revenge.

WILLMORE: Faith, Sir, I know not what you wou'd do, but I believe the Priest within has been so kind.

PEDRO: How! my Sister Married?

WILLMORE: I hope by this time he is, and bedded too, or he has not My longings about him.

PEDRO: Dares he do this! does he not fear my Pow'r?

WILLMORE: Faith not at all, if you will go in, and thank him for the favour he has done your Sister, so, if not, Sir, my Pow'rs greater in this house than yours, I have a damn'd surly Crew here, that will keep you till the next Tide, and then clap you on bord for Prise; my Ship lies but a League off the *Molo*, and we shall show your Donship a damn'd *Tramontana* Rovers Trick.

*Enter* BELVILE

BELVILE: This Rogue's in some new Mischief—hah *Pedro* return'd!

PEDRO: Colonel *Belvile*, I hear you have Married my Sister?

BELVILE: You have heard truth then, Sir.

PEDRO: Have I so; then, Sir, I wish you joy.

BELVILE: How!

PEDRO: By this imbrace I do, and I am glad on't.

BELVILE: Are you in earnest?

PEDRO: By our long Friendship and my obligations to thee, I am,
The sudain change, I'le give you reasons for anon,
Come lead me to my Sister,
That she may know, I now approve her choice.

*Exeunt Belvile with Pedro. Willmore goes to follow them. Enter* HELLENA *as before in Boys Clothes, and pulls him back*

WILLMORE: Ha! my Gipsie:—now a thousand blessings on thee for this kindness, Egad Child I was e'en in dispair of ever seeing thee again; my Friends are all provided for within, each Man his kind Woman.

HELLENA: Hah! I thought they had serv'd me some such trick!

WILLMORE: And I was e'en resolv'd to go aboard, and condemn my self to my lone Cabin, and the thoughts of thee.

HELLENA: And cou'd you have left me behind, wou'd you have been so ill natur'd?

WILLMORE: Whe twou'd have broke my Heart Child:—but since we are met again, I defie foul weather to part us.

HELLENA: And wou'd you be a Faithful Friend, now if a Maid shou'd trust you?

WILLMORE: For a Friend I cannot promise, thou art of a form so Excellent a Face and Humour, too good for cold dull Friendship; I am parlously afraid of being in Love Child, and you have not forgot how severely you have us'd me?

HELLENA: That's all one, such usage you must still look for, to find out all your Haunts, to raile at you to all that Love you, till I have made you love only me in your own defence, because no body else will love.

WILLMORE: But hast thou no better quality, to recommend thy self by.

HELLENA: Faith none Captain:—whe 'twill be the greater Charity to take me for thy Mistress. I am a lone Child, a kind of Orphan Lover, and why I shou'd dye a Maid, and in a Captains hands too, I do not understand,

WILLMORE: Egad, I was never claw'd away with Broad-sides from any Female before, thou hast one Vertue I Adore, good Nature; I hate a Coy demure Mistress, she's as troublesome as a Colt, I'l break none; no give me a mad Mistress when Mew'd, and in flying, one I dare trust upon the wing, that whil'st she's kind will come to the Lure.

HELLENA: Nay as kind as you will good Captain whil'st it lasts, but let's lose no time,

WILLMORE: My time's as precious to me, as thine can be, therefore dear creature, since we are so well agreed, let's retire to my Chamber, and if ever thou wert treated with such Savory Love!—come—my beds prepar'd for such a guest all clean and Sweet as thy fair self, I love to steal a Dish and a Bottle with a Friend, and hate long Graces—come let's retire and fall too.

HELLENA: 'Tis but getting my consent, and the bus'ness is soon done, let but old Gaffer *Himen* and his Priest, say amen to't, and I dare lay my Mothers daughter by as proper a Fellow as your Father's Son, without fear or blushing,

WILLMORE: Hold, hold, no Bugg words Child, Priest and *Hymen*, prithee add a Hangman to 'em to make up the consort,—no, no, we'l have no Vows but Love, Child, nor witness but the Lover, the kind Deity injoyn naught but Love! and injoy! *Himen* and priest wait still upon Portion, and Joynture; Love and Beauty have their own Ceremonies; Marriage is as certain a bane to Love, as lending Money is to Friendship: I'l neither ask nor give a Vow,—tho' I cou'd be content to turn Gipsie, and become a left-handed bride-groom, to have the pleasure of working that great Miracle of making a Maid a Mother, if you durst venture; 'tis upse Gipsie that, and if I miss, I'l lose my Labour.

HELLENA: And if you do not lose, what shall I get? a cradle full of noise and mischief, with a pack of repentance at my back? can you teach me to weave Incle to pass my time with? 'tis upse Gipsie that too.

WILLMORE: I can teach thee to Weave a true loves knot better.

HELLENA: So can my dog.

WILLMORE: Well, I see we are both upon our Guards, and I see there's no way to conquer good Nature, but by yielding,—here—give me thy hand—one kiss and I am thine;—

HELLENA: One kiss! how like my Page he speaks; I am resolv'd you shall have none, for asking such a sneaking sum,—he that will be satisfied with one kiss, will never dye of that longing; good Friend, single kiss, is all your talking come to this?—a kiss, a caudle! farewel Captain, single kiss. *Going out he stays her*

WILLMORE: Nay if we part so, let me dye like a bird upon a bough, at the Sheriffs charge, by Heaven both the *Indies*, shall not buy thee from me. I adore thy Humour and will marry thee, and we are so of one Humour, it must be a bargain—give me thy hand.— *Kisses her Hand*

And now let the blind ones (Love and Fortune) do their worst.

HELLENA: Whe God-a-mercy Captain!

WILLMORE: But harkey—the bargain is now made; but is it not fit we shou'd know each others Names? that when we have reason to curse one another hereafter (and People ask me who 'tis I give to the Devil) I may at least be able to tell, what Family you came of.

HELLENA: Good reason, Captain; and where I have cause, (as I doubt not but I shall have plentiful) that I may know at whom to throw my—blessings—I beseech ye your Name.

WILLMORE: I am call'd *Robert the Constant.*

HELLENA: A very fine name; pray was it your Faulkner or Butler that Ch[r]isten'd you? do they not use to Whistle when they call you?

WILLMORE: I hope you have a better, that a man may name without crossing himself, you are so merry with mine.

HELLENA: I am call'd *Hellena the Inconstant.*

*Enter* PEDRO, BELVILE, FLORINDA, FREDERICK, VALERIA

PEDRO: Hah! *Hellena*!

FLORINDA: *Hellena*!

HELLENA: The very same—hah my Brother! now Captain shew your Love and Courage; stand to your Arms, and defend me bravely, or I am lost for Ever.

PEDRO: What's this I hear! false Girle, how came you hither, and what's your bus'ness? Speak. *Goes roughly* to *her*

WILLMORE: Hold off Sir, you have leave to parly only. *Puts himself between*

HELLENA: I had e'en as good tell it, as you guess it; Faith Brother my bus'ness, is the same with all living Creatures of my Age, to love, and be beloved, and here's the Man.

PEDRO: Perfidious Maid, hast thou deceiv'd me too, deceiv'd thy self and Heaven;

HELLENA: 'Tis time enough to make my peace with that,
Be you but kind let me alone with Heaven,

PEDRO: *Belvile*, I did not expect this false play from you; was't not enough you'd gain *Florinda* (which I pardon'd) but your lewd Friends too must be inricht with the spoyls of a Noble Family?

BELVILE: Faith Sir, I am as much surpriz'd at this as you can be: Yet Sir, my Friends are Gentlemen, and ought to be Esteem'd for their Misfortunes, since they have the Glory to suffer with the best of Men and Kings; 'tis true, he's a Rover of Fortune, Yet a Prince, aboard his little wooden World.

PEDRO: What's this to the maintenance of a Woman of her Birth and Quality.

WILLMORE: Faith Sir, I can boast of nothing but a Sword which does me right where e're I come, and has defended a worse Cause than a Womans; and since I lov'd her before I either knew her Birth or Name, I must pursue my resolution, and marry her.

PEDRO: And is all your holy intent of becoming a Nun, debauch't into a desire of Man?

HELLENA: Whe— I have consider'd the matter Brother, and find, the Three hundred thousand Crowns my Uncle left me (and you cannot keep from me) will be better laid out in Love than in Religion, and turn to as good an account,—let most voyces carry it, for Heaven or the Captain?

ALL *cry*: A Captain[!] a Captain[!]

HELLENA: Look yee Sir, 'tis a clear case.

PEDRO: Oh I am mad—if I refuse, my lifes in danger— *Aside*
—Come—there's one motive induces me—take her—I shall now be free from fears of her Honour, guard it you now, if you can, I have been a slave to't long enough, *Gives her to him*

WILLMORE: Faith Sir, I am of a Nation, that are of opinion a womans Honour is not worth guarding when she has a mind to part with it.

HELLENA: Well said Captain.

PEDRO: This was your Plot Mistress, but I hope you have married one that will revenge my quarrel to you— *To Valeria*

VALERIA: There's no altering Destinie, Sir.

PEDRO: Sooner than a Womans Will, therefore I forgive you all—and wish you may get my Father's Pardon as Easily; which I fear.

*Enter* BLUNT *drest in a Spanish Habit, looking very ridiculously; his* MAN *a[d]justing his Band*

MAN: 'Tis very well Sir—

BLUNT: Well Sir, 'dshearlikins I tell you 'tis damnable Ill Sir,—a *Spanish* habit good Lord! Cou'd the Devil and my Taylor devise no other punishment for me, but the Mode of a Nation I abominate?

BELVILE: What's the matter *Ned*?

BLUNT: Pray view me round, and judge,— *Turns round*

BELVILE: I must confess thou art a kind of an odd Figure.

BLUNT: In a *Spanish* habit with a Vengeance! I had rather be in the Inquisition for Judaisme, than in this Doublet and Breeches, a Pillory were an easie Coller, to this three handfuls high; and these Shoes too, are worse, than the stocks with the sole an Inch shorter than my Foot: In fine, Gentlemen, methinks I look altogether like a Bag of Bayes stufft full of Fooles flesh.

BELVILE: Methinks 'tis well, and makes thee look en Cavalier:
Come Sir, settle your face, and salute our Friends, Lady—

BLUNT: Hah!—say'st thou so my Little Rover— *To Hellena*
Lady—(if you be one) give me leave to kiss your hand, and tell you adshearlikins for all I look so, I am your humble Servant,—a Pox of my *Spanish* habit.

WILLMORE: Hark—what's this? *Musick is heard to play*

*Enter* BOY

BOY: Sir, as the Custome is, the gay people in Masquerade who make every mans House their own, are coming up:

*Enter several* MEN *and* WOMEN *in Masquing Habits with Musick, they put themselves in order and Dance*

BLUNT: Adsheartlikins, wou'd 'twere lawful to pull off their false faces,
That I might see if my Doxie were not amongst e'm.

BELVILE: Ladies and Gentlemen, since you are come so *apropo*, you must take a small Collation with us. *To the Masquero's*

WILLMORE: Whilst we'le to the Good Man within, who stayes to give us a Cast of his Office.—Have you no trembling at the near approach? *To Hellena*

HELLENA: No more than you have in an Engagement or a Tempest.

WILLMORE: Egad thou'rt a brave Girle, and I admire thy Love and Courage.
Lead on, no other Dangers they can dread,
Who Venture in the Storms o'th' Marriage Bed. *Exeunt*

THE END

## EPILOGUE

*The Banisht Cavaliers! a Roving Blade!*
*A Popish Carnival! a Masquerade!*
*The Devel's in't if this will please the Nation,*
*In these our blessed times of Reformation,*
*When Conventickling is so much in fashon.*
*And yet—*
*That Mutinous Tribe less Factions do beget,*
*Than your continual differing in Wit;*
*Your Judgment's (as your Passion's) a disease:*
*Nor Muse nor Miss your Appetite can please;*
*Your grown as Nice as queasie Consciences,*
*Who's each Convulsion, when the Spirit moves,*
*Damns every thing, that Maggot disapproves.*
*With Canting Rule you wou'd the Stage refine,*
*And to Dull Method and all our Sense confine.*
*With th' Insolence of Common-Wealths you rule,*
*Where each gay Fop, and Politick grave Fool*
*On Monarch Wit impose, without controul.*
*As for the last, who seldom sees a Play,*
*Unless it be the old Black Fryers way,*
*Shaking his empty Noddle o're* Bamboo,
*He Crys,—Good Faith, these Playes will never do.*
*—Ah, Sir, in my young days, what lofty Wit,*
*What high strain'd Scenes of Fighting there were Writ:*
*These are slight airy Toys. But tell me, pray,*
*What has the* House of Commons *done to day?*
*Then shews his Politicks, to let you see,*
*Of State Affairs he'l judge as notably,*
*As he can do of Wit and Poetry.*

*The younger Sparks, who hither do resort,*
*Cry,—*
*Pox o' your gentile things, give us more Sport;*
*—Damn me, I'm sure 'twill never please the Court.*
*Such Fops are never pleas'd unless the Play*
*Be stuft with Fools, as brisk and dull as they:*
*Such might the Half-Crown spare, and in a Glass*
*At home, behold a more Accomplisht Ass,*
*Where they may set their Cravats, Wigs and Faces,*
*And Practice all their Buffonry Grimasses:*
*See how this — Huff becomes,— this Damny,— stare,—*
*Which they at home may act, because they dare,*
*But—must with prudent caution do elsewhere.*
*Oh that our* Nokes, *or* Tony Lee *cou'd show*
*A Fop but half so much to th' life as you.*

FINIS

1677

# Henrik Ibsen

## 1828–1906

Born in Skien, Norway, a small town where his father was then a successful merchant, Henrik Ibsen grew up amid the painful circumstances that were brought about by the decline of his father's business, which ended in bankruptcy when Henrik was eight years old. His family was then forced to move from their large and comfortable home to a small attic apartment, and by the time Ibsen was 16 he had been sent off to another town to make his own way as a druggist's apprentice. When he was 22 he moved to Christiana (now Oslo), hoping to study medicine at the city's university, but his failure to gain admission led him to make a career out of the playwriting that he had begun several years earlier. During the next 16 years, he was influenced largely by the nationalistic and romantic movement in Norwegian theatre, and thus gave himself over mostly to writing blank verse plays on subjects drawn from Norwegian myth and history. But in 1869, with *The League of Youth*, a play exposing the corruption of provincial politics and politicians, Ibsen began to write realistic prose plays about the social problems of his time. His best-known problem plays—*A Doll's House* (1879) and *Ghosts* (1881)—were highly controversial in his own time, especially among his Norwegian compatriots, who regarded them as attacking such traditional values as marriage and the family. Social reformers then and now have hailed them as eloquent pleas in defence of women's rights. These plays may also be seen as foreshadowing his late dramatic studies of psychologically troubled men and women in *Rosmersholm* (1886) and *Hedda Gabler* (1890).

# Hedda Gabler[1]

## *CHARACTERS*

JÖRGEN TESMAN, the holder of a University Fellowship in cultural history
MRS HEDDA TESMAN, his wife
MISS JULIANE TESMAN, his aunt
MRS ELVSTED
MR BRACK, a judge
EJLERT LÖVBORG
BERTE, the Tesmans' maid

*The action takes place in Tesman's villa on the west side of the town*

## ACT I

*A spacious, handsome, and tastefully appointed reception room, decorated in dark colours. In the back wall there is a wide doorway with the hangings pulled back. This opening leads to a smaller room in the same style as the reception room. In the wall to the right of the outer room is a folding door leading to the hall. In the opposite wall, to the left, is a glass door, also with the curtains drawn aside. Through the windows we see part of a covered verandah outside, and trees in autumn colours. In the foreground stands an oval table, covered with a heavy cloth, and with chairs around it. Downstage by the right wall are a large, dark, porcelain stove, a high-backed armchair, an upholstered footrest, and two stools. Up in the right-hand corner, a corner sofa and a small round table. Downstage on the left, a little away from the wall, a sofa. Above the glass door, a piano. On either side of the doorway at the back is a whatnot with objects in terra-cotta and majolica.— By the back wall of the inner room are a sofa, a table, and a couple of chairs. Over this sofa hangs the portrait of a handsome, elderly man in the uniform of a general. Over the table, a hanging lamp with a matte, milky-white glass shade.— All around the reception room there are numerous bunches of flowers arranged in vases and glasses. More lie on the tables. The floors of both rooms are covered with thick carpets.— Morning light. The sun is shining in at the glass door.*

*Miss Juliane Tesman, with hat and parasol, comes in from the hall, followed by Berte, who carries a bunch of flowers wrapped in paper. Miss Tesman is a good-looking lady of benevolent aspect, some 65 years old, neatly but simply dressed in a grey costume. Berte is a serving-maid getting on in years, with a plain and somewhat countrified exterior.*

MISS TESMAN [*stops just inside the room, listens and speaks softly*]: Well, I declare! I don't believe they are up yet.

BERTE [*similarly subdued*]: Why, that's what I said, Miss. So late the steamer was last night. And then afterwards! Gracious . . . all the things the young mistress wanted unpacked before she could get off to bed.

1 translated by Jens Arup

MISS TESMAN: Well, well . . . let them have a good rest and welcome. But we'll give them a breath of the fresh morning air when they do come down.

*She crosses to the glass door and throws it wide open.*

BERTE [*by the table, not knowing what to do with the flowers in her hand*]: I'm sure there isn't a decent place left for them. Maybe I'd better put them here, Miss.

*She places the flowers on the front of the piano.*

MISS TESMAN: And so now you've got yourself a new mistress, Berte my dear. The Lord knows, I found it more than hard to let you go.

BERTE [*close to tears*]: And what about me then, Miss? What am I to say! For so many years now I've been with you and Miss Rina.

MISS TESMAN: We must make the best of it, Berte. There's really no other way. Jörgen must have you in the house with him, you see. He simply must. You've always looked after him, ever since he was a little boy.

BERTE: Yes but, Miss, I get so worried about her, too, lying at home. The poor dear, she's quite helpless. And then with that new girl, now! She'll never learn to make things right for the poor lady, she won't.

MISS TESMAN: Oh, I'll soon get her into the way of it. And I'll see to most things myself, you may be sure. You needn't be so anxious for my poor sister's sake, my dear Berte.

BERTE: Yes, but then there's another thing too, Miss. I'm really so scared I'll never give satisfaction to the young mistress.

MISS TESMAN: Oh, Heavens . . . just to begin with of course there might be this and that. . . .

BERTE: Because she's ever so particular.

MISS TESMAN: Why, of course she is. General Gabler's daughter. The way she was used to having things in the General's time. Do you remember her riding along the road with her father? In that long black habit? And with a feather in her hat?

BERTE: I should think I would remember! . . . But I declare, I never once dreamed they'd make a match of it, her and Mr Jörgen, not in those days I didn't.

MISS TESMAN: Nor I. . . . But now here's a point, Berte, while I remember it: you mustn't say mister about Jörgen from now on. He's a doctor.

BERTE: Yes, the lady did say about that too . . . last night . . . soon as they came in at the door. Is it really true then, Miss?

MISS TESMAN: Why certainly it's true. Just fancy, Berte . . . they made him a doctor abroad. Now, on the journey, you know. And I never knew the first thing about it . . . till he told me down there on the quay.

BERTE: Well, I should think he could get to be anything at all, he could. He's that clever. But I'd never have thought he'd have taken to doctoring people, too.

MISS TESMAN: Oh no, he's not that sort of doctor. . . . [*She nods significantly.*] And by the way, you'll probably have to call him something even finer pretty soon.

BERTE: Well I never! What sort of thing, Miss?

MISS TESMAN [*smiles*]: Hm . . . wouldn't you like to know! . . . [*emotionally*] Ah, dear God . . . if my sainted brother could look up from the grave and see what's become of his little boy! [*She looks around.*] But what's this, Berte . . . why on earth have you done that? Taken all the loose covers off?

BERTE: The lady told me to do it. She doesn't like loose covers on the chairs, she said.

MISS TESMAN: But will they be coming in here . . . I mean for every day?

BERTE: That's what it sounded like. The lady, that is. As for himself . . . the doctor . . . he didn't say anything.

*Jörgen Tesman enters from the right of the inner room, humming a tune and carrying an open, empty suitcase. He is a man of 33, of middle height and youthful appearance; slightly plump, his face round, open, and cheerful. Fair hair and beard. He wears glasses, and is dressed in comfortable, slightly slovenly, indoor clothes.*

MISS TESMAN: Good morning, good morning, Jörgen!

TESMAN [*in the doorway*]: Aunt Julle! Dear Aunt Julle! [*goes over and pumps her hand*] Come all this way . . . so early in the morning! Eh?

MISS TESMAN: Well, of course I had to come and see how you've all settled in.

TESMAN: And you never even had a proper night's rest!

MISS TESMAN: Oh, that won't do me any harm.

TESMAN: Well, well, and you managed all right getting home from the quay, I hope? Eh?

MISS TESMAN: Oh yes, I did very well . . . thank Heavens. Mr Brack was so very kind as to take me right to the door.

TESMAN: We were so dreadfully sorry we couldn't take you in the cab. But you could see for yourself. . . . Hedda had so many cases that had to come.

MISS TESMAN: Yes, she really did have a great many cases.

BERTE [*to Tesman*]: Should I maybe go in and ask the mistress whether she wants me for anything?

TESMAN: No thank you, Berte . . . I don't think you'd better. If there is anything she'll ring, she said.

BERTE [*crossing to the right*]: All right, then.

TESMAN: Hey, wait a moment . . . take this along, will you.

BERTE [*taking the suitcase*]: I'll put it up in the loft. [*She goes out at the hall door.*]

TESMAN: Just think, Auntie . . . the whole of that case was crammed full of nothing but notes. It's quite incredible, really, all the things I managed to dig up round about in those old archives. Fantastic old things that no one knew anything about. . . .

MISS TESMAN: Well to be sure, I don't expect you wasted your time on your honeymoon, did you, Jörgen?

TESMAN: I can assure you I didn't. But do take your hat off, Auntie. There now! Let me undo that ribbon. Eh?

MISS TESMAN [*as he does so*]: Oh, my dear . . . it's just as though you were home with us still.

TESMAN [*turning the hat around in his hand*]: My, my . . . that's a fine and fancy hat you've given yourself!

MISS TESMAN: I bought it because of Hedda.

TESMAN: Because of Hedda? Eh?

MISS TESMAN: Yes, so Hedda won't be ashamed of me, if we should happen to walk together in the street.

TESMAN [*patting her cheek*]: You always think of everything, don't you, Auntie Julle. [*He puts the hat on a chair by the table.*] And now . . . there we are . . . now we'll sit down on the sofa here. And we'll have a little chat until Hedda turns up.

*They sit down. She puts her parasol in the corner by the sofa.*

MISS TESMAN [*takes both his hands and looks at him*]: How wonderfully good it is to see you here again, as well as ever, and full of life, Jörgen! Ah . . . sainted Joachim's little boy!

TESMAN: For me too! To be with you again, Auntie Julle! You've always been both father and mother to me.

MISS TESMAN: Yes, I know you'll always have a soft spot in your heart for your old aunts.

TESMAN: But there's absolutely no improvement in Auntie Rina. Eh?

MISS TESMAN: Oh no, dear . . . we don't expect any, poor thing. She just lies there as she has done all these years. But God grant that I may keep her a little while yet! I don't know what I'd do without her, Jörgen. Especially now, you know, when I haven't got you to cope with any more.

TESMAN [*patting her back*]: There now, Auntie! . . .

MISS TESMAN [*suddenly switching to another tone*]: Well just think of it, so now you're a married man, Jörgen! . . . And to think that you'd be the one to walk off with Hedda Gabler! The lovely Hedda Gabler. Imagine it! So many admirers she always had around her!

TESMAN [*hums a bit and smirks*]: Yes I dare say there are one or two of my good friends who wouldn't mind being in my shoes. Eh?

MISS TESMAN: And then that you were able to take such a honeymoon, too! Five months . . . almost six. . . .

TESMAN: Oh well . . . for me it was a sort of academic trip too, you know. I had to look through all those old records. And the books I had to plough through!

MISS TESMAN: Yes, I suppose you did. [*lowers her voice confidentially*] But tell me, no, Jörgen . . . isn't there anything . . . any other news you can tell me?

TESMAN: From the trip, you mean?

MISS TESMAN: Yes.

TESMAN: Well, I don't think there's much I didn't get into my letters. I was given a doctorate . . . but I told you about that last night.

MISS TESMAN: Oh, all those things, yes. But I mean to say . . . haven't you any . . . as it were . . . any prospects of . . . ?

TESMAN: Prospects?

MISS TESMAN: Oh, good Heavens, Jörgen . . . after all I am your old aunt!

TESMAN: Why certainly I can talk of prospects.

MISS TESMAN: Oh!

TESMAN: I have the best prospect in the world of becoming a professor, one of these days.

MISS TESMAN: Oh yes, professor. . . .

TESMAN: Or . . . I may as well say I'm certain to get it. But dear Auntie Julle . . . you know all this yourself!

MISS TESMAN [*suppressing a smile*]: Why, to be sure I do. You're quite right. [*changing the subject*] . . . But you were telling me about the journey. . . . It must have cost a pretty penny, Jörgen?

TESMAN: Oh well, the cost . . . that big fellowship helped quite a bit, you know.

MISS TESMAN: But I just can't imagine how you could make it do for both of you.

TESMAN: No, I suppose that would need a bit of imagination. Eh?

MISS TESMAN: And then when you're travelling with a lady. That makes everything so very much more expensive, I'm told.

TESMAN: Oh of course . . . it's bound to make a bit of difference. But Hedda had to have that trip, Aunt! She really had to. I couldn't do less.

MISS TESMAN: No, I suppose not. A honeymoon trip, that seems to be part of the trimmings, these days. . . . But tell me now . . . have you had a good look round the house?

TESMAN: Indeed I have. I've been up and about since dawn.

MISS TESMAN: Well, and how do you like it all?

TESMAN: Very much! Oh, very much indeed! There's just one thing, I don't quite know what we're going to do about those two empty rooms, you know, between the back room there and Hedda's bedroom.

MISS TESMAN [*with a smile*]: Ah, my dear Jörgen, you might find a use for them . . . when the time comes.

TESMAN: Why yes, Auntie Julle, you've got something there! As I gradually add to my collection of books, then. . . . Eh?

MISS TESMAN: Precisely, my dear boy. I was thinking of your books.

TESMAN: Most of all I'm pleased for Hedda, though. Before we got engaged she always said that old Lady Falk's villa was the only house she'd really like to live in.

MISS TESMAN: Yes, think of it . . . and then just after you'd gone away it came up for sale.

TESMAN: Yes, Aunt Julle, we really were lucky. Eh?

MISS TESMAN: But expensive, my dear Jörgen! It'll be a terrible expense for you . . . all this.

TESMAN [*looks at her rather crestfallen*]: Why yes, I suppose it will, Auntie?

MISS TESMAN: Oh my dear!

TESMAN: How much, do you think? Approximately? Eh?

MISS TESMAN: I simply can't tell you, before all the bills have come in.

TESMAN: Oh well, luckily Brack was able to get very favourable terms for me. He said as much when he wrote to Hedda.

MISS TESMAN: Yes, don't you worry about that, my boy. . . . Anyway, I've given security for the furniture and all the carpets.

TESMAN: Security? You have? But Auntie Julle . . . what sort of security could you offer?

MISS TESMAN: I made out a mortgage on the annuity.

TESMAN [*leaps up*]: What! On your . . . and Aunt Rina's annuity!

MISS TESMAN: Well, there didn't seem to be any other way of doing it, you know.

TESMAN [*places himself in front of her*]: But have you gone out of your mind, Auntie! That annuity . . . you and Aunt Rina, it's the only thing you've got to live on.

MISS TESMAN: There now . . . don't get so excited about it. It's just a formality, you know. Mr Brack said so too, and he's a judge. He was the one who helped me to arrange the whole thing. Just a formality, he said.

TESMAN: Yes, that's all very well. But all the same . . .

MISS TESMAN: And now you're getting your own salary to draw on. And good gracious, if we did have to spend a little . . . ? A helping hand, just to begin with . . . ? Why, we'd be only too happy.

TESMAN: Oh, Auntie . . . you'll never stop sacrificing yourself for me!

MISS TESMAN [*rises and puts her hands on his shoulders*]: Isn't it the only joy I have in this world, to help you along your road, my darling boy? You, who have neither father nor mother to look to? And now we're very nearly there, my boy! There were some black days among the rest. But, thanks be to God, you've made good, Jörgen!

TESMAN: Yes, it's queer, really, the way it all turned out.

MISS TESMAN: Yes . . . and the people who stood in your way . . . and wanted to keep you back . . . you outran them all. They've fallen by the wayside, Jörgen! And your most dangerous adversary, he fell lower than any of them, he did. . . . And now he must lie on the bed he's made for himself . . . the poor depraved creature.

TESMAN: Have you heard anything of Ejlert? Since I went off, I mean.

MISS TESMAN: Only that he's supposed to have published a new book.

TESMAN: What's that! Ejlert Lövborg? Just recently, you mean? Eh?

MISS TESMAN: Yes, so they say. Do you think it's likely to amount to anything much? Now when your new book arrives . . . that'll be another matter, Jörgen! What's it going to be about?

TESMAN: It will be an account of the domestic crafts of mediaeval Brabant.

MISS TESMAN: Just think . . . and you can write about things like that!

TESMAN: Incidentally, it may be quite a while before I get it finished. There are all these extensive collections of material, you know, they all have to be sorted out first.

MISS TESMAN: Yes, collecting things and sorting them out . . . you've always been good at that. You're not Joachim's son for nothing!

TESMAN: I'm ever so keen to get going on it. Especially now, with my own comfortable and charming house to sit and work in.

MISS TESMAN: Ah, and most of all, now that you've won the wife of your heart, dear Jörgen.

TESMAN [*embracing her*]: Oh yes, Auntie Julle! Hedda . . . that's the most wonderful thing of all! [*looks towards the doorway*] But here she is, isn't she? Eh?

*Hedda comes in from the left of the back room. She is a lady of 29. Her face and her figure are aristocratic and elegant in their proportions. He complexion is of an even pallor. Her eyes are steel grey, and cold, clear, and dispassionate. Her hair is an attractive medium brown in colour, but not particularly ample. She is dressed in a tasteful, somewhat loose-fitting morning gown.*

MISS TESMAN [*goes to meet her*]: Good morning, dear Hedda! A very good morning to you!

HEDDA [*offers her hand*]: Good morning, dear Miss Tesman! Such an early visit. So very kind.

MISS TESMAN [*appearing somewhat put out*]: Well, and did the young mistress sleep well in her new home?

HEDDA: Thank you, I slept tolerably well.

TESMAN [*laughs*]: Tolerably! That's a good one, Hedda! You were sleeping like a log, you were, when I got up.

HEDDA: How fortunate. But then, Miss Tesman, one always has to get used to new things. Bit by bit. [*looks towards the window*] Ugh . . . the maid's been and opened the verandah door. The place is flooded with sunlight.

MISS TESMAN [*moving towards the door*]: Well, let's shut it.

HEDDA: Oh no, don't do that! Dear Tesman, go and draw the curtains. That gives a softer light.

TESMAN [*at the door*]: So be it . . . so be it. . . . There you are, Hedda . . . now you've got both shade and fresh air.

HEDDA: Yes, we can do with a bit of fresh air. All these blessed flowers. . . . But dear Miss Tesman . . . won't you take a seat?

MISS TESMAN: No, thank you very much. Now I know everything's all right . . . thanks be to God! And I'd better be thinking of getting home again. To her, lying and waiting so patiently, poor dear.

TESMAN: You'll give her my love, won't you. And say I'll pop in to see her later in the day.

MISS TESMAN: Yes, yes, I'll tell her. Oh, here's another thing, Jörgen . . . [*She feels in her skirt pocket.*] I almost went and forgot it. I've got a little something for you.

TESMAN: What can it be, Aunt? Eh?

MISS TESMAN [*extracts a flat object wrapped in newspaper and hands it to him*]: There you are, my boy.

TESMAN [*opens it*]: Oh my goodness! . . . So you kept them for me, Auntie Julle! Hedda! Now isn't that nice of her, Hedda! Eh?

HEDDA [*by the right-hand whatnot*]: Of course, dear. What is it?

TESMAN: My old house shoes! My slippers, Hedda!

HEDDA: Ah yes. You mentioned them quite frequently on the trip, I remember.

TESMAN: Yes, I did miss them so. [*He goes to her.*] Here, just take a look at them, Hedda!

HEDDA [*crossing to the stove*]: Thank you, they wouldn't appeal to me.

TESMAN [*following her*]: Think of it . . . Aunt Rina lay there and embroidered them for me. Weak as she was. Oh, you can't imagine how many memories they have for me.

HEDDA [*by the table*]: But not for me, particularly.

MISS TESMAN: Why, Hedda's quite right about that, Jörgen.

TESMAN: Yes, but I do think, now that she's one of the family . . .

HEDDA [*interrupts*]: We'll never be able to manage with that maid, Tesman.

MISS TESMAN: Not manage with Berte?

TESMAN: My dear . . . why on earth should you say that? Eh?

HEDDA [*points*]: Look at that! She's left her old hat lying on the chair there.

TESMAN [*appalled, drops the slippers on the floor*]: But . . . but Hedda . . . !

HEDDA: Just think . . . somebody might come in and see it.

TESMAN: No but Hedda . . . that . . . that's Auntie Julle's hat!

HEDDA: Is it?

MISS TESMAN [*takes the hat*]: Yes indeed it's mine. And as it happens it isn't so very old either, my dear young lady.

HEDDA: I really didn't look at it so very closely, Miss Tesman.

MISS TESMAN [*ties on the hat*]: As a matter of fact I'm wearing it for the very first time. And that's the God's truth.

TESMAN: And an awfully fine hat it is too. Really smart!

MISS TESMAN: Oh, that's as it may be, my dear Jörgen. [*looks around*] And my parasol . . . ? Here it is. [*She takes it.*] Because that happens to be mine too. [*under her breath*] Not Berte's.

TESMAN: A new hat and a new parasol! Think of that, Hedda!

HEDDA: Yes, really charming.

TESMAN: Yes, aren't they just? Eh? But Aunt, take a good look at Hedda before you go! Charming's the word for her, eh?

MISS TESMAN: Oh my dear, that's nothing new. Hedda's been lovely all her life.

[*She nods and starts across to the right.*]

TESMAN [*following her*]: Yes, but have you noticed how well and bonny she looks? I declare she's filled out beautifully on the trip.

HEDDA [*moves irritably*]: Oh, do you have to . . . !

MISS TESMAN [*has stopped and turned*]: Filled out?

TESMAN: Yes, Aunt Julle, you don't notice it so much when she's wearing that dress, But I . . . well, I have occasion to . . .

HEDDA [*at the verandah door, impatiently*]: Oh, you don't have occasion for anything!

TESMAN: It must be the mountain air in the Tyrol. . . .

HEDDA [*curtly interrupting*]: I'm exactly the same as I was when we left.

TESMAN: Yes, that's what you say. But you aren't, you know. Can't you see it too, Auntie?

MISS TESMAN [*She has folded her hands and gazes at Hedda.*]: Lovely . . . lovely . . . lovely Hedda. [*She goes to Hedda, takes her head and inclines it towards her with both hands, and kisses her hair.*] God bless you and keep you, Hedda Tesman. For Jörgen's sake.

HEDDA [*frees herself*]: Oh . . . ! Leave me be!

MISS TESMAN [*in quiet rapture*]: Every single day I'll come and visit you both.

TESMAN: Yes, Auntie, that'll be wonderful! Eh?

MISS TESMAN: Goodbye . . . goodbye!

*She goes out at the hall door. Tesman follows her out. The door stays half open, and we hear Tesman repeating his message of love to Aunt Rina, and thanking again for the slippers.*

*While this is going on Hedda walks about the room, raises her arms and clenches her fists as though in a frenzy. Then she draws the curtains back from the verandah door, stands there, and looks out.*

*After a while Tesman comes back and shuts the door behind him.*

TESMAN [*picking up the slippers from the floor*]: What are you looking at, Hedda?

HEDDA [*calm and collected once more*]: I'm just looking at the leaves on the trees. They're so yellow. And so withered.

TESMAN [*rewraps the slippers and lays them on the table*]: Yes, well, it's September now, you know.

HEDDA [*ill at ease again*]: Why yes . . . already it's . . . it's September.

TESMAN: Don't you think Aunt Julle was odd, dear? Almost affected? What can have got into her, do you think? Eh?

HEDDA: Well, I hardly know her. Isn't she usually like that?

TESMAN: Why, no, not like she was just now.

HEDDA [*leaving the window*]: Do you think she was very put out about that hat business?

TESMAN: Oh, not so particularly. Perhaps a little just for a moment. . . .

HEDDA: Well, what manner of behaviour is that, anyway, flinging her hat just anywhere in the drawing room! It's not done.

TESMAN: Well, you may be quite sure that Aunt Julle won't do it again.

HEDDA: Oh, never mind. I'll propitiate her.

TESMAN: Oh my dear, sweet Hedda, if only you would!

HEDDA: When you go down there later you can invite her over for this evening.

TESMAN: Yes, certainly I will. And there's another thing, Hedda, that would make her so very happy.

HEDDA: Well?

TESMAN: Couldn't you bring yourself to give her a kiss when you meet? For my sake, Hedda? Eh?

HEDDA: Oh, don't ask me, Tesman, for God's sake. I've told you before, I just couldn't. I'll try to call her Aunt. And she'll have to be content with that.

TESMAN: Oh well . . . I just thought, now that you belong to the family, you . . .

HEDDA: Hm . . . I'm not at all sure . . . [*She goes upstage towards the doorway.*]

TESMAN [*after a pause*]: Is there anything the matter with you, Hedda? Eh?

HEDDA: I was just looking at my old piano. It doesn't go with the rest of the things.

TESMAN: As soon as I get my first cheque, we'll see about getting it changed.

HEDDA: Oh no . . . not changed. I don't want to part with it. We'd better put it in the back room, there. And then we can get another one for this room. At a suitable moment, I mean.

TESMAN [*rather put out*]: Yes . . . I suppose that would be an alternative.

HEDDA [*takes the bunch of flowers from the piano*]: These flowers weren't here last night when we arrived.

TESMAN: Aunt Julle probably brought them.

HEDDA [*looks into the bouquet*]: A card. [*takes it out and reads*] 'Will come again later today.' Can you guess who it's from.

TESMAN: No. Who is it from? Eh?

HEDDA: It says 'Mrs Carl Elvsted'.

TESMAN: Really! Mrs Elvsted! Miss Rysing, as she used to be.

HEDDA: Exactly. That woman with the provoking hair that everyone made such a fuss of. An old flame of yours, too, I'm told.

TESMAN [*laughs*]: Oh, it didn't last long. And besides, that was before I met you, Hedda. But just think . . . that she should be back in town.

HEDDA: It's odd that she should come here. I hardly know her, apart from school.

TESMAN: No, and I haven't seen her for . . . oh good Lord, it must be years. I don't know how she can bear to be stuck right up there, so many miles away. Eh?

HEDDA [*thinks a moment, then suddenly speaks*]: I say, Tesman . . . wasn't it up there somewhere that he went . . . that . . . Ejlert Lövborg?

TESMAN: Yes, it must be just about there.

*Berte appears at the hall door.*

BERTE: She's here again, ma'am, the lady who looked in with the flowers earlier on. [*She points.*] The ones you're holding, ma'am.

HEDDA: She is, is she. Well, be so good as to let her in.

*Berte opens the door to Mrs Elvsted and goes out herself.—Mrs Elvsted is a slight woman with soft, attractive features. Her eyes are light blue, large, round, and somewhat protruding, with a scared, questioning expression. Her hair is strikingly fair, almost whitish-yellow, and unusually rich and wavy. She is a couple of years younger than Hedda. She wears a dark going-out dress, tastefully styled but not quite in the latest fashion.*

HEDDA [*goes to meet her in a friendly manner*]: Good morning, my dear Mrs Elvsted. How nice to see you once again.

MRS ELVSTED [*nervous, trying to control herself*]: Yes, it's a long time now since we met.

TESMAN [*offering his hand*]: And since we met, too. Eh?

HEDDA: Thank you for your lovely flowers. . . .

MRS ELVSTED: Oh, thank you. . . . I would have come here at once, yesterday afternoon. But then I heard you were abroad. . . .

TESMAN: You've just arrived in town? Eh?

MRS ELVSTED: Yes. I got in about lunch time yesterday. Oh, I was quite in despair when I heard you were away.

HEDDA: In despair! But why?

TESMAN: But my dear Mrs Rysing—Mrs Elvsted I mean to say . . .

HEDDA: I hope there isn't anything wrong?

MRS ELVSTED: Yes, there is. And I don't know another soul here, not anyone I could turn to, apart from you.

HEDDA [*puts the flowers on the table*]: Come . . . we'll sit here on the sofa. . . .

MRS ELVSTED: Oh, I can hardly keep still, let alone sit down!

HEDDA: Of course you can. Come along.

*She persuades Mrs Elvsted onto the sofa, and sits beside her.*

TESMAN: Well? What is it then . . . ?

HEDDA: Is it something that's happened up at your place?

MRS ELVSTED: Well . . . it both is and yet isn't. Oh, I do so hope you won't misunderstand me.

HEDDA: Well, in that case you'd better tell us all about it, from the beginning, Mrs Elvsted.

TESMAN: After all, that's the reason why you came. Eh?

MRS ELVSTED: Yes . . . yes of course it is. And so I'd better tell you . . . if you don't already know it . . . that Ejlert Lövborg is also in town.

HEDDA: Lövborg is . . . !

TESMAN: What, Ejlert Lövborg back again! Think of that, Hedda!

HEDDA: Yes, yes, I heard!

MRS ELVSTED: He's been here now for about a week. Think of it . . . a whole week! In this dangerous place. Alone! And all the bad influences there are here.

HEDDA: But . . . excuse me, Mrs Elvsted, but how can this possibly concern you?

MRS ELVSTED [*gives her a scared look, then speaks quickly*]: He used to come and teach the children.

HEDDA: Your children?

MRS ELVSTED: My husband's. I haven't got any.

HEDDA: Stepchildren, then.

MRS ELVSTED: Yes.

TESMAN [*slightly incoherent*]: But was he sufficiently . . . I don't quite know how to put it . . . sort of . . . well, regular in his life and habits, so that he could be trusted with . . . ? Eh?

MRS ELVSTED: For the last two years, there's been nothing that anyone could hold against him.

TESMAN: Hasn't there really? Think of that, Hedda!

HEDDA: Yes, I'm listening.

MRS ELVSTED: Nothing at all, I assure you. Not in any way. But all the same . . . Now that I know he's down here . . . in the big city . . . I'm so dreadfully worried about him.

TESMAN: Well, why didn't he stay where he was, then? With you and your husband? Eh?

MRS ELVSTED: When the book came out, you see, he just couldn't contain himself any more, up there.

TESMAN: Why yes of course . . . Aunt Julle said he'd published a new book.

MRS ELVSTED: Yes, a big new book, dealing with cultural development . . . sort of altogether. It's a fortnight ago, now. And then when it sold so many copies . . . and caused such an enormous stir . . .

TESMAN: Did it! Did it indeed? I suppose it was something he had tucked away from his good period, then.

MRS ELVSTED: From before, you mean?

TESMAN: Yes.

MRS ELVSTED: No, he wrote the whole thing while he was with us. Just now . . . during the last year.

TESMAN: Well, that really is good news, Hedda! Think of that!

MRS ELVSTED: Oh yes, if only everything's all right!

HEDDA: Have you seen him here in town?

MRS ELVSTED: No, not yet. It was so difficult, trying to discover his address. But this morning I got it at last.

HEDDA [*gives her a searching glance*]: You know, it seems a little odd that your husband . . . hm . . .

MRS ELVSTED [*with a nervous start*]: That my husband? What?

HEDDA: That he should send you down to town on this errand. That he didn't come in himself to look after his friend.

MRS ELVSTED: Oh no, no . . . my husband doesn't have the time. And then there was . . . some shopping I had to do.

HEDDA [*with a little smile*]: Oh, well, that's different, then.

MRS ELVSTED [*gets up quickly, ill at ease*]: And now I beg of you, Mr Tesman, please . . . receive Ejlert Lövborg well, if he comes here! And he's sure to. I know . . . you were such good friends before. And then you're both interested in the same subject. The same field of studies . . . so far as I understand it.

TESMAN: Well, it used to be before, anyway.

MRS ELVSTED: Yes, and that's why I ask you so particularly, . . . please do . . . please would you keep an eye on him as well. You will, won't you Mr Tesman . . . you promise you will.

TESMAN: Yes of course, I'll be only too happy, Mrs Rysing . . .

HEDDA: Elvsted.

TESMAN: I'll certainly do absolutely everything I can for Ejlert. You may be sure of that.

MRS ELVSTED: Oh, how very kind you are! [*She presses his hands.*] Thank you, Mr Tesman, thank you! [*alarmed*] Yes, because my husband is so particularly fond of him!

HEDDA [*rising*]: You ought to write to him, Tesman. Perhaps he won't come on his own initiative.

TESMAN: Yes, wouldn't that be the best idea, Hedda? Eh?

HEDDA: And the sooner the better. You'd better do it now, at once.

MRS ELVSTED [*beseechingly*]: Yes, if only you would!

TESMAN: I'll do it right away. Do you have his address, Mrs . . . Mrs Elvsted?

MRS ELVSTED: Yes. [*She takes a piece of paper from her pocket and hands it to him.*] I wrote it there.

TESMAN: Good, good. I'll go in, then . . . [*He looks around.*] Oh yes, what happened to . . . ? Oh, there they are.

*He picks up the packet with the slippers and is about to go.*

HEDDA: Now be sure to write something really warm and friendly. A good long letter.
TESMAN: Yes, I'll do that.
MRS ELVSTED: But for goodness sake don't say that I asked you to invite him!
TESMAN: No, of course not . . . that goes without saying. Eh?

*He goes out to the right through the back room.*

HEDDA [*goes over to Mrs Elvsted, smiles, and speaks in a low voice*]: There! Two birds with one stone.
MRS ELVSTED: What do you mean by that?
HEDDA: Couldn't you see that I wanted him to leave us?
MRS ELVSTED: Yes, to write the letter . . .
HEDDA: And so that I could speak to you alone.
MRS ELVSTED [*flustered*]: What, about all this?
HEDDA: Exactly.
MRS ELVSTED [*scared*]: But there isn't anything else, Mrs Tesman! Really, nothing more to say!
HEDDA: Oh there is indeed. There's a great deal more. That's perfectly obvious. Come here . . . we'll sit down and have a nice talk about it.

*She forces Mrs Elvsted into the armchair by the stove, and sits down herself on one of the stools.*

MRS ELVSTED [*anxious, looking at her watch*]: But Mrs Tesman, please . . . I should have left long ago.
HEDDA: Oh, you can't be in such an enormous hurry. . . . Well, then. Now you tell me a bit about your life at home.
MRS ELVSTED: Oh, that's just the one thing I really didn't want to talk about.
HEDDA: But you can tell me, my dear . . . ? After all, we were at school together.
MRS ELVSTED: Yes, but you were in the class above. Oh, I was dreadfully frightened of you in those days!
HEDDA: Frightened? Of me?
MRS ELVSTED: Oh, dreadfully frightened. When we met on the steps you always used to pull my hair.
HEDDA: No, did I really?
MRS ELVSTED: Yes, and you once said you were going to burn it off.
HEDDA: Oh, that was just something I said, you know.
MRS ELVSTED: Yes, but I was such a fool in those days. . . . And anyway, since then . . . we've grown such miles apart. We don't meet the same sort of people at all.
HEDDA: Well, we must try to bridge the gap again. We spoke freely to each other at school, at least, and we always called each other by our Christian names. . . .
MRS ELVSTED: Oh, I'm sure you're wrong about that.

HEDDA: Oh no I'm not! I remember it perfectly. And so we'll be good friends again, like we were in the old days. [*She moves her chair closer.*] There! [*She kisses her cheek.*] From now on you're to call me Hedda.

MRS ELVSTED [*presses and pats her hand*]: Oh, you're so kind and good to me! I'm just not used to such kind treatment.

HEDDA: There, now! And I'm going to call you my darling Thora.

MRS ELVSTED: I'm called Thea.

HEDDA: Quite right. Of course. Thea, I meant. [*looks at her sympathetically*] And so you're not accustomed to kind treatment, my poor Thea? Not even in your own home!

MRS ELVSTED: Oh, if only I had a home! But I haven't got one. Never had one.

HEDDA [*looks at her a little*]: I rather thought it must be something like that.

MRS ELVSTED [*stares helplessly in front of her*]: Yes . . . yes . . . yes.

HEDDA: I don't quite remember how it was, now. But didn't you go up there in the first place as Mr Elvsted's housekeeper?

MRS ELVSTED: Oh, actually I was meant to be a governess. But his wife . . . in those days . . . she was an invalid . . . and usually stayed in bed. So I had to look after the house as well.

HEDDA: But then . . . after that . . . you became the mistress of the house.

MRS ELVSTED [*heavily*]: Yes, I became his wife.

HEDDA: Let me see. . . . About how long ago would that be, now?

MRS ELVSTED: That I got married?

HEDDA: Yes.

MRS ELVSTED: That was five years ago.

HEDDA: That's right, five years it must be.

MRS ELVSTED: Oh, those five years . . . ! Well, the last two or three at least. Oh, if only you knew, Mrs Tesman . . .

HEDDA [*hits her lightly on the hand*]: Mrs Tesman? Now that's naughty, Thea.

MRS ELVSTED: Oh no, I'm sorry . . . Hedda. I'll try. But if only you could imagine what it was like. . . .

HEDDA [*casually*]: Ejlert Lövborg's been up there about three years, hasn't he?

MRS ELVSTED [*looks at her uncertainly*]: Ejlert Lövborg? Yes . . . so he has.

HEDDA: Did you know him before that? From town?

MRS ELVSTED: Hardly at all. Well, that is . . . I'd heard of him, of course.

HEDDA: But then up there . . . he used to come to your house quite often?

MRS ELVSTED: Yes, he came over every day. He had to come and read with the children. Because in the long run I couldn't manage it all by myself.

HEDDA: No indeed, I can imagine. . . . And your husband . . . ? I suppose he travels quite a bit in his position?

MRS ELVSTED: Well, of course . . . he's in charge of the whole administration of the district, so he has to keep an eye on things.

HEDDA [*leaning against the arm of the chair*]: Thea . . . poor, sweet Thea . . . now you must tell me all about it . . . as it really is.

MRS ELVSTED: Well, what do you want to know?

HEDDA: Tell me, what's your husband really like, Thea? I mean, well . . . to be with? Does he treat you well?

MRS ELVSTED [*evasively*]: He thinks he does everything for the best.

HEDDA: It just seems to me that he must be a little old for you. Over twenty years older, isn't he?

MRS ELVSTED [*roused*]: Oh, that as well. Just everything about him! There's simply nothing . . . we just haven't a thought in common. We don't share a thing, he and I.

HEDDA: But isn't he fond of you all the same? In his own way?

MRS ELVSTED: Oh, I don't know what he is. I think he just finds me useful. And then it doesn't cost much to keep me. I'm cheap.

HEDDA: That's foolish of you.

MRS ELVSTED [*shakes her head*]: Can't be anything else. Not with him. I don't believe he thinks of anyone except himself. And then perhaps a bit the children.

HEDDA: And then he's fond of Ejlert Lövborg, Thea.

MRS ELVSTED [*looks at her*]: Of Ejlert Lövborg! What gives you that idea?

HEDDA: But my dear . . . it seems to me that when he sends you all this way to town to look for him . . . [*smiles almost imperceptibly*] And besides, you told Tesman so yourself.

MRS ELVSTED [*with a nervous laugh*]: Did I? Well, I suppose I did. [*a subdued outburst*] No . . . I may as well make a clean breast of it at once! It's bound to come out anyway, in the end.

HEDDA: But Thea, my dear . . . ?

MRS ELVSTED: Brief and to the point, then! I never told my husband I was leaving.

HEDDA: What are you saying! Didn't he know you were leaving!

MRS ELVSTED: Of course not. Anyway he wasn't at home. He'd gone on a tour of inspection. Oh, I just couldn't bear it any longer, Hedda! Not another minute! So terribly alone I'd have been, up there, from now on.

HEDDA: Well! And then?

MRS ELVSTED: I just packed up a few of my belongings. The essentials. Without letting anyone see. And then I left.

HEDDA: Just like that?

MRS ELVSTED: Yes. And took the train to town.

HEDDA: But my dear, sweet Thea . . . I don't know how you dared!

MRS ELVSTED [*gets up from the chair and walks across the floor*]: Well what on earth else would you have me do?

HEDDA: But what do you think your husband will say when you go back?

MRS ELVSTED: Back up there?

HEDDA: Yes, yes.

MRS ELVSTED: I'll never go back up there.

HEDDA [*gets up, and goes closer to her*]: Then you've really . . . in all seriousness . . . run away from it all?

MRS ELVSTED: Yes. I didn't think there was anything else I could do.

HEDDA: And then . . . that you left so openly.

MRS ELVSTED: Oh, there's no hiding that sort of thing, anyway.

HEDDA: But what do you think people will say about you, Thea?

MRS ELVSTED: Oh, they'll just have to say what they please. [*She sits depressed and exhausted on the sofa.*] I simply had to do what I did.

HEDDA [*after a short pause*]: And what's going to happen to you now? What are you going to do with yourself?

MRS ELVSTED: I don't know yet. I just know that I must live here, where Ejlert Lövborg's living. . . . If I have to live at all.

HEDDA [*moves a chair across from the table, sits by her, and strokes her hands*]: Tell me, Thea . . . how did it come about, this . . . this familiarity between you and Ejlert Lövborg?

MRS ELVSTED: Oh, it just happened, bit by bit. I got a sort of control over him.

HEDDA: Really?

MRS ELVSTED: He left off his old ways. Not because I asked him to. I never dared to do that. But he knew all right that I didn't like that sort of thing. And then he gave it up.

HEDDA [*concealing an involuntary sneer*]: And so you've reclaimed the prodigal . . . as they say . . . little Thea.

MRS ELVSTED: Well, that's what he says, anyway. And he . . . for his part . . . he's made me into a sort of real person. Taught me to think . . . and to understand quite a lot of things.

HEDDA: Did he give you lessons too, then?

MRS ELVSTED: No, not lessons, like that. But he talked to me. Talked of so fantastically many things. And then came that beautiful, happy time, when I shared his work! Was allowed to help him!

HEDDA: He let you help him?

MRS ELVSTED: Yes! When he wrote anything, we always had to do it together.

HEDDA: Like two good companions, then.

MRS ELVSTED [*animated*]: Companions! Yes, imagine, Hedda . . . that's what he used to say! . . . Oh, I ought to be so wonderfully happy. But I can't be, quite. For I can't be sure that it will really last.

HEDDA: Are you still so uncertain of him, then?

MRS ELVSTED [*heavily*]: There's the shadow of a woman who stands between us.

HEDDA [*looks at her with keen interest*]: Who might that be?

MRS ELVSTED: Don't know. Someone or other from . . . from his past. Someone he can't really forget.

HEDDA: What has he told you . . . about this?

MRS ELVSTED: He's only ever once . . . sort of indirectly . . . touched on it.

HEDDA: Well! And what did he say?

MRS ELVSTED: He said that when they parted, she threatened to shoot him with a pistol.

HEDDA [*cold and collected*]: Oh rubbish! People don't have such things here.

MRS ELVSTED: No. And that's why I think it must be that red-haired singer, whom he once . . .

HEDDA: Yes, I suppose that's possible.

MRS ELVSTED: Because I can remember someone telling me that she carried a loaded pistol.

HEDDA: Oh well . . . then it must be her, then.

MRS ELVSTED [*wrings her hands*]: Yes but just think, Hedda . . . now I hear that the woman . . . she's in town again! Oh . . . I'm quite distracted. . . .

HEDDA [*glancing towards the back room*]: Sh! Here's Tesman coming. [*gets up, and whispers*] Thea . . . all this must be just between you and me.

MRS ELVSTED [*jumping up*]: Oh yes . . . yes! For God's sake . . . !

*Jörgen Tesman, with a letter in his hand, comes from the right of the inner room.*

TESMAN: There now . . . the epistle is signed and sealed.

HEDDA: That's splendid. But I think Mrs Elvsted wants to go now. I won't be a moment. I'm just going as far as the garden gate.

TESMAN: Oh Hedda . . . do you think Berte could see to this?

HEDDA [*takes the letter*]: I'll tell her.

*Berte comes in from the hall.*

BERTE: Mr Brack is here and says please may he come in.

HEDDA: Yes, ask Mr Brack to step inside. And then . . . I say, . . . then put this letter in the post box.

BERTE [*takes the letter*]: Yes, ma'am.

*She opens the door for Mr Brack, and goes out herself. Brack is a gentleman of 45. Stocky, but well built and elastic in his movements. His face roundish, with a good profile. Hair short, still almost black, and carefully dressed. Eyes lively and playful. Thick eyebrows, thick moustache cut short at the ends. He is dressed in a stylish walking suit, perhaps a little too youthful in cut for a man of his age. He uses an eyeglass, which he now and again allows to fall.*

BRACK [*bowing, his hat in his hand*]: Is it permissible to call so early in the day?

HEDDA: Of course it is.

TESMAN [*takes his hand*]: We're always glad to see you. [*He introduces.*] Mr Brack . . . Miss Rysing . . .

HEDDA: Oh . . . !

BRACK [*bows*]: Ah . . . delighted to make your acquaintance. . . .

HEDDA [*looks at him and laughs*]: How charming to view you by daylight, Mr Brack!

BRACK: You find me . . . perhaps a little changed?

HEDDA: Yes, you look rather younger, I think.

BRACK: Accept my humble gratitude.

TESMAN: But what do you say to Hedda, then! Eh? Isn't she blossoming? She's positively . . .

HEDDA: Oh, pray leave me out of this. You'd do better to thank Mr Brack for all the trouble he's taken . . .

BRACK: Oh, not at all . . . I do assure you it was a pleasure. . . .

HEDDA: Yes, you're a loyal soul. But my friend's standing here and dying to get away. Au revoir, Mr Brack. I'll be back in a moment.

*Mutual leave-taking. Mrs Elvsted and Hedda leave by the hall door.*

BRACK: Well, now . . . and does everything come up to the lady's expectations?

TESMAN: Oh yes, and we can't thank you enough. That is . . . a little shifting back and forth may be necessary, I gather. And there are one or two things missing. We'll doubtless have to acquire a few trifles yet.

BRACK: Oh, will you? Really?

TESMAN: But we won't be putting you to any further trouble. Hedda said she'd take care of the necessary purchases herself. . . . But I say, shan't we sit down? Eh?

BRACK: Thank you, just for a moment. [*sits by the table*] There's a little matter I'd like to talk to you about, my dear Tesman.

TESMAN: Oh? Ah, I'm with you! [*He sits down.*] The entertainment has its serious side, no doubt. Eh?

BRACK: Oh, as yet there's no tearing hurry about the financial side. Though incidentally, I should be happier if we'd arranged things a little more modestly.

TESMAN: But that would have been quite out of the question! Think of Hedda, man! You, who know her so well. . . . I couldn't possibly have expected her to put up with a genteel suburb!

BRACK: Ah, no . . . there's the rub.

TESMAN: And then . . . fortunately . . . it can't be long before I get that appointment.

BRACK: Well, you know . . . these things have a habit of taking their time.

TESMAN: Perhaps you've heard some more about it? Eh?

BRACK: Nothing in any way definite, but . . . [*He breaks off.*] Oh, by the way, I do have one piece of news for you.

TESMAN: Oh?

BRACK: Your old friend Ejlert Lövborg is back in town.

TESMAN: I know that already.

BRACK: Oh? How did you come to know it?

TESMAN: She told us, the lady who just went out with Hedda.

BRACK: She did. What was her name again? I didn't quite catch . . .

TESMAN: Mrs Elvsted.

BRACK: Aha . . . so that's who it was, then. Yes . . . I believe he stayed with them up there.

TESMAN: And just think . . . I was so delighted to hear that he's become quite a sober citizen again!

BRACK: Yes, that's what they say.

TESMAN: And he's supposed to have published a new book. Eh?

BRACK: Yes, by God he has!

TESMAN: And what's more, it's been very well received!

BRACK: It's been quite exceptionally well received.

TESMAN: Just think . . . isn't that wonderfully good news? That fellow, with all his extraordinary talents. . . . I was terribly convinced that he'd gone to the dogs for good.

BRACK: Yes, pretty nearly everyone thought the same.

TESMAN: But I just can't imagine what he's going to do with himself now! What on earth can he possibly find to live on? Eh?

*During the last speech, Hedda has come in from the hall.*

HEDDA [*to Brack, laughing a little scornfully*]: Tesman's forever worrying about what people are going to find to live on.

TESMAN: Oh Heavens . . . we're sitting here talking about poor Ejlert Lövborg, my dear.

HEDDA [*looks at him quickly*]: Oh yes? [*sits down in the armchair by the stove and asks indifferently*] What's the matter with him?

TESMAN: Well . . . he must have spent all the money he inherited ages ago. And I don't suppose he can write a new book every year. Eh? Well, then . . . I really can't for the life of me see how he's going to exist at all.

BRACK: Perhaps I could tell you a little about that.

TESMAN: Oh?

BRACK: You must remember that he's got relations with quite a lot of influence.

TESMAN: Oh well, his relations . . . I'm afraid they've disowned him entirely.

BRACK: They used to regard him as the white hope of the family.

TESMAN: Yes, they used to, yes! But he's been and dished all that himself.

HEDDA: Who knows? [*She smiles faintly.*] Up at the Elvsteds' they've been busy reclaiming him. . . .

BRACK: And then there's this new book he's written. . . .

TESMAN: Oh well, I hope to goodness they will help him to get something. I've just written to him. Oh, Hedda, I asked him to come round this evening.

BRACK: But my dear Tesman, you're coming to my bachelor party this evening. You promised last night on the quay.

HEDDA: Had you forgotten, Tesman?

TESMAN: Yes, by all that's holy.

BRACK: In any case, I think you may rely on him to find an excuse.

TESMAN: Why should you think that? Eh?

BRACK [*a little hesitantly, rising and leaning his hands on the back of the chair*]: My dear Tesman . . . And you too, madam. . . . I can no longer allow you to remain in ignorance of something that . . . that . . .

TESMAN: Something to do with Ejlert . . . ?

BRACK: Both him and yourself.

TESMAN: But come on then, Mr Brack!

BRACK: You ought to prepare yourself for the discovery that your appointment may not come quite as soon as you hope and expect.

TESMAN [*jumps up in alarm*]: Has something happened to delay it? Eh?

BRACK: The appointment to the professorship might conceivably be contested by another candidate. . . .

TESMAN: Another candidate! Think of that, Hedda!

HEDDA [*leans further back in her chair*]: Ah, yes . . . yes!

TESMAN: But who on earth! Surely not . . . ?

BRACK: Quite correct. Ejlert Lövborg.

TESMAN [*clasps his hands together*]: No, no . . . this is quite unthinkable! Quite impossible! Eh?

BRACK: Hm . . . we may very well find it happening, all the same.

TESMAN: Oh but my dear sir . . . but that would be quite incredibly inconsiderate of him! [*He flings his arms about.*] Yes, because . . . just think . . . I'm a married man! We got married on our expectations, Hedda and I. Been and borrowed vast sums. We're in debt to Auntie Julle, too! Because, good God . . . the post was as good as promised to me. Eh?

BRACK: Come, come, come . . . you'll most probably get it, too. But only after a bit of competition.

HEDDA [*immobile in her chair*]: Just think, Tesman . . . it'll be quite a sporting event.

TESMAN: But my dearest Hedda, how can you take it all so calmly!

HEDDA [*as before*]: Oh, I don't at all. I await the result with breathless expectation.

BRACK: Well, anyway, Mrs Tesman, it's as well that you should know how matters stand. I mean . . . before you embark on those little purchases you apparently threaten to make.

HEDDA: This can't change anything so far as that's concerned.

BRACK: No? Well, that's all right, then. I'll say goodbye! [*to Tesman*] When I take my constitutional this afternoon I'll step in and fetch you, shall I?

TESMAN: Oh yes, yes . . . I hardly know where I am.

HEDDA [*reclining, stretching out her hand*]: Goodbye, Mr Brack! We look forward to your return.

BRACK: Many thanks. Goodbye, goodbye.

TESMAN [*escorting him to the door*]: Goodbye, my dear Mr Brack! You really must excuse all this. . . .

*Brack goes out at the hall door.*

TESMAN [*trails across the floor*]: Ah, Hedda . . . one should never go building castles in the air. Eh?

HEDDA [*looks at him and smiles*]: And do you?

TESMAN: Yes . . . it can't be denied . . . it was idiotically romantic to go and get married, and buy a house, just on expectations alone.

HEDDA: You may be right about that.

TESMAN: Well . . . at least we have got out lovely house, Hedda! Just think . . . the house we'd both set out hearts on. Our dream house, I might almost call it. Eh?

HEDDA [*rises slowly and tiredly*]: The agreement was that we were to live a social life. Entertain.

TESMAN: Yes, oh Heavens . . . I was so looking forward to it! Just think, to see you as the hostess . . . presiding over a select group of friends! Eh? . . . Well, well, well . . . for the time being we'll just have to be the two of us, Hedda. Just see Aunt Julle once in a while. . . . Oh, for you everything should have been so very . . . very different . . . !

HEDDA: And I suppose I won't get my footman just yet awhile.

TESMAN: Oh no . . . a manservant, you must see that that's quite out of the question.
HEDDA: And the saddle-horse I was to have had . . .
TESMAN [*appalled*]: The saddle-horse!
HEDDA: . . . I suppose I daren't even think of that, now.
TESMAN: No, God preserve us . . . that goes without saying!
HEDDA [*moving across*]: Oh, well . . . I've got one thing at least that I can pass the time with.
TESMAN [*ecstatic*]: Oh, thank the good Lord for that! And what might that be, Hedda? Eh?
HEDDA [*at the centre doorway, looking at him with concealed contempt*]: My pistols . . . Jörgen.
TESMAN [*alarmed*]: Pistols!
HEDDA [*with cold eyes*]: General Gabler's pistols.

*She goes out to the left through the back room.*

TESMAN [*runs to the doorway and shouts after her*]: No, for the love of God, my darling Hedda . . . don't touch those dangerous contraptions! For my sake, Hedda! Eh?

## ACT II

*The room at the Tesmans' as in the first Act, except that the piano has been removed and an elegant little writing-desk with a bookshelf put in its place. A small table has been placed by the sofa on the left. Most of the flowers have been removed. Mrs Elvsted's bunch of flowers stands on the large table in the foreground. . . . It is afternoon.*

*Hedda, now dressed to receive visitors, is alone in the room. She is standing by the open glass door, loading a revolver-type pistol. Its companion lies in an open case on the writing-desk.*

HEDDA [*looks down into the garden and shouts*]: Hullo again, Mr Brack!
BRACK [*down in the garden some distance away*]: Good afternoon to you, Mrs Tesman!
HEDDA [*raises the pistol and takes aim*]: I'm going to shoot you, sir!
BRACK [*shouting down below*]: No-no-no! Don't stand there aiming right at me!
HEDDA: That's what comes of sneaking round the back!

*She fires.*

BRACK [*closer*]: Are you quite mad . . . !
HEDDA: Oh good Lord . . . did I hit you perhaps?
BRACK [*still outside*]: Stop fooling about, I tell you!
HEDDA: Come inside then, Mr Brack.

*Mr Brack, already dressed for the evening's occasion, comes in through the glass door. He carries a light overcoat on his arm.*

BRACK: What the devil . . . do you still play at that game? What are you shooting at?

HEDDA: Oh, I just stand here and shoot into the blue.

BRACK [*eases the pistol out of her hand*]: By your leave, my lady. [*looks at it*] Ah yes . . . I seem to recognize this fellow. [*looks around*] Now then, where's the case? Ah, here. [*He replaces the pistol and shuts the case.*] And now we won't play with those toys any more today.

HEDDA: Well, what in God's name do you want me to do with myself?

BRACK: Haven't you had any visitors?

HEDDA [*shuts the verandah door*]: Not a soul. I suppose the crowds are all in the country still.

BRACK: And Tesman's not in either, perhaps?

HEDDA [*at the writing-desk, puts the pistol in the drawer*]: No. As soon as he'd eaten he ran off to his aunts. He didn't expect you so soon.

BRACK: Hm . . . and I didn't think of that. Stupid of me.

HEDDA [*turns her head and looks at him*]: Why stupid?

BRACK: Because then I could have come out here . . . even a little earlier.

HEDDA [*crosses the floor*]: And then you'd have found no one at all, I've been in my room, changing after lunch.

BRACK: And isn't there the minutest chink in the door that would have permitted communication?

HEDDA: Why, you forgot to arrange one of those.

BRACK: That was also stupid of me.

HEDDA: Well, we'd better sit down here then. And wait. Because Tesman won't be home in a hurry.

BRACK: Well, well, good Heavens, I shall be patient.

*Hedda sits in the corner of the sofa. Brack lays his coat over the nearest chair and seats himself, but keeps his hat in his hand. A short pause. They look at one another.*

HEDDA: Well?

BRACK [*in the same tone*]: Well?

HEDDA: I asked first.

BRACK [*leans forward slightly*]: Well, my lady, what do you say to a comfortable little gossip.

HEDDA [*leans further back in the sofa*]: Doesn't it seem to you that it's an eternity since we talked together? Oh . . . I don't count those few words last night and this morning.

BRACK: But . . . between ourselves? Just the two of us, you mean?

HEDDA: Well, yes. More or less.

BRACK: I've gone around here day after day longing for you to come back again.

HEDDA: And for the matter of that, I've been longing for the same thing.

BRACK: You have? Really, my lady? And I was convinced you were having a wonderful time on the trip!

HEDDA: Oh, magnificent!

BRACK: But Tesman was always saying so in his letters.

HEDDA: Yes, he was! He's absolutely in his element if he's given leave to grub around in libraries. And sit copying out ancient parchments . . . or whatever they are.

BRACK [*a little maliciously*]: After all, that is his particular *raison d'être.* Part of it, anyway.

HEDDA: Yes, that's it. So it was all very fine for him. . . . But for me! Oh no, my dear Brack . . . for me it was horribly tedious.

BRACK [*sympathizing*]: Was it really as bad as all that?

HEDDA: Oh yes, use your imagination . . . ! For six months on end, never meeting anyone who knew anybody in our circle. Who could talk about our own affairs.

BRACK: Well, no . . . I'd have felt the want of that myself.

HEDDA: And then the most unbearable thing of all . . .

BRACK: Well?

HEDDA: . . . everlastingly having to be together with . . . with the selfsame person. . . .

BRACK [*nods assentingly*]: Day in and day out . . . yes. Think of it . . . at all possible times of the . . .

HEDDA: I said everlastingly.

BRACK: So be it. But I should have thought that in the case of our estimable Tesman, it would have been possible to . . .

HEDDA: Tesman is . . . an academic, my dear sir.

BRACK: Undeniably.

HEDDA: And academics aren't a bit amusing as travelling companions. Not in the long run, anyway.

BRACK: Not even . . . the academic with whom one happens to be . . . in love?

HEDDA: Ugh . . . don't use that glutinous word!

BRACK [*pulled up*]: What's this, my lady!

HEDDA [*half laughingly, half bitterly*]: Well, you ought to have a try at it! Hearing about the history of civilization day in and day out. . . .

BRACK: Everlastingly.

HEDDA: Yes-yes-yes! and then this stuff about mediaeval domestic crafts . . . ! That's the most sickening of the lot!

BRACK [*looks at her inquiringly*]: But, tell me . . . how am I then to account for the fact that . . . ? Hm. . . .

HEDDA: That Jörgen Tesman and I made a match of it, you mean?

BRACK: Well, let's put it that way.

HEDDA: Oh, Heavens, does it seem to you so strange, then?

BRACK: Both yes and no . . . my lady.

HEDDA: I'd really danced myself tired, my dear sir. I had had my day. . . . [*She gives a little shudder.*] Oh, no . . . I'm not going to say that. Nor think it, either.

BRACK: With respect, madam, you've no reason to.

HEDDA: Oh . . . reason. . . . [*She sums him up with her look.*] And Jörgen Tesman . . . you must allow that he's a most worthy person in every way.

BRACK: Oh, solid worth. Heaven preserve us.

HEDDA: And I can't see that there's anything specifically ridiculous about him. . . . Or what do you say?

BRACK: Ridiculous? No-o . . . I wouldn't say that exactly. . . .

HEDDA: Well. But then he's a most diligent research worker, at any rate! . . . And after all, he might get somewhere with it in time, in spite of everything.

BRACK [*looks at her a little uncertainly*]: But I thought you believed, like everybody else, that he'd make a really outstanding man.

HEDDA [*with a tired expression*]: Yes, so I did. . . . And then when he came along and was so pathetically eager to be allowed to support me. . . . I don't really see why I shouldn't let him?

BRACK: Well of course, if you put it like that. . . .

HEDDA: It was more than any of my other gallant friends were prepared to do, dear Mr Brack.

BRACK [*laughs*]: Ah, I regret I can't answer for all the others. But as for myself, as you know I've always observed a . . . a certain respect for the bonds of holy matrimony. In a general sort of way, my lady.

HEDDA [*banteringly*]: Well no, I never really had any very high hopes of you.

BRACK: I demand no more than a nice intimate circle of acquaintances, where I can rally round with advice and assistance, and where I'm allowed to come and go as . . . as a trusted friend. . . .

HEDDA: Of the master of the house, you mean?

BRACK [*inclines his head*]: Candidly . . . of the lady, for choice. But naturally of the man as well. D'you know . . . this sort of . . . let me put it, this sort of triangular relationship . . . it's really highly convenient for all concerned.

HEDDA: Yes, I'd have been glad of a third on the trip, often enough. Ugh . . . sitting there, just two people alone in the compartment . . . !

BRACK: Fortunately, the nuptial journey is at an end. . . .

HEDDA [*shakes her head*]: The journey'll be a long one . . . a long one yet. I've just come to a stopping-place on the line.

BRACK: Well, then you jump out. And move around a little, my lady.

HEDDA: I'll never jump out.

BRACK: Are you quite sure?

HEDDA: Yes. Because there's always someone there who'll . . .

BRACK [*laughing*]: . . . who'll look at your legs, you mean?

HEDDA: Exactly.

BRACK: Oh well, good Lord. . . .

HEDDA [*with a gesture of dismissal*]: Don't like it. . . . Then I'd sooner stay where I am . . . in the compartment. Two people alone together.

BRACK: Well then, if somebody else climbs into the compartment.

HEDDA: Ah yes . . . that's quite another thing!

BRACK: A trusted and sympathetic friend . . .

HEDDA: . . . who can converse on all manner of lively topics . . .

BRACK: . . . and who's not in the least academic!

HEDDA [*with an audible sigh*]: Yes, that really is a relief.

BRACK [*hears the front door opening and listens*]: The triangle is completed.

HEDDA [*half aloud*]: And the train drives on.

*Jörgen Tesman, in a grey walking suit and with a soft hat, comes in from the hall. He has quite a number of unbound books under his arm and in his pockets.*

TESMAN [*goes up to the table by the corner sofa*]: Poof . . . hot work dragging all these around. [*He puts down the books.*] To put it elegantly, I'm sweating, Hedda. Why, what's this . . . you're here already, Mr Brack? Eh? Berte didn't tell me anything about that.

BRACK [*gets up*]: I came up through the garden.

HEDDA: What are those books you've got there?

TESMAN [*turns a few pages*]: Oh, new academic publications that I simply had to have.

HEDDA: Academic publications?

BRACK: Aha, they're academic publications, Mrs Tesman.

*Brack and Hedda exchange a knowing smile.*

HEDDA: Do you need still more academic publications?

TESMAN: Oh yes, my dear Hedda . . . can't get too many of those. One must keep up with everything that's written.

HEDDA: Yes, I suppose one must.

TESMAN [*searching among the books*]: And look here . . . here we are, I've got hold of Ejlert Lövborg's new book, too. [*He holds it out.*] Perhaps you'd like to have a look at it, Hedda? Eh?

HEDDA: No thank you. Or . . . yes, perhaps I will, later on.

TESMAN: I glanced at a few pages on my way up.

BRACK: Well, and what did you think of it, then? . . . From the academic point of view?

TESMAN: I think it's remarkable how soberly he's argued it. He never used to write like this before. [*gathers up the books*] But now I'm going to go in with all this. It'll be a joy to cut the pages . . . ! And then I'll have to get into some other clothes. [*to Brack*] I take it we don't have to leave straight away, do we? Eh?

BRACK: No indeed . . . there's no hurry for a long while yet.

TESMAN: Ah well, I'll take my time then. [*goes with the books, but stops in the doorway and turns*] Oh, while I think of it, Hedda . . . Aunt Julle won't be able to come this evening.

HEDDA: Won't she? Is it because of that affair with the hat, perhaps?

TESMAN: Oh, good gracious! How can you think that of Auntie Julle? Just think . . . ! But the thing is Aunt Rina's so very ill, you see.

HEDDA: She always is.

TESMAN: Yes, but today she was quite exceptionally bad, poor thing.

HEDDA: Well, then it's only reasonable that the other one should stay with her. I'll have to make the best of it.

TESMAN: And you can't imagine, Hedda, how overjoyed Aunt Julle was in spite of everything . . . because you looked so well from the trip!

HEDDA [*half under her breath, getting up*]: Oh, these everlasting aunts!

TESMAN: Eh?

HEDDA [*crossing to the glass door*]: Nothing.

TESMAN: Oh, all right then. [*He goes out through the back room to the right.*]

BRACK: What was that about a hat?

HEDDA: Oh, it was to do with Miss Tesman this morning. She'd put her hat down there on the chair. [*looks at him and smiles*] And I pretended I thought it was the maid's.

BRACK [*shakes his head*]: But my dearest lady, how could you do such a thing! To that harmless old soul!

HEDDA [*nervously, walking across*]: Oh, you know how it is . . . these things just suddenly come over me. And then I can't resist them. [*flings herself down in the armchair by the stove*] Oh, I don't know myself how to explain it.

BRACK [*behind the armchair*]: You're not really happy . . . that's probably what it is.

HEDDA [*looking straight ahead*]: And I don't really know why I should be . . . happy. Or perhaps you might be able to tell me?

BRACK: Yes . . . among other things, because you've got just the home you wanted.

HEDDA [*looks up at him and laughs*]: Do you also believe that fairy story?

BRACK: Why, isn't there anything in it?

HEDDA: Oh yes . . . there's something in it.

BRACK: Well?

HEDDA: There's this much in it, that I used Tesman as an escort to take me home from evening parties last summer. . . .

BRACK: Ah, regrettably . . . I had to go quite a different way.

HEDDA: True enough, you were going a rather different way, last summer.

BRACK [*laughs*]: Touché, my lady! Well . . . but you and Tesman, then . . . ?

HEDDA: Yes, well then we came past this house one evening. And Tesman, poor fellow, was floundering and dithering. Because he couldn't think of anything to talk about. So I felt sorry for the poor erudite man. . . .

BRACK [*smiles skeptically*]: Did you? Hm. . . .

HEDDA: Yes, by your leave sir, I did. And then . . . to help him along a bit . . . I happened to say, just on the impulse, that I'd like to live here in this villa.

BRACK: No more than that?

HEDDA: Not that particular evening.

BRACK: But afterwards, then?

HEDDA: Ah yes. My impulsiveness had its consequences, my dear Mr Brack.

BRACK: Unfortunately . . . impulsiveness does that only too frequently, my lady.

HEDDA: Thank you! But in this ardour for Lady Falk's villa Jörgen Tesman and I met in mutual understanding, you see! It brought on engagement and marriage and honeymoon and the whole lot. Ah well, Mr Brack . . . as one makes one's bed one must lie on it . . . I almost said.

BRACK: But this is delicious! And perhaps you didn't really care about the place at all?

HEDDA: No, God knows I did not.

BRACK: Well, but now, then? Now that we've arranged everything a bit comfortably for you!

HEDDA: Ugh . . . I think it smells of lavender and pot-pourri in all the rooms. . . . But perhaps Auntie Julle brought that smell in with her.

BRACK [*laughs*]: No, I think it's more probably a relic of the late lamented Lady Falk.

HEDDA: Yes, it has a sort of odour of death. Like a bouquet the day after a ball. [*clasps her hands at the back of her neck, leans back in the chair and looks at him*] Ah, dear Mr Brack . . . you just can't imagine how excruciatingly bored I'll be, out here.

BRACK: Don't you think that for you too, my lady, life might have something or other up its sleeve?

HEDDA: Anything . . . in any way inviting?

BRACK: Well of course that would be best.

HEDDA: Lord knows what sort of thing that would be. I often wonder whether . . . [*She breaks off.*] But that wouldn't be any good either.

BRACK: Who knows? Let me hear about it.

HEDDA: Whether I could get Tesman to go in for politics, I mean.

BRACK [*laughs*]: Tesman! Oh now seriously . . . anything like politics, he wouldn't be any . . . manner of use at that.

HEDDA: No, I don't suppose he would. . . . But don't you think I might get him to do it, all the same?

BRACK: Well . . . what possible satisfaction could that give you? When he's no good? Why should you want him to?

HEDDA: Because I'm bored, d'you hear! [*after a pause*] So you think it would be quite out of the question for Tesman to end up as Prime Minister?

BRACK: Hm . . . you know, my lady . . . to do that he'd have to be quite a rich man, for a start.

HEDDA [*rises impatiently*]: Yes, there we have it! It's these paltry circumstances I've landed up in . . . ! [*She moves across.*] That's what makes life so pitiful! So positively ludicrous! . . . Because that's what it is.

BRACK: I think it's something else that's the trouble.

HEDDA: What, then?

BRACK: You've never had to go through any really stirring experience.

HEDDA: Anything serious, you mean?

BRACK: Yes, I suppose one could put it that way too. But now . . . it might come.

HEDDA [*tosses her head*]: Oh, you're thinking of all the commotion about this wretched professorship! But that'll be Tesman's own affair. I'm not going to give it a thought.

BRACK: No-no, well we won't talk about that. But then when you're faced with . . . what I may . . . perhaps a little pompously . . . refer to as a sacred and . . . and exacting responsibility? [*smiles*] A new responsibility, my little lady.

HEDDA [*angry*]: Be quiet! You'll never see anything of the sort!

BRACK [*carefully*]: We'll talk about it in a year's time . . . at the very latest.

HEDDA [*shortly*]: I've no aptitude for any such thing, Mr Brack. No responsibilities for me, thank you!

BRACK: Why shouldn't you, like most other women, have a natural aptitude for a vocation that . . . ?

HEDDA [*at the glass door*]: Oh, be quiet, I say! . . . I've often thought there's only one thing in the world I'm any good at.

BRACK [*moves closer*]: And what might that be, may I venture to ask?

HEDDA [*standing and looking out*]: Boring myself to death. So now you know. [*turns, looks towards the inner room, and laughs*] Ah yes, right enough! Here comes the professor.

BRACK [*cautioning her in a low voice*]: Now, now, now, my lady!

*Jörgen Tesman, dressed for the party, holding his gloves and his hat, comes in from the right of the back room.*

TESMAN: Hedda . . . did Ejlert Lövborg send to say he wasn't coming? Eh?

HEDDA: No.

TESMAN: Well then, you'll see, he'll be here in a moment.

BRACK: Do you really think he'll come?

TESMAN: Yes, I'm almost sure of it. Because I don't think you can have been right about what you said this morning.

BRACK: Oh?

TESMAN: Well at any rate Auntie Julle said she couldn't see how he could possibly think of putting himself up against me, as things are. Think of that!

BRACK: Well, then everything's perfectly all right.

TESMAN [*puts his hat, with the gloves inside, on a chair to the right*]: Yes, but you won't mind if we give him as long as possible.

BRACK: Oh, we've got any amount of time. Nobody'll be coming to my place until seven or half past.

TESMAN: Well, we can keep Hedda company until then. And see what happens. Eh?

HEDDA [*carrying Brack's overcoat and hat over to the corner sofa*]: And if the worst comes to the worst Mr Lövborg can always stay here with me.

BRACK [*wants to carry his things himself* ]: Allow me, Mrs Tesman! . . . What do you mean by the worst?

HEDDA: If he won't go with you and Tesman.

TESMAN [*looks at her uncertainly*]: But, dearest Hedda . . . do you think it would be quite the thing for him to stay with you? Eh? Remember Aunt Julle can't come.

HEDDA: No, but Mrs Elvsted's coming. And we'll all three have a nice cup of tea together.

TESMAN: Oh well, then, that's quite all right!

BRACK [*smiles*]: And perhaps that arrangement would be the most wholesome thing for him.

HEDDA: How so?

BRACK: Oh, come, Mrs Tesman, you've twitted me often enough about my little bachelor parties. Only to be recommended, wasn't it, to men of the most steadfast principles?

HEDDA: But surely Mr Lövborg is steadfast enough now. A prodigal reformed. . . .

*Berte appears at the hall door.*

BERTE: Ma'am, there's a gentleman who wants to come in. . . .

HEDDA: Let him come.

TESMAN [*quietly*]: I'm sure it's him! Think of it!

*Ejlert Lövborg comes in from the hall. He is slim and lean; the same age as Tesman, but looks older and a little haggard. Hair and beard dark brown, face longish and pale, patches of colour on either cheekbone. He is dressed in an elegant, black, and quite new suit. Dark gloves and a top hat in his hands. He remains standing close to the door and bows hurriedly. He seems a little embarrassed.*

TESMAN [*goes to him and pumps his hand*]: My dear Ejlert . . . so we meet again in spite of everything!

EJLERT LÖVBORG [*speaks in a low voice*]: Thanks for the letter, Tesman. [*approaches Hedda*] May I take your hand as well, Mrs Tesman?

HEDDA [*taking the hand he offers*]: So pleased you came, Mr Lövborg. [*with a gesture*] I wonder if you two gentlemen . . . ?

LÖVBORG [*with a slight inclination*]: Mr Brack, I believe.

BRACK [*following suit*]: How do you do. Some years ago now. . . .

TESMAN [*to Lövborg, his hands on Lövborg's shoulders*]: And now you must behave just as if you were at home, Ejlert! Isn't that right, Hedda? . . . And I hear you're going to settle here in town again? Eh?

LÖVBORG: That is so.

TESMAN: Well, and why not indeed? Hey listen . . . I've got hold of your new book. But I just haven't had a moment to read it yet.

LÖVBORG: You might as well save yourself the bother.

TESMAN: Why do you say that?

LÖVBORG: Because there's nothing much to it.

TESMAN: Oh but . . . what a thing for you to say!

BRACK: But it's been enormously praised, they tell me.

LÖVBORG: That was just what I wanted. So I wrote a book that nobody could disagree with.

BRACK: Very sensible.

TESMAN: Yes but, my dear Ejlert . . . !

LÖVBORG: Because I'm trying now to build up a position for myself. Starting over again.

TESMAN [*a bit embarrassed*]: Why yes, I suppose you are? Eh?

LÖVBORG [*smiles, puts down his hat and pulls a packet wrapped in paper from his coat pocket*]: But when this one comes out . . . Jörgen Tesman . . . then you're to read it. Because this is the real thing. I put some of myself into this one.

TESMAN: Really? And what's that about?

LÖVBORG: It's the continuation.

TESMAN: The continuation? Of what?

LÖVBORG: Of the book.

TESMAN: The new one?

LÖVBORG: Of course.

TESMAN: Yes but, my dear Ejlert . . . it carries on right to the present day!

LÖVBORG: That is so. And this one deals with the future.

TESMAN: With the future! But ye gods, we don't know anything about that!

LÖVBORG: No. But there are one or two things to be said about it, all the same. [*opens the packet*] Here, look at this. . . .

TESMAN: But that isn't your writing.

LÖVBORG: I dictated it. [*turns the leaves*] It's in two sections. The first is about the social forces involved, and this other bit . . . [*he ruffles the pages further on*] . . . that's about the future course of civilization.

TESMAN: Amazing! It just wouldn't enter my head to write about anything like that.

HEDDA [*at the glass door, drumming her fingers on the pane*]: Hm. . . . No-no.

LÖVBORG [*wraps up the papers again, and puts the packet on the table*]: I brought it along so that I could read you a bit this evening.

TESMAN: Well yes, that was frightfully decent of you, old man. But this evening . . . ? [*looks at Brack*] I don't really know if we can manage it. . . .

LÖVBORG: Well, some other time then. There's no hurry.

BRACK: I ought to tell you, Mr Lövborg . . . there's going to be a little entertainment at my place this evening. More or less in honour of Tesman, you understand. . . .

LÖVBORG [*looks for his hat*]: Ah . . . in that case I won't . . .

BRACK: No, just a moment. Wouldn't you do me the very great honour of joining us?

LÖVBORG [*shortly and firmly*]: No, I'm afraid I can't. Thank you very much indeed.

BRACK: Oh, come along! Do be persuaded. We'll be quite a small and select gathering. And I guarantee that it'll be 'lively', as my la— . . . as Mrs Tesman expresses it.

LÖVBORG: I don't doubt it. But all the same . . .

BRACK: Then you could bring along your manuscript and read to Tesman over at my place. There are plenty of rooms.

TESMAN: Yes, just think, Ejlert . . . what about that! Eh?

HEDDA [*intervenes*]: But my dear, when Mr Lövborg doesn't want to! I'm sure that Mr Lövborg would far sooner stay where he is and take a bit of supper with me.

LÖVBORG [*looks at her*]: With you, Mrs Tesman?

HEDDA: And then with Mrs Elvsted.

LÖVBORG: Oh. . . . [*casually*] I met her for a moment this afternoon.

HEDDA: Did you? Well, she's coming out here. And so you'll almost have to stay, Mr Lövborg. Because otherwise there'll be no one to see her home.

LÖVBORG: That's true. Well, thank you very much, Mrs Tesman . . . I'll stay here then.

HEDDA: Then I'll just have a word with the maid. . . .

*She goes to the hall door and rings. Berte comes in. Hedda speaks to her quietly and points towards the inner room. Berte nods and goes out again.*

TESMAN [*while this is going on, to Lövborg*]: Tell me, Ejlert . . . is it this new subject . . . this business about the future . . . that you'll be lecturing about?

LÖVBORG: Yes.

TESMAN: Because I heard at the bookseller's that you're giving a series of lectures here this autumn.

LÖVBORG: I am. You mustn't hold it against me, Tesman.

TESMAN: No, no, of course I wouldn't dream of it. But . . . ?

LÖVBORG: I can see that for you this must be rather an embarrassment.

TESMAN [*dejected*]: Oh well, I can't possibly expect you to . . .

LÖVBORG: But I shall wait till you've received your appointment.

TESMAN: You'll wait till . . . ! Yes but . . . yes but . . . aren't you going to compete for it? Eh?

LÖVBORG: No. I only intend to outshine you. In reputation.

TESMAN: But, good heavens . . . so Auntie Julle was right after all! There . . . I said she would be! Hedda! Just think, Hedda . . . Ejlert Lövborg isn't going to stand in our way at all!

HEDDA [*shortly*]: Our way? Leave me out of it.

*She goes upstage towards the back room, where Berte is placing a tray with decanters and glasses on the table. Hedda nods her approval and comes forward again. Berte goes out.*

TESMAN [*while this is going on*]: Well, Mr Brack, what about that! . . . What do you say? Eh?

BRACK: Well, I say that honour and reputation . . . hm . . . these things certainly have their appeal. . . .

TESMAN: Yes of course they do. But all the same . . .

HEDDA [*looks at Tesman with a cold smile*]: You stand there looking as if you'd been struck by lightning.

BRACK: And it was quite a thunderstorm that passed over us, Mrs Tesman.

HEDDA [*points to the back room*]: Now, would all you gentlemen like to go inside and take a glass of cold punch?

BRACK [*looks at his watch*]: By way of an hors d'oeuvre? That wouldn't be a bad idea.

TESMAN: Excellent, Hedda! Just what we need! I really feel in the mood for something now.

HEDDA: You'll have some too, Mr Lövborg.

LÖVBORG [*dismissing the subject*]: No thank you. Not for me.

BRACK: But good Lord . . . there's nothing lethal about cold punch, let me tell you.

LÖVBORG: Not perhaps for everyone.

HEDDA: Well then, I'll entertain Mr Lövborg in the meanwhile.

TESMAN: All right, dear Hedda, you do that.

*Tesman and Brack go into the inner room, sit down, drink punch, smoke cigarettes, and carry on an animated conversation during the following scene. Ejlert Lövborg remains standing by the stove. Hedda goes to the desk.*

HEDDA [*in a slightly loud voice*]: And now if you like I'll show you some photographs. We took an excursion through the Tyrol . . . Tesman and I . . . on our way home.

*She produces an album, and, laying it on the small table, sits down at the upper end of the sofa. Ejlert Lövborg comes closer, stops, and looks at her. Then he takes a chair and sits on her left, with his back to the inner room.*

HEDDA [*opens the album*]: Do you see this range of mountains, Mr Lövborg? That is the Ortler Group. Tesman wrote it underneath the picture. There you are: The Ortler Group at Meran.

LÖVBORG [*who has not once taken his eyes off her, says softly and slowly*]: Hedda . . . Gabler!

HEDDA [*with a quick sidelong glance at him*]: Now! Sh!

LÖVBORG [*softly repeats*]: Hedda Gabler!

HEDDA [*looks in the album*]: That was once my name. When . . . when we two used to know each other.

LÖVBORG: And from now on . . . and for the rest of my life . . . I must stop saying Hedda Gabler.

HEDDA [*still turning the pages*]: Yes, you must. And I think you'd better start practising at once. The sooner the better, I should say.

LÖVBORG [*with bitterness in his voice*]: Hedda Gabler married. And married to . . . Jörgen Tesman!

HEDDA: Yes . . . that's the way of it.

LÖVBORG: Oh Hedda . . . darling Hedda, how could you throw yourself away like that?

HEDDA [*with a sharp look*]: Now. None of that!

LÖVBORG: None of what?

*Tesman comes in and goes towards the sofa.*

HEDDA [*hears him coming and says indifferently*]: And this, Mr Lövborg, was taken in the Ampezzo Valley. Just look at those rock formations. [*looks amiably up at Tesman*] What were those peculiar mountains called, dear?

TESMAN: Let me look. Ah, those are the Dolomites.

HEDDA: That's right! . . . those are the Dolomites, Mr Lövborg.

TESMAN: Oh, Hedda . . . I just wanted to ask you if you wouldn't like a little punch in here all the same? For yourself at least. Eh?

HEDDA: Yes, thank you very much. And maybe a few cakes.

TESMAN: No cigarettes?

HEDDA: No.

TESMAN: Very good.

*He goes into the back room and away to the right. Brack sits within, occasionally keeping an eye on Hedda and Lövborg.*

LÖVBORG [*quietly, as before*]: Answer me then, dearest Hedda, how could you go and do such a thing?

HEDDA [*apparently immersed in the album*]: If you continue to address me like that I shan't speak to you at all.

LÖVBORG: Even when we're alone, won't you let me?

HEDDA: I can't dictate your thoughts, Mr Lövborg. But you will speak to me with respect.

LÖVBORG: Ah, I see. Because of your love . . . for Jörgen Tesman.

HEDDA [*glances sideways at him and smiles*]: Love? That's good!

LÖVBORG: Not love, then!

HEDDA: But no kind of unfaithfulness! I'll have none of that.

LÖVBORG: Hedda . . . answer one single question. . . .

HEDDA: Sh!

*Tesman, with a tray, comes in from the back room.*

TESMAN: Here we are! This is what you've been waiting for! [*He puts the tray on the table.*]

HEDDA: Why don't you leave that to the maid?

TESMAN [*fills the glasses*]: Because I think it's such fun to wait on you, Hedda.

HEDDA: But now you've filled them both. And Mr Lövborg doesn't want . . .

TESMAN: No, but Mrs Elvsted must be here soon.

HEDDA: Oh yes, that's true . . . Mrs Elvsted. . . .

TESMAN: Had you forgotten her? Eh?

HEDDA: We're so taken up with this. [*shows him a picture*] Do you remember that little village?

TESMAN: Ah, that's the one below the Brenner Pass! That was where we stayed the night . . .

HEDDA: . . . and met all those lively summer visitors.

TESMAN: Yes, that's the place. Just think . . . if only you could have been with us, Ejlert! Well then! [*He goes in again and sits down by Brack.*]

LÖVBORG: Answer me just this one question, Hedda . . .

HEDDA: Well?

LÖVBORG: Was there no love in your relationship to me either? Not a trace . . . not a suspicion of love in that either?

HEDDA: Can there have been, I wonder? My memory is that we were two good companions. Really sincere friends. [*smiles*] You were especially candid.

LÖVBORG: You were the one who wanted it like that.

HEDDA: When I think back to that time, wasn't there something beautiful, something attractive . . . something courageous too, it seems to me . . . about this . . . this secret intimacy, this companionship that no one even dreamed of.

LÖVBORG: There was, Hedda, wasn't there! . . . When I came up to your father's in the afternoons. . . . And the General used to sit by the window, reading papers . . . his back towards us . . .

HEDDA: And we sat in the corner sofa . . .

LÖVBORG: Always with the same magazine in front of us . . .

HEDDA: Yes . . . for want of an album.

LÖVBORG: Yes, Hedda . . . and then when I used to confess to you . . . ! Told you things about myself that none of the others knew at that time. Sat there and admitted that I'd been out on the razzle for whole days and nights. For days on end. Oh, Hedda . . . what power was it in you that forced me to reveal all those things?

HEDDA: Do you think it was a power in me?

LÖVBORG: Well, how else can I explain it? And all those . . . those roundabout questions you used to put to me . . .

HEDDA: And which you were so quick to understand. . . .

LÖVBORG: That you could sit and ask like that! Quite confidently!

HEDDA: Roundabout questions, if you please.

LÖVBORG: Yes, but confidently all the same, Cross-examine me about . . . about all those things!

HEDDA: And that you could answer, Mr Lövborg.

LÖVBORG: Yes, that's just what I find so incredible . . . now afterwards. But tell me then, Hedda . . . wasn't it love at the back of it all? Wasn't it on your part a desire to absolve me . . . when I came to you and confessed? Wasn't that a part of it?

HEDDA: No, not exactly.

LÖVBORG: Why did you do it, then?

HEDDA: Do you find it so hard to understand that a young girl . . . when it can happen like that . . . in secret . . .

LÖVBORG: Well?

HEDDA: That she should want to find out about a world that . . .

LÖVBORG: That . . . ?

HEDDA: . . . that she isn't supposed to know anything about?

LÖVBORG: So that was it?

HEDDA: That as well . . . I rather think it was that as well.

LÖVBORG: Our common lust for life. But then why couldn't that at least have gone on?

HEDDA: That was your own fault.

LÖVBORG: It was you who broke it off.

HEDDA: Yes, because there was an imminent danger that the game would become a reality. Shame on you, Ejlert Lövborg, how could you offer such violences to . . . to your confidential companion!

LÖVBORG [*presses his fists together*]: Oh, why didn't you play it out! Why didn't you shoot me down, as you threatened!

HEDDA: I'm too much afraid of a scandal.

LÖVBORG: Yes, Hedda, at bottom you're a coward.

HEDDA: An awful coward. [*in a different tone*] Which was lucky for you. And now you've consoled yourself so beautifully up at the Elvsteds'.

LÖVBORG: I know what Thea's told you.

HEDDA: And perhaps you told her something about us?

LÖVBORG: Not a word. She's too stupid to understand anything like that.

HEDDA: Stupid?

LÖVBORG: She's stupid about things like that.

HEDDA: And I'm a coward. [*leans a little closer to him, and without meeting his eyes says softly*] But now I'm going to confess something to you.

LÖVBORG [*in suspense*]: What?

HEDDA: That I didn't dare to shoot you . . .

LÖVBORG: Yes!

HEDDA: . . . that wasn't my worst cowardice . . . that evening. . . .

LÖVBORG [*looks at her for a moment, takes her meaning, and whispers passionately*]: Oh Hedda! Hedda Gabler! Now I think I see what it was that lay behind our companionship! You and I . . . ! So it was your lust for life . . .

HEDDA [*quietly with a sharp glance at him*]: Have a care! Don't assume any such thing!

*It has started to get dark. The hall door is opened by Berte.*

HEDDA [*clasps the album shut and cries out with a smile*]: At last! Thea, my dear . . . come in then!

*Mrs Elvsted comes in from the hall. She is dressed for a social occasion. The door shuts behind her.*

HEDDA [*on the sofa, stretching out her arms towards Mrs Elvsted*]: Dearest Thea . . . you can't imagine how I've been longing for you to come!

*Mrs Elvsted, in passing, exchanges a greeting with the gentlemen in the inner room; then crosses to the table and gives Hedda her hand. Ejlert Lövborg has stood up. He and Mrs Elvsted exchange a nod of greeting without speaking.*

MRS ELVSTED: Shouldn't I go in and have a word with your husband?
HEDDA: Oh, don't worry. Let them stay where they are. They'll be gone soon.
MRS ELVSTED: Are they going?
HEDDA: Yes, they're going out on the spree.
MRS ELVSTED [*quickly, to Lövborg*]: But not you?
LÖVBORG: No.
HEDDA: Mr Lövborg . . . he'll stay here with us.
MRS ELVSTED [*takes a chair and makes to sit down beside Lövborg*]: Oh, it's good to be here!
HEDDA: No you don't, Thea my pet! Not there! You come over here like a good girl. I want to be in the middle.
MRS ELVSTED: All right, just as you please.

*She goes round the table and sits on the sofa on Hedda's right. Lövborg resumes his chair.*

LÖVBORG [*after a little pause, to Hedda*]: Isn't she lovely to sit and look at?
HEDDA [*passes a hand lightly over Mrs Elvsted's hair*]: Just to look at?
LÖVBORG: Yes. Because we two . . . she and I . . . we're really good companions. We trust each other completely. And so we can sit and talk together in full confidence.
HEDDA: Nothing roundabout, Mr Lövborg?
LÖVBORG: Oh, well . . .
MRS ELVSTED [*quietly, clinging to Hedda*]: Oh, how happy I am, Hedda! Because, do you know what he also says . . . he says I've inspired him, too.
HEDDA [*looking at her with a smile*]: Does he really say that, Thea?
LÖVBORG: And then she has the courage to act, Mrs Tesman!
MRS ELVSTED: Oh Heavens . . . me, courage!
LÖVBORG: Infinite courage . . . for her companion.
HEDDA: Oh courage . . . oh yes! If only one had that.
LÖVBORG: What, then, do you mean?

HEDDA: Then life might be liveable, in spite of everything. [*switches to another tone*] But now, Thea my dear . . . now you must let me give you a glass of cold punch.

MRS ELVSTED: No thank you . . . I never drink anything like that.

HEDDA: Well, then you must, Mr Lövborg.

LÖVBORG: Thank you, not for me either.

MRS ELVSTED: No, he doesn't either!

HEDDA [*looks at him steadily*]: But when I want you to?

LÖVBORG: Makes no difference.

HEDDA [*laughs*]: And so I've got no power over you at all? Is that it?

LÖVBORG: Not where that's concerned.

HEDDA: But quite seriously, I do think you should have some all the same. For your own sake.

MRS ELVSTED: Oh, but Hedda . . . !

LÖVBORG: How do you mean?

HEDDA: Or rather, because of other people.

LÖVBORG: Oh?

HEDDA: Otherwise people might so easily get the idea that you're not . . . not really confident, really sure of yourself.

MRS ELVSTED [*quietly*]: Oh, no Hedda, no . . . !

LÖVBORG: People can think whatever they like . . . for the time being.

MRS ELVSTED [*happy*]: Yes, that's right!

HEDDA: It was so obvious with Mr Brack just now.

LÖVBORG: What do you mean?

HEDDA: He smiled so contemptuously when you didn't dare to join them in there at the table.

LÖVBORG: Didn't I dare! I quite naturally preferred to stay here and talk to you.

MRS ELVSTED: Of course he did, Hedda!

HEDDA: Well, Mr Brack wasn't to know that. And I also saw the way he smiled and glanced at Tesman when you didn't dare to go along to this wretched little party, either.

LÖVBORG: Dare! Do you say I didn't dare!

HEDDA: I don't. But that's the way Mr Brack understood it.

LÖVBORG: Let him.

HEDDA: So you're not going?

LÖVBORG: I'll stay with you and Thea.

MRS ELVSTED: Yes, Hedda . . . of course he's going to stay!

HEDDA [*nods and smiles approvingly at Lövborg*]: Firm as a rock, then. A man who is steadfast in his principles. Well, that's how a man should be! [*turns to Mrs Elvsted and pats her*] There, wasn't that what I said this morning when you came in here in such a state of desperation. . . .

LÖVBORG [*pulled up*]: Desperation?

MRS ELVSTED [*in a panic*]: Hedda . . . oh but Hedda . . . !

HEDDA: Just look at him! There isn't the slightest need for you to go about in mortal terror . . . [*She breaks off.*] There! Now we can all be lively!

LÖVBORG [*shocked*]: But . . . what is all this, Mrs Tesman?

MRS ELVSTED: Oh God, oh God, Hedda! What are you saying? What are you trying to do?

HEDDA: Hush, now! That odious Mr Brack has got his eye on you.

LÖVBORG: So you were in mortal terror. On my account.

MRS ELVSTED [*quietly wailing*]: Oh, Hedda . . . now you've really made me unhappy!

LÖVBORG [*looks at her steadily for a moment. His face is tense.*]: So that was my companion's confident belief in me.

MRS ELVSTED [*piteously*]: Oh, my dear, you must let me explain . . . !

LÖVBORG [*takes one of the full punch glasses, raises it, and says quietly, in a hoarse voice*]: Your health, Thea!

[*He empties the glass, puts it down, and picks up the other.*]

MRS ELVSTED [*quietly*]: Oh Hedda, Hedda . . . how could you have wanted this to happen?

HEDDA: I wanted it? Don't be absurd!

LÖVBORG: And yours too, Mrs Tesman! Thanks for the truth. Here's to it!

[*He drinks and makes to refill the glass.*]

HEDDA [*putting her hand on his arm*]: Now, now . . . no more for the moment. Remember you're going to a party.

MRS ELVSTED: No, no, no!

HEDDA: Quiet! They're sitting looking at you.

LÖVBORG [*puts down the glass*]: Thea . . . be honest with me. . . .

MRS ELVSTED: Yes!

LÖVBORG: Did your husband know you were coming down to look for me?

MRS ELVSTED [*wrings her hands*]: Oh Hedda . . . did you hear what he asked me?

LÖVBORG: Did you arrange it between you that you should come to town to keep an eye on me? Or maybe it was the old man himself who suggested it? Aha, now I've got it . . . he wanted me back in the office again! Or was he short of a fourth at cards?

MRS ELVSTED [*quietly, painfully*]: Oh Lövborg . . . !

LÖVBORG [*grabs a glass and starts to fill it*]: And here's one to old Elvsted, too!

HEDDA [*firmly*]: No more now. Remember you're going out to read to Tesman.

LÖVBORG [*quietly, putting down the glass*]: I'm sorry, Thea. I've made a fool of myself. Taking it like that, I mean. Don't be angry with me, my dear . . . dear companion. I'll show you . . . both you and the others . . . that however worthless I may have been in the past, I . . . I've found my feet again! With your help, Thea.

MRS ELVSTED [*ecstatically happy again*]: Oh, thank God . . . !

*In the meanwhile Brack has been looking at his watch. He and Tesman get up and come into the drawing room.*

BRACK [*taking his hat and coat*]: Well, Mrs Tesman, our time is up.

HEDDA: I suppose it is.

LÖVBORG [*getting up*]: Mine too, Mr Brack.

MRS ELVSTED [*quietly and imploringly*]: Oh Lövborg . . . don't do it!

HEDDA [*pinches her arm*]: They can hear you!

MRS ELVSTED [*crying out faintly*]: Ow!

LÖVBORG [*to Brack*]: You were so kind as to invite me.

BRACK: Oh, so you've changed your mind?

LÖVBORG: Yes, if I may.

BRACK: A very great pleasure. . . .

LÖVBORG [*pockets his manuscript and addresses Tesman*]: Because there are one or two things I'd like to show you before I hand it in.

TESMAN: Just think . . . that'll be wonderful! . . . But I say, Hedda, how will you get Mrs Elvsted home then? Eh?

HEDDA: Oh, we'll manage somehow.

LÖVBORG [*looking at the ladies*]: Mrs Elvsted? Why, naturally I'll come back and fetch her. [*goes closer*] Somewhere about ten o'clock, Mrs Tesman. Will that suit you?

HEDDA: Yes, that'll be splendid.

TESMAN: Oh well, then everything's in order. But you mustn't expect me so early, Hedda.

HEDDA: Oh that's all right. Just you stay as long as . . . ever you like.

MRS ELVSTED [*with suppressed anxiety*]: Mr Lövborg . . . I'll stay here then, till you come.

LÖVBORG [*his hat in his hand*]: Why of course.

BRACK: And now, gentlemen, let the revels commence! I trust it will be lively, as a certain lovely lady has it.

HEDDA: Ah, if only that lovely lady could come along as an invisible onlooker . . . !

BRACK: Why invisible?

HEDDA: So as to hear a little of your liveliness . . . unexpurgated, Mr Brack.

BRACK [*laughs*]: Ah, now that's something I wouldn't recommend to the lovely lady!

TESMAN [*also laughing*]: That's a good one, Hedda! Think of that!

BRACK: Well, goodbye, goodbye, ladies!

LÖVBORG [*bowing in departure*]: About ten, then.

*Brack, Lövborg, and Tesman go out at the hall door. Simultaneously Berte comes in from the back room with a lighted lamp, which she places on the large table, and goes out the way she came.*

MRS ELVSTED [*has got up, and wanders uneasily about the room*]: Hedda . . . Hedda . . . how is all this going to end!

HEDDA: Ten o'clock . . . and back he'll come. I can just see him. With vine leaves in his hair. Flushed and confident . . .

MRS ELVSTED: Yes, oh I do so hope it's like that.

HEDDA: And then, my dear . . . then he'll be master of himself again. He'll be a free man for the rest of his life.

MRS ELVSTED: Oh yes, oh God . . . if only he would come back, just as you see him.

HEDDA: He'll come . . . just exactly like that! [*She gets up and goes closer to her.*] You may doubt him as much as you please. I believe in him. And then we'll be able to see . . .

MRS ELVSTED: You've got some reason for all this, Hedda!

HEDDA: Yes, I have. For once in my life I want to feel that I control a human destiny.

MRS ELVSTED: But surely you do already?

HEDDA: I don't, and I never have done.

MRS ELVSTED: But what about your husband?

HEDDA: Yes, that would really be something, wouldn't it. Oh, if only you knew how destitute I am. And you're allowed to be rich! [*She passionately grips Mrs Elvsted in her arms.*] I think I'll burn your hair off after all.

MRS ELVSTED: Let me go! Let me go! I'm frightened of you, Hedda!

BERTE [*in the doorway*]: Everything's ready, ma'am, in the dining room.

HEDDA: Good. We're coming.

MRS ELVSTED: No, no, no! I'd sooner go home alone! Now, at once!

HEDDA: Nonsense! First you're going to have some tea, you little goose. And then . . . at ten o'clock . . . then Ejlert Lövborg will come . . . with vine leaves in his hair.

[*She pulls Mrs Elvsted towards the doorway almost by main force.*]

## ACT III

*The room at the Tesmans'. The curtains are drawn across the centre doorway, and also at the glass door. The lamp, with a shade, and half turned down, is alight on the table. The door of the stove stands open; the fire within has almost burnt itself out.*

*Mrs Elvsted, wrapped in a large shawl and with her feet on a footstool, is reclining in the armchair close to the stove. Hedda, still fully dressed, is lying asleep on the sofa with a rug over her.*

MRS ELVSTED [*after a pause, starts up in the chair and listens anxiously. Then she sinks back wearily and wails quietly*]: Still not back! Oh God . . . oh God . . . still not back!

*Berte comes tiptoeing carefully in at the hall door. She carries a letter in her hand.*

MRS ELVSTED [*turns and whispers urgently*]: Well . . . has anybody come?

BERTE [*quietly*]: Yes, a young woman just came with this letter.

MRS ELVSTED [*quickly, stretching out her hand*]: A letter! Give it to me!

BERTE: No, ma'am, it's for Dr Tesman.

MRS ELVSTED: Oh. . . .

BERTE: It was Miss Tesman's maid who brought it. I'll put it on the table here.

MRS ELVSTED: Yes, do that.

BERTE [*puts down the letter*]: Perhaps I'd best put out the lamp. It's smoking a bit.

MRS ELVSTED: Yes, put it out. It'll soon be light now.

BERTE [*dousing the lamp*]: It's broad daylight.

MRS ELVSTED: Yes, daylight! And still not back . . . !

BERTE: Oh, bless you, ma'am . . . I knew this would happen.

MRS ELVSTED: You knew it?

BERTE: Yes, when I saw that a certain person was back in town. . . . And then when he went off with them. We know what to expect of that gentleman.

MRS ELVSTED: Not so loud. You'll wake Mrs Tesman.

BERTE [*looks at the sofa and sighs*]: Oh the poor dear . . . let her have her sleep. . . . Shan't I put a bit more on the fire?

MRS ELVSTED: Thank you, not on my account.

BERTE: All right, then. [*She goes out quietly at the hall door.*]

HEDDA [*is woken by the closing of the door and looks up*]: What's that . . . !

MRS ELVSTED: It was just the maid. . . .

HEDDA [*looks around*]: Here . . . ! Oh yes, I remember . . . [*Sits up on the sofa, stretches and rubs her eyes.*] What's the time, Thea?

MRS ELVSTED [*looks at her watch*]: It's gone seven.

HEDDA: When did Tesman come in?

MRS ELVSTED: He isn't back yet.

HEDDA: Not back yet?

MRS ELVSTED [*getting up*]: No one came at all.

HEDDA: And we sat there watching and waiting till four in the morning. . . .

MRS ELVSTED [*wringing her hands*]: Oh, and how I did wait for him!

HEDDA [*yawns, and speaks with her hand over her mouth*]: Ah well . . . we could have saved ourselves the trouble.

MRS ELVSTED: Did you sleep at all?

HEDDA: Oh yes . . . I think I slept quite well. Didn't you?

MRS ELVSTED: Not a wink. I just couldn't, Hedda! It was quite impossible.

HEDDA [*gets up and goes towards her*]: Now, now, now! There's nothing to worry about. It's quite obvious what's happened.

MRS ELVSTED: Well, what has happened, then? Just tell me that!

HEDDA: Well, naturally, they must have carried on till all hours at Mr Brack's . . .

MRS ELVSTED: Yes, oh God . . . I suppose they did. But all the same . . .

HEDDA: And then of course Tesman didn't want to come home and make a din and ring the bell in the middle of the night. [*laughs*] Perhaps he didn't want to show himself either . . . right on top of a night like that.

MRS ELVSTED: But for goodness sake . . . where else could he have gone?

HEDDA: He obviously went along up to the aunts to sleep it off there. They still have his old room.

MRS ELVSTED: No, there at least he can't be. Because just now a letter came for him from Miss Tesman. It's lying there.

HEDDA: Oh? [*looks at the writing on the envelope*] Yes, it's from Auntie Julle all right, in her own fair hand. Well, he must have stopped over at Mr Brack's, then. And Ejlert Lövborg, he's sitting there reading aloud . . . with vine leaves in his hair.

MRS ELVSTED: Oh, Hedda, you're just saying all this, you don't really believe it yourself.

HEDDA: You really are a little ninny, Thea.

MRS ELVSTED: Yes, I suppose I am, really.

HEDDA: And you look tired to death.

MRS ELVSTED: Yes, I am tired to death.

HEDDA: And so you're to do as I tell you. You're to go into my room and lie down on the bed for a little while.

MRS ELVSTED: Oh no, no . . . anyway I wouldn't sleep.

HEDDA: Of course you would.

MRS ELVSTED: Yes, but your husband must be back soon. And then I must hear at once . . .

HEDDA: I'll let you know when he comes.

MRS ELVSTED: Do you promise me, Hedda?

HEDDA: Yes, yes, that's all right. Just you go in and sleep till then.

MRS ELVSTED: Thank you. Well, I'll try, then. [*She goes out through the inner room.*]

*Hedda goes over to the glass door and draws the curtains aside. Full daylight streams into the room. She then takes a small looking-glass from the desk, inspects herself and arranges her hair. Then she crosses to the hall door and presses the bell.*

*After a short while Berte comes to the door.*

BERTE: Did you ring, ma'am?

HEDDA: Yes, be so good as to put some more on the stove. I'm cold.

BERTE: Gracious . . . straight away, ma'am . . . I'll have it hot in a moment.

*She rakes the embers together and puts in a piece of wood.*

BERTE [*stops and listens*]: That was the front door, ma'am.

HEDDA: Then go and attend to it. I'll look after the fire myself.

BERTE: It'll soon burn up. [*She goes out at the hall door.*]

*Hedda kneels on the footstool and puts more wood into the stove.*

*After a little while Jörgen Tesman comes in from the hall. He looks tired and rather serious. Creeps on tiptoe towards the doorway, and is about to slip in through the curtains.*

HEDDA [*at the stove, without looking up*]: Good morning.

TESMAN [*turning*]: Hedda! [*comes closer*] But what on earth . . . are you up already! Eh?

HEDDA: Yes, I was up very early this morning.

TESMAN: And I was so sure you'd be sound asleep still! Think of that, Hedda!

HEDDA: Don't talk so loudly. Mrs Elvsted is lying down in my room.

TESMAN: Did Mrs Elvsted stay the night!

HEDDA: Well, nobody came to fetch her.

TESMAN: No, I suppose not.

HEDDA [*shuts the stove door and gets up*]: Well, and did you have a good time at Mr Brack's?

TESMAN: Were you worried about me? Eh?

HEDDA: Good gracious no . . . I wouldn't dream of it. But I asked if you'd had a good time.

TESMAN: Yes, I suppose. For once in a way. . . . But most to begin with, I thought. Then Ejlert read to me. We got there an hour too soon . . . think of that! And Brack had to arrange things. But then Ejlert read to me.

HEDDA [*sits to the right of the table*]: Well? Tell me about it. . . .

TESMAN [*sits on a stool by the stove*]: Oh Hedda, you've no idea, it's going to be ever so good! One of the most remarkable books ever written, I'd almost say. Think of that!

HEDDA: Yes, yes, I don't care so much about that . . .

TESMAN: There's something I'm bound to confess, Hedda. When he'd finished reading . . . something ugly came over me.

HEDDA: Something ugly?

TESMAN: I sat and envied Ejlert that he'd been able to write such a thing. Think of that, Hedda!

HEDDA: Yes, yes, I'm thinking.

TESMAN: And then to know that . . . with all his talents . . . unfortunately he's quite beyond hope of reform, all the same.

HEDDA: I suppose you mean he's got more courage than the rest?

TESMAN: No, good Lord . . . he just can't keep himself under control at all, you know.

HEDDA: Well, and what happened then . . . in the end?

TESMAN: Yes, well, I'd almost have described it as an orgy, Hedda.

HEDDA: Did he have vine leaves in his hair?

TESMAN: Vine leaves? No, I didn't see anything like that. But he made a long and incoherent speech about the woman who had inspired him in his work. Yes, that's how he expressed it.

HEDDA: Did he say who that was?

TESMAN: No, he didn't. But I can only imagine that it must have been Mrs Elvsted. You mark my words!

HEDDA: Well . . . and where did you part company with him?

TESMAN: On the way back to town. We broke up . . . the last of us . . . all together. And Brack came along too to get some fresh air. And then, you see, we agreed that we'd better see Ejlert home. Well, you know, he had quite a few drinks inside him!

HEDDA: I suppose he had.

TESMAN: But now comes the most remarkable thing, Hedda! Or the saddest, I suppose I should say. Oh . . . I'm almost ashamed . . . on Ejlert's behalf . . . to tell you about it. . . .

HEDDA: Well, then . . . ?

TESMAN: Yes, well as we were going along, you see, I happened to fall back a bit behind the others. Just for a minute or two . . . think of it!

HEDDA: Yes, yes, good Lord, but . . . ?

TESMAN: And then as I was hurrying along to catch up . . . well, do you know what I found in the gutter? Eh?

HEDDA: How on earth should I know?

TESMAN: Don't tell anyone, will you, Hedda. Do you hear? Promise me that, for Ejlert's sake! [*He pulls a packet wrapped in paper out of his coat pocket.*] Just think . . . I found this.

HEDDA: Isn't that the packet he had with him here yesterday?

TESMAN: That's it, it's his precious, irreplaceable manuscript! And he's just gone along and dropped it . . . without noticing. Just think of it, Hedda! It's quite pathetic. . . .

HEDDA: But why didn't you give the packet back to him at once?

TESMAN: No, I didn't dare to do that . . . when he was in that condition. . .

HEDDA: Didn't you tell any of the others that you'd found it either?

TESMAN: Oh no, no. You must see I couldn't have done that, for Ejlert's sake.

HEDDA: So nobody knows at all that you've got Ejlert Lövborg's papers?

TESMAN: No. And no one must get to know it.

HEDDA: What did you talk to him about, afterwards?

TESMAN: I didn't get to talk to him at all. Because as we got into the town we quite lost him . . . him and two or three others. Think of that!

HEDDA: Oh? I suppose they saw him home, then.

TESMAN: Yes, so it seemed. And Brack went off, too.

HEDDA: And what did you get up to then . . . afterwards?

TESMAN: Oh, I went with some of the others, and one of the fellows took us to his place and gave us morning coffee. Or night coffee, I suppose I should say. Eh? But now as soon as I've rested a bit . . . and when poor old Ejlert has had a chance to sleep it off . . . I must go in and give him this.

HEDDA [*stretches out her hand for the packet*]: No . . . don't give it back! Not straight away, I mean. Let me read it first.

TESMAN: No, my dear, sweet Hedda, I swear I just daren't do that.

HEDDA: You daren't?

TESMAN: No . . . because you can just imagine, he'll be quite desperate when he wakes up and finds he's lost his manuscript. Because this is the only copy he's got, you know! He told me so himself.

HEDDA [*looks at him keenly*]: But can't a thing like that be rewritten? Over again, I mean?

TESMAN: No, I don't think that would do at all. Because the inspiration . . . you see . . .

HEDDA: Yes, yes . . . that's it, I suppose . . . [*casually*] Oh, by the way . . . there's a letter for you.

TESMAN: A letter? Just think . . . !

HEDDA [*passes it to him*]: It came early this morning.

TESMAN: From Aunt Julle! What can it be? [*He puts the manuscript down on the other stool, opens the letter, glances through it, and jumps up.*] Oh, Hedda . . . she writes that poor Auntie Rina is at the point of death!

HEDDA: Well, it was to be expected.

TESMAN: And if I want to see her again, I must hurry. I'll rush over at once.

HEDDA [*suppressing a smile*]: You'll rush, will you?

TESMAN: Oh Hedda, my dearest . . . if only I could persuade you to come too! Just think!

HEDDA [*gets up and answers tiredly but firmly*]: No, no, don't ask me. I don't want to look at sickness and death. I must be free of everything that's ugly.

TESMAN: Oh well, for God's sake then . . . ! [*rushes about*] My hat . . . ! My coat . . . ? Oh, in the hall. . . . Oh, I do so hope I'm not going to be too late, Hedda? Eh?

HEDDA: You'd better rush, then. . . .

*Berte appears at the hall door.*

BERTE: Mr Brack is outside and asks if he can come in.
TESMAN: Now! No, I can't possibly see him now.
HEDDA: But I can. [*to Berte*] Ask Mr Brack to come inside.

*Berte goes.*

HEDDA [*quickly, whispering*]: The papers, Tesman! [*She whips the packet off the stool.*]
TESMAN: Yes, give them to me!
HEDDA: No, no, I'll look after them till you come back.

*She goes to the desk and puts the packet in the bookshelf. Tesman stands there in a flap, unable to get his gloves on.*

*Mr Brack comes in from the hall.*

HEDDA [*nods to him*]: Well, you are an early bird.
BRACK: Yes, am I not? [*to Tesman*] Are you going out again?
TESMAN: Yes, I have to go to the aunts. Just think . . . the one who's ill, she's dying, poor thing.
BRACK: Good Lord, is she really? But then you musn't stand here talking to me. At such a serious moment. . . .
TESMAN: Yes, I really must rush. . . . Goodbye! Goodbye!
[*He hurries out at the hall door.*]
HEDDA [*comes closer*]: It seems it was decidedly lively at your place last night, Mr Brack.
BRACK: I haven't even had time to change my clothes, my lady.
HEDDA: You haven't either?
BRACK: As you see. But what has Tesman told you of the events of the night?
HEDDA: Oh, nothing much. That he went somewhere and drank coffee.
BRACK: Yes, I know about the coffee party. Ejlert Lövborg wasn't there though, I believe?
HEDDA: No, they'd seen him home first.
BRACK: Tesman too?
HEDDA: No, but a few of the others, he said.
BRACK [*smiles*]: Jörgen Tesman really is a credulous soul, my lady.
HEDDA: Yes, God knows he is. But is there something behind all this?
BRACK: Yes, you might say there is.
HEDDA: Well! Let's sit down, dear Mr Brack. Then you'll tell it better.

*She sits to the left of the table. Brack sits down at the table close to her.*

HEDDA: Well, then?
BRACK: There were particular reasons why I wanted to keep track of my guests . . . or rather, of certain of my guests last night.
HEDDA: And perhaps Ejlert Lövborg was among them?
BRACK: I have to confess . . . he was.
HEDDA: Now you really begin to intrigue me. . . .
BRACK: Do you know where he and a few of the others spent what was left of the night, my lady?

HEDDA: Tell me . . . if it bears telling.

BRACK: Oh yes, it may be told. Well, they adorned a particularly animated soirée.

HEDDA: One of the lively kind?

BRACK: One of the very liveliest.

HEDDA: A bit more about this, Mr Brack . . .

BRACK: Lövborg had also been invited earlier. I happened to know about it. But at that time he declined the invitation. Because now he's put on a new man, as you know.

HEDDA: Up at the Elvsteds', yes. But he went all the same?

BRACK: Well you see, my lady . . . most unfortunately the inspiration took him up at my place last night. . . .

HEDDA: Yes, the spirit did move him, so I'm told.

BRACK: Moved him somewhat vehemently. And, well . . . then he had second thoughts about it, I assume. Because we men, you know, we're not always so firm in our principles as we ought to be.

HEDDA: Oh, I don't doubt that you provide an exception, Mr Brack. But Lövborg . . . ?

BRACK: Well, to cut a long story short . . . he finally adjourned to Mademoiselle Diana's salon.

HEDDA: Mademoiselle Diana's?

BRACK: Mademoiselle Diana was giving the aforesaid soirée. For a select circle of friends and admirers.

HEDDA: Is that a red-haired woman?

BRACK: Most decidedly.

HEDDA: A sort of a . . . singer?

BRACK: Oh yes . . . among other things. And moreover a mighty huntress . . . of men . . . my lady. You must have heard of her. Ejlert Lövborg was one of her most ardent champions . . . in the days of his glory.

HEDDA: And how did it all end, then?

BRACK: Not altogether amicably, it appears. Mademoiselle Diana, I understand, passed from the tenderest possible welcome to actual violence.

HEDDA: Against Lövborg?

BRACK: Yes. He maintained that she, or one of the members of her entourage, had robbed him. He said that he'd lost a pocket-book. And other things as well. In short, he appears to have kicked up the devil of a row.

HEDDA: And what happened then?

BRACK: What happened then was a general mêlée, involving both ladies and gentlemen. Fortunately the police arrived at last.

HEDDA: The police came, too?

BRACK: Yes. But I fear this will have been a costly interlude for that imbecile Lövborg.

HEDDA: Oh!

BRACK: Apparently he put up a spirited resistance. Struck an officer of the law over the head, and tore his tunic. So he had to go along to the police station too.

HEDDA: How do you know all this?

BRACK: The police told me themselves.

HEDDA [*looking away*]: So that was how it was. He didn't have vine leaves in his hair.

BRACK: Vine leaves, my lady?

HEDDA [*in a different voice*]: But tell me now, Mr Brack . . . why should you show such an elaborate interest in Ejlert Lövborg?

BRACK: In the first place, I can't be altogether indifferent if it comes out, when the case is heard, that he came straight from my place.

HEDDA: There'll be a court case, then?

BRACK: Naturally. But it isn't really that so much. No, the fact is I felt it my duty, as a friend of the house, to give you and your husband a full account of his nocturnal escapades.

HEDDA: And why should you feel that, Mr Brack?

BRACK: Well, I have a pretty shrewd suspicion that he intends to use you as a sort of screen.

HEDDA: Why, what gives you that idea?

BRACK: Oh good Heavens . . . we're not blind, my lady. Use your eyes! This Mrs Elvsted person, she won't be leaving town in such a hurry.

HEDDA: Well, and if there is anything between those two, I suppose there are plenty of other places where they can meet.

BRACK: No private household. From now on every decent home will be closed to Ejlert Lövborg once again.

HEDDA: And mine ought to be too, you mean?

BRACK: Yes. I must admit I'd find it extremely awkward if this fellow were to become a constant visitor here. If this superfluous and . . . and unsuitable individual were to insinuate himself into . . .

HEDDA: Into the triangle?

BRACK: Just so. For me it would be like becoming homeless.

HEDDA [*looks at him with a smile*]: So . . . you want to be the only cock in the yard, is that it?

BRACK [*nods slowly and lowers his voice*]: Yes, that's what I want. And I'll fight for that end . . . with every means at my disposal.

HEDDA [*her smile fading*]: You're quite a formidable person . . . when it comes to the point.

BRACK: You think so?

HEDDA: Yes, I'm beginning to think so, now. And I'm content . . . so long as you don't have any sort of hold over me.

BRACK [*laughs equivocally*]: Ah yes, my lady . . . you may be right about that. Who knows, in such a case I might be capable of . . . one thing and another.

HEDDA: Really, Mr Brack! You sound almost as though you mean to threaten me.

BRACK [*rising*]: Oh, far from it! This triangle . . . well, you know, it's best when it's fortified and defended by mutual consent.

HEDDA: I agree with you.

BRACK: Well, now I've said what I wanted to say. And I'd better see about getting back home. Goodbye, my lady! [*He moves towards the glass door.*]

HEDDA [*getting up*]: Are you going through the garden?

BRACK: Yes, it's a bit nearer for me.

HEDDA: Yes, and then it's round the back way.

BRACK: Very true. I've no objection to going round the back way. At times it can be quite stimulating.

HEDDA: When there's target practice going on, you mean?

BRACK [*at the door, laughing*]: Oh, nobody shoots their tame farmyard cocks!

HEDDA [*also laughing*]: Ah no, when they've only got one of them. . . .

*Laughing, they nod their farewells. He leaves. She shuts the door behind him.*

*Hedda stands for a moment with a serious expression, looking out. Then she crosses to the centre doorway and looks in through the curtains. Then moves to the desk, takes Lövborg's packet out of the bookcase, and is about to look at the papers. Berte's voice, raised in altercation, is heard from the hall. Hedda turns and listens. Then she quickly locks the manuscript away in a drawer and puts the key on the writing-pad.*

*Ejlert Lövborg, wearing his overcoat and holding his hat, flings open the hall door. He looks somewhat confused and excited.*

LÖVBORG [*turned towards the hall*]: And I tell you that I must go in! And that's that!

*He shuts the door, turns, and sees Hedda. He controls himself at once, and bows.*

HEDDA [*at the desk*]: Well, Mr Lövborg, you're a little late in calling for Thea.

LÖVBORG: Or a little early in calling on you. I apologize.

HEDDA: How do you know she's still here?

LÖVBORG: They told me at her lodgings that she'd been out all night.

HEDDA [*crosses to the table*]: Did you notice anything in particular when they told you that?

LÖVBORG [*looks at her questioningly*]: Notice anything?

HEDDA: I mean, did they seem to be drawing any inference at all?

LÖVBORG [*suddenly understands*]: Oh yes, of course, you're right! I'm dragging her down with me! But as it happened I didn't notice anything. . . . I suppose Tesman isn't up yet?

HEDDA: No . . . I don't think . . .

LÖVBORG: When did he come in?

HEDDA: Very late.

LÖVBORG: Did he tell you anything?

HEDDA: Yes, he said it was a very gay party at Mr Brack's.

LÖVBORG: Nothing else?

HEDDA: No, I don't think so. But I was frightfully sleepy. . . .

*Mrs Elvsted comes in through the curtains at the back.*

MRS ELVSTED [*comes towards him*]: Oh, Lövborg! At last . . . !

LÖVBORG: Yes, at last. And too late.

MRS ELVSTED [*looks at him anxiously*]: What's too late?

LÖVBORG: Everything's too late now. I'm finished.

MRS ELVSTED: Oh, no, no . . . don't say that!

LÖVBORG: You'll say the same yourself when you hear. . . .

MRS ELVSTED: I don't want to hear anything!

HEDDA: Perhaps you'd prefer to speak to her alone? Because if so I'll go.

LÖVBORG: No, stay . . . I beg you to stay.

MRS ELVSTED: But I don't want to hear about it, I tell you!

LÖVBORG: I'm not going to talk about what happened last night.

MRS ELVSTED: What is it then . . . ?

LÖVBORG: It's just this, that it's all over between us now.

MRS ELVSTED: All over!

HEDDA [*involuntarily*]: I knew it!

LÖVBORG: Because I have no use for you any more, Thea.

MRS ELVSTED: And you can stand there and say that! No use for me any more! Can't I help you now as I did before? Aren't we going to go on working together?

LÖVBORG: I don't intend to do any more work.

MRS ELVSTED [*yielding to despair*]: What am I to do with my life, then?

LÖVBORG: You must try to live your life as though you had never known me.

MRS ELVSTED: Oh, but I can't!

LÖVBORG: See if you can, Thea. You must go back home. . . .

MRS ELVSTED [*in rebellion*]: That I'll never do! Wherever you are, that's where I want to be! I won't be packed off like this! I want to be right here! To be together with you when the book comes out.

HEDDA [*half aloud, tensely*]: Ah yes . . . the book!

LÖVBORG [*looks at her*]: My book and Thea's. Because that's what it is.

MRS ELVSTED: Yes, that's what I feel that it is. And therefore I have a right to be together with you when it comes! I want to see you praised and honoured again. And the joy . . . I want to share the joy of it with you.

LÖVBORG: Thea . . . our book will never be published.

HEDDA: Ah!

MRS ELVSTED: Not published!

LÖVBORG: It's impossible now.

MRS ELVSTED [*in dreadful foreboding*]: Lövborg . . . what have you done to the manuscript!

HEDDA [*looks at him in suspense*]: Yes, the manuscript . . . ?

MRS ELVSTED: Where is it?

LÖVBORG: Oh Thea. . . . Don't ask me to tell you that.

MRS ELVSTED: Yes, yes, I want to know. I've got the right to know. At once.

LÖVBORG: The manuscript. . . . Well, then . . . I've torn the manuscript into a thousand pieces.

MRS ELVSTED [*shrieks*]: Oh no, no . . . !

HEDDA [*involuntarily*]: But that's not . . . !

LÖVBORG [*looks at her*]: Not true, you think?

HEDDA [*collects herself*]: Oh well . . . of course. If you say so yourself. But it sounded so fantastic. . . .

LÖVBORG: True all the same.

MRS ELVSTED [*wrings her hands*]: Oh God . . . oh God, Hedda . . . torn his own work to pieces!

LÖVBORG: I've torn my own life to pieces. So I might as well tear up my life's work as well.

MRS ELVSTED: And you did that last night!

LÖVBORG: Yes, I tell you. Into a thousand pieces. And scattered them out in the fjord. A long way out. At least the water's clean and salt out there. They'll drift with the current and the wind. And after a while they'll sink. Deeper and deeper. Like I will, Thea.

MRS ELVSTED: I want you to know, Lövborg, what you've done to the book. . . . For the rest of my life it'll be for me as though you'd killed a little child.

LÖVBORG: You're right. It was like killing a child.

MRS ELVSTED: But how could you then . . . ! The child was mine, it was also mine.

HEDDA [*almost inaudibly*]: The child . . .

MRS ELVSTED [*sighs deeply*]: So there's an end of it. Well, I'm leaving now, Hedda.

HEDDA: But you're not going back . . . ?

MRS ELVSTED: Oh, I don't know myself what I'll do. There's nothing but darkness ahead of me. [*She goes out at the hall door.*]

HEDDA [*stands for a while and waits*]: So you're not going to take her home, Mr Lövborg?

LÖVBORG: I? Through the streets? And let everybody see her walking with me?

HEDDA: Well, I don't know what else happened last night. But was it so utterly irrevocable?

LÖVBORG: It won't stop at last night. I know that well enough. But then there's another thing, I just can't be bothered with that kind of a life either. Not now again. She's broken my courage, and my defiance.

HEDDA [*looking straight ahead*]: So that silly little fool has had her fingers in a man's destiny. [*looks at him*] But how could you treat her so callously, all the same?

LÖVBORG: Oh, don't say I was callous!

HEDDA: To destroy everything that's filled her mind and her heart for all this long time! Don't you call that callous?

LÖVBORG: I can tell you the truth, Hedda.

HEDDA: The truth?

LÖVBORG: Promise me first . . . give me your word that Thea will never know what I'm going to tell you now.

HEDDA: I give you my word.

LÖVBORG: Well. Then I'll tell you that what I was saying just now wasn't the truth.

HEDDA: About the manuscript?

LÖVBORG: Yes. I didn't tear it up. And I didn't throw it in the fjord, either.

HEDDA: No. . . . But . . . where is it then?

LÖVBORG: I've destroyed it all the same. Destroyed it utterly, Hedda!

HEDDA: I don't understand this.

LÖVBORG: Thea said that for her it was as though I had killed a child.

HEDDA: Yes . . . so she did.

LÖVBORG: But to kill his child . . . that's not the worst thing a father can do.

HEDDA: Not the worst?

LÖVBORG: No. I wanted to spare Thea the worst.

HEDDA: And what is this worst thing, then?

LÖVBORG: Look, Hedda, suppose a man . . . in the early hours of the morning . . . came home to his child's mother after a wild and senseless debauch and said: now listen . . . I've been here and I've been there. To all sorts of places. And I had our child along with me. All over the place. And I've lost him. Just like that. Christ alone knows where he's got to, or who's got hold of him.

HEDDA: Oh but . . . when all's said and done . . . this was only a book. . . .

LÖVBORG: Thea's soul was in that book.

HEDDA: Yes, I can understand that.

LÖVBORG: And so you must understand also that Thea and I . . . that there isn't any future for us any more.

HEDDA: And what are you going to do, then?

LÖVBORG: Nothing. Just put an end to it all. The sooner the better.

HEDDA [*takes a step towards him*]: Ejlert Lövborg . . . listen to me. . . . Couldn't you let it happen . . . beautifully?

LÖVBORG: Beautifully! [*smiles*] Crowned with vine leaves, as you used to imagine?

HEDDA: Oh no. I don't believe in those vine leaves any more. But beautifully all the same! Just for this once! . . . Goodbye. You must go now. And never come here again.

LÖVBORG: Goodbye, Mrs Tesman. And remember me to your husband.

[*He is about to leave.*]

HEDDA: No, wait! I want to give you something to remember me by.

*She goes to the desk and opens the drawer, and takes out the pistol case. Then she comes back to Lövborg with one of the pistols.*

LÖVBORG [*looks at her*]: That! Is that what you want me to have?

HEDDA [*nods slowly*]: Do you recognize it? It was aimed at you, once.

LÖVBORG: You should have used it then.

HEDDA: Well . . . ! You use it now.

LÖVBORG [*sticking the pistol in his breast pocket*]: Thank you.

HEDDA: And beautifully, Ejlert Lövborg. Promise me that!

LÖVBORG: Goodbye, Hedda Gabler. [*He goes out at the hall door.*]

*Hedda listens at the door for a moment. Then she goes to the desk and takes out the packet with the manuscript, peeps inside the wrappers for a moment, takes some of the leaves half way out and looks at them. Then she takes it all over to the armchair by the stove and sits down. After a while she opens the stove door, and unwraps the packet.*

HEDDA [*throws one of the folded sheets into the fire and whispers to herself*]: Now I'm burning your child, Thea! With your curly hair! [*throws a few more sheets into the stove*] Your child and Ejlert Lövborg's. [*throws in the rest*] I'm burning . . . burning your child.

## ACT IV

*The same room at the Tesmans'. It is evening. The outer room is in darkness. The lamp over the table in the inner room is alight. The curtains at the glass door are drawn.*

*Hedda, dressed in black, is walking aimlessly about the darkened room. Then she goes into the inner room and is lost to view to the left of the doorway. A few chords from the piano are heard. Then she emerges again and goes back into the reception room.*

*Berte comes in from the right of the inner room, carrying a lighted lamp, which she places on the table by the corner sofa in the reception room. Her eyes show signs of weeping, and she has black bands in her cap. Goes out quietly and carefully to the right. Hedda crosses to the glass door, draws the curtains aside a little, and looks out into the darkness.*

*After a little while Miss Tesman comes in from the hall, dressed in mourning and wearing a hat and veil. Hedda goes to meet her and gives her her hand.*

MISS TESMAN: Yes, Hedda, I come dressed in the colour of mourning. For now my poor sister has passed away at last.

HEDDA: I am already aware of it, as you see. Tesman sent me a note.

MISS TESMAN: Yes, he promised he would. But I felt all the same that here to Hedda . . . in this house of life . . . I must bring the tidings of death myself.

HEDDA: That was extremely kind of you.

MISS TESMAN: Oh, but Rina shouldn't have been taken just now. This is no time for mourning, not in Hedda's house.

HEDDA [*avoiding the subject*]: She died quite peacefully, Miss Tesman?

MISS TESMAN: Oh, she passed over so quietly . . . and so gently. And it was such a blessed joy to her that she could see Jörgen once again. And could say goodbye to him properly. He isn't home yet?

HEDDA: No. He wrote that I wasn't to expect him straight away. But do sit down.

MISS TESMAN: No, thank you, my dear . . . dear Hedda. I should have liked to. But I have so little time. Now I have to attend to her and prepare her as well as I may. She shall go to her grave looking her best.

HEDDA: Is there nothing I can do?

MISS TESMAN: Oh, you mustn't think of it! No, that's not fit work for Hedda Tesman's hands. Nor a fit subject for her thoughts, either. Not at this time.

HEDDA: Oh thoughts . . . they can't be curbed so easily. . . .

MISS TESMAN [*continuing*]: Ah yes, dear God, that's how it goes. We'll be sewing linen for poor Rina; and soon there'll be sewing to be done here too, I fancy. But that'll be of a different kind . . . thanks be to God.

*Jörgen Tesman comes in at the hall door.*

HEDDA: Well, so you're here at last.

TESMAN: You here, Auntie Julle? With Hedda? Think of that!

MISS TESMAN: I was just going away again, my dear boy. Well, and did you manage to see to it all?

TESMAN: Oh, I'm awfully afraid I'll have forgotten the half of it. I'll have to dash over and see you again tomorrow. I'm all at sixes and sevens today. I just can't think straight.

MISS TESMAN: But Jörgen, my own boy, you mustn't take it like that.

TESMAN: I mustn't? Well, how else, then?

MISS TESMAN: You must be glad, even in your grief. Glad of what has come to pass. As I am.

TESMAN: Oh yes, yes. You're thinking of Auntie Rina.

HEDDA: It will be a little lonely for you now, Miss Tesman.

MISS TESMAN: Why yes, just to begin with. But not for so very long, I sincerely hope. Poor Rina's little room won't be left empty, you may be sure of that!

TESMAN: Oh? Who are you thinking of putting in there, then? Eh?

MISS TESMAN: Oh, there's always some poor invalid or other who needs a bit of care and attention, unfortunately.

HEDDA: Would you really take on another burden of that kind?

MISS TESMAN: Burden! Oh, God forgive you, child . . . this hasn't been a burden to me.

HEDDA: But in the case of a total stranger . . .

MISS TESMAN: Oh, you soon get friendly with people when they're sick. And besides, I also do need to have someone to live for. Ah well, God is good . . . and I fancy there'll soon be a few things for an old aunt to do here in this house, too.

HEDDA: Oh, don't think about us.

TESMAN: Yes, just think how fine it would be if we all three. . . . Yes . . . if only . . .

HEDDA: If only . . . ?

TESMAN [*ill at ease*]: Oh, never mind. It'll all turn out all right, I expect. Let's hope so. Eh?

MISS TESMAN: Well, well. I expect you young people have lots of things you want to talk about. [*smiles*] And perhaps Hedda has something to tell you, too, Jörgen. Goodbye, my dears! I must get back home to Rina. [*She turns at the door.*] Yes, dear God, how strange to think! Now Rina's both here with me, and also with sainted Joachim.

TESMAN: Yes, just think of that, Auntie Julle! Eh?

*Miss Tesman goes out at the hall door.*

HEDDA [*coldly appraising Tesman*]: I almost think you're more upset about this death than she is.

TESMAN: Oh, it's not just Aunt Rina. I'm so frightfully worried about Ejlert.

HEDDA [*quickly*]: Have you heard anything about him?

TESMAN: I was going to run over to see him this afternoon, to tell him that the manuscript's in good hands.

HEDDA: Well? Didn't you catch him?

TESMAN: No. He wasn't at home. But afterwards I met Mrs Elvsted, and she said he'd been here early this morning.

HEDDA: Yes, just after your left.

TESMAN: And that he said that he'd torn up the manuscript. Eh?

HEDDA: Yes, that's what he said.

TESMAN: But, good Heavens above, the man must have been raving! And then you didn't dare let him have it back, I suppose, Hedda?

HEDDA: No, he didn't get it.

TESMAN: But you did tell him we'd got it?

HEDDA: No. [*quickly*] Did you tell Mrs Elvsted?

TESMAN: No. I didn't like to. But you ought to have said it to him. Just think, he might go and do something desperate! Give me the manuscript, Hedda! I'll rush over with it at once. Where have you got it?

HEDDA [*cold and immobile, supporting herself on the armchair*]: I haven't got it any more.

TESMAN: You haven't got it! But for God's sake . . . what do you mean?

HEDDA: I've burnt it up . . . all of it.

TESMAN [*jumps up in alarm*]: Burnt . . . you've burnt it! Burnt Ejlert Lövborg's manuscript!

HEDDA: Don't shout like that. The maid might hear you.

TESMAN: Burnt! But good God! . . . No, no, no . . . this is quite impossible!

HEDDA: Well, it's true, for all that.

TESMAN: Yes, but . . . do you know what it is that you've done, Hedda? It's a felony . . . it's misappropriation of lost property! Think of that! Yes, you just go and ask Mr Brack, he'll tell you.

HEDDA: I think you'd be well advised not to talk about it . . . either to Mr Brack or anyone else.

TESMAN: But how could you go and do anything so utterly fantastic! How on earth did you come to do such a thing? What got into you? Answer me, Hedda! Eh?

HEDDA [*suppressing an almost imperceptible smile*]: I did it for your sake, Jörgen.

TESMAN: For my sake!

HEDDA: When you came home this morning and told me how he'd read to you . . .

TESMAN: Yes, yes, what about it?

HEDDA: You admitted that you envied him for it.

TESMAN: Oh Heavens above, I didn't mean it so literally.

HEDDA: All the same I couldn't bear the thought that someone else should put you in the shade.

TESMAN [*exclaiming, torn between doubt and happiness*]: Hedda . . . oh gracious . . . is this really true! . . . Yes, but . . . yes, but . . . I never knew you loved me like that, Hedda, not in that way. Think of that!

HEDDA: Well, then I suppose I'd better tell you that . . . that just at this time . . . [*breaks off passionately*] Oh no, no . . . you can go and ask your Auntie Julle. She'll tell you all about it.

TESMAN: Oh, I almost think I know what it is, Hedda! [*claps his hands together*] Oh good Heavens . . . is it really possible! Eh!

HEDDA: Don't shout like that. The maid can hear you.

TESMAN [*laughing in the excess of his joy*]: The maid! Oh, Hedda, you really are priceless! The maid . . . why that's Berte! I'll go out and tell Berte myself!

HEDDA [*clenches her hands as though in desperation*]: Oh, it'll kill me . . . it'll kill me, all this!

TESMAN: All what, Hedda? Eh?

HEDDA [*coldly, in control again*]: All this . . . this farce . . . Jörgen.

TESMAN: Farce? But it's just that I'm so happy. But, perhaps. . . . Well, perhaps I'd better not tell Berte, then.

HEDDA: Oh yes . . . why not do the thing properly.

TESMAN: No, no, not just yet. But at least I'll have to tell Aunt Julle. And that you've started to call me Jörgen, too! Think of it. Oh, Auntie Julle really will be pleased!

HEDDA: When she hears that I've burnt Ejlert Lövborg's papers . . . for your sake?

TESMAN: Oh, good Lord yes . . . the papers! No, of course, nobody must get to know about that. But your burning zeal on my behalf, Hedda . . . Auntie Julle really must hear about that! I say though, I wonder, is that sort of thing usual with young wives, d'you think? Eh?

HEDDA: I think it would be a good idea if you asked Auntie Julle about that, too.

TESMAN: Yes, yes, I'll do that some time. [*looks uneasy and thoughtful again*] No, but this business with the manuscript! Good Lord, it's . . . it's quite awful, really, to think of poor Ejlert.

*Mrs Elvsted, dressed as for her first visit, with hat and coat, comes in the hall door.*

MRS ELVSTED [*greets them hurriedly and speaks in agitation*]: Oh my dear Hedda, do excuse me for coming back again.

HEDDA: What's happened to you, Thea?

TESMAN: Is it something to do with Ejlert Lövborg again? Eh?

MRS ELVSTED: Oh yes . . . I'm so dreadfully afraid that he may have met with an accident.

HEDDA [*grips Mrs Elvsted's arm*]: Oh . . . do you think so!

TESMAN: Oh, but good Heavens . . . why should you think that, Mrs Elvsted?

MRS ELVSTED: Oh, yes, I heard them talking about him at the lodging house . . . just as I came in. There are the most incredible rumours about him going around today.

TESMAN: Yes, just think, I heard something too! And yet I can testify that he went straight off home to bed. Think of that!

HEDDA: Well . . . what were they saying then, at the boarding house?

MRS ELVSTED: Oh, I didn't really discover anything at all. Either because they didn't really know the particulars or else. . . . They all stopped talking when they saw me. And I didn't dare to ask.

TESMAN [*anxiously pacing around*]: We can only hope . . . we can only hope you were mistaken, Mrs Elvsted!

MRS ELVSTED: No, no I'm sure it was him they were talking about. And then I heard one of them say something that sounded like hospital or . . .

TESMAN: Hospital!

HEDDA: Oh no . . . that can't be possible!

MRS ELVSTED: Oh, I was so horribly frightened for him. And then I went to his lodgings and asked after him there.

HEDDA: You could bring yourself to do that, Thea!

MRS ELVSTED: Well, and what else was I to do? Because it seemed to me I just couldn't go on, not knowing.

TESMAN: But I suppose you didn't find him there, either? Eh?

MRS ELVSTED: No. And the people knew nothing whatever about him. He hadn't been home since yesterday afternoon, they said.

TESMAN: Yesterday! Fancy their saying that!

MRS ELVSTED: Oh God, I'm so sure that something must have happened to him!

TESMAN: I say, Hedda. . . . what if I go into town, and make a few inquiries round about . . . ?

HEDDA: No, no . . . you'd better not get mixed up in this.

*Mr Brack, carrying his hat in his hand, comes in at the hall door, which Berte opens and closes again behind him. He looks serious and bows without speaking.*

TESMAN: Oh, Mr Brack, you're here are you? Eh?

BRACK: Yes, I had to come up to see you again this evening.

TESMAN: I can see that you've heard from Aunt Julle.

BRACK: Yes, I also received her message.

TESMAN: Isn't it terribly sad? Eh?

BRACK: Oh, my dear Tesman, that's as you choose to take it.

TESMAN [*looks at him uneasily*]: Is there something else, perhaps?

BRACK: Yes, there is.

HEDDA [*in suspense*]: Bad news, Mr Brack?

BRACK: Also as you choose to take it, Mrs Tesman.

MRS ELVSTED [*in a spontaneous outburst*]: Oh, it's to do with Ejlert Lövborg!

BRACK [*looks at her*]: Why should you think that, madam? Perhaps you know something already . . . ?

MRS ELVSTED [*confused*]: No, no, I know absolutely nothing; but . . .

TESMAN: Well, good gracious man, let's have it then!

BRACK [*shrugs his shoulders*]: Well then . . . I regret to say . . . Ejlert Lövborg has been taken to the hospital. He is not expected to live.

MRS ELVSTED [*crying out*]: Oh my God, my God . . . !

TESMAN: To the hospital! And not expected . . . !

HEDDA [*involuntarily*]: So soon . . . !

MRS ELVSTED [*wailing*]: And we . . . we weren't even reconciled when we parted, Hedda!

HEDDA [*whispers*]: Now Thea . . . Thea!

MRS ELVSTED [*taking no notice of her*]: I must go to him! I must see him alive!

BRACK: It's no use, madam. No one is allowed to see him.

MRS ELVSTED: Oh, but at least tell me what's happened to him! What's the matter with him?

TESMAN: Surely he can't have . . . himself . . . ! Eh?

HEDDA: Yes, I'm certain he did.

MRS ELVSTED: Oh Hedda . . . how can you . . . !

BRACK [*who is watching her all the time*]: Regrettably your guess is correct, Mrs Tesman.

MRS ELVSTED: Oh, but how dreadful!

TESMAN: Did it himself! Think of that!

HEDDA: Shot himself!

BRACK: Correctly guessed again, Mrs Tesman.

MRS ELVSTED [*trying to pull herself together*]: When did this happen, Mr Brack?

BRACK: This afternoon. Between three and four.

TESMAN: Yes, but, good Lord . . . where did he do it, then? Eh?

BRACK [*a little uncertainly*]: Where? Well, I . . . suppose it was at his lodgings.

MRS ELVSTED: No, that can't be right. I was there myself at about half past six.

BRACK: Well, somewhere else then. I don't exactly know about that. I just know that he was found. . . . He had shot himself . . . in the breast.

MRS ELVSTED: Oh, but how dreadful! That he should end like that!

HEDDA [*to Brack*]: He was shot in the breast?

BRACK: Yes . . . as I said.

HEDDA: Not in the temple?

BRACK: In the breast, Mrs Tesman.

HEDDA: Well . . . the breast is good, too.

BRACK: I beg your pardon, Mrs Tesman?

HEDDA [*evasively*]: Oh no . . . nothing.

TESMAN: And the wound may be fatal, you say? Eh?

BRACK: The wound will undoubtedly be fatal. Most probably it's all over already.

MRS ELVSTED: Yes, yes, I feel that it is! It's all over! All over! Oh, Hedda . . . !

TESMAN: Yes but tell me then . . . how did you come to hear of all this?

BRACK [*briefly*]: Through the police, a . . . man there I had to see.

HEDDA [*triumphantly*]: At last . . . a really courageous act!

TESMAN [*alarmed*]: But good Lord . . . what are you saying, Hedda?

HEDDA: I say that there is beauty in this deed.

BRACK: Hm, Mrs Tesman . . .

TESMAN: Beauty! Think of that!

MRS ELVSTED: Oh, Hedda, how can you call a thing like that beautiful?

HEDDA: Ejlert Lövborg has settled accounts with himself. He had the courage to do . . . what had to be done.

MRS ELVSTED: Oh no, it couldn't possibly have been like that! He must have done what he did in a fit of madness.

TESMAN: In desperation, it must have been!

HEDDA: It wasn't like that. I am quite certain of it.

MRS ELVSTED: Yes, it was! A fit of madness! Like when he tore our book to pieces!

BRACK [*pulled up*]: The book? The manuscript, you mean? Did he tear it to pieces?

MRS ELVSTED: Yes, he did that last night.

TESMAN [*whispering softly*]: Oh Hedda, we'll never get clear of this.

BRACK: Hm, how very extraordinary.

TESMAN [*drifting about the stage*]: Think of it! That Ejlert should end his life like that! And not even to leave behind him the work that would have made his name immortal. . . .

MRS ELVSTED: Oh, if only it could be put together again!

TESMAN: Yes, if only it could! I'd give anything on earth . . .

MRS ELVSTED: Perhaps it can, Mr Tesman.

TESMAN: What do you mean?

MRS ELVSTED [*searching in her skirt pocket*]: Look here. I kept the notes, all the notes he used when he dictated.

HEDDA [*a step closer*]: Ah . . . !

TESMAN: You kept them, Mrs Elvsted! Eh?

MRS ELVSTED: Yes, they're all here. I took them with me when I left. And they've just stayed in my pocket. . . .

TESMAN: Oh, let me see them!

MRS ELVSTED [*gives him a handful of small papers*]: But they're in such a muddle. All just anyhow.

TESMAN: Just think, if we could manage it all the same! Perhaps if we two were to have a go at it between us . . .

MRS ELVSTED: Oh, yes, let's try at least . . .

TESMAN: It must be done! It shall be done! I'll devote my life to this work!

HEDDA: You, Jörgen? Your life?

TESMAN: Yes, or at any rate the time I have at my disposal. My own material will just have to wait. Hedda . . . you understand me? Eh? I owe this to Ejlert's memory.

HEDDA: Perhaps you do.

TESMAN: And now, my dear Mrs Elvsted, we must pull ourselves together. God knows, there's no point in crying over spilt milk. Eh? We must try to contemplate the matter calmly. . . .

MRS ELVSTED: Yes, Mr Tesman, I'll do my best.

TESMAN: Well, come along then. We must look at these jottings at once. Now, where shall we sit? Here? No, there, in the back room. You'll excuse us, Mr Brack! You come along with me, Mrs Elvsted.

MRS ELVSTED: Oh God . . . if only it could be done!

*Tesman and Mr Elvsted go into the inner room. She removes her hat and coat. They both sit at the table under the hanging lamp, and immerse themselves in an eager examination of the papers. Hedda goes across to the stove and sits in the armchair. After a while Mr Brack joins her.*

HEDDA: Ah, Mr Brack . . . what a sense of release it gives, this affair of Ejlert Lövborg.

BRACK: Release, my lady? Well, of course, for him it's a release. . . .

HEDDA: I mean, for me. It's a liberation to know that an act of spontaneous courage is yet possible in this world. An act that has something of unconditional beauty.

BRACK [*smiles*]: Hm . . . my very dear lady . . .

HEDDA: Oh, I know what you're going to say. Because you're something of an academic too, in your own line, like . . . well!

BRACK [*looks at her steadily*]: Ejlert Lövborg was more to you perhaps than you are willing to admit, even to yourself. Or am I mistaken?

HEDDA: I don't answer that kind of question. I just know that Ejlert Lövborg had the courage to live his life in his own fashion. And then now . . . this! This beautiful act. That he had the courage to take his leave of life . . . so early.

BRACK: It pains me, my lady . . . but I am compelled to disabuse you of a beautiful illusion.

HEDDA: Illusion?

BRACK: Which you would in any case have been deprived of fairly soon.

HEDDA: And what might that be?

BRACK: He didn't shoot himself . . . intentionally.

HEDDA: Not intentionally!

BRACK: No. This business with Ejlert Lövborg didn't happen quite as I described it.

HEDDA [*in suspense*]: Did you keep something back? What is it?

BRACK: For the sake of that poor Mrs Elvsted I made use of a few circumlocutions.

HEDDA: What, then?

BRACK: In the first place, he is already dead.

HEDDA: At the hospital?

BRACK: Yes. Without recovering consciousness.

HEDDA: And what else?

BRACK: That the affair did not take place at his lodgings.

HEDDA: Well, that doesn't really make any difference.

BRACK: Does it not? Because as it happens . . . Ejlert Lövborg was found shot in . . . in Mademoiselle Diana's boudoir.

HEDDA [*is about to jump up, but sinks back again*]: No, that's impossible, Mr Brack! He can't have gone there again today!

BRACK: He went there this afternoon. He wanted to recover something that he said they'd taken. He was talking wildly about a child that had been lost. . . .

HEDDA: Oh . . . so that was why . . .

BRACK: I imagined that he might have been referring to his manuscript. But that he apparently destroyed himself. So it must have been his pocket-book, then.

HEDDA: I suppose so. . . . And so . . . he was found there.

BRACK: Yes, there. With a discharged pistol in his breast pocket. The bullet had wounded him fatally.

HEDDA: In the breast.

BRACK: No . . . he was shot in the abdomen.

HEDDA [*looks up with an expression of revulsion*]: That as well! Oh. . . . Everything I touch seems destined to turn into something mean and farcical.

BRACK: There is a further detail, my lady. Another circumstance that might be classified as somewhat distasteful.

HEDDA: And what is that?

BRACK: The pistol that was found on his body . . .

HEDDA [*holding her breath*]: Well! What about it!

BRACK: It must have been stolen.

HEDDA [*jumps up*]: Stolen! No! That isn't true!

BRACK: There is no possible alternative. He must have stolen it. . . . Sh!

*Tesman and Mrs Elvsted have got up from the table in the inner room and come out to the reception room.*

TESMAN [*with papers in both hands*]: Oh Hedda . . . it's almost impossible for me to see in there under the lamp. Think of that!

HEDDA: Yes, I'm thinking.

TESMAN: Do you think we might be allowed to sit at your desk for a bit? Eh?

HEDDA: Yes, of course you can. [*quickly*] No, wait a moment! Let me clear away some of these things first.

TESMAN: No, no, let me take all these away. I'll put them on the piano. There you are!

*She has pulled an object, covered with sheets of music, out of the bookcase; she adds a few more sheets and carries the whole pile off to the left of the inner room. Tesman puts the papers on the desk, and brings over the lamp from the corner table. He and Mrs Elvsted sit down and proceed with their work. Hedda returns.*

HEDDA [*behind Mrs Elvsted's chair, lightly caressing her hair*]: Well, Thea, my sweet . . . and how is the Ejlert Lövborg memorial getting on?

MRS ELVSTED [*looks up at her, discouraged*]: Oh goodness . . . it's going to be dreadfully difficult to sort out.

TESMAN: It must be possible. It simply has to be. And this . . . putting other people's papers in order . . . that's just the sort of thing I'm good at.

*Hedda goes across to the stove and sits on one of the stools. Brack stands over her, leaning against the armchair.*

HEDDA [*whispers*]: What were you saying about the pistol?

BRACK [*quietly*]: That it must have been stolen.

HEDDA: And why must it have been?

BRACK: Because any other explanation ought to be impossible, my lady.

HEDDA: Indeed.

BRACK [*looks at her*]: Ejlert Lövborg was evidently here this morning. Isn't that so?

HEDDA: Yes.

BRACK: Were you alone with him?

HEDDA: Yes, for a while.

BRACK: And did you not leave the room while he was here?

HEDDA: No.

BRACK: Think carefully. Were you not out of the room even for a moment?

HEDDA: Yes, perhaps just for a moment . . . out in the hall.

BRACK: And where was the case with your pistols during this time?

HEDDA: It was locked in . . .

BRACK: Well, my lady?

HEDDA: The case was standing over there on the writing table.

BRACK: Have you looked at it since then to see whether both pistols are still in place?

HEDDA: No.

BRACK: You don't need to look. I saw the pistol that was found on Lövborg. And I recognized it immediately, from yesterday. And from before that, too.

HEDDA: Have you got the pistol?

BRACK: No, it is in the hands of the police.

HEDDA: And what will the police do with it?

BRACK: Try to discover who owns it.

HEDDA: And do you think they will be successful?

BRACK [*bends over her and whispers*]: No, Hedda Gabler . . . not if I hold my tongue.

HEDDA [*looks at him apprehensively*]: And if you don't . . . what then?

BRACK [*shrugs his shoulders*]: There is always the possibility that the pistol was stolen.

HEDDA [*with determination*]: I'd sooner die!

BRACK [*smiles*] People say such things. But they don't do them.

HEDDA [*without answering*]: And so . . . as the pistol was not stolen. And when the owner is discovered. What happens then?

BRACK: There will be an unpleasant scandal . . . Hedda.

HEDDA: A scandal!

BRACK: Yes, a scandal . . . the thing you are afraid of. You will of course be required to go into the witness box. Both you and Mademoiselle Diana. She will have to explain how the event took place. Whether the wound was inflicted accidentally or deliberately. Was he about to pull the pistol out of his pocket in order to threaten her? And did it then go off? Or did she seize the pistol out of his hand, shoot him down, and then stick the weapon back in his pocket? I wouldn't put it past her. She's a spirited wench, is this Mademoiselle Diana.

HEDDA: But all this revolting business has nothing to do with me.

BRACK: No. But you will be obliged to tell the court why you gave Ejlert Lövborg the pistol. And what inference will be drawn from the fact that you did give it to him?

HEDDA [*lowers her head*]: That's true. I didn't think of that.

BRACK: Well, fortunately there is nothing to fear so long as I keep silence.

HEDDA [*looks up at him*]: And so I am in your power, Mr Brack. From now on I am at your mercy.

BRACK [*whispers more softly*]: Dearest Hedda . . . believe me . . . I shall not abuse the position.

HEDDA: In your power, all the same. Subject to your will and your demands. No longer free! [*She gets up violently.*] No! That's a thought that I'll never endure! Never.

BRACK [*looks at her half tauntingly*]: One generally acquiesces in what is inevitable.

HEDDA [*returns the look*]: Perhaps you're right.

*She crosses to the writing desk.*

HEDDA [*suppresses an involuntary smile, and imitates Tesman's intonation*]: Well? Is it going to work out, Jörgen? Eh?

TESMAN: Heaven knows, my love. At any rate it's going to take us months.

HEDDA [*as before*]: Well, think of that! [*She passes her fingers lightly through Mrs Elvsted's hair.*] Isn't this strange for you, Thea? Now you're sitting here together with Tesman . . . as you used to sit with Ejlert Lövborg.

MRS ELVSTED: Oh yes, oh God . . . if only I could inspire your husband in the same way.

HEDDA: Oh, I expect it will come . . . in time.

TESMAN: Yes, d'you know what, Hedda . . . it really does seem to me that I'm beginning to feel something of the sort. But you go and sit down again, now, with Mr Brack.

HEDDA: And is there nothing I can do to help you two?

TESMAN: No, nothing at all. [*turns his head*] We'll just have to rely on you, dear Mr Brack, to keep Hedda company!

BRACK [*with a look to Hedda*]: It will be a pleasure indeed.

HEDDA: Thank you. But tonight I'm tired. I'm going to go in and lie down a bit on the sofa.

TESMAN: Yes, you do that my dear. Eh?

*Hedda goes into the inner room and pulls the curtains together behind her. A short pause. Suddenly she is heard to play a wild dance tune on the piano.*

MRS ELVSTED [*starts up from her chair*]: Oh . . . what's that!

TESMAN [*runs to the doorway*]: But Hedda, my dear . . . don't play dance music, not tonight! Do think of Aunt Rina! And of Ejlert, too!

HEDDA [*puts her head out between the curtains*]: And of Auntie Julle. And of all the rest of them. . . . I shall be silent in future. [*She draws the curtains together again.*]

TESMAN [*at the desk*]: I don't think it's good for her to see us at this melancholy task. I'll tell you what, Mrs Elvsted . . . you'll have to move in to Aunt Julle's. Then I'll come up in the evenings. And then we can sit and work there. Eh?

MRS ELVSTED: Yes, perhaps that would be best. . . .

HEDDA [*from the inner room*]: I can hear what you're saying, Tesman. And how am I supposed to survive the evenings out here?

TESMAN [*leafing through the papers*]: Oh, I expect Mr Brack will be kind enough to look in now and again.

BRACK [*in the armchair, shouts cheerfully*]: I'll gladly come every single evening, Mrs Tesman! Don't you worry, we'll have a fine time out here together!

HEDDA [*clearly and distinctly*]: Yes, you're looking forward to that, aren't you, Mr Brack? Yourself as the only cock in the yard. . . .

*A shot is heard within. Tesman, Mrs Elvsted, and Brack all start to their feet.*

TESMAN: Oh, now she's playing about with those pistols again.

*He pulls the curtains aside and runs in. Mrs Elvsted follows. Hedda lies stretched out dead on the sofa. Confusion and shouting. Berte, in alarm, comes in from the right.*

TESMAN [*yelling at Brack*]: Shot herself! Shot herself in the temple! Think of that!

BRACK [*half prostrate in the armchair*]: But, good God Almighty . . . people don't do such things!

1890

# Oscar Wilde
## 1854–1900

Playwright and poet, novelist and critic, Oscar Wilde was born in Dublin, Ireland. After majoring in classics at Trinity College, Dublin, he won a scholarship to Oxford University. By the time of his graduation from Oxford in 1878 he was already well known for his commitment to 'art for art's sake' and for his eccentricities in dress and manners. Convinced that 'industry is the root of all ugliness', he sought to raise the taste of his audiences. Between 1892 and 1895 he wrote a series of comedies for the stage—'trivial comedies for serious people', he called them—whose plots were then regarded as scandalous and whose dialogue glistened with his clever wit. In 1895 he was found guilty of homosexual conduct and sentenced to two years in prison with hard labour. His imprisonment led him to write his poem *The Ballad of Reading Gaol* and his prose confession *De Profundis.* After his release from jail he emigrated to France, where he spent his last five years living under an assumed name. *The Importance of Being Earnest* had its premiere at St James's Theatre in London on 14 February 1895.

## The Importance of Being Earnest

### *CHARACTERS*

JOHN WORTHING, JP
ALGERNON MONCRIEFF
REV. CANON CHASUBLE, DD
MIRRIMAN, butler
LANE, manservant
LADY BRACKNELL
HON. GWENDOLEN FAIRFAX
CECILY CARDEW
MISS PRISM, governess

### ACT I

*The Scene: Morning room in Algernon's flat in Half-Moon Street. The room is luxuriously and artistically furnished. The sound of a piano is heard in the adjoining room. Lane is arranging the afternoon tea on the table, and after the music has ceased, Algernon enters.*

ALGERNON: Did you hear what I was playing, Lane?

LANE: I didn't think it polite to listen, sir.

ALGERNON: I'm sorry for that, for your sake. I don't play accurately—any one can play accurately—but I play with wonderful expression. As far as the piano is concerned, sentiment is my forte. I keep science for Life.

LANE: Yes, sir.

ALGERNON: And, speaking of the science of Life, have you got the cucumber sandwiches cut for Lady Bracknell?

LANE: Yes, sir. [*Hands them on a salver.*]

ALGERNON [*inspects them, takes two, and sits down on the sofa*]: Oh! . . . by the way, Lane, I see from your book that on Thursday night, when Lord Shoreman and Mr Worthing were dining with me, eight bottles of champagne are entered as having been consumed.

LANE: Yes, sir; eight bottles and a pint.

ALGERNON: Why is it that at a bachelor's establishment the servants invariably drink the champagne? I ask merely for information.

LANE: I attribute it to the superior quality of the wine, sir. I have often observed that in married households the champagne is rarely of a first-rate brand.

ALGERNON: Good Heavens! Is marriage so demoralizing as that?

LANE: I believe it is a very pleasant state, sir. I have had very little experience of it myself up to the present. I have only been married once. That was in consequence of a misunderstanding between myself and a young person.

ALGERNON [*languidly*]: I don't know that I am much interested in your family life, Lane.

LANE: No sir; it is not a very interesting subject. I never think of it myself.

ALGERNON: Very natural, I am sure. That will do, Lane, thank you.

LANE: Thank you, sir. [*Lane goes out.*]

ALGERNON: Lane's views on marriage seem somewhat lax. Really, if the lower orders don't set us a good example, what on earth is the use of them? They seem, as a class, to have absolutely no sense of moral responsibility.

*Enter Lane.*

LANE: Mr Ernest Worthing.

*Enter Jack. Lane goes out.*

ALGERNON: How are you, my dear Ernest? What brings you up to town?

JACK: Oh, pleasure, pleasure! What else should bring one anywhere? Eating as usual, I see, Algy!

ALGERNON [*stiffly*]: I believe it is customary in good society to take some slight refreshment at five o'clock. Where have you been since last Thursday?

JACK [*sitting down on the sofa*]: In the country.

ALGERNON: What on earth do you do there?

JACK [*pulling off his gloves*]: When one is in town one amuses oneself. When one is in the country one amuses other people. It is excessively boring.

ALGERNON: And who are the people you amuse?

JACK [*airily*]: Oh, neighbours, neighbours.

ALGERNON: Got nice neighbours in your part of Shropshire?

JACK: Perfectly horrid! Never speak to one of them.

ALGERNON: How immensely you must amuse them! [*Goes over and takes sandwich.*] By the way, Shropshire is your country, is it not?

JACK: Eh? Shropshire? Yes, of course. Hallo! Why all these cups? Why cucumber sandwiches? Why such reckless extravagance in one so young? Who is coming to tea?

ALGERNON: Oh! merely Aunt Augusta and Gwendolen.

JACK: How perfectly delightful!

ALGERNON: Yes, that is all very well; but I am afraid Aunt Augusta won't quite approve of your being here.

JACK: May I ask why?

ALGERNON: My dear fellow, the way you flirt with Gwendolen is perfectly disgraceful. It is almost as bad as the way Gwendolen flirts with you.

JACK: I am in love with Gwendolen. I have come up to town expressly to propose to her.

ALGERNON: I thought you had come up for pleasure? . . . I call that business.

JACK: How utterly unromantic you are!

ALGERNON: I really don't see anything romantic in proposing. It is very romantic to be in love. But there is nothing romantic about a definite proposal. Why, one may be accepted. One usually is, I believe. Then the excitement is all over. The very essence of romance is uncertainty. If ever I get married, I'll certainly try to forget the fact.

JACK: I have no doubt about that, dear Algy. The Divorce Court was specially invented for people whose memories are so curiously constituted.

ALGERNON: Oh! there is no use speculating on that subject. Divorces are made in Heaven—[*Jack puts out his hand to take a sandwich, Algernon at once interferes.*] Please don't touch the cucumber sandwiches. They are ordered specially for Aunt Augusta. [*Takes one and eats it.*]

JACK: Well, you have been eating them all the time.

ALGERNON: That is quite a different matter. She is my aunt. [*Takes plate from below.*] Have some bread and butter. The bread and butter is for Gwendolen. Gwendolen is devoted to bread and butter.

JACK [*advancing to table and helping himself* ]: And very good bread and butter it is too.

ALGERNON: Well, my dear fellow, you need not eat as if you were going to eat it all. You behave as if you were married to her already. You are not married to her already, and I don't think you ever will be.

JACK: Why on earth do you say that?

ALGERNON: Well, in the first place, girls never marry the men they flirt with. Girls don't think it right.

JACK: Oh, that is nonsense!

ALGERNON: It isn't. It is a great truth. It accounts for the extraordinary number of bachelors that one sees all over the place. In the second place, I don't give my consent.

JACK: Your consent!

ALGERNON: My dear fellow, Gwendolen is my first cousin. And before I allow you to marry her, you will have to clear up the whole question of Cecily. [*Rings bell.*]

JACK: Cecily! What on earth do you mean? What do you mean, Algy, by Cecily! I don't know anyone of the name of Cecily.

*Enter Lane.*

ALGERNON: Bring me that cigarette case Mr Worthing left in the smoking room the last time he dined here.

LANE: Yes, sir. [*Lane goes out.*]

JACK: Do you mean to say you have had my cigarette case all this time? I wish to goodness you had let me know. I have been writing frantic letters to Scotland Yard about it. I was very nearly offering a large reward.

ALGERNON: Well, I wish you would offer one. I happen to be more than usually hard up.

JACK: There is no good offering a large reward now that the thing is found.

*Enter Lane with the cigarette case on a salver. Algernon takes it at once. Lane goes out.*

ALGERNON: I think that is rather mean of you, Ernest, I must say. [*Opens case and examines it.*] However, it makes no matter, for, now that I look at the inscription inside, I find that the thing isn't yours after all.

JACK: Of course it's mine. [*Moving to him.*] You have seen me with it a hundred times, and you have no right whatsoever to read what is written inside. It is a very ungentlemanly thing to read a private cigarette case.

ALGERNON: Oh! it is absurd to have a hard and fast rule about what one should read and what one shouldn't. More than half of modern culture depends on what one shouldn't read.

JACK: I am quite aware of the fact, and I don't propose to discuss modern culture. It isn't the sort of thing one should talk of in private. I simply want my cigarette case back.

ALGERNON: Yes; but this isn't your cigarette case. The cigarette case is a present from someone of the name of Cecily, and you said you didn't know anyone of that name.

JACK: Well, if you want to know, Cecily happens to be my aunt.

ALGERNON: Your aunt?

JACK: Charming old lady she is, too. Lives at Tunbridge Wells. Just give it back to me, Algy.

ALGERNON [*retreating to back of sofa*]: But why does she call herself little Cecily if she is your aunt and lives at Tunbridge Wells. [*Reading*] 'From little Cecily with her fondest love.'

JACK [*moving to sofa and kneeling upon it*]: My dear fellow, what on earth is there in that? Some aunts are tall, some aunts are not tall. That is a matter that surely an aunt may be allowed to decide for herself. You seem to think that every aunt should be exactly like your aunt! That is absurd. For Heaven's sake give me back my cigarette case. [*Follows Algernon round the room.*]

ALGERNON: Yes. But why does your aunt call you her uncle? 'From little Cecily, with her fondest love to her dear Uncle Jack.' There is no objection, I admit, to an aunt being a small aunt, but why an aunt, no matter what her size may be, should call her own nephew her uncle, I can't quite make out. Besides, your name isn't Jack at all; it is Ernest.

JACK: It isn't Ernest; it's Jack.

ALGERNON: You have always told me it was Ernest. I have introduced you to everyone as Ernest. You answer to the name Ernest. You look as if your name was Ernest. You are the most earnest-looking person I ever saw in my life. It is perfectly absurd your saying that your name isn't Ernest. It's on your cards. Here is one of them [*taking it from case*]. 'Mr Ernest Worthing, B.4, The Albany.' I'll keep this as a proof that your name is Ernest if ever you attempt to deny it to me, or to Gwendolen, or to anyone else. [*Puts the card in his pocket.*]

JACK: Well, my name is Ernest in town and Jack in the country, and the cigarette case was given to me in the country.

ALGERNON: Yes, but that does not account for the fact that your small Aunt Cecily, who lives at Tunbridge Wells, calls you her dear uncle. Come, old boy, you had much better have the thing out at once.

JACK: My dear Algy, you talk exactly as if you were a dentist. It is very vulgar to talk like a dentist when one isn't a dentist. It produces a false impression.

ALGERNON: Well, that is exactly what dentists always do. Now, go on! Tell me the whole thing. I may mention that I have always suspected you of being a confirmed and secret Bunburyist; and I am quite sure of it now.

JACK: Bunburyist? What on earth do you mean by a Bunburyist?

ALGERNON: I'll reveal to you the meaning of that incomparable expression as soon as you are kind enough to inform me why you are Ernest in town and Jack in the country.

JACK: Well, produce my cigarette case first.

ALGERNON: Here it is. [*Hands cigarette case.*] Now produce your explanation, and pray make it improbable. [*Sits on sofa.*]

JACK: My dear fellow, there is nothing improbable about my explanation at all. In fact it's perfectly ordinary. Old Mr Thomas Cardew, who adopted me when I was a little boy, made me in his will guardian to his granddaughter, Miss Cecily Cardew. Cecily, who addresses me as her uncle from motives of respect that you could not possibly appreciate, lives at my place in the country under the charge of her admirable governess, Miss Prism.

ALGERNON: Where is that place in the country, by the way?

JACK: That is nothing to you, dear boy. You are not going to be invited. . . . I may tell you candidly that the place is not in Shropshire.

ALGERNON: I suspected that, my dear fellow! I have Bunburyed all over Shropshire on two separate occasions. Now, go on. Why are you Ernest in town and Jack in the country?

JACK: My dear Algy, I don't know whether you will be able to understand my real motive. You are hardly serious enough. When one is placed in the position of guardian, one has to adopt a very high moral tone on all subjects. It's one's duty to do so. And as a high moral tone can hardly be said to conduce very much to either one's health or one's happiness, in order to get up to town I have always pretended to have a younger brother of the name of Ernest, who lives in Albany, and gets into the most dreadful scrapes. That, my dear Algy, is the whole truth pure and simple.

ALGERNON: The truth is rarely pure and never simple. Modern life would be very tedious if it were either, and modern literature a complete impossibility!

JACK: That wouldn't be at all a bad thing.

ALGERNON: Literary criticism is not your forte, my dear fellow. Don't try it. You should leave that to the people who haven't been at a University. They do it so well in the daily papers. What you really are is a Bunburyist. I was quite right in saying you are a Bunburyist. You are one of the most advanced Bunburyists I know.

JACK: What on earth do you mean?

ALGERNON: You have invented a very useful younger brother called Ernest, in order that you may be able to come up to town as often as you like. I have invented an invaluable permanent invalid called Bunbury, in order that I may be able to go down into the country whenever I choose. Bunbury is perfectly invaluable. If it wasn't for Bunbury's extraordinary bad health, for instance, I wouldn't be able to dine with you at Willis's tonight, for I have been really engaged to Aunt Augusta for more than a week.

JACK: I haven't asked you to dine with me anywhere tonight.

ALGERNON: I know. You are absurdly careless about sending out invitations. It is very foolish of you. Nothing annoys people so much as not receiving invitations.

JACK: You had better dine with your Aunt Augusta.

ALGERNON: I haven't the smallest intention of doing anything of the kind. To begin with, I dined there on Monday, and once a week is quite enough to dine with one's own relations. In the second place, whenever I do dine there I am always treated as a member of the family, and sent down with either no woman at all, or two. In the third place, I know perfectly well whom she will place me next to, tonight. She will place me next Mary Farquhar, who always flirts with her own husband across the dinner table. That is not very pleasant. Indeed, it is not even decent . . . and that sort of thing is enormously on the increase. The amount of women in London who flirt with their own husbands is perfectly scandalous. It looks so bad. It is simply washing one's clean linen in public. Besides, now that I know you to be a confirmed Bunburyist I naturally want to talk to you about Bunburying. I want to tell you the rules.

JACK: I'm not a Bunburyist at all. If Gwendolen accepts me, I am going to kill my brother, indeed I think I'll kill him in any case. Cecily is a little too interested in him. It is rather a bore. So I am going to get rid of Ernest. And I strongly advise you to do the same with Mr . . . with your invalid friend who has the absurd name.

ALGERNON: Nothing will induce me to part with Bunbury, and if you ever get married, which seems to me extremely problematic, you will be very glad to know Bunbury. A man who marries without knowing Bunbury has a very tedious time of it.

JACK: That is nonsense. If I marry a charming girl like Gwendolen, and she is the only girl I ever saw in life that I would marry, I certainly won't want to know Bunbury.

ALGERNON: Then your wife will. You don't seem to realize, that in married life three is company and two is none.

JACK [*sententiously*]: That, my dear young friend, is the theory that the corrupt French Drama has been propounding for the last fifty years.

ALGERNON: Yes; and that the happy English home has proved in half the time.

JACK: For heaven's sake, don't try to be cynical. It's perfectly easy to be cynical.

ALGERNON: My dear fellow, it isn't easy to be anything nowadays. There's such a lot of beastly competition about. [*The sound of an electric bell is heard.*] Ah! that must be Aunt Augusta. Only relatives, or creditors, ever ring in that Wagnerian manner. Now, if I get her out of the way for ten minutes, so that you can have an opportunity of proposing to Gwendolen, may I dine with you tonight at Willis's?

JACK: I suppose so, if you want to.

ALGERNON: Yes, but you must be serious about it. I hate people who are not serious about meals. It is so shallow of them.

*Enter Lane*

LANE: Lady Bracknell and Miss Fairfax.

*Algernon goes forward to meet them. Enter Lady Bracknell and Gwendolen.*

LADY BRACKNELL: Good afternoon, dear Algernon, I hope you are behaving very well.

ALGERNON: I'm feeling very well, Aunt Augusta.

LADY BRACKNELL: That's not quite the same thing. In fact the two things rarely go together. [*Sees Jack and bows to him with icy coldness.*]

ALGERNON [*to Gwendolen*]: Dear me, you are smart!

GWENDOLEN: I am always smart! Am I not, Mr Worthing?

JACK: You're quite perfect, Miss Fairfax.

GWENDOLEN: Oh! I hope I am not that. It would leave no room for developments, and I intend to develop in many directions. [*Gwendolen and Jack sit down together in the corner.*]

LADY BRACKNELL: I'm sorry if we are a little late, Algernon, but I was obliged to call on dear Lady Harbury. I hadn't been there since her poor husband's death. I never saw a woman so altered; she looks quite twenty years younger. And now I'll have a cup of tea and one of those nice cucumber sandwiches you promised me.

ALGERNON: Certainly, Aunt Augusta. [*Goes over to tea table.*]

LADY BRACKNELL: Won't you come and sit here, Gwendolen?

GWENDOLEN: Thanks, mamma, I'm quite comfortable where I am.

ALGERNON [*picking up empty plate in horror*]: Good heavens! Lane! Why are there no cucumber sandwiches? I ordered them specially.

LANE [*gravely*]: There were no cucumbers in the market this morning, sir. I went down twice.

ALGERNON: No cucumbers!

LANE: No, sir. Not even for ready money.

ALGERNON: That will do, Lane, thank you.

LANE: Thank you, sir. [*Goes out.*]

ALGERNON: I am greatly distressed, Aunt Augusta, about there being no cucumbers, not even for ready money.

LADY BRACKNELL: It really makes no matter, Algernon. I had some crumpets with Lady Harbury, who seems to me to be living entirely for pleasure now.

ALGERNON: I hear her hair has turned quite gold from grief.

LADY BRACKNELL: It certainly has changed its colour. From what cause I, of course, cannot say. [*Algernon crosses and hands tea.*] Thank you, I've quite a treat for you tonight, Algernon. I am going to send you down with Mary Farquhar. She is such a nice woman, and so attentive to her husband. It's delightful to watch them.

ALGERNON: I am afraid, Aunt Augusta, I shall have to give up the pleasure of dining with you tonight after all.

LADY BRACKNELL [*frowning*]: I hope not, Algernon. It would put my table completely out. Your uncle would have to dine upstairs. Fortunately he is accustomed to that.

ALGERNON: It is a great bore, and, I need hardly say, a terrible disappointment to me, but the fact is I have just had a telegram to say that my poor friend Bunbury is very ill again. [*Exchanges glances with Jack.*] They seem to think I should be with him.

LADY BRACKNELL: It is very strange. This Mr Bunbury seems to suffer from curiously bad health.

ALGERNON: Yes; poor Bunbury is a dreadful invalid.

LADY BRACKNELL: Well, I must say, Algernon, that I think it is high time that Mr Bunbury made up his mind whether he was going to live or to die. This shilly-shallying with the question is absurd. Nor do I in any way approve of the modern sympathy with invalids. I consider it morbid. Illness of any kind is hardly a thing to be encouraged in others. Health is the primary duty of life. I am always telling that to your poor uncle, but he never seems to take much notice . . . as far as any improvement in his ailments goes. I should be much obliged if you would ask Mr Bunbury, from me, to be kind enough not to have a relapse on Saturday, for I rely on you to arrange my music for me. It is my last reception, and one wants something that will encourage conversation, particularly at the end of the season when everyone has practically said whatever they had to say, which, in most cases, was probably not much.

ALGERNON: I'll speak to Bunbury, Aunt Augusta, if he is still conscious, and I think I can promise you he'll be all right by Saturday. Of course the music is a great difficulty. You see, if one plays good music, people don't listen, and if one plays bad music, people don't talk. But I'll run over the program I've drawn out, if you will kindly come into the next room for a moment.

LADY BRACKNELL: Thank you, Algernon. It is very thoughtful of you. [*Rising, and following Algernon.*] I'm sure the program will be delightful, after a few expurgations. French songs I cannot possibly allow. People always seem to think that they are improper, and either look shocked, which is vulgar, or laugh, which is worse. But German sounds a thoroughly respectable language, and, indeed I believe is so. Gwendolen, you will accompany me.

GWENDOLEN: Certainly, mamma.

*Lady Bracknell and Algernon go into the music room; Gwendolen remains behind.*

JACK: Charming day it has been, Miss Fairfax.

GWENDOLEN: Pray don't talk to me about the weather, Mr Worthing. Whenever people talk to me about the weather, I always feel quite certain that they mean something else. And that makes me so nervous.

JACK: I do mean something else.

GWENDOLEN: I thought so. In fact, I am never wrong.

JACK: And I would like to be allowed to take advantage of Lady Bracknell's temporary absence. . . .

GWENDOLEN: I would certainly advise you to do so. Mamma has a way of coming back suddenly into a room that I have often had to speak to her about.

JACK [*nervously*]: Miss Fairfax, ever since I met you I have admired you more than any girl . . . I have ever met since . . . I met you.

GWENDOLEN: Yes, I am quite aware of the fact. And I do often wish that in public, at any rate, you had been more demonstrative. For me you have always had an irresistible fascination. Even before I met you I was far from indifferent to you. [*Jack looks at her in amazement.*] We live, as I hope you know, Mr Worthing, in an age of ideals. The fact is constantly mentioned in the more expensive monthly magazines, and has reached the provincial pulpits, I am told; and my ideal has always been to love someone of the name of Ernest. There is something in that name that inspires absolute confidence. The moment Algernon first mentioned to me that he had a friend called Ernest, I knew I was destined to love you.

JACK: You really love me, Gwendolen?

GWENDOLEN: Passionately!

JACK: Darling! You don't know how happy you've made me.

GWENDOLEN: My own Ernest!

JACK: But you don't really mean to say that you couldn't love me if my name wasn't Ernest!

GWENDOLEN: But your name is Ernest.

JACK: Yes, I know it is. But supposing it was something else? Do you mean to say you couldn't love me then?

GWENDOLEN [*glibly*]: Ah! that is clearly a metaphysical speculation, and like most metaphysical speculations has very little reference at all to the actual facts of real life, as we know them.

JACK: Personally, darling, to speak quite candidly, I don't much care about the name of Ernest. . . . I don't think the name suits me at all.

GWENDOLEN: It suits you perfectly. It is a divine name. It has a music of its own. It produces vibrations.

JACK: Well, really, Gwendolen, I must say that I think there are lots of other much nicer names. I think Jack, for instance, a charming name.

GWENDOLEN: Jack? . . . No, there is very little music in the name Jack, if any at all, indeed. It does not thrill. It produces absolutely no vibrations. . . . I have known several Jacks, and they all, without exception, were more than usually plain. Besides, Jack is a notorious domesticity for John! And I pity any woman who is married to a man called John. She would probably never be allowed to know the entrancing pleasure of a single moment's solitude. The only really safe name is Ernest.

JACK: Gwendolen, I must get christened at once—I mean we must get married at once. There is no time to be lost.

GWENDOLEN: Married, Mr Worthing?

JACK [*astounded*]: Well . . . surely. You know that I love you, and you led me to believe, Miss Fairfax, that you were not absolutely indifferent to me.

GWENDOLEN: I adore you. But you haven't proposed to me yet. Nothing has been said at all about marriage. The subject has not even been touched on.

JACK: Well . . . may I propose to you now?

GWENDOLEN: I think it would be an admirable opportunity. And to spare you any possible disappointment, Mr Worthing, I think it only fair to tell you quite frankly beforehand that I am fully determined to accept you.

JACK: Gwendolen!

GWENDOLEN: Yes, Mr Worthing, what have you got to say to me?

JACK: You know what I have got to say to you.

GWENDOLEN: Yes, but you don't say it.

JACK: Gwendolen, will you marry me? [*Goes on his knees.*]

GWENDOLEN: Of course I will, darling. How long you have been about it! I am afraid you have had very little experience in how to propose.

JACK: My own one, I have never loved anyone in the world but you.

GWENDOLEN: Yes, but men often propose for practice. I know my brother Gerald does. All my girl friends tell me so. What wonderfully blue eyes you have, Ernest! They are quite, quite blue. I hope you will always look at me just like that, especially when there are other people present.

*Enter Lady Bracknell.*

LADY BRACKNELL: Mr Worthing! Rise, sir, from this semi-recumbent posture. It is most indecorous.

GWENDOLEN: Mamma! [*He tries to rise; she restrains him.*] I must beg you to retire. This is no place for you. Besides, Mr Worthing has not quite finished yet.

LADY BRACKNELL: Finished what, may I ask?

GWENDOLEN: I am engaged to Mr Worthing, Mamma. [*They rise together.*]

LADY BRACKNELL: Pardon me, you are not engaged to anyone. When you do become engaged to someone, I, or your father, should his health permit him, will inform you of the fact. An engagement should come on a young girl as a surprise, pleasant or unpleasant, as the case may be. It is hardly a matter that she could be allowed to arrange for herself. . . . And now I have a few questions to put to you, Mr Worthing. While I am making these inquiries, you, Gwendolen, will wait for me below in the carriage.

GWENDOLEN [*reproachfully*]: Mamma!

LADY BRACKNELL: In the carriage, Gwendolen! [*Gwendolen goes to the door. She and Jack blow kisses to each other behind Lady Bracknell's back. Lady Bracknell looks vaguely about as if she could not understand what the noise was. Finally turns round.*] Gwendolen, the carriage!

GWENDOLEN: Yes, Mamma. [*Goes out, looking back at Jack.*]

LADY BRACKNELL [*sitting down*]: You can take a seat, Mr Worthing. [*Looks in her pocket for notebook and pencil.*]

JACK: Thank you, Lady Bracknell, I prefer standing.

LADY BRACKNELL [*pencil and notebook in hand*]: I feel bound to tell you that you are not down on my list of eligible young men, although I have the same list as the dear Duchess of Bolton has. We work together, in fact. However, I am quite ready to enter your name, should your answers be what a really affectionate mother requires. Do you smoke?

JACK: Well, yes, I must admit I smoke.

LADY BRACKNELL: I am glad to hear it. A man should always have an occupation of some kind. There are far too many idle men in London as it is. How old are you?

JACK: Twenty-nine.

LADY BRACKNELL: A very good age to be married at. I have always been of the opinion that a man who desires to get married should know either everything or nothing. Which do you know?

JACK [*after some hesitation*]: I know nothing, Lady Bracknell.

LADY BRACKNELL: I am pleased to hear it. I do not approve of anything that tampers with natural ignorance. Ignorance is like a delicate exotic fruit; touch it and the bloom is gone. The whole theory of modern education is radically unsound. Fortunately in England, at any rate, education produces no effect whatsoever. If it did, it would prove a serious danger to the upper classes, and probably lead to acts of violence in Grosvenor Square. What is your income?

JACK: Between seven and eight thousand a year.

LADY BRACKNELL [*makes a note in her book*]: In land, or in investments?

JACK: In investments, chiefly.

LADY BRACKNELL: That is satisfactory. What between the duties expected of one during one's lifetime, and the duties exacted from one after one's death, land has ceased to be either a profit or a pleasure. It gives one position, and prevents one from keeping it up. That's all that can be said about land.

JACK: I have a country house with some land, of course, attached to it, about fifteen hundred acres, I believe; but I don't depend on that for my real income. In fact, as far as I can make out, the poachers are the only people who make anything out of it.

LADY BRACKNELL: A country house! How many bedrooms? Well, that point can be cleared up afterwards. You have a town house, I hope? A girl with a simple, unspoiled nature, like Gwendolen, could hardly be expected to reside in the country.

JACK: Well, I own a house in Belgrave Square, but it is let by the year to Lady Bloxham. Of course, I can get it back whenever I like, at six months' notice.

LADY BRACKNELL: Lady Bloxham? I don't know her.

JACK: Oh, she goes out very little. She is a lady considerably advanced in years.

LADY BRACKNELL: Ah, nowadays that is no guarantee of respectability of character. What number in Belgrave Square?

JACK: 149.

LADY BRACKNELL [*shaking her head*]: The unfashionable side. I thought there was something. However, that could easily be altered.

JACK: Do you mean the fashion, or the side?

LADY BRACKNELL [*sternly*]: Both, if necessary, I presume. What are your politics?

JACK: Well, I am afraid I really have none. I am a Liberal Unionist.

LADY BRACKNELL: Oh, they count as Tories. They dine with us. Or come in the evening, at any rate. Now to minor matters. Are your parents living?

JACK: I have lost both my parents.

LADY BRACKNELL: To lose one parent, Mr Worthing, may be regarded as a misfortune; to lose both looks like carelessness. Who was your father? He was evidently a man of some wealth. Was he born in what the Radical papers call the purple of commerce, or did he rise from the ranks of the aristocracy?

JACK: I am afraid I really don't know. The fact is, Lady Bracknell, I said I had lost my parents. It would be nearer the truth to say that my parents seem to have lost me. . . . I don't actually know who I am by birth. I was . . . well, I was found.

LADY BRACKNELL: Found!

JACK: The late Mr Thomas Cardew, an old gentleman of a very charitable and kindly disposition, found me and gave me the name of Worthing, because he happened to have a first-class ticket for Worthing in his pocket at the time. Worthing is a place in Sussex. It is a seaside resort.

LADY BRACKNELL: Where did the charitable gentleman who had a first-class ticket for this seaside resort find you?

JACK [*gravely*]: In a handbag.

LADY BRACKNELL: A handbag?

JACK [*very seriously*]: Yes, Lady Bracknell. I was in a handbag—a somewhat large, black leather handbag, with handles on it—an ordinary handbag in fact.

LADY BRACKNELL: In what locality did this Mr James, or Thomas, Cardew come across this ordinary handbag?

JACK: In the cloakroom at Victoria Station. It was given to him in mistake for his own.

LADY BRACKNELL: The cloakroom at Victoria Station?

JACK: Yes, the Brighton line.

LADY BRACKNELL: The line is immaterial. Mr Worthing, I confess I feel somewhat bewildered by what you have just told me. To be born, or at any rate bred, in a handbag, whether it had handles or not, seems to me to display a contempt for the ordinary decencies of family life that reminds one of the worst excesses of the French Revolution. And I presume you know what that unfortunate movement led to? As for the particular locality in which the handbag was found, a cloakroom at a railway station might serve to conceal a social indiscretion—has probably, indeed, been used for that purpose before now—but it could hardly be regarded as an assured basis for a recognized position in good society.

JACK: May I ask you then what you would advise me to do? I need hardly say I would do anything in the world to ensure Gwendolen's happiness.

LADY BRACKNELL: I would strongly advise you, Mr Worthing, to try and acquire some relations as soon as possible, and to make a definite effort to produce at any rate one parent, of either sex, before the season is quite over.

JACK: Well, I don't see how I could possibly manage to do that. I can produce the handbag at any moment. It is in my dressing room at home. I really think that should satisfy you, Lady Bracknell.

LADY BRACKNELL: Me, sir! What has it to do with me? You can hardly imagine that I and Lord Bracknell would dream of allowing our only daughter—a girl brought up with the utmost care—to marry into a cloakroom, and form an alliance with a parcel. Good morning, Mr Worthing!

[*Lady Bracknell sweeps out in majestic indignation.*]

JACK: Good morning! [*Algernon, from the other room, strikes up the Wedding March. Jack looks perfectly furious, and goes to the door.*] For goodness' sake don't play that ghastly tune, Algy! How idiotic you are!

*The music stops and Algernon enters cheerily.*

ALGERNON: Didn't it go off all right, old boy? You don't mean to say Gwendolen refused you? I know it is a way she has. She is always refusing people. I think it is most ill-natured of her.

JACK: Oh, Gwendolen is as right as a trivet. As far as she is concerned, we are engaged. Her mother is perfectly unbearable. Never met such a Gorgon. . . . I don't really know what a Gorgon is like, but I am quite sure that Lady Bracknell is one. In any case, she is a monster, without being a myth, which is rather unfair. . . . I beg your pardon, Algy, I suppose I shouldn't talk about your own aunt in that way before you.

ALGERNON: My dear boy, I love hearing my relations abused. It is the only thing that makes me put up with them at all. Relations are simply a tedious pack of people who haven't got the remotest knowledge of how to live, or the smallest instinct about when to die.

JACK: Oh, that is nonsense!

ALGERNON: It isn't!

JACK: Well, I won't argue about the matter. You always want to argue about things.

ALGERNON: That is exactly what things were originally made for.

JACK: Upon my word, if I thought that, I'd shoot myself. . . . [*A pause.*] You don't think there is any chance of Gwendolen becoming like her mother in about a hundred and fifty years, do you, Algy?

ALGERNON: All women become like their mothers. That is their tragedy. No man does. That's his.

JACK: Is that clever?

ALGERNON: It is perfectly phrased! and quite as true as any observation in civilized life should be.

JACK: I am sick to death of cleverness. Everybody is clever nowadays. You can't go anywhere without meeting clever people. The thing has become an absolute public nuisance. I wish to goodness we had a few fools left.

ALGERNON: We have.

JACK: I should extremely like to meet them. What do they talk about?

ALGERNON: The fools? Oh! about the clever people, of course.

JACK: What fools.

ALGERNON: By the way, did you tell Gwendolen the truth about your being Ernest in town, and Jack in the country?

JACK [*in a very patronizing manner*]: My dear fellow, the truth isn't quite the sort of thing one tells to a nice, sweet, refined girl. What extraordinary ideas you have about the way to behave to a woman!

ALGERNON: The only way to behave to a woman is to make love to her, if she is pretty, and to someone else, if she is plain.

JACK: Oh, that is nonsense.

ALGERNON: What about your brother? What about the profligate Ernest?

JACK: Oh, before the end of the week I shall have got rid of him. I'll say he died in Paris of apoplexy. Lots of people die of apoplexy, quite suddenly, don't they?

ALGERNON: Yes, but it's hereditary, my dear fellow. It's a sort of thing that runs in families. You had much better say a severe chill.

JACK: You are sure a severe chill isn't hereditary, or anything of that kind?

ALGERNON: Of course it isn't!

JACK: Very well, then. My poor brother Ernest is carried off suddenly, in Paris, by a severe chill. That gets rid of him.

ALGERNON: But I thought you said that . . . Miss Cardew was a little too much interested in your poor brother Ernest? Won't she feel his loss a great deal?

JACK: Oh, that is all right. Cecily is not a silly romantic girl, I am glad to say. She has got a capital appetite, goes on long walks, and pays no attention at all to her lessons.

ALGERNON: I would rather like to see Cecily.

JACK: I will take very good care you never do. She is excessively pretty, and she is only just eighteen.

ALGERNON: Have you told Gwendolen yet that you have an excessively pretty ward who is only eighteen?

JACK: Oh! one doesn't blurt these things out to people. Cecily and Gwendolen are perfectly certain to be extremely great friends. I'll bet you anything you like that half an hour after they have met, they will be calling each other sister.

ALGERNON: Women only do that when they have called each other a lot of other things first. Now, my dear boy, if we want to get a good table at Willis's, we really must go and dress. Do you know it is nearly seven?

JACK [*irritably*]: Oh! it always is nearly seven.

ALGERNON: Well, I'm hungry.

JACK: I never knew you when you weren't. . . .

ALGERNON: What shall we do after dinner? Go to a theatre?

JACK: Oh no! I loathe listening.

ALGERNON: Well, let us go to the Club?

JACK: Oh, no! I loathe talking.

ALGERNON: Well, we might trot round to the Empire at ten?

JACK: Oh, no! I can't bear looking at things. It is so silly.

ALGERNON: Well, what shall we do?

JACK: Nothing!

ALGERNON: It is awfully hard work doing nothing. However, I don't mind hard work where there is no definite object of any kind.

*Enter Lane.*

LANE: Miss Fairfax.

*Enter Gwendolen. Lane goes out.*

ALGERNON: Gwendolen, upon my word!

GWENDOLEN: Algy, kindly turn your back. I have something very particular to say to Mr Worthing.

ALGERNON: Really, Gwendolen, I don't think I can allow this at all.

GWENDOLEN: Algy, you always adopt a strictly immoral attitude towards life. You are not quite old enough to do that. [*Algernon retires to the fireplace.*]

JACK: My own darling.

GWENDOLEN: Ernest, we may never be married. From the expression on mamma's face I fear we never shall. Few parents nowadays pay any regard to what their children say to them. The old-fashioned respect for the young is fast dying out. Whatever influence I ever had over mamma, I lost at the age of three. But although she may prevent us from becoming man and wife, and I may marry someone else, and marry often, nothing that she can possibly do can alter my eternal devotion to you.

JACK: Dear Gwendolen!

GWENDOLEN: The story of your romantic origin, as related to me by mamma, with unpleasing comments, has naturally stirred the deeper fibres of my nature. Your Christian name has an irresistible fascination. The simplicity of your character makes you exquisitely incomprehensible to me. Your town address at the Albany I have. What is your address in the country?

JACK: The Manor House, Woolton, Hertfordshire.

*Algernon, who has been carefully listening, smiles to himself, and writes the address on his shirt cuff. Then picks up the Railway Guide.*

GWENDOLEN: There is a good postal service, I suppose? It may be necessary to do something desperate. That of course will require serious consideration. I will communicate with you daily.

JACK: My own one!

GWENDOLEN: How long do you remain in town?

JACK: Till Monday.

GWENDOLEN: Good! Algy, you may turn around now.

ALGERNON: Thanks, I've turned around already.

GWENDOLEN: You may also ring the bell.

JACK: You will let me see you to your carriage, my own darling?

GWENDOLEN: Certainly.

JACK [*to Lane, who now enters*]: I will see Miss Fairfax out.

LANE: Yes, sir. [*Jack and Gwendolen go off.*]

*Lane presents several letters on a salver to Algernon. It is to be surmised that they are bills, as Algernon, after looking at the envelopes, tears them up.*

ALGERNON: A glass of sherry, Lane.

LANE: Yes, sir.

ALGERNON: Tomorrow, Lane, I'm going Bunburying.

LANE: Yes, sir.

ALGERNON: I shall probably not be back till Monday. You can put up my dress clothes, my smoking jacket, and all the Bunbury suits . . .

LANE: Yes, sir. [*Handing sherry.*]

ALGERNON: I hope tomorrow will be a fine day, Lane.

LANE: It never is, sir.

ALGERNON: Lane, you're a perfect pessimist.

LANE: I do my best to give satisfaction, sir.

*Enter Jack, Lane goes off.*

JACK: There's a sensible, intelligent girl! the only girl I ever cared for in my life. [*Algernon is laughing moderately.*] What on earth are you so amused at?

ALGERNON: Oh, I'm a little anxious about poor Bunbury, that is all.

JACK: If you don't take care, your friend Bunbury will get you into a serious scrape some day.

ALGERNON: I love scrapes. They are the only things that are never serious.

JACK: Oh, that's nonsense, Algy. You never talk anything but nonsense.

ALGERNON: Nobody ever does.

*Jack looks indignantly at him, and leaves the room. Algernon lights a cigarette, reads his shirt-cuff, and smiles.*

## ACT II

*Garden at the Manor House. A flight of grey stone steps leads up to the house. The garden, an old-fashioned one, full of roses. Time of year, July. Basket chairs, and a table covered with books, are set under a large yew tree.*

*Miss Prism discovered seated at the table. Cecily is at the back, watering flowers.*

MISS PRISM [*calling*]: Cecily, Cecily! Surely such a utilitarian occupation as the watering of flowers is rather Moulton's duty than yours? Especially at a moment when intellectual pleasures await you. Your German grammar is on the table. Pray open it at page fifteen. We will repeat yesterday's lesson.

CECILY [*coming over very slowly*]: But I don't like German. It isn't at all a becoming language. I know perfectly well that I look quite plain after my German lesson.

MISS PRISM: Child, you know how anxious your guardian is that you should improve yourself in every way. He laid particular stress on your German, as he was leaving for town yesterday. Indeed, he always lays stress on your German when he is leaving for town.

CECILY: Dear Uncle Jack is so very serious! Sometimes he is so serious that I think he cannot be quite well.

MISS PRISM [*drawing herself up*]: Your guardian enjoys the best of health, and his gravity of demeanour is especially to be commended in one so comparatively young as he is. I know no one who has a higher sense of duty and responsibility.

CECILY: I suppose that is why he often looks a little bored when we three are together.

MISS PRISM: Cecily! I am surprised at you. Mr Worthing has many troubles in his life. Idle merriment and triviality would be out of place in his conversation. You must remember his constant anxiety about that unfortunate young man his brother.

CECILY: I wish Uncle Jack would allow that unfortunate young man, his brother, to come down here sometimes. We might have a good influence over him, Miss Prism. I am sure you certainly would. You know German, and geology, and things of that kind influence a man very much. [*Cecily begins to write in her diary.*]

MISS PRISM [*shaking her head*]: I do not think that even I could produce any effect on a character that according to his own brother's admission is irretrievably weak and vacillating. Indeed I am not sure that I would desire to reclaim him. I am not in favour of this modern mania for turning bad people into good people at a moment's notice. As a man sows so let him reap. You must put away your diary, Cecily. I really don't see why you should keep a diary at all.

CECILY: I keep a diary in order to enter the wonderful secrets of my life. If I didn't write them down, I should probably forget all about them.

MISS PRISM: Memory, my dear Cecily, is the diary that we all carry about with us.

CECILY: Yes, but it usually chronicles the things that have never happened, and couldn't possibly have happened. I believe that Memory is responsible for nearly all the three-volume novels that Mudie sends us.

MISS PRISM: Do not speak slightingly of the three-volume novel, Cecily. I wrote one myself in earlier days.

CECILY: Did you really, Miss Prism? How wonderfully clever you are! I hope it did not end happily? I don't like novels that end happily. They depress me so much.

MISS PRISM: The good ended happily, and the bad unhappily. That is what Fiction means.

CECILY: I suppose so. But it seems very unfair. And was your novel ever published?

MISS PRISM: Alas, no. The manuscript unfortunately was abandoned. [*Cecily starts.*] I use the word in the sense of lost or mislaid. To your work, child, these speculations are profitless.

CECILY [*smiling*]: But I see dear Dr Chasuble coming up through the garden.

MISS PRISM [*rising and advancing*]: Dr Chasuble! This is indeed a pleasure.

*Enter Canon Chasuble.*

CHASUBLE: And how are we this morning? Miss Prism, you are, I trust, well?

CECILY: Miss Prism has just been complaining of a slight headache. I think it would do her so much good to have a short stroll with you in the Park, Dr Chasuble.

MISS PRISM: Cecily, I have not mentioned anything about a headache.

CECILY: No, dear Miss Prism, I know that, but I felt instinctively that you had a headache. Indeed I was thinking about that, and not about my German lesson, when the Rector came in.

CHASUBLE: I hope, Cecily, you are not inattentive.

CECILY: Oh, I am afraid I am.

CHASUBLE: That is strange. Were I fortunate enough to be Miss Prism's pupil, I would hang upon her lips. [*Miss Prism glares.*] I spoke metaphorically.—My metaphor was drawn from bees. Ahem! Mr Worthing, I suppose, has not returned from town yet?

MISS PRISM: We do not expect him till Monday afternoon.

CHASUBLE: Ah yes, he usually likes to spend his Sunday in London. He is not one of those whose sole aim is enjoyment, as, by all accounts, that unfortunate young man his brother seems to be. But I must not disturb Egeria and her pupil any longer.

MISS PRISM: Egeria? My name is Laetitia, Doctor.

CHASUBLE [*bowing*]: A classical allusion merely, drawn from the Pagan authors. I shall see you both no doubt at Evensong?

MISS PRISM: I think, dear Doctor, I will have a stroll with you. I find I have a headache after all, and a walk might do it good.

CHASUBLE: With pleasure, Miss Prism, with pleasure. We might go as far as the schools and back.

MISS PRISM: That would be delightful. Cecily, you will read your Political Economy in my absence. The chapter on the Fall of the Rupee you may omit. It is somewhat too sensational. Even these metallic problems have their melodramatic side.

[*Goes down the garden with Dr Chasuble.*]

CECILY [*picks up books and throws them back on the table*]: Horrid Political Economy! Horrid Geography! Horrid, horrid German!

*Enter Merriman with a card on a salver.*

MERRIMAN: Mr Ernest Worthington has just driven over from the station. He has brought his luggage with him.

CECILY [*takes the card and reads it*]: 'Mr Ernest Worthing, B.4, The Albany, W.' Uncle Jack's brother! Did you tell him Mr Worthing was in town?

MERRIMAN: Yes, Miss. He seemed very much disappointed. I mentioned that you and Miss Prism were in the garden. He said he was anxious to speak to you privately for a moment.

CECILY: Ask Mr Ernest Worthing to come here. I suppose you had better talk to the housekeeper about a room for him.

MERRIMAN: Yes, Miss. [*Merriman goes off.*]

CECILY: I have never met any really wicked person before. I feel rather frightened. I am so afraid he will look just like everyone else.

*Enter Algernon, very gay and debonair.*

He does!

ALGERNON [*raising his hat*]: You're my little cousin Cecily, I'm sure.

CECILY: You are under some strange mistake. I am not little. In fact, I believe I am more than usually tall for my age. [*Algernon is rather taken back.*] But I am your cousin Cecily. You, I see from your card, are Uncle Jack's brother, my cousin Ernest, my wicked cousin Ernest.

ALGERNON: Oh! I am not really wicked at all, Cousin Cecily. You mustn't think that I am wicked.

CECILY: If you are not, then you have certainly been deceiving us all in a very inexcusable manner. I hope you have not been leading a double life, pretending to be wicked and being really good all the time. That would be hypocrisy.

ALGERNON [*looks at her in amazement*]: Oh! Of course I have been rather reckless.

CECILY: I am glad to hear it.

ALGERNON: In fact, now you mention the subject, I have been very bad in my own small way.

CECILY: I don't think you should be so proud of that, though I am sure it must have been very pleasant.

ALGERNON: It is much pleasanter being here with you.

CECILY: I can't understand how you are here at all. Uncle Jack won't be back till Monday afternoon.

ALGERNON: That is a great disappointment. I am obliged to go up by the first train on Monday morning. I have a business appointment that I am anxious . . . to miss!

CECILY: Couldn't you miss it anywhere but in London?

ALGERNON: No: the appointment is in London.

CECILY: Well, I know, of course, how important it is not to keep a business engagement, if one wants to retain any sense of the beauty of life, but still I think you had better wait till Uncle Jack arrives. I know he wants to speak to you about your emigrating.

ALGERNON: About my what?

CECILY: Your emigrating. He has gone up to buy your outfit.

ALGERNON: I certainly wouldn't let Jack buy my outfit. He has no taste in neckties at all.

CECILY: I don't think you will require neckties. Uncle Jack is sending you to Australia.

ALGERNON: Australia! I'd sooner die.

CECILY: Well, he said at dinner on Wednesday night, that you would have to choose between this world, the next world, and Australia.

ALGERNON: Oh, well! The accounts I have received of Australia and the next world are not particularly encouraging. This world is good enough for me, Cousin Cecily.

CECILY: Yes, but are you good enough for it?

ALGERNON: I'm afraid I'm not that. That is why I want you to reform me. You might make that your mission, if you don't mind, Cousin Cecily.

CECILY: I'm afraid I've no time, this afternoon.

ALGERNON: Well, would you mind my reforming myself this afternoon?

CECILY: It is rather Quixotic of you. But I think you should try.

ALGERNON: I will. I feel better already.

CECILY: You are looking a little worse.

ALGERNON: That is because I am hungry.

CECILY: How thoughtless of me. I should have remembered that when one is going to lead an entirely new life, one requires regular and wholesome meals. Won't you come in?

ALGERNON: Thank you. Might I have a buttonhole first? I never have any appetite unless I have a buttonhole first.

CECILY: A Maréchal Niel? [*Picks up scissors.*]

ALGERNON: No, I'd sooner have a pink rose.

CECILY: Why? [*Cuts a flower.*]

ALGERNON: Because you are like a pink rose, Cousin Cecily.

CECILY: I don't think it can be right for you to talk to me like that. Miss Prism never says such things to me.

ALGERNON: Then Miss Prism is a shortsighted old lady. [*Cecily puts the rose in his buttonhole.*] You are the prettiest girl I ever saw.

CECILY: Miss Prism says that all good looks are a snare.

ALGERNON: They are the snare that every sensible man would like to be caught in.

CECILY: Oh, I don't think I would care to catch a sensible man. I shouldn't know what to talk to him about.

*They pass into the house. Miss Prism and Dr Chasuble return.*

MISS PRISM: You are too much alone, dear Dr Chasuble. You should get married. A misanthrope I can understand—a womanthrope, never!

CHASUBLE [*with a scholar's shudder*]: Believe me, I do not deserve so neologistic a phrase. The precept as well as the practice of the Primitive Church was distinctly against matrimony.

MISS PRISM [*sententiously*]: That is obviously the reason why the Primitive Church has not lasted up to the present day. And you do not seem to realize, dear Doctor, that by persistently remaining single, a man converts himself into a permanent public temptation. Men should be more careful; this very celibacy leads weaker vessels astray.

CHASUBLE: But is a man not equally attractive when married?

MISS PRISM: No married man is ever attractive except to his wife.

CHASUBLE: And often, I've been told, not even her.

MISS PRISM: That depends on the intellectual sympathies of the woman. Maturity can always be depended on. Ripeness can be trusted. Young women are green. [*Dr Chasuble starts.*] I spoke horticulturally. My metaphor was drawn from fruits. But where is Cecily?

CHASUBLE: Perhaps she followed us to the schools.

*Enter Jack slowly from the back of the garden. He is dressed in the deepest mourning, with crepe hatband and black gloves.*

MISS PRISM: Mr Worthing!

CHASUBLE: Mr Worthing?

MISS PRISM: This is indeed a surprise. We did not look for you till Monday afternoon.

JACK [*shakes Miss Prism's hand in a tragic manner*]: I have returned sooner than I expected. Dr Chasuble, I hope you are well?

CHASUBLE: Dear Mr Worthing, I trust this garb of woe does not betoken some terrible calamity?

JACK: My brother.

MISS PRISM: More shameful debts and extravagance?

CHASUBLE: Still leading his life of pleasure?

JACK [*shaking his head*]: Dead!

CHASUBLE: Your brother Ernest dead?

JACK: Quite dead.

MISS PRISM: What a lesson for him! I trust he will profit by it.

CHASUBLE: Mr Worthing, I offer you my sincere condolence. You have at least the consolation of knowing that you were always the most generous and forgiving of brothers.

JACK: Poor Ernest! He had many faults, but it is a sad, sad blow.

CHASUBLE: Very sad indeed. Were you with him at the end?

JACK: No. He died abroad; in Paris, in fact. I had a telegram last night from the manager of the Grand Hotel.

CHASUBLE: Was the cause of death mentioned?

JACK: A severe chill, it seems.

MISS PRISM: As a man sows, so shall he reap.

CHASUBLE [*raising his hand*]: Charity, dear Miss Prism, charity! None of us are perfect. I myself am peculiarly susceptible to draughts. Will the interment take place here?

JACK: No. He seems to have expressed a desire to be buried in Paris.

CHASUBLE: In Paris! [*Shakes his head.*] I fear that hardly points to any very serious state of mind at the last. You would no doubt wish me to make some light allusion to this tragic domestic affliction next Sunday. [*Jack presses his hand convulsively.*] My sermon on the meaning of the manna in the wilderness can be adapted to almost any occasion, joyful, or, as in the present case, distressing. [*All sigh.*] I have preached it at harvest celebrations, christenings, confirmations, on days of humiliation and festal days. The last time I delivered it was in the Cathedral, as a charity sermon on behalf of the Society for the Prevention of Discontent among the Upper Orders. The Bishop, who was present, was much struck by some of the analogies I drew.

JACK: Ah! that reminds me, you mentioned christenings I think, Dr Chasuble? I suppose you know how to christen all right? [*Dr Chasuble looks astounded.*] I mean, of course, you are continually christening, aren't you?

MISS PRISM: It is, I regret to say, one of the Rector's most constant duties in this parish. I have often spoken to the poorer classes on the subject. But they don't seem to know what thrift is.

CHASUBLE: But is there any particular infant in whom you are interested, Mr Worthing? Your brother was, I believe, unmarried, was he not?

JACK: Oh, yes.

MISS PRISM [*bitterly*]: People who live entirely for pleasure usually are.

JACK: But it is not for any child, dear Doctor. I am very fond of children. No! the fact is, I would like to be christened myself, this afternoon, if you have nothing better to do.

CHASUBLE: But surely, Mr Worthing, you have been christened already?

JACK: I don't remember anything about it.

CHASUBLE: But have you any grave doubts on the subject?

JACK: I certainly intend to have. Of course I don't know if the thing would bother you in any way, or if you think I am a little too old now.

CHASUBLE: Not at all. The sprinkling, and, indeed, the immersion of adults is a perfectly canonical practice.

JACK: Immersion!

CHASUBLE: You need have no apprehensions. Sprinkling is all that is necessary, or indeed I think advisable. Our weather is so changeable. At what hour would you wish the ceremony performed?

JACK: Oh, I might trot round above five if that would suit you.

CHASUBLE: Perfectly, perfectly! In fact I have two similar ceremonies to perform at that time. A case of twins that occurred recently in one of the outlying cottages on your own estate. Poor Jenkins the carter, a most hard-working man.

JACK: Oh! I don't see much fun in being christened along with other babies. It would be childish. Would half-past five do?

CHASUBLE: Admirably! Admirably! [*Takes out watch.*] And now, dear Mr Worthing, I will not intrude any longer into a house of sorrow. I would merely beg you not to be too much bowed down by grief. What seem to us bitter trials are often blessings in disguise.

MISS PRISM: This seems to be a blessing of an extremely obvious kind.

*Enter Cecily from the house.*

CECILY: Uncle Jack! Oh, I am pleased to see you back. But what horrid clothes you have got on. Do go and change them.

MISS PRISM: Cecily!

CHASUBLE: My child! My child! [*Cecily goes toward Jack; he kisses her brow in a melancholy manner.*]

CECILY: What is the matter, Uncle Jack? Do look happy! You look as if you had toothache, and I have got such a surprise for you. Who do you think is in the dining room? Your brother!

JACK: Who?

CECILY: Your brother Ernest. He arrived about half an hour ago.

JACK: What nonsense! I haven't got a brother.

CECILY: Oh, don't say that. However badly he may have behaved to you in the past he is still your brother. You couldn't be so heartless as to disown him. I'll tell him to come out. And you will shake hands with him, won't you, Uncle Jack? [*Runs back into the house.*]

CHASUBLE: These are very joyful tidings.

MISS PRISM: After we had all been resigned to his loss, his sudden return seems to me peculiarly distressing.

JACK: My brother is in the dining room? I don't know what it all means. I think it is perfectly absurd.

*Enter Algernon and Cecily hand in hand. They come slowly up to Jack.*

JACK: Good heavens! [*Motions Algernon away.*]

ALGERNON: Brother John, I have come down from town to tell you that I am very sorry for all the trouble I have given you, and that I intend to lead a better life in the future. [*Jack glares at him and does not take his hand.*]

CECILY: Uncle Jack, you are not going to refuse your own brother's hand?

JACK: Nothing will induce me to take his hand. I think his coming down here disgraceful. He knows perfectly well why.

CECILY: Uncle Jack, do be nice. There is some good in everyone. Ernest has just been telling me about his poor invalid friend Mr Bunbury whom he goes to visit so often. And surely there must be much good in one who is kind to an invalid and leaves the pleasures of London to sit by a bed of pain.

JACK: Oh! he has been talking about Bunbury, has he?

CECILY: Yes, he has told me about poor Mr Bunbury, and his terrible state of health.

JACK: Bunbury! Well, I won't have him talk to you about Bunbury or about anything else. It is enough to drive one perfectly frantic.

ALGERNON: Of course I admit that the faults were all on my side. But I must say that I think that Brother John's coldness to me is peculiarly painful. I expected a more enthusiastic welcome, especially considering it is the first time I have come here.

CECILY: Uncle Jack, if you don't shake hands with Ernest I will never forgive you.

JACK: Never forgive me?

CECILY: Never, never, never!

JACK: Well, this is the last time I shall ever do it. [*Shakes hand with Algernon and glares.*]

CHASUBLE: It's pleasant, is it not, to see so perfect a reconciliation? I think we might leave the two brothers together.

MISS PRISM: Cecily, you will come with us.

CECILY: Certainly, Miss Prism. My little task of reconciliation is over.

CHASUBLE: You have done a beautiful action today, dear child.

MISS PRISM: We must not be premature in our judgments.

CECILY: I feel very happy. [*They all go off except Jack and Algernon.*]

JACK: You young scoundrel, Algy, you must get out of this place as soon as possible. I don't allow Bunburying here.

*Enter Merriman.*

MERRIMAN: I have put Mr Ernest's things in the room next to yours, sir. I suppose that is all right?

JACK: What?

MERRIMAN: Mr Ernest's luggage, sir. I have unpacked it and put in the room next to your own.

JACK: His luggage?

MERRIMAN: Yes, sir. Three portmanteaus, a dressing case, two hat boxes, and a large luncheon basket.

ALGERNON: I am afraid I can't stay more than a week this time.

JACK: Merriman, order the dogcart at once. Mr Ernest has been suddenly called back to town.

MERRIMAN: Yes, sir. [*Goes back into the house.*]

ALGERNON: What a fearful liar you are, Jack. I have not been called back to town at all.

JACK: Yes, you have.

ALGERNON: I haven't heard anyone call me.

JACK: Your duty as a gentleman calls you back.

ALGERNON: My duty as a gentleman has never interfered with my pleasures in the smallest degree.

JACK: I can quite understand that.

ALGERNON: Well, Cecily is a darling.

JACK: You are not to talk of Miss Cardew like that. I don't like it.

ALGERNON: Well, I don't like your clothes. You look perfectly ridiculous in them. Why on earth don't you go up and change? It is perfectly childish to be in deep mourning for a man who is actually staying for a whole week with you in your house as a guest. I call it grotesque.

JACK: You are certainly not staying with me for a whole week as a guest or anything else. You have got to leave . . . by the four-five train.

ALGERNON: I certainly won't leave you so long as you are in mourning. It would be most unfriendly. If I were in mourning you would stay with me, I suppose. I should think it very unkind if you didn't.

JACK: Well, will you go if I change my clothes?

ALGERNON: Yes, if you are not too long. I never saw anybody take so long to dress, and with such little result.

JACK: Well, at any rate, that is better than being overdressed as you are.

ALGERNON: If I am occasionally a little overdressed, I make up for it by being always immensely over-educated.

JACK: Your vanity is ridiculous, your conduct an outrage, and your presence in my garden utterly absurd. However, you have got to catch the four-five, and I hope you will have a pleasant journey back to town. This Bunburying, as you call it, has not been a great success for you. [*Goes into the house.*]

ALGERNON: I think it has been a great success. I'm in love with Cecily, and that is everything.

*Enter Cecily at the back of the garden. She picks up the can and begins to water the flowers.*

But I must see her before I go, and make arrangements for another Bunbury. Ah, there she is.

CECILY: Oh, I merely came back to water the roses. I thought you were with Uncle Jack.

ALGERNON: He's gone to order the dogcart for me.

CECILY: Oh, is he going to take you for a nice drive?

ALGERNON: He's going to send me away.

CECILY: Then have we got to part?

ALGERNON: I am afraid so. It's a very painful parting.

CECILY: It is always painful to part from people whom one has known for a very brief space of time. The absence of old friends one can endure with equanimity. But even a momentary separation from anyone to whom one has just been introduced is almost unbearable.

ALGERNON: Thank you.

*Enter Merriman.*

MERRIMAN: The dogcart is at the door, sir. [*Algernon looks appealing at Cecily.*]

CECILY: It can wait, Merriman . . . for . . . five minutes.

MERRIMAN: Yes, miss. [*Exit Merriman.*]

ALGERNON: I hope, Cecily, I shall not offend you if I state quite frankly and openly that you seem to me to be in every way the visible personification of absolute perfection.

CECILY: I think your frankness does you great credit, Ernest. If you will allow me, I will copy your remarks into my diary. [*Goes over to table and begins writing in diary.*]

ALGERNON: Do you really keep a diary? I'd give anything to look at it. May I?

CECILY: Oh no. [*Puts her hand over it.*] You see, it is simply a very young girl's record of her own thoughts and impressions, and consequently meant for publication. When it appears in volume form I hope you will order a copy. But pray, Ernest, don't stop. I delight in taking down from dictation. I have reached 'absolute perfection'. You can go on. I am quite ready for more.

ALGERNON [*somewhat taken aback*]: Ahem! Ahem!

CECILY: Oh, don't cough, Ernest. When one is dictating one should speak fluently and not cough. Besides, I don't know how to spell a cough. [*Writes as Algernon speaks.*]

ALGERNON [*speaking very rapidly*]: Cecily, ever since I first looked upon your wonderful and incomparable beauty, I have dared to love you wildly, passionately, devotedly, hopelessly.

CECILY: I don't think that you should tell me that you love me wildly, passionately, devotedly, hopelessly. Hopelessly doesn't seem to make much sense, does it?

ALGERNON: Cecily.

*Enter Merriman.*

MERRIMAN: The dogcart is waiting, sir.

ALGERNON: Tell it to come round next week, at the same hour.

MERRIMAN [*looks at Cecily, who makes no sign*]: Yes, sir. [*Merriman retires.*]

CECILY: Uncle Jack would be very much annoyed if he knew you were staying on till next week, at the same hour.

ALGERNON: Oh, I don't care about Jack. I don't care for anybody in the whole world but you. I love you, Cecily. You will marry me, won't you?

CECILY: You silly boy! Of course. Why, we have been engaged for the last three months.

ALGERNON: For the last three months?

CECILY: Yes, it will be exactly three months on Thursday.

ALGERNON: But how did we become engaged?

CECILY: Well, ever since Uncle Jack first confessed to us that he had a younger brother who was very wicked and bad, you of course have formed the chief topic of conversation between myself and Miss Prism. And of course a man who is much talked about is always very attractive. One feels there must be something in him, after all. I daresay it was foolish of me, but I fell in love with you, Ernest.

ALGERNON: Darling. And when was the engagement actually settled?

CECILY: On the 14th of February last. Worn out by your entire ignorance of my existence, I determined to end the matter one way or the other, and after a long struggle with myself I accepted you under this dear old tree here. The next day I bought this little ring in your name, and this is the little bangle with the true lovers' knot I promised you always to wear.

ALGERNON: Did I give you this? It's very pretty, isn't it?

CECILY: Yes, you've wonderfully good taste, Ernest. It's the excuse I've always given for your leading such a bad life. And this is the box in which I keep all your dear letters. [*Kneels at table, opens box, and produces letters tied up with blue ribbon.*]

ALGERNON: My letters! But, my own sweet Cecily, I have never written you any letters.

CECILY: You need hardly remind me of that, Ernest. I remember only too well that I was forced to write your letters for you. I wrote always three times a week, and sometimes oftener.

ALGERNON: Oh, do let me read them, Cecily?

CECILY: Oh, I couldn't possibly. They would make you far too conceited. [*Replaces box.*] The three you wrote me after I had broken off the engagement are so beautiful, and so badly spelled, that even now I can hardly read them without crying a little.

ALGERNON: But was our engagement ever broken off?

CECILY: Of course it was. On the 22nd of last March. You can see the entry if you like. [*Shows diary.*] 'Today I broke off my engagement with Ernest. I feel it is better to do so. The weather still continues charming.'

ALGERNON: But why on earth did you break it off? What had I done? I had done nothing at all. Cecily, I am very much hurt indeed to hear you broke it off. Particularly when the weather was so charming.

CECILY: It would hardly have been a really serious engagement if it hadn't been broken off at least once. But I forgave you before the week was out.

ALGERNON [*crossing to her, and kneeling*]: What a perfect angel you are, Cecily.

CECILY: You dear romantic boy, [*He kisses her, she puts her fingers through his hair.*] I hope your hair curls naturally, does it?

ALGERNON: Yes, darling, with a little help from others.

CECILY: I am so glad.

ALGERNON: You'll never break off our engagement again, Cecily?

CECILY: I don't think I could break it off now that I have actually met you. Besides, of course, there is the question of your name.

ALGERNON: Of course. [*Nervously.*]

CECILY: You must not laugh at me, darling, but it had always been a girlish dream of mine to love someone whose name was Ernest. [*Algernon rises, Cecily also.*] There is something in that name that seems to inspire absolute confidence. I pity any poor married woman whose husband is not called Ernest.

ALGERNON: But, my dear child, do you mean to say you could not love me if I had some other name?

CECILY: But what name?

ALGERNON: Oh, any name you like—Algernon—for instance . . .

CECILY: But I don't like the name of Algernon.

ALGERNON: Well, my own dear, sweet, loving little darling, I really can't see why you should object to the name of Algernon. It is not at all a bad name. In fact, it is rather an aristocratic name. Half of the chaps who get into the Bankruptcy Court are called Algernon. But seriously, Cecily . . . [*moving to her*] if my name was Algy, couldn't you love me?

CECILY [*rising*]: I might respect you, Ernest, I might admire your character, but I fear that I should not be able to give you my undivided attention.

ALGERNON: Ahem! Cecily! [*Picking up hat.*] Your Rector here is, I suppose, thoroughly experienced in the practice of all the rites and ceremonials of the Church?

CECILY: Oh, yes. Dr Chasuble is a most learned man. He has never written a single book, so you can imagine how much he knows.

ALGERNON: I must see him at once on a most important christening—I mean on most important business.

CECILY: Oh!

ALGERNON: I shan't be away more than half an hour.

CECILY: Considering that we have been engaged since February the 14th, and that I only met you today for the first time, I think it is rather hard that you should leave me for so long a period as half an hour. Couldn't you make it twenty minutes?

ALGERNON: I'll be back in no time. [*Kisses her and rushes down the garden.*]

CECILY: What an impetuous boy he is! I like his hair so much. I must enter his proposal in my diary.

*Enter Merriman.*

MERRIMAN: A Miss Fairfax just called to see Mr Worthing. On very important business, Miss Fairfax states.

CECILY: Isn't Mr Worthing in his library?

MERRIMAN: Mr Worthing went over in the direction of the Rectory some time ago.

CECILY: Pray ask the lady to come out here; Mr Worthing is sure to be back soon. And you can bring tea.

MERRIMAN: Yes, Miss. [*Goes out.*]

CECILY: Miss Fairfax! I suppose one of the many good elderly women who are associated with Uncle Jack in some of his philanthropic work in London. I don't quite like women who are interested in philanthropic work. I think it is so forward of them.

*Enter Merriman.*

MERRIMAN: Miss Fairfax.

*Enter Gwendolen. Exit Merriman.*

CECILY [*advancing to meet her*]: Pray let me introduce myself to you. My name is Cecily Cardew.

GWENDOLEN: Cecily Cardew? [*Moving to her and shaking hands.*] What a very sweet name! Something tells me that we are going to be great friends. I like you already more than I can say. My first impressions of people are never wrong.

CECILY: How nice of you to like me so much after we have known each other such a comparatively short time. Pray sit down.

GWENDOLEN [*still standing up*]: I may call you Cecily, may I not?

CECILY: With pleasure!

GWENDOLEN: And you will always call me Gwendolen, won't you?

CECILY: If you wish.

GWENDOLEN: Then that is all quite settled, is it not?

CECILY: I hope so. [*A pause. They both sit down together.*]

GWENDOLEN: Perhaps this might be a favourable opportunity for my mentioning who I am. My father is Lord Bracknell. You have never heard of Papa, I suppose?

CECILY: I don't think so.

GWENDOLEN: Outside the family circle, Papa, I am glad to say, is entirely unknown. I think that is quite as it should be. The home seems to me to be the proper sphere for the man. And certainly once a man begins to neglect his domestic duties he becomes painfully effeminate, does he not? And I don't like that. It makes men so very attractive. Cecily, mamma, whose views on education are remarkably strict, has brought me up to be extremely short-sighted; it is part of her system; so do you mind my looking at you through my glasses?

CECILY: Oh! not at all, Gwendolen, I am very fond of being looked at.

GWENDOLEN [*after examining Cecily carefully through a lorgnette*]: You are here on a short visit, I suppose.

CECILY: Oh no! I live here.

GWENDOLEN [*severely*]: Really? Your mother, no doubt, or some female relative of advanced years, resides here also?

CECILY: Oh no! I have no mother, nor, in fact, any relations.

GWENDOLEN: Indeed?

CECILY: My dear guardian, with the assistance of Miss Prism, has the arduous task of looking after me.

GWENDOLEN: Your guardian?

CECILY: Yes, I am Mr Worthing's ward.

GWENDOLEN: Oh! It is strange he never mentioned to me that he had a ward. How secretive of him! He grows more interesting hourly. I am not sure, however, that the news inspires me with feelings of unmixed delight. [*Rising and going to her.*] I am very fond of you, Cecily; I have liked you ever since I met you! But I am bound to state that now that I know that you are Mr Worthing's ward, I cannot help expressing a wish you were—well, just a little older than you seem to be—and not quite so very alluring in appearance. In fact, if I may speak candidly—

CECILY: Pray do! I think that whenever one has anything unpleasant to say, one should always be quite candid!

GWENDOLEN: Well, to speak with perfect candour, Cecily I wish that you were fully forty-two, and more than usually plain for your age. Ernest has a strong upright nature. He is the very soul of truth and honour. Disloyalty would be as impossible to him as deception. But even men of the noblest possible moral character are extremely susceptible to the influence of the physical charms of others. Modern, no less than Ancient History, supplies us with many most painful examples of what I refer to. If it were not so, indeed, History would be quite unreadable.

CECILY: I beg your pardon, Gwendolen, did you say Ernest?

GWENDOLEN: Yes.

CECILY: Oh, but it is not Mr Ernest Worthing who is my guardian. It is his brother—his elder brother.

GWENDOLEN [*sitting down again*]: Ernest never mentioned to me that he had a brother.

CECILY: I am sorry to say they have not been on good terms for a long time.

GWENDOLEN: Ah! that accounts for it. And now that I think of it I have never heard any man mention his brother. The subject seems distasteful to most men. Cecily, you have lifted a load from my mind. I was growing almost anxious. It would have been terrible if any cloud had come across a friendship like ours, would it not? Of course you are quite, quite sure that it is not Mr Ernest Worthing who is your guardian?

CECILY: Quite sure. [*A pause.*] In fact, I am going to be his.

GWENDOLEN [*inquiringly*]: I beg your pardon?

CECILY [*rather shy and confidingly*]: Dearest Gwendolen, there is no reason why I should make a secret of it to you. Our little country newspaper is sure to chronicle the fact next week. Mr Ernest Worthing and I are engaged to be married.

GWENDOLEN [*quite politely, rising*]: My darling Cecily, I think there must be some slight error. Mr Ernest Worthing is engaged to me. The announcement will appear in the *Morning Post* on Saturday at the latest.

CECILY [*very politely, rising*]: I am afraid you must be under some misconception. Ernest proposed to me exactly ten minutes ago. [*Shows diary.*]

GWENDOLEN [*examines diary through her lorgnette carefully*]: It is very curious, for he asked me to be his wife yesterday afternoon at 5:30. If you would care to verify the incident, pray do so. [*Produces diary of her own.*] I never travel without my diary. One should always have something sensational to read in the train. I am so sorry, dear Cecily, if it is any disappointment to you, but I am afraid I have the prior claim.

CECILY: It would distress me more than I can tell you, dear Gwendolen, if it caused you any mental or physical anguish, but I feel bound to point out that since Ernest proposed to you he clearly has changed his mind.

GWENDOLEN [*meditatively*]: If the poor fellow has been entrapped into any foolish promise I shall consider it my duty to rescue him at once, and with a firm hand.

CECILY [*thoughtfully and sadly*]: Whatever unfortunate entanglement my dear boy may have gotten into, I will never reproach him with it after we are married.

GWENDOLEN: Do you allude to me, Miss Cardew, as an entanglement? You are presumptuous. On an occasion of this kind it becomes more than a moral duty to speak one's mind. It becomes a pleasure.

CECILY: Do you suggest, Miss Fairfax, that I entrapped Ernest into an engagement? How dare you? This is no time for wearing the shallow mask of manners. When I see a spade I call it a spade.

GWENDOLEN [*satirically*]: I am glad to say that I have never seen a spade. It is obvious that our social spheres have been widely different.

*Enter Merriman, followed by the footman. He carries a salver, tablecloth, and plate stand. Cecily is about to retort. The presence of the servants exercises a restraining influence, under which both girls chafe.*

MERRIMAN: Shall I lay tea here as usual, Miss?

CECILY [*sternly, in a calm voice*]: Yes, as usual.

*Merriman begins to clear table and lay cloth. A long pause. Cecily and Gwendolen glarew at each other.*

GWENDOLEN: Are there many interesting walks in the vicinity, Miss Cardew?

CECILY: Oh! yes! a great many. From the top of one of the hills quite close one can see five counties.

GWENDOLEN: Five counties! I don't think I should like that; I hate crowds.

CECILY [*sweetly*]: I suppose that is why you live in town?

*Gwendolen bites her lip, and beats her foot nervously with her parasol.*

GWENDOLEN [*looking around*]: Quite a well-kept garden this is, Miss Cardew.

CECILY: So glad you like it, Miss Fairfax.

GWENDOLEN: I had no idea there were any flowers in the country.

CECILY: Oh, flowers are as common here, Miss Fairfax, as people are in London.

GWENDOLEN: Personally I cannot understand how anybody manages to exist in the country, if anybody who is anybody does. The country always bores me to death.

CECILY: Ah! This is what the newspapers call agricultural depression, is it not? I believe the aristocracy are suffering very much from it just at present. It is almost an epidemic amongst them, I have been told. May I offer you some tea, Miss Fairfax?

GWENDOLEN [*with elaborate politeness*]: Thank you. [*Aside.*] Detestable girl! But I require tea!

CECILY [*sweetly*]: Sugar?

GWENDOLEN [*superciliously*]: No, thank you. Sugar is not fashionable any more.

*Cecily looks angrily at her, takes up the tongs and puts four lumps of sugar into the cup.*

CECILY [*severely*]: Cake or bread and butter?

GWENDOLEN [*in a bored manner*]: Bread and butter, please. Cake is rarely seen at the best houses nowdays.

CECILY [*cuts a very large slice of cake and puts it on the tray*]: Hand that to Miss Fairfax.

*Merriman does so, and goes out with the footman. Gwendolen drinks the tea and makes a grimace. Puts down cup at once, reaches out her hand to the bread and butter, looks at it, and finds it is cake. Rises in indignation.*

GWENDOLEN: You have filled my tea with lumps of sugar, and though I asked most distinctly for bread and butter, you have given me cake. I am known for the gentleness of my disposition, and the extraordinary sweetness of my nature, but I warn you, Miss Cardew, you may go too far.

CECILY [*rising*]: To save my poor, innocent, trusting boy from the machinations of any other girl there are no lengths to which I would not go.

GWENDOLEN: From the moment I saw you I distrusted you. I felt that you were false and deceitful. I am never deceived in such matters. My first impressions of people are invariably right.

CECILY: It seems to me, Miss Fairfax, that I am trespassing on your valuable time. No doubt you have many other calls of a similar character to make in the neighbourhood.

*Enter Jack.*

GWENDOLEN [*catches sight of him*]: Ernest! My own Ernest!

JACK: Gwendolen! Darling! [*Offers to kiss her.*]

GWENDOLEN [*drawing back*]: A moment! May I ask if you are engaged to be married to this young lady? [*Points to Cecily.*]

JACK [*laughing*]: To dear little Cecily! Of course not! What could have put such an idea into your pretty little head?

GWENDOLEN: Thank you. You may! [*Offers her cheek.*]

CECILY [*very sweetly*]: I knew there must be some misunderstanding, Miss Fairfax. The gentleman whose arm is at present round your waist is my dear guardian, Mr John Worthing.

GWENDOLEN: I beg your pardon?

CECILY: This is Uncle Jack.

GWENDOLEN [*receding*]: Jack! Oh!

*Enter Algernon.*

CECILY: Here is Ernest.

ALGERNON [*goes straight over to Cecily without noticing anyone else*]: My own love! [*Offers to kiss her.*]

CECILY [*drawing back*]: A moment, Ernest! May I ask you—are you engaged to be married to this young lady?

ALGERNON [*looking around*]: To what young lady? Good heavens! Gwendolen!

CECILY: Yes: to good heavens, Gwendolen, I mean to Gwendolen.

ALGERNON [*laughing*]: Of course not. What could have put such an idea into your pretty little head?

CECILY: Thank you. [*Presenting her cheek to be kissed.*] You may. [*Algernon kisses her.*]

GWENDOLEN: I felt there was some slight error, Miss Cardew. The gentleman who is now embracing you is my cousin, Mr Algernon Moncrieff.

CECILY [*breaking away from Algernon*]: Algernon Moncrieff! Oh! [*The two girls move towards each other and put their arms round each other's waists as if for protection.*]

CECILY: Are you called Algernon?

ALGERNON: I cannot deny it.

GWENDOLEN: Is your name really John?

JACK [*standing rather proudly*]: I could deny it if I liked. I could deny anything if I liked. But my name certainly is John. It has been John for years.

CECILY [*to Gwendolen*]: A gross deception has been practised on both of us.

GWENDOLEN: My poor wounded Cecily!

CECILY: My sweet wronged Gwendolen!

GWENDOLEN [*slowly and seriously*]: You will call me sister, will you not? [*They embrace. Jack and Algernon groan and walk up and down.*]

CECILY [*rather brightly*]: There is just one question I would like to be allowed to ask my guardian.

GWENDOLEN: An admirable idea! Mr Worthing, there is just one question I would like to be permitted to put to you. Where is your brother Ernest? We are both engaged to be married to your brother Ernest, so it is a matter of some importance to us to know where your brother Ernest is at present.

JACK [*slowly and hesitatingly*]: Gwendolen—Cecily—it is very painful for me to be forced to speak the truth. It is the first time in my life that I have been reduced to such a painful position, and I am really quite inexperienced in doing anything of the kind. However, I will tell you quite frankly that I have no brother Ernest. I have no brother at all. I never had a brother in my life, and I certainly have not the smallest intention of ever having one in the future.

CECILY [*surprised*]: No brother at all?

JACK [*cheerily*]: None!

GWENDOLEN [*severely*]: Had you never a brother of any kind?

JACK [*pleasantly*]: Never. Not even of any kind.

GWENDOLEN: I am afraid it is quite clear, Cecily, that neither of us is engaged to be married to anyone.

CECILY: It is not a very pleasant position for a young girl suddenly to find herself in. Is it?

GWENDOLEN: Let us go into the house. They will hardly venture to come after us there.

CECILY: No, men are so cowardly, aren't they?

[*They return into the house with scornful looks.*]

JACK: This ghastly state of things is what you call Bunburying, I suppose?

ALGERNON: Yes, and a perfectly wonderful Bunbury it is. The most wonderful Bunbury I have ever had in my life.

JACK: Well, you've no right whatsoever to Bunbury here.

ALGERNON: That is absurd. One has a right to Bunbury anywhere one chooses. Every serious Bunburyist knows that.

JACK: Serious Bunburyists? Good heavens!

ALGERNON: Well, one must be serious about something, if one wants to have any amusement in life. I happen to be serious about Bunburying. What on earth you are serious about I haven't got the remotest idea. About everything, I should fancy. You have such an absolutely trivial nature.

JACK: Well, the only small satisfaction I have in the whole of this wretched business is that your friend Bunbury is quite exploded. You won't be able to run down to the country quite so often as you used to do, dear Algy. And a very good thing too.

ALGERNON: Your brother is a little off colour, isn't he, dear Jack? You won't be able to disappear to London quite so frequently as your wicked custom was. And not a bad thing either.

JACK: As for your conduct towards Miss Cardew, I must say that your taking in a sweet, simple, innocent girl like that is quite inexcusable. To say nothing of the fact that she is my ward.

ALGERNON: I can see no possible defence at all for your deceiving a brilliant, clever, thoroughly experienced young lady like Miss Fairfax. To say nothing of the fact that she is my cousin.

JACK: I wanted to be engaged to Gwendolen, that is all. I love her.

ALGERNON: Well, I simply wanted to be engaged to Cecily. I adore her.

JACK: There is certainly no chance of your marrying Miss Cardew.

ALGERNON: I don't think there is much likelihood, Jack, of you and Miss Fairfax being united.

JACK: Well, that is no business of yours.

ALGERNON: If it was my business, I wouldn't talk about it. [*Begins to eat muffins.*] It is very vulgar to talk about one's business. Only people like stockbrokers do that, and then merely at dinner parties.

JACK: How you can sit there calmly eating muffins when we are in this horrible trouble, I can't make out. You seem to me to be perfectly heartless.

ALGERNON: Well, I can't eat muffins in an agitated manner. The butter would probably get on my cuffs. One should always eat muffins quite calmly. It is the only way to eat them.

JACK: I say it's perfectly heartless your eating muffins at all, under the circumstances.

ALGERNON: When I am in trouble, eating is the only thing that consoles me. Indeed, when I am in really great trouble, as any one who knows me intimately will tell you, I refuse everything except food and drink. At the present moment I am eating muffins because I am unhappy. Besides, I am particularly fond of muffins. [*Rising.*]

JACK [*rising*]: Well, there is no reason why you should eat them all in that greedy way. [*Takes muffins from Algernon.*]

ALGERNON [*offering teacake*]: I wish you would have teacake instead. I don't like teacake.

JACK: Good heavens! I suppose a man may eat his own muffins in his own garden.

ALGERNON: But you have just said it is perfectly heartless to eat muffins.

JACK: I said it was perfectly heartless of you, under the circumstances. That is a very different thing.

ALGERNON: That may be. But the muffins are the same. [*He seizes the muffin dish from Jack.*]

JACK: Algy, I wish to goodness you would go.

ALGERNON: You can't possibly ask me to go without having some dinner. It's absurd. I never go without my dinner. No one ever does, except vegetarians and people like that. Besides I have just made arrangements with Dr Chasuble to be christened at a quarter to six under the name of Ernest.

JACK: My dear fellow, the sooner you give up that nonsense the better. I made arrangements this morning with Dr Chasuble to be christened myself at 5:30, and I naturally will take the name of Ernest. Gwendolen would wish it. We can't both be christened Ernest. It's absurd. Besides, I have a perfect right to be christened if I like. There is no evidence that I have ever been christened by anybody. I should think it extremely probable I never was, and so does Dr Chasuble. It is entirely different in your case. You have been christened already.

ALGERNON: Yes, but I have not been christened for years.

JACK: Yes, but you have been christened. That is the important thing.

ALGERNON: Quite so. So I know my constitution can stand it. If you are not quite sure about your ever having been christened, I must say I think it rather dangerous your venturing on it now. It might make you very unwell. You can hardly have forgotten that someone very closely connected with you was very nearly carried off this week in Paris by a severe chill.

JACK: Yes, but you said yourself that a severe chill was not hereditary.

ALGERNON: It usen't to be, I know—but I daresay it is now. Science is always making wonderful improvements in things.

JACK [*picking up the muffin dish*]: Oh, that is nonsense; you are always talking nonsense.

ALGERNON: Jack, you are at the muffins again! I wish you wouldn't. There are only two left. [*Takes them.*] I told you I was particularly fond of muffins.

JACK: But I hate teacake.

ALGERNON: Why on earth then do you allow teacake to be served up for your guests? What ideas you have of hospitality!

JACK: Algernon! I have already told you to go. I don't want you here. Why don't you go!

ALGERNON: I haven't finished my tea yet! and there is still one muffin left.

*Jack groans, and sinks into a chair. Algernon still continues eating.*

## ACT III

*Morning room at the Manor House. Gwendolen and Cecily are at the window, looking out into the garden.*

GWENDOLEN: The fact that they did not follow us at once into the house, as any one else would have done, seems to me to show that they have some sense of shame left.

CECILY: They have been eating muffins. That looks like repentance.

GWENDOLEN [*after a pause*]: They don't seem to notice us at all. Couldn't you cough?

CECILY: But I haven't got a cough.

GWENDOLEN: They're looking at us. What effrontery!

CECILY: They're approaching. That's very forward of them.

GWENDOLEN: Let us preserve a dignified silence.

CECILY: Certainly. It's the only thing to do now.

*Enter Jack followed by Algernon. They whistle some dreadful popular air from a British opera.*

GWENDOLEN: This dignified silence seems to produce an unpleasant effect.

CECILY: A most distasteful one.

GWENDOLEN: But we will not be the first to speak.

CECILY: Certainly not.

GWENDOLEN: Mr Worthing, I have something very particular to ask. Much depends on your reply.

CECILY: Gwendolen, your common sense is invaluable. Mr Moncrieff, kindly answer me the following question. Why did you pretend to be my guardian's brother?

ALGERNON: In order that I might have an opportunity of meeting you.

CECILY [*to Gwendolen*]: That certainly seems a satisfactory explanation, does it not?

GWENDOLEN: Yes, dear, if you can believe him.

CECILY: I don't. But that does not affect the wonderful beauty of his answer.

GWENDOLEN: True. In matters of grave importance, style, not sincerity, is the vital thing. Mr Worthing, what explanation can you offer to me for pretending to have a brother? Was it in order that you might have an opportunity of coming up to town to see me as often as possible?

JACK: Can you doubt it, Miss Fairfax?

GWENDOLEN: I have the gravest doubts upon the subject. But I intend to crush them. This is not the moment for German skepticism. [*Moving to Cecily.*] Their explanations appear to be quite satisfactory, especially Mr Worthing's. That seems to me to have the stamp of truth upon it.

CECILY: I am more than content with what Mr Moncrieff said. His voice alone inspires one with absolute credulity.

GWENDOLEN: Then you think we should forgive them?

CECILY: Yes. I mean no.

GWENDOLEN: True! I had forgotten. There are principles at stake that one cannot surrender. Which of us should tell them? The task is not a pleasant one.

CECILY: Could we not speak at the same time?

GWENDOLEN: An excellent idea! I nearly always speak at the same time as other people. Will you take the time from me?

CECILY: Certainly. [*Gwendolen beats time with uplifted finger.*]

GWENDOLEN and CECILY [*speaking together*]: Your Christian names are still an insuperable barrier. That is all!

JACK and ALGERNON [*speaking together*]: Our Christian names! Is that all! But we are going to be christened this afternoon.

GWENDOLEN [*to Jack*]: For my sake you are prepared to do this terrible thing?

JACK: I am.

CECILY [*to Algernon*]: To please me you are ready to face this fearful ordeal?

ALGERNON: I am!

GWENDOLEN: How absurd to talk of the equality of the sexes! Where questions of self-sacrifice are concerned, men are infinitely beyond us.

JACK: We are. [*Clasps hands with Algernon.*]

CECILY: They have moments of physical courage of which we women know absolutely nothing.

GWENDOLEN [*to Jack*]: Darling!

ALGERNON [*to Cecily*]: Darling! [*They fall into each other's arms*]

*Enter Merriman. When he enters he coughs loudly, seeing the situation.*

MERRIMAN: Ahem! Ahem! Lady Bracknell.

JACK: Good heavens!

*Enter Lady Bracknell. The couples separate in alarm. Exit Merriman.*

LADY BRACKNELL: Gwendolen! What does this mean?

GWENDOLEN: Merely that I am engaged to be married to Mr Worthing, mamma.

LADY BRACKNELL: Come here. Sit down. Sit down immediately. Hesitation of any kind is a sign of mental decay in the young, of physical weakness in the old. [*Turns to Jack.*] Apprised, sir, of my daughter's sudden flight by her trusty maid, whose confidence I purchased by means of a small coin, I followed her at once by a luggage train. Her unhappy father is, I am glad to say, under the impression that she is attending a more than usually lengthy lecture by the University Extension Scheme on the Influence of a permanent income on Thought. I do not propose to undeceive him. Indeed I have never undeceived him on any question. I would consider it wrong. But of course, you will clearly understand that all communication between yourself and my daughter must cease immediately from this moment. On this point, as indeed on all points, I am firm.

JACK: I am engaged to be married to Gwendolen, Lady Bracknell!

LADY BRACKNELL: You are nothing of the kind, sir. And now as regards Algernon! . . . Algernon!

ALGERNON: Yes, Aunt Augusta.

LADY BRACKNELL: May I ask if it is in this house that your invalid friend Mr Bunbury resides?

ALGERNON [*stammering*]: Oh! No! Bunbury doesn't live here. Bunbury is somewhere else at present. In fact, Bunbury is dead.

LADY BRACKNELL: Dead! When did Mr Bunbury die? His death must have been extremely sudden.

ALGERNON [*airily*]: Oh! I killed Bunbury this afternoon. I mean poor Bunbury died this afternoon.

LADY BRACKNELL: What did he die of?

ALGERNON: Bunbury? Oh, he was quite exploded.

LADY BRACKNELL: Exploded! Was he the victim of a revolutionary outrage? I was not aware that Mr Bunbury was interested in social legislation. If so, he is well punished for his morbidity.

ALGERNON: My dear Aunt Augusta, I mean he was found out! The doctors found out that Bunbury could not live, that is what I mean—so Bunbury died.

LADY BRACKNELL: He seems to have had great confidence in the opinion of his physicians. I am glad, however, that he made up his mind at the last to some definite course of action, and acted under proper medical advice. And now that we have finally got rid of this Bunbury, may I ask, Mr Worthing, who is that young person whose hand my nephew Algernon is now holding in what seems to me a peculiarly unnecessary manner?

JACK: That Lady is Miss Cecily Cardew, my ward. [*Lady Bracknell bows coldly to Cecily.*]

ALGERNON: I am engaged to be married to Cecily, Aunt Augusta.

LADY BRACKNELL: I beg your pardon?

CECILY: Mr Moncrieff and I are engaged to be married, Lady Bracknell.

LADY BRACKNELL [*with a shiver, crossing to the sofa and sitting down.*]: I do not know whether there is anything peculiarly exciting in the air of this particular part of Hertfordshire, but the number of engagements that go on seems to me considerably above the proper average that statistics had laid down for our guidance. I think some preliminary inquiry on my part would not be out of place. Mr Worthing, is Miss Cardew at all connected with any of the larger railway stations in London? I merely desire information. Until yesterday I had no idea that there were any families or persons whose origin was a Terminus. [*Jack looks perfectly furious, but restrains himself.*]

JACK [*in a cold, clear voice*]: Miss Cardew is the granddaughter of the late Mr Thomas Cardew of 149 Belgrave Square, S.W.; Gervase Park, Dorking, Surrey; and the Sporran, Fifeshire, N.B.

LADY BRACKNELL: That sounds not unsatisfactory. Three addresses always inspire confidence, even in tradesmen. But what proof have I of their authenticity?

JACK: I have carefully preserved the Court Guides of the period. They are open to your inspection, Lady Bracknell.

LADY BRACKNELL [*grimly*]: I have known strange errors in that publication.

JACK: Miss Cardew's family solicitors are Messrs Markby, Markby, and Markby.

LADY BRACKNELL: Markby, Markby, and Markby? A firm of the very highest position in their profession. Indeed I am told that one of the Mr Markbys is occasionally to be seen at dinner parties. So far I am satisfied.

JACK [*very irritably*]: How extremely kind of you, Lady Bracknell! I have also in my possession, you will be pleased to hear, certificates of Miss Cardew's birth, baptism, whooping cough, registration, vaccination, confirmation, and the measles; both the German and the English variety.

LADY BRACKNELL: Ah! A life crowded with incident, I see; perhaps somewhat too exciting for a young girl. I am not myself in favour of premature experiences. [*Rises, looks at her watch.*] Gwendolen! the time approaches for our departure. We have not a moment to lose. As a matter of form, Mr Worthing, I had better ask you if Miss Cardew has any little fortune?

JACK: Oh! about a hundred and thirty thousand pounds in the Funds. That is all. Good-bye, Lady Bracknell. So pleased to have seen you.

LADY BRACKNELL [*sitting down again*]: A moment, Mr Worthing. A hundred and thirty thousand pounds! And in the Funds! Miss Cardew seems to be a most attractive young lady, now that I look at her. Few girls of the present day have any really solid qualities, any of the qualities that last, and improve with time. We live, I regret to say, in an age of surfaces. [*To Cecily*] Come over here, dear. [*Cecily goes across.*] Pretty child! your dress is sadly simple, and your hair seems almost as Nature might have left it. But we can soon alter all that. A thoroughly experienced French maid produces a really marvellous result in a very brief space of time. I remember recommending one to young Lady Lancing, and after three months her own husband did not know her.

JACK: And after six months nobody knew her.

LADY BRACKNELL [*glares at Jack for a few moments. Then bends, with a practiced smile, to Cecily.*]: Kindly turn round, sweet child. [*Cecily turns completely around.*] No, the side view is what I want. [*Cecily presents her profile.*] Yes, quite as I expected. There are distinct social possibilities in your profile. The two weak points in our age are its want of principle and its want of profile. The chin a little higher, dear. Style largely depends on the way the chin is worn. They are worn very high, just at present. Algernon!

ALGERNON: Yes, Aunt Augusta!

LADY BRACKNELL: There are distinct social possibilities in Miss Cardew's profile.

ALGERNON: Cecily is the sweetest, dearest, prettiest girl in the whole world. And I don't care twopence about social possibilities.

LADY BRACKNELL: Never speak disrespectfully of Society, Algernon. Only people who can't get into it do that. [*To Cecily*] Dear child, of course you know that Algernon has nothing but his debts to depend upon. But I do not approve of mercenary marriages. When I married Lord Bracknell I had no fortune of any kind. But I never dreamed for a moment of allowing that to stand in my way. Well, I suppose I must give my consent.

ALGERNON: Thank you, Aunt Augusta.

LADY BRACKNELL: Cecily, you may kiss me!

CECILY [*kisses her*]: Thank you, Lady Bracknell.

LADY BRACKNELL: You may also address me as Aunt Augusta for the future.

CECILY: Thank you, Aunt Augusta.

LADY BRACKNELL: The marriage, I think, had better take place quite soon.

ALGERNON: Thank you, Aunt Augusta.

CECILY: Thank you, Aunt Augusta.

LADY BRACKNELL: To speak frankly, I am not in favour of long engagements. They give people the opportunity of finding out each other's character before marriage, which I think is never advisable.

JACK: I beg your pardon for interrupting you, Lady Bracknell, but this engagement is quite out of the question. I am Miss Cardew's guardian, and she cannot marry without my consent until she comes of age. That consent I absolutely decline to give.

LADY BRACKNELL: Upon what grounds, may I ask? Algernon is an extremely, I may almost say an ostentatiously eligible young man. He has nothing, but he looks everything. What more can one desire?

JACK: It pains me very much to have to speak frankly to you, Lady Bracknell, about your nephew, but the fact is that I do not approve at all of his moral character. I suspect him of being untruthful. [*Algernon and Cecily look at him in indignant amazement.*]

LADY BRACKNELL: Untruthful! My nephew Algernon? Impossible! He is an Oxonian.

JACK: I fear there can be no possible doubt about the matter. This afternoon during my temporary absence in London on an important question of romance, he obtained admissions to my house by means of the false pretense of being my brother. Under an assumed name he drank, I've just been informed by my butler, an entire pint bottle of my Perrier-Jouet, Brut, '89; wine I was specially reserving for myself. Continuing his disgraceful deception, he succeeded in the course of the afternoon in alienating the affections of my only ward. He subsequently stayed to tea, and devoured every single muffin. And what makes his conduct all the more heartless is, that he was perfectly well aware from the first that I have no brother, that I never had a brother, and that I don't intend to have a brother, not even of any kind. I distinctly told him so myself yesterday afternoon.

LADY BRACKNELL: Ahem! Mr Worthing, after careful consideration I have decided entirely to overlook my nephew's conduct to you.

JACK: That is very generous of you, Lady Bracknell. My own decision, however, is unalterable. I decline to give my consent.

LADY BRACKNELL [*to Cecily*]: Come here, sweet child. [*Cecily goes over.*] How old are you, dear?

CECILY: Well, I am really only eighteen, but I always admit to twenty when I go to evening parties.

LADY BRACKNELL: You are perfectly right in making some slight alteration. Indeed, no woman should ever be quite accurate about her age. It looks so calculating. . . . [*In a meditative manner.*] Eighteen, but admitting to twenty at evening parties. Well, it will not be very long before you are of age and free from the restraints of tutelage. So don't think your guardian's consent is, after all, a matter of any importance.

JACK: Pray excuse me, Lady Bracknell, for interrupting you again, but it is only fair to tell you that according to the terms of her grandfather's will Miss Cardew does not come legally of age till she is thirty-five.

LADY BRACKNELL: That does not seem to be a grave objection. Thirty-five is a very attractive age. London society is full of women of the very highest birth who have, of their own free choice, remained thirty-five for years. Lady Dumbleton is an instance in point. To my own knowledge she has been thirty-five ever since she arrived at the age of forty, which was many years ago now. I see no reason why our dear Cecily should not be even still more attractive at the age you mention than she is at present. There will be a large accumulation of property.

CECILY: Algy, could you wait for me till I was thirty-five?

ALGERNON: Of course I could, Cecily. You know I could.

CECILY: Yes, I felt it instinctively, but I couldn't wait all that time. I hate waiting even five minutes for anybody. It always makes me rather cross. I am not punctual myself, I know, but I do like punctuality in others, and waiting, even to be married, is quite out of the question.

ALGERNON: Then what is to be done, Cecily?

CECILY: I don't know, Mr Moncrieff.

LADY BRACKNELL: My dear Mr Worthing, as Miss Cardew states positively that she cannot wait till she is thirty-five—a remark which I am bound to say seems to me to show a somewhat impatient nature—I would beg of you to reconsider your decision.

JACK: But my dear Lady Bracknell, the matter is entirely in your own hands. The moment you consent to my marriage with Gwendolen, I will most gladly allow your nephew to form an alliance with my ward.

LADY BRACKNELL [*rising and drawing herself up*]: You must be quite aware that what you propose is out of the question.

JACK: Then a passionate celibacy is all that any of us can look forward to.

LADY BRACKNELL: That is not the destiny I propose for Gwendolen. Algernon, of course, can choose for himself. [*Pulls out her watch.*] Come, dear [*Gwendolen rises*], we have already missed five, if not six, trains. To miss any more might expose us to comment on the platform.

*Enter Dr Chasuble.*

CHASUBLE: Everything is quite ready for the christenings.

LADY BRACKNELL: The christenings, sir! Is not that somewhat premature?

CHASUBLE [*looking rather puzzled, and pointing to Jack and Algernon*]: Both these gentlemen have expressed a desire for immediate baptism.

LADY BRACKNELL: At their age? The idea is grotesque and irreligious! Algernon, I forbid you to be baptized. I will not hear of such excesses. Lord Bracknell would be highly displeased if he learned that that was the way in which you wasted your time and money.

CHASUBLE: Am I to understand then that there are to be no christenings at all this afternoon?

JACK: I don't think that, as things are now, it would be of much practical value to either of us, Dr Chasuble.

CHASUBLE: I am grieved to hear such sentiments from you, Mr Worthing. They savour of the heretical views of the Anabaptists, views that I have completely refuted in four of my unpublished sermons. However, as your present mood seems to be one peculiarly secular, I will return to the church at once. Indeed, I have just been informed by the pew-opener that for the last hour and a half Miss Prism has been waiting for me in the vestry.

LADY BRACKNELL [*starting*]: Miss Prism! Did I hear you mention a Miss Prism?

CHASUBLE: Yes, Lady Bracknell. I am on my way to join her.

LADY BRACKNELL: Pray allow me to detain you for a moment. This matter may prove to be one of vital importance to Lord Bracknell and myself. Is this Miss Prism a female of repellent aspect, remotely connected with education?

CHASUBLE [*somewhat indignantly*]: She is the most cultivated of ladies, and the very picture of respectability.

LADY BRACKNELL: It is obviously the same person. May I ask what position she holds in your household?

CHASUBLE [*severely*]: I am a celibate, madam.

JACK [*interposing*]: Miss Prism, Lady Bracknell, has been for the last three years Miss Cardew's esteemed governess and valued companion.

LADY BRACKNELL: In spite of what I hear of her, I must see her at once. Let her be sent for.

CHASUBLE [*looking off*]: She approaches; she is nigh.

*Enter Miss Prism hurriedly.*

MISS PRISM: I was told you expected me in the vestry, dear Canon. I have been waiting for you there for an hour and three-quarters. [*Catches sight of Lady Bracknell, who has fixed her with a stony glare. Miss Prism grows pale and quails. She looks anxiously round as if desirous to escape.*]

LADY BRACKNELL [*in a severe, judicial voice*]: Prism! [*Miss Prism bows her head in shame.*] Come here, Prism! [*Miss Prism approaches in a humble manner.*] Prism! Where is that baby? [*General consternation. The Canon starts back in horror. Algernon and Jack pretend to be anxious to shield Cecily and Gwendolen from hearing the details of a terrible public scandal.*] Twenty-eight years ago, Prism, you left Lord Bracknell's house, Number 104, Upper Grosvenor Square, in charge of a perambulator that contained a baby of the male sex. You never returned. A few weeks later, through the elaborate investigations of the Metropolitan police, the perambulator was discovered at midnight standing by itself in a remote corner of Bayswater. It contained the manuscript of a three-volume novel of more than usually revolting sentimentality. [*Miss Prism starts in involuntary indignation.*] But the baby was not there. [*Everyone looks at Miss Prism.*] Prism! Where is that baby? [*A pause.*]

MISS PRISM: Lady Bracknell, I admit with shame that I do not know. I only wish I did. The plain facts of the case are these. On the morning of the day you mentioned, a day that is forever branded on my memory, I prepared as usual to take the baby out in its perambulator. I had also with me a somewhat old, but capacious handbag in which I had intended to place the manuscript of a work of fiction that I had written during my few unoccupied hours. In a moment of mental abstraction, for which I can never forgive myself, I deposited the manuscript in the bassinette and placed the baby in the handbag.

JACK [*who has been listening attentively*]: But where did you deposit the handbag?

MISS PRISM: Do not ask me, Mr Worthing.

JACK: Miss Prism, this is a matter of no small importance to me. I insist on knowing where you deposited the handbag that contained that infant.

MISS PRISM: I left it in the cloakroom of one of the larger railway stations in London.

JACK: What railway station?

MISS PRISM [*quite crushed*]: Victoria. The Brighton line. [*Sinks into a chair.*]

JACK: I must retire to my room for a moment. Gwendolen, wait here for me.

GWENDOLEN: If you are not too long, I will wait here for you all my life. [*Exit Jack in great excitement.*]

CHASUBLE: What do you think this means, Lady Bracknell?

LADY BRACKNELL: I dare not even suspect, Dr Chasuble. I need hardly tell you that in families of high position strange coincidences are not supposed to occur. They are hardly considered the thing. [*Noises heard overhead as if someone was throwing trunks about. Every one looks up.*]

CECILY: Uncle Jack seems strangely agitated.

CHASUBLE: Your guardian has a very emotional nature.

LADY BRACKNELL: This noise is extremely unpleasant. It sounds as if he was having an argument. I dislike arguments of any kind. They are always vulgar, and often convincing.

CHASUBLE [*looking up*]: It has stopped now. [*The noise is redoubled.*]

LADY BRACKNELL: I wish he would arrive at some conclusion.

GWENDOLEN: This suspense is terrible. I hope it will last.

*Enter Jack with a handbag of black leather in his hand.*

JACK [*rushing over to Miss Prism*]: Is this the handbag, Miss Prism? Examine it carefully before you speak. The happiness of more than one life depends on your answer.

MISS PRISM [*calmly*]: It seems to be mine. Yes, here is the injury it received through the upsetting of a Gower Street omnibus in younger and happier days. Here is the strain on the lining caused by the explosion of a temperance beverage, an incident that occurred at Leamington. And here, on the lock, are my initials. I had forgotten that in an extravagant mood I had them placed there. The bag is undoubtedly mine. I am delighted to have it so unexpectedly restored to me. It has been a great inconvenience being without it all these years.

JACK [*in a pathetic voice*]: Miss Prism, more is restored to you than this handbag. I was the baby you placed in it.

MISS PRISM [*amazed*]: You?

JACK [*embracing her*]: Yes . . . mother!

MISS PRISM [*recoiling in indignant astonishment*]: Mr Worthing. I am unmarried!

JACK: Unmarried! I do not deny that is a serious blow. But after all, who has the right to cast a stone against one who has suffered? Cannot repentance wipe out an act of folly? Why should there be one law for men, and another for women? Mother, I forgive you. [*Tries to embrace her again.*]

MISS PRISM [*still more indignant*]: Mr Worthing, there is some error. [*Pointing the Lady Bracknell.*] There is the lady who can tell you who you really are.

JACK [*after a pause*]: Lady Bracknell, I hate to seem inquisitive, but would you kindly inform me who I am?

LADY BRACKNELL: I am afraid that the news I have to give you will not altogether please you. You are the son of my poor sister, Mrs Moncrieff, and consequently Algernon's elder brother.

JACK: Algy's elder brother! Then I have a brother after all. I knew I had a brother! I always had a brother! Cecily,—how could you have ever doubted that I had a brother. [*Seizes hold of Algernon.*] Dr Chasuble, my unfortunate brother. Miss Prism, my unfortunate brother. Gwendolen, my unfortunate brother. Algy, you young scoundrel, you will have to treat me with more respect in the future. You have never behaved to me like a brother in all your life.

ALGERNON: Well, not till today, old boy, I admit. I did my best, however, though I was out of practice. [*Shakes hands.*]

GWENDOLEN [*to Jack*]: My own! But what own are you? What is your Christian name now that you have become someone else?

JACK: Good heavens! . . . I had quite forgotten that point. Your decision on the subject of my name is irrevocable, I suppose?

GWENDOLEN: I never change except in my affections.

CECILY: What a noble nature you have, Gwendolen!

JACK: Then the question had better be cleared up at once. Aunt Augusta, a moment. At the time when Miss Prism left me in the handbag, had I been christened already?

LADY BRACKNELL: Every luxury that money could buy, including christening, had been lavished on you by your fond and doting parents.

JACK: Then I was christened! That is settled. Now, what name was I given? Let me know the worst.

LADY BRACKNELL: Being the eldest son you were naturally christened after your father.

JACK [*irritably*]: Yes, but what was my father's Christian name?

LADY BRACKNELL [*meditatively*]: I cannot at the present moment recall what the General's Christian name was. But I have no doubt he had one. He was eccentric, I admit. But only in later years. And that was the result of the Indian climate, and marriage, and indigestion, and other things of that kind.

JACK: Algy! Can't you recollect what our father's Christian name was?

ALGERNON: My dear boy, we were never even on speaking terms. He died before I was a year old.

JACK: His name would appear in the Army Lists of the period, I suppose, Aunt Augusta?

LADY BRACKNELL: The General was essentially a man of peace, except in his domestic life. But have no doubt his name would appear in any military directory.

JACK: The Army Lists of the last forty years are here. These delightful records should have been my constant study. [*Rushes to bookcase and tears the books out.*] M. General . . . Mallan, Maxbohm, Magley—what ghastly names they have—Markby, Migsby, Mobbs, Moncrieff! Lieutenant 1840, Captain, Lieutenant-Colonel, Colonel, General 1869, Christian names, Ernest John. [*Puts book very quietly down and speaks quite calmly.*] I have always told you, Gwendolen, my name was Ernest, didn't I? Well it is Ernest after all. I mean it naturally is Ernest.

LADY BRACKNELL: Yes, I remember now that the General was called Ernest. I knew I had some particular reason for disliking the name.

GWENDOLEN: Ernest! My own Ernest! I felt from the first you could have no other name!

JACK: Gwendolen, it is a terrible thing for a man to find out suddenly that all his life he has been speaking nothing but the truth. Can you forgive me?

GWENDOLEN: I can. For I feel that you are sure to change.

JACK: My own one!

CHASUBLE [*to Miss Prism*]: Laetitia! [*Embraces her.*]

MISS PRISM [*enthusiastically*]: Frederick! At last!

ALGERNON: Cecily! [*Embraces her.*] At last!

JACK: Gwendolen! [*Embraces her.*] At last!

LADY BRACKNELL: My nephew, you seem to be displaying signs of triviality.

JACK: On the contrary, Aunt Augusta, I've now realized for the first time in my life the vital Importance of Being Earnest.

*Tableau*

1899

# George Bernard Shaw

## 1856–1950

Born and raised in Dublin, Ireland, George Bernard Shaw was the youngest child of an unhappy marriage between his drunken, joke-telling father and his artistic, undomestic mother. He dropped out of school when he was 15 and worked briefly at an office job in Dublin. When he was 20 he moved to London, where he lived with his mother, who helped to support him out of her income as a private music teacher while he tried unsuccessfully to make his way as a novelist. During his late twenties he discovered the economic and political theories of Karl Marx and was so inspired by them that he joined a socialist group known as the Fabians and quickly became one of their leading spokesmen, lecturing and writing pamphlets to reform local government, to revise the poor laws, to promote trade unions, and to support women's rights. By his mid-thirties he had also become a well-known art, literature, and music critic through his reviews for various London newspapers, and he had published his first book, *The Quintessence of Ibsenism* (1891), a manifesto celebrating the socially conscious drama of Ibsen. Having proclaimed the English need for a 'new drama' of social ideas, Shaw took up playwriting in 1892, and from then until his death wrote 47 full-length plays promoting his ideas and opinions about economics, politics, society, morality, religion, science, and literature. Most of his plays are comedies, which feature witty men and equally witty women who engage in lively debates that illustrate Shaw's belief in 'free vitality' and the 'life force' as the primary sources of 'creative evolution' within human beings and their social institutions. Among his best-known plays are *Candida* (1895), *Man and Superman*

(1903), *Major Barbara* (1907), *Pygmalion* (1913), and *Saint Joan* (1924).

Shaw expounded his views not only in his plays but also in prefaces that he wrote for the published versions of his plays. By means of these prefaces, which were sometimes as long as the plays themselves, Shaw used his incisive prose style to explicate his characters, plots, and themes, as well as to gain a wider audience for his ideas than was possible in the theatre alone. Published versions of his plays also allowed him to demonstrate some of the spelling reforms he championed (and insisted upon with his publishers), including contractions without apostrophes and words that are spaced out rather than italicized to convey emphasis. These changes have been retained in the text printed here.

# Pygmalion

## Preface

### A Professor of Phonetics

As will be seen later on, Pygmalion needs, not a preface, but a sequel, which I have supplied in its due place.

The English have no respect for their language, and will not teach their children to speak it. They cannot spell it because they have nothing to spell it with but an old foreign alphabet of which only the consonants—and not all of them—have any agreed speech value. Consequently no man can teach himself what it should sound like from reading it; and it is impossible for an Englishman to open his mouth without making some other Englishman despise him. Most European languages are now accessible in black and white to foreigners: English and French are not thus accessible even to Englishmen and Frenchmen. The reformer we need most today is an energetic phonetic enthusiast: that is why I have made such a one the hero of a popular play.

There have been heroes of that kind crying in the wilderness for many years past. When I became interested in the subject towards the end of the eighteen-seventies, the illustrious Alexander Melville Bell, the inventor of Visible Speech, had emigrated to Canada, where his son invented the telephone; but Alexander J. Ellis was still a London patriarch, with an impressive head always covered by a velvet skull cap, for which he would apologize to public meetings in a very courtly manner. He and Tito Pagliardini, another phonetic veteran, were men whom it was impossible to dislike. Henry Sweet, then a young man, lacked the sweetness of character: he was about as conciliatory to conventional mortals as Ibsen or Samuel Butler. His great ability as a phonetician (he was, I think, the best of them all at his job) would have entitled him to high official recognition, and perhaps enabled him to popularize his subject, but for his Satanic contempt for all academic dignitaries and persons in general who thought more of Greek than of phonetics. Once, in the days when the Imperial Institute rose in South Kensington, and Joseph Chamberlain was booming the Empire, I induced the editor of a leading monthly review to commission an article from Sweet on the imperial importance of his subject. When it arrived, it contained nothing but a savagely derisive attack on a professor of language and literature whose chair Sweet regarded as proper to a phonetic expert only. The article, being libellous, had to be returned as impossible; and I had to renounce my dream of dragging its author into the limelight. When I met him afterwards, for the first time in many years, I found to my astonishment that he, who had been a quite tolerably presentable young man, had actually managed by sheer scorn to alter his personal appearance until he had become a sort of walking repudiation of Oxford and all its traditions. It must have been largely in his own despite that he was squeezed into something called a Readership of phonetics there. The future of phonetics rests probably with his pupils, who all swore by him; but nothing could bring the man himself into any sort of compliance with the university to which he nevertheless clung by divine right in an intensely Oxonian way. I daresay his papers, if he has left any, include some satires that may be published without too destructive results fifty years hence. He was, I believe, not in the least an ill-natured man: very much the opposite, I should say; but he would not suffer fools gladly; and to him all scholars who were not rabid phoneticians were fools.

Those who knew him will recognize in my third act the allusion to the Current Shorthand in which he used to write postcards. It may be acquired from a four and sixpenny manual published by the Clarendon Press. The postcards which Mrs Higgins describes are such as I have received from Sweet. I would decipher a sound which a cockney would represent by *zerr*, and a Frenchman by *seu*, and then write demanding with some heat what on earth it meant. Sweet, with boundless contempt for my stupidity, would reply that it not only meant but obviously was the word Result, as no other word containing that sound, and capable of making sense with the context, existed in any language spoken on earth. That less expert mortals should require fuller indications was beyond Sweet's patience. Therefore, though the whole point of his current Shorthand is that it can express every sound in the language perfectly, vowels as well as consonants, and that your hand has to make no stroke except the easy and current ones with which you write m, n, and u, l, p, and q, scribbling them at whatever angle comes easiest to you, his unfortunate determination to make this remarkable and quite legible script serve also as a shorthand reduced it in his practice to the most inscrutable of cryptograms. His true objective was the provision of a full, accurate, legible script for our language; but he was led past that by his contempt for the popular Pitman system of shorthand, which he called the Pitfall system. The triumph of Pitman was a triumph of business organization: there was a weekly paper to persuade you to learn Pitman: there were cheap textbooks and exercise books and transcripts of speeches for you to copy, and schools where experienced teachers coached you up to the necessary proficiency. Sweet could not organize his market in that fashion. He might as well have been the Sybil who tore up the leaves of prophecy that nobody would attend to. The four and sixpenny manual, mostly in his lithographed handwriting, that was never vulgarly advertised, may perhaps some day be taken up by a syndicate and pushed upon the public as The Times pushed the Encyclopaedia Britannica; but until then it will certainly not prevail against Pitman. I have bought three copies of it during my lifetime; and I am informed by the publishers that its cloistered existence is still a steady and healthy one. I actually learned the system two several times; and yet the shorthand in which I am writing these lines is Pitman's. And the reason is, that my secretary cannot transcribe Sweet, having been perforce taught in the schools of

Pitman. In America I could use the commercially organized Gregg shorthand, which has taken a hint from Sweet by making its letters writable (current, Sweet would have called them) instead of having to be geometrically drawn like Pitman's; but all these systems, including Sweet's, are spoilt by making them available for verbatim reporting, in which complete and exact spelling and word division are impossible. A complete and exact phonetic script is neither practicable nor necessary for ordinary use; but if we enlarge our alphabet to the Russian size, and make our spelling as phonetic as Spanish, the advance will be prodigious.

Pygmalion Higgins is not a portrait of Sweet, to whom the adventure of Eliza Doolittle would have been impossible; still, as will be seen, there are touches of Sweet in the play. With Higgins's physique and temperament Sweet might have set the Thames on fire. As it was, he impressed himself professionally on Europe to an extent that made his comparative personal obscurity, and the failure of Oxford to do justice to his eminence, a puzzle to foreign specialists in his subject. I do not blame Oxford, because I think Oxford is quite right in demanding a certain social amenity from its nurslings (heaven knows it is not exorbitant in its requirements!); for although I well know how hard it is for a man of genius with a seriously underrated subject to maintain serene and kindly relations with the men who underrate it, and who keep all the best places for less important subjects which they profess without originality and sometimes without much capacity for them, still, if he overwhelms them with wrath and disdain, he cannot expect them to heap honours on him.

Of the later generations of phoneticians I know little. Among them towered Robert Bridges, to whom perhaps Higgins may owe his Miltonic sympathies, though here again I must disclaim all portraiture. But if the play makes the public aware that there are such people as phoneticians, and that they are among the most important people in England at present, it will serve its turn.

I wish to boast that Pygmalion has been an extremely successful play, both on stage and screen, all over Europe and North America as well as at home. It is so intensely and deliberately didactic, and its subject is esteemed so dry, that I delight in throwing it at the heads of the wiseacres who repeat the parrot cry that art should never be didactic. It goes to prove my contention that great art can never be anything else.

Finally, and for the encouragement of people troubled with accents that cut them off from all high employment, I may add that the change wrought by Professor Higgins in the flower-girl is neither impossible nor uncommon. The modern concierge's daughter who fulfils her ambition by playing the Queen of Spain in Ruy Blas at the Théâtre Français is one of many thousands of men and women who have sloughed off their native dialects and acquired a new tongue. Our West End shop assistants and domestic servants are bilingual. But the thing has to be done scientifically, or the last state of the aspirant may be worse than the first. An honest slum dialect is more tolerable than the attempts of phonetically untaught persons to imitate the plutocracy. Ambitious flower-girls who read this play must not imagine that they can pass themselves off as fine ladies by untutored imitation. They must learn their alphabet over again, and different, from a phonetic expert. Imitation will only make them ridiculous.

## *CHARACTERS*

CLARA EYNSFORD HILL
MRS EYNSFORD HILL
A BYSTANDER
FREDDY EYNSFORD HILL
ELIZA DOOLITTLE
COLONEL PICKERING
HENRY HIGGINS
A SARCASTIC BYSTANDER
MRS PEARCE
ALFRED DOOLITTLE
MRS HIGGINS
PARLOUR-MAID

## ACT I

*London at 11:15 p.m. Torrents of heavy summer rain. Cab whistles blowing frantically in all directions. Pedestrians running for shelter into the portico of St Paul's church (not Wren's cathedral but Inigo Jones's church in Covent Garden vegetable market), among them a lady and her daughter in evening dress. All are peering out gloomily at the rain, except one man with his back turned to the rest, wholly preoccupied with a notebook in which he is writing.*

*The church clock strikes the first quarter.*

THE DAUGHTER [*in the space between the central pillars, close to the one on her left*]: I'm getting chilled to the bone. What can Freddy be doing all this time? He's been gone twenty minutes.

THE MOTHER [*on her daughter's right*]: Not so long. But he ought to have got us a cab by this.

A BYSTANDER [*on the lady's right*]: He wont get no cab not until half-past eleven, missus, when they come back after dropping their theatre fares.

THE MOTHER: But we must have a cab. We cant stand here until half-past eleven. It's too bad.

THE BYSTANDER: Well, it aint my fault, missus.

THE DAUGHTER: If Freddy had a bit of gumption, he would have got one at the theatre door.

THE MOTHER: What could he have done, poor boy?

THE DAUGHTER: Other people got cabs. Why couldnt he?

*Freddy rushes in out of the rain from the Southampton Street side, and comes between them closing a dripping umbrella. He is a young man of twenty, in evening dress, very wet round the ankles.*

THE DAUGHTER: Well, havnt you got a cab?

FREDDY: Theres not one to be had for love or money.

THE MOTHER: Oh, Freddy, there must be one. You cant have tried.

THE DAUGHTER: It's too tiresome. Do you expect us to go and get one ourselves?

FREDDY: I tell you theyre all engaged. The rain was so sudden: nobody was prepared; and everybody had to take a cab. Ive been to Charing Cross one way and nearly to Ludgate Circus the other; and they were all engaged.

THE MOTHER: Did you try Trafalgar Square?

FREDDY: There wasnt one at Trafalgar Square.

THE DAUGHTER: Did you try?

FREDDY: I tried as far as Charing Cross Station. Did you expect me to walk to Hammersmith?

THE DAUGHTER: You havnt tried at all.

THE MOTHER: You really are very helpless, Freddy. Go again; and dont come back until you have found a cab.

FREDDY: I shall simply get soaked for nothing.

THE DAUGHTER: And what about us? Are we to stay here all night in this draught, with next to nothing on? You selfish pig—

FREDDY: Oh, very well: I'll go, I'll go.

*He opens his umbrella and dashes off Strandwards, but comes into collision with a flower girl who is hurrying in for shelter, knocking her basket out of her hands. A blinding flash of lightning, followed instantly by a rattling peal of thunder, orchestrates the incident.*

THE FLOWER GIRL: Nah then, Freddy: look wh' y' gowin, deah.

FREDDY: Sorry. [*He rushes off.*]

THE FLOWER GIRL [*picking up her scattered flowers and replacing them in the basket*]: Theres menners f' yer! Tə-oo banches o voylets trod into the mad.

*She sits down on the plinth of the column, sorting her flowers, on the lady's right. She is not at all a romantic figure. She is perhaps eighteen, perhaps twenty, hardly older. She wears a little sailor hat of black straw that has long been exposed to the dust and soot of London and has seldom if ever been brushed. Her hair needs washing rather badly: its mousy colour can hardly be natural. She wears a shoddy black coat that reaches nearly to her knees and is shaped to her waist. She has a brown skirt with a coarse apron. Her boots are much the worse for wear. She is no doubt as clean as she can afford to be; but compared to the ladies she is very dirty. Her features are no worse than theirs; but their condition leaves something to be desired; and she needs the services of a dentist.*

THE MOTHER: How do you know that my son's name is Freddy, pray?

THE FLOWER GIRL: Ow, eez yə-ooa san, is e? Wal, fewd dan y' də-ooty bawmz a mather should, eed now bettern to spawl a pore gel's flahrzn than ran awy athaht pyin. Will ye-oo py me f'them? [*Here, with apologies, this desperate attempt to represent her dialect without a phonetic alphabet must be abandoned as unintelligible outside London.*]

THE DAUGHTER: Do nothing of the sort, mother. The idea!

THE MOTHER: Please allow me, Clara. Have you any pennies?

THE DAUGHTER: No. Ive nothing smaller than sixpence.

THE FLOWER GIRL [*hopefully*]: I can give you change for a tanner, kind lady.

THE MOTHER [*to Clara*]: Give it to me. [*Clara parts reluctantly.*] Now [*to the girl*]: This is for your flowers.

THE FLOWER GIRL: Thank you kindly, lady.

THE DAUGHTER: Make her give you the change. These things are only a penny a bunch.

THE MOTHER: Do hold your tongue, Clara. [*to the girl*]: You can keep the change.

THE FLOWER GIRL: Oh, thank you, lady.

THE MOTHER: Now tell me how you know that young gentleman's name.

THE FLOWER GIRL: I didnt.

THE MOTHER: I heard you call him by it. Dont try to deceive me.

THE FLOWER GIRL [*protesting*]: Who's trying to deceive you? I called him Freddy or Charlie same as you might yourself if you was talking to a stranger and wished to be pleasant.

THE DAUGHTER: Sixpence thrown away! Really, mamma, you might have spared Freddy that. [*She retreats in disgust behind the pillar.*]

*An elderly gentleman of the amiable military type rushes into the shelter, and closes a dripping umbrella. He is in the same plight as Freddy, very wet about the ankles. He is in evening dress, with a light overcoat. He takes the place left vacant by the daughter.*

THE GENTLEMAN: Phew!

THE MOTHER [*to the gentleman*]: Oh sir, is there any sign of its stopping?

THE GENTLEMAN: I'm afraid not. It started worse than ever about two minutes ago. [*He goes to the plinth beside the flower girl; puts up his foot on it; and stoops to turn down his trouser ends.*]

THE MOTHER: Oh dear! [*She retires sadly and joins her daughter.*]

THE FLOWER GIRL [*taking advantage of the military gentleman's proximity to establish friendly relations with him*]: If it's worse, it's a sign it's nearly over. So cheer up, Captain; and buy a flower off a poor girl.

THE GENTLEMAN: I'm sorry. I havnt any change.

THE FLOWER GIRL: I can give you change, Captain.

THE GENTLEMAN: For a sovereign? Ive nothing less.

THE FLOWER GIRL: Garn! Oh do buy a flower off me, Captain. I can change half-a-crown. Take this for tuppence.

THE GENTLEMAN: Now dont be troublesome: theres a good girl. [*trying his pockets*] I really havnt any change—Stop: heres three hapence, if thats any use to you. [*He retreats to the other pillar.*]

THE FLOWER GIRL [*disappointed, but thinking three halfpence better than nothing*]: Thank you, sir.

THE BYSTANDER [*to the girl*]: You be careful: give him a flower for it. Theres a bloke here behind taking down every blessed word youre saying. [*All turn to the man who is taking notes.*]

THE FLOWER GIRL [*springing up terrified*]: I aint done nothing wrong by speaking to the gentleman. Ive a right to sell flowers if I keep off the kerb. [*hysterically*] I'm a respectable girl: so help me, I never spoke to him except to ask him to buy a flower off me.

*General hubbub, mostly sympathetic to the flower girl, but deprecating her excessive sensibility. Cries of* Dont start hollerin. Who's hurting you? Nobody's going to touch you. Whats the good of fussing? Steady on. Easy easy, etc., *come from the elderly staid spectators, who pat her comfortingly. Less patient ones bid her shut her head, or ask her roughly what is wrong with her. A remoter group, not knowing what the matter is, crowd in and increase the noise with question and answer:* Whats the row? What-she do? Where is he? A tec taking her down. What! him? Yes: him over there: Took money off the gentleman, etc.

THE FLOWER GIRL [*breaking through them to the gentleman, crying wildly*]: Oh, sir, dont let him charge me. You dunno what it means to me. Theyll take away my character and drive me on the streets for speaking to gentlemen. They—

THE NOTE TAKER [*coming forward on her right, the rest crowding after him*]: There! there! there! there! who's hurting you, you silly girl? What do you take me for?

THE BYSTANDER: It's aw rawt: e's a genleman: look at his bə-oots. [*explaining to the note taker*] She thought you was a copper's nark, sir.

THE NOTE TAKER [*with quick interest*]: Whats a copper's nark?

THE BYSTANDER [*inapt at definition*]: It's a—well, it's a copper's nark, as you might say. What else would you call it? A sort of informer.

THE FLOWER GIRL [*still hysterical*]: I take my Bible oath I never said a word—

THE NOTE TAKER [*overbearing but good-humoured*]: Oh, shut up, shut up. Do I look like a policeman?

THE FLOWER GIRL [*far from reassured*]: Then what did you take down my words for? How do I know whether you took me down right? You just shew me what youve wrote about me. [*The note taker opens his book and holds it steadily under her nose, though the pressure of the mob trying to read it over his shoulders would upset a weaker man.*] Whats that? That aint proper writing. I cant read that.

THE NOTE TAKER: I can. [*reads, reproducing her pronunciation exactly*] 'Cheer ap, Keptin; n' baw y flahr orf a pore gel.'

THE FLOWER GIRL [*much distressed*]: It's because I called him Captain. I meant no harm. [*to the gentleman*]: Oh, sir, dont let him lay a charge agen me for a word like that. You—

THE GENTLEMAN: Charge! I make no charge. [*to the note taker*]: Really, sir, if you are a detective, you need not begin protecting me against molestations by young women until I ask you. Anybody could see that the girl meant no harm.

THE BYSTANDERS GENERALLY [*demonstrating against police espionage*]: Course they could. What business is it of yours? You mind your own affairs. He wants promotion, he does. Taking down people's words! Girl never said a word to him. What harm if she did? Nice thing a girl cant shelter from the rain without being insulted, etc., etc., etc. [*She is conducted by the more sympathetic demonstrators back to her plinth, where she resumes her seat and struggles with her emotion.*]

THE BYSTANDER: He aint a tec. He's a blooming busybody: thats what he is. I tell you, look at his bə-oots.

THE NOTE TAKER [*turning on him genially*]: And how are all your people down at Selsey?

THE BYSTANDER [*suspiciously*]: Who told you my people come from Selsey?

THE NOTE TAKER: Never you mind. They did. [*to the girl*] How do you come to be up so far east? You were born in Lisson Grove.

THE FLOWER GIRL [*appalled*]: Oh, what harm is there in my leaving Lisson Grove? It wasnt fit for a pig to live in; and I had to pay four-and-six a week [*in tears*]: Oh, boo—hoo—oo—

THE NOTE TAKER: Live where you like; but stop that noise.

THE GENTLEMAN [*to the girl*]: Come, come! he cant touch you: you have a right to live where you please.

A SARCASTIC BYSTANDER [*thrusting himself between the note taker and the gentleman*]: Park Lane, for instance. I'd like to go into the Housing Question with you, I would.

THE FLOWER GIRL [*subsiding into a brooding melancholy over her basket, and talking very low-spiritedly to herself* ]: I'm a good girl, I am.

THE SARCASTIC BYSTANDER [*not attending to her*]: Do you know where I come from?

THE NOTE TAKER [*promptly*]: Hoxton.

*Titterings. Popular interest in the note taker's performance increases.*

THE SARCASTIC ONE [*amazed*]: Well, who said I didnt? Bly me! you know everything, you do.

THE FLOWER GIRL [*still nursing her sense of injury*]: Aint no call to meddle with me, he aint.

THE BYSTANDER [*to her*]: Of course he aint. Dont you stand it from him. [*to the note taker*]: See here: what call have you to know about people what never offered to meddle with you?

THE FLOWER GIRL: Let him say what he likes. I dont want to have no truck with him.

THE BYSTANDER: You take us for dirt under your feet, dont you? Catch you taking liberties with a gentleman!

THE SARCASTIC BYSTANDER: Yes: tell him where he come from if you want to go fortune-telling.

THE NOTE TAKER: Cheltenham, Harrow, Cambridge, and India.

THE GENTLEMAN: Quite right.

*Great laughter. Reaction in the note taker's favour. Exclamations of* He knows all about it. Told him proper. Hear him tell the toff where he come from? etc.

THE GENTLEMAN: May I ask, sir, do you do this for your living at a music hall?

THE NOTE TAKER: Ive thought of that. Perhaps I shall some day.

*The rain has stopped; and the persons on the outside of the crowd begin to drop off.*

THE FLOWER GIRL [*resenting the reaction*]: He's no gentleman, he aint, to interfere with a poor girl.

THE DAUGHTER [*out of patience, pushing her way rudely to the front and displacing the gentleman, who politely retires to the other side of the pillar*]: What on earth is Freddy doing? I shall get pneumownia if I stay in this draught any longer.

THE NOTE TAKER [*to himself, hastily making a note of her pronunciation of 'monia'*]: Earlscourt.

THE DAUGHTER [*violently*]: Will you please keep your impertinent remarks to yourself.

THE NOTE TAKER: Did I say that out loud? I didnt mean to. I beg your pardon. Your mother's Epsom, unmistakeably.

THE MOTHER [*advancing between her daughter and the note taker*]: How very curious! I was brought up in Largelady Park, near Epsom.

THE NOTE TAKER [*uproariously amused*]: Ha! Ha! What a devil of a name! Excuse me. [*to the daughter*]: You want a cab, do you?

THE DAUGHTER: Dont dare speak to me.

THE MOTHER: Oh please, please, Clara. [*Her daughter repudiates her with an angry shrug and retires haughtily.*] We should be so grateful to you, sir, if you found us a cab. [*The note taker produces a whistle.*] Oh, thank you. [*She joins her daughter.*]

*The note taker blows a piercing blast.*

THE SARCASTIC BYSTANDER: There! I knowed he was a plainclothes copper.

THE BYSTANDER: That aint a police whistle: thats a sporting whistle.

THE FLOWER GIRL [*still preoccupied with her wounded feelings*]: He's no right to take away my character. My character is the same to me as any lady's.

THE NOTE TAKER: I dont know whether youve noticed it; but the rain stopped about two minutes ago.

THE BYSTANDER: So it has. Why didnt you say so before? and us losing our time listening to your silliness! [*He walks off towards the Strand.*]

THE SARCASTIC BYSTANDER: I can tell where you come from. You come from Anwell. Go back there.

THE NOTE TAKER [*helpfully*]: Hanwell.

THE SARCASTIC BYSTANDER [*affecting great distinction of speech*]: Thenk you, teacher. Haw haw! So long. [*He touches his hat with mock respect and strolls off.*]

THE FLOWER GIRL: Frightening people like that! How would he like it himself?

THE MOTHER: It's quite fine now, Clara. We can walk to a motor bus. Come. [*She gathers her skirts above her ankles and hurries off towards the Strand.*]

THE DAUGHTER: But the cab—[*her mother is out of hearing.*] Oh, how tiresome! [*She follows angrily.*]

*All the rest have gone except the note taker, the gentleman, and the flower girl, who sits arranging her basket, and still pitying herself in murmurs.*

THE FLOWER GIRL: Poor girl! Hard enough for her to live without being worrited and chivied.

THE GENTLEMAN [*returning to his former place on the note taker's left*]: How do you do it, if I may ask?

THE NOTE TAKER: Simply phonetics. The science of speech. Thats my profession: also my hobby. Happy is the man who can make a living by his hobby! You can spot an Irishman or a Yorkshireman by his brogue. *I* can place any man within six miles. I can place him within two miles in London. Sometimes within two streets.

THE FLOWER GIRL: Ought to be ashamed of himself, unmanly coward!

THE GENTLEMAN: But is there a living in that?

THE NOTE TAKER: Oh yes. Quite a fat one. This is an age of upstarts. Men begin in Kentish Town with £80 a year, and end in Park Lane with a hundred thousand. They want to drop Kentish Town; but they give themselves away every time they open their mouths. Now I can teach them—

THE FLOWER GIRL: Let him mind his own business and leave a poor girl—

THE NOTE TAKER [*explosively*]: Woman: cease this detestable boohooing instantly; or else seek the shelter of some other place of worship.

THE FLOWER GIRL [*with feeble defiance*]: Ive a right to be here if I like, same as you.

THE NOTE TAKER: A woman who utters such depressing and disgusting sounds has no right to be anywhere—no right to live. Remember that you are a human being with a soul and the divine gift of articulate speech: that your native language is the language of Shakespeare and Milton and The Bible; and dont sit there crooning like a bilious pigeon.

THE FLOWER GIRL [*quite overwhelmed, looking up at him in mingled wonder and deprecation without daring to raise her head*]: Ah-ah-ah-ow-ow-ow-oo!

THE NOTE TAKER [*whipping out his book*]: Heavens! what a sound! [*He writes; then holds out the book and reads, reproducing her vowels exactly*]: Ah-ah-ah-ow-ow-ow-oo!

THE FLOWER GIRL [*tickled by the performance, and laughing in spite of herself*]: Garn!

THE NOTE TAKER: You see this creature with her kerbstone English: the English that will keep her in the gutter to the end of her days. Well, sir, in three months I could pass that girl off as a duchess at an ambassador's garden party. I could even get her a place as lady's maid or shop assistant, which requires better English.

THE FLOWER GIRL: Whats that you say?

THE NOTE TAKER: Yes, you squashed cabbage leaf, you disgrace to the noble architecture of these columns, you incarnate insult to the English language: I could pass you off as the Queen of Sheba. [*to the Gentleman*]: Can you believe that?

THE GENTLEMAN: Of course I can. I am myself a student of Indian dialects; and—

THE NOTE TAKER [*eagerly*]: Are you? Do you know Colonel Pickering, the author of Spoken Sanscrit?

THE GENTLEMAN: I am Colonel Pickering. Who are you?

THE NOTE TAKER: Henry Higgins, author of Higgins's Universal Alphabet.

PICKERING [*with enthusiasm*]: I came from India to meet you.

HIGGINS: I was going to India to meet you.

PICKERING: Where do you live?

HIGGINS: 27A Wimpole Street. Come and see me tomorrow.

PICKERING: I'm at the Carlton. Come with me now and lets have a jaw over some supper.

HIGGINS: Right you are.

THE FLOWER GIRL [*to Pickering, as he passes her*]: Buy a flower, kind gentleman. I'm short for my lodging.

PICKERING: I really havnt any change. I'm sorry. [*He goes away.*]

HIGGINS [*shocked at the girl's mendacity*]: Liar. You said you could change half-a-crown.

THE FLOWER GIRL [*rising in desperation*]: You ought to be stuffed with nails, you ought. [*flinging the basket at his feet*] Take the whole blooming basket for sixpence.

*The church clock strikes the second quarter.*

HIGGINS [*hearing in it the voice of God, rebuking him for his Pharisaic want of charity to the poor girl*]: A reminder. [*He raises his hat solemnly; then throws a handful of money into the basket and follows Pickering.*]

THE FLOWER GIRL [*picking up a half-crown*]: Ah-ow-ooh! [*picking up a couple of florins*] Aaah-ow-ooh! [*picking up several coins*] Aaaaaah-ow-ooh! [*picking up a half-sovereign*] Aaaaaaaaaaaah-ow-ooh!!!

FREDDY [*springing out of a taxicab*]: Got one at last. Hallo! [*to the girl*]: Where are the two ladies that were here?

THE FLOWER GIRL: They walked to the bus when the rain stopped.

FREDDY: And left me with a cab on my hands! Damnation!

THE FLOWER GIRL [*with grandeur*]: Never mind, young man. *I*'m going home in a taxi. [*She sails off to the cab. The driver puts his hand behind him and holds the door firmly shut against her. Quite understanding his mistrust, she shews him her handful of money.*] A taxi fare aint no object to me, Charlie. [*He grins and opens the door.*] Here. What about the basket?

THE TAXIMAN: Give it here. Tuppence extra.

LIZA: No: I dont want nobody to see it. [*She crushes it into the cab and gets in, continuing the conversation through the window.*]: Goodbye, Freddy.

FREDDY [*dazedly raising his hat*]: Goodbye.

TAXIMAN: Where to?

LIZA: Bucknam Pellis [*Buckingham Palace*].

TAXIMAN: What d'ye mean—Bucknam Pellis?

LIZA: Dont you know where it is? In the Green Park, where the King lives. Goodbye, Freddy. Dont let me keep you standing there. Goodbye.

FREDDY: Goodbye. [*He goes.*]

TAXIMAN: Here? Whats this about Bucknam Pellis? What business have you at Bucknam Pellis?

LIZA: Of course I havnt none. But I wasnt going to let him know that. You drive me home.

TAXIMAN: And wheres home?

LIZA: Angel Court, Drury Lane, next Meiklejohn's oil shop.

TAXIMAN: That sounds more like it, Judy. [*He drives off.*]

* * *

*Let us follow the taxi to the entrance to Angel Court, a narrow little archway between two shops, one of them Meiklejohn's oil shop. When it stops there, Eliza gets out, dragging her basket with her.*

LIZA: How much?
TAXIMAN [*indicating the taximeter*]: Cant you read? A shilling.
LIZA: A shilling for two minutes!!
TAXIMAN: Two minutes or ten: it's all the same.
LIZA: Well. I dont call it right.
TAXIMAN: Ever been in a taxi before?
LIZA [*with dignity*]: Hundreds and thousands of times, young man.
TAXIMAN [*laughing at her*]: Good for you, Judy. Keep the shilling darling, with best love from all at home. Good luck! [*He drives off.*]
LIZA [*humiliated*]: Impidence!

*She picks up the basket and trudges up the alley with it to her lodging: a small room with very old wall paper hanging loose in the damp places. A broken pane in the window is mended with paper. A portrait of a popular actor and a fashion plate of ladies' dresses, all wildly beyond poor Eliza's means, both torn from newspapers, are pinned up on the wall. A birdcage hangs in the window; but its tenant died long ago: it remains as a memorial only.*

*These are the only visible luxuries: the rest is the irreducible minimum of poverty's needs: a wretched bed heaped with all sorts of coverings that have any warmth in them, a draped packing case with a basin and jug on it and a little looking glass over it, a chair and table, the refuse of some suburban kitchen, and an American alarum clock on the shelf above the unused fireplace: the whole lighted with a gas lamp with a penny in the slot meter. Rent: four shillings a week.*

*Here Eliza, chronically weary, but too excited to go to bed, sits, counting her new riches and dreaming and planning what to do with them, until the gas goes out, when she enjoys for the first time the sensation of being able to put in another penny without grudging it. This prodigal mood does not extinguish her gnawing sense of the need for economy sufficiently to prevent her from calculating that she can dream and plan in bed more cheaply and warmly than sitting up without a fire. So she takes off her shawl and skirt and adds them to the miscellaneous bedclothes. Then she kicks off her shoes and gets into bed without any further change.*

## ACT II

*Next day at 11 a.m. Higgins's laboratory in Wimpole Street. It is a room on the first floor, looking on the street, and was meant for the drawing room. The double doors are in the middle of the back wall; and persons entering find in the corner to their right two tall file cabinets at right angles to one another against the walls. In this corner stands a flat writing-table, on which are a phonograph, a laryngoscope, a row of tiny organ pipes with a bellows, a set of lamp chimneys for singing flames with burners attached to a gas plug in the wall by an indiarubber tube, several tuning-forks of different sizes, a life-size image of half a human head, shewing in section the vocal organs, and a box containing a supply of wax cylinders for the phonograph.*

*Further down the room, on the same side, is a fireplace, with a comfortable leather-covered easy-chair at the side of the hearth nearest the door, and a coal-scuttle. There is a clock on the mantel-piece. Between the fireplace and the phonograph table is a stand for newspapers.*

*On the other side of the central door, to the left of the visitor, is a cabinet of shallow drawers. On it is a telephone and the telephone directory. The corner beyond, and most of the side wall, is occupied by a grand piano, with the keyboard at the end furthest from the door, and a bench for the player extending the full length of the keyboard. On the piano is a dessert dish heaped with fruit and sweets, mostly chocolates.*

*The middle of the room is clear. Besides the easy-chair, the piano bench, and two chairs at the phonograph table, there is one stray chair. It stands near the fireplace. On the walls, engravings: mostly Piranesis and mezzotint portraits. No paintings.*

*Pickering is seated at the table, putting down some cards and a tuning-fork which he has been using. Higgins is standing up near him, closing two or three file drawers which are hanging out. He appears in the morning light as a robust, vital, appetizing sort of man of forty or thereabouts, dressed in a professional-looking black frock-coat with a white linen collar and black silk tie. He is of the energetic, scientific type, heartily, even violently interested in everything that can be studied as a scientific subject, and careless about himself and other people, including their feelings. He is, in fact, but for his years and size, rather like a very impetuous baby 'taking notice' eagerly and loudly, and requiring almost as much watching to keep him out of unintended mischief. His manner varies from genial bullying when he is in a good humour to stormy petulance when anything goes wrong; but he is so entirely frank and void of malice that he remains likeable even in his least reasonable moments.*

HIGGINS [*as he shuts the last drawer*]: Well, I think thats the whole show.

PICKERING: It's really amazing. I havnt taken half of it in, you know.

HIGGINS: Would you like to go over any of it again?

PICKERING [*rising and coming to the fireplace, where he plants himself with his back to the fire*]: No, thank you: not now. I'm quite done up for this morning.

HIGGINS [*following him, and standing beside him on his left*]: Tired of listening to sounds?

PICKERING: Yes. It's a fearful strain. I rather fancied myself because I can pronounce twenty-four distinct vowel sounds: but your hundred and thirty beat me. I cant hear a bit of difference between most of them.

HIGGINS [*chuckling, and going over to the piano to eat sweets*]: Oh, that comes with practice. You hear no difference at first; but you keep on listening, and presently you find theyre all as different as A from B.

*Mrs Pearce looks in: she is Higgins's housekeeper.*

Whats the matter?

MRS PEARCE [*hesitating, evidently perplexed*]: A young woman asks to see you, sir.

HIGGINS: A young woman! What does she want?

MRS PEARCE: Well, sir, she says youll be glad to see her when you know what she's come about. She's quite a common girl, sir. Very common indeed. I should have sent her away, only I thought perhaps you wanted her to talk into your machines. I hope Ive not done wrong; but really you see such queer people sometimes—youll excuse me, I'm sure, sir—

HIGGINS: Oh, thats all right, Mrs Pearce. Has she an interesting accent?

MRS PEARCE: Oh, something dreadful, sir, really. I dont know how you can take an interest in it.

HIGGINS [*to Pickering*]: Lets have her up. Shew her up, Mrs Pearce. [*He rushes across to his working table and picks out a cylinder to use on the phonograph.*]

MRS PEARCE [*only half resigned to it*]: Very well, sir. It's for you to say. [*She goes downstairs.*]

HIGGINS: This is rather a bit of luck. I'll shew you how I make records. We'll set her talking; and I'll take it down first in Bell's Visible Speech; then in broad Romic; and then we'll get her on the phonograph so that you can turn her on as often as you like with the written transcript before you.

MRS PEARCE [*returning*]: This is the young woman, sir.

*The flower girl enters in state. She has a hat with three ostrich feathers, orange, sky-blue, and red. She has a nearly clean apron, and the shoddy coat has been tidied a little. The pathos of this deplorable figure, with its innocent vanity and consequential air, touches Pickering, who has already straightened himself in the presence of Mrs Pearce. But as to Higgins, the only distinction he makes between men and women is that when he is neither bullying nor exclaiming to the heavens against some feather-weight cross, he coaxes women as a child coaxes its nurse when it wants to get anything out of her.*

HIGGINS [*brusquely, recognizing her with unconcealed disappointment, and at once, babylike, making an intolerable grievance of it*]: Why, this is the girl I jotted down last night. She's no use: Ive got all the records I want of the Lisson Grove lingo; and I'm not going to waste another cylinder on it. [*to the girl*]: Be off with you: I dont want you.

THE FLOWER GIRL: Dont you be so saucy. You aint heard what I come for yet. [*to Mrs Pearce, who is waiting at the door for further instructions*]: Did you tell him I come in a taxi?

MRS PEARCE: Nonsense, girl! what do you think a gentleman like Mr Higgins cares what you came in?

THE FLOWER GIRL: Oh, we *are* proud! He aint above giving lessons, not him: I heard him say so. Well, I aint come here to ask for any compliment; and if my money's not good enough I can go elsewhere.

HIGGINS: Good enough for what?

THE FLOWER GIRL: Good enough for yə-oo. Now you know, dont you? I'm come to have lessons, I am. And to pay for em tə-oo: make no mistake.

HIGGINS [*stupent*]: Well!!! [*recovering his breath with a gasp*] What do you expect me to say to you?

THE FLOWER GIRL: Well, if you was a gentleman, you might ask me to sit down, I think. Dont I tell you I'm bringing you business?

HIGGINS: Pickering: shall we ask this baggage to sit down, or shall we throw her out the window?

THE FLOWER GIRL [*running away in terror to the piano, where she turns at bay*]: Ah-ah-oh-ow-ow-ow-oo! [*wounded and whimpering*] I wont be called a baggage when Ive offered to pay like any lady.

*Motionless, the two men stare at her from the other side of the room, amazed.*

PICKERING [*gently*]: But what is it you want?

THE FLOWER GIRL: I want to be a lady in a flower shop stead of sellin at the corner of Tottenham Court Road. But they wont take me unless I can talk more genteel. He said he could teach me. Well, here I am ready to pay him—not asking any favour—and he treats me zif I was dirt.

MRS PEARCE: How can you be such a foolish ignorant girl as to think you could afford to pay Mr Higgins?

THE FLOWER GIRL: Why shouldnt I? I know what lessons cost as well as you do; and I'm ready to pay.

HIGGINS: How much?

THE FLOWER GIRL [*coming back to him, triumphant*]: Now youre taking! I thought youd come off it when you saw a chance of getting back a bit of what you chucked at me last night. [*confidentially*]: Youd had a drop in, hadnt you?

HIGGINS [*peremptorily*]: Sit down.

THE FLOWER GIRL: Oh, if youre going to make a compliment of it—

HIGGINS [*thundering at her*]: Sit down.

MRS PEARCE [*severely*]: Sit down, girl. Do as youre told.

THE FLOWER GIRL: Ah-ah-ah-ow-ow-oo! [*She stands, half rebellious, half bewildered.*]

PICKERING [*very courteous*]: Wont you sit down? [*He places the stray chair near the hearthrug between himself and Higgins.*]

LIZA [*coyly*]: Dont mind if I do. [*She sits down. Pickering returns to the hearthrug.*]

HIGGINS: Whats your name?

THE FLOWER GIRL: Liza Doolittle.

HIGGINS [*declaiming gravely*]: Eliza, Elizabeth, Betsy and Bess,
They went to the woods to get a bird's nes':

PICKERING: They found a nest with four eggs in it:

HIGGINS: They took one apiece, and left three in it.

*They laugh heartily at their own fun.*

LIZA: Oh, dont be silly.

MRS PEARCE [*placing herself behind Eliza's chair*]: You mustnt speak to the gentleman like that.

LIZA: Well, why wont he speak sensible to me?

HIGGINS: Come back to business. How much do you suppose to pay me for the lessons?

LIZA: Oh, I know whats right. A lady friend of mine gets French lessons for eighteenpence an hour from a real French gentleman. Well, you wouldnt have the face to ask me the same for teaching me my own language as you would for French; so I wont give more than a shilling. Take it or leave it.

HIGGINS [*walking up and down the room rattling his keys and his cash in his pockets*]: You know, Pickering, if you consider a shilling, not as a simple shilling, but as a percentage of this girl's income, it works out as fully equivalent to sixty or seventy guineas from a millionaire.

PICKERING: How so?

HIGGINS: Figure it out. A millionaire has about £150 a day. She earns about half-a-crown.

LIZA [*haughtily*]: Who told you I only—

HIGGINS [*continuing*]: She offers me two-fifths of her day's income for a lesson. Two-fifths of a millionaire's income for a day would be somewhere about £60. It's handsome. By George, it's enormous! it's the biggest offer I ever had.

LIZA [*rising, terrified*]: Sixty pounds! What are you talking about? I never offered you sixty pounds. Where would I get—

HIGGINS: Hold your tongue.

LIZA [*weeping*]: But I aint got sixty pounds. Oh—

MRS PEARCE: Dont cry, you silly girl. Sit down. Nobody is going to touch your money.

HIGGINS: Somebody is going to touch you with a broomstick, if you dont stop snivelling. Sit down.

LIZA [*obeying slowly*]: Ah-ah-ah-ow-oo-o! One would think you was my father.

HIGGINS: If I decide to teach you, I'll be worse than two fathers to you. Here! [*He offers her his silk handkerchief.*]

LIZA: Whats this for?

HIGGINS: To wipe your eyes. To wipe any part of your face that feels moist. Remember: thats your handkerchief; and thats your sleeve. Dont mistake the one for the other if you wish to become a lady in a shop.

*Liza, utterly bewildered, stares helplessly at him.*

MRS PEARCE: It's no use talking to her like that, Mr Higgins: she doesnt understand you. Besides, youre quite wrong: she doesnt do it that way at all. [*She takes the handkerchief.*]

LIZA [*snatching it*]: Here! You give me that handkerchief. He gev it to me, not you.

PICKERING [*laughing*]: He did. I think it must be regarded as her property, Mrs Pearce.

MRS PEARCE [*resigning herself*]: Serve you right, Mr Higgins.

PICKERING: Higgins: I'm interested. What about the ambassador's garden party? I'll say youre the greatest teacher alive if you make that good. I'll bet you all the expenses of the experiment you cant do it. And I'll pay for the lessons.

LIZA: Oh, you are real good. Thank you, Captain.

HIGGINS [*tempted, looking at her*]: It's almost irresistible. She's so deliciously low—so horribly dirty—

LIZA [*protesting extremely*]: Ah-ah-ah-ah-ow-ow-oo-oo!!! I aint dirty: I washed my face and hands afore I come, I did.

PICKERING: Youre certainly not going to turn her head with flattery, Higgins.

MRS PEARCE [*uneasy*]: Oh, dont say that, sir: theres more ways than one of turning a girl's head; and nobody can do it better than Mr Higgins, though he may not always mean it. I do hope, sir, you wont encourage him to do anything foolish.

HIGGINS [*becoming excited as the idea grows on him*]: What is life but a series of inspired follies? The difficulty is to find them to do. Never lose a chance: it doesnt come every day. I shall make a duchess of this draggletailed guttersnipe.

LIZA [*strongly deprecating this view of her*]: Ah-ah-ah-ow-ow-oo!

HIGGINS [*carried away*]: Yes: in six months—in three if she has a good ear and quick tongue—I'll take her anywhere and pass her off as anything. We'll start today: now! this moment! Take her away and clean her, Mrs Pearce. Monkey Brand, if it wont come off any other way. Is there a good fire in the kitchen?

MRS PEARCE [*protesting*]: Yes; but—

HIGGINS [*storming on*]: Take all her clothes off and burn them. Ring up Whiteley or somebody for new ones. Wrap her up in brown paper til they come.

LIZA: Youre no gentleman, youre not, to talk of such things. I'm a good girl, I am; and I know what the like of you are, I do.

HIGGINS: We want none of your Lisson Grove prudery here, young woman. Youve got to learn to behave like a duchess. Take her away, Mrs Pearce. If she gives you any trouble, wallop her.

LIZA [*springing up and running between Pickering and Mrs Pearce for protection*]: No! I'll call the police, I will.

MRS PEARCE: But Ive no place to put her.

HIGGINS: Put her in the dustbin.

LIZA: Ah-ah-ah-ow-ow-oo!

PICKERING: Oh come, Higgins! be reasonable.

MRS PEARCE [*resolutely*]: You must be reasonable, Mr Higgins: really you must. You cant walk over everybody like this.

*Higgins, thus scolded, subsides. The hurricane is succeeded by a zephyr of amiable surprise.*

HIGGINS [*with professional exquisiteness of modulation*]: *I* walk over everybody! My dear Mrs Pearce, my dear Pickering, I never had the slightest intention of walking over anyone. All I propose is that we should be kind to this poor girl. We must help her prepare and fit herself for her new station in life. If I did not express myself clearly it was because I did not wish to hurt her delicacy, or yours.

*Liza, reassured, steals back to her chair.*

MRS PEARCE [*to Pickering*]: Well, did you ever hear anything like that, sir?

PICKERING [*laughing heartily*]: Never, Mrs Pearce: never.

HIGGINS [*patiently*]: Whats the matter?

MRS PEARCE: Well, the matter is, sir, that you cant take a girl up like that as if you were picking up a pebble on the beach.

HIGGINS: Why not?

MRS PEARCE: Why not! But you dont know anything about her. What about her parents? She may be married.

LIZA: Garn!

HIGGINS: There! As the girl very properly says, Garn! Married indeed. Dont you know that a woman of that class looks a worn out drudge of fifty a year after she's married?

LIZA: Whood marry me?

HIGGINS [*suddenly resorting to the most thrillingly beautiful low tones in his best elocutionary style*]: By George, Eliza, the streets will be strewn with the bodies of men shooting themselves for your sake before Ive done with you.

MRS PEARCE: Nonsense, sir. You mustnt talk like that to her.

LIZA [*rising and squaring herself determinedly*]: I'm going away. He's off his chump, he is. I dont want no balmies teaching me.

HIGGINS [*wounded in his tenderest point by her insensibility to his elocution*]: Oh, indeed! I'm mad, am I? Very well, Mrs Pearce: you neednt order the new clothes for her. Throw her out.

LIZA [*whimpering*]: Nah-ow. You got no right to touch me.

MRS PEARCE: You see now what comes of being saucy. [*indicating the door*] This way, please.

LIZA [*almost in tears*]: I didnt want no clothes. I wouldnt have taken them. [*She throws away the handkerchief.*] I can buy my own clothes.

HIGGINS [*deftly retrieving the handkerchief and intercepting her on her reluctant way to the door*]: Youre an ungrateful wicked girl. This is my return for offering to take you out of the gutter and dress you beautifully and make a lady of you.

MRS PEARCE: Stop, Mr Higgins. I wont allow it. It's you that are wicked. Go home to your parents, girl; and tell them to take better care of you.

LIZA: I aint got no parents. They told me I was big enough to earn my own living and turned me out.

MRS PEARCE: Wheres your mother?

LIZA: I aint got no mother. Her that turned me out was my sixth stepmother. But I done without them. And I'm a good girl, I am.

HIGGINS: Very well, then, what on earth is all this fuss about? The girl doesnt belong to anybody—is no use of anybody but me. [*He goes to Mrs Pearce and begins coaxing.*] You can adopt her, Mrs Pearce: I'm sure a daughter would be a great amusement to you. Now dont make any more fuss. Take her downstairs; and—

MRS PEARCE: But whats to become of her? Is she to be paid anything? Do be sensible, sir.

HIGGINS: Oh, pay her whatever is necessary: put it down in the housekeeping book. [*impatiently*] What on earth will she want with money? She'll have her food and her clothes. She'll only drink if you give her money.

LIZA [*turning on him*]: Oh you are a brute. It's a lie: nobody ever saw the sign of liquor on me. [*to Pickering*]: Oh, sir: youre a gentleman: dont let him speak to me like that.

PICKERING [*in good-humoured remonstrance*]: Does it occur to you, Higgins, that the girl has some feelings?

HIGGINS [*looking critically at her*]: Oh no, I dont think so. Not any feelings that we need bother about. [*cheerily*]: Have you, Eliza?

LIZA: I got my feelings same as anyone else.

HIGGINS [*to Pickering, reflectively*]: You see the difficulty?

PICKERING: Eh? What difficulty?

HIGGINS: To get her to talk grammar. The mere pronunciation is easy enough.

LIZA: I dont want to talk grammar. I want to talk like a lady in a flower-shop.

MRS PEARCE: Will you please keep to the point, Mr Higgins. I want to know on what terms the girl is to be here. Is she to have any wages? And what is to become of her when youve finished your teaching? You must look ahead a little.

HIGGINS [*impatiently*]: Whats to become of her if I leave her in the gutter? Tell me that, Mrs Pearce.

MRS PEARCE: Thats her own business, not yours, Mr Higgins.

HIGGINS: Well, when Ive done with her, we can throw her back into the gutter; and then it will be her own business again; so thats all right.

LIZA: Oh, youve no feeling heart in you: you dont care for nothing but yourself. [*She rises and takes the floor resolutely.*] Here! Ive had enough of this. I'm going. [*making for the door*] You ought to be ashamed of yourself, you ought.

HIGGINS [*snatching a chocolate cream from the piano, his eyes suddenly beginning to twinkle with mischief*]: Have some chocolates, Eliza.

LIZA [*halting, tempted*]: How do I know what might be in them? Ive heard of girls being drugged by the likes of you.

*Higgins whips out his penknife; cuts a chocolate in two; puts one half into his mouth and bolts it; and offers her the other half.*

HIGGINS: Pledge of good faith, Eliza. I eat one half: you eat the other. [*Liza opens her mouth to retort: he pops the half chocolate into it.*] You shall have boxes of them, barrels of them, every day. You shall live on them. Eh?

LIZA [*who has disposed of the chocolate after being nearly choked by it*]: I wouldnt have ate it, only I'm too ladylike to take it out of my mouth.

HIGGINS: Listen, Eliza. I think you said you came in a taxi.

LIZA: Well, what if I did? Ive as good a right to take a taxi as anyone else.

HIGGINS: You have, Eliza; and in future you shall have as many taxis as you want. You shall go up and down and round the town in a taxi every day. Think of that, Eliza.

MRS PEARCE: Mr Higgins: youre tempting the girl. It's not right. She should think of the future.

HIGGINS: At her age! Nonsense! Time enough to think of the future when you havnt any future to think of. No, Eliza: do as this lady does: think of other people's futures; but never think of your own. Think of chocolates, and taxis, and gold, and diamonds.

LIZA: No: I dont want no gold and no diamonds. I'm a good girl, I am. [*She sits down again, with an attempt at dignity.*]

HIGGINS: You shall remain so, Eliza, under the care of Mrs Pearce. And you shall marry an officer in the Guards, with a beautiful moustache: the son of a marquis, who will disinherit him for marrying you, but will relent when he sees your beauty and goodness—

PICKERING: Excuse me, Higgins; but I really must interfere. Mrs Pearce is quite right. If this girl is to put herself in your hands for six months for an experiment in teaching, she must understand thoroughly what she's doing.

HIGGINS: How can she? She's incapable of understanding anything. Besides, do any of us understand what we are doing? If we did, would we ever do it?

PICKERING: Very clever, Higgins; but not to the present point. [*to Eliza*]: Miss Doolittle—

LIZA [*overwhelmed*]: Ah-ah-ow-oo!

HIGGINS: There! Thats all youll get out of Eliza. Ah-ah-ow-oo! No use explaining. As a military man you ought to know that. Give her her orders: thats enough for her. Eliza: you are to live here for the next six months, learning how to speak beautifully, like a lady in a florist's shop. If youre good and do whatever youre told, you shall sleep in a proper bedroom, and have lots to eat, and money to buy chocolates and take rides in taxis. If youre naughty and idle you will sleep in the back kitchen among the black beetles, and be walloped by Mrs Pearce with a broom stick. At the end of six months you shall go to Buckingham Palace in a carriage, beautifully dressed. If the King finds out youre not a lady, you will be taken by the police to the Tower of London, where your head will be cut off as a warning to other presumptuous flower girls. If you are not found out, you shall have a present of seven-and-sixpence to start life with as a lady in a shop. If you refuse this offer you will be a most ungrateful wicked girl; and the angels will weep for you. [*To Pickering*]: Now are you satisfied, Pickering? [*to Mrs Pearce*]: Can I put it more plainly and fairly, Mrs Pearce?

MRS PEARCE [*patiently*]: I think youd better let me speak to the girl properly in private. I dont know that I can take charge of her or consent to the arrangement at all. Of course I know you dont mean her any harm; but when you get what you call interested in people's accents, you never think or care what may happen to them or you. Come with me, Eliza.

HIGGINS: Thats all right. Thank you, Mrs Pearce. Bundle her off to the bathroom.

LIZA [*rising reluctantly and suspiciously*]: Youre a great bully, you are. I wont stay here if I dont like. I wont let nobody wallop me. I never asked to go to Bucknam Palace, I didnt. I was never in trouble with the police, not me. I'm a good girl—

MRS PEARCE: Dont answer back, girl. You dont understand the gentleman. Come with me. [*She leads the way to the door, and holds it open for Eliza.*]

LIZA [*as she goes out*]: Well, what I say is right. I wont go near the King, not if I'm going to have my head cut off. If I'd known what I was letting myself in for, I wouldnt have come here. I always been a good girl; and I never offered to say a word to him; and I dont owe him nothing; and I dont care; and I wont be put upon; and I have my feelings the same as anyone else—

*Mrs Pearce shuts the door; and Eliza's plaints are no longer audible.*

* * *

*Eliza is taken upstairs to the third floor greatly to her surprise, for she expected to be taken down to the scullery. There Mrs Pearce opens a door and take her into a spare bedroom.*

MRS PEARCE: I will have to put you here. This will be your bedroom.

LIZA: O-h, I couldnt sleep here, missus. It's too good for the likes of me. I should be afraid to touch anything. I aint a duchess yet, you know.

MRS PEARCE: You have got to make yourself as clean as the room: then you wont be afraid of it. And you must call me Mrs Pearce, not missus. [*She throws open the door of the dressing-room, now modernized as a bathroom.*]

LIZA: Gawd! whats this? Is this where you wash clothes? Funny sort of copper I call it.

MRS PEARCE: It is not a copper. This is where we wash ourselves, Eliza, and where I am going to wash you.

LIZA: You expect me to get into that and wet myself all over! Not me. I should catch my death. I knew a woman did it every Saturday night; and she died of it.

MRS PEARCE: Mr Higgins has the gentlemen's bathroom downstairs; and he has a bath every morning, in cold water.

LIZA: Ugh! He's made of iron, that man.

MRS PEARCE: If you are to sit with him and the Colonel and be taught you will have to do the same. They wont like the smell of you if you dont. But you can have the water as hot as you like. There are two taps: hot and cold.

LIZA [*weeping*]: I couldnt. I dursnt. Its not natural: it would kill me. Ive never had a bath in my life: not what youd call a proper one.

MRS PEARCE: Well, dont you want to be clean and sweet and decent, like a lady? You know you cant be a nice girl inside if youre a dirty slut outside.

LIZA: Boohoo!!!!

MRS PEARCE: Now stop crying and go back into your room and take off all your clothes. Then wrap yourself in this [*taking down a gown from its peg and handing it to her*] and come back to me. I will get the bath ready.

LIZA [*all tears*]: I cant. I wont. I'm not used to it. Ive never took off all my clothes before. It's not right: it's not decent.

MRS PEARCE: Nonsense, child. Dont you take off all your clothes every night when you go to bed?

LIZA [*amazed*]: No. Why should I? I should catch my death. Of course I take off my skirt.

MRS PEARCE: Do you mean that you sleep in the underclothes you wear in the daytime?

LIZA: What else have I to sleep in?

MRS PEARCE: You will never do that again as long as you live here. I will get you a proper nightdress.

LIZA: Do you mean change into cold things and lie awake shivering half the night? You want to kill me, you do.

MRS PEARCE: I want to change you from a frowzy slut to a clean respectable girl fit to sit with the gentlemen in the study. Are you going to trust me and do what I tell you or be thrown out and sent back to your flower basket?

LIZA: But you dont know what the cold is to me. You dont know how I dread it.

MRS PEARCE: Your bed wont be cold here: I will put a hot water bottle in it. [*pushing her into the bedroom*] Off with you and undress.

LIZA: Oh, if only I'd a known what a dreadful thing it is to be clean I'd never have come. I didnt know when I was well off. I—[*Mrs Pearce pushes her through the door, but leaves it partly open lest her prisoner should take to flight.*]

*Mrs Pearce puts on a pair of white rubber sleeves, and fills the bath mixing hot and cold, and testing the result with the bath thermometer. She perfumes it with a handful of bath salts and adds a palmful of mustard. She then takes a formidable looking long handled scrubbing brush and soaps it profusely with a ball of scented soap.*

*Eliza comes back with nothing on but the bath gown huddled tightly around her, a piteous spectacle of abject terror.*

MRS PEARCE: Now come along. Take that think off.

LIZA: Oh I couldnt, Mrs Pearce: I reely couldnt. I never done such a thing.

MRS PEARCE: Nonsense. Here: step in and tell me whether it's hot enough for you.

LIZA: Ah-oo! Ah-hoo! It's too hot.

MRS PEARCE [*deftly snatching the gown away and throwing Eliza down on her back*]: It wont hurt you.

*She sets to work with the scrubbing brush.*

*Eliza's screams are heartrending.*

* * *

*Meanwhile the Colonel has been having it out with Higgins about Eliza. Pickering has come from the hearth to the chair and seated himself astride of it with his arms on the back to cross-examine him.*

PICKERING: Excuse the straight question, Higgins. Are you a man of good character where women are concerned?

HIGGINS [*moodily*]: Have you ever met a man of good character where women are concerned?

PICKERING: Yes: very frequently.

HIGGINS [*dogmatically, lifting himself on his hands to the level of the piano, and sitting on it with a bounce*]: Well, I havnt. I find that the moment I let a woman make friends with me, she becomes jealous, exacting, suspicious, and a damned nuisance. I find that the moment I let myself make friends with a woman, I become selfish and tyrannical. Women upset everything. When you let them into your life, you find that the woman is driving at one thing and youre driving at another.

PICKERING: At what, for example?

HIGGINS [*coming off the piano restlessly*]: Oh, Lord knows! I suppose the woman wants to live her own life; and the man wants to live his; and each tries to drag the other on to the wrong track. One wants to go north and the other south; and the result is that both have to go east, though they both hate the east wind. [*He sits down on the bench at the keyboard.*] So here I am, confirmed old bachelor, and likely to remain so.

PICKERING [*rising and standing over him gravely*]: Come, Higgins! You know what I mean. If I'm to be in this business I shall feel responsible for that girl. I hope it's understood that no advantage is to be taken of her position.

HIGGINS: What! That thing! Sacred, I assure you. [*rising to explain*] You see, she'll be a pupil; and teaching would be impossible unless pupils were sacred. Ive taught scores of American millionairesses how to speak English: the best looking women in the world. I'm seasoned. They might as well be blocks of wood. I might as well be a block of wood. It's—

*Mrs Pearce opens the door. She has Eliza's hat in her hand. Pickering retires to the easy-chair at the hearth and sits down.*

HIGGINS [*eagerly*]: Well, Mrs Pearce: is it all right?

MRS PEARCE [*at the door*]: I just wish to trouble you with a word, if I may, Mr Higgins.

HIGGINS: Yes, certainly. Come in. [*She comes forward.*] Dont burn that, Mrs Pearce. I'll keep it as a curiosity. [*He takes the hat.*]

MRS PEARCE: Handle it carefully, sir, *please*. I had to promise her not to burn it; but I had better put it in the oven for a while.

HIGGINS [*putting it down hastily on the piano*]: Oh! thank you. Well, what have you to say to me?

PICKERING: Am I in the way?

MRS PEARCE: Not at all, sir. Mr Higgins: will you please be very particular what you say before the girl?

HIGGINS [*sternly*]: Of course. I'm always particular about what I say. Why do you say this to me?

MRS PEARCE [*unmoved*]: No, sir: youre not at all particular when youve mislaid anything or when you get a little impatient. Now it doesnt matter before me: I'm used to it. But you really must not swear before the girl.

HIGGINS [*indignantly*]: *I* swear! [*most emphatically*]: I never swear. I detest the habit. What the devil do you mean?

MRS PEARCE [*stolidly*]: Thats what I mean, sir. You swear a great deal too much. I dont mind your damning and blasting, and *what* the devil and *where* the devil and *who* the devil—

HIGGINS: Mrs Pearce: this language from your lips! Really!

MRS PEARCE [*not to be put off* ]—but there is a certain word I must ask you not to use. The girl used it herself when she began to enjoy the bath. It begins with the same letter as bath. She knows no better; she learnt it at her mother's knee. But she must not hear it from your lips.

HIGGINS [*loftily*]: I cannot charge myself with having ever uttered it, Mrs Pearce. [*She looks at him steadfastly. He adds, hiding an uneasy conscience with a judicial air*]: Except perhaps in a moment of extreme and justifiable excitement.

MRS PEARCE: Only this morning, sir, you applied it to your boots, to the butter, and to the brown bread.

HIGGINS: Oh, that! Mere alliteration, Mrs Pearce, natural to a poet.

MRS PEARCE: Well, sir, whatever you choose to call it, I beg you not to let the girl hear you repeat it.

HIGGINS: Oh, very well, very well. Is that all?

MRS PEARCE: No, sir. We shall have to be very particular with this girl as to personal cleanliness.

HIGGINS: Certainly. Quite right. Most important.

MRS PEARCE: I mean not to be slovenly about her dress or untidy in leaving things about.

HIGGINS [*going to her solemnly*]: Just so. I intended to call your attention to that. [*He passes on to Pickering, who is enjoying the conversation immensely.*] It is these little things that matter, Pickering. Take care of the pence and the pounds will take care of themselves is as true of personal habits as of money. [*He comes to anchor on the hearthrug, with the air of a man in an unassailable position.*]

MRS PEARCE: Yes, sir. Then might I ask you not to come down to breakfast in your dressing-gown, or at any rate not to use it as a napkin to the extent you do, sir. And if you would be so good as not to eat everything off the same plate, and to remember not to put the porridge saucepan out of your hand on the clean tablecloth, it would be a better example to the girl. You know you nearly choked yourself with a fishbone in the jam only last week.

HIGGINS [*routed from the hearthrug and drifting back to the piano*]: I may do these things sometimes in absence of mind; but surely I dont do them habitually. [*angrily*] By the way: my dressing-gown smells most damnably of benzine.

MRS PEARCE: No doubt it does, Mr Higgins. But if you will wipe your fingers—

HIGGINS [*yelling*]: Oh very well, very well: I'll wipe them in my hair in future.

MRS PEARCE: I hope youre not offended, Mr Higgins.

HIGGINS [*shocked at finding himself thought capable of an unamiable sentiment*]: Not at all, not at all. Youre quite right, Mrs Pearce: I shall be particularly careful before the girl. Is that all?

MRS PEARCE: No, sir. Might she use some of those Japanese dresses you brought from abroad? I really cant put her back into her old things.

HIGGINS: Certainly. Anything you like. Is *that* all?

MRS PEARCE: Thank you, sir. Thats all. [*She goes out.*]

HIGGINS: You know, Pickering, that woman has the most extraordinary ideas about me. Here I am, a shy, diffident sort of man. Ive never been able to feel really grown-up and tremendous, like other chaps. And yet she's firmly persuaded that I'm an arbitrary overbearing bossing kind of person. I cant account for it.

*Mrs Pearce returns.*

MRS PEARCE: If you please, sir, the trouble's beginning already. Theres a dustman downstairs, Alfred Doodlittle, wants to see you. He says you have his daughter here.

PICKERING [*rising*]: Phew! I say!

HIGGINS [*promptly*]: Send the blackguard up.

MRS PEARCE: Oh, very well, sir. [*She goes out.*]

PICKERING: He may not be a blackguard, Higgins.

HIGGINS: Nonsense. Of course he's a blackguard.

PICKERING: Whether he is or not, I'm afraid we shall have some trouble with him.

HIGGINS [*confidently*]: Oh no: I think not. If theres any trouble he shall have it with me, not I with him. And we are sure to get something interesting out of him.

PICKERING: About the girl?

HIGGINS: No. I mean his dialect.

PICKERING: Oh!

MRS PEARCE [*at the door*]: Doolittle, sir. [*She admits Doolittle and retires.*]

*Alfred Doolittle is an elderly but vigorous dustman, clad in the costume of his profession, including a hat with a back brim covering his neck and shoulders. He has well marked and rather interesting features, and seems equally free from fear and conscience. He has a remarkably expressive voice, the result of a habit of giving vent to his feelings without reserve. His present pose is that of wounded honour and stern resolution.*

DOOLITTLE [*at the door, uncertain which of the two gentlemen is his man*]: Professor Iggins?

HIGGINS: Here. Good morning. Sit down.

DOOLITTLE: Morning, Governor. [*He sits down magisterially.*] I come about a very serious matter, Governor.

HIGGINS [*to Pickering*]: Brought up in Hounslow. Mother Welsh. I should think. [*Doolittle opens his mouth, amazed. Higgins continues*]: What do you want, Doolittle?

DOOLITTLE [*menacingly*]: I want my daughter: thats what I want. See?

HIGGINS: Of course you do. Youre her father, arnt you? You dont suppose anyone else wants her, do you? I'm glad to see you have some spark of family feeling left. She's upstairs. Take her away at once.

DOOLITTLE [*rising, fearfully taken aback*]: What!

HIGGINS: Take her away. Do you suppose I'm going to keep your daughter for you?

DOOLITTLE [*remonstrating*]: Now, now, look here, Governor. Is this reasonable? Is it fairity to take advantage of a man like this? The girl belongs to me. You got her. Where do I come in? [*He sits down again.*]

HIGGINS: Your daughter had the audacity to come to my house and ask me to teach her how to speak properly so that she could get a place in a flower-shop. This gentleman and my housekeeper have been here all the time. [*bullying him*] How dare you come here and attempt to blackmail me? You sent her here on purpose.

DOOLITTLE [*protesting*]: No, Governor.

HIGGINS: You must have. How else could you possibly know that she is here?

DOOLITTLE: Dont take a man up like that, Governor.

HIGGINS: The police shall take you up. This is a plant—a plot to extort money by threats. I shall telephone for the police. [*He goes resolutely to the telephone and opens the directory.*]

DOOLITTLE: Have I asked you for a brass farthing? I leave it to the gentleman here: have I said a word about money?

HIGGINS [*throwing the book aside and marching down on Doolittle with a poser*]: What else did you come for?

DOOLITTLE [*sweetly*]: Well, what *would* a man come for? Be human, Governor.

HIGGINS [*disarmed*]: Alfred: did you put her up to it?

DOOLITTLE: So help me, Governor, I never did. I take my Bible oath I aint seen the girl these two months past.

HIGGINS: Then how did you know she was here?

DOOLITTLE [*'most musical, most melancholy'*]: I'll tell you, Governor, if youll only let me get a word in. I'm willing to tell you. I'm wanting to tell you. I'm waiting to tell you.

HIGGINS: Pickering: this chap has a certain natural gift of rhetoric. Observe the rhythm of his native woodnotes wild. 'I'm willing to tell you: I'm wanting to tell you: I'm waiting to tell you.' Sentimental rhetoric! thats the Welsh strain in him. It also accounts for his mendacity and dishonesty.

PICKERING: Oh, *please*, Higgins: I'm west country myself. [*to Doolittle*] How did you know the girl was here if you didnt send her?

DOOLITTLE: It was like this, Governor. The girl took a boy in the taxi to give him a jaunt. Son of her landlady, he is. He hung about on the chance of her giving him another ride home. Well, she sent him back for her luggage when she heard you was willing for her to stop here. I met the boy at the corner of Long Acre and Endell Street.

HIGGINS: Public house. Yes?

DOOLITTLE: The poor man's club, Governor: why shouldnt I?

PICKERING: Do let him tell his story, Higgins.

DOOLITTLE: He told me what was up. And I ask you, what was my feelings and my duty as a father? I says to the boy, 'You bring me the luggage,' I says—

PICKERING: Why didnt you go for it yourself?

DOOLITTLE: Landlady wouldnt have trusted me with it, Governor. She's that kind of woman: *you* know. I had to give the boy a penny afore he trusted me with it, the little swine. I brought it to her just to oblige you like, and make myself agreeable. Thats all.

HIGGINS: How much luggage?

DOOLITTLE: Musical instrument, Governor. A few pictures, a trifle of jewellery, and a bird-cage. She said she didnt want no clothes. What was I to think from that, Governor? I ask you as a parent what was I to think?

HIGGINS: So you came to rescue her from worse than death, eh?

DOOLITTLE [*appreciatively: relieved at being so well understood*]: Just so, Governor. Thats right.

PICKERING: But why did you bring her luggage if you intended to take her away?

DOOLITTLE: Have I said a word about taking her away? Have I now?

HIGGINS [*determinedly*]: Youre going to take her away, double quick. [*He crosses to the hearth and rings the bell.*]

DOOLITTLE [*rising*]: No, Governor. Dont say that. I'm not the man to stand in my girl's light. Heres a career opening for her, as you might say; and—

*Mrs Pearce opens the door and awaits orders.*

HIGGINS: Mrs Pearce: this is Eliza's father. He has come to take her away. Give her to him. [*He goes back to the piano, with an air of washing his hands of the whole affair.*]

DOOLITTLE: No. This is a misunderstanding. Listen here—

MRS PEARCE: He cant take her away, Mr Higgins: how can he? You told me to burn her clothes.

DOOLITTLE: Thats right. I cant carry the girl through the streets like a blooming monkey, can I? I put it to you.

HIGGINS: You have put it to me that you want your daughter. Take your daughter. If she has no clothes go out and buy her some.

DOOLITTLE [*desperate*]: Wheres the clothes she come in? Did I burn them or did your missus here?

MRS PEARCE: I am the housekeeper, if you please. I have sent for some clothes for your girl. When they come you can take her away. You can wait in the kitchen. This way, please.

*Doolittle, much troubled, accompanies her to the door; then hesitates; finally turns confidentially to Higgins.*

DOOLITTLE: Listen here, Governor. You and me is men of the world aint we?

HIGGINS: Oh! Men of the world, are we? Youd better go, Mrs Pearce.

MRS PEARCE: I think so, indeed, sir. [*She goes, with dignity.*]

PICKERING: The floor is yours, Mr Doolittle.

DOOLITTLE [*to Pickering*]: I thank you, Governor. [*to Higgins, who takes refuge on the piano bench, a little overwhelmed by the proximity of his visitor; for Doolittle has a professional flavour of dust about him.*] Well, the truth is, Ive taken a sort of fancy to you, Governor; and if you want the girl, I'm not so set on having her back home again but what I might be open to an arrangement. Regarded in the light of a young woman, she's a fine handsome girl. As a daughter she's not worth her keep;

and so I tell you straight. All I ask is my rights as a father; and youre the last man alive to expect me to let her go for nothing; for I can see youre one of the straight sort, Governor. Well, whats a five-pound note to you? and whats Eliza to me? [*He turns to his chair and sits down judicially.*]

PICKERING: I think you ought to know, Doolittle, that Mr Higgins's intentions are entirely honourable.

DOOLITTLE: Course they are, Governor. If I thought they wasnt, I'd ask fifty.

HIGGINS [*revolted*]: Do you mean to say that you would sell your daughter for £50?

DOOLITTLE: Not in a general way I wouldnt; but to oblige a gentleman like you I'd do a good deal, I do assure you.

PICKERING: Have you no morals, man?

DOOLITTLE [*unabashed*]: Cant afford them, Governor. Neither could you if you was as poor as me. Not that I mean any harm, you know. But if Liza is going to have a bit out of this, why not me too?

HIGGINS [*troubled*]: I dont know what to do, Pickering. There can be no question that as a matter of morals it's a positive crime to give this chap a farthing. And yet I feel a sort of rough justice in his claim.

DOOLITTLE: Thats it, Governor. Thats all I say. A father's heart, as it were.

PICKERING: Well, I know the feeling; but really it seems hardly right—

DOOLITTLE: Dont say that, Governor. Dont look at it that way. What am I, Governors both? I ask you, what *am* I? I'm the one of the undeserving poor: thats what I am. Think of what that means to a man. It means that he's up agen middle class morality all the time. If theres anything going, and I put in for a bit of it, it's always the same story: 'Youre undeserving; so you cant have it.' But my needs is as great as the most deserving widow's that ever got money out of six different charities in one week for the death of the same husband. I dont need less than a deserving man: I need more. I dont eat less hearty than him; and I drink a lot more. I want a bit of amusement, cause I'm a thinking man. I want cheerfulness and a song and a band when I feel low. Well, they charge me just the same for everything as they charge the deserving. What is middle class morality? Just an excuse for never giving me anything. Therefore, I ask you, as two gentlemen, not to play that game on me. I'm playing straight with you. I aint pretending to be deserving. I'm undeserving; and I mean to go on being undeserving. I like it; and thats the truth. Will you take advantage of a man's nature to do him out of the price of his own daughter what he's brought up and fed and clothed by the sweat of his brow until she's growed big enough to be interesting to you two gentlemen? Is five pounds unreasonable? I put it to you; and I leave it to you.

HIGGINS [*rising, and going over to Pickering*]: Pickering: if we were to take this man in hand for three months, he could choose between a seat in the Cabinet and a popular pulpit in Wales.

PICKERING: What do you say to that, Doolittle?

DOOLITTLE: Not me, Governor, thank you kindly. Ive heard all the preachers and all the prime ministers—for I'm a thinking man and game for politics or religion or social reform same as all the other amusements—and I tell you it's a dog's life any way you look at it. Undeserving poverty is my line. Taking one station in society with another, it's—it's—well, it's the only one that has any ginger in it, to my taste.

HIGGINS: I suppose we must give him a fiver.

PICKERING: He'll make a bad use of it, I'm afraid.

DOOLITTLE: Not me, Governor, so help me I wont. Dont you be afraid that I'll save it and spare it and live idle on it. There wont be a penny of it left by Monday: I'll have to go to work same as if I'd never had it. It wont pauperize me, you bet. Just one good spree for myself and the missus, giving pleasure to ourselves and employment to others, and satisfaction to you to think it's not been throwed away. You couldnt spend it better.

HIGGINS [*taking out his pocket book and coming between Doolittle and the piano*]: This is irresistible. Lets give him ten. [*He offers two notes to the dustman.*]

DOOLITTLE: No, Governor. She wouldnt have the heart to spend ten; and perhaps I shouldnt either. Ten pounds is a lot of money: it makes a man feel prudent like; and then goodbye to happiness. You give me what I ask you, Governor: not a penny more, and not a penny less.

PICKERING: Why dont you marry that missus of yours? I rather draw the line at encouraging that sort of immorality.

DOOLITTLE: Tell her so, Governor: tell her so. *I*'m willing. It's me that suffers by it. Ive no hold on her. I got to be agreeable to her. I got to give her presents. I got to buy her clothes something sinful. I'm a slave to that woman, Governor, just because I'm not her lawful husband. And she knows it too. Catch her marrying me! Take my advice, Governor: marry Eliza while she's young and dont know no better. If you dont youll be sorry for it after. If you do, *she'll* be sorry for it after; but better her than you, because youre a man, and she's only a woman and dont know how to be happy anyhow.

HIGGINS: Pickering: if we listen to this man another minute, we shall have no convictions left. [*to Doolittle*]: Five pounds I think you said.

DOOLITTLE: Thank you kindly, Governor.

HIGGINS: Youre sure you wont take ten?

DOOLITTLE: Not now. Another time, Governor.

HIGGINS [*handing him a five-pound note*]: Here you are.

DOOLITTLE: Thank you, Governor, Good morning. [*He hurries to the door, anxious to get away with his booty. When he opens it he is confronted with a dainty and exquisitely clean young Japanese lady in a simple blue cotton kimono printed cunningly with small white jasmine blossoms. Mrs Pearce is with her. He gets out of her way deferentially and apologizes.*] Beg pardon miss.

THE JAPANESE LADY: Garn! Dont you know your own daughter?

DOOLITTLE: } *exclaiming* { Bly me! it's Eliza!
HIGGINS: } *simul-* { Whats that? This!
PICKERING: } *taneously* { By Jove!

LIZA: Dont I look silly?

MRS PEARCE [*at the door*]: Now, Mr Higgins, please dont say anything to make the girl conceited about herself.

HIGGINS [*conscientiously*]: Oh! Quite right, Mrs Pearce. [*to Eliza*]: Yes: damned silly.

MRS PEARCE: Please, sir.

HIGGINS [*correcting himself* ]: I mean extremely silly.

LIZA: I should look all right with my hat on. [*She takes up her hat; puts it on; and walks across the room to the fireplace with a fashionable air.*]

HIGGINS: A new fashion, by George! And it ought to look horrible!

DOOLITTLE [*with fatherly pride*]: Well, I never thought she'd clean up as good looking as that, Governor. She's a credit to me, aint she?

LIZA: I tell you, it's easy to clean up here. Hot and cold water on tap, just as much as you like, there is. Woolly towels, there is; and a towel horse so hot, it burns your fingers. Soft brushes to scrub yourself, and a wooden bowl of soap smelling like primroses. Now I know why ladies is so clean. Washing's a treat for them. Wish they could see what it is for the like of me!

HIGGINS: I'm glad the bathroom met with your approval.

LIZA: It didnt: not all of it; and I dont care who hears me say it. Mrs Pearce knows.

HIGGINS: What was wrong, Mrs Pearce?

MRS PEARCE [*blandly*]: Oh, nothing, sir. It doesnt matter.

LIZA: I had a good mind to break it. I didnt know which way to look. But I hung a towel over it, I did.

HIGGINS: Over what?

MRS PEARCE: Over the looking-glass, sir.

HIGGINS: Doolittle: you have brought your daughter up too strictly.

DOOLITTLE: Me! I never brought her up at all, except to give her a lick of a strap now and again. Dont put it on me. Governor. She aint accustomed to it, you see: thats all. But she'll soon pick up your free-and-easy ways.

LIZA: I'm a good girl, I am; and I wont pick up no free-and-easy ways.

HIGGINS: Eliza: if you say again that youre a good girl, your father shall take you home.

LIZA: Not him. You dont know my father. All he come here for was to touch you for some money to get drunk on.

DOOLITTLE: Well, what else would I want money for? To put into the plate in church, I suppose. [*She puts out her tongue at him. He is so incensed by this that Pickering presently finds it necessary to step between them.*] Dont you give me none of your lip; and dont let me hear you giving this gentleman any of it either, or youll hear from me about it. See?

HIGGINS: Have you any further advice to give her before you go, Doolittle? Your blessing, for instance.

DOOLITTLE: No, Governor: I aint such a mug as to put up my children to all I know myself. Hard enough to hold them in without that. If you want Eliza's mind improved, Governor, you do it yourself with a strap. So long, gentlemen. [*He turns to go.*]

HIGGINS [*impressively*]: Stop. Youll come regularly to see your daughter. It's your duty, you know. My brother is a clergyman; and he could help you in your talks with her.

DOOLITTLE [*evasively*]: Certainly, I'll come, Governor. Not just this week, because I have a job at a distance. But later on you may depend on me. Afternoon, gentlemen. Afternoon, maam. [*He touches his hat to Mrs Pearce, who disdains the salutation and goes out. He winks at Higgins, thinking him probably a fellow sufferer from Mrs Pearce's difficult disposition, and follows her.*]

LIZA: Dont you believe the old liar. He'd as soon you set a bulldog on him as a clergyman. You wont see him again in a hurry.

HIGGINS: I dont want to, Eliza. Do you?

LIZA: Not me. I dont want to see him again, I dont. He's a disgrace to me, he is, collecting dust, instead of working at his trade.

PICKERING: What is his trade, Eliza?

LIZA: Talking money out of other people's pockets into his own. His proper trade's a navvy; and he works at it sometimes too—for exercise—and earns good money at it. Aint you going to call me Miss Doolittle any more?

PICKERING: I beg your pardon, Miss Doolittle. It was a slip of the tongue.

LIZA: Oh, I dont mind; only it sounded so genteel. I *should* just like to take a taxi to the corner of Tottenham Court road and get out there and tell it to wait for me, just to put the girls in their place a bit. I wouldnt speak to them, you know.

PICKERING: Better wait til we get you something really fashionable.

HIGGINS: Besides, you shouldnt cut your old friends now that you have risen in the world. Thats what we call snobbery.

LIZA: You dont call the like of them my friends now, I should hope. Theyve took it out of me often enough with their ridicule when they had the chance; and now I mean to get a bit of my own back. But if I'm to have fashionable clothes, I'll wait. I should like to have some. Mrs Pearce says youre going to give me some to wear in bed at night different to what I wear in the daytime; but it do seem a waste of money when you could get something to shew. Besides, I never could fancy changing into cold things on a winter night.

MRS PEARCE [*coming back*]: Now, Eliza. The new things have come for you to try on.

LIZA: Ah-ow-oo-ooh! [*She rushes out.*]

MRS PEARCE [*following her*]: Oh, dont rush about like that, girl. [*She shuts the door behind her.*]

HIGGINS: Pickering: we have taken on a stiff job.

PICKERING [*with conviction*]: Higgins: we have.

* * *

*There seems to be some curiosity as to what Higgins's lessons to Eliza were like. Well, here is a sample: the first one.*

*Picture Eliza, in her new clothes, and feeling her inside put out of step by a lunch, dinner, and breakfast of a kind to which it is unaccustomed, seated with Higgins and the Colonel in the study, feeling like a hospital out-patient at a first encounter with the doctors.*

*Higgins, constitutionally unable to sit still, discomposes her still more by striding restlessly about. But for the reassuring presence and quietude of her friend the Colonel she would run for her life, even back to Drury Lane.*

HIGGINS: Say your alphabet.

LIZA: I know my alphabet. Do you think I know nothing? I dont need to be taught like a child.

HIGGINS [*thundering*]: Say your alphabet.

PICKERING: Say it, Miss Doolittle. You will understand presently. Do what he tells you; and let him teach you in his own way.

LIZA: Oh well, if you put it like that—Ahyee, bəyee, cəyee, dəyee—

HIGGINS [*with a roar of a wounded lion*]: Stop. Listen to this, Pickering. This is what we pay for as elementary education. This unfortunate animal has been locked up for nine years in school at our expense to teach her to speak and read the language of Shakespeare and Milton. And the result is Ahyee, Bə-yee, Cə-yee, Də-yee. [*to Eliza*]: Say A, B, C, D.

LIZA [*almost in tears*]: But I'm sayin it. Ahyee, Bəyee, Cə-yee—

HIGGINS: Stop. Say a cup of tea.

LIZA: A cappətə-ee.

HIGGINS: Put your tongue forward until it squeezes against the top of your lower teeth. Now say cup.

LIZA: C-c-c—I cant. C-Cup.

PICKERING: Good. Splendid, Miss Doolittle.

HIGGINS: By Jupiter, she's done it at the first shot. Pickering: we shall make a duchess of her. [*to Eliza*]: Now do you think you could possibly say tea? Not tə-yee, mind: if you ever say bə-yee cə-yee də-yee again you shall be dragged round the room three times by the hair of your head. [*fortissimo*] T, T, T, T.

LIZA [*weeping*]: I cant hear no difference cep that it sound more genteel-like when you say it.

HIGGINS: Well, if you can hear that difference, what the devil are you crying for? Pickering: give her a chocolate.

PICKERING: No, no. Never mind crying a little, Miss Doolittle: you are doing very well; and the lessons wont hurt. I promise you I wont let him drag you round the room by your hair.

HIGGINS: Be off with you to Mrs Pearce and tell her about it. Think about it. Try to do it by yourself: and keep your tongue well forward in your mouth instead of trying to roll it up and swallow it. Another lesson at half-past four this afternoon. Away with you.

*Eliza, still sobbing, rushes from the room.*

*And that is the sort of ordeal poor Eliza has to go through for months before we meet her again on her first appearance in London society of the professional class.*

## ACT III

*It is Mrs Higgins's at-home day. Nobody has yet arrived. Her drawing room, in a flat on Chelsea Embankment, has three windows looking on the river; and the ceiling is not so lofty as it would be in an older house of the same pretensions. The windows are open, giving access to a balcony with flower pots. If you stand with your face to the windows, you have the fireplace on your left and the door in the right-hand wall close to the corner nearest the windows.*

*Mrs Higgins was brought up on Morris and Burne Jones; and her room, which is very unlike her son's room in Wimpole Street, is not crowded with furniture and little tables and nicknacks. In the middle of the room there is a big ottoman; and this, with the carpet, the Morris wall-papers, and the Morris chintz window curtains and brocade covers of the ottoman and its cushions, supply all the ornament, and are much too handsome to be hidden by odds and ends of useless things. A few good oil-paintings from the exhibitions in the Grosvenor Gallery thirty years ago (the Burne Jones, not the Whistler side of them) are on the walls. The only landscape is a Cecil Lawson on the scale of a Rubens. There is a portrait of Mrs Higgins as she was when she defied fashion in her youth in one of the beautiful Rossettian costumes which, when caricatured by people who did not understand, led to the absurdities of popular estheticism in the eighteen-seventies.*

*In the corner diagonally opposite the door Mrs Higgins, now over sixty and long past taking the trouble to dress out of the fashion, sits writing at an elegantly simple writing-table with a bell button within reach of her hand. There is a Chippendale chair further back in the room between her and the window nearest her side. At the other side of the room, further forward, is an Elizabethan chair roughly carved in the taste of Inigo Jones. On the same side a piano in a decorated case. The corner between the fireplace and the window is occupied by a divan cushioned in Morris chintz.*

*It is between four and five in the afternoon.*

*The door is opened violently; and Higgins enters with his hat on.*

MRS HIGGINS [*dismayed*]: Henry! [*scolding him*] What are you doing here today? It is my at-home day: you promised not to come. [*As he bends to kiss her, she takes his hat off, and presents it to him.*]

HIGGINS: Oh bother! [*He throws the hat down on the table.*]

MRS HIGGINS: Go home at once.

HIGGINS [*kissing her*]: I know, mother. I came on purpose.

MRS HIGGINS: But you mustnt. I'm serious, Henry. You offend all my friends: they stop coming whenever they meet you.

HIGGINS: Nonsense! I know I have no small talk; but people dont mind. [*He sits on the settee.*]

MRS HIGGINS: Oh! dont they? Small talk indeed! What about your large talk? Really, dear, you mustnt stay.

HIGGINS: I must. Ive a job for you. A phonetic job.

MRS HIGGINS: No use, dear. I'm sorry; but I cant get round your vowels; and though I like to get pretty postcards in your patent shorthand, I always have to read the copies in ordinary writing you so thoughtfully send me.

HIGGINS: Well, this isnt a phonetic job.

MRS HIGGINS: You said it was.

HIGGINS: Not your part of it. Ive picked up a girl.

MRS HIGGINS: Does that mean that some girl has picked *you* up?

HIGGINS: Not at all. I dont mean a love affair.

MRS HIGGINS: What a pity!

HIGGINS: Why?

MRS HIGGINS: Well, you never fall in love with anyone under forty-five. When will you discover that there are some rather nice-looking young women about?

HIGGINS: Oh, I cant be bothered with young women. My idea of a lovable woman is somebody as like you as possible. I shall never get into the way of seriously liking young women: some habits lie too deep to be changed. [*rising abruptly and walking about, jingling his money and his keys in his trouser pockets*] Besides, theyre all idiots.

MRS HIGGINS: Do you know what you would do if you really loved me, Henry?

HIGGINS: Oh bother! What? Marry, I suppose.

MRS HIGGINS: No. Stop fidgeting and take your hands out of your pockets. [*With a gesture of despair, he obeys and sits down again.*] Thats a good boy. Now tell me about the girl.

HIGGINS: She's coming to see you.

MRS HIGGINS: I dont remember asking her.

HIGGINS: You didnt. *I* asked her. If youd known her you wouldnt have asked her.

MRS HIGGINS: Indeed! Why?

HIGGINS: Well, it's like this. She's a common flower girl. I picked her off the kerbstone.

MRS HIGGINS: And invited her to my at-home?

HIGGINS [*rising and coming to her to coax her*]: Oh, thatll be all right. Ive taught her to speak properly; and she has strict orders as to her behaviour. She's to keep to two subjects: the weather and everybody's health—Fine day and How do you do, you know—and not to let herself go on things in general. That will be safe.

MRS HIGGINS: Safe! To talk about our health! about our insides! perhaps about our outsides! How could you be so silly, Henry?

HIGGINS [*impatiently*]: Well, she must talk about something. [*He controls himself and sits down again.*] Oh, she'll be all right: dont you fuss. Pickering is in it with me. Ive a sort of bet on that I'll pass her off as a duchess in six months. I started on her some months ago; and she's getting on like a house on fire. I shall win my bet. She has a quick ear; and she's been easier to teach than my middle-class pupils because she's had to learn a complete new language. She talks English almost as you talk French.

MRS HIGGINS: Thats satisfactory, at all events.

HIGGINS: Well, it is and it isnt.

MRS HIGGINS: What does that mean?

HIGGINS: You see, Ive got her pronunciation all right; but you have to consider not only *how* a girl pronounces, but *what* she pronounces; and thats where—

*They are interrupted by the parlour-maid, announcing guests.*

THE PARLOUR-MAID: Mrs and Miss Eynsford Hill. [*She withdraws.*]

HIGGINS: Oh Lord! [*He rises; snatches his hat from the table; and makes for the door; but before he reaches it his mother introduces him.*]

*Mrs and Miss Eynsford Hill are the mother and daughter who sheltered from the rain in Covent Garden. The mother is well bred, quiet, and has the habitual anxiety of straitened means. The daughter has acquired a gay air of being very much at home in society: the bravado of genteel poverty.*

MRS EYNSFORD HILL [*to Mrs Higgins*]: How do you do? [*They shake hands.*]

MISS EYNSFORD HILL: How d'you do? [*She shakes.*]

MRS HIGGINS [*introducing*]: My son Henry.

MRS EYNSFORD HILL: Your celebrated son! I have so longed to meet you, Professor Higgins.

HIGGINS [*glumly, making no movement in her direction*]: Delighted. [*He backs against the piano and bows brusquely.*]

MRS EYNSFORD HILL [*going to him with confident familiarity*]: How do you do?

HIGGINS [*staring at her*]: Ive seen you before somewhere. I havnt the ghost of a notion where; but Ive heard your voice. [*drearily*] It doesnt matter. Youd better sit down.

MRS HIGGINS: I'm sorry to say that my celebrated son has no manners. You mustnt mind him.

MISS EYNSFORD HILL [*gaily*]: I dont. [*She sits in the Elizabethan chair.*]

MRS EYNSFORD HILL [*a little bewildered*]: Not at all. [*She sits on the ottoman between her daughter and Mrs Higgins, who has turned her chair away from the writing-table.*]

HIGGINS: Oh, have I been rude? I didnt mean to be.

*He goes to the central window, through which, with his back to the company, he contemplates the river and the flowers in Battersea Park on the opposite bank as if they were a frozen desert.*

*The parlour-maid returns, ushering in Pickering.*

THE PARLOUR-MAID: Colonel Pickering. [*She withdraws.*]

PICKERING: How do you do, Mrs Higgins?

MRS HIGGINS: So glad youve come. Do you know Mrs Eynsford Hill—Miss Eynsford Hill?

*Exchange of bows. The Colonel brings the Chippendale chair a little forward between Mrs Hill and Mrs Higgins, and sits down.*

PICKERING: Has Henry told you what weve come for?

HIGGINS [*over his shoulder*]: We were interrupted: damn it!

MRS HIGGINS: Oh Henry, Henry, really!

MRS EYNSFORD HILL [*half rising*]: Are we in the way?

MRS HIGGINS [*rising and making her sit down again*]: No, no. You couldnt have come more fortunately: we want you to meet a friend of ours.

HIGGINS [*turning hopefully*]: Yes, by George! We want two or three people. Youll do as well as anybody else.

*The parlour-maid returns, ushering Freddy.*

THE PARLOUR-MAID: Mr Eynsford Hill.

HIGGINS [*almost audibly, past endurance*]: God of Heaven! another of them.

FREDDY [*shaking hands with Mrs Higgins*]: Ahdedo?

MRS HIGGINS: Very good of you to come. [*introducing*] Colonel Pickering.

FREDDY [*bowing*]: Ahdedo?

MRS HIGGINS: I dont think you know my son, Professor Higgins.

FREDDY [*going to Higgins*]: Ahdedo?

HIGGINS [*looking at him much as if he were a pickpocket*] I'll take my oath Ive met *you* before somewhere. Where was it?

FREDDY: I dont think so.

HIGGINS [*resignedly*]: It dont matter, anyhow. Sit down. [*He shakes Freddy's hand, and almost slings him on to the ottoman with his face to the windows; then comes round to the other side of it.*]

HIGGINS: Well, here we are, anyhow! [*He sits down on the ottoman next Mrs Eynsford Hill on her left.*] And now what the devil are we going to talk about until Eliza comes?

MRS HIGGINS: Henry: you are the life and soul of the Royal Society's soirées; but really youre rather trying on more commonplace occasions.

HIGGINS: Am I? Very sorry. [*beaming suddenly*] I suppose I am, you know. [*uproariously*] Ha, ha!

MISS EYNSFORD HILL [*who considers Higgins quite eligible matrimonially*]: I sympathize. I havnt any small talk. If people would only be frank and say what they really think!

HIGGINS [*relapsing into gloom*]: Lord forbid!

MRS EYNSFORD HILL: [*taking up her daughter's cue*]: But why?

HIGGINS: What they think they ought to think is bad enough, Lord knows; but what they really think would break up the whole show. Do you suppose it would be really agreeable if I were to come out now with what *I* really think?

MISS EYNSFORD HILL [*gaily*]: Is it so very cynical?

HIGGINS: Cynical! Who the dickens said it was cynical? I mean it wouldnt be decent.

MRS EYNSFORD HILL [*seriously*]: Oh! I'm sure you dont mean that, Mr Higgins.

HIGGINS: You see, we're all savages, more or less. We're supposed to be civilized and cultured—to know all about poetry and philosophy and art and science, and so on; but how many of us know even the meanings of these names? [*to Miss Hill*]: What do *you* know of poetry? [*to Mrs Hill*]: What do *you* know of science? [*indicating Freddy*]: What does *he* know of art or science or anything else? What the devil do you imagine I know of philosophy?

MRS HIGGINS [*warningly*]: Or of manners, Henry?

THE PARLOUR-MAID [*opening the door*]: Miss Doolittle. [*She withdraws.*]
HIGGINS [*rising hastily and running to Mrs Higgins*]: Here she is, mother.

*He stands on tiptoe and makes signs over his mother's head to Eliza to indicate to her which lady is her hostess.*

*Eliza, who is exquisitely dressed, produces an impression of such remarkable distinction and beauty as she enters that they all rise, quite fluttered. Guided by Higgins's signals, she comes to Mrs Higgins with studied grace.*

LIZA [*speaking with pedantic correctness of pronunciation and great beauty of tone*]: How do you do, Mrs Higgins? [*She gasps slightly in making sure of the H in Higgins, but is quite successful.*] Mr Higgins told me I might come.
MRS HIGGINS [*cordially*]: Quite right: I'm very glad indeed to see you.
PICKERING: How do you do, Miss Doolittle?
LIZA [*shaking hands with him*]: Colonel Pickering, is it not?
MRS EYNSFORD HILL: I feel sure we have met before, Miss Doolittle. I remember your eyes.
LIZA: How do you do? [*She sits down on the ottoman gracefully in the place just left vacant by Higgins.*]
MRS EYNSFORD HILL [*introducing*]: My daughter Clara.
LIZA: How do you do?
CLARA [*impulsively*]: How do you do? [*She sits down on the ottoman besides Eliza, devouring her with her eyes.*]
FREDDY [*coming to their side of the ottoman*]: Ive certainly had the pleasure.
MRS EYNSFORD HILL [*introducing*]: My son Freddy.
LIZA: How do you do? [*Freddy bows and sits down in the Elizabethan chair, infatuated.*]
HIGGINS [*suddenly*]: By George, yes: it all comes back to me! [*They stare at him.*] Covent Garden! [*lamentably*] What a damned thing!
MRS HIGGINS: Henry, please! [*He is about to sit on the edge of the table.*] Dont sit on my writing-table: youll break it.
HIGGINS [*sulkily*]: Sorry.

*He goes to the divan, stumbling into the fender and over the fire-irons on his way; extricating himself with muttered imprecations; and finishing his disastrous journey by throwing himself so impatiently on the divan that he almost breaks it. Mrs Higgins looks at him, but controls herself and says nothing.*

*A long and painful pause ensues.*

MRS HIGGINS [*at last, conversationally*]: Will it rain, do you think?
LIZA: The shallow depression in the west of these islands is likely to move slowly in an easterly direction. There are no indications of any great change in the barometrical situation.
FREDDY: Ha! ha! how awfully funny!
LIZA: What is wrong with that, young man? I bet I got it right.

FREDDY: Killing!

MRS EYNSFORD HILL: I'm sure I hope it wont turn cold. Theres so much influenza about. It runs right through our whole family regularly every spring.

LIZA [*darkly*]: My aunt died of influenza: so they said.

MRS EYNSFORD HILL [*clicks her tongue sympathetically*]: !!!

LIZA [*in the same tragic tone*]: But it's my belief they done the old woman in.

MRS HIGGINS [*puzzled*]: Done her in?

LIZA: Y-e-e-e-es, Lord love you! Why should she die of influenza? She come through diphtheria right enough the year before. I saw her with my own eyes. Fairly blue with it, she was. They all thought she was dead; but my father he kept ladling gin down her throat til she came to so sudden that she bit the bowl off the spoon.

MRS EYNSFORD HILL [*startled*]: Dear me!

LIZA [*piling up the indictment*]: What call would a woman with that strength in her have to die of influenza? What become of her new straw hat that should have come to me? Somebody pinched it; and what I say is, them as pinched it done her in.

MRS EYNSFORD HILL: What does doing her in mean?

HIGGINS [*hastily*]: Oh, thats the new small talk. To do a person in means to kill them.

MRS EYNSFORD HILL [*to Eliza, horrified*]: You surely dont believe that your aunt was killed?

LIZA: Do I not! Them she lived with would have killed her for a hatpin, let alone a hat.

MRS EYNSFORD HILL: But it cant have been right for your father to pour spirits down her throat like that. It might have killed her.

LIZA: Not her. Gin was mother's milk to her. Besides, he'd poured so much down his own throat that he knew the good of it.

MRS EYNSFORD HILL: Do you mean that he drank?

LIZA: Drank! My word! Something chronic.

MRS EYNSFORD HILL: How dreadful for you!

LIZA: Not a bit. It never did him no harm what I could see. But then he did not keep it up regular. [*cheerfully*] On the burst, as you might say, from time to time. And always more agreeable when he had a drop in. When he was out of work, my mother used to give him four-pence and tell him to go out and not come back until he'd drunk himself cheerful and loving-like. Theres lots of women has to make their husbands drunk to make them fit to live with. [*now quite at her ease*] You see, it's like this. If a man has a bit of a conscience, it always takes him when he's sober; and then it makes him low-spirited. A drop of booze just takes that off and makes him happy. [*to Freddy, who is in convulsions of suppressed laughter*]: Here! what are you sniggering at?

FREDDY: The new small talk. You do it awfully well.

LIZA: If I was doing it proper, what was you laughing at? [*to Higgins*]: Have I said anything I oughtnt?

MRS HIGGINS [*interposing*]: Not at all, Miss Doolittle.

LIZA: Well, thats a mercy, anyhow. [*expansively*] What I always say is—

HIGGINS [*rising and looking at his watch*]: Ahem!

LIZA [*looking round at him; taking the hint; and rising*]: Well: I must go. [*They all rise. Freddy goes to the door.*] So pleased to have met you. Goodbye. [*She shakes hands with Mrs Higgins.*]

MRS HIGGINS: Goodbye.

LIZA: Goodbye, Colonel Pickering.

PICKERING: Goodbye, Miss Doolittle. [*They shake hands.*]

LIZA [*nodding to the others*]: Goodbye, all.

FREDDY [*opening the door for her*]: Are you walking across the Park, Miss Doolittle? If so—

LIZA [*with perfectly elegant diction*]: Walk! Not bloody likely. [*sensation*] I am going in a taxi. [*She goes out.*]

*Pickering gasps and sits down. Freddy goes out on the balcony to catch another glimpse of Eliza.*

MRS EYNSFORD HILL [*suffering from shock*]: Well, I really cant get used to the new ways.

CLARA [*throwing herself discontentedly into the Elizabethan chair*]: Oh, it's all right, mamma, quite right. People will think we never go anywhere or see anybody if you are so old-fashioned.

MRS EYNSFORD HILL: I daresay I am very old-fashioned; but I do hope you wont begin using that expression, Clara. I have got accustomed to hear you talking about men as rotters, and calling everything filthy and beastly; though I do think it horrible and unladylike. But this last is really too much. Dont you think so, Colonel Pickering?

PICKERING: Dont ask me. Ive been away in India for several years; and manners have changed so much that I sometimes dont know whether I'm at a respectable dinner-table or in a ship's forecastle.

CLARA: It's all a matter of habit. Theres no right or wrong in it. Nobody means anything by it. And it's so quaint, and gives such a smart emphasis to things that are not in themselves very witty. I find the new small talk delightful and quite innocent.

MRS EYNSFORD HILL [*rising*]: Well, after that, I think it's time for us to go.

*Pickering and Higgins rise.*

CLARA [*rising*]: Oh yes: we have three at-homes to go to still. Goodbye, Mrs Higgins. Goodbye, Colonel Pickering. Goodbye, Professor Higgins.

HIGGINS [*coming grimly at her from the divan, and accompanying her to the door*]: Goodbye. Be sure you try on that small talk at the three at-homes. Dont be nervous about it. Pitch it in strong.

CLARA [*all smiles*]: I will. Goodbye. Such nonsense, all this early Victorian prudery!

HIGGINS [*tempting her*]: Such damned nonsense!

CLARA: Such bloody nonsense!

MRS EYNSFORD HILL [*convulsively*]: Clara!

CLARA: Ha! ha! [*She goes out radiant, conscious of being thoroughly up to date, and is heard descending the stairs in a stream of silvery laughter.*]

FREDDY [*to the heavens at large*]: Well, I ask you—[*He gives it up, and comes to Mrs Higgins.*] Goodbye.

MRS HIGGINS [*shaking hands*]: Goodbye. Would you like to meet Miss Doolittle again?

FREDDY [*eagerly*]: Yes, I should, most awfully.

MRS HIGGINS: Well, you know my days.

FREDDY: Yes, thanks awfully. Goodbye. [*He goes out.*]

MRS EYNSFORD HILL: Goodbye, Mr Higgins.

HIGGINS: Goodbye. Goodbye.

MRS EYNSFORD HILL [*to Pickering*]: It's no use. I shall never be able to bring myself to use that word.

PICKERING: Dont. It's not compulsory, you know. Youll get on quite well without it.

MRS EYNSFORD HILL: Only, Clara is so down on me if I am not positively reeking with the latest slang. Goodbye.

PICKERING: Goodbye. [*They shake hands.*]

MRS EYNSFORD HILL [*to Mrs Higgins*]: You mustnt mind Clara. [*Pickering, catching from her lowered tone that this is not meant for him to hear, discreetly joins Higgins at the window.*] We're so poor! and she gets so few parties, poor child! She doesnt quite know. [*Mrs Higgins, seeing that her eyes are moist, takes her hand sympathetically and goes with her to the door.*] But the boy is nice. Dont you think so?

MRS HIGGINS: Oh, quite nice. I shall always be delighted to see him.

MRS EYNSFORD HILL: Thank you, dear. Goodbye. [*She goes out.*]

HIGGINS [*eagerly*]: Well? Is Eliza presentable? [*He swoops on his mother and drags her to the ottoman, where she sits down in Eliza's place with her son on her left. Pickering returns to his chair on her right.*]

MRS HIGGINS: You silly boy, of course she's not presentable. She's a triumph of your art and of her dressmaker's; but if you suppose for a moment that she doesnt give herself away in every sentence she utters, you must be perfectly cracked about her.

PICKERING: But dont you think something might be done? I mean something to eliminate the sanguinary element from her conversation.

MRS HIGGINS: Not as long as she is in Henry's hands.

HIGGINS [*aggrieved*]: Do you mean that my language is improper?

MRS HIGGINS: No, dearest: it would be quite proper—say on a canal barge, but it would not be proper for her at a garden party.

HIGGINS [*deeply injured*]: Well I must say—

PICKERING [*interrupting him*]: Come, Higgins: you must learn to know yourself. I havnt heard such language as yours since we used to review the volunteers in Hyde Park twenty years ago.

HIGGINS [*sulkily*]: Oh, well, if *you* say so, I suppose I dont always talk like a bishop.

MRS HIGGINS [*quieting Henry with a touch*]: Colonel Pickering: will you tell me what is the exact state of things in Wimpole Street?

PICKERING [*cheerfully: as if this completely changed the subject*]: Well, I have come to live there with Henry. We work together at my Indian Dialects; and we think it more convenient—

MRS HIGGINS: Quite so. I know all about that: it's an excellent arrangement. But where does this girl live?

HIGGINS: With us, of course. Where *should* she live?

MRS HIGGINS: But on what terms? Is she a servant? If not, what is she?

PICKERING [*slowly*]: I think I know what you mean, Mrs Higgins.

HIGGINS: Well, dash me if *I* do! Ive had to work at the girl every day for months to get her to her present pitch. Besides, she's useful. She knows where my things are, and remembers my appointments and so forth.

MRS HIGGINS: How does your housekeeper get on with her?

HIGGINS: Mrs Pearce? Oh, she's jolly glad to get so much taken off her hands; for before Eliza came, *she* used to have to find things and remind me of my appointments. But she's got some silly bee in her bonnet about Eliza. She keeps saying 'You dont think, sir': doesnt she, Pick?

PICKERING: Yes: thats the formula. 'You dont think, sir.' Thats the end of every conversation about Eliza.

HIGGINS: As if I ever stop thinking about the girl and her confounded vowels and consonants. I'm worn out, thinking about her, and watching her lips and her teeth and her tongue, not to mention her soul, which is the quaintest of the lot.

MRS HIGGINS: You certainly are a pretty pair of babies, playing with your live doll.

HIGGINS: Playing! The hardest job I ever tackled: make no mistake about that, mother. But you have no idea how frightfully interesting it is to take a human being and change her into a quite different human being by creating a new speech for her. It's filling up the deepest gulf that separates class from class and soul from soul.

PICKERING [*drawing his chair closer to Mrs Higgins and bending over to her eagerly*]: Yes: it's enormously interesting. I assure you, Mrs Higgins, we take Eliza very seriously. Every week—every day almost—there is some new change. [*closer again*] We keep records of every stage—dozens of gramophone disks and photographs—

HIGGINS [*assailing her at the other ear*]: Yes, by George: it's the most absorbing experiment I ever tackled. She regularly fills our lives up: doesnt she, Pick?

PICKERING: We're always talking Eliza.

HIGGINS: Teaching Eliza.

PICKERING: Dressing Eliza.

MRS HIGGINS: What!

HIGGINS: Inventing new Elizas.

| | | |
|---|---|---|
| HIGGINS: | [*speaking* | You know, she has the most extraordinary quickness of ear: |
| PICKERING: | *together*] | I assure you, my dear Mrs Higgins, that girl |
| HIGGINS: | | just like a parrot. Ive tried her with every |
| PICKERING: | | is a genius. She can play the piano quite beautifully. |
| HIGGINS: | | possible sort of sound that a human being can make |
| PICKERING: | | We have taken her to classical concerts and to music |

HIGGINS: Continental dialects, African dialects, Hottentot<br>
PICKERING: halls; and its all the same to her: she plays everything

HIGGINS: clicks, things it took me years to get hold of; and<br>
PICKERING: she hears right off when she comes home, whether it's

HIGGINS: she picks them up like a shot, right away, as if she had<br>
PICKERING: Beethoven and Brahms or Lehar and Lionel Monckton;

HIGGINS: been at it all her life.<br>
PICKERING: though six months ago, she'd never as much as touched a piano—

MRS HIGGINS [*putting her fingers in her ears, as they are by this time shouting one another down with an intolerable noise*]: Sh-sh-sh-sh!

*They stop.*

PICKERING: I beg your pardon. [*He draws his chair back apologetically.*]

HIGGINS: Sorry. When Pickering starts shouting nobody can get a word in edgeways.

MRS HIGGINS: Be quiet, Henry. Colonel Pickering: dont you realize that when Eliza walked into Wimpole Street, something walked in with her?

PICKERING: Her father did. But Henry soon got rid of him.

MRS HIGGINS: It would have been more to the point if her mother had. But as her mother didnt something else did.

PICKERING: But what?

MRS HIGGINS [*unconsciously dating herself by the word*]: A problem.

PICKERING: Oh, I see. The problem of how to pass her off as a lady.

HIGGINS: I'll solve that problem. Ive half solved it already.

MRS HIGGINS: No, you two infinitely stupid male creatures: the problem of what is to be done with her afterwards.

HIGGINS: I dont see anything in that. She can go her own way, with all the advantages I have given her.

MRS HIGGINS: The advantages of that poor woman who was here just now! The manners and habits that disqualify a fine lady from earning her own living without giving her a fine lady's income! Is that what you mean?

PICKERING [*indulgently, being rather bored*]: Oh, that will be all right, Mrs Higgins. [*He rises to go.*]

HIGGINS [*rising also*]: We'll find her some light employment.

PICKERING: She's happy enough. Dont you worry about her. Goodbye. [*He shakes hands as if he were consoling a frightened child, and makes for the door.*]

HIGGINS: Anyhow, theres no good bothering now. The thing's done. Goodbye, mother. [*He kisses her, and follows Pickering.*]

PICKERING [*turning for a final consolation*]: There are plenty of openings. We'll do whats right. Goodbye.

HIGGINS [*to Pickering as they go out together*]: Lets take her to the Shakespeare exhibition at Earls Court.

PICKERING: Yes: lets. Her remarks will be delicious.

HIGGINS: She'll mimic all the people for us when we get home.

PICKERING: Ripping.

*Both are heard laughing as they go downstairs.*

MRS HIGGINS [*rises with an impatient bounce, and returns to her work at the writing-table. She sweeps a litter of disarranged papers out of her way; snatches a sheet of paper from her stationery case; and tries resolutely to write. At the third line she gives it up; flings down her pen; grips the table angrily and exclaims*]: Oh, men! men!! men!!!

* * *

*Clearly Eliza will not pass as a duchess yet; and Higgins's bet remains unwon. But the six months are not yet exhausted; and just in time Eliza does actually pass as a princess. For a glimpse of how she did it imagine an Embassy in London one summer evening after dark. The hall door has an awning and a carpet across the sidewalk to the kerb, because a grand reception is in progress. A small crowd is lined up to see the guests arrive.*

*A Rolls-Royce car drives up. Pickering in evening dress, with medals and orders, alights, and hands out Eliza, in opera cloak, evening dress, diamonds, fan, flowers and all accessories. Higgins follows. The car drives off; and the three go up the steps and into the house, the door opening for them as they approach.*

*Inside the house they find themselves in a spacious hall from which the grand staircase rises. On the left are the arrangements for the gentlemen's cloaks. The male guests are depositing their hats and wraps there.*

*On the right is a door leading to the ladies' cloakroom. Ladies are going in cloaked and coming out in splendour. Pickering whispers to Eliza and points out the ladies' room. She goes into it. Higgins and Pickering take off their overcoats and take tickets for them from the attendant.*

*One of the guests, occupied in the same way, has his back turned. Having taken his ticket, he turns round and reveals himself as an important looking young man with an astonishingly hairy face. He has an enormous moustache, flowing out into luxuriant whiskers. Waves of hair cluster his brow. His hair is cropped closely at the back, and glows with oil. Otherwise he is very smart. He wears several worthless orders. He is evidently a foreigner, guessable as whiskered Pandour from Hungary; but in spite of the ferocity of his moustache he is amiable and genially voluble.*

*Recognizing Higgins, he flings his arms wide apart and approaches him enthusiastically.*

WHISKERS: Maestro, maestro. [*He embraces Higgins and kisses him on both cheeks.*] You remember me?

HIGGINS: No I dont. Who the devil are you?

WHISKERS: I am your pupil: your first pupil, your best and greatest pupil. I am little Nepommuck, the marvellous boy. I have made your name famous throughout Europe. You teach me phonetic. You cannot forget ME.

HIGGINS: Why dont you shave?

NEPOMMUCK: I have not your imposing appearance, your chin, your brow. Nobody notice me when I shave. Now I am famous: they call me Hairy Faced Dick.

HIGGINS: And what are you doing here among all these swells?

NEPOMMUCK: I am interpreter. I speak 32 languages. I am indispensable at these international parties. You are great cockney specialist: you place a man anywhere in London the moment he open his mouth. I place any man in Europe.

*A footman hurries down the grand staircase and comes to Nepommuck.*

FOOTMAN: You are wanted upstairs. Her Excellency cannot understand the Greek gentleman.

NEPOMMUCK: Thank you, yes, immediately.

*The footman goes and is lost in the crowd.*

NEPOMMUCK [*to Higgins*]: This Greek diplomatist pretends he cannot speak nor understand English. He cannot deceive me. He is the son of a Clerkenwell watchmaker. He speaks English so villainously that he dare not utter a word of it without betraying his origin. I help him to pretend; but I make him pay through the nose. I make them all pay. Ha Ha! [*He hurries upstairs.*]

PICKERING: Is this fellow really an expert? Can he find out Eliza and blackmail her?

HIGGINS: We shall see. If he finds her out I lose my bet.

*Eliza comes from the cloakroom and joins them.*

PICKERING: Well, Eliza, now for it. Are you ready?

LIZA: Are you nervous, Colonel?

PICKERING: Frightfully. I feel exactly as I felt before my first battle. It's the first time that frightens.

LIZA: It is not the first time for me, Colonel. I have done this fifty times—hundreds of times—in my little piggery in Angel Court in my day-dreams. I am in a dream now. Promise me not to let Professor Higgins wake me; for if he does I shall forget everything and talk as I used to in Drury Lane.

PICKERING: Not a word, Higgins. [*to Eliza*]: Now, ready?

LIZA: Ready.

PICKERING: Go.

*They mount the stairs, Higgins last. Pickering whispers to the footman on the first landing.*

FIRST LANDING FOOTMAN: Miss Doolittle, Colonel Pickering, Professor Higgins.

SECOND LANDING FOOTMAN: Miss Doolittle, Colonel Pickering, Professor Higgins.

*At the top of the staircase the Ambassador and his wife, with Nepommuck at her elbow, are receiving.*

HOSTESS [*taking Eliza's hand*]: How d'ye do?

HOST [*same play*]: How d'ye do? How d'ye do, Pickering?

LIZA [*with a beautiful gravity that awes her hostess*]: How do you do? [*She passes on to the drawing room.*]

HOSTESS: Is that your adopted daughter, Colonel Pickering? She will make a sensation.

PICKERING: Most kind of you to invite her for me. [*He passes on.*]

HOSTESS [*to Nepommuck*]: Find out all about her.

NEPOMMUCK [*bowing*]: Excellency—[*He goes into the crowd.*]

HOST: How d'ye do, Higgins? You have a rival here tonight. He introduced himself as your pupil. Is he any good?

HIGGINS: He can learn a language in a fortnight—knows dozens of them. A sure mark of a fool. As a phonetician, no good whatever.

HOSTESS: How d'ye do, Professor?

HIGGINS: How do you do? Fearful bore for you this sort of thing. Forgive my part in it. [*He passes on.*]

*In the drawing room and its suite of salons the reception is in full swing. Eliza passes through. She is so intent on her ordeal that she walks like a somnambulist in a desert instead of a débutante in a fashionable crowd. They stop talking to look at her, admiring her dress, her jewels, and her strangely attractive self. Some of the younger ones at the back stand on their chairs to see.*

*The Host and Hostess come in from the staircase and mingle with their guests. Higgins, gloomy and contemptuous of the whole business, comes into the group where they are chatting.*

HOSTESS: Ah, here is Professor Higgins: he will tell us. Tell us all about the wonderful young lady, Professor.

HIGGINS [*almost morosely*]: What wonderful young lady?

HOSTESS: You know very well. They tell me there has been nothing like her in London since people stood on their chairs to look at Mrs Langtry.

*Nepommuck joins the group, full of news.*

HOSTESS: Ah, here you are at last, Nepommuck. Have you found out all about the Doolittle lady?

NEPOMMUCK: I have found out all about her. She is a fraud.

HOSTESS: A fraud! Oh no.

NEPOMMUCK: YES, yes. She cannot deceive me. Her name cannot be Doolittle.

HIGGINS: Why?

NEPOMMUCK: Because Doolittle is an English name. And she is not English.

HOSTESS: Oh, nonsense! She speaks English perfectly.

NEPOMMUCK: Too perfectly. Can you shew me any English woman who speaks English as it should be spoken? Only foreigners who have been taught to speak it speak it well.

HOSTESS: Certainly she terrified me by the way she said How d'ye do. I had a schoolmistress who talked like that; and I was mortally afraid of her. But if she is not English what is she?

NEPOMMUCK: Hungarian.

ALL THE REST: Hungarian!

NEPOMMUCK: Hungarian. And of royal blood. I am Hungarian. My blood is royal.

HIGGINS: Did you speak to her in Hungarian?

NEPOMMUCK: I did. She was very clever. She said 'Please speak to me in English: I do not understand French.' French! She pretends not to know the difference between Hungarian and French. Impossible: she knows both.

HIGGINS: And the blood royal? How did you find that out?

NEPOMMUCK: Instinct, maestro, instinct. Only the Magyar races can produce that air of the divine right, those resolute eyes. She is a princess.

HOST: What do you say, Professor?

HIGGINS: I say an ordinary London girl out of the gutter and taught to speak by an expert. I place her in Drury Lane.

NEPOMMUCK: Ha ha ha! Oh, maestro, maestro, you are mad on the subject of cockney dialects. The London gutter is the whole world for you.

HIGGINS [*to the Hostess*]: What does your Excellency say?

HOSTESS: Oh, of course I agree with Nepommuck. She must be a princess at least.

HOST: Not necessarily legitimate, of course. Morganatic perhaps. But that is undoubtedly her class.

HIGGINS: I stick to my opinion.

HOSTESS: Oh, you are incorrigible.

*The group breaks up, leaving Higgins isolated. Pickering joins him.*

PICKERING: Where is Eliza? We must keep an eye on her.

*Eliza joins them.*

LIZA: I dont think I can bear much more. The people all stare so at me. An old lady has just told me that I speak exactly like Queen Victoria. I am sorry if I have lost your bet. I have done my best; but nothing can make me the same as these people.

PICKERING: You have not lost it, my dear. You have won it ten times over.

HIGGINS: Let us get out of this. I have had enough of chattering to these fools.

PICKERING: Eliza is tired; and I am hungry. Let us clear out and have supper somewhere.

## ACT IV

*The Wimpole Street laboratory. Midnight. Nobody in the room. The clock on the mantelpiece strikes twelve. The fire is not alight: it is a summer night.*

*Presently Higgins and Pickering are heard on the stairs.*

HIGGINS [*calling down to Pickering*]: I say, Pick: lock up, will you? I shant be going out again.

PICKERING: Right. Can Mrs Pearce go to bed? We dont want anything more, do we?

HIGGINS: Lord, no!

*Eliza opens the door and is seen on the lighted landing in all the finery in which she has just won Higgins's bet for him. She comes to the hearth, and switches on the electric lights there. She is tired: her pallor contrasts strongly with her dark eyes and hair; and her expression is almost tragic. She takes off her cloak; puts her fan and gloves on the piano; and sits down on the bench, brooding and silent. Higgins, in evening dress, with overcoat and hat, comes in, carrying a smoking jacket which he has picked up downstairs. He takes off the hat and overcoat; throws them carelessly on the newspaper stand; disposes of his coat in the same way; puts on the smoking jacket; and throws himself wearily into the easy-chair at the hearth. Pickering, similarly attired, comes in. He also takes off his hat and overcoat, and is about to throw them on Higgins's when he hesitates.*

PICKERING: I say: Mrs Pearce will row if we leave these things lying about in the drawing room.

HIGGINS: Oh, chuck them over the bannisters into the hall. She'll find them there in the morning and put them away all right. She'll think we were drunk.

PICKERING: We are, slightly. Are there any letters?

HIGGINS: I didnt look. [*Pickering takes the overcoats and hats and goes downstairs. Higgins begins half singing half yawning an air from La Fanciulla del Golden West. Suddenly he stops and exclaims*]: I wonder where the devil my slippers are!

*Eliza looks at him darkly; then rises suddenly and leaves the room.*
*Higgins yawns again, and resumes his song.*
*Pickering returns, with the contents of the letter-box in his hand.*

PICKERING: Only circulars, and this coroneted billet-doux for you. [*He throws the circulars into the fender, and posts himself on the hearthrug, with his back to the grate.*]

HIGGINS [*glancing at the billet-doux*]: Money-lender. [*He throws the letter after the circulars.*]

*Eliza returns with a pair of down-at-heel slippers. She places them on the carpet before Higgins, and sits as before without a word.*

HIGGINS [*yawning again*]: Oh Lord! What an evening! What a crew! What a silly tomfoolery! [*He raises his shoe to unlace it, and catches sight of the slippers. He stops unlacing and looks at them as if they had appeared there of their own accord.*] Oh! theyre there, are they?

PICKERING [*stretching himself*]: Well, I feel a bit tired. It's been a long day. The garden party, a dinner party, and the reception! Rather too much of a good thing. But youve won your bet, Higgins. Eliza did the trick, and something to spare, eh?

HIGGINS [*fervently*]: Thank God it's over!

*Eliza flinches violently; but they take no notice of her; and she recovers herself and sits stonily as before.*

PICKERING: Were you nervous at the garden party? *I* was. Eliza didnt seem a bit nervous.

HIGGINS: Oh, she wasnt nervous. I knew she'd be all right. No: it's the strain of putting the job through all these months that has told on me. It was interesting enough at first, while we were at the phonetics; but after that I got deadly sick of it. If I hadnt backed myself to do it I should have chucked the whole thing up two months ago. It was a silly notion: the whole thing has been a bore.

PICKERING: Oh come! the garden party was frightfully exciting. My heart began beating like anything.

HIGGINS: Yes, for the first three minutes. But when I saw we were going to win hands down, I felt like a bear in a cage, hanging about doing nothing. The dinner was worse: sitting gorging there for over an hour, with nobody but a damned fool of a fashionable woman to talk to! I tell you, Pickering, never again for me. No more artificial duchesses. The whole thing has been simple purgatory.

PICKERING: Youve never been broken in properly to the social routine. [*strolling over to the piano*] I rather enjoy dipping into it occasionally myself: it makes me feel young again. Anyhow, it was a great success: an immense success. I was quite frightened once or twice because Eliza was doing it so well. You see, lots of the real people cant do it at all: theyre such fools that they think style comes by nature to people in their position; and so they never learn. Theres always something professional about doing a thing superlatively well.

HIGGINS: Yes: thats what drives me mad: the silly people dont know their own silly business. [*rising*] However, it's over and done with; and now I can go to bed at last without dreading tomorrow.

*Eliza's beauty becomes murderous.*

PICKERING: I think I shall turn in too. Still, it's been a great occasion: a triumph for you. Goodnight. [*He goes.*]

HIGGINS [*following him*]: Goodnight. [*over his shoulder, at the door*] Put out the lights, Eliza; and tell Mrs Pearce not to make coffee for me in the morning: I'll take tea. [*He goes out.*]

*Eliza tries to control herself and feel indifferent as she rises and walks across to the hearth to switch off the lights. By the time she gets there she is on the point of screaming. She sits down in Higgins's chair and holds on hard to the arms. Finally she gives way and flings herself furiously on the floor, raging.*

HIGGINS [*in despairing wrath outside*]: What the devil have I done with my slippers? [*He appears at the door.*]

LIZA [*snatching up the slippers, and hurling them at him one after the other with all her force*]: There are your slippers. And there. Take your slippers; and may you never have a day's luck with them!

HIGGINS [*astounded*]: What on earth—! [*He comes to her.*] Whats the matter? Get up. [*He pulls her up.*] Anything wrong?

LIZA [*breathless*]: Nothing wrong—with *you*. Ive won your bet for you, havnt I? Thats enough for you. *I* dont matter, I suppose.

HIGGINS: *You* won my bet! You! Presumptuous insect! *I* won it. What did you throw those slippers at me for?

LIZA: Because I wanted to smash your face. I'd like to kill you, you selfish brute. Why didnt you leave me where you picked me out of—in the gutter? You thank God it's all over, and that now you can throw me back again there, do you? [*She crisps her fingers frantically.*]

HIGGINS [*looking at her in cool wonder*]: The creature is nervous, after all.

LIZA [*gives a suffocated scream of fury, and instinctively darts her nails at his face*]: !!

HIGGINS [*catching her wrists*]: Ah! would you? Claws in, you cat. How dare you shew your temper to me? Sit down and be quiet. [*He throws her roughly into the easy-chair.*]

LIZA [*crushed by superior strength and weight*]: Whats to become of me? Whats to become of me?

HIGGINS: How the devil do I know whats to become of you? What does it matter what becomes of you?

LIZA: You dont care. I know you dont care. You wouldnt care if I was dead. I'm nothing to you—not so much as them slippers.

HIGGINS [*thundering*]: *Those* slippers.

LIZA [*with bitter submission*]: Those slippers. I didnt think it made any difference now.

*A pause. Eliza hopeless and crushed. Higgins a little uneasy.*

HIGGINS [*in his loftiest manner*]: Why have you begun going on like this? May I ask whether you complain of your treatment here?

LIZA: No.

HIGGINS: Has anybody behaved badly to you? Colonel Pickering? Mrs Pearce? Any of the servants?

LIZA: No.

HIGGINS: I presume you dont pretend that *I* have treated you badly?

LIZA: No.

HIGGINS: I am glad to hear it. [*He moderates his tone.*] Perhaps youre tired after the strain of the day. Will you have a glass of champagne? [*He moves towards the door.*]

LIZA: No. [*recollecting her manners*] Thank you.

HIGGINS [*good-humoured again*]: This has been coming on you for some days. I suppose it was natural for you to be anxious about the garden party. But thats all over now. [*He pats her kindly on the shoulder. She writhes.*] Theres nothing more to worry about.

LIZA: No. Nothing more for *you* to worry about. [*She suddenly rises and gets away from him by going to the piano bench, where she sits and hides her face.*] Oh God! I wish I was dead.

HIGGINS [*staring after her in sincere surprise*]: Why? In heaven's name, why? [*reasonably, going to her*] Listen to me, Eliza. All this irritation is purely subjective.

LIZA: I dont understand. I'm too ignorant.

HIGGINS: It's only imagination. Low spirits and nothing else. Nobody's hurting you. Nothing's wrong. You go to bed like a good girl and sleep it off. Have a little cry and say your prayers: that will make you comfortable.

LIZA: I heard your prayers. 'Thank God it's all over!'

HIGGINS [*impatiently*]: Well, *dont* you thank God it's all over? Now you are free and can do what you like.

LIZA [*pulling herself together in desperation*]: What am I fit for? What have you left me fit for? Where am I to go? What am I to do? Whats to become of me?

HIGGINS [*enlightened, but not at all impressed*]: Oh, thats whats worrying you, is it? [*He thrusts his hands into his pockets, and walks about in his usual manner, rattling the contents of his pockets, as if condescending to a trivial subject out of pure kindness.*] I shouldnt bother about it if I were you. I should imagine you wont have much difficulty in settling yourself somewhere or other, though I hadnt quite realized that you were going away. [*She looks quickly at him: he does not look at her, but examines the dessert stand on the piano and decides that he will eat an apple.*] You might marry, you know. [*He bites a large piece out of the apple and munches it noisily.*] You see, Eliza, all men are not confirmed old bachelors like me and the Colonel. Most men are the marrying sort (poor devils!); and youre not bad-looking: it's quite a pleasure to look at you sometimes—not now, of course, because youre crying and looking as ugly as the very devil; but when youre all right and quite yourself, youre what I should call attractive. That is, to the people in the marrying line, you understand. You go to bed and have a good nice rest; and then get up and look at yourself in the glass; and you wont feel so cheap.

*Eliza again looks at him speechless, and does not stir.*

*The look is quite lost on him: he eats his apple with a dreamy expression of happiness, as it is quite a good one.*

HIGGINS [*a genial afterthought occuring to him*]: I daresay my mother could find some chap or other who would do very well.

LIZA: We were above that at the corner of Tottenham Court Road.

HIGGINS [*waking up*]: What do you mean?

LIZA: I sold flowers. I didnt sell myself. Now youve made a lady of me I'm not fit to sell anything else. I wish youd left me where you found me.

HIGGINS [*slinging the core of the apple decisively into the grate*]: Tosh, Eliza. Dont you insult human relations by dragging all this cant about buying and selling into it. You neednt marry the fellow if you dont like him.

LIZA: What else am I to do?

HIGGINS: Oh, lots of things. What about your old idea of a florist's shop? Pickering could set you up in one: he has lots of money. [*chuckling*] He'll have to pay for all those togs you have been wearing today; and that, with the hire of the jewellery, will make a big hole in two hundred pounds. Why, six months ago you would have thought it the millennium to have a flower shop of your own. Come! youll be all right. I must clear off to bed: I'm devilish sleepy. By the way, I came down for something: I forget what it was.

LIZA: Your slippers.

HIGGINS: Oh yes, of course. You shied them at me. [*He picks them up, and is going out when she rises and speaks to him.*]

LIZA: Before you go, sir—

HIGGINS [*dropping the slippers in his surprise at her calling him Sir*]: Eh?

LIZA: Do my clothes belong to me or to Colonel Pickering?

HIGGINS [*coming back into the room as if her question were the very climax of unreason*]: What the devil use would they be to Pickering?

LIZA: He might want them for the next girl you pick up to experiment on.

HIGGINS [*shocked and hurt*]: Is *that* the way you feel towards us?

LIZA: I dont want to hear anything more about that. All I want to know is whether anything belongs to me. My own clothes were burnt.

HIGGINS: But what does it matter? Why need you start bothering about that in the middle of the night?

LIZA: I want to know what I may take away with me. I dont want to be accused of stealing.

HIGGINS [*now deeply wounded*]: Stealing! You shouldnt have said that, Eliza. That shews a want of feeling.

LIZA: I'm sorry. I'm only a common ignorant girl; and in my station I have to be careful. There cant be any feelings between the like of you and the like of me. Please will you tell me what belongs to me and what doesnt?

HIGGINS [*very sulky*]: You may take the whole damned houseful if you like. Except the jewels. Theyre hired. Will that satisfy you? [*He turns on his heel and is about to go in extreme dudgeon.*]

LIZA [*drinking in his emotion like nectar, and nagging him to provoke a further supply*]: Stop, please. [*She takes off her jewels.*] Will you take these to your room and keep them safe? I dont want to run the risk of their being missing.

HIGGINS [*furious*]: Hand them over. [*She puts them into his hands.*] If these belonged to me instead of the jeweller, I'd ram them down your ungrateful throat. [*He perfunctorily thrusts them into his pockets unconsciously decorating himself with the protruding ends of the chains.*]

LIZA [*taking a ring off*]: This ring isnt the jeweller's: it's the one you bought me in Brighton. I dont want it now. [*Higgins dashes the ring violently into the fireplace, and turns on her so threateningly that she crouches over the piano with her hands over her face and exclaims*]: Dont you hit me.

HIGGINS: Hit you! You infamous creature, how dare you accuse me of such a thing? It is you who have hit me. You have wounded me to the heart.

LIZA [*thrilling with hidden joy*]: I'm glad. Ive got a little of my own back, anyhow.

HIGGINS [*with dignity, in his finest professional style*]: You have caused me to lose my temper: a thing that has hardly ever happened to me before. I prefer to say nothing more tonight. I am going to bed.

LIZA [*pertly*]: Youd better leave a note for Mrs Pearce about the coffee; for she wont be told by me.

HIGGINS [*formally*]: Damn Mrs Pearce; and damn the coffee; and damn you; and [*wildly*] damn my own folly in having lavished my hard-earned knowledge and the treasure of my regard and intimacy on a heartless guttersnipe. [*He goes out with impressive decorum, and spills it by slamming the door savagely.*]

*Eliza goes down on her knees on the hearthrug to look for the ring. When she finds it she considers for a moment what to do with it. Finally she flings it down on the dessert stand and goes upstairs in a tearing rage.*

* * *

*The furniture of Eliza's room has been increased by a big wardrobe and a sumptuous dressing-table. She comes in and switches on the electric light. She goes to the wardrobe; opens it; and pulls out a walking dress, a hat, and a pair of shoes, which she throws on the bed. She takes off her evening dress and shoes; then takes a padded hanger from the wardrobe; adjusts it carefully in the evening dress; and hangs it in the wardrobe, which she shuts with a slam. She puts on her walking shoes, her walking dress, and hat. She takes her wrist watch from the dressing-table and fastens it on. She pulls on her gloves; takes her vanity bag; and looks into it to see that her purse is there before hanging it on her wrist. She makes for the door. Every movement expresses her furious resolution.*

*She takes a last look at herself in the glass.*

*She suddenly puts out her tongue at herself; then leaves the room, switching off the electric light at the door.*

*Meanwhile, in the street outside, Freddy Eynsford Hill, lovelorn, is gazing up at the second floor, in which one of the windows is still lighted.*

*The light goes out.*

FREDDY: Goodnight, darling, darling, darling.

*Eliza comes out, giving the door a considerable bang behind her.*

LIZA: Whatever are you doing here?

FREDDY: Nothing. I spend most nights here. It's the only place where I'm happy. Dont laugh at me, Miss Doolittle.

LIZA: Dont you call me Miss Doolittle, do you hear? Liza's good enough for me. [*She breaks down and grabs him by the shoulders.*] Freddy: you dont think I'm a heartless guttersnipe, do you?

FREDDY: Oh no, no, darling: how can you imagine such a thing? You are the loveliest, dearest—

*He loses all self-control and smothers her with kisses. She, hungry for comfort, responds. They stand in one another's arms.*

*An elderly police constable arrives.*

CONSTABLE [*scandalized*]: Now then! Now then!! Now then!!!

*They release one another hastily.*

FREDDY: Sorry, constable. Weve only just become engaged.

*They run away.*

*The constable shakes his head, reflecting on his own courtship and on the vanity of human hopes. He moves off in the opposite direction with slow professional steps.*

*The flight of the lovers takes them to Cavendish Square. There they halt to consider their next move.*

LIZA [*out of breath*]: He didnt half give me a fright, that copper. But you answered him proper.

FREDDY: I hope I havnt taken you out of your way. Where were you going?

LIZA: To the river.

FREDDY: What for?

LIZA: To make a hole in it.

FREDDY [*horrified*]: Eliza, darling. What do you mean? Whats the matter?

LIZA: Never mind. It doesnt matter now. Theres nobody in the world now but you and me, is there?

FREDDY: Not a soul.

*They indulge in another embrace, and are again surprised by a much younger constable.*

SECOND CONSTABLE: Now then, you two! Whats this? Where do you think you are? Move along here, double quick.

FREDDY: As you say, sir, double quick.

*They run away again, and are in Hanover Square before they stop for another conference.*

FREDDY: I had no idea the police were so devilishly prudish.

LIZA: It's their business to hunt girls off the streets.

FREDDY: We must go somewhere. We cant wander about the streets all night.

LIZA: Cant we? I think it'd be lovely to wander about for ever.

FREDDY: Oh, darling.

*They embrace again, oblivious of the arrival of a crawling taxi. It stops.*

TAXIMAN: Can I drive you and the lady anywhere, sir?

*They start asunder.*

LIZA: Oh, Freddy, a taxi. The very thing.

FREDDY: But, damn it, Ive no money.

LIZA: I have plenty. The Colonel thinks you should never go out without ten pounds in your pocket. Listen. We'll drive about all night; and in the morning I'll call on old Mrs Higgins and ask her what I ought to do. I'll tell you all about it in the cab. And the police wont touch us there.

FREDDY: Righto! Ripping. [*to the Taximan*]: Wimbledon Common. [*They drive off.*]

## ACT V

*Mrs Higgins's drawing room. She is at her writing-table as before. The parlour-maid comes in.*

THE PARLOUR-MAID [*at the door*]: Mr Henry, maam, is downstairs with Colonel Pickering.

MRS HIGGINS: Well, shew them up.

THE PARLOUR-MAID: Theyre using the telephone, maam. Telephoning to the police, I think.

MRS HIGGINS: What!

THE PARLOUR-MAID [*coming further in and lowering her voice*]: Mr Henry is in a state, maam. I thought I'd better tell you.

MRS HIGGINS: If you had told me that Mr Henry was not in a state it would have been more surprising. Tell them to come up when theyve finished with the police. I suppose he's lost something.

THE PARLOUR-MAID: Yes, maam. [*going*]

MRS HIGGINS: Go upstairs and tell Miss Doolittle that Mr Henry and the Colonel are here. Ask her not to come down til I send for her.

THE PARLOUR-MAID: Yes, maam.

*Higgins bursts in. He is, as the parlour-maid has said, in a state.*

HIGGINS: Look here, mother: heres a confounded thing!

MRS HIGGINS: Yes, dear. Good morning. [*He checks his impatience and kisses her, whilst the parlour-maid goes out.*] What is it?

HIGGINS: Eliza's bolted.

MRS HIGGINS [*calmly continuing her writing*]: You must have frightened her.

HIGGINS: Frightened her! nonsense! She was left last night, as usual, to turn out the lights and all that; and instead of going to bed she changed her clothes and went right off: her bed wasnt slept in. She came in a cab for her things before seven this morning; and that fool Mrs Pearce let her have them without telling me a word about it. What am I to do?

MRS HIGGINS: Do without, I'm afraid, Henry. The girl has a perfect right to leave if she chooses.

HIGGINS [*wandering distractedly across the room*]: But I cant find anything. I dont know what appointments Ive got. I'm—

*Pickering comes in. Mrs Higgins puts down her pen and turns away from the writing-table.*

PICKERING [*shaking hands*]: Good morning, Mrs Higgins. Has Henry told you? [*He sits down on the ottoman.*]

HIGGINS: What does that ass of an inspector say? Have you offered a reward?

MRS HIGGINS [*rising in indignant amazement*]: You dont mean to say you have set the police after Eliza.

HIGGINS: Of course. What are the police for? What else could we do? [*He sits in the Elizabethan chair.*]

PICKERING: The inspector made a lot of difficulties. I really think he suspected us of some improper purpose.

MRS HIGGINS: Well, of course he did. What right have you to go to the police and give the girl's name as if she were a thief, or a lost umbrella, or something? Really! [*She sits down again, deeply vexed.*]

HIGGINS: But we want to find her.

PICKERING: We cant let her go like this, you know, Mrs Higgins. What were we to do?

MRS HIGGINS: You have no more sense, either of you, than two children. Why—

*The parlour-maid comes in and breaks off the conversation.*

THE PARLOUR-MAID: Mr Henry: a gentleman wants to see you very particular. He's been sent on from Wimpole Street.

HIGGINS: Oh, bother! I cant see anyone now. Who is it?

THE PARLOUR-MAID: A Mr Doolittle, sir.

PICKERING: Doolittle! Do you mean the dustman?

THE PARLOUR-MAID: Dustman! Oh no, sir: a gentleman.

HIGGINS [*springing up excitedly*]: By George, Pick, it's some relative of hers that she's gone to. Somebody we know nothing about. [*to the parlour-maid*]: Send him up, quick.

THE PARLOUR-MAID: Yes, sir. [*She goes.*]

HIGGINS [*eagerly, going to his mother*]: Genteel relatives! now we shall hear something. [*He sits down in the Chippendale chair.*]

MRS HIGGINS: Do you know any of her people?

PICKERING: Only her father: the fellow we told you about.

THE PARLOUR-MAID [*announcing*]: Mr Doolittle. [*She withdraws.*]

*Doolittle enters. He is resplendently dressed as for a fashionable wedding, and might, in fact, be the bridegroom. A flower in his buttonhole, a dazzling silk hat, and patent leather shoes complete the effect. He is too concerned with the business he has come on to notice Mrs Higgins. He walks straight to Higgins, and accosts him with vehement reproach.*

DOOLITTLE [*indicating his own person*]: See here! Do you see this? *You* done this.

HIGGINS: Done what, man?

DOOLITTLE: This, I tell you. Look at it. Look at this hat. Look at this coat.

PICKERING: Has Eliza been buying you clothes?

DOOLITTLE: Eliza! not she. Why would she buy me clothes?

MRS HIGGINS: Good morning, Mr Doolittle. Wont you sit down?

DOOLITTLE [*taken aback as he becomes conscious that he has forgotten his hostess*]: Asking your pardon, maam. [*He approaches her and shakes her proffered hand.*] Thank you. [*He sits down on the ottoman, on Pickering's right.*] I am that full of what has happened to me that I cant think of anything else.

HIGGINS: What the dickens h a s happened to you?

DOOLITTLE: I shouldnt mind if it had only *happened* to me: anything might happen to anybody and nobody to blame but Providence, as you might say. But this is something that *you* done to me: yes, *you*, Enry Iggins.

HIGGINS: Have you found Eliza?

DOOLITTLE: Have you lost her?

HIGGINS: Yes.

DOOLITTLE: You have all the luck, you have. I aint found her; but she'll find me quick enough now after what you done to me.

MRS HIGGINS: But what has my son done to you. Mr Doolittle?

DOOLITTLE: Done to me! Ruined me. Destroyed my happiness. Tied me up and delivered me into the hands of middle class morality.

HIGGINS [*rising intolerantly and standing over Doolittle*]: Youre raving. Youre drunk. Youre mad. I gave you five pounds. After that I had two conversations with you, at half-a-crown an hour. Ive never seen you since.

DOOLITTLE: Oh! Drunk am I? Mad am I? Tell me this. Did you or did you not write a letter to an old blighter in America that was giving five million to found Moral Reform Societies all over the world, and that wanted you to invent a universal language for him?

HIGGINS: What! Ezra D. Wannafeller! He's dead. [*He sits down again carelessly.*]

DOOLITTLE: Yes: he's dead; and I'm done for. Now did you or did you not write a letter to him to say that the most original moralist at present in England, to the best your knowledge, was Alfred Doolittle, a common dustman?

HIGGINS: Oh, after your first visit I remember making some silly joke of the kind.

DOOLITTLE: Ah! you may well call it a silly joke. It put the lid on me right enough. Just give him the chance he wanted to shew that Americans is not like us: that they reckonize and respect merit in every class of life, however humble. Them words is in his blooming will, in which, Henry Higgins, thanks to your silly joking, he leaves me a share of his Predigested Cheese Trust worth three thousand a year on condition that I lecture for his Wannafeller Moral Reform World League as often as they ask me up to six times a year.

HIGGINS: The devil he does! Whew! [*Brightening suddenly*] What a lark!

PICKERING: A safe thing for you, Doolittle. They wont ask you twice.

DOOLITTLE: It aint the lecturing I mind. I'll lecture them blue in the face, I will, and not turn a hair. It's making a gentleman of me that I object to. Who asked him to make a gentleman of me? I was happy. I was free. I touched pretty nigh everybody for money when I wanted it, same as I touched you, Enry Iggins. Now I am worrited; tied neck and heels; and everybody touches *me* for money. It's a fine thing for you, says my solicitor. Is it? says I. You mean it's a good thing for you, I says. When I was a poor man and had a solicitor once when they found a pram in the dust cart, he got me off, and got shut of me and got me shut of him as quick as he could. Same with the doctors: used to shove me out of the hospital before I could hardly stand on my legs, and nothing to pay. Now they finds out that I'm not a healthy man and cant live unless they looks after me twice a day. In the house I'm not let do a hand's turn for myself: somebody else must do it and touch me for it. A year ago I hadnt a relative in the world except two or three that wouldnt speak to me. Now Ive fifty, and not a decent week's wages among the lot of them. I have to live for others and not for myself: thats middle class morality. You talk of losing Eliza. Dont you be anxious: I bet she's on my doorstep by this: she that could support herself easy by selling flowers if I wasnt respectable. And the next one to touch me will be you, Enry Iggins. I'll have to learn to speak middle class language from you, instead of speaking proper English. Thats where youll come in; and I daresay thats what you done it for.

MRS HIGGINS: But, my dear Mr Doolittle, you need not suffer all this if you are really earnest. Nobody can force you to accept this bequest. You can repudiate it. Isnt that so, Colonel Pickering?

PICKERING: I believe so.

DOOLITTLE [*softening his manner in deference to her sex*]: Thats the tragedy of it, maam. It's easy to say chuck it; but I havnt the nerve. Which of us has? We're all intimidated. Intimidated, maam: thats what we are. What is there for me if I chuck it but the workhouse in my old age? I have to dye my hair already to keep my job as a dustman. If I was one of the deserving poor, and had put by a bit, I could chuck it; but then why should I, acause the deserving poor might as well be millionaires for all the happiness they ever has. They dont know what happiness is. But I, as one of the undeserving poor, have nothing between me and the pauper's uniform but this here blasted three thousand a year that shoves me into the middle class. (Excuse the expression, maam; youd use it yourself if you had my provocation.) Theyve got you every way you turn: it's a choice between the Skilly of the workhouse and the Char Bydis of the middle class; and I havnt the nerve for the workhouse. Intimidated: thats what I am. Broke. Bought up. Happier men than me will call for my dust, and touch me for their tip; and I'll look on helpless, and envy them. And thats what your son has brought me to. [*He is overcome by emotion.*]

MRS HIGGINS: Well, I'm glad youre not going to do anything foolish, Mr Doolittle. For this solves the problem of Eliza's future. You can provide for her now.

DOOLITTLE [*with melancholy resignation*]: Yes, maam: I'm expected to provide for everyone now, out of three thousand a year.

HIGGINS [*jumping up*]: Nonsense! he cant provide for her. He shant provide for her. She doesnt belong to him. I paid him five pounds for her. Doolittle: either youre an honest man or a rogue.

DOOLITTLE [*tolerantly*]: A little of both, Henry, like the rest of us: a little of both.

HIGGINS: Well, you took that money for the girl; and you have no right to take her as well.

MRS HIGGINS: Henry: dont be absurd. If you want to know where Eliza is, she is upstairs.

HIGGINS [*amazed*]: Upstairs!!! Then I shall jolly soon fetch her downstairs. [*He makes resolutely for the door.*]

MRS HIGGINS [*rising and following him*]: Be quiet, Henry. Sit down.

HIGGINS: I—

MRS HIGGINS: Sit down, dear; and listen to me.

HIGGINS: Oh very well, very well, very well. [*He throws himself ungraciously on the ottoman, with his face towards the windows.*] But I think you might have told us this half an hour ago.

MRS HIGGINS: Eliza came to me this morning. She told me of the brutal way you two treated her.

HIGGINS [*bounding up again*]: What!

PICKERING [*rising also*]: My dear Mrs Higgins, she's been telling you stories. We didnt treat her brutally. We hardly said a word to her; and we parted on particularly good terms. [*turning to Higgins*] Higgins: did you bully her after I went to bed?

HIGGINS: Just the other way about. She threw my slippers in my face. She behaved in the most outrageous way. I never gave her the slightest provocation. The slippers came bang into my face the moment I entered the room—before I had uttered a word. And used perfectly awful language.

PICKERING [*astonished*]: But why? What did we do to her?

MRS HIGGINS: I think I know pretty well what you did. The girl is naturally rather affectionate, I think. Isnt she, Mr Doolittle?

DOOLITTLE: Very tender-hearted, maam. Takes after me.

MRS HIGGINS: Just so. She had become attached to you both. She worked very hard for you, Henry. I dont think you quite realize what anything in the nature of brain work means to a girl of her class. Well, it seems that when the great day of trial came, and she did this wonderful thing for you without making a single mistake, you two sat there and never said a word to her, but talked together of how glad you were that it was all over and how you had been bored with the whole thing. And then you were surprised because she threw your slippers at you! I should have thrown the fire-irons at you.

HIGGINS: We said nothing except that we were tired and wanted to go to bed. Did we, Pick?

PICKERING [*shrugging his shoulders*]: That was all.

MRS HIGGINS [*ironically*]: Quite sure?

PICKERING: Absolutely. Really, that was all.

MRS HIGGINS: You didnt thank her, or pet her, or admire her, or tell her how splendid she'd been.

HIGGINS [*impatiently*]: But she knew all about that. We didnt make speeches to her, if thats what you mean.

PICKERING [*conscience stricken*]: Perhaps we were a little inconsiderate. Is she very angry?

MRS HIGGINS [*returning to her place at the writing-table*]: Well, I'm afraid she wont go back to Wimpole Street, especially now that Mr Doolittle is able to keep up the position you have thrust on her; but she says she is quite willing to meet you on friendly terms and to let bygones be bygones.

HIGGINS [*furious*]: Is she, by George? Ho!

MRS HIGGINS: If you promise to behave yourself, Henry, I'll ask her to come down. If not, go home; for you have taken up quite enough of my time.

HIGGINS: Oh, all right. Very well. Pick: you behave yourself. Let us put on our best Sunday manners for this creature that we picked out of the mud. [*He flings himself sulkily into the Elizabethan chair.*]

DOOLITTLE [*remonstrating*]: Now, now, Enry Iggins! Have some consideration for my feelings as a middle class man.

MRS HIGGINS: Remember your promise, Henry. [*She presses the bell-button on the writing-table.*] Mr Doolittle: will you be so good as to step out on the balcony for a moment. I dont want Eliza to have the shock of your news until she has made it up with these two gentlemen. Would you mind?

DOOLITTLE: As you wish, lady. Anything to help Henry to keep her off my hands. [*He disappears through the window.*]

*The parlour-maid answers the bell. Pickering sits down in Doolittle's place.*

MRS HIGGINS: Ask Miss Doolittle to come down, please.

THE PARLOUR-MAID: Yes, maam. [*She goes out.*]

MRS HIGGINS: Now, Henry: be good.

HIGGINS: I am behaving myself perfectly.

PICKERING: He is doing his best, Mrs Higgins.

*A pause. Higgins throws back his head; stretches out his legs; and begins to whistle.*

MRS HIGGINS: Henry, dearest, you dont look at all nice in that attitude.

HIGGINS [*pulling himself together*]: I was not trying to look nice, mother.

MRS HIGGINS: It doesnt matter, dear. I only wanted to make you speak.

HIGGINS: Why?

MRS HIGGINS: Because you cant speak and whistle at the same time.

*Higgins groans. Another very trying pause.*

HIGGINS [*springing up, out of patience*]: Where the devil is that girl? Are we to wait here all day?

*Eliza enters, sunny, self-possessed, and giving a staggeringly convincing exhibition of ease of manner. She carries a little work-basket, and is very much at home. Pickering is too much taken aback to rise.*

LIZA: How do you do, Professor Higgins? Are you quite well?

HIGGINS [*choking*]: Am I—[*He can say no more.*]

LIZA: But of course you are: you are never ill. So glad to see you again, Colonel Pickering. [*He rises hastily; and they shake hands.*] Quite chilly this morning, isnt it? [*She sits down on his left. He sits beside her.*]

HIGGINS: Dont you dare try this game on me. I taught it to you; and it doesnt take me in. Get up and come home; and dont be a fool.

*Eliza takes a piece of needlework from her basket, and begins to stitch at it, without taking the least notice of this outburst.*

MRS HIGGINS: Very nicely put, indeed, Henry. No woman could resist such an invitation.

HIGGINS: You let her alone, mother. Let her speak for herself. You will jolly soon see whether she has an idea that I havnt put into her head or a word that I havnt put into her mouth. I tell you I have created this thing out of the squashed cabbage leaves of Covent Garden; and now she pretends to play the fine lady with me.

MRS HIGGINS [*placidly*]: Yes, dear; but youll sit down, wont you?

*Higgins sits down again, savagely.*

LIZA [*to Pickering, taking no apparent notice of Higgins, and working away deftly*]: Will *you* drop me altogether now that the experiment is over, Colonel Pickering?

PICKERING: Oh dont. You mustnt think of it as an experiment. It shocks me, somehow.

LIZA: Oh, I'm only a squashed cabbage leaf—

PICKERING [*impulsively*]: No.

LIZA [*continuing quietly*]—but I owe so much to you that I should be very unhappy if you forgot me.

PICKERING: It's very kind of you to say so, Miss Doolittle.

LIZA: It's not because you paid for my dresses. I know you are generous to everybody with money. But it was from you that I learnt really nice manners; and that is what makes one a lady, isnt it? You see it was so very difficult for me with the example of Professor Higgins always before me. I was brought up to be just like him, unable to control myself, and using bad language on the slightest provocation. And I should never have known that ladies and gentlemen didnt behave like that if you hadnt been there.

HIGGINS: Well!!

PICKERING: Oh, thats only his way, you know. He doesnt mean it.

LIZA: Oh, *I* didnt mean it either, when I was a flower girl. It was only my way. But you see I did it; and thats what makes the difference after all.

PICKERING: No doubt. Still, he taught you to speak; and I couldnt have done that, you know.

LIZA [*trivially*]: Of course: that is his profession.

HIGGINS: Damnation!

LIZA [*continuing*]: It was just like learning to dance in the fashionable way: there was nothing more than that in it. But do you know what began my real education?

PICKERING: What?

LIZA [*stopping her work for a moment*]: Your calling me Miss Doolittle that day when I first came to Wimpole Street. That was the beginning of self-respect for me. [*She resumes her stitching.*] And there were a hundred little things you never noticed, because they came naturally to you. Things about standing up and taking off your hat and opening doors—

PICKERING: Oh, that was nothing.

LIZA: Yes: things that shewed you thought and felt about me as if I were something better than a scullery-maid; though of course I know you would have been just the same to a scullery-maid if she had been let into the drawing room. You never took off your boots in the dining room when I was there.

PICKERING: You mustnt mind that. Higgins takes off his boots all over the place.

LIZA: I know. I am not blaming him. It is his way, isnt it? But it made such a difference to me that you didnt do it. You see, really and truly, apart from the things anyone can pick up (the dressing and the proper way of speaking, and so on), the difference between a lady and a flower girl is not how she behaves, but how she's treated. I shall always be a flower girl to Professor Higgins, because he always treats me as a flower girl, and always will; but I know I can be a lady to you, because you always treat me as a lady, and always will.

MRS HIGGINS: Please dont grind your teeth, Henry.

PICKERING: Well, this is really very nice of you, Miss Doolittle.

LIZA: I should like you to call me Eliza, now, if you would.

PICKERING: Thank you. Eliza, of course.

LIZA: And I should like Professor Higgins to call me Miss Doolittle.

HIGGINS: I'll see you damned first.

MRS HIGGINS: Henry! Henry!

PICKERING [*laughing*]: Why dont you slang back at him? Dont stand it. It would do him a lot of good.

LIZA: I cant. I could have done it once; but now I cant go back to it. You told me, you know, that when a child is brought to a foreign country, it picks up the language in a few weeks, and forgets its own. Well, I am a child in your country. I have forgotten my own language, and can speak nothing but yours. Thats the real break-off with the corner of Tottenham Court Road. Leaving Wimpole Street finishes it.

PICKERING [*much alarmed*]: Oh! but youre coming back to Wimpole Street, arnt you? Youll forgive Higgins?

HIGGINS [*rising*]: Forgive! Will she, by George! Let her go. Let her find out how she can get on without us. She will relapse into the gutter in three weeks without me at her elbow.

*Doolittle appears at the centre window. With a look of dignified reproach at Higgins, he comes slowly and silently to his daughter, who, with her back to the window, is unconscious of his approach.*

PICKERING: He's incorrigible, Eliza. You wont relapse, will you?

LIZA: No: not now. Never again. I have learnt my lesson. I dont believe I could utter one of the old sounds if I tried.

[*Doolittle touches her on her left shoulder. She drops her work, losing her self-possession utterly at the spectacle of her father's splendour.*]

A-a-a-a-a-ah-ow-ooh!

HIGGINS [*with a crow of triumph*]: Aha! Just so. A-a-a-a-ahowooh! A-a-a-a-ahowooh! A-a-a-a-ahowooh! Victory! Victory! [*He throws himself on the diva, folding his arms, and spraddling arrogantly.*]

DOOLITTLE: Can you blame the girl? Dont look at me like that, Eliza. It aint my fault. Ive come into money.

LIZA: You must have touched a millionaire this time, dad.

DOOLITTLE: I have. But I'm dressed something special today. I'm going to St George's, Hanover Square. Your stepmother is going to marry me.

LIZA [*angrily*]: Youre going to let yourself down to marry that low common woman!

PICKERING [*quietly*]: He ought to, Eliza. [*to Doolittle*]: Why has she changed her mind?

DOOLITTLE [*sadly*]: Intimidated, Governor. Intimidated. Middle class morality claims its victim. Wont you put on your hat, Liza, and come and see me turned off?

LIZA: If the Colonel says I must, I—I'll [*almost sobbing*] I'll demean myself. And get insulted for my pains, like enough.

DOOLITTLE: Dont be afraid: she never comes to words with anyone now, poor woman! respectability has broke all the spirit out of her.

PICKERING [*squeezing Eliza's elbow gently*]: Be kind to them, Eliza. Make the best of it.

LIZA [*forcing a little smile for him through her vexation*]: Oh well, just to shew theres no ill feeling. I'll be back in a moment. [*She goes out.*]

DOOLITTLE [*sitting down beside Pickering*]: I feel uncommon nervous about the ceremony, Colonel. I wish youd come and see me through it.

PICKERING: But youve been through it before, man. You were married to Eliza's mother.

DOOLITTLE: Who told you that, Colonel?

PICKERING: Well, nobody told me. But I concluded—naturally—

DOOLITTLE: No: that aint the natural way, Colonel: it's only the middle class way. My way was always the undeserving way. But dont say nothing to Eliza. She dont know: I always had a delicacy about telling her.

PICKERING: Quite right. We'll leave it so, if you dont mind.

DOOLITTLE: And youll come to the church, Colonel, and put me through straight?

PICKERING: With pleasure. As far as a bachelor can.

MRS HIGGINS: May I come, Mr Doolittle? I should be very sorry to miss your wedding.

DOOLITTLE: I should indeed be honoured by your condescension, maam; and my poor old woman would take it as a tremenjous compliment. She's been very low, thinking of the happy days that are no more.

MRS HIGGINS [*rising*]: I'll order the carriage and get ready.

[*The men rise, except Higgins.*]

I shant be more than fifteen minutes.

[*As she goes to the door Eliza comes in, hatted and buttoning her gloves.*]

I'm going to the church to see your father married, Eliza. You had better come in the brougham with me. Colonel Pickering can go on with the bridegroom.

*Mrs Higgins goes out. Eliza comes to the middle of the room between the centre window and the ottoman. Pickering joins her.*

DOOLITTLE: Bridegroom! What a word! It makes a man realize his position, somehow. [*He takes up his hat and goes towards the door.*]

PICKERING: Before I go, Eliza, do forgive Higgins and come back to us.

LIZA: I dont think dad would allow me. Would you, dad?

DOOLITTLE [*sad but magnanimous*]: They played you off very cunning, Eliza, them two sportsmen. If it had been only one of them, you could have nailed him. But you see, there was two; and one of them chaperoned the other, as you might say. [*to Pickering*]: It was artful of you, Colonel: but I bear no malice: I should have done the same myself. I been the victim of one woman after another all my life; and I dont grudge you two getting the better of Eliza. I shant interfere. It's time for us to go, Colonel. So long, Henry. See you in St George's, Eliza. [*He goes out.*]

PICKERING [*coaxing*]: Do stay with us, Eliza. [*He follows Doolittle.*]

*Eliza goes out on the balcony to avoid being alone with Higgins. He rises and joins her there. She immediately comes back into the room and makes for the door; but he goes along the balcony quickly and gets his back to the door before she reaches it.*

HIGGINS: Well, Eliza, youve had a bit of your own back, as you call it. Have you had enough? and are you going to be reasonable? Or do you want any more?

LIZA: You want me back only to pick up your slippers and put up with your tempers and fetch and carry for you.

HIGGINS: I havnt said I wanted you back at all.

LIZA: Oh, indeed. Then what are we talking about?

HIGGINS: About you, not about me. If you come back I shall treat you just as I have always treated you. I cant change my nature; and I dont intend to change my manners. My manners are exactly the same as Colonel Pickering's.

LIZA: Thats not true. He treats a flower girl as if she was a duchess.

HIGGINS: And I treat a duchess as if she was a flower girl.

LIZA: I see. [*She turns away composedly, and sits on the ottoman, facing the window.*] The same to everybody.

HIGGINS: Just so.

LIZA: Like father.

HIGGINS [*grinning, a little taken down*]: Without accepting the comparison at all points, Eliza, it's quite true that your father is not a snob, and that he will be quite at home in any station of life to which his eccentric destiny may call him. [*seriously*] The great secret, Eliza, is not having bad manners or good manners or any other particular sort of manners, but having the same manners for all human souls: in short, behaving as if you were in Heaven, where there are no third-class carriages, and one soul is as good as another.

LIZA: Amen. You are a born preacher.

HIGGINS [*irritated*]: The question is not whether I treat you rudely, but whether you ever heard me treat anyone else better.

LIZA [*with sudden sincerity*]: I dont care how you treat me. I dont mind your swearing at me. I shouldnt mind a black eye: Ive had one before this. But [*standing up and facing him*] I wont be passed over.

HIGGINS: Then get out of my way; for I wont stop for you. You talk about me as if I were a motor bus.

LIZA: So you are a motor bus: all bounce and go, and no consideration for anyone. But I can do without you: dont think I cant.

HIGGINS: I know you can. I told you you could.

LIZA [*wounded, getting away from him to the other side of the ottoman with her face to the hearth*]: I know you did, you brute. You wanted to get rid of me.

HIGGINS: Liar.

LIZA: Thank you. [*She sits down with dignity.*]

HIGGINS: You never asked yourself, I suppose, whether I could do without you.

LIZA [*earnestly*]: Dont you try to get round me. Youll *have* to do without me.

HIGGINS [*arrogant*]: I can do without anybody. I have my own soul: my own spark of divine fire. But [*with sudden humility*] I shall miss you, Eliza. [*He sits down near her on the ottoman.*] I have learnt something from your idiotic notions: I confess that humbly and gratefully. And I have grown accustomed to your voice and appearance. I like them, rather.

LIZA: Well, you have both of them on your gramophone and in your book of photographs. When you feel lonely without me, you can turn the machine on. It's got no feelings to hurt.

HIGGINS: I cant turn your soul on. Leave me those feelings; and you can take away the voice and the face. They are not you.

LIZA: Oh, you are a devil. You can twist the heart in a girl as easy as some could twist her arms to hurt her. Mrs Pearce warned me. Time and again she has wanted to leave you; and you always got round her at the last minute. And you dont care a bit for her. And you dont care a bit for me.

HIGGINS: I care for life, for humanity; and you are a part of it that has come my way and been built into my house. What more can you or anyone ask?

LIZA: I wont care for anybody that doesnt care for me.

HIGGINS: Commercial principles, Eliza. Like [*reproducing her Covent Garden pronunciation with professional exactness*] s'yollin voylets [selling violets], isn't it?

LIZA: Dont sneer at me. It's mean to sneer at me.

HIGGINS: I have never sneered in my life. Sneering doesnt become either the human face or the human soul. I am expressing my righteous contempt for Commercialism. I dont and wont trade in affection. You call me a brute because you couldnt buy a claim on me by fetching my slippers and finding my spectacles. You were a fool: I think a woman fetching a man's slippers is a disgusting sight: did I ever fetch *your* slippers? I think a good deal more of you for throwing them in my face. No use slaving for me and then saying you want to be cared for: who cares for a slave? If you come back, come back for the sake of good fellowship; for youll get nothing else. Youve had a thousand times as much out of me as I have out of you; and if you dare to set up your little dog's tricks of fetching and carrying slippers against my creation of a Duchess Eliza, I'll slam the door in your silly face.

LIZA: What did you do it for if you didnt care for me?

HIGGINS [*heartily*]: Why, because it was my job.

LIZA: You never thought of the trouble it would make for me.

HIGGINS: Would the world ever have been made if its maker had been afraid of making trouble? Making life means making trouble. Theres only one way of escaping trouble; and thats killing things. Cowards, you notice, are always shrieking to have troublesome people killed.

LIZA: I'm no preacher: I dont notice things like that. I notice that you dont notice me.

HIGGINS [*jumping up and walking about intolerantly*]: Eliza: youre an idiot. I waste the treasures of my Miltonic mind by spreading them before you. Once for all, understand that I go my way and do my work without caring twopence what happens to either of us. I am not intimidated, like your father and your stepmother. So you can come back or go to the devil: which you please.

LIZA: What am I to come back for?

HIGGINS [*bouncing up on his knees on the ottoman and leaning over it to her*]: For the fun of it. Thats why I took you on.

LIZA [*with averted face*]: And you may throw me out tomorrow if I dont do everything you want me to?

HIGGINS: Yes; and you may walk out tomorrow if I dont do everything y o u want me to.

LIZA: And live with my stepmother?

HIGGINS: Yes, or sell flowers.

LIZA: Oh! if I only *could* go back to my flower basket! I should be independent of both you and father and all the world! Why did you take my independence from me? Why did I give it up? I'm a slave now, for all my fine clothes.

HIGGINS: Not a bit. I'll adopt you as my daughter and settle money on you if you like. Or would you rather marry Pickering?

LIZA [*looking fiercely round at him*]: I wouldnt marry *you* if you asked me; and youre nearer my age than what he is.

HIGGINS [*gently*]: Than he is: not 'Than what he is.'

LIZA [*losing her temper and rising*]: I'll talk as I like. Youre not my teacher now.

HIGGINS [*reflectively*]: I dont suppose Pickering would, though. He's as confirmed an old bachelor as I am.

LIZA: Thats not what I want; and dont you think it. Ive always had chaps enough wanting me that way. Freddy Hill writes to me twice and three times a day, sheets and sheets.

HIGGINS [*disagreeably surprised*]: Damn his impudence! [*He recoils and finds himself sitting on his heels.*]

LIZA: He has a right to if he likes, poor lad. And he does love me.

HIGGINS [*getting off the ottoman*]: You have no right to encourage him.

LIZA: Every girl has a right to be loved.

HIGGINS: What! By fools like that?

LIZA: Freddy's not a fool. And if he's weak and poor and wants me, may be he'd make me happier than my betters that bully me and dont want me.

HIGGINS: Can he *make* anything of you? Thats the point.

LIZA: Perhaps I could make something of him. But I never thought of us making anything of one another; and you never think of anything else. I only want to be natural.

HIGGINS: In short, you want me to be as infatuated about you as Freddy? Is that it?

LIZA: No I dont. Thats not the sort of feeling I want from you. And dont you be too sure of yourself or of me. I could have been a bad girl if I'd liked. Ive seen more of some things than you, for all your learning. Girls like me can drag gentlemen down to make love to them easy enough. And they wish each other dead the next minute.

HIGGINS: Of course they do. Then what in thunder are we quarrelling about?

LIZA [*much troubled*]: I want a little kindness. I know I'm a common ignorant girl, and you a book-learned gentleman; but I'm not dirt under your feet. What I done [*correcting herself*] what I did was not for the dresses and the taxis: I did it because we were pleasant together and I come—came—to care for you; not to want you to make love to me, and not forgetting the difference between us, but more friendly like.

HIGGINS: Well, of course. Thats just how I feel. And how Pickering feels. Eliza: youre a fool.

LIZA: Thats not a proper answer to give me. [*She sinks on the chair at the writing-table in tears.*]

HIGGINS: It's all youll get until you stop being a common idiot. If youre going to be a lady, youll have to give up feeling neglected if the men you know dont spend half their time snivelling over you and the other half giving you black eyes. If you cant stand the coldness of my sort of life, and the strain of it, go back to the gutter. Work til youre more a brute than a human being; and then cuddle and squabble and drink til you fall asleep. Oh, it's a fine life, the life of the gutter. It's real: it's warm: it's violent: you can feel it through the thickest skin: you can taste it and smell it without any training or any work. Not like Science and Literature and Classical Music and Philosophy and Art. You find me cold, unfeeling, selfish, dont you? Very well: be off with you to the sort of people you like. Marry some sentimental hog or other with lots of money, and a thick pair of lips to kiss you with and a thick pair of boots to kick you with. If you cant appreciate what youve got, youd better get what you can appreciate.

LIZA [*desperate*]: Oh, you *are* a cruel tyrant. I cant talk to you: you turn everything against me: I'm always in the wrong. But you know very well all the time that youre nothing but a bully. You know I cant go back to the gutter, as you call it, and that I have no real friends in the world but you and the Colonel. You know very well I couldnt bear to live with a low common man after you two; and it's wicked and cruel of you to insult me by pretending I could. You think I must go back to Wimpole Street because I have nowhere else to go but father's. But dont you be too sure that you have me under your feet to be trampled on and talked down. I'll marry Freddy, I will, as soon as I'm able to support him.

HIGGINS [*thunderstruck*]: Freddy!!! that young fool! That poor devil who couldnt get a job as an errand boy even if he had the guts to try for it! Woman: do you not understand that I have made you a consort for a king?

LIZA: Freddy loves me: that makes him king enough for me. I dont want him to work: he wasnt brought up to it as I was. I'll go and be a teacher.

HIGGINS: What'll you teach, in heaven's name?

LIZA: What you taught me. I'll teach phonetics.

HIGGINS: Ha! ha! ha!

LIZA: I'll offer myself as an assistant to that hairy-faced Hungarian.

HIGGINS [*rising in a fury*]: What! That impostor! that humbug! that toadying ignoramus! Teach him *my* methods! *my* discoveries! You take one step in his direction and I'll wring your neck. [*He lays hands on her.*] Do you hear?

LIZA [*defiantly non-resistant*]: Wring away. What do I care? I knew youd strike me some day.

[*He lets her go, stamping with rage at having forgotten himself, and recoils so hastily that he stumbles back into his seat on the ottoman.*]

Aha! Now I know how to deal with you. What a fool I was not to think of it before! You cant take away the knowledge you gave me. You said I had a finer ear than you. And I can be civil and kind to people, which is more than you can. Aha! [*Purposely dropping her aitches to annoy him.*] Thats done you, Enry Iggins, it az. Now I dont care *that* [*snapping her fingers*] for your bullying and your big talk. I'll advertize it in the papers that your duchess is only a flower girl that you taught, and that she'll teach anybody to be a duchess just the same in six months for a thousand guineas. Oh, when I think of myself crawling under your feet and being trampled on and called names, when all the time I had only to lift up my finger to be as good as you, I could just kick myself.

HIGGINS [*wondering at her*]: You damned impudent slut, you! But it's better than snivelling; better than fetching slippers and finding spectacles, isnt it? [*rising*] By George, Eliza, I said I'd make a woman of you; and I have. I like you like this.

LIZA: Yes: you turn round and make up to me now that I'm not afraid of you, and can do without you.

HIGGINS: Of course I do, you little fool. Five minutes ago you were like a millstone round my neck. Now youre a tower of strength: a consort battleship. You and I and Pickering will be three old bachelors together instead of only two men and a silly girl.

*Mrs Higgins returns, dressed for the wedding. Eliza instantly becomes cool and elegant.*

MRS HIGGINS: The carriage is waiting, Eliza. Are you ready?

LIZA: Quite. Is the Professor coming?

MRS HIGGINS: Certainly not. He cant behave himself in church. He makes remarks out loud all the time on the clergyman's pronunciation.

LIZA: Then I shall not see you again, Professor. Goodbye. [*She goes to the door.*]

MRS HIGGINS [*coming to Higgins*]: Goodbye, dear.

HIGGINS: Goodbye, mother. [*He is about to kiss her, when he recollects something.*] Oh, by the way, Eliza, order a ham and a Stilton cheese, will you? And buy me a pair of reindeer gloves, number eights, and a tie to match that new suit of mine. You can choose the colour. [*His cheerful, careless, vigorous voice shews that he is incorrigible.*]

LIZA [*disdainfully*]: Number eights are too small for you if you want them lined with lamb's wool. You have three new ties that you have forgotten in the drawer of your washstand. Colonel Pickering prefers double Gloucester to Stilton; and you dont notice the difference. I telephoned Mrs Pearce this morning not to forget the ham. What you are to do without me I cannot imagine. [*She sweeps out.*]

MRS HIGGINS: I'm afraid youve spoilt that girl, Henry. I should be uneasy about you and her if she were less fond of Colonel Pickering.

HIGGINS: Pickering! Nonsense: she's going to marry Freddy. Ha ha! Freddy! Freddy!! Ha ha ha ha ha!!!!! [*He roars with laughter as the play ends.*]

* * *

The rest of the story need not be shewn in action, and indeed, would hardly need telling if our imaginations were not so enfeebled by their lazy dependence on the ready-mades and reach-me-downs of the ragshop in which Romance keeps its stock of 'happy endings' to misfit all stories. Now, the history of Eliza Doolittle, though called a romance because the transfiguration it records seems exceedingly improbable, is common enough. Such transfigurations have been achieved by hundreds of resolutely ambitious young women since Nell Gwynne set them the example by playing queens and fascinating kings in the theatre in which she began by selling oranges. Nevertheless, people in all directions have assumed, for no other reason than that she became the heroine of a romance, that she must have married the hero of it. This is unbearable, not only because her little drama, if acted on such a thoughtless assumption, must be spoiled, but because the true sequel is patent to anyone with a sense of human nature in general, and of feminine instinct in particular.

Eliza, in telling Higgins she would not marry him if he asked her, was not coquetting: she was announcing a well-considered decision. When a bachelor interests, and dominates, and teaches, and becomes important to a spinster, as Higgins with Eliza, she always, if she has character enough to be capable of it, considers very seriously indeed whether she will play for becoming that bachelor's wife, especially if he is so little interested in marriage that a determined and devoted woman might capture him if she set herself resolutely to do it. Her decision will depend a good deal on whether she is really free to choose; and that, again, will depend on her age and income. If she is at the end of her youth, and has no security for her livelihood, she will marry him because she must marry somebody who will provide for her. But at Eliza's age a good-looking girl does not feel that pressure: she feels free to pick and choose. She is therefore guided by her instinct in the matter. Eliza's instinct tells her not to marry Higgins. It does not tell her to give him up. It is not in the slightest doubt as to his remaining one of the strongest personal interests in her life. It would be very sorely strained if there was another woman likely to supplant her with him. But as she feels sure of him on that last point, she has no doubt at all as to her course, and would not have any, even if the difference of twenty years of age, which seems so great to youth, did not exist between them.

As our own instincts are not appealed to by her conclusion, let us see whether we cannot discover some reason for it. When Higgins excused his indifferences to young women on the ground that they had an irresistible rival in his mother, he gave the clue to his inveterate old-bachelordom. The case is uncommon only to the extent that remarkable mothers are uncommon. If an imaginative boy has a sufficiently rich mother who has intelligence, personal grace, dignity of character without harshness, and a cultivated sense of the best art of her time to enable her to make her house beautiful, she sets a standard for him against which very few women can struggle, besides effecting for him a disengagement of his affections, his sense of beauty, and his idealism from his specifically sexual impulses. This makes him a standing puzzle to the huge number of uncultivated people who have been brought up in tasteless homes by commonplace or disagreeable parents, and to whom, consequently, literature, painting, sculpture, music, and affectionate personal relations come as modes of sex if they come at all. The word passion means nothing else to them; and that Higgins could have a passion for phonetics and idealize his mother instead of Eliza, would seem to them absurd and unnatural. Nevertheless, when we look round and see that hardly anyone is too ugly or disagreeable to find a wife or a husband if he or she wants one, whilst many old maids and bachelors are above the average in quality and culture, we cannot help suspecting that the disentanglement of sex from the associations with which it is so commonly confused, a disentanglement which persons of genius achieve by sheer intellectual analysis, is sometimes produced or aided by parental fascination.

Now, though Eliza was incapable of thus explaining to herself Higgins's formidable powers of resistance to the charm that prostrated Freddy at the first glance, she was instinctively aware that she could never obtain a complete grip on him, or come between him and his mother (the first necessity of the married woman). To put it shortly, she knew for some mysterious reason he had not the makings of a married man in him, according to her conception of a husband as one to whom she would be his nearest and fondest and warmest interest. Even had there been no mother-rival, she would still have refused to accept an interest in herself that was secondary to philosophic interests. Had Mrs Higgins died, there would still have been Milton and the Universal Alphabet. Landor's remark that to those who have the greatest power of loving, love is a secondary affair, would not have recommended Landor to Eliza. Put that along with her resentment of Higgins's domineering superiority, and her mistrust of his coaxing cleverness in getting around her and evading her wrath when he had gone too far with his impetuous bullying, and you will see that Eliza's instinct had good grounds for warning her not to marry her Pygmalion.

And now, whom did Eliza marry? For if Higgins was a predestinate old bachelor, she was most certainly not a predestinate old maid. Well, that can be told very shortly to those who have not guessed it from the indications she has herself given them.

Almost immediately after Eliza is stung into proclaiming her considered determination not to marry Higgins, she mentions the fact that young Mr Frederick Eynsford

Hill is pouring out his love for her daily through the post. Now Freddy is young, practically twenty years younger than Higgins: he is a gentleman (or, as Eliza would qualify him, a toff), and speaks like one. He is nicely dressed, is treated by the Colonel as an equal, loves her unaffectedly, and is not her master, nor ever likely to dominate her in spite of his advantage of social standing. Eliza has no use for the foolish romantic tradition that all women love to be mastered, if not actually bullied and beaten. 'When you go to women' says Nietzsche 'take your whip with you.' Sensible despots have never confined that precaution to women: they have taken their whips with them when they have dealt with men, and been slavishly idealized by the men over whom they have flourished the whip much more than by women. No doubt there are slavish women as well as slavish men; and women, like men, admire those that are stronger than themselves. But to admire a strong person and to live under that strong person's thumb are two different things. The weak may not be admired and hero-worshipped; but they are by no means disliked or shunned; and they never seem to have the least difficulty in marrying people who are too good for them. They may fail in emergencies; but life is not one long emergency: it is mostly a string of situations for which no exceptional strength is needed, and with which even rather weak people can cope if they have a stronger partner to help them out. Accordingly, it is a truth everywhere in evidence that strong people, masculine or feminine, not only do not marry stronger people, but do not shew any preference for them in selecting their friends. When a lion meets another with a louder roar 'the first lion thinks the last a bore.' The man or woman who feels strong enough for two, seeks for every other quality in a partner than strength.

The converse is also true. Weak people want to marry strong people who do not frighten them too much; and this often leads them to make the mistake we describe metaphorically as 'biting off more than they can chew'. They want too much for too little; and when the bargain is unreasonable beyond all bearing, the union becomes impossible: it ends in the weaker party being either discarded or borne as a cross, which is worse. People who are not only weak, but silly or obtuse as well, are often in these difficulties.

This being the state of human affairs, what is Eliza fairly sure to do when she is placed between Freddy and Higgins? Will she look forward to a lifetime of fetching Higgins's slippers or to a lifetime of Freddy fetching hers? There can be no doubt about the answer. Unless Freddy is biologically repulsive to her, and Higgins biologically attractive to a degree that overwhelms all her other instincts, she will, if she marries either of them, marry Freddy.

And that is just what Eliza did.

Complications ensued; but they were economic, not romantic. Freddy had no money and no occupation. His mother's jointure, a last relic of the opulence of Largelady Park, had enabled her to struggle along in Earlscourt with an air of gentility, but not to procure any serious secondary education for her children, much less give the boy a profession. A clerkship at thirty shillings a week was beneath Freddy's dignity, and extremely distasteful to him besides. His prospects consisted of a hope that if he kept up appearances somebody would do something for him. The something appeared vaguely to his imagination as a private secretaryship or a sinecure of some sort. To his mother it perhaps appeared as a marriage to some lady of means who could not resist her boy's niceness. Fancy her feelings when he married a flower girl who had become disclassed under extraordinary circumstances which were now notorious!

It is true that Eliza's situation did not seem wholly ineligible. Her father, though formerly a dustman, and now fantastically disclassed, had become extremely popular in the smartest society by a social talent which triumphed over every prejudice and every disadvantage. Rejected by the middle class, which he loathed, he had shot up at once into the highest circles by his wit, his dustmanship (which he carried like a banner), and his Nietzschean transcendence of good and evil. At intimate ducal dinners he sat on the right hand of the Duchess; and in country houses he smoked in the pantry and was made much of by the butler when he was not feeding in the dining room and being consulted by cabinet ministers. But he found it almost as hard to do all this on four thousand a year as Mrs Eynsford Hill to live in Earlscourt on an income so pitiably smaller that I have not the heart to disclose its exact figure. He absolutely refused to add the last straw to his burden by contributing to Eliza's support.

Thus Freddy and Eliza, now Mr and Mrs Eynsford Hill, would have spent a penniless honeymoon but for a wedding present of £500 from the Colonel to Eliza. It lasted a long time because Freddy did not know how to spend money, never having any to spend, and Eliza, socially trained by a pair of bachelors, wore her clothes as long as they held together and looked pretty, without the least regard to their being many months out of fashion. Still, £500 will not last two young people for ever; and they both knew, and Eliza felt as well, that they must shift for themselves in the end. She could quarter herself on Wimpole Street because it had come to be her home; but she was quite aware that she ought not to quarter Freddy there, and that it would not be good for his character if she did.

Not that the Wimpole Street bachelors objected. When she consulted them, Higgins declined to be bothered about her housing problem when that solution was so simple. Eliza's desire to have Freddy in the house with her seemed of no more importance than if she had wanted an extra piece of bedroom furniture. Pleas as to Freddy's character, and the moral obligation on him to earn his own living, were lost on Higgins. He denied that Freddy had any character, and declared that if he tried to do any useful work some competent person would have the trouble of undoing it: a procedure involving a net loss to the community, and great unhappiness to Freddy himself, who was obviously intended by Nature for such light work as amusing Eliza, which, Higgins declared, was a much more useful and honourable occupation than working in the city. When Eliza referred again to her project of teaching phonetics, Higgins abated not a jot of his violent opposition to it. He said she was not within ten years of being qualified to meddle with his pet subject; and as it was evident that the Colonel agreed with him, she felt she could not go against them in this grave matter, and that she had no right, without Higgins's consent, to exploit the knowledge he had given her; for his knowledge seemed to her as much his private property as his watch: Eliza was no communist. Besides, she was superstitiously devoted to them both, more entirely and frankly after her marriage than before it.

It was the Colonel who finally solved the problem, which had cost him much perplexed cogitation. He one day asked Eliza, rather shyly, whether she had quite given up her notion of keeping a flower shop. She replied that she had thought of it, but had put it out of her head, because the Colonel had said, that day at Mrs Higgins's, that it would never do. The Colonel confessed that when he said that, he had not quite recovered from the dazzling impression of the day before. They broke the matter to Higgins that evening. The sole comment vouchsafed by him very nearly led to a serious quarrel with Eliza. It was to the effect that she would have in Freddy an ideal errand boy.

Freddy himself was next sounded on the subject. He said he had been thinking of a shop himself; though it had presented itself to his pennilessness as a small place in which Eliza should sell tobacco at one counter whilst he sold newspapers at the opposite one. But he agreed that it would be extraordinarily jolly to go early every morning with Eliza to Covent Garden and buy flowers on the scene of their first meeting: a sentiment which earned him many kisses from his wife. He added that he had always been afraid to propose anything of the sort, because Clara would make an awful row about a step that must damage her matrimonial chances, and his mother could not be expected to like it after clinging for so many years to that step of the social ladder on which retail trade is impossible.

This difficulty was removed by an event highly unexpected by Freddy's mother. Clara, in the course of her incursions into those artistic circles which were the highest within her reach, discovered that her conversational qualifications were expected to include a grounding in the novels of Mr H.G. Wells. She borrowed them in various directions so energetically that she swallowed them all within two months. The result was a conversion of a kind quite common today. A modern Acts of the Apostles would fill fifty whole Bibles if anyone were capable of writing it.

Poor Clara, who appeared to Higgins and his mother as a disagreeable and ridiculous person, and to her own mother as in some inexplicable way a social failure, had never seen herself in either light; for, though to some extent ridiculed and mimicked in West Kensington like everybody else there, she was accepted as a rational and normal—or shall we say inevitable?—sort of human being. At worst they called her The Pusher; but to them no more than to herself had it ever occurred that she was pushing the air, and pushing it in a wrong direction. Still, she was not happy. She was growing desperate. Her one asset, the fact that her mother was what the Epsom greengrocer called a carriage lady, had no exchange value, apparently. It had prevented her from getting educated, because the only education she could have afforded was education with the Earlscourt greengrocer's daughter. It had led her to seek the society of her mother's class; and that class simply would not have her, because she was much poorer than the greengrocer, and, far from being able to afford a maid, could not afford even a housemaid, and had to scrape along at home with an illiberally treated general servant. Under such circumstances nothing could give her an air of being a genuine product of Largelady Park. And yet its tradition made her regard a marriage with anyone within her reach as an unbearable humiliation. Commercial people and professional people in a small way were odious to her. She ran after painters and novelists; but she did not charm them; and her bold attempts to pick up and practise artistic and literary talk irritated them. She was, in short, an utter failure, an ignorant, incompetent, pretentious, unwelcome, penniless, useless little snob; and though she did not admit these disqualifications (for nobody ever faces unpleasant truths of this kind until the possibility of a way out dawns on them) she felt their effects too keenly to be satisfied with her position.

Clara had a startling eyeopener when, on being suddenly wakened to enthusiasm by a girl of her own age who dazzled her and produced in her a gushing desire to take her for a model, and gain her friendship, she discovered that this exquisite apparition had graduated from the gutter in a few months time. It shook her so violently, that when Mr H.G. Wells lifted her on the point of his puissant pen, and placed her at the angle of view from which the life she was leading and the society to which she clung appeared in its true relation to real human needs and worthy social structure, he effected a conversion and a conviction of sin comparable to the most sensational feats of General Booth or Gypsy Smith. Clara's snobbery went bang. Life suddenly began to move with her. Without knowing how or why, she began to make friends and enemies. Some of the acquaintances to whom she had been a tedious or indifferent or ridiculous affliction, dropped her: others became cordial. To her amazement she found that some 'quite nice' people were saturated with Wells, and that this accessibility to ideas was the secret of their niceness. People she had thought deeply religious, and had tried to conciliate on that track with disastrous results, suddenly took an interest in her, and revealed a hostility to conventional religion which she had never conceived possible except among the most desperate characters. They made her read Galsworthy; and Galsworthy exposed the vanity of Largelady Park and finished her. It exasperated her to think that the dungeon in which she had languished for so many unhappy years had been unlocked all the time, and that the impulses she had so carefully struggled with and stifled for the sake of keeping well with society, were precisely those by which alone she could have come into any sort of sincere human contact. In the radiance of these discoveries, and the tumult of their reaction, she made a fool of herself as freely and conspicuously as when she so rashly adopted Eliza's expletive in Mrs Higgins's drawing room; for the new-born Wellsian had to find her bearings almost as ridiculously as a baby; but nobody hates a baby for its ineptitudes, or thinks the worse of it for trying to eat the matches; and Clara lost no friends by her follies. They laughed at her to her face this time; and she had to defend herself and fight it out as best she could.

When Freddy paid a visit to Earlscourt (which he never did when he could possibly help it) to make the desolating announcement that he and his Eliza were thinking of blackening the Largelady scutcheon by opening a shop, he found the little household already convulsed by a prior announcement from Clara that she also was going to work in an old furniture shop in Dover Street, which had been started by a fellow Wellsian. This appointment Clara owed, after all, to her old social accomplishment of Push. She had made up her mind that, cost what it might, she would see Mr Wells in the flesh; and she had achieved her end at a garden party. She had better luck than so rash an enterprise deserved. Mr Wells came up to her expectations. Age had not withered him, nor could custom stale his infinite variety in half an hour. His pleasant neatness and compactness, his small hands and feet, his teeming ready brain, his unaffected accessibility, and a certain fine apprehensiveness which stamped him as susceptible from his topmost hair to his tipmost toe, proved irresistible. Clara talked of nothing else for weeks and weeks afterwards. And as she happened to talk to the lady of the furniture shop, and that lady also desired above all things to know Mr Wells and sell pretty things to him, she offered Clara a job on the chance of achieving that end through her.

And so it came about that Eliza's luck held, and the expected opposition to the flower shop melted away. The shop is in the arcade of a railway station not very far from the Victoria and Albert Museum; and if you live in that neighbourhood you may go there any day and buy a buttonhole from Eliza.

Now here is a last opportunity for romance. Would you not like to be assured that the shop was an immense success, thanks to Eliza's charms and her early business experience in Covent Garden? Alas! the truth is the truth: the shop did not pay for a long time, simply because Eliza and her Freddy did not know how to keep it. True, Eliza had not to begin at the very beginning: she knew the names and prices of the cheaper flowers; and her elation was unbounded when she found that Freddy, like all youths educated at cheap, pretentious, and thoroughly inefficient schools, knew a little Latin. It was very little, but enough to make him appear to her a Porson or Bentley, and to put him at ease with botanical nomenclature. Unfortunately he knew nothing else; and Eliza, though she could count money up to eighteen shillings or so, and had acquired a certain familiarity with the language of Milton from her struggles to qualify herself for winning Higgins's bet, could not write out a bill without utterly disgracing the establishment. Freddy's power of stating in Latin that Balbus built a wall and that Gaul was divided into three parts did not carry with it the slightest knowledge of accounts or business: Colonel Pickering had to explain to him what a cheque book and a bank account meant. And the pair were by no means easily teachable. Freddy backed up Eliza in her obstinate refusal to believe that they could save money by engaging a bookkeeper with some knowledge of the business. How, they argued, could you possibly save money by going to extra expense when you already could not make both ends meet? But the Colonel, after making ends meet over and over again, at last gently insisted; and Eliza, humbled to the dust by having to beg from him so often, and stung by the uproarious derision of Higgins, to whom the notion of Freddy succeeding at anything was a joke that never palled, grasped the fact that business, like phonetics, has to be learned.

On the piteous spectacle of the pair spending their evenings in shorthand schools and polytechnic classes, learning bookkeeping and typewriting with incipient junior clerks, male and female, from the elementary schools, let me not dwell. There were even classes at the London School of Economics, and a humble personal appeal to the director of that institution to recommend a course bearing on the flower business. He, being a humorist, explained to them the method of the celebrated Dickensian essay of Chinese Metaphysics by the gentleman who read an article on China and an article on Metaphysics and combined the information. He suggested that they should combine the London School with Kew Gardens. Eliza, to whom the procedure of the Dickensian gentleman seemed perfectly correct (as in fact it was) and not in the least funny (which was only her ignorance), took the advice with entire gravity. But the effort that cost her the deepest humiliation was a request to Higgins, whose pet artistic fancy, next to Milton's verse, was caligraphy, and who himself wrote a most beautiful Italian hand, that he would teach her to write. He declared that she was congenitally incapable of forming a single letter worthy of the least of Milton's words; but she persisted; and again he suddenly threw himself into the task of teaching her with a combination of stormy intensity, concentrated patience, and occasional bursts of interesting disquisition on the beauty and nobility, the august mission and destiny, of human handwriting. Eliza ended by acquiring an extremely uncommercial script which was a positive extension of her personal beauty, and spending three times as much on stationary as anyone else because certain qualities and shapes of paper became indispensable to her. She could not even address an envelope in the usual way because it made the margins all wrong.

Their commercial schooldays were a period of disgrace and despair for the young couple. They seemed to be learning nothing about flower shops. At last they gave it up as hopeless, and shook the dust of the shorthand schools, and the polytechnics, and the London School of Economics from their feet for ever. Besides, the business was in some mysterious way beginning to take care of itself. They had somehow forgotten their objections to employing other people. They came to the conclusion that their own way was the best, and that they had really a remarkable talent for business. The Colonel, who had been compelled for some years to keep a sufficient sum on current account at his bankers to make up their deficits, found that the provision was unnecessary: the young people were prospering. It is true that there was not quite fair play between them and their competitors in trade. Their week-ends in the country cost them nothing, and saved them the price of their Sunday dinners; for the motor car was the Colonel's; and he and Higgins paid the hotel bills. Mr F. Hill, florist and greengrocer (they soon discovered that there was money in asparagus; and asparagus led to other vegetables), had an air which stamped the business as classy; and in private life he was Frederick Eynsford Hill, Esquire. Not that there was any swank about him: nobody but Eliza knew that he had been christened Frederick Challoner. Eliza herself swanked like anything.

That is all. That is how it has turned out. It is astonishing how much Eliza still manages to meddle in the housekeeping at Wimpole Street in spite of the shop and her own family. And it is notable that though she never nags her husband, and frankly loves the Colonel as if she were his favourite daughter, she has never got out of the habit of nagging Higgins that was established on the fatal night when she won his bet for him. She snaps his head off on the faintest provocation, or on none. He no longer dares to tease her by assuming an abysmal inferiority of Freddy's mind to his own. He storms and bullies and derides; but she stands up to him so ruthlessly that the Colonel has to ask her from time to time to be kinder to Higgins; and it is the only request of his that brings a mulish expression into her face. Nothing but some emergency or calamity great enough to break down all likes and dislikes, and throw them both back on their common humanity—and may they be spared any such trial!—will ever alter this. She knows that Higgins does not need her, just as her father did not need her.

The very scrupulousness with which he told her that day that he had become used to having her there, and dependent on her for all sorts of little services, and that he should miss her if she want away (it would never have occurred to Freddy or the Colonel to say anything of the sort) deepens her inner certainty that she is 'no more to him than them slippers'; yet she has a sense, too, that his indifference is deeper than infatuation of commoner souls. She is immensely interested in him. She has even secret mischievous moments in which she wishes she could get him alone, on a desert island, away from all ties and with nobody else in the world to consider, and just drag him off his pedestal and see him making love like any common man. We all have private imaginations of that sort. But when it comes to business, to the life that she really leads as distinguished from the life of dreams and fancies, she likes Freddy and she likes the Colonel; and she does not like Higgins and Mr Doolittle. Galatea never does quite like Pygmalion: his relation to her is too godlike to be altogether agreeable.

*The End*

1913

# Samuel Beckett
## 1906–1989

Born and raised near Dublin, where his father was a well-to-do purveyor, Samuel Beckett was sent to a boarding school at the age of 14, and went on to receive a BA at Trinity College, Dublin, where he distinguished himself as a scholar of French and Italian. His academic distinction won him a lectureship in Paris, where he met and became the literary disciple of James Joyce, and began writing experimental poetry and fiction. After receiving his MA from Trinity College in 1931, he gave up academic life, returned to the continent, and continued to write fiction, while travelling around France and Germany, leading a vagabond existence. He settled in Paris in 1937 and subsequently became a member of the French resistance movement. At the end of the Second World War he began writing the plays that were to make him internationally famous as the first and leading practitioner of absurdist drama. His best-known plays, *Waiting for Godot* (1953), *Endgame* (1957), and *Krapp's Last Tape* (1958), repeatedly challenge conventional dramatic expectations through their depiction of bizarre vaudeville-like characters in outlandish settings, engaged in purposeless activities, exchanging frequently illogical and comically nonsensical dialogue with each other or with themselves. And in challenging traditional forms of theatre, they ultimately challenge traditional views of human existence, suggesting that it may be as illogical, as absurd, as the dramatic spectacles they portray.

# Krapp's Last Tape

*A late evening in the future.*

*Krapp's den.*

*Front centre a small table, the two drawers of which open towards audience. Sitting at the table, facing front, i.e. across from the drawers, a wearish old man: Krapp.*

*Rusty black narrow trousers too short for him. Rusty black sleeveless waistcoat, four capacious pockets. Heavy silver watch and chain. Grimy white shirt open at the neck, no collar. Surprising pair of dirty boots, size ten at least, very narrow and pointed.*

*White face. Purple nose. Disordered grey hair. Unshaven.*

*Very near-sighted (but unspectacled). Hard of hearing.*

*Crackled voice. Distinctive intonation.*

*Laborious walk.*

*On the table a tape-recorder with microphone and a number of cardboard boxes containing reels of recorded tapes.*

*Table and immediately adjacent area in strong white light. Rest of stage in darkness.*

*Krapp remains a moment motionless, heaves a great sigh, looks at his watch, fumbles in his pockets, takes out an envelope, puts it back, fumbles, takes out a small bunch of keys, raises it to his eyes, chooses a key, gets up and moves to front of table. He stoops, unlocks first drawer, peers into it, feels about inside it, takes out a reel of tape, peers at it, puts it back, locks drawer, unlocks second drawer, peers into it, feels about inside it, takes out a large banana, peers at it, locks drawer, puts keys back in his pocket. He turns, advances to edge of stage, halts, strokes banana, peels it, drops skin at his feet, puts end of banana in his mouth and remains motionless, staring vacuously before him. Finally he bites off the end, turns aside, and begins pacing to and fro at edge of stage, in the light, i.e. not more than four or five paces either way, meditatively eating banana. He treads on skin, slips, nearly falls, recovers himself, stoops and peers at skin and finally pushes it, still stooping, with his foot over the edge of the stage into pit. He resumes his pacing, finishes banana, returns to table, sits down, remains a moment motionless, heaves a great sigh, takes keys from his pockets, raises them to his eyes, chooses key, gets up and moves to front of table, unlocks second drawer, takes out a second banana, peers at it, locks drawer, puts back keys in his pocket, turns, advances to edge of stage, halts, strokes banana, peels it, tosses skin into pit, puts end of banana in his mouth and remains motionless, staring vacuously before him. Finally he has an idea, puts banana in his waistcoat pocket, the end emerging, and goes with all the speed he can muster backstage into darkness. Ten seconds. Loud pop of cork. Fifteen seconds. He comes back into light carrying an old ledger and sits down at table. He lays ledger on table, wipes his mouth, wipes his hands on the front of his waistcoat, brings them smartly together and rubs them.*

KRAPP [*briskly*]: Ah! [*He bends over ledger, turns the pages, finds the entry he wants, reads.*] Box . . . thrree . . . spool . . . five. [*He raises his head and stares front. With relish.*] Spool! [*Pause.*] Spooool! [*Happy smile. Pause. He bends over table, starts peering and poking at the boxes.*] Box . . . thrree . . . thrree . . . four . . . two . . . [*with surprise*] nine! good God! . . . seven . . . ah! the little rascal! [*He takes up box, peers at it.*] Box thrree. [*He lays it on table, opens it and peers at spools inside.*] Spool . . . [*he peers at ledger*] . . . five [*he peers at spools*] . . . five . . . five! . . . ah! the little scoundrel! [*He takes out a spool, peers at it.*] Spool five. [*He lays it on table, closes box three, puts it back with the others, takes up the spool.*] Box thrree, spool five. [*He bends over the machine, looks up. With relish.*] Spooool! [*Happy smile. He bends, loads spool on machine, rubs his hands.*] Ah! [*He peers at ledger, reads entry at foot of page.*] Mother at rest at last . . . Hm . . . The black ball . . . [*He raises his head, stares blankly in front. Puzzled.*] Black ball? . . . [*He peers again at ledger, reads.*] The dark nurse . . . [*He raises his head, broods, peers again at ledger, reads.*] Slight improvement in bowel condition . . . Hm . . . Memorable . . . what? [*He peers closer.*] Equinox, memorable equinox. [*He raises his head, stares blankly front. Puzzled.*] Memorable equinox? . . . [*Pause. He shrugs his shoulders, peers again at ledger, reads.*] Farewell to—[*he turns the page*]—love.

*He raises his head, broods, bends over machine, switches on and assumes listening posture, i.e. leaning forward, elbows on table, hand cupping ear towards machine, face front.*

TAPE [*strong voice, rather pompous, clearly Krapp's at a much earlier time*]: Thirty-nine today, sound as a—[*Settling himself more comfortably he knocks one of the boxes off the table, curses, switches off, sweeps boxes and ledger violently to the ground, winds tape back to beginning, switches on, resumes posture.*] Thirty-nine today, sound as a bell, apart from my old weakness, and intellectually I have now every reason to suspect at the . . . [*hesitates*] . . . crest of the wave—or thereabouts. Celebrated the awful occasion, as in recent years, quietly at the Winehouse. Not a soul. Sat before the fire with closed eyes, separating the grain from the husks. Jotted down a few notes, on the back of an envelope. Good to be back in my den, in my old rags. Have just eaten I regret to say three bananas and only with difficulty refrained from a fourth. Fatal things for a man with my condition. [*Vehemently.*] Cut 'em out! [*Pause.*] The new light above my table is a great improvement. With all this darkness round me I feel less alone. [*Pause.*] In a way. [*Pause.*] I love to get up and move about in it, then back here to . . . [*hesitates*] . . . me. [*Pause.*] Krapp.

*Pause.*

The grain, now what I wonder do I mean by that, I mean . . . [*hesitates*] . . . I suppose I mean those things worth having when all the dust has—when all my dust has settled. I close my eyes and try and imagine them.

*Pause. Krapp closes his eyes briefly.*

Extraordinary silence this evening, I strain my ears and do not hear a sound. Old Miss McGlome always sings at this hour. But not tonight. Songs of her girlhood, she says. Hard to think of her as a girl. Wonderful woman though. Connaught, I fancy. [*Pause.*] Shall I sing when I am her age, if I ever am? No. [*Pause.*] Did I sing as a boy? No. [*Pause.*] Did I ever sing? No.

*Pause.*

Just been listening to an old year, passages at random. I did not check in the book, but it must be at least ten or twelve years ago. At that time I think I was still living on and off with Bianca in Kedar Street. Well out of that, Jesus yes! Hopeless business. [*Pause.*] Not much about her, apart from a tribute to her eyes. Very warm. I suddenly saw them again. [*Pause.*] Incomparable! [*Pause.*] Ah well . . . [*Pause.*] These old PMs are gruesome, but I often find them—[*Krapp switches off, broods, switches on*]—a help before embarking on a new . . . [*hesitates*] . . . retrospect. Hard to believe I was ever that young whelp. The voice! Jesus! And the aspirations! [*Brief laugh in which Krapp joins.*] And the resolutions! [*Brief laugh in which Krapp joins.*] To drink less, in particular. [*Brief laugh of Krapp alone.*] Statistics. Seventeen hundred hours, out of the preceding eight thousand odd, consumed on licensed premises alone. More than 20 per cent, say 40 per cent of his waking life. [*Pause.*] Plans for a less . . . [*hesitates*] . . . engrossing sexual life. Last illness of his father. Flagging pursuit of happiness. Unattainable laxation. Sneers at what he calls his youth and thanks to God that it's over. [*Pause.*] False ring there. [*Pause.*] Shadows of the opus . . . magnum. Closing with a—[*brief laugh*]—yelp to Providence. [*Prolonged laugh in which Krapp joins.*] What remains of all that misery? A girl in a shabby green coat, on a railway-station platform? No?

*Pause.*

When I look—

*Krapp switches off, broods, looks at his watch, gets up, goes backstage into darkness. Ten seconds. Pop of cork. Ten seconds. Second cork. Ten seconds. Third cork. Ten seconds. Brief burst of a quavering song.*

KRAPP [*sings*]: Now the day is over,
Night is drawing nigh-igh,
Shadows—

*Fit of coughing. He comes back into the light, sits down, wipes his mouth, switches on, resumes his listening posture.*

TAPE: —back on the year that is gone, with what I hope is perhaps a glint of the old eye to come, there is of course the house on the canal where mother lay a-dying, in the late autumn, after her long viduity [*Krapp gives a start*], and the—[*Krapp switches off, winds back tape a little, bends his ear closer to machine, switches on*]—a-dying, after her long viduity, and the—

*Krapp switches off, raises his head, stares blankly before him. His lips move in the syllables of 'viduity'. No sound. He gets up, goes backstage into darkness, comes back with an enormous dictionary, lays it on table, sits down and looks up the word.*

KRAPP [*reading from dictionary*]: State—or condition of being—or remaining—a widow—or widower. [*Looks up. Puzzled.*] Being—or remaining? . . . [*Pause. He peers again at dictionary. Reading.*] 'Deep weeds of viduity' . . . Also of an animal, especially a bird . . . the vidua or weaver-bird . . . Black plumage of male . . . [*He looks up. With relish.*] The vidua-bird!

*Pause. He closes the dictionary, switches on, resumes listening posture.*

TAPE: —bench by the weir from where I could see her window. There I sat, in the biting wind, wishing she were gone. [*Pause.*] Hardly a soul, just a few regulars, nursemaids, infants, old men, dogs. I got to know them quite well—oh by appearance of course I mean! One dark young beauty I recollect particularly, all white and starch, incomparable bosom, with a big black hooded perambulator, most funereal thing. Whenever I looked in her direction she had her eyes on me. And yet when I was bold enough to speak to her—not having been introduced—she threatened to call a policeman. As if I had designs on her virtue! [*Laugh. Pause.*] The face she had! The eyes! Like . . . [*hesitates*] . . . chrysolite! [*Pause.*] Ah well . . . [*Pause.*] I was there when—[*Krapp switches off, broods, switches on again*]—the blind went down, one of those dirty brown roller affairs, throwing a ball for a little white dog, as chance would have it. I happened to look up and there it was. All over and done with, at last. I sat on for a few moments with the ball in my hand and the dog yelping and pawing at me. [*Pause.*] Moments. Her moments, my moments. [*Pause.*] The dog's moments. [*Pause.*] In the end I held it out to him and he took it in his mouth, gently, gently. A small, old, black, hard, solid rubber ball. [*Pause.*] I shall feel it, in my hand, until my dying day. [*Pause.*] I might have kept it. [*Pause.*] But I gave it to the dog.

*Pause.*

Ah well . . .

*Pause.*

Spiritually a year of profound gloom and indigence until that remarkable night in March, at the end of the jetty, in the howling wind, never to be forgotten, when suddenly I saw the whole thing. The vision, at last. This I fancy is what I have chiefly to record this evening, against the day when my work will be done and perhaps no place left in my memory, warm or cold, for the miracle that . . . [*hesitates*] . . . for the fire that set it alight. What I suddenly saw then was this, that the belief I had been going on all my life, namely—[*Krapp switches off impatiently, winds tape forward, switches on again*]—great granite rocks the foam flying up in the light of the lighthouse and the wind-gauge spinning like a propellor, clear to me at last that the dark I have always struggled to keep under is in reality my most—[*Krapp curses, switches off, winds tape forward, switches on again*]—unshatterable association until my dissolution of storm and night with the light of the understanding and the fire—[*Krapp curses louder, switches off, winds tape forward, switches on again*]—my face in her breasts and my hand on her. We lay there without moving. But under us all moved, and moved us, gently, up and down, and from side to side.

*Pause.*

Past midnight. Never knew such silence. The earth might be uninhabited.

*Pause.*

Here I end—

*Krapp switches off, winds tape back, switches on again.*

—upper lake, with the punt, bathed off the bank, then pushed out into the stream and drifted. She lay stretched out on the floorboards with her hands under her head and her eyes closed. Sun blazing down, bit of a breeze, water nice and lively. I noticed a scratch on her thigh and asked her how she came by it. Picking gooseberries, she said. I said again I thought it was hopeless and no good going on, and she agreed, without opening her eyes. [*Pause.*] I asked her to look at me and after a few moments—[*pause*]—after a few moments she did, but the eyes just slits, because of the glare. I bent over her to get them in the shadow and they opened. [*Pause. Low.*] Let me in. [*Pause.*] We drifted in among the flags and stuck. The way they went down, sighing, before the stem! [*Pause.*] I lay down across her with my face in her breasts and my hand on her. We lay there without moving. But under us all moved, and moved us, gently, up and down, and from side to side.

*Pause.*

Past midnight. Never knew—

*Krapp switches off, broods. Finally he fumbles in his pockets, encounters the banana, takes it out, peers at it, puts it back, fumbles, brings out the envelope, fumbles, puts back envelope, looks at his watch, gets up and goes backstage into darkness. Ten seconds. Sound of bottle against glass, then brief siphon. Ten seconds. Bottle against glass alone. Ten seconds. He comes back a little unsteadily into light, goes to front of table, takes out keys, raises them to his eyes, chooses key, unlocks first drawer, peers into it, feels about inside, takes out reel, peers at it, locks drawer, puts keys back in his pocket, goes and sits down, takes reel off machine, lays it on dictionary, loads virgin reel on machine, takes envelope from his pocket, consults back of it, lays it on table, switches on, clears his throat and begins to record.*

KRAPP: Just been listening to that stupid bastard I took myself for thirty years ago, hard to believe I was ever as bad as that. Thank God that's all done with anyway. [*Pause*] The eyes she had! [*Broods, realizes he is recording silence, switches off, broods. Finally.*] Everything there, everything, all the—[*Realizes this is not being recorded, switches on.*] Everything there, everything on this old muckball, all the light and dark and famine and feasting of . . . [*hesitates*] . . . the ages! [*In a shout.*] Yes! [*Pause.*] Let that go! Jesus! Take his mind off his homework! Jesus! [*Pause. Weary.*] Ah well, maybe he was right. [*Pause.*] Maybe he was right. [*Broods. Realizes. Switches off. Consults envelope.*] Pah! [*Crumples it and throws it away. Broods. Switches on.*] Nothing to say, not a squeak. What's a year now? The sour cud and the iron stool. [*Pause.*] Revelled in the word spool. [*With relish.*] Spooool! Happiest moment of the past half million. [*Pause.*] Seventeen copies sold, of which eleven at trade price to free circulating libraries beyond the seas. Getting known. [*Pause.*] One pound six and something, eight I have little doubt. [*Pause.*] Crawled out once or twice, before the summer was cold. Sat shivering in the park, drowned in dreams and burning to be gone. Not a soul. [*Pause.*] Last fancies. [*Vehemently.*] Keep 'em under! [*Pause.*] Scalded the eyes out of me reading Effie again, a page a day, with tears again. Effie . . . [*Pause.*] Could have been happy with her, up there on the Baltic, and the pines, and the dunes. [*Pause.*] Could I? [*Pause.*] And she? [*Pause.*] Pah! [*Pause.*] Fanny came in a couple of times. Bony old ghost of a whore. Couldn't do much, but I suppose better than a kick in the crutch. The last time wasn't so bad. How do you manage it, she said, at your age? I told I'd been saving up for her all my life. [*Pause.*] Went to Vespers once, like when I was in short trousers. [*Pause. Sings.*]

Now the day is over.
Night is drawing nigh-igh,
Shadows—[*coughing, then almost inaudible*]—of the evening
Steal across the sky.

[*Gasping.*] Went to sleep and fell off the pew. [*Pause.*] Sometimes wondered in the night if a last effort mightn't—[*Pause.*] Ah finish your booze now and get to your bed. Go on with this drivel in the morning. Or leave it at that. [*Pause.*] Leave it at that. [*Pause.*] Lie propped up in the dark—and wander. Be again in the dingle on a Christmas Eve, gathering holly, the red-berried. [*Pause.*] Be again on Croghan on a Sunday morning, in the haze, with the bitch, stop and listen to the bells. [*Pause.*] And so on. [*Pause.*] Be again, be again. [*Pause.*] All that old misery. [*Pause.*] Once wasn't enough for you. [*Pause.*] Lie down across her.

*Long pause. He suddenly bends over machine, switches off, wrenches off tape, throws it away, puts on the other, winds it forward to the passage he wants, switches on, listens staring front.*

TAPE: —gooseberries, she said. I said again I thought it was hopeless and no good going on, and she agreed, without opening her eyes. [*Pause.*] I asked her to look at me and after a few moments—[*pause*]—after a few moments she did, but the eyes just slits, because of the glare. I bent over her to get them in the shadow and they opened. [*Pause. Low.*] Let me in. [*Pause.*] We drifted in among the flags and stuck. The way they went down, sighing, before the stem! [*Pause.*] I lay down across her with my face in her breasts and my hand on her. We lay there without moving. But under us all moved, and moved us, gently, up and down, and from side to side.

*Pause. Krapp's lips move. No sound.*

Past midnight. Never knew such silence. The earth might be uninhabited.

*Pause.*

Here I end this reel. Box—[*pause*]—three, spool—[*pause*]—five. [*Pause.*] Perhaps my best years are gone. When there was a chance of happiness. But I wouldn't want them back. Not with the fire in me now. No, I wouldn't want them back.

*Krapp motionless staring before him. The tape runs on in silence.*

*Curtain*

1958

# Edward Albee

*b.* 1928

Born in Washington, DC, Edward Albee attended a series of private schools before graduating from Choate School in Wallingford, Connecticut. He went to Trinity College, Hartford, for 18 months, then moved to New York City, which became his home. His grim yet frequently humorous plays, usually classified as theatre of the absurd, strip their characters of their pretense and hypocrisy and force them to confront less pleasant aspects of their lives. *Who's Afraid of Virginia Woolf?* (1962) remains the most successful of his more than 20 plays. *The Zoo Story*, his first produced play, had its premiere at the Schiller Theater Werkstatt in Berlin on 28 September 1959. It received its first American production four months later at the Provincetown Playhouse in New York City on a double bill with Samuel Beckett's *Krapp's Last Tape.*

# The Zoo Story

## *PLAYERS*

PETER, *a man in his early forties, neither fat nor gaunt, neither handsome nor homely. He wears tweeds, smokes a pipe, carries horn-rimmed glasses. Although he is moving into middle age, his dress and his manner would suggest a man younger.*

JERRY, *a man in his late thirties, not poorly dressed, but carelessly. What was once a trim and lightly muscled body has begun to go to fat; and while he is no longer handsome, it is evident that he once was. His fall from physical grace should not suggest debauchery; he has, to come closest to it, a great weariness.*

*The Scene: It is Central Park; a Sunday afternoon in summer; the present. There are two park benches, one toward either side of the stage; they both face the audience. Behind them: foliage, trees, sky. At the beginning, Peter is seated on one of the benches.*

*(As the curtain rises. Peter is seated on the bench stage-right. He is reading a book. He stops reading, cleans his glasses, goes back to reading. Jerry enters.)*

JERRY: I've been to the zoo. [*Peter doesn't notice.*] I said, I've been to the zoo. MISTER, I'VE BEEN TO THE ZOO!

PETER: Hm? . . . What? . . . I'm sorry, were you talking to me?

JERRY: I went to the zoo, and then I walked until I came here. Have I been walking north?

PETER [*puzzled*]: North? Why . . . I . . . I think so. Let me see.

JERRY [*pointing past the audience*]: Is that Fifth Avenue?

PETER: Why yes; yes, it is.

JERRY: And what is that cross street there; that one, to the right?

PETER: That? Oh, that's Seventy-fourth Street.

JERRY: And the zoo is around Sixty-fifth Street; so, I've been walking north.

PETER [*anxious to get back to his reading*]: Yes; it would seem so.

JERRY: Good old north.

PETER [*lightly, by reflex*]: Ha, ha.

JERRY [*after a slight pause*]: But not due north.

PETER: I . . . well, no, not due north; but, we . . . call it north. It's northerly.

JERRY [*watches as Peter, anxious to dismiss him, prepares his pipe*]: Well, boy; you're not going to get lung cancer, are you?

PETER [*looks up, a little annoyed, then smiles*]: No, sir. Not from this.

JERRY: No, sir. What you'll probably get is cancer of the mouth, and then you'll have to wear one of those things Freud wore after they took one whole side of his jaw away. What do they call those things?

PETER [*uncomfortable*]: A prosthesis?

JERRY: The very thing! A prosthesis. You're an educated man, aren't you? Are you a doctor?

PETER: Oh, no; no. I read about it somewhere; *Time* magazine, I think. [*He turns to his book.*]

JERRY: Well, *Time* magazine isn't for blockheads.

PETER: No, I suppose not.

JERRY [*after a pause*]: Boy, I'm glad that's Fifth Avenue there.

PETER [*vaguely*]: Yes.

JERRY: I don't like the west side of the park much.

PETER: Oh. [*then, slightly wary, but interested*] Why?

JERRY [*offhand*]: I don't know.

PETER: Oh. [*He returns to his book.*]

JERRY [*He stands for a few seconds, looking at Peter, who finally looks up again, puzzled.*]: Do you mind if we talk?

PETER [*obviously minding*]: Why . . . no, no.

JERRY: Yes you do; you do.

PETER [*puts his book down, his pipe out and away, smiling*]: No, really, I don't mind.

JERRY: Yes you do.

PETER [*finally decided*]: No; I don't mind at all, really.

JERRY: It's . . . it's a nice day.

PETER [*stares unnecessarily at the sky*]: Yes. Yes, it is; lovely.

JERRY: I've been to the zoo.

PETER: Yes, I think you said so . . . didn't you?

JERRY: You'll read about it in the papers tomorrow, if you don't see it on your TV tonight. You have TV, haven't you?

PETER: Why yes, we have two; one for the children.

JERRY: You're married!

PETER [*with pleased emphasis*]: Why, certainly.

JERRY: It isn't a law, for God's sake.

PETER: No . . . no, of course not.

JERRY: And you have a wife.

PETER [*bewildered by the seeming lack of communication*]: Yes!

JERRY: And you have children.

PETER: Yes; two.

JERRY: Boys?

PETER: No, girls . . . both girls.

JERRY: But you wanted boys.

PETER: Well . . . naturally, every man wants a son, but . . .

JERRY [*lightly mocking*]: But that's the way the cookie crumbles?

PETER [*annoyed*]: I wasn't going to say that.

JERRY: And you're not going to have any more kids, are you?

PETER [*a bit distantly*]: No. No more. [*then back, and irksome*] Why did you say that? How would you know about that?

JERRY: The way you cross your legs, perhaps; something in the voice. Or maybe I'm just guessing. Is it your wife?

PETER [*furious*]: That's none of your business! [*A silence.*] Do you understand? [*Jerry nods. Peter is quiet now.*] Well you're right. We'll have no more children.

JERRY [*softly*]: That *is* the way the cookie crumbles.

PETER [*forgiving*]: Yes . . . I guess so.

JERRY: Well, now; what else?

PETER: What were you saying about the zoo . . . that I'd read about it, or see . . . ?

JERRY: I'll tell you about it, soon. Do you mind if I ask you questions?

PETER: Oh, not really.

JERRY: I'll tell you why I do it; I don't talk to many people—except to say like: give me a beer, or where's the john, or what time does the feature go on, or keep your hands to yourself, buddy. You know—things like that.

PETER: I must say I don't . . .

JERRY: But every once in a while I like to talk to somebody, really talk; like to get to know somebody, know all about him.

PETER [*lightly laughing, still a little uncomfortable*]: And am I the guinea pig for today?

JERRY: On a sun-drenched Sunday afternoon like this? Who better than a nice married man with two daughters and . . . uh . . . a dog? [*Peter shakes his head.*] No? Two dogs. [*Peter shakes his head again.*] Hm. No dogs? [*Peter shakes his head, sadly.*] Oh, that's a shame. But you look like an animal man. CATS? [*Peter nods his head, ruefully.*] Cats! But, that can't be your idea. No, sir. Your wife and daughters? [*Peter nods his head.*] Is there anything else I should know?

PETER [*He has to clear his throat.*]: There are . . . there are two parakeets. One . . . uh . . . one for each of my daughters.

JERRY: Birds.

PETER: My daughters keep them in a cage in their bedroom.

JERRY: Do they carry disease? The birds.

PETER: I don't believe so.

JERRY: That's too bad. If they did you could set them loose in the house and the cats could eat them and die, maybe. [*Peter looks blank for a moment, then laughs.*] And what else? What do you do to support your enormous household?

PETER: I . . . uh . . . I have an executive position with a . . . a small publishing house. We . . . uh . . . we publish textbooks.

JERRY: That sounds nice; very nice. What do you make?

PETER [*still cheerful*]: Now look here!

JERRY: Oh, come on.

PETER: Well, I make around eighteen thousand a year, but I don't carry more than forty dollars at any one time . . . in case you're a . . . a holdup man . . . ha, ha, ha.

JERRY [*ignoring the above*]: Where do you live? [*Peter is reluctant.*] Oh, look; I'm not going to rob you, and I'm not going to kidnap your parakeets, your cats, or your daughters.

PETER [*too loud*]: I live between Lexington and Third Avenue, on Seventy-fourth Street.

JERRY: That wasn't so hard, was it?

PETER: I didn't mean to seem . . . ah . . . it's that you don't really carry on a conversation; you just ask questions. And I'm . . . I'm normally . . . uh . . . reticent. Why do you just stand there?

JERRY: I'll start walking around in a little while, and eventually I'll sit down. [*recalling*] Wait until you see the expression on his face.

PETER: What? Whose face? Look here; is this something about the zoo?

JERRY [*distantly*]: The what?

PETER: The zoo; the zoo. Something about the zoo.

JERRY: The zoo?

PETER: You've mentioned it several times.

JERRY [*still distant, but returning abruptly*]: The zoo. Oh, yes; the zoo. I was there before I came here. I told you that. Say, what's the dividing line between upper-middle-middle-class and lower-upper-middle-class?

PETER: My dear fellow, I . . .

JERRY: Don't my dear fellow me.

PETER [*unhappily*]: Was I patronizing? I believe I was; I'm sorry. But you see, your question about the classes bewildered me.

JERRY: And when you're bewildered you become patronizing?

PETER: I . . . I don't express myself too well, sometimes. [*He attempts a joke on himself.*] I'm in publishing, not writing.

JERRY [*amused, but not at the humour*]: So be it. The truth is: I was being patronizing.

PETER: Oh, now; you needn't say that. [*It is at this point that Jerry may begin to move about the stage with slowly increasing determination and authority, but pacing himself, so that the long speech about the dog comes at the high point of the arc.*]

JERRY: All right. Who are your favourite writers? Baudelaire and J.P. Marquand?

PETER [*wary*]: Well, I like a great many writers; I have a considerable . . . catholicity of taste, if I may say so. Those two men are fine, each in his way. [*warming up*] Baudelaire, of course . . . uh . . . is by far the finer of the two, but Marquand has a place . . . in our . . . uh . . . national . . .

JERRY: Skip it.

PETER: I . . . sorry.

JERRY: Do you know what I did before I went to the zoo today? I walked all the way up Fifth Avenue from Washington Square; all the way.

PETER: Oh; you live in the Village! [*This seems to enlighten Peter.*]

JERRY: No, I don't. I took the subway down to the Village so I could walk all the way up Fifth Avenue to the zoo. It's one of those things a person has to do; sometimes a person has to go a very long distance out of his way to come back a short distance correctly.

PETER [*almost pouting*]: Oh, I thought you lived in the Village.

JERRY: What were you trying to do? Make sense out of things? Bring order? The old pigeonhole bit? Well, that's easy; I'll tell you. I live in a four-story brownstone rooming-house on the upper West Side between Columbus Avenue and Central Park West. I live on the top floor; rear; west. It's a laughably small room, and one of my walls is made of beaverboard; this beaverboard separates my room from another laughably small room, so I assume that the two rooms were once one room, a small room, but not necessarily laughable. The room beyond my beaverboard wall is occupied by a coloured queen who always keeps his door open; well, not always but *always* when he's plucking his eyebrows, which he does with Buddhist concentration. This coloured queen has rotten teeth, which is rare, and he has a Japanese kimono, which is also pretty rare; and he wears this kimono to and from the john in the hall, which is pretty frequent. I mean, he goes to the john a lot. He never bothers me, and he never brings anyone up to his room. All he does is pluck his eyebrows, wear his kimono and go to the john. Now, the two front rooms on my floor are a little larger, I guess; but they're pretty small, too. There's a Puerto Rican family in one of them, a husband, a wife, and some kids; I don't know how many. These people entertain a lot. And in the other front room, there's somebody living there, but I don't know who it is. I've never seen who it is. Never. Never ever.

PETER [*embarrassed*]: Why . . . why do you live there?

JERRY [*from a distance again*]: I don't know.

PETER: It doesn't sound like a very nice place . . . where you live.

JERRY: Well, no; it isn't an apartment in the East Seventies. But, then again, I don't have one wife, two daughters, two cats and two parakeets. What I do have, I have toilet articles, a few clothes, a hot plate that I'm not supposed to have, a can opener, one that works with a key, you know; a knife, two forks, and two spoons, one small, one large; three plates, a cup, a saucer, a drinking glass, two picture frames, both empty, eight or nine books, a pack of pornographic playing cards, regular deck, an old Western Union typewriter that prints nothing but capital letters, and a small strongbox without a lock which has in it . . . what? Rocks! Some rocks . . . sea-rounded rocks I picked up on the beach when I was a kid. Under which . . . weighed down . . . are some letters . . . please letters . . . please why don't you do this, and please when will you do that letters. And when letters, too. When will you write? When will you come? When? These letters are from more recent years.

PETER [*stares glumly at his shoes, then*]: About those two empty picture frames . . . ?

JERRY: I don't see why they need any explanation at all. Isn't it clear? I don't have pictures of anyone to put in them.

PETER: Your parents . . . perhaps . . . a girl friend . . .

JERRY: You're a very sweet man, and you're possessed of a truly enviable innocence. But good old Mom and good old Pop are dead . . . you know? . . . I'm broken up about it, too . . . I mean really. BUT. That particular vaudeville act is playing the cloud circuit now, so I don't see how I can look at them, all neat and framed. Besides, or, rather, to be pointed about it, good old Mom walked out on good old Pop when I was ten and a half years old; she embarked on an adulterous turn of our southern states . . . a journey of a year's duration . . . and her most constant companion . . . among others, among many others . . . was a Mr Barleycorn. At least, that's what good old Pop told me after he went down . . . came back . . . brought her body north. We'd received the news between Christmas and New Year's, you see, that good old Mom had parted with the ghost in some dump in Alabama. And, without the ghost . . . she was less welcome. I mean, what was she?

A stiff . . . a northern stiff. At any rate, good old Pop celebrated the New Year for an even two weeks and then slapped into the front of a somewhat moving city omnibus, which sort of cleaned things out family-wise. Well no; then there was Mom's sister, who was given neither to sin nor the consolations of the bottle. I moved in on her, and my memory of her is slight excepting I remember still that she did all things dourly: sleeping, eating, working, praying. She dropped dead on the stairs to her apartment, my apartment then, too, on the afternoon of my high school graduation. A terribly middle-European joke, if you ask me.

PETER: Oh, my; oh, my.

JERRY: Oh, your what? But that was a long time ago, and I have no feeling about any of it that I care to admit to myself. Perhaps you can see, though, why good old Mom and good old Pop are frameless. What's your name?

PETER: I'm Peter.

JERRY: I'd forgotten to ask you. I'm Jerry.

PETER [*with a slight, nervous laugh*]: Hello, Jerry.

JERRY [*nods his hello*]: And let's see now; what's the point of having a girl's picture, especially in two frames? I have two picture frames, you remember. I never see the pretty little ladies more than once, and most of them wouldn't be caught in the same room with a camera. It's odd, and I wonder if it's sad.

PETER: The girls?

JERRY: No. I wonder if it's sad that I never see the little ladies more than once. I've never been able to have sex with, or, how is it put? . . . make love to anybody more than once. Once; that's it. . . . Oh, wait, for a week and a half, when I was fifteen . . . and I hang my head in shame that puberty was late . . . I was a h-o-m-o-s-e-x-u-a-l. I mean, I was queer . . . [*very fast*] . . . queer, queer, queer . . . with bells ringing, banners snapping in the wind. And for those eleven days, I met at least twice a day with the park superintendent's son . . . a Greek boy, whose birthday was the same as mine, except he was a year older. I think I was very much in love . . . maybe just with sex. But that was the jazz of a very special hotel, wasn't it? And now; oh, do I love the little ladies; really, I love them. For about an hour.

PETER: Well, it seems perfectly simple to me. . . .

JERRY [*angry*]: Look! Are you going to tell me to get married and have parakeets?

PETER [*angry himself*]: Forget the parakeets! And stay single if you want to. It's no business of mine. I didn't start this conversation in the . . .

JERRY: All right, all right. I'm sorry. All right? You're not angry?

PETER [*laughing*]: No, I'm not angry.

JERRY [*relieved*]: Good. [*now back to his previous tone*] Interesting that you asked me about the picture frames. I would have thought that you would have asked me about the pornographic cards.

PETER [*with a knowing smile*]: Oh, I've seen those cards.

JERRY: That's not the point. [*Laughs.*] I suppose when you were a kid you and your pals passed them around, or you had a pack of your own.

PETER: Well, I guess a lot of us did.

JERRY: And you threw them away just before you got married.

PETER: Oh, now; look here. I didn't need anything like that when I got older.

JERRY: No?

PETER [*embarrassed*]: I'd rather not talk about these things.

JERRY: So? Don't. Besides, I wasn't trying to plumb your post-adolescent sexual life and hard times; what I wanted to get at is the value difference between pornographic playing cards when you're a kid, and pornographic playing cards when you're older. It's that when you're a kid you use the cards as a substitute for a real experience, and when you're older you use real experience as a substitute for the fantasy. But I imagine you'd rather hear about what happened at the zoo.

PETER [*enthusiastic*]: Oh, yes; the zoo. [*then, awkward*] That is . . . if you . . .

JERRY: Let me tell you about why I went . . . well, let me tell you some things. I've told you about the fourth floor of the rooming-house where I live. I think the rooms are better as you go down, floor by floor. I guess they are; I don't know. I don't know any of the people on the third and second floors. Oh, wait! I do know that there's a lady living on the third floor, in the front. I know because she cries all the time. Whenever I go out or come back in, whenever I pass her door, I always hear her crying, muffled, but . . . very determined. Very determined indeed. But the one I'm getting to, and all about the dog, is the landlady. I don't like to use words that are too harsh in describing people. I don't like to. But the landlady is a fat, ugly, mean, stupid, unwashed, misanthropic, cheap, drunken bag of garbage. And you may have noticed that I very seldom use profanity, so I can't describe her as well as I might.

PETER: You describe her . . . vividly.

JERRY: Well, thanks. Anyway, she has a dog, and I will tell you about the dog, and she and her dog are the gatekeepers of my dwelling. The woman is bad enough; she leans around in the entrance hall, spying to see that I don't bring in things or people, and when she's had her midafternoon pint of lemon-flavoured gin she always stops me in the hall, and grabs ahold of my coat or my arm, and she presses her disgusting body up against me to keep me in a corner so she can talk to me. The smell of her body and her breath . . . you can't imagine it . . . and somewhere, somewhere in the back of that pea-sized brain of hers, an organ developed just enough to let her eat, drink, and emit, she has some foul parody of sexual desire. And I, Peter, I am the object of her sweaty lust.

PETER: That's disgusting.That's . . . horrible.

JERRY: But I have found a way to keep her off. When she talks to me, when she presses to my body and mumbles about her room and how I should come there, I merely say: but, Love; wasn't yesterday enough for you, and the day before? Then she puzzles, she makes slits of her tiny eyes, she sways a little and then, Peter . . . and it is at this moment that I think I might be doing some good in that tormented house . . . a simple-minded smile begins to form on her unthinkable face, and she giggles and groans as she thinks about yesterday and the day before; and she believes and relives what never happened. Then, she motions to that black monster of a dog she has, and she goes back to her room. And I am safe until our next meeting.

PETER: It's so . . . unthinkable. I find it hard to believe that people such as that really are.

JERRY [*lightly mocking*]: It's for reading about, isn't it?

PETER [*seriously*]: Yes.

JERRY: And fact is better left to fiction. You're right, Peter. Well, what I have been meaning to tell you about is the dog; I shall, now.

PETER [*nervously*]: Oh, yes; the dog.

JERRY: Don't go. You're not thinking of going, are you?

PETER: Well . . . no, I don't think so.

JERRY [*as if to a child*]: Because after I tell you about the dog, do you know what then? Then . . . then I'll tell you about what happened at the zoo.

PETER [*laughing faintly*]: You're . . . you're full of stories, aren't you?

JERRY: You don't have to listen. Nobody is holding you here; remember that. Keep that in mind.

PETER [*irritably*]: I know that.

JERRY: You do? Good. [*The following long speech, it seems to me, should be done with a great deal of action, to achieve a hypnotic effect on Peter, and on the audience, too. Some specific actions have been suggested, but the director and the actor playing Jerry might best work it out for themselves.*] ALL RIGHT. [*as if reading from a huge bill-board*] THE STORY OF JERRY AND THE DOG! [*natural again*]: What I am gong to tell you has something to do with how sometimes it's necessary to go a long distance out of the way in order to come back a short distance correctly; or, maybe I only think that it has something to do with that. But, it's why I went to the zoo today, and why I walked north . . . northerly, rather . . . until I came here. All right. The dog, I think I told you, is a black monster of a beast: an oversized head, tiny, tiny ears, and eyes . . . bloodshot, infected, maybe; and a body you can see the ribs through the skin. The dog is black, all black; all black except for the bloodshot eyes, and . . . yes . . . and an open sore on its . . . *right* forepaw; that is red, too. And, oh yes; the poor monster, and I do believe it's an old dog . . . it's certainly a misused one . . . almost always has an erection . . . of sorts. That's red, too. And . . . What else? . . . oh, yes; there's a grey-yellow-white colour, too, when he bares his fangs. Like this: Grrrrrrr! Which is what he did when he saw me for the first time . . . the day I moved in. I worried about that animal the very first minute I met him. Now, animals don't take to me like Saint Francis had birds hanging off him all the time. What I mean is: animals are indifferent to me . . . like people [*He smiles slightly.*] . . . most of the time. But this dog wasn't indifferent. From the very beginning he'd snarl and then go for me, to get one of my legs. Not like he was rabid, you know; he was sort of a stumbly dog, but he wasn't half-assed, either. It was a good, stumbly run; but I always got away. He got a piece of my trouser leg, look, you can see right here, where it's mended; he got that the second day I lived there; but, I kicked free and got upstairs so fast, so that was that. [*Puzzles.*] I still don't now to this day how the other roomers manage it, but you know what I think: I think it had to do only with me. Cozy. So. Anyway, this went on for over a week, whenever I came in; but never when I went out. That's funny. Or, it was funny. I could pack up and live in the street for all the dog cared. Well, I thought about it up in my room one day, one of the times after I'd bolted upstairs, and I made up my mind. I decided: First, I'll kill the dog with kindness, and if that doesn't work . . . I'll just kill him. [*Peter winces.*] Don't react, Peter; just listen. So, the next day I went out and bought a bag of hamburgers, medium rare, no catsup, no onion; and on the way home I threw away all the rolls and kept just the meat. [*Action for the following, perhaps.*] When I got back to the rooming-house the dog was waiting for me. I half opened the door that led into the entrance hall, and there he was; waiting for me. It figured. I went in, very cautiously, and I had the hamburgers, you remember; I opened the bag, and I set the meat down about twelve feet from where the dog was snarling at me. Like so! He snarled; stopped snarling; sniffed; moved slowly; then faster; then faster toward the meat. Well, when he got to it he stopped, and he looked at me. I smiled; but tentatively, you understand. He turned his face back to the hamburgers, smelled, sniffed some more, and then . . . RRRAAAAGGGGGHHHH, like that . . . he tore into them. It was as if he had never eaten anything in his life before, except like garbage. Which might very well have been the truth. I don't think the landlady ever eats anything but garbage. But. He ate all the hamburgers, almost all at once, making sounds in his throat like a woman. *Then*, when he'd finished the meat, the hamburger, and tried to eat the paper, too, he sat down and smiled. I think he smiled; I know cats do. It was a very gratifying few moments. Then BAM, he snarled and made for me again. He didn't get me this time, either. So, I got upstairs, and I lay down on my bed and started to think about the dog again. To be truthful, I was offended, and I was damn mad, too. It was six perfectly good hamburgers with not enough pork in them to make it disgusting. I was offended. But, after a while, I decided to try it for a few more days. If you think about it, this dog had what amounted to an antipathy toward me; really. And, I wondered if I mightn't overcome this antipathy. So, I tried it for five more days, but it was always the same: snarl, sniff; move; faster; stare; gobble; RAAGGGHHH; smile; snarl; BAM. Well, now; by this time Columbus Avenue was strewn with hamburger rolls and I was less offended than disgusted. So, I decided to kill the dog. [*Peter raises a hand in protest.*] Oh, don't be so alarmed, Peter; I didn't succeed. The day I tried to kill the dog I bought only one hamburger and what I thought was a murderous portion of rat poison. When I bought the hamburger I asked the man not to bother with the roll, all I wanted was the meat. I expected some reaction from him, like: we don't sell no hamburgers without rolls; or, wha' d'ya wanna do, eat it out'a ya han's? But no; he smiled benignly, wrapped up the hamburger in waxed paper, and said: A bite for ya pussy-cat? I wanted to say: No, not really; it's part of a plan to poison a dog I know. But, you can't say 'a dog I know' without sounding funny; so I said, a little too loud, I'm afraid, and too formally: YES, A BITE FOR MY PUSSY-CAT. People looked up. It always happens when I try to simplify things; people look up. But that's neither hither nor thither. So. On my way back to the rooming-house, I kneaded the hamburger and the rat poison together between my hands, at that point feeling as much sadness as disgust. I opened the door to the entrance hall, and there the monster was, waiting to take the offering and then jump me. Poor bastard; he never learned that the moment he took to smile before he went for me gave me time enough to get out of range. BUT, there he was; malevolence with an erection, waiting. I put the poison patty down, moved toward the stairs and watched. The poor animal gobbled the food down as usual, smiled, which made me almost sick, and then, BAM. But, I sprinted up the stairs, as usual, and the dog didn't get me, as usual. AND IT CAME TO PASS THAT THE BEAST WAS DEATHLY ILL. I knew this because he no longer attended me, and because the landlady sobered up. She stopped me in the hall the same evening of the attempted murder and confided the information that God had struck her puppy-dog a surely fatal blow. She had forgotten her bewildered lust, and her eyes were wide open for the first time. They looked like the dog's eyes. She snivelled and implored me to pray for the animal. I wanted to say to her: Madam, I have myself to pray for, the coloured queen, the Puerto Rican family, the person in the front room whom I've never seen, the woman who cries deliberately behind her closed door, and the rest of the people in all rooming-houses, everywhere; besides, Madam, I don't understand how to pray. But . . . to simplify things . . . I told her I would pray. She looked up. She said that I was a liar, and that I probably wanted the dog to die. I told her, and there was so much truth here, that I didn't want the dog to die. I didn't, and not just because I'd poisoned him. I'm afraid that I must tell you I wanted the dog to live so that I could see what our new relationship might come to. [*Peter indicates his increasing displeasure and slowly growing antagonism.*] Please understand, Peter; that sort of thing is important. You must believe me; it is important. We have to know the effect of our actions. [*another deep sigh*] Well, anyway; the dog recovered. I have no idea why, unless he was a descendant of the puppy that guarded the gates of hell or some such resort. I'm not up on my mythology. [*He pronounces the word myth-o*-logy.] Are you? [*Peter sets to thinking, but Jerry goes on.*] At any rate, and you've missed the eight-thousand-dollar question, Peter; at any rate, the dog recovered his health and the landlady recovered her thirst, in no way altered by the bow-wow's deliverance. When I came home from a movie that was playing on Forty-second Street, a movie I'd seen, or one that was very much like one or several I'd seen, after the landlady told me puppykins was better, I was so hoping for the dog to be waiting for me. I was . . . well, how would you put it . . . enticed? . . . fascinated? . . . no, I don't think so . . . heart-shatteringly anxious, that's it; I was heart-shatteringly anxious to confront my friend again. [*Peter reacts scoffingly.*] Yes, Peter; friend. That's the only word for it. I was heart-shatteringly et cetera to confront my doggy friend again. I came in the door and advanced, unafraid, to the centre of the entrance hall. The beast was there . . . looking at me. And, you know, he looked better for his scrape with the nevermind. I stopped; I looked at him; he looked at me. I think . . . I think we stayed a long time that way . . . still, stone-statue . . . just looking at one another. I looked more into his face than he looked into mine. I mean, I can concentrate longer at looking into a dog's face than a dog can concentrate at looking into mine, or into anybody else's face, for that matter. But during that twenty seconds or two hours that we looked into each other's face, we made contact. Now, here is what I had wanted to happen: I loved the dog now, and I wanted him to love me. I had tried to love, and I had tried to kill, and both had been unsuccessful by themselves. I hoped . . . and I don't really know why I expected the dog to understand anything, much less my motivations . . . I hoped that the dog would understand. [*Peter seems to be hypnotized.*] It's just . . . it's just that . . . [*Jerry is abnormally tense, now.*] . . . it's just that if you can't deal with people, you have to make a start somewhere. WITH ANIMALS! [*much faster now, and like a conspirator*] Don't you see? A person has to have some way of dealing with SOMETHING. If not with people . . . if not with people . . . SOMETHING. With a bed, with a cockroach, with a mirror . . . no, that's too hard, that's one of the last steps. With a cockroach, with a . . . with a . . . with a carpet, a roll of toilet paper . . . no, not that, either . . . that's a mirror, too; always check bleeding. You see how hard it is to find things? With a street corner, and too many lights, all colours reflecting on the oily-wet streets . . . with a wisp of smoke, a wisp . . . of smoke . . . with . . . with pornographic playing cards, with a strongbox . . . WITHOUT A LOCK . . . with love, with vomiting, with crying, with fury because the pretty little ladies aren't pretty little ladies, with making money with your body which is an act of love and I could prove it, with howling because you're alive; with God. How about that? WITH GOD WHO IS A COLOURED QUEEN WHO WEARS A KIMONO AND PLUCKS HIS EYEBROWS, WHO IS A WOMAN WHO CRIES WITH DETERMINATION BEHIND HER CLOSED DOOR . . . with God who, I'm told, turned his back on the whole thing some time ago . . . with . . . some day, with people. [*Jerry sighs the next word heavily.*] People. With an idea; a concept. And where better, where ever better in this humiliating excuse for a jail, where better to communicate one single, simple-minded idea than in an entrance hall? Where? It would be A START! Where better to make a beginning . . . to understand and just possibly be understood . . . a beginning of an understanding, than with . . . [*Here Jerry seems to fall into almost grotesque fatigue.*] . . . than with A DOG. Just that; a dog. [*Here there is a silence that might be prolonged for a moment or so; then Jerry wearily finishes his story.*] A dog. It seemed like a perfectly sensible idea. Man is a dog's best friend, remember. So: the dog and I looked at each other. I longer than the dog. And what I was then has been the same ever since. Whenever the dog and I see each other we both stop where we are. We regard each other with a mixture of sadness and suspicion, and then we feign indifference. We walk past each other safely; we have an understanding. It's very sad, but you'll have to admit that it is an understanding. We had made many attempts at contact, and we had failed. The dog has returned to garbage, and I to solitary but free passage. I have not returned. I mean to say, I have *gained* solitary free passage, if that much further loss can be said to be gain. I have learned that neither kindness nor cruelty by themselves, independent of each other, creates any effect beyond themselves; and I have learned that the two combined, together, at the same time, are the teaching emotion. And what is gained is loss. And what has been the result: the dog and

I have attained a compromise; more of a bargain, really. We neither love nor hurt because we do not try to reach each other. And, *was* trying to feed the dog an act of love? And, perhaps, was the dog's attempt to bite me *not* an act of love? If we can so misunderstand, well then, why have we invented the word love in the first place? [*There is silence. Jerry moves to Peter's bench and sits down beside him. This is the first time Jerry has sat down during the play.*] The Story of Jerry and the Dog: the end. [*Peter is silent.*] Well, Peter? [*Jerry is suddenly cheerful.*] Well, Peter? Do you think I could sell that story to the *Reader's Digest* and make a couple of hundred bucks for *The Most Unforgettable Character I've Ever Met*? Huh? [*Jerry is animated, but Peter is disturbed.*] Oh, come on now, Peter; tell me what you think.

PETER [*numb*]: I . . . I don't understand what . . . I don't think I . . . [*now, almost tearfully*] Why did you tell me all of this?

JERRY: Why not?

PETER: I DON'T UNDERSTAND!

JERRY [*furious, but whispering*]: That's a lie.

PETER: No. No, it's not.

JERRY [*quietly*]: I tried to explain it to you as I went along. I went slowly; it all has to do with . . .

PETER: I DON'T WANT TO HEAR ANYMORE. I don't understand you, or your landlady, or her dog. . . .

JERRY: *Her* dog! I thought it was my . . . No. No, you're right. It *is* her dog. [*Looks at Peter intently, shaking his head.*] I don't know what I was thinking about; of course you don't understand. [*in a monotone, wearily*] I don't live in your block; I'm not married to two parakeets, or whatever your setup is. I am a *permanent transient*, and my home is the sickening rooming-houses on the West Side of New York City, which is the greatest city in the world. Amen.

PETER: I'm . . . I'm sorry; I didn't meant to . . .

JERRY: Forget it. I suppose you don't quite know what to make of me, eh?

PETER [*a joke*]: We get all kinds in publishing. [*Chuckles.*]

JERRY: You're a funny man. [*He forces a laugh.*] You know that? You're a very . . . a richly comic person.

PETER [*modestly, but amused*]: Oh, now, not really [*still chuckling*].

JERRY: Peter, do I annoy you, or confuse you?

PETER [*lightly*]: Well, I must confess that this wasn't the kind of afternoon I'd anticipated.

JERRY: You mean, I'm not the gentleman you were expecting.

PETER: I wasn't expecting anybody.

JERRY: No, I don't imagine you were. But I'm here, and I'm not leaving.

PETER [*consulting his watch*]: Well, you may not be, but I must be getting home soon.

JERRY: Oh, come on; stay a while longer.

PETER: I really should get home; you see . . .

JERRY [*Tickles Peter's ribs with his fingers.*]: Oh, come on.

PETER [*He is very ticklish; as Jerry continues to tickle him his voice becomes falsetto.*]: No. I . . . OHHHHH! Don't do that. Stop, Stop. Ohhh, no, no.

JERRY: Oh, come on.

PETER [*as Jerry tickles*]: Oh, hee, hee, hee. I must go. I . . . hee, hee, hee. After all, stop, stop, hee, hee, hee, after all, the parakeets will be getting dinner ready soon. Hee, hee. And the cats are setting the table. Stop, stop, and, and . . . [*Peter is beside himself now.*] . . . and we're having . . . hee, hee . . . uh . . . ho, ho, ho. [*Jerry stops tickling Peter, but the combination of the tickling and his own mad whimsy has Peter laughing almost hysterically. As his laughter continues, then subsides, Jerry watches him, with a curious fixed smile.*]

JERRY: Peter?

PETER: Oh, ha, ha, ha, ha, ha. What? What?

JERRY: Listen, now.

PETER: Oh, ho, ho. What . . . what is it, Jerry? Oh, my.

JERRY [*mysteriously*]: Peter, do you want to know what happened at the zoo?

PETER: Ah, ha, ha. The what? Oh, yes; the zoo. Oh, ho, ho. Well, I had my own zoo there for a moment with . . . hee, hee, the parakeets getting dinner ready, and the . . . ha, ha, whatever it was, the . . .

JERRY [*calmly*]: Yes, that was very funny, Peter. I wouldn't have expected it. But do you want to hear about what happened at the zoo, or not?

PETER: Yes. Yes, by all means; tell me what happened at the zoo. Oh, my. I don't know what happened to me.

JERRY: Now I'll let you in on what happened at the zoo; but first, I should tell you why I went to the zoo. I went to the zoo to find out more about the way people exist with animals, and the way animals exist with each other, and with people too. It probably wasn't a fair test, what with everyone separated by bars from everyone else, the animals for the most part from each other, and always the people from the animals. But, if it's a zoo, that's the way it is. [*He pokes at Peter on the arm.*] Move over.

PETER [*friendly*]: I'm sorry, haven't you enough room? [*He shifts a little.*]

JERRY [*smiling slightly*]: Well, all the animals are there, and all the people are there, and it's Sunday and all the children are there. [*He pokes Peter again.*] Move over!

PETER [*patiently, still friendly*]: All right. [*He moves some more, and Jerry has all the room he might need.*]

JERRY: And it's a hot day, so all the stench is there, too, and all the balloon sellers, and all the ice cream sellers, and all the seals are barking, and all the birds are screaming. [*Pokes Peter harder.*] Move over!

PETER [*beginning to be annoyed*]: Look here, you have more than enough room! [*But he moves more, and is now fairly cramped at one end of the bench.*]

JERRY: And I am there, and it's feeding time at the lions' house, and the lion keeper comes into the lion cage, one of the lion cages, to feed one of the lions. [*Punches Peter on the arm, hard.*] MOVE OVER!

PETER [*very annoyed*]: I can't move over any more, and stop hitting me. What's the matter with you?

JERRY: Do you want to hear the story? [*Punches Peter's arm again.*]

PETER [*flabbergasted*]: I'm not so sure! I certainly don't want to be punched in the arm.

JERRY [*Punches Peter's arm again.*]: Like that?

PETER: Stop it! What's the matter with you?

JERRY: I'm crazy, you bastard.

PETER: That isn't funny.

JERRY: Listen to me, Peter. I want this bench. You go sit on the bench over there, and if you're good I'll tell you the rest of the story.

PETER [*flustered*]: But . . . whatever for? What is the matter with you? Besides, I see no reason why I should give up this bench. I sit on this bench almost every Sunday afternoon, in good weather. It's secluded here; there's never anyone sitting here, so I have it all to myself.

JERRY [*softly*]: Get off this bench, Peter; I want it.

PETER [*almost whining*]: No.

JERRY: I said I want this bench, and I'm going to have it. Now get over there.

PETER: People can't have everything they want. You should know that; it's a rule; people can have some of the things they want, but they can't have everything.

JERRY [*laughs*]: Imbecile! You're slow-witted!

PETER: Stop that!

JERRY: You're a vegetable! Go lie down on the ground.

PETER [*intense*]: Now you listen to me. I've put up with you all afternoon.

JERRY: Not really.

PETER: LONG ENOUGH. I've put up with you long enough. I've listened to you because you seemed . . . well, because I thought you wanted to talk to somebody.

JERRY: You put things well; economically, and, yet . . . oh, what is the word I want to put justice to your . . . JESUS, you make me sick . . . get off here and give me my bench.

PETER: MY BENCH!

JERRY [*pushes Peter almost, but not quite, off the bench*]: Get out of my sight.

PETER [*regaining his position*]: God da . . . mn you. That's enough! I've had enough of you. I will not give up this bench; you can't have it, and that's that. Now, go away. [*Jerry snorts but does not move.*] Go away, I said. [*Jerry does not move.*] Get away from here. If you don't move on . . . you're a bum . . . that's what you are. . . . If you don't move on, I'll get a policeman here and make you go. [*Jerry laughs, stays.*] I warn you, I'll call a policeman.

JERRY [*softly*]: You won't find a policeman around here; they're all over on the west side of the park chasing fairies down from trees or out of the bushes. That's all they do. That's their function. So scream your head off; it won't do you any good.

PETER: POLICE! I warn you, I'll have you arrested.

JERRY: You look ridiculous: a grown man screaming for the police on a bright Sunday afternoon in the park with nobody harming you. If a policeman *did* fill his quota and come sludging over this way he'd probably take you in as a nut.

PETER [*with disgust and impotence*]: Great God, I just came here to read, and now you want me to give up the bench. You're mad.

JERRY: Hey, I got news for you, as they say. I'm on your precious bench, and you're never going to have it for yourself again.

PETER [*furious*]: Look, you; get off my bench. I don't care if it makes any sense or not. I want this bench to myself; I want you OFF IT!

JERRY [*mocking*]: Aw . . . look who's mad.

PETER: GET OUT!

JERRY: No.

PETER: I WARN YOU!

JERRY: Do you know how ridiculous you look now?

PETER [*His fury and self-consciousness have possessed him.*]: It doesn't matter. [*He is almost crying.*] GET AWAY FROM MY BENCH!

JERRY: Why? You have everything in the world you want; you've told me about your home, and your family, and *your* own little zoo. You have everything, and now you want this bench. Are these the things men fight for? Tell me, Peter, is this bench, this iron and this wood, is this your honour? Is this the thing in the world you'd fight for? Can you think of anything more absurd?

PETER: Absurd? Look, I'm not going to talk to you about honour, or even try to explain it to you. Besides, it isn't a question of honour; but even if it were, you wouldn't understand.

JERRY [*contemptuously*]: You don't even know what you're saying, do you? This is probably the first time in your life you've had anything more trying to face than changing your cats' toilet box. Stupid! Don't you have any idea, not even the slightest, what other people *need*?

PETER: Oh, boy, listen to you; well, you don't need this bench. That's for sure.

JERRY: Yes; yes, I do.

PETER [*quivering*]: I've come here for years; I have hours of great pleasure, great satisfaction, right here. And that's important to a man. I'm a responsible person, and I'm a GROWNUP. This is my bench, and you have no right to take it away from me.

JERRY: Fight for it, then. Defend yourself; defend your bench.

PETER: You've *pushed* me to it. Get up and fight.

JERRY: Like a man?

PETER [*still angry*]: Yes, like a man, if you insist on mocking me even further.

JERRY: I'll have to give you credit for one thing: you *are* a vegetable, and a slightly nearsighted one, I think . . .

PETER: THAT'S ENOUGH . . .

JERRY: . . . but, you know, as they say on TV all the time—you know—and I mean this, Peter, you have a certain dignity; it surprises me . . .

PETER: STOP!

JERRY [*rises lazily*]: Very well, Peter, we'll battle for the bench, but we're not evenly matched. [*He takes out and clicks open an ugly looking knife.*]

PETER [*suddenly awakening to the reality of the situation*]: You are mad! You're stark raving mad! YOU'RE GOING TO KILL ME! [*But before Peter has time to think what to do, Jerry tosses the knife at Peter's feet.*]

JERRY: There you go. Pick it up. You have the knife and we'll be more evenly matched.

PETER [*horrified*]: No!

JERRY [*Rushes over to Peter, grabs him by the collar; Peter rises; their faces almost touch.*]: Now you pick up that knife and you fight with me. You fight for your self-respect; you fight for that goddamned bench.

PETER [*struggling*]: No! Let . . . let go of me! He . . . Help!

JERRY [*Slaps Peter on each 'fight'.*]: You fight, you miserable bastard; fight for that bench; fight for your parakeets; fight for your cats, fight for your two daughters; fight for your wife; fight for your manhood, you pathetic little vegetable. [*Spits in Peter's face.*] You couldn't even get your wife with a male child.

PETER [*Breaks away, enraged.*]: It's a matter of genetics, not manhood, you . . . you monster. [*He starts down, picks up the knife and backs off a little; he is breathing heavily.*] I'll give you one last chance; get out of here and leave me alone! [*He holds the knife with a firm arm, but far in front of him, not to attack, but to defend.*]

JERRY [*sighs heavily*]: So be it! [*With a rush he charges Peter and impales himself on the knife. Tableau: For just a moment, complete silence, Jerry impaled on the knife at the end of Peter's still firm arm. Then Peter screams, pulls away, leaving the knife in Jerry. Jerry is motionless, on point. Then he, too, screams, and it must be the sound of an infuriated and fatally wounded animal. With the knife in him, he stumbles back to the bench that Peter had vacated. He crumbles there, sitting, facing Peter, his eyes wide in agony, his mouth open.*]

PETER [*whispering*]: Oh my God, oh my God, oh my God . . . [*He repeats these words many times, very rapidly.*]

JERRY [*Jerry is dying; but now his expression seems to change. His features relax, and while his voice varies, sometimes wrenched with pain, for the most part he seems removed from his dying. He smiles.*]: Thank you, Peter. I mean that, now; thank you very much. [*Peter's mouth drops open. He cannot move; he is transfixed.*] Oh, Peter, I was so afraid I'd drive you away. [*He laughs as best he can.*] You don't know how afraid I was you'd go away and leave me. And now I'll tell you what happened at the zoo. I think . . . I think this is what happened at the zoo . . . I think. I think that while I was at the zoo I decided that I would walk north . . . northerly, rather . . . until I found you . . . or somebody . . . and I decided that I would talk to you . . . I would tell you things . . . and things that I would tell you would . . . Well, here we are. You see? Here we are. But . . . I don't know . . . could I have planned all this? No . . . no, I couldn't have. But I think I did. And now I've told you what you wanted to know, haven't I? And now you know all about what happened at the zoo. And now you will know what you'll see in your TV, and the face I told you about . . . you remember . . . the face I told you about . . . my face, the face you see right now. Peter . . . Peter? . . . Peter . . . thank you. I came unto you [*He laughs, so faintly.*] and you have comforted me. Dear Peter.

PETER [*almost fainting*]: Oh my God!

JERRY: You'd better go now. Somebody might come by, and you don't want to be here when anybody comes.

PETER [*does not move, but begins to weep*]: Oh my God, oh my God.

JERRY [*most faintly, now; he is very near death*]: You won't be coming back here any more, Peter; you've been dispossessed. You've lost your bench, but you've defended your honour. And Peter, I'll tell you something now; you're not really a vegetable; it's all right, you're an animal. You're an animal, too. But you'd better hurry now, Peter. Hurry, you'd better go . . . see? [*Jerry takes a handkerchief and with great effort and pain wipes the knife handle clean of fingerprints.*] Hurry away, Peter. [*Peter begins to stagger away.*] Wait . . . wait, Peter. Take your book . . . book. Right here . . . beside me . . . on your bench . . . my bench, rather. Come . . . take your book. [*Peter starts for the book, but retreats.*] Hurry . . . Peter. [*Peter rushes to the bench, grabs his book. Retreats.*] Very good, Peter . . . very good. Now . . . hurry away. [*Peter hesitates for a moment, then flees, stage-left.*] Hurry away . . . [*His eyes are closed now.*] Hurry away, your parakeets are making the dinner . . . the cats . . . are setting the table . . .

PETER [*off stage, a pitiful howl*]: OH MY GOD!

JERRY [*His eyes still closed, he shakes his head and speaks; a combination of scornful mimicry and supplication.*]: Oh . . . my . . . God. [*He is dead.*]

*Curtain*

1959

# Sharon Pollock
## *b.* 1936

Playwright, actress, and director Sharon Pollock was born in Fredericton, New Brunswick. The daughter of a physician, she spent her early years in Quebec's Eastern Townships before returning to Fredericton to attend the University of New Brunswick for two years. She began her acting career in amateur theatre in New Brunswick, later moving to Calgary to join the touring company Prairie Players. Her first play, *A Compulsory Option*, won the 1971 Alberta Playwriting Competition. She has written plays for children, several radio and television scripts, and many plays for the theatre. Her early plays focus mostly on social issues; for example, *The Komagatu Maru Incident*, about a ship of Sikh immigrants that is denied permission to land in Vancouver, explores racism in the early twentieth century. Her more recent plays, such as *Doc*, focus on familial and personal conflicts. She has taught playwriting at the University of Alberta, headed the Playwrights' Colony at the Banff Centre, been playwright-in-residence at Calgary's Alberta Theatre Projects, and served as artistic director of Theatre Calgary. Based loosely on her own family background, *Doc* had its premiere at Theatre Calgary in April 1984.

# Doc

## *THE CHARACTERS*

EV, an elderly man in his seventies
CATHERINE, his daughter, in her mid-thirties
KATIE, Catherine, as a young girl
BOB, Ev's wife, Catherine's mother
OSCAR, Ev's best friend

## *PLAYWRIGHT NOTES*

Much of the play consists of the sometimes shared, sometimes singular memories of the past, as relived by Ev and Catherine, interacting with figures from the past. Structurally, shifts in time do not occur in a linear, chronological fashion, but in an unconscious and intuitive patterning of the past by Ev and Catherine. A stage direction [*Shift*] marks these pattern changes which are often, but not always, time shifts as well. In production, music has been used to underscore the pattern shifts, however the characters' shifts from one pattern to another must be immediate. They do not 'hold' for the music. The physical blocking must accommodate this immediacy and the stage setting facilitate it.

The 'now' of the play takes place in the house in which Catherine grew up and in which Ev now lives alone. The play is most effective when the set design is not a literal one, and when props and furniture are kept to a minimum. I think of the setting as one which has the potential to explode time and space while simultaneously serving certain naturalistic demands of the play.

A kaleidoscope of memory constitutes the dialogue and action of the opening sequence. It is followed by a scene set more firmly in the 'now'. Ev is 'old' during these two segments, as he is at the opening and closing of Act II. Although Ev relives the past as a younger man, we never see Catherine any age but in her mid-thirties. She is able to speak across time to her father, to her mother, and to her younger self. Catherine and Katie blend, sharing a sense of one entity, particularly in the scenes with her father's best friend, Oscar. This should not be interpreted to mean that Catherine and Katie share one mind or are always in accord. They are often in conflict.

Oscar is first seen in the opening sequence wearing a Twenties-era hockey uniform. He is a young man about to enter medical school. Oscar's scenes with Katie cover a four-year period prior to and ending with Bob's death. In the scenes he shares with Bob and Ev there is a longer, more chronological unfolding of time. For the most part, we see him as a man in his mid-thirties.

We see Bob in her mid-twenties to mid-thirties. She wears a dressing gown which has a belt or tie at the waist, and under this she wears a slip. The material of the gown is satin or satin-like; the gown itself has the look of a tailored long dinner gown when appropriately belted. On other occasions, undone and flapping, it has the appearance of a sloppy kimono. Is it necessary to say that her descent into alcoholism, despair, and self-disgust must be carefully charted?

Ev as an old man wears glasses and a worn cardigan sweater.

There are liquor bottles on stage in Act I; they have been removed from the set in Act II. A trunk is useful on stage; it holds photos and memorabilia; as well, it provides a storage place in Act I for Oscar's hockey uniform, and the clothing into which he and Ev will change.

In some productions all characters are always on stage with the exception of Ev, who is free to exit and enter during the play, and Katie, Bob, and Oscar who exit near the end of the play. In other productions there has been a greater freedom of movement re characters' exists and entrances. The script indicates where a character 'may enter' or 'may exit'. If this is not indicated, the character must remain on stage.

## ACT I

*In the black there is a subtle murmuring of voices, with the odd phrase and word emerging quite clearly. They are repeats of bits and pieces of dialogue heard later in the play. The voices are those of Katie, Oscar, Bob, and the young Ev; they often speak on top of each other.*

*Light grows on Ev, who is seated by the open trunk. He holds an unopened letter. A match flares as Bob lights a cigarette in the background. Light grows on Bob, on Oscar who is smoothing tape on his hockey stick, and on Katie who concentrates on moving one foot back and forth slowly and rhythmically. Ev slowly closes the trunk, his focus still on the envelope he holds.*

*Catherine enters. She carries an overnight bag as well as her shoulder bag. She puts the overnight bag down. She sees Katie. She watches Katie for a moment, and then speaks to Katie's rhythmic movement.*

CATHERINE: Up-on the carpet . . . you shall kneel . . . while the grass . . . grows in the field

*Katie's motion turns into skipping as Katie turns an imaginary skipping rope and jumps to it.*

Stand up straight
Upon your feet

KATIE [*speaks with Catherine. The murmuring of voices can still be heard but they are fading*]:
Choose the one you love so sweet
Now they're married wish them well
First a girl, gee that's swell

*Katie's voice is growing louder, taking over from Catherine.*

KATIE and CATHERINE: Seven years after, seven to come

KATIE [*alone*]:

Fire on the mountain kiss and run
[*jumps 'pepper' faster and faster*]
Tinker, tailor, soldier, sailor,
Rich man, poor man, beggar man thief

BOB: Doctor
KATIE: Doc-tor!!! [*stops skipping*]
CATHERINE [*removing her gloves*]: Daddy?
EV [*looks up from the envelope*]: Katie? [*stands up*] Is that you, Katie?
KATIE [*skipping towards Ev singing*]: La da da da daah.

*Katie continues her 'la dahs' skipping away from Ev as Oscar speaks.*

OSCAR: Hey, you and me, Ev.

*Ev looks at the letter and sits back down.*

Best friends. Ev and Oscar, Oscar and Ev—and if we weren't—I think I'd hate you.
KATIE [*stops skipping but continues*]: La dada da daaah
BOB: Why don't you open it?
OSCAR: You see, Ev—you're just too good at things.
BOB: Go on, open it.

*The murmuring voices have faded out.*

OSCAR: It makes people nervous.

*Sound of an approaching train whistle.*

It makes me nervous.
BOB: Listen.

*The train whistle is growing in volume. Katie stops her 'la la la dahs'.*

Your Gramma, Katie, his mother. She'd set her clock by that train. Set her clock by the junction train crossing the railway bridge into Devon. Must be what? Three-quarters of a mile of single track spanning the river? And midnight, every night, that train coming down from the junction—half-way across three-quarters of a mile of single track its whistle would split the night . . . and that night do you know what she did?
EV [*his focus on the letter*]: No.
BOB: She walked out to meet it.
EV: No.
BOB: You wanna know something, Katie?
KATIE: No.
BOB: Your father's mother, your grandmother, killed herself . . . Katie!
KATIE: What!
BOB: She walked across the train bridge at midnight and the train hit her.

KATIE: That's an accident.

BOB: She left a letter, and the letter tells him why she did it.

KATIE: There isn't any letter.

BOB: What's that?

KATIE: Daddy?

BOB: And he won't open it cause he's afraid, he's afraid of what she wrote.

KATIE: Is that true, Daddy?

EV: No.

KATIE: Is that the letter?

EV: Your grandmother was walking across the Devon bridge—

KATIE: What for?

EV: Well—it was a kind of short cut.

BOB: Short cut?

EV: And she got caught in the middle of a span and she was hit and killed.

CATHERINE: I stayed with her once when I was little . . . I can hardly remember.

EV [*continuing to talk to Katie*]: It was after your mother had Robbie.

KATIE: Why didn't I stay with you and Robbie and Mummy?

EV: Your mother was sick so you stayed with your Gramma.

CATHERINE: Yes . . . and she made me soft-boiled runny eggs, and she'd feed me them and tell me stories about Moses in the bulrushes, and I . . . and I . . . would peel the wallpaper off behind the door, and she'd get angry.

EV: That's right.

CATHERINE: Why didn't she jump?

OSCAR: A hat trick! Ev! Everybody screaming—everybody on their feet—what's it feel like, Ev?

BOB: He doesn't care. He doesn't care about anything except his 'prac-tice' and his 'off-fice' and his 'off-fice nurse' and all those stupid, stupid people who think he's God.

EV [*to Katie*]: Don't listen to her.

BOB: You're not God.

EV: Your mother's sick.

KATIE: No she isn't.

OSCAR: God, you're good. You fly, Ev.

KATIE: Why do you keep saying she's sick?

OSCAR: You don't skate, you fly.

KATIE: She's not sick.

EV: Your mother's—

KATIE: Why do you keep saying that!

EV: Katie—

KATIE: No!

CATHERINE: For a long time I prayed to God. I asked him to make her stop. I prayed and prayed. I thought, I'm just a little girl. Why would God want to do this to a little girl? I thought it was a mistake. I thought maybe he didn't know. I don't know what I thought. I prayed and prayed. . . . Now, I don't believe in God.

KATIE: And if there is a God, then I don't like him.

EV: She isn't well.

*Bob slowly opens a drawer, feels inside it, and runs her hand along a chair cushion. She continues to quietly, unobtrusively look for something as Katie and Ev speak.*

KATIE: Tell Robbie that. He wants to believe that. I want the truth.

EV: I'm telling you the truth.

KATIE: No! Do you know what I did yesterday? She kept going to the bathroom and going to the bathroom and I went in and looked all over and I found it. In the clothes hamper with all the dirty clothes and things. And I took it and I poured it down the sink and I went downstairs and I threw the empty bottle in the garbage so don't tell me she's sick!

BOB: It's gone.

*Bob looks at Katie. In the following sequence, although Catherine is the speaker, Bob will act out the scene with Katie.*

CATHERINE: No. No, don't.

BOB: It's gone.

CATHERINE: No.

BOB: You.

CATHERINE: No.

BOB: You took it and I want it back.

*Bob grabs Katie.*

I want it back.

CATHERINE: It's gone now and you can't have it.

BOB: Where? You tell me where?

CATHERINE: I poured it out.

BOB: No.

CATHERINE: Down the sink.

BOB: No.

CATHERINE: It's gone, forget it.

BOB: It's mine, I want it back!

CATHERINE: Gone.

BOB: No fair!

*Bob struggles with Katie.*

CATHERINE: Let me go!

BOB: No right!

CATHERINE: Let me go!

BOB: You had no right!

*Katie strikes Bob, knocking her down.*

CATHERINE: Daddy!

EV: Katie?

*Ev gets up from his chair and moves to look for Catherine. Oscar may follow him. Ev does not see Catherine, nor she him.*

OSCAR: You know my father wishes I were you. He does. He wishes I were you. 'Oscar,' he says, 'Oscar, look at Ev—why can't you be like Ev.'

BOB: Look at what your father did.

KATIE: You lie.

OSCAR: I say nothing. There's nothing to be said. 'You got to have that killer instinct on the ice,' he says. I play goalie—what the hell's a killer instinct in a goalie? Then he says, 'Oscar,' he says, 'Oscar, you are goin' into medicine.'

EV: Katie?

OSCAR: My Dad's a doctor so I gotta be a doctor.

BOB: Your father hit me and I fell.

KATIE: You're always lying.

BOB: See?

KATIE: He didn't hit you.

BOB: See?

KATIE: I hit you!—Get away from me!

OSCAR: What's so funny is you're the one so bloody keen on medicine—you'd kill for medicine. [*laughs*] Hey Ev, kills for medicine, eh. [*laughs*]

BOB: You father's mother, your Gramma, killed herself and he's afraid to open it.

KATIE [*covers her ears*]:

Now they're married
wish them joy
First a girl for a toy
Seven year after, seven to come
Fire on the mountain, kiss and run

*Ev returns from his search for Catherine. Oscar follows him. Katie sees Catherine, and moves towards her, speaking the verse to her.*

On the mountain berries sweet
Pick as much as you can eat
By the berries bitter bark
Fire on the mountain break your heart.

KATIE and CATHERINE: Years to come—kiss and run—bitter bark—

*Catherine sees Ev, who sees Catherine. Catherine speaks softly, almost to herself.*

CATHERINE: Break your heart . . .
It's me, Daddy.

EV: Katie?

KATIE: When I was little, Daddy.

CATHERINE: It's Catherine now, call me Catherine . . . well . . . aren't you going to say anything?

EV: You're home.

CATHERINE: Ah-huh . . . a hug, a big hug, Daddy, come on.

*Catherine and Ev embrace.*

Ooh.

EV: What.

CATHERINE: How long has it been?

EV: Be ah . . .

CATHERINE: Four years, right? Medical convention in where? Vancouver, right?

EV: That's right. Vancouver.

CATHERINE: Montreal, Toronto, Calgary, Van, where haven't we met, eh?

EV: Here.

CATHERINE: Yup. Not . . . not met here.

*Catherine notices the envelope in Ev's hand.*

What're you doing with that?

EV: Oh—just goin' through things. Clearin' things out.

*Catherine, getting out a cigarette, turns away from Ev.*

BOB: Katie's afraid of what she wrote.

KATIE [*to Catherine*]: Is that true?

EV: Are you here for this hoopla tomorrow?

CATHERINE: Not really.

EV: There's gonna be speeches and more speeches. I lay the cornerstone, and dinner I think.

CATHERINE: Ah-huh.

EV: I got it all written down with the times.

CATHERINE: Ah-huh.

EV: I got it downstairs. . . . You wanna take a look? . . . Not here for that, eh?

CATHERINE: No. I came home to see you.

EV: Pretty sad state of affairs when your own daughter's in town and can't attend a sod-turnin' in honour of her father.

CATHERINE: So I'll go, I'll be there.

EV: Coulda sent a telegram. Saved the air fare.

CATHERINE: Christ Daddy, don't be so stupid.

EV: Sound like your mother.

CATHERINE: I learned the four-letter words from you.

EV: Bullshit.

CATHERINE: I said I'd go, I said I'd be there. So. [*pause*] I'm proud of you, Daddy.

EV: Did you know it was a write-in campaign?

CATHERINE: Oh?

EV: The niggers from Barker's Point, the mill workers from Marysville, they're the ones got this hospital named after me. Left to the politicians God knows what they'd have called it.

CATHERINE: Well, I'm proud.

EV: Some goddamn French name I suppose—what?

CATHERINE: Proud, you must be proud having the hospital named after you.

EV: The day I first started practice, that day I was proud. Was the day after you were born. . . . There was a scarlet fever epidemic that year, you remember?

CATHERINE: No Daddy.

EV: Somebody . . . some couple came in, they were carryin' their daughter, what was she? Two, maybe three? I took her in my arms . . . could see they'd left it too late. I remember that child. I passed her back to her mother. Hold her tight, I said. Hold her tight till she goes. . . . Do you remember that woman holdin' that child in the hallway?

CATHERINE: No Daddy.

EV: No. That was you mother . . . that was your mother.

BOB: Blueberries, Katie.

EV: You were just little then.

BOB: Blueberries along the railway tracks, and every year we'd pick them and sell them. I was the youngest, and Mama was always afraid I'd get lost, but I never got lost.

*Catherine looks at Bob.*

Not once.

*Pause.*

EV: What are you thinkin'?

CATHERINE [*looks away from Bob*]: Nothing. . . . You've lost weight.

EV: Of course I lost. I damn near died. You didn't know that, did you.

CATHERINE: No. No, nobody told me.

EV: Well it was that goddamn heart man. It was him gave me a heart attack.

CATHERINE: Really?

EV: What the hell's his name?

CATHERINE: Whose?

EV: The heart man's!

CATHERINE: I wouldn't know, Daddy.

EV: Demii—no, Demsky. I go to him, I tell him I been gettin' this pain in my ticker, and he has me walkin' up and down this little set a stairs, and runnin' on treadmills. Jesus Christ, I said to him, I'm not tryin' out for a sports team, I'm here because I keep gettin' this pain in my ticker! For Christ's sake, I said, put a stethoscope to my chest before you kill me with these goddamn stairs!

CATHERINE: So how are you now?

EV: It would've served the bastard right if I'd died right there in his office—do you remember how good Valma was with your mother?

CATHERINE: I remember.

EV: Every statutory holiday your mother's killin' herself or seein' things crawlin' on the walls or some goddamn thing or other, and Valma is like a rock, isn't that right?

CATHERINE: I guess so.

EV: So I come home from Demsky's, and I get the pain in my ticker and I wait all night for it to go away, and long about four or four-thirty, I phone Valma. Valma,

I say, I'm havin' a heart attack, Valma—and she drops the phone nearly breakin' my ear drum and I can't phone out and I'm damned if I'm gonna get in that car and die all alone on Charlotte Street like that foolish Hazel Arbeton—If you were livin' in town, I'd have phoned you.

CATHERINE: You couldn't if Valma dropped the phone, Daddy.

EV: I'd have phoned you first.

CATHERINE: Would you?

EV: Well if I'd known she was gonna drop that goddamn phone I would have.

CATHERINE: What about Robbie?

EV: Who?

CATHERINE: Your son—Robbie.

EV: I'm not senile, I know who the hell Robbie is, what about him?

CATHERINE: You could have phoned him.

EV: I couldn't phone anyone! I was connected to Valma and I couldn't get disconnected!

CATHERINE: Would you have phoned him if you could?

EV: He wouldn't be home.

CATHERINE: How do you know?

EV: He's never home.

CATHERINE: Do you see him much?

EV: How the hell could I if he's never home?

CATHERINE: Do you *try* to see him!

EV: Of course I try! Have you seen him, phoned him, been over to visit?

CATHERINE: For Christ's sake Daddy, I just got in.

EV: Do you write?

CATHERINE: To Robbie?

EV: Yes to Robbie! You sure as hell don't write to me!

CATHERINE: I don't have the time.

EV: Some people make time.

CATHERINE: Why don't you?

EV: I'm busy.

CATHERINE: So am I.

EV: Mn. [*pause*] Does he ever write you?

CATHERINE: No.

EV: Do you wonder why?

CATHERINE: He's busy! Everyone's busy!

EV: Bullshit. It's that woman of his.

CATHERINE: It isn't.

EV: Paula.

CATHERINE: Who's Paula?

EV: She thinks we're all crazy.

CATHERINE: Well maybe we are, who in hell's Paula?

EV: His wife!

CATHERINE: You mean Corinne.

EV: What did I say?

CATHERINE: You said Paula.

EV: Well I meant Corinne! [*pause*] Paula. Who the hell's Paula? [*pause*]

BOB: Pauline.

EV: Pauline now, that was a friend of your mother's. Died a cancer, died in your room, and where did you sleep?

CATHERINE: In this room

EV: because

CATHERINE: the maid had left

EV: and your mother nursed Pauline right through to the end. Didn't touch a drop for three months.

*As Catherine turns away, she sees Bob.*

BOB: Not a drop for three months, Katie.

*Pause.*

EV: Best . . . best office nurse . . . I—ever had.

CATHERINE: Who, Mummy?

EV: Not Mummy, no. Valma. She ran that office like Hitler rollin' through Poland, and good with your mother—

CATHERINE [*turns back to Ev*]: I know, forty years like a rock.

EV: That's right, like a rock, but I call her with that heart attack and she goes hysterical. I never saw that in her before. It was a surprise. It was a goddamn disappointment. She comes runnin' into the house and up the stairs and huffin' and puffin' and blue in the face and—I'm on the bathroom floor by this time. She sees that, and gets more hysterical. She's got to run next door—my phone not workin' bein' connected to her phone which she dropped breakin' my ear drum—and she phones the hospital. And then we sit—I lie, she sits—and we wait for the goddamn ambulance, her holdin' my hand and bawlin'.

CATHERINE: Poor Valma.

EV: Poor Valma be damned! If I'd had the strength I'd have killed her. I kept tellin' her two things, I said it over and over—one, you keep that Demsky away from me—and you know what she does?

CATHERINE: She is sixty-seven.

EV: I'm seventy-three, you don't see me goin' hysterical! And I'm the one havin' the heart attack!

CATHERINE: Alright.

EV: You know the first thing I lay eyes on when I wake up in that hospital bed? Well, do you!

CATHERINE: No, I don't know, no.

EV: First thing I see is that goddamn Demsky hangin' over me like a vulture. Demsky who gave me the heart attack! . . . Next death bed wish I make I sure as hell won't make it to Valma.

CATHERINE: Well . . . it wasn't a real death bed wish, Daddy. You're still here.

EV: No thanks to her!

*Pause.*

CATHERINE: So?

EV: So what?

CATHERINE: Jesus Daddy, so how are you now?

EV: I don't read minds, I'm not a mind reader!

CATHERINE: How are you!

EV: I'm fine.

CATHERINE: Good.

EV: What?

CATHERINE: I said good. Great. I'm glad that you're fine.

EV: Got the nitro pills . . . pop a couple of them. Slow down they say. Don't get excited, don't talk too fast, don't walk too fast, don't, don't, don't, just pop a pill.

CATHERINE: Is it hard?

EV: Is what hard?

CATHERINE: Is it hard to slow down?

EV: . . . The nurses could always tell when I'd started my rounds. They could hear my heels hittin' the floor tiles, hear me a wing away.

*Oscar starts to laugh quietly.*

Did I ever tell you . . .

OSCAR: That's what you call a Cuban heel, Ev.

EV: . . . 'Bout those white woman's shoes I bought on St Lawrence?

CATHERINE: For the OR.

EV: That's right. They were on sale, real cheap, but they fit my foot cause my foot is so narrow.

OSCAR: Still, a woman's shoe, Ev?

EV: A good shoe for the OR was hard to find then!

CATHERINE: So you bought two pair.

EV: And I wore them.—How did you know?

CATHERINE: You told me.

EV: I told you.

CATHERINE: Don't you remember? You and Uncle Oscar would act that whole story out. . . . Do you see Uncle Oscar? [*pause*] Daddy? [*pause*] Well . . . anyway . . . so, what was the other thing?

EV: Mn?

CATHERINE: The other thing. You kept telling Valma two things, Demsky, and what was the other?

EV: Don't tell Katie. I musta said that a dozen times. I could hear myself. You're not to tell Katie. You're not to tell Katie.

CATHERINE: Why not?

EV: Because I didn't want you to know.

CATHERINE: Why not?

EV: Because I knew, even if you did know, you wouldn't come—and my heart would've burst from that pain.

*Catherine and Ev look at each other. Catherine looks away.*

Look at me—look at me! . . .

*Catherine looks at Ev.*

You knew. That goddamn Valma, she told you.

CATHERINE: No—

EV: You think I don't know a lie when I hear it, I see it, right in your goddamn eyes I can see it.

CATHERINE: Alright, alright, Valma did write—

EV: Ignores every goddamn thing I tell her.

CATHERINE: You could have died, Daddy.

EV: If you gave a damn you'd have been here!

CATHERINE: I don't want to fight.

EV: You afraid?

CATHERINE: No.

EV: I'm not afraid.

CATHERINE: God.

EV: Looked death in the face in that goddamn bathroom. It's not easy starin' death down with Valma bawlin' beside you. Every bit a your bein' directed, concentrated on winnin', not lettin' go. . . . [*gets out nitro pills; unscrews top while talking; takes pill by placing it under his tongue during speech*] Hated, hated losin'! Always. Hockey, politics, surgery, never mattered to me, just had to win. Could never let go. Do you know . . . do you know I saved Billy Barnes' life by hangin' onto his hand? I would not let him go till the sulpha took hold. I hung onto his hand, and I said Billy, goddamn it, you fight! And he did. They said it was the sulpha that saved him, miracle drug in those days, but you could never convince Billy of that. 'Goddamn it, Doc, it was you!' . . . I opened his belly two or three years ago. Opened his belly and closed his belly. Inoperable carcinoma. . . . 'Are you tellin' me this thing is gonna kill me, Doc?' I reached out my hand and he took it. . . . Hung . . . onto my hand. . . .

CATHERINE: I would have come, but you didn't want me to know.

EV: But you did know, didn't you. That goddamn Valma, she told you, and you didn't come.

CATHERINE: I'm here now.

EV: Bit of free time, drop in and see the old man, eh?

CATHERINE: No.

EV: But if this ticker gives out and catches you typin', too bad.

CATHERINE: Don't.

EV: So were you workin' or weren't you workin'?

CATHERINE: I'm always working.

EV: And that's more important than your own father.

CATHERINE: Don't start.

EV: A woman your age should be raisin' a family.

CATHERINE: What family did you ever raise? You were never home from one day to the next so who are you to talk to me about family?

EV: Your father, that's who. The one damn near died with no one but an office nurse by his side.

CATHERINE: Valma loves you!

EV: That's not what we're talkin' about here. We're talkin' about you and your work and your father dyin', that's what we're talkin' about!

CATHERINE: Are we?

EV: That's what I'm talking about—I don't know what the hell you're on about—I don't know what the hell you're doin' here!

CATHERINE: I just came home to see you, I wanted to see you . . . have you got any idea how hard it was for me to come home, to walk in that door, to, to come home? . . . Have you? . . . and when I leave here . . . my plane . . . could fall out of the sky, you could get another pain in your ticker, we could never talk again . . . all of the things never said, do you ever think about that?

EV: You mean dyin'?

CATHERINE: No, more than that, I mean . . . I don't know what I mean.

*Pause.*

EV: Are you still with that . . . whatshisname?

CATHERINE: Sort of.

EV: What's his name?

CATHERINE: What's it matter, you never remember.

EV: What's his name? Dugan? or Dougan?

CATHERINE: That was before, years before, Daddy.

EV: You should get one and hang onto one, Katie. Then I'd remember.

CATHERINE: I . . .

EV: What?

CATHERINE: I said it's difficult to keep a relationship goin' when you're busy, right?

EV: Why don't you marry this whosits?

CATHERINE: Yeah, well. . . . Whosits talks about that.

EV: I'm still waitin' for a grandson you know.

CATHERINE: I'm too old for that.

EV: You're soon gonna be—how old are you anyway?

CATHERINE: Besides I'd only have girls.

EV: Robbie's got girls . . . girls are alright. . . . You can have girls if you want.

CATHERINE: I said I don't know if I want.

EV: But get married first.

CATHERINE: Actually—I've been thinking . . . of . . . of maybe calling it quits with whosits.

EV: Quits?

CATHERINE: Ah-huh.

EV: You're callin' it quits.

CATHERINE: The work you know. Makes it hard.

EV: I thought this was the one. What the hell was his name, Sturgeon or Stefan or—

CATHERINE: His name doesn't matter.

EV: Stupid goddamn name—an actor, an actor for Christ's sake.

CATHERINE: We're not goin' to get into whosits and me and marriage and me and kids and me, all right?

EV: You go through men like boxes of Kleenex.

CATHERINE: I don't want to talk about it!

EV: Jesus Christ, I can't keep up.

CATHERINE: No you can't! You can't even remember his name!

EV: Burgess Buchanan, that was his name! And you sat in the lounge at the Bayside and you said, 'Oh Daddy, you just got to meet him, he's such a nice fella, he's so understanding, and he's so this and he's so that and he's. . . . So explain to me what went wrong this time.

CATHERINE: Why do we always end up yelling and screaming, why do we do that?

EV: I care 'bout you! . . . I want to see you settled, Katie. Happy. I want you to write, letters, not . . . I want you close.

CATHERINE: . . . I do write somebody you know. I write Uncle Oscar . . . every once in a while . . . when the spirit moves me.

EV: Not often.

CATHERINE: No. Not often. But I do. Write letters to someone. I do make the time. I know you and he don't keep in touch any more but I like to.

EV: Not lately.

CATHERINE: No, not lately. I . . . why do you say that?

EV: He was fly-fishin'. He slipped and fell in the Miramichi with his waders on.

CATHERINE [*pause*]: No . . . Did—did you see him?

EV: At the morgue when they brought him in.

CATHERINE: I mean before. Did you see him before? Were the two of you talking?

*Ev shakes his head.*

Why not?

EV: Too late.

CATHERINE: Now it's too late.

EV: Too late even then. Even before. Too much had been said.

CATHERINE: I wish you'd have told me.

EV: Would you have come home for him?

CATHERINE: . . . Probably not.

EV: So what difference does it make?

CATHERINE: I like to know these things. Whether I can come or not. I can't help it if I'm in the middle of things.

EV: You make sure you're always in the middle of something. It's an excuse. How old are you now?

CATHERINE: Stop asking me that.

EV: You're gonna end up a silly old woman with nothin' but a cat for company.

CATHERINE: It'll be a live-in cat which is more than you've got with Valma.

EV: If I wanted Valma here, she'd be here.

CATHERINE: So you don't want her here, eh? You like it alone. Sitting up here all alone.

EV: I'm not alone!

CATHERINE: You and Robbie, the same city, you never see Robbie!

EV: Go on! Why doncha go on! You got so goddamn much to say, why don't you say it! I am alone and it's you left me alone! My own daughter walkin' out and leavin' her father alone!

CATHERINE: How many years before you noticed my bed wasn't slept in?

EV: Don't go pointin' your finger at me! Look at yourself! What the hell do you do? Work, work, work—at what, for Christ's sake?

CATHERINE: I write! I'm good at it!

EV: Writing, eh Katie?

CATHERINE: Don't call me Katie!

EV: I'll call you by the name we gave you and that name is Katie.

CATHERINE: It's Catherine now.

EV: Oh, it's Catherine now, and you write Literature, don't you? And that means you can ignore your brother and your father and dump this Buchanan jerk and forget kids and family, but your father who gave his life to medicine because he believed in what he was doin' is an asshole!

CATHERINE: I never said that!

EV: My whole family never had a pot to piss in, lived on porridge and molasses when I was a kid.

CATHERINE: Alright!

EV: And fought for every goddamn thing I got!

CATHERINE: And it all comes down to you sitting up here alone with Gramma's letter!

EV: I am goin' through things!

CATHERINE: Why won't you open it?

EV: I know what it says.

CATHERINE: Tell me.

EV: You want it, here, take it.

*Catherine grabs letter from Ev. She almost rips it open, but stops and turns it in her hand. Pause.*

CATHERINE: Did Gramma really walk out to meet it?

EV: It was an accident.

CATHERINE: What was Mummy?

EV: You blame me for that.

CATHERINE: No.

EV: It was all my fault, go on, say it, I know what you think.

CATHERINE: It was my fault.

EV: Oh for Christ's sake.

*Ev moves away from Catherine. He sits, takes off his glasses and rubs the bridge of his nose. He looks at Catherine, then back to the glasses which he holds in his hand.*

. . . Your mother . . .

CATHERINE: Yes?

EV: Your mother and I—

CATHERINE: Tell me. Explain it to me.

BOB: There were eight of us, Katie, eight of us.

OSCAR [*softly*]: Go, go.

BOB: How did my mama manage?

*Oscar stands up, holding two hockey sticks. He is looking at Ev, whose back is to him. Ev puts his glasses in his pocket.*

OSCAR: Go.

BOB: All older than me, all born before he went to war.

OSCAR: Go.

BOB: Him, her husband, my father, your grandfather, Katie.

OSCAR: Go. Go!

BOB: And her with the eight of us and only the pension.

OSCAR: Go!! Go!!

BOB: How did my mama manage?

*Bob may exit. Shift.*

OSCAR: Go!!! Go!!!

*Oscar throws a hockey stick at Ev who stands, turns, plucking it out of the air at the last minute. They are catapulted back in time, rough-housing after a game.*

Go!!! The Devon Terror has got the puck, out of his end, across the blue line, they're mixing it up in the corner and he's out in front, he shoots! He scores! Rahhhh!

*Oscar has ended up on the floor with his hockey sweater pulled over his head. Ev, who's scored, raises his arms in acknowledgement of the crowd's 'Rah!'. Ev helps Oscar up.*

You know somethin' Ev? This is the truth. Honest to God. Are you listenin'?

EV: Yeah.

*Ev takes off his 'old man' sweater and hangs it on the back of a chair. During the following dialogue, Oscar changes out of his hockey clothes, putting them in the trunk. He removes a jacket, pants, and shoes for Ev, and a suit of clothes plus shoes for himself.*

OSCAR: When I think of medicine I get sick. Yeah. The thought of medicine makes me ill. Physically ill. Do you think that could be my mother in me?

*Ev slips out of his slippers and removes his pants. Oscar will put the pants in the trunk.*

EV: Maybe.

OSCAR: My father says its my mother in me. At least she had the good sense to get out. Leaving me with him. How could she do that?

EV: I dunno. [*puts on suit jacket*]

OSCAR: The old man calls her a bitch. And now nuthin' for it but I got to go into medicine.

EV: So tell him no.

OSCAR: I can't.

EV: Stand up to him.

OSCAR: I can't.

EV: Just tell him.

OSCAR: It'd break his heart.

EV: Shit Oscar, it's your life, you can't think about that.

OSCAR: Yeah.

EV: You just gotta tell him what you really want to do . . . how does that look?

OSCAR: Great.

EV: Which is?

OSCAR: Which is what?

*Oscar throws Ev a tie.*

EV: What you really want to do.

OSCAR: Oh.

EV: What do you really want to do?

OSCAR: I dunno.

EV: Come on.

OSCAR: Live someplace where it's hot.

EV: Come onnn . . .

OSCAR: New Orleans, I'd like to live in New Orleans.

EV: Oscar—

OSCAR: How hot is New Orleans anyway?

EV: And *do what*—in New Orleans, Oscar?

OSCAR: Do what. I dunno. Something. Anything. Not medicine.

*Oscar reties Ev's tie for him.*

EV: Look, if you're gonna tell your father you don't want to do what he wants you to do, you can't just say your life's ambition is to live someplace where it's hot.

OSCAR: What if it is?

EV: That is not gonna work, Oscar.

OSCAR: You're like my Dad, Ev. The two of you. You're always . . .

EV: What?

OSCAR: Forging *ahead.*

EV: What's wrong with that? [*puts on pants*]

OSCAR: Nothing. Forging is fine. I admire forging, I do, I admire it. It's just—not for me; do you think that could be my mother in me?

EV: Forget your mother. Concentrate on what you're gonna tell your father—and New Orleans is out.

OSCAR: It's honest, don't I get points for honest?

EV: Belt?
OSCAR: No points for honest.
EV: Or suspenders?
OSCAR: What's honest, honest is nothing, nobody wants honest.
EV: Honest is good, New Orleans is bad, belt or suspenders?
OSCAR: Belt.

*Oscar throws Ev a belt.*

EV: Thanks.
OSCAR: It's not fair.
EV: I don't wanna hear about fair.
OSCAR: Right.
EV: Face it, you're a lazy son of a bitch.
OSCAR: I know.
EV: You've got no drive.
OSCAR: I know.
EV: You've got no push.
OSCAR: I know.
EV: I worked my ass off last summer in construction, what did you do?
OSCAR: I lay in the sun.
EV: That's right.
OSCAR: I'm a loser.
EV: And a whiner.
OSCAR: Right. [*pause*] Why are we friends?
EV: Eh?
OSCAR: I agree with everything you say, it's the truth, what can I say? So why are we friends?—I figure it's the car and the clothes.

*Ev puts on shoes. By the end of the scene he is dressed in a suit, tie, and shoes.*

EV: That's a pretty shitty thing to imply.
OSCAR: I wasn't implying, I was just wondering.
EV: You've got other qualities.
OSCAR: Name one.
EV: We grew up together.
OSCAR: Go on.
EV: So we've known each other for a long time.
OSCAR: Yeah.
EV: Since Grade One.

*Pause.*

OSCAR: Well I figure it's the car and the clothes and the fact the old man dotes on you.
EV: Jesus Oscar.
OSCAR: Everybody knows I'm just a—
EV: Don't whine!

OSCAR: I'm not whining. I'm analyzing!

EV: I'm tryin' to help, Oscar. Now you must have some ambition, some desire, something you're at least vaguely interested in, that you could propose to your father as a kinda alternative to medicine, eh?

OSCAR: You mean apart from New Orleans.

EV: That's what I mean.

OSCAR: My mother might have gone to New Orleans.

EV: Forget your mother! Alternative to medicine! Not New Orleans!

OSCAR: Algeria.

EV: Oscar!

OSCAR: I know.

EV: I try to look out for you and it's like pissing on a forest fire.

OSCAR: I'm telling you exactly how I feel. I don't have ambitions and desires and goals in life. I don't need 'em. My old man has my whole life mapped out for me and I know what I'm supposed to do. I'm supposed to read and follow the map. That's it.

*Ev moves away from Oscar.*

EV: There is no wardrobe and no car and no amount of dotage from your old man that would compensate a person for putting up with you!

*Shift.*

CATHERINE: Uncle Oscar?

*Oscar looks at Katie as if it was she who had spoken. Katie holds her shoe out to him.*

Fix my shoe.

KATIE: It's got about a million knots—but keep talking.

CATHERINE: I want to know everything.

OSCAR: Construction work in the summer, hockey in the winter, and when we went to McGill, they'd bring him home on the overnight train to play the big games, the important games—and that's how he paid his way through medical school.

KATIE: Keep talking.

OSCAR: My father was their family doctor—I was there at his house the night his brother George died from the influenza—and that left him, and his sister Millie and his Mum and Dad.

CATHERINE: My Gramma.

KATIE: What was she like?

OSCAR: Proper. United Church. Poor and proper.

*Oscar gives Katie back her shoe.*

That's all I remember.

*Katie hits Oscar with the shoe.*

KATIE: Remember more!

OSCAR: I think your father got his drive from your Gramma and you get yours from him.
KATIE: Are you saying I'm like her?
OSCAR: In some ways perhaps.
KATIE: I would never walk across a train bridge at midnight!
OSCAR: You might.
KATIE: I would not!
OSCAR: Well it was an accident she—
KATIE: What do you mean I might!
OSCAR: It was a short cut.
KATIE: I'm not like her! I would never do that!
OSCAR: It wasn't anything she did.
KATIE: I'm too smart to do that!
OSCAR: It was just something that happened.
KATIE: You don't know! You don't know anything!
OSCAR: Katie—
KATIE: Get away from me!
CATHERINE: Stop.

*Shift.*

EV: If you want to know about this crazy bastard—if you want to know about him—When I needed a friend at my back, in a fight, in a brawl? This silly son of a bitch in sartorial splendour has saved my ass more than once—and me his—I'm gonna tell you a story. Now listen—we used to drink at this hole in the wall, this waterin' hole for whores and medical students, eh? An' we'd sit there and nurse a beer all night and chat it up with the whores who'd come driftin' in well after midnight, towards mornin' really, and this was in winter, freeze a Frenchman's balls off—and the whores would come in off the street for a beer and we'd sit there all talkin' and jokin' around. They were nice girls these whores, all come to Montreal from Three Rivers and Chicoutimi and a lotta places I never heard tell of, and couldn't pronounce. Our acquaintance was strictly a pub acquaintance, we students preferin' to spend our money on beer thus avoidin' a medical difficulty which intimacy with these girls would most likely entail. So—this night we're stragglin' home in the cold walkin' and talkin' to a bunch a these whores, and as we pass their house, they drop off there up the steps yellin' 'Goo-night goo-night.'. . . Bout a block further on, someone says: 'Where the hell's Oscar?' Christ, we all start yellin': 'Where the hell's Oscar? Oscar! Oscar!' Searchin' in gutters, snowbanks, and alleys, but the bugger's gone, disappeared! Suddenly it comes to me. Surer than hell he's so pissed that he's just followed along behind the girls when they peeled off to go home and he's back there inside the cat house. So back I go. Bang on the door. This giant of a woman, uglier than sin, opens it up. Inside is all this screamin' and cryin' and poundin' and I say: 'Did a kinda skinny fellow'—and she says: 'Get that son of a bitch outa here!' 'Where is he?' I say. 'Upstairs, he's locked himself in one of the rooms with Janette! He's killin' her for Christ's sake!' She takes me up to the room, door locked, girl inside screamin' bloody murder and I can hear Oscar makin' a kinda intent diabolical ahhhhhin' and oohhhin' sound. 'Oscar! Oscar! For Christ's sake, open up!' The girl's pleadin' with him to stop, beggin' him, chill your blood to the bone to hear her. And still that aaahhhhin'! and ooohhhhhin'! Nothin' for it but I got to throw myself at the door till either it gives or my shoulder does. Finally Boom! I'm in. I can see Oscar is not. He's got Janette tied to the bed, staked right out, naked and nude. He's straddlin' her but he's fully clothed, winter hat, scarf, boots and all, and he's wieldin' his blue anatomy pencil. He's drawin' all of her vital organs, he's outlinin' them on her skin with his blue anatomy pencil. He's got her kidneys and her lungs, her trachea and her liver all traced out. Takes four of us to pull him off—me and three massive brutes who've appeared. Janette is so upset they sent her back to Rivière-du-Loup for two weeks to recover, Oscar has to turn pimp till he pays back the price of the door, and everyone swears it's the worst goddamn perversion and misuse of a whore ever witnessed in Montreal . . . what in God's name did you think you were doin' that night?

*Oscar shrugs and smiles. Ev is taking out a letter and opening it as he speaks.*

Jesus Christ . . . silly bastard . . .

*Shift.*

It's from Mum . . . the old man's been laid off.

OSCAR: She sound worried?

EV: She says go ahead with the Royal Vic.

OSCAR: The General would be closer to home.

EV: What good would that do?

OSCAR: I don't know.

EV: No money to be made in post-graduate work anywhere.

OSCAR: I thought moral support, you know, being close.

EV: The Vic's the best in the country.

OSCAR: I know that.

EV: Mum would probably kill me if I gave up the Royal Vic.

OSCAR: She definitely would. . . . What about Millie?

EV: Millie?

OSCAR: Yeah.

EV: What about her?

OSCAR: I guess she could probably help out. Get a job.

EV: There's no jobs anywhere. Besides Millie's still in school.

OSCAR: Will she quit?

EV: What the hell do you want me to do?

OSCAR: I don't want you to do anything. I just wondered if Millie would quit school to help out at home, that's all.

EV: What the hell're you tryin' to say to me? Are you sayin' I should quit?

OSCAR: No, I just meant there are hospitals closer to home.

*Oscar may exit. Ev calls after him.*

EV: You can't be serious. The Vic's the best post-graduate training in the country. I've worked goddamn hard for it and I won't give it up—not for Mum if she asked me. Not for Millie! Not for anyone!

CATHERINE: But you did, Daddy.

*Ev looks at Catherine.*

You gave it up for her.

EV: If . . . if you could have seen her.

*Shift. Bob may enter. She carries a music box.*

BOB: He would step off the elevator—every nurse on the floor, 'Yes Doctor'—'No Doctor'—'Is there anything else' dramatic pause, sighhhh, 'I can *do* for you, Doctor?' Even Matron. Yes, Matron! And the goo-goo eyes—I remember those eyes.

EV: Do you know what they said?

CATHERINE: What did they say?

EV: Forget her, she is immune to the charms of the predatory male.

BOB: They were right.

EV: No fraternization between doctors and nurses on pain of dismissal.

CATHERINE: So why did you ask her?

EV: I—

BOB: He couldn't resist me—and I—

*Bob passes Catherine the jewellery box to hold. Bob opens the box. It plays 'Smoke Gets in Your Eyes'. Bob takes out a pair of earrings and puts them on as she's speaking. The lid of the box remains up and the music box plays during the scene.*

I don't give a fig for regulation or rules, only ones I make myself. And if in the past I chose to observe that regulation, it was only because a suitable occasion to break it hadn't arisen.

EV: Be serious.

BOB: My goodness, here I am without two pennies to rub together, and I rush out and buy a new sweater for a bar date with you, and you don't call that serious?

EV: When our eyes first met over what? . . . A perforated ulcer, were you serious then?

BOB: Do you know how many floors my mama scrubbed for that sweater?

*'Smoke Gets in Your Eyes' played by big band fades in.*

CATHERINE [*closes jewellery box*]: Was she really like that?

EV: If you could have seen her.

*Oscar may enter.*

OSCAR: Why risk it?

EV: Wait till you meet her.

*Ev moves towards Bob, who is swaying to the music.*

OSCAR: I don't need to meet her. For Christ's sake, Ev, you're . . . Ev? . . . Ev!

*Ev and Bob dance to a medley of Thirties tunes. Oscar watches, drawn into that warm atmosphere. Ev and Oscar take turns cutting in on each other, as they ballroom dance with Bob. They're all very good dancers, and Oscar is as captivated as Ev by Bob. Oscar dances with Bob. She is looking over his shoulder at Ev. Shift.*

KATIE [*interrupts, a sudden scream*]: Stop that! You stop it!

*The dancers stop; a soft freeze.*

I know things! I can figure things out!

*The soft freeze breaks. Shift.*

OSCAR: Have you told your mother?
EV: Not yet.
OSCAR: She had her heart set on a specialist.
EV: She'll settle for a grandson.
CATHERINE: But that's not what you got, you got me.

*Shift.*

KATIE: Why did he marry her?
OSCAR: He loved her.
KATIE: Why didn't you marry her?
OSCAR: She loved him.
KATIE: They didn't want to have me.
OSCAR: That isn't true.
KATIE: Did your mother want to have you?

*Shift.*

BOB: Your mother, ooohhh, your poor father, Ev.
EV: I know.
BOB: And Millie—you never told me about Millie.
EV: I mentioned her once or twice.
BOB: If you were only Catholic she could be a nun.
EV: Don't judge her by what you've seen tonight.
BOB: And your mother could be Pope.
EV: She liked you.
BOB: She hated me.
EV: When you get to know her, it'll be different.
BOB: I don't want to know her. Look at Millie under her thumb.
EV: Millie isn't under her thumb.
BOB: And your father.

*There is a sense of intimacy, rather than irritation, between Ev and Bob.*

EV: Look, you saw them for the first time for what—four or five hours—you can't make generalizations based on that.

BOB: You were there. You heard her. 'Poor Ev. Giving up the Vic.' You'd think a general practice was the end of the earth—And why've you fallen so far?

EV: She never said any of those things.

BOB: She implied I'd caught you by the oldest trick in the book.

EV: She didn't.

BOB: 'Why does a girl go into nursing?' Why to marry a doctor, of course! And Millie nodding away and your father smiling away—I wanted to stand up and scream.

EV: You're tired.

BOB: And you, you're there, way up there, the shining light, can do nothing wrong, except one thing is wrong, we are wrong!

EV: She had certain expectations, I'm not defending her, I'm just trying to explain how things are, or have been—Bob? . . . Bob!

BOB: For years she's been practising, 'I'd like you to meet my son, The Specialist.'

EV: Things haven't been that easy, you know. You've seen Dad, he's a good man but he's—when Georgie died, the old man wept on her—there was no one for her to weep on. It was hard on her losin' Georgie, and now all of her hopes for me and for Georgie are all pinned on me. . . . You can understand that.

BOB: She'll be counting the months.

EV: Let her.

*Ev kisses Bob.*

Again.

*Ev kisses Bob.*

Again.

BOB: You.

EV: You smile that smile at my Mum and she'll love you. It's a beautiful smile.

BOB: We aren't wrong, are we?

EV: We'll have a boy and we'll call him George after my brother. She'll like that.

BOB: Or William, after my brother Bill.

EV: And he'll have a beautiful smile.

BOB: And he'll have a nose like yours.

EV: And he'll . . .

*Shift. Ev and Bob may exit.*

CATHERINE: I notice this thing about having boys first. I mean what is that all about?

KATIE: Who was I named after?

OSCAR: Kate was your grandmother's name.

KATIE: Nobody calls me Kate.

OSCAR: That's your name.

KATIE: It's an ugly name. Why did they call me that? Couldn't they think of anything else?

OSCAR: Kate isn't ugly.

KATIE: Do I look like a Kate to you?

OSCAR: What's a Kate look like?

KATIE: Do you think names are like dogs?

OSCAR: In what way like dogs?

KATIE: I read dogs start to look like their owners or their owners start to look like their dogs. Do you think if you get an ugly name you start to look like your name?

CATHERINE: Or be like who you were named after?

*Shift. Ev and Bob may enter. Bob carries Ev's suitcoat. Ev carries a doctor's bag. Bob will help Ev on with his jacket.*

BOB: I want to go back to work.

EV: Where would you work?

BOB: I'm an RN, I'll apply at a hospital.

EV: No.

CATHERINE: Why not?

EV: I don't want her there.

CATHERINE: Why not?

EV: A matter of policy.

CATHERINE: Whose?

EV: What about Katie?

BOB: What about her?

EV: You should be home with her.

BOB: Why?

EV: You're her mother.

BOB: You're her father, you're not home from one day to the next. What am I supposed to do, rattle around with a four-month-old baby to talk to?

EV: So get somebody in.

BOB: Let me work, Ev.

EV: I don't want you down at the hospital.

BOB: Why not?

EV: Because as a surgeon operating out of that hospital, I don't want my wife on staff. I don't want any surgeon's wife on staff. And I don't know any surgeon who wants his wife on staff.

*Shift.*

KATIE: They were fighting last night.

OSCAR: Oh?

KATIE: Do you want to know what they were fighting about, if you don't already know.

OSCAR: How would I know?

KATIE: How do you think! Someone would tell you! Behind Daddy's back they would tell you! They would whisper.

OSCAR: That doesn't happen.

CATHERINE: Then why, Uncle Oscar, did you spend so much time talking to me if you didn't want to find out about them?

*Shift.*

BOB: I could work at the office. [*pours herself a drink*]

EV: No.

BOB: McQuire's wife—

EV: is a silly bitch who keeps McQuire's office in an uproar from the time she comes in in the morning till she leaves at night.

BOB: I'm not Marg McQuire.

EV: I have an office nurse, she does a good job and she needs the job and I don't intend letting her go.

BOB: I could work for someone else!

EV: I don't know what doctor would hire another doctor's wife as an office nurse.

BOB: Why not?

EV: Look, you're not just an RN anymore.

BOB: No.

EV: You're not Eloise Roberts, you're not Bob any more.

BOB: Who am I?

EV: My wife.

CATHERINE: Daddy.

EV: You're working the OR, the surgeon hits a bleeder, starts screaming for clamps, you're slow off the mark, and when the whole mess is under control, he turns round to give you shit, you take off your surgical mask and who does he see? Not a nurse, another surgeon's wife. My wife. Is he gonna give you shit?

BOB: I'm not slow off the mark in the OR.

EV: That's not the point, you're my wife, is he gonna give you shit?

BOB: That's his problem, not mine.

EV: I'm in the OR. I hit a bleeder. I scream for a clamp. I look at the nurse who's too fuckin' slow and who do I see? My wife!

BOB: I'm not slow! I'm good in the OR.

EV: That's not the point.

CATHERINE: Why don't you just say you don't want her there instead of all this bullshit?

EV: Jesus Christ I said it! I don't want her there!

*Shift. Katie is holding her wrist. She speaks to Oscar.*

KATIE: My father works hard! My father works really hard!

CATHERINE: I know. I know.

KATIE: You don't work as hard as my father. My father is never home. He goes to the hospital before we're up and when he comes home we're asleep.

CATHERINE: Robbie's asleep.

KATIE: I'm surprised Daddy knows who Robbie is. I'm surprised Robbie knows who Daddy is . . . I hate Robbie.

OSCAR: How did this happen?

KATIE: I dunno.

OSCAR: Yes you do.

KATIE: I'm accident-prone. Some people are you know. Accident-prone. I do dangerous things. I like doing dangerous things.
OSCAR: How did you do this?
KATIE: It was just something that happened.
OSCAR: Ah-huh.

*Oscar is taping Katie's wrist.*

KATIE: I do lots of things. Last Sunday when we were supposed to be in Sunday School, Robbie and I, do you know what we did?
OSCAR: Might hurt.
KATIE: Won't hurt. We went to the freight yards and played. I crawled under the train cars twice and Robbie crawled over where they're hitched together. He was too scared to crawl under. I wasn't scared.
OSCAR: You shouldn't do that.
KATIE: We decided together, Robbie and I. I didn't make him. Do you believe that?
OSCAR: What?
KATIE: That Robbie and I decided together to go to the freight yards instead of to Sunday School, do you believe that?
OSCAR: No.
KATIE: Anyway we had these gloves on. You know the ones Mummy made out of kid or leather the last time she was away? She made about a million pair. She probably gave a pair to you.

*Shift.*

BOB: It's not my fault if other people don't know who I am! It's not my fault if all they can see is your wife!
EV: Aren't you my wife?
BOB: That's not all I am!
EV: Don't yell at me.
BOB: Who do I yell at?
EV: Half the nurses in that goddamn hospital are lookin' for a doctor to marry so they can sit on their ass, and here you are screamin' cause you're not on your feet twelve hours a day bein' overworked and underpaid.
BOB: I am on my feet twelve hours a day!
EV: So let me get somebody in.
BOB: I feel funny with somebody in. . . . If I'm here, I feel I should be doing it.
EV: You want to get out more.
BOB: I know I'm a good nurse. I'm as good as anyone. When I'm out . . . I'm never sure what fork to use.
EV: Who gives a shit which fork you use? Whichever one comes to hand.
BOB: When you 'go out' that fork's important.
EV: Get Oscar to teach you how to play bridge. First year of university that's all he did.
BOB: I feel as if I wasted something.

*Shift. Katie is still with Oscar.*

KATIE: I don't know how she is supposed to get better by making gloves and painting pictures. Her pictures are awful. It costs a fortune to send her there and it never works! . . . Anyway . . . I got black all over my gloves and it wouldn't come off so I made Robbie give me his cause Mummy never gets mad at him and that's one of the reasons I hate him, and as soon as we got home do you know what he did?

CATHERINE: Told.

KATIE: He told. He said I *made* him go to the freight yards and then I *made* him change gloves. He's always telling and that's another reason I hate him.

OSCAR: You're the oldest—you should look out for Robbie.

KATIE: I'm trying to teach Robbie to look out for *himself!* I am! . . . She didn't even ask and he told. She's always saying Robbie's just like her side of the family and I'm just like Daddy's—Have you met my Uncle Bill?

OSCAR: I might have.

KATIE: Well I wouldn't want to be like her side of the family. I'd rather be like his!

*Shift.*

BOB: Nobody else in my family finished high school, did I tell you that?

*No one is listening to Bob.*

CATHERINE: Was she a good nurse, Daddy?

EV: That's not the point, Katie.

CATHERINE: Was she?

EV: I'm late for my rounds.

BOB: I was the smartest.

EV: You get some sleep now.

*Ev may exit.*

CATHERINE: Daddy?

BOB: And I always won, Katie! Because I played so hard! Played to win! And school—*first*, always first! 'Our valedictorian is Eloise Roberts.'

*Catherine moves away from Bob, who continues speaking with the drink in her hand.*

Eloise Roberts, and they called me Bob, and I could run faster and play harder and do better than any boy I ever met! And my hair? It was all the way down to there! And when I asked my Mama—Mama?—She said, we have been here since the Seventeen Hundreds, Eloise, and in your blood runs the blood of Red Roberts! Do you know who he is? A pirate, with flamin' red hair and a flamin' red beard who harboured off a cove in PEI! A pirate! And inside of me—just bustin' to get out! To reach out! To grow! . . . And when I sat on our front porch and I looked out—I always looked *up*, cause lookin' up I saw the sky, and the sky went on forever! And I picked and sold my berries, and my Mama cleaned house for everyone all around, and my sisters and my one brother Bill, everything for one thing. For me. For Eloise Roberts. For Bob.

*Shift. Ev enters, carrying his bag. He is speaking to Oscar.*

EV: You know somethin'!? The goddamn health care services in this province are a laugh!

BOB: Katie?

EV: I had a woman come into my office yesterday. I've never seen her before, but she's got a lump in her breast and she's half out of her mind with worry. Surer than hell it's cancer, but there's nothin' I can do till I damn well find out it *is* cancer. So what do I have to do? I gotta take a section and ship that tissue to Saint John on the bus, for Christ's sake! And then what? I got to wait for three days to maybe a week to hear. Do you know how often I get a replay of that scenario? She's a mother or she works for a living or she's at home looking after her old man and I can't tell her what's wrong or what we have to do till I get that goddamn report back from Saint John! We need a medical laboratory in this town, and by God, I'm gonna see that we get one!

OSCAR: Have you seen Bob?

EV: When?

OSCAR: Do you know you've a son?

EV: Georgie, we're callin' him Georgie, a brother for Katie. Hell of a good-lookin' boy, have you seen him?

OSCAR: I popped into the nursery.

EV: Looks like his old man.

OSCAR: Where were you?

EV: Had a call in Keswick.

OSCAR: What the hell would take you to Keswick when your wife's in labour?

EV: I hear it went as smooth as silk.

OSCAR: Ev?

EV: . . . Frank Johnston's kid fell under a thresher.

OSCAR: Bad?

EV: Bad as it can get.

OSCAR: You . . . could have sent someone else.

EV: Frank's been a patient of mine since I started the practice. Who the hell else could I send?

OSCAR: What about Bob?

EV: Valma was with her.

OSCAR: She didn't want Valma, she wanted you.

EV: Look, I brought Frank Johnston's kid into the world—and eight hours ago I saw him out, kneelin' in a field, with the kid's blood soaking my pants. . . . And afterwards, I sat in the kitchen with his mother, and before I left, I shared a mickey of rum with Frank.

OSCAR: It was important to Bob you be here, she needed you.

*Oscar may exit. Ev calls after him.*

EV: Well Frank Johnston needed me more!

*Ev looks at Catherine.*

The last baby I delivered was in a tarpaper shack. They paid me seven eggs, and when the crabapples fall, the mother's bringin' some round. Would you like to talk need to that woman? . . .

*Catherine looks away.*

She's got the best maternity care this province provides, and the best obstetrician in town. She's got a private nurse, and a baby boy. What the hell else does she want?

*Ev carries a chair over near Bob.*

CATHERINE: She wants you.
EV: She's got me.

*Ev sits beside Bob. Shift.*

BOB: I like Robert.
EV: I thought it was George or William.
BOB: Robbie's better.
EV: What's wrong with George?
BOB: Nothing's wrong with it, I like Robbie best.
EV: George was my brother's name.
BOB: I know.
EV: Robert George?
BOB: Robert Dann.
EV: Where the hell did you get that name?
BOB: Out of my head.
EV: Well, you can stick George in someplace, can't you?
BOB: I'm not calling him George.
EV: It's my goddamn brother's name!
BOB: I know.
EV: It means a lot to my mother.
BOB: I know.
EV: So stick it someplace!
BOB: No.
EV: Jesus Christ do you have to make an issue outa every little thing?
BOB: I don't like George.
EV: What the hell harm does it do to stick George in somewhere! Robert Dann George, George Robert Dann, George Damn Robert.
BOB: He's my son.
EV: He's our son.
BOB: So register him whatever you like.

EV: I will. [*stands up*]

BOB: I'm calling him Robbie.

EV [*returns chair to original position*]: I work my ass off. Why do I do it if it's not for her?

CATHERINE: Why?

EV: For her. Oscar?

*Shift. Oscar may enter.*

OSCAR: Ah-huh?

EV: What're your evenings like?

OSCAR: What're your evenings like?

EV: I'm doing rounds at night and squeezin' in house calls after that—could you drop over to see her till she comes round a bit?

OSCAR: What about my house calls?

EV: You never made a house call in your life.

OSCAR: I made one once.

EV: You lazy son of a bitch. If it weren't for the remnants of your old man's practice, you'd starve to death. What'll you do when the last of his patients die off?

OSCAR: Move someplace where it's hot.

EV: Listen, what she needs is someone to talk to, play a little golf, shit, the Medical Ball's comin' up next month, take her to that. I'm too goddamn busy.

OSCAR: When do you sleep?

EV: I don't.

OSCAR: How the hell did she ever get pregnant?

EV: I didn't say I never laid down.

*Ev may exit with bag. Shift.*

BOB: I want to go to New York next month. Go to New York and see the shows—do you want to do that?

*Sound of Forties dance music.*

OSCAR: Can Ev get away?

BOB: We'll ask.

*Oscar lights Bob's cigarette.*

Look around us. Look at all these pursey little lips. Look at all these doctors' wives. Do I look like that? Do I?

OSCAR: Not a bit.

BOB [*holding a glass*]: Well thas good. Look at them. . . . D'you know I joined the IODE? The IODE. I joined it. And do you wanna know what's really frightenin'? I could prolly, after a bit, I could prolly achully—forget. I could get to like the IODE. Isn't tha' frightening? . . . Isn't tha' frightening! . . . Ah, you're as bad as Everett. Whasa matter with doctors, you're a doctor, you tell me, so busy savin' lives you've forgotten how to talk? Talk!

OSCAR: The IODE eh?

BOB: Thas right . . . next year I might run as Grand Something. . . . The IODE does some very importan' work you know.

*Oscar smiles and casually takes the glass from her.*

. . . I don't like anybody here, do you? . . .

*Bob takes the glass back as casually, takes a drink.*

Do you know my mother . . . and all my sisters . . . and my one brother Bill who taught me how to fish—hey! We could go fishing some time if you want.

OSCAR: Bob.

BOB: Everett doesn't fish! Everett doesn't do anything except go . . . round . . .

OSCAR: Bob.

BOB: Anyway—so all these people, mother, sisters, Bill, they all worked to put me through nursing, wasn't that wonderful of them? . . . And now Ev, he lent Bill the money for something Bill thinks he wants to do and it'll all be a disaster cause it's about the tenth time he'd done it, but Ev's always giving money to his mother, so I don't care. Why should I care? But you know what I don't like? Do you?

OSCAR: What don't you like?

BOB: I don't like the cleanin' lady. Because every time . . . the cleanin' lady comes in, I think of my Mama who cleaned all around so I could go into nursing.

*Music out; silence.*

And you want to know what's worse? My Mama's so happy I married a doctor. I'm successful you see. I made something of myself. [*moves away smiling; lifting her glass in a toast*] I married a doctor.

*Shift. Katie carries a hairbrush.*

KATIE: Why don't you get married?

OSCAR: I'm waiting for you.

KATIE: I'm not related to you.

OSCAR: No.

KATIE: But you're always here, you're always about. . . . Do you love my mother?

OSCAR: I love you.

KATIE: Do you want to brush my hair?

OSCAR: If you want me to.

KATIE: You can if you want.

*Katie gives Oscar the brush, and sits at his feet. He brushes her hair. She enjoys it for a moment before speaking.*

I'm named after my Gramma, but I'm not like my Gramma. . . . I know when trains are coming . . . and when they're coming, I don't go that way then. . . . Do you like brushing my hair?

OSCAR: It needs it.

KATIE: I don't care if it's messy. It's how you are inside that counts.
OSCAR: That's true.
KATIE: I'm surprised you don't know that.
CATHERINE: Did you love my mother, Uncle Oscar?
OSCAR: When your mother's not well, you should think about that.
KATIE: About what?
OSCAR: How she feels inside.
KATIE: . . . I wonder—what my father sees in you. [*grabs the hairbrush*] You're not a very good doctor. What does he see in you?
OSCAR: Katie—
KATIE: Do you like brushing my hair?
Do you like brushing my hair!
OSCAR: Katie—
KATIE: I hate you!

*Katie moves away from Oscar, who follows her. Shift. Bob moves to the liquor and refills her glass. It is late, and she drinks while she waits.*

BOB: Ev! . . . is that you, Ev?

*Ev may enter. He will sit, his bag at his feet, with his head back and his eyes closed.*

EV: Yeah.
BOB: What time is it? . . . Where were you?
EV: Just left the hospital. They brought in some kid with a ruptured spleen . . . car accident . . . took out every guard rail on that big turn on River Road . . . damn near bled out when we got him.
BOB: How is he?
EV: Mnn?
BOB: I said, how is he?
EV: Bout half a million pieces . . .
BOB: . . . Ev?
EV: What time is it?
BOB: Late.
EV: Takin' out a stomach in the mornin'.
BOB: . . . Can we talk?
EV: Talk away . . .
BOB: I let the maid go today. It wasn't working out—
EV: Medjuck call?
BOB: What?
EV: Did Sam Medjuck call?
BOB: I said I let the maid go today—
EV: Mn?
BOB [*moves to refill her drink*]: Valma phoned and said he'd called her.
EV: Christ. [*gets up; picks up his bag*]
BOB: Why would he phone Valma's looking for you?

EV: He knows her, she kids him along.
CATHERINE: Were you over at Valma's?
EV: I was takin' out a spleen!
CATHERINE: Should I believe that?
EV: I was takin' out a spleen.
BOB: I said I let the maid go today!
EV: How many's that?
BOB: She was a smarmy bitch and I fired her!
EV: I said how many's that?

*Ev may exit.*

BOB: Where're you going?
EV [*offstage*]: House call to Medjuck's!
BOB: It's the middle of the night!
EV [*offstage*]: It's morning!
BOB: Ev! Ev!
CATHERINE: He's gone.
BOB: You'll fall asleep, Ev! You'll fall asleep and run off the road!
KATIE: Shut up Mummy!
BOB: Ev!
KATIE: Why don't you shut up and let people sleep!
BOB: Oscar!
CATHERINE: He isn't here, Mummy!
BOB: Count on Oscar!
KATIE: He's not here, Mummy!
OSCAR: When you need me you call, I'll be there.
CATHERINE: Daddy!

*Ev may enter, isolated on stage. Music filters in, 'Auld Lang Syne'.*

EV: Buy a Packard I always say! Best goddamn car on the road!
CATHERINE: Do something.
EV: I'd be drivin' along, middle of the night—
BOB: It's seven maids, that's how many!
EV: All of a sudden, swish, swish, swish, tree branches hittin' the car, look around—
BOB: And I'll fire the next seven whenever I damn well feel like it!
CATHERINE: Daddy!
EV: Car's in the middle of a goddamn orchard.
BOB: Oscar!
EV: I've fallen asleep and failed to navigate a turn and here's me and the car travellin' through this goddamn orchard.

*Bob is joined by Oscar. They dance to 'Auld Lang Syne', as Katie watches. Catherine's focus slowly switches, from her father to Bob and Oscar.*

BOB: Oscar.

EV: And me without a clue in the world as to where I'm headed. Black as pitch, not a light to be seen, and me drivin' over bumps and skirtin' fences and tryin' to remember where in the hell I'm goin'. Then I catch a glimpse of this little light, almost like a low-lyin' star in the sky.

*Bob kisses Oscar.*

EV: . . . head for that—what the hell—could end up on Venus! Door opens and someone is standin' there—

*Bob sees Katie watching.*

'We've been waiting for you, Doc.'

BOB: What do you want?

EV: 'Is the coffee hot?'

BOB: What do you want!

EV: 'Melt a spoon.'

KATIE [*screams*]: Don't! You don't!

*Katie launches herself at Oscar and Bob.*

EV: 'We've been waitin' for you, Doc.'

*Katie hits Oscar and Bob and Bob steps away from Oscar. During all the action she continues to scream.*

KATIE: You! You! Get away! Get away! I hate you! I hate you! You don't! Get away!

*Catherine runs to Katie and tries to restrain her.*

CATHERINE: Stop. Stop. Daddy. Daddy!!

*Katie collapses against Catherine.*

Help me.

*End of Act One*

## ACT II

*The house is silent. Ev and Catherine are most prominent on stage. Katie is not far from Catherine. Bob and Oscar are in the background. Catherine looks at Ev, who is wearing an old cardigan and glasses. Catherine holds Gramma's letter.*

CATHERINE: . . . Go on.

EV: . . . When I was little, Katie . . . when I was a kid, I saw my own father get smaller and smaller, physically smaller, cause he was nothin', no job, no . . . nothin'. I was only a kid but I saw him . . . get smaller like that. . . . Georgie now, he was the one in our family would have gone places.

CATHERINE: Haven't you 'gone places'?

EV: Seen half this province from their mother's belly to the grave.

CATHERINE: Was it worth it?

EV: . . . When that goddamn Demsky let me up, I'd wander all round that hospital. I'd look in the wards, Intensive Care. . . . You get to be my age, the only place better than a hospital for meetin' people you know is a mortuary . . . Frank Johnston died while I was there in his room. They had him hooked up to all these goddamn monitors. And do you know how they knew he was dead? Straight lines and the sound from the monitors. Nobody looked down at Frank. Just at the monitors. . . . And that is the kinda hospital they're gonna put my name on? . . . I wouldn't like to go like Frank.

CATHERINE: You won't go for ages, Daddy.

EV: If I can keep away from that Demsky I got a chance . . .

CATHERINE: Daddy?

EV: What?

CATHERINE: About Mummy.

EV: . . . If I could—I'm gonna show you somethin', I want you to see this . . . you see this, you'll understand. [*opens trunk and begins to sort through it*] Six or seven kids standin' by the car, and the car outside this Day Clinic . . . Valma and I, we were doing these check-ups and physicals and what-have-you . . . where the hell . . . we were doin' that one day a week in Minto, families a miners, poor goddamn buggers, most of 'em unemployed at the time. And this bunch a little rag-tag snotty-nosed kids, smellin' a wet wool and Javex, were impressed all to hell by the car—and Valma, out with the goddamn camera, and she took this here picture . . . it's in here, where the hell is it? [*stops looking for the snapshot*] . . . I don't care about this hospital thing, I don't care about . . . I care about those little kids! I looked into their faces, and I saw my own face when I was a kid . . . was I wrong to do that? So goddamn much misery—should I have tended my own little plot when I looked round and there was so damn much to do—so much I could do—I did do! Goddamn it, I did it! You tell me, was I wrong to do that!

*Pause. Ev is about to look again for the picture.*

CATHERINE: It isn't there, Daddy.

EV: I had to rely on myself cause there was fuckin' little else to rely on, I made decisions when decisions had to be made, I chose a road, and I took it, and I never looked back.

CATHERINE: You've always been so sure of things, haven't you.

*Ev watches Catherine as she looks down at the envelope, and turns it over in her hands.*

EV: . . . You're like her, Katie.

CATHERINE: Like Gramma?

EV: Like your mother. [*removes his glasses*]

CATHERINE: She always said I was just like you.

EV: Like her.

CATHERINE: Don't say that.

KATIE: Am I like Gramma, Daddy?

EV: You're like yourself, Katie.

KATIE: Why don't you open it, Daddy?

*Katie is looking at the letter Catherine holds.*

EV: I will.

CATHERINE: When I was little I stayed with her once.

*Catherine looks at Katie.*

EV: After your mother had Robbie.

KATIE: And I swore, and she said, 'You never say those words, Katie, only in church,' and when I dropped my prayer book I said, 'Jesus Christ, Gramma,' and she said 'Ka-Ty!'

CATHERINE: And I said, 'But we are in church, Gramma.'

*Katie and Catherine laugh. Ev takes off the old cardigan and hangs it over his chair as he speaks.*

EV: She'd write that kinda thing in a letter. That's all that she'd write. That's what's in this letter. [*exits*]

CATHERINE [*to Katie*]: I don't want to be like her, and I don't want to be like Mummy.

KATIE [*sings to Catherine*]:

K-K-K-Katie, my beautiful Katie,
You're the only G-G-G-Girl that I adore
When the M-M-M-Moon shines
[*Katie looks at a note book; she has not carried one before.*]
I'll be waiting . . .
K-K-K-Katie . . . Katie . . .

*Shift. Oscar is watching Katie.*

[*to Catherine*]: Everything's down in here. I write it all down. And when I grow up, I'll have it all here.

CATHERINE: Will it be worth it?

KATIE: I used to pray to God, but I don't anymore. I write it all down in here. I was just little then and now—

*Katie senses Oscar is watching her.*

Are you interested in this, Uncle Oscar? Cause if you aren't, why do you listen?

OSCAR: For you.

KATIE: I don't like people doing things for me. I can do things for myself . . .

*Katie starts to write in the book, the only time she does so.*

'Now Mummy has a "medical problem" p-r-ob.' Did you know that, Uncle Oscar? Mummy has a *medical problem*—that's apart from her *personal problems*, did you know that?

OSCAR: No.
KATIE: Really?

*Shift. Ev enters with bag and suit jacket. Oscar may help him on with it.*

EV: I thought you knew.
OSCAR: How the hell would I know?
EV: I'm sending her to the Royal Vic.
OSCAR: Who to?
EV: You remember Bob Green from McGill?
OSCAR: Bit quick to cut, isn't he?
EV: You never liked him.
OSCAR: Neither did you.
EV: So he's an asshole, was, is, and will be, but he's goddamn good at his job.
OSCAR: He's too quick to cut.
EV: And the best gynecologist in the country.
OSCAR: He'll have her in surgery before the ink on her train ticket dries.
EV: This is your professional opinion, is it, based on your *extensive* practice?
OSCAR: There's gotta be other options.
EV: We could go someplace where it's hot and lie in the sun till she grows a tumour the size of a melon—why don't we do that?
OSCAR: I—
EV: You wanna look at her medical records? Go talk to Barney, tell him I said to pull 'em and show you—fibrous uterus, two opinions.
OSCAR: Green'll go for radical surgery and—
EV: What the hell do you want me to do?
OSCAR: Does she know?
EV: Of course she knows! What the hell do you mean, does she know?
OSCAR: You gotta take some time with her, she's gonna need that.
EV: I got no time.
OSCAR: What's wrong with just takin' off—the two of you go just as soon as she's able.
EV: I can't.
OSCAR: Look, you lie on the sand in the sun and you relax for Christ's sake.
EV: I got patients been waitin' for a bed for months, I can't just leave 'em to whoever's on call.
OSCAR: I'll take 'em, you go.
EV: They count on me bein' there, Oscar.
OSCAR: The population of this province will not wither and die if you take a three-week vacation—I'll handle your patients.
EV: I'd go nuts doin' nothin'.
OSCAR: You're doin' it for her.
EV: I'd go nuts.
OSCAR: You're drivin' her nuts!
EV: Were that true, three weeks in the sun wouldn't change it.

OSCAR: Don't think of her as your wife—think of her as a patient who's married to an insensitive son-of-a-bitch.

EV: I was an insensitive son-of-a-bitch when she met me; I haven't changed.

OSCAR: I give up.

EV: OK, OK, I'm thinking . . . I'm thinking. . . . I'm thinking you like sand and sun, you could take her.

OSCAR: I didn't marry her.

EV: You like her.

OSCAR: I like her.

EV: She likes you.

OSCAR: Listen to yourself! You're asking me to take your wife on a three-week vacation to recover from major surgery, do you realize that?

EV: She needs to get away, I can't take the time, you can.

OSCAR: It's one thing I'm not gonna do for you.

EV: So do it for her.

OSCAR: No.

EV: It makes sense to me.

OSCAR: No.

EV: Why not?

OSCAR: No, I said no.

EV: You're the one suggested it.

OSCAR: I didn't.

*Ev looks at his watch.*

We're not leaving it there!

EV: Look. There's an alumnae thing in six or seven months, I can schedule around it and the three of us'll go and have one hell of a good bash, but right now I cannot get away so I'm askin' you to do me this favour. How often do I ask for a favour? Take her to one of those islands you go to, eat at the clubs, lie in the sun, and—Christ, Oscar, I got to go, so gimme an answer, yes or no? [*pause*] You make the arrangements, I'll pick up the tab.

OSCAR: Half the tab.

EV: Fifty-fifty all the way.

OSCAR: Are you sure you don't want me to check her into the Vic, observe the surgery, hang around the recovery room and generally be there?

EV: I can clear three or four days for that.

*Oscar is silent. As Ev is about to leave he notices Oscar's silence and stops.*

Say—how did that burn case go?

OSCAR: That was four months ago, Ev.

EV: Seems like yesterday, so how did it go?

OSCAR: Zip, kaput.

EV: What the hell did you do?

OSCAR: Did it ever occur to you that I might find Bob very attractive?

EV: I know she's attractive, hell, I married her, didn't I?

OSCAR: That she might find me very attractive?

EV: Don't let it go to your head.

OSCAR: You know rumours fly.

EV: I'm too damned busy to listen to rumours.

OSCAR: Your mother isn't. She listens. After that, she phones.

EV: Who?

OSCAR: Me. She phones me. To talk about you. She's a remnant of my old man's practice, remember?

EV: Last time I saw her she didn't—

OSCAR: When was that anyway?

EV: Oh I was over—no—ah—

OSCAR: She can't remember either. I've seen you, you son-of-a-bitch, I've seen you take time with some old biddy, you laugh, you hang onto her hand, and she leaves your office thinking she's Claudette Colbert, and has just stolen a night with you at the Ritz—and I—I get phone calls from your mother who is reduced to writing you letters and crying to me on the phone. You don't call, you don't visit, you don't . . . and now she's got it into her head that . . .

EV: What?

OSCAR: Rumours fly.

EV: So you reassure her. I gotta go, Oscar.

OSCAR: What if I can't reassure her?

EV: Then you laugh, hang onto her hand, and make Mum think she's Claudette Colbert at the Ritz.

OSCAR: It's not that simple.

*Ev is moving away from Oscar.*

I do find Bob very attractive.

EV: Total agreement.

OSCAR: You never think for one minute there could be one iota of truth in those rumours?

EV: I just don't believe you'd do that to me.

OSCAR: How can you be so sure?

EV: I know you.

OSCAR: Better than I know myself?

EV: I must. [*speaking as he exits*] Barbados eh, or someplace like that.

*Shift.*

BOB: I don't plan on having any more children.

CATHERINE: No more children.

BOB: I didn't plan, didn't.

CATHERINE: No children.

BOB: Don't have to plan now. All taken care of. Are you listenin' to me?

*Shift. Katie and Catherine will end up together, a mirror image.*

KATIE: I'll tell you what she does. What she does is, she starts doing something. Something big. That's how I can tell. She's all right for awhile—then she decides she's gonna paint all of the downstairs—or we're gonna put in new cupboards—or knock out a wall! . . . We got so many walls knocked out, the house started to fall down in the middle! Can you believe that?—And we had to get a big steel beam put through in the basement! Can you believe that?

CATHERINE: It's true.

KATIE: And before she gets finished one of those big jobs—she starts.

CATHERINE: And she never finishes. Someone else comes in, and they finish.

KATIE: But that's how I can tell when she's gonna start. And I try to figure out

CATHERINE: I ask myself

KATIE: Does the big job make her start—or does she start the big job because she knows she's gonna start?

CATHERINE: But that's how I could tell, that's the beginning.

*Shift.*

BOB: So . . . why does it . . . why do I feel that it matters? Two were enough, Katie and Robert, so why do I feel that it matters? I don't want any more . . . Oscar!

OSCAR: I'm here.

BOB: Does it matter?

OSCAR: Well . . . from the medical—

BOB: Medical, medical, medical, I don't wanna talk about medical.

OSCAR: It affects—

BOB: Me! Me! I'm talkin' about me! Why do I feel like, why do I feel—we didn't want any more children! I can't have any more children! Me, the part of me that's important, here, inside here—Me! That's the same. I'm the same. So . . . why do I feel that it matters?

OSCAR: It doesn't matter.

BOB: Why don't you listen? I'm trying to explain. We didn't want any more, I can't have any more, so why does it matter?

OSCAR: It doesn't matter.

BOB: It does matter! . . . I'm the same. Inside I'm the same. I'm Eloise Roberts and they called me Bob and I can run faster and do better than any boy I ever met!

OSCAR: It's all right.

BOB: No.

OSCAR: Come here.

BOB: I try to figure it out and I just keep going round.

CATHERINE: It's all right.

BOB: I need to do more, I need to . . . I need . . .

CATHERINE: Why don't you just do what you want?

BOB: Sometimes I want to scream. I just want to stand there and scream, to hit something, to reach out and smash things—and hit and smash and hit and smash and . . . and then . . . I would feel very tired and I could lie down and sleep.

OSCAR: Do you want to sleep now?

BOB: No. I'm not tired now. I want a drink now. Want a drink, and then we'll . . . what will we do?

CATHERINE: Why couldn't you leave.

BOB: Leave?

CATHERINE: Just leave!

BOB: Katie and Robbie.

CATHERINE: Did you care about them?

BOB: And your father?

*Shift. Ev enters, carrying a bag. He is isolated on stage.*

EV: We had the worst polio epidemic this province has seen, eleven years ago. We had an outbreak this year. You are lookin' at the attendin' physician at the present Polio Clinic—it is a building that has been condemned by the Provincial Fire Marshall, it has been condemned by the Provincial Health Officer, it has been condemned by the Victoria Public Hospital, it's infested by cockroaches, it's overrun by rats, it's the worst goddamn public building in this province! When is the government gonna stop building liquor stores and give the doctors of this province a chance to save a few fuckin' lives!

BOB: Haven't you got enough?

EV: Enough of what?

BOB: Enough! Enough everything!

EV: You're drunk.

BOB: You'll never get enough, will you?

EV: Did Valma phone?

BOB: I don't answer the phone, just let it ring and ring—

*Ev starts to exit.*

Where're you going?

EV: Valma's.

BOB: What for?

EV: To pick up the messages that she'd give me by phone if you'd answer the phone.

BOB: Maid could answer it. Does answer it, but she's not good with messages, no.

EV: You run them through the house so goddamn fast they don't have time to pick up a phone. Why don't you get one and keep one?

BOB: Interviewin' them gives me somethin' to do. I enjoy interviewin' them. Purpose and direction to my life! Where're you goin'?

EV [*exiting*]: Valma's.

BOB: Stay.

CATHERINE: Stay.

*Ev stops.*

Don't go. Sit for a little while.

*There is a moment of silence.*

CATHERINE: Talk.
EV: If I sit down . . . my head will start to nod.
CATHERINE: That'd be all right. She wouldn't mind. You'd be here.

*Ev puts down his bag. He moves to Bob and sits beside her. He takes his hat off and takes her hand. Bob smiles and strokes Ev's hand, then holds it against her face.*

BOB: Do you remember . . . sometimes I . . . we had some good times, didn't we?
EV: We can still have good times.
BOB: I don't know.
EV: You've got to get hold of things.
BOB: I try.
EV: I know I'm busy.
BOB: Always busy.
EV: I know.
BOB: If I could do something.
EV: There's the house and the kids. Just tell me what you want and I'll get it.
BOB: I can't do anything.
EV: You can.
BOB: No. There's nothing I can do.
EV: Sure there is.

*Bob slowly shakes her head.*

Come on . . . hey, listen, did you know the Hendersons were sellin' their camp on Miramichi?

*Pause.*

Well they are. What say we buy it? You'd like that, wouldn't you? You could get away from the kids and the house, do some fishin', you like fishin' don't you?

*Bob nods her head.*

Well, that's what we'll do. [*checks his watch*] Shit. You get to bed. Get some sleep. [*exits*]

BOB: Can't sleep.

*There is the sound of a train whistle; Bob listens to it. It fades away. Shift.*

. . . Half-way across three-quarters of a mile of single track . . . its whistle would split the night, and that night . . . do you know what she did?
CATHERINE: No, and neither to you.
BOB: She walked out to meet it.
CATHERINE: And you say I'm like his side of the family, you say I'm like her?
BOB: She did.
CATHERINE: I would never do that!

*Shift.*

KATIE: Mummy didn't like her. I could have gone to see her with Daddy, but Daddy was always too busy to go, so it was all his fault I didn't see her. . . . I guess that's true.

CATHERINE: She would phone, she would ask for me.

KATIE: But I could never think of anything to say. . . . They're the ones I'm supposed to be like, his side of the family, so it would have been nice to see her . . . was she old? . . .

*Catherine doesn't answer.*

KATIE: Is that what she died of? . . .

*Catherine doesn't answer.*

What did she die of, Uncle Oscar?

OSCAR: It was an accident.

CATHERINE: We know 'accidents', don't we?

KATIE: I never saw anybody dead before. I don't know if I wanted to see her dead . . . it didn't matter because they didn't take us anyway—I was a bit happy not to go because I don't like to go anywhere with Mummy when she's like that. She said Gramma was a bitch who went around saying bad things about her and Mummy was glad she was dead—and Daddy just kept getting dressed and pretended Mummy wasn't talking—You can only pretend for so long.

CATHERINE: And when they came home he went out.

KATIE: And Mummy phoned all over but he wasn't any place she could find, and . . .

CATHERINE: . . . then she tripped at the top of the stairs and she fell. I went to my bedroom as soon as that happened . . .

KATIE: . . . and Robbie screamed and cried and screamed and cried and . . .

CATHERINE: . . . the maid got up and put her to bed—she'll be leaving soon and we'll get a new one . . .

KATIE: . . . you'd think if a person kept falling down stairs it would hurt them!

CATHERINE: It never did a thing to her.

*Shift.*

BOB: Katie! . . . Katie! You wanna know somethin'?

KATIE: No.

BOB: Your father's mother killed herself! . . .

*Pause. Katie stares at Bob.*

You look at me . . . you look at me and what are you thinking?

KATIE: Nothing.

BOB: This isn't me you know. This isn't really me. This is someone else. . . . What are you thinking?

KATIE: I don't think anything.

BOB: Katie!

CATHERINE: Leave her alone!

BOB: You know what your father's mother said?

CATHERINE: Leave her alone!

BOB: Do you know?

KATIE: No!

BOB: Why would a nurse—to catch a doctor, that's why. Why would he marry me, eh? Why would a brilliant young man, whole life ahead of him, why would he marry me? Eh? Do you know why? Do you know!

KATIE: No.

BOB: Why would he do that?!

KATIE: I don't know.

BOB: Answer me!

KATIE: I don't know!

BOB: No! You don't know! Nobody knows!

KATIE: I know. Inside I know. He had to.

CATHERINE: Don't.

KATIE: Inside I do know. Because of me—and that's what went wrong.

CATHERINE: He loved her and she loved him, Uncle Oscar says.

KATIE: No.

CATHERINE: That's true, Katie!

KATIE: Do you believe that?

*Ev enters in his shirt sleeves.*

Daddy!

*Katie runs to Ev and he puts his arms around her.*

EV: Your mother sometimes says things that she doesn't mean. She's sick and she—

KATIE: She isn't sick!

EV: She loves you.

KATIE: I don't love her.

*Katie quickly moves away. Ev starts after her.*

EV: Yes you do.

*Shift.*

BOB: Valma, Valma, Valma, Valma, Valma, Valma I am so sick of that woman's name. What're you and her doing, that's what I'd like to know!

EV: Nothing. [*sits*]

BOB: Oooh, you don't tell me that! I know better than that! She's like your right arm, your left arm, part of your leg!

EV: Leave Valma out of it.

BOB: I don't wanna leave Valma out of it! She'd do anything for you—put your wife to bed, get her up—why does she do that, eh? Tell me why?

EV: She's the best office nurse in the city and I couldn't run that office without her. Why the Christ don't you go to bed?

BOB: Why the Christ don't you go to bed?

EV: Go to bed.

BOB: Gonna go over to Valma's and go to bed? You don't love me, you never loved me! You never loved me.

EV: Go to bed.

BOB: You don't even see me. You look at me and there's nobody there. You don't see anybody but those stupid stupid people who think you're God. You're not God!

*Catherine and Katie are together and Bob moves towards them. Bob grabs Catherine's hand.*

And it's so funny . . . do you know what he's done, do you know? . . . If I . . . If I go into the liquor store, do you know what happens? They say . . . sorry, but the Doc says no. He says . . . they're not to . . . and they don't. They don't. He tells them don't sell it to her the Doc says don't do that and they don't. But what's so funny is . . . every drunk in the city goes into that office on Saturday and they say . . . 'Jeez Chris Doc, spent the whole cheque on booze, the old lady's gonna kill me,' and he gives them money. . . . Gives them money.

*Katie moves away.*

And Valma says he says maybe one of them takes it home instead of just buyin' more, can you believe that? . . . And when I go in, they say, 'The Doc says no' . . . but I don't have to worry. [*moves to refill her glass*] So long as I keep interviewin' the maids . . . I don't have to worry about a thing.

*Shift.*

KATIE: You don't have any family.

OSCAR: You're my family.

KATIE: I'm not related to you, and you're not related to me, you can't be family, Uncle Oscar.

*Shift.*

BOB [*leaves her glass*]: Hey! Do you want to know what a bastard he is?

*Catherine turns her head away as Bob advances on Ev.*

Well I don't care if you want to know or not—I'm gonna tell you. I put the clothes out, put the suit out for the cleaners and I went through his pockets, and do you know what I found, do you know? It was something he didn't need for me, something he wouldn't use with me, because I can't have any more, no, I've been fixed like the goddamn cat or the dog so what the hell did you have it for?

EV: If you found it, that means I didn't use it, so what the hell's your problem?

*Bob runs at Ev.*

BOB: You bastard!

*Bob strikes at Ev's chest. He grabs her wrists.*

You bastard you.

*Bob attempts to strike Ev several times before collapsing against Ev's chest. He picks her up, carries her to her chair, and puts her in it. He looks down at her for a moment, then moves away, to sit isolated on the stage. Oscar joins him. Shift.*

OSCAR: She tells me you're bangin' Valma.

EV: If I wanted to bang someone, it sure as hell wouldn't be Valma.

OSCAR: So who are you bangin'?

EV: Has she posted that condom story in the staff room, or is it just you she told?

OSCAR: I asked you a question.

EV: I'm not bangin' anyone! Who the hell are you bangin'! . . . I . . . I lost Jack Robinson the other night. . . . I felt so goddamn bad. I thought he was gonna make it and then everything started shuttin' down. He gets pneumonia, we get that under control, then his heart starts givin' us problems, we get that solved, then his goddamn kidneys go—I don't know why, just one thing after another. Someone was callin' his name and I couldn't do a damn thing about it . . . and I felt so bad, I thought . . . I don't want to go home, you can see what she's like so . . . you know what I did? I bought a mickey of rum and that goddamn condom and I . . . I drove around for a coupla hours. And that was it. . . . That was it.

OSCAR: Things can't go on.

EV: Don't start on that give her more time shit. Her problem's got nothin' to do with time nor work nor any other goddamn thing.

OSCAR: Her problem is the crazy son-of-a-bitch she's married to.

EV: Who the hell is crazy here? I'm the one can't keep a bottle of booze in the house, I'm the one's gotta put the fear of God in the help so they're too damn scared to buy it for her—and now she's into the vanilla or any other goddamn thing she can pour down her throat! I can't keep pills in the bag and she'd let the kids starve to death if it weren't for the maid! I'm the one goin' eighteen hours a day tryin' to hold the fuckin' fort so I can hear you say what!? . . . That I'm crazy! I'm not a goddamn machine!!! I thought if anyone would understand, it would be you . . . and you . . . [*exits*]

OSCAR: Ev. Ev!

*Oscar may exit after him. Shift. Bob runs her hand along the cushion in the chair. She gets on her knees, lifts the cushion up. Catherine watches her search. Katie observes, from a distance. Bob continues her search.*

BOB: Everyone has something hidden in this house. I hid it and he hides it and you hide it.

CATHERINE: Do something.

BOB: Do something. Just like your father. Do, do, do.

CATHERINE: Just stop!

BOB: Just stop. [*finds the bottle of pills*] Stop doing. [*unscrews bottle; pours pills in hand; looks at Catherine*] Stop. [*swallows pills; settles back in chair; shuts eyes*]

*Shift. Katie slowly approaches Bob. She and Catherine stand, looking at Bob. Pause.*

KATIE: She was blue. . . . I'd never seen anybody blue before. Robbie went in the kitchen and cried. I stood at the bottom of the stairs and watched them bring her down on a stretcher. I didn't cry. . . . I don't know what she took—was it the pills that made her sleep?

CATHERINE: Uncle Oscar said.

KATIE: She was asleep all right. And really blue. I thought . . . I thought . . .

CATHERINE: Go on, you can say it.

KATIE: I thought maybe she was dead. [*moves away*] . . . and now she's going to Connecticut? Will she be better then?

*Catherine joins Katie.*

CATHERINE: Uncle Oscar said.

KATIE: All better?

*Catherine doesn't answer.*

I wonder . . . do you know what I wonder? I wonder, did she take the pills to sleep like she sometimes does, or did she . . .

CATHERINE: It was

KATIE: An accident? . . . Sometimes I look . . .

CATHERINE: . . . in the mirror, I look in the mirror . . .

KATIE: . . . and I see Mummy and I see . . .

CATHERINE: . . . Gramma, and Mummy and me . . .

KATIE: . . . I don't want to be like them.

*Shift. Oscar may enter. Bob is sitting. She will get up and very carefully tie her gown. There is a certain formality, seriousness, alienation, and deliberation about her. She moves and speaks somewhat slowly. Oscar stands a distance from her, still and watching.*

BOB: You have to get hold of things. Routine's important. Get out. Get around. Do things. The IODE, Bridge. . . . The doctors' wives have this sort of club that meets on a regular basis, I . . .

OSCAR: Tired?

BOB: No. Feeling fine. How do I look?

OSCAR: Good.

*Bob moves to another chair and sits. Oscar remains in the same position, watching her. Bob doesn't speak till seated. She does not look at Oscar.*

BOB: Leisure activity is big. Structured leisure activity. Very big. [*pause*] Painting. I paint now. You know. [*pause*] Pictures. [*pause; speaks softly*] What else? [*pause*] Gorgeous place. If you'd been there, it would have been perfect. [*pause; speaks softly*] What else. [*pause*] Psychiatrists, psychiatrists. They ask you obvious things and you give them obvious answers. It's all very obvious. . . . Obvious . . . [*softly*] what else. [*long pause; softly*] Nothing . . . nothing else . . . I can't think of . . . anything else.

*Bob sits very still. Oscar stands watching her. Bob begins to rock back and forth very slightly and sings very softly to herself. She is not singing words, but merely making sounds. Oscar moves to her. He stands behind her looking down for a moment. He slowly places a hand on her shoulder. She reaches up and holds his hand pressing it to her shoulder. She continues to rock slightly but the words of the song can be heard. She is singing 'Auld Lang Syne'. Oscar moves around her without letting go of her hand and draws her up to dance, which they do rather formally.*

BOB [*sings*]: Should auld acquaintance be forgot
and never brought to mind
Should auld acquaintance
Be forgot—and auld lang syne
an auld lang syne m'dear
an auld lang syne

*Bob begins to cry but continues singing and dancing.*

Let's drink a cup of kindness up
For auld lang syne.

*Shift. Ev enters. He is isolated on stage. He carries his bag, and his hat is pushed back on his head. There is an air of powerful relaxation and poise about him. He might almost be standing in a glow of golden sunshine. When he speaks Bob and Oscar stop dancing. They turn to stare at him and Oscar will step away from Bob. Bob is drawn towards Ev, who does not acknowledge her.*

EV: I say three or four of us go in together. I mean look at the situation now. A patient comes in from Durham Bridge, and has to run all over this Christless city, GP here, lab tests there, pediatrician someplace else. I've got my eye on a place on the hill. We renovate it—

BOB: Bar date with him.

EV: And we open a Medical Clinic, lab, X-ray, everything in that one building—

BOB: And you don't call that—

EV: We solicit the best specialists we can to take office space there. We give the people of this goddamn province the medical care they deserve, without havin' to run all over hell and hackety to get it!

BOB: And I laughed—and he said—and it was so funny—such a long time ago . . .

*Shift.*

KATIE: You lied to me.

OSCAR: When?

KATIE: People do lie to me quite a bit. They think I don't know it, but I do.

OSCAR: I didn't mean to lie.

KATIE: You didn't tell the truth.

OSCAR: What did I lie about?

KATIE: Guess—one guess?

BOB: S'funny thing.

KATIE: You promised me she'd get better, Uncle Oscar! You promised and you lied.

*Shift. Bob lights a cigarette during her speech. By the end of her speech it is apparent she's been drinking.*

BOB: The more you do of certain things, the less it seems you do. You fill your time up, my time's filled up. I sit at these tea luncheons, s'always . . . sherry. I hate sherry. I never have any sherry. I know what they think, but that's not the reason. I just don't like sherry. No. No sherry. [*pause*] Children are important. [*pause*] And the IODE . . . I go to—and bridshe, play a lot of bridshe, I'm good at that. Win, always win. . . . I like bridshe. And ahh [*pause*] I don't really like them but—everything's working for them and everything can work for me too. I can be them. It isn't hard, I can do it. If I . . . if I want to.

*Bob moves to drawer, opens it and feels inside. She is looking for a bottle, slowly and methodically. She becomes aware of Katie watching her.*

BOB: What do you want?

KATIE: I don't want anything.

BOB: What're you doing?

KATIE: I'm watching you.

BOB: Your father tell you to do that?

KATIE: No.

BOB: Then why are you watchin'?

KATIE: I want to remember.

BOB: Remember what?

KATIE: Remember you.

BOB: I know what you're thinking. It's all right. You can say it . . . do you want me to say it?

KATIE: No.

BOB: I'm not afraid. I can say it.

KATIE: If I were you—I wouldn't let Robbie see me like that. It makes him feel bad. He has to pretend that you're sick.

BOB: What do you pretend, Katie?

KATIE: I don't have to pretend anymore.

CATHERINE: Katie.

*Bob stops her search, turns to Katie.*

BOB: Did you take something of mine?

KATIE: Did I?

BOB: You took something of mine and I want it back.

KATIE: You can't have it back.

BOB: I want it back!

KATIE: It's gone.
BOB: No.
KATIE: I poured it out, let go!
BOB: Give it back!
CATHERINE: Don't.

*Bob and Katie struggle.*

BOB: You had no right you . . .
KATIE: Let go!
BOB: No.
CATHERINE: Let her go.
BOB: Give it to me.
KATIE: Let go, let go!
BOB: You you no right!
KATIE: Go!

*Katie strikes Bob, knocking her down.*

I'm not gonna cry. I'm not gonna cry!
BOB: I tried. I really did try.
CATHERINE: I'm not gonna cry.
BOB: Listen.

*Bob grabs Catherine's hand.*

Listen Katie. I want . . . I want to tell you—when—when I was little, do you know, do you know I would sit on our front porch, and I would look up, look up at the sky, and the sky, the sky went on forever. And I just looked up. That was me, Katie. That was me.
CATHERINE: I'm holding my breath and my teeth are together and my tongue, I can feel my tongue, it presses hard on the back of my teeth and the roof of my mouth . . .
KATIE: . . . and I hang on really tight. Really tight, and then . . . I don't cry.
CATHERINE: I never cried . . . [*to Bob*] but I couldn't listen like that.

*Bob releases Catherine's hand and moves away from her. Catherine runs after her as she speaks.*

CATHERINE: It's one of those things you can't do like that!
KATIE: It's better not to cry than to listen.
CATHERINE: Is it?
KATIE: It's how you keep on. It's one of the ways. I'm surprised you don't know that.

*Katie moves away from Catherine, who then follows her. Shift.*

EV: Close this time.
OSCAR: How close?

EV: Too damn close. We pumped her stomach and prayed. The kids spent Christmas Day at Valma's. . . . I think . . . I think the psychiatrist she sees is nuttier than she is. . . . I'm alright . . .

*Ev sits in the same chair he sat in as 'Old Ev', at the start of the play. Pause.*

Did you know . . . what the hell is their name . . . live over on King Street, married someone or other, moved to Toronto. . . . I'm alright. [*pause*] Some silly son of a whore didn't look close enough, she kept tellin' him she had this lump in her breast. . . . I'm alright. . . . She's got a three-month-old kid and she's come home to die. . . . Thing is no one's got around to tellin' her that's how it is. They asked me to come over and tell her . . . patients of mine . . . come home to die . . .

*Oscar may exit. Pause. Ev takes Gramma's letter out of his pocket and looks at it.*

EV: I'm alright . . .

*Shift.*

BOB: Open it! Go on, open it!
EV: You're drunk.
BOB: I'm drunk. So I'm drunk. What the hell are you, what's your excuse? What's his excuse, Katie?
EV: Leave her alone.
BOB: Why don't you open it!
EV: What for?
BOB: To see what it says.
EV: Says nothing.
BOB: Your father's mother killed herself, Katie. She walked across the train bridge at midnight and—
KATIE: That's an accident!
BOB: She left a letter and the letter tells him why she did it.
KATIE: What's in the letter, Daddy?
EV: Your Gramma—

*Oscar may unobtrusively enter, and stand silently in the background.*

BOB: She killed herself because of him!
KATIE: Because of you!
EV: Your Gramma loved us.
KATIE: Why don't you open it?
EV: She didn't see us so she'd write.
BOB: So open it!
EV: That's all it is.
BOB: Pretending! He's pretending!
KATIE: He is not!
BOB: He pretends a lot!

KATIE: You do!
BOB: Valma! Valma! Valma!
KATIE: I hate you!
BOB: Not afraid to say it!
KATIE: I hate you and I wish that you were dead!
CATHERINE: No.
KATIE: It's true!
CATHERINE: No.
KATIE: I wish and wish and
CATHERINE: No.
KATIE: someday you will be dead and I'll be happy!
OSCAR: It's alright, Katie!
KATIE [*to Ev*]: You all say she's sick, she isn't sick.
BOB [*to Katie*]: Katie!
KATIE: She's a drunk and that's what we should say!
BOB [*to Catherine*]: Katie!?
CATHERINE: Stop.
KATIE: And if I find her next time, I won't call for Daddy!
CATHERINE: No.
KATIE: I won't call for anyone!
CATHERINE: Stop Katie please.
KATIE [*sits*]: I'll go back downstairs and I'll sit in the kitchen and I'll pretend that I don't know, I'll pretend that everything's all right, I'll shut my eyes, and I'll pretend!
BOB: Katie! [*retreats*]
KATIE [*chants*]: Now they're married wish them joy
BOB: Katie. [*exits*]
KATIE [*puts hands over ears; chants louder*]:
First a girl for a toy
Seven years after seven years to come
BOB [*voice-over on mike, offstage*]: Katie!
KATIE [*chants louder*]: Fire on the mountain
kiss and run
on the mountains berries sweet
BOB [*on mike, offstage*]: Katie!
KATIE [*chants*]: Pick as much as you can eat
By the berries bitter bark
BOB [*on mike, offstage*]: Katie!
KATIE [*chants louder*]: Fire on the mountain break your heart
Years to come—kiss and run
bitter bark—break your heart

*Katie slowly takes her hands from her ears. There is silence. Pause.*

I don't hear you! [*pause*] I don't hear you! [*pause*]! I don't!

*Katie jumps up and whirls around, to look over at where she last saw Bob. Pause.*

KATIE [*softly*]: I don't hear you at all.
CATHERINE: You can cry, Katie . . . it's all right to cry . . .
KATIE: Would you want to have me?
CATHERINE: Yes, yes I would.

*Shift.*

EV: All over now.

*Ev gets up from the chair and moves to the table where Catherine left the jewellery box in Act One. He stands, looking down at it.*

CATHERINE: No, Daddy.
OSCAR: When was it we played scrub hockey on the river ice. . . . Ev and Oscar, Oscar, Ev. . . . 'We're rough, we're tough, we're from Devon, that's enough' . . .

*Ev lifts the lid of the music box. It plays 'Smoke Gets in Your Eyes'.*

. . . driving my old man's car, watering his whisky, Ev and Oscar . . .
EV: Ever since Grade One.
OSCAR: I knew you then, and I knew you after that, and then I got to know you less and less—and here we are. . . . I said why risk it? And I saw her and knew why . . . well, she's gone now. . . . What the hell does that mean to you, Ev. That's something I want to know. What's it mean? . . . For Christ's sake, say something, say anything.
EV: There's nothing to say.
OSCAR: It shouldn't have happened.
EV: It did. [*closes the music box*]
OSCAR: She asked for goddamn little and you couldn't even give her that.
EV: You got no more idea of what she wanted that I have.
OSCAR: You never knew her and you don't know me.
EV: How can you say that? I carried you on my back since Grade One cause I liked you, I loved you, like a brother.
OSCAR: I could see it in my father, I can see it in you. You got your eyes fixed on some goddamn horizon, and while you're striding towards that, you trample on every goddamn thing around you!
EV: The biggest dream you ever had, what the hell was it? What was it, Oscar? New Orleans! New Orleans.
OSCAR: She understood what that meant.
EV: Bullshit. You been a pseudo-doctor for your old man, a pseudo-husband to my wife, and a pseudo-father to my kids! I gave you that, Oscar, like I gave you everything else cause I knew you'd never have the goddamn gumption to get it for yourself!
OSCAR: I should have taken your wife.
EV: My wife wouldn't have you!

*Oscar starts to leave. Ev calls after him.*

She knew you! She knew what you were! And because of that you say I killed her! It was all my fault?

*Oscar stops. Ev moves to him.*

Supposin' it were, her death my fault, put a figure on it, eh? Her death my fault on one side—and the other any old figure, thousand lives the figure—was that worth it?

*Oscar exits.*

Was it? I'm askin' you a question! Was that worth it!

*Silence. Shift. Katie approaches Ev. As he removes his overcoat, he speaks to her.*

What the hell do you mean?

KATIE: I don't know what I mean.

EV: Where the hell would you go?

KATIE: I don't know. Away. Away to some school.

EV: I don't want you to go.

KATIE: Send me anyway. For me, Daddy. Do it for me.

EV: What if I said no?

KATIE: You won't say no.

EV: You wanna hear me say no!

KATIE: I'm like you Daddy. I just gotta win—and you just gotta win—and if you say no—you'll have lost. [*exiting as she speaks*] I'll come back . . . every once in a while . . . I'll come back . . .

EV: Katie? [*screams*] Katie!

CATHERINE: I'm here.

*Shift. Catherine and Ev are alone on stage. As Catherine speaks, Ev puts on his old cardigan, which was hanging on the back of his chair. He puts on his glasses. Catherine has Gramma's letter.*

Do you remember when she gathered together all the photographs and snapshots, all the pictures of her, and she sat in the living room, and she ripped them all up? So . . . after she died, we had no pictures of her. . . . And Oscar, remember Oscar came over with one . . . it was taken at a nightclub somewhere, and she was feeding this little pig—a stupid little pig standing on the table and she—she was feeding it with a little bottle like a baby's bottle . . .

EV: Her with . . .

CATHERINE: . . . a baby bottle feeding the pig with a bottle . . .

EV [*small chuckle*]: Her and Oscar at some goddamn Caribbean nightclub feedin' a pig . . .

CATHERINE: Like a baby. She was looking up at the camera. She was smiling a bit. You could see her teeth. She didn't look happy, or unhappy. She looked like she was waiting. Just waiting.

EV: For what?

CATHERINE: I don't know. But whatever it was, she couldn't grab it.

EV: Do you know what you want?

CATHERINE: . . . Yes . . . Yes, I do.

EV: Then you grab it.

CATHERINE [*Pause; looks at Gramma's letter, which she is holding in her hand*]: What are you gonna do with this?

EV: Do you wanna open it?

CATHERINE: I can. Do you want me to?

EV: I know what's in it.

*Pause. Catherine strikes a match. She looks at Ev.*

CATHERINE: Should I? . . . should I? . . .

*Catherine blows the match out and gives the letter to Ev. He sits looking at it for a moment.*

EV: Burn the goddamn thing.

*Ev holds the letter out. Catherine sets it on fire and it flares up as Ev holds it.*

CATHERINE: Be careful!

EV: I am bein' careful.

*Ev drops the burning envelope into an ashtray. Lights are fading.*

Two minutes home and you're as bad as Valma.

CATHERINE: Bullshit, Daddy.

EV: Jesus Christ I hate to hear a woman talk like that.

*As the lights fade to black, Catherine looks to Ev and smiles. Black except for the dying flame of the letter.*

*The End*

1986

# Michel Tremblay

*b.* 1942

Born in Montreal, Michel Tremblay wrote his first play, *Le Train*, which won first prize in Radio-Canada's Young Authors' Competition, at the age of 16. His first staged play, *Les Belles-soeurs* (1968), revolutionized Quebec theatre with its use of *joual*, the language of working-class Montrealers, and its forthright presentation of marginalized characters. For all of its verbal comedy and abundant farce, it depicts the sheer emptiness of contemporary urban existence and the bitter alienation of the Quebec people. The play has been translated into many languages and staged throughout the world. The novels of his 'Chroniques du Plateau Mont-Royal' series are semi-autobiographical fictions that further explore the world created in his plays. *For the Pleasure of Seeing Her Again*, which premiered in English on 1 October 1998 in Montreal, explores the relationship between Tremblay and his mother in the conversations between the narrator and Nana.

## For the Pleasure of Seeing Her Again[1]

*The stage is empty.*

*The narrator enters, sits down on a chair where he will stay until the end.*

*He can move, gesticulate, cross his arms and legs, but he should not leave the chair until the last few minutes of the play.*

*Nana, on the other hand, takes over the stage the minute she arrives, she fills it, dominates it, makes it her kingdom.*

*It is her space.*

NARRATOR: Tonight, no one will rage and cry: 'My kingdom for a horse!' No ghost will come to haunt the battlements of a castle in the kingdom of Denmark where, apparently, something is rotten. Nor will anyone wring her hands and murmur: 'Leave, I do not despise you.' Three still young women will not retreat to a dacha, whispering the name of Moscow, their beloved, their lost hope. No sister will await the return of her brother to avenge the death of their father, no son will be forced to avenge an affront to his father, no mother will kill her three children to take revenge on their father. And no husband will see his doll-like wife leave him out of contempt. No one will turn into a rhinoceros. Maids will not plot to assassinate their mistress, after denouncing her lover and having him jailed. No one will fret about 'the rain in Spain!' No one will emerge from a large garbage pail to tell an absurd story. Italian families will not leave for the seashore. No soldier will return from World War II and bang on his father's bedroom door, protesting the presence of a new wife in his mother's bed. No evanescent blonde will drown. No Spanish

1 translated by Linda Gaboriau

nobleman will seduce a thousand and three women, nor will an entire family of Spanish women writhe beneath the heel of the fierce Bernarda Alba. You won't see a brute of a man rip his sweat-drenched t-shirt, shouting: 'Stella! Stella!' and his sister-in-law will not be doomed the minute she steps off the streetcar named Desire. Nor will you see a stepmother pine away for her new husband's youngest son. The plague will not descend upon the city of Thebes, and the Trojan War will not take place. No king will be betrayed by his ungrateful daughters. There will be no duels, no poisonings, no wracking coughs. No one will die, or, if someone must die, it will become a comic scene. No, there will be none of the usual theatrics. What you will see tonight is a very simple woman, a woman who will simply talk. . . . I almost said, about her life, but the lives of others will be just as important: her husband, her sons, her relatives and neighbours. Perhaps you will recognize her. You've often run into her at the theatre, in the audience and on stage, you've met her in life, she's one of you. She was born, it's true, during a specific era in this country and lived her life in a city that resembles this city, but, I am convinced, she is everywhere. She is universal. She is Rodrigue's aunt, Electra's cousin, Ivanov's sister, Caligula's stepmother, Mistress Quickly's little niece, the mother of Ham or of Clov, or perhaps of both. And when she speaks in her own words, people who speak differently will understand her, in their own words. She has existed throughout the ages and in every culture. She always has been present and always will be. I wanted the pleasure of seeing her again. The pleasure of hearing her. So she could make me laugh and cry. One more time, if I may. [*He looks towards the wings.*] Aha, I hear her coming. Get ready, she'll talk a blue streak, because words have always been her most effective weapon. [*He smiles.*] As they say in the classics: 'Hark, she cometh this way!'

*Enter Nana.*

*She is visibly furious.*

NANA: Go to your room. Right this minute! How could you do such a thing? At your age! Ten years old, you should know better! No, it's not true, how can I say that, at ten, you can't be expected to know much. Maybe you've reached the age of reason, but you're inexperienced. At ten, you're just a stupid kid, and you act like a stupid kid! But still, I thought you'd be smart enough to know not to do something like this!

NARRATOR: I didn't do it on purpose.

NANA: You didn't do it on purpose?! You threw a chunk of ice under a moving car, don't try to tell me you didn't do it on purpose! That chunk of ice didn't take off by itself.

NARRATOR: Everybody was doing it!

NANA: Listen to that! How smart can you get! Everybody was doing it! Since when do you have to act like everybody else? If everybody decides to go lick a frozen fence post, are you going to risk tearing off the tip of your tongue and lisping for the rest of your life, just to act like everybody else?

NARRATOR: If I hadn't done it—

NANA: If you hadn't done it, none of this would have happened, and I wouldn't have been so ashamed of you! Do you realize what I just went through? Eh? Do you? You don't seem very upset. There I was quietly doing my wash, pulling your father's drawers through the wringer, listening to the radio, I think I was even singing, and the doorbell rings. I didn't have time to go to the door, besides I thought it was the kid from Provost's Market who'd come to deliver the meat, so I yelled: 'C'mon in, door's not locked!' as loud as I could, hoping he'd hear me, and I kept pulling stuff through the wringer. But nothing happened, so I turned around. I thought maybe the kid from Provost's was too shy to walk through to the kitchen. . . . And what do I see burst into my dining room? A policeman! A policeman in uniform! In my own dining room! With his cap on his head and his heavy winter coat! Barefoot 'cause he had the decency to take his boots off in the hall! A policeman standing barefoot in my dining room, how do you think I felt! Of course, you're nowhere in sight, you're hiding in your room, so how was I supposed to know he'd come for you! Do you know what I thought? I thought someone had died! I thought someone was *dead!* Your father, or one of your brothers, or you! Do you know what went through my mind, eh, have you any idea? Maybe it only lasted a few seconds, who knows, but I saw a corpse, covered with a plaid blanket, cut in two by a streetcar or squashed by a bus, and that corpse was one of you! All I could see was a hand sticking out from under that blanket and I had to guess whose hand it was! Do you realize how that makes a mother feel? Eh? Answer me!

NARRATOR: You're pretty melodramatic, Ma.

NANA: Don't you talk to me like that! Just wait till a bare-socked policeman brings me back cut in two under a plaid wool blanket, young man, then we'll see which one of us is more melodramatic! I could've got my arm caught in the wringer! Right up to the elbow! Up to my armpit! Like your Aunt Gertrude!

NARRATOR: Aunt Gertrude—

NANA: Forget your Aunt Gertrude and listen to me, I haven't finished! So there I am, my jaw hanging open, facing the policeman, with one of your father's drawers caught in the wringer, spinning round and round, and I felt like the kitchen floor was about to cave in and I was going to end up downstairs, lying spreadeagle on Madame Forget's kitchen table with bits of baloney sandwiches stuck to my back!

*The narrator laughs.*

Don't laugh, it's not funny!

NARRATOR: Don't tell me you thought about the baloney sandwiches, Ma, you just added that now—

NANA: Maybe they weren't baloney sandwiches, but I felt them sticking to my back just the same!

NARRATOR: Ma. . . .

NANA: Shut up and listen to me! I can never get a word in edgewise around here!

*The narrator shakes his head and tries not to smile.*

I didn't dare ask him who had died, you hear me, I was afraid I'd collapse and die right there myself. . . . Two deaths in the family, the same day, that's one too many! But no! Nobody died! It was just . . . just that my stupid kid had been arrested like a highway robber because he was fooling around with his stupid friends, throwing chunks of ice under the cars going by! Imagine how ashamed I was! Ten years old! Ten years old and a delinquent already! Do you know what went through my mind when he told that? Any idea? Do you know what I saw?

*The narrator raises his eyes to heaven.*

Don't roll your eyes like that, how many times do I have to tell you, I hate it when you do that! While he was telling me about your little . . . mishap, there I was, picturing you locked up in jail for the rest of your life! I could see you, my own kid, behind bars for the rest of your days. I saw you growing up, getting married, having kids. . . . [*She realizes what she just said.*] I don't mean you got married and had kids in jail, I mean, I saw you spending the rest of your days, in and out of jail, and then. . . . Oh, now I'm all mixed up. I know you're laughing at me, and that always makes me upset! I don't feel like spending the rest of my life with a bag of oranges in one hand and a hankie in the other, every Sunday afternoon, visiting you in some jail, is that clear?

NARRATOR: It wasn't that serious, what I did, Ma, you shouldn't get all upset like that . . . and the policeman didn't come just because of the chunk of ice—

NANA: So why did he come, then, just to scare the wits out of me? Just to upset me?

NARRATOR: Didn't he tell you what happened?

NANA: Maybe he did, but he could've been speaking Chinese, I wouldn't have noticed, I was so upset. . . .

NARRATOR: Listen, I'll tell you what happened.

NANA: Make it fast. You always go into too much detail.

NARRATOR: But I don't want you to punish me. . . .

NANA: Well, I'll be the judge of that, young man, you hear me?

NARRATOR: I should have kept my mouth shut. If you didn't listen to him, you don't know what happened—

NANA [*threateningly*]: I promise I'll listen to every word you have to say.

NARRATOR: And I'm gonna get it afterwards. . . .

NANA: You were asking for it. Go on, I'm listening.

NARRATOR: Oh, God!

NANA: Don't take the Lord's name in vain! Not in front of me! How many times do I have to tell you, it's just as bad as swearing! You're looking for trouble, buster.

NARRATOR: Now I'm not so sure I want to tell you what happened.

NANA: Well, now I want to know! Let's hear it!

NARRATOR: It's true that me and my friends were throwing chunks of ice, but we weren't throwing them under the cars. We were aiming in front of the cars, before they arrived, to see how the drivers would react, to see if they'd slam on the brakes or just slow down. . . . It was only a game, Ma . . . it wasn't serious. . . . Most of the time, the drivers didn't even notice because the chunks of ice were too small. Then, when it was my turn, I chose a chunk that was a bit bigger, to make sure the guy driving down the street would see it . . . that's when Jean-Paul Jodoin held my arm. I struggled, finally pulled away from him, and the chunk of ice landed too late, it rolled under the back wheels of the car . . . and the guy thought he had run over a kid.

NANA: So that's the bit about the run-over kid! I knew there was something about a run-over kid! He got out of his car thinking he had run over a kid, and all he found was a chunk of ice! No wonder he called the cops! Can you imagine how he felt? Eh? Can you imagine what he went through, the poor guy, thinking he'd driven over the body of some poor little kid who was trying to cross the street! Maybe crawling across the street on all fours! He probably thought it was a baby who'd escaped from his mother and was crawling across the street on all fours! Good heavens! Poor man! You're lucky he didn't strangle you right on the spot! That's what I would have done, for sure, I would've driven over you with my car! And I'm not kidding! Well, believe you me, you're going to pay for this, I'm not going to forget this in a hurry!

NARRATOR: I didn't do it on purpose, Ma!

NANA: Stop saying that! If you weren't such a copycat, things like this wouldn't happen!

NARRATOR: It's the first time it's happened!

NANA: That's no excuse! Can't you think for yourself? Can't you tell when your friends are saying stupid things, when they're doing stupid things? Do I always have to be standing beside you telling you what to do, saying do this, that's fine, don't do that, it's dangerous?

NARRATOR: They'd played this game before and they said it was fun. . . .

NANA: Great, here we go again! If they told you it was fun to put your neck through the wringer, I suppose you'd believe them!

NARRATOR [*sarcastically*]: Maybe it is fun to put your neck through the wringer!

NANA: Hey, don't get smart with me! Your wisecracks aren't going to work today, I'm warning you! When I think of that poor little kid squished under the tires of that big car. . . . And the poor mother!

NARRATOR: Ma, there wasn't any run-over kid. . . .

NANA: A good thing, too! That's all I needed! A criminal in the family! The embarrassment! The relatives! The neighbours! I'd have to wear more than a little veil to Sunday mass, I'd have to wear a gas mask! Next time your friends talk about playing some stupid game, think of your poor mother who doesn't feel like wearing a gas mask to church on Sunday, just because she's ashamed of her ten year old son!

NARRATOR: Stop saying you're ashamed of me, I hate that!

NANA: You can't expect me to say I'm proud of you, there's a poor man who almost died of a heart attack because you made him think he left some kid flat as a pancake! No wonder he called the police! If it had been me, I would've taken care of you myself! And believe you me, it's not the chunk of ice that would be in bad shape! Arghh, there's no point in arguing with you, we always end up going round in circles, and there's no end to it. All I'm asking is, in the future, just think twice before you do something stupid like that! And if your friends make fun of you 'cause you don't do what they say, tell them you don't want to be a copycat, you don't want to waste your life doing what other people tell you to do, acting like a smart aleck, just so you can end up spending your life in Bordeaux jail!

NARRATOR: Did you really imagine me in jail?

NANA: With a skullcap on your head, and a pair of striped pyjamas! And believe me, you were dragging your tail between your legs!

*The narrator smiles.*

NARRATOR: The other day, Jean-Paul Jodoin's mother asked me where I got my imagination. . . .

NANA: Next time, you tell her that imagination can help a person avoid a lot of trouble! I'd rather imagine the worst and be relieved, than imagine nothing, and be surprised when trouble strikes! In the meantime, go pick up my order at Provost's, looks like the kid went on vacation!

NARRATOR: You're not going to punish me? A little while ago, you said you were going to punish me.

NANA: Were you scared when that guy jumped out of his car?

NARRATOR: Sure, I was.

NANA: And when the policeman showed up?

NARRATOR: Even more.

NANA: Well, that's enough punishment for today. The police, that's the worst punishment!

*She heads for the wings and pauses.*

By the way, how did that guy figure out it was you who threw the chunk of ice under his car?

NARRATOR: The other kids told on me.

*She stares at him briefly.*

NANA: I guess I don't have to say any more, eh? That says a lot about your friends' solidarity!

*She heads for the wings and pauses again.*

If that guy takes us to court, I'll deny that you're my son, I'll say I adopted you, that your real parents were bandits and I'm not responsible for your stupid behaviour. And don't count on me to come visiting you in Reform School!

*She turns to face him.*

Reform School! You know what that means? *She exits.*

NARRATOR: Need I say that the threat of Reform School hung over my entire childhood?

*Nana reenters.*

NANA: That's where they send stupid kids like you, the wiseguys, the tough guys, the hotheads, the birdbrains, the copycats, and they shave their heads and stick them in a pair of pyjamas made of burlap sacks and sentence them to hard labour!

Instead of going to school, they crush stones with pickaxes, you think you'd enjoy that!? In your case, I'll tell them you prefer chunks of ice. *She exits.*

NARRATOR: She'll be back. She's got something on her mind.

*Nana returns.*

NANA: Did I ever tell you what really happened to Aunt Gertrude?

NARRATOR: Yes, Ma, lots of times.

NANA: Listen to this. She was doing her wash, just like me this morning, and like me, she'd reached the point where she was pulling it through the wringer. But her washing machine wasn't as modern as mine, mine's electric, so she had to keep turning this big handle with her right hand while she slipped the wet clothes through the wringer with her left. You follow me?

*She mimes the gestures she has just described.*

NARRATOR: Sure, it's clear.

NANA: Good. She says she was daydreaming, I say she's crazy. Anyway. Apparently the phone rang and she wanted to finish pushing your Uncle Alfred's pyjama bottoms through the wringer before she answered, but she got all nervous—you know how she is—and she caught the tip of her left hand in the wringer. So far, it's not so bad, it happens to all of us. A little pinch, you pull your hand out, you blow on it, and you go back to work. But not her, she's so crazy she forgot to stop turning the handle with her right hand! How dumb can you get! So she keeps cranking away and the phone keeps on ringing . . . and before you know it she's put her whole arm through the wringer, and it wasn't even automatic, right up to the armpit! Can you believe it, she cranked her own arm through the wringer! She's so crazy, if it was possible, I'm sure she would've put her whole body through, and her husband would've come home from work and found her in the wet laundry basket, all wrung out, flat as a pancake! They had to stitch her up, from the tip of her indexed finger right up to her armpit! When she came over, after that, she showed us her operation, and I'm telling you, I almost lost unconsciousness, it was so ugly! Imagine, she had stitching that ran all the way up . . . through the fat part of her arm, and you know how flabby the fat part of her arm is . . . all she has to do is give it a little tap and it starts shaking like a bowl of jello. . . . She might be my sister-in-law, but I'm telling you, she's no genius. . . . *She exits.*

NARRATOR: My Aunt Gertrude only pinched the tips of her index and middle fingers, and they were bruised for a few days—

*Nana returns.*

NANA: Did you believe everything I just told you?

NARRATOR: I knew there was more to come.

NANA: I'm talking to you!

NARRATOR: No, Ma, I didn't believe everything you just told me.

NANA: Good, I'm glad. You're not as gullible as I thought. Next time your friends tell you crazy stories, and they promise you the world if you do what they say, just remember the story of Aunt Gertrude. Divide everything by ten, and that'll give you an idea of how much fun is really in store for you! *She exits.*

*The narrator smiles.*

NARRATOR: Sometimes she was the only one who understood the point of her stories.

*He takes out a copy of Patira by Raoul de Navery, places it on his lap.*

*Nana returns.*

NANA: You finished it already?

NARRATOR: It doesn't take forever to read that kind of book, Ma—

NANA: But you had three of them to read.

NARRATOR: One day each, it's enough.

NANA: Beautiful books, aren't they?

NARRATOR: Hmmmm, yeah.

NANA: You don't seem so sure—

NARRATOR: Oh, they're beautiful. Real beautiful, but—

NANA: There are no buts about it! They're beautiful, period. Anyway, I loved every page of them. So don't start criticizing them in front of me, you understand?

NARRATOR: I wasn't criticizing, Ma, I didn't say anything!

NANA: You didn't say anything yet, but I can see it coming!

NARRATOR: C'mon, Ma! I told you I thought they were beautiful! But there were some things I didn't understand—

NANA: Oh, well . . . If that's the problem. . . . What didn't you understand? Seems to me they're pretty easy to understand.

NARRATOR: The story's easy to follow, but. . . . How come, in all French novels, there are always some abandoned children?

NANA: What do you mean? Are there that many?

NARRATOR: If you ask me, yes. In *Guardian Angel Inn*, both kids have been abandoned, in *The Foundling*, little Rémi was abandoned, it's always happening in fairy tales. . . . And now, in *Patira*—

NANA: Poor little Patira, doesn't he just break your heart—

NARRATOR: Sure he does, but. . . . Do the French really go around abandoning their kids like that? Their books make it sound like the roads of France are full of abandoned children who are starving to death and filthy dirty—

NANA: They're only books—

NARRATOR: I know they're only books, but still, it seems to happen all the time—

NANA: These books take place in the past. . . . Maybe in the past, I don't know, maybe people in France abandoned their kids more than today, because they couldn't support them—

NARRATOR: Sure, but there are poor people here, too, and you don't see abandoned kids on every street corner! C'mon, people don't abandon their kids like that! I don't believe it! Didn't those people ever get arrested?

NANA: Well, as far as that goes. . . . Listen. . . . There are books where mothers abandon their babies on the church steps. Nobody can catch them that way, for sure! You can't ask a newborn baby to remember his father or his mother! Especially when the mother's an unmarried mother who dumped him there the day after he was born!

NARRATOR: I don't see how you can defend them—

NANA: I'm not defending them, I find it as awful as you do, but what can I say? I'm trying to find an explanation! You asked me a question, I'm trying to find an answer. Maybe there are lots of abandoned children in novels because it's an interesting way to start a story! We want to find out where they come from, why their parents didn't want them. . . . Take little Patira, when he's abandoned by those jugglers who raised him without even knowing where he came from, it makes you want to know where he comes from right away! So you go on reading the book! And . . . how do I know?! What kind of a question is that anyway?

NARRATOR: If you had been poor, you never would've abandoned me on the church steps!

NANA: I was poor, believe me!

NARRATOR: So, you see!

NANA: Maybe I just didn't have the guts!

NARRATOR: Ma!

NANA: C'mon, I'm just kidding! I never would've abandoned you, I wanted you too badly! But had I known—

NARRATOR: Very funny!

NANA: Anyway, things are different in France!

NARRATOR: That's what I wanted to know.

NANA: Now don't you make me say things I don't mean!

NARRATOR: You just admitted that things are different in France!

NANA: I don't mean that the French go around abandoning their kids, so don't you dare repeat that, I know you, yakety-yakking everywhere, and I'll look like a real shrew. Maybe the French only do that in their books.

NARRATOR: Aren't books supposed to be like real life?

NANA: Now you're testing my patience!

NARRATOR: I'm not testing your patience, I'm asking you a simple question!

NANA: What do you expect me to say? I'm no expert on literature! I just enjoy reading books, I like following the story and I cry when it's sad and I laugh when it's funny. I don't stop to ask myself a thousand questions after every sentence. I'd never get to the end of Chapter One! I can tell if I like a story or not, and I read it or I don't, period! What do I care if the French abandon their kids or not, as long as the story about Patira makes me cry! And believe you me, I cried so much reading *Patira*, I felt like I'd lost ten pounds by the time I finished the book, so I was very happy, you hear me!

NARRATOR: You always cry when you read.

NANA: I like sad books.

NARRATOR: Well, you got your money's worth this time!

NANA: Sure did! When poor Blanche de Coed-Queen. . . .

NARRATOR: Coëtquen, Ma.

NANA: That's what I said.

NARRATOR: You said Coed-Queen.

NANA: I got used to reading it that way, it was easier to remember. Anyway, when poor Blanche however you say it gave birth to her baby in the dungeon of the castle because her two brothers-in-law had kept her locked up there for the past six months, the heartless creeps, and when Patira arrived with his little file to saw the thick bars, and Blanche passed her baby through the cellar window, then Patira put the baby on some reeds tied together like a raft, what can I say—

NARRATOR: The whole story is kind of ridiculous—

NANA: What do you mean, ridiculous—

NARRATOR: Well, locking a poor pregnant woman up in a dungeon in the middle of winter—

NANA: Heartless creeps don't wait for warm weather, young man. They were jealous because they said she had usurped, that's the word they used, that she had usurped her title of Marquise, and they wanted to get rid of her, no matter what! They were prepared to do anything, and they did!

NARRATOR: Ma! Blanche de Coëtquen spends the *whole* winter locked up in a dungeon so damp water trickles down the walls, she sleeps on a straw mat on a wooden shelf, all she eats is black bread and stagnant water, there are floods in the spring, the cold water comes up to her chin, she can't change her clothes, she gives birth to her baby lying there in the dark on her wooden shelf, with no doctor to help her, she saws the bars of her prison with a tiny little file, she scrapes her hands so bad they're bleeding, she doesn't have any mercurochrome to put on her cuts, *and she doesn't die!*

NANA: What do you mean, she doesn't die! She certainly does die! She dies at the end of the first book, and it's so sad I thought I'd never recover!

NARRATOR: But before she dies, she's released by someone sleepwalking, she's reunited with her child *in the middle* of a fire that is devouring him and Jeanne, the crazy woman who's been taking care of him without knowing who he was, and—here we go again!—she's saved for the second time by Patira. Then she passes away peacefully, after kissing her child on the forehead and giving everyone her blessing! I mean, really!

NANA: If you didn't cry during that death, kiddo, you've got a heart of stone.

NARRATOR: Well, I guess I've got a heart of stone!

NANA: Don't say that! You're my son. No son of mine can have a heart of stone! When she realizes, just before she dies, that her hair had turned completely white while she was locked up, even though she's only *eighteen years old*, I thought I was going to die myself. . . . Don't tell me you didn't feel anything?

NARRATOR: I thought it made no sense at all. Eighteen years old and her hair's all white! C'mon!

NANA: Maybe it didn't make sense, but it was sad anyway.

NARRATOR: You see, you admit it didn't make sense!

NANA: Maybe it wouldn't have made sense in real life, but so what, it made sense in the book! And that's all that matters! All that nonsense you read, the adventures of Biggles, and those novels by Jules Verne, and your Tintins, and the Scarlet Pimpernels, do you think all that would make sense in real life? Eh? No! But you believe it anyway.

NARRATOR: I want you to know that Jules Verne is based on science! But not this! Hey! She's locked up in a *castle*, it's not the size of Montreal, and nobody ever hears her calling for help!?

NANA: She's at the far end of the castle, in the depths of the moat, *in the dungeon*, it's explained very clearly, you have to admit that.

NARRATOR: And nobody ever goes near there!

NANA: Of course not! There are pools of water and mud, there are frogs and bugs. . . .

NARRATOR: C'mon! She could've called for help a little louder and everybody would've heard her!

NANA: People hear her when she yells, but they think it's a ghost! You're thirteen years old, don't you know how to read? They think it's the ghost of Lady Coed-Queen! There's a song about it in the book, 'n' everything! Did you skip some parts, or what?

NARRATOR: Of course not.

NANA: So you must've understood that when they hear her wailing, they're scared to death!

NARRATOR: How dumb can you get?

NANA: Okay, I think we better stop right here, or I'm going to lose my temper!

NARRATOR: Besides, doesn't that woman ever have to go to the bathroom?

NANA: What do you mean, go to the bathroom?

NARRATOR: Simon, the jailer, he brings her a pitcher of water every day, don't tell me she pees in the pitcher! And . . . where does she pooh?

NANA: Are you losing your mind? They're not about to tell us in books where people pooh!

NARRATOR: Why not? Didn't you ever wonder where she made pooh in her dungeon?

NANA: Not for one minute! I couldn't care less!

NARRATOR: Well, I care!

NANA: That figures! You and your father, you're all pee, pooh, snot, farts, and private parts, we know that! You love that kind of talk, makes you split a gut laughing! In your books by Jules Verne, do they say where people do all that?

NARRATOR: No, but when the characters are lost in the Amazon jungle, or in the back of beyond in the steppes of Russia, you can guess the answer, it's no big mystery. But her, c'mon, Ma! She spends the whole winter in a damp dungeon! She can't be constipated for six months! And if she's not constipated, and she does it in a corner of her cell, it must smell to high heaven after a few weeks, if Simon doesn't clean it up!

NANA: I refuse to let you make fun of one of my favourite books of all times, you hear me?

NARRATOR: I'm not making fun of it! I just would've liked to have that information, that's all!

NANA: Well, I wouldn't! First of all, it never even occurred to me that Blanche Coed-Queen would do such a thing! And how do you expect the author to describe that?

'She crouched in a corner and did her business. The jailer promptly arrived with a shovel and removed the little pile.' It's a novel, we don't need to know that! Last year, when you read *The Count of Monte Cristo*, and for two months straight you thought you were Edmond Dantès and wanted to take revenge on every human being you'd met in your life, did Alexandre Dumas tell you where his hero did that in **his** dungeon?

NARRATOR: No, I guess you're right.

NANA: And did you wonder?

NARRATOR: I guess not.

NANA: So, you see! You only wonder about that when it suits you! You wonder about it in *Patira* because I loved the book! You're just trying to make me mad! Well, you won't succeed! You can be so dishonest, sometimes!

NARRATOR: I'm not being dishonest, Ma, it's the first time I ever asked myself the question, that's all. Besides, the whole bit about her two brothers-in-law being jealous, I didn't believe all that. C'mon!

NANA: And why not?

NARRATOR: They never accepted her because she wasn't a real princess, and because she wasn't a real princess, she didn't deserve to belong to their family! Do *you* believe in that stuff?

NANA: Of course, I do! There are snobs everywhere! We've got one right here in this neighbourhood, a couple of blocks away, on Cartier Street! I could give you her name! But I'm a charitable soul, so I'll keep my mouth shut! She thinks she's a princess, puts on airs, struts around, dresses up like a Sunday mass day in and day out, and she forgets she came into this world under the Jacques-Cartier Bridge just like the rest of us!

NARRATOR: You didn't come into this world under the Jacques-Cartier Bridge, Ma.

NANA: You're right. I came into this world in the middle of the plains of Saskatchewan. . . . But I've been here so long I feel like a real Montrealer. . . . And believe you me, I don't think I'm a princess! That's one thing nobody can accuse me of! Unlike some people I know—

NARRATOR: Who are you talking about?

NANA: Never mind, it's not interesting.

NARRATOR: I'm interested—

NANA: Oh, I know you're interested! The minute there's a bit of gossip, you're right there. . . . Forget all that princess business, and concentrate on Patira's adventures!

NARRATOR: What is a real princess, anyway?

NANA: What do you mean, what is a real princess?

NARRATOR: I mean, what makes someone a real princess?

NANA: Well, she's the daughter of a king and a queen, it's as simple as that. You know that as well as I do.

NARRATOR: And what about her parents, how did they know they were a real king and a real queen?

NANA: It was the same for them, their parents were nobility.

NARRATOR: What does that mean, their parents were nobility?

NANA: You read French novels till they come out your ears, you must know what nobility is, don't make me waste my breath! It's people who have blue blood.

NARRATOR: Blue blood!

NANA: Right!

NARRATOR [*dubiously*]: When they cut themselves, it comes out blue!

NANA: No, it's a manner of speaking! It's an expression, their blood isn't really blue—but it's noble blood.

NARRATOR: I don't get it.

NANA: Listen. I'm no expert on French History, they taught us Canadian History out in Saskatchewan, but the way I understand it . . . when the first king of France appeared—

NARRATOR: And how did he know he was the king of France?

NANA: Listen, that's what I'm trying to explain to you! If I remember correctly, he was a Louis! They were all Louis, I think, the kings of France. . . . He must've been Louis One, or Louis the First. Anyway, the Good Lord appeared to him—

NARRATOR: The Good Lord appeared to him!

NANA: That's what they say.

NARRATOR [*jeering*]: He doesn't usually show up in person, he sends somebody else to represent him . . . like the Virgin Mary, or the angels—

NANA [*starting to lose her patience*]: Right, well, this time was special, it was for the king of France! And stop interrupting me! Anyway, apparently the Lord told him he'd been chosen to be the king of France, and from that moment on, so that everybody would recognize them, he and his descendants would have blue blood!

NARRATOR: But you told me their blood wasn't really blue!

NANA: I'm trying to explain to you that it's just an expression!

NARRATOR: Okay, but how can they know they have blue blood, if it isn't really blue?

NANA: They know, because they pass it on, from father to son! Like you, for instance, you have your father's name, well, you'd have blue blood if your father had had blue blood before you! Now do you understand?

NARRATOR: So that means Blanche de Coëtquen, when her name was still Blanche Halgan, didn't have blue blood because her father was just a ship's captain?

NANA: That's right. And since it's frowned upon for nobility—people with blue blood—to marry somebody who isn't nobility, the two Tanguy de Coed-Queen brothers can't forgive their brother for marrying the daughter of a ship's captain, instead of somebody more important.

NARRATOR: But when she married him, did her blood become blue?

NANA: No, that's the point! You don't get blue blood from your husband, you get it from your father!

NARRATOR: And their baby was born in the dungeon, I suppose his blood was half 'n' half?! That's stupid!

NANA: It's not stupid. It comes from the Good Lord!

NARRATOR: Honestly! All I'd have to do is claim that the Good Lord appeared to tell me he'd appointed me king of Canada, and then my blood would be blue?

NANA: Don't worry, if you said that, nobody would believe you!

NARRATOR: Exactly! So why did they believe him?
NANA: Because for him, it was true!
NARRATOR: It could be true for me, too!
NANA: I'm your mother, I'd know it wasn't true. Mothers know everything.
NARRATOR: Well he must've had a mother, too! And she believed him, and you say you wouldn't believe me!
NANA: How do I know, maybe he was a hero, maybe he saved his country from thieves and bandits, from the plague and dragons! And you haven't saved a darn thing!
NARRATOR: Give me time!
NANA: Okay, stop trying to get me going.
NARRATOR: You believe everything you read in your books!
NANA: Well, believe you me, it's a lot more interesting than arguing with you!
NARRATOR: It's like your stories about Aunt Gertrude, eh, Ma, you can't believe everything.
NANA: You've been asking questions since the day you were born, it's reached the point, a person doesn't know what to make up anymore!
NARRATOR: Ah ha! You just admitted it, sometimes you make things up!
NANA: If I lined up all the answers I've made up to answer all the questions you've asked since you were born, I might be a great novelist myself! And I'd make a fortune! And believe you me, we wouldn't stay cooped up on Cartier Street facing Mount-Royal Convent another day longer!
NARRATOR: What about the girls who go to the Mount-Royal Convent School, Ma, they're rich, aren't they?
NANA: I guess so! You can tell by the cars that deliver them every Sunday night!
NARRATOR: Do they have blue blood?
NANA: Of course not! Nobody has blue blood in America! Only in Europe!
NARRATOR: How come?
NANA: Don't ask me! Maybe because they've been around for longer than us. If we had been around earlier, maybe we'd have some blue bloods, too!
NARRATOR: What about your family . . . your grandparents were Cree from Saskatchewan—
NANA: On my mother's side.
NARRATOR: And they'd settled here a long time before the Europeans arrived—
NANA: I know—
NARRATOR: So how come the Good Lord never appeared to tell them they had blue blood? How come he just appeared in Europe? I don't think that's fair! There must've been a Cree somewhere who deserved to be declared noble like those guys on the other side.
NANA: It's true, actually, it's not fair. As far as that goes, you're right. But what do you expect, it comes from the Good Lord and the Cree didn't know the Lord. Or maybe he didn't know them.
NARRATOR: The Europeans are the ones who claim it comes from the Good Lord. Do we have to believe them? Did the Good Lord appear to tell you it was true, that he'd told all the first kings in Europe they had blue blood?

NANA: Listen, it all happened so long ago, somebody must've found proof, after all these years.

NARRATOR: Nobody's ever seen that proof.

NANA: Are you trying to tell me that the first one, there, Louis One, might've made all that up just to become the King of France, and that all the people who believed him were a bunch of dummies? That the kings of France were *usurpers*? Right up to the French Revolution?

NARRATOR: I don't know, I'm just asking—

NANA: That all the Louis, up to Louis . . . how many Louis were there, all together? Anyway, that they were all liars? You're such a doubting Thomas! Well, now there aren't any more kings of France. So that settles that.

NARRATOR: But there's still nobility.

NANA: Maybe—

NARRATOR: And there's still lots of blue bloods.

NANA: Not lots, but there are some left.

NARRATOR: There are lots of them in *Paris Match* magazine.

NANA: Maybe.

NARRATOR: There's even a queen in Belgium. And a brand new beautiful queen in England.

NANA: Oh yes, my pretty Princess Elizabeth who became queen so young! And her sister, Princess Margaret-Rose, too pretty for her own good! Don't you start criticizing them, you know how much I admire them! They might have blue blood, but those two girls aren't snobs, not one bit. They know how to behave, how to speak in public, and I'm telling you, they know how to wear a crown. They deserve to be noble, I can tell you that!

NARRATOR: Don't try to change the subject, Ma, I know how much you love the English royal family, you talk about them as if you'd grown up together, like they were next of kin! So, if I follow your logic, the Good Lord appeared to the first king of England, as well?

NANA: I guess so.

NARRATOR: And he told him the same thing as the other guy?

NANA: Probably, yes.

NARRATOR: In English!

NANA: If he spoke French to the other one, he must've spoken English to him! And Spanish to the King of Spain. And Italian . . . wait, is there a king of Italy?

NARRATOR: He sure speaks a lot of languages!

NANA: He's God! He's the one who invented them all at the Tower of Babel!

NARRATOR: Do you really believe all that?

NANA: I'm beginning to wonder, you know . . . I never thought about it that way. When you get right down to it, there must've been a Cree who deserved it, too.

NARRATOR: So, if we trace it back to the first king of France, nobility is something you deserve!

NANA: Right!

NARRATOR: So, Blanche de Coëtquen would've deserved to have blue blood when she married Tanguy, even if she wasn't born with it. . . .

NANA: Of course!

NARRATOR: And her two brothers-in-law, Florent and Gaël, were real bastards because they made their poor sister-in-law suffer like that!

NANA: That's what I've been trying to tell you!

NARRATOR: Blue blood or not. . . .

NANA: Right, and believe you me, I was happy when they paid for their crimes! I kissed the book, I held it to my heart—

NARRATOR: So, maybe the French Revolution was a good thing after all—

NANA: Of course, it was a good thing! I never said it wasn't! The poor people were dying of hunger while the nobility, the blue bloods, were stuffing their faces! Marie-Antoinette was gorging herself on Viennese pastry while the country was yelling their lungs out at the gates of Versailles, with their shovels, and scythes, and whips and torches! We saw the whole thing, in that film with Norma Shearer! But, wait, how come you're talking about the French Revolution all of a sudden? What's that got to do with anything?

NARRATOR: Because Raoul de Navery says the opposite in *The Treasure of the Abbey*, his sequel to *Patira*. . . . Now you're the one who skipped some parts. . . . He describes the revolutionaries as bloodthirsty monsters, they're all hunchbacks, ugly as sin, one-eyed cripples, they stink like the devil, and they kill all the poor blue bloods. . . . They're only interested in taking their place—

NANA: Now, just a minute, don't get me going again. . . . That's enough talk for this afternoon, we'll settle the problem of the French Revolution some other day. If you don't mind, we'll tackle volume two tomorrow! That's that trouble, when a person starts talking with you, there's no knowing where it will end!

NARRATOR: I wonder who I get that from—

NANA: Pardon me?

NARRATOR: I didn't say a thing—

NANA: If you didn't say a thing, you said it pretty loud, 'cause I heard you!

NARRATOR: Then why did you ask me to repeat it?

NANA: To see if you had the courage! To see if you deserved blue blood! And you flunked the test, you'll never become king, so go do the errands at Steinberg's instead, there's nothing in the house for supper. Anyway, next time I read a good book, I won't tell you! I'll keep it to myself, that way, I'll be sure to go on liking it.

*She turns to exit, then turns back to him.*

While you're out, you can stop by Shiller's and take these buttons back. They're too big for your father's buttonholes. And ask for my money back. If he asks any questions, just say: '*The woman* says she doesn't want them.'

NARRATOR: I hate it when you ask me to do that!

NANA: Why?

NARRATOR: Don't you think he knows it's my mother who's sent me? He's not crazy, he recognizes me!

NANA: I hope you never admitted it to him!

NARRATOR: You always told me never to lie!

NANA: Well, that's not a lie.

NARRATOR: Ma! Is it true? No. So, it's a lie.

NANA: Am I a woman or not? 'The woman says she doesn't want them'—it could be your mother or some other woman. That's what my mother used to call 'a little white lie'. Little insignificant lies we tell to protect ourselves.

NARRATOR: To protect ourselves?

NANA: Listen, if you say: 'My mother says she doesn't want them,' he won't listen and I'll never get my money back. But if you say: 'The woman says she doesn't want them,' he won't know if it's me or some other woman who stopped you on the street and asked you to do an errand for her, so he'll feel like he has to reimburse you!

NARRATOR: But he's not crazy, he knows you're the one who sent me!

NANA: I know, but I'm not crazy either! Since he can't be really sure, he'll give you the money back, it's less complicated for him and I win all down the line.

NARRATOR: Oh, my God!

NANA: Hey! What did I say! No swearing in this house!

NARRATOR: Saying, oh, my God, isn't swearing.

NANA: In my house it is! And as long as you're in my house, you follow my rules.

NARRATOR: Oh, my gosh!

NANA: That's no better, you just replace the 'sh' with a 'd' and you've got God.

NARRATOR: Oh, golly, then? Holly golly? Molly? What do you prefer?

NANA: Molly's fine. It's far enough away from Oh, my God. Now, get moving, get your gangly legs going down Mount Royal Street, and stop arguing. . . . Stop wagging your tongue and use your legs instead, it'll do you good. It'll do us both good! Here's the list for supper, I wrote everything out, and here's the buttons. Don't forget: 'The woman says she doesn't want them. . . .' [*She laughs.*] Good luck!

*She exits laughing.*

NARRATOR: Oh, goddamn!

*She returns.*

NANA: What a night! Couldn't fall asleep for the life of me! I lay there thinking. . . . Looking at the clock every ten minutes, knowing how hard it would be to get up this morning. . . . I couldn't stop thinking about that TV drama we watched together last night. You have to admit it was beautiful, 'nuff to make you cry. The sets . . . the costumes. Just like Russia last century. And such a beautiful story. . . . Really, for me to go to bed that late on a Sunday night. . . . But. . . . It's funny. . . . I don't know why . . . it's the first time I ever thought about it. . . . I lay down beside your father, and for once he wasn't snoring, for once I could've fallen asleep right away without having to smack him or shake him . . . but I was thinking about Huguette Oligny! You know, we were talking about her before we went to bed, but I couldn't stop thinking about her—that woman talked for almost two and a half hours straight, non-stop! Here we go, let me change costumes, here I am giving a party, now I've got a scene with this one, then a scene with that one. . . . She laughed, she cried, she got mad, she made up, she had love scenes, she was a flirt, she was tragic, she didn't stop once! And you told me it was all done live, like at the theatre, and that while we sat there watching her, she was performing in some studio down on Dorchester Street and they were filming it. . . . That she changed sets by ducking behind the cameras, that she changed costumes while the others were doing a scene while she was changing costumes. . . . And . . . I don't know. . . . It never occurred to me before, but . . . I guess it's because you've started to write plays you don't want me to read. . . . It's alright, don't worry, I understand, at sixteen it's normal not to want to tell your mother everything. . . . But that's not what I was thinking about, I was thinking about Huguette Oligny. . . . And I wondered. . . . Who is Huguette Oligny? You know what I mean? We always see her on TV. . . . She's always disguised as somebody else. . . . Yesterday she was a woman from Russia, last year, in that play that rhymed, you know, what's it called, she always wore the same long nightgown and it took place in Greece. . . . Anyway. Sometimes she's comical, sometimes she's amusing, she always has tons of lines to say. . . . but who is she, really? I mean, in real life? I know she's married, but when I see a picture of her in the TV guide, with her husband and kids, I don't find her as real as in 'A Month in the Country', last night. Strange, eh? I feel like she's playing some role in the photograph. We were wondering last night how she managed to learn all that by heart, two and a half hours of talk, how does she do it, but I went farther than that, I wondered . . . where was she when she learned all that by heart? I realize she must've been at home, she must have a house like everybody else, but where is she when she learns all that by heart? Is she sitting on a sofa, lying in her bed, soaking in her bath? Is she cooking supper? Doing the dishes? Is it easy? Does she find it hard? Does she have somebody help her? Does she talk out loud? Does she go over it in her head? Does she enjoy learning those lines, or does it drive her crazy? Believe me, I couldn't sleep a wink! At one point, your father woke up and I had to smack him in the back 'cause he lit up a cigarette. You know how I hate it when he smokes in bed. . . . He fell back to sleep, and I still couldn't stop thinking about it. When actors are rehearsing their plays, where do they do it? In the studio? Do they always wear their costumes? And how do they do it? How does it work? I never thought about all that before, you understand? I watch those shows as if they came out of the blue and disappeared back into the blue! I usually turn off the television set, and none of it exists anymore. No kidding! Last night I realized that the actors only exist for me when I see them on television! When Huguette Oligny finished her two and a half hour show last night, she stopped existing for us, at least, for me, even though we went on talking about her! As if your Aunt Gertrude and Uncle Alfred stopped existing when they leave the house after our Saturday night card game. Mind you, there are times when I wish they would, they drive me crazy, but that's beside the point. But what did she do last night, Huguette Oligny, when she finished taking off her makeup and changing her clothes? Did she go out with the other actors, or were they all too tired? Does she have a car? The woman who wore all those beautiful gowns, did she step on the gas to get home faster? That woman's been coming into my home since television began, and before that her voice was already here on the radio dramas and the Ford Theatre on Thursday nights, and I don't even know who she is! Then . . . it's strange, eh . . . really late, in the middle of the night, I lay there and wondered if she ever asked herself the same question about me. How crazy can you get! You know, they're there, they come into our homes every night. . . . Now don't you go thinking that I believe they can see us, you know I'm not as dumb as those people who get all dressed up to watch 'Concert Hour' on Sunday night, 'cause they think Jean Deslauriers can see them! Oh, no. But I said to myself, if I wonder who she is, does she ever wonder who I am, once in a while? I mean, not me personally, she doesn't know me, but the people who watch her spend a month in the country, or die in a Greek nightgown? Do the actors ever think about us? They can't see us, but they're staring into cameras, they know they're coming right into our homes. . . . Do they ever wonder: 'Where are they? In their living room? In the dining room? How many are there? Do they have company? Do they talk while we're saying our lines? Do they get up to go to the bathroom during the best scenes?' Or are we just like a great big empty black hole they carry on in front of, simply to earn a living? Is it clear, what I mean? I mean, they exist because we can see them, even though they're not in colour, but do we exist for them, too? Even the ones who act on stage, they might know there are people in the audience, but do they wonder what those people do after? Or does the audience stop existing for them the minute they walk out of the theatre? And the actors who work on television and on the radio, they have no contact with us, do they completely forget that we exist? You must think I'm crazy wondering about stuff like that, eh? But, you see, last night I was lying there beside my husband, thinking about Huguette Oligny, what a great actress she is, how beautiful she looks in those gowns, and I said to myself, I'd like to think that sometimes, when she's lying next to her husband, she wonders about me. I'd like to be as important in her life as she is in mine. But I guess that's too much to hope for. I don't dare ask what you think about all that, I know you want to land on the other side, part of their world, I've known that for a long time. . . . Once you're there, if you ever manage to get there, think about it and try to find an answer for me. . . . *She exits.*

NARRATOR: She never saw the wings of a theatre or a television studio, she never attended a rehearsal, a costume fitting, a preview or an opening night. She left without knowing how it all works. It's one of the greatest regrets in my life. I would have loved to introduce her to Huguette Oligny, so the possibility that Madame Oligny might think of her from time to time could exist.

*Nana returns.*

NANA: I'm telling you, there's no escaping that woman! Impossible! I don't know how she manages, I never see her coming, honestly, never! She cooks it up behind my back, then, I, dummy, fall right into it! Every time! And it's been going on for thirty years! More! *She always gets me to invite her to supper!* Can you tell me why?

There's always some point where I hear myself say: 'Why don't you come for supper Saturday night?' Why do I say it? Do I feel obligated because her husband is your father's brother? Do I just say it to get off the phone because she talks so loud? Search me! It's a real mystery! Maybe she has hypnotical powers in her voice and I don't realize it! It just happened again, right now, do you believe it? She calls me supposedly just to say hello, I say to myself, 'Careful, it's Thursday, Saturday's right around the corner, watch out!' And sure enough! I don't know what she was rattling on about, how she roped me in, but the next thing I know, I'm saying that good goshdarn sentence, and they're coming for Saturday night supper again! I'm stuck with your aunt Gertrude, your Uncle Alfred and their boring daughter Lucille for another Saturday night supper! I know you like your cousin Lucille, but I'm telling you, that child sets my teeth on edge!

NARRATOR: She's not a child anymore, Ma.

NANA: How old are you now? Eighteen? Well, she's seventeen, it's true she's not a child anymore. Makes it all the worse!

NARRATOR: I know she bothers you because she's got some tics, but—

NANA: Tics? That kid is like a Christmas tree, blinking away non-stop! During her awkward stage, every time she left here with her parents, my face would go on twitching for hours!

NARRATOR: Ma. . . .

NANA: Ma, what?

NARRATOR: You promised you'd try not to exaggerate so much.

NANA: I tried, and I thought I was going to die of boredom! Things are never interesting enough when you describe them as is, c'mon! Just thinking about them showing up on Saturday night makes me want to pack my bags and take off for the planet Mars. How's that for an exaggeration, eh?

NARRATOR: Not bad—

NANA: If I didn't exaggerate, you'd think I was boring!

NARRATOR: That's true, but—

NANA: So don't nag me. I can see it all now. Your Uncle Alfred will take your father's place at the end of the table, and your father's too much of a coward to say anything, your uncle will light his damn pipe that smells like the devil who hasn't taken a bath since the Messiah appeared, and he'll start yakking about Fernandel! That man can only talk about one thing: *Fernandel!* Did you ever see anything like it? I ask you! Men his age, I don't know, seems to me they talk about Marilyn Monroe, or Lana Turner, or even hockey, but not him, he bends our ear about Fernandel! When he starts going on about the last Fernandel film he's seen, I don't know if you ever noticed, but I leave the room! I pretend I have to do something in the kitchen or I say I have to make a phone call, and I end up chatting with nobody at the other end of the line, but I have to do something, otherwise I'll smack him on the head! He talks like Fernandel, he imitates Fernandel's sissy gestures, and he *sings* like Fernandel! Oooff, when he starts singing with his Marseillais accent. . . . Look, just talking about it gives me hot flashes! If he tells us the story, if he acts out 'Coeur de coq' once more, I'm gonna have such a fit, they'll hear me all the way to Ausable Chasm!

*They both laugh.*

I'm pretty funny today, eh?

NARRATOR: Yes, you're in fine form!

NANA: No choice, otherwise I'd explode.

NARRATOR: How would you explode? Usually, you add an image—

NANA: Wait. . . . [*proud of herself* ] I'd explode like a pressure cooker that was left on the burner so long, you'd all have to scrape me off the ceiling!

*They laugh even harder.*

Ah, that feels better! Look, your Uncle Alfred might be your father's brother, but believe you me, he's not the guy who hitched the lanterns to the fireflies' backsides!

*They split a gut laughing.*

It's Mr Gagnon, from Saint-Pacôme, a friend of your grandparents on your father's side, who used to say that. Funny, eh?

NARRATOR: Yeah, it's really great. I'm going to use it some day.

NANA [*more seriously*]: I'm sure you will. We should talk about that. . . . But her! *THAT ONE!* She's been coming to supper for thirty years now, and lately you know what she's been saying to me, as she leaves?

NARRATOR: I know, but—

NANA: 'The tea was very good.' The tea! She does me the honour of liking my tea!

NARRATOR: It's her idea of a joke, Ma—

NANA: A joke that's been going on for three years is no joke, it's sick! Her husband with Fernandel, her with her tea, and their daughter with her twitches, I'm telling you they're quite the family! I guess they don't get a few laughs every day like us!

NARRATOR: You always make roast beef when they come. . . .

NANA: People say my roast beef is the best roast beef this side of the Rockies!

NARRATOR: I know, but you always make it rare. . . . Maybe she like it well-done, I don't know. . . .

NANA: What's that supposed to mean? Did she ever say anything to you?

NARRATOR: Well, no—

NANA: Tell me the truth! Did your Aunt Gertrude ever complain about my roast beef?

NARRATOR: I told you, no. . . . I'm just saying that some people probably like it more well-done—

NANA: Well, listen to that! Would you be talking about yourself there?

NARRATOR: Well. . . .

NANA: You've hated my roast beef for eighteen years, and you never even told me!

NARRATOR: I never said I hated your roast beef, Ma. . . .

NANA: You've been eating roast beef that makes you sick for eighteen years, and you never had the courage to tell me.

NARRATOR: Ma, you've been boasting about your roast beef for so long, it's pretty hard to contradict you!

NANA: I don't believe it! He doesn't like my cooking!

*She puts her hand to her heart.*

He's going to kill me. How about my potatoes, are they cooked enough for you? Are my peas hot enough? Are my carrots chopped too big? Is my gravy thick enough? Maybe there's too much tea in it? Is there anything I cook right, or is it all like my roast beef, awful?!

NARRATOR: Ma, I never said I didn't like your cooking. . . . Gosh, it's hard to talk to you!

NANA: You go eat at your friend's houses where they eat baloney sandwiches day in and day out, and then, believe you me, you'll miss your mother's cooking!

NARRATOR: Ma, listen to me, please. I was just trying to say that to my taste, that's just me, you don't cook your roast beef long enough. That's all. No more, no less! It's no big deal! No tragedy!

NANA: *Well, maybe, but your father likes his beef so rare it can get up, moo, and walk away from the plate!*

NARRATOR: I know, but we don't all have to share his taste! You've just closed the oven door, and it's time to take it out again!

NANA: Now look who's exaggerating!

NARRATOR: But it's true. You put it in, what, for half an hour at 400? The outside is burnt to a crisp and inside it's still alive!

NANA: So just ask me for the end piece!

NARRATOR: Listen, when I was little, I was the youngest kid of all the families who came to dinner, so, Saturday nights, I was always the last one to be served. . . . You'd buy a huge roast beef, you'd hardly cook it, and I'd end up with the middle, you see, the middle of the roast, the least cooked, the rawest, the cow was practically still breathing in my plate. It was red, full of blood, and it tasted like a wet facecloth! I felt like there was a cow in the bathroom and you'd just gone to slice off a piece of thigh and put it in my plate!

NANA: And you never said anything.

NARRATOR: You would've killed me.

NANA: If you said it in front of other people, maybe, but—

NARRATOR: It doesn't matter, Ma, this Saturday you'll give me the end piece and we'll forget the whole thing. . . . If I'm home for supper.

NANA: What do you mean, *if* you're home for supper?

NARRATOR: Well, I don't really feel like spending another evening with Fernandel's official imitator! C'mon, Ma, I've got other things to do with my life!

NANA: First of all, that's not true, just this morning you asked me what I was making for supper Saturday night . . . and besides, you have to keep your favourite cousin Lucille company while she blinks her lights. . . .

NARRATOR: Ma, I'm eighteen years old, I'm not ten anymore, I'm a consenting adult and I can do what I want!

NANA: If you don't mind my saying so . . . you've been staying out pretty late these days . . . and hanging out with some pretty . . . strange people! You can go out when it's time for them to leave, period.

NARRATOR: And if they leave after midnight, like they usually do?

NANA [*after some hesitation*]: You'll leave along with them.
NARRATOR: And you won't say anything?
NANA [*after another hesitation*]: No.
NARRATOR: Okay!
NANA: Would you mind telling me where you go, and what you do with those weirdos, so late at night? You come home smelling of cigarettes, and you don't even smoke! I'd like to know what kind of a dive you're hanging out in!
NARRATOR: Ma!
NANA: Okay! Okay! We'll drop the subject! But you better sit there beside your cousin Lucille and mind your p's and q's.
NARRATOR: It's a deal!
NANA: You see what I mean? I feel like you just pulled the wool over my eyes, just like your Aunt Gertrude! *She exits.*

*Then returns.*

Did I ever tell you about your cousin Lucille's recital?
NARRATOR: Thousands of times, Ma.
NANA: Listen to this. You'll get a kick out of it.

*He raises his eyes to heaven.*

Don't raise your eyes to heaven like that, you're not ten years old anymore! [*She coughs into her fist, as if about to begin a song.*] You have to realize that your Aunt Gertrude had been bending my ear about her daughter's recital for months and months! I absolutely had to attend, I absolutely had to see it, she had made Lucille's costume herself, she'd bought the material at the Shiller's in her neighbourhood. . . . Mind you, I should've realized, your Aunt Gertrude's never had good taste in clothes, but anyway. . . . It went on for months! She acted like her daughter Lucille was the first human being who had ever taken ballet lessons in the History of Humanity! The fact that she was taking her ballet lessons in an elocution school, I should've known . . . but anyway, I finally gave in and promised I'd go, she must've hypnotized me, as usual. . . . So I arrive, the night of the recital. It was in a church basement, you can imagine the atmosphere! I sit down on a hard church pew, beside your aunt who smelled so strong I felt like I was sitting in the middle of a garden of dead roses. . . . It begins with some sketch about Cinderella, with the little 8–10 year old girls. . . . Your aunt leans over and tells me this is the scene Lucille's in. I found that a bit strange 'cause your cousin Lucille was almost fifteen at the time. . . anyway, I grin and bear it. . . . Cinderella is really miserable, her stepmother and her stepsisters are really mean, she's crying her eyes out, the others leave for the ball. . . . Normally, I admit, I might've thought it was cute, I like that kinda thing, kids playacting, but that night I must've decided to hate it, so I was bored stiff. . . . I kept thinking, don't tell me Lucille's going to play Prince Charming, her mother told me she'd be wearing a dress! Then comes the moment where Cinderella's fairy godmother is supposed to appear. Cinderella is sprawled out in the cardboard pumpkins and she's crying her heart out, the mothers of the artists pull out their hankies because they think she's great, poor things, then the curtain in the background opens . . . and Lucille arrives on points, disguised like a fairy. Honestly, she was three times taller than Cinderella! And with her toeshoes, she looked like a horse trying to do ballet! Your aunt didn't dare make her a tutu 'cause she's kind of bowlegged, so she settled for these rags in blue and pink tulle, draped over a really stiff petticoat. . . . It was supposed to be chic, but it looked poorer than Cinderella's costume! It made her look like she was the one who should change her clothes to go to the ball! It was no magical apparition, it was a vision of horror! That's when your Uncle Alfred, the president of Fernandel's fan club, tries to get everyone to clap! But he's the only one clapping because only three of us in the hall realize that it's his daughter, Lucille, who's just appeared, and he looks like a damn fool! But he doesn't care how crazy he looks, the stubborn goat, he goes on clapping harder and harder! Your cousin Lucille starts to wobble on her long bowlegs, because her father won't stop clapping and she feels like she has to stay on her tiptoes till the applause stops! It was so embarrassing! It was no prima ballerina who'd appeared, for crying out loud, it was just a poor kid who'd taken a few months of ballet in an elocution school! If I'd had an axe with me, believe you me, your Uncle Alfred's arms would've grown shorter that night. He'd be imitating Fernandel with two stumps! He finally stopped clapping, but by then, there were five hundred heads turned toward us! Talk about being embarrassed! And then, Lucille, who's still tottering on her tired pins, takes a few steps, still on points, she lowers her magic wand, poof, the pumpkin turns into a carriage and she exits! That was it! I'd just attended your cousin Lucille's *recital*! She appears, poof, she waves her wand, and that's all, folks! Maybe she was on stage for a grand total of two minutes, maximum, and her career was over! Not everyone's cut out for a career on stage, you know! Your uncle was wiping his eyes, your aunt was holding her heart with both hands, and I was thinking: 'Go ahead, die a natural death, both of you, before I feel I have to kill you with my own two hands.' At intermission, I found some excuse, a bus to take or a headache, I can't remember, and I took off like a coward! Never, you hear me, never did I tell your aunt that I liked her daughter's recital! She did everything, she tried everything, but for once she didn't succeed! Maybe it's cost me tons of roast beef, and I always get roped in when she wants to be invited to supper, *but never as long as I live will I tell her I enjoyed that evening*!

NARRATOR: And you wonder why she only says tea was good when she leaves the house!

*Nana freezes briefly.*

NANA: Well, I'll be. . . . You. . . . Well, I never. . . . *She exits.*

*She returns.*

I've changed my mind. I'm going to cook a ham Saturday night. You boil ham for ages, it should be well-done enough for you, right? *She exits.*

NARRATOR: They never made up. I mean, my Aunt Gertrude and my mother. Because my Aunt Gertrude died suddenly of a heart attack. My mother always used to say: 'Your fat Aunt Gertrude never had time to waste away.'

*Nana returns.*

NANA: It could happen to me, too, you know, if you all don't start being nicer to me. You've got nothing to say? Usually, you react, when I say stupid things like that!

NARRATOR: I've learned to let you talk, it's funnier.

NANA: Well, look at that, the great twenty-year-old philosopher trying to show his mother a thing or two!

NARRATOR: I'm not trying to—

NANA [*laughing*]: You see, you're not letting me talk!

*He lets out a sigh of exasperation.*

Apparently he just stood there puffing on his pipe and watched her die. Your Uncle Alfred. He's a real case! I just hope he wasn't doing one of his Fernandel imitations while she was calling for help! Don't laugh.

NARRATOR: How do you know he kept puffing on his pipe while she was dying?! You weren't there.

NANA: He said so himself! He seems proud of it! Did I ever tell you how it happened? It's awful! It was a Saturday morning. Like every Saturday morning, she was on her hands and knees waxing her floor, while your Uncle Alfred stood there puffing on his pipe, watching her. Don't ask me why she always waited till Saturday morning to wash her floor, but anyway. Maybe she was hoping that some day he'd offer to help, that he'd feel sorry for her, down on her hands and knees on the linoleum, and that he'd say: 'Stop, Gertrude, let me do that.' Did I ever tell you that woman was really naive? Anyway. He says he was in the middle of telling her something. . . . Maybe she died just to avoid another description of Fernandel cutting Suzy Delair's hair. . . . Anyway. All of a sudden, she starts doing the hula on all fours. That's how he put it . . . doing the hula. I don't know how he came up with that, but anyway. He thought she was fooling around, or something, so he went on talking until she fell flat on her face in her puddle of wax. End of story. He watched her die without even realizing it. I always said he was really thick. You want a glass of milk? My stomach's hurting, again. . . . *She exits.*

NARRATOR: She never tackled important subjects directly, she never asked a simple question when she wanted to know something or when something was bothering her. No, out of discretion or shyness, she'd make up stories, she'd beat around the bush, she'd talk a blue streak to hide her concerns, all the while keeping an eye on the person she was talking to, watching for their reactions, trying to read their expressions for a kind of understanding, I guess. An understanding she rarely found, because her ranting was often incomprehensible. People would have had to interpret her monologues, decipher her stories to understand the real meaning, but her wit submerged everything and all too often we allowed ourselves to be mesmerized by this irresistible flow of words, delighted by her punch lines, enthralled by her humour. For example, her last story, her absurd version of my Aunt Gertrude's death, had a very precise meaning which unfortunately I didn't grasp right away, I was too busy trying to understand why my mother made up a comical death for someone she had never liked, I was almost shocked by her cruelty. Until one day—it was in the spring, I remember that because it was during final exams my last year at the Graphic Arts Institute—for the first time in her life, with me at least, she opened up, all of a sudden. And for once, her monologue took the form of a confession.

*Nana enters, walks over to the narrator, stands behind him, puts her arms around his shoulders.*

NANA: Will you take care of your father for me when I'm gone?

*Silence.*

NARRATOR: Uhh . . . yes. Why are you asking me that?
NANA: I've really spoiled him, you know, and he's not always easy to get along with.

*Silence.*

NARRATOR: It depends on what you mean by taking care of him. I can't do everything you do. You can't expect me to give him his spoonful of Milk of Magnesia every day before he leaves for work.
NANA: Don't joke about this, I'm serious.
NARRATOR: Well, yes, I'll try, but you know that nobody will ever be able to replace you in his life, Ma!

*She starts with pain, and tries to hide it.*

*The narrator hesitates before asking his question.*

Does it really hurt?
NANA: Yes, but it will go away. It's going already. [*to change the subject*] Do you remember when I used to hold you like this when you were little?
NARRATOR: Of course, I do. But in those days, you weren't standing behind me, you were sitting down, and I was on your lap.
NANA: Hmmm, you really loved it.
NARRATOR: I still like it, you know.

*She gives him a little slap on the shoulder.*

NANA: You should've said so before, I've been holding back for years! When I'm gone, it'll be too late.

*Heavy, embarrassed silence.*

Have you thought about what will happen around the house when I'm gone?
NARRATOR: No.
NANA: You better start thinking about it, eh?
NARRATOR: I know. But I can't. It's . . . unthinkable.
NANA: Nonsense. Housekeeping isn't the end of the world. Don't worry, I'm not asking you to do the housekeeping when I'm gone. I suppose the three of you will

chip in, you, your father and your brother. . . . You'll manage, you'll see. Nobody's irreplaceable.

NARRATOR: Yes, you are.

NANA: Oh, you're sweet. Did I ever tell you how sweet you are?

NARRATOR: Oh, no. You were more apt to tell me how stupid I was and yell your head off at me.

NANA: You deserved it, too, you stupid kid! But behind all that, couldn't you tell how I felt about you?

NARRATOR: I guess so. But not always. Sometimes, when you got carried away about nothing, you scared me. I used to think it wasn't normal to make such a scene over stupid little incidents.

NANA: It's true, I can get pretty melodramatic.

NARRATOR: She finally admits it!

*Nana smiles, stands up straight.*

*He looks at her, he is smiling, too.*

NANA: I'm really worried about you, you know.

NARRATOR: Why?

NANA: I don't know. I feel as if I've managed to get all the men in my life settled, except you.

NARRATOR: Settled?

NANA: Maybe it's not the right word. . . . Anyway. . . . What I mean is. . . . your father's going to retire soon, he'll be able to take it easy at last, he's worked so hard all his life. . . . Your oldest brother is a teacher, he's got a good job, even if we don't hear from him much. Your other brother has the same trade as your father, he earns a good living, he's got a wife and kids. . . .

NARRATOR: Ma, you're not going to start up about the wife and kids again—

NANA: No . . . I haven't talked about that for years, I realized a long time ago that you'll never have a wife and kids, that's not what I mean, even if it is one of the things that worries me most. . . . What I mean is what I just said, there's no other word. . . . I don't feel as if you're settled, and that's going to be one of my greatest regrets when I leave. . . . Not knowing what's going to happen to you. Not even being sure that something will happen to you.

NARRATOR: Ma, please, don't worry about me. Think about yourself. For once, just think about yourself.

NANA: I know, but what are you going to do with your life?

NARRATOR: I don't know, but for the time being, it doesn't matter.

NANA: How can you say it doesn't matter! It's *your life*!

NARRATOR: I'll manage, Ma!

NANA: It's not true! You've never managed! Never! You've always been a dreamer! Always off in your own dreamworld! Don't tell me you're going to spend the rest of your days dreaming about a life for yourself!

NARRATOR: Maybe I prefer that to being settled, as you say.

NANA: Don't say that, you'll make me even more worried! That's nonsense! Saying stuff like that at your age!

*He puts his arm around her waist, places his head on her stomach.*

NARRATOR: Let me live the life I want.

NANA: You know very well you're not living the life you want! You can't kid me! Don't make me lose my temper! Everything you've been doing in that school for the past three years, that's what I call marking time! Postponing things. Playing with fire! You're playing with fire, that's what you're doing! You're doing nothing to get ahead in life, just hoping that something will save you. You're waiting for someone or something to come along and save you!

NARRATOR: I'm really convinced that something or someone will come along—

NANA: Suddenly you'll realize that you're forty, fifty years old, and nothing will have happened, and—

NARRATOR: I still won't be settled—

NANA: Don't make fun of that either, I'm serious! I let you daydream too much! I encouraged you to dream too much, I let you read anything you wanted too young, I watched too many TV dramas with you, knowing perfectly well it was getting under your skin like some kind of poison—maybe you'll never end up on the other side, on the artists' side, on the side of the ones who write, who act, who dance, who make movies, the way you'd like to! Maybe you'll never make anything of your life because I let you dream too much, and it's all going to be my fault.

NARRATOR: Don't say that! I'll always be grateful to you for letting me dream, Ma! Everything I have, I got from you! I'm melodramatic, too, Ma, I love getting carried away in the long monologues I make up, and just like you, I'm willing to make fun of everything to avoid facing reality! It's not a weakness, Ma, it's a strength, and maybe that's what will save me!

NANA: If only I could believe you—

NARRATOR: Believe me, I swear it's true. If I make something of my life, I'll owe it all to you!

NANA: And if you fail?

NARRATOR: You want me to tell you something important? Listen carefully. I'm only going to say it once: I have no intention of failing. Do you hear me?

NANA: But how do you expect me to believe you? Maybe you're just saying that to comfort me, so I don't worry.

NARRATOR: Just decide to believe me!

NANA: I can't.

NARRATOR: Ma, please try, for once. . . . I'm asking you to believe in me.

*She stares at him for a long moment.*

NANA: Okay. I'm going to believe in you. But you know I'm capable of coming back to haunt you, if what you make of your life doesn't suit me, right?

NARRATOR: Oh, yes. If you come back to twist my toes, I'll know why and I'll change direction!

*She kisses him on the forehead.*

Can I tell you how empty the house is going to be without you?

NANA: Oh, if you only knew how I need to hear that. . . .

NARRATOR: The house is going to be horribly empty, Ma. We're going to miss . . . everything you did, everything you said, even the worst stuff. I'm going to miss everything, even the worst, Ma, I swear!

NANA: Even my stubbornness that used to make you so mad?

NARRATOR: Yes.

NANA: Even my unfairness?

NARRATOR: You're hardly ever unfair, Ma.

NANA: Thanks for talking about me in the present tense.

NARRATOR: You haven't left yet, Ma.

NANA: No, but believe me, I'm on my last legs.

*She puts her hands on her stomach, and leans against him lightly.*

NARRATOR: Is it starting again?

NANA: Yes.

NARRATOR: If you only knew how useless I feel.

NANA: When I was carrying you kids, it hurt there. The same place. The exact same place. That's what makes me the saddest. I feel like . . . I feel like I'm carrying my death. Like I'm pregnant with my own death. Like I'm preparing to give birth to my death. Do you understand? Sometimes, it's the same symptoms. I mean, when the pain starts, it hurts in the same place, a bit the same way . . . but not afterwards, not when the pain gets worse, when it becomes unbearable. You kids never hurt like that, even if all five of you were big babies. . . . I don't know how to explain it. . . . It's a presence, like being pregnant, you can feel that something is feeding off you, something that's growing, trying to kick . . . but . . . it's not life. . . . You can't . . . you can't imagine what's it's like knowing that you're carrying your own death inside you! And knowing, because it hurts in a specific place, exactly where in your body death will overcome you. . . . I look at myself the way I did when I was pregnant, twenty years after my last baby, like this, you know, with my head bent over, my hands on my belly, and I know that it's my death that's there! There, where five times—

NARRATOR: Don't talk about it, Ma, it will only make you feel bad. . . .

NANA: Don't stop me, maybe it will do me good, bring some relief . . . not from the pain, but the. . . . I don't know . . . from the weight that's made my heart so heavy since I found out.

*Silence.*

NANA: You know what? I would've preferred to joke about all this, as usual. . . . You know, make up a story, act crazy or dramatic. . . . I tried, at first, with the story about your Aunt Gertrude's death, but. . . . No. I can't do it anymore. You can't . . . imagine . . . the anxiety. It's as if . . . you know that expression: a sinking feeling, the sense of sinking, like a ship . . . [*She raises her arms, as if she were going to fly away.*] . . . but me, I feel as if I'm going to fly away with anxiety. The pain is horribly heavy, but I feel as if I'm going to fly away, as if I'm being lifted up, as if the fear, the fear of suffering, the fear of dying, was making me lighter. As if punishment, hell, were above us, instead of below us! Good heavens! Maybe I'm being blasphemous, without realizing it!

NARRATOR: No, don't worry, go on if it makes you feel better. . . .

NANA: I don't know if it makes me feel better! I don't know! I'm so afraid! I refuse to leave, you understand? I refuse to leave! Not because I'm afraid of death itself, but because your father needs his spoonful of Milk of Magnesia every day, and if I'm not here, he won't take it! No, that's not true. Not true. It's death I'm afraid of. I'm afraid of dying, there's no sense in trying to deny it. I'm afraid of the black hole if there's nothing, afraid of the eternal flames if there is something!

NARRATOR: You certainly won't go to hell. . . .

NANA: Well, I certainly won't go to heaven! They don't need a pain in the neck like me.

*She almost doubles over with pain.*

Help! Help me! It hurts so bad. No, no, never mind, it's stupid of me to ask, you can't do anything for me—

NARRATOR: I don't want you to suffer like that, Ma!

NANA: It will go away. . . . It will go away. . . . It's going away already. . . .

*The narrator gets up from his chair.*

NARRATOR: Listen, you can't leave like this. . . . I can't let you suffer like this. . . . I've prepared a surprise for you. . . .

NANA: A surprise!

*The pain seems to subside.*

NARRATOR: Yes. Come here, I'll show you.

*He leads her to the edge of the stage.*

Turn around.

*Nana turns to face the back of the stage.*

Everything's possible, in the theatre, Ma, and I've prepared an exit worthy of you . . .

*He signals.*

*Magnificent music is heard—perhaps Händel—while from the wings and the heavens a superb trompe-l'oeil set appears, stage machinery and false perspectives, depicting the plains of Saskatchewan with a rippling lake in the background.*

NANA: Oh, how beautiful! Really, how beautiful! It looks like back home, in Saskatchewan! And look, look at the ripples on the lake, and everything!

NARRATOR: It's the stagehands, in the wings, who make it move.

*She walks toward the back of the stage, then turns around.*

NANA: Good heavens! It's so ugly from behind! They didn't paint both sides?
NARRATOR: It's made to be seen from the audience, Ma. . . .
NANA: Oh, right. . . . There's no point. . . . Strange, eh, I never would've imagined it that way. . . .
NARRATOR: But that's not all. . . . Come back here.

*Nana returns to the edge of the stage and turns around again.*

*The narrator signals again and an enormous pair of angel wings holding a wicker basket descend from on high.*

NANA: Oh, now I understand. That's for me, right? For my . . . departure? My . . . exit?
NARRATOR: Yes.
NANA: You're sweet. It's going to be wonderful, leaving like that! Can I go now?
NARRATOR: Of course, that's what it's here for. . . .

*They walk over to the basket, the narrator opens the little door to let Nana enter.*

NANA: I feel like I'm going for a balloon ride!
NARRATOR: Yes, and I promise you, there's no anxiety awaiting you up there, Ma. Anxiety doesn't come from on high!
NANA: I'm not worried about that anymore, I'm too happy!

*He holds her in his arms.*

NARRATOR: Don't be afraid to come back, if I do things that don't suit you. . . .
NANA: It's a promise.

*The music can be heard again.*

*The basket begins to rise, slowly.*

NARRATOR: You look good, Ma, with angel wings!
NANA: I don't know if I'm headed for heaven, but, oh, my God!, I'm having a good time!
NARRATOR: Oh, my God?
NANA: Oh, my God!

*She blows kisses and waves goodbye, before disappearing into the heavens.*

1998

# Tomson Highway

*b.* 1951

Born in a tent on his father's trapline on the remote island of Maria Lake in northern Manitoba, Tomson Highway grew up in a family devoted to the art of storytelling. He attended high school in Winnipeg, then studied piano for two years at the University of Manitoba. He obtained his BA in music (1975) and then completed his courses for a second BA in general studies (1976) at the University of Western Ontario. After his graduation he devoted himself to the service of Aboriginal people, working for many First Nations social and cultural organizations. *The Rez Sisters* (1986), his first play, won the Dora Mavor Moore Award for Best Play of the Toronto Season, then toured across Canada to sold-out audiences and represented Canada at the Edinburgh Festival. His next play, *Dry Lips Oughta Move to Kapuskasing* (1989), is the flip-side to *The Rez Sisters*, featuring seven men and a female Nanabush. Highway has also written a novel, *Kiss of the Fur Queen* (1998).

## The Rez Sisters

### *PRODUCTION NOTES*

The role of Nanabush in *The Rez Sisters* is to be played by a male dancer—modern, ballet, or traditional. Stage directions for this mostly silent Nanabush are indicated very sparingly in this script. Only his most 'essential' appearances are explicitly set out.

The music for *The Rez Sisters*, in its first productions, was provided by a musician who played at least thirty different percussion instruments from drum kit to bells to rattles, etc. This is the way I find the 'soundscape' and the rhythm of this piece to be most effectively underlined.

Both Cree and Ojibway are used freely in this text for the reasons that these two languages, belonging to the same linguistic family, are very similar and that the fictional reserve of Wasaychigan Hill was a mixture of both Cree and Ojibway residents.

### *A NOTE ON NANABUSH*

The dream world of North American Indian mythology is inhabited by the most fantastic creatures, beings, and events. Foremost among these things is the 'Trickster', as pivotal and important a figure in the Native world as Christ is in the realm of Christian mythology. 'Weesageechak' in Cree, 'Nanabush' in Ojibway, 'Raven' in others, 'Coyote' in still others, the Trickster goes by many names and many guises. In fact, he can assume any guise he chooses. Essentially a comic, clownish sort of character, he teaches us about the nature and the meaning of existence on the planet Earth; he straddles the consciousness of man and that of God, the Great Spirit.

Some say that 'Nanabush' left this continent when the white man came. We believe he is still among us—albeit a little the worse for wear and tear—having assumed other guises. Without him—and without the spiritual health of this figure—the core of Indian culture would be gone forever.

## *CAST OF CHARACTERS*

PELAJIA PATCHNOSE, 53
PHILOMENA MOOSETAIL, 49, sister of Pelajia
MARIE-ADELE STARBLANKET, 39, half-sister of Pelajia & Philomena
ANNIE COOK, 36, sister of Marie-Adele & half-sister of the other two
EMILY DICTIONARY, 32, sister of Annie & ditto
VERONIQUE ST PIERRE, 45, sister-in-law of all the above
ZHABOONIGAN PETERSON, 24, mentally disabled adopted daughter of Veronique
NANABUSH—who plays the Seagull (the dancer in white feathers), the Nighthawk (the dancer in dark feathers), and the Bingo Master.

*Time: Late summer, 1986*

*Place: The Wasaychigan Hill Indian Reserve, Manitoulin Island, Ontario. (Note: 'Wasaychigan' means 'window' in Objibway.)*

## ACT I

*It is mid-morning of a beautiful late August day on the Wasaychigan Hill Indian Reserve, Manitoulin Island, Ontario. Pelajia Patchnose is alone on the roof of her house, nailing shingles on. She wears faded blue denim men's cover-alls and a baseball cap to shade her eyes from the sun. A brightly-coloured square cushion belonging to her sister, Philomena Moosetail, rests on the roof beside her. The ladder to the roof is off-stage.*

PELAJIA: Philomena. I wanna go to Toronto.

PHILOMENA [*from offstage*]: Oh, go on.

PELAJIA: Sure as I'm sitting away up here on the roof of this old house. I kind of like it up here, though. From here, I can see half of Manitoulin Island on a clear day. I can see the chimneys, the tops of apple trees, the garbage heap behind Big Joey's dumpy little house. I can see the seagulls circling over Marie-Adele Starblanket's white picket fence. Boats on the North Channel I wish I was on, sailing away somewhere. The mill at Espanola, a hundred miles away . . . and that's with just a bit of squinting. See? If I had binoculars, I could see the superstack in Sudbury. And if I were Superwoman, I could see the CN Tower in Toronto. Ah, but I'm just plain old Pelajia Rosella Patchnose and I'm here in plain, dusty, boring old Wasaychigan Hill . . . Wasy . . . waiting . . . waiting . . . nailing shining shingles with my trusty silver hammer on the roof of Pelajia Rosella Patchnose's little two-bedroom welfare house. Philomena. I wanna go to Toronto.

*Philomena Moosetail comes up the ladder to the roof with one shingle and obviously hating it. She is very well-dressed, with a skirt, nylons, even heels, completely impractical for the roof.*

PHILOMENA: Oh, go on.

PELAJIA: I'm tired, Philomena, tired of this place. There's days I wanna leave so bad.

PHILOMENA: But you were born here. All your poop's on this reserve.

PELAJIA: Oh, go on.

PHILOMENA: You'll never leave.

PELAJIA: Yes, I will. When I'm old.

PHILOMENA: You're old right now.

PELAJIA: I got a good 30 years to go . . .

PHILOMENA: . . . and you're gonna live every one of them right here beside me . . .

PELAJIA: . . . maybe 40 . . .

PHILOMENA: . . . here in Wasy. [*tickles Pelajia on the breasts*] Chiga-chiga-chiga.

PELAJIA [*yelps and slaps Philomena's hand away*]: Oh, go on. It's not like it used to be.

PHILOMENA: Oh, go on. People change, places change, time changes things. You expect to be young and gorgeous forever?

PELAJIA: See? I told you I'm not old.

PHILOMENA: Oh, go on. You.

PELAJIA: 'Oh, go on. You.' You bug me like hell when you say that.

PHILOMENA: You say it, too. And don't give me none of this 'I don't like this place. I'm tired of it.' This place is too much inside your blood. You can't get rid of it. And it can't get rid of you.

PELAJIA: Four thirty this morning, I was woken by . . .

PHILOMENA: Here we go again.

PELAJIA: . . . Andrew Starblanket and his brother, Matthew. Drunk. Again. Or sounded like . . .

PHILOMENA: Nothing better to do.

PELAJIA: . . . fighting over some girl. Heard what sounded like a baseball bat landing on somebody's back. My lawn looks like the shits this morning.

PHILOMENA: Well, I like it here. Myself, I'm gonna go to every bingo and I'm gonna hit every jackpot between here and Espanola and I'm gonna buy me that toilet I'm dreaming about at night . . . big and wide and very white . . .

PELAJIA: Aw-ni-gi-naw-ee-dick.[1]

PHILOMENA: I'm good at bingo.

PELAJIA: So what! And the old stories, the old language. Almost all gone . . . was a time Nanabush and Windigo and everyone here could rattle away in Indian fast as Bingo Betty could lay her bingo chips down on a hot night.

1 Oh, go on. (Ojibway)

PHILOMENA: Pelajia Rosella Patchnose. The sun's gonna drive you crazy.

*[And she descends the ladder.]*

PELAJIA: Everyone here's crazy. No jobs. Nothing to do but drink and screw each other's wives and husbands and forget about our Nanabush.

*From off stage Philomena screams. She fell down the ladder.*

Philomena! [*as she looks over the edge of the roof* ] What are you doing down there?

PHILOMENA: What do you think? I fell.

PELAJIA: Bring me some of them nails while you're down there.

PHILOMENA [*whining and still from offstage, from behind the house*]: You think I can race up and down this ladder? You think I got wings?

PELAJIA: You gotta wear pants when you're doing a man's job. See? You got your skirt ripped on a nail and now you can see your thighs. People gonna think you just came from Big Joey's house.

PHILOMENA [*She comes up the ladder in a state of disarray.*] Let them think what they want. That old cow Gazelle Nataways . . . always acting like she thinks she's still a spring chicken. She's got them legs of hers wrapped around Big Joey day and night . . .

PELAJIA: Philomena. Park your tongue. My old man has to go the hundred miles to Espanola just to get a job. My boys. Gone to Toronto. Only place educated Indian boys can find decent jobs these days. And here I sit all broken-hearted.

PHILOMENA: Paid a dime and only farted.

PELAJIA: Look at you. You got dirt all over your backside. [*turning her attention to the road in front of her house and standing up for the first and only time*] And dirt roads! Years now that old chief's been making speeches about getting paved roads 'for my people' and still we got dirt roads all over.

PHILOMENA: Oh, go on.

PELAJIA: When I win that jackpot next time we play bingo in Espanola . . .

PHILOMENA [*examining her torn skirt, her general state of disarray, and fretting over it*]: Look at this! Will you look at this! Ohhh!

PELAJIA: . . . I'm gonna put that old chief to shame and build me a nice paved road right here in front of my house. Jet black. Shiny. Make my lawn look real nice.

PHILOMENA: My rib-cage!

PELAJIA: And if that old chief don't wanna make paved roads for all my sisters around here . . .

PHILOMENA: There's something rattling around inside me!

PELAJIA: . . . I'm packing my bags and moving to Toronto. [*sits down again*]

PHILOMENA: Oh, go on. [*She spies Annie Cook's approach a distance up the hill.*] Why, I do believe that cloud of dust over there is Annie Cook racing down the hill, Pelajia.

PELAJIA: Philomena. I wanna go to Toronto.

PHILOMENA: She's walking mighty fast. Must be excited about something.

PELAJIA: Never seen Annie Cook walk slow since the day she finally lost Eugene to Marie-Adele at the church 19 years ago. And even then she was walking a little too fast for a girl who was supposed to be broken-heart . . . [*stopping just in time and laughing*] . . . heart-broken.

*Annie Cook pops up the top of the ladder to the roof.*

ANNIE [*all cheery and fast and perky*]: Halloooo! Watchyou doing up here?
PELAJIA: There's room for only so much weight up here before we go crashing into my kitchen, so what do you want?
ANNIE: Just popped up to say hi.
PELAJIA: And see what we're doing?
ANNIE: Well . . .
PELAJIA: Couldn't you see what we're doing from up where you were?
ANNIE [*confidentially, to Philomena*]: Is it true Gazelle Nataways won the bingo last night?
PHILOMENA: Annie Cook, first you say you're gonna come with me and then you don't even bother showing up. If you were sitting beside me at that bingo last night you would have seen Gazelle Nataways win that big pot again with your own two eyes.
ANNIE: Emily Dictionary and I went to Little Current to listen to Fritz the Katz.
PELAJIA: What in God's name kind of a band might that be?
ANNIE: Country rock. My favourite. Fritz the Katz is from Toronto.
PELAJIA: Fritzy . . . ritzy . . . Philomena! Say something.
PHILOMENA: My record player is in Espanola getting fixed.
ANNIE: That's nice.
PHILOMENA: Good.
ANNIE: Is it true Gazelle Nataways plans to spend her bingo money to go to Toronto with . . . with Big Joey?
PHILOMENA: Who wants to know? Emily Dictionary?
ANNIE: I guess so.
PELAJIA: That Gazelle Nataways gonna leave all her babies behind and let them starve to death?
ANNIE: I guess so. I don't know. I'm asking you.
PELAJIA and PHILOMENA: We don't know.
ANNIE: I'm on my way to Marie-Adele's to pick her up.
PELAJIA: Why? Where you gonna put her down?

*Pelajia and Philomena laugh.*

ANNIE: I mean, we're going to the store together. To the post office. We're going to pick up a parcel. They say there's a parcel for me. They say it's shaped like a record. And they say it's from Sudbury. So it must be from my daughter, Ellen . . .
PELAJIA and PHILOMENA: . . . 'who lives with this white guy in Sudbury' . . .
ANNIE: How did you know?
PHILOMENA: Everybody knows.

ANNIE: His name is Raymond. Not Raymond. But Raymond. Like in Bon Bon. [*Philomena tries out 'bon bon' to herself.*]
He's French.

PELAJIA: Oh?

ANNIE: Garage mechanic. He fixes cars. And you know, talking about Frenchmen, that old priest is holding another bingo next week and when I win . . . [*to Philomena*]: Are you going?

PELAJIA: Does a bear shit in the woods?

ANNIE: . . . When I win, I'm going to Espanola and play the bingo there. Emily Dictionary says that Fire Minklater can give us a ride in her new car. She got it through Raymond's garage. The bingo in Espanola is bigger. And it's better. And I'll win. And then I'll go to Sudbury, where the bingos are even bigger and better. And then I can visit my daughter, Ellen . . .

PELAJIA: . . . 'Who lives with this white guy in Sudbury' . . .

ANNIE: . . . and go shopping in the record stores and go to the hotel and drink beer quietly—not noisy and crazy like here—and listen to the live bands. It will be so much fun. I hope Emily Dictionary can come with me.

PHILOMENA: It's true. I've been thinking . . .

PELAJIA: You don't say.

PHILOMENA: It's true. The bingos here are getting kind of boring . . .

ANNIE: That old priest is too slow and sometimes he gets the numbers all mixed up and the pot's not big enough.

PHILOMENA: And I don't like the way he calls the numbers. [*nasally*] B 12, O 64.

ANNIE: When Little Girl Manitowabi won last month . . .

PHILOMENA: She won just enough to take a taxi back to Buzwah.

ANNIE: That's all.

*Both Annie and Philomena pause to give a quick sigh of yearning.*

PHILOMENA: Annie Cook, I want that big pot.

ANNIE: We all want big pots.

PELAJIA: Start a revolution!

PHILOMENA and ANNIE: Yes!

ANNIE: All us Wasy women. We'll march up the hill, burn the church hall down, scare the priest to death, and then we'll march all the way to Espanola, where the bingos are bigger and better . . .

PHILOMENA: We'll hold big placards!

ANNIE: They'll say: 'Wasy women want bigger bingos!'

PELAJIA: And one will say: 'Annie Cook Wants Big Pot!'

PHILOMENA: . . . and the numbers at those bingos in Espanola go faster and the pots get bigger by the week. Oh, Pelajia Patchnose, I'm getting excited just thinking about it!

ANNIE: I'm going.

PELAJIA: You are, are you?

ANNIE: Yes. I'm going. I'm running out of time. I'm going to Marie-Adele's house and then we'll walk to the store together and pick up the parcel—I'm sure there'll be a letter in it, and Marie-Adele is expecting mail, too—and we'll see if Emily Dictionary is working today and we'll ask her if Fire Minklater has her new car yet so we can go to Espanola for that big pot. [*She begins to descend the ladder.*]

PELAJIA: Well, you don't have much to do today, do you?

ANNIE: Well. Toodle-oo! [*And she pops down the ladder and is gone.*]

PELAJIA: Not bad for someone who was in such a hurry to get her parcel. She talks faster than she walks. [*Noticing how dejected and abandoned Philomena looks, she holds up her hammer.*] Bingo money. Top quality. $24.95.

PHILOMENA: It's true. Bingos here in Wasy are getting smaller and smaller all the time. Especially now when the value of the dollar is getting lesser and lesser. In the old days, when Bingo Betty was still alive and walking these dirt roads, she'd come to every single bingo and she'd sit there like the Queen of Tonga, big and huge like a roast beef, smack-dab in the middle of the bingo hall. One night, I remember, she brought two young cousins from the city—two young women, dressed real fancy, like they were going to Sunday church—and Bingo Betty made them sit one on her left, with her three little bingo cards, and one on her right, with her three little ones. And Bingo Betty herself sat in the middle with 27 cards. Twenty seven cards! Amazing.

[*Pelajia starts to descend the ladder, and Philomena, getting excited, steps closer and closer to the edge of the roof.*]

And those were the days when they still used bingo chips, not these dabbers like nowadays, and everyone came with a little margarine container full of these bingo chips. When the game began they started calling out the numbers, Bingo Betty was all set, like a horse at the race-track in Sudbury, you could practically see the foam sizzling and bubbling between her teeth. Bingo Betty! Bingo Betty with her beady little darting eyes, sharp as needles, and her roly-poly jiggledy-piggledy arms with their stubby little claws would go: chiga-chiga-chiga-chiga-chiga-chiga arms flying across the table smooth as angel's wings chiga-chiga-chiga-chiga-chiga-chiga-woosh! Cousin on the left chiga-chiga, cousin on the right chiga, chiga-eeee! [*She narrowly misses falling off the roof and cries out in terror.*]

PELAJIA: Philomena!

PHILOMENA [*scrambling on hands and knees to Pelajia, and coming to rest in this languorous pose, takes a moment to regain her composure and catch her breath*]: And you know, to this very day, they say that on certain nights at the bingo here in Wasy, they say you can see Bingo Betty's ghost, like a mist, hovering in the air above the bingo tables, playing bingo like it's never been played before. Or since.

PELAJIA: Amazing! She should have gone to Toronto.

*Black-out.*

*The same day, same time, in Wasaychigan Hill. Marie-Adele Starblanket is standing alone outside her house, in her yard, by her 14-post white picket fence. Her house is down the hill from Pelajia Patchnose's, close to the lake. A seagull watches her from a distance away. He is the dancer in white feathers. Through this whole section, Nanabush (i.e. Nanabush in the guise of the seagull), Marie-Adele, and Zhaboonigan play 'games' with each other. Only she and Zhaboonigan Peterson can see the spirit inside the bird and can sort of (though not quite) recognize him for who he is. A doll belonging to a little girl lies on the porch floor. Marie-Adele throws little stones at the seagull.*

MARIE-ADELE: Awus! Wee-chee-gis. Ka-tha pu-g'wun-ta oo-ta pee-wee-sta-ta-gu-mik-si. Awus! Neee. U-wi-nuk oo-ma kee-tha ee-tee-thi-mi-soo-yin holy spirit chee? Awus! Hey, maw ma-a oop-mee tay-si-thow u-wu seagull bird. I-goo-ta poo-goo ta-poo. Nu-gu-na-wa-pa-mik. Nu-gu-na-wa-pa-mik.

NANABUSH: As-tum.

MARIE-ADELE: Neee. Moo-tha ni-gus-kee-tan tu-pi-mi-tha-an. Moo-tha oo-ta-ta-gwu-na n'tay-yan. Chees-kwa. [*Pause.*] Ma-ti poo-ni-mee-see i-goo-ta wee-chi-gi-seagull bird come shit on my fence one more time and you and anybody else look like you cook like stew on my stove. Awus![2]

*Veronique St Pierre 'passes by' with her adopted daughter Zhaboonigan Peterson.*

VERONIQUE: Talking to the birds again, Marie-Adele Starblanket?

MARIE-ADELE: Aha. Veronique St Pierre. How are you today?

VERONIQUE: Black Lady Halked's sister-in-law Fire Minklater, Fire Minklater's husband, just bought Fire Minklater a car in Sudbury.

MARIE-ADELE: New?

VERONIQUE: Used. They say he bought it from some Frenchman, some garage. Cray-<u>on</u>.

MARIE-ADELE: Ray<u>mond</u>.

VERONIQUE: These Frenchmen are forever selling us their used cars. And I'm sure that's why Black Lady Halked has been baring those big yellow teeth of hers, smiling all over the reserve recently. She looks like a hound about to pounce on a mouse, she smiles so hard when she smiles. I'd like to see her smile after plastic surgery. Anyway. At the bingo last night she was hinting that it wouldn't be too long before she would be able to go to the bingo in Espanola more frequently. Unfortunately, a new game started and you know how Black Lady Halked has to concentrate when she plays bingo—her forehead looks like corduroy, she concentrates so hard—so I didn't get a chance to ask her what she meant. So. Fire Minklater has a used car. Imagine! Maybe I can make friends with her again. NO! I wouldn't be caught dead inside her car. Not even if she had a brand-new Cadillac. How are your children? All 14 of them.

MARIE-ADELE: Okay, I guess.

2 MARIE-ADELE: Go away! You stinking thing. Don't come messing around here for nothing. Go away! Neee. Who the hell do you think you are, the Holy Spirit? Go away! Hey, but he won't fly away, this seagull bird. He just sits there. And watches me. Watches me.
NANABUSH: Come.
MARIE-ADELE: Neee. I can't fly away. I have no wings. Yet. [*Pause.*] Will you stop shitting all over the place you stinking seagull bird etc. (Cree)
(Note: 'Neee' is a very common Cree expression with the approximate meaning of 'Oh you.')

VERONIQUE: Imagine. And all from one father. Anyway. Who will take care of them after you . . . ahem . . . I mean . . . when you go to the hospital?
MARIE-ADELE: Eugene.
ZHABOONIGAN: Is he gentle?
MARIE-ADELE: Baby-cakes. How are you?
ZHABOONIGAN: Fine. [*giggles*]
VERONIQUE: She's fine. She went berry-picking yesterday with the children.
ZHABOONIGAN: Where's Nicky?
MARIE-ADELE: Nicky's down at the beach.
ZHABOONIGAN: Why?
MARIE-ADELE: Taking care of Rose-Marie.
ZHABOONIGAN: Oh.
MARIE-ADELE: Yup.
ZHABOONIGAN: Me and Nicky, ever lots of blueberries!
MARIE-ADELE: Me and Nicky picked lots of blueberries.
ZHABOONIGAN: I didn't see you there.
MARIE-ADELE: When?
ZHABOONIGAN: Before today.
MARIE-ADELE: How come Nicky didn't come home with any?
ZHABOONIGAN: Why?

*Marie-Adele shrugs. Zhaboonigan imitates this, and then pretends she is stuffing her mouth with berries.*

MARIE-ADELE: Aw, yous went and made pigs of yourselves.
ZHABOONIGAN: Nicky's the pig.
MARIE-ADELE: Neee.
ZHABOONIGAN: Are you going away far?
MARIE-ADELE: I'm not going far.
ZHABOONIGAN: Oh. Are you pretty?

*Marie-Adele, embarrassed for a moment, smiles and Zhaboonigan smiles, too.*

MARIE-ADELE: You're pretty, too.
[*Zhaboonigan tugs at Marie-Adele's shoelaces.*]
Oh, Zhaboonigan. Now you have to tie it up. I can't bend too far cuz I get tired.

*Zhaboonigan tries to tie the shoelaces with great difficulty. When she finds she can't she throws her arms up and screams.*

ZHABOONIGAN: Dirty trick! Dirty trick! [*She bites her hand and hurts herself.*]
MARIE-ADELE: Now, don't get mad.
VERONIQUE: Stop it. Stop it right now.
ZHABOONIGAN: No! No!
MARIE-ADELE: Zha. Zha. Listen. Listen.
ZHABOONIGAN: Stop it! Stop it right now!
MARIE-ADELE: Come on Zha. You and I can name the koo-koos-suk.[3] All 14 of them.

ZHABOONIGAN: Okay. Here we go.

*Marie-Adele leads Zhaboonigan over to the picket fence and Veronique follows them.*

ZHABOONIGAN [*to Veronique*]: No.

*Veronique retreats, obviously hurt.*

MARIE-ADELE [*taking Zhaboonigan's hand and counting on the 14 posts of her white picket fence*]: Simon, Andrew, Matthew, Janie, Nicky, Ricky, Ben, Mark, Ron, Don, John, Tom, Pete, and Rose-Marie. There.

*Underneath Marie-Adele's voice, Zhaboonigan has been counting.*

ZHABOONIGAN: One, two, three, four, five, six, seven, eight, nine, ten, eleven, twelve, thirteen, fourteen. [*giggles*]

MARIE-ADELE: Ever good counter you, Zhaboonigan.

ZHABOONIGAN: Yup.

VERONIQUE: This reserve, sometimes I get so sick of it. They laugh at me behind my back, I just know it. They laugh at me and Pierre St Pierre because we don't have any children of our own. 'Imagine, they say, she's on her second husband already and she still can't have children!' They laugh at Zhaboonigan Peterson because she's crazy, that's what they call her. They can't even take care of their own people, they'd rather laugh at them. I'm the only person who would take Zhaboonigan after her parents died in that horrible car crash near Manitowaning on Saturday November 12 1964 may they rest in peace. [*She makes a quick sign of the cross without skipping a beat.*] I'm the only one around here who is kind enough. And they laugh at me. Oh, I wish I had a new stove, Marie-Adele. My stove is so old and broken down, only two elements work anymore and my oven is starting to talk back at me.

MARIE-ADELE: Get it fixed.

VERONIQUE: You know that Pierre St Pierre never has any money. He drinks it all up. [*She sighs longingly.*] Some day! Anyway. Zhaboonigan here wanted to go for a swim so I thought I'd walk her down—drop by and see how you and the children are doing—it will do my weak heart good, I was saying to myself.

MARIE-ADELE: Awus!

*As she throws a pebble at the seagull on the stone, Veronique, for a second, thinks it's her Marie-Adele is shooing away. There is a brief silence broken after awhile by Zhaboonigan's little giggle.*

VERONIQUE: Anyway, I was walking down by that Big Joey's shameless little shack just this morning when guess who pokes her nose out the window but Gazelle Nataways—the nerve of that woman. I couldn't see inside but I'm sure she was only half-dressed, her hairdo was all mixed up and she said to me: 'Did you know, Veronique St Pierre, that Little Girl Manitowabi told me her daughter, June Bug

3 The little pigs. (Cree)

McLeod, just got back from the hospital in Sudbury where she had her tubes tied and told her that THE BIGGEST BINGO IN THE WORLD is coming to Toronto?'

MARIE-ADELE: When?

VERONIQUE: I just about had a heart attack.

MARIE-ADELE: When?

VERONIQUE: But I said to Gazelle anyway: Is there such a thing as a BIGGEST BINGO IN THE WORLD? And she said: Yes. And she should know about these things because she spends all her waking and sleeping hours just banging about in bed with the biggest thing on Manitoulin Island, I almost said.

MARIE-ADELE: This bingo. When?

VERONIQUE: She didn't know. And now that I think of it, I don't know whether to believe her. After all, who should believe a woman who wrestles around with dirt like Big Joey all night long leaving her poor babies to starve to death in her empty kitchen? But if it's true, Marie-Adele, if it's true that THE BIGGEST BINGO IN THE WORLD is coming to Toronto I'm going and I want you to come with me.

MARIE-ADELE: Well . . .

VERONIQUE: I want you to come shopping with me and help me choose my new stove after I win.

MARIE-ADELE: Hang on . . .

VERONIQUE: They have good stoves in Toronto.

MARIE-ADELE: Let's find out for sure. Then we start making plans.

VERONIQUE: Maybe we should go back and ask that Gazelle Nataways about this. If she's sure.

MARIE-ADELE: Maybe we should go and ask June Bug McLeod herself.

VERONIQUE: We can't walk to Buzwah and I'm too old to hitch-hike.

MARIE-ADELE: There's Eugene's van. He'll be home by six.

VERONIQUE: I want to find out NOW. But what if people see us standing at Big Joey's door?

MARIE-ADELE: What do you mean? We just knock on the door, march right in, ask the bitch, and march right out again.

VERONIQUE: Zhaboonigan dear, wait for me over there. [*She waits until Zhaboonigan is safely out of earshot and then leans over to Marie-Adele in a conspiratorial whisper.*] Anyway. You must know, Marie-Adele, that there's all kinds of women who come streaming out of that house at all hours of the day and night. I might be considered one of them. You know your youngest sister, Emily Dictionary, was seen staggering out of that house in the dead of night two nights ago?

MARIE-ADELE: Veronique St Pierre, what Emily Dictionary does is Emily's business.

*Annie Cook enters, walking fast and comes to a screeching halt.*

ANNIE: Hallooooo! Whatchyou doin'?

VERONIQUE [*giving Annie the baleful eye*]: How are you?

ANNIE: High as a kite. Just kidding. Hi, Zha.

ZHABOONIGAN: Hi. [*giggles. She runs toward Marie-Adele, bumping into Annie en route.*]

ANNIE: Hey, Marie-Adele.

ZHABOONIGAN: Marie-Adele. How's your cancer? [*giggles and scurries off laughing*]

VERONIQUE: Shkanah, Zhaboonigan, sna-ma-bah . . .[4]

MARIE-ADELE: Come on, before the post office closes for lunch.

VERONIQUE: You didn't tell me you were going to the store.

ANNIE: Well, we are. [*to Marie-Adele*]: Hey, is Simon in? I'm sure he's got my Ricky Skaggs album. You know the one that goes [*sings*] 'Honeee!' [*calling into the house*] Yoo-hoo, Simon!

MARIE-ADELE: He's in Espanola with Eugene.

VERONIQUE: Expecting mail, Annie Cook?

ANNIE: A parcel from my daughter, Ellen, who lives with this white guy in Sudbury . . .

VERONIQUE: So I've heard.

ANNIE: And my sister here is expecting a letter, too.

VERONIQUE: From whom?

ANNIE: From the doctor, about her next check-up.

VERONIQUE: When?

MARIE-ADELE: We don't know when. Or where. Annie, let's go.

ANNIE: They say it's shaped like a record.

VERONIQUE: Maybe there'll be news in that parcel about THE BIGGEST BINGO IN THE WORLD! [*shouts toward the lake, in a state of great excitement*] Zhaboonigan! Zhaboonigan! We're going to the store!

ANNIE: THE BIGGEST BINGO IN THE WORLD?

VERONIQUE: In Toronto. Soon. Imagine! Gazelle Nataways told me. She heard about it from Little Girl Manitowabi over in Buzwah who heard about it from her daughter June Bug McLeod who just got back from the hospital in Sudbury where she had her tubes tied I just about had a heart attack!

ANNIE: Toronto?

MARIE-ADELE: We gotta find out for sure.

ANNIE: Right.

MARIE-ADELE: We could go to Big Joey's and ask Gazelle Nataways except Veronique St Pierre's too scared of Gazelle.

VERONIQUE: I am not.

ANNIE: You are too.

MARIE-ADELE: We could wait and borrow Eugene's van . . .

VERONIQUE: I am not.

ANNIE: . . . drive over to Buzwah . . .

MARIE-ADELE: . . . and ask June Bug McLeod . . .

ANNIE: . . . but wait a minute! . . .

MARIE-ADELE and ANNIE: Maybe there IS news in that parcel about this BIGGEST BINGO IN THE WORLD!

MARIE-ADELE: Come on.

VERONIQUE [*shouting toward the lake*]: Zhaboonigan! Zhaboonigan!

4 Shush, Zhaboonigan, don't say that. (Ojibway)

ANNIE: And here I was so excited about the next little bingo that old priest is holding next week. Toronto! Oh, I hope it's true!

VERONIQUE: Zhaboonigan! Zhaboonigan! Zhaboonigan! Dammit! We're going to the store!

*And the 'march' to the store begins, during which Nanabush, still in the guise of the seagull, follows them and continues to play tricks, mimicking their hand movements, the movement of their mouths, etc. The three women appear each in her own spot of light at widely divergent points on the stage area.*

ANNIE: When I go to THE BIGGEST BINGO IN THE WORLD, in Toronto, I will win. For sure, I will win. If they shout the B 14 at the end, for sure I will win. The B 14 is my lucky number after all. Then I will take all my money and I will go to every record store in Toronto. I will buy every single one of Patsy Cline's records, especially the one that goes [*sings*] 'I go a-walking, after midnight,' oh I go crazy every time I hear that one. Then I will buy a huge record player, the biggest one in the whole world. And then I will go to all the taverns and all the night clubs in Toronto and listen to the live bands while I drink beer quietly—not noisy and crazy like here—I will bring my daughter Ellen and her white guy from Sudbury and we will sit together. Maybe I will call Fritz the Katz and he will take me out. Maybe he will hire me as one of his singers and I can [*sings*] 'Oooh,' in the background while my feet go [*shuffles her feet from side to side*] while Fritz the Katz is singing and the lights are flashing and the people are drinking beer and smoking cigarettes and dancing. Ohhh, I could dance all night with that Fritz the Katz. When I win, when I win THE BIGGEST BINGO IN THE WORLD!

MARIE-ADELE: When I win THE BIGGEST BINGO IN THE WORLD, I'm gonna buy me an island. In the North Channel, right smack-dab in the middle—eem-shak min-stik[5]—the most beautiful island in the world. And my island will have lots of trees—great big bushy ones—and lots and lots and lots of sweetgrass. MMMMM! And there's gonna be pine trees and oak trees and maple trees and big stones and little stonelets—neee—and, oh yeah, this real neat picket fence, real high, long and very, very, very white. No bird shit. Eugene will live there and me and all my Starblanket kids. Yup, no more smelly, stinky old pulp and paper mill in Espanola for my Eugene—pooh!—my 12 Starblanket boys and my two Starblanket girls and me and my Eugene all living real nice and comfy right there on Starblanket Island, the most beautiful incredible goddamn island in the whole goddamn world. Eenshak min-stik! When I win THE BIGGEST BINGO IN THE WORLD!

VERONIQUE: Well, when I win the BIGGEST BINGO IN THE WORLD. No! After I win THE BIGGEST BINGO IN THE WORLD, I will go shopping for a brand-new stove. In Toronto. At the Eaton Centre. A great big stove. The kind Madame Benoit has. The kind that has the three different compartments in the oven alone. I'll have the biggest stove on the reserve. I'll cook for all the children on the reserve. I'll adopt

5 A great big island. (Cree)

all of Marie-Adele Starblanket's 14 children and I will cook for them. I'll even cook for Gazelle Nataways' poor starving babies while she's lolling around like a pig in Big Joey's smelly, sweaty bed. And Pierre St Pierre can drink himself to death for all I care. Because I'll be the best cook on all of Manitoulin Island! I'll enter competitions. I'll go to Paris and meet what's-his-name Cordon Bleu! I'll write a cookbook called 'The Joy of Veronique St Pierre's Cooking' and it will sell in the millions! And I will become rich and famous! Zhaboonigan Peterson will wear a mink while she eats steak tartare-de-frou-frou! Madame Benoit will be so jealous she'll suicide herself. Oh, when I win THE BIGGEST BINGO IN THE WORLD.

*Zhaboonigan comes running in from swimming, 'chasing' after the other three women, counting to herself and giggling.*

ZHABOONIGAN: One, two, three, four, five, six, seven, eight, nine, ten, eleven, twelve, thirteen, fourteen.

*At the store. Annie Cook, Marie-Adele Starblanket, Veronique St Pierre, and Zhaboonigan Peterson have arrived. Emily Dictionary makes a sudden appearance, carrying a huge bag of flour on her shoulder. She is one tough lady, wearing cowboy boots, tight blue jeans, a black leather jacket—all three items worn to the seams—and she sports one black eye.*

EMILY: [*in a loud, booming voice that paralyzes all movement in the room while she speaks*]: Zhaboonigan Peterson! What in Red Lucifer's name ever possessed you to be hangin' out with a buncha' dizzy old dames like this?

*Bag of flour hits the floor with a 'doof'.*

MARIE-ADELE: Emily. Your eye.

EMILY: Oh, bit of a tussle.

VERONIQUE: With who?

EMILY: None of your goddamn business.

MARIE-ADELE: Emily, please.

ANNIE [*following Emily about the store while Veronique tries, in vain, to hear what she can*]: I wasn't able to find out from Pelajia Patchnose or Philomena Moosemeat if Gazelle Nataways is going to Toronto this weekend with . . . Big Joey . . . they didn't know . . . Gazelle did win the bingo last night though.

EMILY: Aw shit. Veronique St Pierre, you old bag. Is it true Gazelle Nataways is takin' off for Toronto with that hunk Big Joey?

VERONIQUE: It WAS you coming out of that house two nights ago. I walked by as quickly as I could . . .

EMILY: . . . shoulda come out and nailed your big floppy ears to the door . . .

VERONIQUE: . . . and I would have called the police but I was too scared Big Joey might come after me and Zhaboonigan later . . .

EMILY: . . . yeah, right.

ZHABOONIGAN: Yeah, right.

VERONIQUE: . . . and I have a weak heart, you know? Who hit you? Big Joey? Or Gazelle Nataways?

EMILY: The nerve of this woman.

VERONIQUE: Well?

EMILY [*calls Zhaboonigan, who is behind the counter, on the floor, playing with the merchandise*]: Zhaboonigan Peterson! Where in Red Lucifer's name is that dozy pagan?

VERONIQUE: You keep hanging around that house and you're gonna end up in deep trouble. You don't know how wicked and vicious those Nataways women can get. They say there's witchcraft in their blood. And with manners like yours, Emily Dictionary, you'd deserve every hex you got.

EMILY: Do I know this woman? Do I know this woman?

VERONIQUE: [*During this speech, Marie-Adele and Annie sing 'Honeee' tauntingly.*] I'm sorry I have to say this in front of everyone like this but this woman has just accused my daughter of being a pagan. I didn't call her Zhaboonigan. The people on this reserve, who have nothing better to do with their time than call each other names, they called her that. Her name is Marie-Adele. Marie-Adele Peterson. You should talk. I should ask you where in Red . . . Red . . . whatever, you got a circus of a name like Emily Dictionary.

*Emily grabs Veronique and throws her across the room. Veronique goes flying right into Pelajia, who has entered the store during the latter part of this speech.*

PELAJIA: Veronique St Pierre! Control yourself or I'll hit you over the head with my hammer.

VERONIQUE [*blows a 'raspberry' in Pelajia's face*]: Bleah!

ANNIE: No, Pelajia, no.

EMILY: Go ahead, Pelajia. Make my day.

ANNIE: Down, put it down.

PHILOMENA [*as she comes scurrying into the store*]: I have to use the toilet. [*running to Emily*] I have to use the toilet. [*and goes scurrying into the toilet*]

ANNIE [*to Pelajia*]: Remember, that's Veronique St Pierre and if you get on the wrong side of Veronique St Pierre she's liable to spread rumours about you all over kingdom come and you'll lose every bit of respect you got on this reserve. Don't let those pants you're wearing go to your head.

PELAJIA [*catching Annie by the arm as she tries to run away*]: Annie Cook! You got a mouth on you like a helicopter.

ANNIE: Veronique's mad at you, Emily, because you won't tell her what happened the other night at Big Joey's house. And she's jealous of Gazelle Nataways because Gazelle won the bingo again last night and she hopes you're the one person on this reserve who has the guts to stand up to Gazelle.

VERONIQUE [*making a lunge at Annie, who hides behind Emily*]: What's that! What's that! Ohhh! Ohhh!

ANNIE: Leave me alone, you old snoop. All I wanna know is is this big bingo really happening in Toronto.

VERONIQUE: Annie Cook. You are a little suck.

EMILY [*to Veronique*]: Someday, someone oughta stick a great big piece of shit into that mouth of yours.

PELAJIA [*to Emily*]: And someday, someone ought to wash yours out with soap.

PHILOMENA [*Throwing the toilet door open, she sits there in her glory, panties down to her ankles.*]: Emily Dictionary. You come back to the reserve after all these years and you strut around like you own the place. I know Veronique St Pierre is a pain in the ass but I don't care. She's your elder and you respect her. Now shut up, all of you, and let me shit in peace.

*And slams the washroom door. Veronique, scandalized by this, haughtily walks through toward the door, bumping into Pelajia en route.*

PELAJIA: Philomena. Get your bum out here. Veronique St Pierre is about to lose her life. [*She raises her hammer at Veronique.*]

VERONIQUE [*to Pelajia*]: Put that hammer away. And go put a skirt on, for heaven's sake, you look obscene in those tight pants.

ANNIE: Hit her. Go on. Hit the bitch. One good bang is all she needs.

EMILY: Yeah, right. A gang-bang is more like it.

*And a full-scale riot breaks out, during which the women throw every conceivable insult at each other. Emily throws open the toilet door and Philomena comes stomping out, pulling her panties on and joining the riot. All talk at the same time, quietly at first, but then getting louder and louder until they are all screaming.*

PHILOMENA [*to Annie*]: What a slime. Make promises and then you go do something else. And I always have to smile at you. What a slime. [*to Emily*]: All that tough talk. I know what's behind it all. You'll never be big enough to push me around. [*to Marie-Adele*]: Fourteen kids! You look like a wrinkled old prune already. [*to Pelajia*]: At least I'm a woman. [*to Veronique*]: Have you any idea how, just how offensive, how obnoxious you are to people? And that halitosis. Pooh! You wouldn't have it if you didn't talk so much.

EMILY [*to Philomena*]: So damned bossy and pushy and sucky. You make me sick. Always wanting your own way. [*to Veronique*]: Goddamned trouble-making old crow. [*to Pelajia*]: Fuckin' self-righteous old bitch. [*to Marie-Adele*]: Mental problems, that's what you got, princess. I ain't no baby. I'm the size of a fuckin' church. [*to Annie*]: You slippery little slut. Brain the size of a fuckin pea. Fuck, man, take a Valium.

VERONIQUE [*to Emily*]: You have no morals at all. You sick pervert. You should have stayed where you came from, where all the other perverts are. [*to Pelajia*]: Slow turtle. Talk big and move like Jell-o. [*to Annie*]: Cockroach! [*to Philomena*]: You big phony. Flush yourself down that damned toilet of yours and shut up. [*to Marie-Adele*]: Hasn't this slimy little reptile [*referring to Annie*] ever told you that sweet little Ellen of hers is really Eugene's daughter? Go talk to the birds in Sudbury and find out for yourself.

PELAJIA [*to Veronique*]: This reserve would be a better place without you. I'm tired of dealing with people like you. Tired. [*to Marie-Adele*]: You can't act that way.

This here's no time to be selfish. You spoiled brat. [*to Philomena*]: You old fool. I thought you were coming back to help me and here you are all trussed up like a Thanksgiving turkey, putting on these white lady airs. [*to Annie*]: Annie Cook. Move to Kapuskasing! [*to Emily*]: 'Fuck, fuck, fuck!' Us women got no business talking like that.

MARIE-ADELE [*to Pelajia*]: You don't have all the answers. You can't fix everything. [*to Annie*]: White guys. Slow down a minute and see how stupid you look. [*to Emily*]: Voice like a fog-horn. You ram through everything like a truck. You look like a truck. [*to Veronique*]: Some kind of insect, sticking insect claws into everybody's business. [*to Philomena*]: Those clothes. You look like a giant Kewpie doll. You make me laugh.

ANNIE [*to Marie-Adele*]: You always make me feel so . . . small . . . like a little pig or something. You're no better than me. [*to Philomena*]: Why can't you go to bingo by yourself, you big baby? At least I got staying power. Piss off. [*to Veronique*]: Sucking off everybody else's life like a leech because you got nothing of your own. Pathetic old coot. Just buzz off. [*to Emily*]: You call me names. I don't call you names. You think you're too smart. Shut up. [*to Pelajia*]: 'Queen of the Indians,' you think that's what you are. Well, that stupid hammer of yours doesn't scare me. Go away. Piss me off.

*Then Pelajia lifts her hammer with a big loud 'Woah'! And they come to a sudden dead stop. Pause. Then one quick final volley, all at once, loudest of all.*

PHILOMENA [*to Annie*]: You slimy buck-toothed drunken worm!

EMILY [*to Veronique*]: Fuckin' instigator!

VERONIQUE [*to Marie-Adele*]: Clutching, clinging vine!

PELAJIA [*to Veronique*]: Evil no-good insect!

MARIE-ADELE [*to Veronique*]: Maggot-mouthed vulture!

ANNIE [*to Philomena*]: Fat-assed floozy, get off the pot!

*Marie-Adele, stung to the quick, makes a vicious grab for Veronique by the throat. In a split-second, all freeze. Lights out in store interior. Lights on on Zhaboonigan, who has run out in fright during the riot, outside the store. Nanabush, still in his guise as the seagull, makes a grab at Zhaboonigan. Zhaboonigan begins talking to the bird.*

ZHABOONIGAN: Are you gentle? I was not little. Maybe. Same size as now. Long ago it must be? You think I'm funny? Shhh. I know who you are. There, there. Boys. White boys. Two. Ever nice white wings, you. I was walking down the road to the store. They ask me if I want ride in car. Oh, I was happy I said, 'Yup.' They took me far away. Ever nice ride. Dizzy. They took all my clothes off me. Put something up inside me here. [*pointing to her crotch, underneath her dress*] Many, many times. Remember. Don't fly away. Don't go. I saw you before. There, there. It was a. Screwdriver. They put the screwdriver inside me. Here. Remember. Ever lots of blood. The two white boys. Left me in the bush. Alone. It was cold.

And then. Remember. Zhaboonigan. Everybody calls me Zhaboonigan. Why? It means needle. Zhaboonigan. Going-through-thing. Needle Peterson. Going-through-thing Peterson. That's me. It was a screwdriver. Nice. Nice. Nicky Ricky Ben Mark. [*as she counts, with each name, feathers on the bird's wing*] Ever nice. Nice white birdie you.

*During this last speech, Nanabush goes through agonizing contortions. Then lights change instantly back to the interior of the store. The six women spring back into action. Philomena stomps back into the toilet.*

MARIE-ADELE [*to Veronique*]: Fine. And the whole reserve knows the only reason you ever adopted Zhaboonigan is for her disability cheque.

ANNIE: You fake saint.

*Annie, Marie-Adele, and Emily start pushing Veronique, round-robin, between the three of them, laughing tauntingly until Veronique is almost reduced to tears.*

VERONIQUE [*almost weeping*]: Bastards. The three of you.

*Marie-Adele grabs Veronique by the throat and lifts her fist to punch her in the face. But the exertion causes her body to weaken, almost to the point of collapse, from her illness. At this point, Philomena emerges from the toilet.*

PHILOMENA [*crinkling her nose*]: Emily. Your toilet.

WOMEN: Shhhh.

MARIE-ADELE [*holding her waist, reeling, barely audible*]: Oh, shit.

PHILOMENA: I can't get it to flush.

WOMEN: Shhhh.

PELAJIA [*rushing to Marie-Adele*]: Marie-Adele. You're not well.

MARIE-ADELE [*screams*]: Don't touch me.

*Complete silence from all while Marie-Adele weaves and struggles to keep herself from collapsing. Annie scurries offstage, to the back part of the store, where the post office would be.*

EMILY [*to Veronique*]: You f'in' bitch!

PHILOMENA: What did I just tell you? Who did that to your eye?

VERONIQUE: Big Joey.

EMILY [*to Veronique*]: Look here, you old buzzard. I'll tell you a few things. You see this fist? You see these knuckles? You wanna know where they come from? Ten years. Every second night for 10 long ass-fuckin' years that goddamn Yellowknife asshole Henry Dadzinanare come home to me so drunk his eyes was spittin' blood like Red Lucifer himself and he'd beat me purple.

VERONIQUE: I wish I'd been there to see it all.

EMILY: Yeah, scumbag. I wish you'd been there to watch me learn to fight back like you've never seen a woman fight for her life before. Take a look at this eye. I earned it, Veronique St Pierre, I earned it.

PHILOMENA: Henry Dadzinanare, Big Joey. They're all the same. Emily, use your brains.

EMILY: Use my brains. Yeah, right. I used them alright the night he came at me with an axe and just about sank it into my spine, I grabbed one bag, took one last look at the kids, and walked out of his life forever.

ANNIE [*from offstage*]: And she took the bus to San Francisco.

PHILOMENA: And gets herself mixed up with a motorcycle gang, for God's sake.

EMILY [*now addressing all in the room*]: Rosabella Baez, Hortensia Colorado, Liz Jones, Pussy Commanda. And me. The best. 'Rose and the Rez Sisters', that's us. And man, us sisters could weave knuckle magic.

VERONIQUE: So why did you bother coming back?

PHILOMENA: You stay out of this.

EMILY: Come back to the Rez for a visit, get all wedged up with that hunk Big Joey one night . . . [*grunts*]

PHILOMENA: I give up.

EMILY: . . . and I was hooked. Couldn't leave. Settlin' back on a couple beers with Big Joey the other night when Gazelle Nataways come sashayin' in like she's got half the Rez squished down the crack of her ass. She was high. I was high. Hell, we were all high. Get into a bit of a discussion, when she gets me miffed and I let fly, she let fly, Big Joey let fly, misses that nympho and lands me one in the eye instead.

VERONIQUE: So it was Big Joey.

EMILY: Damn rights. And that's as close as he got cuz I put him out for the night right then and there. Just one of these. [*brandishing her fist*] One. That's all it took.

*Veronique runs off to look for Zhaboonigan.*

ANNIE and PHILOMENA [*Philomena with exasperation, Annie with adulation, from offstage*]: Emily Dictionary.

ANNIE: You're amazing!

EMILY: Not Dictionary. Dadzinanare. Henry Dadzinanare. The man who made me learn to fight back. Never let a man raise one dick hair against me since.

VERONIQUE [*calling out to Zhaboonigan*]: Zhaboonigan. Don't you be talking to the birds like that again. You're crazy enough as it is.

ANNIE [*as she comes running back in from the post office with her parcel, already unwrapped, and two letters, one for herself, already unfolded, and one still in its envelope*]: See? I told you. It's a record. Patsy Cline.

PHILOMENA: Never mind Patsy Cline.

ANNIE [*as she hands Marie-Adele the letter in the envelope*]: Hey, Marie-Adele.

EMILY: Read your friggin' letter, Annie Cook.

ANNIE: Listen to this.

*Zhaboonigan walks back in as Annie reads her own letter very haltingly.*

Dear Mom: Here is the record you wanted. I thought you'd like the picture of Patsy Cline on the cover. [*Annie shows off her record.*] See? It's Patsy Cline. [*returns to her letter*] I also thought you might like to know that there is a bingo called THE BIGGEST BINGO IN THE WORLD. Can you fu . . . ture that?

EMILY [*who has been looking over Annie's shoulder*]: Feature. Feature.

ANNIE: Can you . . . feature . . . that? . . . that's coming to Toronto. The jackpot is $500,000. It's on Saturday, September 8. Raymond's Mom was in Toronto. Aunt Philomena will hit the roof when she hears this. Much love, your daughter Ellen. [*Annie announces once more.*]

*There is a brief electric silence followed by an equally electric scream from all the women. Even Zhaboonigan screams. Excitement takes over completely.*

VERONIQUE: So it's true! It's true!

PHILOMENA: The Espanola bingo. Piffle. Mere piffle.

VERONIQUE: My new stove!

PHILOMENA: My new toilet! White! Spirit white!

EMILY [*grabbing Zhaboonigan and dancing around the room with her*]: I'd take the money, come back to the Rez, beat the shit out of Gazelle Nataways and take you down to Frisco with me. Whaddaya think?

ZHABOONIGAN: Yup.

MARIE-ADELE [*in the background, where she has been reading her letter quietly to herself*]: September 10.

ANNIE [*taking the letter from Marie-Adele*]: Look, Pelajia. Marie-Adele's tests are in Toronto just two days after THE BIGGEST.

*There is a brief embarrassed silence.*

MARIE-ADELE: Kill two birds with one stone. [*to Nanabush*]: I wanna go. [*to Pelajia and Philomena*]: I wanna go.

VERONIQUE: Goood!

EMILY [*mimicking Veronique*]: Goood! Now how the hell are you guys gonna get down to Toronto? You're all goddamn welfare cases.

ANNIE: Fire Minklater.

VERONIQUE: Mary, mother of Jesus! I refuse, I absolutely refuse to be seen anywhere near that sorceress! We'll chip in and rent a car.

EMILY: Zhaboonigan Peterson here gonna chauffeur you down?

ZHABOONIGAN: Yup.

VERONIQUE: Don't you make fun of my daughter.

EMILY: What kind of stove you gonna buy, Veronique St Pierre? Westinghouse? Electrolux? Yamaha? Kawasaki?

VERONIQUE: Oh my god, Marie-Adele, I never thought about it. They will have so many stoves in Toronto, I'll get confused.

ANNIE: If you go to Toronto and leave Wasy for even one day, Emily, you'll lose Big Joey forever . . .

VERONIQUE: To that witch!

ANNIE: . . . and then whose thighs will you have to wrestle around with in the dead of night? You'll dry up, get all puckered up and pass into ancient history.

EMILY: Annie Cook. I don't know what the fuck you're yatterin' on about now but I'd like to hear you say two words of French to that white guy in Sudbury you're so damn proud of.

ANNIE: Oh my god, Marie-Adele, she's right. I won't know what to say to this Raymond. I've never met him. I can't speak French. All I can say in French is Raymond and Bon Bon and I don't even know what that means. I can't go and live with them, not even after I win THE BIGGEST BINGO IN THE WORLD. What am I gonna do?

[*She collapses on the floor and rolls around for a bit.*]

EMILY: And Philomena Moosemeat's so fulla shit she'd need five toilets to get it all out.

PHILOMENA [*going at Emily*]: And just who do you think you're talking to, Miss Dictionary, just who the hell do you think you're talking to?

*With a resounding belly butt from Emily, they begin to wrestle.*

PELAJIA [*banging her hammer on the counter*]: Alright, alright. It's obvious we've got a problem here.

EMILY [*throwing Philomena off to the side*]: I'll say.

MARIE-ADELE: It's true. None of us has any money.

*But Veronique, standing behind Pelajia, winks at the others and makes a hand motion indicating that Pelajia, for one, does have money. All the other women slowly surround Pelajia. But Pelajia catches the drift and quickly collects herself to meet the onslaught. During Pelajia's speech, the women respond at periodic intervals with a 'yoah' and 'hmmm,' etc., as when a chief speaks at a council meeting.*

PELAJIA: I say we all march down to the Band Office and ask the Band Council for a loan that will pay for the trip to this bingo. I know how to handle that tired old chief. He and I have been arguing about paved roads for years now. I'll tell him we'll build paved roads all over the reserve with our prize money. I'll tell him the people will stop drinking themselves to death because they'll have paved roads to walk on. I'll tell him there'll be more jobs because the people will have paved roads to drive to work on. I'll tell him the people will stop fighting and screwing around and Nanabush will come back to us because he'll have paved roads to dance on. There's enough money in there for everyone, I'll say. And if he doesn't lend us the money. I'll tell him I'm packing my bags and moving to Toronto tomorrow.

EMILY: That oughta twist his arm but good.

PELAJIA: And if he still says no, I'll bop him over the head with my hammer and we'll attack the accountant and take the money ourselves. Philomena, we're going to Toronto!

*The seven women have this grand and ridiculous march to the band office, around the set and all over the stage area, with Pelajia leading them forward heroically, her hammer just a-swinging in the air. Nanabush trails merrily along in the rear of the line. They reach the 'band office'—standing in one straight line square in front of the audience. The 'invisible' chief 'speaks': cacophonous percussion for about seven beats, the women listening more and more incredulously. Finally, the percussion comes to a dead stop.*

PELAJIA: No?

*Pelajia raises her hammer to hit the 'invisible' chief, Nanabush shrugs a 'don't ask me, I don't know,' Emily fingers a 'fuck you, man.' Blackout. End of Act I.*

## ACT II

*All seven women are holding a meeting in the basement of Pelajia Patchnose's house. This is a collection of chairs and stools off to the side of the stage area. The only light comes from an old, beat-up trilight pole lamp. Some have tea, Emily and Annie a beer.*

VERONIQUE: We should have met at the priest's house.

PELAJIA: No! We're gonna work this out on our own. Right here. Emily Dictionary, you chair. [*And she lends Emily her hammer.*]

VERONIQUE: She's good at ordering people around.

PHILOMENA: Shut up.

EMILY: First. When are we leaving? [*She bangs the hammer regularly throughout the meeting.*]

VERONIQUE: How much is the trip going to cost?

EMILY: When are we leaving?

PHILOMENA: How long to Toronto?

ANNIE: Four hours.

EMILY: When are we leaving?

PHILOMENA: The only human being who can make it in four hours is Annie Cook.

VERONIQUE: I'm not dying on the highway.

PHILOMENA: Eight hours.

PELAJIA: No way we're gonna stop at every toilet on the highway.

MARIE-ADELE: Six hours. Eugene's driven there.

VERONIQUE: Maybe we can borrow his van.

ANNIE: Maybe we can borrow Big Joey's van. [*a quick little aside to Pelajia*]: Hey, can I have another beer?

PELAJIA: No.

VERONIQUE: What about Gazelle Nataways?

EMILY: We're gonna borrow his van, not his buns, for Chris'sakes.

MARIE-ADELE: The only thing we have to pay for is the gas.

ANNIE: Philomena's got gas.

EMILY: Right! Six hours. Eugene's van.

MARIE-ADELE: We still don't know when we're leaving.

PHILOMENA: Bingo's on Saturday night.

ANNIE: Leave Saturday morning.

VERONIQUE: Oh! I'll be so tired for the bingo. I'll get confused. Wednesday. Rest on Thursday.

ANNIE: And rest again on Friday? Too much resting. I can't go for that.

PELAJIA: And we can't afford such a long stay.
PHILOMENA: Where are we gonna stay?
EMILY: Whoa!

*Pause.*

PELAJIA: Friday night.
EMILY: Right. Leave Friday night. Next.
PHILOMENA: Coming home right after the bingo.
MARIE-ADELE: And leave me behind? Remember my tests Monday morning.
EMILY: Right. Monday noon, we come back. Next.
VERONIQUE: Don't go so fast. My mind is getting confused.
EMILY: Goood! Next.
MARIE-ADELE: Where are we gonna stay?
ANNIE: The Silver Dollar!
MARIE-ADELE: You can't stay there.
ANNIE: There's rooms upstairs.
PELAJIA: You wanna sleep in a whorehouse?
VERONIQUE: Zhaboonigan! Don't listen to this part.
PELAJIA: There's room at my son's.
PHILOMENA: Two washrooms! He's got a wonderful education.
EMILY: Next.
VERONIQUE: Who's going to drive?
ANNIE: Emily. She can drive anything.
VERONIQUE: I believe it.
ANNIE: But I can drive, too.
VERONIQUE: Oh my god.
ANNIE: Long as I don't have to drive in the city. You drive the city.
VERONIQUE: Me?
ANNIE and MARIE-ADELE: No!
PELAJIA: Long as you don't drive too fast, Annie Cook.
PHILOMENA: And we'll pack a lunch for the trip and then eat in restaurants. Chinese.
PELAJIA: Can't afford it. We chip in, buy groceries and cook at my son's.
VERONIQUE: I'll give $10.
EMILY: You old fossil. You want us to starve?
PHILOMENA: $50 a day. Each.
EMILY: Philomena Moosemeat! That's $50 times seven people times four days. That's over a $1,000 worth of groceries.
VERONIQUE: Imagine!
MARIE-ADELE: Okay. Veronique St Pierre. You cook. $20 apiece. Right?
EMILY: Right. Next.
PHILOMENA: Anybody writing this down?
ANNIE: I'm gonna go to Sam the Recordman.
MARIE-ADELE: I'll make the grocery list.
PELAJIA: How much for gas?

VERONIQUE [*still in dreamland over the groceries*]: $1,000!
PHILOMENA [*flabbergasted*]: Nooo! You goose.
ANNIE: $40.
EMILY: $150. Period. Next.
PELAJIA: We got 10 days to find this money.
MARIE-ADELE: What's it cost to get into the bingo?
VERONIQUE: All the Indians in the world will be there!
PHILOMENA: $50.
ANNIE: And we're gonna be the only Indians there.
PELAJIA: Silence.

[*There is a long, thoughtful silence, broken only after awhile by a scream from Zhaboonigan. Nanabush has knocked her off her stool. The women laugh.*]

Can't think of anything else.
PHILOMENA: Add it up. [*She hands a pencil to Emily.*]
EMILY [*calculates*]: $1,400. You guys need $200 each.
VERONIQUE: Where am I going to get $400?
EMILY: Make it. End of meeting.

*And the women start their fundraising activities with a vengeance. The drive is underlined by a wild rhythmic beat from the musician, one that gets wilder and wilder with each successive beat, though always underpinned by this persistent, almost dance-like pulse. The movement of the women covers the entire stage area, and like the music, gets wilder and wilder, until by the end it is as if we are looking at an insane eight-ring circus, eight-ring because through all this, Nanabush, as the seagull, has a holiday, particularly with Marie-Adele's lines of laundry, as Marie-Adele madly strings one line of laundry after another all over the set, from Pelajia's roof to Emily's store, etc. For the garage sale, Annie sells off Pelajia's lamp, chairs, etc., so that Pelajia's 'basement' simply dissolves into the madness of the fundraising drive.*

*Beat one.*

*Pelajia is hammering on the roof.*
*Emily is at the store cash register and rings up each sale as Annie, Philomena, Marie-Adele, Zhaboonigan, and Veronique stand shoulder to shoulder and pass the following from one side of the stage to the other:*
*seven large sacks marked 'FLOUR'*
*two giant tubs marked 'LARD'*
*one bushel of apples*

*Beat two.*

*Zhaboonigan brings small table on and puts it stage left.*
*Annie brings table on and puts it stage right.*
*Philomena brings a basket full of beer bottles to centre and empties it. She has a baby attached to her.*

*Veronique comes on with cloth and Windex and starts 'cleaning windows' rhythmically, listening to whatever gossip she can hear.*
*Marie-Adele strings two lines of clothing across the stage.*
*Pelajia hammers on her roof.*
*Emily brings on several empty beer cases and fills them with Philomena's bottles.*

*Beat three.*

*Zhaboonigan brings in six quarts of blueberries and then takes over window cleaning from Veronique.*
*Annie brings on basket of old clothes and a broken kitchen chair.*
*Philomena brings on another basket full of beer bottles, empties it. She now has two babies attached to her, like a fungus.*
*Emily fills beer cases rapidly, expertly.*
*Pelajia gets down off roof, hammering everything until she is on hands and knees, hammering the floor.*
*Marie-Adele strings third and fourth lines of laundry across the stage.*
*Veronique comes in burdened with seven apple pies and puts them on Annie's table.*

*Beat four.*

*Pelajia hammers as she crawls across the floor.*
*Zhaboonigan washes windows like a person possessed.*
*Emily runs and rings up a sale on the cash register and then brings on more empty beer cases and loads them up.*
*Philomena brings on a third load of bottles. Three babies are now attached to her.*
*Annie brings on an old trilight pole lamp and an old record player, which she opens and stacks alongside the rest of her stuff.*
*Annie and Emily sing a line of their song with very bad harmony.*
*Marie-Adele strings fifth and sixth lines of laundry across stage.*
*Veronique comes on with seven loaves of bread and puts them neatly by the pies.*

*Beat five.*

*Pelajia hammers as she crawls across the floor, hammering everything in sight. The women protect their poor feet.*
*Zhaboonigan washes windows even faster; she's starting to cry.*
*Emily and Philomena work together filling the empty beer cases as fast as they can.*
*Emily runs to the register, rings in seven sales and sings a bit of song with Annie, better this time. Philomena now has four kids attached to her body.*
*Annie comes on with a small black and white TV with rabbit ears and an old toaster.*
*Veronique comes on with six dozen buns and dumps them out of their tins all over the table.*
*Pelajia hammers faster and faster.*
*Zhaboonigan is now working like a maniac and is sobbing.*
*Marie-Adele strings seventh and eight lines of laundry across the stage.*

*Beat six.*

*Emily goes to cash register and tallies their earnings; she works the register with tremendous speed and efficiency all this beat.*
*Zhaboonigan continues washing windows.*
*Philomena sticks a sign in beer bottles: World's Biggest Bottle Drive. She now has five babies attached to her.*
*Veronique sticks a sign on her table: World's Biggest Bake Sale.*
*Annie sticks a sign up around her stuff: World's Biggest Garage Sale.*
*Marie-Adele sticks a sign up on Zha's table: Big Blueberries and Laundry While You Wait.*
*Pelajia begins hammering the air. She may have lost her marbles.*

*Beat seven.*

EMILY: Whoa!

*The 'music' comes to a sudden stop. The women all collapse. The women look at each other. They then quickly clear the stage of everything they've brought on as Pelajia speaks, consulting her list. By the end of Pelajia's speech, the stage area is clear once more, except for a microphone stand that one of the women has brought on as part of the 'clean-up' activities.*

PELAJIA: Bottle drive. Ten cents a bottle, 24 bottles a case, equals two dollars and 40 cents. 777 bottles collected divided by 24 is 32 cases and nine singles that's 32 times \$2.40 equals \$77.70. Blueberries equals \$90. Good pickin' Zha and the Starblanket kids. Washing windows at \$5.00 a house times 18 houses. Five eights are 40, carry the four and add the five is 90 bucks less two on account of that cheap Gazelle Nataways only gave three dollars. That's \$88. Household repairs is four roofs including the Chief's and one tiled floor is \$225. Garage sale brung in \$246.95, the bake sale equals \$83 after expenses, we make 110 bucks on doing laundry, 65 bucks babysitting, 145 from Emily doing a double shift at the store and I have generously donated \$103 from my savings. That brings us to a grand total of \$1233.75. So!

*Emily and Annie move forward as the music starts up. They are lit only by tacky floor flood-lighting, and are, in effect, at the Anchor Inn, Little Current. Emily speaks into the microphone.*

EMILY: Thank-you. Thank-you, ladies and gentlemen. I thank you very much. And now for the last song of the night, ladies and gents, before we hit the road. A song that's real special to me in my heart. A song I wrote in memory of one Rosabella Baez, a Rez Sister from way back. And Rose baby, if you're up there tonight, I hope you're listenin' in. Cuz it's called: 'I'm Thinkin' of You.' Here goes . . .

*Emily and Annie grab their microphones; Emily sings lead, Annie sings backup. And it's 'country' to the hilt.*

I'm thinkin' of you every moment,
As though you were here by my side;
I'll always remember the good times,
So darlin' please come back to me.

I'm dreamin' of you every night,
That we were together again;
If time can heal up our partin'
Then love can remove all this pain.

*Instrumental—dance break*

If love is the secret of livin',
Then give me that love, shinin' light;
When you are again by my side,
Then livin' will once more be right.

*The audience claps. Emily says, 'Thank-you.' And then she and Annie join the other women, who have, during the song, loaded themselves, their suitcases, and their lunches into the 'van'. This van consists of three battered old van seats stuck to the walls of the theatre, on either side and up high. The back seat is on the 'stage left' side of the theatre and the other two are on the other side, the middle seat of the van towards the back of the theatre, the front seat, complete with detachable steering wheel, just in front and 'stage right' of the stage area. Each seat is lit by its own light.*

EMILY: How much did me and Annie take in singin' at the Anchor Inn?
PELAJIA: $330 at the door.
MARIE-ADELE: Solid packed house, eh? Shoulda charged more.
ANNIE: Fifty bucks for the oom-chi-cha machine. Twenty bucks for Ronnie's guitar. That's our only costs.
EMILY: Ha! We're laughin'.

*A capella reprise of a verse of their song, which fades into the highway sounds, and they drive, for a few moments, in silence.*

*In the van, driving down the highway to Toronto, at night. The women have intimate conversations, one on one, while the rest are asleep or seated at the other end of the van. Annie is driving. Emily sits beside her listening to her Walkman, while Marie-Adele is 'leaning' over Annie's shoulder from her place in the middle seat. Veronique sits beside Marie-Adele, sleeping. Pelajia and Philomena are in the very back seat with Zhaboonigan between them.*

MARIE-ADELE: Nee, Annie, not so fast.
[*Pause. Annie slows down.*]
So. You couldn't get Ellen and Raymond to come along? I'd like to meet this Raymond someday.

ANNIE [*angrily insisting on the correct pronunciation*]: Raymond! Ellen says he's got a whole library full of cassette tapes.

MARIE-ADELE: Annie. You ever think about getting married again?

ANNIE: Not really. I can hear the band at the Silver Dollar already.

MARIE-ADELE: Do you still think about . . . Eugene?

ANNIE: What're you talkin' about? Of course, I think about him, he's my brother-in-law, ain't he?

MARIE-ADELE: He made his choice.

ANNIE: Yeah. He picked you.

MARIE-ADELE: Annie. I never stole him off you.

ANNIE: Drop dead. Shit! I forgot to bring that blouse. I mean. In case I sing. Shit.

MARIE-ADELE: If I'm gone and Eugene if he starts drinkin' again. I see you going for him.

ANNIE: Why would I bother? I had my chance 20 years ago. Christ!

MARIE-ADELE: Twenty years ago, I was there.

ANNIE: Why would I want 14 kids for?

MARIE-ADELE: That's exactly what I'm scared of. I don't want them kids to be split up. You come near Eugene you start drinking messing things up me not here I come back and don't matter where you are . . .

ANNIE: I don't want him. I don't want him. I don't want him. I don't want him. I don't want him.

EMILY: Put us all in the fuckin' ditch!

PELAJIA: Hey, watch your language up there.

ANNIE: Shit! I don't care. There's nothing more to say about it. Why don't you take your pills and go to sleep.

*Pelajia and Philomena begin talking.*

PHILOMENA: September 8 again.

PELAJIA: Hmmm? What about September 8?

PHILOMENA: You don't remember?

PELAJIA: What?

PHILOMENA: How could you?

PELAJIA: Mama died?

PHILOMENA: No! Remember?

PELAJIA: I can't remember. Got so much on my mind. So many things to forget.

ZHABOONIGAN [*to Philomena*]: You like me?

PHILOMENA: Yes, Zhaboonigan. I like you.

ZHABOONIGAN: I like the birdies.

PHILOMENA: You like talking to the birdies?

ZHABOONIGAN: Yup. [*She falls asleep.*]

PHILOMENA: Zhaboonigan . . . sometimes I wonder . . .

PELAJIA: It's dark . . . warm . . . quiet . . .

PHILOMENA: Toronto. Had a good job in Toronto. Yeah. Had to give it all up. Yeah. Cuz mama got sick. Philomena Margaret Moosetail. Real live secretary in the garment district. He'd come in and see my boss. Nice man, I thought. That big, red, fish-tail Caddy. Down Queen Street. He liked me. Treated me like a queen. Loved me. Or I thought he did. I don't know. Got pregnant anyway. Blond, blue-eyed, six foot two. And the way he smelled. God! His wife walks in on us.

[*Long silence.*]

He left with her.

[*Long silence.*]

I don't even know to this day if it was a boy or a girl. I'm getting old. That child would be . . . 28 . . . 28 years old. September 8. You know what I'm gonna do with that money if I win? I'm gonna find a lawyer. Maybe I can find that child. Maybe I wouldn't even have to let him . . . her . . . know who I am. I just . . . want to see . . . who . . .

PELAJIA: I hope you win.

*Annie and Emily, at the front of the van with Annie driving, are laughing and singing, 'I'm a little Indian who loves fry bread'. From time to time, they sneak each other a sip of this little bottle of whisky Annie has hidden away inside her purse.*

I'm a little Indian who loves fry bread,
Early in the morning and when I go to bed;
Some folks say I'm crazy in the head,
Cuz I'm a little Indian who loves fry bread.

Now, some folks say I've put on a pound or two,
My jeans don't fit the way they used to do;
But I don't care, let the people talk,
Cuz if I don't get my fry bread, you'll hear me squawk.

ANNIE: So tell me. What's it like to go to a big bar like . . . I mean like . . . the Silver Dollar.

EMILY: Lotta Nishnawbs.[6]

ANNIE [*disappointed*]: Yeah? Is the music good?

EMILY: Country rock.

ANNIE [*screams gleefully*]: Yee-haw! Maybe the band will ask me up to sing, eh? I'll sing something fast.

EMILY: You would, too.

ANNIE [*sings real fast*]: 'Well, it's 40 below and I don't give a fuck, got a heater in my truck and I'm off to the rodeo. Woof!' Something like that.

EMILY: Yup. That's pretty fast.

ANNIE: Hey. Maybe Fritz the Katz will be there. Never know. Might get laid, too, eh? Remember Room 20 at the Anchor Inn? Oh, that Fritz! Sure like singin' with him. Crazy about the way . . .

[*Emily starts singing Patsy Cline's famous 'Crazy . . . crazy for feelin' so lonely . . .' all the way through Annie's next speech.*]

. . . he stands there with his guitar and his 10-gallon hat. Is that what you call them hats? You know the kind you wear kind of off to the side like this? That's what

6 Indians. (Ojibway)

he does. And then he winks at me. [*sings*] 'Crazy . . .' Oooh, I love, just love the way the lights go woosh woosh in your eyes and kinda' wash over your body. Me standing there shuffling my feet side to side, dressed real nice and going [*sings*] 'Oooh darlin' . . .' with my mike in my hand just so. Oh! And the sound of that band behind me. And Fritz. [*sings*] 'Crazy, crazy for feelin' so lonely . . .'

EMILY: Yeah. You look good on stage.

ANNIE: Yeah?

EMILY: How come you're so keen on that guy anyway?

ANNIE: Sure Veronique St Pierre isn't just pretending to be asleep back there?

*Emily and Marie-Adele check Veronique in the middle seat.*

MARIE-ADELE: Nah. Out like a lamp.

EMILY: Hey! We'll get her drunk at the Silver Dollar and leave her passed out under some table. Take two beers to do that.

ANNIE: Hey. Too bad Big Joey had to come back from Toronto before we got there, eh?

EMILY: Man! That dude's got buns on him like no other buns on the face of God's entire creation. Whooo! No to mention a dick that's bigger than a goddamn breadbox.
[*Annie screams gleefully.*]
How about Fritz? What's his look like?

ANNIE [*after an awkward pause*]: He's Jewish, you know.

EMILY [*laughing raucously*]: World's first Jewish country singer!

ANNIE: Don't laugh. Those Jews make a lot of money, you know.

EMILY: Not all of them.

ANNIE: Fritz buys me jeans and things. I'm gonna be one of them Jewish princesses.

EMILY: What's wrong with being an Indian princess?

ANNIE: Aw, these white guys. They're nicer to their women. Not like Indian guys. Screw you, drink all your money, and leave you flat on your ass.

EMILY: Yeah, right. Apple Indian Annie. Red on the outside. White on the inside.

ANNIE: Emily!

EMILY: Keep your eye on the road.

ANNIE: Good ol' highway 69.

EMILY: Hey. Ever 69 with Fritz?

MARIE-ADELE: Neee.

ANNIE: White guys don't make you do things to them. You just lie there and they do it all for you. Ellen's real happy with her Ray<u>mond</u>. You can tell the way she sounds on the phone. Maybe someday I'll just take off with a guy like Fritz.

EMILY: Then what? Never come back to the rez?
[*Annie is cornered. Emily then slaps her playfully on the arm.*]
Hey. Know what?
[*sings*]

When I die, I may not go to heaven,
I don't know if they let Indians in;
If they don't, just let me go to Wasy, lord,
Cuz Wasy is as close as I've been.

ANNIE: Lots of white people at this Silver Dollar?
EMILY: Sometimes. Depends.
ANNIE: How much for beer there?
EMILY: Same as up here. Nah! Don't need money, Annie Cook. You just gotta know how to handle men. Like me and the Rez Sisters down in Frisco.
ANNIE: Yeah?
EMILY: I'll take care of them.
ANNIE: Maybe we can find a party, eh? Maybe with the band.
EMILY: Whoa! Slow down, Annie Cook! Easy on the gas!
MARIE-ADELE: Annie!

*Pow. Black-out. They have a flat tire.*

*The flat tire. Everything now happens in complete darkness.*

VERONIQUE: Bingo!
PHILOMENA: What was that? What happened?
ANNIE: I don't know. Something just went 'poof'!
EMILY: Alright. Everybody out. We got a fuckin' flat.

*They all climb out of the van.*

VERONIQUE: Oh my god! We'll never get to the bingo.
ZHABOONIGAN: Pee pee.
PELAJIA: I can't fix a flat tire.
ANNIE: Emily can.
PELAJIA: Get the jack. Spare tire.
ANNIE: Philomena's wearing one.
ZHABOONIGAN: Pee pee.
PHILOMENA: This is all your fault, Annie Cook.
MARIE-ADELE: It's in the back.
ANNIE: So what do we do?
PELAJIA: What's the matter with Zha?
PHILOMENA: Gotta make pee pee.
VERONIQUE: I knew there was something wrong with this van the moment I set eyes on it. I should have taken the bus.
PHILOMENA: Oh shut up. Quack, quack, quack.
ANNIE: Don't look at me. It's not my fault the tires are all bald.
PHILOMENA: Nobody's blaming you.
ANNIE: But you just did.
PHILOMENA: Quack, quack, quack.
VERONIQUE: Where are we?
ANNIE: The Lost Channel. This is where you get off.
VERONIQUE [*groans*]: Ohhh!
EMILY: Yeah, right.
PHILOMENA: Shhh!

PELAJIA: Jack's not working too well.
EMILY: Okay. Everybody. Positions.
VERONIQUE: Not me. My heart will collapse.
EMILY: You wanna play bingo?
VERONIQUE [*groans*]: Ohhh!
ANNIE: Hurry up! Hurry up!
EMILY: Okay. One, two, three lift.

*Everybody lifts and groans.*

PELAJIA: Put the jack in there.

*All lift, except Marie-Adele and Zha, who wander off into the moonlight darkness. Dim light on them.*

ZHABOONIGAN: Ever dark.
MARIE-ADELE: You'll be fine, Zhaboonigan.

*Suddenly, a nighthawk—Nanabush, now in dark feathers—appears, darting in the night.*

ZHABOONIGAN: The birdies!
MARIE-ADELE: Yes, a birdie.
ZHABOONIGAN: Black wings!

*Marie-Adele begins talking to the bird, almost if she were talking to herself. Quietly, at first, but gradually—as the bird begins attacking her—growing more and more hysterical, until she is shrieking, flailing, and thrashing about insanely.*

MARIE-ADELE: Who are you? What do you want? My children? Eugene? No! Oh no! Me? Not yet. Give me time. Please. Don't. Please don't. Awus! Get away from me. Eugene! Awus! You fucking bird! Awus! Awus! Awus! Awus!

*And she has a total hysterical breakdown.*

*Zhaboonigan, at first, attempts to scare the bird off by running and flailing her arms at it. Until the bird knocks her down and she lies there on the ground, watching in helpless astonishment and abject terror. Underneath Marie-Adele's screams, she mumbles to herself, sobbing.*

ZHABOONIGAN: One, two, three, four, five, six, seven . . . Nicky Ricky Ben Mark . . . eight, nine, ten, eleven, twelve . . . [*until the other women come running. Total darkness again.*]
EMILY: What the . . .
ANNIE: Marie-Adele!
PELAJIA: Stop her! Hold her!
VERONIQUE: What's happening?
PHILOMENA: Marie-Adele. Now, now . . . come . . . come . . .
EMILY [*in the background*]: Stop that fucking screaming will ya, Marie-Adele!

PHILOMENA: Emily. There's no need to talk to her like that now.
PELAJIA: Help us get her in the van.
PHILOMENA: Come . . . come, Marie-Adele . . . everything's fine . . . you'll be fine . . . come . . . shhh . . . shhh . . .

*And they ease Marie-Adele back into the van. Once all is beginning to settle down again:*

PELAJIA: Everything okay now?
PHILOMENA: Yes. She's fine now.
PELAJIA: Emily, take over.
VERONIQUE: Yes. I don't trust that Annie Cook. Not for one minute.
EMILY: All set?
MARIE-ADELE: What time is it?
PELAJIA: Twenty after four.
ANNIE: Oh! We're over two hours behind schedule. Hurry up. Hurry up.
VERONIQUE: I'll be exhausted for the bingo tomorrow night. Maybe I should just take 15 cards.
EMILY: You can rest your heart. And your mouth. All day tomorrow. All set? [*And she starts up the van. The van lights come back on.*]

*The dialogues resume. Marie-Adele now sits in the front with Emily, who is driving. Zhaboonigan sits between them. Pelajia and Philomena are now in the middle seat, Annie and Veronique in the back.*

EMILY: You scared the shit out of me out there.
[*silence*]
Don't do that again.
[*silence*]
Feeling better now?
[*silence*]
MARIE-ADELE: I could be really mad, just raging mad just wanna tear his eyes out with my nails when he walks in the door and my whole body just goes 'k-k-k-k'. . . . He doesn't talk when something goes wrong with him, he doesn't talk, shuts me out, just disappears. Last night he didn't come home. Again, it happened. I couldn't sleep. You feel so ugly. He walks in this morning. Wanted to be alone, he said. The curve of his back, his breath on my neck. 'Adele, ki-sa-gee-ee-tin oo-ma,'[7] making love, always in Indian, only. When we still could. I can't even have him inside me anymore. It's still growing there. The cancer. Pelajia, een-pay-seek-see-yan.[8]
PELAJIA: You know one time, I knew this couple where one of them was dying and the other one was angry at her for dying. And she was mad because he was gonna be there when she wasn't and she had so much left to do. And she'd lie there in bed and tell him to do this and do that and he'd say 'Okay, okay.' And then he'd go

7 Adele, I love you. (Cree)
8 Pelajia, I'm scared to death. (Cree)

into the kitchen and say to me, 'She's so this and she's so that and she's so damned difficult.' And I watched all this going on. That house didn't have room for two such angry people. But you know, I said to her, 'You gotta have faith in him and you gotta have faith in life. He loves you very much but there's only so much he can do. He's only human.' There's only so much Eugene can understand, Marie-Adele. He's only human.

EMILY: Fuckin' right. Me and the Rez Sisters, okay? Cruisin' down the coast highway one night. Hum of the engine between my thighs. Rose. That's Rosabella Baez, leader of the pack. We were real close, me and her. She was always thinkin' real deep. And talkin' about bein' a woman. An Indian woman. And suicide. And alcohol and despair and how fuckin' hard it is to be an Indian in this country.

[*Marie-Adele shushes her gently.*]

No goddamn future for them, she'd say. And why, why, why? Always carryin' on like that. Chris'sakes. She was pretty heavy into the drugs. Guess we all were. We had a fight. Cruisin' down the coast highway that night. Rose in the middle. Me and Pussy Commanda off to the side. Big 18-wheeler come along real fast and me and Pussy Commanda get out of the way. But not Rose. She stayed in the middle. Went head-on into that truck like a fly splat against a windshield. I swear to this day I can still feel the spray of her blood against my neck. I drove on. Straight into daylight. Never looked back. Had enough gas money on me to take me far as Salt Lake City. Pawned my bike off and bought me a bus ticket back to Wasy. When I got to Chicago, that's when I got up the nerve to wash my lover's dried blood from off my neck. I loved that woman, Marie-Adele, I loved her like no man's ever loved a woman. But she's gone. I never wanna go back to San Francisco. No way, man.

MARIE-ADELE [*comforting the crying Emily*]: You should get some rest. Let Annie take over.

EMILY: I'll be fine. You go to sleep. Wake you up when we get to Toronto.

*Emily puts her Walkman on and starts to sing along quietly to 'Blue Kentucky Girl' by Emmylou Harris with its 'I swear I love you . . .' while Marie-Adele leans her head against the 'window' and falls asleep.*

*After a few moments, Zhaboonigan, who has been dozing off between Emily and Marie-Adele in the front seat, pokes her head up and starts to sing along off-key. Then she starts to play with Emily's hair.*

EMILY [*shrugging Zhaboonigan's hand off*]: Don't bug me. My favourite part's comin' up.

*Initiated by Zhaboonigan, they start playing 'slap.' The game escalates to the point where Emily almost bangs Zhaboonigan over the head with her elbow.*

EMILY: Yeah, right. You little retard.

[*Mad at this, Zhaboonigan hits Emily in the stomach.*]

Don't hit me there, you little. . . . Hey, man, like ummm . . . I'm sorry, Zha.

ZHABOONIGAN: Sorry.

EMILY [*Emily feels her belly thoughtfully. After a brief silence*]: You gonna have kids someday, Zha?

ZHABOONIGAN: Ummm . . . buy one.

EMILY: Holy! Well, kids were alright. Aw geez, Zha, that man treated me real bad. Ever been tied to a bed post with your arms up like this? Whoa! [*grabbing the steering wheel*] Maybe you should drive.

ZHABOONIGAN: Scary.

EMILY: Aw, don't be scared. Fuck.

ZHABOONIGAN: Fuck.

EMILY: Zhaboonigan Peterson! Your ma'll give me a black eye.

*Zhaboonigan turns her head toward the back seat, where Veronique sits sleeping, and says one more time, really loud.*

ZHABOONIGAN: Fuck!

EMILY: Shhh! Look, Zha. You don't let any man bother you while we're down in T.O. You just stick close to me.

ZHABOONIGAN: Yup.

EMILY: We're sisters, right? Gimme five.
[*They slap hands.*]
Alright. Bingo!!!

*Instantly, the house lights come on full blast. The Bingo Master—the most beautiful man in the world—comes running up the centre aisle, cordless mike in hand, dressed to kill: tails, rhinestones, and all. The entire theatre is now the bingo palace. We are in: Toronto!!!!*

BINGO MASTER: Welcome, ladies and gentlemen, to the biggest bingo the world has ever seen! Yes, ladies and gentlemen, tonight, we have a very special treat for you. Tonight, ladies and gentlemen, you will be witness to events of such gargantuan proportions, such cataclysmic ramifications, such masterly and magnificent manifestations that your minds will reel, your eyes will nictitate, and your hearts will palpitate erratically.

Because tonight, ladies and gentlemen, you will see the biggest, yes, ladies and gentlemen, the very biggest prizes ever known to man, woman, beast, or appliance. And the jackpot tonight? The jackpot, ladies and gentlemen, is surely the biggest, the largest, the hugest, and the most monstrous jackpot ever conceived of in the entire history of monstrous jackpots as we know them. $500,000! Yes, ladies and gentlemen, $500,000 can be yours this very night! That's half a million—A HALF MILLION SMACKEROOS!!! IF you play the game right.

And all you have to do, ladies and gentlemen, is reach into your programs and extract the single bingo card placed therein. Yes, ladies and gentlemen, the single bingo card placed therein, which bingo card will entitle you to one chance at winning the warm-up game for a prize of $20. $20! And all you have to do is poke holes in that single bingo card. Yes, ladies and gentlemen, just poke holes in that single bingo card and bend the numbers backward as the numbers are called. And don't forget the free hole in the middle of the card. Twenty dollars, ladies and gentlemen, that's one line in any direction. That means, of course, ladies and gentlemen, that the first person to form one line, just one straight line in any direction on their card, will be the very lucky winner of the $20 prize. $20! Are you ready, ladies and gentlemen? Are you ready? Then let the game begin! Under the G 56. Etc. . . .

*The audience plays bingo, with the seven women, who have moved slowly into the audience during the Bingo Master's speech, playing along. Until somebody in the audience shouts, 'Bingo!'*

BINGO MASTER: Hold your cards, ladies and gentlemen, bingo has been called.

*The Bingo Master and the assistant stage manager check the numbers and the prize money is paid out.*

BINGO MASTER: And now for the game you've all been waiting for, ladies and gentlemen. Now for the big game. Yes, ladies and gentlemen, get ready for THE BIGGEST BINGO IN THE WORLD! For the grand jackpot prize of $500,000! Full house, ladies and gentlemen, full house! Are you ready? Are you ready? Then let the game begin!

*The house lights go out. And the only lights now are on the bingo balls bouncing around in the bingo machine—an eery, surreal sort of glow—and on the seven women who are now playing bingo with a vengeance on centrestage, behind the Bingo Master, where a long bingo table has magically appeared with Zhaboonigan at the table's centre banging a crucifix Veronique has bought along for good luck. The scene is lit so that it looks like 'The Last Supper'.*

*The women face the audience. The bingo table is covered with all the necessary accoutrements: bags of potato chips, cans of pop, ashtrays (some of the women are smoking), etc. The Bingo Master calls out number after number—but not the B 14—with the women improvising responses. These responses—Philomena has 27 cards!—grow more and more raucous: 'B 14? Annie Cook? One more number to go! The B 14! Where is that B 14? Gimme that B 14! Where the fuck is that B 14?!!!' etc. Until the women have all risen from the table and come running downstage, attacking the bingo machine and throwing the Bingo Master out of the way. The women grab the bingo machine with shouts of: 'Throw this fucking machine into the lake! It's no damn good!' etc. And they go running down centre aisle with it and out of the theatre. Bingo cards are flying like confetti. Total madness and mayhem. The music is going crazy.*

*And out of this chaos emerges the calm, silent image of Marie-Adele waltzing romantically in the arms of the Bingo Master. The Bingo Master says 'Bingo' into her ear. And the Bingo Master changes, with sudden bird-like movements, into the nighthawk, Nanabush in dark feathers. Marie-Adele meets Nanabush.*

*During this next speech, the other women, one by one, take their positions around Marie-Adele's porch, some kneeling, some standing. The stage area, by means of 'lighting magic', slowly returns to its Wasaychigan Hill appearance.*

MARIE-ADELE: U-wi-nuk u-wa? U-wi-nuk u-wa? Eugene? Neee. U-wi-nuk ma-a oo-ma kee-tha? Ka. Kee-tha i-chi-goo-ma so that's who you are . . . at rest upon the rock . . . the master of the game . . . the game . . . it's me . . . nee-tha . . . come . . . come . . . don't be afraid . . . as-tum . . . come . . . to . . . me . . . ever soft wings . . . beautiful soft . . . soft . . . dark wings . . . here . . . take me . . . as-tum . . . as-tum . . . pee-na-sin . . . wings . . . here . . . take me . . . take . . . me . . . with . . . pee-na-sin . . .[9]

*As Nanabush escorts Marie-Adele into the spirit world, Zhaboonigan, uttering a cry, makes a last desperate attempt to go with them. But Emily rushes after and catches her at the very last split second. And the six remaining women begin to sing the Ojibway funeral song. By the beginning of the funeral song, we are back at the Wasaychigan Hill Indian Reserve, at Marie-Adele's grave.*

WOMEN:
Wa-kwing, wa-kwing,
Wa-kwing nin wi-i-ja;
Wa-kwing, wa-kwing,
Wa-kwing nin wi-i-ja.[10]

*At Marie-Adele's grave. During Pelajia's speech, the other women continue humming the funeral song until they fade into silence. Pelajia drops a handful of earth on the grave.*

PELAJIA: Well, sister, guess you finally hit the big jackpot. Best bingo game we've ever been to in our lives, huh? You know, life's like that, I figure. When all is said and done. Kinda' silly, innit, this business of living? But. What choice do we have? When some fool of a being goes and puts us Indians plunk down in the middle of this old earth, dishes out this lot we got right now. But. I figure we gotta make the most of it while we're here. You certainly did. And I sure as hell am giving it one good try. For you. For me. For all of us. Promise. Really. See you when that big bird finally comes for me.[*whips out her hammer one more time, holds it up in the air and smiles*] And my hammer.

*Back at the store in Wasaychigan Hill. Emily is tearing open a brand-new case of the small cans of Carnation milk, takes two cans out and goes up to Zhaboonigan with them.*

9 MARIE-ADELE: Who are you? Who are you? Eugene? Nee. Then who are you really? Oh. It's you, so that's who you are . . . at rest upon the rock . . . the master of the game . . . the game . . . it's me . . . me . . . come . . . come . . . don't be afraid . . . come . . . come . . . to . . . me . . . ever . . . soft wings . . . beautiful soft . . . soft . . . darkwings . . . here . . . take me . . . come . . . come . . . come and get me . . . wings here . . . take me . . . take . . . me . . . with . . . come and get me . . . (Cree)

10 WOMEN: Heaven, heaven, heaven, I'm going there; Heaven, heaven, heaven, I'm going there. (Ojibway)

EMILY: See, Zha? The red part up here and the white part down here and the pink flowers in the middle?

ZHABOONIGAN: Oh.

EMILY: Carnation milk.

ZHABOONIGAN: Carnation milk.

EMILY: And it goes over here where all the other red and white cans are, okay?

ZHABOONIGAN: Yup.

*Zhaboonigan rushes to Emily and throws her arms around her affectionately. Emily is embarrassed and struggles to free herself. Just then, Annie enters. She's lost some of her speed and frenetic energy. There's obviously something wrong with her.*

ANNIE: Halloo! Whatchyou doing.

EMILY: Red Lucifer's whiskers! It's Annie Cook.

ANNIE: Well, we seem to have survived the biggest bingo in the world, eh? Well . . . ummm . . . not all of us . . . not Marie-Adele . . . but she knew she was . . . but we're okay. [*laughs*] . . . us? . . .

EMILY: Annie Cook. Sometimes you can be so goddamn ignorant. [*pause*] Too bad none of us won, eh.

ANNIE: Philomena Moosemeat won $600. That's something.

EMILY: Yup. That's one helluva jazzy toilet she's got there, eh?

ANNIE: She's got eight-ply toilet paper. Dark green. Feels like you're wiping your ass with moss!

EMILY: Holy!

ANNIE: I'm singing back-up for Fritz weekends. 25 bucks a gig. That's something, eh?

EMILY: Katz's whore . . .

ANNIE: What?

EMILY: You heard me.

ANNIE: The Katz's what?

EMILY: Chris'sakes. Wake up.

ANNIE: I love him, Emily.

EMILY: You been drinkin'.

ANNIE: Please, come with me tonight.

EMILY: Have to wait for the old buzzard to come pick up this dozy daughter of hers and that's not 'til seven.

ANNIE: Okay?

EMILY: Alright. But we're comin' right back to the Rez soon as the gig's over. Hear?

ANNIE: Thanks. Any mail today?

EMILY: Sorry.

ANNIE: That's okay. See you at seven. [*And she exits.*]

ZHABOONIGAN: Why . . . why . . . why do you call me that?

EMILY: Call you what?

ZHABOONIGAN: Dozy dotter.

*Awkward silence, broken after awhile by Zhaboonigan's little giggle.*

EMILY: Look, Zha. Share a little secret with you, okay?

ZHABOONIGAN: Yup.

EMILY: Just you and me, promise?

ZHABOONIGAN: Yup.

EMILY: Gazelle Nataways'll see fit to kill . . . but I'm gonna have a baby.

ZHABOONIGAN [*drops the Carnation milk cans she's been holding all this time and gasps*]: Ohhh! Big Joey!

EMILY [*in exasperation*]: This business of having babies . . .

*And the last we see of them is Zhaboonigan playfully poking Emily in the belly and Emily slapping Zhaboonigan's hand away.*

*At Eugene Starblanket's house. Veronique St Pierre is sitting on the steps, glowing with happiness, looking up at the sky as though looking for seagulls. She sees none so she picks up the doll that lies under her chair and cradles it on her lap as though it were a child. At this point, Annie Cook enters.*

ANNIE: Halloo! [*surprised to see Veronique sitting there*] Veronique St Pierre. What are you doing here?

VERONIQUE: Annie Cook. Haven't you heard I'm cooking for Eugene and the children these days? It's been four days since the funeral as you know may she rest in peace [*makes a quick sign of the cross without missing beat*] but I was the only person on this reserve who was willing to help with these 14 little orphans.

ANNIE: That's nice. But I came to see if Simon Star . . .

VERONIQUE: The stove is so good. All four elements work and there is even a timer for the oven. As I was saying to Black Lady Halked at the bingo last night, 'Now I don't have to worry about burning the fried potatoes or serving the roast beef half-raw.'

ANNIE: Well, I was about to . . .

VERONIQUE: Yes, Annie Cook. I bought a roast beef just yesterday. A great roast beef. Almost 16 pounds. It's probably the biggest roast beef that's been seen on this reserve in recent years. The meat was so heavy that Nicky, Ricky, Ben, and Mark had to take turns carrying it here for me. Oh, it was hard and slippery at first, but I finally managed to wrestle it into my oven. And it's sitting in there at this very moment just sizzling and bubbling with the most succulent and delicious juices. And speaking of succulent and delicious juices, did you come to call on Eugene? Well, Eugene's not home.

ANNIE: Yeah, right. I came to see if Simon had that new record.

VERONIQUE: Why?

ANNIE: I'm singing in Little Current tonight and I gotta practise this one song.

VERONIQUE [*contemptuously*]: That Ritzie Ditzie character.

ANNIE: It's Fritz the Katz, Veronique St Pierre. FREDERICK STEPHEN KATZ. He's a very fine musician and a good teacher.

VERONIQUE: Teacher?! Of what?! As I was saying to Little Girl Manitowabi and her daughter June Bug McLeod at the bingo last night, 'You never know about these non-Native bar-room types.' I said to them, 'We have enough trouble right here on this reserve without having our women come dragging these shady white characters into the picture.' Before you know it, you will end up in deep trouble and bring shame and disrespect on the name of Pelajia Patchnose and all your sisters, myself included.

ANNIE: Myself included, my ass! Veronique St Pierre. I wish you would shut that great big shitty mouth of yours at least once a year!

VERONIQUE [*stunned into momentary silence. Then*]: Simon Starblanket is not at home. [*With this, she bangs the doll down viciously.*]

ANNIE: Good day, Veronique St Pierre. [*And exits.*]

*Veronique, meanwhile, just sits there in her stunned state, mouth hanging open and looking after the departing Annie.*

*On Pelajia Patchnose's roof. As at the beginning of the play, Pelajia is alone, nailing shingles on. But no cushion this time.*

PELAJIA: Philomena. Where are those shingles?

PHILOMENA [*from offstage*]: Oh, go on. I'll be up in just a minute.

PELAJIA [*coughs*]: The dust today. It's these dirt roads. Dirt roads all over. Even the main street. If I were chief around here, that's the very first thing I would do is . . .

PHILOMENA [*coming up the ladder with one shingle and the most beautiful pink, lace-embroidered, heart-shaped pillow you'll ever see*]: Oh, go on. You'll never be chief.

PELAJIA: And why not?

PHILOMENA: Because you're a woman.

PELAJIA: Bullshit! If that useless old chief of ours was a woman, we'd see a few things get done around here. We'd see our women working, we'd see our men working, we'd see our young people sober on Saturday nights, and we'd see Nanabush dancing up and down the hill on shiny black paved roads.

*Annie Cook pops up at the top of the ladder.*

ANNIE: Pelajia for chief! I'd vote for you.

PHILOMENA: Why, Annie Cook. You just about scared me off the edge of this roof.

PELAJIA: Someday, we'll have to find you a man who can slow you down. So what do you want this time, Annie Cook?

ANNIE: Well, to tell you the truth, I came to borrow your record player, Philomena Moosemeat . . . I mean, Moosetail. I'm going to practise this one song for tonight. Emily Dictionary is coming to Little Current to watch me sing with the band.

PELAJIA: It's back from Espanola.

PHILOMENA [*to Pelajia*]: Pelajia Rosella Patchnose! [*to Annie*]: It's still not working very well. There's a certain screeching, squawking noise that comes out of it every time you try to play it.

PELAJIA: That's okay, Philomena. There's a certain screechy, squawky noise that comes out of Annie Cook every time she opens her mouth to sing anyway.

PHILOMENA: Yes, Annie Cook. You can borrow it. But only for one night.

ANNIE: Good. Hey, there's a bingo in Espanola next week and Fire Minklater is driving up in her new car. There might be room. [*to Philomena*]: Would you like to go?

PELAJIA: Does a bear shit in the woods?

PHILOMENA [*glares at Pelajia first*]: Yes. [*then quickly to Annie*]: Make . . . make sure you don't leave me behind.

ANNIE: I'll make sure. Well. Toodle-oo! [*And she pops down the ladder again, happy, now that she's finally got her record player.*]

PELAJIA: That Annie Cook. Records and bingo. Bingo and records.

PHILOMENA: You know, Pelajia, I'd like to see what this Fritz looks like. Maybe he IS the man who can slow her down, after all.

PELAJIA: Foolishness! Annie Cook will be walking fast right up until the day she dies and gets buried beside the two of us in that little cemetery beside the church.

PHILOMENA: Oh, go on.

[*Pause. As Philomena sits down beside her sister, leaning with her elbow on her heart-shaped pillow.*]

So, Pelajia Patchnose. Still thinking about packing your bags and shipping off to Toronto?

PELAJIA: Well . . . oh . . . sometimes, I'm not so sure I would get along with him if I were to live down there. I mean my son Tom. He was telling me not to play so much bingo.

PHILOMENA: His upstairs washroom. Mine looks just like it now.

PELAJIA: Here we go again.

PHILOMENA: Large shining porcelain tiles in hippity-hoppity squares of black and white . . . so clean you can see your own face, like in a mirror, when you lean over to look into them. It looks so nice. The shower curtains have a certain matching blackness and whiteness to them—they're made of a rich, thick plasticky sort of material—and they're see-through in parts. The bathtub is beautiful, too. But the best, the most wonderful, my absolute most favourite part is the toilet bowl itself. First of all, it's elevated, like on a sort of . . . pedestal, so that it makes you feel like . . . the Queen . . . sitting on her royal throne, ruling her Queendom with a firm yet gentle hand. And the bowl itself—white, spirit white—is of such a shape, such an exquisitely soft, perfect oval shape that it makes you want to cry. Oh!!! And it's so comfortable you could just sit on it right up until the day you die!

*After a long, languorous pause, Philomena snaps out of her reverie when she realizes that Pelajia, all this time, has been looking at her disbelievingly and then contemptuously. Pelajia cradles her hammer as though she'd like to bang Philomena's head with it. Philomena delicately starts to descend the ladder. The last we see of her is her Kewpie-doll face. And beside it, the heart-shaped pillow, disappearing like a setting sun behind the edge of the roof. Once she's good and gone, Pelajia dismisses her.*

PELAJIA: Oh, go on!

[*Then she pauses to look wistfully at the view for a moment.*]

Not many seagulls flying over Eugene Starblanket's house today.

*And returns once more to her hammering on the roof as the lights fade into black-out. Split seconds before complete black-out, Nanabush, back once more in his guise as the seagull, 'lands' on the roof behind the unaware and unseeing Pelajia Patchnose. He dances to the beat of the hammer, merrily and triumphantly.*

*End of Play*

1988

# Glossary of Critical Terms

## Fiction

ALLEGORY a story in which the events and characters are symbolic of another order of meaning, in a frame of reference outside that of the fictional world, the way slaying a dragon may symbolize defeating the devil.

CHARACTER a name (or title) and a set of qualities that make up a fictional person.

COMEDY the story of a person's rise to a higher station in life through education or improvement of personality.

DESIGN the shape of a story when it is considered as a completed object rather than an ongoing process.

DIALOGUE the parts of a story in which the words of characters are reported directly.

FABULATION fiction that violates normal probabilities to make some point about the nature of existence.

FACT a thing that has been done, or a true statement.

FANTASY a story of events that violate our sense of natural possibilities in this world; the more extreme the violation, the more *fantastic* the story is said to be.

FICTION something made up, usually a made-up story.

HISTORY the events of the past, or a retelling of those events in the form of a story; the most factual kind of fiction.

IRONY the result of some difference in the point of view or values of a character in fiction and those of the narrator or reader.

JUXTAPOSITION the way episodes or elements of a plot are located next to one another to contribute to the design of a story.

METAFICTION a kind of fabulation that calls into question the nature of fiction itself.

METAPHOR a method of conveying rich and complex thoughts by linking different images and ideas.

NARRATION the parts of a story that summarize events and conversations.

NARRATOR the person who tells a story.

PATHOS the emotion generated by the story of a character's fall or persecution through no fault of his or her own.

PICARESQUE a word used to describe a kind of story that blends comedy and satire to narrate the adventures of a rogue through a low or debased version of contemporary reality.

PLOT the order of events in a story as an ongoing process.

POINT OF VIEW the voice and vision through which the events of a story reach the reader.

REALISM a mode of fiction that is not specifically factual but presents a world recognizably bound by the same laws as the world of the author.

REPETITION a means of drawing attention to the thematic point by presenting certain features or elements of a story more than once.

ROMANCE a story that is neither wildly fantastic nor bound by the conventions of realism, but that offers a heightened version of reality.

SATIRE a story that offers a world that is debased in relation to the world of the author.

STORY a complete sequence of events, as told about a single character or a group of characters.

STREAM OF CONSCIOUSNESS a technique of narrative fiction in which the thoughts of a character are entirely open to the reader, usually being presented as a flow of ideas and feelings apparently without logical organization.

SYMBOL a particular object or event in a story that acquires thematic value through its function or the way it is presented.

THEME the ideas, values, or feelings that are developed or questioned in a work of fiction.

TONE the way in which attitudes are conveyed through language without being presented directly as statements, as in sarcasm.

TRAGEDY the story of a character's fall from a high position through some flaw of personality.

## Poetry

ACCENT the rhythm of alternating light and heavy (soft and loud) sounds in verse. (*See also* stress.)

ALLITERATION the use of the same sound at the beginning of two or more words in the same line (or two adjacent lines) of verse.

ANIMATION the endowment of inanimate objects with some of the qualities of living creatures. (*Compare* personification.)

ASSONANCE the repetition of vowel sounds in two or more words in the same line (or adjacent lines).

BALLAD a poem that tells a story, usually meant to be sung.

BLANK VERSE unrhymed iambic pentameter lines. (*See also* foot; line.)

CAESURA the point or points within a line of verse where a pause is noticeable.

CONCEIT an elaborate and sometimes farfetched metaphor.

DESCRIPTION in poetry, the use of visual images and appeals to other senses. (*Compare* imagery.)

DRAMA the quality of poetry that is like theatrical drama, requiring the reader to grasp the nature of speaker, listener, and situation.

DRAMATIC MONOLOGUE a poem in which a single speaker addresses remarks to one or more listeners at some significant moment in the speaker's life.

END-STOPPED describing a line of verse that ends where one would normally pause in speech or punctuate in writing.

ENJAMBMENT the use of run-on lines in verse. (*See* run-on line.)

FEMININE RHYME a rhyme of two words that end in unaccented syllables (e.g., *yellow* and *fellow*), in which two rhyming sounds are required.

FOOT a unit of metre or rhythm. Five kinds of metrical foot are normally recognized: the iamb (da-*dum*), the anapest (da-da-*dum*), the trochee (*dum*-da), the dactyl (*dum*-da-da), and the spondee (*dum-dum*). (*See* metre.)

FREE VERSE unrhymed lines in which no particular metre is maintained. (*See* metre.)

HEROIC COUPLET a rhymed pair of iambic pentameter lines, both of which are typically end-stopped, with a period or other full stop at the end of the second line. (*See* end-stopped.)

IMAGERY the use in poetry of sensory details (*images*), such as sounds, scents, tastes, textures, and especially sights. (*Compare* description.)

IRONY a deliberate gap or disparity between the language in which a thing is discussed and the language usually considered appropriate for that particular subject.

LINE the line of verse as it is normally printed on a page. Lines may be divided into feet and labelled according to the number of feet per line. In English metrical verse the most common lines are pentameter (five feet) and tetrameter (four feet). (*See* foot; metre.)

MEDITATION in poetry, the movement from images to ideas.

METAPHOR the discovery and presentation of likeness or similarity in different things — a major resource of poetical expression.

METRE the rhythm of a piece of poetry, determined by the kind and number of feet in a line. (*See* foot.)

METRICS the aspect of poetry that has to do with sound rather than sense.

NARRATION the quality of poetry that is like fiction, requiring the reader to follow shifts in time and space, and to observe significant details, in order to understand a poem as a kind of story.

NARRATOR the character who tells a story.

PERSONIFICATION the endowment of non-human things or creatures with distinctly human qualities. (*Compare* animation.)

PUN a word used in a context in which it carries two conflicting meanings.

RHYME a sound pattern in which both vowel and consonant sounds at the end of words match (as in *rhyme* and *chime*), especially when these words come at the ends of nearby lines.

RUN-ON LINE a line of verse that ends where one would not normally pause in speech or punctuate in writing.

SCANSION the act of determining the metrical structure and rhyme scheme of a poem. (*See* metre.)

SIMILE a kind of metaphor in which the likeness of two things is made explicit by such words as *like*, *as*, *so*. (*See* metaphor.)

SITUATION in a narrative or dramatic poem, the circumstances of the character or speaker.

SONNET a verse form featuring intricate rhyming, typically consisting of fourteen iambic pentameter lines.

STANZA a regularly repeated metrical pattern of the same number of lines in groups throughout a poem, sometimes including repeated patterns of rhyme as well.

STRESS the ways in which verse sounds are accented. Three types of stress are recognized in poetry: *grammatical stress*, which is the normal pronunciation of a word or phrase; *rhetorical stress*, which involves a change in pronunciation to emphasize some part of the meaning of an utterance; and *poetical stress*, the regular rhythm established in metrical verse.

SYMBOL an extension of metaphor in which one thing is implicitly discussed by means of the explicit discussion of something else.

TACT a reader's ability to observe the conventions operating in any particular poem and to pay attention to the idiom of every poet.

## Drama

ABSURDIST DRAMA a mode of drama that does not provide any rational source of explanation for the behaviour and fate of its characters and thus expresses the possibility that human existence may be meaningless.

BLOCKING the arrangement of characters on stage during any particular moment in the production of a play.

CHARACTER a dramatic being, known by name, word, and deed.

CHORIC CHARACTER a character who takes part in the action of a play but is not directly involved in the outcome of the action, and thus can provide commentary upon it.

CHORIC COMMENTARY commentary upon characters and events of a play provided either by a chorus or by choric characters.

CHORUS (*or* CHORAGOS) a group of characters who comment upon the action of a play but do not take part in it.

CLOSET DRAMA drama written to be read either privately or aloud in a small group, rather than performed on stage.

COMEDY the dramatization of a hero's and heroine's change in fortune (from frustration to satisfaction) brought about not only by the effort of the hero and heroine themselves but also by some element of chance, coincidence, or luck.

COSTUME a piece of physical apparel worn by actors to create a visual illusion appropriate to the characters they are pretending to be.

CUE a word, phrase, or statement in the text of a play that provides explicit or implicit information relevant to the theatrical production of the play.

DIALOGUE a specialized form of conversation in drama that is designed to convey everything about the imaginative world of a play as well as to provide all the cues necessary for production of the play.

DISCOVERY a change from ignorance to knowledge on the part of a dramatic hero and/or heroine, which brings about a significant change in the fortune of the hero and/or heroine. (*Compare* reversal.)

DRAMA imitative action created through the words of imaginary beings talking to one another rather than to a reader or spectator.

DRAMATIC UNIT a segment of the scenario that is determined by the entrance or exit of a character or group of characters. (*See* scenario.)

EXPOSITION dialogue at the beginning of a play that includes background information about characters and events in the imaginative world of a play.

GESTURE a physical movement made by actors appropriate to the attitudes and intentions of the characters they are pretending to be.

INTERACTION verbal and physical deeds performed by dramatic characters in relation to one another.

INTONATION the particular manner (including pronunciation, rhythm, and volume) in which actors deliver the lines of the characters they are pretending to be.

MEDITATIVE DRAMA a form of drama that is primarily concerned with representing the internalized thoughts and feelings of its characters.

NARRATION an element in drama that is like the act of storytelling in that it tells about characters and events, or comments upon characters and events, rather than showing them directly. (*See also* choric commentary; exposition; reported action; retrospection.)

NATURALISTIC DRAMA a mode of drama that embodies a view of humans as being influenced by psychological, social, and economic forces beyond their control and comprehension.

PACING the tempo of activity on stage during any particular moment in the production of a play.

PERSUASIVE DRAMA a form of drama that uses dialogue, plot, and character primarily as a means of testing ideas, expounding ideas, or demonstrating the superiority of one set of ideas over another.

PLOT a specialized form of experience that consists of a wholly interconnected system of events, deliberately selected and arranged to fulfill both the imaginative and the theatrical purposes of a play. (*Compare* scenario.)

PROP any physical item (apart from costume and set) that is used by actors on stage during the production of a play.

REPORTED ACTION action taking place during the time of the play that is reported by one or more of the characters rather than presented directly.

REPRESENTED ACTION action taking place during the time of the play that is presented directly rather than reported by one or more of the characters.

RETROSPECTION post-expository dialogue in which characters survey, explore, and attempt to understand action that has taken place well before the time of the play.

REVERSAL an incident or sequence of incidents that goes contrary to the expectations of a hero and/or heroine. (*Compare* discovery.)

ROMANCE a mode of drama that uses characters and events to present an intensified but not completely idealized view of human excellence.

SATIRE a mode of drama that uses characters and events to present an intensified but not completely negative view of human imperfection.

SCENARIO action that is presented directly and thus embodies everything that takes place in the imaginative world of a play (i.e. the plot).

SCRIPT the text of a play interpreted as a set of cues for theatrical production.

SET a physical construction placed on stage to represent an interior or exterior location in the imaginative world of a play.

SOLILOQUY lines spoken by a character but meant to represent his or her unspoken thoughts and feelings.

SPECTACLE sights and sounds of performance by means of which the imaginative world of a play is brought to life in the theatre. (*See also* blocking; costume; gesture; intonation; pacing; prop; set.)

TRAGEDY the dramatization of a hero's or heroine's change in fortune (from prosperity to catastrophe) brought about by some great error in judgment on the part of the hero or heroine.

TRAGICOMEDY a mode of drama that does not embody a clear-cut pattern of catastrophe or rebirth (as in tragedy or comedy) or present clear-cut images of good or evil (as in romance or satire), and thus presents an ambiguous and problematic view of human experience. (*See also* absurdist drama; naturalistic drama.)

# Acknowledgements


Edward Albee *The Zoo Story*. Copyright © 1960 Edward Albee, copyright renewed © 1987 Edward Albee, copyright © 2008 Edward Albee. Published in 2011 by The Overlook Press, New York, NY. All rights reserved. www.overlookpress.com.

Margaret Atwood "At the tourist centre in Boston", "Progressive Insanities of a Pioneer", Variations on the Word *LOVE*", "Variations on the Word *SLEEP*", and "Interlunar", from *Selected Poems 1966–1984* by Margaret Atwood. Copyright © 1990 Oxford University Press Canada. Reprinted by permission of the publisher. • "The Door", from *The Door* by Margaret Atwood. Copyright © 2007 O.W. Toad Ltd. Reprinted by permission of McClelland & Stewart, a division of Random House of Canada Limited, a Penguin Random House Company.

W.H. Auden "Musée des Beaux Arts," "The Unknown Citizen," "Lullaby (1937)," "In Memory of W.B. Yeats," and "As I Walked Out One Evening," copyright © 1940 and renewed 1968 by W.H. Auden; and "Who's Who," copyright © 1937 and renewed 1965 by W.H. Auden; from W.H. Auden COLLECTED POEMS by W.H. Auden. Used by permission of Random House, an imprint and division of Penguin Random House LLC. All rights reserved.

Margaret Avison "Snow", "New Year's Poem", "The Swimmer's Moment", "Butterfly Bones: Sonnet Against Sonnets", "In a Season of Unemployment", and "We the Poor Who Are Always with Us", from *Always Now: The Collected Poems* (in three volumes) by Margaret Avison by permission of The Porcupine's Quill. Copyright © The Estate of Margaret Avison, 2003.

Samuel Beckett *Krapp's Last Tape* by Samuel Beckett. Copyright © 1958 by the Estate of Samuel Beckett. Used by permission of Grove/Atlantic, Inc. Any third party use of this material, outside this publication, is prohibited.

Elizabeth Bishop "The Map", "First Death in Nova Scotia", "In the Waiting Room", and "One Art", from *The Complete Poems: 1927–1979* by Elizabeth Bishop. Copyright © 2011 by The Alice H. Methfessel Trust.

Christian Bök "Chapter I" and "Vowels" from *Eunoia* © Christian Bök, 2001. Reprinted with the permission of Coach House Books.

Dionne Brand "Islands Vanish", from *Land to Light On* by Dionne Brand. Copyright © 1997 Dionne Brand. Reprinted by permission of McClelland & Stewart, a division of Random House of Canada Limited, a Penguin Random House Company. • "Poem I", "Poem II", and "Poem III", from *thirsty* by Dionne Brand. Copyright © 2002 Dionne Brand. Reprinted by permission of McClelland & Stewart, a division of Random House of Canada Limited, a Penguin Random House Company.

Robert Bringhurst "Essay on Adam", "The Stonecutter's Horses", and "Leda and the Swan", from *Selected Poems* by Robert Bringhurst. Copyright © Robert Bringhurst. Reprinted with the permission of Gaspereau Press Limited, Printers & Publishers.

Morley Callaghan "A Cap for Steve" appears in *The Complete Stories, Volume One*, by Morley Callaghan, pages 96–110, published by Exile Editions, © 2012.

John Cheever "The Swimmer", from *The Stories of John Cheever* by John Cheever. Copyright © 1978 by John Cheever. Used by permission of Alfred A. Knopf, an imprint of the Knopf Doubleday Publishing Group, a division of Random House LLC. All rights reserved.

George Elliott Clarke "Look Homeward, Exile", "Bees' Wings", and "Blank Sonnet", from *Whylah Falls*, published in 2010 by Gaspereau Press. Reprinted with the permission of Gaspereau Press Limited, Printers & Publishers. • "Le Tombeau de Bishop", "Paris Annapolis", and "Burning Poems", from *Blue*, published in published in 2011 by Gaspereau Press. Rerpinted with the permission of Gaspereau Press Limited, Printers & Publishers.

LEONARD COHEN "A Kite is a Victim", "Prayer for Messiah", "Snow is Falling", and "What I'm Doing Here" from *Stranger Music: Selected Poems and Songs* by Leonard Cohen. Copyright © 1993 Leonard Cohen. Reprinted by permission of McClelland & Stewart, a division of Random House of Canada Limited, a Penguin Random House Company. • "I Threw Open the Shutters" from *The Energy of Slaves* by Leonard Cohen. Copyright © 1972 Leonard Cohen. Reprinted by permission of McClelland & Stewart, a division of Random House of Canada Limited, a Penguin Random House Company. • "I Threw Open the Shutters" from *The Energy of Slaves* by Leonard Cohen. Copyright © 1972 Leonard Cohen. Reprinted by permission of McClelland & Stewart, a division of Random House of Canada Limited, a Penguin Random House Company.

TAMAS DOBOZY "The Ghosts of Budapest" originally appeared in *Siege 13*, (Thomas Allen Publishers, 2002) by permission of Dundurn Press Limited.

T.S. ELIOT "The Love Song of J. Alfred Prufrock", "The Hollow Men", "Journey of the Magi", and "Marina", from *Collected Poems 1909–1962* (London: Faber and Faber, 1963), reprinted with permission.

LOUISE ERDRICH "Fleur", from *Tracks* by Louise Erdrich. Copyright © 1988 by Louise Erdrich. Reprinted by permission of Henry Holt and Company, LLC. All right reserved.

WILLIAM FAULKNER "A Rose for Emily", from *Collected Stories of William Faulkner* by William Faulkner. Copyright 1930 and renewed 1958 by William Faulkner. Used by permission of Random House, Inc.

ROBERT FROST "Mending Wall", "After Apple-Picking", "Design", "Provide, Provide", "Stopping by Woods on a Snowy Evening", and "Birches", from *The Poetry of Robert Frost*, edited by Edward Connery Lathem. Copyright 1923, 1930, 1939, 1947, 1969 by Henry Holt and Company, copyright 1936, 1951, 1958 by Robert Frost, copyright 1964, 1967, 1975 by Lesley Frost Ballantine. Reprinted by arrangement with Henry Holt and Company, LLC.

MAVIS GALLANT "The Ice Wagon Going Down the Street" by Mavis Gallant. Copyright © 1963, 1981 by Mavis Gallant. Originally appeared in *The New Yorker* (14 December 1953). Reprinted by permission of Georges Borchardt, Inc., on behalf of the Mavis Gallant Estate.

SEAMUS HEANEY "Requiem for the Croppies" from *Opened Ground: Poems 1966–1996* by Seamus Heaney, published in 2002 by Faber and Faber Ltd. First published in *Door into the Dark* (1969, Faber and Faber Ltd.). Reprinted by permission. • "Traditions" from *Opened Ground: Poems 1966–1996* by Seamus Heaney, published in 2002 by Faber and Faber Ltd. First published in *Wintering Out* (1972, Faber and Faber Ltd.). Reprinted by permission. • "The Crossing", "Seeing Things", and "The School Bag" from *Opened Ground: Poems 1966–1996* by Seamus Heaney, published in 2002 by Faber and Faber Ltd. First published in *Seeing Things* (1991, Faber and Faber Ltd.). Reprinted by permission.

TOMSON HIGHWAY Copyright © 1998 by Tomson Highway. Published by Fifth House Ltd., Canada. Reprinted with permission

HENRIK IBSEN *Hedda Gabler*, from *Henrik Ibsen: Four Major Plays*, translated by James McFarlane and Jens Arup, published by Oxford University Press. By permission of Oxford University Press, Inc.

THOMAS KING "Borders", from *One Good Story, That One* (HarperCollins, 1993; New Edition, 1999). Copyright © 1993 Dead Dog Café Productions Inc. Reprinted with permission of the author.

A.M. KLEIN Excerpt from "Portrait of the Poet as Landscape" by A.M. Klein, from Complete Poems, edited by Zailig Pollock, © University of Toronto Press, 1990. • "Soiree of Velvel Kleinburger", "The Rocking Chair", and "Portrait of the Poet as Landscape", from *Complete Poems*, edited by Zailig Pollock (Toronto: University of Toronto Press, 1990), reprinted by permission of the publisher.

ROBERT KROETSCH "The Poet's Mother", from *Completed Field Notes: The Long Poems of Robert Kroetsch* by Robert Kroetsch (McClelland & Stewart, 1989). Copyright © 1989 Robert Kroetsch. Reprinted with permission of the author. • "Hornbook #43" and "Hornbook #45", from *The Hornbooks of Rita K* by Robert Kroetsch (The University of Alberta Press, 2001). Copyright © 2001 Robert Kroetsch. Reprinted with permission of the author.

MARGARET LAURENCE "A Bird in the House", from *A Bird in the House* by Margaret Laurence. Copyright © 1963, 1964, 1965, 1966, 1967, 1970. Reprinted by permission of McClelland & Stewart, a division of Random House of Canada Limited, a Penguin Random House Company.

IRVING LAYTON "The Cold Green Element", "Berry Picking", "Whatever Else Poetry Is Freedom", and "Keine Lazarovitch 1870–1959", from *The Collected Poems of Irving Layton* by Irving Layton, published by McClelland & Stewart Ltd. Used with permission of the publisher.

DORIS LESSING "A Sunrise on the Veld". Copyright © 1973 Doris Lessing. Reprinted by kind permission of Jonathan Clowes Ltd, London, on behalf of Doris Lessing.

ROBERT LOWELL "To Speak of Woe That Is in Marriage", "Skunk Hour", "Water", and "For the Union Dead", from *Collected Poems* by Robert Lowell. Copyright © 1976 by Robert Lowell.

ALISTAIR MACLEOD "The Boat", from *Island: The Collected Stories of Alistair MacLeod* by Alistair MacLeod. Copyright © 2002 Alistair MacLeod. Reprinted by permission of McClelland & Stewart, a division of Random House of Canada Limited, a Penguin Random House Company.

BERNARD MALAMUD "The Magic Barrel", from *The Magic Barrel* by Bernard Malamud. Copyright © 1950, 1958, renewed 1977, 1986 by Bernard Malamud.

ROY MIKI "make it new", "attractive", "subversion in tokyo", and "on the sublime", from *Surrender* (Toronto: The Mercury Press, 2001).

ARTHUR MILLER *The Price*. Copyright © 1968 by Arthur Miller and Ingeborg M. Miller, Trustee. Used by permission of Viking Penguin, a division of Penguin Group (USA) Inc.

ROHINTON MISTRY "The Collectors", from *Tales from Firozsha Baag* by Rohinton Mistry. Copyright © 1997 Rohinton Mistry. First published 1987 by Penguin Books Canada. Reprinted by permission of McClelland & Stewart, a division of Random House of Canada Limited, a Penguin Random House Company.

MARIANNE MOORE "Poetry", an excerpt from "Poetry", "The Fish", and "A Jelly-Fish", from *The Poems of Marianne Moore* by Marianne Moore, edited by Grace Schulman. Copyright © 2003 by Marianne Craig Moore, Executor of the Estate of Marianne Moore. Used by permission of Viking Penguin, a division of Penguin Group (USA) LLC "Nevertheless", from *The Collected Poems of Marianne Moore* by Marianne Moore, reprinted with the permission of Scribner, a Division of Simon & Schuster, Inc. Copyright © 1944 by Marianne Moore, renewed 1972 by Marianne Moore. All rights reserved.

BHARATI MUKHERJEE "The Lady from Lucknow", originally published in *Darkness*. Copyright © 1985 by Bharati Mukherjee. Reprinted by permission of the author.

ALICE MUNRO "Child's Play" from *Too Much Happiness* by Alice Munro. Copyright © 2009 Alice Munro. Reprinted by permission of McClelland & Stewart, a division of Random House of Canada Limited, a Penguin Random House Company.

MICHAEL ONDAATJE "Bearhug", "Letters and Other Worlds", "Elizabeth", and "The Cinnamon Peeler" copyright © 2008 by Michael Ondaatje, reprinted by permission of Michael Ondaatje.

P.K. PAGE, "The Stenographers", "Photos of a Salt Mine", "Arras", "The New Bicycle", and "Deaf-mute in a Pear Tree", from *The Hidden Room* (in two volumes) by P.K. Page, reprinted by permission of the Porcupine's Quill. Copyright © The Estate of P.K. Page, 1997.

ROBERT PINSKY "The Figured Wheel", "From the Childhood of Jesus", "Shirt", and "At Pleasure Bay" from *The Figured Wheel: New and Collected Poems 1966–1996* by Robert Pinsky. Copyright © 1996 by Robert Pinsky. Reprinted by permission of Farrar, Straus and Giroux, LLC.

SYLVIA PLATH "Sheep in Fog", "Daddy", "Kindness", "Edge", and "Worlds", from *Collected Poems*, edited by Ted Hughes published by Faber and Faber Ltd, 1981 and 2003. Reprinted with permission.

SHARON POLLOCK *Doc.* Copyright © 1984 Sharon Pollock, revised edition copyright © 2003 Sharon Pollock. Reprinted by permission of Broadview Press.

E.J. PRATT "The Shark", "Erosion", "One Hour of Life", "Silences", and "The Dead", from *E.J. Pratt: The Complete Poems,* edited by Sandra Djwa and R.J. Moyles (Toronto: University of Toronto Press, 1989), reprinted by permission of the publisher.

ADRIENNE RICH "The Afterwake", "Novella", "Night-Pieces: For a Child", and "Moving in Winter", from *Collected Early Poems: 1950–1970* by Adrienne Rich. Copyright © 1993 by Adrienne Rich. Copyright © 1967, 1963, 1962, 1961, 1960, 1959, 1958, 1957, 1956, 1955, 1954, 1953, 1952, 1951 by Adrienne Rich. Copyright © 1984, 1975, 1971, 1969, 1966 by W.W. Norton & Company, Inc. Used by permission of the author and W.W. Norton & Company, Inc. • "Rape". Copyright © 2002 by Adrienne Rich. Copyright © 1973 by W.W. Norton & Company, Inc., from *The Fact of a Doorframe: Selected Poems 1950–2001* by Adrienne Rich. Used by permission of the author and W.W. Norton & Company, Inc.

SINCLAIR ROSS "The Painted Door", from *The Lamp at Noon and Other Stories* by Sinclair Ross. Copyright © 1968 Sinclair Ross. Reprinted by permission of McClelland & Stewart, a division of Random House of Canada Limited, a Penguin Random House Company.

WILLIAM SHAKESPEARE *King Lear,* edited by Ralph E.C. Houghton, M.A., sometime Fellow and Tutor of St Peter's Hall and Lecturer of Oriel College, Oxford. Notes reprinted with permission of the estate of Ralph E.C. Houghton.

SOPHOCLES *Oedipus Rex,* from *Sophocles, The Oedipus Cycle: An English Version* by Dudley Fitts and Robert Fitzgerald. Copyright 1939 by Houghton Mifflin Harcourt Publishing Company. Copyright © Renewed 1967 by Dudley Fitts and Robert Fitzgerald. Reprinted by permission of Houghton Mifflin Harcourt Publishing Company. All rights reserved. All professional, amateur, motion picture, recitation, lecturing, performance, public reading, radio, and television rights are strictly reserved. Inquiries on all rights should be sent to Houghton Mifflin Harcourt.

MADELEINE THIEN "Simple Recipes", from *Simple Recipes* by Madeleine Thien. Copyright © 2001 Madeleine Thien. Reprinted by permission of McClelland & Stewart, a division of Random House of Canada Limited, a Penguin Random House Company.

MICHEL TREMBLAY *For the Pleasure of Seeing Her Again,* translated by Linda Gaboriau. Copyright 1998 © Michel Tremblay and Linda Gaboriau, Talonbooks, Vanvouver, BC. Used by permission of Talon Books Ltd. Any third party use of this material, outside of this publication, is prohibited.

PHYLLIS WEBB "Marvell's Garden", "Lament", "To Friends Who Have Also Considered Suicide", and "The Days of the Unicorns", from *The Vision Tree.* Copyright 1982 © Phyllis Webb, Talonbooks, Vancouver, BC. Used by permission of Talon Books Ltd. Any third party use of this material, outside of this publication, is prohibited.

EUDORA WELTY "Why I Live at the P.O.", from *A Curtain of Green and Other Stories.* Copyright © 1941 and renewed 1969 by Eudora Welty, reprinted by permission of Houghton Mifflin Harcourt Publishing Company. All rights reserved.

Every effort has been made to determine and contact copyright holders. In the case of any omissions, the publisher will be pleased to make suitable acknowledgement in future editions.

# Index